MAKING AMERICA

A History of the United States

SIXTH EDITION

Carol Berkin
Baruch College, City University of New York

Christopher L. Miller
The University of Texas—Pan American

Robert W. Cherny
San Francisco State University

James L. Gormly
Washington and Jefferson College

WADSWORTH
CENGAGE Learning™

Australia • Brazil • Japan • Korea • Mexico • Singapore • Spain • United Kingdom • United States

WADSWORTH
CENGAGE Learning

Making America: A History of the United States, Sixth Edition, Advantage Edition
Carol Berkin, Christopher L. Miller, Robert W. Cherny and James L. Gormly

Senior Publisher: Suzanne Jeans

Senior Sponsoring Editor: Ann West

Director of Development: Jeff Greene

Development Editor: Jan Fitter

Assistant Editor: Megan Chrisman

Editorial Assistant: Patrick Roach

Managing Media Editor: Lisa Ciccolo

Marketing Coordinator: Lorreen Towle

Marketing Communications Manager: Glenn McGibbon

Art and Cover Direction, Production Management, and Composition: PreMediaGlobal

Senior Manufacturing Planner: Sandee Milewski

Rights Acquisition Director: Tim Sisler

Cover Image: Benton, Thomas Hart (1889–1975) © VAGA, NY *Wheat*, 1967. Oil on canvas, 20 × 21 in. (50.8 × 53.5 cm). Gift of Mr. and Mrs. James A. Mitchell. © Copyright VAGA, NY. Smithsonian American Art Museum, Washington, DC, U.S.A. Smithsonian American Art Museum, Washington, DC/Art Resource, NY/ © T. H. Benton and R. P. Benton Testamentary Trusts/ UMB Bank Trustee/Licensed by VAGA, New York, NY

Library of Congress Control Number: 2011935728

ISBN-13: 978-0-8400-2871-6

ISBN-10: 0-8400-2871-7

Wadsworth
20 Channel Center Street
Boston, MA 02210
USA

Cengage Learning is a leading provider of customized learning solutions with office locations around the globe, including Singapore, the United Kingdom, Australia, Mexico, Brazil and Japan. Locate your local office at **international.cengage.com/region**

Cengage Learning products are represented in Canada by Nelson Education, Ltd.

For your course and learning solutions, visit **www.cengage.com**.

Purchase any of our products at your local college store or at our preferred online store **www.cengagebrain.com**.

Instructors: Please visit **login.cengage.com** and log in to access instructor-specific resources.

Printed in the United States of America
1 2 3 4 5 6 7 15 14 13 12 11

Brief Contents

Contents

4

THE ENGLISH COLONIES IN THE EIGHTEENTH CENTURY, 1689–1763   77

5

DECIDING WHERE LOYALTIES LIE, 1763–1776   107

Maps

Preface

Like all history teachers, the authors of this book have heard the groans that arise from a class as students open the textbook. They see page after page of densely packed information, destined to be highlighted or underlined, memorized, and then quickly forgotten. We all agreed: There must be a better way, a way to convey the excitement, the human drama, the surprising twists and turns, the individual and collective stories of success and failure that made our American past. This complex story should be told clearly and engagingly. And "how we know," as much as "what we know," should be shared with students, so that as soon as they begin to read Chapter 1, they too are historians, playing an active role in reconstructing the past. This conviction—that a textbook can challenge students intellectually and spark their curiosity about the past as well as provide them with necessary information—has been, and remains, the guiding principle behind *Making America*.

To achieve our goal, we had to know our students. As professors in large public universities located on three of the nation's borders—the Pacific Ocean, the Atlantic, and the Rio Grande—we are keenly aware that today's classroom reflects our cultural diversity, our mix of native-born students and recent immigrants, those for whom English is a first language and those for whom it is a second or even a third tongue. Every class may include a significant number of serious-minded men and women whose formal skills lag behind their interest and enthusiasm for learning. Thus, from its first edition to its present one, we made certain that our textbook built on certain key elements. It offers a chronological, historical narrative that does not assume or demand a lot of prior knowledge about the American past. It does not rely solely on words to tell this story, for we know that people, places, and events can be brought to life through maps, paintings, photos, and cartoons, as well as the written word. Our book speaks to students in a voice that strives to communicate rather than impress, sharing with them the difficult questions we seek to answer in each chapter. Perhaps most importantly, this book offers a full array of integrated and supportive learning aids to help students at every level of preparedness comprehend what they read.

Over the years we have remained learners as well as teachers. In each edition of *Making America* we have listened to its readers, both professors and students, and made changes to improve the book. Thus, this sixth edition has eliminated elements that did not prove effective and added features that we believe will help us convey the pleasure and value of understanding the people of the past and their role in making America.

The Approach

Professors and students who have used the previous editions of *Making America* will recognize immediately that we have preserved many of its central features. We have again set the nation's complex story within an explicitly political chronology, relying on a basic and familiar structure that is nevertheless broad enough to accommodate generous attention to social, economic, and diplomatic aspects of our national history. Because our own scholarly research often focuses on the experiences of women, immigrants,

African Americans, and Native Americans, we would not have been content with a framework that marginalized their history. *Making America* continues to be built on the premise that all Americans are historically active figures, playing significant roles in creating the history of our nation's development. We have also continued what is now a tradition in *Making America*, that is, providing pedagogical tools for students that allow them to master complex material and enable them to develop analytical skills.

THEMES

The sixth edition continues to weave five central themes through the narrative. The first of these themes, the political development of the nation, is evident in the text's coverage of the creation and revision of the federal and local governments, the contests waged over domestic and diplomatic policies, the internal and external crises faced by the United States and its political institutions, and the history of political parties and elections.

The second theme is the diversity of a national citizenry created by both Native Americans and immigrants. To do justice to this theme, *Making America* explores not only English and European immigration during the early settling of the country but the full array of groups immigrating to the North American continent from Paleolithic times to the present. The text attends to the tensions and conflicts that arise in a diverse population, but it also examines the shared values and aspirations that define middle-class American lives.

Making America's third theme is the significance of regional subcultures and economies. This regional theme is developed for society before European colonization and for the colonial settlements of the seventeenth and eighteenth centuries. It is evident in our attention to the striking social and cultural divergences that existed between the American Southwest and the Atlantic coastal regions and between the antebellum South and North, as well as significant differences in social and economic patterns in the West.

A fourth theme is the rise and impact of large social movements, from the Great Awakening in the 1740s to the rise of youth cultures in the post–World War II generations, movements prompted by changing material conditions or by new ideas challenging the status quo.

The fifth theme is the relationship of the United States to other nations. In *Making America* we explore in depth the causes and consequences of this nation's role in world conflict and diplomacy, whether in the era of colonization of the Americas, the eighteenth-century independence movement, the removal of Indian nations from their traditional lands, the impact of the rhetoric of manifest destiny, American policies of isolationism and interventionism, or the modern role of the United States as a dominant player in world affairs. Viewing American history in a global context, we point out the parallels and the contrasts between our society and those of other nations.

LEARNING FEATURES

The chapters in *Making America* provide students with essential study aids. The first page of each chapter begins with a topical **outline** of the material students will encounter in the chapter.

Each chapter concludes with **"Study Tools,"** which include a summary that reinforces the most important themes and information covered in the chapter; a chronology that lists key events discussed in the chapter; focus questions that cover each section; and finally, a list of key study terms. These tools can help students gain a firmer understanding of the material they have just read.

Within each chapter students will encounter several distinctive features that will help them get the most out of their reading. First, *Making America* provides a unique on-page glossary that defines basic vocabulary—words that might trip up some students. The glossary defines words such as "allegory," "impeach," and "dividend" and each word's historical context to assure that students understand the full meaning of a discussion. The second type of term highlighted on the page includes major historical events, people, phrases, and documents. These historical key terms are included in the "Study Tools" section as a list for review. We believe that this approach will help students simultaneously build their vocabularies and review for tests; it reflects our concern about communicating fully with student readers without sacrificing the complexity of the history we are relating.

The sixth edition also retains the popular feature "**It Matters Today**" in most of the chapters, which points out critical connections between current events and past ones. This feature includes discussion and reflection questions that challenge students to examine and evaluate these connections. We hope that these brief essays will also provide a spark for faculty and students to generate their own additional "It Matters Today" discussions on other key issues within the chapter.

Finally, the illustrations in each chapter were chosen carefully to provide a visual connection to the past that is useful rather than simply decorative. The captions that accompany these illustrations analyze the subject of the painting, photograph, or artifact—and relate it to the narrative. For this edition we have selected many new illustrations to reinforce or illustrate the themes of the narrative.

NEW TO THIS EDITION

In this new edition we have preserved what our colleagues and their students considered the best and most useful aspects of *Making America*, including the strong narrative voice, the respect for chronology, and focus questions. We have replaced what was less successful, revised what could be improved, and added new elements to strengthen the book.

Our most significant new feature is the end-of-chapter "Study Tools," which, as described above, provides students with the tools they will need to review what they have learned and to formulate their own analysis of its significance.

We have made important changes in the text itself. Many of these changes are based on reviewer feedback, and all of them reflect our commitment to incorporating the newest scholarship and to producing a coherent narrative, rather than an oversimplified one. Perhaps the most significant change to this edition was made as part of our ongoing effort to pace the content in a way that reflects current teaching needs. The four chapters covering the period from 1865 to 1900 have been reduced to three chapters. Details about how this was accomplished—and other chapter revisions—are as follows:

Chapter 2
- An added discussion reflects new scholarship on the Protestant role in establishing New France.

Chapter 3
- Coverage of the Jamestown settlement has been revised and updated.

Chapter 4
- Added discussion of support among a minority in British politics for the colonists' position on government policies.

Chapter 7
- Streamlined and tightened throughout.

Chapter 8
- New "It Matters Today" feature on the peaceful transition of power.
- New coverage of Gabriel's rebellion.
- Addition on Jefferson's attitude toward women.

Chapter 9
- New coverage of Denmark Vesey's conspiracy.

Chapter 10
- Discussion of Jackson's administration reorganized.

Chapter 12
- The section on the Mexican War has been moved to Chapter 13.

Chapter 13
- Coverage of the Mexican War has been moved into this chapter.
- Added explanation of the beginning of the Free Soil Party and the outcome of the 1848 election.
- Discussion of the Know-Nothings has been revised and tightened.

Chapters 16–18 combine and consolidate material covered in Chapters 16–19 of the fifth edition, reducing four chapters to three. In addition, the following revisions have been made:

Chapter 16 The Nation Industrializes, 1865–1900
- Chapter 16 now focuses largely on the emergence of an industrial economy, including the role of specific entrepreneurs, the rise of big business, and the roles of technology and finance.
- Discussion of the economic transformation of the West (previously in a separate chapter) is now integrated into a chapter that addresses the whole national economy.
- Similarly, additional coverage of the South emphasizes economic developments, including advocacy of a New South.

Chapter 17 Life in the Gilded Age, 1865–1900
- Chapter 17 now focuses largely on new social and cultural patterns, especially urbanization, immigration, ethnic and racial relations, and changing gender roles.
- A new section has been added on changing social patterns in the New South.

Chapter 18 Politics and Foreign Relations in a Rapidly Changing Nation, 1865–1902
- This chapter now focuses centrally on domestic politics and foreign relations, including the dominant role of political parties in the 1870s and 1880s, various radical and reform groups, Populism, and short-term and long-term results of the election of 1896.

Chapter 19 (formerly 20)
- New coverage added on Southern Progressivism.

Chapter 20 (formerly 21)
- Analysis of Wilson's decision to go to war has been revised.
- New data regarding civilian deaths in World War I.

Chapter 22 (formerly 23)
- This chapter has been significantly expanded and revised throughout.
- Text revisions include new statistics on 1929 suicide rates and the effect of the Crash on the Dow Jones average; expanded discussion of the role of installment buying; tightened and clarified discussion of banks and credit; expanded attention to the U.S. Communist Party; new analysis of the First Hundred Days; expanded coverage of labor action in 1934; expanded coverage of the Second Hundred Days; more on cultural expression during this period.
- New "It Matters Today" feature discusses lessons applied in 2008–2009 to avoid another depression.

Chapter 23 (formerly 24)
- Provides new information on U.S. economic and security preparations as the Roosevelt administration responded to the conflicts in Europe and Asia.
- Provides new discussion and examples of women's role in the wartime economy.

Chapter 24 (formerly 25)
- Material on Latino postwar experiences has been expanded.
- Material on the origins of the Cold War has been revised and incorporates Kennan's "Long Telegram" as part of the text; an excerpt of Novikov's long telegram remains as an insert to provide a Soviet perspective.

Chapter 25 (formerly 26)
- Provides expanded information on the economic changes and concerns of the 1950s, including the movement toward conglomerates.

Chapter 26 (formerly 27)
- Provides a new discussion of student activism involved in the Students for a Democratic Society and in the Free Speech movements.

Chapter 27 (formerly 28)
- Sections on Nixon's domestic programs and Watergate are revised and expanded.
- Discussion of environmental issues includes material on Rachel Carson and a new "It Matters Today" feature focuses on DDT.

Chapter 28 (formerly 29)
- The chapter has been reorganized and includes a new section, "New Economic and Political Alignments, 1976–1992."

- Expanded coverage of the Americans with Disabilities Act.
- A new "It Matters Today" explores the topic of migrant workers.

Chapter 29 (formerly 30)
- New chapter title, "Entering a New Century, 1992–2010," reflects revised and updated coverage and focus.
- Revised coverage of the Clinton administration includes the Clinton/Mitchell role in the Northern Ireland peace process.
- The "It Matters Today" feature on Islamic fundamentalism is now in this chapter.
- Updated through Obama's first year and a half in office, including material on the Great Recession and the recovery plans offered by Bush and Obama, the struggle over the passage of a national healthcare plan, the Tea Party movement, and the Gulf disaster.

We, the authors of *Making America,* believe that this new edition will be effective in the history classroom. Please let us know what you think.

Learning and Teaching Ancillaries

The program for this edition of *Making America* includes a number of useful learning and teaching aids. These ancillaries are designed to help students get the most from the course and to provide instructors with useful course management and presentation tools.

Kelly Woestman has been involved with *Making America* through previous editions and has taken an even more substantive role in the sixth edition. We suspect that no other technology author has been so well integrated into the author team as Kelly has been with our team, and we are certain that this will add significantly to the value of these resources.

Instructor Resources

Instructor Companion Site Instructors will find here all the tools they need to teach a rich and successful U.S. history survey course. The protected teaching materials include the Instructor's Resource Manual, customizable Microsoft® PowerPoint® slides of both lecture outlines and images from the text, and JoinIn® PowerPoint® slides with clicker content. The companion website also provides instructors with access to HistoryFinder and to the Wadsworth American History Resource Center (see descriptions below). Go to www.cengagebrain.com to access this site.

PowerLecture DVD with ExamView® and JoinIn® This dual-platform, all-in-one multimedia resource includes the Instructor's Resource Manual, Test Bank in Word and PDF formats, customizable Microsoft® PowerPoint® slides of both lecture outlines and images from the text, and *JoinIn®* PowerPoint® slides with clicker content. Also included is ExamView, an easy-to-use assessment and tutorial system that allows instructors to create, deliver, and customize tests in minutes.

HistoryFinder This searchable online database allows instructors to quickly and easily search and download selections from among thousands of assets, including art, photographs, maps, primary sources, and audio/video clips. Each asset downloads directly into a Microsoft® PowerPoint® slide, allowing instructors to easily create exciting PowerPoint presentations for their classrooms.

eInstructor's Resource Manual Prepared by Kelly Woestman of Pittsburg State University, this manual includes instructional objectives, chapter outlines and summaries, lecture suggestions, suggested debate and research topics, cooperative learning activities, and suggested readings and resources. Available on the instructor's companion website and from the PowerLecture DVD.

WebTutor™ on Blackboard® and WebCT® With WebTutor's text-specific, preformatted content and total flexibility, instructors can easily create and manage their own custom course website. WebTutor's course management tool gives instructors the ability to provide virtual office hours, post syllabi, set up threaded discussions, track student progress with the quizzing material, and much more. For students, WebTutor offers real-time access to a full array of study tools, including audio chapter summaries, practice quizzes, glossary flashcards, and weblinks.

CourseMate Cengage Learning's CourseMate brings course concepts to life with interactive learning, study, and exam preparation tools that support the printed textbook. Watch student comprehension soar as your class works with the printed textbook and the *Making America* CourseMate site with interactive teaching and learning tools and EngagementTracker, a first-of-its-kind tool that monitors student engagement in the course. Learn more at www.cengagebrain.com.

STUDENT RESOURCES

CourseMate For students, the *Making America* CourseMate website provides an additional source of interactive learning, study, and exam preparation outside the classroom. Students will find outlines and objectives, focus questions, flashcards, quizzes, primary source links, and video clips. The CourseMate site also includes an integrated *Making America* eBook. Students taking quizzes will be linked directly to relevant sections in the ebook for additional information. The ebook is fully searchable and students can even take notes and save them for later review. In addition, the ebook links to rich media assets such as video and MP3 chapter summaries, primary source documents with critical thinking questions, and interactive (zoomable) maps. Students can use the ebook as their primary text or as a companion multimedia support. Available at www.cengagebrain.com.

Wadsworth American History Resource Center This gives your students access to a "virtual reader" with hundreds of primary sources, including speeches, letters, legal documents and transcripts, poems, maps, simulations, timelines, and additional images that bring history to life, along with interactive assignable exercises. A map feature including Google Earth™ coordinates and exercises will aid in student comprehension of geography and use of maps. Students can compare the traditional textbook map with an aerial view of the location today. It's an ideal resource for study, review, and research. In addition to this map feature, the resource center also provides blank maps for student review and testing. Ask your sales representative for more information on how to bundle access to the HRC with your text.

cengagebrain.com Save your students time and money. Direct them to www. cengagebrain.com for choice in formats and savings and a better chance to succeed in class. Students have the freedom to purchase à la carte exactly what they need when they need it. There, students can purchase a downloadable ebook or electronic access to the American History Resource Center, the premium study tools and interactive ebook in the *Making America* CourseMate, or eAudio modules from *The History Handbook* (see below). Students can save 50 percent on the electronic textbook and can pay as little as $1.99 for an individual eChapter.

The History Handbook, 2e Written by Carol Berkin of Baruch College, City University of New York, and Betty Anderson of Boston University, this book teaches students both basic and history-specific study skills such as how to take notes, get the most out of lectures and readings, read primary sources, research historical topics, and correctly cite sources. Substantially less expensive than comparable skill-building texts, *The History Handbook* also offers tips for Internet research and evaluating online sources. Additionally, students can purchase and download the **eAudio** version of *The History Handbook* or any of its eighteen individual units at www.cengagebrain.com to listen to on-the-go.

Doing History: Research and Writing in the Digital Age, 1e Prepared by Michael J. Galgano, J. Chris Arndt, and Raymond M. Hyser of James Madison University. Whether you're starting down the path as a history major, or simply looking for a straightforward and systematic guide to writing a successful paper, you'll find this text to be an indispensable handbook to historical research. This text's "soup to nuts" approach to researching and writing about history addresses every step of the process, from locating your sources and gathering information, to writing clearly and making proper use of various citation styles to avoid plagiarism. You'll also learn how to make the most of every tool available to you—especially the technology that helps you conduct the process efficiently and effectively.

Reader Program Cengage Learning publishes a number of readers, some containing exclusively primary sources, others a combination of primary and secondary sources, and many designed to guide students through the process of historical inquiry. Visit www.cengage.com/history for a complete list of readers or ask your sales representative to recommend a reader that would work well for your specific needs.

CUSTOM OPTIONS

Nobody knows your students like you, so why not give them a text that is tailor-fit to their needs? Cengage Learning offers custom solutions for your course—whether it's making a small modification to *Making America* to match your syllabus or combining multiple sources to create something truly unique. You can pick and choose chapters, include your own material, and add additional map exercises along with the Rand McNally Atlas (including questions developed around the maps in the atlas) to create a text that fits the way you teach. Ensure that your students get the most out of their textbook dollar by giving them exactly what they need. Contact your Cengage Learning representative to explore custom solutions for your course.

CourseReader Our new CourseReader lets you create a customized electronic reader in minutes! With our easy-to-use interface and assessment tool, you can choose exactly what your students will be assigned—simply search or browse Cengage Learning's extensive document database to preview and select your customized collection of readings.

Once you've made your choice, students will always receive the pedagogical support they need to succeed with the materials you've chosen: each source document includes a descriptive headnote that puts the reading into context, and every selection is further supported by both critical thinking and multiple-choice questions designed to reinforce key points.

Rand McNally Atlas of American History, 2e This comprehensive atlas features more than eighty maps, with new content covering global perspectives, including events in the Middle East from 1945 to 2005, as well as population trends in the United States and around the world. Additional maps document voyages of discovery; the settling of the colonies; major U.S. military engagements, including the American Revolution and World Wars I and II; and sources of immigrations, ethnic populations, and patterns of economic change.

ACKNOWLEDGMENTS

The authors of *Making America* have benefited greatly from the critical reading of this edition of the book by instructors from across the country. We would like to thank these scholars and teachers who provided feedback for this current revision:

Tom Angle, *Metropolitan Community College*
Anthony Beninati, *Valencia Community College*
Martha Bonte, *Clinton Community College, Eastern Iowa Community College District*
Scott Buchanan, *South Plains College*
Thomas Clarkin, *San Antonio College*
Robert Cray, *Montclair State University*
Latangela Crossfield, *Paine College*
Jeffrey Davis, *Bloomsburg University of Pennsylvania*
Julian DelGaudio, *Long Beach City College*
Gretchen Eick, *Friends University*
Jennifer Fry, *King's College*
Michael Gabriel, *Kutztown University*
Leah Hagedorn, *Tidewater Community College*
Stephen Katz, *Community College of Philadelphia*
Kurt Kortenhof, *Saint Paul College*
Mark Kuss, *Our Lady of Holy Cross College*
Margaret Lowe, *Bridgewater State College*
Mark McCarthy, *Southern New Hampshire University Online*
Suzanne McCormack, *Community College of Rhode Island*
Todd Menzing, *Saddleback College*
Rebecca Montgomery, *Texas State University*
Bryant Morrison, *South Texas College*

David Parker, *California State University–Northridge*
Laura Perry, *The University of Memphis*
Steven Rauch, *Augusta State University*
Kathryn Rokitski, *Old Dominion University*
James Seaman, *Saddleback College*
Carey Shellman, *Armstrong Atlantic State University*

Carol Berkin, who is responsible for Chapters 3 through 7, wants to acknowledge the colleagues and students who suggested interesting new primary sources for her chapters. She also thanks the many teachers across the country whom she met as she participated in Teaching American History grant programs for their excellent ideas about what makes a textbook useful in the classroom. She offers special thanks to Margaret Crocco and Barbara Winslow, her co-editors on a new book on teaching women's history, for the long conversations about how to make history exciting to students of all ages. As always, she thanks her children, Hannah and Matthew, for their support as she revised this book.

Christopher L. Miller, who is responsible for Chapters 1 and 2 and 8 through 14, is indebted to the community at the University of Texas—Pan American for providing the constant inspiration to innovate. Colleagues, including David Carlson, Amy M. Hay, and Kristine Wirts, were particularly helpful. Colleagues on various H-Net discussion lists as always were generous with advice, guidance, and often abstruse points of information. As in each of our collaborative projects, thanks are owed to Carol Berkin, Bob Cherny, and Jim Gormly and to Kelly Woestman.

Robert W. Cherny, who is responsible for Chapters 15 through 22, wishes to thank his students who, over the years, have provided the testing ground for much that is included in these chapters, and especially to thank his colleagues and research assistants who have helped with the previous editions and Sarah Alexander, his research assistant for this edition. Much of the revision was done while in residence as a Fulbright Scholar at the Heidelberg Center for American Studies, University of Heidelberg, and thanks are due to the faculty and staff there, especially Mischa Honeck. The staff of the Leonard Library at San Francisco State has always been most helpful. Rebecca Marshall Cherny, Sarah Cherny, and Lena Hobbs Kracht Cherny have been unfailing in their encouragement, inspiration, and support.

James L. Gormly, who is responsible for Chapters 23 through 30, would like to acknowledge the support and encouragement he received from Washington and Jefferson College. He wants to give a special thanks to Sharon Gormly, whose support, ideas, advice, and critical eye have helped to shape and refine his chapters.

As always, this book is a collaborative effort between authors and the editorial staff of Wadsworth, Cengage Learning. We would like to thank Ann West, senior sponsoring editor; Megan Chrisman, assistant editor; Carol Newman, senior content project manager; Bruce Carson, who helped us fill this edition with remarkable illustrations, portraits, and photographs; and Charlotte Miller, who helped us improve the maps in the book. Finally, but far from least, we thank Jan Fitter, our always patient and tactful text editor, who made our prose clearer and more concise in every chapter. These talented, committed members of the publishing world encouraged us and generously assisted us every step of the way.

A Note for the Students

YOUR GUIDE TO *MAKING AMERICA*

Dear Student:

History is about people—brilliant and insane, brave and treacherous, lovable and hateful, murderers and princesses, daredevils and visionaries, rule breakers and rule makers. It has exciting events, major crises, turning points, battles, and scientific breakthroughs. We, the authors of *Making America*, believe that knowing about the past is critical for anyone who hopes to understand the present and chart the future. In this book, we want to tell you the story of America from its earliest settlement to the present and to tell it in a language and format that helps you enjoy learning that history.

This book is organized and designed to help you master your American History course. The narrative is chronological, telling the story as it happened, decade by decade or era by era. We have developed special tools to help you learn. In the following pages, we'll introduce you to the unique features of this book that will not only help you understand the complex and fascinating story of American history but also provide you the tools to "do" history yourself.

At the back of the book, you will find some additional resources. In the Appendix you will find reprinted two of the most important documents in American history: the Declaration of Independence and the Constitution. Finally, you will see the index, which will help you locate a subject quickly if you want to read about it.

In addition, you will find a number of useful study tools on the *Making America* Coursemate website. These include map and chronology exercises, chapter quizzes, and primary sources—all geared to help you study, do research, and take tests effectively. Here, now, is some additional advice on how to approach your learning experience.

HOW TO SUCCEED IN YOUR HISTORY COURSE

We know that, at first glance, a history textbook can seem overwhelming. There is so much to learn, so much to remember, so much to think about. The features of *Making America* are all designed to help you conquer your anxiety and enjoy your journey through the American past. Here are a few tips to make this a smoother trip:

- Follow all the clues the authors provide. How many of the key topics in the chapter outline are familiar to you—and which ones are new? Don't just pay attention to the unfamiliar material; read carefully how the authors describe those events you have encountered before. Surprises may be in store.
- Don't skip over unfamiliar words in the text. Use the glossary to help you understand the reading—and to increase your vocabulary. That vocabulary will come in handy if you are asked to write an exam essay.

- Use the study tools feature to test your own strengths and weaknesses as you prepare for an exam. Would your own summary of the chapter be similar to the summary the authors provide? Can you remember the context for the events that appear in the chapter chronology? Can you answer the focus questions now that you have read and taken notes on the chapter? Would you be able to identify and explain the significance of the key terms if your professor required you to do so? If not, page numbers will help you review and strengthen your command of the material.

Making America offers you a wealth of primary sources on its website, and your professor is likely to distribute some in the class. Practice analyzing some primary sources, asking questions such as: Who was the person who created this source? Under what circumstances was it created? What prompted this person to write this document or to paint this portrait or to build this house or make this piece of clothing or this tool or weapon? Was the author a reliable witness or was he or she a participant in the event being described? Does this source agree with or contradict other sources you have found? Does it challenge the interpretations you have read in history books?

This type of analysis is not only useful for success in a history class. It will also benefit you as you read the newspaper, watch today's news on the Web or TV, or listen to the critical arguments of your own day. It will help you form your own independent judgments about the world around you.

We hope that our textbook conveys to you our own fascination with the American past and sparks your curiosity about the nation's history. We invite you to share your feedback on the book: you can reach us through Wadsworth Cengage's **Making America CourseMate website**, which you'll find initially at www.cengagebrain.com.

Carol Berkin, Chris Miller,
Bob Cherny, and Jim Gormly

About the Authors

CAROL BERKIN

Born in Mobile, Alabama, Carol Berkin received her undergraduate degree from Barnard College and her Ph.D. from Columbia University. Her dissertation won the Bancroft Award. She is now Presidential Professor of history at Baruch College and the Graduate Center of City University of New York. She has written *Jonathan Sewall: Odyssey of an American Loyalist* (1974); *First Generations: Women in Colonial America* (1996); *A Brilliant Solution: Inventing the American Constitution* (2002); *Revolutionary Mothers: Women in the Struggle for America's Independence* (2005); and *Civil War Wives: The Lives and Times of Angelina Grimke Weld, Varina Howell Davis, and Julia Dent Grant* (2009). She has edited *Women of America: A History* (with Mary Beth Norton, 1979); *Women, War and Revolution* (with Clara M. Lovett, 1980); *Women's Voices, Women's Lives: Documents in Early American History* (with Leslie Horowitz, 1998); *Looking Forward/Looking Back: A Women's Studies Reader* (with Judith Pinch and Carole Appel, 2005); and *Clio in the Classroom: A Guide to Teaching U.S. Women's History* (with Margaret Crocco and Barbara Winslow, 2009). Professor Berkin edits *History Now*, an online journal for teachers sponsored by The Gilder Lehrman Institute of American History. She has appeared in the PBS series *Liberty! The American Revolution; Ben Franklin;* and *Alexander Hamilton;* and The History Channel's *Founding Fathers.* She has served on the Planning Committee for the U.S. Department of Education's National Assessment of Educational Progress, and chaired the CLEP Committee for Educational Testing Service. She currently serves on the Board of Trustees of The Gilder Lehrman Institute of American History and The National Council for History Education and is an elected member of the American Antiquarian Society and The Society of American Historians.

CHRISTOPHER L. MILLER

Born and raised in Portland, Oregon, Christopher L. Miller received his bachelor of science degree from Lewis and Clark College and his Ph.D. from the University of California, Santa Barbara. He is currently associate professor of history at the University of Texas—Pan American. He is the author of *Prophetic Worlds: Indians and Whites on the Columbia Plateau* (1985), which was republished (2003) as part of the Columbia Northwest Classics Series by the University of Washington Press. His articles and reviews have appeared in numerous scholarly journals and anthologies as well as standard reference works. Dr. Miller is also active in contemporary Indian affairs, having served, for example, as a participant in the American Indian Civics Project funded by the Kellogg Foundation. He has been a research fellow at the Charles Warren Center for Studies in American History at Harvard University and was the Nikolay V. Sivachev Distinguished Chair in American History at

Lomonosov Moscow State University (Russia). Professor Miller has also been active in projects designed to improve history teaching, including programs funded by the Meadows Foundation, the U.S. Department of Education, and other agencies.

ROBERT W. CHERNY

Born in Marysville, Kansas, and raised in Beatrice, Nebraska, Robert W. Cherny received his B.A. from the University of Nebraska and his M.A. and Ph.D. from Columbia University. He is professor of history at San Francisco State University. His books include *Competing Visions: A History of California* (with Richard Griswold del Castillo and Gretchen Lemke Santangelo, 2005); *American Politics in the Gilded Age, 1868–1900* (1997); *San Francisco, 1865–1932: Politics, Power, and Urban Development* (with William Issel, 1986); *A Righteous Cause: The Life of William Jennings Bryan* (1985, 1994); and *Populism, Progressivism, and the Transformation of Nebraska Politics, 1885–1915* (1981). He is co-editor of *California Women and Politics from the Gold Rush to the Great Depression* (with Mary Ann Irwin and Ann Marie Wilson, 2011) and of *American Labor and the Cold War: Unions, Politics, and Postwar Political Culture* (with William Issel and Keiran Taylor, 2004). In 2000, he and Ellen Du Bois co-edited a special issue of the *Pacific Historical Review* that surveyed woman suffrage movements in nine locations around the Pacific Rim. Most of his thirty articles in journals and anthologies have dealt with politics and labor in the late nineteenth and early twentieth centuries. He has been an NEH Fellow, Distinguished Fulbright Lecturer at Lomonosov Moscow State University (Russia), Visiting Research Scholar at the University of Melbourne (Australia), and Senior Fulbright Scholar at the Heidelberg Center for American Studies, University of Heidelberg (Germany). He has served as president of H-Net (an association of more than one hundred electronic networks for scholars in the humanities and social sciences), the Society for Historians of the Gilded Age and Progressive Era, and the Southwest Labor Studies Association; as treasurer of the Organization of American Historians; and as a member of the council of the American Historical Association, Pacific Coast Branch.

JAMES L. GORMLY

Born in Riverside, California, James L. Gormly received a B.A. from the University of Arizona and his M.A. and Ph.D. from the University of Connecticut. He is now professor of history and chair of the history department at Washington and Jefferson College. He has written *The Collapse of the Grand Alliance* (1970) and *From Potsdam to the Cold War* (1979). His articles and reviews have appeared in *Diplomatic History, The Journal of American History, The American Historical Review, The Historian, The History Teacher,* and *The Journal of Interdisciplinary History.*

1

MAKING A "NEW" WORLD, TO 1588

CHAPTER OUTLINE

• A World of Change • Exploiting Atlantic Opportunities • The Challenges of Mutual Discovery • Study Tools

---

A WORLD OF CHANGE

Christopher Columbus's accidental encounter with the Western Hemisphere came after nearly a thousand years of increasing restlessness and dramatic change that affected all of the areas surrounding the Atlantic Ocean. After **millennia** of relative isolation, the natural and human environments in America were opened to the flow of people, animals, and goods from the rest of the Atlantic world. During the centuries before 1492, Christian monarchs and church leaders conducted a series of **Crusades** to wrest control of the **Holy Land** from the **Muslims**. As armies of Crusaders pushed their way into the region, they came into contact with many desirable commodities—fine silks, exotic spices, and precious stones and metals. As word spread of the finery Muslims obtained through trade with Africa and Asia, enterprising individuals began looking for ways to profit by supplying such luxuries to European consumers. At the same time, northern European **Vikings** were extending their holdings throughout many parts of Europe and westward all the way to North America. Both Crusaders and Vikings came into contact with equally restless and vibrant societies in Africa and the Western Hemisphere, lending greater impetus to continuing exploration.

American Origins

It might be said that the process of Making America actually began about 2.5 million years ago with the onset of the Great Ice Age. During the height of the Ice Age, great sheets

---

millennia The plural of *millennium*, a period of one thousand years.

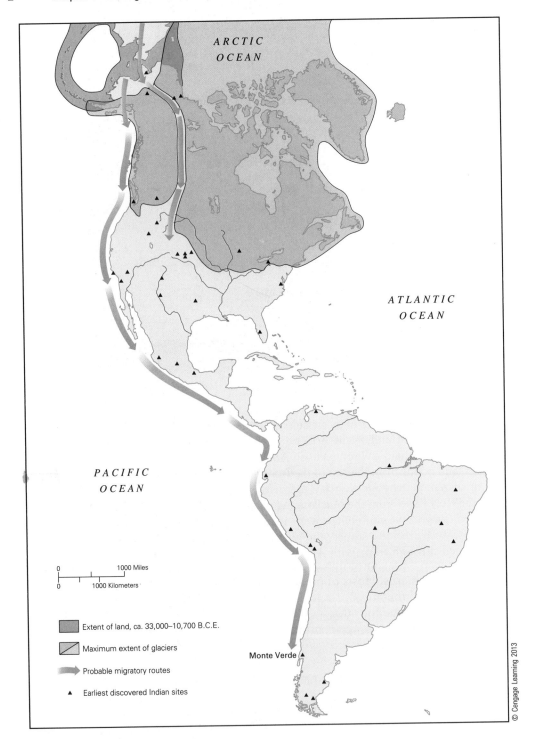

ARCTIC
OCEAN

ATLANTIC
OCEAN

PACIFIC
OCEAN

0   1000 Miles
0   1000 Kilometers

Extent of land, ca. 33,000–10,700 B.C.E.

Maximum extent of glaciers

Probable migratory routes

▲ Earliest discovered Indian sites

Monte Verde

© Cengage Learning 2013

MAP 1.1 The Peopling of the Americas

Scientists postulate two probable routes by which the earliest peoples reached America. By 9500 B.C.E., they had settled throughout the Western Hemisphere.

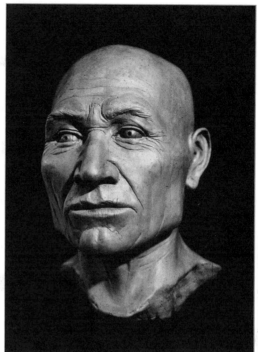

Although some archaeologists and many Native Americans dispute the accuracy of this forensic reconstruction, many experts consider this bust of the Kenniwick Man, based on a skull discovered on the banks of the Columbia River in 1996, to be the best indication of both the deep antiquity and diversity of Native American peoples.

James Chatters and Thomas McClelland

of ice advanced and withdrew across the world's continents. During the last ice advance, the Wisconsin glaciation, a sheet of ice more than 8,000 feet thick covered the northern half of both Europe and North America and so much water was frozen into the glaciers that sea levels dropped as much as 450 feet. Migratory animals found vast regions closed to them by the imposing ice fields and ventured into areas exposed by the receding sea. One such region, Beringia, lay between present-day Siberia on the Asian continent and Alaska in North America. Now covered by the waters of the Bering Sea and Arctic Ocean, Beringia during the Ice Age was a dry, frigid grassland—between 70,000 and 10,000 years ago, it was a perfect grazing ground for animals such as giant bison and huge-tusked woolly mammoths. Hosts of predators, including large wolves and saber-toothed cats, followed them.

What was true for other species may also have been true for humans. Each of the indigenous peoples who continue to occupy this hemisphere has its own account of its origins, some of which involve migration while others do not. Biological evidence suggests that the majority of Native Americans did migrate here and are descended from a common genetic line. Though science paints a clear picture of this process, a great many anomalies exist. Recent archaeological finds and isolated discoveries such as that of the **Kenniwick Man** suggest that many different groups of migrating or truly indigenous people may have coexisted or succeeded each other over this 60,000-year period.

Beginning about 9,000 years ago temperatures warmed, leading to the extinction of the large Ice Age animals. As these staple meat sources disappeared, people everywhere in North America abandoned big-game hunting and began to explore newly emerging local environments for new sources of food, clothing, shelter, and tools. In the forests that grew up to cover the eastern half of the continent, they developed finely polished stone tools, which they used to make functional and beautiful implements out of wood, bone, shell, and other materials. There and along the Pacific shore, people hollowed out massive tree trunks, making boats from which they could harvest food from inland waterways and from the sea. During this time, domesticated dogs were introduced into North America also. With boats for river transportation and dogs to help carry loads on land, Native American people were able to make the best use of their local environments by moving around to different spots during different seasons of the year, following an annual round of movement from camp to camp—perhaps collecting shellfish for several weeks at the mouth of a river, then moving on to where wild strawberries were ripening, and later in the summer relocating to fields in which maturing wild onions or sunflower seeds could be harvested.

Although these ancestors of modern Native Americans believed in and celebrated the animating spirits of the plants and animals that they depended on for survival, they nonetheless engaged in large-scale environmental engineering. They used fire to clear forests of unwanted scrub and to encourage the growth of berries and other plants they found valuable. In this way they produced vegetables for themselves and also provided food for browsing animals such as deer, which increased in number while other species, less useful to people, declined. They also engaged in genetic engineering. A highly significant example comes from north-central Mexico, where, beginning perhaps 7,000 years ago, human intervention helped a wild strain of grass develop bigger seedpods with more nutritious seeds. Such intervention eventually transformed a fairly unproductive plant into an enormously nourishing and prolific food crop: **maize**.

Maize (corn), along with other engineered plants like beans, squash, and chilies, formed the basis for an agricultural revolution in North America, allowing many people to settle in larger villages for longer periods. Successful adaptation—including plant cultivation and eventually agriculture—along with population growth and the constructive use of spare time allowed some Indians in North America to build large, ornate cities. The map of ancient America is dotted with such centers. Beginning about 3,000 years ago, the Ohio and Mississippi Valleys became the home for a number of **mound builder** societies whose cities became trading and ceremonial centers that had enormous economic and social outreach. Large quantities of both practical and purely decorative artifacts from all over North America have been found at these sites. Then, about 800 years ago, midwestern mound builder sites fell into decline, and the people who once had congregated there withdrew to separated villages or bands. No single satisfactory explanation accounts for why this happened.

maize   Corn; the word *maize* comes from an Indian word for this plant.

IT MATTERS TODAY

Native Americans Shape a New World

It may be hard to imagine why understanding the original peopling of North America and how native cultures evolved during the millennia before Columbus could possibly matter to the history of the United States or, more specifically, to how we live our lives today. Without this chapter in our history, there likely would have been no U.S. history at all. Europeans in the fifteenth century lacked the tools, the organization, the discipline, and the economic resources to conquer a true wilderness—such a feat would have been the equivalent of our establishing a successful colony on the moon today. But the environmental and genetic engineering conducted through the millennia of North American history created a hospitable environment into which European crops, animals, and people could easily transplant themselves. And while the descendants of those Europeans may often suppose that they constructed an entirely new world in North America, the fact is that they simply grafted new growth onto ancient rootstock, creating the unique hybrid that is today's America.

- Describe what you think it would take technologically, economically, and politically for the United States to establish a successful permanent colony on the moon. How would the presence of a biologically identical indigenous population change those requirements?
- In what ways are the Indian heritages of America still visible in our society today?

Change and Restlessness in the Atlantic World

During the few centuries following the death of the prophet Mohammed in 632, Muslim Arabs, Turks, and **Moors** made major inroads into western Asia and northern Africa, eventually encroaching on Europe's southern and eastern frontiers. During these same years, Scandinavian Vikings, who controlled the northern frontiers of Europe, began expanding southward and westward. Accomplished and fearless seamen, the Vikings swept down Europe's western shore and through Russia by river to the Mediterranean. They also began colonizing Iceland and Greenland. And, according to Viking sagas, these sailors launched their first expedition to North America in the year 1000. Over the decades that followed, Vikings established several American colonies.

By about the year 1000, then, the heartland of Europe was surrounded by dynamic societies that served as conduits to a much broader world. Although Europeans resented and resisted both Viking and Islamic invasion, the newcomers brought with them tempting new technologies, food items, and expansive knowledge. These contributions not only enriched European culture but also improved the quality of life. For example, new farming methods increased food production so much that Europe began to experience a population explosion. Soon Europeans would begin turning this new knowledge and these new tools against the people who brought them.

Iberians launched a **Reconquista**, an effort to break Islamic rule on the peninsula, and in 1096, European Christians launched the first in a series of Crusades to sweep the Muslims from the Holy Land and elsewhere. With the aid of English Crusaders, Portugal attained independence in 1147. In the Holy Land, hordes of Crusaders captured key points only to be expelled by Muslim counterattacks. The effort to dislodge Islamic forces from Jerusalem and other sacred sites came largely to an end in 1291, but the struggle continued in the Iberian Peninsula. By 1380 Portugal's King John I had united that country's various principalities under his rule. In Spain, unification took much longer, but in 1469 **Ferdinand and Isabella**, heirs to the rival thrones of Aragon and Castile, married and created a united state in Spain. Twenty-three years later, in 1492, the Spanish subdued the last Moorish stronghold on the peninsula, completing the Reconquista.

Dealings with the Vikings in the north took a somewhat different turn. Although they maintained trading contacts with North America for several hundred years, the Vikings began to retreat in the middle of the 1300s. By 1450 or so, they had withdrawn entirely from their transatlantic colonies. The most likely cause of their departure was a shift in climate. Although experts disagree about the exact timing, it appears that at some time between 1350 and 1450 a significant climatic shift called the Little Ice Age began to affect the entire world. In the Arctic and subarctic, temperatures fell, snowfall increased, and sea ice became a major hazard to navigation. This shift made it impossible for the Vikings to practice the herding, farming, and trading that supported their economy in Greenland and elsewhere. Finding themselves cut off from a vibrant North Atlantic empire, Viking settlements in the British Isles, Russia, France, and elsewhere merged with local populations.

Like Native Americans at the same time, these Viking refugees often joined with their neighbors in recognizing the value of large-scale political organization. Consolidation began in France in around 1480, when Louis XI took control of five rival provinces to create a unified kingdom. Five years later in England, Henry Tudor and the House of Lancaster defeated the rival House of York in the Wars of the Roses, ending nearly a hundred years of civil war. Tudor, now styling himself King Henry VII, cemented this victory by marrying into the rival house, wedding Elizabeth of York to finally unify the English throne. As in Spain and Portugal, the formation of unified states in France and England opened the way to new expansive activity that would accelerate the creation of an Atlantic world.

**The Complex
World of Indian
America**

The world into which Vikings first sailed at the beginning of the second millennium and into which other Europeans would intrude half a millennium later was not some static realm stuck in the Stone Age. Native American societies were every bit as progressive, adaptable, and historically dynamic as those that would invade their homes. In fact, adaptive flexibility characterized Indian life throughout North America; the vast variety in environmental conditions that characterized the continent led to the emergence of enormous differences between various Indian groups. **Anthropologists** have tried to make the extremely complicated cultural map of North America understandable by dividing the continent into a series of culture areas—regions where the similarities among native societies were greater than the differences.

In the southeastern region of North America, peoples speaking Siouan, Caddoan, and Muskogean languages formed vibrant agricultural and urban societies with ties to exchange centers farther north as well as to traders from Mexico. At places like Natchez, fortified cities housed gigantic pyramids, and farmland radiating outward provided food for large residential populations. These were true cities and, like their counterparts in Europe and Asia, were magnets attracting ideas, technologies, and religious notions from the entire continent.

Farther north, in the region called the Eastern Woodlands, people lived in smaller villages and combined agriculture with hunting and gathering. The Iroquois, for example, lived in towns numbering three thousand or more people, changing locations only as soil fertility, firewood, and game became exhausted. Each town was made up of a group of **longhouses**, structures often 60 feet or more in length.

A tradition that may go back to the time when the Iroquois lived as nomadic hunters and gatherers dictated that men and women occupy different spheres of existence. The women's world was the world of plants, healing, nurturing, and order. The men's was the world of animals, hunting, and war. By late **pre-Columbian** times, the Iroquois had become strongly agricultural, and because plants were in the women's sphere, women occupied places of high social and economic status in Iroquois society, ruling over domestic politics. Families were matrilineal, meaning that they traced their descent through the mother's line, and matrilocal, meaning that a man left his home to move in with his wife's family upon marriage. Women distributed the rights to cultivate specific fields and controlled the harvest.

Variations on the Iroquois economic and social pattern were typical throughout the Eastern Woodlands and in the neighboring Great Plains and Southwest. Having strong ties with agriculturalists in the east, Plains groups such as the Mandans began settling on bluffs overlooking the many streams that eventually drain into the Missouri River. Living in substantial houses insulated against the cold winters, these people divided their time among hunting, crop raising, and trade. Over a five-hundred-year period, populations increased, and agricultural settlements expanded. By 1300, such villages could be found along every stream ranging southward from North Dakota into present-day Kansas.

In the Southwest, groups with strong ties to Mexico began growing corn as early as 3,200 years ago, but they continued to follow a migratory life until about

anthropologists   Scholars who study human behavior and culture in the past or the present.

longhouses   Communal dwellings, usually built of poles and bark and having a central hallway with family apartments on either side.

pre-Columbian   Existing in the Americas before the arrival of Columbus.

400 C.E., when they began building larger and more substantial houses and limiting their migrations. The greatest change, however, came during the eighth century, when a shift in climate made the region drier and a pattern of late-summer thunderstorms triggered dangerous and erosive flash floods.

There seem to have been two quite different responses to this change in climate. A group called the Anasazi expanded their agricultural ways, cooperating to build flood-control dams and irrigation canals. The need for cooperative labor meant forming larger communities, and between about 900 and 1300 the Anasazi built whole cities of multistory apartment houses along the high cliffs, safe from flooding

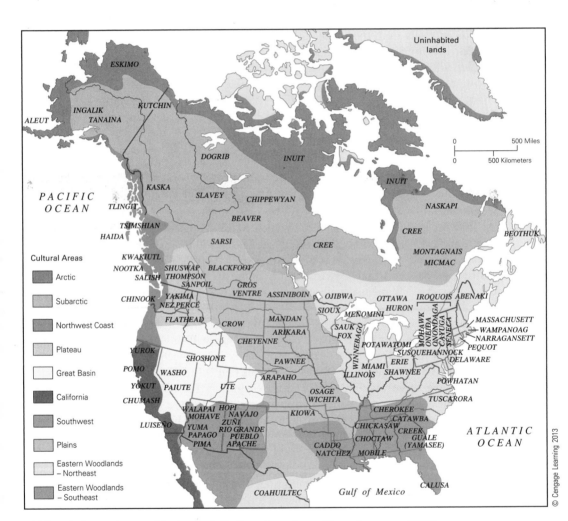

MAP 1.2 Locations of Selected Native American Peoples, A.D. 1500

Today's Indian nations were well established in homelands across the continent when Europeans first arrived. Many would combine with others or move in later centuries, either voluntarily or because they were forced.

but near their irrigated fields. In these densely populated towns Anasazi craft specialists manufactured goods such as pots, textiles, and baskets for the community while farmers tended fields and priests attended to the spiritual needs of the society.

Another contingent of southwestern Indians abandoned the region, moving southward into Mexico. Here they came upon the remnants of classical city-states like Teotihuacán. One of several highly developed societies of central Mexico, Teotihuacán was the largest city-state in the Western Hemisphere, with a population of nearly 200,000. However, by around the year 600, urban Mexican societies were in decline. Over the next several hundred years, migrants from southwestern North America—so-called Chichimecs or "wild tribes"—borrowed architectural and agricultural skills from the fallen societies and built new monumental cities. One of these groups, the **Aztecs,** arrived in the Valley of Mexico soon after 1200, settling on a small island in the middle of a brackish lake. From this unappealing center, a series of strong leaders used a combination of diplomacy and brutal warfare to establish a **tributary empire** that eventually ruled as many as 6 million people.

Other major changes occurred in the Southwest after 1300. During the last quarter of the thirteenth century, a long string of summer droughts and bitterly cold winters forced the Anasazi to abandon their cities. They disappeared as a people, splitting into smaller communities that eventually became the various Pueblo groups. At the same time, an entirely new population entered the region. These hunter-gatherers brought new technologies, including the bow and arrow, into the Southwest. About half of them continued to be hunter-gatherers, while the rest borrowed cultivating and home-building techniques from the Pueblos. Europeans who later entered the area called the hunter-gatherers Apaches and the settled agriculturalists Navajos.

In other regions agriculture was practiced only marginally, if at all. In areas like the Great Basin, desert conditions made agriculture too risky, and in California, the Northwest Coast, and the Intermountain Plateau, the bounty of available wild foods made it unnecessary. In these regions, hunting and gathering remained the chief occupations. For example, the Nez Perces and their neighbors living in the Plateau region occupied permanent village sites in the winter but did not stay together in a single group all year. Rather, they formed task groups—temporary villages that came together to share the labor required to harvest a particular resource—and then went their separate ways when the task was done. These task groups brought together not only people who lived in different winter villages but often people from different tribes and even different language groups. In such groups, political authority passed among those who were best qualified to supervise particular activities. If the task group was hunting, the best and most senior hunters—almost always men—exercised political authority. If the task group was

---

tributary empire An empire in which subjects rule themselves but are required to contribute goods and labor, called tribute, to an imperial government in return for protection and services.

gathering roots, then the best and most senior diggers—almost always women—ruled. Thus among such hunting-gathering people, political organization changed from season to season, and social status depended on what activities were most important to the group at a particular time.

As these examples illustrate, variations in daily life and social arrangements in pre-Columbian North America reflected variations in climate, soil conditions, food supplies, and cultural heritages from place to place across the vast continent. But despite the enormous size of the continent and the amazing variety of cultures spread across it, economic and social connections within and between ecological regions tied the people together in complex ways. For example, varieties of shell found only along the Northwest Pacific Coast were traded to settlements as far away as Florida, having been passed from hand to hand over thousands of miles of social and physical space.

A World of Change in Africa

Like North America, Africa was home to an array of societies that developed in response to varying natural and historical conditions. But unlike contemporary Indian groups, Africans maintained continual if perhaps only sporadic contacts with societies in Europe and Asia.

In ancient times tendrils of trade tied the Mediterranean and **sub-Saharan Africa** together, but over the last five thousand years increasing desertification cut off most of Africa from the fertile areas of the Mediterranean coast. The people living south of the desert were forced to largely reinvent civilization in response to changing conditions. They abandoned the wheat and other grain crops that had predominated in earlier economies, domesticating new staples such as **millet** and native strains of rice. They also abandoned the cattle and horses that had been common in earlier times, adopting sheep and goats, which were better suited to arid environments. Depending on immediate conditions, groups could establish large villages and live on a balance of vegetables, meat, and milk or, if necessary, shift over to a purely nomadic lifestyle following their herds.

Social organization tended to follow a similar adaptive strategy. The most common social structure was based on the belief that large geographically and linguistically related groups were descended from a common **fictive ancestor**. These larger organizations were then subdivided into smaller and smaller groups, each independent—as a modern nuclear family might be—but tied through an elaborate family tree to hundreds or even thousands of other similar groups.

sub-Saharan Africa   The region of Africa south of the Sahara Desert.

millet   A large family of grain grasses that produce nutritious, carbohydrate-rich seeds used for both human and animal feed.

fictive ancestor   A mythical figure believed by a social group to be its founder, from whom all members are biologically descended.

The status of each group was determined by seniority in the line of descent—those descended from the oldest offspring of the common ancestor were socially and politically superior to those descended from younger branches. This fundamental hierarchy created an organizational structure that permitted large-group cooperation and management when appropriate but also permitted each small band to function independently when conditions required. Within each group, seniority also determined political and social status: the eldest descendant of the common ancestor within each group held superior power.

Sometime between two and three thousand years ago, sub-Saharan groups appear to have discovered iron smelting. Inventing a furnace shaped like a long tube that permitted both the high heat and the air draft necessary for melting iron ore, craftsmen were able to make use of abundant raw iron deposits in southern Africa to produce tools, vessels, and weapons. Often, large cities with elaborate social hierarchies grew in neighborhoods where iron and other ores were particularly abundant. These would then become centers for trade as well as political hubs, the seeds from which later kingdoms and empires would sprout.

These trading centers became particularly important when Islamic expansion brought new, outside sources for trade into the sub-Saharan world. The first mention of trade between Islamic adventurers and African communities stems from the eighth century, and it seems to have developed slowly over the next several hundred years. One catalyst of the trade growth was the introduction of the camel as a draft animal. Native to Asia and the Arabian Peninsula, camels were ideally suited for crossing the inhospitable desert, making it possible to establish regular caravan routes that linked sub-Saharan trading centers with the outside world. Increasingly after 1100, iron, gold, precious gems, and slaves were carried

Introducing camels as draft animals made it possible for Arab and other traders to penetrate the forbidding Sahara Desert to open up a highly profitable trade with sub-Saharan states that were rich with gold, ivory, and other valuable commodities. This gold and diamond miniature (the sculpture is only about two-and-a-half inches tall) celebrates the riches that these animals carried out of Africa.

Indian, Mughal period, ca. 1800. Camel: gold enamel, diamond chips, ivory. Gr. H. 2-5/8 in. (6.7 cm). L. 2-3/4 in. (7.0 cm). Diam. 1-3/16 in. (3.0 cm). The Metropolitan Museum of Art, New York, N.Y., U.S.A. Gift of The Shaw Foundation, Inc., 1959 (59.44.1). Photograph © 1996 The Metropolitan Museum of Art/Art Resource, New York across the desert by Arab, Berber, and other Muslim traders, who gave African middlemen silks, spices, and other foreign goods in exchange. This trade tended to enhance the power of African elites, leading to ever larger and more elaborate states.

Exploiting Atlantic Opportunities

Dynamic forces in America, Europe, Africa, and beyond were drawing the disparate societies that occupied the Atlantic shore into a complex world of mutual experience. But this process was not automatic. Enterprising people throughout the globe seized opportunities created by the spirit of restlessness and the merging of historical streams, advancing the process and giving it peculiar shape. Generally seeking profits for themselves and advancement for their own nations, tribes, or classes, those who sought to exploit the emerging new world nonetheless had enormous impact on the lives of all who occupied it. The process of outreach and historical evolution that helped launch the American experience grew directly from these efforts at exploitation.

The Portuguese, Africa, and Plantation Slavery   The first of the European states to pull itself together was also the first to challenge Islamic dominance in both the Asian and African trade. Portugal's John I encouraged exploration by establishing a school of navigation on his kingdom's southwestern shore; the school sent numerous expeditions in search of new sources of wealth. By the 1430s, the Portuguese had discovered and taken control of islands off the western shore of Africa, and within thirty years had pushed their way to Africa itself, opening relations with the Songhai Empire.

The **Songhai Empire** was typical of the sub-Saharan trading states that emerged through Muslim contacts. As was common in the region, the Songhai state consisted of numerous smaller societies, all related through a common ancestor and organized along hierarchical lines. Society remained largely village based, with slaves at the bottom, skilled craftsmen in the middle, and a small noble class at the top. These nobles assembled in Timbuktu, a trading hub and the Songhai capital, which became a cosmopolitan center where African and Islamic influences met. Its art and architecture and the accomplishments of its scholars impressed all who ventured there. From Timbuktu, Songhai traders shipped valuable trade goods across the Sahara by means of caravans. The Portuguese, however, offered speedier shipment and higher profits by carrying trade goods directly to Europe by sea.

By the end of the fifteenth century, Portuguese navigators had gained control over the flow of prized items such as gold, ivory, and spices out of West Africa, and Portuguese colonizers were growing sugar and other crops on the newly conquered Azores and Canary Islands. From the beginning of the sixteenth century onward, the Portuguese also became increasingly involved in slave trafficking, at first to their own plantations and then to Europe itself. By 1550, Portuguese ships were carrying African slaves throughout the world.

The Continued Quest for Asian Trade	Meanwhile, the Portuguese continued to venture outward. In 1487, Bartolomeu Dias became the first European to reach the **Cape of Good Hope** at the southern tip of Africa. Ten

years later Vasco da Gama sailed around the cape and launched the Portuguese exploration of eastern Africa and the Indian Ocean.

By the end of the fifteenth century, England, Spain, and France were vying with Portugal to find the shortest, cheapest, and safest sea route between Europe and Asia. Because of its early head start, Portugal remained fairly cautious in its explorations, hugging the coast around Africa before crossing the ocean to India. As latecomers, Spain and England could not afford to take such a conservative approach to exploration. Voyagers from those countries took advantage of borrowed technologies to expand their horizons. From China, Europeans acquired the magnetic compass, which allowed mariners to determine direction even when out of sight of land. An Arab invention, the astrolabe, allowed seafarers to calculate the positions of heavenly bodies and determine their latitude (their distance north or south of the equator). These inventions, together with improvements in steering mechanisms and hull design, made voyages much less risky.

A number of visionary navigators longed for the opportunity to seek new routes. One, an ambitious sailor from the Italian port city of Genoa, **Christopher Columbus**, approached a number of European governments to support a voyage westward from Europe across the Atlantic to the East Indies, but found no one willing to fund him. Finally, in 1492, Ferdinand and Isabella's defeat of the Moors provided Columbus with an opportunity.

Eager to break into overseas trading, dominated in the east by the Arabs and in the south and west by the Portuguese, Ferdinand and Isabella agreed to equip three ships in exchange for a short, safe route to the Orient. On August 3, 1492, Columbus and some ninety sailors departed on the *Niña, Pinta,* and *Santa Maria* for the uncharted waters of the Atlantic. More than three months later, they finally made landfall. Columbus thought he had arrived at the East Indies, but in fact he had reached the islands we now call the **Bahamas**.

Over the next ten weeks, Columbus explored the mysteries of the Caribbean, making landfalls on the islands now known as Cuba and Hispaniola. He collected spices, coconuts, bits of gold, and some native captives. Columbus then returned to Spain, where he was welcomed with great celebration and rewarded with backing

Cape of Good Hope   A point of land at the southern tip of Africa around which European mariners had to sail to reach the Indian Ocean and trade with Asia.

Bahamas   A group of islands in the Atlantic Ocean east of Florida and Cuba.

for three more voyages. Over the next several years, the Spanish gained a permanent foothold in the region that Columbus had discovered and became aware that the area was a world entirely new to them.

England, like Spain, was jealous of Portugal's trade monopoly, and in 1497 Henry VII commissioned another Italian mariner, Giovanni Caboto, to search for a sea route to India. John Cabot, as the English called him, succeeded in crossing the North Atlantic, arriving in the area that Vikings had colonized nearly five hundred years earlier. Shortly thereafter, another Italian, **Amerigo Vespucci**, sailing under the Spanish flag, sighted the northeastern shore of South America and sailed northward into the Caribbean in search of a passage to the East. Finally, in 1524, Giovanni da Verrazano, sailing for France, explored the Atlantic coast of North America, charting the coastline of what later became the thirteen English mainland colonies.

A New Transatlantic World

At first, European monarchs greeted the discovery of a new world as bad news: they wanted access to the riches of Asia, not contact with some undiscovered place. As knowledge of the New World spread, the primary goal of exploration became finding a route around or through it. Yet even before Verrazano, ambitious adventurers from western Europe began exploring the fertile fishing grounds off the northern shores of North America. By 1506, such voyages became so common that the king of Portugal placed a 10 percent tax on fish imported from North America. But these voyages did more than feed the European imagination and the continent's appetite for seafood. Europeans, even relatively poor fishermen, had many things that the Indians lacked: copper pots, jewelry, woolen blankets, and hundreds of other novelties. For their part, the Indians provided firewood, food, ivory, and furs. Apparently the trade grew quickly. By 1534, when Jacques Cartier made the first official exploration of the Canadian coast for the French government, he was approached by party after party of Indians offering to trade furs for the goods he carried. He could only conclude that many other Europeans had come before him.

The presence of explorers such as Verrazano and Cartier and of unknown numbers of anonymous fishermen and part-time traders had several effects on the native population. The Mi'kmaqs, Hurons, and other northeastern Indian groups approached the invading Europeans in friendship, eager to trade and to learn more about the strangers. In part this response was a sign of natural curiosity, but it also reflected some serious changes taking place in the native world of North America.

As we have noted, the onset of the Little Ice Age had far-reaching effects. The deteriorating climate made it more difficult for Indian villages to depend on their corn crops for food. Forced to rely more on hunting and gathering, they had to expand their territory, and in doing so came into conflict with their neighbors. As warfare became more common, groups increasingly formed alliances for mutual defense—systems like the Powhatan Confederacy, a thirty-village alliance in present-day Virginia. And Indians often found it beneficial to welcome European newcomers into their midst—as trading partners bearing new tools, as allies

Left: "Adoration of the Magi" by Master of Viseu, Museum Nacional de Arte Antiga, Lisbon, Portugal/Scala/White Images/Art Resource, New York; right: "Inferno" anonymous, Portuguese. Giraudon/Art Resource. New York

Europeans had trouble fitting American Indians into their preconceived ideas about the world. Native Americans were sometimes cast as noble savages and other times as devils. The Brazilian Indian shown in these two works illustrates the conflicting views. In one, the feather-clad Indian is shown as a wise magus paying homage to the Christ-child; in the other, an Indian devil wears the same costume while presiding over the tortures of Hell.

in the evolving conflicts with neighboring Indian groups, and as powerful magicians whose **shamans** might provide explanations and remedies for the hard times that had befallen them.

THE CHALLENGES OF MUTUAL DISCOVERY

Europeans approached the New World with certain ideas in mind and defined what they found there in terms that reflected what they already believed. American Indians approached Europeans in the same way. Both of these groups—as well as Africans—were thrown into a new world of understanding that challenged many of

shamans   People who act as a link between the visible material world and an invisible spirit world; a shaman's duties include healing, conducting religious ceremonies, and foretelling the future.

their fundamental assumptions. They also exchanged material goods that affected their physical well-being profoundly.

A Meeting of Minds in America   Most Europeans had a firm sense of how the world was arranged, who occupied it, and how they had come to be where they were. The existence of America—and even more the presence there of American Indians—challenged that secure knowledge. In the first stages of mutual discovery in America, most Europeans were content mentally to reshape what they found in the New World to fit with what they expected to find. Columbus expected to find India and Indians, and he believed that was precisely what he had found. Other Europeans understood that America was a new land and that the Indians were a new people, but they attempted to fit both into the cosmic map outlined in the Bible.

Columbus's initial comments about the American Indians set the tone for many future encounters. "Of anything that they possess, if it be asked of them, they never say no," Columbus wrote; "on the contrary, they invite you to share it and show as much love as if their hearts went with it." Such writings were widely circulated in Europe and led to a perception of the Indians as noble savages, men and women free from the temptations and vanities of modern civilization. On the other hand, Amerigo Vespucci found them far from noble. "They marry as many wives as they please," he explained. "The son cohabits with mother, brother with sister, male cousin with female, and any man with the first woman he meets.... Beyond the fact that they have no church, no religion and are not **idolaters**, what more can I say?"

In some ways, Europeans may have been easier for American Indians to understand than the existence of American Indians was for Europeans. To Indians, the world was alive, animated by a spiritual force that was both universal and intelligent. This force took on many forms. Some of these forms were visible in the everyday world of experience, some were visible only at special times, and some were never visible. Social ties based on fictive kinship and **reciprocal trade** linked all creatures—human and nonhuman—together into a common cosmos. These connections were chronicled in myth, maintained through ritual, and graphically recorded in forms like the Powhatan Mantle. Their formation and continuity often involved the exchange of ceremonial items believed to have spiritual value. In the pre-Columbian trading world, such prized goods passed from society to society, establishing a spiritual bond between the initial givers and the eventual receivers, even though the two groups might never meet.

Europeans and European goods slipped easily into this ceremonial trading system. The trade items that the Europeans generally offered to American Indians on first contact—glass beads, mirrors, brass bells—resembled closely the items that the

---

idolater   A person who worships symbols or objects, idol worship, a practice forbidden in the Judeo-Christian and Muslim traditions.

Indians traditionally used to establish friendly spiritual and economic relations with strangers. The perceived similarity of the trade goods offered by the Europeans led Indians to accept the newcomers as simply another new group in the complex social cosmos uniting the spiritual and material worlds.

On the other hand, Europeans perceived such items as worthless trinkets, valuing instead Indian furs and Indian land. This difference in perception became a major source of misunderstanding and conflict. To the Indians, neither the furs nor the land was of much value because by their understanding they did not "own" either. According to their beliefs, all things had innate spirits and belonged to themselves. Thus passing animal pelts along to Europeans was simply extending the social connection that had brought the furs into Indian hands in the first place. Similarly, according to Indian belief, land was seen as a living being—a mother—who feeds, clothes, and houses people as long as she receives proper respect. The idea of buying or selling land was therefore unthinkable. When Europeans offered spiritually significant objects in exchange for land on which to build, farm, or hunt, Indians perceived the offer as an effort to join an already existing relationship, and not as a contract transferring ownership.

The Columbian Exchange   Even though Europeans and American Indians saw some similarities in each other, their worlds differed greatly, sometimes in ways hidden to both groups. The natural environments of these worlds were different, and the passage of people, plants, and animals among Europe, Africa, and North America wrought profound changes in all three continents. Historians call this process the **Columbian Exchange.**

Perhaps the most tragic trade among the three continents came about as the direct and unavoidable consequence of human contact. During the period leading up to the age of exploration, many Europeans lost their lives to epidemic diseases. The Black Death of the fourteenth century, for example, wiped out over a third of Europe's population. Exposure to smallpox, measles, typhus, and other serious diseases had often had devastating results, but Europeans gradually developed resistance to infection. In contrast, the Indian peoples whom Columbus and other European explorers encountered lived in an environment in which contagious diseases were never a serious threat until the Europeans arrived. They had no **acquired immunity** to the various bacteria and viruses that Europeans carried. As a result, the new diseases spread very rapidly and were much more deadly among the native peoples than they were among Europeans.

Controversy rages over the number of Indians killed by imported European diseases. Estimates of how many people lived in America north of Mexico in 1492 run from a high of 25 million to a low of 1 million. At the moment, most scholars accept a range of from 3 to 10 million. Even if the most conservative estimate is correct, the raw numbers of people who died of imported diseases were enormous. Between 90 and 95 percent of the native population appears to have died of disease during the first century of contact. Although the percentage was probably lower in areas where contact was infrequent and where native populations were sparse, disease took a terrible toll as it followed the lines of kinship and trade that held native North America together.

Disease, however, did not flow in only one direction. Some diseases that originated in Africa found their way to both North America and Europe. At least one, syphilis, may have originated in the Western Hemisphere and migrated eastward. Less immediate but perhaps equally extreme ecological effects arose from the passage of plants among Europe, North America, and Africa. The introduction of plants into the New World extended a process that had been taking place for centuries in the Old World. Trade with Asia had carried exotic plants such as bananas, sugarcane, and rice into Africa as early as 2,300 years ago. From Africa, these plants were imported to Iberian-claimed islands such as the Canaries and eventually to America, where, along with cotton, indigo, coffee, and other imports, they would become cash crops on European-controlled plantations. Grains such as wheat, barley, and millet were readily transplanted to some areas in North America, as were grazing grasses and various vegetables, including turnips, spinach, and cabbage.

North American plants also traveled from west to east in the Columbian Exchange. Leading the way in economic importance was tobacco, a stimulant used widely in North America for ceremonial purposes and broadly adopted by Europeans and Africans as a recreational drug. In addition, New World vegetables helped to revolutionize world food supplies. Remarkably easy to grow, maize thrived virtually everywhere. In addition, the white potato, tomato, manioc, squash, and beans native to the Western Hemisphere were soon cultivated throughout the world. Animals also moved in the Columbian Exchange. Europeans brought horses, pigs, cattle, oxen, sheep, goats, and domesticated fowl to America, where their numbers soared.

The transplanting of European grain crops and domesticated animals reshaped the American landscape. Changing the contours of the land by clearing trees and undergrowth and by plowing and fencing altered the flow of water, the distribution of seeds, the nesting of birds, and the movement of native animals. Gradually, imported livestock pushed aside native species, and imported plants choked out indigenous ones.

Probably the most important and far-reaching environmental impact of the Columbian Exchange was its overall influence on human populations. Although exchanged diseases killed many millions of Indians and lesser numbers of Africans and Europeans, the transplantation of North American plants significantly expanded food production in what had been marginal areas of Europe and Africa. At the same time, the environmental changes that Europeans wrought along the

---

syphilis   An infectious disease usually transmitted through sexual contact; if untreated, it can lead to paralysis and death.

cash crops   A crop raised in large quantities for sale rather than for local or home consumption.

manioc   Also called cassava and tapioca, a root vegetable native to South America that became a staple food source throughout the tropical world after 1500.

Atlantic shore of North America permitted the region to support many more people than it had sustained under Indian cultivation. The overall result in Europe and Africa was a population explosion that eventually spilled over to repopulate a devastated North America.

New Worlds in Africa and America As the Columbian Exchange redistributed plants, animals, and populations among Europe, Africa, and North America, it permanently altered the history of both hemispheres. In North America, for example, the combination of disease, environmental transformation, and immigrant population pressure changed American Indian life and culture in profound ways.

Clearly, imported disease had the most ruinous influence on the lives of Indians. Cooperative labor was required for hunting and gathering, and native groups faced extinction if disease caused a shortage of labor. Also, most societies in North America were **nonliterate** and wholesale death by disease wiped out the elders and storytellers who preserved practical, religious, and cultural knowledge, resulting in confusion and disorientation among survivors. In an effort to avert extinction, remnant groups banded together to share labor and lore. Members of formerly self-sustaining kinship groups joined together in composite villages or, in some cases, intertribal leagues or confederacies. And the devastation that European diseases wrought eased the way for the deeper penetration of Europeans into North America as Indians sought alliances with the newcomers to gain new tools, new sources of information, and new military partners, pushing Indians into increasingly tangled relationships with Europeans.

The Columbian Exchange also severely disrupted life in Africa. Africa had long been a key supplier of labor in the Old World. Perhaps as many as 4 million slaves were carried across the desert by Muslim traders between 800 and the time the Portuguese redirected the trade in the sixteenth century, which introduced European technology, wealth, and ideas that fostered the development of aggressive centralized states along the **Slave Coast** on the shore of West Africa's Gulf of Guinea. Armed with European firearms, aggressive tribes engaged in large-scale raiding deep into the Niger and Congo river regions. These raiders captured millions of prisoners, whom they herded back to the coast and sold to Portuguese, Spanish, Dutch, and other European traders to supply labor for mines and plantations in the New World.

The most recent estimates suggest that more than 9.5 million enslaved Africans arrived in the New World between 1500 and 1800. And they were only a small portion of the total number of Africans victimized by the system. On average, between 10 and 20 percent of the slaves shipped to the Americas died in transit. Adding in the numbers who were shipped to other locations in the Eastern

---

nonliterate Lacking a system of reading and writing, relying instead on storytelling and mnemonic (memory-assisting) devices such as pictures.

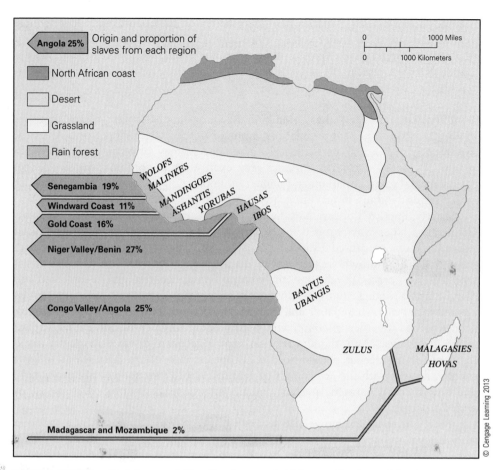

MAP 1.3 Major Origins and Destinations of Africans Enslaved in the Americas

As this schematic map shows, enslaved Africans were drawn from many regions of western Africa (with some coming from the interior of the continent) and were shipped to areas throughout the Americas.

Hemisphere, who were kept in slavery within Africa, and who died during the raids and on the marches to the coast yields a staggering total.

A New World in Europe   The discovery of America and the Columbian Exchange also had staggering repercussions on life in Europe. New economic opportunities and new ideas demanded new kinds of political and economic organization. The discovery of the New World clearly forced a new and more modern society onto Europeans.

Europe's population was already rising when potatoes, maize, and other New World crops began to revolutionize food production. Populations then began to soar despite nearly continuous wars and a flood of migration to the New World. European rulers and their advisers saw that centralized states offered the most promising device for harnessing the riches of the New World while controlling ever-increasing numbers of people at home. The sons and daughters of Europe's first generation of **absolute monarchs** chose to continue the consolidation of authority begun by their parents.

As Europeans responded to social, political, and economic changes, traditional patterns of authority broke down, especially in the realm of religion. A generation of theologians who were dissatisfied with the perceived corruption and superstition they found in the medieval Catholic Church launched the period known as the **Reformation**. Known as **Protestantism**, the doctrines adopted by these reformers launched an ideology that appealed to a broad audience in the rapidly changing European world of the sixteenth century. Ever critical of entrenched authority, the new doctrines attracted lawyers, bureaucrats, merchants, and manufacturers, whose economic and political status was on the rise, thanks to increased prosperity generated by the Columbian Exchange. But many in the ruling classes also found aspects of the new theology attractive. In Germany, the Protestant challenge to Catholic authority led many local princes to question the **divine right** claimed by the ruler of the **Holy Roman Empire**. Similarly, **Henry VIII** of England, at one time a critic of Protestant ideas, found Protestantism convenient when he wanted to resist the authority of the pope and expand English national power.

Henry VIII, the son of Henry VII and Elizabeth of York, was the first undisputed heir to the English throne in several generations, and he was consumed with the desire to avoid renewed civil war. When his wife, Catherine of Aragon, failed to bear a son who might inherit the throne, Henry demanded in 1527 that Pope Clement VII grant him a divorce and permission to marry someone else. Clement refused, and in desperation, Henry launched an English Reformation by seizing the Catholic Church in England, gaining complete control of it by 1535.

For Henry, the idea of unifying religious and civil authority under his personal control was appealing. He needed Protestant support in his war against the pope's authority, so he reluctantly opened the door to Protestant practices in his newly created Church of England.

After Henry's death, his very young son ascended the throne as Edward VI. In the absence of a strong king, Protestants had virtual free rein, and the pace

absolute monarch   The ruler of a kingdom in which every aspect of national life—including politics, religion, the economy, and social affairs—comes under royal authority.

divine right   The idea that monarchs derive their authority to rule directly from God and are accountable only to God.

Holy Roman Empire   A political entity, authorized by the Catholic Church in 1356, unifying central Europe under an emperor elected by four princes and three Catholic archbishops.

of reform quickened. Edward, however, died after ruling for only six years, and Mary, his oldest sister, succeeded him. Married to Philip II of Spain and a devout Roman Catholic, Mary attempted to reverse the reforming trend, cruelly suppressing Protestantism by executing several hundred leading reformers. But her brutality only drove the movement underground and made it more militant. By the time her half-sister Elizabeth, who was born and raised a Protestant, inherited the crown in 1558, the Protestant underground had become powerful and highly motivated. In fact, **Elizabeth I** spent her entire half-century reign trying to reach a workable settlement with Protestant **dissenters** that would permit them free worship without endangering her control over church and state.

STUDY TOOLS

SUMMARY

Making America began many thousands of years ago. Over millennia the continent's residents continually crafted economic strategies, social arrangements, and political systems to preserve and enhance their lives. The result was a rich and flourishing world of different cultures, linked by common religious and economic bonds.

At first, the arrival of Europeans only added another society to an already cosmopolitan sphere. The Vikings came and went, as perhaps did other non-Indians. But ultimately, the dynamic European society that arose after the Crusades became more intrusive. As a result, Native Americans faced challenges that they had never imagined: economic crises, disease, war, and the unfolding environmental changes wrought by the Europeans who followed Columbus.

In addition, influences from the New World reached out to accelerate processes that were already affecting the Old. The flow of wealth and food out of the West was increasing populations, and this growth, with the accompanying rise of powerful kings and unified nations, led to continuing conflict over newfound resources. In Africa, strong coastal states raided weaker neighboring groups, more than doubling the flow of slaves out of Africa. This, in turn, influenced further developments in America. As disease destroyed millions of Indians, newcomers from the entire Atlantic rim poured in to replace them. These newcomers came from very different physical environments and had distinctly foreign ideas about nature. Their novel practices and ideas helped to create a new America on top of the old, rendering drastic changes to the landscape. Continuing interactions among these various newcomers, and between them and the survivors of America's original people, would launch the process of Making America.

---

dissenters   People who do not accept the doctrines of an established or national church.

CHRONOLOGY

THE NEW WORLD

ca. 70,000–8000 B.C.E.	Human migration from Asia into Beringia
ca. 7000 B.C.E.	Plant cultivation begins in North America
ca. 34 C.E.	Death of Jesus of Nazareth and beginning of Christianity
632	Death of Mohammed and beginning of Islamic expansion
ca. 750	Islamic caravans travel to West Africa; African slave trade begins
ca. 500–1000	Rise of Hopewell culture
ca. 800–1700	Rise of Mississippian culture
ca. 1000–1400	Vikings in North America
1096–1291	The Crusades
ca. 1200	Aztecs arrive in the Valley of Mexico
ca. 1400	Beginning of Little Ice Age
1492	Reconquista completed; Columbus's first voyage
1500	Portuguese begin to transport and trade African slaves
1527–1535	Henry VIII initiates English Reformation
ca. 1550	Formation of the Powhatan Confederacy
1558	Elizabeth I becomes queen of England

Note: B.C.E. means "before the common era."

FOCUS QUESTIONS

If you have mastered this chapter, you should be able to answer these questions and identify the terms that follow the questions.

1. How did environmental changes influence the development of various societies in North America during the millennia before the emergence of the Atlantic world?
2. What forces came into play in the centuries before 1500 that would launch Europeans on a program of outward exploration?
3. What factors in sub-Saharan African history helped lead to the development of the slave trade?
4. How did the Atlantic world change as a result of efforts to exploit new discoveries leading up to and following 1492?
5. How did Native Americans and Africans respond initially to European expansion?
6. How did Native Americans and Europeans respond to increasing contact with each other?
7. What global changes occurred through the process called the Columbian Exchange?

KEY TERMS

Crusades (*p.* 1)

Holy Land (*p.* 1)

Muslims (*p.* 1)

Vikings (*p.* 1)

Kenniwick Man (*p.* 3)

mound builder (*p.* 4)

Moors (*p.* 5)

Reconquista (*p.* 6)

Ferdinand and Isabella (*p.* 6)

Aztecs (*p.* 9)

Songhai Empire (*p.* 12)

Christopher Columbus (*p.* 13)

Amerigo Vespucci (*p.* 14)

reciprocal trade (*p.* 16)

Columbian Exchange (*p.* 17)

acquired immunity (*p.* 17)

Slave Coast (*p.* 19)

Reformation (*p.* 21)

Protestantism (*p.* 21)

Henry VIII (*p.* 21)

Elizabeth I (*p.* 22)

2

A CONTINENT ON THE MOVE, 1400–1725

CHAPTER OUTLINE

• The New Europe and the Atlantic World • European Empires in America
• Indians and the European Challenge • Conquest and Accommodation in a
Shared New World • Study Tools

THE NEW EUROPE AND THE ATLANTIC WORLD

Expansion into the New World and the subsequent economic and political pressures of colonization aggravated the crisis of authority in Europe. Eager to enlist political allies against Protestants, popes during this era used land grants in the New World as rewards to faithful monarchs. At the same time, Henry VIII and Elizabeth I, constantly fearful of being outflanked by Catholic adversaries, promoted the development of a powerful English navy and geographical exploration as defensive measures.

Spanish Expansion in America

Spain's entry into Atlantic exploration first sparked a diplomatic crisis between the Spanish and Portuguese. Portugal feared that Spain's intrusion might endanger its hard-won trading enterprises in Africa and the Atlantic islands. Spain, however, claimed the right to explore freely. In 1493, the pope settled the dispute by drawing a line approximately 300 miles west of Portugal's westernmost holdings, declaring that Spanish exploration was to be confined to areas west of the line. A year later, Spain and Portugal updated the agreement in the **Treaty of Tordesillas**, which moved the line an additional 1,000 miles westward. Most of the Western Hemisphere then fell exclusively to Spain, at least in the eyes of Roman Catholics.

Over the next several decades the Spanish monarchs recruited hardened veterans of the Reconquista to lead their New World colonization efforts. **Hernando Cortés**

The differences between European and Native American styles and conceptions of warfare were often striking. This scene, from the Codex Durán, *illustrates a Spanish force besieged by Aztec warriors. Note the contrast in clothing, for example. For most Indian groups, warfare was a highly spiritual affair surrounded by ceremony, often involving colorful and fanciful costumes. The European battle dress, however, bespeaks a very different conception of warfare: practical and deadly.*

was one such figure. In 1519, Cortés landed on the mainland of Mexico with an army of six hundred soldiers. Within three years he and his small force had conquered the mighty Aztec Empire. Crucially, smallpox and other European germs weakened the Aztecs during the two years in which Cortés maintained strained but peaceful relations with them. However, good relations with Indians who were subjects of the Aztec Empire also proved critical to the effort. An Indian woman whom he called Doña Marina served as his translator and cultural adviser, and with her help the **conquistadores** gained military support from numerous tribes of Mexican Indians who resented the Aztecs' power and their continuous demands for tribute.

The Spanish Crown supported many other exploratory ventures designed to bring new regions under Spain's control. In 1513 and again in 1521, Juan Ponce de León led expeditions to Florida. Following up on these voyages, Pánfilo de Narváez embarked on a colonizing mission to Florida in 1527. When his party became stranded, local Indians killed most of its members but took a few captives. One of these captives, Álvar Núñez Cabeza de Vaca, escaped with three others in 1534. The stories they told upon returning to Mexico led the Spanish to send Hernando de Soto to claim the Mississippi River, and he penetrated into the heart of the mound builders' territory in present-day Louisiana and Mississippi. One year later, **Francisco Vásquez de Coronado** left Mexico to look for seven cities that Cabeza de Vaca had heard glittered with gold. Coronado eventually crossed what are now the states of New

conquistadores Spanish soldiers who conquered Indian civilizations in the New World.

Mexico, Arizona, Colorado, Oklahoma, and Kansas. These explorations were but a few of the ambitious adventures undertaken by Spanish conquistadores.

Coronado never found Cabeza de Vaca's "cities of gold," but other Spaniards did locate enormous sources of mineral wealth. Enslaving local Indians for labor, Spanish officials everywhere in the New World quickly moved to rip precious metals both out of the ground and out of what they characterized as "heathen temples." Between 1545 and 1660, Indian and later African slaves extracted over 7 million pounds of silver from Spanish-controlled areas, twice the volume of silver held by all of Europe before 1492. In the process, Spain became the richest nation in Europe, perhaps in the world.

Dreams of an English Eden   Given the stormy political and religious climate that prevailed during the sixteenth century, it is not surprising that Spain's early successes in the New World stirred up conflict with the other emerging states in Europe. To England, France, and other European countries, the massive flow of wealth made Spanish power a growing threat that had to be checked. The continuing religious controversies that accompanied the Reformation worsened the situation. Economic, religious, and political warfare was the rule throughout the century. One of the most celebrated of these early conflicts involved Spain and England.

Tension between Spain and England had been running high ever since Henry VIII had divorced his Spanish wife, Catherine of Aragon. That he quit the Catholic Church to do so and began permitting Protestant reforms in England added to the affront. Firmly wedded to the Catholic Church politically and religiously, Spain was aggressive in denouncing England. For his part, Henry was concerned primarily with domestic issues and steered away from direct confrontations with Spain or any of the other outraged Catholic countries.

Henry did, however, move to bring Ireland firmly under his control through colonization and land confiscation. During the years to come, England's rulers continued a systematic policy of colonization in Ireland. In the process, British authorities instituted a new set of colonial offices and encouraged generations of military adventurers, both of which would shape and advance later ventures in North America.

During the reign of Henry's younger daughter, Elizabeth, the continuing flow of New World wealth into Spain and that nation's anti-Protestant aggression led to an upturn in hostile activity. When Philip II of Spain, Elizabeth's brother-in-law and most vehement critic, sent an army of twenty thousand soldiers to root out Protestantism in the nearby **Netherlands**, the English queen began providing covert aid to the **Dutch** rebels. Elizabeth also struck at Philip's most valuable and vulnerable possession: his New World empire. In 1577, Elizabeth secretly authorized English **privateer**

Netherlands/Holland/Dutch   The first two terms, often used interchangeably, refer to the low-lying area in western Europe on the coast north of France and Belgium; the Dutch are the inhabitants of the Netherlands.

privateer   A ship captain who owned his own boat, hired his own crew, and was authorized by his government to attack and capture enemy ships.

Queen Elizabeth I used her charm and intelligence to turn England into a major world power and restored order to a kingdom shaken by religious and political turmoil following the death of her father, Henry VIII. This pendant from the 1570s not only captures the queen's elegance and austere grace but also was a powerful political statement. Note the intertwining of white and red roses—emblems of the Houses of York and Lancaster, respectively— symbolizing the unified monarchy forged by her grandfather. On the reverse is an image of a phoenix rising from the flames of its nest, symbolizing the renewal of the true monarchy.

and explorer Francis Drake to attack Spanish ships. Drake carried out his task with enthusiasm, seizing tons of gold and silver during a three-year cruise around the world.

Elizabeth was open to virtually any venture that might vex her troublesome brother-in-law. New World colonizing efforts promised to do that and had the potential to enrich the kingdom as well. Although Elizabeth's father had confiscated and redistributed large tracts of church-owned land during his reign, farmland was becoming extremely scarce, and members of both the traditional nobility and the **gentry**—a class that was becoming increasingly important because of its investments in manufacturing and trading ventures—wanted more space for expansion. A relatively small island, England could acquire more territory only by carving it out of the New World.

Thus in 1578, Elizabeth granted Sir Humphrey Gilbert permission to settle two hundred colonists between the St. Lawrence River and the mythical land of Norumbega in what is now Newfoundland. One disaster after another plagued the

gentry   The class of English landowners ranking just below the nobility.

effort, and Gilbert himself died at sea while trying to return to England. Thereafter, Gilbert's half-brother, **Sir Walter Raleigh**, took over the colonizing effort. This time, Elizabeth commanded Raleigh to locate farther south on the border of Spanish Florida, where an English base would facilitate raids on Philip's treasure fleets. Raleigh chose an island off the coast of present-day North Carolina. He advertised **Roanoke Island** as an "American Eden," where "the earth bringeth forth all things in abundance, as in the first Creation, without toile or labour." To honor his benefactor, he decided to call this paradise Virginia, tribute to the unwed, and thus officially virgin, queen.

In 1585 Elizabeth further angered the Spanish king by openly sending an army of six thousand troops to aid the Dutch rebels. In the meantime, Philip was supporting various Catholic plots within England, as well as in Scotland and Ireland, to subvert Elizabeth's authority and bring down the Protestant state. As tensions increased, so did English piracy. In 1586 Drake intensified his campaign, not only raiding Spanish ships at sea but attacking settlements in the Caribbean. By 1586, war between the two powers loomed.

The Decline of Spanish Power   The enormous inflow of wealth from the New World brought Spain power that no European country since the Roman Empire had enjoyed, but such rapid enrichment was a mixed blessing. Starting in Spain and radiating outward, prices began to climb as the growth of the money supply outpaced the growth of European economies. Too much money was chasing too few goods. Between 1550 and 1600, prices doubled in much of Europe, and **inflation** continued to soar for another half-century.

In addition, the social impact of the new wealth was forcing European monarchs to expand geographically and crack down domestically. As prices rose, the traditional landholding classes earned enormous profits from the sale of food and other necessities. Other groups fared less well. Artisans, laborers, and landless peasants—by far the largest class of people in Europe—found the value of their labor constantly shrinking. Throughout Europe, social unrest increased as formerly productive and respected citizens were reduced to poverty and begging. Overseas expansion seemed an inviting solution to the problem of an impoverished population. It was a safety valve that relieved a potentially dangerous source of domestic pressure while opening opportunities for enhancing national wealth through the development of colonies.

Sitting at the center of the new economy, Philip's Spain had the most to lose from rapid inflation and popular unrest. It also had the most to lose from New World expansion by any other European nation. Each New World claim asserted by England, France, or some other country represented the loss of a piece of

Sir Walter Raleigh   English courtier, soldier, and adventurer who attempted to establish the Virginia Colony.

inflation   Rising prices that occur when the supply of currency or credit grows faster than the available supply of goods and services.

treasure that Spain claimed as its own. Philip finally chose to confront building tensions by taking a desperate gamble: he would destroy England. This ploy, he thought, would effectively remove the Protestant threat, rid him of Elizabeth's ongoing harassment, and demonstrate to the rest of Europe that Spain intended to exercise absolute authority over the Atlantic world. In the spring of 1585, when tensions were at their peak, Philip began massing what was to be the largest marine force Europe had ever witnessed.

In 1588 Philip launched 132 warships carrying more than three thousand cannons and an invasion force of thirty thousand men. Arriving off the shores of England in July, the so-called "Invincible **Spanish Armada**" ran up against small, maneuverable British defense ships commanded by Elizabeth's skilled pirate captains. Drake and his fleet harassed the Spanish ships, preventing them from launching a successful attack. Then a storm blowing down from the North Sea scattered the Spanish fleet. Though Spanish power remained great for some time to come, the Armada disaster effectively ended Spain's near-monopoly over New World colonization.

EUROPEAN EMPIRES IN AMERICA

In the seventeenth and eighteenth centuries, Spain, France, England, and a number of other European nations vied for control of the Americas and for domination of the transatlantic trade. For reasons explained in Chapter 3, England was somewhat delayed in its colonizing efforts, and by the time it became deeply involved in New World ventures, Spain, France, and Holland had already made major progress toward establishing empires in America. These European settlements not only affected England's colonization process profoundly, but through their interactions among themselves and with the Native Americans, they also created unique societies in North America whose presence influenced the entire course of the continent's history.

The Troubled Spanish Colonial Empire   Although the destruction of the Armada in 1588 struck a terrible blow at Spain's military power and its New World monopoly, the Spanish Empire continued to grow. By the end of the seventeenth century, it stretched from New Mexico southward through Central America and much of South America into the Caribbean islands and northward again into Florida. Governing such a vast empire was difficult, and periodic efforts to reform the system usually failed. Two agencies in Spain, the House of Trade and the Council of the Indies, set Spanish colonial policy. In the colonies, Crown-appointed viceroys wielded military and political power in each of the four divisions of the empire. The Spanish colonies set up local governments as well; each town had a **cabildo secular**, a municipal council, as well as judges and other minor officials. The colonial administrators were appointed rather than elected, and most were envoys from Spain rather than native-born individuals.

Over the centuries, as the layers of bureaucracy developed, corruption and inefficiency developed as well. One major source of corruption and unrest stemmed from a persistent New World problem: the shortage of labor. The Spanish had adapted traditional institutions to address the demand for workers in mines and on plantations. In Spain, work was directed by **feudal** landlords, *encomenderos*, whose military service to the king entitled them to harness the labor of Spanish peasants. In New Spain, Indians took the place of the peasants in what was called the *encomienda* system. Under a law passed in 1512, when the Spanish first encountered an Indian group, the conquistador was required to explain to them that they were subject to the Spanish king and to the Catholic Church, offering to absorb them peacefully. Having satisfied this *requerimiento*, the *encomenderos* gained the right to use the Indians' labor for nine months each year. For his part, the *encomendero* paid a tax to the Crown for each Indian he received and agreed to teach his workers the Catholic faith, Spanish language, and a "civilized" vocation.

Despite some commitment to uplifting local Indians, the system in reality was brutally exploitative. As Bartolomé de Las Casas, a bishop of Chiapas and a former conquistador and encomendero, reported both to the Council of the Indies and to the king himself, landlords frequently overworked their Indian **serfs** and failed in their "civilizing" responsibilities. As the result of Las Casas's appeal, the *Leyes Nuevas*, a series of new laws signed by Charles V in 1542, turned Indian relations in New Spain over to the church, and priests were assigned to enforce the laws. As Las Casas soon discovered, however, colonists often ignored even these slim protections.

The Dutch Enterprise   Interestingly, it was a former Spanish colony, the Netherlands, that presented one of the most serious threats to Spain's New World monopoly. The Armada disaster in 1588 had tipped the scales in favor of Dutch Protestant rebels, and the newly independent nation quickly developed a thriving commercial economy. Holland's first serious claim to American territory came in 1609, when Dutch sea captain **Henry Hudson** explored the East Coast in search of a passage eastward toward east Asia. He sailed up a large river that he hoped would lead him west to the Pacific. After realizing that he had not found the hoped-for route to the Far East, he returned to Holland and reported that the territory surrounding this river—which he named after himself—was "pleasant with Grasse & Flowers and Goodly Trees" and that the Indians were friendly. Surely, he added, profits could be made there. Hudson's employers did not share his enthusiasm for settlement; however, a fashion trend that seized Europe late in the sixteenth century provided a powerful incentive for some investment in the region. The immense

feudal   Relating to a system in which landowners held broad powers over peasants or tenant farmers, providing protection in exchange for loyalty and labor.

serfs   Peasants who were bound to a particular estate but, unlike slaves, were not the personal property of the estate owner and received traditional feudal protections.

popularity of the broad-brimmed beaver felt hat created a nearly insatiable demand for fur, and the experiences of early explorers and fishermen along America's North Atlantic shore indicated that a near endless supply was ripe for the trapping. Seeking to tap in on this "brown gold," the Dutch built a trading post on the Hudson River at Albany and an export station on Manhattan Island in 1614. Real Dutch efforts at New World colonization, however, did not begin until investors formed the **Dutch West India Company** in 1621.

In 1626, the company instructed official Peter Minuit to negotiate a lease for the entire island of Manhattan from the Manhates Indians, but the focus remained upriver; the company did nothing to attract settlers. By 1629, only three hundred colonists had spread themselves in a thin ribbon from Manhattan Island upriver to Albany. The situation began to change, however, when the Dutch West India Company drew up a comprehensive business plan to maximize profits and minimize dependence on local Indians for food and other support. To encourage the agricultural development necessary to support the fur industry, the company offered huge estates called **patroonships** to any company stockholder willing to bring fifty colonists to **New Netherland** at his own expense. In exchange, the patroons would enjoy near-feudal powers over their tenants. But few prosperous Dutchmen were interested in becoming New World barons. Rensselaerswyck, the estate of Kilian van Rensselaer, was the only patroonship that resembled the company's plan. The colony's development came to rely instead on many poorer migrants who were drawn by unofficial promises of land ownership and economic betterment.

Settlers from just about anywhere were welcome in New Netherland—the colony attracted an extremely diverse population, including German and French Protestants, free and enslaved Africans, Catholics, Jews, and Muslims. In 1638 the Dutch even encouraged Swedish fur traders to create their own colony, New Sweden, within New Netherland's boundaries. Local government in such a disparate community was a persistent problem. Although the Dutch West India Company was officially in charge, day-to-day affairs were actually run by an elite group of **burghers**, men in New Amsterdam whose economic and political successes gave them significant influence. To reassert its power, the company reorganized its New World operations in 1645, appointing Peter Stuyvesant to manage all of its affairs in the Western Hemisphere. Stuyvesant immediately came into conflict with the local burghers in New Amsterdam, who in 1647 forced him to create a compromise government that gave the burghers an official voice through a council of nine appointed representatives. Six years later, Stuyvesant and the council created a municipal government modeled on those back in Holland. Despite this nod to democratic government, Stuyvesant ran company affairs with an iron hand, significantly tightening operations throughout the colony. In 1655 he even invaded and rooted out the Swedes, eliminating that source of dissension and competition.

burghers   In New Amsterdam, men who were not Dutch West India Company officials, but who governed civic affairs through their political influence.

The Felt Hat Fad

Changes in fashion come and go, and we seldom give much thought to them as being historically significant. But the sudden popularity of felt hats in the late sixteenth century had a profound impact on not just America's history, but the history of the entire world. The flood of new wealth flowing into Europe from America permitted people of means—not just the nobility, but the landed gentry and even urban craftsmen and small business owners—to keep up with the latest fashions. Being in style became increasingly important to status-conscious merchants, manufacturers, and other beneficiaries of the New World boom. Demand for the beaver fur to make the felt became so steep that virtually the entire population of Old World beavers was wiped out, and entire industries arose in France, the

Netherlands, Great Britain, and Russia to import this "brown gold" from the Americas. Fur drew Europeans up virtually every waterway in North America, leading to the founding of many of the most prominent cities in America today. It is safe to say that without this seemingly silly fashion trend, little in the United States would be as we know it today.

- Another important trade item during this era was deerskins. Research the demand for deerskins and then discuss what this tells us about socioeconomic changes during this era.
- Identify a current fashion trend and discuss its impact on global society. What differences do you think this trend will make on the future?

The French Presence in America

Although France made a number of efforts to compete with Spain's New World projects during the sixteenth century, Spanish power was sufficient to prevent any major successes. For example, when a force of French Protestants established a colony in Florida in 1564, Spanish authorities sent an army to root them out. This led to increased Spanish vigilance, prompting Pedro Menéndez de Aviles to build the city of **Saint Augustine** the following year.

Unable to penetrate Spain's defenses in the south, the French concentrated their efforts farther north. In 1599, French Protestants facing an increasingly discriminatory environment at home began seeking investment opportunities in the New World. Pierre Chauvin and **Pierre Dugua de Mons** established a year-round trading post at Tadoussac, northeast of the eventual site of Quebec City. De Mons went back to France but in 1604 returned with **Samuel de Champlain,** establishing a string of settlements in what would be called **New France**. In 1608 de Mons and Champlain founded the city of Quebec and formed an enduring alliance with the Huron Indians. Two years later, King Henri IV was assassinated, setting off a wave of religious violence in France and destabilizing the French settlement in America. Over the next decade, French colonial authorities took little interest in overseas enterprises.

Although this scene in Quebec was not painted until 1820, back streets in the old part of the city still looked very much as they had during the heyday of the French coureurs de bois. So did the people. Shops, like the one on the left, sold provisions and tools—often on credit—to the outward-bound runners of the woods, binding them to bring their next load of furs back to satisfy their debt. Thus, while the French Crown did little to encourage it, the fur business formed the core of Canada's woodland and urban economies.

With permission of the Royal Ontario Museum © ROM

Finally in 1627 French minister Cardinal Richelieu chartered the **Company of New France**, awarding a group of the king's favorites licenses to establish plantations in Canada, but the venture failed to attract much interest. Frustrated by the lack of profits, Richelieu reorganized the Company of New France in 1633, dispatching Champlain, now bearing the title Lieutenant of New France, with three ships of supplies, workmen, and soldiers who, it was hoped, would breathe new life into the colony. In its new form, the company ignored the government's demands that it establish agricultural settlements and focused instead on the fur trade. Setting up posts in Quebec, Montreal, and a few more remote locations, the company became the primary outfitter of and buyer from the *coureurs de bois* and amassed huge profits by reselling the furs in Europe. After Richelieu's death in 1642, queen mother and French regent Anne of Austria acted on complaints filed by both fur trade investors and Jesuit missionaries that the Company of New France was not governing effectively. She chose to empower a new company, the **Community of Habitants of New France**, with a monopoly on the fur trade and

coureurs de bois Literally, "runners of the woods"; independent French fur traders who lived among the Indians and sold furs to the French.

the privilege of granting land claims. Then, in 1647, Anne approved the formation of a council that consisted of the governor, the local director of the Jesuits, the colony's military commandant, and three elected officials. Meanwhile, the Company of New France continued technically to own the land and retained the power to appoint the governor and court officials in the colony.

Local authorities managed most of the colony's affairs until 1663, when the Crown began to intervene seriously in Canada. Having taken the functions of state into his own hands, young Louis XIV gave his finance minister, Jean-Baptiste Colbert, considerable authority over all monetary matters, including colonial enterprises. Seeking to make New France more efficient and to increase its contribution to the empire at large, Colbert founded the **Company of the West**, modeled on the highly successful Dutch West India Company. He also revoked the land titles held by the Company of New France, putting them directly into the king's hands, and overturned the political power of the Community of Habitants, making New France a royal colony.

Although the king reaped enormous profits from the fur trade, his colonial interests ranged beyond this single source of income. In 1673 a French expedition led by Louis Joliet and Jacques Marquette set out on a systematic exploration of New France's many waterways. They discovered what appeared to be a major river, but it fell to **Robert Cavelier, Sieur de La Salle**, to prove the strategic and economic value of that discovery. In 1683 he and a party of French *coureurs de bois* and Indians retraced the earlier expedition and then followed the Mississippi River all the way to the Gulf of Mexico. La Salle immediately claimed the new territory for Louis XIV of France, naming it **Louisiana** in his honor. In 1698 the king sent settlers to the lower Mississippi Valley under the leadership of Pierre Le Moyne d'Iberville, who in 1699 raised Louisiana's first French fort, near present-day Biloxi, Mississippi. In 1718 French authorities built the city of New Orleans to serve as the capital of the new territory.

The acquisition of Louisiana was a major accomplishment for La Salle and for France. The newly discovered river way gave the French a rich, untapped source of furs as well as an alternative shipping route, allowing them to avoid the cold, stormy North Atlantic. Also, if an agricultural venture could be started in the new territory, it might serve as an inexpensive source of supplies to support both the fur trade in Canada and France's sugar plantations in the Caribbean. But perhaps of greatest importance was Louisiana's strategic location between Spain's claims in the Southwest and the Dutch and other colonies along the eastern seaboard. Controlling this piece of real estate gave Louis considerable leverage in international diplomacy.

INDIANS AND THE EUROPEAN CHALLENGE

Native Americans did not sit idly by while the European powers carved out empires in North America. Some joined the newcomers, serving as advisers and companions. Others sought to use the Europeans as allies to accomplish their own economic, diplomatic, or military goals. Still others, overwhelmed by the onset of European diseases and shifting population pressures, withdrew into the interior. The changes in native America created both obstacles and opportunities, giving shape to the patterns of expansion and conflict that characterized the colonial world.

The Indian Frontier in New Spain   Indian assistance had been critical in Spain's successful campaign against the Aztecs. Groups who had been forced to pay tribute to the Aztec Empire gladly allied themselves with the Spanish in what the natives perceived as an opportunity to win their independence. Their hopes were soon dashed when the Spanish simply replaced the Aztecs as the new lords of a tributary empire.

Once Spain's New World empire was firmly rooted, Spanish expansion met little native resistance until 1598, when a particularly brutal conquistador named **Don Juan de Oñate** led a large expedition to the Rio Grande region of New Mexico. When some Pueblos resisted Oñate's efforts to impose Spanish culture and religion, the conquistador chose to make an example of **Ácoma pueblo**. It took Oñate's troops three days to subdue the settlement, but Spanish steel finally overcame Ácoma clubs and stone knives. When the battle was over, Oñate ordered eight hundred Indians executed and made slaves of the nearly seven hundred survivors, mostly women and children. In addition, each male survivor over the age of 25 had one foot chopped off to prevent his escape from slavery. Two **Hopi Indians** who had been visiting Ácoma at the time of the battle had their right hands cut off and then were sent home as examples of the price of resistance.

This blatant cruelty disgusted even the most cynical authorities in New Spain, and both the church and state stepped in. Oñate was removed, and the surviving Indians were placed under joint military and religious protection. Some members of Oñate's company remained, however, founding the town of **Santa Fe** in 1609. Others scattered to set up ranches throughout the region.

Thanks in part to Las Casas's efforts, the church played a key role in developing the colonies, especially in the stark regions along Mexico's northern frontier where there were no gold mines or profitable plantations. The Franciscan order led church efforts in New Mexico and put a peculiar stamp on the pattern of Indian relations. A highly **ascetic** and disciplined order, the Franciscans were particularly offended by Pueblo religion and the Pueblo lifestyle. Indian ceremonies that involved various types of traditional religious objects smacked of idolatry to the Franciscans, and the priests embarked on a wholesale effort to destroy every vestige of the Indians' religion. The priests also interfered in the most intimate social aspects of Pueblo life, imposing foreign ideas about sexual relations and family structure, punishing most of the Pueblos' traditional practices as sinful.

After nearly a century of enduring these assaults on their most fundamental values, the Pueblos struck back. In 1680 a traditional leader named Popé led an uprising that united virtually all of the Indians in New Mexico against Spanish rule. The **Pueblo Revolt** left four hundred Spaniards dead as the rebels captured Santa Fe and drove the invaders from their land. It took almost a decade for the Spanish to regroup sufficiently to reinvade New Mexico. In 1689 troops moved

---

ascetic   Practicing severe abstinence or self-denial, generally in pursuit of spiritual awareness.

back into the region and over the next several years waged a brutal war to recapture the territory. The fighting continued off and on until the end of the century, but Spanish settlers began returning to New Mexico after the recapture of Santa Fe in 1693.

The Indian World in the Southeast

Members of Spanish exploring expeditions under would-be conquistadores such as Ponce de León and Hernando de Soto were the first Europeans to contact the mound builder societies and other Indian groups in the Southeast. Although their residential and ceremonial centers often impressed the Spaniards, these Mississippian agricultural groups had no gold and could not easily be enslaved. The conquistadores moved on without attempting to force Spanish rule or the Catholic religion on them.

Given sufficient incentive, however, the Spanish were quick to strike at Indian independence and culture. In Florida, for example, the need to protect Spanish ships from French settlers led Spain to establish garrisons such as Saint Augustine. With this and other similar military posts in place, Jesuit and Franciscan missionaries ranged outward to bring Catholicism to Indians in the region. By 1600 they had established missions from the Gulf Coast of Florida all the way to Georgia.

Although the Spanish presence in the region was small, its impact was enormous. The Spanish introduced European diseases into the densely populated towns in the Mississippi River region. Epidemics wiped out entire Native American civilizations and forced survivors to abandon their towns and entirely modify their ways of life. Certain groups, among them the Cherokees and Creeks, formed village-based economies that combined agriculture, hunting, and gathering. As had happened earlier in the Northeast among the Iroquois and others, this change in economy led to increasing intergroup warfare. And like the Iroquois, many southeastern groups created formal confederacies as a way of coping. One example is the **Creek Confederacy,** a union of many groups who had survived the Spanish epidemics. Internally, members created an economic and social system in which each population contributed to the welfare of all and differences were settled through athletic competition—a ballgame not unlike modern lacrosse—rather than warfare. And when new Europeans arrived in the seventeenth and eighteenth centuries, the Creeks and other confederacies found it beneficial to welcome them as trading partners and allies, balancing the competing demands of the Spanish and French, and later the English. To some degree, they took advantage of the European rivalries to advance their own interests against those of neighboring confederacies.

The Indian World in the Northeast

By the time Europeans had begun serious exploration and settlement of the Northeast, the economic and cultural changes among northeastern Woodlands Indians had resulted in the creation of two massive—and opposing—alliance systems. On one side were the Hurons, Algonquins, Abenakis, Mi'kmaqs, Ottawas, and several smaller tribes. On the other was the Iroquois League.

The costs and benefits of sustained European contact first fell to the Hurons and their allies. The Abenakis, Mi'kmaqs, and others who lived along the northern shore of the Atlantic were the first groups drawn into trade with the French, and it was among them that the *coureurs de bois* settled and inter-married. These family ties became firm economic bonds when formal French exploration brought these groups into more direct contact with the European trading world. Seeking advantage against the Iroquois, the Hurons and their neighbors created a great wheel of alliance with the fur trade at its hub and France as its axle.

The strong partnership between these Indians and the French posed a serious threat to the Iroquois. Much of the territory being harvested for furs by the Hurons had once belonged to the Iroquois, and the Confederacy wanted it back. The presence of the French and the fur trade made this objective all the more desirable. If they could push the Hurons and their allies out and take control of the St. Lawrence River, the French would then have to trade exclusively with them. But the French presence also complicated the situation in that the Hurons had a ready source for guns, iron arrowheads, and other tools that gave them a military edge.

The arrival of the Dutch in Albany, however, offered the Iroquois an attractive diplomatic alternative. In 1623 the Dutch West India Company invited representa-tives from the Iroquois League to a meeting at **Fort Orange,** offering them friend-ship and trade. The Iroquois responded enthusiastically, but in a way that the Dutch had not anticipated. They began a bloody war with the **Mohicans,** who had been the Dutch traders' main source for furs in the Hudson Valley. By 1627 the Iroquois had driven the Mohicans out of the Hudson Valley and had taken control over the flow of furs.

Trade was so vigorous that the Iroquois soon wiped out fur supplies in their own territory and began a serious push to acquire new sources. Beginning in the late 1630s, the Iroquois Confederacy entered into a long-term aggressive war against the Hurons and their allies in New France; against the Munsees, Delawares, and other groups in the Susquehanna and Delaware River valleys to the south; and even against the Iroquois-speaking Eries to the west.

The New Indian World of the Plains   Though largely unexplored and untouched by Europeans, the vast area of the Great Plains also underwent profound transformation during the period of initial contacts. Climate change, the pressure of shifting populations, and the intro-duction of novel European goods through lines of kinship and trade created an altogether new culture and economy among the Indians in this region.

Before about 1400, Indians living on the plains rarely strayed far from the waterways that form the Missouri River drainage, where they lived in villages sus-tained by agriculture, hunting, and gathering. The climate cooldown that affected their neighbors to the east had a similar effect on the Plains Indians: growing seasons became shorter, and the need to hunt became greater. But at the same time, this shift in climate produced an increase in one food source: **buffalo.**

A survivor of the great ice ages, the American bison is particularly well adapted to cold climates. Although buffalo had long been a presence on the plains, the cold weather during the Little Ice Age spurred a massive increase in their numbers. Between 1300 and 1800, herds numbering in the millions emerged in the new environment created by the climate change.

Some groups—such as the **Caddoan**-speaking Wichitas, Pawnees, and Arikaras—virtually abandoned their agricultural villages and became hunters. Others, such as the Hidatsas, split in two: a splinter group calling themselves Crows went off permanently to the grasslands to hunt, while the remainder stayed in their villages growing corn and tobacco. These and others who chose to continue their agricultural ways, the Mandans, for example, established a thriving trade with the hunters, exchanging vegetables and tobacco for fresh meat and other buffalo products.

The increase in buffalo not only provided a welcome resource for the Indians already on the Great Plains but also drew new populations to the area. The Blackfeet and other Indians swept down from the subarctic Northeast to hunt on the plains. Other Algonkian-speaking Indians, including the Gros Ventres, Cheyennes, and Arapahos, soon followed, to be joined by other northeastern groups fleeing the violence and disease that were becoming endemic in the Eastern Woodlands. The **Lakotas**, for example, once the westernmost family of Siouan agriculturalists, were pushed onto the plains by continuing pressure from the east, but they maintained close relations with their **Dakota** neighbors in Minnesota, who continued to farm and harvest wild rice and other crops. This continued tie, like that between the Crows and Hidatsas, increased both the hunters' and the farmers' chances for survival in an ever more hostile world: intergroup trade became the key to the welfare of all.

The buffalo also began to play an important role on the southern plains. There, groups such as the Apaches, Comanches, and Kiowas specialized in hunting the ever-increasing herds and then exchanging part of their kill for village-based products from their neighbors and kin, the Navajos, Hopis, and Pueblos. And it was in these intergroup trades that the Plains Indians acquired a new advantage in their efforts to expand their hunting economy: the horse.

One unintentional outcome of the Pueblo Revolt was the liberation of thousands of Spanish horses. The Pueblos had little use for these animals, but their trading partners, the Kiowas and Comanches, quickly adopted them. Horses could carry much larger loads than dogs and could survive on a diet of grass rather than taking a share of the meat. In less than a generation, horses became a mainstay of the buffalo-hunting cultures on the southern plains. And from there, horses spread quickly to other hunting people.

buffalo   The American bison, a large member of the ox family, native to North America and the staple of the Plains Indian economy between the fifteenth and mid-nineteenth centuries.

Caddoan   A family of languages spoken by several groups of Plains Indians.

Northern plains dwellers such as the Shoshones quickly began acquiring horses from their southwestern kin. Following a northward path along the eastern flank of the Rocky Mountains, horses were passed from one group to another in the complex trading system that had come into existence in the plains region. Well adapted to grasslands and virtually free from natural predators or diseases, horses greatly increased in number. By 1730, virtually all of the plains hunting peoples had some horses and were clamoring for more.

The steady demand for horses and hunting grounds created a new dynamic on the Great Plains and set a new economy into motion. After the Spanish reconquest of New Mexico, Indians could obtain horses only through warfare and trade, and both increased significantly. Surprise raids to steal horses from neighboring Indian groups and European settlements brought both honor and wealth to those who were successful.

CONQUEST AND ACCOMMODATION IN A SHARED NEW WORLD

Old World cultures, Native American historical dynamics, and New World environmental conditions combined to create vibrant new societies in European pioneer settlements. Despite the regulatory efforts of Spanish bureaucrats, French royal officials, and Dutch company executives, life in the colonies developed in its own peculiar ways. Entire regions in what would become the United States assumed cultural contours that would shape all future developments in each.

New Spain's Northern Frontiers   After suppressing the Pueblo Revolt during the 1690s, Spaniards began drifting back into New Mexico. Unlike areas to the south, New Mexico offered no rich deposits of gold or silver, and the climate was unsuitable for large-scale agriculture. With neither mines nor plantations to support the *encomienda* system, the basic underpinnings of the traditional ruling order never emerged. Even so, the Spanish colonial bureaucracy followed conventional imperial procedures and made Santa Fe the official municipal center for the region. But there were no *encomenderos* to provide wealth. The church, which was channeling money to missions, and the Spanish government, which allocated both military and civic support funds, were the only major employers in the region. Those in neither church's nor state's employ had to scramble for a living.

Under Pueblo control following the revolt, the small flocks of sheep abandoned by the fleeing Spanish had grown dramatically, and sheep ranching had become a reliable way to make a living. Thus, rather than concentrating near the municipal center in Santa Fe, the population in New Mexico spread out across the land, forming two sorts of communities. South of Santa Fe, people settled on scattered ranches. Elsewhere, they gathered in small villages along streams and pooled their labor to make a living from irrigated **subsistence farming**.

Like colonists elsewhere in Spain's New World empire, the New Mexico colonists were almost entirely male. Isolated on sheep ranches or in small villages, these men sought Indian companionship and married into local populations. These marriages gave birth not only to a new hybrid population but also to lines of kinship, trade, and authority that were in sharp contrast to the imperial ideal. For example, when Navajo or Apache raiding parties struck, ranchers and villagers turned to their Indian relatives for protection rather than to Spanish officials in Santa Fe.

Far away from the imperial economy centered in Mexico City, New Mexicans looked northward for trading opportunities. Southern Plains Indians—Apaches, Comanches, Kiowas, and their kin—needed a continuous supply of horses. They could obtain them by raiding Spanish ranches, but doing so brought reprisals by ranchers and their Indian relatives. Trade was a safer option. Facing labor shortages, New Mexicans accepted Indian slaves—especially children—in exchange for horses. Soon, these young captives became another important commodity in the already complex trading and raiding system that prevailed among the southwestern Indians and Spanish New Mexicans.

In this frontier world, unlike the rest of Spanish America, a man's social status came to depend less on his Spanish connections than on his ability to work effectively in the complicated world of kinship that prevailed in the Indian community. The people who eventually emerged as the elite class in New Mexico were those who best perfected these skills. Under their influence, Santa Fe was transformed from a traditional mission and imperial town into a cosmopolitan frontier trading center. During the next two centuries, this multiethnic elite absorbed first French and then Anglo-American newcomers while maintaining its own social, political, and economic style.

The Dutch Settlements   Few of the wealthy stockholders in the Dutch West India Company wanted to trade their lives as successful gentleman investors for a pioneering existence on a barely tamed frontier. The economy in Holland was booming, and only the most desperate or adventurous wanted to leave. But having no one to pay their way, even the few who were willing were hard-pressed to migrate to the colony.

Desperate to draw settlers, the Dutch West India Company created an alternative to patroonship, agreeing to grant a tract of land to any free man who would agree to farm it. This offer appealed to many groups in Europe who were experiencing hardship in their own countries but who, for one reason or another, were unwelcome in the colonies of their homelands. French Protestants,

---

subsistence farming Farming that produces enough food for survival but no surplus that can be sold.

for example, were experiencing terrible persecution in France but were forbidden to go to Canada or Louisiana. Roman Catholics, Quakers, Jews, Muslims, and a wide variety of others also chose to migrate to New Netherland. Most of the colonists settled on small farms, called *bouweries* in Dutch, and engaged in the same agricultural pursuits they had practiced in Europe. Thus New Netherland was dotted with little settlements, each having its own language, culture, and internal economy.

Farming was the dominant activity among the emigrants, but some followed the example of the French *coureurs de bois* and went alone or in small groups into the woods to live and trade with the Indians. Called **bosch loopers**, these independent traders traveled through the forests, trading cheap brandy and rum for the Indians' furs, which they then sold for enormous profits. Although both tribal leaders and legitimate traders complained about the *bosch loopers'* illegal activities, company officials could not control them.

In fact, the Dutch West India Company was unable to control much of anything in New Netherland. The incredible diversity of the settlers no doubt contributed to this administrative impotence. For example, Dutch law and company policy dictated that the **Dutch Reform Church** was to be the colony's official and only religion. But instead of drawing everyone into one congregation, the policy had the opposite effect. As late as 1642 not a single church of any denomination had been planted. Poor leadership and unimaginative policies also contributed to the general air of disorder. Following Peter Minuit's dismissal by the company in 1631, a long line of incompetent governors ruled the colony. In the absence of any legislative assembly or other local body to help keep matters on track, for years one bad decision followed another. It took a major reorganization by the West India Company and its appointment of Peter Stuyvesant in 1645 to turn the colony around.

Life in French Louisiana   France's colony in Louisiana had many of the same qualities and faced many of the same problems as Holland's and Spain's North American possessions. Like most European settlements, Louisiana suffered from a critical shortage of labor, leading first to dependence on the Indians and eventually to the wholesale adoption of African slavery. And like all Europeans who settled in North America, Louisianans found themselves embroiled in a complicated Native American world that usually defied European understanding.

Despite the territory's strategic location, fertile soils, and fur-bearing animals, few Frenchmen showed any interest in settling there. In the first years of the colony's existence, the population consisted primarily of three groups: military men, who were generally members of the lower nobility; *coureurs de bois* from Canada looking for new and better sources of furs; and French craftsmen seeking economic independence in the New World. The men in each group had little in common with those in the other groups, and more important, none had knowledge of or interest in food production. In the absence of an agricultural

The French had difficulty persuading settlers to come to their New World province in Louisiana. As a result, the region's development depended on a mixture of various European refugees, native Indians, and imported Africans for labor. Alexander de Batz's 1735 painting gives us a good idea of what the population around New Orleans looked like at that time. As in neighboring New Mexico, a multiracial and multicultural society emerged in Louisiana that left a permanent legacy in the region.

establishment, the small number of settlers in Louisiana had to depend on imported food. At first, ships from France carried provisions to the colonies, but war in Europe frequently interrupted this source. In desperation, the colonists turned to the Indians.

The **Natchez, Chickasaws,** and **Choctaws** were all close by and well provisioned. The Chickasaws refused to deal with the French, and the Natchez, divided into quarreling factions, were sometimes helpful and sometimes hostile. But the Choctaws, locked into a war with the Chickasaws and a tense relationship with the Natchez, found the prospect of an alliance with the French quite attractive. In the realignment process, the Choctaws helped shape France's Indian policies and expansion plans. For example, they were able to convince the French to expand onto Natchez land rather than in Choctaw territory. When the Natchez resisted French incursion, the Choctaws helped their European allies destroy the tribe. The Choctaws also assisted the French in a thirty-year-long conflict with the Chickasaws, though with less success.

Despite the Choctaw alliance, which guaranteed ample food supplies and facilitated territorial acquisitions, Louisiana remained unappealing to Frenchmen. Increasingly, settlers in Louisiana followed their Spanish neighbors' example by importing African slaves to do necessary work. By 1732, slaves made up two-thirds of the population.

STUDY TOOLS

SUMMARY

Spain's opening ventures in the Americas had been wildly successful, making the Iberian kingdom the envy of the world. Hoping to cash in on the bounty, other European nations challenged Spain's monopoly on American colonization, creating an outward explosion. Although slow to consolidate an imperial presence in North America, England was the first to confront the Spanish in force, wounding them severely. France and the Netherlands took advantage of the situation to begin building their own American empires.

For Native Americans, the entry of Europeans into their realms combined with other forces to create an air of crisis. Presented with a series of new challenges, Indians sought new ways to solve their problems and created altogether new societies. This often involved difficult choices: perhaps allying with the newcomers, resisting them, or fleeing. As different groups exercised different options, the outcome was a historically dynamic world of interaction involving all of the societies that were coming together in North America.

This dynamic interaction yielded interesting fruit. In New Spain, New France, Louisiana, New Netherland, and throughout the Great Plains, truly cosmopolitan societies emerged. Bearing cultural traits and material goods from throughout the world, these new transatlantic societies set the tone for future development in North America. As we see in Chapter 3, societies on the Atlantic coast, too, were evolving as English colonists interacted with the land and its many occupants. The outcome of such interchange, over the centuries, was the emergence of a multicultural, multiethnic, and extraordinarily rich culture—an essential element in Making America.

CHRONOLOGY

NEW WORLD COLONIES AND NATIVE AMERICANS	
1494	Treaty of Tordesillas
1512	Creation of the *encomienda* system
1519–1521	Hernando Cortés invades Mexico
1551	Council of Valladolid rules that American Indians are human beings with souls
1558	Elizabeth I becomes queen of England
1565	Spanish found St. Augustine in present-day Florida
1588	English defeat Spanish Armada
1598	Don Juan de Oñate destroys Ácoma pueblo

1608	French-Huron alliance
1609	Spanish found Santa Fe in present-day New Mexico
1627	Creation of Company of New France
1680	Pueblo Revolt
1683	La Salle expedition down the Mississippi River to the Gulf of Mexico
ca. 1700	Beginning of French-Choctaw alliance

Focus Questions

If you have mastered this chapter, you should be able to answer these questions and explain the terms that follow the questions.

1. Why did European rulers promote exploration and colonization in North America?
2. How did religious and political rivalries influence each European power's approach to New World colonization?
3. What similarities and differences characterized Spanish, French, and Dutch patterns of empire building in North America? What role did colonists' experiences play?
4. How did natural environments help shape the colonial enterprises?
5. How did changes in the natural environment affect Indian societies during the early colonial period?
6. How did the arrival of Europeans influence continuing adaptations by Native American groups?
7. How did settlers and American Indians adapt to changing conditions in the different regions of colonial occupation?

Key Terms

Treaty of Tordesillas (*p.* 25)

Hernando Cortés (*p.* 25)

Francisco Vásquez de Coronado (*p.* 26)

Roanoke Island (*p.* 29)

Spanish Armada (*p.* 30)

cabildo secular (*p.* 30)

requerimiento (*p.* 31)

Henry Hudson (*p.* 31)

Dutch West India Company (*p.* 32)

patroonships (*p.* 32)

New Netherland (*p.* 32)

Saint Augustine (*p.* 33)

Pierre Dugua de Mons (*p.* 33)

Samuel de Champlain (*p.* 33)

New France (*p.* 33)

Company of New France (*p.* 34)

Community of Habitants of New France (*p.* 34)

Company of the West (*p.* 35)

Robert Cavelier, Sieur de La Salle (*p.* 35)

Louisiana (*p.* 35)

Don Juan de Oñate (*p.* 36)

3

Founding the English Mainland Colonies, 1585–1732

England and Colonization

Unlike France or Spain, the English government was not willing to finance the creation of an American empire. No conquering army and no church-supported missionaries would be provided to aid colonists hoping to settle along the North American coastline. Instead, the Crown relied on private citizens to take on the risks of colonization. Sometimes the king helped by providing huge grants of land to the risk-takers, but the royal treasury was not tapped to create the thirteen colonies that eventually emerged on the mainland.

England's First Attempts at Colonization   The first and perhaps the most foolhardy Englishman to take up the challenge of colonization was the poet and courtier Sir Walter Raleigh. Spurred by patriotism and a sense of grand adventure, Raleigh risked his personal fortune in an effort to establish a colony off the coast of what became North Carolina. In 1584, Raleigh sent a small group to test the viability of a settlement on Roanoke Island. The test failed: before the year was out, these men had eagerly headed home to England. Undaunted by this initial failure, Raleigh tried again in 1587. He spent most of his remaining resources to finance the settlement of a hundred colonists at Roanoke. Unfortunately, by 1588 England was locked in naval warfare with Spain, and Raleigh was unable to send supplies to his colony for over three years. When a supply ship finally reached Roanoke, the men on board could find no trace of the colonists. Instead, they found abandoned ruins and a single word carved into the bark of a nearby tree: "Croatan." Whether the Roanoke colonists had fled from an attack by the Croatan Indians, been murdered by them, or rescued by them in the face of starvation, epidemic, or some other natural disaster, no one knows. But news of the mysterious disappearance of the colony spread rapidly. So too did news that Sir Walter Raleigh's wealth had disappeared in the process. It would be almost sixteen years before anyone else dared to establish an English colony in North America.

Turmoil and Tensions in England   No one will ever know what crisis the Roanoke settlers faced, but the crises plaguing English life in the seventeenth century were all too clear. Economic upheaval, bitter religious disagreements, and a political challenge to the Crown that ended in civil war all contributed to decades of unrest, violence, and misery. These crises played an important role in reviving the dream of colonization.

The strains of economic change were apparent everywhere in England. The rise of the woolens industry and the transformation of farmland into sheep pastures left thousands of tenant farm families homeless. "Sheep eat men" became the bitter cry of farmers who, overnight, had become vagabonds, roaming from countryside to cities in search of work. Many turned to crime or prostitution to survive. The nation's more fortunate citizens began to discuss the merits of America as a "dumping ground" for the poor and desperate among them; the poor and desperate began to consider a dangerous ocean voyage and the unknown terrors of the New World a better choice than life on the streets of London or Bristol.

Religious tensions troubled the nation as well. Although the official **Church of England** that Henry VIII had created in 1531 was Protestant, a movement to "purify" the church had grown steadily in the early seventeenth century, led by Protestants who believed that the church had kept too many Catholic rituals and customs. To the monarchs of the Stuart dynasty, this **Puritan** criticism smacked of treason as well as heresy, for the king was not only head of the nation but head of the Anglican Church. The mistrust between Puritan reformers and their kings grew during the reigns of James I and his son Charles I, for both men were rumored to be secretly practicing Catholicism.

The political situation was equally tense. A power struggle between the Crown and **Parliament**, which was the legislative branch of the English government, erupted into open warfare in 1642. This civil war brought together many of the threads of religious and political discontent and conflict, pitting Puritans, merchants, and members of the rising middle class against the Stuart king. A Puritan army, led by Oliver Cromwell, overthrew the monarchy and, in 1649, Cromwell took the radical step of executing Charles I. This execution established the supremacy of Parliament. Cromwell headed the new **Commonwealth** government until his death in 1658, but he proved no more popular than the former king. In 1660, the Stuart family was invited to take the throne once again. For the next twenty-five years, a period called the **Restoration**, Charles II ruled England. But when the crown passed to his brother, James II, who openly practiced Catholicism, a second revolution began. This time, there was little bloodshed, for James wisely fled to the safety of France. His Protestant daughter Mary and her

Dutch husband, William, then came to the English throne. This **Glorious Revolution** of 1688 ended almost a century of political, ideological, and economic instability. But by that time, thousands of English men and women had journeyed across the Atlantic Ocean and twelve colonies covered the mainland shores.

SETTLING THE CHESAPEAKE

Fears of financial ruin had prevented any Englishman from following in Sir Walter Raleigh's footsteps. But by the beginning of the seventeenth century, English **entrepreneurs** had developed a new method of financing high-risk ventures, the **joint-stock company**. In 1603, King James I granted a charter to two such companies eager to establish colonies on mainland North America. The Plymouth Company's settlement quickly failed, for the frigid rocky coast of Maine proved uninviting and the local Indians unfriendly. It thus fell to the remaining Virginia Company to create the first successful English colony in North America.

The Jamestown Colony   The 101 men and four boys sent by the Virginia Company found themselves crammed aboard three small ships, the *Susan Constant,* the *Godspeed,* and the *Discovery.* Tempers grew short as the months at sea grew long, and trouble erupted on the *Susan Constant.* One of the troublemakers, an adventurer named John Smith, landed in the ship's brig for his role in attempting to organize a mutiny. The colonists had more to worry about than Mr. Smith's temper, however. The Spanish had proven eager to repel any European competitors from the vast territory stretching from Florida to Maine that the pope had granted them in the sixteenth century. French Huguenots seeking refuge in Florida had learned this all too well when Spanish forces brutally massacred the small band of Protestants who dared to settle there. And although the Indians had been friendly on the Caribbean Islands where the English colonists had stopped for provisions, the colonists were far from certain of the reception they would receive when they reached their destination.

The three ships entered Chesapeake Bay five months after they had set sail. The colonists decided to establish themselves on a small peninsula that jutted out from a river they named the James, in honor of their king, calling their little foothold **Jamestown.** As they explored their surroundings and met the local Indians, the Englishmen concluded that prospects looked good for forging a peaceful and profitable relationship.

entrepreneur   A person who organizes and manages a business enterprise that involves risk and requires initiative.

joint-stock company   A business financed through the sale of shares of stock to investors; the investors share in both the profits and losses from a risky venture.

Yet even the least insightful among them should have recognized the wide chasm that separated Englishmen from Indians. To the local tribes, the land on which the colonists had set up their tents and begun to build their fortifications was not Virginia but Tsenacommacah, and it belonged to the confederation of some thirty Algonkian-speaking tribes dominated by the Powhatan chieftain Wahunsunacock. If the English found the Indians exotic—in their body and face paints, their relative nakedness, their religious ceremonies, and their weaponry— the Pamunkeys, Arrohatecks, and Mattoponis found the cumbersome dress and the noisy but less than effective weaponry of the new arrivals equally odd. Each viewed their own culture as superior and, for a brief period, seemed willing to tolerate the misguided beliefs and behaviors of the other. The colonists were thus convinced that they had met the instructions given them to "take great care not to offend the naturals."

If the English men and boys had known what lay in store for them in the next decade, they might have sailed for home at once. For even without attacks from Indians or the Spanish, the settlers soon faced a seemingly endless series of survival challenges. The site of their encampment proved unhealthy, and one by one, colonists fell ill, suffering from typhus, malaria, or dysentery. Few of them had the skills needed to survive in what was proving to be a hostile and alien environment. Many lacked the experience or the motivation needed to clear fields, plant crops, or build fortifications. These adventurers, as one Englishman bluntly put it, "never knew what a day's labour meant."

The disease, starvation, and exposure to the elements that threatened to destroy the colony were temporarily relieved when the former troublemaker, John Smith, took command. Smith was hardly a well-liked man: he was overconfident and self-centered, full of exaggerated tales of his heroic deeds as a mercenary in exotic lands. He had narrowly escaped execution on the voyage from England. Smith did have some survival knowledge, however, and he did know how to discipline men. He established a "no work, no food" policy, and he negotiated with the Powhatans for corn and other supplies. When Smith left in 1609, the discipline and order he had established quickly collapsed. The original colonists and those who joined them the following spring remembered that winter as "the starving time." The desperate colonists burned their housing to keep warm and ate dogs, cats, mice, snakes, even shoe leather in their struggle to survive. Only sixty settlers were alive at winter's end.

The Powhatans had little sympathy for the desperate colonists. Even before Smith had departed, cooperation between the two groups had begun to disintegrate, for despite all their problems, the English exhibited a sense of superiority and entitlement that alienated Wahunsunacock and his confederacy. By 1609 tension and resentment had turned to bloodshed, and raids and counterattacks defined Anglo-Indian relationships for over a decade. Wahunsunacock made several efforts to establish peace, but English encroachments on Indian lands made any lasting truce impossible. Wahunsunacock and his successor, Opechancanough, the chief of the Pamunkeys, recognized that dealing with the English colonists would require warfare, not words.

If the settlers were learning hard lessons in survival, the Virginia Company was learning hard lessons, too. The colony was hanging on by a thread, but the

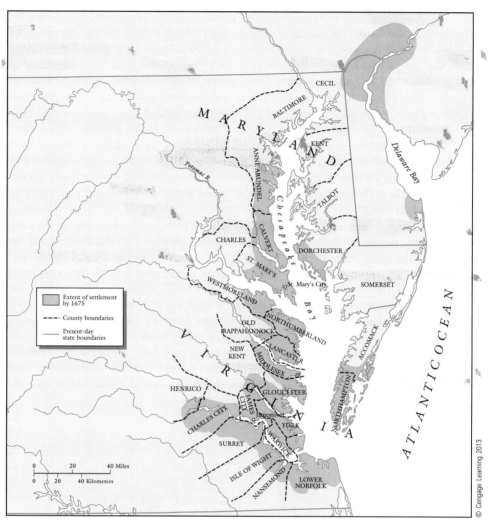

MAP 3.1 Virginia and Maryland, circa 1675

Nearly 70 years after the founding of Jamestown, settlement remained confined to the tidewater and the eastern shore.

stockholders saw no profits, only their yearly expenses of passage for new colonists and supplies for old ones. The Virginia Company seemed caught in an investor's nightmare, pumping good money after bad in hopes of delaying a total collapse. Prospects seemed bleak: the only gold the colonists had found was "fool's gold," and the investors could see nothing else of economic value in the Chesapeake.

Fortunately the investors were wrong. Tobacco, a weed native to the Americas, proved to be the colony's salvation. Pipe smoking had been a steady habit in England since the mid-sixteenth century, and Englishmen were a steady market for this "brown gold." The local strain of tobacco in Virginia was too harsh for English tastes, but one of the colonists, an enterprising young planter named John Rolfe, managed to transplant a milder strain of West Indian tobacco to the colony. This success changed Rolfe's life, earning him both wealth and the admiration of his neighbors. Rolfe made a second contribution to the colony soon afterward, easing the strained Indian-white relationships by his marriage to an Indian princess, Pocahontas, who John Smith insisted had saved his life.

By 1612, the Virginia Colony's settlers were engaged in a mad race to plant and harvest as many acres of tobacco as possible. Yet the Virginia Company was unable to take full advantage of this unexpected windfall, for it had changed its policies in an effort to ease its financial burdens. In the beginning the company owned all the land but also bore all the costs of colonization. By 1618, however, the company's new policy allowed individual colonists to own land if they paid their own immigration expenses. This **head right system** granted each male colonist a deed for 50 acres of land for himself and for every man, woman, or child whose voyage he financed. In this way the Virginia Company shifted the cost of populating and developing the colony to others. But the head rights also ended the company's monopoly on the suddenly valuable farmland.

Other important concessions to the colonists soon followed. The military-style discipline instituted by John Smith and continued by later leaders was abandoned. At the same time, a measure of self-government was allowed. In 1618 the company created an elected, representative lawmaking body called the **House of Burgesses**, which gave the landholders—tobacco planters—of Virginia some control over local political matters. In effect, a business enterprise had finally become a colonial society.

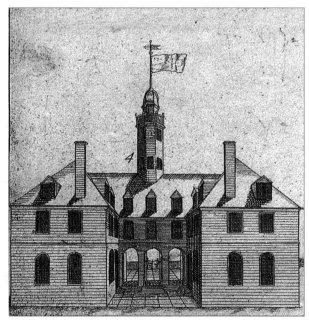

The Virginia House of Burgesses was the first representative assembly to be established in the British colonies. The legislators held their first session in a small Jamestown church, but by 1669, the tobacco planters who served in this assembly had moved into elegant quarters in the colonial capital of Williamsburg. The imposing building sent a clear message to all Virginians that government was the proper domain of gentlemen of wealth and social standing.

Library of Congress

The Virginia Company did retain one of the colony's earliest traditions: a bad relationship with the Powhatan Indians. By 1622, the English seemed to have the upper hand, for the population had grown and tobacco had brought a measure of prosperity. As Virginia planters pressed farther inland, seizing Indian land along local rivers, the new Powhatan chief, Opechancanough, decided to strike back. On what the Christian settlers called Good Friday, he mounted a deadly attack on Jamestown, killing a quarter of the colonists in a single day. The company responded as quickly as it could, sending weapons to the Virginians. For two years, war raged between Indians and the English. Although the bloodshed became less frequent by 1625, a final peace was not reached for a decade. By that time, disease and violence had taken its toll on the Powhatans. Once over forty thousand strong, they had dwindled to fewer than five hundred people.

The Good Friday Massacre, as the English called it, brought important changes for the colony. King James I had already begun an investigation of the Virginia Company's management record—and the colony's growing profit potential. When he learned of the renewed conflict between Indians and colonists, the king took away the company's charter and declared Virginia to be a royal possession.

If the king's advisers had tallied the cost in human life for planting this first English colony in the same manner that the company tallied expenses in pence and pounds, they would have found the outcome sobering. By 1624, only 1,275 of the 8,500 settlers who had arrived since 1607 remained alive. Fortunately, no other English colony would pay such a price for its creation.

| Maryland: A Catholic Refuge | As Virginians spread out along the river ways of their colony, searching for good tobacco land, plans for a second Chesapeake colony were brewing in England. The man |

behind this project was not a merchant or entrepreneur, and profit was not his motive. George Calvert, a wealthy Catholic whom King Charles I had just made Lord Baltimore, envisioned a religious refuge in America for fellow Catholics suffering growing harassment and discrimination at home. Calvert acquired a charter from the king for a generous tract of land east and north of Chesapeake Bay. Here, he planned to establish a highly traditional society, dominated by powerful noblemen and populated by obedient tenant farmers. Thus, in the 1630s, George Calvert was a reactionary thinker with a radical vision.

Calvert died before a single colonist could be recruited for his Maryland. His oldest son, Cecilius Calvert, the second Lord Baltimore, took on the task of establishing the colony. To Calvert's surprise, few English Catholics showed any enthusiasm for the project. When the first boatload of colonists sailed up the Chesapeake Bay in 1634, most of the two hundred volunteers were young Protestants seeking a better life. Calvert wisely adopted the head right system developed by the Virginia Company to attract additional settlers. The lure of land ownership, he realized, was the key to populating Maryland.

Calvert's colony quickly developed along the same lines as neighboring Virginia. Marylanders immediately turned to planting the profitable **staple crop,**

---

staple crop   A basic or necessary agricultural item, produced for sale or export.

George Calvert, Lord Baltimore, hoped to create a refuge for English Catholics in America. But Maryland soon filled with Protestants, hoping for a new start in a new world. Conflict between colonists of the two faiths soon followed.

© Northwind Picture Archives

tobacco, and joined the scramble for good riverfront land. Like the Virginians, these colonists used trickery, threats, and violence to pry acres of potential farmland from resisting Indians. By midcentury, the two Chesapeake colonies could claim a modest prosperity, even though their populations grew slowly. But they could not claim a peaceful existence. The political crises that shook England during the mid-seventeenth century sent shock waves across the Atlantic Ocean to American shores. These crises intertwined with local tensions among colonists or between colonists and Indians to produce rebellions, raids, and civil wars.

Troubles on the Chesapeake   In Maryland, tensions ran high between the Catholic minority, who had political influence beyond their numbers because of Lord Baltimore's support, and the Protestant majority in the colony. But with the rise to power of the Puritan leader Oliver Cromwell, Calvert realized that his power to protect Maryland's Catholics was in jeopardy. Hoping to avoid persecution of the Catholic colonists, Calvert offered religious toleration to all Marylanders. In 1649 he issued the innovative Toleration Act, protecting all Christians from being "troubled [or] molested … in respect of his or her religion." Cromwell, however, promptly repealed the act. In 1654, Parliament took Maryland away from the Calvert family and established a Protestant assembly in the colony. As Calvert had feared, a wave of anti-Catholic persecution swept over Maryland.

Within a year, a bloody civil war was raging in Maryland. Protestant forces won the fiercely fought Battle of the Severn, but their victory proved futile when Oliver Cromwell died and the monarchy was restored. Charles II returned Maryland to the Calvert family, who had always been loyal supporters of the Stuart dynasty. Despite this reversal of fortunes, Protestants in Maryland continued their struggle, organizing unsuccessful rebellions in 1659, 1676, and again in 1681. Then, in 1689, the Glorious Revolution prompted Maryland's Protestants to rally once again. Led by an unlikely looking hero, the stooped and nearly crippled minister **John Coode**, these colonists formed an army they called the Protestant Association. By 1691, Coode had persuaded the Crown to make Maryland a royal colony. The story did not end there, however. In 1715 the fourth Lord Baltimore gave up the Catholic faith and joined the Church of England. Maryland was once again returned to the Calverts.

Virginia was less affected by religious controversy than its neighbor. There, colonists were primarily Anglicans although small communities of Quakers, Puritans, and even members of the radical Dutch Labadist sect were scattered throughout Virginia. Religious differences, however, did not spark hostilities. Instead, the fault lines in Virginia society developed between the wealthy planters of the **tidewater** region and the ambitious newcomers seeking to make their fortunes in the backcountry. It was this tension that led to Bacon's Rebellion.

In 1674, a charismatic young Englishman named Nathaniel Bacon arrived in Virginia. He was wealthy enough to buy a large plantation near Jamestown and a large tract of land on the frontier, and he was quickly appointed to Governor William Berkeley's elite advisory council. When Indians attacked his frontier farm, Bacon demanded that the governor raise a militia to rid the area of all Indians. The governor refused—and Bacon took matters into his own hands. He raised a vigilante army and began a war against all nearby Indians, even the peaceful tribes. The amazed and enraged governor branded Bacon a traitor. Bacon quickly struck back. Over five hundred men flocked to join "General" Bacon, and together they seized control of the colony's capital. By mid-October, Bacon's rebels controlled over two thirds of Virginia. Then tragedy struck. On October 26, 1676, Nathaniel Bacon suddenly died of dysentery. Without his leadership, the revolution faltered and by the spring of 1677, it had been crushed. Many of the ideas behind this failed rebellion would resurface one hundred years later during the events leading up to the Revolutionary War.

| Colonial Chesapeake Life | Every aspect of life in the Chesapeake colonies, observers noted, seemed to be shaped by tobacco. Its cultivation set rhythms of work and play. Planting, tending, harvesting, and drying tobacco leaves took almost ten months of the year, |

tidewater   Low coastal land drained by tidal streams in Maryland and Virginia.

Grassroots Movements, Then and Now

Bacon's Rebellion is one of the first instances of a grassroots movement in American history. These movements often give voice to people who feel they are not being heard by the government on important issues. Many things we take for granted today began as demands by grassroots movements, including the end to slavery, the direct election of senators, and women's suffrage. The antiwar movement of the 1960s, the environmental movement of the 1990s, and the antismoking movement of today are recent examples of grassroots movements. Often grassroots movements provide insights into changing values in American society and, equally often, they arise as part of a cluster of reform movements.

- Research a modern grassroots movement. What tactics has it employed to win support? How successful do you think these tactics have been?

- Do you think grassroots protest is a valuable part of the American political process today, or do we have institutions and political processes that make such protests unnecessary?

beginning in late winter and ending just before Christmas. In the short period between the holiday and the start of a new planting cycle, Chesapeake planters, their families, and their servants worked frantically to catch up on other, neglected farm chores. They did repairs, sewed and mended, built new cabins and sheds, cut timber and firewood. They also compressed what meager social life they had into these winter weeks, engaging—whenever possible—in hasty courtships followed by marriage.

Because tobacco quickly exhausted the soil in which it grew, planters moved frequently to new acres on their estates or to newly acquired lands farther west. Since they rarely stayed in one place very long, planters placed little value on permanent homes or on creating permanent social institutions such as schools. Throughout the century, Chesapeake colonists sacrificed many of the familiar forms of community life to the demands of their profitable crop.

Planters needed a labor force large enough and cheap enough to ensure their profits. As long as poverty and social unrest plagued England, they found the workers they needed in their homeland. Over 175,000 young, single, and impoverished immigrants flooded the Chesapeake during the seventeenth century, their passages paid by the ship captain or the planter. In exchange for their transatlantic voyage, these **indentured servants** worked for several years in the tobacco fields without pay. Planters preferred a male work force, for they shared the general European assumption that farming was a masculine activity. As a result, these colonies had an unusual population profile: men outnumbered women in most areas of Virginia and Maryland by 3 to 1. In some areas, the ratio was a remarkable 6 to 1 until the end of the century.

For indentured servants, and often for their masters as well, life was short and brutal. They spent long, backbreaking days in the fields. Their food rations were meager, their clothing and bedding inadequate, and their shoulders frequently scarred by the master's whip. Servants wrote letters home describing their miserable existence. "People cry out day, and night," wrote one young man, who told his father that most servants would give up "any limb to be in England again."

Most servants also expressed doubts that they would survive to win their freedom. In many cases, they were correct. Disease and malnutrition took the lives of perhaps a quarter of these bound laborers. Free colonists fared little better than servants. Typhus, dysentery, and malaria killed thousands. Over one-quarter of the infants born in the Chesapeake did not live to see their first birthdays; another quarter of the population died before reaching the age of 20. Early death, the skewed ratio of men to women, and high infant mortality combined to create a **demographic disaster** that continued until the last decades of the century.

By the end of the 1600s, the labor force had become increasingly biracial. The steady supply of English workers dried up as economic conditions in England improved. At the same time, the cost of purchasing an African slave declined. During the next century, the shift from English servants to African slaves would be completed.

NEW ENGLAND: COLONIES OF DISSENTERS

While Captain John Smith was barking orders at the settlers in Jamestown, some religious dissenters in a small English village were preparing to escape King James's wrath. These residents of Scrooby Village were people of modest means, without powerful political allies or a popular cause. But they had gone one step further than the majority of Puritans, who continued to be members of the Anglican Church despite their criticisms of it. The Scrooby villagers had left the church altogether, forming a separate sect of their own. James I despised these **separatists** and declared his intention to drive them out of England—or worse.

The Scrooby separatists took James's threats seriously. In 1611 they fled to the Netherland city of Leyden. They saw themselves as **Pilgrims** on a spiritual journey to religious freedom. The Dutch welcomed them warmly, but several Pilgrims feared that the comfortable life they had found in Holland was diminishing their devotion to God. By 1620, **William Bradford** was leading a small group of these transplanted English men and women on a second pilgrimage—to America.

demographic disaster   The outcome of a high death rate and an unbalanced ratio of men to women in the Chesapeake colonies.

separatists   English Protestants who chose to leave the Church of England because they believed it was corrupt.

The Plymouth Colony

The Leyden Pilgrims were joined by other separatists in England. Together, they set sail on an old, creaky ship called the *Mayflower*. On board, too, were a band of "strangers," outsiders to the religious sect who simply wanted passage to America. Crammed together in close and uncomfortable quarters, Pilgrims and strangers weathered a nightmare voyage of violent storms and choppy waters. After nine weeks at sea, the captain anchored the *Mayflower* at Cape Cod, almost 1,000 miles north of the original Virginia destination. The exhausted passengers did not complain; they fell to the ground to give thanks. Once the thrill of standing on dry land had passed, however, many of them sank into depression. The early winter landscape of New England was dreary, alien, and disturbingly empty. William Bradford's own wife, Dorothy, may have committed suicide in the face of this bleak landscape.

Talk of setting sail for Virginia spread through the ranks of the ship's crew and the passengers. Mutiny was in the air. To calm the situation, Bradford negotiated an unusual contract with every man aboard the ship—Pilgrim, crew, servant, and stranger. This document, known as the **Mayflower Compact**, granted political rights to any man willing to remain and to abide by whatever laws the new colony enacted. Here was an unheard-of opportunity for poor men to participate in governing themselves. All agreed, and the new colony of Plymouth Plantations began to prepare for the long winter ahead.

In Plymouth Plantations, as in Virginia, the first winter brought sickness, hunger, and death. Half of the colonists did not survive. When a Patuxet Indian, **Squanto**, came upon the remaining men and women in the spring of 1621, he found them huddled in flimsy shelters, trapped between a menacing forest and a dangerous ocean. Squanto sympathized with their confusion and their longings for home, for he had crossed the Atlantic in 1605 aboard an English trading ship and spent several years in an alien environment. He also understood what it meant to be a survivor, for the Pilgrims had settled where his own village had once stood. His entire family and tribe had been wiped out by diseases carried by English traders and fishermen.

Squanto helped the colonists, teaching them how to plant corn, squash, and pumpkins. Perhaps his greatest service, however, was in helping William Bradford negotiate a peace treaty with Massasoit, leader of the local Wampanoag Indians. The combined efforts of Squanto and Massasoit saved the Plymouth Colony, and in the fall of 1621, English settlers and Indian guests sat down together in a traditional harvest celebration of thanksgiving.

Plymouth grew slowly, its colonists earning their livings by farming, fishing, and lumbering. A few Pilgrims grew wealthy by developing a fur trade with the Indians. Unlike the Jamestown settlers, the Plymouth community purchased land rather than seizing it, and they were strong allies when warfare broke out between Massasoit's people and their enemies. In fact, the colonists proved to be such ferocious fighters that they were known as Wotoroguenarge, or "Cutthroats."

Massachusetts Bay and Its Settlers

A second colony soon appeared beside Plymouth Plantations. In 1629 a group of prosperous Puritans, led by the 41-year-old lawyer and landowner **John Winthrop**, secured a charter for their Massachusetts Bay Company from King Charles I. These Puritans had grown increasingly worried about the government's policies toward

The Bible was the most cherished book, and often the only book, in a colonist's home. To safeguard this treasure, many Pilgrims stored their Bibles in hand-carved boxes like this one belonging to William Bradford. This box, once decorated with the lion and unicorn symbol of England, was politicized during the American Revolution, when the British lion was scraped off.

Courtesy of the Pilgrim Hall Museum, Plymouth, Massachusetts

dissenters. Harassment, coupled with a deepening economic depression in England, spurred them to set sail for New England. Advertising their colony as "a refuge for many who [God] means to save out of the general calamity," Winthrop and his colleagues had no trouble recruiting like-minded Puritans to migrate. As religious tensions and economic distress increased in England, Massachusetts attracted thousands of settlers. This **Great Migration** continued until Oliver Cromwell's Puritan army took control of England.

While profit motivated the Virginia colonists and a desire to worship in peace prompted the Pilgrims to sail to America, the Puritans of Massachusetts were people with a mission. They hoped to create a model Christian community, a "city upon a hill" that would persuade all English men and women that the reforms they proposed in the Anglican Church were correct. John Winthrop set out their mission in a speech to the passengers aboard the *Arabella*. "The eyes of all peoples are upon us," Winthrop warned, and, more importantly, God, too, was watching them. If they abandoned or forgot their mission, the consequences would surely include divine punishment.

This sense of mission influenced the physical as well as spiritual shape of the colony. Massachusetts colonists created tight-knit farming villages and small seaport towns in which citizens could monitor one another's behavior as well as come together in prayer. This settlement pattern fit well with the realities of New England's climate and terrain, since the short growing season and the rocky soil made large, isolated plantations based on staple crops impossible. The colonists, homesick for English villages in regions such as East Anglia, did their best to reproduce familiar architecture and placement of public buildings. The result was often a hub-and-spoke design, with houses tightly clustered around a village green or common pasture, a church beside this green, and most of the fields and farms within walking distance of the village center. This design set natural limits on the size of any village because beyond a certain point—usually measured in a winter's walk to church—a farm family was considered outside the community circle. As a town's population grew and the available farmland was farther from the village green, settlers on the outer rim of the town usually chose to create a new community for themselves. The Puritans called this process of establishing a new village "hiving off."

Massachusetts and other New England settlements that followed were societies of families. Many of the colonists arriving during the Great Migration came as members of a family. Of course, each ship carried unmarried male and female servants too, but unlike in the Chesapeake, the gender ratio in the northern colonies was never dramatically skewed. And unlike their Chesapeake counterparts, New Englanders never endured a demographic disaster. The cool temperatures and clean drinking water made the region a healthy place for Europeans, healthier than England itself. Infant mortality was low, and most children lived to marry and produce families of their own. A couple could expect to live a long life together and raise a family of five to seven children. One outcome of this longevity was a rare phenomenon in the seventeenth-century English world: grandparents.

Both Puritans and neighboring Pilgrims spoke of the family as "a little commonwealth," the building block on which the larger society was constructed. And, like the larger society, the family was a **hierarchy**. Children were to obey parents; wives were to obey husbands. "Wives," Puritan ministers preached, "are part of the House and Family, and ought to be under a Husband's Government." A husband, however, was bound by sacred obligations to care for and be respectful toward his wife. Marriage involved many practical duties as well. Wives were expected to strive to be "notable housewives"—industrious, economical managers of resources and skilled at several crafts. They were to spin yarn, sew, cook, bake, pickle, butcher farm animals, cure meat, churn butter, and set cheeses. Husbands were expected to labor in the fields or in the shop to provide for their families.

Although obligated to be tender and loving, the husband controlled the resources of the family. This was true in all English colonies, although in the Chesapeake, a husband's early death often left the wife in charge of the family farm or shop and its profits until sons came of age. Under English law, a married woman, as a *femme couverte*, lost many of her legal rights because, in law, she came under the protection and governance of her husband. Married women could not acquire, sell, or bequeath property to another person. They could not sue or be sued or claim the use of any wages they earned. They could gain such basic legal rights only through special contracts made with their husbands. Puritan communities, however, frowned on any such arrangements. A husband also represented the family's interests in the realm of politics. No matter how wise or wealthy a woman might become, she did not have a political voice.

hierarchy A system in which people or things are ranked above one another.

femme couverte From the French for "covered woman"; a legal term for a married woman; this legal status limited women's rights, denying them the right to sue or be sued, own or sell property, or earn wages.

Government in Puritan Massachusetts

To create the "city upon a hill" the directors of the Massachusetts Bay Company needed, and expected, the full cooperation of all colonists. However, John Winthrop made it clear that the "wilderness Zion" was not intended to be an **egalitarian** society. Like most of his audience, Winthrop believed that it was natural and correct for some people to be rich and some to be poor. Other colonies denied women, children, servants, young men, and adult men without property a political voice, but Massachusetts further limited political participation. No man in Massachusetts had a full political voice unless he was an acknowledged church member, not just a churchgoer. Church membership, or **sainthood**, was granted only after a person testified to an experience of "saving grace," a moment of intense awareness of God's power and a reassuring conviction of personal salvation. Thus Massachusetts made religious qualifications as important as gender or economic status in the colony's political life.

Massachusetts differed from the Chesapeake colonies in other significant ways. The colony's government enforced biblical law as well as English civil and criminal law. This meant that the government regulated a colonist's religious beliefs and practices, style of dress, sexual conduct, and personal behavior. For example, every colonist was required to attend church and to observe the Sabbath as Puritan custom dictated. The church played a role in supervising business dealings, parent-child relationships, and marital life.

In the early decades of the colony, the Puritan sense of mission left little room for religious toleration. Colonial leaders saw no reason to welcome anyone who disagreed with their religious views. English America was large, they argued, and people of other faiths could settle elsewhere. Winthrop's government was particularly aggressive against members of a new sect called the **Quakers**, who came to Massachusetts on a mission of their own—to convert Puritans to their faith. Quakers entering the colony were beaten, imprisoned, or branded with hot irons, and thrown out. If they returned, they were hanged. Puritan leaders showed just as little tolerance toward members of their own communities who criticized or challenged the rules of the Bay Colony or the beliefs of its church. They drove out men and women they perceived to be **heretics**, or religious traitors.

Almost anyone could be labeled a heretic—even a popular Puritan minister like **Roger Williams**. Williams, the assistant minister of the Salem church, attracted a devoted following with his electrifying sermons and his impressive knowledge of scripture. But he soon attracted the attention of local authorities as well, for his sermons were highly critical of the colonial government. From his pulpit, Williams condemned political leaders for seizing Indian land, calling their tactics of intimidation and violence a "National Sinne." He also denounced laws requiring church attendance.

egalitarian   Believing in human equality.

sainthood   Full membership in a Puritan church.

heretic   A person who does not behave in accordance with an established attitude, doctrine, or principle, usually in religious matters.

In 1635 John Winthrop's government banished Roger Williams from the colony. With snow thick on the ground, Williams left Salem and sought refuge with the Narragansett Indians. When spring came, many of his Salem congregation joined him in exile. Together, in 1635, they created a community called Providence that welcomed dissenters of all kinds, including Quakers, Jews, and Baptists. Providence also attracted other Massachusetts colonists tired of the tight controls imposed on their lives by Winthrop and his colleagues. In 1644 the English government granted Williams a charter for his colony, which he eventually called Rhode Island. Within their borders, Rhode Islanders firmly established the principle of separation of church and state.

Soon after the Massachusetts authorities rid the colony of Roger Williams, a new challenge arose. In 1634 a merchant named William Hutchinson arrived in Massachusetts with his family. His wife, **Anne Hutchinson**, had received an exceptionally fine education from her father and was eloquent, witty, and well versed in scripture. In addition, she was clearly knowledgeable about the religious debates of the day. Like Williams, Hutchinson put little stock in the power of a minister or in any rules of behavior to assist an individual in the search for salvation.

Hutchinson's opinions, aired in popular meetings at her home, disturbed the Puritan authorities. That she was a woman made her outspoken defiance even more shocking. Men like John Winthrop believed that women ought to be silent in the church and had no business criticizing male authorities. A surprising number of Puritans, however, were untroubled by Hutchinson's sex. Male merchants and craftsmen who lacked political rights because they were not members of the saintly elect welcomed her attacks on the authorities. Hutchinson also attracted Puritan saints who resented the tight grip of the colonial government on their business, personal, and social lives.

In the end, none of Hutchinson's supporters could protect her against the determined opposition of the Puritan leadership. In 1637 she was arrested and brought to trial. John Winthrop and his colleagues declared her a heretic, "unfit to our society." They banished her from Massachusetts.

Many Puritans who left Massachusetts did so by choice, not because they were banished. For example, in 1636 the Reverend Thomas Hooker and his entire Newton congregation abandoned Massachusetts and resettled in the Connecticut River valley. Other Puritan congregations followed. In 1644 the Connecticut Valley towns of Hartford, Wethersfield, and Windsor united with the Saybrook settlement at the mouth of the Connecticut River to create the colony of Connecticut. In 1660 the independent New Haven community joined them. Other Bay colonists, searching for new or better lands, made their way north to what later became Maine and New Hampshire. New Hampshire settlers won a charter for their own colony in 1679, but Maine remained part of Massachusetts until it became a state in 1820.

Indian
Suppression

Although the Puritan colonists hoped to create a godly community, they were often motivated by greed and jealousy. Between 1636 and the 1670s, New Englanders came into

This statue of Anne Hutchinson conveys her as a courageous and determined woman. Massachusetts Bay's Puritan officials would not have approved. They considered her a dangerous heretic who overstepped her proper place as a woman by challenging the established religious and political authorities. Like Roger Williams, Anne Hutchinson was exiled from the colony for her unorthodox views.

Collection of Picture Research Consultants

conflict with one another over desirable land. They also waged particularly violent warfare against the Indians of the region.

When the Connecticut Valley towns sprang up, for example, Winthrop tried to assert Bay Colony authority over them. His motives were personal: he and his friends had expected to develop the valley area lands themselves someday. The Connecticut settlers ignored Winthrop's claims and blocked his attempts to prevent their independence from Massachusetts. But they could not ignore the Indians of the area, who understood clearly the threat that English settlers posed to their territories and their way of life. Sassacus, leader of the Pequots, hoped that an armed struggle would break out between Winthrop and the new Connecticut towns, destroying them both. Instead, however, the two English rivals concentrated on destroying the Pequots.

By 1636, the **Pequot War** had begun, with the Indians under attack from both Massachusetts and Connecticut armies and their Indian allies, the Narragansetts and the Mohicans. Mounting a joint effort, the colonists, under Captain John

Mason, attacked the Pequot town of Mystic Village, although the village was defenseless and contained only civilians. Captain John Underhill of the Massachusetts army recorded the slaughter with obvious satisfaction: "Many [Pequots] were burnt in the fort, both men, women, and children." When the survivors tried to surrender to the Narragansetts, Puritan soldiers killed them. The brutal war did not end until all the Pequot men had been killed and the women and children sold into slavery. If the Narragansett Indians believed their alliance with Winthrop would protect them, they were mistaken. Within five years the Puritans had assassinated the Narragansett chief, an act of insurance against problems with these Indian allies.

An uneasy peace followed, despite the ongoing struggle over the land. By 1675, however, new Pilgrim demands for Indian lands had so eroded the friendship between the Plymouth colonists and the Wampanoags that Chief **Metacomet**, known to the English as King Philip, made the difficult decision to resist. Employing **guerrilla tactics**, Metacomet's early, devastating raids on white settlements terrified the colonists, but soon the casualties grew on both sides. Atrocities were committed by everyone involved in this struggle, which the English called King Philip's War. With the help of Iroquois troops sent by the governor of New York, the colonists finally defeated the Wampanoags. The victors murdered Metacomet and impaled his head on a stick.

Indian objections to colonial expansion in New England had been silenced. Indeed, few native peoples remained to offer resistance of any sort. Several tribes had been wiped out entirely in the war, or their few survivors sold into slavery in the Caribbean. Those who escaped enslavement or death scattered to the north and the west. The victory had cost the English dearly also. More than two thousand New England colonists lost their lives as the war spread from Plymouth to nearby settlements. And the war left a legacy of hate that prompted Indian tribes west of Massachusetts to block Puritan expansion whenever possible. The costs of New England's Indian policy prompted colonial leaders in other regions to try less aggressive tactics in dealing with local Indians. For the Wampanoags, the Narragansetts, and the Pequots, however, this decision came too late.

Change and Reaction in England and New England   The rise of England's Puritan Commonwealth during the 1640s was celebrated in New England. But Cromwell's victory had unexpected consequences for "the city upon a hill." Many Puritans returned to England to enjoy Cromwell's success. Many of the newcomers to the colony during the rest of the century were not Puritans at all, but men and women eager to improve their fortunes. Among those Puritans who remained, religious zeal seemed to fade. Few native-born colonists petitioned for full membership, or sainthood, in their local churches as their parents had done, perhaps because of their growing involvement with commerce or

---

guerrilla tactics   A method of warfare in which small bands of fighters in occupied territory harass and attack their enemies, often in surprise raids; the Indians used these tactics during King Philip's War.

No portrait of Metacomet, or King Philip, was painted during his lifetime. In this nineteenth-century painting, Metacomet wears traditional New England Indian clothing, yet he is armed with a European musket, providing a stark reminder that even the bitterest enemies borrowed from one another's culture.

Getty Images

because their mission seemed to have been fulfilled by Cromwell and his followers. By 1662, anxious members of the older, saintly generation approved a compromise to ensure that their sons would enjoy political rights despite their failure to recount a conversion experience. The resulting **Half-Way Covenant** kept political power in the hands of Puritans—for the moment.

Pressures from England could not be dealt with so easily, however. After the Restoration in 1660, Charles II cast a doubtful eye on a colony that sometimes ignored English civil law if it conflicted with biblical demands. In 1683 Charles insisted that the Bay Colony revise its charter to weaken the influence of biblical teachings and eliminate the stringent voting requirements. The Massachusetts government said no. With that, Charles revoked the charter. Massachusetts remained in political limbo until 1685, when James II came to the throne. Then conditions grew far worse.

In an effort to centralize administration of his growing American empire, King James decided on a massive reorganization of the mainland colonial world. He combined several of the northern colonies into one large unit under direct royal control. This megacolony, the **Dominion of New England**, included Massachusetts, Rhode Island, Connecticut, Plymouth Plantations, and the newly acquired colonies of New Jersey and New York. James expected the Dominion to increase the

Dominion of New England A megacolony created in 1686 by James II that brought Massachusetts, Plymouth Plantations, Connecticut, Rhode Island, New Jersey, and New York under the control of one royal governor; William and Mary dissolved the Dominion when they came to the throne in 1689.

patronage, or political favors, he could provide to his loyal supporters—favors such as generous land grants or colonial administrative appointments. He also expected to increase revenues by imposing duties and taxes on colonial goods in the vast region he now controlled.

What King James did not expect was how strongly colonists resented his Dominion and the man he chose to govern it: the arrogant and greedy Sir Edmund Andros. Andros immediately offended New England Puritans by establishing the Church of England as the official religion of the new colony. Then he added insult to injury by commandeering a Puritan church in Boston for Anglican worship. Andros also alienated many non-Puritans in Massachusetts by abolishing the representative assembly there. Non-Puritan men had been struggling to be included in the assembly, not to have the assembly destroyed. Andros's high-handed tactics united Massachusetts colonists who had been at odds with each other. One sign of this cooperation surfaced when the Dominion governor imposed new taxes: saints and nonsaints alike refused to pay them.

When Boston citizens received news of the Glorious Revolution, they imprisoned Edmund Andros and shipped him back to England to stand trial as a traitor to the nation's new Protestant government. Massachusetts Puritans hoped to be rewarded for their patriotism, but although William and Mary abolished the Dominion, they chose not to restore the Bay Colony charter. In 1691 Massachusetts became a royal colony, its governor appointed by the Crown. **Suffrage**, or voting rights, was granted to all free males who met an English **property requirement**. Church membership would never again be a criterion for citizenship in the colony.

Over the course of its sixty-year history, Massachusetts had undergone many significant changes. The Puritan ideal of small, tightly knit farming communities whose members worshiped together and shared common values and goals had been replaced for many colonists by an emerging "Yankee" ideal of trade and commerce, bustling seaport cities, diverse beliefs, and a more secular, or nonreligious, orientation to daily life. This transition increased tensions in every community, especially during the difficult years of the 1680s. Those tensions contributed to one of the most dramatic events in the region's history: the Salem witch trials.

In 1692 a group of young women and girls in Salem Village began to show signs of what seventeenth-century society diagnosed as bewitchment. They fell into violent fits, contorting their bodies and showing great emotional distress. Under questioning, they named several local women, including a West Indian slave named Tituba, as their tormentors. The conviction that the devil had come to Massachusetts spread quickly, and the number of people accused of witchcraft mushroomed. Within months, more than a hundred women, men, and children were crowded into local jails, awaiting trial. Accusations, trials, and even

---

patronage   Jobs or favors distributed by political leadership, usually as rewards for loyalty or service.

suffrage   The right to vote.

property requirement   The limitation of voting rights to citizens who own certain kinds or amounts of property.

executions—nineteen in all—continued until the new royal governor, Sir William Phips, arrived in the colony and forbade any further arrests. Phips dismissed the court that had passed judgment based on "spectral evidence"—that is, testimony by the alleged victims that they had seen the spirits of those tormenting them. In January 1693, Phips assembled a new court that acquitted the remaining prisoners.

What had prompted this terrible episode in colonial history? Seventeenth-century people throughout Europe and America widely believed that the devil and his disciples could work great harm in a community. But in part, the Salem witch trials played out a struggle between Puritan farmers of Salem Village and the town's more worldly merchants, for the accusers were often members of the farming community while the accused were often associated with commercial activities. In part, the trials reflected that despite the busy port towns and the prosperity of the older farming communities, danger continued to lurk nearby. French and Indian attacks on the border settlements were frequent and brutal, and refugees from this violence could be seen in many older towns. In the despair that followed these attacks, colonists looked for someone to blame for their losses. It was easy to conclude that hostile Indians were the agents of the devil in Massachusetts.

THE PLURALISM OF THE MIDDLE COLONIES

Between the Chesapeake and New England lay the vast stretch of forest and farm-land called New Netherland, a Dutch colony that was home to settlers from Holland, Sweden, Germany, and France. In the 1660s, Charles II seized the area and drove the Dutch from the Atlantic coast of North America. The English divided the conquered territory into three colonies: New York, New Jersey, and Pennsylvania. Although the region changed hands, it did not change its character: the Middle Colonies remained a multicultural, commercially oriented, and competitive society no matter whose flag flew over them.

From New Netherland to New York
By 1652, England and Holland had become bitter rivals, fighting three naval wars to decide who would control the transatlantic trade in raw materials and manufactured goods. After each war, the Dutch lost ground, and their decline made it likely that their New Netherland settlement would be abandoned.

King Charles II of England wanted New Netherland very much, and James, Duke of York (later King James II), was eager to satisfy his brother's desires. In 1664 Charles agreed to give James control of the region lying between the Connecticut and Delaware Rivers—if James could wrest it from the Dutch. The promise and the prize amounted to a declaration of war on New Netherland.

When the duke's four armed ships arrived in New Amsterdam harbor and aimed their cannons at the town, Governor Peter Stuyvesant tried to rally the local residents to resist. They refused. Life under the English, they reasoned, would

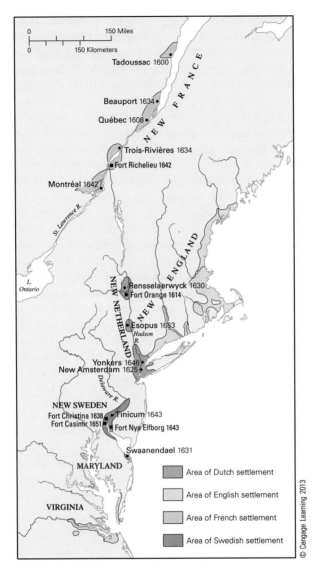

MAP 3.2 European Colonization in the Middle and North Atlantic, circa 1650

North of Spanish Florida, four European powers competed for territory and trade with Native Americans in the early seventeenth century. Swedish and Dutch colonization was the foundation upon which England's middle colonies were built.

probably be no worse than life under the Dutch. Perhaps it might be better. The humiliated governor surrendered the colony, and in 1664 New Netherland became New York without a shot being fired.

In many ways, James proved to be a very liberal ruler, allowing the Dutch and other European colonists to keep their lands, practice their religions, and conduct their business in their native languages. But the duke's generosity and tolerance did not extend to taxation matters. James saw his colonists much as his brother the king saw every colonist: as a source of personal revenue. James taxed New Yorkers heavily and allowed no representative assembly that might interfere with his use of the treasury. All political offices in the new colony, high or low, went to the duke's friends, creating a patronage system that impressed even King Charles.

James's colony did not develop as he had hoped, however. Settlement did not expand to the north and east as he wished. He could not enlist the aid of influential New Yorkers in his expansion plans, even though he offered them the incentive of a representative assembly in 1682. By 1685, James—now king of England—had lost interest in the colony, abandoning his schemes for its growth and abolishing the representative assembly as well.

Leisler's Rebellion   Although James viewed New York as a failure, the colony actually grew rapidly during his rule. The population doubled between 1665 and 1685, reaching fifteen thousand the year the duke ascended to the English throne. These new settlers added to the cultural diversity that had always characterized the region. The colony became a religious refuge for French Protestants, English Quakers, and Scottish **Presbyterians**. New York's diverse community, however, did not always live in harmony. English, Dutch, and German merchants competed fiercely for control of New York City's trade and for dominance in the city's cultural life. An equally intense rivalry existed between Manhattan's merchants and Albany's fur traders. Only one thing united these competitors: a burning resentment of James's political control and the men he chose to enforce his will. Their anger increased when James created the Dominion of New England.

In 1689 news of the Glorious Revolution prompted a revolt in New York City similar to the one that shook Boston. **Jacob Leisler**, a German merchant, emerged as its leader. Although Leisler lacked the charisma and commanding presence that had allowed Nathaniel Bacon to rise to power in 1676, he was able to take control of the entire colony. When William and Mary sent a new governor to New York, Leisler refused to surrender the reins of government. This time, the abrasive, headstrong merchant found few supporters, and eventually he was forced to step down. To Leisler's surprise, he was then arrested and charged with treason. Both he and his son-in-law were tried, found guilty, and executed. As befit traitors in the seventeenth century, the two rebels were hanged, disemboweled while still alive, and then beheaded. Afterward, their mutilated bodies were quartered. In death, Leisler became a hero and a martyr. Popular anger was so great that to quiet the discontent, the new governor had to permit the formation of a representative assembly. Several of the men elected to this new legislature were ardent Leislerians, and for many years New York politics remained a battleground between home rule advocates and supporters of the royal governor and the king.

Presbyterians   Members of a Protestant sect that eventually became the established church of Scotland but that in the seventeenth century was sometimes persecuted by Scotland's rulers.

William Penn's Holy Experiment   More than most dissenting sects, Quakers had paid a high price for their strongly held convictions. Members of the Society of Friends had been jailed in England and Scotland and harassed by their neighbors throughout the empire. Quaker leaders had strong motives to create a refuge for members of their beleaguered sect. In the 1670s, a group of wealthy Friends purchased New Jersey from its original **proprietors** and offered religious freedom and generous political rights to its current and future colonists, many of whom were, in fact, Puritans. The best known of these Quaker proprietors was **William Penn**, who had given up a life of privilege, luxury, and self-indulgence in Restoration society and embraced the morally demanding life of the Friends.

Penn's father, Admiral Sir William Penn, was one of England's naval heroes and a political adviser to King Charles II. The senior Penn and his son had little in common except their loyalty to the king and their willingness to provide liberal loans to support their monarch's extravagant lifestyle. Eventually, Charles rewarded the Penns' devotion. In 1681, he granted the younger Penn a charter to a huge area west of the Delaware River. This gave Penn the opportunity to create a refuge for Quakers that fully embodied their religious principles.

Penn called his new colony Pennsylvania, meaning "Penn's Woods," in memory of his father. (The southernmost section of Penn's grant, added later by Charles II, developed independently of Penn's control and in 1776 became the state of Delaware.) Like most colonial proprietors, Penn expected to profit from his charter, and he set a quitrent, or small fee, on all land purchased within his colony. But his religious devoutness ensured that he would not govern by whim. Instead, Quaker values and principles were the basis for his "holy experiment." At the heart of the Quaker faith was the conviction that the divine spirit, or "inner light," resided in every human being. Quakers thus were expected to respect all individuals. By their plain dress and their refusal to remove their hats in the presence of their social "betters," Quakers demonstrated their belief that all men and women were equal. In keeping with their egalitarian principles, Quakers also recognized no distinctions of wealth or social status in their places of worship. At the strikingly simple Quaker meeting, or worship service, any member who felt moved to speak was welcome to participate, no matter how poor or uneducated and no matter what sex or age. Although they actively sought converts, Quakers were always tolerant of other religions.

Pennsylvania's political structure reflected this egalitarianism. All free male residents had the right to vote during Penn's lifetime, and the legislature they elected had full governing powers. Penn honored the legislature's decisions even when they disturbed or amazed him. The political quarrels that developed in Pennsylvania's assembly actually shocked Penn, but his only action was to urge political leaders not to be "so noisy, and open, in your dissatisfactions."

Penn's land policy also reflected Quaker principles. Unlike many proprietors, he wanted no politically powerful landlords and no economically dependent

---

proprietor   In colonial America, a proprietor was a wealthy Englishman who received a large grant of land in America from the king or queen in order to create a new colony.

tenant farmers. Instead, he actively promoted a society of independent, landowning farm families. Penn also insisted that all land be purchased fairly from the Indians, and he pursued a policy of peaceful coexistence between the two cultures. William Penn took an active role in making Pennsylvania a multicultural society, recruiting non- English settlers through pamphlets that stressed the religious and political freedoms and economic opportunities his colony offered. More than eight thousand immigrants poured into the colony in the first four years. Many did come from England, but Irish, Scottish, Welsh, French, Scandinavian, and German settlers came as well. To their English neighbors who did not speak German, newcomers from Germany such as the Mennonites and Amish were known as the "Pennsylvania Dutch" (*Deutsch,* meaning "German," would have been correct).

When William Penn died in 1717, he left behind a successful, dynamic colony. Philadelphia was already emerging as a great shipping and commercial center, rivaling the older seaports of Boston and New York City. But this success came at some cost to Penn's original vision and to his Quaker principles. The commercial orientation here, as in Puritan Massachusetts, attracted colonists who were more secular in their interests and objectives than the colony's founders. Many newcomers saw Penn's Indian policy as a check on their ambitions and preferred to seize land from the Indians rather than purchase it. The demand for military protection from Indians by these land-hungry farmers in the western part of the colony, similar to the demands made decades before by Nathaniel Bacon and his followers, became a major political issue and a matter of conscience for Quakers, whose religious principles included **pacifism**. Eventually many Quakers chose to resign from the colonial government rather than struggle to uphold a holy experiment their neighbors did not support.

Colonies of the Lower South

In 1663 King Charles II surprised eight of his favorite supporters by granting them several million acres lying south of Virginia and stretching from the Atlantic to the Pacific Ocean. The gesture was both grand and calculated. France, Spain, Holland, and the Indian tribes that inhabited this area all laid claim to it, and Charles thought it would be wise to secure England's control of the region by colonizing it. The eight new colonial proprietors named their colony Carolina to honor the king's late father, who had lost his head to the Puritan Commonwealth (and whose name in Latin was Carolus).

The Carolina Colony   The proprietors' plan for Carolina, called the Fundamental Constitution, was similar to Lord Baltimore's medieval dream. It was an elaborate blueprint for a society of great landowners, **yeomen** (small, independent farmers), and serfs (agricultural laborers) bound to work for their landlords. Like the Calverts, however, the Carolina

pacifism   Opposition to war or violence of any kind.
yeoman   Independent landowner entitled to suffrage.

proprietors discovered that few English people were willing to travel three thousand miles across the ocean to become serfs. Bowing to reality, the proprietors offered the incentive of the head right system.

The early settlers in Carolina, many of them relocating from the Caribbean island of Barbados, made their way to the southeastern portion of the colony, drawn there by the fine natural harbor of the port city, Charles Town (later Charleston), and its fertile surroundings. Despite the dangers of the Spanish to the south in Florida and the Yamasee Indians to the southwest, Charles Town grew rapidly, becoming the most important city in the southern colonies. The early Carolinians experimented with several moneymaking activities: they traded with the Indians for deerskins and for captive victims of tribal warfare, whom the colonists sold as slaves in the Caribbean; they produced naval stores from the region's pine forests and experimented with several cash crops, such as sugarcane, tobacco, silk, cotton, ginger, and olives. The colonists' first real success turned out to be cattle raising, a skill they learned from African slaves brought into the colony by the settlers from Barbados. But by the 1680s rice cultivation became the road to riches. In 1719, Carolina's elite rice planters took control of the southern section of the colony from the original proprietors and named it South Carolina. These planters quickly became the richest English colonists on the mainland.

The northern region of Carolina did not fare as well. Bordered by the Great Dismal Swamp to the north and by smaller swamps to the south, this isolated area attracted few colonists. The land around Albemarle Sound was fertile enough, but the remaining coastline was cut off from the Atlantic by a chain of barrier islands that blocked access to oceangoing vessels. Despite all these constraints, some poor farm families and freed white indentured servants had drifted in from Virginia, searching for unclaimed land and a fresh start. They had modest success in growing tobacco and producing naval stores.

In 1729 the Albemarle colonists followed the lead of their elite neighbors around Charleston and rid themselves of proprietary rule. These North Carolinians then officially separated from the rice-rich southern section of the colony. Thus both South Carolina and North Carolina had become royal colonies.

Georgia, the Last Colony

In 1732 **James Oglethorpe**, a wealthy English social reformer, and several of his friends requested a charter for a colony on the Florida border. Their goal was to provide a new, moral life for English men and women imprisoned for minor debts. King George II had other motives for granting the charter, however. He was anxious to create a protective buffer between the valuable rice-producing colony of South Carolina and the Spanish in Florida. The king inserted a clause in the Georgia charter requiring military service from every male settler. Thus he guaranteed that the poor men of Georgia would protect the rich men of South Carolina.

Oglethorpe and his associates added their own special restrictions on the lives of the Georgia colonists. Because they believed that poverty was the result of a weak character or, worse, of an addiction to vice, they did not think debtors could govern themselves. They forbade a representative assembly and denied the settlers a voice in selecting political leaders and military officers. In an effort to reform the character of their colonists, the trustees set other rules, including a ban on all alcoholic beverages. To ensure that these settlers worked hard, they kept individual land grants small, and they banned slavery.

Oglethorpe interviewed many imprisoned debtors, searching for members of the "deserving poor" who would benefit from Georgia. But few of these debtors met his standards. In the end, most of the colony's settlers turned out to be middle-class English immigrants and South Carolinians looking for new land. These colonists did not welcome the trustees' paternalistic attitudes, and they soon challenged all the restrictive rules and regulations in the charter. They won the right to accumulate and sell land. They introduced slave labor in defiance of the trustees. By the 1740s, illegal slave auctions were a common sight in Georgia's largest town, Savannah. By 1752, Oglethorpe and his fellow trustees had lost enthusiasm for their reform project and, with relief, returned Georgia to the king.

Study Tools

Summary

In 1607, the English created their first permanent colony at Jamestown. By 1732, thirteen English colonies hugged the coast of the Atlantic Ocean. Some, like Maryland, Pennsylvania, and Massachusetts, were founded as religious refuges; others were founded for profit. Four distinct regions soon emerged, based primarily on how the settlers made their livings.

Virginia and Maryland made up the Chesapeake region. Here tobacco shaped every aspect of life. Thousands of poor young Englishmen were brought over to work in the tobacco fields. They came as indentured servants, working without pay in exchange for passage to America. Few women were recruited, and the combination of an unbalanced sex ratio and frequent deaths caused by an unhealthy climate, grueling labor, and poor diet produced what historians call a "demographic disaster" in the seventeenth-century Chesapeake.

The colonies of the Lower South, the Carolinas and Georgia, were established many decades after the Chesapeake by two groups of wealthy Englishmen. Carolina's proprietors tried to create a feudal society, and Georgia's founders wanted to build a haven for debtors. In the end, however, neither goal was achieved. After experiments in cattle raising and other enterprises, the settlers of what became South Carolina focused on rice production, using African slave labor, and these planters became the richest group in the colonies. North Carolinians were poorer, growing tobacco and farming.

Plymouth Plantations, Massachusetts, Rhode Island, Connecticut, and later New Hampshire made up the New England colonies, with their small farms and shipping and lumbering industries. Here, the earliest settlers were dissenters who sought religious freedom. In 1620, separatists known as the Pilgrims founded the first New England colony, Plymouth Plantations. Their leaders drafted a radical document known as the Mayflower Compact, which assured broad political rights to all the men on board their ship, including the crew and servants. In 1630,

Massachusetts Bay was founded by Puritans who intended it to be a model Protestant community. They demanded conformity to their religious views and drove out those who challenged them, especially Quakers. When Puritans like Roger Williams and Anne Hutchinson challenged the colony's leadership and its religious practices, they too were exiled. Williams went on to found Rhode Island on the principle of separation of church and state. Other colonists left Massachusetts voluntarily and founded Connecticut. In 1691, Massachusetts was taken over by the King, and the Puritans' religious experiment ended. The anxiety produced by this political change coupled with economic tensions and dangers on the frontier contributed to the Salem witch hunts of 1691.

The Middle Colonies region was originally settled by the Dutch and the Swedes, but the English seized the area in 1664. New Sweden and New Netherland became New Jersey and New York. In 1681 William Penn created the colony of Pennsylvania, west of New Jersey, as a home for Quakers. Unlike the Puritans, however, he welcomed people of all faiths into his "holy experiment." The Middle Colonies, where many colonists grew wheat and exported it through the major ports of Philadelphia and New York, were noted for their diverse populations and policies of religious toleration.

Religious, economic, and political conflicts were common back in England, and it was often no more peaceful in the colonies. In Maryland, Protestants and Catholics warred with each other and in Virginia, poor backcountry farmers, led by Nathaniel Bacon, rose up against the wealthier coastal planters in 1676. The desire for land also led to bloodshed. Land-hungry colonists in Virginia and New England made war against the Indians. Finally, English policies prompted rebellions, as colonists in Boston and New York rose up to overthrow the hated Dominion of New England in 1689.

As you will see in Chapter 4, most colonists continued to think of England as "home" even as they developed their own societies and their own institutions. Some developments, like widespread African slavery, would seem to widen the differences among the colonial regions; some, like the rise of local representative government, would seem to bring them together. Slowly, however, colonists in all regions developed interests and goals that conflicted with the policies of the Mother Country. One thing was certain: great changes would take place in the eighteenth century.

CHRONOLOGY

SETTLING THE MAINLAND COLONIES	
1585	English colonize Roanoke Island
1607	Virginia Company founds Jamestown
1619	Virginia House of Burgesses meets
1620	Pilgrims found Plymouth Plantations
1625	Charles I becomes king of England
1630	Puritans found Massachusetts Bay Colony
1634	Lord Baltimore establishes Maryland

1635	Roger Williams founds Providence
1636	Anne Hutchinson banished from Massachusetts Pequot War in New England Connecticut settled
1642–1648	English civil war
1649	Charles I executed; Cromwell and Puritans come to power in England
1655	Civil war in Maryland
1660	Restoration of English monarchy
1663	Carolina chartered
1664	New Netherland becomes New York
1675	King Philip's War in New England
1676	Bacon's Rebellion in Virginia
1681	Pennsylvania chartered
1685	James II becomes king of England
1686	Dominion of New England established
1688	Glorious Revolution in England
1689	Leisler's Rebellion in New York
1691	Massachusetts becomes royal colony
1692	Salem witch trials
1732	Georgia chartered

FOCUS QUESTIONS

If you have mastered this chapter, you should be able to answer these questions and explain the terms that follow the questions.

1. What circumstances or conditions in England affected people's willingness to join England's colonizing efforts?
2. What were the goals of the Virginia Company and of the Calvert family in creating their Chesapeake colonies? Did the colonies achieve these goals?
3. What events illustrate the racial, class, and religious tensions in the Chesapeake?
4. What type of society did the Puritans create in Massachusetts?
5. What troubles confronted New England colonists, and how did they respond?
6. How did New Netherland develop under English control, and what cultural and economic tensions came to a head in Leisler's Rebellion?
7. What made William Penn's vision for Pennsylvania so distinctive?
8. What type of society did the founders of Carolina hope to create? How did the colony differ from their expectations?
9. Why did philanthropists create Georgia? Why did the king support this project?

KEY TERMS

Church of England (*p.* 48)

Puritan (*p.* 48)

Parliament (*p.* 48)

Commonwealth (*p.* 48)

Restoration (*p.* 48)

Glorious Revolution (*p.* 49)

Jamestown (*p.* 49)

head right system (*p.* 52)

House of Burgesses (*p.* 52)

John Coode (*p.* 55)

indentured servants (*p.* 56)

Pilgrims (*p.* 57)

William Bradford (*p.* 57)

Mayflower Compact (*p.* 58)

Squanto (*p.* 58)

John Winthrop (*p.* 58)

Great Migration (*p.* 59)

Quakers (*p.* 61)

Roger Williams (*p.* 61)

Anne Hutchinson (*p.* 62)

Pequot War (*p.* 63)

Metacomet (*p.* 64)

Half-Way Covenant (*p.* 65)

Jacob Leisler (*p.* 69)

William Penn (*p.* 70)

James Oglethorpe (*p.* 72)

4

THE ENGLISH COLONIES IN THE EIGHTEENTH CENTURY, 1689–1763

THE ENGLISH TRANSATLANTIC COMMUNITIES OF TRADE

Although the English spoke of "the colonial trade," British America did not have a single, unified economy. Instead, four distinctive regional economies had developed on the mainland, concentrated along the Atlantic coastline and bordered on the west by the primarily **subsistence society** that was commonly found on the edge of white settlement. To the south, the sugar islands of the Caribbean made up a fifth unique regional economy. Each of these economies was shaped by environmental conditions, natural resources, English commercial policy, the available labor force, and the available technological know-how.

Regions of Commerce   The sugar-producing islands of the West Indies were the brightest jewels in the English imperial crown. Spain had first laid claim to most of these islands, but England had slowly gobbled up many of them, and thus, by the eighteenth century, the English flag flew over St. Kitts, Barbados, Nevis, Montserrat, and Jamaica. Here, English plantation owners built fabulous fortunes on the sugar that African slaves produced. While the

---

subsistence society A society that produces the food and supplies necessary for its survival but that does not produce a surplus for market.

absentee planters lived in luxury in England, black slaves lived—and died in staggering numbers—on the islands, working the cane fields and tending the fires that burned day and night under the sugar vats of the boiling houses where the raw sugar, or molasses, was produced.

Few mainland colonists enjoyed the wealth of this "Sugar Interest." Still, in the Lower South, planters of South Carolina and Georgia, amassed considerable fortunes by growing rice in the lowlands along the Atlantic coast. By the 1730s, this American rice was feeding the people of the Mediterranean, Portugal, and Spain. By midcentury, planters were making additional profits from indigo crops. Like the sugar planters, Carolina and Georgia rice growers based their production on slave labor, but unlike the island moguls, these plantation masters never became permanently absent landowners.

Tobacco or "brown gold" continued to dominate the economy of the Chesapeake, although the high taxes placed on this crop prompted many eighteenth-century planters to diversify. They began producing wheat and other grains for export. Tobacco production shifted west to the area along the Potomac, the James River valley, and the **piedmont** foothills. The second major shift came in the labor force used in tobacco cultivation. By the eighteenth century, African slaves had replaced indentured servants in the fields. Planters who could afford to purchase a number of slaves enjoyed a competitive advantage over their neighbors in both the old and the new tobacco areas because they had enough workers to plant and harvest bigger crops. This large-scale production kept tobacco the number one export of the mainland colonies.

Together, these two southern regions provided the bulk of the mainland's agricultural exports to Great Britain. In contrast, the New England regional economy depended far less on Britain as a market. Except in the Connecticut River valley, where tobacco was grown, the region's rocky soil made large-scale farming unfeasible for New Englanders. Instead, shipbuilding and the ambitious **carrying trade** dominated New England's economy. Colonists made great profits from an extensive shipping network that carried colonial exports across the Atlantic and to the Caribbean and distributed foreign goods and English manufactured products to the colonies. Some merchant-shippers—the slave traders of Newport, Rhode Island, for example—specialized in a certain commodity, but most were willing to carry any cargo that promised a profit. An economy based on the carrying trade made New Englanders rivals of English merchants rather than useful sources of profit for the Mother Country.

Sandwiched between the South and New England, the colonies of New York, New Jersey, Pennsylvania, and later Delaware developed their own regional economy, which combined the successes of their neighbors to the north and south. They created profits from both staple-crop farming and trade. The forests of the

---

absentee planter   An estate owner who collects profits from farming or rent but does not live on the land or help cultivate it.

piedmont   Land lying at the foot of a mountain range.

Pocono Mountains and upper New York were a source of wood and wood products for the shipbuilding industry, and locally harvested flaxseed was exported to Ireland for its linen industry. The central crop, however, was wheat. Fortunately for the colonists of this area, the price of wheat rose steadily during the eighteenth century. The carrying trade was equally important in this region's mixed economy. Ships carrying cargoes of grain and flour across the Atlantic and into the Caribbean crossed paths with other colonial ships bringing manufactured goods and luxury items from Europe to the region's two major port cities, New York and Philadelphia.

Not everyone in the colonies participated in the market-oriented activity, of course. In the older coastal settlements of each region, harbors and river ways provided the necessary transportation routes for the shipment of crops, goods, and supplies. But most colonies had an inland backcountry that was sparsely populated and farmed by European immigrants, ex-servants, or the families of younger sons from older communities. There, on what white settlers thought of as the frontier and Indians called the invasion line, colonists struggled to produce enough for survival. They lacked both the labor force to clear and work sufficient acreage for a marketable crop and the transport to get a crop to market. And they had no financial or political resources that might help overcome these obstacles. This belt of subsistence extended like a border from Maine to western Pennsylvania, to inland Carolina, along every region of the mainland colonies. But even these backcountry farms had a fragile link to the world of international trade, for settlers brought with them the farm tools and basic household supplies that had been manufactured in England or imported through colonial ports.

The Cords of Commercial Empire   England's mainland colonists traded with many European nations and their colonies. Salt, wine, and spices reached colonial tables from southern Europe, and sugar, rum, and cotton came to their households from the West Indies. But the deepest channels in the transatlantic trade were those that connected the Mother Country and the colonies. The British purchased over half of all the crops, furs, and mined resources that colonists produced for market and supplied 90 percent of all colonial imports. The English mainland colonies were also bound to one another, despite a deserved reputation for dispute, disagreement, and endless rivalries. New Englanders might exchange insults with Pennsylvanians, but in the shops and on the wharfs, Pennsylvania flour, Massachusetts mackerel, Carolina rice, and scores of domestic products and produce changed hands in a lively and cheerful commerce. Domestic trade was greater in volume, although lower in value, than all foreign trade in this eighteenth-century world.

COMMUNITY AND WORK IN COLONIAL SOCIETY

Despite the belief of many observers that there was an "American character," visitors could not fail to note striking differences as they traveled from New England to the Lower South. Moving from the carefully laid-out towns of New England, through the crowded seaport cities of the Middle Colonies, and into the isolated rural worlds of the plantation South, they could see that the Yankee culture of Connecticut differed strikingly from the lifestyle and social attitudes of South Carolina's elegant planter elite.

The Emergence of the "Yankee"   In the early eighteenth century, New England's seaport towns and cities grew steadily in size and economic importance. With the rise of a profitable international commerce, the Puritan culture of the village gave way to a more secular "Yankee" culture. In this atmosphere, a wealthy man could rise politically without any need to demonstrate his piety. Economic competition and the pursuit of profit eclipsed older notions that the well-being of the community came before the gains of the individual. This shift to a "Yankee" mentality was reflected in the law: Puritan laws regulating prices and interest rates, for example, were repealed or simply ignored. Still, some sense of obligation to the community remained in New Englanders' willingness to create and maintain public institutions such as schools and colleges. In 1701, for example, Yale College opened its doors in New Haven, Connecticut, giving the sons of elite New Englanders an alternative to Massachusetts's Harvard College, founded in 1636. And New Englanders supported newspapers and printing presses that kept their communities informed about local, regional, and international events.

Even in more traditional New England villages, changes were evident. By the eighteenth century, fathers no longer had enough farmland to provide adequately for all their sons. Thus many younger sons left their families and friends behind to seek their fortunes. Some chose to push the frontier of settlement westward as they searched for fertile land. Others went north, to less developed areas such as Maine, causing the number of backcountry New England towns to grow steadily until the end of the colonial period. Still other young men abandoned farming entirely and relocated to the commercial cities of the region. Urban life often disappointed them, for inequality of wealth and opportunity went hand in hand with the overall prosperity. In Boston, a growing number of poor widows and landless young men scrambled for employment and often wound up dependent on public charity. As news spread about the scarcity of farmland in the countryside and the poverty and competition for work in the cities, European immigrants to America tended to bypass New England and settle in the Middle Colonies or along the southern frontier.

Planter Society and Slavery   Southern society was changing as dramatically as New England's. By the end of the seventeenth century, the English economy was improving, and young men who might once have signed on as indentured servants in Virginia or Maryland now chose to remain at home. Those who did immigrate preferred to indenture themselves to farmers and merchants of the Middle Colonies, where work conditions were bearable and economic opportunities were brighter. While the supply of indentured servants was declining, however, a different labor supply was growing: enslaved Africans.

Although a small number of Africans had been brought to Virginia as early as 1619, the legal distinctions between black and white workers remained vague until the 1660s. As the number of African workers slowly increased, white colonists began to adopt the different and harsher treatment that defined slavery in the Caribbean and South America. By midcentury, it became the custom in the Chesapeake to hold black servants for life terms, although their children were still considered free. By the 1660s, colonists turned these customs of **discrimination** into law. In 1662, Virginia took a major step toward making slavery an inherited condition by declaring that "all children born in this country shall be held bond or free according to the condition of the mother."

Southern planters had long been well aware of the advantages of slave labor over indentured servitude. First, a slave, bound for life, would never compete with his former master the way freed white servants did. Second, most white colonists did not believe that the English customs regulating a master's treatment of servants had to be applied to African workers. For example, Christian holidays need not be honored for African laborers, and the workday itself could be lengthened without any outcry from white neighbors. Until the end of the 1600s, though, Chesapeake planters found investment in African laborers both too costly and too risky. Dutch control of the slave trade kept purchase prices high and the supply low, and the disease environment of the Chesapeake cut human life short. In the 1680s, however, mortality rates fell in the Chesapeake, and the English broke the Dutch monopoly on the slave trade. Fierce competition among English slavers drove prices down and at the same time ensured a steady supply of slaves. Under these conditions, the demand for slaves in the Chesapeake grew rapidly. Although only 5 percent of the roughly 9.5 million Africans brought to the Americas came to the North American mainland colonies, their numbers in Virginia and Maryland rose dramatically in the eighteenth century. By 1700, 13 percent of the Chesapeake population was African or of African descent. In Virginia, where only 950 Africans had lived in 1660, the black population grew to 120,000 by 1756. At the end of the colonial period, blacks made up 40 percent of Virginia's population.

Chesapeake colonists who could not afford to purchase African slaves now moved west, and new immigrants to the colonies avoided the coastal and piedmont plantation society altogether. Colonial merchants and skilled craftspeople also avoided the Chesapeake, for the planters purchased goods directly from England or used slave labor to manufacture barrels, bricks, and other products. As a result, few towns or cities developed in this region. The Chesapeake region remained a

discrimination Treatment that denies opportunity or rights because of class, gender, or racial category; sometimes called *prejudice*.

rural society, dominated by a planter class whose prosperity rested on the labor of enslaved African Americans.

If tobacco provided a comfortable life for an eighteenth-century planter, rice provided a luxurious one. The Lower South, too, was a plantation society, dominated by the wealthiest mainland colonists. Members of South Carolina's elite never fully became absentee planters but they did move each summer to Charles Town to avoid the heat, humidity, and unhealthy environment of their lowland plantations. With its beautiful townhouses, theaters, and parks, Charles Town was the single truly cosmopolitan city of the South and perhaps the most sophisticated of all mainland cities in North America.

The prosperity that these Lower South planters enjoyed was based on the forced labor of slaves. Indeed, the families from Barbados who settled South Carolina had arrived with slaves from their Caribbean plantations. By 1708, one-half of the colonial population in Carolina was black, and by 1720, Africans and African Americans outnumbered their white masters. Farther south, in Georgia, the colonists openly defied the trustees' ban on slavery until that ban was finally lifted.

Slave Experience and Slave Culture   Most slaves brought to the mainland colonies did not come directly from Africa but were reexported to the Chesapeake or the Lower South after a short period of **seasoning** in the tropical climate of the West Indies. But all imported slaves, whether seasoned or new to the Americas, began their bondage when African slavers, often armed with European weapons, captured men, women, and children and delivered them in chains to European ships anchored along the coast of West Africa. While many of those enslaved were considered war captives, others were simply kidnap victims. The slave trader John Barbot recounted the theft of "little Blacks" who had been sent by their parents to "scare away the devouring small birds" in the family cornfield. Even before these captives reached the European slave ships, they were introduced to the horrors of slavery. Their captors treated them "severely and barbarously," beating and wounding them. The many who died on the long march from the interior to the coast were left unburied, their bodies to be "devoured by … beasts of prey." As the surviving captives were branded and then rowed to the waiting ships, some committed suicide, leaping overboard into the ocean waters. Slave traders tried to prevent these suicides—every death meant a smaller profit—but were not surprised by them. The slaves, they commented, dreaded life in America more than their captors dreaded hell.

The slaves' transatlantic voyage, or **middle passage**, was a nightmare of death, disease, suicide, and sometimes mutiny. The casualties included the white officers and crews of the slave ships, who died of diseases in such great numbers that the waters near Benin in West Africa were known as the "white man's grave." But the

---

seasoning   A period during which slaves from Africa were held in the West Indies so they could adjust to the climate and disease environment of the American tropics.

TEN DOLLARS

REWARD.

RAN away, on the 23d inft. a handfome active *Mulatto* flave, named A R C H, about 21 years of age, is flender built and of middle ftature, talks fenfible and artful, but if clofly examined is apt to tremble, has a ridge or fcar on

Advertisements like this one were common in the eighteenth century colonies, both north and south. Rewards were usually offered to encourage colonists to turn in the enslaved men and women seeking their freedom.

loss of black lives was far greater. Slave ships were breeding grounds for scurvy, yellow fever, malaria, dysentery, smallpox, measles, and typhus—each bringing painful death. When smallpox struck his slave ship, one European recorded that "we hauled up eight or ten slaves dead of a morning. The flesh and skin peeled off their wrists when taken hold of." Perhaps 18 percent of all the Africans who began the middle passage died on the ocean.

Until the 1720s, most Chesapeake slaves worked alone on a tobacco farm with the owner and his family or in small groups of two or three in a system known as "gang labor." This isolation made both the creation of a family and the emergence of a slave community almost impossible. Even on larger plantations, community formation was discouraged by the division of women and men into separate gangs. The steady influx of newly imported slaves, or "outlanders," during the first decades of the eighteenth century also made it difficult for African Americans to work together to create a culture of their own. The new arrivals had to be taught to speak English and to adapt to the demands of slavery. Slowly, however, these involuntary immigrants from different African societies, speaking different languages, practicing different religions, and surviving under the oppressive conditions of slavery, did create a sense of community, weaving together African and European traditions. The result was an African American culture that gave meaning to, and a sense of identity within, the slave's oppressive world.

In the Lower South, slaves were concentrated on large plantations where they had limited or no contact with white society. This isolation from the dominant society allowed them an earlier opportunity to develop a creole, or native, culture. In contrast to gang labor, here a "task labor" system prevailed. Slaves were assigned certain chores to be completed within a certain time period, and this gave rice plantation slaves some control over their pace of work and some opportunities to manage their free time. Local languages evolved that mixed a basic English vocabulary with words from a variety of African tongues. One of these languages, Gullah, spoken on the Sea Islands off the coast of Georgia and South Carolina, remained the local dialect until the end of the nineteenth century.

For many slaves, the bonds of community became a form of resistance to enslavement. But African Americans also developed other ways to show their hatred of slavery. The diary of Virginia planter William Byrd is filled with accounts of daily resistance: slaves who challenged orders, field hands who broke tools and staged work slowdowns, men who pretended sickness and women who claimed pregnancies, household servants who stole supplies and damaged property, and slaves who ran away to the woods for a day or two or to the slave quarters of a neighboring plantation. African Americans with families, and those who understood the odds against escape, preferred to take disruptive actions like these rather than risk almost certain death in open rebellion.

The Urban Culture of the Middle Colonies   The small family farms of Pennsylvania, with their profitable wheat crops, earned the colony its reputation as the "best poor man's country." Tenant farmers, hired laborers, and even African slaves were not unknown in eastern Pennsylvania, but the colony boasted more comfortable or middle-class farm families than neighboring New York or New Jersey. In New York great estates along the Hudson River controlled much of the colony's good land, and in New Jersey wealthy owners dominated the choicest acreage, which often resulted in tensions between the landlords and their tenants in both colonies.

But what made the Middle Colonies distinctive was the dynamic urban life of the two major cities, New York and Philadelphia. Although only 3 percent of the colonial population lived in the eighteenth-century cities, they were a magnet for young men and women, widows, free African Americans and slaves, and some of the immigrant population pouring into the colonies from Europe. By 1770, Philadelphia's forty thousand residents made it the second-largest city in the British Empire. In the same year, twenty-five thousand people crowded onto the tip of New York's Manhattan Island.

New York residents shared their cramped living spaces with chickens and livestock and their streets with roving packs of dogs and pigs. On the narrow cobblestone or gravel streets, pedestrians jostled one another and struggled to avoid being run down by carts, carriages, men on horseback, or cattle being driven to slaughter. Although colonial cities were usually thought to be cleaner than European cities, with better sewage and drainage systems, garbage and excrement left to rot on the streets provided a feast for flies and scavenging animals.

City residents faced more serious problems than runaway carts and snarling dogs. Sailors on the ships docked at Philadelphia or New York often carried venereal diseases. These and other communicable diseases spread rapidly in overcrowded areas. Fires also raced through these cities of wooden houses, wharfs, and shops. And urban dwellers were no strangers to crime—especially robbery and assault—in a community where taverns, brothels, and gambling houses were common.

Despite the dangers, colonial cities attracted many a farmer's daughter or son because they offered a wide range of occupations and experiences. These newcomers were sometimes overwhelmed by city life. One farm boy wrote to his father: "I must confess, the jolts of Waggons, the Ratlings of Coaches, the crying of meat for the Market, the [hollering] of negroes and the ten thousand junggles and Noises, that continually Surround us in every Part almost of the Town, confuse my Thinking."

Young men who could endure the noise and confusion sought work as **apprentices** in scores of artisan trades ranging from the luxury crafts of silver-smithing and goldsmithing or cabinet making to the profitable trades of shipbuilding, blacksmithing, or butchering, to the more modest occupations of ropemaking, baking, barbering, or shoemaking. The poorest might find work on the docks or as servants, or they might go to sea. Young women had fewer choices because few trades were open to them. Some might become dressmakers or **milliners**, but domestic service or prostitution were more likely choices. In the Middle Colony cities, as in Boston, widowed farm wives came seeking jobs as nurses, laundresses, teachers, or seamstresses. A widow or an unmarried woman who had a little money could open a shop or set up a tavern or a boarding house.

New York City had the highest concentration of African Americans in the northern colonies. While few northern farmers owned slaves, New York's merchants and shippers found enslaved manual laborers valuable on their docks and wharfs. Many free black men and women also made their way to New York City. Only perhaps 5 percent of all mainland colony African Americans were free. Many remained in the South, although they faced social and legal harassment—for example, striking a white person in self-defense could cost a black man his life. Others, though, made their way to the cities of New England and the Middle Colonies, making a living as laborers and servants or sailors.

Life in the Backcountry	Thomas Malthus, a well-known English analyst of **demographics**, believed the eighteenth-century population explosion in the English mainland colonies was "without parallel

apprentice A person bound by legal agreement to work for a craftsman for a specific length of time in exchange for instruction in a trade, craft, or business.

milliner A maker or designer of hats.

demographics The physical characteristics of a population such as age, sex, marital status, family size, education, geographic location, and occupation; usually in the form of statistics.

in history." The colonial white population climbed from 225,000 in 1688 to over 2 million in 1775, and the number of African Americans reached 500,000 in the same year. Natural increase accounted for much of this growth, and over half of the colonists were under age 16 in 1775. But hundreds of thousands of white immigrants arrived during the eighteenth century, risking hunger, thirst, discomfort, fear, and death on the transatlantic voyage to start life over in America. The majority of these immigrants ended up in the colonial backcountry.

Migration westward gradually shifted the population center of mainland society. Newcomers from Europe and Britain, as well as descendants of original New England settlers and the younger sons of the tidewater Chesapeake, all saw their best opportunities in the sparsely settled regions of western New York, northern New England, western Pennsylvania, Virginia's Shenandoah Valley, or the Carolina backcountry. Many of these settlers were squatters who cleared a few acres and laid claim by their presence to a promising piece of land.

The westward flow of settlers was part of the American landscape throughout the century, but it became a flood after 1760. A seemingly endless train of carts, sledges, and wagons moved along Indian paths to the west, and the rivers were crowded with rafts and canoes carrying families, farm tools, and livestock. Many of these new immigrants traveled south from Pennsylvania along a wagon road that ran eight hundred miles from Philadelphia all the way to Augusta, Georgia. Others chose to remain in the Middle Colonies. New York's population rose 39 percent between 1760 and 1776, and in 1769, on the day the land office opened at Fort Pitt (Pittsburgh), over twenty-seven hundred applicants showed up to register for land.

By 1760, perhaps 700,000 new arrivals had made their homes in the mainland colonies. In the early part of the century, the largest immigrant group was the **Scots-Irish**. Later, German settlers dominated. Some 100,000 German Protestants, fleeing persecution by Catholic rulers, made the long and grim journey down the Rhine to Rotterdam, then to English port cities, and finally across the Atlantic Ocean to the colonies. But an occasional traveler on the wagon roads might be Italian, Swiss, Irish, Welsh, or a European Jew. Most striking, the number of British immigrants swelled after 1760. What prompted this transatlantic population shift was not always desperation or oppression. Many arrived with enough resources to finance their new life in the colonies. Some became indentured servants only to preserve those savings. While unemployment, poverty, the oppression of landlords, and crop failures pushed men and women out of Europe or Britain, it is also true that the availability of cheap land, a greater likelihood of religious freedom, and the chance to pursue a craft pulled others toward the colonies.

Scots-Irish Protestant Scottish settlers in British-occupied northern Ireland, many of whom migrated to the colonies in the eighteenth century.

CONFLICTS AMONG THE COLONISTS

The strains of economic inequality in every region of mainland British America frequently erupted into violent confrontations. At the same time, tensions between Indians and colonists continued, and tensions between black and white colonists increased as both slave and free black populations grew during the eighteenth century. In almost every decade, blood was shed as colonist battled colonist over economic opportunity, personal freedom, western lands, or political representation.

Slave Revolts, North and South Southern planters thus took elaborate precautions to prevent slave rebellions, assembling armed patrols that policed the roads and woods near their plantations. These patrols were usually efficient, and the punishment they inflicted was deadly. Even if rebels escaped immediate capture, few safe havens were available to them. Despite the terrible odds, slaves continued to seek their liberty, often timing their revolts to coincide with epidemics or imperial wars that distracted the white community.

The most famous slave revolt of the eighteenth century, the **Stono Rebellion**, took place in the midst of a yellow-fever epidemic in Charles Town and just as news of war between England and Spain reached South Carolina. Early on a Sunday morning in September 1739, about twenty slaves gathered at the Stono River, south of Charles Town. Their leader, Jemmy, had been born in Africa, possibly in the Congo but more likely Angola, for twenty or more of those who eventually joined the revolt were Angolan. The rebels seized guns and gunpowder, killed several planter families and storekeepers, and then headed south. But rather than traveling quietly through the woods, they marched boldly in open view, beating drums to invite slaves on nearby plantations to join them in their flight to Spanish Florida. Other slaves answered the call, and the Stono rebels' ranks grew to almost one hundred. Alerted to the rebellion, Charles Town planters gathered to put an end to the uprising. By late Sunday afternoon white militias had overtaken and surrounded the escaping slaves. The Stono rebels stood and fought, but the militiamen killed almost thirty of them. Those who were captured were executed. Those who escaped into the countryside were hunted down.

The Stono Rebellion terrified white South Carolinians, who hurried to make the colony's already harsh slave codes even more brutal. The government increased both the size and frequency of the slave patrols. It also raised the rewards offered for the capture of runaways to make sure that fleeing slaves taken alive and unharmed, or brought in dead and scalped, were worth hunting down.

In the crowded environment of New York City, white residents showed the same fear of slave rebellions as Carolina or Virginia planters. Even before the Stono Rebellion, New Yorkers' fears had become reality. At midnight on April 6, 1712, two dozen blacks, armed with guns, hatchets, and swords, set fire to a downtown building. Startled white colonists who rushed to keep the flames from spreading were attacked by the rebels, leaving nine people shot, stabbed, or beaten to death. Six more were wounded. Militia units were called out to quell the riot and to cut off any hope of escape for the rebels. Realizing the hopelessness of their situation, six committed suicide. Those who were taken alive suffered horrible punishment. According to the colonial governor, Robert Hunter, "some were burnt, others were hanged, one broke on the wheel, and one hung alive in chains in the town." Twenty-nine years later, the mere rumor of a conspiracy by African Americans to commit arson was enough to move white residents to violent reprisals. Despite the lack of any evidence to support the charge, 101 of the city's black residents were arrested—18 of them were hanged and 18 burned alive.

Clashes Between the Rich and the Poor   Most often, class tensions erupted into violence as tenant farmers battled landlords and backcountry farmers took up arms against the elite planters who dominated their colonial governments. In New York tenant farmers frequently mounted "land riots" against their powerful landlords. Tenants in Essex County, New Jersey, angered by attempts to raise their rents, rioted when three of their neighbors were arrested by local authorities. Such tenant uprisings in both colonies continued during the 1750s and 1760s, as these men expressed their resentment and frustration at their inability to acquire land of their own.

In the backcountry, settlers were likely to face two enemies: Indians and the established political powers of their own colonies. Often the clashes with the colonial government were about Indian policy, just as Bacon's Rebellion had been. Eighteenth-century colonial legislatures and governors preferred diplomacy to military action, but western settlers wanted a more aggressive program to push Indians out of the way. Even when frontier hostilities led to bloodshed, the colonists of the coastal communities were reluctant to spend tax money to provide protection along the settlement line.

The revolt by Pennsylvania's **Paxton Boys** was the most dramatic eighteenth-century episode. Pennsylvania's Quaker-dominated government had consistently encouraged settlers to find peaceful ways to coexist with local tribes, but the eighteenth-century Scots-Irish settlers did not share the Quaker commitment to pacifism. Philadelphians often spoke of these settlers as savages, but the frontiersmen saw themselves as sacrificing their own safety to expand the colonial frontier. To them, every Indian was a potential enemy, even those who pledged friendship or had adapted to English culture. In 1763, when the government failed to provide protection against Indian raids on their isolated homesteads, the frustrated settlers of Paxton, Pennsylvania, vented their anger on a village of peaceful Conestoga Indians. Although the murder of these Indians solved nothing and could not be justified, hundreds of western colonists supported this vigilante group known as the Paxton Boys. The group marched on Philadelphia to press their demands for an aggressive Indian policy. Philadelphia residents feared their city would be attacked and looted, but the popular printer and political leader Benjamin Franklin met the Paxton Boys on the outskirts of the city and negotiated a truce. The outcome was a dramatic shift in Pennsylvania Indian policy, illustrated by an official bounty for Indian scalps.

Vigilante action, however, was not always connected to Indian conflicts. In South Carolina, trouble arose because coastal planters refused to provide basic government services to the backcountry. Settlers in western South Carolina paid their taxes, but because their counties had no courts, they had to travel long distances to register land transactions or file lawsuits. The government provided no sheriffs either, and outlaws preyed on these communities. Since the coastal planters refused to admit any backcountry representatives to the colonial legislature, settlers could do little but complain, petition, and demand relief. In the 1760s, the farmers took matters into their own hands, choosing to "regulate" backcountry affairs themselves through vigilante action. These **Regulators** pursued and punished backcountry outlaws, dispensing justice without the aid of courts or judges.

In North Carolina, a similar power struggle led to a brief civil war. Here, a Regulator movement was organized against legal outlaws, a collection of corrupt local officials in the backcountry appointed because of their political connections to the colony's slaveholding elite. These officials awarded contracts to friends for building roads and bridges; charged exorbitant fees to register deeds, surveys, or even the sale of cattle; and set high annual taxes on their backcountry neighbors. The North Carolina Regulators wanted these men removed, and when the Regulators' demands were ignored, they mounted a taxpayers' rebellion. When tax collection dried up, the governor raised a militia of twelve hundred men who met the rebels in 1771 near the Alamance River, where the governor's army easily

Vision/Historic Accuracy Credit: Jeff Bright; Artist rendering: Wayne Feamster

When North Carolina backcountry farmers rose up in rebellion against their colonial government, the wealthy tidewater planters called on Governor Tryon to crush the revolt. At the Battle of Alamance, the farmers proved no match for the newly organized but better trained militia.

defeated the two thousand poorly armed Regulators. The brief east-west war ended in North Carolina, but the bitterness remained. During the Revolutionary War, when most of North Carolina's coastal elite cast their lot for independence, many farmers of the backcountry—disgusted with colonial government—sided with England.

REASON AND RELIGION IN COLONIAL SOCIETY

Trade routes tied the eighteenth-century colonial world to parent societies across the Atlantic. The bonds of language and custom tied the immigrant communities in America to their homelands too. In addition to these economic and cultural ties, the flow of ideas and religious beliefs helped sustain a transatlantic community.

The Impact of the Enlightenment At the end of the seventeenth century, a new intellectual movement arose in Europe: the **Enlightenment**. Enlightenment thinkers argued that reason, or rational thinking, rather than divine revelation, tradition, intuition, or established authority, was the true path to reliable knowledge and to human progress. A group of brilliant French thinkers called **philosophes**, including Voltaire, Rousseau, Diderot, Buffon, and Montesquieu, were among the central figures of the Enlightenment, along with English intellectuals such as John Locke and Isaac Newton and Scotland's David Hume. These philosophers, political theorists, and scientists disagreed about many issues, but all embraced the belief that nature could provide for all human wants and that human nature was basically good rather than flawed by original sin. Human beings, they insisted, were rational and capable of making progress toward a perfect society if they studied nature, unlocked its secrets, and carefully nurtured the best human qualities in themselves and their children. This belief in progress and perfectibility became a central Enlightenment theme.

Only the colonial elite had access to the books and essays that Europe's Enlightenment philosophers produced. Elite colonists were particularly drawn to two aspects of Enlightenment thought: its new religious philosophy of **deism** and the political theory of the "social contract." Deists believed that the universe operated according to logical, natural laws, without divine intervention. They denied the existence of any miracles after the Creation and rejected the value of prayer in this rational universe. Deism appealed to colonists such as the Philadelphia scientist, writer, and political leader Benjamin Franklin and Virginia planters George Washington and Thomas Jefferson, men who were intensely interested in science and the scientific method.

philosophe Any of the popular French intellectuals or social philosophers of the Enlightenment, such as Voltaire, Diderot, or Rousseau.

The most widely accepted Enlightenment ideas in the colonies were those of the English political theorist John Locke, who published his *Essay Concerning Human Understanding* in 1690 and *Two Treatises of Government* in 1691. In his political essays Locke argued that human beings have certain natural rights, which include the right to own themselves and their own labor and the right to own that part of nature on which they have labored productively—that is, their property. However, in exchange for the government's protection of their natural rights to life, liberty, and property, people make a social contract to give up absolute freedom and to live under a rule of law. According to Locke, the government created by this **social contract** receives its political power from the consent of those it governs, and it cannot claim a divine right to rule. In Locke's scheme, the people express their will, or their demands and interests, through a representative assembly, and the government is obligated to protect and respect the natural rights of its citizens and serve their interests. If the government fails to do this, Locke said, the people have a right, even a duty, to rebel. Locke's theory was especially convincing because it meshed with political developments in England from the civil war to the Glorious Revolution that were familiar to the colonists.

Religion and Religious Institutions

Many eighteenth-century Americans were impressed by the growing religious diversity of their society. Some colonists began to see religious toleration as a practical matter. The commitment to religious toleration did not come at an even pace, of course, nor did it extend to everyone. No colony allowed Catholics to vote or hold elective office after Rhode Island disfranchised Catholics in 1729, and even Maryland did not permit Catholics to celebrate Mass openly until Baltimore's Catholics broke the law and founded a church in 1763. Connecticut granted freedom of worship to "sober dissenters" such as Anglicans, Quakers, and Baptists as early as 1708, but in 1750 its legislature declared it a felony to deny the **Trinity**. When colonists spoke of religious toleration, they did not mean the separation of church and state. On the contrary, the tradition of an **established church** supported by taxes went unchallenged in the southern colonies, where Anglicanism was established, and in Massachusetts and Connecticut, where **Congregationalism** was established.

As the diversity in churches was growing, the number of colonists who did not regularly attend any church at all was growing too. Some colonists were more preoccupied with secular concerns than with spiritual ones. Others were losing their devotion to churches where the sermons were more intellectual than impassioned and the worship service was more formal than inspiring.

Trinity   In Christian doctrine, the belief that God has three divine aspects—Father, Son, and Holy Spirit.

Congregationalism   A form of Protestant church government in which the local congregation is independent and self-governing; in the colonies, the Puritans were Congregationalists.

Into this moment stepped that group of **charismatic** preachers who denounced the obsession with profit and wealth they saw around them, condemned the sinfulness and depravity of all people, warned of the terrible punishments of eternal hellfires, and praised the saving grace of Jesus Christ. In a society divided by regional disputes, racial conflicts, and economic competition, these preachers held out a promise of social harmony based on the surrender of individual pride and a renewed love and fear of God. In voices filled with "Thunder and Lightning," they called for a revival of basic Protestant belief.

The Great Awakening   The religious revival of the eighteenth century was based as much on a new approach to preaching as on the message itself. This new-style preaching first appeared in New Jersey and Pennsylvania in the 1720s, when two **itinerant** preachers—Theodore Frelinghuysen and William Tennent Jr.—accused local churches of a lack of devotion to God and "cold" preaching. Tennent established what he called a "log college" to train fiery preachers who could spread a Christian revival throughout the colonies. Soon afterward, Jonathan Edwards introduced the revival to Massachusetts. The revival, or **Great Awakening**, spread rapidly throughout the colonies, carried from town to town by wandering ministers called "awakeners." These preachers stirred entire communities to renewed religious devotion.

The Great Awakening's success was ensured in 1740 when the English minister **George Whitefield** toured the colonies from Charles Town to Maine. Everywhere this young preacher went, crowds gathered to hear him. His impact was electric. "Hearing him preach gave me a heart wound," wrote one colonist, and even America's most committed deist, Benjamin Franklin, confessed that Whitefield's sermons moved him. Whitefield himself recorded his effect on a crowd: "A wonderful power was in the room and with one accord they began to cry out and weep most bitterly for the space of half an hour."

The Great Awakening did not go unchallenged. Many ministers were angered by the criticisms of their preaching and suggestions that they themselves were unsaved. They launched a counterattack against the revivalists and their "beastly brayings." Members of the colonial elite, disturbed by the Awakening's loud condemnation of their worldly amusements, such as dancing, gambling, drinking, the theater, and elegant clothing, were roused to political action against the revivalists. In Connecticut, for example, the assembly passed a law banning would-be itinerant ministers from preaching outside their own parishes.

Bitter fights within congregations and denominations also developed. "Old Light" Congregationalists upheld the established service but "New Lights" chose

charismatic Having a spiritual power or personal quality that stirs enthusiasm and devotion in large numbers of people.

itinerant Traveling from place to place.

Evangelist George Whitefield drew huge crowds each time he preached, and the men and women in his audiences often fainted or cried out in ecstasy. As the leading figure of the Great Awakening, Whitefield was loved by thousands but criticized by ministers who opposed the religious enthusiasm he represented.

revivalism, and "Old Side" Presbyterians similarly battled "New Sides." Congregations split, and the minority groups hurriedly formed new churches. Many awakened believers left their own **denominations** entirely, joining the Baptists or the Methodists. Antirevivalists also left their strife-ridden churches and became Anglicans. These religious conflicts frequently became intertwined with secular disputes. Colonists who had long-standing disagreements over Indian policy or economic issues lined up on opposite sides of the Awakening. Class tensions influenced religious loyalties, as poor colonists pronounced judgment on their rich neighbors using religious vocabulary that equated luxury, dancing, and gambling with sin.

denomination   A group of religious congregations that accept the same doctrines and are united under a single name.

Thus, the Great Awakening increased rather than eliminated strife and tension among colonists. Yet it had positive effects as well. For example, the Awakening spurred the growth of higher education. During the complicated theological arguments between Old Lights and Awakeners, the revivalists came to see the value of theological training. They founded new colleges, including Rutgers, Brown, Princeton, and Dartmouth, to prepare their clergy just as the Old Lights relied on Harvard and Yale to train theirs. One of the most important effects of the Great Awakening was also one of the least expected. The resistance to authority, the activism involved in creating new institutions, the participation in debate and argument—these experiences reinforced a sense that protest and resistance were acceptable, not just in religious matters but in the realm of politics as well.

GOVERNMENT AND POLITICS IN THE MAINLAND COLONIES

The English mainland colonies were part of a large and complex empire, and the English government had created many agencies to set and enforce imperial policy. Parliament passed laws regulating colonial affairs, the royal navy and army determined colonial defense, and English diplomats decided which foreign nations were friends and which were foes. But from the beginning, kings and proprietors like the Calverts had also found it convenient to create local colonial governments to handle day-to-day affairs. Virginia's House of Burgesses was the first locally elected legislative body in the colonies, but by 1700 every mainland colony boasted a representative assembly.

In the first half of the eighteenth century, the British government decided to restructure its colonial administration, hoping to make it more efficient, but the government remained notably lax in enforcing colonial regulations. Even so, colonists often objected to the constraints of imperial law and challenged the role of the king or the proprietors in shaping local political decisions. This **insubordination** led to a long and steady struggle for power between colonial governors and colonial assemblies. Over the first half of the century, the colonists did wrest important powers from the governors. But the British government remained adamant that ultimate power, or **sovereignty**, rested with the king and Parliament.

Imperial Institutions and Policies   By the eighteenth century, the British government had divided responsibility for colonial regulation and management among several departments, commissions, and agencies. The potential for conflict among all these bureaucracies was great. But the overarching British indifference to colonial affairs helped to preserve harmony.

Parliament set the tone for colonial administration in the eighteenth century with a policy that came to be known unofficially as **salutary neglect**. Salutary, or

---

insubordination   Resistance to authority; disobedience.
sovereignty   The ultimate power in a nation or a state.

healthy, neglect meant the government was satisfied with lax enforcement of most regulations as long as the colonies remained dutifully loyal in military and economic matters. As long as specific, or **enumerated**, colonial raw materials continued to flow into British hands and the colonists continued to rely on British manufactured goods, salutary neglect satisfied the king, Parliament, and most government officials. Looking the other way when rules were broken was, after all, cheaper than hiring scores of customs inspectors and courtroom officials to see that every rule was always obeyed.

Salutary neglect did not mean that the colonists were free to do exactly as they pleased. Even in purely domestic matters the colonial governments could not operate as freely as many of them desired. The most intense political conflicts before the 1760s centered on the colonial assemblies' power to govern local affairs as they chose.

Local Colonial Government The eighteenth-century mainland colonies remained a mixture of royal, proprietary, and corporate colonies, although most were held directly by the king. Whatever the form of ownership, however, the colonies were strikingly similar in the structure and operation of their governments. Each colony had a governor appointed by the king or the proprietor or, in Connecticut and Rhode Island (the two **corporate colonies**), elected to executive office. Each had a council, usually appointed by the governor, though sometimes elected by the assembly, which served as an advisory body to the governor. And each had an elected representative assembly with lawmaking and taxing powers.

The governor, who represented royal authority and imperial interests in the local setting, was the linchpin of colonial government. In theory, his powers were impressive. He alone could call the assembly into session, and he had the power to dismiss it. He also could veto any act passed by the assembly. He had the sole power to appoint and dismiss judges, justices of the peace, and all government officials. He could grant pardons and reprieves. The governor made all land grants, oversaw all aspects of colonial trade, and conducted all diplomatic negotiations with the Indians. Because he was commander in chief of the military and naval forces of the colony, he decided what action, if any, to take in conflicts between colonists and Indians. Armed with such extensive powers, the man who sat in the English colonial governor's seat ought to have been respected—or at least obeyed.

A closer look, however, reveals that the governor was not so powerful after all. First, in many cases he was not free to exercise his own judgment because he was bound by a set of instructions written by England's Board of Trade. Though highly detailed and specific, these instructions often bore little relation to the realities the governor encountered in his colony. Instead, by limiting his ability to improvise and

---

enumerated   Added to the list of regulated goods or crops.

corporate colony   A self-governing colony, not directly under the control of proprietors or the Crown.

compromise, they proved more burdensome than helpful to many a frustrated governor.

Second, the governor's own skills and experience were often limited. Few men in the prime of their careers sought posts in the provinces, three thousand miles from England. Thus governorships went to **bureaucrats** nearing the end of sometimes unimpressive careers or to younger men who were new to the rough-and-tumble games of politics. Many colonial governors were honorable and competent, but enough of them were fools, scoundrels, or eccentrics to give the office a poor reputation.

Finally, most governors served brief terms, sometimes too brief for them to learn which local issues were critical or to discern friend from foe in the colonial government. For many, the goal was simply to survive the ordeal. They were willing to surrender much of their authority to the local assemblies in exchange for a calm, uneventful, and, they hoped, profitable term in office.

Even the most ignorant or incompetent governor might have managed to dominate colonial politics had he been able to apply the grease that oiled eighteenth-century political wheels: patronage. The kings of England had learned that political loyalty could be bought on the floor of Parliament with royal favors. By midcentury, over half of the members of Parliament held Crown offices or had received government contracts. Unfortunately for the colonial governor, he had few favors to hand out. The king could also bribe voters or intimidate them to ensure the election of his supporters to Parliament, but the governor lacked this option as well. The number of eligible voters in most colonies was far too great for a governor's resources.

The most significant restraint on the governor's authority was not his rigid instructions, his inexperience, or his lack of patronage, but that the colonial assembly paid his salary. England expected the colonists to foot the bill for local government, including compensation for the governor. Governors who challenged the assembly too strongly or too often usually found a sudden, unaccountable budget crisis delaying or diminishing their allowances, while those who bent to assembly wishes could expect bonuses in the form of cash or grants of land.

While the governors learned that their great powers were not so great after all, the assemblies in every colony were making an opposite discovery: they learned they could broaden their powers far beyond the king's intent. They fought for and won more freedom from the governor's supervision and influence, gaining the right to elect their own speaker of the assembly, make their own procedural rules, and settle contested elections. They also increased their power over raising and spending revenues or, in eighteenth-century parlance, their **power of the purse**.

In their pursuit of power, these local political leaders had several advantages besides the governor's weakness. They came from a small social and economic elite who were regularly elected to office for both practical and social reasons.

bureaucrat   A government official, usually appointed, who is deeply devoted to the details of administrative procedures.

First, they could satisfy the high property qualifications set for most officeholding. Second, they could afford to accept an office that cost more to win and to hold than its modest salary could cover. Third, a habit of **deference** toward the more educated and wealthy men in a community won them office. Although as many as 50 to 80 percent of adult free white males in a colony could vote, few were considered suitable to hold office. Generations of fathers and sons from elite families thus dominated political offices. These men knew one another well, and although they fought among themselves for positions and power, they could effectively unite against outsiders such as an arrogant governor or rebellious backcountry settlers. Finally, through long careers in the legislature they honed the political, administrative, and even **oratorical** skills that would enable them to contend successfully with the royal appointees.

Conflicting Views of the Assemblies

The king and Parliament gave local assemblies the authority to raise taxes, pay government salaries, direct the care of the poor, and maintain bridges and roads. To the colonists, this division of authority indicated acceptance of a two-tiered system of government: (1) a central government based in England that created and executed imperial policy and (2) a set of local governments that managed colonial domestic affairs. If these levels of government were not equal in their power and scope, the colonists believed they were equally legitimate. Most British leaders disagreed. They did not acknowledge a multilevel system. They saw a single vast empire ruled by one government consisting of king and Parliament. The colonial governments may have acquired the power to establish temporary operating procedures and to pass minor laws, but these British leaders did not believe they had acquired a share of the British government's sovereign power. As the governor of Pennsylvania put it in 1726, the assembly's actions and decisions should in "no ways interfere ... with the Legal Prerogative of the Crown or the true Legislative Power of the Mother State." Yet a vocal if small minority in English politics supported the colonists' view. For example, Thomas Pownall, who served as governor of Massachusetts in the 1750s and later as governor of South Carolina, believed that political powers must be shared between Parliament and the colonial assemblies. This notion of a dominion government shocked eighteenth-century members of Parliament, yet by the next century it had become the blueprint of the British empire.

North America and the Struggle for Empire

During the 1600s, most of the violence and warfare in colonial America arose from struggles either between Indians and colonists over land or among colonists over political power and the use of revenues and resources. These struggles continued to be important during the 1700s, but by 1690 the most persistent dangers to

deference   Yielding respectfully to the judgment or wishes of a social or intellectual superior.
oratorical   Related to the art of persuasive and eloquent public speaking.

colonial peace and safety came from the fierce rivalries between the French, Spanish, and English. Between 1688 and 1763, these European powers waged five bloody and costly wars. Most of these conflicts were motivated by politics within Europe, although colonial ambitions spurred the last and most decisive of them. No matter where these worldwide wars began, or what their immediate cause, colonists were usually drawn into them.

When imperial wars included fighting in America, English colonists relied on Indian allies and faced Indian enemies as well as European ones. For example, until the mid-seventeenth century, the Huron-dominated confederacy to the north supported the French while the Hurons' rivals, the Iroquois League, gave their support to the English and their colonists. The southern English colonists turned to the Creek Confederacy when wars with Spain erupted. Yet the colonists' own land hunger always worked to undermine—if not unravel—these Indian alliances. Thus the southern tribes' support was unreliable, and the Iroquois, wary of English westward expansion, often chose to pursue an independent strategy of neutrality.

The wars that raged from 1688 until 1763 were part of a grand effort by rival European nations to control the balance of power at home and abroad. The colonists often felt like pawns in the hands of the more powerful players, and resentment sometimes overshadowed their patriotic pride when England was victorious. Whatever their views on imperial diplomacy, few colonists escaped the impact of this nearly century-long power struggle, for periods of peace were short and the long shadow of war hung over the colonies until Britain's major triumph in 1763.

An Age of Imperial Warfare

To begin what seemed like an endless series of wars, colonists were enlisted to fight in 1689 against the French in what Europeans called the War of the League of Augsburg but colonists called simply King William's War. In this war, New England and northern New York bore the brunt of what quickly became vicious fighting in the colonies. As reports of atrocities mounted, the governments of Massachusetts, Plymouth, Connecticut, and New York made a rare attempt at cooperation. Their goal was to capture Canada, but when few participants made good on their promises of men or money, assaults on Montreal and Quebec both failed. When the war finally ended with the Treaty of Ryswick in 1697, 659 New Englanders had died in battle, in raids, or in captivity. The death toll for their Iroquois allies was between 600 and 1300. The lessons of the war were apparent. First, colonists paid a high price for their lack of cooperation. Second, no New Englander could ever feel secure until the French had been driven out of Canada. Third, the colonists needed the aid of the English army and navy to effectively drive the French away.

The colonists had little time to enjoy peace. Five years later, in 1702, the conflict colonists called Queen Anne's War began, once again pitting France, with its now dependent ally Spain, against England, Holland, and Austria. In this eleven-year struggle, colonists faced enemies on both their southern and northern borders. Once again, those enemies included Indians. Between 1711 and 1713, southern colonists were caught up in fierce warfare with the Tuscaroras, who were angered by North Carolina land seizures. The casualties were staggering, and both sides outdid one another in cruelty, running stakes through women's bodies and murdering children; colonists roasted Indian captives alive. When the war ended, the Tuscaroras had been decimated. Many of their survivors were sold into slavery, while others took refuge in the land of the Iroquois.

The war in the north was just as deadly. Indian and French raids, such as the one on Deerfield, Massachusetts, cost the lives of many New Englanders. Indeed, the high death toll of King William's War and Queen Anne's War was staggering: nearly one of every four soldiers in uniform had died. The financial cost was equally devastating. Four-fifths of Massachusetts revenues in 1704–1705 went for military expenses. Homeowners in Boston saw their taxes rise 42 percent between 1700 and 1713. Beggars filled the city's streets and widows occupied its homes. In Connecticut and Massachusetts, colonists spoke bitterly of the Mother Country's failure to protect them. Yet England's victory in 1713 brought tangible gains to New Englanders. The English flag now flew over Nova Scotia, Newfoundland, and Hudson Bay, which meant that Maine settlers no longer had to fear enemy raids. New England fleets could fish the cod-rich waters of Newfoundland more safely. And colonial fur traders could profit from Hudson Bay's resources.

For a generation, Europeans kept the peace. In America, however, violence continued along the line of settlement, with New Englanders battling Indian allies of the French and southern colonists making war on their own former allies, the Yamasees. The short but ferociously fought Yamasee War of 1715 left four hundred of South Carolina's five thousand colonists dead in the first twelve months of fighting, a higher death rate than white Massachusetts had sustained in King Philip's War.

Events at the end of the 1730s fractured the calm in Europe. By 1740, France, Spain, and Prussia were at war with England and its ally Austria. This war, known in the colonies as King George's War, again meant enemy attacks on both the northern and southern colonies. New Englanders, swept up in the Great Awakening, viewed the war as a Protestant crusade against Catholicism, a holy war designed to rid the continent of religious enemies. Yet when the war ended in 1748, Catholic France still retained its Canadian territories.

The Great War for Empire   Despite three major wars and countless border conflicts, the map of North America had changed very little. Colonial efforts to capture Canada or to rid the southwest of Indian enemies had not succeeded. Yet veterans of the wars and their civilian colonial supporters spoke with pride of the colonial armies as excellent military forces. Without assistance from British regulars or the British navy, militiamen and volunteer armies had defended their communities, defeated Indian enemies, and captured important French forts.

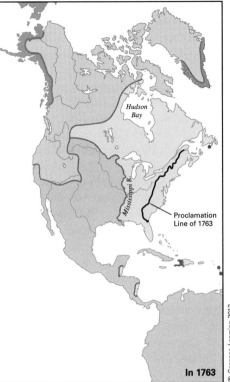

MAP 4.1 European Claims in North America

The dramatic results of the British victory in the Seven Years' (French and Indian) War are vividly demonstrated in these maps, which depict the abandonment of French claims to the mainland after the Treaty of Paris in 1763.

Many colonists remained angry and bewildered, however, by the Mother Country's military neglect. From their perspective, they were being dragged into European wars that did not concern them. Then, in 1756, the tables seemed to turn: this time, Europe was dragged into a colonial war. Westward expansion deeper into North America triggered a great war for empire, referred to in Europe as the Seven Years War and in the colonies as the **French and Indian War**.

The problem began in the 1740s, as the neutral zone between the French colonial empire and the British mainland settlements began to shrink. As thousands of new immigrants poured into the English colonies, the colonists pressed farther westward, toward the Ohio Valley. Virginia land speculators began to woo the Indians of the region with trading agreements. The English colonial interest in the valley alarmed the French, who had plans to unite their mainland empire, connecting Canada and Louisiana with a chain of forts, trading posts, and missions across the Ohio Valley.

Virginia's governor, Robert Dinwiddie, was troubled by French military buildup in the Ohio Valley. He warned the British that a potential crisis was developing thousands of miles from London. In 1754 Britain responded; the government agreed to send an expedition to assess French strength and warn the French to abandon a new fort on French Creek. Dinwiddie chose an inexperienced Virginia planter and colonial militia officer, Major George Washington, to lead the expedition. When Washington conveyed the warning, the French commander responded with insulting sarcasm. Tensions escalated rapidly. Dinwiddie later sent Major Washington to challenge the French at Fort Duquesne, near present-day Pittsburgh, but the French forced him to surrender.

Fearing another war, colonial political leaders knew it was time to act decisively—and to attempt cooperation. In June 1754, seven colonies sent representatives to Albany, New York, to organize a united defense. Unfortunately this effort at cooperation failed. When the Albany Plan of Union was presented to the individual colonial assemblies, not one was willing to approve it. Instead, American colonists looked to Britain to act. This time, Britain did. Parliament sent Major General Edward Braddock, a battle-hardened veteran, to drive the French out of Fort Duquesne. A French ambush routed Braddock's force and killed the general. Braddock's humiliating failure was only the first of many for the English in America.

English and French forces engaged each other in battle four times before war was officially declared in 1756. Soon, every major European power was involved, and the fighting spread rapidly across Europe, the Philippines, Africa, India, the Caribbean, and North America. In America, France's Indian allies joined the war more readily than England's. Iroquois tribes opted for neutrality, waiting until 1759 to throw in their lot with the English. In the south, the Cherokees played the French and English against each other. Given these circumstances, a British defeat seemed likely.

In 1756 the worried British government turned over the direction of the war to the ardent imperialist William Pitt. More than willing to take drastic steps, Pitt committed the British treasury to the largest war expenditures the nation had ever known and then put together the largest military force that North America had ever seen, combining twenty-five thousand colonial troops with twenty-four thousand British regulars. The fortunes of war soon reversed. By the end of 1759, the upper Ohio Valley had been taken from the French. And in August of that year, a force led by British General James Wolfe captured the French fortress city of Quebec. Both Wolfe and the French commander, Louis-Joseph, Marquis de Montcalm, died in the battle on Quebec's Plains of Abraham. In 1760 the city of Montreal also fell to the British. With that, the French governor surrendered the whole of New France to his enemies, and the war in North America was over. The fighting in this most global of eighteenth-century wars continued elsewhere until 1763. Spain entered the struggle as a French ally in 1761, but English victories in India, the Caribbean, and the Pacific squelched any hopes the French had. The **Treaty of Paris** established the supremacy of the British Empire.

The Outcomes of the Great War for Empire The war had redrawn the map of the world (see Table 4.1). The French Empire had shriveled, with nothing remaining of New France but two tiny islands between Nova Scotia and Newfoundland. Ten thousand Acadians—French colonists of Nova Scotia—were refugees of the war. Deported from their homes by the English because their loyalty was suspect, these Acadians either relocated to France, settled in New England, or made the exhausting trek to French-speaking Louisiana. The only other remnants of the French Empire in the Western Hemisphere were the sugar islands of Guadeloupe, Martinique, and St. Domingue, left to France because England's so-called Sugar Interest wanted no further competition in the British market. Across the ocean, France lost trading posts in Africa, and on the other side of the world, the French presence in India vanished.

The 1763 peace treaty dismantled the French Empire but did not destroy France itself. Although the nation's treasury was empty, its borders were intact and its alliance with Spain held firm. Britain was victorious but did not escape

TABLE 4.1 | IMPERIAL AND COLONIAL WARS

Name	Date	Participants	Treaty
In colonies: King William's War *In Europe:* War of the League of Augsburg	1688–1697	*In Europe:* France vs. England, Holland, Sweden, and Spain *In North America:* Colonists and their Iroquois allies vs. French and their Indian allies *Area:* New England and Northern New York	Treaty of Ryswick (1697) *Results* Port Royal in Acadia (Nova Scotia) is returned to France France is still a presence in North America
In colonies: Queen Anne's War *In Europe:* War of the Spanish Succession	1702–1713	*In Europe:* England, Holland, and Austria vs. France and Spain *In North America:* English colonists vs. French and Spanish powers in North and South and their Indian allies	Treaty of Utrecht (1713) *Results* France renounces plans to unite with Spain under one crown England gains Caribbean islands, St. Kitts, Gibraltar, and Minorca English flag flies over Nova Scotia, Newfoundland, and Hudson Bay War takes a financial toll on the colonies

Table 4.1	Imperial and Colonial Wars (continued)		
Name	**Date**	**Participants**	**Treaty**
War of Jenkins's Ear	1739–1740	*In Europe:* England vs. Spain *In North America:* English colonists clash with Spanish in interior regions (Georgia, South Carolina, Virginia)	None—Conflict expands into King George's War
In colonies: King George's War *In Europe:* War of the Austrian Succession	1740–1748	*In Europe:* Austria and England vs. Prussia, France, and Spain *In North America:* English colonists in New England vs. French and their Indian allies	Treaty of Aix-la-Chapelle (1748) *Results* England returns Louisbourg to French in exchange for Madras (in India)
In colonies: French and Indian War *In Europe:* Seven Years War	1756–1763	*In Europe:* England and Prussia vs. France and Austria *In North America:* English colonists vs. French and their Indian allies *Area:* Global war; in colonies, all regions	Treaty of Paris (1763) *Results* French Empire shrinks France's presence in North America is greatly reduced France loses trading posts in Africa and exits India Britain takes Florida from Spain and Canada from France France gives up Louisiana to Spain for compensation for Florida British government is deeply in debt The borders of Britain's North American colonies are secured

unharmed. The British government was deeply in debt and faced new problems associated with managing and protecting its greatly enlarged empire.

In the mainland colonies, people lit bonfires and staged parades to celebrate Britain's victory and the safety of their own borders. But the tension of being both members of a colonial society and citizens of a great empire could not be easily dismissed. The war left scars, including memories of the British military's arrogance toward provincial soldiers and lingering resentment over the quartering of British soldiers at colonial expense. The colonists were aware that the British had grounds for resentment also, particularly the profitable trade some Americans had carried on with the enemy even in the midst of the war. Suspicion and resentment, a growing sense of difference, a tug of loyalties between the local community and the larger empire—these were the unexpected outcomes of a glorious victory.

Study Tools

Summary

Important changes emerged in the British mainland colonies during the eighteenth century. In New England, increased commercial activity produced a shift from a "Puritan" culture to a more secular "Yankee" culture. In the South, the planter elite shifted from a labor force of indentured servants to one of African slaves. By midcentury, these enslaved workers had begun to develop their own community life and their own African American culture. The Middle Colonies developed a lively urban culture that contrasted with the backcountry culture of newly arrived immigrants.

Intellectual life in the eighteenth century also changed. The colonial elite embraced the Enlightenment notion that progress would come through the application of reason rather than faith. They developed a skepticism about religious dogmas and accepted John Locke's theory of natural rights. At the same time, the Great Awakening unleashed a second, and opposing, intellectual current aimed at renewing the quest for religious salvation among ordinary colonists. Their message had radical implications, for these "awakeners" challenged all authority except the individual spirit.

A similar challenge to authority emerged in politics and imperial relations. Despite England's policy of salutary neglect in governing the colonies, colonial assemblies resented royal officials and asserted their own claims to power as the legitimate representatives of the local interests.

England, France, and Spain fought five major wars between 1688 and 1763. Colonists were expected to defend their own borders in most of the wars. In the French and Indian War, however, the British played an active role in driving the French out of mainland America. Their victory in 1763 altered the colonial map of North America and changed power relations throughout the European world.

Dramatic events like the British victory often have unexpected consequences. As you will see in the next chapter, that victory carried with it a long trail of problems for the British government. Where would the government find the money to operate its vastly increased empire? What policies should it pursue toward the French colonists in Canada and the Indians of the Ohio Valley? Perhaps most surprising, tensions between the English colonists and the Mother Country intensified as colonial celebration and appreciation quickly turned into resentment, protest, and resistance. How this happened is the focus of Chapter 5.

CHRONOLOGY

FROM SETTLEMENTS TO SOCIETIES

1690–1691	John Locke's essays *Concerning Human Understanding* and *Two Treatises of Government*
1702	Queen Anne's War begins
1704	Pro-French Indians attack Deerfield, Massachusetts; Tuscarora War begins in North Carolina
1712	New York City slave revolt
1715	Colonists defeat Creek and Yamasee Indians of Georgia
1734	Great Awakening spreads to New England
1739	Stono Rebellion in South Carolina
1740	King George's War begins; George Whitefield begins his preaching tour
1756	Great War for Empire begins
1763	Treaty of Paris
1771	North Carolina Regulator movement defeated

FOCUS QUESTIONS

If you have mastered this chapter, you should be able to answer these questions and explain the terms that follow the questions.

1. What were the main regional differences in colonial commerce, and what kind of economic choices did each region offer colonists?
2. How did the Yankee society of early eighteenth-century New England differ from Puritan society?
3. Why did colonists in the Chesapeake and Lower South shift to slave labor? What problems faced Africans in slavery?
4. What distinguished life in the Middle Colonies?
5. What motivated colonists to migrate to the backcountry?
6. What events illustrated the tensions between races in colonial society?
7. What conflicts arose between elites and poorer colonists?
8. What political and personal expectations arose from Enlightenment philosophy?
9. What was the impact of the Great Awakening on colonial attitudes toward authority?
10. What factors affected the struggle for power between the colonial assemblies and the colonial governors?
11. What were the diplomatic and military goals of Europeans and American Indians in North America, and what role did American colonists play in the fighting?
12. How did the English victory in 1763 affect people in North America?

KEY TERMS

carrying trade (*p.* 78)

middle passage (*p.* 82)

Stono Rebellion (*p.* 87)

Paxton Boys (*p.* 88)

Regulators (*p.* 89)

Enlightenment (*p.* 90)

deism (*p.* 90)

social contract (*p.* 91)

established church (*p.* 91)

Great Awakening (*p.* 92)

George Whitefield (*p.* 92)

salutary neglect (*p.* 94)

power of the purse (*p.* 96)

French and Indian War (*p.* 100)

Treaty of Paris (*p.* 101)

5

DECIDING WHERE LOYALTIES LIE,
1763–1776

CHAPTER OUTLINE

• Victory's New Problems • Asserting American Rights • The Crisis
Renewed • The Decision for Independence • Study Tools

VICTORY'S NEW PROBLEMS

In the midst of the French and Indian War, King George II died in his bed. Loyal subjects mourned the old king and in 1760 welcomed his grandson **George III**. At 22, the new monarch was hardworking but highly self-critical, and he was already showing the symptoms of an illness that produced **delusions** and severe depression. Although he was inexperienced in matters of state, George III meant to rule—even if he had to deal with politicians, whom he distrusted, and engage in politics, which he disliked. He chose **George Grenville**, a no-nonsense, practical man, to assist him. Grenville's two most pressing postwar tasks were negotiating England's victory treaty with France and designing Britain's peacetime policies.

At the peace table with France, England had the opportunity to decide what the spoils of war would be: a French Caribbean sugar island or the mainland territory of Canada. English sugar planters opposed adding a new competitor to their profitable market and so the government opted for the vast region north and west of the thirteen colonies. American colonists could not help but be pleased. With one sweep of the pen, their worst enemies had been eliminated from their borders. The treaty also held out the promise of profitable fishing off the Newfoundland coast and new farmlands in the fertile Ohio Valley. By the end of 1763, George III and his subjects could look with pride on an empire that had grown in physical size, on a nation that dominated the markets of Europe, and on a navy that ruled the seas.

---

delusion A false belief strongly held in spite of evidence to the contrary.

Unfortunately, victory also brought new problems. First, the new English glory did not come cheaply. To win the war, William Pitt had spent vast sums of money, leaving the new king with an enormous war debt. English taxpayers, who had groaned under the wartime burden, now demanded tax relief, not tax increases. Second, the new Canadian territory posed serious governance problems because the Indians were unwilling to pledge their allegiance to the English king and the French Canadians were unwilling to abandon their traditions, their laws, or the Catholic Church.

Dealing with Indian and French Canadian Resistance

Both the Canadian tribes and Spain's former Indian allies along the southeastern borders of the English colonies felt threatened by Britain's victory. For decades, Indian diplomats had protected their lands by playing European rivals against one another, but with the elimination of France and the weakening of Spain in mainland America, this strategy was now impossible. Warfare rather than diplomacy had become their only option. When settlers from the southern colonies poured into Creek and Cherokee lands, the Cherokees mounted a full-scale, but ultimately futile, resistance along the Virginia and Carolina western settlement line. Defeated, the Cherokee leaders were forced to sign treaties opening up their lands to both English settlement and military bases.

In the Ohio Valley, Indian tribes were determined to resist not only the settlers' invasion of their homelands but also the increase in the price British traders set on tools, clothing, and liquor. Together, Senecas, Ojibwas, Potawatomis, Hurons, Ottawas, Delawares, Shawnees, and Mingoes formed an alliance known as the **Covenant Chain**. Led by the Ottawa chief **Pontiac**, the Indians mounted their attack on British forts and colonial settlements in the spring of 1763. By fall, however, their resistance had evaporated, and the Covenant Chain tribes were forced to acknowledge British control of the Ohio Valley.

The British realized that their victories did not mean a permanent peace in the West. As long as the "middle ground" between Indian and colonial populations continued to shrink, Indians would rise up against what Creeks bluntly called "people greedily grasping after the lands of red people." Settlers would then demand expensive military protection as they pushed westward. If the army did not respond, settlers were ready to take vigilante action on their own. Violence would lead to violence—unless Grenville could keep Indians and settlers at arm's length. Grenville's solution was a proclamation, issued in 1763, temporarily banning all colonial settlement west of the Appalachian Mountains.

Grenville's **Proclamation Line of 1763** outraged colonists hoping to move west and wealthy land speculators hoping to reap a profit from their western investments. Most colonists simply ignored the Proclamation Line. Over the next decade, areas such as Kentucky began to fill with eager homesteaders, creating a wedge that divided northern from southern Indian tribes and increasing Indian anxiety about their own futures.

In this 1710 portrait, Tao Yec Neen Ho Gar Ton, Emperor of the Six Nations, holds a wampum belt, a woven or beaded belt that often represented treaty agreements or other diplomatic decisions. The British government courted the support of the Iroquois confederation, whose alliance of six Indian nations made them a critical force in the military and territorial rivalries between France and England in North America.

Private Collection/The Bridgeman Art Library International

Because of their long tradition of anti-Catholic sentiment, American colonists also objected to Grenville's strategy of winning over Britain's new French-speaking Catholic Canadian subjects rather than strong-arming them. To balance their loss of fishing and fur-trading industries, Grenville promised the Canadians the right to preserve their religious and cultural way of life. American colonists were scandalized by this concession to the losers in the war.

Demanding More from the Colonists

Colonists were not the only ones growing discontented. In London, the king and many members of Parliament were impatient with colonial behavior and attitudes. Hadn't the colonists benefited more than anyone from the French defeat? asked George Grenville. And hadn't they contributed less than anyone to securing that victory? Such questions revealed the subtle but important rewriting of the motives and goals of the French and Indian War. Although Britain had waged the war to win dominance in European affairs, not to benefit the colonies, Grenville now declared that the war had been fought to protect the colonists and to expand their opportunities for settlement.

This new interpretation fit well with the government's increasing sense that something had gone wrong in the economic relationship between England and its mainland colonies. Colonial cities such as Boston, Philadelphia, and New York had grown considerably, yet their growth did not make England as rich as **mercantile theory** said it should. One reason was that in every colony locally produced goods competed with English-made goods. A more important reason, however, was widespread illegal trade with Britain's rivals. In fact, to English amazement, colonials had continued to trade with the French Caribbean islands throughout the French and Indian War. In peacetime, colonists avoided paying the required **import duties** on foreign goods by bribing customs officials or landing cargoes where no customs officers were stationed.

What Grenville discovered when he examined the imperial trade books proved shocking. By the 1760s, the Crown had collected less than £2,000 in revenue from colonial trade with other nations, yet the cost of collecting these duties was over £7,000 a year. Such discoveries fueled British suspicions that the colonies were underregulated and undergoverned, not to mention ungrateful and uncooperative. When the strong doubts about colonial loyalty met the reality of British government debts and soaring expenses, something drastic could be expected to follow. And it did. In 1764, Parliament approved Grenville's dramatic reforms of colonial trade policy. Colonists greeted these new policies with shock and alarm.

Separately, each of Grenville's measures addressed a loophole in the proper relationship between Mother Country and colonies. For example, a **Currency Act** outlawed the use of paper money as legal tender in the colonies. Grenville reasoned that this would drive colonial manufacturers, who were paid with paper money, out of business and ensure that colonists bought their manufactured goods from England. But Grenville's main focus was the widespread practice of colonial smuggling.

Lawbreakers were so common, and customs officers so easily bribed, that smuggling had become an acceptable, even respectable form of commerce. To halt this illegal traffic, Grenville created the American Revenue Act. This 1764 act increased the powers of the customs officers, allowing them to use blanket warrants, called writs of assistance, to search ships and warehouses for smuggled goods. He also changed the regulations regarding key foreign imports, including sugar, wine, and coffee. This startling shift in policy, known popularly as the **Sugar Act**, revealed Grenville's practical bent. He knew that any attempt to stop the flow of French sugar into the colonies was a waste of time and resources. So he decided to make a profit for the Crown from this trade. He would lower the tax on imported sugar—but he would make sure it was collected. He would also change the way in which alleged smugglers were brought to justice. Until 1764, a colonist accused of smuggling was tried before a jury of his neighbors in a

---

mercantile theory The economic notion that a nation should amass wealth by exporting more than it imports; colonies are valuable in a mercantile system as a source of raw materials and as a market for manufactured goods.

import duties Taxes on imported goods.

civil court. He expected, and usually got, a favorable verdict from his peers. Grenville now declared that anyone caught smuggling would be tried in a juryless **vice-admiralty court,** where a conviction was far more likely. Once smuggling became too costly and too risky, Grenville reasoned, American shippers would declare their cargoes of French sugar and pay the Crown for the privilege of importing them.

The Colonial Response   Grenville's reforms were spectacularly ill timed as far as Americans were concerned. The colonial economy was suffering from a postwar **depression,** brought on in part by the loss of the British army as a steady market for American supplies and of British soldiers as steady customers who paid in hard currency rather than paper money. In 1764 unemployment was high among urban artisans, dockworkers, and sailors, and colonial merchants were caught in a credit squeeze—unable to pay their debts to British merchants because their colonial customers had no cash to pay for their purchases. These colonists were not likely to cheer a Currency Act that shut off a source of money or a Sugar Act that established a new get-tough policy on foreign trade. In the eyes of many anxious colonists, the English government was turning into a greater menace than the French army had ever been.

Protests and proposals for action soon filled the pages of colonial newspapers. This concern suggested that Grenville's reforms had raised profound issues about the rights of citizens and of the relationship between Parliament and the colonial governments—issues that needed to be resolved. The degree to which Parliament had, or ought to have, power over colonial economic and political life required serious, public pondering. Years later, with the benefit of hindsight, Massachusetts lawyer and revolutionary John Adams stressed the importance of the Sugar Act in starting America down the road to independence. "I know not why we should blush to confess," wrote Adams, "that molasses [liquid sugar] was an essential ingredient in American independence." But in 1764 colonists were far from agreement over the issue of parliamentary and local political powers. They were not even certain how to respond to the Sugar Act.

The Stamp Act   Did Grenville stop to consider the possibility of "great events" arising from his postwar policies? Probably not. He was hardly a stranger to protest and anger, for he had often heard British citizens grumble about taxes and assert their rights against the government. As he saw it, his duty was to fill the treasury, reduce the nation's staggering debt, arm its troops, and keep the royal

---

civil court   Any court that hears cases regarding the rights of private citizens.

vice-admiralty court   Nonjury British court in which a judge heard cases involving shipping.

depression   A period of drastic economic decline, marked by decreased business activity, falling prices, and high unemployment.

navy afloat. The duty of loyal British citizens, he believed, was to obey the laws of their sovereign government. Grenville had no doubt that the measures he and Parliament were taking to regulate the colonies and their revenue-producing trade were constitutional. Some colonists, however, had doubts. To settle the issue, Grenville proposed another piece of legislation designed not only to raise revenue but to assert the principle of parliamentary sovereignty. The new law was called the Stamp Act.

The **Stamp Act** of 1765 was to be the first **direct tax** ever laid on the colonies by Parliament. There was nothing startling or novel about this revenue-collecting method. A stamp tax raised money by requiring the use of government "stamped paper" on certain goods or as part of the cost for certain services. It was simple and efficient, and several colonial legislatures used this method themselves. What was startling, however, was that this tax had nothing to do with foreign trade. Until 1765, Parliament had passed many acts regulating colonial trade, and if these regulations generated revenue for the Crown, the colonists did not complain. They accepted this as a form of **external taxation**. But colonists were convinced that only their local assemblies had the power to impose direct taxation like the stamp tax. Grenville's Stamp Act was a sharp break with the traditional understanding of the relationship between Mother Country and colonies, and it challenged the distribution of political power between colonial assemblies and Parliament. Did Parliament realize what it had done?

Most members of Parliament did not. They saw the Stamp Act as an efficient and modest redistribution of the burdens of the empire—and a constitutional one. Colonists were certainly not being asked to shoulder the entire burden, since the estimated £160,000 in revenue from the stamped paper would cover only one-fifth of the cost of maintaining a British army in North America.

The new law, passed in February 1765, was set to go into effect in November. The nine-month delay was necessary, for Grenville needed time to print the stamped paper, arrange for its shipment across the Atlantic, and appoint agents to receive and distribute the stamps in each colony. News of the tax, however, crossed the ocean rapidly and was greeted with outrage and anger. Virtually every free man and woman was affected by a tax that required stamps on all legal documents, newspapers and pamphlets, playing cards and dice. Grenville was reaching into the pockets of the rich, who would need stamped paper to draw up wills and property deeds and to bring suit in court. And he was emptying the pockets of the poor, who would feel the pinch when dealing a hand of cards in a tavern or buying a printed **broadside** filled with advertising. Colonial merchants and ship captains would have to use stamped clearances for all shipments or risk the seizure of their cargoes by the royal navy. Lawyers feared the loss of clients if they had to add the cost of the stamps to their fees. Thus, with the stamp tax Grenville united northern

---

direct tax   A tax imposed to raise revenue rather than to regulate trade.

external taxation   Revenue raised in the course of regulating trade with other nations.

broadside   An advertisement, public notice, or other publication printed on one side of a large sheet of paper.

merchants and southern planters and rural women and urban workingmen, and he riled the most articulate and argumentative of all Americans: lawyers and newspaper publishers.

The Popular   Many colonists proved ready to resist the new legislation.
Response   Massachusetts, whose smugglers were already choking on
                     the new customs regulations, and whose assembly had a long
history of struggle with local Crown officers, led the way. During the summer of
1765, a group of Bostonians formed a secret resistance organization called the
Sons of Liberty. The Sons were led by the irrepressible **Samuel Adams**, a Harvard-
educated member of a prominent Massachusetts family who preferred the company
of local working men and women to the conversation of the elite. More at home in
the dockside taverns than in the comfortable parlors of his relatives, Adams was a
quick-witted, dynamic champion of working-class causes. He had a genius for
writing propaganda and for mobilizing popular sentiment on political and community issues. Most members of the Sons of Liberty were artisans and shopkeepers,
and the group's main support came from men of the city's laboring classes who had
been hard hit by the postwar depression and would suffer from the stamp tax.
These colonists had little influence in the legislature or with Crown officials, but
they compensated by staging public demonstrations and protests to make their
opinions known. By January 1765, New York City also had a Sons of Liberty
organization, and by August, the Sons could be found in other cities and towns
across the colonies.

Demonstrations and protests were soon mounted, and Boston led the way. On
August 14, shoemaker **Ebenezer McIntosh** led a crowd to protest the appointment
of the colony's stamp agent, the wealthy merchant Andrew Oliver. The crowd
included a number of the city's gentlemen, disguised as workingmen. Together
with the workingmen, they paraded through the city streets carrying an effigy of
Oliver. The crowd then destroyed Oliver's dockside warehouse and went on to
break all the windows in his home. The message was clear—and Oliver understood
it well. The following day Andrew Oliver resigned as stamp agent. Boston Sons of
Liberty celebrated by declaring the tree on which they hanged Oliver's effigy the
"liberty tree."

But Oliver's resignation did not end the protest. Customs officers and other
Crown officials living in Boston were threatened with words and worse. The chief
target of abuse, however, was the wealthy merchant and political office holder
Thomas Hutchinson, resented by many of the ambitious younger political leaders
because he monopolized appointive offices in the colony's government and hated
by the working men because of his disdain for ordinary people. Late one August
evening, a large crowd surrounded Hutchinson's elegant brick mansion. Hutchinson and his family, warned of trouble, had wisely fled, escaping just before rocks
began to shatter the parlor windows. By dawn, the house was in ruins, and Hutchinson's furniture, clothing, and personal library had been trashed. The attack on
Hutchinson revealed that sometimes protests were not simply over British policies
but over local issues and against local elites as well. It was not surprising, therefore,
that prosperous merchants and shippers soon saw a potential danger in the

mobilization of lower-class crowds like the Sons of Liberty. For elites like Hutchinson, crowd protest was a double-edged sword, a useful weapon that could be deadly in the wrong hands.

The campaign against the stamp agents spread like a brushfire across the colonies. Agents in Connecticut, Rhode Island, Maryland, and New York were mercilessly harassed. Most stamp agents resigned. When the stamps reached colonial ports in November, only the young and conservative colony of Georgia could produce anyone willing to distribute them. Colonial governors retaliated by refusing to allow any colonial ships to leave port. They hoped this disruption of trade would persuade local merchants to help end the resistance. Their strategy backfired. Violence increased as hundreds of unemployed sailors took to the streets, terrorizing customs officers and any colonists suspected of supporting the king's taxation policy.

Political Debate   While the Sons of Liberty and their supporters demonstrated in the streets, colonial political leaders were proceeding with caution. Virginia lawyer and planter **Patrick Henry** briefly stirred the passions of his colleagues in the House of Burgesses when he suggested that the Stamp Act was evidence of the king's tyranny. Not everyone agreed with him that the measure was so serious. Many did agree, however, that the heart of the matter was not stamped paper but parliamentary sovereignty versus the rights of colonial citizens. "No taxation without representation"—the principle that citizens cannot be taxed by a government unless they are represented in it—was a fundamental assumption of free white Englishmen on both sides of the Atlantic. The crucial question was, Did the House of Commons represent the colonists even though no colonist sat in the House and none voted for its members? If the answer was no, then the Stamp Act violated the colonists' most basic "rights of Englishmen."

Stating the issue in this way led to other concerns. Could colonial political leaders oppose a single law such as the Stamp Act without completely denying the authority of the government responsible for its passage? Massachusetts lawyer James Otis pondered this question when he sat down to write his *Rights of the British Colonists Asserted and Proved.* Any opposition to the Stamp Act, he decided, was ultimately a challenge to parliamentary authority over the colonies, and it would surely lead to colonial rebellion and a declaration of colonial independence. He, for one, was not prepared to become a rebel. Instead he proposed that Parliament give seats in the government to colonial representatives.

Like Otis, most political leaders shrank from denying Parliament's authority. But his suggestion that Parliament admit colonial representatives satisfied no one. A small contingent of colonial members of Parliament would have little power and was likely to find its views ignored. The only solution seemed to be to protest against the Stamp Act, demand its repeal, and warn Parliament that Americans would resist further efforts to infringe on their rights and liberties.

When Parliament enacted the Stamp Act of 1765, the government designed this special embossed tax stamp to be used on the items that came under the new law. These items included newspapers, most legal documents, playing cards, and dice. The Stamp Act provoked the first major protest and boycott by colonists against the Mother Country.

Yet many members of the colonial legislatures felt more was needed than strong words and implicit threats. Their own authority was at stake, for if Parliament acted on its assertion that it had the right to govern the colonies directly, their powers would be diminished. These men had much to lose—status, prestige, and the many benefits that came from deciding how tax monies would be allocated. Thus, when Massachusetts put out a call for an intercolonial meeting of delegates to discuss the Stamp Act crisis, the idea was greeted with enthusiasm.

Grenville's policies appeared to be bringing about what had once seemed impossible: united political action by the colonies. Until the Stamp Act, competition among the colonial governments was far more common than cooperation. Yet in the fall of 1765 delegates from nine colonies met in New York "to consider a general and unified, dutiful, loyal and humble Representation [petition]" to the king and Parliament. The petitions this historic **Stamp Act Congress** ultimately produced were far bolder than the delegates first intended. They were powerful, tightly argued statements that conceded parliamentary authority over the colonies but denied Parliament's right to impose any direct taxes on them. "No taxes," the Congress said, "ever have been, or can be Constitutionally imposed" on the colonies "but by their respective Legislatures." Clearly Americans expected this tradition to be honored.

Repeal of the Stamp Act   Neither the protest in the streets nor the arguments of the Stamp Act Congress moved the king or Parliament to repeal the stamp tax. But economic pressure did. Thus the most powerful weapon in the colonial arsenal was a refusal to purchase English goods, for English manufacturers relied heavily on their colonial markets. On Halloween night, just one day before the stamp tax officially went into effect, two hundred New York merchants announced that they would not import any new British goods. Local artisans and laborers rallied to support this **boycott**. A mixture of patriotism and self-interest motivated both of these groups. The merchants saw the possibility of emptying warehouses bulging with unsold goods because of the postwar depression. Unemployed and underemployed artisans and laborers saw the chance to sell their own products if the supply of cheaper English-made goods dried up. The same combination of interests existed in other colonial cities, and thus the movement for a boycott, which they called nonimportation and nonconsumption, spread quickly. By the end of November, several colonial assemblies had publicly endorsed the boycott agreements signed by local merchants. Popular support widened as well.

English exporters complained bitterly of the damage done to their businesses and pressured Parliament to take colonial protest seriously. The Grenville government reluctantly conceded that enforcement of the Stamp Act had failed miserably. Even in colonies where royal officials dared to distribute the stamped paper, Americans refused to purchase it. Colonists simply ignored the hated law and continued to sue their neighbors, sell their land, publish their newspapers, and buy their playing cards as if the stamped paper and the Stamp Act did not exist.

By winter's end, Grenville had been replaced by Lord Rockingham, and for the new prime minister the critical issue was how to repeal the Stamp Act without appearing to cave in to colonial pressure. In 1766, the government came up with a satisfactory solution. Great Britain repealed the Stamp Act but at the same time passed a **Declaratory Act**, which asserted that the colonies were "subordinate unto, and dependent upon the imperial Crown and parliament of Great Britain." Thus Parliament's right to pass legislation for and raise taxes from the North American colonies was reaffirmed as absolute.

Colonists celebrated the repeal with public outpourings of loyalty to England that were as impressive as their public protests had been. There were cannon salutes, bonfires, parades, speeches, and public toasts to the king and Rockingham. In Boston, Sons of Liberty built a pyramid and covered its three sides with patriotic poetry. In Anne Arundel County, Maryland, colonists erected a "liberty pillar" and buried "Discord" beneath it. And in a spectacular but poorly executed gesture, the Liberty Boys of Plymouth, Massachusetts, tried

---

boycott   An organized political protest, used by the colonists to protest British taxation, in which people refuse to buy goods from a nation or group of people whose actions they oppose; also called *nonimportation*.

to move Plymouth Rock to the center of town. When the famous rock on which the Pilgrims were said to have landed split in two, half of it was carried to Liberty Pole Square, where it remained until 1834. As for the Declaratory Act, colonists greeted it with indifference. Those who commented on it at all dismissed it as a face-saving device. To a degree, they were correct. But the Declaratory Act expressed the views of powerful men in Parliament, and within a year they put it to the test.

ASSERTING AMERICAN RIGHTS

By the summer of 1766, William Pitt had returned to power within George III's government. But Pitt was old and preoccupied with his failing health. A young playboy named Charles Townshend, serving as chancellor of the exchequer, rushed in to fill the leadership void. This brash young politician wasted little time foisting a new package of taxes on the colonies.

The Townshend Acts and Colonial Protest   During the Stamp Act crisis, Benjamin Franklin had assured Parliament that American colonists accepted indirect taxation through trade regulations, even if they violently protested a direct tax such as the Stamp Act. In 1767 Townshend decided to test this distinction by proposing new regulations on a variety of imported necessities and luxuries. But unlike any import taxes the colonies had ever seen, the **Townshend Acts** taxed products made within the British empire.

The Townshend Acts taxed glass, paper, paint, and lead products, all made in England. The acts also placed a three-penny tax on tea, considered a necessity by virtually all colonists. Townshend wanted to be certain these taxes were collected, so he ordered new customs boards in the colonies and created new vice-admiralty courts in the major port cities of Boston, Charleston, and Philadelphia to try cases of smuggling or tax evasion. In case Americans tried to harass customs officials, Townshend ordered British troops transferred from the western regions to the major colonial port cities. To help finance this military occupation of key cities, Townshend invoked the 1766 Quartering Act, a hated law requiring colonists to provide room and board; "candles, firing, bedding, cooking utensils, salt and vinegar"; and a ration of beer, cider, or rum to troops stationed in their midst. Clearly taking every precaution to avoid the embarrassment Grenville had suffered in the Stamp Act disaster, Townshend relied on the presence of uniformed soldiers—known as "redcoats" because of their scarlet jackets—to keep the peace.

When news of the new regulations reached the colonies, however, the response was immediate, determined, and well-organized resistance. Newspaper accounts indicate that the colonists were united in their opposition to the Townshend Acts and the repressive enforcement policies. Some once again angrily invoked the principle of "no taxation without representation." In Boston, Samuel Adams voiced his outrage: "Is it possible to form an idea of Slavery, more compleat, more miserable, more disgraceful than that of a people, where justice is administer'd, government exercis'd, and a standing army maintain'd at the expense of the people, and yet without the least dependence upon them?" Others worried more about the economic burden of new taxes and quartering troops than about political rights. Boston lawyer Josiah Quincy, Jr., asked readers of the *Boston Gazette*: "Is not the bread taken out of the children's mouths and given unto the Dogs?"

John Dickinson, a well-respected Pennsylvania landowner and lawyer, laid out the basic American position on imperial relations in his pamphlet *Letters from a Farmer in Pennsylvania* (1767). Direct taxation without representation violated the colonists' rights as English citizens, Dickinson declared. But by imposing any tax that did not regulate foreign trade, Parliament also violated those rights. Dickinson also considered, and rejected, the British claim that Americans were represented in the House of Commons. According to the British argument, colonists enjoyed "virtual representation" because the House of Commons represented the interests of all citizens in the empire who were not members of the nobility, whether those citizens participated directly in elections to the House or not. Like most Americans, Dickinson discounted virtual representation. What Englishmen were entitled to, he wrote, was *actual* representation by men they had elected to government to protect their interests. For qualified voters in the colonies, who enjoyed actual representation in their local assemblies, virtual representation was nothing more than a weak excuse for exclusion and exploitation. As one American quipped: "Our privileges are all virtual, our sufferings are real."

Popular resistance began when Samuel Adams set in motion a massive boycott of British goods to begin on January 1, 1768. Some colonists who worried about the growing **materialism** among their neighbors welcomed the chance for a boycott to "mow down luxury and high living." But simple economics also contributed forcefully to support for the boycott. Boston artisans remained enthusiastic about any action that stopped the flow of inexpensive English-made goods to America. Small-scale merchants who had little access to British goods were also eager to see nonimportation enforced. The large-scale merchants who had led the 1765 boycott were not enthusiastic, however. By 1767, their warehouses were no longer overflowing with unsold English stock, and the boycott might cut off their livelihoods. Many of these elite merchants delayed signing the agreements. Others did not sign at all.

Those who opposed resistance to the Townshend Acts most strongly were colonists holding Crown-appointed government offices. These fortunate few—including judges and customs men—shared their neighbors' sensitivity to abuse or exploitation by the Crown, but they had sworn to uphold the policies of the British government. Because their careers and their identities were closely tied to the authority of the Crown, they were inclined to see British policymakers as well intentioned, and they saw acceptance of British policy as a patriotic duty. Jonathan

---

materialism   Excessive interest in worldly matters, especially in acquiring goods.

Samuel Adams, whose family owned a Boston brewery, was the undisputed leader of the popular protest movement in Massachusetts during the 1760s and 1770s. Adams was one of the organizers of the Sons of Liberty, a group responsible for many of the demonstrations against British policies as well as some of the violence against British officials. After the Revolution, he served as governor of Massachusetts.

The Granger Collection, New York

Sewall, the king's attorney general in Massachusetts, was perhaps typical of these royal officeholders.

Sewall had deep roots in his colonial community, for his family went back many generations and included lawyers, judges, merchants, and assemblymen. His closest friend was John Adams, cousin of Samuel Adams, and the wealthy Boston merchant and smuggler John Hancock would soon become his brother-in-law. Yet Sewall became a staunch public defender of Crown policy. In his newspaper articles he urged his neighbors to ignore the call to resistance, and he questioned the motives of the leading activists, suggesting that greed, thwarted ambition, and envy rather than high-minded principles motivated the rabble-rousers. But despite their prestige and their positions of authority, Crown officers like Sewall were unable to prevent the boycott or slow the spread of resistance.

The 1768 boycott brought politics into the lives of women just as the Stamp Act mobilized working-class men. Women's boycott of English cloth was critically important and many women rose to the challenge, resurrecting the tedious skill of spinning yarn for cloth. Taking a bold political stance, women, including wealthy mothers and daughters, formed groups called the Daughters of Liberty and staged large public spinning bees to show support for the boycott. Wearing clothing made of "homespun" became a mark of honor and a political statement. As one male observer noted, "The ladies ... while they vie with each other in skill and industry in their profitable employment, may vie with the men in contributing to the preservation and prosperity of their country and equally share in the honor of it." Through the boycott, politics had entered the domestic circle.

The British Humiliated	Although the Townshend Acts met with defiance in almost every colony, Massachusetts provided the greatest embarrassment for Parliament and the king.

The colonial governor Francis Bernard had lost his control over local politics ever since the assembly defied him by issuing a Circular Letter to other colonies, calling for united protest against the Townshend Acts. The helpless governor could do nothing to save face except dismiss the assembly, leaving the colony without any representative government. Bernard's ability to ensure law and order eroded rapidly after this. Throughout 1768, enforcers of the boycott roamed the streets of Boston, intimidating pro-British merchants and harassing anyone wearing British-made clothing. Boston mobs of men and women openly threatened customs officials, and the Sons of Liberty protected the colony's thriving business in smuggling foreign goods and the items listed in the hated Townshend Acts. One of the town's most notorious smugglers, the flamboyant John Hancock, grew more popular with his neighbors each time he unloaded his illegal cargoes of French and Spanish wines or West Indian sugar. When customs officers seized Hancock's vessel, aptly named the *Liberty,* in June 1768, protesters beat up senior customs men, and mobs visited the homes of other royal officials. The now-desperate Governor Bernard sent an urgent plea for help to the British government.

In October 1768, four thousand troops arrived in Boston. The Crown clearly believed that the presence of one soldier for every four citizens would be enough to restore order quickly. John Adams marveled at what he considered British thickheadedness. The presence of so many young soldiers, far from home and surrounded by a hostile community, was certain to worsen the situation. Military occupation of Boston, Adams warned, made more violence inevitable. Adams was right. With time on their hands, the soldiers passed the hours courting any local women who would speak to them and pestering those who would not. They angered local dockworkers by moonlighting in the shipyards when off duty and taking jobs away from colonists by accepting lower pay. For their part, civilians taunted the sentries, insulted the soldiers, and refused the military any sign of hospitality. News of street-corner fights and tavern brawls inflamed feelings on both sides. Samuel Adams and his friends did their best to fan the flames of hatred, publishing daily accounts of both real and imaginary confrontations in which soldiers threatened the honor or endangered the safety of innocent townspeople.

The military occupation dragged on through 1769 and early 1770. On March 5, the major confrontation most people expected occurred. An angry crowd began throwing snowballs—undoubtedly laced with bricks and rocks—at British sentries guarding the customs house. The redcoats, under strict orders not to fire on civilians, issued a frantic call for help in withdrawing to safety. When Captain Thomas Preston and his men arrived to rescue the sentries, the growing crowd immediately enveloped them. How, and under whose orders, Preston's soldiers began to fire is unknown, but they killed five men and wounded eight other colonists. Four of the five victims were white laborers. The fifth, Crispus Attucks, was a free black sailor.

Massachusetts protest leaders immediately labeled the confrontation the **Boston Massacre**. Their account appeared in colonial newspapers everywhere and included a dramatic anti-British illustration engraved by silversmith Paul Revere. A jury of colonists later cleared Preston and all but two of his men of the charges against them. But nothing that was said at their trial—no sworn testimony, no lawyer's arguments—could erase the image of British brutality against British subjects.

Even before the bloodshed of March 5, Edmund Burke, a member of Parliament known for his sympathy to the colonial cause, had warned the House of Commons that the relationship between Mother Country and colonies was both desperate and tragic. "The Americans," Burke said, "have made a discovery, or think they have made one, that we mean to oppress them; we have made a discovery, or think we have made one, that they intend to rise in rebellion. We do not know how to advance; they do not know how to retreat." Burke captured well the growing American conviction of a conspiracy by Parliament to deprive the colonists of their rights and liberties. He also captured the British government's growing sense that a rebellion was being hatched. But Parliament was ready to act to ease the crisis and make a truce possible. A new minister, Frederick, Lord North, was given the reins of government, and on the very day Captain Preston's men fired on the crowd at Boston, Lord North repealed the Townshend Acts and allowed the hated Quartering Act to expire. Yet Lord North wanted to give no ground on the question of parliamentary control of the colonies. For this reason, he kept the tax on tea—to preserve a principle rather than fill the king's treasury.

Success Weakens Colonial Unity   Repeal of the Townshend Acts allowed the colonists to return to the ordinary routine of their lives. But it was not true that all tensions had vanished. Troubling ones remained—and they were largely among the colonists themselves. Struggling artisans and laborers now found themselves at odds with their former allies, the merchants. In fact, many elite colonists gladly abandoned the radical activism they had shown in the 1760s in favor of social conservatism. Their fear of British tyranny dimmed, but their fear of the lower classes' clamor for political power grew. The tyranny that some of them opposed seemed to them to be close to home. "Many of the poorer People," observed one supporter of expanded political participation, "deeply felt the Aristocratic Power, or rather the intolerable Tyranny of the great and opulent." The new political language in which common men justified their demands made their social superiors uneasy. Their own impassioned appeals for rights and liberties were returning to haunt some of the colonial elite.

The Crisis Renewed

Lord North's government took care not to disturb the calm created by the repeal of the Townshend Acts. Between 1770 and 1773, North proposed no new taxes on the colonists and made no major changes in colonial policy. American political leaders took equal care not to make any open challenges to British authority. Both sides recognized that their political truce had its limits. It did not extend to smugglers and customs men, who continued to lock horns; it did not end the bitterness of southern colonists who wished to settle beyond the Proclamation Line; nor did it erase the distrust colonial political leaders and the British government felt for each other.

Disturbing the Peace of the Early 1770s
The British effort to crack down on American smuggling continued to disturb New England merchants whose fortunes were built on trade with the Caribbean. They resented the sight of customs officers at the docks and of customs ships patrolling the coastline. Rhode Island merchants took revenge against the determined—and highly effective—customs operation in their colony. One June day in 1772, the customs patrol boat *Gaspée* ran aground as it chased an American vessel off Rhode Island. That evening a band of colonists boarded the *Gaspée*, taunted the stranded customs men, and then set fire to their boat.

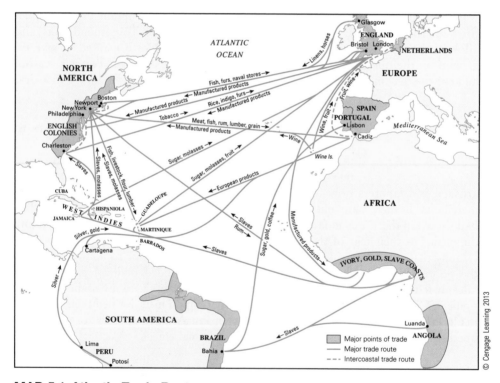

MAP 5.1 Atlantic Trade Routes

By the late seventeenth century, an elaborate trade network linked the countries and colonies bordering the Atlantic Ocean. The most valuable commodities exchanged were enslaved people and the products of slave labor.

Rhode Islanders called the burning of the *Gaspée* an act of political resistance. The English called it an act of vandalism and appointed a royal commission to investigate. To their amazement, no witnesses came forward, and no evidence could be gathered to support any arrests. The British found the conspiracy of silence among the Rhode Islanders appalling.

Many American political leaders found the royal commission equally appalling. They were convinced that the British government had intended to bring its suspects to England for trial and thus deprive them of a jury of their peers. They read this as further evidence of the plot to destroy American liberty, and they decided to keep in close contact to monitor British moves. Following the Virginia assembly's lead, five colonies organized a communications network called the **committees of correspondence**, instructing each committee to circulate detailed accounts of any questionable royal activities in its colony. These committees of correspondence were also a good mechanism for coordinating protest or resistance should the need arise. Thus the colonists put in place their first permanent machinery of protest.

The Tea Act and the Tea Party   During the early 1770s, colonial activists worked to keep the political consciousness of the 1760s alive. They commemorated American victories over British policy and observed the anniversary of the Boston Massacre with solemn speeches and sermons. Without major British provocation, however, a revival of mass action was unlikely.

In 1773 Parliament provided that provocation. This time the government was not setting new colonial policy but trying to save a major commercial enterprise, the East India Tea Company. Mismanagement, coupled with the American boycott and the tendency of colonists to buy smuggled Dutch tea, had left the company in serious financial trouble, its warehouses bursting with unsold tea.

The company directors had a plan: if Parliament allowed them to ship their tea directly to the colonial market, eliminating the English merchants who served as middlemen, they could lower their prices and compete effectively against the smuggled Dutch tea. Even with the three-penny tax on tea that remained from the Townshend era, smart consumers would see this as a bargain. Lord North liked the plan and saw in it the opportunity for vindication: Americans who purchased the cheaper English tea would be confirming Parliament's right to tax the colonies. With little debate, Parliament made the company's arrangement legal through passage of the Tea Act. No one expected the colonists to object.

Once again, British politicians had seriously misjudged the impact of their decisions. Colonists read the Tea Act as an insult, a challenge, another chilling sign of a conspiracy against their well-being and their liberty. They distrusted the arrangement, believing that the East India Tea Company would raise its prices dramatically once all foreign teas were driven off the market. And they were concerned that if other British companies marketing products in the colonies followed the East India Tea Company's example, prices for scores of products would soar. These objections, however, paled beside the colonists' immediate grasp of Lord North's strategy: purchasing cheaper English tea would confirm Parliament's right to tax the colonies. The tea that Americans drank might be cheap, but the price of conceding the legitimacy of the tea tax was too high.

Colonists mobilized their resistance in 1773 with the skill acquired from a decade of experience. In several cities, crowds met the ships carrying the East India tea and prevented the unloading of their cargoes. They used the threat of violence to persuade ship captains to return to England with the tea still on board. As long as both the captains and the local royal officials gave in to these pressures, no serious confrontation occurred. But in Massachusetts, the most famous victim of mob violence, now Governor Thomas Hutchinson, was not willing to give in. A stalemate resulted: colonists refused to allow crews to unload the tea, but Hutchinson refused to allow the tea ships to depart without unloading. Boston activists broke the stalemate on December 16, 1773, when some sixty men, thinly disguised as Mohawk Indians, boarded the tea ships. Working calmly and methodically, they dumped 342 chests of tea, worth almost £10,000, into the waters of Boston harbor.

The Intolerable Acts (Coercive Acts)   The Boston Tea Party delighted colonists everywhere. The Crown, however, failed to see the humor in this deliberate destruction of valuable private property. The tea chests had barely settled into the harbor mud before Parliament retaliated. The king and his minister meant to make an example of everyone in Boston, the source of so much trouble and embarrassment over the past decade. Americans on the scene in England warned friends and family back home of the growing rage against the colonies. Arthur Lee, serving in London as Massachusetts's colonial agent, drew a gloomy picture of the dangers ahead in a letter to his brother. "The storm, you see, runs high," he wrote, "and it will require great prudence, wisdom and resolution, to save our liberties from shipwreck."

The four acts known as the Coercive Acts that Parliament passed in 1774 to discipline Massachusetts were as harsh and uncompromising as Arthur Lee predicted. The colonists called them the **Intolerable Acts**. The Port Act closed the port of Boston to all trade until the citizens compensated the East India Tea Company fully for its losses. This was a devastating blow to the colony's economy. The Massachusetts Government Act transferred much of the power of the colony's assembly to the royal governor, including the right to appoint judges, sheriffs, and members of the colonial legislature's upper house. The colony's town meetings, which had served as forums for anti-British sentiment and protests, also came under the governor's direct control. A third measure, the Justice Act, allowed royal officials charged with capital crimes to stand trial in London rather than before local juries. And a new Quartering Act gave military commanders the authority to house troops in private homes. To see that these laws were enforced, the king named General Thomas Gage, commander of the British troops in North America, as the acting governor of Massachusetts.

At the same time that Parliament passed these punitive measures, the British government issued a comprehensive plan for the government of Canada. The timing of the Quebec Act may have been a coincidence, but its provisions infuriated Americans. The Quebec Act granted the French in Canada the right to worship as Catholics, retain their language, and keep many of their legal practices—all marks of a tolerance that the Crown had refused to show its English colonists. The Quebec Act also expanded the borders of Canada into the Ohio Valley at the expense of the English-speaking colonies' claim to western land. This dealt a harsh blow to Virginia planters who hoped to profit from land speculation in the region. The king expected the severe punishment of Massachusetts to isolate that colony from its neighbors. But the Americans resisted this divide-and-conquer strategy. In every colony, newspaper essays and editorials urged readers to see Boston's plight as their own. "This horrid attack upon the town of Boston," said the *South Carolina Gazette*, "we consider not as an attempt upon that town singly, but upon the whole Continent." George Washington, by now an influential Virginia planter and militia officer, declared that "the cause of Boston now is and ever will be the cause of America." Indeed, the Intolerable Acts produced a wave of sympathy for the beleaguered Bostonians, and relief efforts sprang up across the colonies.

In pamphlets and political essays, colonists placed the Intolerable Acts into the larger context of systematic oppression by the Mother Country. Political writers referred to the British government as the "enemy," conspiring to deprive Americans of their liberty, and urged colonists to defend themselves against the "power and cunning of our adversaries." This unity of sentiment, however, was more fragile than it appeared. In the cities, bitter divisions quickly developed, and artisans struggled with merchants to control the mass meetings that would make strategy choices. Samuel Adams and the radical artisans and workers of Boston suggested what might be at stake in this struggle between elites and ordinary citizens when they formed a "solemn league and covenant" to lead a third intercolonial boycott of British goods. As most Bostonians knew, the words *solemn league* referred to a pact between the Scottish Presbyterians and English Puritans who had overthrown royal government in the 1640s and beheaded a king. Adams and his allies had made their choice: armed rebellion. Yet even in crisis-torn Boston, not everyone wanted matters to go that far. And in the southern colonies, planters worried that slave revolts and class antagonisms between the elite and the poorer farmers might be the ultimate outcome of escalating protest.

Creating a National Forum: The First Continental Congress   On September 5, 1774, delegates from every colony but Georgia gathered in Philadelphia for a continental congress. Few of the delegates or the people they represented thought of themselves as revolutionaries. "We want no revolution," a North Carolina delegate bluntly stated. Yet in the eyes of their British rulers, he and other colonists were treading dangerously close to treason. After all, neither the king nor Parliament had authorized the congress, which was intent on resisting acts of Parliament and defying the king. English men and women had been hanged as traitors for far less serious betrayals of the English government.

Some of the most articulate political leaders in the colonies attended this **First Continental Congress**. Conservative delegates such as Joseph Galloway of Pennsylvania hoped to slow the pace of colonial resistance by substituting petitions to Parliament for the total boycott proposed by Samuel Adams. Their radical opponents—including Samuel Adams and his cousin John, Patrick Henry, and delegates from the artisan community of Philadelphia—demanded the boycott and more. Most of the delegates were desperately searching for a third choice: a way to express their grievances and demand that injustices be corrected without further eroding their relationship with England.

The mounting crisis in Massachusetts diminished the chances of a moderate solution. Rumors spread that the royal navy was planning to bombard Boston and that General Gage was preparing to invade the countryside. Thousands of Massachusetts militiamen had begun mustering in Cambridge. The growing conflict drove many delegates into the radical camp. In this atmosphere of dread and anxiety, the Continental Congress approved the Continental Association, a boycott of all English goods to begin on December 1, 1774. The Congress also passed strong resolutions demanding the repeal of the Intolerable Acts.

The First Continental Congress had chosen radical tactics, but many delegates were torn between loyalty to Mother Country and loyalty to colony. Thomas Jefferson, a young Virginia planter and intellectual, tried to find a way out of this dilemma by separating loyalty to the king from resistance to Parliament. He argued that the colonists owed allegiance to the nation's king, not to Parliament, and that each colony did indeed have the right to legislate for itself. Not everyone agreed.

If no compromise could be reached, the delegates—and Americans everywhere—would have to choose where their strongest loyalties lay. Joseph Galloway believed that he had worked out the necessary compromise. In his Plan of Union, Galloway called for a Grand Council, elected by each colonial legislature, that would share with Parliament the right to originate laws for the colonies.

Congress rejected Galloway's compromise by the narrowest of margins. Then it was John Adams's turn to propose a solution. Under his skillful urging and direction, the Congress adopted the Declaration of Rights and Grievances, which politely but firmly established the colonial standard for acceptable legislation by Parliament. Colonists, said the declaration, would consent to acts meant to regulate "our external commerce." But they absolutely denied the legitimacy, or lawfulness, of an "idea of taxation, internal or external, for raising revenue on the subjects of America, without their consent."

The delegates knew that the force behind the declaration came from the unspoken but nevertheless real threat that rebellion would occur if the colonists' demands were not met. To make this threat clearer, Congress endorsed a set of resolutions rushed to Philadelphia from Suffolk County, Massachusetts. These Suffolk Resolves called on the residents of that county to arm themselves and prepare to resist British military action. Congressional support for these resolves sent an unmistakable message that American leaders were willing to choose rebellion if politics failed.

The delegates adjourned and headed home, bringing news of the Congress's decisions with them to their families and their communities. There was nothing to do now but wait for the Crown's response. When it came, it was electric. "Blows must decide," declared King George III, "whether they are to be subject to this country or independent."

THE DECISION FOR INDEPENDENCE

Americans were anxious while they waited for the king and Parliament to respond to the Declaration of Rights and Grievances, but they were not idle. In most colonies, a transfer of political power was occurring as the majority of Americans recognized the authority of anti-British, patriot governments.

Taking Charge and Enforcing Policies   Imperial control broke down as communities in each colony refused to obey royal laws or acknowledge the authority of royal officers. For example, when General Thomas Gage, the acting governor of Massachusetts, refused to convene the Massachusetts assembly, its members met anyway. Their first order of business was to prepare for military resistance to Gage and his army. While the redcoats occupied Boston, the rebellious assembly openly ordered the colonists to stockpile military supplies near the town of Concord.

The transition from royal to patriot political control was peaceful in communities where anti-British sentiment was strong. Where it was weak, or where the community was divided, radicals used persuasion, pressure, and open intimidation to advance the patriot cause. In most colonial cities and towns, patriot committees arose to enforce compliance with the boycott of British goods. These committees publicly exposed those who did not obey the Continental Association, publishing violators' names in local newspapers and calling on the community to shun them. These tactics were effective against merchants who wanted to break the boycott and consumers willing to purchase English goods if they could find them. When public shaming did not work, most committees were ready to use threats of physical violence and to make good on them.

Colonists suspected of sympathizing with the British were brought before committees and made to swear oaths of support for the patriot cause. Such political pressure often gave way to violence. In Connecticut a group of patriots hauled a 70-year-old Anglican man from his bed, dragged him naked into the winter night, and beat him brutally because his loyalty to the Church of England made him suspect. In New England, many pro-British citizens, or loyalists, came to fear for their lives. In the wake of the Intolerable Acts, hundreds of them fled to the city of Boston, hoping General Gage could protect them from their neighbors.

The Shot Heard 'Round the World   King George continued to believe that resistance in most colonies would fade if the Massachusetts radicals were crushed. In January 1775, he ordered General Gage to arrest the most notorious leaders of rebellion in that colony,

Samuel Adams and John Hancock. Gage made plans to send redcoats to Concord with orders to seize the rapidly growing stockpile of weapons and arrest the two radical leaders along the way.

The patriots, of course, had their spies in Boston. Reports of the arrest orders and of suspicious troop preparations reached the militias gathered outside the occupied city. The only question was when and where Gage would attack. The Americans devised a warning system: as soon as Gage's troops began to move out of Boston, spies would signal the route with lanterns hung in the bell tower of the North Church. On April 18, 1775, riders waiting outside Boston saw one lantern, then another, flash from the bell tower. Within moments, silversmith Paul Revere and his fellow messengers rode off to give news of the British army's approach to the militia and the people living in the countryside.

Around sunrise on April 19, an advance guard of a few hundred redcoats reached the town of Lexington, where they expected to apprehend Adams and Hancock. In the pale light, they saw about seventy colonial militiamen waiting on the village green. As the badly outnumbered colonists began to disperse, eager and nervous redcoats broke ranks and rushed forward, sending up a triumphant cheer. No order came to fire, but in the confusion shots rang out. Eight Americans were killed, most of them shot in the back as they ran for safety. Nine more were wounded. Later Americans who told the story of the skirmish at Lexington would insist that the first musket fired there sounded a "shot heard 'round the world."

The British troops marched from Lexington to Concord. Surprised to find the town nearly deserted, they began a methodical search for weapons. All they uncovered were five hundred musket balls, which they dumped into a nearby pond. They then burned the town's liberty tree. Ignoring this act of provocation, the Concord **Minutemen**, in hiding nearby, waited patiently. When the moment seemed right, they swooped down on the unsuspecting British troops guarding the town's North Bridge.

The sudden attack by the Americans shocked the redcoats, who fled in a panic back toward Boston. The Minutemen followed, gathering more men along the path of pursuit. Together, these American farmers, artisans, servants, and shopkeepers terrorized the young British soldiers, firing on them from behind barns, stone walls, and trees; 73 redcoats were killed, 174 were wounded, and 26 were missing. The day after the **Battles of Lexington and Concord**, thousands of New England militiamen poured in from the surrounding countryside, dug trenches, and laid siege to Boston. As far as they and thousands of other Americans were concerned—including the loyalist refugees crowded into the city—war had begun.

The Second Continental Congress   When the Continental Congress reconvened in May 1775, it began at once to ready the colonies for war. This Second Continental Congress authorized the printing of American paper money for the purchase of supplies and appointed a

---

Minutemen   Nickname first given to the Concord militia because of their speed in assembling and later applied generally to colonial militia during the Revolution.

committee to oversee foreign relations. It approved the creation of a Continental Army and chose George Washington, the Virginia veteran of the French and Indian War, to serve as its commander.

The Congress was clearly ready to defend Americans' rights and protect their liberties. But was it ready to declare a complete break with England? Some delegates still hoped to find a peaceful solution to the crisis, despite the bloodshed at Lexington and Concord. This sentiment led the Congress to draft the **Olive Branch Petition**, which offered the king a choice: the colonists would end their armed resistance if the king would withdraw the British military and revoke the Intolerable Acts. Many delegates must have doubted the king's willingness to make such concessions, for the very next day the Congress issued a public statement in defense of the war preparations. This "Declaration of the Causes and Necessity of Taking Up Arms" boldly accused the British government of tyranny. It stopped short, however, of declaring colonial independence.

Across the Atlantic, British leaders struggled to find some negotiating points despite the king's refusal to bend. Almost two months before the battles at Lexington and Concord, Lord North had drafted a set of Conciliatory Propositions for Parliament and the American Continental Congress to consider. North's proposals gave no ground on Parliament's right to tax the colonies, but they did offer to suspend taxation if Americans would raise funds for their own military defense. Members of Parliament who were sympathetic toward the Americans also pressed for compromise. They insisted that it made better sense to keep the colonies as a market for English goods than to lose them in a battle over raising revenue.

Cooler heads, however, did not prevail. Americans rejected Lord North's proposals in July 1775. The king, loathe to compromise, rejected the Olive Branch Petition. George III then persuaded Parliament to pass an **American Prohibitory Act** instructing the royal navy to seize American ships engaged in any form of trade, "as if the same were the ships ... of open enemies." For all intents and purposes, King George III declared war on his colonies before the colonies declared war on their king.

The Impact of *Common Sense*   War was a fact, yet few American voices were calling for a complete political and emotional break with Britain. Even the most ardent patriots continued to justify their actions as upholding the British constitution. They were rebelling, they said, to preserve the rights guaranteed English citizens, not to establish an independent nation. Their drastic actions were necessary because a corrupt Parliament and corrupt ministers were trampling on those rights.

If any American political leaders believed the king was as corrupt as his advisers and his Parliament, they did not make this view public. Then, in January 1776, Thomas Paine, an Englishman who had emigrated to America a few years earlier, published a pamphlet he called ***Common Sense***. Paine's pamphlet broke the silence about King George III.

Tom Paine was a corset maker by trade but a political radical by temperament. Soon after settling in Philadelphia, he wrote *Common Sense,* directed at ordinary citizens, not their political leaders. Like the preachers of the Great Awakening, Paine rejected the formal language of the elite, adopting instead a plain, urgent, and emotional vocabulary and writing style designed to reach a mass audience.

Common Sense was unique in its content as well as its style. Paine made no excuses for his revolutionary zeal. He expressed no admiration for the British constitution or reverence for the British political system. Instead, he attacked the **sanctity** of the monarchy head-on. He challenged the idea of a hereditary ruler, questioned the value of monarchy as an institution, and criticized the personal character of the men who ruled as kings. Paine put it bluntly and sarcastically: "Of more worth is one honest man to society, and in the sight of God, than all the crowned ruffians that ever lived." He dismissed George III as nothing more than a "Royal Brute," and he urged Americans to establish their own **republic**.

Common Sense sold 120,000 copies in its first three months in print. The impact of Paine's words resounded in the taverns and coffeehouses, where ordinary farmers, artisans, shopkeepers, and laborers took up his call for independence and the creation of a republic. Political leaders acknowledged Paine's importance, although some begrudged the popular admiration lavished on this poorly educated artisan whose flamboyant writing style they found unsuitable.

Declaring Independence   The Second Continental Congress, lagging far behind popular sentiment, inched its way toward a formal declaration of independence. John Adams fumed at its snail's pace. But finally, on June 7, 1776, Adams's close ally, Virginia lawyer Richard Henry Lee, rose on the floor of the Congress and offered this straightforward motion: "That these United Colonies are, and of right ought to be, free and independent States, that they are absolved from all allegiance to the British Crown, and that all political connection between them and the State of Great Britain is, and ought to be, totally dissolved."

Lee's resolution was no more than a statement of reality, yet the Congress chose to postpone its final vote until July. The delay would give members time to win over the few fainthearted delegates from the Middle Colonies. It also would allow the committee appointed to draft a formal declaration of independence time to complete its work.

Congress had chosen an all-star group to draft the declaration, including John Adams, Connecticut's Roger Sherman, Benjamin Franklin, and New York

---

sanctity Saintliness or holiness; the quality of being sacred or beyond criticism.

republic A nation in which supreme power resides in the citizens, who elect representatives to govern them.

landowner Robert Livingston. But these men delegated the task of writing the document to the fifth and youngest member of the committee, Thomas Jefferson. The 33-year-old Virginian was not a social radical like Samuel Adams and Tom Paine. He was not an experienced politician like John Adams and Benjamin Franklin. And he lacked the reputation of fellow Virginians George Washington and Richard Henry Lee. But the committee members recognized that Jefferson could draw on a deep and broad knowledge of political theory and philosophy. He had read the works of Enlightenment philosophers, classical theorists, and seventeenth-century English revolutionaries. And though shy and somewhat halting in his speech, Thomas Jefferson was a master of written prose. Jefferson began the **Declaration of Independence** with a defense of revolution based on "self-evident" truths about humanity's "inalienable rights"—rights that included life, liberty, and the pursuit of property. (In a later draft, the rights became "unalienable" and "property" became "happiness.") Jefferson argued that these rights were natural rather than historical. In other words, they came from the "Creator" rather than developing out of human law, government, or tradition. Thus they were broader and more sacred than the specific "rights of Englishmen." With this philosophical groundwork in place, Jefferson moved on to list the grievances that demanded America end its relationship with Britain. He focused on the king's abuse of power rather than on the oppressive legislation passed by Parliament. All government rested on the consent of the governed, Jefferson asserted, and the people had the right to overthrow any government that tyrannized rather than protected them, that threatened rather than respected their unalienable rights.

The genius of Jefferson's Declaration was not that it contained novel ideas but that it contained ideas that were commonly accepted by most colonists. Jefferson gave voice to these beliefs, clearly and firmly. He also gave voice to the sense of abuse and injustice that had been growing in colonial society for several decades.

Declaring Loyalties   Delegates to the Second Continental Congress approved the Declaration of Independence on July 2, 1776, and made their approval public on July 4 (the text of the Declaration is reprinted in the Documents section at the end of this book). As John Adams was fond of saying, "The die had been cast," and Americans had to weigh loyalty to king against loyalty to a new nation. In the face of such a critical choice, many wavered. Throughout the war that followed the Declaration, a surprising number of colonists clung to neutrality, hoping that the breach could be resolved without their having to participate or choose sides.

Those who did commit themselves based their decisions on deeply held beliefs and personal considerations as well as fears. For some of the perhaps 150,000 active loyalists, their commitment was a matter of personal character.

Reluctance to break a solemn oath of allegiance to the king or fear of the chaos and violence that were a real part of revolution could motivate a colonist to remain loyal rather than rebel. Many loyalists believed that tradition and common sense argued for acknowledging parliamentary supremacy and the king's right to rule. These colonists had an abiding respect for the structure of the British government. In addition, in their judgment, the advantages of remaining within the protective circle of Europe's most powerful nation seemed too obvious to debate, and the likelihood of swift and bloody defeat at the hands of the British army and navy too obvious to risk. Many of the men who articulated the loyalist position were members of the colonial elite. They frankly admitted their fears that a revolution would unleash the "madness of the multitude." The tyranny of the mob, they argued, was far more damaging than the tyranny of which the king stood accused.

For many colonists who chose loyalism, however, the deciding issues were economic. Holders of royal offices and merchants who depended on trade with British manufacturers found loyalty the compelling option. The loyalist ranks were also filled with colonists from the "multitude." Many small farmers in the Carolinas and tenant farmers in New York gave their support to the Crown when their political and economic foes—the great planters or the wealthy manor lords—became patriots. The choice of which side to back often hinged, therefore, on local struggles and economic conflicts rather than on beliefs about government and imperial issues.

For African Americans, the rallying call of liberty was familiar long before the Revolution began. Decades of slave resistance and rebellion demonstrated that black colonists did not need the impassioned language of a Patrick Henry to remind them of the value of freedom. Instead, many slaves viewed the Revolution as they viewed epidemics and imperial warfare: as a potential opportunity to gain their own liberty. In the same way, many free blacks saw the Revolution as a possible opportunity to win civil rights they had been denied before 1776.

African Americans had pointed out the inconsistencies of the radical position even before the Declaration of Independence. In 1773, a group of enslaved blacks in Boston petitioned the governor and the assembly for their freedom, "in behalf of all those, who ... are held in a state of SLAVERY, within the bowels of a FREE country." Some white colonists appreciated these sentiments. In 1774, while John Adams debated the threat of political slavery for colonial Englishmen in the First Continental Congress, his wife Abigail observed: "It always appeared a most iniquitous [sinful] scheme to me—to fight ourselves for what we are daily robbing and plundering from those who have as good a right to freedom as we have." Tom Paine agreed. Writing as "Humanus" in a Philadelphia newspaper, Paine urged white patriots to abolish slavery and give freed blacks western land grants.

Other patriots worried that slaves would seek their freedom by supporting the British in the war. Indeed, in 1775 the royal governor of Virginia, Lord Dunmore, expressed his intention to "arm all my own Negroes and receive all others that will come to me whom I shall declare free." Rumors of this plan horrified neighboring

Peter Salem (1750–1816) was an African American soldier who fought in the battle of Concord on April 19, 1775, and later in the Battle of Bunker Hill. He reenlisted in 1776 and fought once again in the battles of Saratoga and Stony Point. After the war, he returned to his home state of Massachusetts where he died in a poorhouse at the age of 66.

Schomburg Center/Art Resource, New York.

Maryland planters, who demanded that their governor issue arms and ammunition to protect against slave **insurrection**. Throughout the South, white communities braced themselves for a black struggle for freedom that would emerge in the midst of the colonial struggle for independence.

When Dunmore did offer freedom to "all indentured Servants, negroes or others ... able and willing to bear Arms who escaped their masters," he was more interested in disrupting the slave-based plantation economy of his American enemies than in African American rights. Yet slaves responded, crossing into British lines in great enough numbers to create an "Ethiopian Regiment" of soldiers. These black loyalists wore a banner across their uniforms that read "Liberty to Slaves." In the southern campaigns of the long war that followed, thousands of black men, women, and children made their way to the British lines. Once in uniform, black soldiers were usually assigned to work in road construction and other manual labor rather than participate in combat. Perhaps as many as fifty thousand slaves gained their freedom during the war as a result of either British policy or the disruptions that made escape possible.

Indians' responses to news of the war were far from uniform. At first, many considered the Revolution a family quarrel that should be avoided. The revolutionaries would have been satisfied to see Indians adopt this policy of neutrality. They knew they were unlikely to win Indian support given the legacy of border warfare and the actions of land-hungry settlers. As early as 1775, the Second Continental Congress issued a proclamation warning Indians to remain neutral. But the British, recognizing their advantage, made strong efforts to win Indian support. Indian leaders proceeded cautiously, however. When a British negotiator boasted to Flying Crow that British victory was inevitable, the Seneca chief was unimpressed. "If you are so strong, Brother, and they but as a weak Boy, why ask

insurrection   An uprising against a legitimate authority or government.

our assistance?" The chief was unwilling to commit his tribe based on issues that divided Crown and colonists but meant little to the welfare of his own people. "You say they are all mad, foolish, wicked, and deceitful—I say you are so and they are wise for you want us to destroy ourselves in your War and they advise us to live in Peace."

The British continued to press for Indian participation in the war, and many Indian tribes and confederations eventually decided that the Crown would better serve their interests and respect their rights than would the colonists. First, the British were much more likely than the colonists to be able to provide a steady supply of the manufactured goods and weapons the Indians relied on in the eighteenth century. Second, colonial territorial ambitions threatened the Indians along the southern and northwestern frontiers. Third, an alliance with the British offered some possibility of recouping land and trading benefits lost in the past. No uniformity emerged, however. Intertribal rivalries and Indians' concerns about the safety of their own villages often determined alignments. Even among the Iroquois, pro-British Senecas burned the crops and houses of Oneidas who had joined forces with the patriots. In the southern backcountry, fierce fighting between Indians and revolutionaries seemed a continuation of the century's many border wars. But there, too, alignments could shift. Although the Cherokees began the war as British allies, a split developed, producing an internal civil war.

Fewer than half of the colonists threw in their lot immediately with the revolutionaries. Among those who did were people whose economic interests made independence seem worth the risk, including artisans and urban laborers as well as merchants who traded outside the British Empire, most large and some small farmers, and many members of the southern planter elite. For these Americans, it was not simply a matter of escaping unfair taxation. A release from Britain's mercantile policies, which restricted colonial trade with other nations, held out the promise of expanded trade and an end to the risks of smuggling. Sometimes the pressure for independence came from below rather than from a colony's political leadership, most notably in Virginia where many elite planters were pressed by more radical ordinary farmers to support independence or lose their positions of authority. Colonists affected by the Great Awakening's message of egalitarianism often chose the patriot side. Americans with a conscious, articulated radical vision of society—the Tom Paines and Samuel Adamses—supported the Revolution and its promise of a republic. Many who became revolutionaries shared the hope for a better life under a government that encouraged its citizens to be virtuous and to live in simplicity.

As Americans—of English, European, Indian, and African heritage—armed themselves or fled from the violence and bloodshed they saw coming, they realized that the conflict wore two faces: this was a war for independence, but it was also a civil war. In the South, it pitted slave against master, Cherokee against Cherokee, and frontier farmer against coastal planter. In New England, it set neighbor against neighbor, forcing scores of loyalist families to flee. In some instances, children were set against parents, and wives refused to support the cause their husbands had chosen. Whatever the outcome of the struggle ahead, Americans knew that it would come at great cost.

STUDY TOOLS

SUMMARY

The British victory in the Great War for Empire produced many new problems. The British had to govern the French population in Canada and maintain security against Indians on a greatly expanded colonial frontier. They had to pay an enormous war debt but continue to finance strong and well-equipped armed forces to keep the empire they had won. To deal with these new circumstances, the English government chose to impose revenue-raising measures on the colonies.

The Sugar Act of 1764 tightened customs collections, the Stamp Act of 1765 placed a direct tax on legal documents, and the Townshend Acts of 1767 set import taxes on English products such as paint and tea. Colonists protested each of these sharp shifts in policy, for they saw Parliament's revenue-raising actions as an abuse of power. Political debate in the colonies began to focus on the possibility that the British government meant to curtail American liberties.

Crowds directed by the Sons of Liberty attacked royal officials, and in Boston five civilians died in a clash with British troops known as the Boston Massacre. But colony-wide boycotts of British goods proved to be the most effective form of protest. They led to the repeal of all three taxes.

Political activists prepared for a quick and united response to any new crises by creating organizations such as the committees of correspondence. In 1773 the British expected little American opposition to the Tea Act, but they were wrong. In Boston a group of activists dumped thousands of pounds' worth of tea into the harbor, enraging British officials, who as a punishment closed the port of Boston to all trade. This and other Intolerable Acts infuriated colonists, and they took united action in support of Massachusetts. A new colonial forum, the First Continental Congress, met in 1774 to debate the colonies' relationship to England and to issue a united protest. A Declaration of Rights and Grievances was sent to the king, but he rejected the colonists' appeal for compromise, instead declaring that "blows must decide."

After British troops fought militiamen at Lexington and Concord, the Second Continental Congress prepared for war. Tom Paine's pamphlet *Common Sense* pushed many reluctant colonists into the revolutionary camp. In July 1776, Congress issued the Declaration of Independence, drafted by Thomas Jefferson, which defended the colonists' right to resist a tyrannical king. In 1776 Americans faced the difficult task of choosing sides: loyalty to the Crown or revolution. African Americans and Indians had to decide whether to support one side or the other or try to remain neutral in the midst of revolution. The outcome was both a war for colonial independence and a civil war that divided families and communities across America. In Chapter 6, you will see how independence was won.

CHRONOLOGY

LOYALTY OR REBELLION?

1763	Treaty of Paris ends French and Indian War
	Pontiac's Rebellion
	Proclamation Line
1764	Sugar Act
1765	Stamp Act
	Sons of Liberty organized
	Stamp Act Congress
	Nonimportation of British goods
1766	Stamp Act repealed
	Declaratory Act
1767	Townshend Acts
1768	Renewed boycott of British goods
1770	Boston Massacre
	Townshend Acts repealed
1773	Tea Act and Tea Party
1774	Intolerable Acts
	First Continental Congress
	Continental Association
	Declaration of Rights and Grievances
1775	Battles of Lexington and Concord
	Second Continental Congress
	Olive Branch Petition
1776	Tom Paine's Common Sense
	Declaration of Independence

FOCUS QUESTIONS

If you have mastered this chapter, you should be able to answer these questions and explain the terms that follow the questions.

1. Why did Prime Minister Grenville expect the colonists to accept part of the burden of financing the British Empire in 1764?
2. How did colonists understand their obligations to the empire?
3. Why were the colonists alarmed by Grenville's 1765 stamp tax?
4. How did the colonists protest Parliament's taxation policies?
5. Why did Charles Townshend expect his revenue-raising measures to be successful?
6. What forms of resistance did the colonists use against Townshend's measures and what were the results?
7. What British policies led Americans to imagine a plot against their rights and liberties?

8. How did the king hope to crush resistance in Massachusetts and how did the Continental Congress respond?
9. What compromises were still available in 1775–1776 and how might the Revolutionary War have been avoided?
10. What motivated some colonists to become loyalists and others to become patriots?

KEY TERMS

George III (*p.* 107)

George Grenville (*p.* 107)

Covenant Chain (*p.* 108)

Pontiac (*p.* 108)

Proclamation Line of 1763 (*p.* 108)

Currency Act (*p.* 110)

Sugar Act (*p.* 110)

Stamp Act (*p.* 112)

Sons of Liberty (*p.* 113)

Samuel Adams (*p.* 113)

Ebenezer McIntosh (*p.* 113)

Thomas Hutchinson (*p.* 113)

Patrick Henry (*p.* 114)

Stamp Act Congress (*p.* 115)

Declaratory Act (*p.* 116)

Townshend Acts (*p.* 117)

Boston Massacre (*p.* 121)

committees of correspondence (*p.* 123)

Intolerable Acts (*p.* 124)

First Continental Congress (*p.* 126)

Battles of Lexington and Concord (*p.* 128)

Olive Branch Petition (*p.* 129)

American Prohibitory Act (*p.* 129)

Common Sense (*p.* 129)

Declaration of Independence (*p.* 131)

6

RECREATING AMERICA: INDEPENDENCE
AND A NEW NATION, 1775–1783

CHAPTER OUTLINE

• The First Two Years of War • Diplomacy Abroad and Profiteering at
Home • From Stalemate to Victory • Republican Expectations in a New
Nation • Study Tools

THE FIRST TWO YEARS OF WAR

In 1775 General **Thomas Gage**, the military governor of Massachusetts and
commander of the British army of occupation there, surely wished he were anywhere
but Boston. The town was unsophisticated by British standards, many of its inhabitants were unfriendly, and its taverns and lodging houses bulged at the seams with
complaining loyalist refugees from the countryside. Gage's army was restless, and his
officers were bored. The American encampments outside the city were growing daily,
filling with local farmers and artisans after the bloodshed of Lexington and Concord.
These thousands of colonial **militiamen** were clearly the military enemy, yet in 1775
they were still citizens of the British Empire, not foreign invaders or foes. Gage, like
his American opponents, was caught up in the dilemma of an undeclared war.

The Battle for   With proper artillery, well placed on the hills surrounding
Boston   the city, the Americans could have done serious damage to
                        Gage's army of occupation. To supply the needed cannon, a
New Haven druggist named **Benedict Arnold** joined forces with a Vermont farmer
named Ethan Allen and, in May 1775, their troops captured Fort Ticonderoga in
New York and began transporting the fort's cannon across hundreds of miles of
mountains and forests to Boston. By the time the artillery reached the city, however,
a bloody battle between Gage and the American militia had already taken place.

---

militiamen Soldiers who were not members of a regular army but ordinary citizens called out in case
of an emergency.

In early June, Gage had issued a proclamation declaring all armed colonists traitors, but he offered **amnesty** to any rebel who surrendered to British authorities. When the militiamen ignored the general's offer, Gage decided a show of force was necessary. On June 17, 1775, Gage's fellow officer **William Howe** led a force of twenty-four hundred soldiers against rebel-held Breed's Hill. Despite the day's oppressive heat and humidity, General Howe ordered his men to advance in full dress uniform, weighed down with wool jackets and heavy knapsacks. Howe also insisted on making a proper frontal attack on the Americans. From the top of the hill, Captain William Prescott's militiamen immediately opened fire on the unprotected redcoats. The result was a near massacre. The tables turned, however, when the Americans ran out of ammunition. Most of Prescott's men fled in confusion, and the British soldiers bayoneted the few who remained to defend their position.

Even battle-worn veterans were shocked at the carnage. The British suffered more casualties that June afternoon than they would in any other battle of the war. The Americans, who retreated to the safety of Cambridge, learned a costly lesson on the importance of an effective supply line of arms and ammunition to their fighting men. Little was gained by either side. That the battle was misnamed the **Battle of Bunker Hill** captured perfectly the confusion and the absurdity of the encounter.

Congress Creates an Army

While militiamen and redcoats turned the Boston area into a war zone, the Continental Congress took its first steps toward recruiting and supplying an army. The "regular" army that took shape was not really a national force. It was a collection of small state armies whose recruits preserved their local or regional identities. While this army was expected to follow the war wherever it led, the Continental Congress still relied on state militias to join in any battles that took place within their own borders.

Congress chose French and Indian War veteran **George Washington** to command the Continental forces. Washington wrote gloomily of the task before him. Nothing he saw when he reached Massachusetts on July 3, 1775, made him more optimistic. A carnival atmosphere seemed to prevail inside the militiamen's camps. Farm boys turned soldiers fired their muskets at random, often using their weapons to start fires or to shoot at geese flying overhead. In the confusion, they sometimes accidentally wounded or killed themselves and others. "Seldom a day passes but some persons are shot by their friends," Washington noted in amazement.

The camps resembled pigsties. The stench from open latrines was terrible, and rotting animal carcasses, strewn everywhere, added to the aroma. The men were dirty and infected with lice, and most soldiers were constantly scratching, trying to relieve an itch that left them covered with scabs and raw, peeling skin. General Washington was disturbed but not surprised by what he saw. He knew that the men in these camps were country boys, away from home for the first time in their lives. The chaos they created resulted from a combination of fear, excitement,

---

amnesty A general pardon granted by a government, especially for political offenses.

boredom, inexperience, and plain homesickness, all brewing freely under poor leadership. Despite his sympathy for these young men, Washington acted quickly to reorganize the militia units, replace incompetent officers, and tighten discipline within the camps.

The British meanwhile laid plans for the evacuation of Boston, spurred in part by the knowledge that Arnold's wagon train of cannon was nearing Massachusetts. In March 1776 a fleet arrived to carry Thomas Gage, his officers, the British army, and almost a thousand loyalist refugees north to the safety of Halifax, Nova Scotia. By this time, His Majesty's war was in the hands of General William Howe and his brother **Richard Howe**, an admiral in the royal navy. With the help of military strategists and the vast resources of the Crown, the Howes were expected to bring the rebellion to a speedy end and restore order to the colonies.

The British Strategy in 1776   General Howe thought the most effective strategy would be to locate areas with high concentrations of loyalists and mobilize them to secure the allegiance of their undecided and even rebellious neighbors. Howe and his advisers targeted two reputed centers of loyalist strength. The first—New York, New Jersey, Pennsylvania—had a legacy of social and economic conflicts, such as the revolt of the Paxton Boys, that had caused many of the region's elite families to fear that independence threatened their prosperity. But loyalism was not confined to the conservative and wealthy. Its second stronghold was among the poor settlers of the Carolina backcountry. There, decades of bitter struggle between the coastal planters and the backcountry farmers had led to the Regulator movement and to intense loyalist sentiment among many of the embattled westerners.

General Howe's strategy had its flaws, however. First, although many people in these two regions were loyal, their numbers were never as great as the British assumed. Second, everywhere they went, British and **Hessian troops** left behind a trail of destruction and memories of abuse that alienated many Americans who might have considered remaining loyal. Howe was not likely to win over families who saw their "cattle killed and lying about the fields and pastures ... household furniture hacked and broken into pieces ... wells filled up and ... tools destroyed."

Nevertheless, in 1776 Howe launched his first major military assaults in the South and the mid-Atlantic region. In North Carolina, loyalists did turn out to fight for the Crown, but the British, directed by General Henry Clinton, failed to provide them the military support they needed. Poorly armed and badly outnumbered, Carolina loyalists were decisively defeated by the rebel militia on February 27 in the Battle of Moore's Creek. Rather than rush to their defense, the British abandoned their loyalist allies in favor of taking revenge on South Carolina. An impressive fleet of fifty ships and three thousand men sailed into Charleston harbor. But the British had unexpected bad luck. As the troops started to wade ashore, they found themselves stranded on small islands surrounded by a sudden rush of tidal waters. The Americans, meanwhile, had unexpected good luck. Working frantically to defend the harbor, they constructed a flimsy fort out of local palmetto wood. To the surprise of both sides, the cannon balls fired by British ships sank harmlessly into the absorbent, pulpy palmetto stockade. The fort—and the city of Charleston—remained standing.

Embarrassed and frustrated, the British abruptly ended the southern campaign, and General Clinton sailed north. The North and South Carolina loyalists, however, could not escape British failures. They had been denounced, mobbed, imprisoned, and sometimes tortured since 1775. Their situation grew even worse after the British withdrew.

Escape from New York

While Clinton was failing in the Carolinas, the Howe brothers were preparing a massive invasion of the mid-Atlantic region. In July 1776, Admiral Howe and General Howe sailed into New York harbor with the largest expeditionary force of the eighteenth century. With thirty thousand men, one-third of them Hessian mercenaries, this British army was larger than the peacetime population of New York City.

The Howes were not eager to demolish New York, however. Unlike most British officers, the brothers were genuinely fond of Americans, and they preferred to be agents of compromise and negotiation rather than of destruction. They hoped that a spectacular show of force and a thorough humiliation of rebel commander George Washington would be enough to bring the Americans to their senses and end the rebellion.

General Washington rushed his army south from Massachusetts to defend the city, but he had few illusions that his twenty-three thousand men, many of them sick and most of them inexperienced at war, could repel the invading British forces. For a month, the Howes made no move on the city. Finally, early in the morning of August 22, 1776, the British began their advance, landing unopposed and moving toward the Brooklyn neck of Long Island. Just as Washington had feared, when fighting began five days later almost all his raw and inexperienced troops surrendered or ran. A single Maryland regiment made a heroic stand against the landing forces but was destroyed by the oncoming British. Washington, at the scene himself, might have been captured had the Howes pressed their advantage. But they withdrew, content that they had made the American commander look foolish.

Washington took advantage of the Howes' delay to bring his troops to the safety of Manhattan Island. But on September 15, a British attack again sent his army into flight. Angry and frustrated, Washington threw his hat to the ground and shouted, "Are these the men with whom I am to defend America!"

Washington's army fled north with the British in hot pursuit. In a skirmish at Harlem Heights, the American commander was relieved to see his men stand their ground and win their first combat victory. He was even more relieved by the strange failure of the British to press their advantage. When the redcoats finally engaged the Continentals again at White Plains, the Americans managed to retreat safely. Soon afterward, Washington took his army across the Hudson River to New Jersey and marched them farther west, across the Delaware River into Pennsylvania.

Winter Quarters and Winter Victories

Following European customs, General Howe established winter quarters for his troops before the cold set in. His men made their camps in the New York area and in Rhode Island that December, expecting Washington to make camp

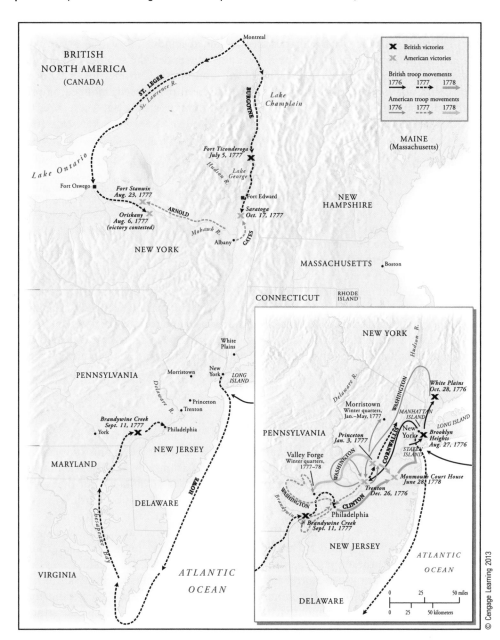

MAP 6.1 Northern Campaigns, 1776–1778

The major revolutionary battles of these years took place in New York, New Jersey, and Pennsylvania. The inset indicates battles in 1776, when the British invaded Long Island and New York City, pushing Washington's troops across New Jersey until they won crucial battles at Trenton and Princeton. The larger map illustrates British offensives in 1777; the 1778 battle at Monmouth Court House appears on the inset.

somewhere as well. But Washington, safe for the moment in Pennsylvania, was too restless to settle in just yet. Enlistment terms in his army would soon be up, and without some encouraging military success he feared few of his soldiers would reenlist. Thus Washington looked eagerly for a good target to attack—and found one. Across the Delaware, on the Jersey side, two or three thousand Hessian troops held a garrison near the town of Trenton.

On Christmas night, amid a howling blizzard, General Washington led twenty-four hundred of his men back across the river. Marching 9 miles, the Americans arrived to find the Hessians asleep. The surprised enemy surrendered immediately. Without losing a single man, Washington had captured nine hundred prisoners and many badly needed military supplies. Taking full advantage of the moment, Washington made a rousing appeal to his men to reenlist. About half of the soldiers agreed to remain.

The **Battle of Trenton** was a crucial victory, but Washington enjoyed his next success even more. In early January he again crossed into New Jersey to attack the British garrison at Princeton. On the way, his advance guard ran into two British regiments. As both sides lined up for battle, Washington rode back and forth in front of his men, shouting encouragement and urging them to stand firm. His reckless behavior put him squarely in the line of fire, but it was effective. When the British turned in retreat, Washington rashly rode after them, clearly delighted to be in pursuit for once in the war.

The Trenton and Princeton victories raised the morale of the Continental Army as it settled at last into its winter quarters near Morristown, New Jersey. They also stirred popular support for the raids that many called Washington's "nine-day wonder." Of course, General Howe was still poised to march on Philadelphia when warm weather returned. And Congress still had few resources to spare for Washington's army. When Washington pleaded for supplies, Congress urged him to commandeer what he needed from civilians nearby. The general wisely refused. English high-handedness and cruelty had turned many people of the area into staunch supporters of the Revolution, and Washington had no intention of alienating them by seizing their livestock, food, or weapons.

Burgoyne's New York Campaign

In July 1777 General William Howe sailed up the Chesapeake Bay toward Philadelphia with fifteen thousand men. The Continental Congress had already fled the city, knowing that Washington could not prevent the enemy occupation, and the British had little difficulty capturing Philadelphia. The problems they did face in 1777 came not from Washington but from the poor judgment of one of their own, a flamboyant young general named **John Burgoyne**.

Burgoyne had won approval for an elaborate plan to separate New England from the rest of the American colonies. He would move his army south from Montreal, while a second army of redcoats and Iroquois, commanded by Colonel Barry St. Leger, would veer east across the Mohawk Valley from Fort Oswego. At the same time, William Howe would send a third force north from New York City. The three armies would rendezvous at Albany, effectively isolating New England and, it was assumed, giving the British a perfect opportunity to crush the rebellion.

On paper, this daring plan seemed to have every chance of success. In reality, however, it had serious flaws. First, neither Burgoyne nor the British officials in England had any knowledge of the American terrain that had to be covered. Second, they badly misjudged the Indian support St. Leger would receive. Third, General Howe, no longer in New York City, knew absolutely nothing of his own critical role in the plan. Blissfully unaware of these problems, Burgoyne led his army from Montreal in high spirits in June 1777. The troops floated down Lake Champlain in canoes and flatbottom boats and easily retook Fort Ticonderoga. From Ticonderoga, the invading army continued to march toward Albany. From this point on, however, things began to go badly for Burgoyne.

In true eighteenth-century British style, Burgoyne chose to travel well rather than lightly. The thirty wagons moving slowly behind the general contained over fifty pieces of artillery for the campaign. They also contained Burgoyne's mistress, her personal wardrobe and his, and a generous supply of champagne. But when the caravan encountered New York's swamps and gullies, movement slowed to a snail's pace. Ethan Allen and his Green Mountain Boys harassed the British as they entered Allen's home region of Vermont. A bloody, head-on battle near Bennington further slowed Burgoyne's progress. When the general's army finally reached Albany in mid-September, neither St. Leger nor Howe were in sight.

The full support St. Leger had counted on from the Iroquois had not materialized, and he met fierce resistance as he made his way to the rendezvous point. When news reached him that Benedict Arnold and an army of a thousand Americans were approaching, St. Leger simply turned around and took his exhausted men to safety at Fort Niagara. Howe, of course, had no idea that he was expected in Albany. This left John Burgoyne stranded in the heart of New York. His supplies dwindling, on September 19 he attacked the American lines hoping to clear a path of retreat toward Canada for his army. The American general, Horatio "Granny" Gates, was neither bold nor particularly clever, but it took little daring or genius to defeat Burgoyne's weary, dispirited British soldiers. On October 17, 1777, General John Burgoyne surrendered.

News that a major British army had been defeated spread quickly on both sides of the Atlantic. It was a powerful boost to American confidence and an equally powerful blow to British self-esteem. The report also reversed the fortunes of American diplomatic efforts. Until the **Battle of Saratoga**, American appeals to the governments of Spain, France, and Holland for supplies, loans, and military support had met with only moderate success. Now, hopes ran high that France would recognize independence and join the war effort.

Winter Quarters in 1777   John Adams, who never wore a uniform, had once toasted a "short and Violent war." After Burgoyne's defeat, many Americans believed that Adams's wish was coming true. General Washington, however, did not share their optimism. French help might be coming, he pointed out, but who knew when? In the meantime, he reminded Congress, his army still needed funds and supplies. Congress ignored all his urgent requests. The result was the long and dreadful winter at Valley Forge. **Valley Forge** was 20 miles from Philadelphia, where General Howe and his army

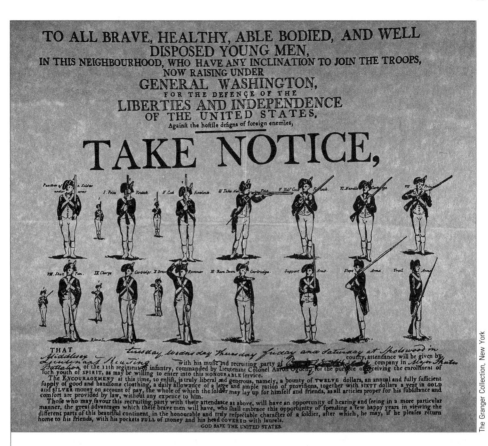

This recruiting poster for the Continental Army invites young men to join in the defense of American liberty and independence. The bounty of $12, along with "good and handsome clothing," a daily allowance of provisions, and $60 a year paid in gold, tempted many poor farm and city boys.

were comfortably housed for the winter. Throughout December 1777, Washington's men labored to build the huts and cabins they needed. While two officers were assigned to share quarters, a dozen enlisted men were expected to crowd into a 14-by-16-foot hut. Rations were a problem from the start. Most soldiers at Valley Forge lived entirely on a diet of fire cakes, made of flour and water baked in the coals or over the fire on a stick. Blankets were scarce, coats were rare, and firewood was precious. An army doctor summed up conditions when he wrote: "Poor food—hard lodgings—cold weather—fatigue—nasty clothes—nasty cookery—vomit half my time—smoked out of my senses—the devil's in it—I can't endure it."

The doctor, however, did endure it. So did the soldiers he tended to daily, men such as the barefoot, half-naked, dirty young man who cried out in despair, "I am sick, my feet lame, my legs are sore, my body covered with this tormenting itch." While civilians mastered the steps of the latest dance craze, "the Burgoyne surrender," soldiers at Valley Forge traded the remains of their uniforms and sometimes their muskets for the momentary warmth and sense of well-being provided by liquor.

The enlisted men who survived the winter at Valley Forge were strangers to luxury even in peacetime. Most were from the humblest social classes: farm laborers, servants, apprentices, even former slaves. But if poverty had driven them into the army, a commitment to see the war through kept them there. The contrast between their own patriotism and the apparent indifference of the civilian population made many of these soldiers bitter. Private Joseph Plumb Martin expressed the feelings of most when he said "a kind and holy Providence" had done more to help the army while it was at Valley Forge "than did the country in whose service we were wearing away our lives by piecemeal."

These suffering soldiers did get one thing they desperately needed—professional military training. In the spring of 1778, an unlikely Prussian volunteer arrived at Valley Forge. **Baron Friedrich von Steuben** was almost 50 years old, dignified, elegantly dressed, with a dazzling gold and diamond medal always displayed on his chest. Like most foreign volunteers, many of whom plagued Washington more than they helped him, the baron claimed to be an aristocrat, to have vast military experience, and to have held high rank in a European army. In truth, he had purchased his title only a short time before fleeing his homeland in bankruptcy, and he had only been a captain in the Prussian army. He had not, however, exaggerated his talent as a military drillmaster. All spring, the baron could be seen drilling Washington's troops, alternately shouting in rage and applauding with delight. Washington had little patience with most foreign volunteers, but he considered von Steuben a most unexpected and invaluable surprise.

In the spring of 1778, Washington received the heartening news that France had formally recognized the independence of the United States. He immediately declared a day of thanks and issued brandy to each enlisted man at Valley Forge. American diplomacy had triumphed; Washington hoped the combined forces of France and America would soon bring victory as well.

DIPLOMACY ABROAD AND PROFITEERING AT HOME

Like most wars, the Revolutionary War was not confined to the battlefields. Diplomacy was essential, and American diplomats hoped to secure supplies, safe harbors for American ships, and if at all possible, formal recognition of independence and the open military assistance that would allow. British diplomats, on the other hand, worked to prevent any formal alliances between European powers and the American rebels. Both sides issued propaganda to ensure continued popular support for the war. General Burgoyne's defeat and the widening of the war into an international struggle affected popular morale in both America and Britain.

The Long Road to Formal Recognition   In 1776, England had many enemies and rivals in Europe who were only too happy to see George III expend his resources and military personnel to quell a colonial rebellion. Although these nations expected the American Revolution to fail, they were more than eager to keep the conflict going as long as possible. Before Saratoga, they preferred to keep their support for the Revolution unofficial.

The Americans hoped for more. In December 1776, Congress sent the printer-politician-scientist **Benjamin Franklin** to Paris in hopes of winning formal recognition of American independence. The charming and witty Franklin was the toast of Paris, adored by aristocrats and common people alike, but even he could not persuade the king to support the Revolution openly. Burgoyne's surrender changed everything. After Saratoga, the British government began scrambling to end a war that had turned embarrassing, and the French government began scrambling to reassess its diplomatic position. French foreign minister Charles Gravier, comte de Vergennes, suspected that the English would quickly send a peace commission to America after Burgoyne's defeat. If the American Congress agreed to a compromise ending the rebellion, France could gain nothing more. But if the French helped keep the war alive, perhaps they could recoup some of the territory and prestige lost to England in the Seven Years' War. This meant, of course, recognizing the United States and entering a war with Britain. Vergennes knew a choice had to be made—but he was not yet certain what to do.

Meanwhile, the English government was indeed preparing a new peace offer for Congress. At the heart of the British offer were two promises that George III considered to be great concessions. First, Parliament would renounce all intentions of ever

In this political cartoon, the members of a British peace commission, sent to America in 1778, make their offers of compromise to America in hopes of ending the revolution. While these men are dressed in wigs and brocade coats—representing luxury and decadence, America appears in the natural simplicity of an Indian woman. Notice, however, that this defender of liberty carries a weapon and sits confidently upon the agricultural bounty of a new nation.

taxing the colonies again. Second, the Intolerable Acts, the Tea Act, and any other objectionable legislation passed since 1763 would be repealed. Many members of Parliament thought these overtures were long overdue, and after Burgoyne's defeat, popular support for compromise grew. The Americans, however, were unimpressed by the offers. For Congress, a return to colonial status was now unthinkable.

Benjamin Franklin knew that Congress would reject the king's offer. But he was too shrewd to relieve the comte de Vergennes's fear that a compromise was in the works. Franklin warned that France must act quickly and decisively or accept the consequences. His gamble worked, and in 1778 France and the United States signed a treaty linking French and American fates tightly together. Under its provisions neither country could make a separate peace with Great Britain. By 1779, Spain had also formally acknowledged the United States, and in 1780 the Netherlands did so too. George III had little choice but to declare war against these European nations.

The Revolution had grown into an international struggle that taxed British resources further and made it impossible for Britain to concentrate all its military might and naval power in America. With ships diverted to the Caribbean and to the European coast, Britain could no longer blockade American ports as effectively as before or transport troops to the American mainland as quickly. Above all, if the Americans could count on the cooperation of the French fleet, a British army could be trapped on American soil, cut off by French ships from supplies, reinforcements, and any chance of escape.

War and the American Public   News of the alliance with France seemed to release an orgy of spending and purchasing by American civilians. The conditions were ripe for such a spree in 1778, for with profits soaring from the sale of supplies to the army, many Americans had more money to spend than ever before. Also, not all of the credit that diplomats had negotiated with European allies went toward military supplies. Some of it was available for the purchase of manufactured goods. This combination of optimism, **cheap money**, and plentiful foreign goods led to a wartime spending bonanza.

Many of the goods imported into America over the next few years were actually British-made. American consumers apparently saw no contradiction between their strong patriotism and the purchase of enemy products. A **black market** in English goods grew rapidly, and profits from it skyrocketed. Abandoning the commitment to "virtuous simplicity" that had led them to dress in homespun, Americans stampeded to purchase tea and other imported luxuries.

Both the government and the military succumbed to this spirit of self-indulgence. Corruption and **graft** grew common as both high- and low-ranking officials sold government supplies for their own profit or charged the army excessive rates for goods and services. Cheating the government and the army was a game civilians could play, too. Wagoners carting pickled meat to military encampments drained the brine from the barrels to lighten their load so they could carry more. The results were spoiled meat, soldiers suffering from food poisoning—and a greater profit for the cartmen.

cheap money   Paper money that is readily available but has declined in value.

black market   The illegal business of buying and selling goods that are banned or restricted.

graft   Misuse of one's position for profit or advantage.

Soldiers became accustomed to defective weapons, defective shoes, and defective ammunition, but many of them joined the profit game by selling off their army-issued supplies to any available buyers. Recruiters pocketed the bounties given to them to attract enlistees. Officers accepted bribes from enlisted men seeking discharges.

Popular optimism and the spending frenzy unleashed by the French treaty contrasted sharply with the financial realities facing Congress. Bluntly put, the government was broke by 1778. The government met the crisis by printing more paper money. The result was rampant inflation. The value of the "continental," as the congressional paper money was called, dropped steadily with each passing day. The government's inability to pay soldiers became widely known—and enlistments plummeted. Both the state militias and the Continental Army resorted to impressment, or forced military service, to fill their ranks. Men forced to serve, however, were men more likely to mutiny or to desert. Officers did not know whether to sympathize with their unpaid and involuntary soldiers or to enforce stricter discipline upon them. Congress acknowledged the justice of the soldiers' complaints by giving them pay raises in the form of certificates that they could redeem—after the war.

From Stalemate to Victory

The French presence in the war did not immediately alter the strategies of British or American military leaders. English generals in the North displayed caution after Burgoyne's surrender, and Washington waited impatiently for signs that the French fleet would come to his aid. The result was a stalemate. The active war shifted to the South once again in late 1778 as the British mounted a second major campaign in the Carolinas.

The War Stalls in the North　**Sir Henry Clinton,** now the commander of the British army in North America, knew that the French fleet could easily blockade the Delaware River and thus cut off supplies to occupied Philadelphia. So, by the time warm weather had set in, his army was on the march, heading east through New Jersey en route to New York. Clinton's slow-moving caravan, burdened by a long train of bulky supply wagons, made an irresistible target—and Washington decided to strike.

Washington entrusted a former British career officer, **General Charles Lee**, with the initial attack. Lee marched his men to Monmouth, New Jersey, and as the British approached, the Americans opened fire. Yet as soon as the British army began to return fire, Lee ordered his men to retreat. When Washington arrived on the scene, the Americans were fleeing and the British troops were closing in.

Washington rallied the retreating Americans, calling on them to re-form their lines and stand their ground. Trained by von Steuben, the men responded well. They moved forward with precision and speed, driving the redcoats back. The **Battle of Monmouth** was not the decisive victory Washington had dreamed of, but it was a fine recovery from what first appeared to be certain defeat. Lee, who had long been a critic and rival of Washington, was discharged from the army.

Monmouth was only the first of several missed opportunities that summer of 1778. In August the French and Americans launched their first joint effort, sending a combined land and naval attack against the British base at Newport, Rhode Island. At the last minute, however, French admiral D'Estaing decided that the casualty rate would be too high. He abruptly gathered up his own men and sailed to safety on the open seas. The American troops were left to retreat as best they could.

Throughout the fall and winter of 1778 Washington waited in vain for French naval support for a major campaign. Early news coming from the western front did little to improve his bleak mood. In Kentucky and western Virginia, deadly Indian attacks had decimated many American settlements. The driving force behind these attacks was a remarkable British official named Harry Hamilton, who had won the nickname "Hair Buyer" because of the bounties he paid for American scalps. In October Hamilton led Indian troops from the Great Lakes tribes into the Illinois-Indiana region and captured the fort at Vincennes. The American counterattack was organized by a stocky young frontiersman, **George Rogers Clark**, whose own enthusiasm for scalping earned him the nickname "Long-Knife." To Washington's relief, Clark and his volunteer forces managed to drive the British from Vincennes.

Border conflict with Britain's Indian allies remained a major problem, and when loyalist troops joined these Indians, the danger increased. So did the atrocities. When patriot General John Sullivan's regular army was badly defeated by local loyalists and the Mohawk chief **Thayendanegea**, known to the Americans as Joseph Brant, Sullivan took revenge by burning forty Indian villages. It was an act of violence and cruelty that deeply shocked and shamed General Washington.

Spring and summer of 1779 passed and still Washington waited for the French navy's cooperation. Fall brought the general the worst possible news: Admiral D'Estaing and his fleet had sailed for the West Indies under orders to protect valuable French possessions in the Caribbean and, if possible, to seize English possessions there. News of D'Estaing's departure spurred a new wave of discipline problems among Washington's idle troops. Mutinies and desertions increased. From his winter headquarters in Morristown Heights, New Jersey, Washington wrote to von Steuben: "The prospect, my dear Baron, is gloomy, and the storm thickens." The real storm, however, was raging not in New Jersey but in the Carolinas.

The Second Carolinas Campaign

Since the fall of 1778, the British had been siphoning off New York–based troops for a new invasion of the South. The campaign began in earnest with the capture of Savannah, Georgia. Then, in the winter of 1779, General Henry Clinton sailed for Charleston, South Carolina, eager to avenge his embarrassing retreat in the 1776 campaign. Five thousand Continental soldiers hurried to join the South Carolina militia in defense of the city. From the Citadel, a fortification spanning the northern neck of the city's peninsula, these American forces bombarded the British with all they could find, firing projectiles made of glass, broken shovels, hatchets, and pickaxes. From aboard their ships, the British answered with a steady stream of mortar shells. On May 12, 1780, after months of deadly bombardment and high

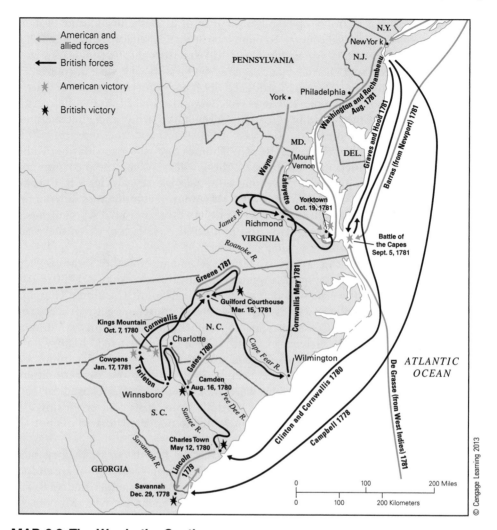

MAP 6.2 The War in the South

The southern war—after the British invasion of Georgia in late 1778—was characterized by a series of British thrusts into the interior, leading to battles with American defenders in both North and South Carolina. Finally, after promising beginnings, Cornwallis's foray into Virginia ended with disaster at Yorktown in October 1781.

casualties on both sides, the Citadel fell. The American commander, General Benjamin Lincoln, surrendered his entire army to the British, and a satisfied General Clinton returned to New York.

Clinton left the southern campaign in the hands of **Charles Cornwallis**, an ambitious and able general who set out with more than eight thousand British regulars, joined by loyalist troops as eager to defeat their enemies as Clinton had been. Since the British had abandoned the South in 1776, small, roving bands of loyalist guerrillas had kept resistance to the Revolution alive. Indeed, in this region the revolution was proving to be a bloody civil war of ambush, arson, and brutality between tidewater and backcountry communities in the Carolinas. By the summer of 1780, the fortunes in this war-within-a-war had reversed: the revolutionaries were now the resistance, using guerrilla tactics against the loyalists who were in control.

The revolutionary resistance produced legendary guerrilla leaders. Patriot **Francis Marion,** known as the "Swamp Fox," organized black and white recruits into raiding bands that steadily harassed Cornwallis's army and effectively cut British lines of communication between Charleston and the interior. While Marion did his best to trouble the British, Thomas Sumter's guerrillas and other resistance forces focused their energies on the loyalists. When these patriots and loyalists met head-on in battle, they honored few of the rules of war. In October 1780, for example, in the **Battle of King's Mountain**, revolutionaries surrounded loyalist troops and picked them off one by one. As this bitter civil war continued, marauding bands terrorized civilians and plundered their farms. Often the worst damage was done by outlaws posing as soldiers.

The regular American army, under the command of the Saratoga hero "Granny" Gates, had little success against Cornwallis. In August 1780, Gates and his men suffered a crushing defeat at Camden, South Carolina. That fall, Washington wisely replaced Gates with a younger, more energetic officer from Rhode Island, **Nathanael Greene**. The fourteen hundred Continental soldiers Greene found when he arrived in South Carolina were tired, hungry, and clothed in rags. They were also, Greene discovered, "without discipline and so addicted to plundering that the utmost exertions of the officers cannot restrain them." Greene's first steps were to ease the strains caused by civil war, raids, and plundering by offering pardons to loyalists and proposing alliances with local Indian tribes. In the end, Greene managed to win all but the Creeks away from the British.

Greene's military strategy was attrition: wear the British out by making them chase his small army across the South. He sent Virginian Daniel Morgan and six hundred riflemen to western South Carolina to tempt troops under the command of Banastre Tarleton into pursuit. Tarleton finally caught up with Morgan on an open meadow called the Cowpens in January 1781. When the outnumbered Americans stood their ground, ready to fight, the tired and frustrated British soldiers panicked and fled. Annoyed by this turn of events, Cornwallis decided to take the offensive. Now Greene led the British on a long, exhausting chase. In March 1781, the two armies finally met at Guilford Courthouse, North Carolina. Although the Americans lost the battle and withdrew, British losses were so great that a disgusted Cornwallis ordered his army northward to Virginia. Perhaps, he mused, he would have better luck there.

Treason and Triumph

In the fall of 1780, the popular general Benedict Arnold, one of Washington's protégés, defected to the British. The Americans foiled Arnold's bold plot to turn over control of the Hudson River to the British by surrendering the fort at **West Point**, New York, but his treason saddened Washington and damaged American morale.

Washington's spirits brightened the following spring, however, when news came that French help was at last on its way. At a strategy session with his French counterpart, General Rochambeau, in May 1781, Washington pressed for an attack on British-occupied New York, but Rochambeau insisted on a move against Cornwallis in Virginia. Since the French general had already ordered Admiral de Grasse and his fleet to the Chesapeake, Washington had little choice but to concur.

Thus, on July 6, 1781, a French army joined Washington's Continental forces just north of Manhattan for the long march to Virginia. The French soldiers, elegant in their sparkling uniforms, were openly amazed and impressed by their bedraggled allies. "It is incredible," wrote one French officer, "that soldiers composed of whites and blacks, almost naked, unpaid, and rather poorly fed, can march so well and stand fire so steadfastly."

Within a few months, General Cornwallis too would be forced to admire the American army's stamina. That summer, however, unaware that a combined army was marching toward him, the British commander moved his army to the peninsula port of **Yorktown**, a choice he would heartily regret.

By September 1781, the combined forces coming from New York had reached Virginia, and Admiral de Grasse's fleet was in place in Chesapeake Bay. General Clinton, still in New York, had been devastatingly slow to realize what the enemy intended. In desperation, he now sent a naval squadron from New York to rescue the trapped Cornwallis. He could do little more, since most of the British fleet was in the Caribbean.

Admiral de Grasse had no trouble fending off Clinton's rescue squadron. Then he turned his naval guns on the redcoats at Yorktown. From his siege positions on land, Washington also directed a steady barrage of artillery fire against the British, producing a deafening roar both day and night. On October 19, 1781, Lord Cornwallis admitted the hopelessness of his situation and surrendered. Despite the stunning turn of events at Yorktown, fighting continued in some areas. Loyalists and patriots continued to make war on each other in the South for another year. Bloody warfare against the Indians also meant more deaths along the frontier. The British occupation of Charleston, Savannah, and New York continued. But after Yorktown the British gave up all hope of military victory against their former colonies. On March 4, 1782, Parliament voted to cease "the further prosecution of offensive war on the Continent of North America, for the purpose of reducing the Colonies to obedience by force." The war for independence had been won.

Winning Diplomatic Independence

What Washington and his French and Spanish allies had won, the American diplomats Benjamin Franklin, John Adams, and John Jay had to preserve. At first glance, these men made an odd trio. The elderly Franklin, witty and sophisticated, had spent most of the war years in Paris, where he earned a deserved reputation as an admirer of French women and French wines. Adams, competitive, self-absorbed, and socially inept, did not hide his distaste for Franklin's flamboyance. Neither man found much comfort in the presence of the prudish, aristocratic John Jay of New York. Yet they proved to be a highly effective combination. Franklin brought a crafty skill and a love of strategy to the team as well as a useful knowledge of French politics. Adams provided the backbone, for in the face of any odds he was stubborn, determined, fiercely patriotic, and a watchdog of American interests. Jay was calm, deliberate, and though not as aggressive as his New England colleague, he matched Adams in patriotism and integrity.

European political leaders expected the Americans to fare badly against the more experienced British and French diplomats. But Franklin, Jay, and Adams were far from naive. They understood what was at stake at the peace table. They knew that their chief ally, France, had its own agenda and that England still wavered on the degree of independence America had actually won at York-town. Thus, despite firm orders from Congress to rely on France at every phase of the negotiations, the American diplomats quickly put their own agenda on the table. They issued a direct challenge to Britain: you must formally recognize American independence as a precondition to any negotiations at all. The British commissioner reluctantly agreed. Negotiations continued for more than a year, with all sides debating, arguing, and compromising until the terms of a treaty were finally set.

In the **Treaty of Paris of 1783** the Americans emerged with two clear victories. First, the boundaries of the new nation were extensive. Second, the treaty granted the United States unlimited access to the fisheries off Newfoundland, a particular concern of New Englander John Adams. It was difficult to measure the degree of success on other issues, however, since the terms for carrying out the agreements were so vague. For example, Britain ceded the Northwest to the United States. But the treaty said nothing about approval of this transfer of power by the Indians of the region, and it failed to set a timetable for British evacuation of the forts in the territory. In other cases, however, the treaty's vague language worked to American advantage. The treaty contained only the most general promise that the American government would not interfere with collection of the large prewar debts southern planters owed to British merchants. The promise to urge the states to return confiscated property to loyalists was equally inexact.

The peacemakers were aware of the treaty's shortcomings and its lack of clarity on key issues. But this was the price for avoiding stalemate and dangerous confrontation on controversial issues. Franklin, Adams, and Jay knew the consequences might be serious, but for the moment they preferred to celebrate rather than to worry.

REPUBLICAN EXPECTATIONS IN A NEW NATION

As an old man, John Adams insisted that the Revolution was more than battlefield victories and defeats. The Revolution took place, he said, "in the hearts and the minds of the people." What he meant was that changes in American social values and political ideas were as critical as artillery, swords, and battlefield strategies in creating the new nation. "The people" were, of course, far more diverse than

Adams was ever willing to admit. And they often differed in their "hearts and minds." Race, region, social class, gender, religion, even the national origin of immigrants all played a part in creating diverse interests and diverse interpretations of the Revolution. Adams was correct, however, that significant changes took place in American thought and behavior during the war and the years immediately after.

The Protection of Fundamental Rights   The Declaration of Independence expressed the commonly held American view that government must protect the fundamental rights of life, liberty, property, and as Jefferson put it, "the pursuit of happiness." The belief that Britain was destroying these rights was a major justification for the Revolution. Thus, whatever form Americans chose for their new, independent government, they were certain to demand the protection of these fundamental rights. This emphasis had many social consequences.

The protection of many individual rights—freedom of speech, assembly, and the press, and the right to a trial by jury—were written into the new constitutions of several states. But some rights were more difficult to define than others. Many Americans supported "freedom of conscience," yet not all of them supported separation of church and state. For example, Virginia's House of Burgesses approved George Mason's Declaration of Rights, which guaranteed its citizens "the free exercise of religion," yet Virginia continued to use tax monies to support the Anglican Church. It was not until 1786 that the Statute of Religious Freedom ended tax-supported churches in Virginia and guaranteed complete freedom of conscience, even for atheists. Other southern states followed Virginia's lead, ending tax support for their Anglican churches.

The battle was more heated in New England, where many wished to continue government support of the Congregational Church. Others simply wished to keep the principle of an established church alive. As a compromise, communities were sometimes allowed to decide which local church received their tax money, although each town was required to make one church the established church. New England did not separate church and state entirely until the nineteenth century.

Protection of Property Rights   In the decade before the Revolution, much of the protest against British policy had focused on the right to private property and the government's duty to protect that right. For free, white, property-holding men—and for those white male servants, tenant farmers, or apprentices who hoped to join their ranks someday—life, liberty, and happiness were interwoven with the right of landownership.

The property rights of some infringed on the freedoms of others, however. Claims made on western lands by white Americans often meant the denial of Indian rights to that land. Masters' rights included a claim to the time and labor of their servants or apprentices. In the white community, a man's property rights usually included the restriction of his wife's right to own or sell land, slaves, and even her own personal possessions. And the institution of slavery transformed human beings into the private property of others.

Even for white men, the right to property was a principle, not a guarantee. Many were unable to acquire land during the revolutionary era or in the decades that followed. When the Revolution began, one-fifth of free American people lived in poverty or depended on the community's charity. For some, taking advantage of opportunities to acquire property was difficult even when those opportunities arose. Washington's Continental soldiers, for example, were promised western lands as delayed payment for their military service. But when they left the army in 1783, most were penniless, jobless, and sometimes homeless. They had little choice but to sell their precious land warrant certificates, trading their future as property owners tomorrow for bread today.

Legal Reforms   Although economic inequality actually grew in the decades after the Revolution, a commitment to the republican belief in social equality led to the end of **primogeniture** and **entail**. In Britain, these inheritance laws ensured the creation of a landed aristocracy. The actual threat they posed in America was small, for few planters ever adopted them. But the principle they represented remained important to republican spokesmen such as Thomas Jefferson, who pressed successfully for their abolition in Virginia and North Carolina.

The passion for social equality—in appearance if not always in fact—affected customs as well as laws. To downplay their elite status as landowners, revolutionaries stopped the practice of adding "**Esquire**" (abbreviated "Esq.") after their names. (George Washington, Esq., became plain George Washington.)

In some states, the principle of social equality had concrete political consequences. Pennsylvania and Georgia eliminated all property qualifications for voting among free white males. Other states lowered their property requirements for voters but refused to go as far as universal white manhood suffrage. They feared that the outcome of such a sweeping reform was unpredictable. Even women might demand a political voice.

Women in the   The war did not erase differences of class, race, region, or age
New Republic   for either men or women. Thus its impact was not uniform
for all American women. Yet some experiences, and the memories of them, were probably shared by the majority of white and even many black women. They would remember the war years as a time of constant danger, anxiety, harassment, and unfamiliar and difficult responsibilities. As their men went off to war, these women took on the task of managing shops and farms in addition to caring for large families and coping with shortages of food and supplies. Some, like the woman who pleaded with her soldier husband to "pray come home," may have feared they would fail in these new circumstances. Yet many spoke with satisfaction about how well they had adapted to new roles. They

---

primogeniture   The legal right of the eldest son to inherit the entire estate of his father.

entail   A legal limitation that prevents property from being divided, sold, or given away.

Esquire   A term used to indicate that a man was a gentleman.

expressed their sense of accomplishment in letters to husbands that no longer spoke of "your farm" and "your crop" but of "our farm" and even "my crop."

Many women found they enjoyed the sudden independence from men and from the domestic hierarchy that men ruled in peacetime. Even women in difficult circumstances experienced this new sense of freedom. Grace Galloway, wife of loyalist exile Joseph Galloway of Pennsylvania, remained in America during the war in an effort to preserve her husband's property. Shunned by her patriot neighbors, reduced from wealth to painful poverty, Grace Galloway nevertheless confided to her diary that "Ye liberty of doing as I please Makes even Poverty more agreable than any time I ever spent since I married." If Galloway experienced new self-confidence and liberty during wartime, not all women were so fortunate. For the victims of rape and physical attack by soldiers on either side, the war meant more traditional experiences of vulnerability. American soldiers sang songs of flirtation and of their hopes for kisses from admiring young women, but occupying armies, guerrilla bands, and outlaws posing as soldiers left trails of abuse, particularly in New Jersey, along the frontier, and in the Carolinas.

For women, just as for men, the war meant adapting traditional behavior and skills to new circumstances. Women who followed the eighteenth-century custom of joining husbands or fathers in army camps took up the familiar domestic chores of cooking, cleaning, laundering, and providing nursing care. Outside the army camps, loyalist and patriot women served as spies or saboteurs and risked their lives by sheltering soldiers or hiding weapons in their cellars. Sometimes they opted to burn their crops or destroy their homes to prevent the enemy from using them. These were conscious acts of patriotism rather than wifely duties. On some occasions, women crossed gender boundaries dramatically. Although few disguised themselves as men to enlist as soldiers, women such as **Mary Ludwig** and Margaret Corbin did engage in military combat. These "Molly Pitchers" carried water to cool down the cannon in American forts across the country and if men fell wounded, they frequently took their place on the firing line. After the war, female veterans of combat, including Corbin, applied to the government for pensions, citing as evidence the wounds they had received in battle.

In the postwar years, members of America's political and social elite engaged in a public discussion of women's role in their new republican society. Spurred by Enlightenment assertions that all humans were capable of rational thought and by the empirical evidence of women's patriotic commitment and behavior, these Americans set aside older colonial notions that women lacked the ability to reason and to make moral choices. They urged a new role for women within the family: the moral upbringing of their children. This training would include the inculcating of patriotism and republican principles. Thus the republic would rely on wives and mothers to sustain its values and to raise a new generation of concerned citizens.

This new ideal, "**republican womanhood**," reflected Enlightenment ideals, but it also had roots in economic and social changes that began before the Revolution, including the growth of a prosperous urban class able to purchase many household necessities. Since prosperous urban wives and mothers no longer

Sheet music such as "The Ladies Patriotic Song" found its way into the parlors of many revolutionary and early republic homes. This song, which celebrates the heroes of independence, George Washington and John Adams, also celebrates what postwar society considered to be feminine virtues: beauty, innocence, and patriotic devotion.

needed to make cloth or candles or butter, they had time to devote to raising children. Republican womanhood probably had little immediate impact in the lives of ordinary free women who remained unable to purchase essential goods or to pay others to do household chores or in the lives of African American or Indian women.

Although women's active role in the education of the next generation was often applauded as a public, political contribution, not simply a private, family duty, it did not lead to formal political participation for female Americans. The Constitution left suffrage qualifications to the state governments, and no state chose to extend voting rights to women. Only one state, New Jersey, failed to stipulate "male" as a condition for suffrage in its first constitution, but this oversight was soon revised.

Although American republicanism expected mothers to instill patriotism in their children, it also expected communities to provide formal education for future citizens. Arguing that a citizen could not be both "ignorant and free," several states allotted tax money for public elementary schools. Some went even further. By 1789, for example, Massachusetts required every town to provide free education to its children. After the Revolution, *children* meant girls as well as boys.

This new emphasis on female education was a radical departure for women. Before the Revolution, the education of daughters was haphazard at best. Colleges

It Matters Today

Tracking Changes in Gender Roles

Eighteenth-century women like Mary Ludwig tested the limits of traditional gender roles, demonstrating bravery on the battlefield and political organizing skills during the American Revolution. But it would be over 140 years before their descendants could vote in a national election and decades more before they could serve in the military. The impact of this social change can be seen today in the accomplishments of women such as Lt. General Claudia J. Kennedy, the United States Army's first female three-star general; Sandra Day O'Connor, the first woman to become a Supreme Court justice; Madeleine Albright, the first woman secretary of state; and Shirley Chisholm, the first woman to run for the presidency of the United States. Tracking major changes in gender roles and examining why those changes occurred is a critical part of the historian's task.

- Do you think a woman president is likely to be elected in your lifetime? Explain the factors on which you base your opinion.

and the preparatory schools that trained young men for college were closed to female students. A woman got what formal knowledge she could by reading her father's or her brother's books. Most women had to be content to learn domestic skills. After the Revolution, however, educational reformers reasoned that mothers must be well versed in history and even political theory if they were to teach their children the essential principles of citizenship. By the 1780s, private academies had opened to educate the daughters of wealthy American families. These privileged young women enjoyed the rare opportunity to study mathematics, history, geography, and political theory. Although their curriculum was often as rigorous as that in a boys' preparatory school, the addition of courses in fancy needlework reminded the girls that their futures lay in marriage and motherhood, not government or the professions.

The War's Impact on Slaves and Slavery

Liberty and freedom were major themes of the Revolution. Yet the denial of liberty was a central reality in the lives of most African Americans. To win their freedom, thousands of slaves had opposed the patriot cause and risked their lives to escape to the British army. In contrast, only about five thousand African American men joined the Continental Army once Congress opened enlistment to them in 1776. Although black soldiers were generally treated better by the British, they received lower pay than white soldiers in both armies and were often assigned to the most dangerous or menial duties. Slaves found other routes to freedom besides military service during the war. Some escaped from farms and plantations to the cities, where they passed as free people. Others fled to the frontier, where they joined sympathetic Indian tribes. Women and

Phillis Wheatley was brought from Africa as a child. The Boston couple who purchased her encouraged her literary talent. Wheatley's patriotic poetry won approval from George Washington and praise from many revolutionary leaders. She died free but in poverty in the 1780s.

Library of Congress.

children, in particular, took advantage of wartime disruptions to flee their masters' control.

With American victory in 1781, thousands of former slaves boarded British transport ships, headed to what they hoped would be a better life in Canada, England, British Florida, or the Caribbean. But their dreams often went unrealized. Three thousand former slaves settled initially in Nova Scotia, but the racism of their white loyalist neighbors led more than a thousand of these veterans to emigrate a second time. Led by an African-born former slave named Thomas Peters, they sailed to Sierra Leone, in West Africa, where they established a free black colony.

During the war, loyalists had taunted patriots, asking, "How is it that we hear the loudest yelps for liberty among the drivers of negroes?" The question made the contradiction between revolutionary ideals and American reality painfully clear, especially in the northern states. Not all slave-owners needed to be shamed by others into grappling with the contradictions between their principles and slavery. In the 1760s and 1770s, influential political leaders such as James Otis, Thomas Paine, and Benjamin Rush campaigned to end slavery. In Boston, Phillis Wheatley, a young African-born slave whose master recognized and encouraged her literary talents, called on the revolutionaries to acknowledge the universality of the wish for freedom. "In every human breast," Wheatley wrote, "God had implanted a Principle, which we call love of freedom; it is impatient of Oppression, and pants for Deliverance...."

Free black Americans joined with white reformers to mobilize antislavery campaigns in Pennsylvania, Massachusetts, Rhode Island, and Connecticut. In Boston and Philadelphia, slaves petitioned on their own behalf to be "liberated from a state of Bondage, and made Freemen of this Community." Of course, these states were home to few slaves, and the regional economy did not depend on unfree labor. Thus it was easier there to acknowledge the truth in the slave's cry: "We have no property! ... we have no children! ... we have no city! ... we have no country!"

Manumission increased during the 1770s, especially in the North. In 1780, Pennsylvania became the first state to pass an emancipation statute, making manumission a public policy rather than a private matter of conscience. Pennsylvania lawmakers, however, compromised on a gradual rather than an immediate end to slavery. Only slaves born after the law was enacted were eligible, and they could not expect to receive their freedom until they had served a twenty-eight-year term of indenture. By 1804, all northern states except Delaware had committed themselves to a slow end to slavery.

Slavery was far more deeply embedded in the South, as a labor system and as a system that regulated race relations. In the Lower South, white Americans ignored the debate over slavery and took immediate steps to replace missing slaves and to restore tight control over work and life on their plantations. Manumission did occur in the Upper South. Free black communities grew in both Maryland and Virginia after the Revolutionary War, and planters openly debated the morality of slavery in a republic and the practical benefits of slave labor. They did not all reach the same conclusions. George Washington freed all his slaves on the death of his wife, but Patrick Henry, who had often stirred his fellow Virginia legislators with his spirited defense of American liberty, justified his decision to continue slavery with blunt honesty. Freeing his slaves, he said, would be inconvenient (see Figure 6.1).

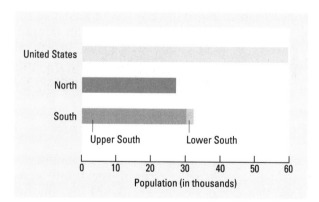

FIGURE 6.1 Free Black Population, 1790

This graph shows the number of free African Americans in the United States in 1790, as well as their regional distribution. These almost 60,000 free people were less than 10 percent of the African American population of the nation. Although 40 percent of northern blacks were members of this free community, only about 5.5 percent of the Upper South African Americans and less than 2 percent of those in the Lower South lived outside the bounds of slavery.

Manumission   Freedom from slavery or bondage.

The Fate of the Loyalists   After 1775, America's loyalists flocked to the safety of British-occupied cities, crowding first into Boston and, as the war dragged on, into New York City and Philadelphia. When the British left an area, the loyalists evacuated with them. More than a thousand Massachusetts loyalists boarded British ships when Boston was abandoned in 1776, and fifteen thousand more sailed out of New York harbor when the war ended in 1781. Altogether, as many as a hundred thousand men, women, and children left their American homes to take up new lives in England, Canada, and the West Indies.

Wealth often determined a loyalist's destination. Rich and influential men such as Thomas Hutchinson of Massachusetts took refuge in England during the war. But life in England was so expensive that it quickly ate up their resources and drove them into debt. Accustomed to comfort, many of these exiles passed their days in seedy boarding houses in the small cities outside London. They lost more than servants and fine clothes, however. In a society dominated by aristocrats and royalty, loyalist men who had enjoyed status and prestige in America suddenly found themselves socially insignificant, with no work and little money. Loyalists in England grew more desperately homesick each day.

When the war ended, most of the loyalists in England departed for Nova Scotia, New Brunswick, or the Caribbean. Many of these exiles were specifically forbidden to return to the United States by the new state governments. Others refused to go back to America because they equated the new republican society with mob rule. Those who were willing to adjust to the new American nation returned slowly.

Less prosperous loyalists, especially those who served in the loyalist battalions during the war, went to Canada after 1781. The separation from family and friends, as much as the bleak climate of Canada, at first caused depression and despair in some exiles. One woman who had bravely endured the war and its deprivations broke down and cried when she landed at Nova Scotia. Like the revolutionaries, these men and women had chosen their political loyalty based on a mixture of principle and self-interest. Unlike the revolutionaries, they had chosen the losing side. They lived with the consequences for the rest of their lives.

Canada became the refuge of another group of loyalists: members of the Indian tribes that had supported the Crown. The British ceded much of the Iroquois land to the United States in the Treaty of Paris, and American hostility toward "enemy savages" made peaceful postwar coexistence unlikely. Thus, in the 1780s, Mohawks, Onondagas, Tuscaroras, Senecas, Oneidas, and Cayugas along with Delawares, Tutelos, and Nanticokes created new, often multiethnic settlements on the banks of the Grand River in Ontario. These communities marked an end to the dislocation and suffering many of these refugees had experienced during the Revolution, when steady warfare depleted Indian resources and made thousands dependent on the British for food, clothing, and military supplies.

STUDY TOOLS

SUMMARY

In 1776, few patriots or loyalists believed that America could win its independence from Britain. The British outnumbered and outgunned the Americans, and their troops were better trained and better equipped. The Americans' major advantage was logistic: they were fighting a war on familiar terrain.

The early British strategy was to invade New York and the southern colonies, where they expected to rally strong loyalist support. This strategy failed, not only because they were waging war on unfamiliar territory but also because they had overestimated loyalist strength and alienated would-be sympathizers. Washington's hit-and-run tactics made it impossible for the British to deliver a crushing blow.

The turning point in the war came in 1777 when British general John Burgoyne's plan to isolate New England from the other rebel colonies failed. Burgoyne was forced to surrender at Saratoga, New York. The surprising American victory led to an alliance between France and the United States and the expansion of the war into an international conflict. The British invaded the South again in 1778, but despite early victories, their campaign ended in disaster. American victory was assured when French and American forces defeated General Cornwallis at Yorktown, Virginia, in October 1781. Fighting continued for a time, but in March 1782, the British Parliament ended the conflict. The Treaty of Paris was negotiated in 1783, and to the surprise of many European diplomats, the Americans gained important concessions.

Victory led to significant transformations in American society. Individual rights were strengthened for free white men. A republican spirit changed the outlook, if not the condition, of many Americans, as customs that fit a hierarchical society gave way to more egalitarian behavior. The wartime experiences of women led American intellectuals to reconsider women's "nature" and their abilities. Although full citizenship was not granted, white women's capacity for rational thought was acknowledged, and their new role as the educators of their children led to expanded formal education for women. Black Americans also made some gains. Fifty thousand slaves won their freedom during the war by fleeing to the British army camps or by serving in the Continental Army. Northern states moved to outlaw slavery, but southern slaveholders decided to preserve the institution despite intense debate. For most loyalists, black or white, the end of the war meant permanent exile from their homeland.

Independence had been won. But could it be preserved? In Chapter 7, you will read about the struggles, not just of the federal governments, but the state governments that could protect the young nation and preserve the liberties its citizens had fought to ensure.

CHRONOLOGY

REBELLION AND INDEPENDENCE

1775   Battle for Boston
George Washington assumes command of Continental Army

1776   Declaration of Independence
British campaigns in South and mid-Atlantic regions

1777   Burgoyne's New York campaign
Battle of Saratoga
Winter at Valley Forge

1778   American-French alliance
British begin second southern campaign

1780   Fall of Charleston
Treason of Benedict Arnold
Pennsylvania enacts manumission statute

1781   Cornwallis surrenders at Yorktown
Loyalists evacuate United States

1782   British Parliament votes to end war

1783   Treaty of Paris signed

FOCUS QUESTIONS

If you have mastered this chapter, you should be able to answer these questions and explain the terms that follow the questions.

1. What were the British and American strategies in the early years of the war?
2. What decisions and constraints kept the British from achieving the quick victory many expected?
3. What strategy did Benjamin Franklin pursue to win recognition from the French?
4. How did the French alliance affect the war effort and wartime spending?
5. What factors produced a stalemate in the war?
6. What characterized warfare in the South and what led to General Cornwallis's surrender at Yorktown?
7. What were the most important results of the peace treaty negotiations?
8. How did the Revolution affect Americans' expectations regarding individual rights, social equality, and the role of women in American society?
9. What opportunities were open to African Americans during and after the Revolution?
10. What was the fate of the loyalists?

KEY TERMS

Thomas Gage (*p.* 138)

Benedict Arnold (*p.* 138)

William Howe (*p.* 139)

Battle of Bunker Hill (*p.* 139)

George Washington (*p.* 139)

Richard Howe (*p.* 140)

Hessian troops (*p.* 140)

Battle of Trenton (*p.* 143)

John Burgoyne (*p.* 143)

Battle of Saratoga (*p.* 144)

Valley Forge (*p.* 144)

Baron Friedrich von Steuben (*p.* 146)

Benjamin Franklin (*p.* 147)

Sir Henry Clinton (*p.* 149)

General Charles Lee (*p.* 149)

Battle of Monmouth (*p.* 149)

George Rogers Clark (*p.* 150)

Thayendanegea (*p.* 150)

Charles Cornwallis (*p.* 151)

Francis Marion (*p.* 152)

Battle of King's Mountain (*p.* 152)

Nathanael Greene (*p.* 152)

West Point (*p.* 152)

Yorktown (*p.* 153)

Treaty of Paris of 1783 (*p.* 154)

Mary Ludwig (*p.* 157)

republican womanhood (*p.* 157)

7

COMPETING VISIONS OF THE VIRTUOUS REPUBLIC, 1770–1796

AMERICA'S FIRST CONSTITUTIONS

The writers of state constitutions were the first to grapple with troubling but fundamental issues—in particular, the definition of citizenship and the extent of political participation. Could landless men, servants, free blacks, or apprentices enjoy a political voice? Should women with property be allowed to vote? These were exactly the kinds of questions John Adams feared might arise in any discussion of voting rights, or suffrage. They raised the specter of democracy, which he and most other revolutionary leaders considered a dangerous system. Once the question was posed, he predicted, "There will be no end of it ... women will demand a vote, lads from twelve to twenty-one will think their rights are not enough attended to, and every man who has not a **farthing** will demand an equal voice with any other in all acts of state."

English political tradition supported Adams's view that political rights were not universal. Under English law, "rights" were, in fact, particular *privileges* that a group enjoyed because of special social circumstances—including age, sex, wealth, or family ties. In their first constitutions, several states extended these privileges to all free white men, a democratic reform but one that still set special conditions of race and sex.

---

farthing   A British coin worth one-fourth of a penny and thus a term used to indicate something of very little value.

The state constitutions reflected the variety of opinion on this matter of democracy within a republic. At one end of the spectrum was Pennsylvania, whose constitution abolished all property qualifications and granted the vote to all white males in the state. At the other end were states such as Maryland, whose constitution continued to link the ownership of property to voting. To hold office, a Marylander had to meet even higher standards of wealth than the voters.

While constitution writers in every state believed that the legislature was the primary branch of government, they were divided over other issues. Should there be a separate executive branch? Should the legislature have one house or two? What qualifications should be set for officeholders? Again, Pennsylvania produced the most democratic answer to this question. Pennsylvania's constitution concentrated all power to make and to administer law in a one-house, or **unicameral**, elected assembly, and it eliminated the executive office. In contrast, Maryland and the other states divided powers among a governor, or executive branch, and a **bicameral** legislature, although the legislature enjoyed the broader powers. Members of the upper house in Maryland's legislature had to meet higher property qualifications than those in the lower house, or assembly. In this manner, political leaders in this state ensured their elite citizens a secure voice in lawmaking.

Pennsylvania and Maryland represented the two ends of the democratic spectrum. The remaining states fell between these poles. The constitutions of New Hampshire, North Carolina, and Georgia followed the democratic tendencies of Pennsylvania. New York, South Carolina, and Virginia chose Maryland's more conservative or traditional approach. New Jersey and Delaware took the middle ground, with at least one surprising result. New Jersey's first constitution, written in 1776, gave the vote to "all free inhabitants" who met certain property qualifications. This requirement denied the ballot to propertyless men but granted voting rights to property-holding women. A writer in the *New York Spectator* in 1797 snidely remarked that New Jersey women "intermeddl[ing] in political affairs" made that state's politics as strange as those of the "emperor of Java [who] never employs any but women in his embassies." Nevertheless, for thirty-one years, at least a few New Jersey women regularly exercised their right to vote.

A state's particular history often determined the type of constitution it produced. For example, coastal elites and lowland gentry had dominated the colonial governments of New Hampshire, South Carolina, Virginia, and North Carolina. These states sought to correct this injustice by ensuring representation to small farming districts in interior and frontier regions. The memory of high-handed colonial governors and elitist upper houses in the legislature led Massachusetts lawmakers to severely limit the powers of their first state government. The constitutions in all of these states reflected the strong political voice that ordinary citizens had acquired during the Revolution.

Beginning in the 1780s, however, many states revised their constitutions, increasing the power of the government. At the same time, they added safeguards they believed would prevent abuse. The 1780 Massachusetts constitution was the

unicameral   Having a single legislative house.
bicameral   Having a legislature with two houses.

model for many of these revisions, building in a system of so-called checks and balances among the legislative, judicial, and executive branches to ensure that no branch of the government could grow too powerful or overstep its assigned duties. Most of these revised constitutions restored wealth as a qualification to govern, although they did not allow the wealthy to tamper with the basic individual rights of citizens. In seven states, these individual rights were safeguarded by a **bill of rights** guaranteeing freedom of speech, religion, and the press as well as the right to assemble and to petition the government.

The Articles of Confederation   There was little popular support for a powerful central government in the early years of the Revolution. Instead, as John Adams later recalled, Americans wanted "a Confederacy of States, each of which must have a separate government." When Pennsylvania's **John Dickinson** submitted a blueprint for a strong national government to the Continental Congress in July of 1776, he watched in wonder and dismay as his colleagues transformed his plan, called **Articles of Confederation**, into a government that preserved the rights and privileges of the states.

Members of the one-house Continental Congress agreed that the new Confederation government should also be a unicameral legislature, without an executive branch or a separate judiciary. Democrats like Tom Paine and Samuel Adams praised the Articles' concentration of lawmaking, administrative, and judicial powers in the hands of an elected assembly, whereas conservatives like John Adams condemned the new government as "too democratical," lacking "any equilibrium" among the social classes.

In any case, the powers of the proposed Confederation government were severely limited. It had no authority to tax or to regulate trade or commerce. These powers remained with the state governments, reflecting the view of many Americans that the behavior of their local governments could be closely monitored. Because it had no taxing power, the Confederation had to depend on the states to finance its operations.

Dickinson's colleagues agreed that the state legislatures, not the voters themselves, should choose the members of the Confederation Congress. But they did not agree on how many members each state should have. Should the states have equal representation or **proportional representation** based on population? Dickinson argued for a one-state, one-vote rule, but fellow Pennsylvanian Benjamin Franklin insisted that large states such as his own deserved more influence in the new government. This time, Dickinson's argument carried the day, and the Articles established that each state, large or small, was entitled to a single vote when the Confederation roll was called. The same jealous protection of state power also shaped the Confederation's amendment process. Any amendment required the unanimous consent of the states.

Arguments over financial issues were as fierce as those over representation and sovereignty. How was each state's share of the federal operating budget to

bill of rights   A formal statement of essential rights and liberties under law.

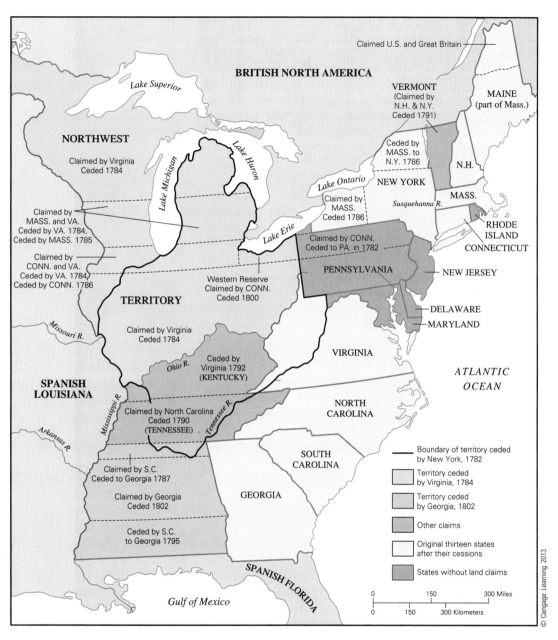

Claimed U.S. and Great Britain

BRITISH NORTH AMERICA

Lake Superior

VERMONT
(Claimed by
N.H. & N.Y.
Ceded 1791)

MAINE
(part of Mass.)

NORTHWEST

Claimed by Virginia
Ceded 1784

Lake Michigan

Lake Huron

Ceded by
MASS. to
N.Y. 1786

N.H.

Claimed by
MASS. and VA.
Ceded by VA. 1784,
Ceded by MASS. 1785

Lake Ontario

NEW YORK

MASS.

Claimed by
MASS.
Ceded 1786

Susquehanna R.

Lake Erie

Claimed by CONN.
Ceded to PA. in 1782

RHODE
ISLAND

CONNECTICUT

Claimed by
CONN. and VA.
Ceded by VA. 1784,
Ceded by CONN. 1786

PENNSYLVANIA

NEW JERSEY

Western Reserve
Claimed by CONN.
Ceded 1800

TERRITORY

Missouri R.

Claimed by Virginia
Ceded 1784

DELAWARE

MARYLAND

Ohio R.

Ceded by
Virginia 1792
(KENTUCKY)

VIRGINIA

ATLANTIC
OCEAN

SPANISH
LOUISIANA

Mississippi R.

Claimed by North Carolina
Ceded 1790
(TENNESSEE)

Tennessee R.

NORTH
CAROLINA

Arkansas R.

Claimed by S.C.
Ceded to Georgia 1787

SOUTH
CAROLINA

Claimed by Georgia
Ceded 1802

GEORGIA

Ceded by S.C.
to Georgia 1795

Boundary of territory ceded
by New York, 1782

Territory ceded
by Virginia, 1784

Territory ceded
by Georgia, 1802

Other claims

Original thirteen states
after their cessions

States without land claims

SPANISH FLORIDA

Gulf of Mexico

| 0 | 150 | 300 Miles |
| 0 | 150 | 300 Kilometers |

© Cengage Learning 2013

MAP 7.1 State Claims to Western Lands, and State Cessions to the Federal Government, 1782–1802

Eastern states' surrender of land claims paved the way for new state governments in the West.

It Matters Today

Having a Vision for the Future

In 1791, Alexander Hamilton outlined his vision for the economic future of the United States. When Hamilton predicted that manufacturing would, and should, overtake agriculture as the basis for the American economy, he knew he would be setting himself against some of the most important people in the nation. Hamilton's *Report on Manufactures* was not adopted by Congress, but the ideas set forth in it would eventually become central to the economy of the United States. Hamilton's belief that a strong central government with broad economic powers could encourage the fledgling manufacturing industries of the new country set the stage for this country to become the economic superpower it is today.

- Presidential candidates often outline their vision for the nation's future in their inaugural addresses. Select one such inaugural address and analyze the vision it offers.
- If you had the chance to put forward your vision of the future, what priorities would you insist upon?

be determined? Dickinson reasoned that a state's contribution should be based on its population, including inhabitants of every age, sex, and legal condition (free or unfree). This proposal brought southern political leaders to their feet in protest. Because their states had large, dependent slave populations, the burden of tax assessment would fall heavily on slave masters and other free white men. In the end, state assessments were based on the value of land, buildings, and improvements rather than on population. The Continental Congress thus shrewdly avoided any final decision on the larger question of whether slaves were property or people.

When Congress finally submitted the Articles to the states for their approval in November of 1777, the fate of the western territories proved to be the major stumbling block to **ratification**. In his draft of the Articles, Dickinson had designated the Northwest Territory as a national domain. But states with colonial charters granting them land from the Atlantic to the Pacific Oceans protested, each claiming the exclusive right to the lands beyond the Appalachian mountains. Delegates from Maryland, a state having no claim to western territory, dug in their heels, insisting that citizens of every state ought to have the right to pioneer the northwestern territories. Maryland's ultimatum—no national domain, no ratification—produced a stalemate until, at last, Virginia agreed to cede all claims to Congress. The other states with claims followed suit, and the crisis was over. In 1781, Maryland became the thirteenth and final state to ratify the Confederation government. Establishing this first national government had taken three and a half years.

ratification The act of approving or confirming a proposal.

CHALLENGES TO THE CONFEDERATION

The members of the first Confederation Congress had barely taken their seats in 1781 when Cornwallis surrendered at Yorktown and peace negotiations began in Paris. Even the most optimistic of the Confederation leaders could see that the postwar problems of the new nation were daunting. The long home-front war had left physical, psychological, and economic scars. In New Jersey and Pennsylvania, communities were still recovering from the rape and looting by the British occupying armies. In the South, where civil war had raged, a steady stream of refugees filled the cities. In New England, the postwar depression and food shortages were made worse by an insect attack that destroyed the local wheat crops.

The postwar economic depression seemed to touch everyone's lives. Four years after the American victory, Thomas Jefferson might boast that Americans "adore [their] country, its climate, its equality, liberty, laws, people and manners." But America's unemployed sailors, debt-ridden farmers, and destitute widows and orphans would have found it difficult to share his enthusiasm.

Depression and Financial Crisis   Financial problems plagued wealthy Americans as well as poor farmers and unpaid Revolutionary War veterans. Many merchants had overextended their credit importing foreign goods after the war, while those who had once imported English goods were forced to close their shops. Land **speculators** had also borrowed too heavily in order to grab confiscated loyalist lands or portions of the Northwest Territory, and planters were hard hit when the demand for staple crops such as rice dropped dramatically after the war. By 1786 the New England fisheries were operating at only about 80 percent of their prewar level. Not surprisingly, the English did nothing to ease the plight of their former colonists. In fact, Britain banned the sale of American farm products in the West Indies and limited the American shipping there. These restrictions hit New England shipbuilding so hard that whole communities were impoverished.

The Confederation government did not create these economic problems, but it had little success in dealing with them. In fact, it was helpless to solve its own most pressing problem—debt. To finance the war, the Continental Congress had printed more than $240 million in paper money backed by "good faith" rather than by the hard currency of gold and silver. As doubts grew that the government could ever **redeem** these continentals for hard currency, their value fell rapidly. The scornful phrase "not worth a continental" indicated popular attitudes about a government that owed money to its own citizens and to allies abroad.

speculator   A person who buys and sells land or some other commodity in the hope of making a profit.

redeem   To pay a specified sum in return for something; in this case, to make good on paper money issued by the government by exchanging it for hard currency, silver or gold.

In 1781 the government turned to Philadelphia shipper and merchant **Robert Morris** for advice on how to raise funds. Morris, known as a financial wizard, came up with a solution: ask the states to approve federal **tariffs**, or import taxes, on certain foreign goods. The tariffs would provide desperately needed income for the Confederation and relieve the states from having to contribute funding many could scarcely afford. But even this modest plan failed. Both Virginia and Rhode Island said no, and, to add insult to injury, some states promptly passed their own tariffs on imported goods. The failure of the tariff strategy prompted one critic of the Confederation government to comment: "Thirteen wheels require a steady and powerful regulation to keep them in good order." Until Congress could act without the unanimous consent of all states, nothing could prevent the machine from becoming useless.

The Northwest Ordinances   The Confederation turned to the sale of western lands to solve its financial problems. Here at least Congress had the authority to act, for it could set policy for the settlement and governance of all national territories. In 1784, 1785, and 1787, a national land policy took shape in three **Northwest Ordinances**.

The 1784 ordinance established that five new states would be carved out of the region, each to stand on an equal footing with the older, original states. In the earliest stages of settlement, each territory would have an appointed governor. As soon as the number of eligible voters in the territory increased sufficiently, however, they could elect a representative assembly, and the territory could begin to govern itself. Once a state constitution was drafted and approved by the territory's voters, the new state could send elected representatives to the Confederation Congress. Ohio, Indiana, Illinois, Michigan, and Wisconsin would each follow this path to full statehood.

The ordinance of 1785 spelled out the terms for sale of the land. Mapmakers divided the region into five districts and subdivided each district into townships. Each township, covering 36 square miles, was broken down in a gridlike pattern of thirty-six 640-acre plots. Congress intended to auction off these plots to individual settlers rather than to land speculators, but when the original selling price of $1 per acre in hard currency proved too high for the average farm family, Congress lowered the price and lifted the ban on sales to speculators.

The ordinance of 1787 established that sixty thousand white males were needed for a territory to apply for admission as a state. Thomas Jefferson, who drafted this ordinance, took care to protect the liberties of the settlers with a bill of rights and to ban slavery north of the Ohio River. Yet these provisions trampled on the rights of American Indians whose claims to the land were ignored.

Diplomatic Problems   The Confederation's diplomatic record was as discouraging as its financial plight. Problems with the British and the Indians arose in the West as settlers began to pour into the Northwest

---

tariff   A tax on imported or exported goods.

Territory. According to the Treaty of Paris, the British were to evacuate their western forts, but they refused to do so until the Americans honored their treaty promises to repay war debts and return confiscated property to loyalists. Instead, the British encouraged Indian resistance by selling arms and supplies to the Shawnees, Miamis, and Delawares. These tribes, and others, denied the legitimacy of the two treaties that turned over the northwest territories to the Americans.

American claims to western lands rested on the 1784 **Treaty of Fort Stanwix** and the 1785 **Hopewell Treaties**. But these treaties had not been approved by all the tribes of either area. The Shawnees and their allies challenged both treaties, asking what right other tribes had to speak for them. Throughout the 1780s, the Confederation and the Indians resorted to warfare rather than negotiation.

The Confederation preferred diplomacy to armed conflict when dealing with European powers. The new nation desperately needed trade concessions from its former Mother Country, for commercial ties with France and Holland had not developed as rapidly as some patriots had predicted. American merchants thus remained economically dependent on England as a source of manufactured goods, and on British possessions in the Caribbean for trade. Congress sent John Adams to Great Britain, but the American bargaining position was weak. Britain had no desire to end America's economic dependency.

The Confederation had problems with allies as well as with enemies. Spain, for example, was alarmed to find thousands of Americans ready to join the almost fifty thousand Americans who had moved into what would become Kentucky and Tennessee. The Spanish government, which controlled access to the Mississippi River and the port of New Orleans, responded to this threat by banning all American traffic on the river. The Confederation appointed **John Jay**, fresh from his success as a Paris peace commissioner, to negotiate with Spain on this and other issues, but Jay could make no headway.

The Confederation had no better luck in dealing with the **Barbary pirates**. For many years, the rulers of Algiers, Tunisia, Tripoli, and Morocco had taken advantage of their location along the Barbary Coast of North Africa to attack European vessels engaged in Mediterranean trade. Most European nations kept this piracy under control by paying blackmail or by providing armed escorts for their merchant ships. The Barbary pirates found a new target in the American merchant marine, for American ships were no longer protected by the royal navy. In 1785 a New England ship was captured, its cargo seized, and the crew stripped and sold into slavery. The Confederation Congress was outraged, but with no navy and no authority to create one, it could do nothing to ensure American safety in the Mediterranean.

A Farmers' Revolt   After the Revolution, the postwar economic depression weighed on backcountry farmers, and these Americans began to protest burdens they had long resented—high rents and land prices, heavy taxes, debts, oppressive legal fees, and the failure of central governments to provide protection from Indian attacks and frontier bandits. They used the language of republicanism to defend their position and to justify the occasional violence that erupted in their areas. "We fought for land & liberty," wrote one

squatter in response to a land speculator's claim to his farm. "Who can have a better right to the land than we who have fought for it, subdued it & made it valuable?" Members of the political and economic elite, who remembered the violence of the Regulator movement and the Paxton Boys revolt, grew uneasy. When farmers in western Massachusetts began an organized protest in 1786, this uneasiness reached crisis proportions.

Western Massachusetts farmers were among those hardest hit by the postwar depression. Many were deeply in debt to creditors who held mortgages on their farms and lands. In the 1780s, these farmers looked to the state government for temporary relief, hoping that it would pass **stay laws** that would temporarily suspend creditors' rights to foreclose on lands and farm equipment. The Massachusetts assembly responded sympathetically but met stubborn resistance from the merchants and creditors who were themselves deeply in debt to foreign manufacturers. The upper house of the state legislature, with its more elite members, sided with the creditors and blocked the passage of stay laws. The Massachusetts government then shocked the farmers by raising taxes.

In 1786 hundreds of farmers revolted. They believed they were protecting their rights and their communities as true republicans must do. To their creditors, though, the farmers appeared to be dangerous rebels threatening the state with "anarchy, confusion, and total ruin." The rebels, led by men such as Revolutionary War veteran **Daniel Shays**, closed several courts and freed a number of their fellow farmers from debtors' prison.

Their actions struck a chord among desperate farmers in other New England states, and fear of a widespread uprising spurred the Massachusetts government to action. It sent a military force of six hundred to Springfield, where more than a thousand farmers, most armed with pitchforks rather than guns, had gathered to close the local courthouse. The troops let loose a cannon barrage that killed four protesters and set the remaining men to flight. Although Daniel Shays managed to escape, by February 4, 1787, the farmers' revolt was over.

Shays's Rebellion revealed the temper of the times. When the government did not respond to their needs, the farmers acted as they had been encouraged to act in the prerevolutionary years. They organized, and they protested—and when government still did not respond, they took up arms against what they considered to be injustice. Across the country, many Americans sympathized with these farmers. But just as many did not. Abigail Adams, adopting language earlier used against her husband by his loyalist opponents, condemned the leaders of the farmers' revolt as "ignorant, restless, desperadoes, without conscience or principles," who were persuading a "deluded multitude to follow their standards."

The revolt stirred up fears of slave rebellions and pitched battles between debtors and creditors, haves and have-nots. Above all, it raised doubts among influential political figures about the ability of either state governments or the Confederation

---

squatter   A person who settles on unoccupied land to which he or she has no legal claim.

stay laws   Laws suspending the right of creditors to foreclose on, or seize, debtors' property; they were designed to protect indebted farmers from losing their land.

to preserve the basic rule of law. To George Washington, Shays's Rebellion was also a tragedy for the reputation of the United States. When the farmers' protest began, Washington wrote to authorities in Massachusetts urging them to act fairly but decisively. "If they have real grievances," he said, the government should acknowledge them. But if not, authorities should "employ the force of government against them at once.... To be more exposed to the eyes of the world, and more contemptible than we already are, is hardly possible."

The Revolt of the "Better Sort"   By 1786, members of the nation's elite, or the "better sort," believed the survival of the nation was in question. Of the Confederation's limited central government, Washington predicted "the worst consequences from a half-starved, limping government, always moving upon crutches and tottering at every step." For him, for Hamilton, and for others like them who thought of themselves as **nationalists**, the solution was clear. "I do not conceive we can long exist as a nation," Washington remarked, "without having lodged somewhere a power which will pervade the whole Union in as energetic a manner as the authority of the State government extends over the several states." Here was a different form of republican government to consider.

Support for a stronger national government grew in the key states of Virginia, Massachusetts, and New York. Leaders in these states wanted to give the central government taxing powers, devise an easier amendment process, and provide some legal means to enforce national government policies that a state might oppose. They wanted a government that could establish stable diplomatic and trade relations with foreign countries. They also wanted a national government able to preserve their property and their peace of mind. Alexander Hamilton was one of the driving forces behind this movement. At Hamilton's urging, in 1786 a group of influential Virginians called for a meeting on problems of interstate trade. With the approval of the Confederation Congress, delegates met at Annapolis, Maryland. But beyond trade issues, the meeting organizers had a second agenda: to test the waters on revising the nation's constitution. Although only a third of the states participated in the Annapolis conference, nationalists were convinced that their position had substantial support. They asked Congress to call a convention in Philadelphia so that political leaders could continue to discuss interstate commerce problems—and other aspects of government reform. Some members of Congress were reluctant, but news of Shays's Rebellion tipped the balance in favor of the convention.

CREATING A NEW CONSTITUTION

Late in May 1787, George Washington called the Constitutional Convention to order in Philadelphia. Before him sat delegates from eleven of the thirteen states (New Hampshire's delegates did not arrive until late July), closeted behind curtained

nationalists Americans who preferred a strong central government rather than the limited government prescribed in the Articles of Confederation.

windows and locked doors in the heat and humidity of a Philadelphia summer. These secrecy precautions stemmed in large part from the delegates' ultimate purpose. Rhode Island, refusing to participate in the deliberations, accused the convention of masquerading as a discussion of interstate trade while intending to drastically revise the national government. The accusation was correct. The fifty-five prominent and prosperous delegates did expect to make significant changes in the structure of the government. This objective and the need to freely debate the compromises it would require were ample reasons to keep the deliberations secret.

Most of the men gathered in that room were lawyers, merchants, or planters—Americans of social standing though not necessarily intellectual achievement. When the absent Thomas Jefferson later referred to the convention members as "demigods," he was probably thinking of the likes of 81-year-old Benjamin Franklin, whose sparkling wit and crafty political style set him apart from his colleagues despite his advanced age; or of the articulate, brilliant Alexander Hamilton of New York, whose reputation as a financial mastermind equal to the Confederation's adviser Robert Morris was well established; or of Pennsylvania's Gouverneur Morris, who was widely admired for his intelligence as well as for his literary skills; or of **James Madison**, the prim Virginia planter who turned out to be the chief architect of a new constitution. Several notable men were absent. Jefferson, author of the Declaration of Independence, was abroad serving as ambassador to France. John Adams was representing the United States in the same capacity in London. And the two great propagandists of the Revolution, Samuel Adams and Thomas Paine, were also absent, for both opposed any revision of the Articles of Confederation.

Revise or Replace?   Most of the delegates were nationalists, but they did not necessarily agree on how best to proceed. Should they revise the Articles or abandon them? Several delegates, including Alexander Hamilton himself, would present blueprints for the new government. But it was the Virginia planter and lawyer Edmund Randolph who first captured the convention's attention with his delegation's proposal, which effectively amended the Articles of Confederation out of existence.

Although Randolph introduced the **Virginia Plan** on the convention floor, James Madison was its guiding spirit. The 36-year-old Madison was no dashing figure. He was small, frail, charmless, and a hypochondriac. But he was highly respected as a scholar of philosophy and history and as an astute political theorist, and his long service as a member of the Virginia legislature and in the Confederation Congress gave him a practical understanding of politics and government. At the convention, Madison brought all his knowledge to bear on one question: What was the best form of government for a strong republic? He concluded, as John Adams had done early in the 1780s, that the fear of tyranny should not rule out a powerful national government. Any dangerous abuse of power could be avoided if internal checks and balances were built into the republican structure.

Madison's Virginia Plan embodied this conviction. It called for a government with three distinct branches—legislative, executive, and judicial—to replace the

Signing of the Constitution of the United States by Thomas Pritchard Rossiter, 1867. Gift of John Schermerhorn Jacobus, 1960. Collection of Fraunces Tavern® Museum, New York City.

In 1867, Thomas Pritchard Rossiter painted his Signing of the Constitution of the United States *honoring a group of statesmen that included James Madison, Alexander Hamilton, and George Washington, who presided over the Constitutional Convention. Thomas Jefferson, absent because of his duties as ambassador to France, later referred to the fifty-five delegates who crafted the Constitution as a gathering of "demigods."*

Confederation's Congress, which was performing all three functions. By dividing power in this way, Madison believed, the plan could prevent an individual or group of men from wielding too much authority, especially for self-interested reasons. Madison's plan also gave Congress the power to **veto** laws passed by the state legislatures and the right to intervene directly if a state acted to interrupt "the harmony of the United States."

The delegates endorsed Madison's notion of a strong government able "to control the governed" but also "obliged to control itself." But they were in sharp disagreement over many specific issues in the Virginia Plan. The greatest controversy swirled around representation in the legislative branch—Congress—a controversy familiar to those who had helped draft the Articles of Confederation. Madison proposed a two-house or bicameral legislature. Membership in both houses would be based on proportional representation. Large states supported the plan, for representation based on population worked to their advantage. Small states objected heatedly, arguing that proportional representation would leave them helpless against a national government dominated by the large ones. Small-state delegates threw their support behind a second proposal, the **New Jersey Plan**, which also called for three branches of government and gave Congress the power to tax and to control national commerce. This plan, however, preserved an equal voice and vote for every state within a unicameral legislature.

Debate over the two plans dragged on through the steamy days of a June heat wave. Tempers flared, and at times the deadlock seemed hopeless. Threats to walk

veto   The power or right of one branch of government to reject the decisions of another branch.

out of the convention came from both sides. Ultimately, a compromise, hammered out by a special committee, was presented by Roger Sherman of Connecticut. This **Great Compromise** proposed a two-house legislature to satisfy both sides, with proportional representation in the lower house (the House of Representatives) and equal representation in the upper house (the Senate).

The Great Compromise resolved the first major controversy at the convention but opened the door to the next one. The delegates had to decide how the representatives in each house were to be elected. A compromise also settled this issue. State legislatures would select senators, and the eligible voters of each state would directly elect their member of the House. This formula allowed the delegates to acknowledge the sovereignty of the state governments but also to accommodate the republican commitment to popular elections in a representative government.

The delegates faced one last stumbling block over representation: Which Americans were to be counted to determine a state's population? This issue remained as divisive as it had been when the Articles of Confederation were drafted. Southern delegates argue that slaves, who composed as much as one-third and sometimes more of each plantation state's residents, should be included in the population count that determined a state's seats in the House of Representatives. Northern delegates protested, declaring that slaves should be considered property. These delegates were motivated by self-interest rather than a desire for consistency, for if slaves were considered property, not people, the North would dominate the lower house.

A compromise that defied reason but made brilliant political sense settled this question. The **Three-Fifths Compromise** established that three-fifths of the slave population would be included in a state's critical headcount. A clause was then added guaranteeing that the slave trade would continue for a twenty-year period. Some southern leaders, especially in South Carolina, wanted this extension badly because they had lost many slaves during the Revolution. But not all slave-owners concurred. Virginia's George Mason, a slave-owner himself, spoke passionately of the harm slavery did to his region. It not only prevented white immigration to the South, Mason said, but infected the moral character of the slave master. "Every master of slaves," Mason argued, "is born a petty tyrant." Slave-owners "bring the judgment of heaven upon a country," particularly one intended as a republic.

Drafting an Acceptable Document   The Three-Fifths Compromise ended weeks of debate over representation. No other issue arose to provoke such controversy, and the delegates proceeded calmly to implement the principle of checks and balances. For example, the president, or executive, was named commander in chief of the armed forces and given primary responsibility for foreign affairs. To balance these **executive powers**, only Congress was given the right to declare war and to raise an army.

---

executive powers   Powers given to the president by the Constitution.

Congress received the critical "power of the purse," but this power to tax and to spend the revenues raised by taxation was checked in part by the president's power to veto congressional legislation. As yet another balance, Congress could override a presidential veto by the vote of a two-thirds majority. Following the same logic of distributing power, the delegates gave authority to the president to name federal court judges, but the Senate had to approve all such appointments.

Occasionally, as in the system for electing the president, the convention chose awkward or cumbersome procedures. For example, many delegates opposed direct popular election of the president. A few agreed with the elitist sentiments of George Mason, who said this "would be as unnatural ... as it would [be] to refer a trial of colours to a blind man." Others simply doubted that the citizens of one state would be familiar enough with a candidate from a distant state to make a valid judgment. In an age of slow communication, few men besides George Washington had a truly national reputation. Should the president be chosen by state legislators who had perhaps worked in government with political leaders from outside their states? Delegates rose to object that this solution threatened too great a concentration of power in the legislators' hands. As a somewhat clumsy compromise, the delegates created the **Electoral College**, a group of special electors to be chosen by the states to vote for presidential candidates. Each state would be entitled to a number of electors equal to the number of its senators and representatives sitting in Congress, but no one serving in Congress at the time of a presidential election would be eligible to be an elector. If two presidential candidates received the same number of Electoral College votes, or if no candidate received a majority of the Electoral College votes, then the House of Representatives would choose the new president. This complex procedure honored the **discretion** of the state governments in appointing the electors but limited the power of individuals already holding office.

The long summer of conflict and compromise ended with a new plan for a national government. Would the delegates be willing to put their names to the document they had created in secrecy and by overreaching their authority? Benjamin Franklin fervently hoped so. Though sick and bedridden, Franklin was carried by friends to the convention floor, where he pleaded for unanimous support for the new government. When a weary George Washington at last declared the meetings adjourned on September 17, 1787, only a handful of delegates left without signing what the convention hoped would be the new American constitution.

RESOLVING THE CONFLICT OF VISION

The framers of the Constitution called for special state **ratifying conventions**, with delegates chosen by voters, to discuss and then vote on the proposed change of government. The framers believed that these conventions would give citizens, including themselves, a more direct role in this important political decision, while

---

discretion   The power or right to act according to one's own judgment.

bypassing the state legislatures, which stood to lose power under the new government and were thus likely to oppose it. The framers added to their advantage by declaring that the approval of only nine states was necessary to establish the Constitution. Reluctantly, the Confederation Congress agreed to all these terms and procedures. By the end of September 1787, Congress had passed the proposed Constitution on to the states, triggering the next round of debates over America's political future.

The Ratification Controversy   As Alexander Hamilton boasted, "The new Constitution has in favor of its success … [the] very great weight of influence of the persons who framed it." Hamilton was correct. Men of wealth, political experience, and frequently great persuasive powers put their skills to the task of achieving ratification. But what Hamilton did not mention was that many revolutionary heroes and political leaders opposed the Constitution with equal intensity—most notably Patrick Henry, Samuel Adams, George Mason, and George Clinton, the popular governor of New York. Boston's most effective

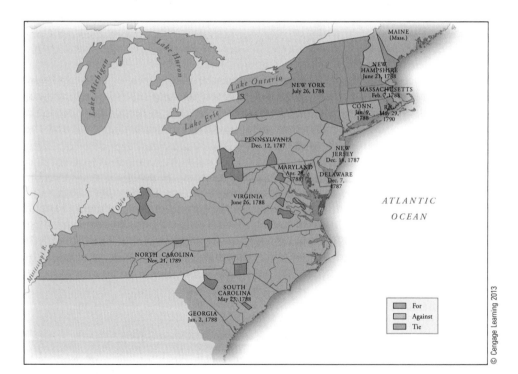

MAP 7.2 Ratification of the Constitution

The pattern of support by relatively small states is visible in the votes of Delaware, New Jersey, Georgia, and Connecticut. In Pennsylvania, Massachusetts, and New York, the more populated urban areas supported ratification.

revolutionary propagandist, Mercy Otis Warren, immediately took up her pen to attack the Constitution and even **canvassed** her neighbors to stand firm against what she called an assault on republican values. Thus the leadership on both sides of the issue was drawn from the political elite of the revolutionary generation.

The pro-Constitution forces won an early and important victory by clouding the language of the debate. They abandoned the label "nationalists," which drew attention to their belief in a strong central government, and chose to call themselves **Federalists**, a name originally associated with a system of strong state governments and limited national government. This shrewd tactic cheated opponents of the Constitution out of their rightful name. The pro-Constitution forces then dubbed their opponents **Antifederalists**. This label implied that their adversaries were negative thinkers and pessimists who lacked a program of their own.

Although the philosophical debate over the best form of government for a republic was an important one, voters considered other, practical factors in choosing a Federalist or Antifederalist position. Voters in states with a stable or recovering economy were likely to oppose the Constitution because the Confederation system gave their states greater independent powers. Those in small, geographically or economically disadvantaged states were likely to favor a strong central government that could protect them from their competitive neighbors. Thus the small states of Delaware and Connecticut ratified the Constitution quickly, but in New York and Virginia ratification was hotly contested.

To some degree, Federalist and Antifederalist camps matched the divisions between the relatively urban, market-oriented communities of the Atlantic coast and the frontier or rural communities of the inland areas. For example, the backcountry of North and South Carolina and the less economically developed areas of Virginia saw little benefit in a stronger central government, especially one that might tax them. But coastal centers of trade and overseas commerce such as Boston, New York City, and Charleston were eager to see an aggressive and effective national policy regarding foreign and interstate trade. In these urban centers, artisans, shopkeepers, and even laborers joined forces with wealthy merchants and shippers to support the Constitution as they had once joined them to make the Revolution. No generalization can explain every political choice, of course. No economic or social group was unified under the Federalist or the Antifederalist banner. On the whole, however, it can be said that the Federalists were better organized, had more resources at their disposal, and campaigned more effectively than the Antifederalists.

Public debates sharply defined the political differences between the Federalists and Antifederalists. Antifederalists rejected the claim that the nation was in a "critical period," facing economic and political collapse. As one New Yorker put it: "I deny that we are in immediate danger of anarchy and commotions. Nothing but the passions of wicked and ambitious men will put us in the least danger." Nevertheless, the Federalists were successful in portraying the moment as a crisis or turning point

canvass   To survey people relating to an issue.

for the young republic—and in insisting that their plan for recovery was better than no plan at all.

The Antifederalists struck hard against the dangerous elitism they believed they saw in the Constitution. They portrayed the Federalists as a privileged, sophisticated minority, ready and able to tyrannize the people if their powerful national government were ratified. Be careful, one Massachusetts man warned, because "these lawyers, and men of learning, and moneyed men, that talk so finely and gloss over matters so smoothly, to make us poor illiterate people swallow down the pill, expect to get into Congress themselves." And New York Antifederalist Melancton Smith predicted that the proposed new government would lead inevitably to rule by a wealthy, unrepresentative minority. The Virginia revolutionary leader Richard Henry Lee was flabbergasted that his generation would even consider ratifying the Constitution. "'Tis really astonishing," he wrote to a New York opponent in the summer of 1788, "that the same people, who have just emerged from a long and cruel war in defense of liberty, should agree to fix an elective **despotism** upon themselves and posterity."

The Antifederalists' most convincing evidence of elitism and its potential for tyranny was that the proposed Constitution lacked a bill of rights. It contained no written guarantees of the people's right to assemble or to worship as they saw fit, and it gave no assurances of a trial by jury in civil cases or the right to bear arms. The framers believed that these rights were secure because most state constitutions contained strong guarantees of them. But Antifederalists put the question to both voters and delegates: What did this glaring omission tell Americans about the framers' respect for republican ideals? The only conclusion, Antifederalists argued, was that the Constitution was a threat to republican principles of representative government, a vehicle for elite rule, and a document unconcerned with the protection of the people's individual liberties. Federalists countered by insisting that the Constitution fulfilled and could preserve the republican ideals of the Revolution far better than the Articles of Confederation had done. Their cause was put forward most convincingly by Alexander Hamilton, James Madison, and John Jay, who entered the newspaper wars over ratification in the key state of New York. Together, they produced a series of essays known today as the **Federalist Papers**. Although these 85 essays were all signed "Publius," Hamilton wrote 51 of them, Madison 29, and Jay 5. Their common theme was the link between American prosperity, American liberties, and a strong central government.

The Federalist Victory   Practical politics rather than political theory seemed to influence the outcome of many of the ratifying conventions. Delaware, New Jersey, Georgia, and Connecticut—all small states—quickly approved the Constitution. In Pennsylvania, Antifederalists in the rural western regions lost control of the convention to the Federalists and thus that state also endorsed the Constitution. In the remaining states, including Massachusetts, Virginia, and New York, the two sides were more evenly matched.

***

despotism   Rule by a tyrant.

Antifederalists were in the majority in the Massachusetts convention, where most of the delegates were small farmers from the western counties and more than twenty of them had participated in Shays's Rebellion. The Federalists' strategy was to make political deals with key delegates, winning over Antifederalists such as Samuel Adams and John Hancock, for example, with promises to demand the addition of a bill of rights to the Constitution. At the final count, a 19-vote margin gave the Federalists a narrow victory in Massachusetts.

After Massachusetts ratified, the fight shifted to New Hampshire. Here, too, Federalists won by a small majority. Rhode Island, true to its history of opposition to strong central authority, rejected the Constitution decisively. But Maryland and South Carolina ratified it, and the tide in favor of the new government influenced the next critical vote: that of Virginia. There, Antifederalist leaders Lee, Henry, and James Monroe focused on the absence of a bill of rights in the proposed Constitution. James Madison and George Washington directed the Federalist counterattack. In the end, the presence of Washington proved irresistible because Virginians knew that this war hero and admired colleague was certain to be the first president of the United States if the Constitution went into effect. When the vote was taken on June 25, 1788, Virginia became the tenth state to ratify the new government.

New York's battle was equally intense. Acknowledging that the absence of a bill of rights was a major political error, Federalist leaders Jay and Hamilton made a public pledge to support its inclusion. By then, however, ten states had already ratified the Constitution, and so the new government was a **fait accompli**. Realizing this, on July 26, 1788, a majority of New York delegates voted yes on ratification.

President George Washington

The election of senators and Congress members was almost complete by February 4, 1789, when presidential electors met in each state to choose the nation's first president. Although George Washington did not seek the position, he knew the nation expected him to serve. He was hailed as the hero of the Revolution, and he looked and acted the part of the dignified, virtuous patriot. Washington became president by a unanimous vote of the Electoral College. For regional balance, New Englander John Adams was chosen vice president.

In April 1789, as Washington made his way from Virginia to his inauguration in New York City, the temporary national capital, Americans thronged to greet him with parades, sharply dressed military escorts, and choruses of church bells and cannon fire. Near Trenton, New Jersey, he passed through a triumphal arch 20 feet high, supported by thirteen pillars, and inscribed in gold with the date of the Battle of Trenton. Thousands of supporters gathered to see him take the oath of office. Yet amid the celebration, Washington and his closest advisers knew the future was uncharted and uncertain. "We are in a wilderness," Madison observed, "without a single footstep to guide us."

Washington agreed and proceeded with caution and deliberation. He labored carefully over each of his selections to the almost one thousand federal

---

fait accompli   An accomplished deed or fact that cannot be reversed or undone.

The unknown artist of "The Federal Procession in New York, 1788," captured the jubilant mood of Americans as they celebrated their new Constitution with parades, bonfires, and banquets. As the "Ship of State" float indicates, New Yorkers were particularly eager to acknowledge the role of their own Alexander Hamilton in launching the new government.

offices waiting to be filled. He took particular care in choosing the men to head four executive departments created with approval from Congress. Naming his **protégé** Alexander Hamilton to the Treasury Department was probably Washington's easiest decision. He asked the Massachusetts military strategist Henry Knox to head the War Department and fellow Virginian Edmund Randolph to serve as attorney general. Washington chose another Virginian, Thomas Jefferson, to be secretary of state. Over time, the president established a pattern of meeting with this **cabinet** of advisers on a regular basis to discuss policy matters. Together, they made major decisions and, as Washington expected, expressed serious disagreements that exposed him to differing viewpoints on policy.

COMPETING VISIONS RE-EMERGE

A remarkable but, as it turned out, short-lived spirit of unity marked the early days of Washington's administration. Federalists had won the overwhelming majority of seats in the new Congress, and this success enabled them to work quickly and efficiently on matters they felt had priority. But the unity was fragile. By 1792, as the government debated foreign policy and domestic affairs, two distinct groups, voicing serious differences of opinion, began to form. Alexander Hamilton's vision for America guided one group, Thomas Jefferson's vision the other.

protégé   An individual whose welfare or career is promoted by an influential person.

cabinet   A body of officials appointed by the president to run the executive departments of the government and to act as the president's advisers.

Unity's Achievements

In addition to creating the four executive departments that became the cabinet, the First Congress passed the **Judiciary Act of 1789**. This act established a Supreme Court, thirteen district courts, and three circuit courts. It also empowered the Supreme Court to review the decisions of state courts and to nullify any state laws that violated either the Constitution or any treaty made by the federal government. President Washington chose John Jay to serve as first chief justice of the Supreme Court.

The First Congress also managed to break the stalemate on the tariff issue. Southern leaders had opposed a tariff because a tax on imports added to the cost of the consumer goods that southern agriculturalists had to purchase. Northeastern leaders had favored tariff legislation because such a tax, by making foreign goods more expensive, would benefit their region's merchants and manufacturers. During Washington's first term, southerner James Madison took the lead in conducting the delicate negotiations over tariffs. The result was an import tax on certain items such as rum, cocoa, and coffee.

Madison also prodded Congress to draft the promised **Bill of Rights** and helped craft the ten amendments that on December 15, 1791, were added to the Constitution. Soon after, both Rhode Island and North Carolina ratified the Constitution and joined the union. Eight of these original constitutional amendments spelled out the government's commitment to protect individual **civil liberties**. They guaranteed that the new national government could not limit free speech, interfere with religious worship, deny U.S. citizens the right to keep or bear arms, force the quartering of troops in private homes, or allow homes to be searched without proper search warrants. The amendments prohibited the government from requiring persons accused of crimes to testify against themselves, nor could it deny citizens the right to a trial by jury. The government also could not deprive a citizen of life, liberty, or property without "due process of law," or impose excessive bail, or administer "cruel and unusual punishments." The Ninth Amendment made clear that the inclusion of these protections and rights did not mean that others were excluded. The Tenth Amendment stated that any powers not given to the federal government or denied to the states belonged solely to the states or the people.

Condensed into these ten amendments was a rich history of struggle for individual rights in the face of abusive power. It was a history that recalled the illegal search and seizure of cargoes in Boston Harbor, the British government's insistence on quartering troops in New York homes, and the religious persecution of men and women who dissented from established churches both in England and in the colonies.

Hamilton and Jefferson's Differences

Alexander Hamilton was consumed by a bold dream: to transform agricultural America into a manufacturing society that rivaled Great Britain. His blueprint for achieving this goal called for protective tariffs designed to assist developing American industry rather than simply raise revenue. It also called for subsidies, or

---

civil liberties Fundamental individual rights such as freedom of speech and religion, protected by law against interference from the government.

government financial support, for new enterprises and for incentives to support new industries. And it relied on strong economic and diplomatic ties with the mercantile interests of England. Hamilton's vision had great appeal in the Northeast but few advocates in the southern states. Indeed, his ambitious development program seemed to confirm Patrick Henry's worst fear that the new government would produce "a system which I have ever dreaded—subserviency of Southern to Northern Interests."

Virginia planters Thomas Jefferson and James Madison offered a different vision of the new nation: a prosperous, agrarian society. Instead of government tariffs designed to encourage American manufacturing, they advocated a national policy of **free trade** to keep consumer prices low. They did not rule out commerce and industry in the United States but believed it should remain only as "a hand-maiden to agriculture." In the same fashion, Hamilton was content to see agriculture thrive as long as it did not stand in the way of commercial or industrial growth. Hamilton and men of similar vision around him spoke of themselves as true **Federalists**. Those who agreed with Jefferson and Madison identified themselves as **Republicans**.

The emergence of two political camps was certain to trouble even the men who played a role in creating them. The revolutionary generation believed that **factions**, or special-interest parties, were responsible for the corruption of English politics. John Adams seemed to speak for all these political leaders when he declared: "A division of the republic into two great parties … is to be dreaded as the greatest political evil." Yet as President Washington was quick to see, **sectionalism** fueled the growth of just such a division.

Hamilton's
Economic Plan
As secretary of the treasury, Alexander Hamilton was expected to seek solutions to the nation's **fiscal** problems, particularly the foreign and domestic debts hanging over America's head. His proposals were the source of much of the conflict that divided Congress in the early 1790s.

In January 1790 Hamilton submitted a ***Report on Public Credit*** to the Congress. In it, he argued that the public debt fell into three categories, each requiring attention: (1) foreign debt, owed primarily to France; (2) state debts, incurred by the individual states to finance their war efforts; and (3) a national debt in the form of government securities (the notorious paper continentals) that had been issued to help finance the war. To establish credit, and thus to be able to borrow money and attract investors in American enterprises, Hamilton declared that the nation had to make good on all it owed.

---

free trade   Trade between nations without any protective tariffs.

factions   A political group with shared opinions or interests.

sectionalism   Competition between regional interests, for example, Southern versus Northern interests.

fiscal   Relating to finances.

Hamilton proposed that the federal government assume responsibility for the repayment of all three categories of debt. He insisted that continentals be redeemed for the amount shown on the certificate, regardless of what their current value might be. And he proposed that *current* holders of continentals should receive that payment regardless of how or when they had acquired them. These recommendations, and the political agenda for economic growth they revealed, raised furious debate within Congress.

Before Hamilton's *Report on Public Credit,* James Madison had been the voice of unity in Congress. Now Madison leapt to his feet to protest the treasury secretary's plan. The government's debt, both financial and moral, Madison argued, was not to the current creditors holding the continentals but to the *original* holders, many of whom were ordinary citizens and Continental soldiers who had sold these certificates to speculators at a tremendous loss during the postwar depression. The state treasuries of New York, Pennsylvania, and Maryland were three of the largest speculators, having bought up great quantities of these bonds when they were disgracefully cheap. If Hamilton's plan were adopted, Madison protested, these speculators, rather than the nation's true patriots, would reap enormous unfair profits.

Although enslaved men and women performed the work done on Madison's plantation, the Virginia planter believed that wealth acquired by productive labor was moral whereas wealth gained by the manipulation of money was corrupt. Hamilton simply sidestepped the moral issue by explaining the difficulty of identifying and locating the original holders of the continentals. Whatever the ethical merits of Madison's argument, Hamilton said, his solution was impractical. Congress supported Hamilton, but the vote reflected the growing rift between regions.

Far from silenced, Madison next led the opposition to Hamilton's proposal that the federal government assume, or take over, the states' debts. Here, Hamilton's motives were quite transparent: as a fierce nationalist, he wished to concentrate both political and economic power in the federal government at the expense of the states. He knew that creditors, who included America's wealthiest citizens, would take a particular interest in the welfare and success of any government that owed them money. By concentrating the debt in the federal government, Hamilton intended to give America's elite a clear stake in that government's success. Hamilton also knew that a sizable debt provided a compelling reason for raising revenue. By assuming the state debts, the federal government could undercut state governments' need for new taxes—and justify its own.

Congress saw the obvious **inequities** of the plan. States such as Maryland and Virginia had paid all their war debts during the 1780s. Their members protested that if the national government assumed state debts and raised taxes to repay them, responsible citizens of Maryland and Virginia would be taxed for the failure of Massachusetts or New York to honor their obligations. Although the Senate approved the assumption of state debts, members of the House strongly objected and deferred a decision. Hamilton, realizing he faced defeat, sought a behind-the-scenes compromise with Madison and his ally Jefferson, using the location of the national capital as a bargaining chip.

---

inequities Unfair circumstances or proceedings.

In 1789 the new government had made New York its temporary home until Congress could settle on a permanent site. Hamilton was willing to put the capital right in Jefferson's backyard in exchange for the Virginian's support on assumption of state debts. Southern regional pride was not the only reason Madison and Jefferson agreed to the deal. Like many good Republicans, they believed it was important to monitor the deliberations of a powerful government. In an age of slow land travel and communication, it was difficult to keep watch from a distance. New Englanders knew that "watching" from nearby meant the chance to influence the government. "The climate of the Potomac," one New Englander quipped, would prove unhealthy, if not deadly, to "northern constitutions." Nevertheless, by trading away the capital location, Hamilton ensured the success of his assumption plan.

As the year 1791 began, Hamilton outlined another controversial proposal— a plan for chartering a national bank, modeled on the Bank of England, to serve as fiscal agent for the federal government. The bank would not be an exclusively public institution but instead would be funded by both the government and private sources in a partnership that fit nicely with Hamilton's plan to tie national prosperity to the interests of private wealth.

Once again, James Madison led the opposition. He argued that the government had neither the express right nor the **implied power** to create a national institution such as the bank. The majority of Congress did not agree, and the bill passed. But Madison's argument that the bank was unconstitutional did cause President Washington to hesitate over signing the bill into law. Turning to his advisers as usual, Washington asked both Secretary of State Jefferson and treasury secretary Hamilton to set down their views on the matter.

Like Madison, Jefferson was at that time a **strict constructionist** in his interpretation of the Constitution. On February 15, 1791, he wrote of the dangers of interpreting the government's powers broadly. "To take a single step beyond the boundaries ... specifically drawn around the powers of Congress," he warned, "is to take possession of a boundless field of power." A **broad constructionist**, Hamilton saw no such danger in the bank. He based his argument on Article 1, Section 8 of the Constitution, which granted Congress the right to "make all Laws which shall be necessary and proper" to exercise its legitimate powers. Because it seemed obvious that "a bank has a natural relation to the power of collecting taxes," Hamilton believed there could be no reasonable constitutional argument against it. As he put it on February 23: "The powers contained in a constitution ... ought to be construed liberally in advancement of the public good." Hamilton's argument persuaded the president, and the **Bank of the United States** was chartered on February 25, 1791, with stock offered for sale by July 4, 1791.

---

implied power   Power that is not specifically granted to the government by the Constitution but can be viewed as necessary to carry out the governing duties that the Constitution does list.

strict constructionist   A person who believes the government has only the powers specifically named in the Constitution.

broad constructionist   A person who believes the government can exercise implied powers in keeping with the spirit of the Constitution.

To complete his vision, Hamilton in 1792 issued his *Report on Manufactures*, a package of aggressive policies aimed to industrialize the nation—including protective tariffs and government incentives and subsidies. But this time his program was too extreme to win support in Congress. Still, the Bank of the United States, which provided much-needed working **capital** for new commercial and manufacturing enterprises, and the establishment of sound national credit, which attracted foreign capital to the new nation, had gone far toward moving the economy in the direction of Hamilton's vision.

Foreign Affairs In 1789, just as George Washington became the first
and Deepening president of the United States, the **French Revolution**
Divisions began. And in the years in which Hamilton was advancing
his economic programs, that revolution stirred new controversy within American politics.

On July 14, 1789, as crowds took to the streets in the name of broad social reform, Parisian radicals stormed the Bastille prison, a symbol of royal oppression, tearing down its walls and liberating its political prisoners. The crowds filling the Paris streets owed some of their political rhetoric and ideals to the American Revolution, a debt the marquis de Lafayette, who had volunteered in the American Revolution, acknowledged when he sent his old friend President Washington the key to the Bastille. Like most Americans in these early days of the French Revolution, Washington was pleased to be identified with this new struggle for the "rights of man." Briefly, enthusiasm for the French Revolution united Hamilton's Federalists and Jefferson's Republicans.

By 1793, however, American public opinion began to divide sharply on the French Revolution. Popular support faded when the revolution's most radical party, the Jacobins, executed King Louis XVI and his wife. Many shocked Americans denounced the revolution completely when the Jacobins, in their **Reign of Terror** against any who opposed their policies, began marching moderate French reformers as well as members of the nobility to the guillotine to be beheaded.

Soon, the Jacobin government vowed to bring "liberty, equality, and brotherhood" to the peoples of Europe, by force if necessary. This campaign to spread the revolution led France into war with England, Spain, Austria, and **Prussia**. At the very least, France expected the Americans to honor the terms of the treaty of 1778, which bound the United States to protect French possessions in the West Indies from enemy attack. The enemy most likely to strike was England, which suddenly made a second war between England and the United States a possibility.

American opinion on a second war with England was contradictory and complex. George Blake, a Boston lawyer and political figure, reminded his fellow citizens, "The [French] cause is half our own, and does not our policy and our honor urge us to most forcibly cherish it?" But others who continued to support the French Revolution, including Thomas Jefferson, did not want the United States to

capital   Money needed to start or sustain a commercial enterprise.
Prussia   A northern European state that became the basis for the German Empire in the late
nineteenth century.

In 1793, French revolutionaries executed both the king and the queen of France. More executions would follow in what came to be known as the years of "The Terror." In this pen and ink drawing, executioners tie the hands of King Louis XVI in preparation for his beheading on the guillotine while soldiers and citizens look on.

become embroiled in a European war. On the other hand, many who condemned the French Revolution were eager to use any excuse to attack the British, who still were occupying forts in the Northwest and restricting American trade in the Caribbean. Political leaders such as Hamilton who were working toward better relations with England were appalled by the French assault on other nations and by the prospect of American involvement in it.

The French, meanwhile, plotted to mobilize American support. In 1793 the new French republic sent a diplomatic minister to the United States. When Citizen **Edmond Genêt** arrived in Charleston, he wasted no time on formal matters such as presenting his **diplomatic credentials** to either the president or the secretary of state. Instead, he immediately launched a campaign to recruit Americans to the war effort. By all accounts, Genêt was charming, affable, and in the words of one observer, so humorous that he could "laugh us into the war." President Washington, however, was not amused. Genêt's total disregard for formal procedures infuriated Washington. Genêt's bold attempts to provoke incidents between the United States and Spain stunned Hamilton. Even Thomas Jefferson grew uncomfortable when the Frenchman used the port of Philadelphia to transform a captured British ship into a French privateer!

On April 22, 1793, Washington decided to act. Publicly, the president issued a proclamation that declared American **neutrality** without actually using the term.

diplomatic credentials Papers certifying that a government has empowered someone to represent it to another government; procedure calls for credentials to be formally presented upon arrival.

neutrality The policy of treating both sides in a conflict the same way and thus favoring neither.

While allowing Washington to avoid a formal **repudiation** of America's treaty with France, the proclamation made clear that the United States would give no military support to the French. Privately, Washington asked the French government to recall Genêt.

The Genêt affair had domestic as well as diplomatic repercussions. For the first time, George Washington came under public attack. A Republican newspaper whose editor was employed by Jefferson in the state department, questioned the president's integrity in refusing to honor the Franco-American treaty. Washington was furious with this assault on his character. Federalist newspapers struck back, insisting that Jefferson and his followers had actively encouraged the outrageous behavior of Genêt. By the end of 1793, Jefferson had resigned from Washington's government, more convinced than ever that Hamilton and his supporters posed a serious threat to the survival of the American republic.

More Domestic Disturbances   Hamilton's Federalists agreed that the republic was in danger—from Jefferson's Republicans. By Washington's second term (he was reelected in 1792), both political groups were trying to rouse popular sentiment for their programs and policies and against those of their opponents. Just as in the prerevolutionary years, these appeals to popular opinion broadened participation in the debate over the future of the nation. In the wake of the French Revolution and British interference in the west and on the seas, organizations rose up to make demands on the government. The most troubling of these to President Washington were the **Democratic-Republican societies**.

Between 1793 and 1794, thirty-five Democratic-Republican societies were created. Made up primarily of craftsmen and men of the "lower orders," these pro-French political groups also had their share of professional men, merchants, and planters. In Philadelphia, for example, noted scientist and inventor David Rittenhouse and Alexander Dallas, secretary to the governor of Pennsylvania, were society members. In Kentucky, which had split from Virginia in 1792, local elites organized their own society, separate from the one made up of western farmers. No matter what the background of the membership, these societies shared a common agenda: to serve as a platform for expressing the public's will. They insisted that political officeholders were "the agents of the people," not their leaders, and thus should act as the people wished.

In 1794, protest turned violent. That July, a crowd in western Pennsylvania, angry about a new federal **excise** tax on the whiskey they produced, ransacked and burned the home of the federal excise inspector and then threatened to march on Pittsburgh if the tax were not repealed.

President Washington, haunted by the memory of Shays's Rebellion and worried that the radical spirit of the French Revolution was spreading throughout America, determined to crush this **Whiskey Rebellion** firmly. Calling up thirteen thousand militiamen, the president marched into the countryside to do battle with

---

repudiation   The act of rejecting the validity or the authority of something.

excise   A tax on goods or services produced and sold within the country.

In 1794, the new federal government passed an excise tax on whiskey, made from grain. Farmers in western Pennsylvania rose up in protest against what they considered an unfair assault on their livelihood. Using tactics straight out of the pre–Revolutionary War era, including tarring and feathering the "revenooer" assigned to collect the taxes, the "Whiskey Rebels" challenged the federal government's authority. President Washington assembled an army of almost thirteen thousand men to put down the Whiskey Rebellion. Critics declared the president's response excessive. Do you agree?

a few hundred citizens armed with rifles and pitchforks. In the face of such an over-whelming military force, the whiskey rebels abruptly dispersed.

Washington publicly laid the blame for the western insurrection on the Democratic-Republican societies. Federalists in Congress rushed to propose a resolution condemning those groups. These societies, one Federalist declared, "arrogantly pretended sometimes to be the people and sometimes the [people's] guardians, the champions of the people." Instead, he said, they represented no one but themselves.

By 1796, the Democratic-Republican organizations had vanished from the American political scene. The president's public condemnation and Congress's censure undoubtedly damaged them. But improvements on the western borders also diminished the farmers' interest in protest organizations. In October 1795, Carolina planter Thomas Pinckney won the concession from Spain that Jay had been unable to obtain in earlier negotiations: free navigation of the Mississippi River. Pinckney's **Treaty of San Lorenzo** not only gave western farmers an outlet to ocean trade through the port of New Orleans but also ensured that Indian attacks would not be launched from Spanish-held territories.

Jay's Treaty   During Washington's second administration, the diplomatic crisis continued to worsen. England resented America's claim to neutrality, believing it helped France. The British, therefore, ignored American claims that "free ships made free goods" and began to seize American vessels trading with the French Caribbean islands. These seizures prompted new calls for war with Great Britain.

Anti-British emotion ran even higher when the governor of Canada actively encouraged Indian resistance to American settlement in the Northwest. Indian relations were dismal enough without such meddling, especially since efforts to crush the Miamis of Ohio had recently ended in two embarrassing American defeats. In February 1794, as General Anthony Wayne headed west for a third attempt against the Miamis, the Canadian governor's fiery remarks were particularly disturbing.

Anti-British sentiment showed itself in the House of Representatives, where Republicans considered restricting trade with England. Outside the government, war hysteria led mobs to attack English seamen and tar and feather Americans expressing pro-British views. What would Washington do?

Early in 1794, the president sent Chief Justice John Jay to England as his special **envoy**. Jay's mission was to produce a compromise that would prevent war. Jay, however, was pessimistic. Britain wanted to avoid war with the United States, but what would British diplomats concede to his weak nation?

Jay's negotiations did resolve some old nagging issues. In the treaty that emerged, Britain agreed to evacuate the western forts, although it did not promise to end support for Indian resistance to American western settlement. Britain also granted some small trade favors to America in the West Indies. For its part, the United States agreed to see that all prewar debts owed to British merchants were at last paid. Jay, a fierce opponent of slavery, did not press for any provision to pay slaveholders for slaves lost during the Revolution. In the end, Jay knew he had given up more than he gained: he had abandoned America's demand for freedom of the seas and acknowledged the British navy's right to remove French property from any neutral ship.

Although Federalists in Congress credited **Jay's Treaty** with preserving the peace, Republicans condemned it as an embarrassment and a betrayal of France. Once again, the president came under attack, and Kentucky settlers threatened rebellion, warning Washington that if he signed Jay's Treaty, "western America is gone forever—lost to the Union." The treaty finally squeaked through the Senate in the spring of 1795 with only two southern senators supporting ratification. Despite the criticism heaped upon him, Jay knew he had accomplished his mission, for American neutrality in the European war continued.

Jay's negotiations with England damaged the prestige and authority of Washington's administration. The president did far better, however, in military and diplomatic affairs in the West. In August 1794, Anthony Wayne's army defeated the northwestern Indians at the **Battle of Fallen Timbers**. Wayne then lived up to his reputation as "Mad Anthony" by rampaging through enemy villages, destroying all he could. These terror tactics helped produce the **Treaty of Greenville** in August 1795. By this treaty, the Indians ceded most of the land that later became the state of Ohio. These victories, combined with the auspicious terms of Pinckney's Treaty of San Lorenzo, won praise for the troubled president.

Washington's Farewell   As his second term drew to a close, George Washington made a precedent-setting decision: he would not seek a third term as president. Instead, in 1796 he would return to his beloved Virginia home, Mount Vernon, and resume the life of a gentleman planter.

---

envoy   A government representative charged with a special diplomatic mission.

When Washington retired, he left behind a nation very different from the one whose independence he had helped win and whose survival he had helped secure. The postwar economic depression was over, and the war raging in Europe had produced a steadily rising demand for American foodstuffs. More fundamentally, in the fifteen years since the Revolution, the U.S. economy had moved decisively in the direction that Alexander Hamilton had envisioned. The values and expectations of a **market economy**—with its stress on maximizing profit and the pursuit of individual economic interests—had captured the imagination and shaped the actions of many white Americans. Hamilton's policies as secretary of the treasury had both reflected and advanced a growing interest in the expansion of trade, the growth of markets, and the development of American manufacturing and industry. In its political life, the republic had been reorganized and the relationships between the states and the central government redefined. The new Constitution granted greater diplomatic and commercial powers to the federal government but protected individual citizens through the Bill of Rights. America's political leaders, though convinced that factions were dangerous to the survival of the republic, had nevertheless created and begun to work within an evolving party system.

In his Farewell Address to the public, Washington expressed his thoughts on many of these changes. Although Jefferson had viewed the president as a **partisan** Federalist, Washington spoke with feeling against parties in a republic, urging the nation to return to nonpartisan cooperation. Washington also warned America and its new leaders not to "interweave our destiny with any part of Europe" or "entangle our peace and prosperity in the toils of European ambition." An honorable country must "observe good faith and justice toward all nations," said the aging Virginian, but Americans must not let any alliance develop that draws the nation into a foreign war. The final ingredient in Washington's formula for America's success and its "permanent felicity" was the continuing virtue of its people.

STUDY TOOLS

SUMMARY

After independence was declared, Americans faced the challenge of creating a new nation out of thirteen distinct states. The new nation faced enormous debt and was still surrounded by real and potential enemies, and its ability to survive seemed doubtful to many.

As colonies became states, they drafted their own constitutions. Some put in place democratic forms of government while others built in more restrictive features such as high property qualifications for officeholding. The first national government, created by the Articles of Confederation, reflected the states' desire to preserve their individual sovereignty. It also embodied the revolutionary generation's opposition to a strong centralized government. The Confederation government thus lacked basic powers: it could not raise taxes or regulate commerce. However,

---

market economy   An economy in which production of goods is geared to sale or profit.

partisan   Taking a strong position on an issue out of loyalty to a political group or leader.

it negotiated the peace treaty of 1783, and it established, through three Northwest Ordinances, the process by which territories became states on an equal footing with the original states. But with limited powers, the Confederation could not resolve the nation's financial problems, deal effectively with foreign nations, or ensure social order within its borders. By the time Massachusetts farmers, hard hit by the post-war depression, rose up in revolt in Shays's Rebellion in 1786, many of the nation's elite political figures were calling for a stronger national government.

In the summer of 1787, these nationalists met in Philadelphia to consider a new constitution. The Constitution they produced, after long months of debate, steered a middle ground between a central government that was too powerful and one that was too limited. It established executive, legislative, and judicial branches, which could "check and balance" one another and thus, it was hoped, safeguard the nation from tyranny. The new government could both raise taxes and regulate commerce. After intense battles between pro-Constitution forces, known as Federalists, and their Antifederalist opponents, the new Constitution was ratified by the states in 1788.

Soon after George Washington took office as the first president, serious differences in political opinion again emerged. Alexander Hamilton's vision of a vigorous commercial and industrial nation conflicted with Thomas Jefferson's desire for an agrarian republic. The two resulting factions disagreed over economic and foreign policy. The French Revolution intensified the divisions: while Hamilton argued against American support for the French in their war with England, Jefferson pressed the administration to support their fellow revolutionaries. Washington managed to steer a neutral course in this European conflict. By the end of Washington's second term, the United States had expanded its borders, negotiated with Spain for access to the Mississippi River, and under Hamilton's guidance, it had established a national bank at the center of an economic system that promoted market-oriented growth. The departing Washington urged Americans to continue to cooperate and cautioned them not to allow competing visions of America's future to harm the new nation.

CHRONOLOGY

FROM REVOLUTION TO NATIONHOOD

1770s	State constitutions developed
1776	Oversight in New Jersey constitution gives property-holding women the right to vote
1781	States ratify Articles of Confederation Cornwallis surrenders at Yorktown
1784–1787	Northwest Ordinances
1786	Annapolis Convention Shays's Rebellion
1787	Constitutional Convention
1787–1788	States ratify U.S. Constitution

1789	First congressional elections
	George Washington inaugurated as first president
	Judiciary Act of 1789
1791	First Bank of the United States chartered
	Bill of Rights added to Constitution
	Alexander Hamilton's *Report on Manufactures*
1792	Washington reelected
1793	Genêt affair
	Jefferson resigns as secretary of state
1794	Whiskey Rebellion in Pennsylvania
	Battle of Fallen Timbers
1795	Congress approves Jay's Treaty
	Treaty of San Lorenzo
1796	Washington's Farewell Address

Focus Questions

If you have mastered this chapter, you should be able to answer these questions and explain the terms that follow the questions.

1. What types of legislatures did the states create?
2. What were the major elements of the Articles of Confederation?
3. What problems arose in ratifying the Articles?
4. What problems faced the Confederation?
5. What gains did nationalists expect from a stronger central government?
6. How did the Confederation establish relations with other nations?
7. What major compromises did the framers make in writing the new constitution?
8. What safeguards did James Madison see in his "checks and balances" system?
9. What were the Antifederalists' arguments against the Constitution? What were the Federalists' arguments in its favor?
10. What was the outcome of the ratification process?
11. How did Alexander Hamilton's expectations for the new nation differ from those of Thomas Jefferson? What were the consequences of this conflict of vision?
12. How did the French Revolution affect Washington's diplomatic policy?

Key Terms

John Dickinson (*p.* 168)

Articles of Confederation (*p.* 168)

proportional representation (*p.* 168)

Robert Morris (*p.* 172)

Northwest Ordinances (*p.* 172)

Treaty of Fort Stanwix (*p.* 173)

Hopewell Treaties (*p.* 173)

John Jay (*p.* 173)

Barbary pirates (*p.* 173)

Daniel Shays (*p.* 174)

James Madison (*p.* 176)
Virginia Plan (*p.* 176)
New Jersey Plan (*p.* 178)
Great Compromise (*p.* 178)
Three-Fifths Compromise (*p.* 178)
Electoral College (*p.* 179)
ratifying conventions (*p.* 179)
Federalists/Antifederalists (*p.* 181)
Federalist Papers (*p.* 182)
Judiciary Act of 1789 (*p.* 185)
Federalists (*p.* 186)
Republicans (*p.* 186)

Report on Public Credit (*p.* 186)
Bank of the United States (*p.* 188)
French Revolution (*p.* 189)
Reign of Terror (*p.* 189)
Edmond Genêt (*p.* 190)
Democratic-Republican societies (*p.* 191)
Whiskey Rebellion (*p.* 191)
Treaty of San Lorenzo (*p.* 192)
Jay's Treaty (*p.* 193)
Battle of Fallen Timbers (*p.* 193)
Treaty of Greenville (*p.* 193)

8

THE EARLY REPUBLIC, 1796–1804

CHAPTER OUTLINE

- Conflict in the Adams Administration • The "Revolution of 1800"
- Republicanism in Action • Challenge and Uncertainty in Jefferson's America • Study Tools

---

CONFLICT IN THE ADAMS ADMINISTRATION

Retiring president George Washington spoke for many in 1796 when he warned in his Farewell Address of "the baneful effects of the spirit of party." Followers of both Hamilton and Jefferson were thoroughgoing republicans, but their conceptions of republicanism were essentially different. Hamiltonians tended to be "classical republicans," and espoused the belief that governments are fragile and must be led by an aristocracy that could protect the people from themselves. Jeffersonians, on the other hand, tended to be "liberal republicans," asserting that the people could care for themselves and that government existed solely to guarantee free and equal participation for citizens. For Federalists, aristocratically led republicanism in England provided the appropriate model; for Republicans, popularly led republicanism in revolutionary France came closer to the ideal. These views were fundamentally incompatible and led each side to the conviction that the other sought to destroy "real" republicanism. These differences led to serious political conflict during the years following Washington's retirement.

The Split Election of 1796 As the broadly accepted leader of the opposition to Hamilton's policies, Thomas Jefferson was the Republicans' logical choice to represent them in the presidential election in 1796. Most people at the time were not surprised that Republicans chose **Aaron Burr**, a brilliant young New York attorney and member of the Senate, to balance the ticket. Though many years apart in age and from vastly different backgrounds, both Jefferson and Burr were veterans of the revolutionary struggles in 1776 and outspoken champions of liberal republicanism.

Although he styled himself a spokesman for the common man, Burr definitely was not one—his grandfather was the famous evangelical minister Jonathan Edwards, and his family continued to have enormous influence. During the Revolutionary War, Burr accepted a commission in the Continental Army, where he found common cause with the radical democrats who had formed the Sons of Liberty. By 1784, he had used his political connections and backing from the Sons of Liberty to win a place in the New York state assembly. In 1791 the New York Sons of Liberty, now calling themselves the Society of St. Tammany, maneuvered Burr's election to the U.S. Senate.

Approaching the election of Washington's successor, most Federalists assumed that Vice President Adams would be their candidate, but Hamilton and some other hardcore party members favored Thomas Pinckney of South Carolina. The younger son of a prestigious South Carolina planter, Pinckney emerged as a major political force when he successfully negotiated the treaty with Spain that opened the Mississippi River to American commerce. This coup won Pinckney the unreserved admiration of both southerners and westerners. Hamilton supported him, though, because he felt he could exercise more influence over the mild-mannered South Carolinian than he could over the stiff-necked Yankee Adams.

Most Federalists, however, aligned behind the old warhorse from Massachusetts. A descendant of New England Puritans, Adams was a man of strong principles, fighting for what he believed was right despite anyone's contrary opinion. Though a thorough Federalist, he remained Thomas Jefferson's close friend: both he and his wife, Abigail, maintained a spirited correspondence with the red-haired Virginian during his stay in Paris. Like Washington, Adams was seen by many old revolutionaries as above politics, as a **statesman** whose conscience and integrity would help the new nation avoid the pitfalls of **factionalism**.

It was precisely Adams's statesmanship that led Hamilton to oppose him, and he sought to use a loophole in the Constitution to rig the election against Adams. According to the Constitution, each member of the Electoral College could cast votes for any two candidates; the highest vote getter became president, and the runner-up became vice president. Hamilton urged Pinckney supporters to cast only one vote—for Pinckney—so that Adams could not get enough votes to win the presidency. But Hamilton made various miscalculations, and he did not expect Adams supporters to learn of the plot; when they did, they withheld votes from Pinckney to make up for the votes being withheld from Adams.

Because of the squabbling within the Federalist faction, Jefferson received the votes of disgruntled Federalist electors as well as electors within Republican ranks. He thus ended up with more votes than Pinckney—and only three fewer than Adams. So the nation emerged from the first truly contested presidential election with a split administration: the president and vice president belonged to different factions and held opposing political philosophies.

---

statesman A political leader who acts out of concern for the public good and not out of self-interest.

factionalism In politics, the emergence of various self-interested parties (factions) that compete to impose their own views onto either a larger political party or the nation at large.

Adams was ill suited to lead a deeply divided nation. Although he disavowed any aristocratic sentiments in his inaugural address, the new president's aloofness did little to put liberal Republicans' fears to rest. In fact, Adams retained ultra-Federalists Oliver Wolcott, James McHenry, and Timothy Pickering from Washington's cabinet. Clearly the divisions between classical and liberal republicans were still alive. This disunity enticed interested parties both at home and abroad to try to undermine Adams's authority and influence.

XYZ: The Power of Patriotism   One group seeking to take advantage of the divisions in the United States was the revolutionary government in France. America's minister in Paris, James Monroe, sympathized with the French cause, but the pro-British impact of Jay's Treaty and the antirevolutionary rhetoric adopted by Federalists led the French to suspect American sincerity. During the election of 1796, France sought to influence American voting by actively favoring the Republican candidates, threatening to terminate diplomatic relations if the vocally pro-British Federalists won. True to its word, the revolutionary government of France broke off relations with the United States as soon as Adams was elected.

Angry at the French, Adams retaliated in 1796 by calling home the sympathetic Monroe and replacing him with devout Federalist **Charles Cotesworth Pinckney**, the older brother of Hamilton's favored candidate for the presidency. The French refused to acknowledge Pinckney as ambassador and began seizing American ships. Faced with what was fast becoming a diplomatic crisis, and possibly a military one as well, Adams wisely chose to pursue two courses simultaneously. Asserting that the United States would not be "humiliated under a colonial spirit of fear and a sense of inferiority," he pressed Congress in 1797 to build up America's military defenses. At the same time, he dispatched John Marshall and Elbridge Gerry to join Pinckney in Paris, where they were to arrange a peaceful settlement of the two nations' differences.

Playing a complicated diplomatic game, French foreign minister **Charles Maurice de Talleyrand-Périgord** declined to receive Pinckney and the peace delegation. As weeks passed, three businessmen residing in Paris, whose international trading profits stood at risk, offered themselves as go-betweens in solving the stalemate. According to Pinckney's report, these men suggested that if the Americans were willing to pay a bribe to key French officials and guarantee an American loan of several million dollars to France, the three businessmen would be able to get them a hearing. Offended at such treatment, Pinckney broke off diplomatic relations. Reporting the affair to President Adams, Pinckney refused to name the would-be go-betweens, calling them only "X," "Y," and "Z."

Americans' response to the **XYZ affair** was overwhelming. France's diplomatic slight seemed a slap in the face to a new nation seeking international respect. In Philadelphia, people paraded in the streets to protest French arrogance. The crowds chanted Pinckney's reported response: "No, no, not a sixpence!" This wave of patriotism overcame the spirit of division that had plagued the Adams administration, giving the president a virtually unified Congress and country. In the heat of the moment,

The majority of Americans were scandalized by the XYZ affair and convinced that French radicalism and corruption threatened their security. In this cartoon from 1798, the French Directory is depicted as a five-headed monster threatening the American delegation with a dagger. In the background, French dignitaries share a feast at the base of the guillotine. Such images ginned up American resentment as the Quasi-War unfolded.

Adams pressed for increased military forces, and in short order Congress created the Department of the Navy and appropriated money to start building a fleet of warships. Then, on July 7, 1798, Congress rescinded all treaties with France and authorized privateering against French ships. Congress also created a standing army of twenty thousand troops and ordered that the militia be expanded to thirty thousand men. Washington added his prestige to the effort by coming out of retirement to lead the new army, with Hamilton as his second-in-command. Although running sea battles between French and American ships resulted in the sinking or capture of many vessels on both sides, Congress shied away from actually declaring war, which led to the conflict being labeled the **Quasi-War**.

The Home Front in the Quasi-War

Federalists immediately seized upon the war as a means to crush their political enemies. In Congress, they began referring to Jefferson and his supporters as the "French Party" and accused the vice president and his faction of treason whenever they advised a moderate course. Arguing that the presence of this "French Party" constituted a danger to national security, congressional Federalists proposed a series of new laws to destroy all opposition to their conception of true republicanism.

One source of opposition was **naturalized** American citizens. The revolutionary promises of "life, liberty, and the pursuit of happiness" had attracted many immigrants to the United States. They were drawn to Jefferson's political rhetoric—especially his stress on equal opportunity and his attacks on aristocracy. In 1798 Federalists in Congress passed three acts designed to counter political activities by immigrants. The Naturalization Act extended the residency requirement for citizenship from five to fourteen years. The Alien Act authorized the president to deport any foreigner he judged "dangerous to the peace and safety of the United States." The Alien Enemies Act permitted the president to imprison or banish any foreigner he considered dangerous during a national emergency. The Naturalization Act was designed to prevent recent immigrants from supporting the Republican cause by barring them from the political process. The other two acts served as a constant reminder that the president or his agents could arbitrarily imprison or deport any resident alien who stepped out of line.

The other source of support for Jefferson was a partisan Republican press, which attempted to balance the biased news and criticism spewing forth from Federalist news sources with biased accounts of its own. To counter this, congressional Federalists passed the Sedition Act. In addition to outlawing conspiracies to block the enforcement of federal laws, the Sedition Act prohibited the publication or utterance of any criticism of the government or its officials that would bring either "into contempt or disrepute." In the words of one Federalist newspaper, "It is patriotism to write in favour of our government, it is **sedition** to write against it." Federalists brandished the law against all kinds of criticism directed toward either the government or the president, including perfectly innocent political editorials. Not surprisingly, most of the defendants in the fifteen cases brought by federal authorities under the Sedition Act were prominent Republican newspaper editors.

Republicans complained that the **Alien and Sedition Acts** violated the Bill of Rights, but Congress and the federal judiciary, controlled as they were by Federalists, paid no attention. Dissidents had little choice but to take their political case to the state governments, which they did in the fall of 1798. One statement, drafted by Madison, came before the Virginia legislature, and another, by Jefferson, was considered in Kentucky.

Madison and Jefferson based their **Virginia and Kentucky Resolutions** on the Tenth Amendment, contending that powers not specifically granted to the federal government under the Constitution or reserved to the people in the Bill of Rights fell to the states. By passing laws such as the Alien and Sedition Acts that were not explicitly permitted in the text of the Constitution, Congress had violated the states' rights. The two authors differed, however, in how the states should respond. For his part, Madison asserted that when the majority of states agreed that a federal law had violated their Tenth Amendment rights, they could collectively overrule federal authority. But Jefferson argued for the principle of

naturalized   Granted full citizenship (after having been born in a foreign country).

sedition   Conduct or language inciting rebellion against the authority of a state.

interposition, recognizing each state's "natural right" to interpose its authority between the federal government and its own citizens.

The Virginia and Kentucky Resolutions passed in their respective state legislatures, but no other states followed suit. Even within Kentucky and Virginia, great disagreement arose over how far state authority should extend. Nevertheless, this response to the Federalists' use of federal power brought the disputed relationship between federal law and **states' rights** into national prominence.

Another bone of contention was the methods used to finance the Quasi-War with France and the impact these methods had on various groups of Americans. Consistent with Hamilton's views on finance, tariffs and excises were to be the primary source of revenue, and they had the greatest impact on people who needed manufactured or imported items but had little hard cash. In addition, Federalists imposed a tax on land, hitting cash-poor farmers especially hard. In 1799 farmers in Northampton County, Pennsylvania, refused to pay the tax and began harassing tax collectors. Several tax resisters were arrested, but local Federalist John Fries raised an armed force to break them out of jail. Later, federal troops sent by Adams to suppress what was characterized as **Fries's Rebellion** arrested Fries and two of his associates. Charged with treason, the three were tried in federal court, found guilty, and condemned to death.

Settlement with France

The Federalists' seeming overreaction to French provocation and domestic protest alienated increasing numbers of Americans. Adams himself was eager to end the conflict, and when Quaker negotiator George Logan sent news from France that Foreign Minister Talleyrand was asking that a new American delegation be sent, Adams seized the opportunity to end the Quasi-War. Telling the Federalist-dominated Congress that he would give them the details later, Adams instructed the American minister to the Netherlands, William Vans Murray, to go immediately to Paris. As rumors of negotiations began to circulate, Hamilton and his supporters became furious, all but accusing Adams of treason. This gave the president the ammunition he needed: he fired Hamilton loyalists Pickering, Wolcott, and McHenry and then embarrassed the Federalist judiciary by granting a presidential pardon to John Fries and his fellow Pennsylvania rebels.

Adams's diplomatic appeal to France was well timed. When Murray and his delegation arrived in Paris in November 1799, they found that whatever ill feeling might have existed toward the United States had been swept away. On November 9, 1799, **Napoleon Bonaparte** had overthrown the government that was responsible for the XYZ affair. Napoleon was more interested in establishing an empire in Europe than in continuing an indecisive conflict with the United States. After some negotiation, Murray and Napoleon drew up and signed the Convention of Mortefontaine, ending the Quasi-War on September 30, 1800.

interposition To Jefferson, the principle of interposition meant that states had the right to use their sovereign power as a barrier between the federal government and the states' citizens when the natural rights of those citizens were at risk.

THE "REVOLUTION OF 1800"

According to the partisan press, the political situation in 1800 was as simple as the contrast between the personalities of the major presidential candidates. The Republican press characterized Adams as an aristocrat and claimed that his efforts to expand the powers of the federal government were really attempts to rob citizens of freedom and turn the United States back into a colony of England. In contrast, the Republican press characterized Jefferson as a man of the people, sensitive to the appeals of southern and western agricultural groups who felt perpetually ignored or abused by northeastern elites. According to Federalist newspapers, however, Vice President Jefferson was a dangerous radical and an atheist. In the eyes of the Federalists, Adams was a man whose policies and steady-handed administration would bring stability and prosperity, qualities that appealed to manufacturers and merchants in New England. The rhetoric became so hateful that even Adams and Jefferson got caught up in it—the old friends stopped speaking to each other; nearly twenty years passed before they renewed their friendship.

The Lesser of Republican Evils As the election of 1800 approached, the split between Adams and Hamilton widened. Both agreed on the necessity of dumping Jefferson as vice president, putting forward Charles Cotesworth Pinckney, hero of the XYZ affair, to replace him. But Adams's behavior in the wake of George Logan's mission to France had angered Federalists; they now wanted Adams to be gone as well. Having gotten Pinckney into the Electoral College balloting, Hamilton again tried to steal the 1800 election. As before, he advised delegates to withhold votes, but this time he engaged in direct lobbying, even writing a pamphlet in which he questioned Adams's suitability for the presidency.

Hamilton's methods backfired again: Federalists cast one more vote for Adams than for Pinckney. But more important, Hamilton's scheming and his faction's consistent promanufacturing stance had so alienated southern Federalists that many chose to support Jefferson. With Jefferson pulling in the southern vote and his running mate—Burr again—pulling in the craftsmen and small-farm vote in New York and Pennsylvania, the Republicans outscored the Federalists by 16 votes in the Electoral College. But that still did not settle the election. Burr and Jefferson won the same number of electoral votes, throwing the contest into the still Federalist-dominated House of Representatives.

Federalists in the House now faced the task of choosing between two men whom most of them viewed as being dangerous radicals bent on destroying the Federalists' hard work. Indecision was plain: in ballot after ballot over six grueling days early in 1801, neither Jefferson nor Burr could win the necessary majority. Eventually, two things combined to break the deadlock. First, Hamilton convinced several Federalists that even though Jefferson's rhetoric was dangerous, the Virginian was a gentleman of property and integrity—a suitable guardian under classical republican theory— whereas Burr was "the most dangerous man of the community." Second, intent on preventing a "legislative usurpation" of the popular will, Virginia and Pennsylvania mobilized their militias. As Delaware senator James Bayard described the situation, "we must risk the Constitution and a Civil War or take Mr. Jefferson." Finally, on the thirty-sixth ballot, on February 17, 1801, Jefferson emerged as the winner.

Federalists and Republicans agreed about very little, but the threat of civil war frightened both factions equally. Not long after Jefferson's election, both parties aligned briefly to pass the **Twelfth Amendment** to the Constitution, which requires separate balloting in the Electoral College for president and vice president, thereby preventing deadlocks like the one that nearly wrecked the nation in 1800.

Federalist Defenses and a Loyal Opposition	The Federalists had outmaneuvered themselves in the election of 1800, but they were not about to leave office without erecting some defenses for the political and economic machinery they had constructed. The Federalist-controlled judiciary, which had proved its clout during the

controversy over the Alien and Sedition Acts, appeared to offer the strongest bulwark to prevent Republicans from tampering with the Constitution. Thus, during their last days in office, the Federalist **lame ducks** in Congress passed the **Judiciary Act of 1801**, which greatly expanded the federal court system. President Adams then rushed to fill all these positions with loyal Federalists, signing appointments right up to midnight on his last day in office. The appointments came in such large numbers and so late in the day that **John Marshall**, Adams's secretary of state, was unable to deliver all the appointment letters before his own term ran out. But Marshall did deliver one letter promptly: the one addressed to himself, making him chief justice of the Supreme Court.

Considering the ill will evident in the Alien and Sedition Acts and the presidential electioneering, Jefferson's inaugural address was oddly **conciliatory**. "We are all Republicans; we are all Federalists," Jefferson said, seeming to abandon partisan politics and align himself with those who had recently labeled him a "contemptible hypocrite." In his mind, all Americans shared the same fundamental principles—the principles of 1776. But even Jefferson considered the election of 1800 a revolution—"as real a revolution in the principles of our government as that of 1776 was in its form."

Jefferson was right in many respects about the revolutionary nature of the election of 1800. Although his inaugural address preached kinship between Federalists and Republicans, the new president repeatedly criticized his opponents for their lack of faith in democracy and the American people. "If there be any among us who would wish to dissolve this Union or to change its republican form," he said,

lame duck   An officeholder who has failed to win, or is ineligible for reelection but whose term in office has not yet ended.

conciliatory   Striving to overcome distrust or to regain good will.

"let them stand undisturbed as monuments of the safety with which error of opinion may be tolerated, where reason is left free to combat it."

As a result of Jefferson's reassuring address, the nation began to share the president's view that "every difference of opinion is not a difference of principles." Even extreme Federalists such as Fisher Ames came to understand that a "party is an association of honest men for honest purposes." Ames went on to describe how a loyal **opposition party** should behave. "We are not to revile or abuse magistrates, or lie even for good cause," he said. "We must act as good citizens, using only truth, and argument, and zeal to impress them." With parties such as these, a system of loyal opposition could become a permanent part of a republican government without risk to security or freedom. And in keeping with the two-party spirit and Jefferson's philosophical commitment to free speech, Congress eliminated the Alien and Sedition Acts.

Jefferson's Vision for America

Jefferson had a strong, positive vision for the nation, and the party made every effort to put his policies into effect. The greatest dangers to a republic, he believed, were (1) high population density and the social evils it generated and (2) the concentration of money and power in the hands of a few. Accordingly, Jefferson wanted to steer America away from the large-scale, publicly supported industry so dear to Hamilton and toward an economy founded on yeoman farmers—men who owned their own land, produced their own food, and were beholden to no one. Such men, Jefferson believed, could make political decisions based solely on pure reason and good sense.

But Jefferson was not naive. He knew Americans would continue to demand the comforts and luxuries found in industrial societies. His solution was simple. In America's vast lands, he said, a nation of farmers could produce so much food that "its surplus [could] go to nourish the now perishing births of Europe, who in return would manufacture and send us in exchange our clothes and other comforts." Overpopulation and **urbanization**—the twin causes of corruption in Europe— would not occur in America, for here, Jefferson said, "the immense extent of uncultivated and fertile lands enables every one who will labor, to marry young, and to raise a family of any size."

Making such a system work, however, would require a radical change in economic policy. The government would have to let businesses make their own decisions and succeed or fail in a marketplace free of government interference. In an economy with absolutely free trade and an open marketplace, the iron law of **supply and demand** would determine the cost of goods and services. This view of the economy was a direct assault on mercantilist notions of governments controlling prices and restricting trade to benefit the nation-state.

opposition party   A political party opposed to the party or government in power.

urbanization   The growth of cities in a nation or region and the shifting of the population from rural to urban areas.

supply and demand   The two factors that determine price in an economy based on private property: (1) how much of a commodity is available (supply) and (2) how many people want it (demand).

REPUBLICANISM IN ACTION

When Jefferson assumed office, he ushered a new spirit into national politics and the presidency. A combination of circumstances moved him to lead a much simpler life than had his predecessors. For one thing, he was the first president to be inaugurated in the new national capital, the still largely uncompleted Washington City, which afforded quite different and much more limited **amenities**. Washington lacked the taverns and entertaining social circles that both previous capitals, New York and Philadelphia, had offered. Personal preferences also moved him in a simpler direction. He refused, for example, to ride in a carriage, choosing to go by horseback through Washington's muddy and rutted streets. He sometimes entertained with startling informality, wearing frayed slippers and work clothes, and seated his guests at a round table so that no one might be seen as more important than the others.

But this show of simplicity and his conciliatory inaugural address were somewhat misleading. Jefferson was a hardworking partisan politician and administrator whose main objective was to turn the nation around to his vision of republican virtue with all possible speed. He quickly launched a program to revamp the American economy and give the United States a place in the international community. Along the way, he captured many Americans' affection and their political loyalty but also alienated those who did not share his vision or who lacked his zeal.

Assault on Federalist Defenses   Aware of the partisan purpose behind the Judiciary Act of 1801 and Adams's midnight appointments, Republicans chose to wage an equally aggressive partisan war to reverse Federalist control of the justice system. In January 1802, Republicans in Congress proposed the repeal of the 1801 Judiciary Act, arguing that the expanded court system was unnecessary. Federalists countered that repealing the act would violate the separation of powers. Congress proceeded anyway, replacing the Judiciary Act of 1801 with the Judiciary Act of 1802, and awaited the response of the Federalist courts.

The **constitutionality** of the new Judiciary Act was never tested, but the power of the judicial branch to interpret and enforce federal law did become a major issue the following year. On taking office, Jefferson's secretary of state, James Madison, held back the appointment letters that John Marshall had been unable to deliver before the expiration of his term. One jilted appointee was William Marbury, who was to have been **justice of the peace** for the newly created District of Columbia in which Washington was located. Marbury, with the support of his

amenities   Conveniences, comforts, and services.

constitutionality   Accordance with the principles or provisions of the Constitution.

justice of the peace   The lowest level of judge in some state court systems, usually responsible for hearing small claims and minor criminal cases; because the District of Columbia is a federal territory rather than a state, the justice of the peace for that district is a federal appointee.

IT MATTERS TODAY

The Peaceful Transit of Power

Beginning with debates over the ratification of the Constitution and continuing with ever-increasing stridency through the Quasi-War, questions about the legitimacy of opposition politics ran rampant. Many among the nation's founders wondered if *loyal* opposition was even a possibility. In 1798, one Federalist in Congress accused the Republican opposition of outright treason, charging that they "believe it to be their duty to do all in their power to overturn the whole system, to effect which, they may think a French army and a French invasion necessary." Republican John Nicholas countered that the Federalists were far more dangerous than the French, seeking to "subvert all the liberties of our country," and many suspected that they were not above using a British army to attain that end. Such charges and countercharges became increasingly strident as the presidential election approached in 1800, and many feared that a truly contested election would result in civil war. Despite these realistic fears, the election came and

went, the Federalists were swept from power, and both parties settled into a comfortable, though seldom affable, pattern of permanent opposition. With a few minor exceptions, the two-party political system has dominated the political process ever since, and while claims of treason or of subverting liberties continue to muddle our political rhetoric, the precedent of a peaceful transit of power set in the election of 1800 remains fundamental to our success as a nation.

- Consider the impact of a two-party political system on national life. Has the impact been generally positive? Why or why not?
- Though the two-party system has dominated politics in the United States, there have been some significant exceptions. Examine a period during which there was either only one political party or more than two parties and analyze what caused this exception and how it played out.

party, filed suit in the Supreme Court. According to Marbury, the Judiciary Act of 1789 gave the federal courts the power to order the executive branch to deliver his appointment.

Marbury v. Madison was Chief Justice Marshall's first major case, and in it he proved his political as well as his judicial ingenuity. Marshall was keenly aware that in a direct confrontation between the executive and judicial branches, the judiciary was sure to lose. Rather than risking a serious blow to the dignity of the Supreme Court, Marshall ruled in 1803 that the Constitution contained no provision for the Supreme Court to issue such orders as the Judiciary Act of 1789 required and that therefore the law was unconstitutional.

This decision put Jefferson and Madison in a difficult political position. On one hand, the authors of the Virginia and Kentucky Resolutions were on record for arguing that the states and not the courts should determine the constitutionality of federal laws. But political realities forced them to accept Marshall's

Suffering a lifelong sensitivity to cold as well as a dislike for formality, Thomas Jefferson usually chose to dress practically, in fairly plain clothes that kept him warm. This 1822 portrait by Thomas Sully captures the former president in his customary greatcoat, unadorned suit, and well-worn boots.

"Thomas Jefferson" by Thomas Sully. West Point Art Collection, United States Military Academy, West Point, New York.

decision in this case if they wanted to block Adams's handpicked men from assuming lifetime appointments in powerful judicial positions. Although this **precedent** for **judicial review** did not immediately invalidate the principles set forth in Jefferson's and Madison's earlier **manifestos**, it established the standard that federal courts, rather than states, could decide the constitutionality of acts of Congress.

Marshall's decision in *Marbury v. Madison* gave the Republicans the power to withhold undelivered letters of appointment from the Adams administration, but it gave them no power to control the behavior of judges whose appointments were already official. Thus, in the aftermath of the Marbury decision, Republican radicals in Congress decided to take aim at particularly partisan Federalist judges.

precedent   An event or decision that may be used as an example in similar cases later on.

judicial review   The power of the Supreme Court to review the constitutionality of laws passed by Congress and by the states.

manifesto   A written statement publicly declaring the views of its author.

John Pickering of New Hampshire was an easy first target. Mentally ill, he was known to rave incoherently both on and off the bench, usually about the evils of Jefferson and liberal republicanism. No one, not even staunch Federalists, doubted that the man was incompetent, but it was far from certain that he had committed the "high crimes and misdemeanors" for which he was **impeached** in 1803. Whether he had or not, the Senate found him guilty and removed him from office.

Emboldened by that easy victory and armed with a powerful precedent, radical Republicans took on Supreme Court justice Samuel Chase. Chase was notorious for making partisan decisions—such as condemning John Fries to death—and for using the federal bench as an anti-Republican soapbox. Unlike Pickering, Chase defended himself very competently, making the political motivations behind the impeachment effort obvious to all observers. In the end, both Federalists and many Republicans voted to dismiss the charges, returning Chase to his position on the Supreme Court. The failure to impeach Chase demonstrated that the political structure was not going to tip decisively to either side and made Jefferson's inaugural statement of principle a guideline for political reality: both sides would have to compromise in charting the course for the nation.

Implementing a New Economy   Still, Republicans were determined on one partisan agenda item: tearing down Hamilton's economic structure and replacing it with a new one more consistent with Jefferson's vision. Responsibility for planning and implementing this economic policy fell to Treasury Secretary **Albert Gallatin**. Gallatin's first effort as Secretary of the Treasury was to try to settle the nation's debts. His ambitious goal was to make the United States entirely debt free by 1817. With Jefferson's approval, Gallatin implemented a radical course of budget cutting, going so far as to close several American embassies overseas to save money. At home, Gallatin and Jefferson pared administrative costs by reducing staff and putting an end to the fancy receptions and other social events that President Adams had so enjoyed. The administration cut the military by half, reducing the army from four thousand to twenty-five hundred men and the navy from twenty-five ships to a mere seven.

But Gallatin's cost cutting did much more than just reduce the national budget. First, Gallatin was able to mask the firing of loyal Federalists still employed in civil service in a seemingly nonpartisan appeal to fiscal responsibility. He accomplished another ideological goal by reducing the overall federal presence, putting more responsibilities onto the states, where Jefferson's philosophy said they belonged. In addition, Gallatin's plan called for a significant change in how the government raised money. In 1802 the Republican Congress repealed all **internal taxes**, leaving customs duties and the sale of western lands as the sole

---

impeach   To formally charge a public official with criminal conduct in office; once the House of Representatives has impeached a federal official, the official is then tried in the Senate on the stated charges.

internal taxes   Taxes collected directly from citizens, like Alexander Hamilton's various excise taxes, as opposed to tariffs or other taxes collected in connection with foreign trade.

sources of federal revenue. With this one sweeping gesture, Gallatin struck a major blow for Jefferson's economic vision by tying the nation's financial future to westward expansion and foreign trade. But this vision would soon face serious challenges.

Threats to Jefferson's Vision   One threat to Jefferson's commitment to foreign trade came from pirates who patrolled the northern coast of Africa from Tangier to Tripoli, controlling access to the Mediterranean Sea. Ever since gaining independence, the United States had in effect been bribing the Barbary pirates not to attack American ships. By 1800, fully a fifth of the federal budget was earmarked for this purpose, a cost Gallatin wished to see eliminated as he tried to balance the nation's books. To Jefferson, principle was as important as financial considerations. Deciding on war, Jefferson asserted presidential privilege as commander in chief to dispatch navy ships to the Mediterranean in 1801.

What followed was a fiasco from anyone's point of view. After some indecisive engagements between the American fleet and the pirates, Jefferson's navy suffered a major defeat with the capture of a prize warship, the *Philadelphia,* and its entire crew. A bold but unsuccessful attempt to invade Tripoli by land across the Libyan Desert led only to a threat to kill the crew of the *Philadelphia* and other hostages. The war dragged along until 1805, when the United States finally negotiated peace terms, agreeing to pay $60,000 for the release of the hostages and accepting the pirates' promise to stop raiding American shipping.

In the meantime, France and Spain posed a serious threat to Jefferson's dream of rapid westward expansion. As settlers continued to pour into the region between the Appalachian Mountains and the Mississippi River, the commercial importance of that inland waterway increased. Whoever controlled the mouth of the Mississippi—the place where it flows past New Orleans and into the Gulf of Mexico and the open seas—would have the power to make or break the interior economy.

In accordance with the Treaty of San Lorenzo (1795), Spain had granted American farmers the right to ship cargoes down the Mississippi without paying tolls and had given American merchants permission to **transship** goods from New Orleans to Atlantic ports without paying export duties. In 1800, however, Napoleon had traded some of France's holdings in southern Europe to Spain in exchange for Spain's land in North America. The United States had no agreement with France concerning navigation on the Mississippi, so the deal between Spain and France threatened to scuttle American commerce on the river. Anxiety over this issue turned to outright panic when, preparatory to the transfer of the land to France, Spanish officials suspended free trade in New Orleans.

---

transship   To ship cargo to a port and then transfer it to other ships for transport to a final destination; cargoes shipped by barge down the Mississippi River to New Orleans were then loaded onto ocean-going vessels bound for American ports along the Atlantic coast.

Jefferson responded on two fronts. Backing away from his usual anti-British position, he announced, "The day France takes possession of New Orleans we must marry ourselves to the British fleet and nation," and he dispatched James Monroe to talk with the British about a military alliance. He also had Monroe instruct the American minister to France, Robert Livingston, that he could spend as much as $2 million to try to purchase New Orleans and as much adjacent real estate as possible.

Napoleon may have been considering the creation of a Caribbean empire when he acquired Louisiana from Spain, but a series of setbacks prevented his following through, including a slave revolt on the island of **Saint-Domingue** led by **François Dominique Toussaint Louverture**.

Stymied in the Caribbean, Napoleon turned his full attention back to extending his holdings in Europe and was seeking funds to finance a continental war. Thus, by the time Monroe and Livingston entered into negotiations with the French in 1803, Napoleon had instructed Foreign Minister Talleyrand to offer the whole of Louisiana to the Americans for $15 million.

Pushing Westward

Although Livingston and Monroe had been authorized to spend only $2 million for the purchase of Louisiana, they jumped at Talleyrand's offer. The president was overjoyed. The deal contained three important benefits for Jefferson and the nation. It removed one European power—France—from the continent and saved Jefferson from having to ally the United States with Britain. It secured the Mississippi River for shipments of American agricultural products to industrial Europe. And it doubled the size of the United States, opening uncharted new expanses for settlement by yeoman farmers.

The **Louisiana Purchase** was immensely popular among most Americans, but it raised significant ideological and constitutional questions. Some Federalists *and* Republicans questioned whether the United States could acquire this territory and its many residents without becoming an empire—something entirely at war with the rhetoric of our Revolution against the British. To this Jefferson responded by spinning the term "empire" into the phrase "empire of liberty," emphasizing that the new territory would aid Americans in securing and extending the benefits of our revolutionary tradition. Members of both parties also pointed out that the framers of the Constitution had made no provision for the acquisition of new territories by the United States, saying that the nation was prohibited from extending westward beyond its then-current boundaries without specific constitutional authorization. Again Jefferson parried with rhetoric, saying: "Strict observance to the written laws is doubtless one of the high duties of a good citizen, but it is not the highest. The laws of necessity, of self-preservation, of saving our country when in danger, are of a higher obligation." In the end, Jefferson got his way: Congress voted overwhelmingly for ratification of the treaty in November 1803.

Even before the Louisiana Purchase, "laws of necessity" had led Jefferson to exert presidential power in an unusual way. Although Spanish, French, and American fur traders, outlaws, and soldiers of fortune had crisscrossed Louisiana over the years, little systematic exploration had been done. When rumors of the land transfer between France and Spain began circulating, Jefferson started preparations for a covert spy mission. In a series of confidential letters, Jefferson instructed his private secretary, **Meriwether Lewis**, to form a party that would pretend to be on a scientific expedition into Louisiana. Their primary mission, however, would be to note the numbers of French, Spanish, and other agents in the area, along with the numbers and condition of the Indians, and to chart major waterways and other important strategic sites. They were also to open the way for direct dealings between the Indians and the United States, undermining the Indians' relations with the Spanish and French whenever possible. Early in 1803, months before ratifying the Louisiana Purchase, Congress secretly granted the funds necessary to finance the mission.

Lewis, his co-commander **William Clark**, and the rest of the Corps of Discovery set out by boat in the spring of 1804. Pushing its way up the Missouri River, the party arrived among the Mandan Indians in present-day North Dakota in the late fall. They chose to winter among the Mandans, a decision that may have ensured the expedition's success. The Mandans were a settled agricultural group who had

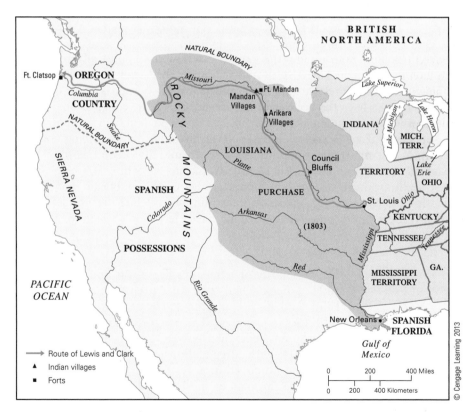

MAP 8.1 The Louisiana Purchase and the Exploration of the West

The explorations of Lewis and Clark demonstrated the vast extent of the area purchased from France.

been farming along the upper Missouri for over a thousand years. Their villages, which offered food and shelter for the wandering hunting tribes, became hubs in the evolving Plains trading and raiding system after the arrival of horses. By wintering with the Mandans, the expedition came into contact with many of the Indian and European groups that participated in the complex economy of the West. Lewis and Clark acted on Jefferson's secret instructions by learning all they could from the Mandans and their visitors about the fur trade, the nature of military alliances, and the tribes that lived farther west.

One particularly important contact Lewis and Clark made during the Mandan winter was with a French trapper named Charbonneau and his Shoshone wife, **Sacajawea**. Between the two of them, Sacajawea and Charbonneau spoke several of the languages understood by the Indians in the Far West and possessed knowledge about the geography and the various peoples in the area. With their help, Lewis and Clark were able to make contact with the Shoshones, who aided them in crossing the Rocky Mountains. From there, the expedition passed from Indian group to Indian group along a chain of friendship. Following this chain of Indian hospitality, the expedition finally reached the Pacific Ocean in November 1805.

CHALLENGE AND UNCERTAINTY IN JEFFERSON'S AMERICA

Jefferson's policies not only put the nation on a new road politically and economically but also brought a new spirit into the land. The Virginian's commitment to opportunity and progress, to openness and frugality, offered a stark contrast in approach and style to the policies of his predecessors. The congressional elections of 1802 and the presidential election in 1804 proved Jefferson's popularity and the Republican Party's strong appeal. Nevertheless, some disturbing social and intellectual undercurrents began to surface during his second term. National expansion strained conventional social institutions as white farmers, entrepreneurs, and adventurers seized the opportunities that Republican economic and expansion policies offered. Adding to the strain was the fact that the Jeffersonian spirit was more of a promise than a commitment: Jefferson's vision for the republic excluded many.

The Heritage of Partisan Politics   The popularity of Jefferson's party was abundantly clear in 1804. Jefferson had won an extremely narrow victory in 1800, and his Republican Party had won significant but hardly overwhelming majorities in Congress. The congressional elections of 1802, however, had virtually eclipsed Federalist power, and Federalists faced the presidential election of 1804 with dread. Former president John Adams commented, "The power of the Administration rests upon the support of a much stronger majority of the people throughout the Union than the former administrations ever possessed since the first establishment of the Constitution."

Despite an abiding faith in the emerging two-party system, staunch Federalist congressman Fisher Ames withdrew from public life, followed by John Jay and other prominent leaders. Charles Cotesworth Pinckney, however, stepped forward to head the Federalists' 1804 presidential ticket. For the vice presidency, the Federalists chose Rufus King, a defender of the notion of loyal opposition and the two-party system. But Federalists had trouble identifying issues on which to build a viable platform. Pinckney accused Jefferson of violating his own political principles by exerting the federal authority to purchase Louisiana, which was not explicitly granted in the Constitution. Beyond that, there was little to complain about: the economy had continued to grow at the same rate during Jefferson's tenure in office as it had under the Federalists. Such economic growth permitted Jefferson to maintain a favorable **balance of payments** throughout his first administration, a feat the Federalists had never achieved. And with Gallatin's help, Jefferson had proved his fiscal responsibility by building up a multimillion-dollar Treasury surplus. The enormous scope of Jefferson's successes and the limited scope of his opponent's platform helped swing the election of 1804 firmly over to the Republicans. Jefferson won 162 electoral votes to Pinckney's 14, carrying every state except Connecticut and Delaware.

Westward Expansion and Social Stress   A baby boom had followed the Revolution, and as new territories opened in the West, young people streamed into the region at a rate that alarmed many. This had an unsettling effect on communities in the East. During the eighteenth century, older people maintained authority by controlling the distribution of land to their children. With only so much worthwhile land to go around, sons and daughters lived with and worked for their parents until their elders saw fit to deed property over to them. As a result, children living in the East generally did not become independent—that is, they did not become church members, marry, or operate their own farms or businesses—until they were in their thirties. Economic opportunities available in the West, however, lessened young people's need to rely on their parents for support and lowered the age at which they began to break away. Breathing the new air of independence, intrepid young people not only migrated west but also challenged their parents' authority at home, upsetting social and political traditionalists. Business interests in the East were also upset as they witnessed westward expansion drawing off population, which in time would drive up the price of labor and reduce profits.

Conditions out west were even less stable as rapid growth put enormous stress on conventional institutions. The population of Ohio, for example, grew from 45,000 in 1800 to 231,000 in 1810, and similar rates of growth occurred in the new states of Tennessee and Kentucky and in territories from Louisiana north to Michigan and west to Missouri. Authorities in the West found these increases challenging as they tried to deal with the practical matters of maintaining governments, economies, and peaceful relations among the new settlers and between the settlers and neighboring Indians.

balance of payments   The difference between a nation's total payments to foreign countries and its total receipts from abroad.

Most of the people who moved west looked forward to achieving the agrarian self-sufficiency that Jefferson advocated, but life in the West was far more complicated. Inexpensive, reliable transportation was impossible in the vast, rugged interior, and Jefferson's notion of breadbasket America trading with industrial Europe was doomed without it. No navigable streams ran eastward from America's interior across the Appalachians to the Atlantic, and the ridges of those mountains made road building extremely difficult.

Only two reliable routes existed for transporting produce from the interior to shipping centers in the East. The Ohio-Mississippi-Missouri drainage system provided a reliable watercourse, and huge cargoes flowed along its stream. Shipping goods on the Mississippi, however, was dangerous and expensive. Because of the river's strong current, loads could be shipped only one way—downstream. Rafts were built for the purpose and then were broken up and sold for lumber in New Orleans. Shippers had to return home by foot. On both legs of the journey, travelers risked attack by river pirates, Indians, and sickness. Moreover, it was virtually impossible for shippers to take manufactured goods back with them because of the condition of the roads and the distances involved. The other river route—the St. Lawrence River, flowing east from the Great Lakes to the northern Atlantic—presented similar problems. In addition, that river passed through British Canada and therefore was closed to American commercial traffic.

As a result of geographical isolation and the rapid pace of settlement, the economy in the West became highly localized. Settlers arriving with neither food nor seed bought surplus crops produced by established farmers. The little capital that was generated in this way supported the development of local industries in hundreds of farming villages. Enterprising craftsmen ranging from **coopers** to **wheelwrights** produced hand-manufactured items on demand. As long as people kept moving into an area, local economies boomed. But when new arrivals slowed and then stopped, the market for surplus crops and local manufactures collapsed, and the economy went bust. Swinging from boom to bust and back again became a way of life in newly settled areas.

Along with economic instability, social instability was also common. The odd mixture of ethnic, religious, and national groups found in western villages did little to bring cohesiveness to community life.

The Religious Response to Social Change	The changes taking place in the young republic stirred conflicting religious currents. One was liberalism in religious thought. The other was a new **evangelicalism**.

cooper   A person who makes or repairs wooden barrels.

wheelwright   A person who makes or repairs wheels for carts, wagons, or other vehicles.

evangelicalism   A Protestant religious persuasion that emphasizes the literal truth of the Gospels and salvation through faith alone; in the early nineteenth century, it became infused with increasing amounts of romantic emotionalism and an emphasis on converting others.

The Mississippi River drainage system was the only reliable transportation route for Americans moving into the West during the early 1800s. Farmers moved produce to market on keelboats like the one depicted here. Above decks, cargo and livestock endured weather and exposure to mosquitoes and other river menaces. Below decks, however, there was a cabin-like environment where people could eat, drink, and sleep in comfort during the trip downriver. One problem with this mode of transport was that the current on the giant river made upstream travel impossible during much of the year, so boats like this one were often sold for lumber after they reached New Orleans.

Born of the Enlightenment in France, Scotland, and England, liberal religious thought emphasized the connection between **rationalism** and faith. To rationalists like both Jefferson and Adams, the possibility that a being as perfect as God might behave irrationally was unthinkable. In fact, for such men, the more plain, reasonable, and verifiable religious claims were, the more likely it was that they emanated from God. Less perfect than God, it was man who had cluttered the plain revealed truth with irrational claims and insolvable mysteries. For his part, Jefferson was so convinced of this logic that he edited his own version of the Bible, keeping only the moral principles and the solid historical facts and discarding anything supernatural.

rationalism   The theory that the exercise of reason, rather than the acceptance of authority or spiritual revelation, is the only valid basis for belief and the best source of spiritual truth.

This liberal creed led many, including Jefferson, to abandon organized religion altogether. Not all liberals were so quick to bolt organized worship, however. John Adams, for example, continued to adhere to New England Congregationalism, but he and others used their influence to promote a young and more liberal clergy who sought to insert a heavy dose of rationalism into the old Puritan structure. Rejecting such traditional mysteries as the **Trinity** and the literal divinity of Christ, **Unitarianism** expanded inside Congregational churches during the years just before and following the American Revolution. Liberal influence within Congregationalism became so prominent in New England that Unitarians were able to engineer the election of their own **Henry Ware** as the senior professor of theology at Harvard College, formerly the educational heart of orthodox American Protestantism. Though outraged, more traditional Congregationalists did little immediately to oust liberals from their churches. In the decades to come, however, doctrinal disagreements between the parties led to virtual religious warfare.

While deism and Unitarianism were gaining strong footholds in eastern cities, disorder, insecurity, and missionizing activities were helping to foster a very different kind of religious response in the West. Although Methodists, Baptists, Presbyterians, and evangelical Congregationalists disagreed on many specific principles, they all emphasized the spirited preaching that could bring about the emotional moment of conversion—the moment of realization that without the saving grace of God, every soul is lost. Each of these denominations concentrated on training a new, young ministry and sending it to preach in every corner of the nation. In this way, another religious awakening swept across America, beginning in Cane Ridge, Kentucky, in 1801 and spreading throughout the South and West.

The new evangelicalism stressed the individual nature of salvation but at the same time emphasized the importance of Christian community. Looking back to the first generation of Puritans in America, evangelicals breathed new life into the old Puritan notion of God's plan for the universe and the leading role that Americans were to play in its unfolding. As early nineteenth-century Presbyterian divine Lyman Beecher put it, "It was the opinion of [Jonathan] Edwards that the millennium would commence in America ... all providential signs of the times lend corroboration to it."

In addition to numerous official evangelical councils and conventions, hundreds of informal associations came together to carry out what they characterized as God's plan for America. These organizations helped counterbalance the forces of extreme individualism and social disorder by providing ideological underpinnings for the expansive behavior of westerners and a sense of mission to ease the insecurities produced by venturing into the unknown. They also provided an institutional framework that brought some stability to communities in which traditional controls were lacking. These attractive features helped evangelicalism to sweep across the West. During the early nineteenth century, it became the dominant religious persuasion in that region.

Trinity   The Christian belief that God consists of three divine persons: Father, Son, and Holy Spirit.

Exceptions in Jefferson's Vision

Jefferson's policies enabled many Americans to benefit from the nation's development, but they certainly did not help everyone. Neither Native Americans nor African Americans had much of a role in Jefferson's republic, and each group was subject to different forms of unequal treatment. And women were to occupy a special, but far from equal place in the envisioned society.

A slaveholder himself, Jefferson expressed strong views about African Americans. In his *Notes on the State of Virginia* (1781), Jefferson asserted that blacks were "inferior to whites in the endowments both of body and mind." Even when presented with contrary evidence, like the case of well-respected African American mathematician, astronomer, and engineer Benjamin Banneker, Jefferson remained unmoved. "I have a long letter from Banneker," Jefferson told his friend Joel Barlow, "which shows him to have had a mind of very common stature indeed."

Jefferson was convinced, and stated publicly on many occasions, that the white and black races could not live together without inevitably polluting both. This was the key reason for what little opposition he voiced to slavery and for his continued involvement in various projects to remove African Americans by colonizing them in Africa. And yet despite this attitude, many of his contemporaries believed that he kept a slave mistress, Sally Hemings, by whom he fathered several children, a contention that modern DNA evidence has demonstrated as credible. Even so, almost no documentary evidence about the relationship exists despite the fact that hundreds of the nation's most prolific writers (and gossips) passed through Jefferson's home regularly. Circumstantial evidence, however, suggests that their relationship was an exclusive one and lasted for a long time. And traditions passed down through generations of Sally Hemings's descendants claim that theirs was a sentimental, even romantic bond.

Given his belief in racial inequality, it seems contradictory that Jefferson could have had a long-term affectionate relationship with an African American woman. If so, it reflects equally deep-seated contradictions that shot through American society at the time. Truly a man of his century and his social class, Jefferson was convinced that women, like slaves, existed to serve and entertain men. For example, when asked if a woman could hold public office, Jefferson replied, "The appointment of a woman to office is an innovation for which the public is not prepared, nor am I." Thus his entanglement with Hemings, who probably was the half-sister of Jefferson's deceased wife, seemed no more unequal or unnatural than his marriage. But while the relationship may have seemed perfectly natural behind closed doors, the race code to which Jefferson gave voice in his various publications and official utterances defined it as entirely unacceptable in public. This rigid separation between public and private behavior led Jefferson to keep the relationship secret, and his friends and family—even most of his political enemies—joined him in a conspiracy of silence. This, too, reflected broader social ambiguities, contradictions that defined the sex lives of masters and slaves in Jefferson's South.

Throughout the Jeffersonian era, the great majority of African Americans lived in that South, and most of them were slaves. But during the late eighteenth century, conditions for slaves underwent some serious modifications and the number of free blacks increased steadily. In northern states like New York and Pennsylvania slavery was in the process of gradual legislative abolition, and even the plantation states showed increasing flexibility in dealing with slavery, as some elite southerners began to recognize the unprofitability, though generally not the immorality, of the institution. After Virginia authorized owners to free their slaves in 1782, Delaware and Maryland soon did likewise. But an event that took place in 1800 revealed that slavery would continue to be a controversial issue and source of enormous anxiety.

In the more relaxed racial atmosphere that was coming into existence in late-eighteenth-century Virginia, skilled slave workers like a blacksmith named Gabriel, owned by a Henrico County planter named Thomas Prosser, exercised significant freedom, hiring himself out for wages and learning to read and write. Gabriel came into contact with a wide variety of people and learned about the promises of greater freedom mouthed by Jeffersonian reformers and of the successful slave revolution in Saint-Domingue. Frustrated by the impotence of Republican rhetoric and emboldened by Toussaint's Louverture's successes, Gabriel enlisted at least two white partners and a number of fellow slaves to wage an armed revolt. On August 30, they armed themselves in preparation to invade nearby Richmond, but torrential rainfall bogged down the effort. Eventually Gabriel, along with his two brothers and twenty-four other slaves, were captured and hanged. It appears that Virginia governor James Monroe was aware that there were white participants, but did not pursue the evidence in fear that the information would hurt Jefferson's election efforts.

Gabriel's Rebellion had a chilling effect on race relations throughout the country. In Virginia and throughout the slave South, new restrictions were placed on the freedoms accorded to both enslaved and free African Americans. Even in northern states blacks were not permitted to testify in court, vote, attend schools, or exercise other fundamental freedoms accorded to whites. Even churches were often closed to blacks who wished to worship.

Some African Americans began to respond to systematic exclusion and to express their cultural and social identity by forming their own institutions. In Philadelphia, tension between white and free black Methodists led former slave Richard Allen to form the Bethel Church for Negro Methodists in 1793. Two years later, Allen became the first black deacon ordained in America. Ongoing tension with the white Methodist hierarchy, however, eventually led Allen to secede from the church and form his own **African Methodist Episcopal Church** (Bethel) in 1816. Similar controversies in New York led black divine James Varick to found an African Methodist Episcopal Church (Zion) in that city in 1821.

African American leadership was not confined to religious and intellectual realms. **James Forten**, for example, a free-born African American, followed up on his experience as a sailor in the Revolutionary navy with a career as a sail maker in Philadelphia. Despite both overt and subtle racial discrimination, he acquired his own company in 1798, eventually becoming a major employer of both African American and white workers. Though himself a Quaker, Forten often cooperated with Richard Allen but did not subscribe to projects designed to separate the races, working consistently—even to the point of petitioning Congress and the Pennsylvania assembly—to pass laws ensuring desegregation and equal treatment. In cooperation with other African American entrepreneurs, such as Boston's Paul Cuffe, Forten invested expertise, capital, and personal influence in an effort to create jobs for black city-dwellers and opportunities for budding black businessmen. Despite these efforts, the overall racial atmosphere in Jefferson's America significantly limited the number of African American leaders who attained positions of wealth or influence.

Jefferson thought differently of Native Americans than he did of African Americans. He considered Indians to be "savages" but was not convinced that they were biologically inferior to Europeans: "They are formed in mind as well as in body," he said, "on the same module with the 'Homo Sapiens Europaeus.' " Jefferson attributed the differences between Indians and Europeans to what he termed the Indians' cultural retardation. He was confident that if whites lifted Indians out of their uncivilized state and put them on an equal footing with Europeans, Indian populations would grow, their physical condition would improve, and they would be able to participate in the yeoman republic on an equal footing with whites.

Jefferson's Indian policy reflected this attitude. Jefferson created a series of government-owned trading posts at which Indians were offered goods at cheap prices. He believed that Indians who were exposed to white manufactures would come to agree that white culture was superior and would make the rational decision to adopt that culture wholesale. At the same time, both the government and right-minded philanthropists should engage in instructing Native Americans in European methods of farming, ensuring that these former "savages" would emerge as good, Republican-voting frontier farmers. Until this process of **acculturation** was complete, however, Jefferson believed the Indians, like children, should be protected from those who might take advantage of them or lead them astray. Also like children, the Indians were not to be trusted to exercise the rights and responsibilities of citizenship. Thus Indian rights were left to the whims of the Senate—which drafted and ratified Indian treaties—and of the army—which enforced those treaties.

The chief problem for Jeffersonian Indian policy was not the Indians' supposed cultural retardation but their rapid modernization. Among groups such as the Cherokees and Creeks, members of a rising new elite led their people toward greater prosperity and diplomatic independence. Alexander McGillivray of the Creeks, for example, deftly manipulated American, French, and Spanish interests to Creek advantage while building a strong economic base founded on both communally and privately owned plantations. In similar fashion, the rising Cherokee elite in 1794 established a centralized government that began pushing the Cherokees into a new era of wealth and power.

Although Jefferson might have greeted such acculturation with enthusiasm, the Indians' white neighbors generally did not. Envisioning all-out war between the states and the Indians—war that his reduced government and shrunken military was helpless to prevent—Jefferson advanced an alternative. Having acquired Louisiana, Jefferson

---

acculturation   Changes in the culture of a group or an individual as a result of contact with a different culture.

Unlike many of his contemporaries, Thomas Jefferson was convinced that the American Indians could eventually become full participants in the American republic. Members of the "Five Civilized Tribes" (Cherokee, Choctaw, Chickasaw, Creek, and Seminole) often owned large plantations and practiced lifestyles not unlike those of their white neighbors. Unfortunately, Jefferson's hopes fell before the racism and greed of white settlers. Even sophisticated leaders like Cherokee chief Tah Chee, pictured here, were driven from their land; he and his band eventually took up residence in Texas to escape persecution in their native Arkansas.

TAH-CHEE
A CHEROKEE CHIEF

Library of Congress

suggested the creation of large reserves to which Indians currently residing within states could relocate, taking themselves out of state jurisdictions and removing themselves from the corrupting influence of the "baser elements" of white society. Although he did not advocate the use of force to move Indians west of the Mississippi, he made every effort to convince them to migrate. This idea of segregating Native Americans from other Americans formed the basis for Indian policy for the rest of the century.

STUDY TOOLS

SUMMARY

Americans faced a difficult choice in 1796: to continue in a Federalist direction with John Adams or to move into new and uncharted regions of republicanism with Thomas Jefferson. Factionalism and voter indecision led to Adams's election as president and Jefferson's as vice president. The split outcome frightened Federalists, and they used every excuse to make war on their political opponents. Diplomatically, they let relations with France sour to the point that the two nations were at war in all but name. At home, they used repressive measures such as the Alien and Sedition Acts to try to silence opponents, and they imposed tariffs and taxes that were hateful to many. Reminded of what they had rebelled against in the Revolution, in 1800 the American people decided to give Jefferson and the Republican faction a chance.

Although Jefferson called the election "the revolution of 1800," even hard-line Federalists such as Hamilton were sure that the general direction in government would not change. Just to be safe, however, Federalists stacked the court system so that Republicans would face insurmountable constraints if they tried to change government too much.

Jefferson's inaugural address in 1801 seemed to announce an end to partisan warfare, but both Madison and hard-line Republicans in Congress attempted to restrict Federalist power in the court system. The Republican program, however, was not entirely negative. Jefferson looked toward a future in which most Americans could own enough land to produce life's necessities for themselves and were beholden to no one and thus free to vote as their consciences and rationality dictated. To attain this end, Jefferson ordered massive reductions in the size of government, the elimination of internal federal taxes, and rapid westward expansion, including the purchase of the vast territory called Louisiana. For some the outcome was a spirit of excitement and optimism, but not everyone was so hopeful. Many were unsure and fearful of the new order's novelty and of the stresses that rapid expansion engendered; social change disrupted lives and communities.

Jefferson clearly wanted most Americans to share in the bounty of an expanded nation, but not all were free to share equally. For American Indians, the very success of Jefferson's expansion policy meant a contraction in their freedom of action. African Americans also found that the equality Jefferson promised to others was not intended for them, though many like Benjamin Banneker and Paul Cuffe grasped for it anyway. As to women, they were encouraged to play an active role in the new nation but were expected to do so only through their roles as wives and mothers.

CHRONOLOGY

PARTISAN TENSION AND JEFFERSONIAN OPTIMISM	
1796	George Washington's Farewell Address First contested presidential election: John Adams elected president, Thomas Jefferson vice president
1797	XYZ affair
1798	Quasi-War with France begins Alien and Sedition Acts Kentucky and Virginia Resolutions George Logan's mission to France
1799	Napoleon seizes control in France
1800	Convention of Mortefontaine ends Quasi-War

1801	Jefferson elected president in House of Representatives; Burr vice president
	Judiciary Act of 1801
	John Marshall becomes chief justice
	War begins between American navy ships and Barbary pirates
	Outdoor revival meeting at Cane Ridge, Kentucky
1802	Congress repeals all internal taxes
	Congress repeals Judiciary Act of 1801
	French invade Saint-Domingue
1803	*Marbury v. Madison*
	Louisiana Purchase
1804	Twelfth Amendment ratified
	Jefferson reelected
1804–1806	Lewis and Clark expedition
1816	African Methodist Episcopal Church formed in Philadelphia

Focus Questions

If you have mastered this chapter, you should be able to answer these questions and explain the terms that follow the questions.

1. How did Federalists manipulate the crisis with France in 1798 for their own political advantage?
2. What steps did Republicans take to counter Federalist manipulations?
3. How did Federalists respond to losing the election of 1800? What does this response reveal about their political attitudes?
4. What did Thomas Jefferson mean by the statement "Every difference of opinion is not a difference of principles"?
5. How did Jefferson's vision for America differ from that of Hamilton, Adams, and other Federalists?
6. What legal maneuvers did Republicans initiate to deal with defenses Federalists put in place in 1801? What were the political and constitutional consequences?
7. What policies did Jefferson pursue to carry out his vision for the country? What obstacles did he encounter?
8. How did American life change during Jefferson's presidency?
9. How did Native Americans and African Americans figure into Jefferson's vision of America? How did each group respond to their circumstances?

Key Terms

Aaron Burr (*p.* 198)

Charles Cotesworth Pinckney (*p.* 200)

Charles Maurice de Talleyrand-Périgord (*p.* 200)

XYZ affair (*p.* 200)

Quasi-War (*p.* 201)

Alien and Sedition Acts (*p.* 202)

Virginia and Kentucky Resolutions (*p.* 202)

states' rights (*p.* 203)

Fries's Rebellion (*p.* 203)

Napoleon Bonaparte (*p.* 203)

Twelfth Amendment (*p.* 205)

Judiciary Act of 1801 (*p.* 205)

John Marshall (*p.* 205)

Marbury v. Madison (*p.* 208)

Albert Gallatin (*p.* 210)

Saint-Domingue (*p.* 212)

François Dominique Toussaint Louverture (*p.* 212)

Louisiana Purchase (*p.* 212)

Meriwether Lewis (*p.* 213)

William Clark (*p.* 213)

Sacajawea (*p.* 214)

Unitarianism (*p.* 218)

Henry Ware (*p.* 218)

Gabriel's Rebellion (*p.* 220)

African Methodist Episcopal Church (*p.* 220)

James Forten (*p.* 220)

9

Increasing Conflict and War, 1805–1815

Troubling Currents in Jefferson's America

Jefferson's successes, culminating in his victory in the 1804 election, seemed to prove that Republicans had absolute control over the nation's political reins. But factions challenging Jefferson's control were forming. A small but vocal coalition of disgruntled Federalists threatened to **secede** from the Union. Even within his own party, Jefferson's supremacy eroded and dissidents emerged. Diplomatic problems joined domestic ones to trouble Jefferson's second administration.

Emerging Factions in American Politics
The Federalists' failure in the election of 1804 nearly spelled the troubled party's demise. With the West and the South firmly in Jefferson's camp, disgruntled New England Federalists found their once-dominant voice being drowned out by those who shared Jefferson's rather than Hamilton's view of America's future. Proclaiming that "the people of the East cannot reconcile their habits, views, and interests with those of the South and West," Federalist leader Timothy Pickering advocated radical changes in the Constitution that he thought might restore balance. Among other things, northeasterners demanded much stricter standards for admitting new states in the West and the elimination of

secede To withdraw formally from membership in a political union; threats of secession were used frequently during the early nineteenth century to bring attention to political issues.

the Three-Fifths Compromise. Pickering brought together a tight political coalition called the **Essex Junto** to press for these changes.

Regional fissures began to open inside Jefferson's party as well. Throughout Jefferson's first administration, some within his party, especially those from the South, criticized the president for turning his back on republican principles by expanding federal power and interfering with states' rights. One of Jefferson's most vocal critics was his cousin **John Randolph.**

On the eve of the 1804 election, the two Virginia Republicans clashed over the **Yazoo affair**, a complicated legal tangle arising from land fraud in Georgia. Traditional Republicans thought the matter should have been worked out at the state level. Jefferson, however, chose to involve the federal courts in the affair. He irritated Randolph again in 1806 by approaching Congress for a $2 million appropriation to be used to win French influence in convincing Spain to sell Florida to the United States. Citing these and other perceived violations of republican principles, Randolph announced, "I found I might co-operate or be an honest man." Randolph chose honesty, splitting with Jefferson to form a third party, the **Tertium Quid**, which fractured the Republicans' united political front.

A second fissure in the party opened over controversial vice president Aaron Burr's political scheming. Upset that Burr had not conceded the presidency immediately after the tied Electoral College vote in 1800, Jefferson snubbed him for four years and then dropped him as vice-presidential nominee in 1804. With Burr in political limbo, Pickering saw an opportunity; he offered to help Burr become governor of New York if Burr would commit the state to the Essex Junto. Mainstream New York Federalists were furious, especially Alexander Hamilton, who was quoted by the press as saying that Burr was "a dangerous man, and one who ought not to be trusted with the reins of government." Burr lost the election in a landslide. Never willing to accept defeat gracefully, he challenged Hamilton to a duel. Hamilton was personally opposed to dueling, but in the honor-driven culture that permeated early nineteenth-century politics, he could not refuse. An excellent shot, Burr put a bullet through Hamilton's liver and into his spine, killing him.

Though his political career was now in shambles, Burr was not finished meddling in the nation's future. Calling in outstanding political favors, he arranged for James Wilkinson to become governor of the Louisiana Territory. To this day, no one is entirely certain what Wilkinson and Burr had in mind, but it appears that they intended to carve out a personal domain in the borderland between American and Spanish territories in the Mississippi region. In 1805, Burr ventured west, sailing down the Mississippi to recruit associates. Amid rumors of intrigue, federal authorities received a letter from Wilkinson late in 1806 implicating Burr in a "deep, dark, wicked, and widespread conspiracy" against the United States. Learning that Wilkinson had turned him in, Burr tried to reach Spanish Florida but was captured early in 1807 and put on trial for treason.

Burr's trial provided an open arena for Jefferson and his critics to air their views on such touchy subjects as presidential power, westward expansion, and national loyalty. Jefferson used the powers of his office to pardon conspirators who would testify against Burr and he leaked information that made his former vice president look guilty. Chief Justice John Marshall presided over the case, and citing Marshall's earlier support for George Washington's assertion of presidential privilege during investigations into Jay's Treaty, Jefferson refused court orders to deliver evidence from presidential records that might have aided Burr's case. Marshall, making clear that he believed Burr was the victim, not the perpetrator, of a conspiracy, retaliated by applying Jefferson's position of strict constitutional constructionism. He advised the jury that treason consisted of, and *only* of, "levying war against the United States or adhering to their enemies." Burr had done neither, and so the jury was forced to acquit, to the glee of Jefferson's critics.

The Problem of American Neutrality   Internal tensions in American politics were matched by growing stress in the nation's diplomatic and economic relations. Jefferson's economic successes had been the product of continuing warfare in Europe. With their fleets engaged in naval battles, their people locked in combat, and their lands crisscrossed by opposing armies, Europeans needed American ships and the fruits of American labor, especially food. American neutrality ensured continued prosperity as long as the contending parties in Europe agreed to recognize that neutrality.

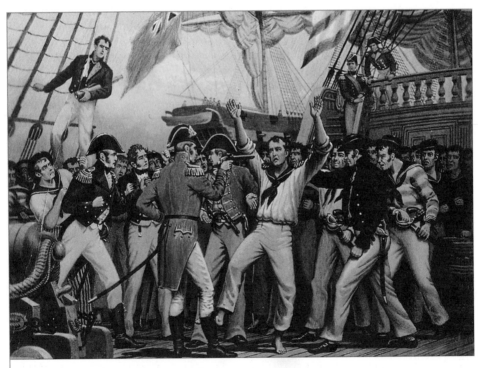

Library of Congress

The impressment of sailors into the British navy from American ships was one of the more prominent causes of the War of 1812. This 1790 engraving shows an American sailor being seized at gunpoint while those who might try to assist him are elbowed aside.

Americans immediately grasped at this opportunity. An upsurge in European campaigning in 1803 helped raise the total value of American exports by over 65 percent. A significant proportion of the increase came from the shipment of foreign goods to foreign markets by way of neutral American ports: sugar from the Caribbean, for example, frequently passed through the United States on its way to Europe. These so-called reexports rose in value from $14 million in 1803 to $60 million in 1807, prompting a rapid growth in earnings for American shipping. In 1790, net income from shipping amounted to a mere $5.9 million; by 1807 the volume had surged to $42.1 million.

Prospects seemed bright for America's economic and diplomatic future and for Jefferson's dream of agricultural America feeding overcrowded, war-torn Europe. But politicians in both England and France cared about their own military victories, not about American prosperity. Their decisions, especially those relating to neutral shipping, constantly threatened to disrupt American trade and created an atmosphere of hostility.

Another source of tension was **impressment**. For decades, British sailors had protested the exceedingly cruel conditions and low pay in His Majesty's navy by jumping ship in American ports and enlisting as merchant sailors on American vessels. Strapped for mariners by renewed warfare, England pursued a vigorous policy of reclaiming British sailors after 1803, even if they were on neutral American ships and, more provocatively, even if they had become citizens of the United States. It is estimated that the British abducted as many as eight thousand sailors from American ships between 1803 and 1812. The loss of so many seamen hurt American shippers economically, but it wounded American pride even more. Like the XYZ affair, impressment seemed to be a direct denial of the United States' status as a legitimate nation.

Economic Warfare

Pressure on American neutrality increased after 1805, when a military deadlock emerged in the European war: Britain was supreme at sea, while France was in control on the ground. The war then changed from one of military campaigning to one of diplomatic and economic maneuvering. Seeking to close off foreign supplies to England, in November 1806 Napoleon issued the **Berlin Decree**, barring ships that had anchored at British harbors from entering ports controlled by France. The British Parliament responded by issuing a series of directives that permitted neutral ships to sail to European ports only if they first called at a British port to pay a transit tax. It was thus impossible for a neutral ship to follow the laws of either nation without violating the laws of the other. All this European blustering, however, had little immediate effect on the American economy. From the issuance of the Berlin Decree to the end of 1807, American exports and shipping rose more than they had risen during any similar period.

But such good fortune was not to last. Seeking to break France's dependence on America as a source for food and other supplies, Napoleon sought an alliance with Russia, and in the spring of 1807 his diplomatic mission succeeded. Having acquired an alternative source for grain and other foodstuffs, Napoleon immediately began enforcing the Berlin Decree, hoping to starve England into submission.

The British countered by stepping up enforcement of their European blockade and aggressively pursuing impressment to strengthen the Royal Navy.

The escalation in both France's and Britain's economic war efforts quickly led to confrontation with Americans and a diplomatic crisis. A pivotal event occurred in June 1807. The British **frigate** *Leopard,* patrolling the American shoreline, confronted the American warship *Chesapeake.* The *Leopard* ordered the American ship to halt and hand over any British sailors on board. When the *Chesapeake*'s captain refused, the *Leopard* fired several **broadsides**, crippling the American vessel, killing three sailors, and injuring eighteen. The British then boarded the *Chesapeake* and dragged off four men, three of whom were naturalized citizens of the United States. Americans were outraged.

Americans were not the only ones galvanized by British aggression. Shortly after the *Chesapeake* affair, word arrived in the United States that Napoleon had responded to Britain's belligerence by declaring a virtual economic war against neutrals. In the **Milan Decree,** he vowed to seize any neutral ship that so much as carried licenses to trade with England. What was worse, the Milan Decree stated that ships that had been boarded by British authorities—even against their crew's will— were subject to immediate French capture.

Many Americans viewed the escalating French and English sanctions as insulting treachery that cried out for an American response. The *Washington Federalist* newspaper observed, "We have never, on any occasion, witnessed ... such a thirst for revenge." But Jefferson stayed calm. He had insisted on inexpensive government, lobbied for American neutrality, and hoped for renewed prosperity through continuing trade with Europe. War would destroy his entire agenda. But clearly Jefferson had to do something.

Believing that Europeans were far more dependent on American goods and ships than Americans were on European money and manufactures, Jefferson chose to violate one of his cardinal principles: the U.S. government would interfere in the economy to force Europeans to recognize American neutral rights. In December 1807, the president announced the **Embargo Act,** which would, in effect, close all American foreign trade as of January 1 unless the Europeans agreed to recognize America's neutral rights.

Crises in the Nation

Jefferson's reaction to European aggression immediately began strangling American trade and with it America's domestic economy. In addition, European countries still had legitimate claims on much of North America, and the Indians who continued to occupy most of the continent could pose a serious threat to the United States if properly motivated. While impressment, blockade, and embargo paralyzed America's Atlantic frontier, a combination of European and Indian hostility along the western frontier added to the air of national emergency. The resulting

frigate   A very fast warship, rigged with square sails and carrying from thirty to fifty cannon on two gun decks.

broadside   The simultaneous discharge of all the guns on one side of a warship.

series of domestic crises played havoc with Jefferson's vision of a peaceful, prosperous nation.

Economic Depression   Although Jefferson felt justified in suspending free trade to protect neutral rights, the result was the worst economic depression since the founding of the British colonies in North America. Critics such as John Randolph pronounced Jefferson's solution worse than the problem—like trying "to cure corns by cutting off the toes." And while Jefferson's "damn-bargo," as critics called it, was only halfheartedly enforced, the economy slumped disastrously. Taken together, all American exports fell from $109 million to $22 million, and net earnings from shipping fell by almost 50 percent. During 1808, earnings from legitimate business enterprise in America declined to less than a quarter of their value in 1807.

The depression shattered economic and social life in many eastern towns. It has been estimated that thirty thousand sailors were thrown out of work and that as many as a hundred thousand people employed in support industries were laid off. During 1808 in New York City alone, 120 businesses went bankrupt, and the combination of unemployment and business failure led to the imprisonment of twelve hundred New Yorkers for debt. New England, where the economy was almost entirely dependent on foreign trade, was hit harder still. In light of Jefferson's policies and the collapsing economy, the extremism expressed by the Essex Junto three years earlier began to sound reasonable.

New Englanders screamed loudest about the impact of the embargo, but southerners and westerners were just as seriously affected by it. The economy of the South had depended on the export of staple crops like tobacco since colonial times and was rapidly turning to cotton. There, embargo meant near-death to all legitimate trade. In response to the loss of foreign markets, tobacco prices fell from $6.75 per hundredweight to $3.25, and cotton from 21 to 13 cents per pound. In the West, wholesale prices for agricultural products spiraled downward also. Overall, the prices of farm products were 16 percent lower between 1807 and 1811 than they had been between 1791 and 1801. At the same time, the price of virtually every consumer item went up. For example, the price of building materials—hardware, glass, and milled lumber—rose 11 percent during the same period, and the price of textiles climbed 20 percent. In fact, the only consumer item that did not go up in price was the one item farmers did not need to buy: food. Faced with dropping incomes and soaring costs, farmers probably felt the trade restrictions more profoundly than others.

Rather than blaming their problems on the Republican administration, however, disaffected farmers directed their anger at the British. Frontiersmen believed, rightly or wrongly, that eliminating British interference with American trade would restore the boom economy that had drawn so many of them to the edge of American settlement. Thus westerners banded together to raise their voices in favor of war against Britain.

Political
Upheaval
Despite the escalating crisis in the country, Jefferson remained popular and powerful, but like Washington, he chose to step down from the presidency after serving two terms, making it clear to party officials that he favored James Madison to replace him. Although Madison and Jefferson had much in common and were longtime friends, they seemed very different from each other. Few could say they knew Madison well, but those who did found him captivating: a man of few words but of piercing intellect and unflinching conviction. Those less well acquainted with him thought the quiet Virginian indecisive: where Jefferson tended to act on impulse, Madison approached matters of state as he approached matters of political philosophy—with caution, patience, and reason.

Dissatisfied with Jefferson's policies, both southern and northeastern party members contested Madison's succession. The Tertium Quid challenged Jefferson's authority in the **party caucus** and tried to secure the nomination for the stately and conservative **James Monroe**. Jefferson managed to hold the party's southern wing in line, but northeasterners, stinging under the pressure of the embargo, bucked the decision of the party caucus and nominated their own presidential candidate: New Yorker George Clinton. Although Clinton polled only six electoral votes, his nomination was a sign of growing divisions over the problems that the United States faced in 1808. Despite all the political contention, Madison also easily defeated his Federalist opponent, Charles Cotesworth Pinckney. But Federalist criticism of Jefferson's policies, especially of the embargo, was finding a growing audience as the depression deepened, and in the congressional elections the Republicans lost twenty-four seats to Federalists.

During Madison's first two years in office, lack of any progress toward resolving the nation's woes seemed to confirm critics' perception of his indecisiveness. Nevertheless, Republicans actually made gains in the congressional elections in 1810: they regained fourteen of the seats they had lost in the House in 1808 and picked up two additional Senate seats. But this was no vote of confidence in Madison. Though the new congressmen were Republicans, sixty-three of them did not support Madison or his commitment to a conciliatory policy toward the British. These new members of Congress were mostly very young, extremely patriotic, and represented frontier constituents who were being ravaged by the agricultural depression. In the months to come, their increasingly strident demands for aggressive action against England earned them the nickname **War Hawks**.

The Rise of
the Shawnee
Prophet
A key reason for War Hawk militancy was the unsettled conditions along the western frontier. Relations with Indians in the West had been peaceful since the Battle of Fallen Timbers in 1794. The Shawnees and other groups had been thrown off their traditional homelands in Ohio by the Treaty of Greenville and

party caucus   A meeting of members of a political party to decide on questions of policy, leadership, or candidates running for office.

forced to move to new lands in Indiana. There, food shortages, disease, and continuing encroachment by settlers caused many young Indians to lose faith in their traditional beliefs and in themselves as human beings.

In the midst of the crisis, one disheartened, diseased alcoholic rose above his afflictions to lead the Indians into a brief new era of hope. Like others of his generation, Lalawethika felt increasingly hopeless, turned to alcohol, and finally in 1805 became critically ill. He claimed that he remembered dying and meeting the Master of Life and then awoke cured of his illness. Launching a full-fledged religious and cultural revival designed to teach the ways revealed to him by the Master of Life, he adopted the name Tenskwatawa ("the Way"). Whites called him **The Prophet.**

Blaming the decline of his people on their adoption of white ways, the Prophet taught them to go back to their traditional lifestyle—to discard whites' clothing, religion, and especially alcohol—and live as their ancestors had lived. He also urged his followers to unify against the temptations and threats of white exploiters and to hold on to what remained of their lands. If they followed his teachings, the Prophet insisted, the whites would vanish from their world. In 1807 the Prophet established a religious settlement, Prophetstown, on the banks of Tippecanoe Creek in Indiana Territory. This community was to serve as a center for the Prophet's activities and as a living model for revitalized Indian life.

Although the Prophet preached a message of ethnic pride, nonviolence, and passive resistance, as white settlers continued to pressure his people, he began to advocate more forceful solutions. In a speech to an intertribal council in April 1807, he suggested for the first time that warriors unite to resist white expansion. Although he did not urge his followers to attack the whites, he made it clear that the Master of Life would defend him and his followers if war were pressed on them.

Prophecy and Politics in the West

While Tenskwatawa continued to stress spiritual means for stopping white aggression, his brother Tecumseh pushed for a more political course of action. Seven years older than the Prophet, Tecumseh had always inclined more toward politics and warfare. Known as a brave fighter and a persuasive political orator, Tecumseh traveled throughout the western frontier, working out political and military alliances designed to put a stop to white expansion once and for all. Although he did not want to start a war against white settlers, Tecumseh exhorted Indians to defend every inch of land that remained to them.

Tecumseh's plan might have brought about his brother's goals. Faced by a unified defensive line of Indians stretching along the American frontier from Canada to the Gulf of Mexico, the United States probably would have found it virtually impossible to expand any farther, and the Indian confederacy would have become a significant force in America's future. Concerns soon led to rumors that the Shawnee leader was a British agent and that his activities were an extension of some hidden international plot. Though wrong, such theories helped to escalate the air of crisis in the West and in the nation at large.

Indiana governor William Henry Harrison had good reason to advance the impression of a conspiracy between Tecumseh and the British. Harrison and men like him believed the United States had the right to control all of North America and, accordingly, to brush aside anything standing in the way. Britain and the Indians were thus linked in their minds. Both were seen as obstacles to national destiny, and many War Hawks prayed for the outbreak of war between the United States and the British with the Indians in between. Such a war would provide an excuse to attack the Indians and dispossess them of their land. In addition, a war would justify invading and seizing Canada, fulfilling what many considered a logical but frustrated objective of the American Revolution. Taking Canada from the British would open rich timber, fur, and agricultural lands for American settlement. More important, it would secure American control of the Great Lakes and St. Lawrence River—potentially a very valuable shipping route for agricultural produce.

Choosing War   With the nation reeling from the economic squeeze of the embargo, Congress replaced it with the **Non-Intercourse Act** early in 1809. The new law forbade trade only with England and France and gave the president the power to reopen trade if either of the combatants lifted its restrictions against American shipping. Even though this act was much less restrictive than the embargo, American merchants were relieved when it expired in the spring of 1810. At that point, Congress passed an even more permissive boycott, **Macon's Bill No. 2**. According to this new law, merchants could trade with the combatants if they wanted to take the risk, but if either France or England lifted its blockade, the United States would stop trading with the other.

Hoping to cut England off from needed outside supplies, Napoleon responded to Macon's Bill in August by promising to suspend French restrictions on American shipping while secretly ordering the continued seizure of American ships. Despite Napoleon's devious intentions, Madison sought to use the French peace overture as a lever: he instructed the American mission in London to tell the British that he would close down trade with them unless they joined France in dropping trade restrictions. Sure that Napoleon was lying, the British refused, backing the president into a diplomatic corner. In February 1811, the provisions of Macon's Bill forced Madison to close trading with Britain for its failure to remove economic sanctions, stepping up tensions all around.

Later in the year, events in the West finally triggered a crisis. The origin of the problem was an agreement, the Fort Wayne Treaty, signed in the fall of 1809 between the United States and representatives of the Miami, Potawatomi, and Delaware Indians. In return for an outright bribe of $5,200 and individual **annuities** ranging from $250 to $500, accommodationists among these three tribes sold over 3 million acres of Indian land in Indiana and Illinois—land already occupied by many other Indian groups.

In August 1810, Tecumseh met with Governor Harrison in Vincennes, Indiana, to denounce the Fort Wayne Treaty. Harrison insisted that the agreement was legitimate. Speaking for those whose lands had been sold out from under them, Tecumseh

---

annuity An allowance or income paid annually.

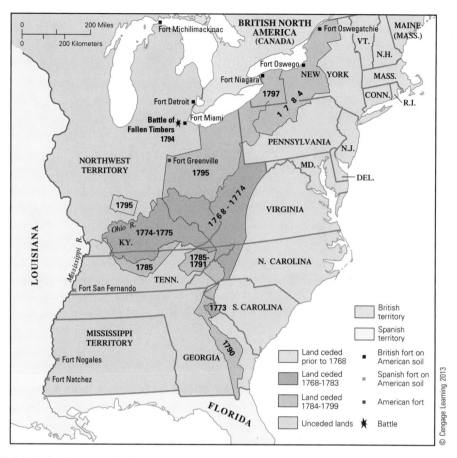

MAP 9.1 Indian Land Cessions, 1768–1799

During the last third of the eighteenth century, Native Americans were forced to give up extensive homelands throughout the eastern backcountry and farther west in the Ohio and Tennessee River valleys.

said, "They want to save that piece of land, we do not wish you to take it.... I want the present boundary line to continue. Should you cross it, I assure you it will be productive of bad consequences." But Harrison refused to budge.

The Vincennes meeting convinced the Indians that they must prepare for a white attack. Tecumseh traveled up and down the American frontier, enlisting additional allies in his growing Indian confederacy. Meanwhile, Harrison grew more and more eager to attack the Indians before they could unite fully. He got his chance when a second peace conference in the summer of 1811 also failed. Citing the failed peace effort and sporadic skirmishes between frontier settlers and renegade bands of Indians, none of which were connected to Tecumseh, Harrison ordered an attack. On November 7, in the so-called **Battle of Tippecanoe**, an army of enraged frontiersmen burned Prophetstown. Then, having succeeded in

Cincinnati Museum Center/Cincinnati Historical Society Library

Although they had enormous respect for each other, Indiana territorial governor William Henry Harrison and Tecumseh were both ferocious when it came to defending their political and diplomatic positions. This painting of their confrontation at the 1810 peace conference held at Vincennes makes this point clearly. The two never actually came to blows at this meeting or at another held one year later, but they never were able to find common ground.

setting the Indian frontier ablaze, Harrison called for a declaration of war against the Indians and the British.

Headlining Harrison's call for war, a Kentucky newspaper proclaimed, "The war on the Wabash is purely BRITISH, the SCALPING KNIFE and TOMAHAWK of British savages, is now, again devastating our frontiers." Coming as it did while Congress was already embroiled in debate over economic sanctions and British impressment, the outbreak of violence on the frontier was finally enough to push Madison into action. Still hoping for some sort of peaceful resolution, the president chose his words carefully when he told Congress, "We behold … on the side of Great Britain, a state of war against the United States; and on the side of the United States, a state of peace toward Britain." As chairman of the House Foreign Relations Committee, however, John C. Calhoun was less circumspect: "The mad ambition, the lust of power, and the commercial avarice of Great Britain have left to neutral nations an alternative only between the base surrender of their rights, and a manly vindication of them." He then introduced a war bill in Congress.

The Battle of Tippecanoe

Many Americans today think that Indians never really mattered in the nation's history. This modern dismissal of Indian significance is entirely incorrect. For years before the Battle of Tippecanoe, William Henry Harrison warned officials in Washington that if Tecumseh was successful he almost certainly would stop American westward expansion. This was not baseless exaggeration. As Harrison himself said of Tecumseh, "He is one of those uncommon geniuses, which spring up occasionally to produce revolutions and overturn the established order of things." We will never know how close Tecumseh came to overturning the established order. We do know that he experienced considerable success in raising a unified defense, and there is no question that such a unified force would have compelled politicians like Jefferson to reconsider their policies. Undoubtedly, America today would be a profoundly different place had Harrison not destroyed Prophetstown and undermined the growing Indian confederacy.

- How might the Jefferson administration have dealt differently with the demands made by Tecumseh and his allies? In what ways would the United States be different today had this alternative course been followed?
- Since the early nineteenth century, the United States has encountered resistance to national expansion on a number of fronts. Choose another situation from later in the nation's history in which such resistance was dealt with. What similarities or differences, or both, do you see between this event and the handling of Tecumseh's resistance movement?

When the vote was finally cast in 1812, the war bill passed 79 to 49 in the House and 19 to 13 in the Senate. Although they seemed to have the most to lose from continued indecisive policies, representatives from the heavily Federalist regions that depended the most on overseas trade—Massachusetts, Connecticut, and New York, for example—voted against war, whereas strongly Republican western and southern representatives voted in favor.

THE NATION AT WAR

With its woefully neglected army and navy, the United States was taking a terrible risk in engaging Britain, a nation that was fast becoming the most awesome military power in the world. Not surprisingly, defeat and humiliation were the main fruits of American efforts as the two nations faced off.

The Fighting Begins

Despite years of agitation, the war's actual arrival in 1812 caught the United States terribly unprepared. Republican cost cutting had virtually disbanded the military during Jefferson's first term in office. Renewed fighting with pirates in the Mediterranean and building tensions in the Atlantic had forced Republicans to increase military spending, but the navy still had fewer than twenty vessels, and the army could field fewer than seven thousand men. And for all its war fever, Congress balked at appropriating new funds even after war had been declared. Thus the first ventures in the war went forward with only grudging financial support.

In line with what the War Hawks wanted, the first military campaign was a three-pronged drive toward Canada and against the Indians. One force, commanded by Harrison, successfully raided undefended Indian villages but was unable to make any gains against British troops. Farther east, a force led by Major General Stephen Van Rensselaer was defeated by a small British and Indian army. Meanwhile, the third force, commanded by Henry Dearborn, lunged at Montreal but nervously withdrew back into U.S. territory after an inconclusive battle against the British.

American sailors fared much better during the war's opening days. Leading the war effort at sea were three frigates: the *Constitution* (popularly known as **Old Ironsides**), the *President,* and the *United States.* In mid-August, the *Constitution* outmaneuvered and eventually captured what the British described as "one of our stoutest frigates," the H.M.S. *Guerrière.* The *United States,* under the command of Stephen Decatur, both endured and delivered horrific broadsides while subduing the British *Macedonian.* The carnage Decatur described when he boarded the crippled vessel was typical of naval warfare at the time: "fragments of the dead scattered in every direction, the decks slippery with blood." American privateers also enjoyed success, capturing 450 British merchant ships valued in the millions during the first six months of the war.

American naval victories were all that kept the nation's morale alive in 1812. Former Treasury secretary Albert Gallatin summarized the nation's humiliating military efforts: "The series of misfortunes exceeds all anticipations made even by those who had least confidence in our inexperienced officers and undisciplined men." The land war had been, as another politician recalled, a "miscarriage, without even the heroism of disaster." Vowing to reverse the situation, Congress increased the size of the army to fifty-seven thousand men and offered a $16 bonus to encourage enlistments.

Thus in 1812 Madison stood for reelection at a time when the nation's military fate appeared uncertain and his own leadership equally so. Although the majority of his party's congressional caucus supported him for reelection, nearly a third of the Republican congressmen—mostly those from New York and New England—rallied around New Yorker DeWitt Clinton. Like his uncle George Clinton, DeWitt Clinton was a Republican who favored Federalist economic policies and agreed with New England Federalists that the war was unnecessary. Most Federalists supported Clinton, and the party did not field a candidate of its own.

The campaign's outcome mirrored the congressional vote on the war bill earlier in the year. New York and New England rallied behind Clinton. The South and West continued to support Madison, the Republicans, and war. Madison won, but his share of electoral votes had fallen from 72 percent in 1808 to 58.9 percent. At the same time, Republican Party strength in the House dropped by over 13 percent, and in the Senate by about 8 percent.

**The War
Continues**

When military campaigning resumed in the spring of 1813, it appeared that the U.S. Army would fare as badly as it had the previous fall. Fighting resumed when British colonel Henry Proctor and Tecumseh, with a joint force of nine hundred British soldiers and twelve hundred Indians, laid siege to Harrison's command camped at Fort Meigs on the Maumee Rapids in Ohio. An army of twelve hundred Kentucky militiamen finally arrived and drove the enemy off but were so disorganized that they lost nearly half their number in pursuing the British and Indian force. Harrison was shocked, proclaiming the Kentuckians' "excessive ardour scarcely less fatal than cowardice." Having escaped virtually unscathed, Proctor and Tecumseh continued to harass American forces through the summer. Then, with winter approaching, the British and Indians withdrew to Canada. Harrison, who had been busy raising additional troops, decided to pursue.

No doubt Harrison's new effort would have proved as fruitless as his earlier ones, but an unexpected event turned the odds in his favor. One key problem plaguing Harrison and other commanders in the field was that the British controlled the Great Lakes and so could depend on an uninterrupted supply line. In contrast, American forces and their supplies moved along undeveloped roads and were easy targets for Indian and British attackers. **Oliver Hazard Perry**, a young naval tactician, had been given command of a small fleet assigned to clear the lakes of British ships. He got his chance at Put-in-Bay on Lake Erie in September 1813. Two hours of cannon fire left Perry's **flagship**, the *Lawrence,* nearly destroyed, and 80 percent of the crew lay dead or wounded. Perry refused to surrender. He slipped off his damaged vessel and took command of another ship standing nearby. What remained of his command then sailed back into the heart of the British force and after three hours of close combat subdued and captured six British ships. Perry immediately sent a note to Harrison stating, "We have met the enemy and they are ours."

Buoyed by this news, Harrison's army closed in on Proctor and Tecumseh at the Thames River, about 50 miles northeast of Detroit, on October 5. The British force faced a piercing cavalry charge and, lacking naval support, abandoned their Indian allies and fled. The Indians held out longer, but when Tecumseh was shot and killed in battle, they melted into the woods, leaving the body of their fallen leader to be mutilated by the victorious Americans.

Another war front had also opened farther south during 1813. Although the Creek Confederacy as a whole wished to remain neutral, one faction calling themselves the Red Sticks had allied with Tecumseh in 1812. In the summer of 1813, Red Stick leader William Weatherford led a force against Fort Mims, killing all but about thirty of the more than three hundred occupants. The so-called Fort Mims massacre enraged whites in the Southeast. In Tennessee, twenty-five hundred militiamen rallied around **Andrew Jackson**, a young brawler and Indian fighter. Already called "Old Hickory" because of his toughness, Jackson made a bold promise: "The blood of our women & children shall not call for

flagship   The ship that carries the fleet commander and bears the commander's flag.

vengeance in vain." In the course of that summer and fall, Jackson's frontier ruffians fought multiple engagements against the Red Stick Creeks, driving them into hiding.

While these battles raged on land, the British shut down American forces at sea. Embarrassed by the success of Old Ironsides and the other American frigates, the British admiralty ordered that "the naval force of the enemy should be quickly and completely disposed of" and sent sufficient ships to do the job. The American naval fleet and **merchant marine** found themselves bottled up in port by the world's strongest navy.

The Politics of War   The war had wound down for the winter by the time Congress reconvened in December 1813, but the outlook was not good. President Madison tried to be optimistic. Recalling the victories during the year, he said, "The war, with its **vicissitudes**, is illustrating the capacity and destiny of the United States to be a great, a flourishing, and a powerful nation." Madison's optimism seemed justified later in December when the British offered to open direct peace negotiations with the Americans. The president quickly formed a peace commission, but until its work was done, Madison and Congress still had to worry about the practical issues of troops and money, both of which were in critically short supply.

Despite increases in army pay and bonuses for new recruits, enlistments were falling off in 1813. Congressional Republicans responded by adding further enticements, including grants of 160 acres of land in the western territories. Congress also authorized the president to extend the term of enlistment for men already in service. By 1814, the army had increased to more than sixty-two thousand men but Congress had not figured out how to pay them.

Traditional enemies of internal taxes, the Republicans faced a dilemma: in the federal budget for 1814 the government's income would be approximately $16 million, but its expenses would amount to over $45 million. Congress had already passed a set of new taxes and could not imagine explaining another increase to their constituents. So congressional Republicans decided to borrow instead, authorizing a $35 million deficit.

Adding to the money problem, the United States, to this point in the war, had permitted neutral nations to trade freely in American ports, carrying American exports to England and Canada and English goods into eastern U.S. ports. As a result American food was rolling directly into British military commissaries, strengthening the enemy's ability and will to fight.

In a secret message to Congress, the president proposed an absolute embargo on all American ships and goods—neither were to leave port. Federalists, especially those from New England, screamed in protest. They called the proposal "an engine of tyranny." But congressional Republicans passed the embargo a mere eight days

merchant marine A nation's commercial ships.

vicissitudes Sudden or unexpected changes in circumstances.

after Madison submitted it. What emerged, the **Embargo of 1813**, was the most far-reaching trade restriction bill ever passed by Congress. It confined all trading ships to port, and even fishing vessels could put to sea only if their masters posted sizable **bonds**. Government officials charged with enforcing the new law had unprecedented **discretionary powers**. The impact was devastating: the embargo virtually shut down the New England and New York economies, and it severely crippled the economy of nearly every other state.

New British Offensives   While Congress debated matters of finance and trade restrictions, events in Europe were changing the entire character of the war. On March 31, 1814, the British and their allies took Paris, forcing Napoleon to abdicate his throne. Napoleon's defeat left the United States as Great Britain's sole military target. Republican Joseph Nicholson expressed a common lament when he observed, "We should have to fight hereafter not for 'free Trade and sailors rights,' not for the Conquest of the Canadas, but for our national Existence." As Nicholson feared, a flood of combat-hardened British veterans began arriving in North America, and the survival of the United States as an independent nation was indeed at issue. By the late summer of 1814, British troop strength in Canada had risen to thirty thousand men. From this position of power, the British prepared a chain of three offensives to bring the war to a quick end.

In the first of these, twenty British warships and several troop transports sailed up Chesapeake Bay toward Washington, D.C. The British arrived outside Washington at midday on August 24. The troops defending the city could not withstand the force of hardened British veterans, but they slowed the invasion long enough for the government to escape. Angered at being foiled, the British sacked the city, torching most of the buildings. They then moved on toward the key port city of Baltimore.

At Baltimore, the British navy had to knock out Fort McHenry and take the harbor before the army could take the city. On September 13, British ships armed with heavy **mortars** and rockets attacked the fort. Despite the pounding, when the sun rose on September 14, the American flag continued to wave over Fort McHenry. The sight moved a young prisoner of war held on a British ship, **Francis Scott Key**, to record the event in a poem that was later set to music and became the national anthem of the United States. Having failed to reduce the fort, the British were forced to withdraw, leaving Baltimore undisturbed.

While this strike at the nation's midsection was raging, Sir George Prevost, governor-general of Canada, massed ten thousand troops for an invasion in the

bond   A sum of money paid as bail or security.

discretionary powers   Powers to be used at one's own judgment; in government, powers given to an administrative official to be used without outside consultation or oversight.

mortar   A portable, muzzle-loading cannon that fires large projectiles; traditionally used against fixed fortifications.

© Bettmann/Corbis

In frustration at failing to capture members of the U.S. government, the British pillaged Washington in August 1814 and then burned the public buildings. This painting captures the disordered scene as city-dwellers try to quench the flames while the capitol building blazes in the background.

north. The British force arrived just north of Plattsburgh, New York, on September 6, where it was to join the British naval fleet that controlled Lake Champlain. However, a small American flotilla under the command of Lieutenant Thomas Macdonough outmaneuvered the imposing British armada and forced a surrender on September 11. Prevost had already begun his attack against the defenders at Plattsburgh, but when he learned that the British lake fleet was defeated, he lost his nerve and ordered his men to retreat.

On yet another front, the British pressed an offensive against the Gulf Coast designed to take pressure off Canada and close transportation on the Mississippi River. The defense of the Gulf Coast fell to Andrew Jackson and his Tennesseans. Having spent the winter raising troops and collecting supplies, in March 1814 Jackson and his army of four thousand militiamen and Cherokee volunteers resumed their mission to punish the Red Stick Creeks. Learning that the Red Sticks had established a camp on the peninsula formed by a bend in the Tallapoosa River, Jackson led his men on a forced march to attack. On March 27 in what was misleadingly called the **Battle of Horseshoe Bend**, Jackson's force trapped the Creeks and slaughtered nearly eight hundred people, destroying Red Stick opposition and severely crippling Indian resistance in the South.

After the massacre at Horseshoe Bend, Jackson moved his army toward the Gulf of Mexico, where a British offensive was in the making. Arriving in New Orleans on December 1, he found the city ill prepared to defend itself. The local militia, consisting mostly of French and Spanish residents, would not obey American officers. "Those who are not for us are against us, and will be dealt with accordingly," Jackson proclaimed. He turned increasingly to unconventional sources of support. Free blacks in the city formed a regular army corps, and Jackson created a special unit of black refugees from Saint-Domingue. He also accepted a company of river pirates under the command of **Jean Lafitte**, awarding them a blanket pardon for all past crimes. "Hellish Banditti," Jackson himself called them, but the pirate commander and the general hit it off so well that Lafitte became Jackson's constant companion during the campaign.

Having pulled his ragtag force together, Jackson settled in to wait for the British attack. On the morning of January 8, 1815, it came. The British force, commanded by General Edward Pakenham, emerged from the fog at dawn, directly in front of Jackson's defenses. Waiting patiently behind hastily constructed barricades, Jackson's men began firing cannon, rifles, and muskets as the British moved within range. According to one British veteran, it was "the most murderous fire I have ever beheld before or since."

When it was all over, more than two thousand British troops had been killed or wounded in the **Battle of New Orleans**. This was by far the most successful battle fought by American forces during the War of 1812. But ironically, it was fought after the war was over.

The War's Strange Conclusion   While the British were closing in on Washington in the summer of 1814, treaty negotiations designed to end the war were beginning in Ghent, Belgium. Confident that their three-pronged attack against the United States would soon knock the Americans out of the war, the British delegates were in no hurry to end it by diplomacy. They refused to discuss substantive issues, insisting that all of the matters raised by Madison's peace commission were nonnegotiable.

At that point, however, domestic politics in England began to play a deciding role. After nearly a generation of armed conflict, British taxpayers were war weary. As one official put it, "Economy & relief from taxation ... are the real objects to which public attention is turned." The failures at Plattsburgh and Baltimore made it appear that the war would drag on at least another year, adding another $44 million to the British tax burden. Moreover, continuation of the American war was interfering with Britain's European diplomacy: "We do not think the Continental Powers will continue in good humour with our Blockade of the whole Coast of America," one British diplomat observed. Speaking for the military, the **Duke of Wellington** reviewed British military successes and failures in the American war and advised his countrymen, "You have no right ... to demand any **concession** ... from America."

In the end, the **Treaty of Ghent**, completed on December 24, 1814, simply restored diplomatic relations between England and the United States to what they had been prior to the outbreak of war. The treaty said nothing about impressment, blockades, or neutral trading rights. Neither military action nor diplomatic finagling netted Canada for the War Hawks. And the treaty did nothing about the alleged conspiracies between Indians and British agents. Although Americans called the War of 1812 a victory, they actually won none of the prizes that Madison's war statement had declared the nation was fighting for.

PEACE AND THE RISE OF NEW EXPECTATIONS

Despite repeated military disasters, loss of life, and diplomatic failure, the war had a number of positive effects on the United States. Just to have survived a war against the British was enough to build national confidence, but to have scored major victories such as those at Plattsburgh, Baltimore, and especially New Orleans was truly worth boasting about. Americans emerged from the conflict with a new sense of national pride and purpose. And many side effects from the fighting itself gave Americans new hopes and stimulated new plans.

New Expectations in the Northeastern Economy   Although trading interests in the Northeast suffered following Jefferson's embargo and were nearly ruined by the war and Madison's embargo, a new avenue of economic expansion opened in New England: cut off from European manufactured goods, Americans started to make more textiles and other items for themselves.

Samuel Slater, an English immigrant who had been trained in manufacturing in Britain, introduced the use of machines for spinning cotton yarn to the United States in 1790. His mill was financially successful, but few others tried to copy his enterprise. Even with shipping expenses, tariffs, and other added costs, buying and selling machine-made British cloth was still more practical than investing large sums at high risk to build competing factories in the United States. And after 1800, Jefferson's economic policies discouraged such investment. But his embargo changed all that. After it went into effect in 1808, British fabrics became increasingly unavailable, and prices soared. Slater and his partners moved quickly to expand their spinning operations to fill the void. And now his inventiveness was widely copied.

---

concession   Something given up during negotiations.

Another entrepreneur, Francis Cabot Lowell, went even further than Slater. On a trip to England in 1810, he engaged in wholesale industrial espionage, making detailed notes and sketches of British textile-manufacturing practices and machinery. Returning to the United States just before war broke out in 1812, Lowell formed the Boston Manufacturing Company. In 1813 the company used the plans Lowell had smuggled back to the United States to build a factory in Waltham, Massachusetts. The new facility included spinning machines, power looms, and all the equipment necessary to **mechanize** every stage in the production of finished cloth, bringing the entire process under one roof. Like Slater's innovations, Lowell's too were soon duplicated by economically desperate New Englanders.

The spread of textile manufacturing was astonishing. Prior to 1808, only fifteen cotton mills had been built in the entire country. But between the passage of the embargo and the end of 1809, eighty-seven additional mills had sprung up, mostly in New England. And when war came, the pace increased, especially when Lowell's idea of a factory mechanizing production through finished cloth proved to be highly efficient and profitable. The number of people employed in manufacturing increased from four thousand in 1809 to perhaps as many as a hundred thousand in 1816. In the years to come, factories in New England and elsewhere supplied more and more of the country's consumer goods.

New Opportunities in the West

Different kinds of development took place in the West following the war. Settlers poured into western regions in astounding numbers. The population of Ohio had already soared from 45,000 in 1800 to 231,000 in 1810, but it more than doubled again by 1820, reaching 581,000. Indiana, Illinois, Missouri, and Michigan experienced similar growth. Most of those who flooded into the newly opened West were small farmers, but subsistence agriculture was not the only economic opportunity that drew expectant Americans into the region.

One of the designs behind the Lewis and Clark expedition had been to gain entry for the United States into the burgeoning economy in North America's interior. That economy was complex, with many commodities being traded, and few entirely understood all of its intricacies. There was one facet, though, that was well known and very desirable to entrepreneurs: the brown gold of beaver, otter, and other animal furs. Even before the War of 1812, John Jacob Astor, a German immigrant, announced that he intended to establish "a range of Posts or Trading houses" along the route that Lewis and Clark had followed from St. Louis to the Pacific.

Another visionary entrepreneur sought a similar fortune in the Southwest. Auguste Chouteau was French by birth, but like many frontiersmen, he changed nationalities as frequently as the borderlands changed owners. Chouteau had helped to found the town of St. Louis and had been instrumental in establishing that city as the capital for a fur-trading empire. He, his brother Pierre, and an extended family of business partners used intermarriage to create a massive kinship

mechanize   To substitute machinery for human labor.

This portrait by noted American painter Gilbert Stuart captures the young (31 years old) and energetic John Jacob Astor. Totally unlike the stereotype of the wild mountain man, Astor combined entrepreneurial daring with sound financial planning to build a fortune based on the fur trade. By the time of his death in 1848, he was the richest man in America.

© Christie's Images/The Bridgeman Art Library International

network that included important French, Spanish, and Indian connections. The Chouteaus were able to extend their reach deep into the Missouri region and establish trade between St. Louis and the Spanish far western trading capital at Santa Fe. As Americans began to penetrate the area, the Chouteaus took the change in stride, inviting William Clark of the Corps of Discovery and fur entrepreneur Andrew Henry to join forces with them in founding the Missouri Fur Company in 1809.

The war disrupted both Astor's and the Missouri Fur Company's operations, but when the war was over, the fur business resumed with increasing vigor. Pierre Chouteau and his various American partners pushed continually farther into the West, using their strategy of forming traditional Indian trading partnerships, often rooted in intermarriage, to expand business. Chouteau also used his kin partnerships and capital from the fur trade to branch into other businesses. He was a cofounder of the Bank of Missouri and served as its president for a number of years. He also operated flour mills and distilleries and speculated in real estate. Members of his extended family later helped to found Kansas City, pioneered mining in Colorado, and financed railroad building in the Dakotas.

Such economic expansion into the West posed a terrible threat to Native Americans. When Harrison's soldiers burned Prophetstown and later killed Tecumseh, they wiped out all hopes for a pan-Indian confederacy. In addition, the civil war among the Creeks, followed by Jackson's victories against the Red Stick faction, removed all meaningful resistance to westward expansion in the South. Many Indian groups continued to wield great power, but accommodationist leaders increasingly suggested that cooperation with federal authorities was the best course. Collaboration helped to prevent renewed warfare, but at enormous cost to the Indians. Within a year of the Battle of Horseshoe Bend, Jackson forced the Creeks to sign the Treaty of Fort Jackson, which confiscated over 20 million acres of land from the Creek Confederacy.

A similar but more gradual assault on Indian landholding began in the Northwest in 1815. In a council meeting at Portage des Sioux in Illinois Territory, the United States signed peace accords with the various tribes that had joined the British during the war. Both sides pledged to live in "perpetual peace and friendship," but the northwestern Indians possessed some 2 million acres of prime real estate between the Illinois and Mississippi Rivers—land that the U.S. government had already given away as enlistment bonuses to white war volunteers. Moving the Indians off that land as quickly as possible thus became a matter of national priority.

Over the next several years, **federal Indian agents** used every tactic they could think of to coerce groups like the Kickapoo Indians into ceding their lands. Finally, in 1819, the Kickapoo Nation signed the Treaty of Edwardsville, turning over most of the land the United States had demanded. Having secured this massive tract, government agents then turned their attention to the vast holdings of more distant tribes—the Sauk, Fox, Chippewa, and Dakota Indians in western Illinois, Wisconsin, and Michigan. As they had done with the Kickapoos, American negotiators used bribery, threat, and manipulation of local tensions to pursue their goal, eventually winning an enormous cession of land in the Prairie du Chien treaties of 1825.

A Revolution in the Southern Economy   Indian dispossession and westward expansion also promised great economic growth for the South. In the years before the War of 1812, the southern economy had been sluggish, and the future of the region's single-crop agricultural system was doubtful. However, the technological and economic changes that came in the war's wake pumped new energy into the South. In only a few decades, an entirely new South emerged.

The mechanization of the British textile industry in the late eighteenth century created an enormous new demand for cotton. Southern planters had been growing the plant and harvesting its fibrous **cotton bolls** since colonial times, but soil and climatic conditions limited the growing area for the sort of **long-staple cotton** that could be harvested and sold economically. Large areas of the South and Southwest had proved suitable for growing **short-staple cotton**, but the time and labor required to pick the sticky seeds from the compact bolls made the crop unprofitable. In 1793 a young Yale College graduate, **Eli Whitney**, was a guest at a plantation in Georgia where he learned about the difficulty of removing the seeds from short-staple cotton. In a matter of weeks, Whitney helped to perfect a machine

cotton boll   The pod of the cotton plant; it contains the plant's seeds surrounded by the fluffy fiber that is spun into yarn.

long-staple cotton   A variety of cotton with long and loosely packed bolls of fiber that is easy to comb out and process.

short-staple cotton   A variety of cotton with short and tightly packed bolls of fiber in which the plant's seeds are tangled.

that allowed a small and unskilled work force to quickly comb out the seeds without damaging the fibers.

The outcome of Whitney's inventiveness was the rapid spread of short-staple cotton throughout inland South Carolina and Georgia. Then, just as it seemed that the southern economy was about to bloom, embargo and war closed down exports to England. Although some cotton growers were able to shift sales from England to the rising new factories in New England, a true explosion of growth in cotton cultivation had to await war's end.

With the arrival of peace and the departure of the British naval blockade, cotton growing began to spread at an astounding rate. Southerners rushed into frontier areas, spreading cotton agriculture into Alabama and Mississippi and then into Arkansas and northern Louisiana. Even the Mississippi River seemed to present no serious barrier to this runaway expansion. In 1821 Spanish authorities gave long-time western land speculator Moses Austin permission to settle three hundred American families within a 200,000-acre tract in Texas between the Brazos and Colorado Rivers. When the elder Austin died, his son, **Stephen F. Austin**, took over the enterprise and was able to offer families large plots of land for a filing fee of only 12½ cents an acre. "I am convinced," he exclaimed, "that I could take on fifteen hundred families as easily as three hundred if permitted to do so." Throughout the 1820s and 1830s, Austin and other *empresarios* helped thousands of hopeful cotton capitalists to expand into Mexican territory. As a result of this expansion, the South's annual cotton crop grew by leaps and bounds. By 1840, annual exports reached nearly a million and a half bales, and increasing volumes were consumed within the United States by the mushrooming textile factories in the Northeast.

Reviving and Reinventing Slavery

Before the emergence of cotton, when the South's agricultural system was foundering, many southerners began to question the use of slaves. In 1784 Thomas Jefferson proposed (but saw defeated) a land ordinance that would have prohibited slavery in all of the nation's territories after 1800. Some southern leaders advocated abolishing slavery and transporting freed blacks to Africa. But the booming southern economy after the War of 1812 required more labor than ever. As a result, African American slavery expanded as never before.

Viewed side by side, a map showing cotton agriculture and one showing slave population would appear nearly identical. In the 1820s, when cotton production was most heavily concentrated in South Carolina and Georgia, the greatest density of slaves occurred in the same area. During the 1840s, as cotton growing spread to the West, slavery followed. By 1860, both cotton growing and slavery formed a continuous belt stretching from the Carolinas through Georgia and Alabama and on to the Mississippi River.

The virtually universal shift to cotton growing throughout the South brought about not only the expansion and extension of slavery but also substantial

---

empresario   In the Spanish colonies, a person who organized and led a group of settlers in exchange for land grants and the right to assess fees.

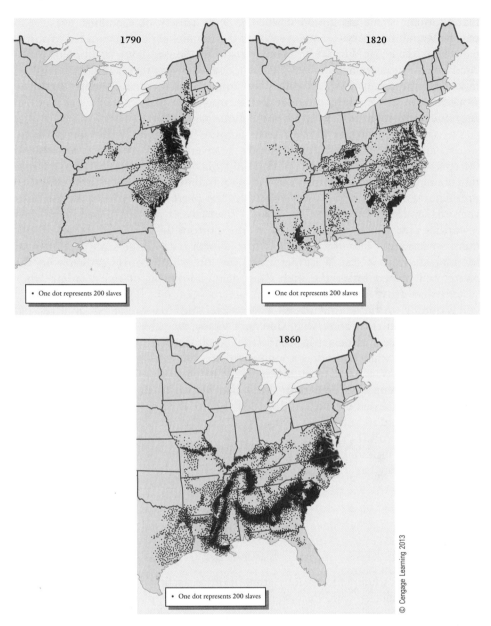

MAP 9.2 Distribution of Slave Population, 1790, 1820, and 1860

In 1790, slaves were concentrated in the Chesapeake and in the South Carolina and Georgia lowcountry. Over the next 70 years, Chesapeake planters put thousands of slaves into the interstate trade, which stretched from the interior of the Carolinas to East Texas.

modifications to the institution itself. The wide variety of economic pursuits in which slave labor had been employed from the colonial period onward led to varied patterns in slave employment. In many parts of the South, slaves traditionally exercised a great deal of control over their work schedules as they completed assigned tasks. But the cotton business called for large gangs of predominantly unskilled workers, and increasingly slaves found themselves regimented like machines in tempo with the demands of cotton production.

At the same time, as northeastern factories were able to provide clothing, shoes, and other manufactured goods at ever more attractive prices and western farmers shipped cheap pork and grain into southern markets, plantation managers found it more practical to purchase such goods rather than to produce them. Thus slaves who formerly had performed various skilled tasks such as milling and weaving found themselves pressed into much less rewarding service as brute labor in the cotton fields. To a large extent, then, specialized manufacturing in the North and large-scale commercial food production in the West permitted an intensified cotton industry in the South and helped foster the increasing dehumanization of the peculiar labor system that drove it.

Naturally, African Americans—both slave and free—resented and resisted increasingly strict conditions. One, **Denmark Vesey**, was able to buy his freedom in 1799 and became a carpenter in Charleston, South Carolina. Over the next two decades, however, white authorities continually harassed Vesey and the African American community: in 1818 and again in 1820 they closed down the African Methodist Episcopal Church that Vesey had helped to build. Angered, in July 1822 Vesey organized a rebellion designed to seize the city of Charleston, but the plot was reported to authorities, who arrested and charged 131 free and enslaved alleged conspirators. In the end, sixty-seven were found guilty, of whom thirty-five were executed, including Vesey. As with Gabriel's Rebellion two decades earlier, Vesey's conspiracy terrorized whites and led to even greater restrictions in the years to come.

STUDY TOOLS

SUMMARY

After Jefferson's triumphal first four years in office, factional disputes at home and diplomatic deadlocks with European powers began to plague the Republicans. Although the Federalists were in full retreat, many within Jefferson's own party rebelled against some of his policies. When Jefferson decided not to run for office in 1808, tapping James Madison as his successor, Republicans in both the Northeast and the South bucked the president, supporting George Clinton and James Monroe, respectively.

To a large extent, the Republicans' problems were the outcome of external stresses. On the Atlantic frontier, the United States tried to remain neutral in the wars that engulfed Europe. On the western frontier, the Prophet and Tecumseh were successfully unifying dispossessed Indians into an alliance devoted to stopping U.S. expansion. Things went from bad to worse when Jefferson's use of economic sanctions gave rise to the worst economic depression since the beginnings of English colonization. The embargo strangled the economy in port cities, and the downward spiral in agricultural prices threatened to bankrupt many in the West and South.

The combination of economic and diplomatic constraints brought aggressive politicians to power in 1808 and 1810. Men such as William Henry Harrison expected that war with England would permit the United States finally to realize independence—forcing freedom of the seas, eliminating Indian resistance, and justifying the conquest of the rest of North America. Despite Madison's continuing peace efforts, southern and western interests finally pushed the nation into war with England in 1812.

Although some glimmering moments of glory heartened the Americans, the war was mostly disastrous. But after generations of fighting one enemy or another, the English people demanded peace. When their final offensive in America failed to bring immediate victory in 1814, the British chose to negotiate. Finally, on Christmas Eve, the two nations signed the Treaty of Ghent, ending the war. From a diplomatic point of view, it was as though the war had never happened.

Nevertheless, in the United States the war created strong feelings of national pride and confidence, and Americans looked forward to even better things to come. In the Northeast, entrepreneurs explored new industries, creating the first stage of an industrial revolution in the country. In the West, the defeat of Indian resistance combined with bright economic opportunities to trigger a wave of westward migration. In the South, the economy was revolutionized by the cotton gin and the growing demand for fiber among English and then American manufacturers. Throughout the country, economic progress promised to improve life for most Americans, but as before, both African Americans and Native Americans bore much of the cost.

CHRONOLOGY

DOMESTIC EXPANSION AND INTERNATIONAL CRISIS

1794	Eli Whitney perfects the cotton gin
1803	Britain steps up impressments
1804	Duel in which Aaron Burr kills Alexander Hamilton
	Jefferson reelected
1807	Burr conspiracy trial
	Prophetstown founded amid Shawnee religious revival
	Chesapeake affair
1808	Embargo of 1808
	Economic depression begins
	James Madison elected president
1809	Non-Intercourse Act
	Fort Wayne Treaty
	Chouteau brothers form Missouri Fur Company

1810	Macon's Bill No. 2
	Vincennes Conference between Harrison and Tecumseh
	War Hawk faction forms
1811	United States suspends trade with Britain
	Battle of Tippecanoe destroys Prophetstown
1812	United States declares war against England, invades Canada
	James Madison reelected
1813	Fort Mims massacre
	Embargo of 1813
	First mechanized textile factory, Waltham, Massachusetts
1814	Battle of Horseshoe Bend
	British burn Washington, D.C.
	Treaty of Ghent
1815	Battle of New Orleans
	Treaty of Fort Jackson
	Portage des Sioux treaties
1819	Treaty of Edwardsville
1825	Prairie du Chien treaties

Focus Questions

If you have mastered this chapter, you should be able to answer these questions and explain the terms that follow the questions.

1. How did varying regional interests complicate Jefferson's political situation during his second term as president?
2. How did European politics affect the American economy between 1804 and 1808?
3. How did Jefferson's economic and Indian policies influence national developments after 1808?
4. How did problems in Europe, coupled with the actions of frontier politicians such as William Henry Harrison, lead the nation into war in 1812?
5. What geographic and economic factors impeded American war efforts?
6. What part did events in Europe and Britain play in ending the war and what were the results from Americans' point of view?
7. How did events during the War of 1812 help to move the American economy in new directions after peace was restored?
8. How did changes in the economy affect the institution of slavery and the lives of slaves?

Key Terms

Essex Junto (*p.* 227)

John Randolph (*p.* 227)

Yazoo affair (*p.* 227)

Tertium Quid (*p.* 227)

impressment (*p.* 229)

Berlin Decree (*p.* 229)

Milan Decree (*p.* 230)

Embargo Act (*p.* 230)

James Monroe (*p.* 232)

War Hawks (*p.* 232)

The Prophet (*p.* 233)

Non-Intercourse Act (*p.* 234)

Macon's Bill No. 2 (*p.* 234)

Battle of Tippecanoe (*p.* 235)

Old Ironsides (*p.* 238)

Oliver Hazard Perry (*p.* 239)

Andrew Jackson (*p.* 239)

Embargo of 1813 (*p.* 241)

Francis Scott Key (*p.* 241)

Battle of Horseshoe Bend (*p.* 243)

Jean Lafitte (*p.* 243)

Battle of New Orleans (*p.* 243)

Duke of Wellington (*p.* 244)

Treaty of Ghent (*p.* 244)

federal Indian agents (*p.* 247)

Eli Whitney (*p.* 247)

Stephen F. Austin (*p.* 248)

Denmark Vesey (*p.* 250)

10

THE RISE OF A NEW NATION,
1815–1836

CHAPTER OUTLINE

• An "Era of Good Feelings" • Dynamic Growth and Political
Consequences • The "New Man" in Politics • The Reign of "King
Andrew" • Study Tools

AN "ERA OF GOOD FEELINGS"

James Madison had been the butt of jokes and the cause of dissension within his
own party during the War of 1812, but he emerged from the war with considerable
political clout. Although his fellow Republicans considered his wartime policies
indecisive, after the war Madison immediately seized the political initiative to inau-
gurate vigorous new diplomatic and domestic programs. His successor, James
Monroe, then picked up the beat, pressing on with a new nationalistic Republican
agenda. The nationalism that arose after the war seemed to bring political dissension to a close; a Federalist newspaper in Boston proclaimed the dawn of an
"Era of Good Feelings."

**The "American
System" and
New Economic
Direction**

The nation was much more unified politically in 1815 than it
had been for years. The war's outcome and the growth that
began to take place immediately following the peace
settlement had largely silenced Madison's critics within the
Republican Party. And during the waning days of the war,
extreme Federalists had so embarrassed their party that they were at a severe
political disadvantage.

The Essex Junto was primarily responsible for the Federalists' embarrassment.
The junto had capitalized on the many military blunders and growing national debt
to cast Republicans in a bad light and was drawing increasing support in the
Northeast. In mid-December 1814 they staged the **Hartford Convention**, voting to

secede from the Union unless Congress repealed the Embargo of 1813 and passed the slate of constitutional reforms the junto had been pushing since its formation. However, many viewed the Federalists' efforts as either foolish or treasonous, and party popularity underwent a steep decline.

Facing no meaningful opposition, Madison chose in December 1815 to launch an aggressive new domestic policy. He challenged Congress to correct the economic ills that had caused the depression and helped to propel the nation into war. He also encouraged the states to invest in the nation's future by financing transportation systems and other internal improvements. Former critics such as **DeWitt Clinton, Henry Clay**, and **John C. Calhoun** quickly rallied behind the president and his nationalistic economic and political agenda.

Clay took the lead. He had come to Congress as one of the War Hawks in 1810 and had quickly become the dominant voice among the younger representatives. Born in Virginia in 1777, Clay had moved to the wilds of Kentucky to practice law and carve out a career in politics. He was fantastically successful, becoming Speaker of the Kentucky state assembly when he was only 30 years old and winning a seat in the House of Representatives four years later. He became Speaker of the House during the prewar crisis. Now aligning himself firmly with the new economic agenda, Clay became its champion, calling it the **American System**.

What congressional Republicans had in mind was to create a national market economy. In the colonial period and increasingly thereafter, local market economies grew up around the trading and manufacturing centers of the Northeast. Individuals in these areas produced single items for cash sale and used the cash they earned to purchase goods produced by others. Specialization was the natural outcome. Farmers, for example, chose to grow only one or two crops and to sell the whole harvest for cash, which they used to buy various items they had once raised or made for themselves. Clay and others wanted to see such interdependence on a much larger scale. They envisioned a time when whole regions would specialize in producing commodities for which the geography, climate, and the temperament of the people was most suitable. Agricultural regions in the West, for example, would produce food for the industrializing Northeast and the fiber-producing South. The North would depend on the South for efficiently produced cotton, and both South and West would depend on the Northeast for manufactured goods. Advocates of the American System were confident that the balance eventually established among regions would free the nation as a whole from economic dependence on Europe.

Nationalists recognized that one of the first steps in bringing all this about would have to be a national banking authority. Republicans had persistently opposed the Bank of the United States and had killed it in 1811, but the postwar call for a unified national economy prompted Republicans to press again for a national currency and for a national bank to regulate its circulation. In 1816 Calhoun introduced legislation chartering a Second Bank of the United States, which Congress approved overwhelmingly. The Second Bank had many of the same powers and responsibilities as the first. Congress provided

$7 million of its $35 million in opening capital and appointed one-fifth of its board of directors. The Second Bank opened for business in Philadelphia on January 1, 1817.

Proponents also saw improvements in transportation and communications as essential. Announcing that they would "bind the republic together with a perfect system of roads and canals," Republicans in Congress put forward a series of proposals designed to achieve this result.

Finally, they advocated **protective tariffs** to help the fledgling industries that had hatched during the war. Helped by the embargoes, American cotton-spinning plants had increased rapidly between 1808 and 1815. But with the return of open trade at war's end, British merchants dumped accumulated inventories of cotton and woolen cloth onto the U.S. market. Although some New

"Travel by Stagecoach Near Trenton, New Jersey" by Pavel Petrovich Svinin (1787/88–1839), 1811–ca. 1813. Watercolor, gouache, and pen and ink on off-white wove paper, 6 7/8 × 9 13/16 in. (17.5 × 24.9 cm). Rogers Fund, 1942 (42.95.11), the Metropolitan Museum of Art, New York, NY, U.S.A. Image © The Metropolitan Museum of Art/Art Resource, NY

Before the transportation revolution, traveling was highly risky and uncomfortable. This painting shows a rather stylish stagecoach, but its well-dressed passengers are clearly being jostled. Note how the man in the front seat is bracing himself, while the man behind him loses his hat under the wheels.

protective tariff   Tax on imported goods intended to make them more expensive than similar domestic goods, thus protecting the market for goods produced at home.

England voices protested tariffs as unfair government interference, most north-easterners supported protection. Most southerners and westerners, however, remained leery of its impact on consumer prices. Still, shouting with nationalistic fervor about American economic independence, westerners like Clay and southerners like Calhoun were able to raise enough support to pass Madison's proposed **Tariff of 1816**, opening the way for continued tariff legislation in the years to come.

The popularity of these measures was apparent in the outcome of the 1816 elections. The Republican caucus nominated Virginian James Monroe who won by a decisive electoral majority: 184 votes to Federalist Rufus King's 34. Congressional Republicans enjoyed a similar sweep, winning more than three-fourths of the seats in the House of Representatives and the Senate. Presented with such a powerful mandate and the political clout necessary to carry it out, Republicans immediately set about expanding on the new nationalistic agenda.

The Transporta-
tion Problem
It was clear to many after the War of 1812 that only the large-scale resources available to state and federal governments could make a practical difference in the transportation picture. Immediately after the war, Calhoun introduced legislation in Congress to finance a national transportation program. Congress approved, but Madison vetoed the bill, stating that the Constitution did not authorize federal spending on projects designed to benefit individual states. But Calhoun finally won Madison's support by convincing the president that a government-funded national road between Cumberland, Maryland, and Wheeling, Virginia, was a military and postal necessity and therefore the initial federal expenditure of $30,000 for the **Cumberland Road** was constitutional. Construction began in 1815.

Although people and light cargoes might move efficiently along the proposed national road, water transportation remained the most economical way to ship bulky freight. Unfortunately, with few exceptions, navigable rivers and lakes did not link up conveniently to form usable transportation networks. Before the War of 1812, some Americans had considered canals as a likely solution, but enormous costs and engineering problems had limited canal construction to less than 100 miles. After the war, however, the entry of the state and federal governments into transportation development opened the way to an era of canal building.

New York State was most successful at canal development. Though Governor DeWitt Clinton hoped to cash in on federal money, Martin Van Buren blocked that move, convincing the state legislature to issue bonds instead. In 1817 the state started work on a canal that would run more than 350 miles from Lake Erie at Buffalo to the Hudson River at Albany. Three thousand workers dug the huge ditch and built the **locks**, dams,

---

lock A section of canal with gates at each end, used to raise or lower boats from one level to another by admitting or releasing water; locks allow canals to compensate for changes in terrain.

and **aqueducts** that would eventually form the **Erie Canal**. The last leg was completed in 1825, and the first barge made its way from Buffalo to Albany and then on to New York City.

Canals were really little more than extensions of natural river courses, and fighting the currents of great rivers remained a problem. Pushed along by current and manpower, a barge could make the trip south from Pittsburgh to New Orleans in about a month. Returning north, against the current, took more than four months, if a boat could make the trip at all. In 1807, however, Robert Fulton's 160-ton steam-powered ship, the *Clermont*, ran upstream from New York City to Albany in an incredibly quick thirty-two hours. Unfortunately, the design of the *Clermont* made it impractical for most of America's rivers. After the war Henry M. Shreve borrowed the hull design of the shallow-draft, broad-beamed keelboats that had been sailing up and down inland streams for generations. Shreve added two lightweight steam engines, each one driving an independent side wheel. He also added an upper deck for passengers, creating the now-familiar multistoried steamboats of southern lore. Funded by merchants in Wheeling, Virginia—soon to be the western terminus for the Cumberland Road—Shreve successfully piloted one of his newly designed boats upriver, from Wheeling to Pittsburgh. Then, in 1816, he made the first successful run south, all the way to New Orleans.

Legal Anchors for New Business Enterprise   President Madison had raised serious constitutional concerns when Henry Clay and his congressional clique proposed spending federal money on road development. Though Calhoun was able to ease the president's mind on this specific matter, many constitutional issues needed clarification if the government was going to play the economic role that nationalists envisioned.

In 1819 the Supreme Court took an important step in clarifying the federal government's role in national economic life. The case arose over an effort by the state of Maryland to raise money by placing **revenue stamps** on federal currency. When a clerk at the Bank of the United States' Baltimore branch, James McCulloch, refused to apply the stamps, he was indicted by the state. In the resulting Supreme Court case, **McCulloch v. Maryland** (1819), the majority ruled that the states could not impose taxes on federal institutions and that McCulloch was right in refusing to comply with Maryland's revenue law. But more important, Chief Justice John Marshall wrote, "The Constitution and the laws made in pursuance thereof are supreme: that they control the constitution and laws of the respective states, and cannot be controlled by them." With this,

---

aqueduct An elevated structure raising a canal to bridge rivers, canyons, or other obstructions.

revenue stamps Stickers affixed to taxed items by government officials indicating that the tax has been paid.

Marshall declared his binding opinion that federal law was superior to state law in all matters.

Marshall reinforced this principle five years later in the landmark case of **Gibbons v. Ogden** (1824). In 1808 the state of New York had recognized Robert Fulton's accomplishments in steamboating by granting him an exclusive contract to run steamboats on rivers in that state. Fulton then used this monopoly power to sell licenses to various operators, including Aaron Ogden, who ran a ferry service between New York and New Jersey. Another individual, Thomas Gibbons, was also running a steamboat service in the same area, but he was operating under license from the federal government. When Ogden accused Gibbons of violating his contractual monopoly in a New York court, Gibbons took refuge in federal court. It finally fell to Marshall's Supreme Court to resolve the conflict. Consistent with its earlier decision, the Court ruled in favor of Gibbons, arguing that the New York monopoly conflicted with federal authority and was therefore invalid. In cases of interstate commerce, it ruled, Congress's authority "is complete in itself" and the states could not challenge it.

But it was going to take more than federal authority and investment to revolutionize the economy. Private money would be needed as well, and that too required some constitutional clarification. At issue were contracts, the basis for all business transactions, and their security from interference by either private or public challengers.

One case from before the war was important in clarifying how federal authorities would deal with matters of contract. The issue was the Yazoo affair, in which the Georgia state legislature had contracted to sell vast tracts of land to private investors. The decision by the legislature to overturn that contract led to a great deal of political fuss, but it created a legal problem also: could a state legislature dissolve an executed contract? This came before Marshall's Court in 1810 with the case of **Fletcher v. Peck** (1810). In this case, the Court ruled that even if the original contract was fraudulently obtained, it still was binding and that the state legislature had no right to overturn it. Nor, it ruled in a later case, could a state modify a standing contract. That case, **Dartmouth College v. Woodward** (1819), involved Dartmouth College's founding charter, which specified that new members of the board of trustees were to be appointed by the current board. In 1816 the New Hampshire state legislature tried to take over the college by passing a bill that would allow the state's governor to appoint board members. The college brought suit, claiming that its charter was a legal contract and that the legislature had no right to abridge it. Announcing the Court's decision, Marshall noted that the Constitution protected the sanctity of contracts and that state legislatures could not interfere with them.

These and other cases helped ease the way for the development of new business ventures. With private contracts and federal financial bureaus safe from state and local meddling and the superiority of Congress in interstate commerce established, businesses had the security they needed to expand into new areas and attempt to turn Clay's dream of a national market economy into a reality. And private investors knew that their involvement in often risky ventures was protected, at least from the whims of politicians.

The Federal Role in Interstate Commerce

Gibbons v. Ogden (1824) established a strong precedent that had far-reaching consequences. At the time of the ruling, interstate commerce was fairly inconsequential; most people in the United States depended on themselves and their immediate neighbors for their needs. But with this ruling in place, as interstate commerce expanded, the power of the federal government expanded, too. It is now virtually impossible to engage in any sort of activity that does not involve interstate commerce. Even in the most private and intimate moments of our lives, objects we use often were manufactured, in whole or in part, in another state; if not, they likely were carried to our local community on interstate highways; and in all cases they were paid for using federal reserve notes. Marshall's decision granting absolute federal authority over interstate commerce thus justified central government jurisdiction over a wide variety of our everyday activities. For example, many civil rights

cases during the 1960s and after landed in federal court because interstate commerce was involved.

- Reflecting upon the development of canal and road systems during the early nineteenth century, how did the Supreme Court's decisions concerning interstate commerce and federal supremacy influence the way the nation developed?

- Choose an activity in which you engage on a regular basis—an athletic event, cultural activity, religious act, or something entirely personal and private; virtually anything—and examine what role interstate commerce plays in it. In what ways might the involvement of interstate commerce give the federal government the right to influence or even control that activity? Do you think that degree of influence is justified?

James Monroe and the Nationalist Agenda

While Congress and the courts were firmly in the hands of forward-looking leaders, the presidency passed in 1816 to the seemingly old-fashioned James Monroe. Personally conservative, Monroe nonetheless was a strong nationalist as well as a graceful statesman. He had served primarily as a diplomat during the contentious period that preceded the War of 1812, and as president he turned his diplomatic skills to the task of calming political disputes. He was the first president since Washington to take a national goodwill tour, during which he persistently urged various political factions to merge their interests for the benefit of the nation at large.

Monroe's cabinet was well chosen to carry out the task of smoothing political rivalries while flexing nationalistic muscles. He selected John Quincy Adams, son and heir of Yankee Federalist John Adams, as secretary of state because of his diplomatic skill and to win political support in New England. Monroe tapped southern nationalist John C. Calhoun for secretary of war and balanced his appointment with that of southern states' rights advocate William C. Crawford as secretary of the treasury. With his team assembled, Monroe launched the nation on a course designed to increase its control over the North American continent and improve its position in world affairs.

Madison had already taken steps toward initiating a more aggressive diplomatic policy, setting the tone for the years to come. Taking advantage of U.S. involvement in the War of 1812, Barbary pirates had resumed their raiding activity against American shipping. In June 1815, Madison ordered a military force back to the Mediterranean to put an end to those raids. Naval hero Stephen Decatur returned to the region with a fleet of ten warships. Training his guns on the port of Algiers itself, Decatur threatened to level the city if the pirates did not stop raiding American shipping. The Algerians and the rest of the Barbary pirates signed treaties ending the practice of exacting **tribute**. They also released all American hostages and agreed to pay compensation for past seizures of American ships. Celebrating the victory, Decatur gave voice to a militant new American nationalism, proclaiming, "Our Country! In her intercourse with foreign nations may she always be in the right; but our country, right or wrong."

Monroe maintained Madison's firm stand as he attempted to resolve important issues not settled by earlier administrations. Secretary of State Adams began negotiating for strict and straightforward treaties outlining America's economic and territorial rights.

The first matter Adams addressed were the loose ends left dangling by the Treaty of Ghent (1814). One problem had been the **demilitarization** of the Great Lakes boundary between the United States and British Canada. In the 1817 Rush-Bagot Agreement, both nations agreed to cut back their Great Lakes fleets to only a few vessels. A year later, the two nations drew up the Convention of 1818: the British agreed to honor American fishing rights in the Atlantic, to recognize the 49th parallel as the boundary between the Louisiana Territory and Canada, and to occupy the Oregon Territory jointly with the United States.

With these northern border issues settled, Adams set his sights on defining the nation's southern and southwestern frontiers. Pirates and other renegades used Florida as a base for launching raids against American settlements and shipping, and runaway slaves found it a safe haven in their flight from southern plantations. Reflecting on the situation in December 1817, General Andrew Jackson wrote to the president advocating the invasion of Spanish Florida. A short time later, Secretary of War Calhoun ordered Jackson to lead a military expedition into southern Georgia, but Jackson crossed the border and forced the Spanish government to flee. Though some recommended that the general be severely disciplined, Adams saw an opportunity to settle the Florida border issue. He announced that Jackson's raid was an act of self-defense that would be repeated unless Spain could police the area adequately. Fully aware that Spain could not guarantee American security, Adams knew that the Spanish would either have to give up Florida or stand by and watch the United States take it by force. Understanding his country's precarious position, Spanish minister Don Luis de Onís chose to cede Florida in the **Adams-Onís Treaty**

tribute   A payment of money or other valuables that one group makes to another as the price of security.

demilitarization   The removal of military forces from a region and the restoration of civilian control.

With a long and distinguished career as a diplomat behind him, the handsome and elegant James Monroe brought a statesmanlike demeanor into the White House. He managed to soothe long-standing disputes between various political factions, ushering in what would be called "The Era of Good Feelings."

The Granger Collection, New York

of 1819. The United States got all of Florida in exchange for releasing Spain from $5 million in damage claims resulting from border raids.

Spain's inability to police its New World territories also led to a more general diplomatic problem. As the result of Spain's weakness, many of its colonies in Latin America had rebelled and established themselves as independent republics. Fearful of the anticolonial example being set in the Western Hemisphere, several European powers were poised to help Spain reclaim its overseas empire. Neither England, which had developed a thriving trade with the new Latin American republics, nor the United States wanted recolonization to occur. In 1823 the British foreign minister proposed that the United States and England form an alliance to end European meddling in Latin America. Adams protested that America would be reduced to a "cock-boat in the wake of the British man-of-war," suggesting instead a **unilateral** statement saying that "the American continents by the free and independent

---

unilateral   Undertaken or issued by only one side and thus not involving an agreement made with others.

condition which they have assumed, and maintain, are henceforth not to be considered as subject for future colonization by any European power."

Monroe remained undecided. He trusted Adams's judgment but did not share the secretary of state's confidence in the nation's ability to fight off European colonization without British help. Monroe nevertheless conceded the nationalistic necessity for the United States to "take a bolder attitude ... in favor of liberty." In November 1823 European support to restore Spain's colonies was faltering, so with the immediate threat removed, Monroe announced that the United States would regard any effort by European countries "to extend their system to any portion of this hemisphere as dangerous to our peace and safety." He went on to define any attempt at European intervention in the affairs of the Western Hemisphere as a virtual act of war against the United States.

The **Monroe Doctrine** was exactly the proud assertion of principle "in favor of liberty" that Monroe had deemed necessary. It immediately won the support of the American people. Like Decatur's "Our country, right or wrong" speech, it seemed to announce the arrival of the United States on the international scene.

DYNAMIC GROWTH AND POLITICAL CONSEQUENCES

After the **Napoleonic wars** ended in 1815, Europeans continued to need American food and manufactures as they rebuilt a peacetime economy. Encouraged by a ready European market and expanding credit offered by both public and private banks, budding southern planters, northern manufacturers, and western and southwestern farmers embarked on a frenzy of speculation. They rushed to borrow against what they were sure was a golden future to buy equipment, land, and slaves.

Although all shared the same sense of optimism, entrepreneurs in the North, West, and South had different ideas about the best course for the American economy. As the American System drew the regions together into increasing mutual dependency, the tensions among them increased as well. As long as economic conditions remained good, there was little reason for conflict, but when the speculative boom collapsed, sectional tensions increased dramatically.

The Panic of 1819   Earlier changes in federal land policy had contributed to the rise of speculation. In 1800 and again in 1804, Congress had passed bills lowering the minimum number of acres of federal land an individual could purchase and the minimum price per acre. After 1804 the minimum purchase became 160 acres and the minimum price, $1.64 per acre. The bill also permitted farmers to pay the government in **installments**. For most Americans, the minimum investment of $262.40 was still out of reach, but the installment option encouraged many to take the risk and buy farms they could barely afford.

Land speculators complicated matters considerably. Taking advantage of the new land prices, they too jumped into the game, buying land on credit. Unlike farmers, however, speculators never intended to put the land into production. They

---

installments   Partial payments of a debt made at regular intervals until the entire debt is repaid.

hoped to subdivide it and sell it to people who could not afford to buy 160-acre lots directly from the government. Speculators also offered installment loans, pyramiding the already huge tower of debt.

Banks—both relatively unsupervised state banks and the Second Bank of the United States—then added to the problem. Farmers who bought land on credit seldom had enough cash to purchase farm equipment, seed, materials for housing, and the other supplies necessary to put the land to productive use. So the banks extended liberal credit on top of the credit already extended by the government and by land developers. Farmers thus had acreage and tools, but they also had an enormous debt.

Several developments in the international economy combined to undermine the nation's tower of debt. The economic optimism that fed the speculative frenzy rested on profitable markets. But as the 1810s drew to a close and recovery began in Europe, the profit bandwagon began to slow, and optimism to slip. Not only was Europe able to supply more of its own needs, but Europeans were also importing from other regions of the globe. Led by Great Britain, European nations were establishing colonies in Asia, Africa, and the Pacific. In addition, the recent independence of many of Europe's Latin American colonies deprived the Europeans of the gold and silver that had driven international economics since the discovery of America. Europe became less and less dependent on American goods and, at the same time, less and less able to afford them. Thus the bottom began to fall out of the international market that had fueled speculation within the United States.

Congress noted the beginning of the collapse late in 1817 and tried to head off disaster by tightening credit. The government stopped installment payments on new land purchases and demanded that they be transacted in hard currency. The Second Bank of the United States followed suit in 1818, demanding immediate repayment of loans in either gold or silver. State banks then followed and were joined by land speculators. Instead of curing the problem, however, tightening credit and recalling loans drove the economy over the edge. The speculative balloon burst, leaving nothing but a mass of debt behind. This economic catastrophe became known as the **Panic of 1819**.

Six years of economic depression followed the panic. As prices declined, individual farmers and manufacturers, unable to repay loans for land and equipment, faced **repossession** and imprisonment for debt. In Cincinnati and other agricultural cities, bankruptcy sales were a daily occurrence. In New England and the West, factories closed, throwing both employees and owners out of work. In New York and other manufacturing and trading cities, the ranks of the unemployed grew steadily. The number of **paupers** in New York City nearly doubled between 1819 and 1820, and in Boston thirty-five hundred people were imprisoned for debt. Shaken by the

---

repossession   The reclaiming of land or goods by the seller or lender after the purchaser fails to pay installments due.

paupers   A term popular in the eighteenth and nineteenth centuries to describe poor people; cities like New York and Boston often registered paupers so as to provide local relief.

Before the adoption of modern bankruptcy laws, it was common for people to be put in prison when they could not pay their debts. One impact of the Panic of 1819 was a huge upturn in such imprisonments. Newspapers like The Remembrancer, or Debtors Prison Recorder, which began publication with this issue on April 8, 1820, called for reform in debtor laws and also reported gruesome stories about the sufferings of previously respectable people who found themselves in debtors' prison through no fault of their own.

THE REMEMBRANCER,
OR
DEBTORS PRISON RECORDER.

" HE WHO'S ENTOMB'D WITHIN A PRISON'S WALLS
ENDURES THE ANGUISH OF A LIVING DEATH "

VOL. I.   NEW-YORK, SATURDAY APRIL 8, 1820.   No. 1.

THE
DEBTORS PRISON RECORDER
IS ISSUED FROM THE PRESS OF
CHARLES N. BALDWIN,
AND PUBLISHED BY
JOHN B. JANSEN,
No. 15 Chatham-street,
NEW-YORK,
At two dollars per annum, payable quarterly in advance.

Persons at a distance may have the paper regularly forwarded to them by mail, provided they forward the requisite advance, *post paid.*

TO THE PUBLIC.

THE chief object of this publication will be to spread before an enlightened public the deplorable effects resulting from the barbarous practice of imprisonment for debt—to exhibit the misery of its wretched victims, and the unfeeling conduct of unpitying creditors. By these means, " with truth as its guide, and justice for its object," it will, it is hoped, gradually prepare the minds of the community for the entire abolition of a law which exists a dishonor to the precepts of Christianity, and as a blot on the statute book.

It will be published weekly, in an octavo form, each number to consist of eight pages, comprising a succinct and correct history of the interesting incidents which daily occur in the debtors prison—a correct Journal of prisoners received and discharged from

time to time, with such remarks as may grow out of peculiar persecution or other causes; nor will it neglect to announce the number of those who are supplied with food from that inestimable body, the Humane Society, to whom the profits of this publication will be faithfully applied, as a small testimonial of the gratitude felt by the unfortunate inmates of the prison, for their distinguished beneficence. It will contain interesting extracts from the latest European and American publications. In its columns will be found a variety of communications on various interesting subjects, from gentlemen without the prison walls, who have kindly volunteered their services to furnish us with essays on the ARTS and SCIENCES, criticisms on the DRAMA, POETRY, &c.

This work will be edited, and its matter carefully revised by several prisoners, who, if they cannot themselves enjoy the benefits of their labor, may at least feel a pleasure in the reflection that after ages will bestow a pitying tear on their sufferings, and bless them for the exertions made to rescue their country from the only vestage of feudal tyranny remaining in a land that boasts of freedom.

The small pittance paid for its perusal, will, it is beleived, procure for it the patronage of a generous public, who will be amply remunerated in performing a duty subserving the great and benign ends of Charity, while in return they are furnished with a species of reading not to be met with in any other publication

Debtors Prison Recorder, Vol. 1., No. 1, New York, Saturday, April 8, 1820

enormity of the problem, John C. Calhoun observed in 1820: "There has been within these two years an immense revolution of fortunes in every part of the Union; enormous numbers of persons utterly ruined; multitudes in deep distress."

Economic Woes and Political Sectionalism

Despite Monroe's efforts to merge southern, northern, and nationalist interests during the Era of Good Feelings, the Panic of 1819 drove a wedge between the nation's geographical sections. The depression touched each of the major regions differently, calling for conflicting solutions. For the next several years, the halls of Congress rang with debates rooted in each section's particular economic needs.

Tariffs were one proven method for handling economic emergencies, and as the Panic of 1819 spread economic devastation throughout the country, legislators from Pennsylvania and the Middle Atlantic states, southern New England, and then Ohio and Kentucky began clamoring for protection. Others disagreed, turning tariffs into the issue that would pit region against region more violently than any other during these years.

Farmers were split on the tariff issue. Irrespective of where they lived, so-called yeoman farmers favored a free market that would keep the price of the manufactures they had to buy as low as possible. In contrast, the increasing number of commercial farmers—those who had chosen to follow Henry Clay's ideas and were specializing to produce cash crops of raw wool, hemp, and wheat—joined mill owners, factory managers, and industrial workers in supporting protection against the foreign dumping of such products. So did those westerners who were producing raw minerals such as iron and tin that were in high demand in the industrializing economy.

Southern commercial farmers, however, did not join with their western counterparts in favoring protection. After supporting the protective Tariff of 1816, Calhoun and other southerners became firm opponents of tariffs. Their dislike of protection reflected a complex economic reality. Britain, not the United States, was the South's primary market for raw cotton and its main supplier of manufactured goods. Protective tariffs raised the price of such goods as well as the possibility that Britain might enact a **retaliatory tariff** on cotton imports from the South. If that happened, southerners would pay more for manufactures but receive less profit from cotton.

When, in 1820, northern congressmen proposed a major increase in tariff rates, small farmers in the West and cotton growers in the South combined to defeat the measure. Northerners then began engaging in **log rolling** with congressmen from the West. The northerners supported one bill that lowered the minimum price of public land to $1.25 per acre and another that allowed farmers who had bought land before 1820 to pay off their debts at the reduced price. The bill also extended the time over which those who were on the installment plan could make payments. Then, in 1822, northerners backed a bill authorizing increased federal spending on the Cumberland Road, an interest vital to westerners. The strategy succeeded: in 1824 western congressmen repaid northern manufacturing interests by voting for a greatly increased tariff.

This victory demonstrated an important new political reality. Of the six western states admitted to the Union after 1800, three—Ohio, Indiana, and Illinois—were predominantly farming states, split between commercial and nonspecialized farming. The other three—Louisiana, Mississippi, and Alabama—were increasingly dominated by cotton growing. As long as northern commercial interests could pull support from Ohio, Indiana, and Illinois, the balance of power in Congress remained relatively even. But new expansion in either the North or South had the

retaliatory tariff   A tariff on imported goods imposed neither to raise revenue nor control commerce but to retaliate against tariffs charged by another nation.

log rolling   The trading of favors, such as vote trading, by legislators to obtain passage of bills that would otherwise lack sufficient votes to pass.

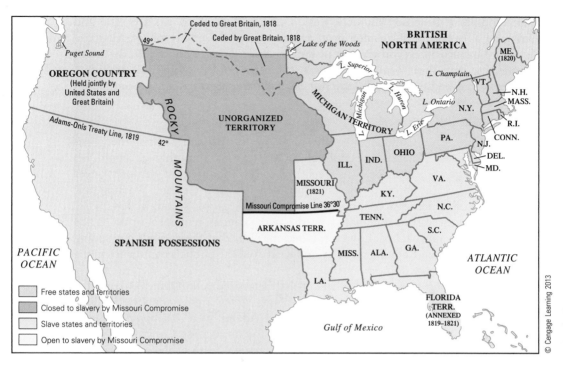

MAP 10.1 The Missouri Compromise, 1820–1821

The Missouri Compromise temporarily quelled controversy over slavery by admitting Maine as a free state and Missouri as a slave state, and by prohibiting slavery in the remainder of the Louisiana Purchase north of 36°30′.

potential to tip the political scale. As all three regions fought to implement specific solutions to the nation's economic woes, the regional balance of power in Congress became a matter of crucial importance.

The Missouri Compromise   The delicate balance in Congress began to wobble immediately in 1819 when the Missouri Territory applied for statehood. New York congressman James Tallmadge, Jr., realized that if Missouri was admitted as a free state, its economy would resemble the economies of states in the Old Northwest, and its congressmen would be susceptible to northern log rolling. This realization led Tallmadge to propose Missouri be closed to slavery. Southerners likewise understood that if Missouri was admitted as a slave state, it would undoubtedly support the southern position on tariffs and other key issues. They unified to oppose the **Tallmadge Amendment**.

Both sides in the debate were deeply entrenched, but in 1820 Henry Clay suggested a compromise. Late in 1819, Maine applied for admission to the United States.

The compromise proposed by Clay was to admit Missouri as a slave state and Maine as a free state. Clay also proposed that after the admission of Missouri, slavery be banned forever in the rest of the Louisiana Territory above 36°30′ north latitude, the line that formed Missouri's southern border. With this provision, Congress approved the **Missouri Compromise**, and the issue of slavery in the territories faded—for a while.

New Politics and the End of Good Feelings   Conducted in the midst of the Missouri crisis, the presidential election of 1820 went as smoothly as could be: Monroe was reelected with the greatest majority ever enjoyed by any president except George Washington. Despite economic depression and sectional strife, the people's faith in Jefferson's party and his successors nominated by the party caucus remained firm. As the election of 1824 approached, however, it became clear that the nation's continuing problems had broken Republican unity and destroyed the public's confidence in the party's ability to solve domestic problems.

Although Monroe and many others probably favored John Quincy Adams, the southern-dominated party caucus tapped Georgia states' rights advocate William Crawford as its candidate. Certainly Clay and Adams were disappointed: each immediately defied party discipline by deciding to run against Crawford without the approval of the caucus. Encouraged by the apparent death of the caucus system for nominating presidential candidates, the Tennessee state legislature chose to put forward its own candidate, Andrew Jackson.

The election that followed was a painful demonstration of how deeply divided the nation had become. Northern regional political leaders rallied behind Adams, southern sectionalists supported Crawford, and northwestern commercial farmers and other backers of the American System lined up behind Clay. But a good portion of the American people—many of them independent yeoman farmers, traditional craftsmen, and immigrants—defied their political leaders by supporting the hero of New Orleans: Jackson.

Though a political **dark horse**, Jackson won the popular election, but the Electoral College vote was another matter. Jackson had 99 electoral votes to Adams's 84, Crawford's 41, and Clay's 37, but although Jackson won a **plurality** of electors, it was not the "majority of the whole number of electors" required by the Constitution. The Constitution specifies that in such cases, a list of the top three vote getters be passed to the House of Representatives for a final decision.

By the time the House had convened to settle the election, Crawford, the third-highest vote getter, had suffered a disabling stroke, so the list of candidates had only two names: John Quincy Adams and Andrew Jackson. Because Clay had

dark horse   A political candidate who has little organized support and is not expected to win.

plurality   In an election with three or more candidates, the number of votes received by the leading candidate but which amount to less than half of the total number of votes cast.

finished fourth, he was not in contention in the **runoff election**, but as Speaker of the House he was in a particularly strategic position to influence the outcome. Adams's and Clay's views on tariffs, manufacturing, foreign affairs, and other key issues were quite compatible. Clay therefore endorsed Adams, who won the House election and in 1825 became the nation's sixth president.

Jackson and his supporters were outraged. They considered Clay a betrayer of western and southern interests, calling him the "Judas of the West." Then when Adams named Clay as his secretary of state—the position that had been the springboard to the presidency for every past Republican who held it—Jacksonians exploded. Proclaiming Adams's election a "corrupt bargain," Jackson supporters withdrew from the party of Jefferson, bringing an end to the one-party system that had emerged under the so-called **Virginia Dynasty** and dealing the knockout blow to the Era of Good Feelings.

THE "NEW MAN" IN POLITICS

Since Washington's day the presidency had been considered an office for gentlemen and statesmen. The first several presidents had tried to maintain an air of polite dignity while in office, and voters were generally pleased with that orderly approach. But with the massive social changes taking place after the War of 1812, the conduct of national politics changed drastically. New voters from new occupations with radically varying political and economic views began making demands. Many felt isolated from a political system that permitted the presidency to pass from one propertied gentleman to another. Clearly, changing times called for political change, and the American people began to press for it in no uncertain terms.

Adams's Troubled Administration   John Quincy Adams may have been the best-prepared man ever to assume the office of president. As the son of former president John Adams, John Quincy had been born and raised in the midst of America's most powerful political circles. By the time of his controversial election in 1825, Adams had been a foreign diplomat, a U.S. senator, a Harvard professor, and an exceptionally effective secretary of state. Adams conducted himself in office as his father had, holding himself above partisan politics and refusing to use political favors to curry support. As a result, Adams had no effective means of rallying those who might have supported him or of pressuring his opponents. Thus, despite his impressive résumé, Adams's administration was a deeply troubled one.

Adams's policy commitments did nothing to boost his popularity. The new president promised to increase tariffs to protect American manufacturing and to raise funds necessary to pay for "the improvement of agriculture, commerce, and manufactures." He also wanted the Second Bank of the United States to stabilize

---

runoff election   A final election held to determine a winner after an earlier election has eliminated the weakest candidates.

the economy while providing ample loans to finance new manufacturing ventures. And he advocated federal spending to improve "the elegant arts" and advance "literature and the progress of the sciences, ornamental and profound." High-sounding though Adams's objectives were, Thomas Jefferson spoke for many when he observed that such policies would establish "a single and splendid govern-ment of an aristocracy ... riding and ruling over the plundered ploughman and beg-gared yeomanry." Jefferson's criticism seemed particularly apt in the economic turmoil that followed the Panic of 1819. Moreover, the increase in federal power implied by Adams's policies frightened southerners, and this fear, combined with their traditional distaste for tariffs, virtually unified opposition to Adams in the South.

Led by John C. Calhoun, Adams's opponents tried to manipulate tariff legis-lation to undercut the president's support. Calhoun proposed an unprecedented increase in tariff rates. Northeastern Jacksonians should then voice support for the increase while Jackson supporters in the West and South opposed them. Calhoun and his colleagues envisioned a win-win situation: northeastern Jackso-nians would win increasing support from manufacturing interests in their region by appearing to support tariffs; southern and western Jackson supporters could take credit for sinking tariff increases, cementing support in their districts; and Adams, who had promised increases as part of his political agenda, would appear ineffectual. But Calhoun and his fellow conspirators had miscalculated: when the tariff package came to the floor in May 1828, key northeastern congressmen engineered its passage. The resulting **Tariff of Abominations** was not what Calhoun had expected, but it served his ends by establishing tariff rates that were unpopular with almost every segment of the population, and the unpopular president would bear the blame.

Democratic Styles and Political Structure   Adams's demeanor and outlook compounded his problems. He seemed more a man of his father's generation than of his own. The enormous economic and demographic changes that occurred during the first decades of the nineteenth century created a new political climate, one in which Adams's archrival Andrew Jackson felt much more at ease than did the stiff Yankee who occupied the White House.

One of the most profound changes in the American political scene was an explosion in the number of voters. Throughout the early years of the republic's history, voting rights were limited to white men who held real estate. In a nation primarily of farmers, most men owned land, so the fact of limited suffrage raised little controversy. But as economic conditions changed, a smaller proportion of the population owned farms, and while bankers, lawyers, manufacturers, and other such men often were highly educated, economically stable, and politically concerned, their lack of real estate barred them from political participation. Not surprisingly, such elite and middle-class men urged suffrage reform. In 1800 only three of the sixteen states had no property qualifications for voting, and another three permitted taxpayers to vote even if they did not own real property. By 1830, only five of the twenty-four states retained property qualifications, nine required tax payment only, and ten made no property demands at all. The raw number of voters grew enormously and rapidly. In 1824, 356,038 men cast ballots for the presidency. Four years later, more than three times that number voted. In addition, states increasingly dropped property qualifications for office-holding as well as voting, opening new opportunities for breaking the gentlemanly monopoly on political power. Of course, all of the states continued to bar women from voting, and most refused the ballot to African Americans, whether free or slave.

Political opportunists were not slow to take advantage of the new situation. Men such as Van Buren quickly came to the fore, organizing political factions into tightly disciplined local and statewide units. Opposing Governor DeWitt Clinton's faction in New York, Van Buren molded disaffected Republicans into the so-called Bucktail faction. In 1820 the Bucktails used a combination of political patronage—the ability of the party in power to distribute government jobs—**influence peddling**, and fiery speeches to draw newly qualified voters into the political process and swept Clinton out of office.

Many new voters were gratified at finally being allowed to participate in politics but sensed that their participation was not having the impact it should. They resented the "corrupt bargain" that had denied the presidency to the people's choice—Andrew Jackson—in the election of 1824. Voters in upstate New York and elsewhere pointed at organizations such as the **Masons**, claiming that they used secret signs and rituals to ensure the election of their own members, thwarting the popular will. In the fall of 1826, William Morgan, a New York bricklayer, decided to publish some of the organization's secrets. Morgan was promptly arrested—charged with owing a debt of $2.69—and jailed. What happened after that remains a mystery. Some unknown person paid Morgan's debt, and he was released. But as he emerged from jail, he was seized, bound and gagged, and dragged into a carriage that whisked him out of town. He was never seen again.

Morgan's disappearance caused a popular outcry, and political outsiders demanded a complete investigation. When no clues turned up, many assumed that a Masonic conspiracy was afoot. Within a year, opportunistic young politicians, including New Yorkers Thurlow Weed and William Seward and Pennsylvanian **Thaddeus Stevens**, had harnessed this political anxiety by forming the **Antimasonic Party**. Based exclusively on the alienation felt by small craftsmen, farmers, and other marginalized groups, the Antimasons had no platform beyond their shared opposition to conspiracies they were sure were directed against political transparency. The Antimasonic Party was, in effect, a political party whose sole cause was to oppose political parties.

What was happening in New York was typical of party and antiparty developments throughout the country. As the party of Jefferson dissolved, a tangle of

influence peddling   Using one's influence with people in authority to obtain favors or preferential treatment for someone else, usually in return for payment.

Masons   An international fraternal organization with many socially and politically prominent members, including a number of U.S. presidents.

political factions broke out across the nation. This was precisely the sort of petty politics that Adams disdained, but the chaos suited a man like Jackson perfectly. So, while the Antimasons were busy pursuing often highly fanciful conspiracy theories, Van Buren was busy forging with the hero of New Orleans an alliance that would fundamentally alter American politics.

The Rise of "King Andrew" Within two years of Adams's election, Van Buren had brought together northern outsiders like himself, dissident southern Republicans like John C. Calhoun, and western spokesmen like **Thomas Hart Benton** of Missouri and John H. Eaton of Tennessee into a new political party. Calling themselves Democratic-Republicans—the **Democratic Party** for short—this party railed against the neofederalism of Clay's and Adams's National Republican platform. The Democrats called for a return to Jeffersonian simplicity, states' rights, and republican principles. Behind the scenes, however, they employed the tight organizational discipline and manipulative techniques that Van Buren had used to such good effect against the Clintons in New York. Lining up behind the recently defeated popular hero Andrew Jackson, the new party appealed to both opportunistic political outsiders and democratically inclined new voters. In the congressional elections of 1826, Van Buren's coalition drew the unqualified support of both groups, unseating enough National Republicans to gain a twenty-five-seat majority in the House of Representatives and an eight-seat advantage in the Senate.

In the presidential election that followed, having Andrew Jackson as a candidate was probably as important to the Democrats' success as their ideological appeal and tight political organization. In many ways, Jackson was a perfect reflection of the new voters. Like many of them, he was born in a log cabin under rustic circumstances. His family had faced more than its share of hardships: his father had died two weeks before Andrew's birth, and he had lost his two brothers and his mother during the Revolutionary War. In the waning days of the Revolution, at the age of 13, Jackson joined a mounted militia company and was captured by the British. His captors beat their young prisoner and then let him go, a humiliation he would never forgive.

At the end of the war, like Van Buren and others, Jackson chose the legal profession as the route to advancement. Driven by an indomitable will and a wealth of native talent, Jackson became the first U.S. congressman from the state of Tennessee and eventually was elected to the Senate. He also was a judge on the Tennessee Supreme Court. Along the way, Jackson's exploits established his solid reputation as a heroic and natural leader: in the popular view, it was Jackson's brashness, not Adams's diplomacy, that had finally won Spanish Florida for the United States.

Jackson's popular image as a rough-hewn man of the people was somehow untarnished by his political alliance with business interests, his activities as a land speculator, and his large and growing personal fortune and stock of slaves. In the eyes of frontiersmen, small farmers, and to some extent urban workingmen, he remained a common man like them. Having started with nothing, Jackson seemed

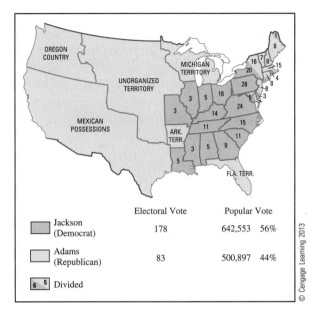

MAP 10.2 The Election of 1828

to have drawn from a combination of will, natural ability, and divine favor to become a man of substance without becoming a snob.

Caricature and image making rather than substantive issues dominated the election campaign of 1828. Jackson supporters accused Adams of being cold, aristocratic, and corrupt in bowing to speculators and **special interests** when defining his tariff and land policies. Adams supporters charged Jackson with being a dueler, an insubordinate military adventurer, and an uncouth backwoodsman. The characterization of Adams as cold was accurate, but charges of corruption were entirely untrue. The charges against Jackson were all too true, but voters saw them as irrelevant: rather than damaging Jackson's image, such talk made him appear romantic and daring. When all was said and done, the Tennessean polled over a hundred thousand more popular votes than did the New Englander and won the vast majority of states, taking every one in the South and West.

As if in response to his supporters' desires and his opponents' fears, Jackson swept into the White House on a groundswell of unruly popular enthusiasm. Ten thousand visitors crammed into the capital to witness Jackson's inauguration on March 4, 1829. Showing his usual disdain for tradition, Jackson took the oath of office and then pushed through the crowd and mounted his horse, galloping off

caricature An exaggerated image of a person, usually enhancing his or her most uncomplimentary features.

special interest A person or organization that seeks to benefit by influencing legislators to support particular policies.

Left: Copy of an 1818 painting by Gilbert Stuart/White House Historical Association (White House Collection): 32; right: ca. 1818 painting by Ralph E.W. Earl/© Smithsonian Institution/Corbis

The presidential election of 1828 pitted two totally opposite kinds of men against each other. The staid John Quincy Adams (left), who had been involved in national politics for over a quarter of a century, represented old-style gentlemanly politics. The flamboyant military hero Andrew Jackson (right), on the other hand, was a political outsider and seemed to have much more in common with the new generation of American voters.

toward the White House followed by a throng of excited onlookers. When they arrived, the mob flowed behind him into the presidential mansion, where a spontaneous party broke out. The new president was finally forced to flee the near-riot by climbing out a back window. Clearly a boisterous new spirit was alive in the nation's politics.

Launching Jacksonian Politics

That he was a political outsider was a major factor in Jackson's popularity. Antimasons and others were convinced that politics consisted primarily of conspiracies among political insiders, and Jackson curried their support by promising **retrenchment** and reform in the federal system. In the process, he initiated a personal style in government unlike that of any of his predecessors in office and alienated many both inside and outside Washington.

Retrenchment was first on the new president's agenda. Jackson challenged the notion that government work required an elite core of professional civil servants. Such duties, Jackson declared, were "so plain and simple that men of intelligence may readily qualify themselves for their performance." And in order to keep such

retrenchment   In government, the elimination of unnecessary jobs or functions for reform or cost-cutting purposes.

men from becoming entrenched, Jackson promised to institute regular rotation in office for federal bureaucrats: appointments in his administration would last only four years, after which civil servants would have to return to "making a living as other people do."

Like many of Jackson's policies, this rotation system was designed to accomplish more than a single goal. Because no new party had come to power since Jefferson's election in 1800, Jackson inherited some ten thousand civil servants who owed their jobs to Republican patronage. Rotation in office gave the president the excuse to fire people whom he associated with the "corrupt bargain" and felt he could not fully trust. It also opened up an unprecedented opportunity for Jackson to reward his loyal supporters by placing them in the newly vacated civil service jobs. The Jacksonian adage became "To the victor belong the **spoils**," and the Democrats made every effort to advance their party's hold on power by distributing government jobs to loyal party members.

Patronage appointments extended to the highest levels in government. Jackson selected cabinet members not for their experience or ability but for their political loyalty and value in satisfying the various factions that formed his coalition. The potential negative impact of these appointments was minimized by Jackson's decision to abandon his predecessors' practice of regularly seeking his cabinet members' advice on major issues: the president called virtually no cabinet meetings and seldom asked for his cabinet's opinion. Instead, he surrounded himself with an informal network of friends and advisers. This so-called **Kitchen Cabinet**, under the deft leadership of Van Buren, worked closely with the president on matters of both national policy and party management.

Jackson's relationship with everyone in government was equally unconventional. He was known to rage, pout, and storm at suspected disloyalty. Earlier presidents had at least pretended to believe in the equal distribution of power among the three branches of government, but Jackson avowed that the president was the only member of the government elected by all the people, making it clear that he would stand in opposition to both private and congressional opponents. Reflecting his generally testy relationship with the legislative branch, he vetoed more bills than all his predecessors combined. Nor did he feel any qualms about standing up to the judiciary. Such arrogant assertions of executive power led Jackson's opponents to call the new president "King Andrew."

THE REIGN OF "KING ANDREW"

Jackson had promised the voters "retrenchment and reform." He delivered retrenchment, but reform was more difficult to arrange. Jackson tried to implement reform in four broad areas: (1) the nation's banking and financial system, (2) internal improvements and public land policy, (3) Indian affairs, and (4) the collection of revenue and enforcement of federal law. The steps that Jackson took appealed to some of his

spoils Jobs and other rewards for political support.

supporters but strongly alienated others. Thus, as Jackson tried to follow through on his promise to reform the nation, he nearly tore the nation apart.

Jackson and   The Second Bank of the United States was an essential part of
the Bank   the American System. In addition to serving as the depository
                         for federal funds, the Second Bank issued national currency,
which could be exchanged directly for gold, and it served as a national clearing-house for notes issued by state and local banks. In that capacity, the Second Bank could regulate currency values and credit rates and help to control the activities of state banks by refusing to honor their notes if the banks lacked sufficient gold to back them. The Second Bank could also police state and local banks by calling in loans and refusing credit—actions that had helped bring on the Panic of 1819 and had made the Second Bank very unpopular.

In 1823 **Nicholas Biddle** became president of the bank. An able administrator and talented economist, Biddle enforced firm and consistent policies that restored some confidence in the bank and its functions. But many Americans still were not ready to accept the notion of an all-powerful central banking authority. The vast majority did not understand the function of the Second Bank, viewing it as just another instrument for helping the rich get richer. These critics tended instinctively to support the use of **specie**. Other critics, including many state bankers, opposed the Second Bank because they felt that Biddle's controls were too strict and that they were not receiving their fair share of federal revenues. Speculators and debtors also opposed the bank: when they gambled correctly, they could benefit from the sort of economic instability the bank was designed to prevent.

Hoping that Democratic Party discipline would break down before the upcoming presidential election, Jackson's opponents in Congress proposed to renew the bank's twenty-year charter four years early. Congress passed the renewal bill, and as expected, Jackson vetoed it, but an anticipated rift between Jackson and congressional Democrats did not open. The president stole the day by delivering a powerful veto message geared to appeal to the mass of Americans on whose support his party's congressmen depended. In line with his political supporters, Jackson denounced the Second Bank for serving the interests of "the few at the expense of the many" and injuring "humbler members of society—the farmers, the mechanics, and laborers—who have neither the time nor the means of securing like favors to themselves."

Although the charter was not renewed, the Second Bank could operate for four more years on the basis of its unexpired charter. Jackson, however, wanted to "deprive the conspirators of the aid which they expect from its money and power." Withdrawing federal deposits would do just that, although doing so was illegal. Jackson nonetheless ordered Treasury Secretary Louis McLane to make the withdrawals. When he refused, the president fired him and replaced him with William J. Duane, who also refused. Jackson quickly fired him too and appointed Kitchen Cabinet member Roger B. Taney to head the Treasury Department. Taney chose to step around the law rather than breaking it by paying the government's

specie Coins minted from precious metals.

bills from existing accounts in the Second Bank while placing all new deposits in so-called **pet banks.**

Powerless to stop Taney's diversion of federal funds, Biddle sought to replace dwindling assets by raising interest rates and calling in loans owed by state banks. In this way, the banker believed, he would not only head off the Second Bank's collapse but also trigger a business panic that might force the government to reverse its course. "Nothing but the evidence of suffering . . . will produce any effect," Biddle said as he pushed the nation toward economic instability. Biddle was correct that there would be "evidence of suffering," but the full effect of the **Bank War** would not be felt until after the reign of "King Andrew" had ended.

The Nullification Crisis   Southern concerns about banking and rising tariffs reflected the South's abiding political and economic posture during the Jackson administration. For years, southerners had complained that tariffs discriminated against them. From their point of view, they were paying at least as much in tariffs as the North and West but were not getting nearly the same economic benefits. The banking system, too, seemed to benefit others more than it did them.

This matter had come to a head in 1829 when the impact of the ill-considered Tariff of Abominations (1828) began to be felt throughout the nation. The new tariffs roused loud protest from states such as South Carolina, where soil exhaustion and declining agricultural prices were putting strong economic pressure on men who were deeply invested in land and slaves. Calhoun, who took office as Jackson's vice president in 1829, spearheaded the protest.

Though it guarded the author's identity, the South Carolina legislature published Calhoun's *South Carolina Exposition and Protest* in 1828, fanning the flames of sectionalism. Calhoun's **nullification** sentiments reflected notions being expressed throughout the nation. And as Calhoun's pamphlet circulated to wider and wider audiences, nationalists such as Clay and Jackson grew more and more anxious about the potential threat to federal power. The test came in 1830, when Senator Robert Y. Hayne of South Carolina and Senator **Daniel Webster** of Massachusetts entered into a debate over Calhoun's ideas. Hayne zealously supported Calhoun; Webster appealed to nationalism. Jackson soon made his opinion known at a political banquet, offering the toast, "Our Federal Union—It must be preserved," indicating that he would brook no nullification arguments. Calhoun, who was sitting near the president, then rose and countered Jackson's toast with one of his own: "The Union—next to our liberty most dear." For Jackson, who valued loyalty above all else, his vice president's insubordination was inexcusable. Still, two years passed before the crisis finally came.

In 1832 nullification advocates in South Carolina called for a special session of the state legislature, which voted overwhelmingly to nullify the despised tariff. The legislature also elected Hayne, nullification's most prominent spokesman, as governor and named Calhoun as his replacement in the Senate. The vice president, who

nullification   Refusal by a state to recognize or enforce a federal law within its boundaries.

realized that he would not be Jackson's running mate in the coming election, finally admitted writing the *Exposition and Protest* and resigned from the vice presidency to lead the pro-nullification forces from the Senate floor.

Jackson quickly proved true to his toast of two years before. Bristling that nullification violated the Constitution and was "destructive of the great object for which it was formed," Jackson immediately reinforced federal forts in South Carolina and sent warships to guarantee the tariff's collection. He also asked Congress to pass a "force bill" giving him the power to invade the rebellious state if doing so proved necessary to carry out federal law. In hopes of placating southerners and winning popular support in the upcoming election, Congress passed a lowered tariff, but it also voted to give Jackson the power he requested.

South Carolina nullifiers immediately called a new convention, which withdrew its nullification of the previous tariff but passed a resolution nullifying the force bill. Because Jackson no longer needed the force bill to apply federal law and collect the new tariff, he chose to ignore this action. Thus there was no real resolution to the problem, and the gash over federal versus states' rights remained unhealed. The wound continued to fester until it was finally cauterized thirty years later by civil war.

Jackson and the West   Although Jackson was a westerner, his views on federal spending for roads, canals, and other internal improvements seemed based more on politics than on ideology or regional interest. For example, when Congress passed a bill calling for federal money to build a road in Kentucky—from Maysville, on the Ohio border, to Lexington—Jackson vetoed it, claiming that it would benefit only one state and was therefore unconstitutional. But three practical political issues influenced his decision. First, party loyalists in places such as Pennsylvania and New York, where Jackson hoped to gain support, opposed federal aid to western states. Second, Lexington was the hub of Henry Clay's political district, and by denying aid that would benefit that city, Jackson was putting his western competitor in political hot water. Finally, Jackson's former congressional district centered on Nashville—already the terminus of a national road and therefore a legitimate recipient of federal funds. Thus Jackson could lavish money on his hometown while seeming to stand by strict constitutional limitations on federal power.

Disposing of the **public domain** was the other persistent problem Jackson faced. By the time he came to power, land policy had become a major factor in sectional politics. Currying support from western voters, Jackson abandoned his predecessors' notion that public land sales should profit the government, taking the position that small farmers should be able to buy federal land for no more than it cost the government to **survey** the plot and process the sale.

public domain   Land owned and controlled by the federal government.

survey   To determine the area and boundaries of land through measurement and mathematical calculation.

Jackson thus directed Congress that "public lands shall cease as soon as practicable to be a source of revenue," and western Jacksonians responded immediately. One of them, Senator Thomas Hart Benton of Missouri, proposed in 1830 that the price of government land be dropped gradually from $1.25 to just 25 cents an acre and that any lands not sold at that price simply be given away. He also suggested that squatters—people who were currently settled illegally on public land—be given the first chance to buy the tract where they were squatting when the government offered it for sale.

Such measures pleased Jackson's western supporters but frightened easterners and southerners. His supporters in the East and South feared that migration would give the West an even bigger say in the nation's economic and political future. In addition, southerners were concerned that Congress would replace revenues lost from the sale of public land by raising tariffs, threatening the South's economic relationship with Europe. Northerners were afraid that as people moved west, the drain on population would drive up the price of labor, increasing the cost of production and lowering profits. The result was nearly three years of debate in Congress. A frustrated Henry Clay, desperate to save any scrap of his economic plans for the nation, suggested that the distribution of public land be turned over to the states. Congress, relieved to have the matter taken out of its hands, passed Clay's bill in 1833, but Jackson vetoed it.

Jackson and the Indians At the end of the War of 1812, the powerful Cherokees, Choctaws, Seminoles, Creeks, and Chickasaws—the so-called **Five Civilized Tribes**—numbered nearly seventy-five thousand people and occupied large holdings within the states of Georgia, North and South Carolina, Alabama, Mississippi, and Tennessee. These Indians had embraced Jefferson's vision of acculturation but were seen as an obstruction to westward migration, especially by grasping planters on the make who coveted Indian land for cotton fields. A similar situation prevailed in the Northwest. Though neither as numerous nor as Europeanized as the Civilized Tribes, groups such as the Peorias, Kaskaskias, Kickapoos, Sauks, Foxes, and Winnebagos were living settled and stable lives along the northern frontier.

Throughout the 1820s, the federal government tried to convince tribes along the frontier to move farther west. Promised money, new land, and relief from white harassment, many Indian leaders agreed. Others, however, resisted, insisting that they stay where they were. The outcome was terrible factionalism within Indian societies as some lobbied to sell out and move west while others fought to keep their lands. Playing on this factionalism, federal Indian agents were able to extract land cessions that consolidated the eastern tribes onto smaller and smaller holdings. One such transaction, the 1825 Treaty of Indian Springs, involved fraud and manipulation so obnoxious that President Adams overturned the ratified treaty and insisted on a new one.

Adams at least paid lip service to honest dealings with the Indians and the sanctity of treaties. Jackson scoffed at both. In 1817 he had told President Monroe, "I have long viewed treaties with the Indians an absurdity not to be reconciled to the principles of our government." As president, Jackson advocated removing all the eastern Indians to the west side of the Mississippi, by force if necessary. Following Jackson's direction, Congress passed the **Indian Removal Act** in 1830, appropriating the funds necessary to purchase all of the lands held by Indian tribes east of the Mississippi River and to pay for their resettlement in the West.

It did not take Jackson long to begin implementing his new authority. When white farmers penetrated Sauk Indian territory during the summer of 1831, the Jackson administration authorized federal troops to forcibly move the entire band of more than a thousand Indian men, women, and children across the Mississippi.

At the same time, whites were exerting similar pressure on the southern tribes. The case of the Cherokees provides an excellent illustration of the new, more aggressive attitude toward Indian policy. Having allied with Jackson against the Creeks in 1813, the Cherokees emerged from the War of 1812 with their lands pretty well intact, and a rising generation of accommodationist leaders pushed strongly for the tribe to embrace white culture. In the early 1820s the Cherokees created a formal government with a bicameral legislature, a court system, and a professional, salaried civil service. In 1827 the tribe drafted and ratified a written

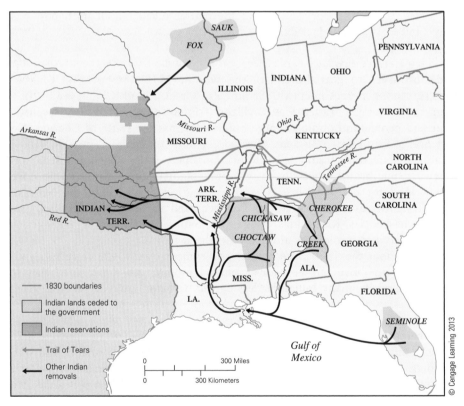

MAP 10.3 The Removal of the Native Americans to the West, 1820–1840

The so-called Trail of Tears, followed by the Cherokees, was one of several routes along which various tribes migrated on their forced removal to reservations west of the Mississippi.

constitution modeled on the Constitution of the United States. In the following year the tribe began publication of its own newspaper, the *Cherokee Phoenix*, printed in both English and Cherokee, using the alphabet devised earlier in the decade by tribal member **George Guess (Sequoyah)**.

Rather than winning the acceptance of their white neighbors, however, those innovations led to even greater friction. From the frontiersmen's point of view, Indians were supposed to be dying out, disappearing into history, not founding new governments and competing successfully for economic power. Thus in 1828 the Georgia legislature nullified the Cherokee constitution. In the following year, gold was found on Cherokee land. As more than three thousand greedy prospectors violated tribal territory, the state of Georgia extended its authority over the Cherokees and ordered all communal tribal lands seized.

That was the first in a series of laws that the Georgia legislature passed to make life as difficult as possible for the Cherokees in hopes of driving them out of the state. When Christian missionaries living with the tribe protested the state's actions and encouraged the Cherokees to seek federal assistance, Georgia passed a law that required teachers among the Indians to obtain licenses from the state—a law expressly designed to eliminate the missionaries' influence. When two missionaries, Samuel Austin Worcester and Elizur Butler, refused to comply, a company of Georgia militia invaded the Cherokee reservation, arrested the teachers, and marched them off to jail.

Two notable lawsuits came out of the combined efforts of the missionaries and Cherokees to get justice. In the first case, **Cherokee Nation v. Georgia** (1831), the Cherokees claimed that Georgia's action in extending authority over them and enforcing state law within Cherokee territory was illegal because they were a sovereign nation in a treaty relationship with the United States. The U.S. Supreme Court refused to hear this case. Speaking for the Court, Chief Justice John Marshall stated that the Cherokee Nation was neither a foreign nor a domestic state but was a "domestic dependent nation" and as such had no standing in federal court.

As American citizens, however, Worcester and Butler did have legitimate standing under federal law, and in 1832 Marshall was able to render a decision in the case of **Worcester v. Georgia**. In this case, the Court ruled that the Cherokee Nation was a distinct political community recognized by federal authority and that Georgia did not have legitimate power to pass laws regulating Indian behavior or to invade Indian land. He thus declared all the laws Georgia had passed to harass the Cherokees null and void and ordered the state to release Worcester and Butler from jail.

Although the Cherokees had grounds for celebration, their joy was short-lived. Jackson refused to use any federal authority to carry out the Court's order. When the Cherokees and their sympathizers pressed Jackson on the matter, he claimed that he was powerless to help and that the only way the Indians could get protection from the Georgians was to relocate west of the Mississippi.

Under this sort of pressure, tribal unity broke down. The majority of Cherokees stood fast with their stalwart leader John Ross, fighting Georgia through the court system. But another faction emerged advocating relocation. Preying on the division, federal Indian agents named the dissenters as the true representatives of the tribe and convinced them to sign the **Treaty of New Echota** (1835), in which the minority faction sold the last 8 million acres of Cherokee land in the East to the U.S. government for $5 million.

A similar combination of pressure, manipulation, and outright fraud led to the dispossession of all the other Civilized Tribes. During the winter of 1831–1832, the Choctaws in Mississippi and Alabama became the first tribe to be forcibly removed from their lands to a designated Indian Territory in what is now Oklahoma. They were joined by the Creeks in 1836 and by the Chickasaws in 1837. John Ross and the other antitreaty Cherokee leaders continued to fight in court and to lobby in Congress, but in 1838 federal troops rounded up the entire Cherokee tribe and force-marched them to Indian Territory. Like all of the Indian groups who were forcibly removed from their native lands, the Cherokees suffered terribly. In the course of the **Trail of Tears**, nearly a fourth of the twenty thousand Cherokees who started the march died of disease, exhaustion, or heartbreak.

Only one of the Civilized Tribes resisted militarily: the Seminoles. Like the other tribes, the Seminoles were deeply divided. Some chose peaceful relocation; others advocated rebellion. After the conciliatory faction signed the Treaty of Payne's Landing in 1832, a group led by **Osceola** broke with the tribe, declaring war on the protreaty group and on the United States. After years of guerrilla swamp fighting, Osceola was finally captured in 1837, but the antitreaty warriors fought on. The struggle continued until 1842, when the United States withdrew its troops, having lost fifteen hundred men during the ten-year conflict. Eventually, even the majority of Osceola's followers agreed to move west, though a small faction of the Seminoles remained in Florida's swamps, justly proud that they were neither conquered nor dispossessed by the United States.

STUDY TOOLS

SUMMARY

With the end of the War of 1812, President Madison and the Republicans promoted a strong agenda for the nation. Joining with former critics such as Henry Clay and John C. Calhoun, Madison pushed for a national market economy by sponsoring federal legislation for a national bank, controlled currency, and tariff protection for American industry. In addition, Madison gave free rein to nationalists such as Stephen Decatur, John Quincy Adams, and Andrew Jackson, who succeeded in enhancing the nation's military reputation and expanding its sphere of influence.

While the nation moved forward in accomplishing its diplomatic goals, the Republicans' economic agenda suffered from a lack of viable transportation and communication systems. Expecting quick and enormous profits, New York built the Erie Canal, the first successful link between the increasingly urban and manufacturing East and the rural, agricultural West. Convinced finally that transportation improvements were necessary for carrying out the work of the government, Madison and his successors joined with state officials to begin the process of building a truly national system of roads and canals.

But what had begun as an age of optimism closed in a tangle of conflict and ill will. A much-hoped-for prosperity dissolved in the face of shrinking markets, resulting in economic panic in 1819 and a collapse in the speculative economy. Economic hard times, in turn, triggered increased competition between the nation's geographical sections, as leaders wrestled for control over federal power in an effort to rid particular areas of economic despair. Supporters of the American System tried to craft a solution, but their compromise did not entirely satisfy anyone. And in the sea of contention that swelled around the Missouri Compromise, the Era of Good Feelings collapsed.

Meanwhile, an army of newly enfranchised voters, common men of moderate means, distressed by what seemed an elite conspiracy to run American affairs, swept the gentlemanly John Quincy Adams out of office and replaced him with the more exciting and presumably more democratic Andrew Jackson. Backed by a political machine composed of northern, western, and southern interests, Jackson had to juggle each region's financial, tariff, and Indian policy demands while trying to hold his political alliance and the nation together. The outcome was a series of regional crises—the Bank War, nullification, and Indian removal—that alienated each region and together constituted a crisis of national proportions.

CHRONOLOGY

NEW OPTIMISM AND A NEW DEMOCRACY

1810	*Fletcher v. Peck*
1814	Treaty of Ghent ends War of 1812
1814–1815	Hartford Convention
1815	Government funds Cumberland Road
	Stephen Decatur defeats Barbary pirates
1816	Tariff of 1816
	First successful steamboat run, Pittsburgh to New Orleans
	James Monroe elected president
1817	Second Bank of the United States opens
1818	Andrew Jackson invades Spanish Florida
1819	*McCulloch v. Maryland*
	Adams-Onís Treaty
	Panic of 1819
1820	Monroe reelected
	Missouri Compromise
1823	Monroe Doctrine
1824–1828	Suffrage reform triples voter population
1825	House of Representatives elects John Quincy Adams president
	Completion of Erie Canal

1826	Disappearance of William Morgan and beginning of Antimasons
1827	Ratification of Cherokee constitution
1828	Tariff of Abominations
	Jackson elected president
	Publication of Calhoun's *The South Carolina Exposition and Protest*
	First issue of the *Cherokee Phoenix*
1830	Webster-Hayne debate
	Indian Removal Act
1831	Federal removal of Sauks and Choctaws
1832	*Worcester v. Georgia*
	Bank War
	Nullification crisis
	Sauk massacred while resisting removal
	Seminole War begins
1836–1838	Federal removal of Creeks, Chickasaws, and Cherokees

FOCUS QUESTIONS

If you have mastered this chapter, you should be able to answer these questions and explain the terms that follow the questions.

1. What were the sources for Americans' optimism as they emerged from the War of 1812 and how did the American government capitalize on this optimism?
2. How did new developments in the nation influence foreign affairs?
3. How did the global economic situation combine with postwar economic optimism to lead to economic panic in 1819?
4. How did economic growth and panic contribute to sectional conflict and political contention?
5. What factors helped change Americans' political options during the mid-1820s?
6. How did the election of Andrew Jackson in 1828 reflect those new options?
7. How did regional conditions influence the national divisions reflected in the Bank War and the nullification crisis?
8. What was President's Jackson role in shaping U.S. Indian policy?

KEY TERMS

"Era of Good Feelings" (*p.* 254)

Hartford Convention (*p.* 254)

DeWitt Clinton (*p.* 255)

Henry Clay (*p.* 255)

John C. Calhoun (*p.* 255)

American System (*p.* 255)

Tariff of 1816 (*p.* 257)

Cumberland Road (*p.* 257)

Erie Canal (*p.* 258)

McCulloch v. Maryland (*p.* 258)

11

THE GREAT TRANSFORMATION: GROWTH AND EXPANSION, 1828–1848

CHAPTER OUTLINE

• The New Cotton Empire in the South • The Manufacturing Empire in the Northeast • A New Empire in the West • Study Tools

---

THE NEW COTTON EMPIRE IN THE SOUTH

The South exploded outward, seeking new lands on which to grow the glamour crop of the century: cotton. In 1820 cotton was being grown heavily in parts of Virginia, South Carolina, and Georgia. Within a matter of decades, the cotton empire had expanded to include most of the South and Southwest. The new dependence on a single crop changed the outlook and experiences not just of large planters but also of the slaves, free blacks, and poor whites whose labor made cotton king.

A New Birth for the Plantation System   Often characterized as the direct heirs of colonial era patriarchs and the conservators of an older, stately way of life, the cotton barons of the **antebellum** South generally were not related to the colonial plantation gentry, but had begun their careers as land speculators, financiers, and rough-and-tumble yeoman farmers whose lucky speculations in the burgeoning cotton market netted large landholdings and armies of slaves. And these planters were far from typical among southerners in general. First, the total number of slaveholders constituted less

---

antebellum The decades before the Civil War, the period from 1815 to 1860; Latin for "before the war."

than one-third of all white southerners. Of the minority who actually owned slaves, nearly three-quarters owned only 80 to 160 acres of land and fewer than ten slaves; another 15 percent owned up to 800 acres and between ten and twenty slaves, leaving only about 12 percent who possessed more than 800 acres and twenty or more slaves. Though few in number, slaveholders in general, and the planter class in particular, controlled the biggest share of productive land and labor. As a result, their economic, political, and social importance was far out of proportion to their numbers.

This is not to say that the image of grand plantations and lavish aristocratic living is entirely false. The owners of cotton plantations made an excellent living from the labor of their slaves. Although they often complained of debt and poor markets, it appears that large-scale planters could expect an annual **return on capital** equivalent to what the most successful northern industrialists were making. Agricultural profits in non-cotton-producing areas were significantly lower, but even there slavery netted white landowners major profits. The enormous demand for workers in the heart of the **Cotton Belt** created a profitable interstate trade in slaves, especially after Congress outlawed the international slave trade in 1808. Thus even planters who did not grow cotton came to have a significant investment in its cultivation and in the labor system that was its cornerstone.

The increasing demand for slaves had a terribly unsettling effect on social stability in the plantation world. Whereas generations of slaves had coexisted with generations of slaveowners on the traditional plantations in the colonial South, now the appeal of quick profits led planters in places like Virginia and Maryland to sell off their slaves, often breaking up families and deeply rooted social connections. This fragmentation of slave society helped to further dehumanize an already dehumanizing institution and drove a deeper wedge between the races.

The enormous profits earned from cotton in the 1840s and 1850s permitted some planters to build elegant mansions and to affect the lifestyle that they associated with a noble past. Voracious readers of romantic literature, planters assumed what they imagined were the ways of medieval knights, adopting courtly manners and the nobleman's **paternalistic** obligation to look out for the welfare of social inferiors, both black and white. Women decked out in the latest gowns flocked to formal balls and weekend parties. Young men were sent to academies where they could learn the twin aristocratic virtues of militarism and honor. Young women attended private "seminaries" where they were taught, in the words of one southern seminary mistress, "principles calculated to render them useful and rational companions." Courtship became highly ritualized, an imitation of imagined medieval court manners.

Practical concerns, however, always threatened to crack this romantic veneer. Although cotton planting might yield huge profits, successful ventures required major capital investment. If land suitable for cotton could be purchased directly

return on capital   The yield on money that has been invested in an enterprise or product.

paternalistic   Treating social dependents as a father treats his children, providing for their needs but denying them rights or responsibilities.

from the federal government, it might be had for as little as 25 cents an acre, but efficient planting called for huge blocks of land, and planters often had to pay a premium to get them. And contrary to popular perception, slave labor was not free: at the height of the slave trade, a healthy male field hand sold for an average of $1,800. Often planters purchased slaves and fields on credit and genuinely feared that their carefully constructed empires and lifestyles might collapse in an instant. Aristocratic parents sought to use marriage as a way to enhance family and economic security. "As to my having any sweethearts that is not thought of," one young southern woman complained. "Money is too much preferred, for us poor Girls to be much caressed."

Even those girls whose fortunes earned caresses faced a strange and often difficult life. Planters' wives bore little resemblance to their counterparts in popular fiction. Far from being frail, helpless creatures, southern plantation mistresses carried a heavy burden of responsibility. A planter's wife was responsible for all domestic matters. She supervised large staffs of slaves, looked out for the health of everyone, and managed all plantation operations in the absence of her husband. All those duties were complicated by a sex code that relegated southern women to a peculiar position in the plantation hierarchy—between white men and black slaves. Southern white women were expected to exercise absolute authority over their slaves while remaining absolutely obedient to white men. "He is master of the house," said plantation mistress Mary Boykin Chesnut about her husband. "To hear [him] is to obey." She also remarked, anxiously, "All the comfort of my life depends upon his being in a good humor." It is little wonder that Chesnut concluded her observations about southern womanhood with the statement, "There is no slave ... like a wife."

And while in some respects planters treated their slaves like machines, slaves were nonetheless human—and sexual—beings, a fact that produced even more stress for planters' wives. Like Thomas Jefferson before them, antebellum planters found that their power over slave women afforded them sexual as well as financial benefits. One southerner rationalized this situation, saying, "The intercourse which takes place with enslaved females is less depraving in its effects [on white men] than when it is carried on with females of their own caste." As a result, a particularly beautiful young slave woman, who like Sally Hemings might herself have been the daughter of such a relationship, could bring as much as $5,000 at auction.

Life among Common Southern Whites   As noted above, fully two-thirds of free southern families owned no slaves. A small number of these families owned stores, craft shops, and other businesses in southern cities. Some were attorneys, teachers, doctors, and other professionals. The great majority, however, were proud small farmers who owned, leased, or simply squatted on the land they farmed.

Often tarred with the label "poor white trash" by their planter neighbors, these people were often productive stock raisers and farmers. They concentrated on producing what they needed to live, but all aspired to produce surpluses or to grow cotton in an effort to raise cash, though they generally could not do so on a large scale. Whatever cash they raised they usually spent on necessary manufactures, as well as on land and slaves.

These small farmers had a shaky relationship with white planters. On the one hand, many wanted to join the ranks of the great planters, hoping they could transform their small holdings into cotton empires. On the other hand, they resented the aristocracy and envied the planters' exalted status and power. They also feared the expansion of large plantations, which often forced smallholders to abandon their hard-won farms and slaves.

Although they seldom rebelled openly against their social superiors, common white people often used the power of the ballot box to make their dissatisfactions known. For despite the enormous power of the plantation elite, they were greatly outnumbered by the lesser class of whites, who had the power to wreck the entire social and economic structure if they became sufficiently disgruntled. Thus the **noblesse oblige** practiced by aristocrats toward poorer whites was as much a practical necessity as it was a romantic affectation.

Large-scale planters also used racial tensions as a device for controlling their contentious neighbors. Although they were not above taking slave concubines or trusting African Americans with positions of authority on plantations, the white elite nonetheless emphasized white supremacy when conversing with their poorer neighbors. They acknowledged that poor farmers felt underprivileged but stressed that slavery spared them from the most demeaning work. Planters asserted that should slavery ever end, whether because of poor white political maneuverings or outside pressures, it would be the farmers who would have the most to lose.

Free Blacks in the South

Caught in the middle between southern planters, slaves, and poor white farmers, African Americans in the South who were not slaves often faced extreme discrimination. Some communities of free blacks could trace their origins back to earliest colonial times, when Africans, like Europeans, served limited terms of indenture. The majority, however, had been freed recently because of diminishing plantation profits during the late 1700s. Most of these people lived not much differently from slaves, working for white employers as day laborers.

Mounting restrictions on free blacks during the first half of the nineteenth century limited their freedom of movement, their economic options, and the protection they could expect to receive by law. In the town of Petersburg, Virginia, for example, when a free black woman named Esther Fells irritated her white neighbor, he took it upon himself to whip her for disturbing his peace. The sheriff did not arrest the assailant but instead took Mrs. Fells into custody, and the court ordered that she be given fifteen more lashes for "being insolent to a white person." Skin color left free African Americans open to abuses and forced them to be extremely careful in their dealings with their white neighbors.

---

noblesse oblige   The belief that members of the elite are duty-bound to treat others charitably, especially those of lower status than themselves.

Still, some opportunities were available for a handful of free blacks who had desirable skills. In the Upper South—Delaware, Maryland, and Virginia—master craftsmen hired young African American boys as apprentices, and those who could stick out their apprenticeship might eventually make an independent living. African American girls, however, had few opportunities as skilled laborers, although some became seamstresses or cooks. Others became washers, and a few grew up to run small groceries, taverns, and restaurants. Folk healing, **midwifery**, and prostitution also led to economic independence for some black women.

Living Conditions for Southern Slaves   A delicate balance between power and profit shaped planters' policies toward slaves and set the tone for slave life. Maintaining profitability prompted slaveowners to enforce severe discipline and exercise careful supervision over slaves, leading southern states to write increasingly harsh **slave codes** during the early nineteenth century, which gave slaveowners virtual life-and-death control over their human property. But slaves were expensive: damaging a healthy slave meant taking a significant financial loss. Still, given the need to keep up productivity, slaveowners readily used measured force. "I always punish according to the crime," one plantation owner declared. "If it is a Large one I give him a genteel flogging with a strop, about 75 Lashes I think is a good whipping." Acknowledging the practical effects of even this "genteel" form of discipline, he continued, "When picking cotton I never put on more than 20 stripes and very frequently not more than 10 or 15." But not all plantation owners were gentle or even practical when it came to discipline. The historical record is filled with accounts of slaveowners who were willing to take a financial loss by beating slaves until they became useless or even died.

In keeping with demands for profitability, housing for slaves was seldom more than adequate. Most slaves lived in one-room log cabins with dirt floors. Mindful of the need to maintain control and keep slaves productive, slaveowners tried to avoid crowding people into slave quarters. Census figures suggest that the average slave cabin housed five or six people. As one slaveowner explained, "The crowding [of] a number into one house is unhealthy. It breeds contention; is destructive of delicacy of feeling, and it promotes immorality between the sexes." The cabins had windows, but generally only wooden shutters and no glass, so that occupants had to choose between shutting out the light or letting in flies in summer and cold in winter. The usual source of artificial light was an open fireplace or stove, also used for heat and cooking. Ever-present fires increased the danger of cabins burning down, especially because chimneys were generally made of sticks held together with dried mud. As one slave commented, "Many the time we have to get up at midnight and push the chimney away from the house to keep the house from burning up."

Furnishings in slave houses were usually fairly crude and often crafted by the residents themselves. Bedding normally consisted of straw pallets stacked on the floor or occasionally mounted on rough bedsteads. Other furnishings were equally

midwifery   The practice of assisting women in childbirth.

This early photograph, taken on a South Carolina plantation before the Civil War, freezes slave life in time, giving us a view of what slave cabins looked like, how they were arranged, how the largest majority of slaves dressed, and how they spent what little leisure time they had.

simple—rough-hewn wooden chairs or benches and plank tables. Clothing was also very basic. One Georgia planter itemized the usual yearly clothing allowance for slaves: "two suits of cotton for spring and summer, and two suits of woolen for winter; four pair of shoes and three hats." Women commonly wore simple dresses or skirts and blouses, while children often went naked in the summer and were fitted with long, loose hanging shirts during the colder months.

It appears that the slave diet, like slave clothing and housing, was sufficient but not particularly pleasing. One slave noted that there was "plenty to eat sich as it was," but in summer flies swarmed all over the food. Her master, she said, would laugh about that, saying the added nutrition provided by the flies "made us fat." Despite justified complaints, slaves in the American South ate significantly more meat than workers in the urban North. In addition to meat, slaves consumed milk and corn, potatoes, peas and beans, molasses, and fish. The planter usually provided this variety of food, but owners also occasionally permitted slaves to hunt and fish and to collect wild roots, berries, and vegetables.

Although the diet provided to slaves kept them alive, the southern diet in general lacked important nutrients, and diet-related diseases plagued southern communities. Slaves were also subject to occupational ailments like hernia, pneumonia,

Collection of William Gladstone

and **lockjaw**. Because of inadequate sanitation, slaves also suffered from dysentery and **cholera**. Cardiovascular (heart and circulatory) diseases were also **endemic** among slaves. Recent research reveals that most slave children were undernourished because slaveowners would not allocate enough food for people who did not work. Once children were old enough to work, however, they had access to a very high-calorie diet. Such early malnutrition followed by an abrupt switch to a high-calorie and often high-fat diet may well have led to the high incidence of heart attacks, strokes, and similar ailments that the historical record indicates among slaves. And given the balance-sheet mentality among plantation owners, this phenomenon may not have been unwelcome. Old people who could not work hard were, like children, a liability; thus having slaves die from circulatory disease in middle age saved planters from unnecessary expenditures later on.

As to the work itself, cotton planting led to increasing concentration in the tasks performed by slaves. A survey of large and medium-size plantations during the height of the cotton boom shows that the majority of slaves (58 percent of the men and 69 percent of the women) were employed primarily as **field hands**. Of the rest, only 2 percent of slave men and 17 percent of slave women were employed as **house slaves**. The remaining 14 percent of slave women were employed in nonfield occupations such as sewing, weaving, and food processing. Seventeen percent of slave men were employed in nonfield activities such as driving wagons, piloting riverboats, and herding cattle. Another 23 percent were managers and craftsmen.

The percentage of slave craftsmen was much higher in cities, where slave **artisans** were often allowed to hire themselves out on the open job market in return for handing part of their earnings over to their owners. In Charleston, Norfolk, Richmond, and Savannah, slave artisans formed **guilds**. Feeling threatened by their solidarity, white craftsmen appealed to state legislatures and city councils for restrictions on slave employment in skilled crafts. Such appeals, and the need for more and more field hands, led to a decline in the number of slave artisans during the 1840s and 1850s.

Whether on large plantations or small farms, the burden of slavery was a source of constant stress for both slaves and masters in the newly evolving South. The precarious nature of family life, the ever-present threat of violence, and the overwhelming sense of powerlessness weighed heavily on slaves. Among masters, the awareness that they often were outnumbered and thus vulnerable to organized slave rebellion was a source of anxiety. Locked into this fear- and hate-laden

---

lockjaw   A popular name for tetanus, an often fatal disease resulting primarily from deep wounds.

cholera   An infectious disease of the small intestines contracted mainly from bacteria in untreated water.

endemic   Present in a particular group of people or geographical area.

field hands   People who did agricultural work such as planting, weeding, and harvesting.

house slaves   People who did domestic work such as cleaning and cooking.

artisan   A person who works at a craft, such as a blacksmith, cabinet maker, or stone mason.

guild   An association of craftspeople with the same skills who join together to protect their common interests.

atmosphere, everyone in the cotton South was drawn into what would become a long-lasting legacy of racial tension and distrust.

THE MANUFACTURING EMPIRE IN THE NORTHEAST

Although the South changed radically during the opening years of the nineteenth century, one thing persisted: the economy remained rooted in households. Before the 1820s, households in the North also produced most of the things they used. For example, more than 60 percent of the clothing that Americans wore was spun from raw fibers and sewn by women in their own homes. Some householders even crafted sophisticated items—furniture, clocks, and tools—but skilled artisans usually made such products. These craftsmen, too, usually worked in their homes, assisted by family members and an extended family of artisan employees: apprentices and **journeymen**.

Beginning with the cotton-spinning plants that sprang up during the War of 1812, textile manufacturing led the way in pushing production out of the home: from 1820 onward, manufacturing increasingly moved into factories, and cities began to grow up around the factories. Such changes severed the intimate ties between manufacturers and workers, and both found themselves surrounded by strangers in the new urban environments. "In most large cities there may be said to be two nations, understanding as little of one another, having as little intercourse, as if they lived in different lands," said one insightful observer. "This estrangement of men from men, of class from class, is one of the saddest features of a great city."

The "American System of Manufacturing" The transition from home manufacturing to factory production did not take place overnight, and the two processes often overlapped. Pioneer manufacturers such as Samuel Slater relied on home workers to carry out major steps in the production of textiles. Using what was called the **putting-out system**, cotton spinners supplied machine-produced yarn to individual households, where families then wove fabric on their own looms during their spare time. Such activities provided much-needed cash to farm families, enabled less productive family members (like the elderly or children) to contribute, and gave entire families worthwhile pastimes during lulls in the farming calendar.

But innovations in manufacturing soon began to displace such home crafting. The factory designs pioneered by Francis Cabot Lowell and his various partners were widely copied during the 1820s and 1830s. Spinning and weaving on machines located in one building significantly cut both the time and the cost of manufacturing. Quality control became easier because the tools of the trade, owned by the manufacturer rather than by the worker, were standardized and employees were under constant supervision. As a result, the putting-out system for

---

journeyman   A person who has finished an apprenticeship to learn a trade or craft and is a qualified worker in the employ of another.

Manufacturing and the Revolution in Time

In 1838, Chauncey Jerome introduced the first mass-produced brass clock to the consumer market at a price that virtually any American could afford. The distribution of clocks and the means by which they were manufactured reinforced each other. Factory production required that workers, clerks, managers, shippers, and others essential to industry be coordinated if factories were going to function effectively. All of these employees, from the highest to the lowest in status, needed to have a reliable way of telling time. Mass-produced clocks provided that reliability, contributing to a revolution in the way Americans began thinking about time itself. Increasingly people looked to mechanical devices to punctuate their lives. Time management, a concept that would have been foreign to a previous generation of Americans, had now

become a reality. Today we are almost entirely dependent on day planners or electronic personal information managers to keep track of time, a heritage of the revolution in timekeeping that was born in 1838 with the introduction of cheap brass clocks.

- How were the lives of Americans in the early nineteenth century changed by the increased regimentation and mechanical perceptions of time that accompanied the manufacturing revolution? In what ways does your life reflect these changes that took place so long ago?
- Try to imagine experiencing one day without referring to any sort of mechanical or electronic time management device. Describe what your day would be like.

turning yarn into cloth went into serious decline, falling off by as much as 90 percent in some areas of New England. Even home production of clothes for family use declined. Women discovered that spending their time producing cheese or eggs or other marketable items could bring in enough cash to purchase clothing and still have money left over. Throughout the 1830s and 1840s, ready-made clothing became standard wearing apparel.

A major technological revolution helped to push factory production into other areas of manufacturing as well during these years. In traditional manufacturing, individual artisans crafted each item one at a time, from the smallest part to the final product. A clock maker, for example, either cast or carved individually by hand all of the clock's internal parts. As a result, the mechanisms of a clock worked together only in the clock for which they had been made. If that clock ever needed repair, new parts had to be custom-made for it. The lack of **interchangeable parts** made manufacturing extremely slow and repairs difficult, and it limited employment in the manufacturing trades to highly skilled professionals.

After years of experimentation, in 1821 an engineer named John H. Hall brought together the necessary skill, financing, and tools at the Harper's Ferry federal armory to prove that manufacturing using interchangeable parts was practical.

Within twenty years this "American system of manufacturing," as it was called, was being used to produce a wide range of products—farm implements, padlocks, sewing machines, and clocks. Formerly, clocks had been a status symbol setting apart people of means from common folks; however, using standardized parts, pioneer manufacturers like Chauncey Jerome revolutionized clock making to the point where virtually all Americans could afford them. Such manufacturing breakthroughs produced a number of goods so inexpensive and reliable that even Europeans began importing them, reversing the long-standing pattern of manufactures moving exclusively from Europe to America and launching a trend that would grow in the years to come.

New Workplaces and New Workers
With machines now producing standardized parts for complex mechanisms such as clocks, the worker's job was reduced to simply assembling premade components. The centuries-old guild organization for artisans—preserved in the hierarchical system of apprentices, journeymen, and master craftsmen—rapidly fell away as extensive training in the manufacturing arts became irrelevant.

At first, owners found they had to use creative means to attract workers into the new factories. Some entrepreneurs developed company towns. In New England these towns resembled traditional New England villages. Families recruited from the economically depressed countryside were installed in neat row houses, each with its own small vegetable garden. The company employed each family member. Women worked on the production line. Men ran heavy machinery and worked as **millwrights**, carpenters, haulers, or as day laborers dredging out the **millraces**. Children did light work in the factories and tended gardens at home.

Lowell's company developed another system at its factories. Hard-pressed to find enough families to leave traditional employment and come to work in the factories, Lowell recruited unmarried farm girls. The company built dormitories to house these young working women, offering cash wages and reasonable prices for room and board, as well as cultural events and educational opportunities. Because most of the girls saw factory work as a transitional stage between girlhood and marriage, Lowell assured them and their families that the company would strictly control the moral atmosphere so that the girls' reputations would remain spotless.

In New York, Philadelphia, and other cities, immigrant slums offered opportunistic manufacturers an alternative source of labor. In the shoe industry, for example, one family would make soles, while a neighboring family made heels, and so forth. This type of operation was not as efficient as large shoe factories, but the money that urban manufacturers saved by not building factories and by paying rock-bottom wages to desperate slum-dwellers made it possible for the companies to compete successfully in the open market.

The combination of machine production and a growing pool of labor proved economically devastating to workers. No longer was the employer a master

millwright   A person who designs, builds, or repairs mills or mill machinery.
millrace   The channel for the fast-moving stream of water that drives a mill wheel.

craftsman or a paternalistic entrepreneur who felt some responsibility to look out for his workers' domestic needs. Factory owners were obligated to investors and bankers and had to squeeze the greatest possible profit out of the manufacturing process. They kept wages low, regardless of the workers' cost of living. As the swelling supply of labor allowed employers to offer lower and lower wages, increasing numbers of working people faced poverty and squalor.

Immigration supplied much of this labor. Between 1820 and 1830 slightly more than 151,000 people immigrated to the United States. In the decade that followed, that number increased to nearly 600,000; between 1840 and 1850, well over a million-and-a-half people moved to the United States from abroad. This enormous increase in immigration changed not only the demographic but also the cultural and economic face of the nation. The flood of immigrants collected in the port and manufacturing cities of the Northeast, where they joined Americans fleeing financial depression in the countryside. Adding to the resulting brew were former master craftsmen, journeymen, and apprentices who no longer had a secure place in the changing economy. Together, though seldom cooperatively, these groups helped to form a new social class in America.

Nearly half of all the immigrants who flooded into the United States between 1820 and 1860 came from Ireland. In the mid-1840s a blight that killed the one staple food source for Irish peasants—the potato—led millions to flee the island. Most Irish immigrants had few marketable skills or more money than the voyage to America cost; they arrived penniless and with little choice when seeking employment.

Similar conditions beset many members of the second most numerous immigrant group: the Germans. Economic change and political upheaval in Germany were putting both peasants and skilled craftsmen to flight. Like Irish peasants, German farmers arrived in America destitute and devoid of opportunities. Trained German craftsmen had a better chance of finding employment, but as unskilled factory workers rather than empowered artisans.

Not only were the new immigrants poor and often unskilled, but also most were culturally different from native-born Americans. Religion was their most notable cultural distinction: the majority were Roman Catholic. This made them suspect in the minds of people steeped in anti-Catholic sentiments handed down from earlier generations of Protestant immigrants. Immigrants' languages, dress, and eating and drinking habits also set them off, making them targets of discrimination.

Such discrimination and a desire to live among people who understood their ways and spoke their language brought new immigrants to neighborhoods where their countrymen had already found places to live. In New York, Philadelphia, and other cities, people with the same culture and religion built churches, stores, pubs or beer halls, and other familiar institutions that helped them cope with the shock of transplantation from Europe and gave them a chance to adapt gradually to life in the United States. They also started **fraternal organizations** and clubs to overcome the loneliness, isolation, and powerlessness they were experiencing.

fraternal organizations   Organizations in which private individuals freely associate as equals for mutually beneficial purposes.

Because the new immigrants were poor, housing in their neighborhoods was often substandard, and living conditions were crowded, uncomfortable, and unsanitary. Desperate for work and eager to make their own way in their new country, these fresh immigrants were willing to do nearly anything to earn money. Lacking the resources to buy farms and the skills to enter professional trades, they were the perfect work force for the newly evolving industrial economy. As the flow of immigrants increased, the traditional labor shortage in America was replaced by a **labor glut**, and the social and economic status of all workers declined accordingly.

Living Conditions in Blue-Collar America

Working conditions for **blue-collar workers** in factories reflected the labor supply, the amount of capital available to the manufacturing company, and the personal philosophy of the factory owner. Girls at Lowell's factories described an environment of familiar paternalism. Factory managers and boarding-house keepers supervised every aspect of their lives in much the same manner that authoritarian fathers saw to the details of life on traditional New England farms. As for the work itself, one mill girl commented that it was "not half so hard as ... attending the dairy, washing, cleaning house, and cooking." What bothered factory workers most was the repetitive nature of the work and the resulting boredom. One of Lowell's employees described the tedium. "The time is often apt to drag heavily till the dinner hour arrives," she reported. "Perhaps some part of the work becomes deranged and stops; the constant friction causes a belt of leather to burst into a flame; a stranger visits the room, and scans the features and dress of its inmates inquiringly; and there is little else to break the monotony."

She went on to note that daydreaming provided relief from the boredom, but daydreaming in front of fast-moving equipment could have disastrous consequences for what a New Jersey magazine called "the human portion of the machine." Inattentive factory workers were likely to lose fingers, hands, or whole arms to whirring, pounding, slashing mechanisms. Not a few lost their lives. Investors vetoed any additional costs that safety devices might have incurred: Samuel Slater, for example, complained bitterly to his investors after a child was chewed up in a factory machine, "You call for yarn but think little about the means by which it is to be made."

Gradually Slater's and Lowell's well-meaning paternalism became rare as factory owners withdrew from overseeing day-to-day operations. The influx of laborers from the depressed countryside and of foreign immigrants wiped out both decent wages and the sorts of incentives the early manufacturing pioneers had employed. Not only did wages fall but laborers were also expected to find their own housing. Soon hulking **tenements** sprang up, replacing the open fields and clusters of small homes that once had dominated the urban landscape. Large houses

labor glut Oversupply of labor in relation to the number of jobs available.

blue-collar workers Workers who wear work clothes, such as coveralls and jeans, on the job; their work is likely to involve manual labor.

tenement An urban apartment house, usually with minimal facilities for sanitation, safety, and comfort.

The Granger Collection, New York

Living conditions for working people in America's new industrializing cities were often terrible, as this illustration of a working class tenement apartment makes clear. "The walls are dark and damp and the miserable room is lighted only by a shallow sash," a New York Tribune *reporter observed. "Here they work, here they cook, they eat, they sleep, they pray."*

formerly occupied by domestic manufacturers and their apprentices were broken up into tiny apartments by profit-hungry speculators who rented them to desperate laborers. Cellars and attics became living spaces like the rest of the building. In cities like New York, laborers lived fifty to a house in some working-class areas. As population soared, sewage disposal, drinking water, and trash removal became difficult to provide. Life in such conditions was grossly unpleasant and extremely unhealthy: epidemics of typhus, cholera, and other crowd diseases swept through the slums periodically.

Investigating living and working conditions, a *New York Tribune* reporter found them deplorable. "The floor is made of rough plank laid loosely down, and the ceiling is not quite so high as a tall man," he reported of a tenement dwelling. "The walls are dark and damp and the miserable room is lighted only by a shallow sash partly projecting above the surface of the ground and by the light that struggles from the steep and rotting stairs." In this dark and tiny space, he observed, "often lives the man and his work bench, the wife, and five or six children of all ages; and perhaps a palsied grandfather and grandmother and often both. Here they work, here they cook, they eat, they sleep, they pray."

Life and Culture among a New Middle Class

Large-scale manufacturing not only changed industrial work but also introduced demands for a new class of skilled managerial and clerical employees. Under the old system of manufacturing, the master craftsman or his wife had managed the company's accounts, hired journeymen and apprentices, purchased raw materials, and seen to the delivery of finished products. The size of the new factories made such direct contact between owners, workers, and products impossible. To fill the void, a new class of professionals came into being. In these days before the invention of the typewriter, firms such as Lowell's Boston Manufacturing Company employed teams of young men as clerks. These clerks kept accounts, wrote orders, and drafted correspondence, all in longhand. As elite owners such as Lowell and his partners became wrapped up in building new factories, pursuing investors, and entering new markets, both clerical and manufacturing employees were increasingly supervised by professional managers.

One distinguishing characteristic of the new **white-collar workers** was their relative youth. These young people, many of them the sons and daughters of rural farmers, had flocked to newly emerging cities in pursuit of formal education. They stayed to seek employment, leaving behind the economic instability and **provincialism** of the farm.

Men too attended school when and where they could get financial assistance and then settled down where they could find employment and the company of others like themselves. Women joined men in moving into new professions. While middle-class men found employment as clerks, bookkeepers, and managers, middle-class women parlayed their formal education and their gender's perceived gift for nurturing children into work as teachers. It became acceptable for women to work as teachers for several years before marriage, and many avoided marriage altogether to pursue their hard-won careers.

Middle-class men and women tended to put off marriage as long as possible while they established themselves socially and economically. They also tended to have fewer children than their parents. In the new urban middle-class setting, parents felt compelled to send their children to school so that they could take their place on the career ladder chosen by their parents. Adding nothing to family income, children thus became economic liabilities rather than assets, and middle-class adults used a combination of late marriage and various forms of birth control to keep families small.

A lack of traditional ties affected the lives of both married and unmarried middle-class people. Many unmarried men and women seeking their fortunes in town boarded in private homes or rooming houses. After marriage, middle-class men and women often moved into private town homes, isolating themselves and their children from perceived dangers in the faceless city but also losing the comforting sociability of traditional country life. Accordingly, these young people crafted new urban structures that might provide the missing companionship and guidance. Many found companionship in **voluntary associations**. Students in colleges and universities formed a variety of discussion groups, preprofessional clubs,

white-collar workers Workers able to wear white shirts on the job because they do no grubby manual labor.

provincialism The limited and narrow perspective thought to be characteristic of people in rural areas.

voluntary association An organization or club through which individuals engage in voluntary service, usually associated with charity or reform.

and benevolent societies. After graduation, groups such as the Odd Fellows and the Masons brought people together for companionship. Such organizations helped enforce traditional values through rigid membership standards stressing moral character, upright behavior, and, above all, order.

The *Odd Fellows' Manual* summarized the philosophy of these organizations well. "In the transaction of our business we pursue strict parliamentary rules, that our members may be qualified for any public stations to which they may be called by their fellow-citizens," the manual asserts. "And when business has been performed, we indulge in social intercourse, and even in cheerful and innocent hilarity and amusement. But all in strict order and decorum, good fellowship and prudence are constantly to be kept in view." In such clubs, people could discuss the latest books or world affairs with others of similar education and lifestyle in an affable setting. As the *Odd Fellows' Manual* went on to say, "Exercise yourself in the discussions of your Lodge not for the purpose of mere debate, contention, or 'love of opposition,' but to improve yourself in suitably expressing your sentiments." Young people also created and joined professional and trade groups. These associations served a social function, but they also became forums for training novices and for setting standards for professional methods and modes of conduct.

Members of the new middle class also used their organizing skills to press for reforms. While the elite class of factory owners and financiers generally formed the leadership for such organizations as the American Tract Society, the American Bible Society, and the American Board of Commissioners for Foreign Missions—each a multimillion-dollar reforming enterprise—young middle-class men and women provided the rank and file of charity workers.

In addition to their youth, another characteristic that prevailed among this newly forming class was deep anxiety. Although their education and skills earned them jobs with greater prestige than those of the average worker, these clerks and supervisors could be laid off or demoted to working-class status at any time. Also, because of the anonymity in the new cities, it was virtually impossible to know if a stranger was truly a member of one's own class or an imposter who might use the trappings of gentility to take advantage of the new urban scene. Such suspicions led to a very strict set of rules for making social connections.

Social Life for a Genteel Class   The changes in lifestyle that affected working-class and middle-class Americans were in large part an outcome of changes in the daily lives of those who owned and operated manufacturing businesses. In earlier years, when journeymen and apprentices had lived with master craftsmen, they were in effect members of a craftsman's extended family. Such working arrangements blurred the distinction between employee and employer. The factory system ended this relationship. The movement of workers out of the owners' homes permitted members of the emerging elite class to develop a **genteel** lifestyle that set them off from the army of factory workers and lesser number of clerks. Genteel families aimed at the complete separation of their

---

genteel   The manner and style associated with elite classes, usually characterized by elegance, grace, and politeness.

private and public lives. Men in the manufacturing elite class spent their leisure time in new activities. Instead of drinking, eating, and playing with their employees, business owners began to socialize with one another in private clubs and in church and civic organizations. Instead of attending the popular theater, elite patrons began endowing opera companies and other highbrow forms of entertainment.

The lives of the factory owners' wives also changed. The mistress of a traditional manufacturing household had been responsible for important tasks in the operation of the business. Genteel women, in contrast, were expected to leave business dealings to men. Ensconced in private houses set apart from the new centers of production and marketing, genteel women found themselves with time on their hands. To give themselves something to do, they sought areas of activity that would provide focus and a sense of accomplishment without imperiling their elite status by involving them in what was now perceived as the crass, masculine world of commerce. Many found outlets for their creative energies in fancy needlework, reading, and art appreciation societies. But some wished for more challenging activities. Sarah Huntington Smith, for example, a member of Connecticut's elite, spoke for many when she complained in 1833, "To make and receive visits, exchange friendly salutations, attend to one's wardrobe, cultivate a garden, read good and entertaining books, and even attend religious meetings for one's own enjoyment; all this does not satisfy me."

One activity that consumed genteel women was motherhood. Magazines and advice manuals, which began appearing during the 1820s and 1830s, rejected the traditional adage of "spare the rod, spoil the child," replacing it with an insistence on gentle nurturing. One leader in this movement was author and teacher Bronson Alcott. Alcott denied the concept of **infant depravity** that had so affected Puritan parents during the colonial era and led them to break their children's will, often through harsh measures. Instead, he stated emphatically that "the child must be treated as a free, self-guiding, self-controlling being." Alcott was equally emphatic that child rearing was the mother's responsibility. As his wife, Abigail, wrote of family management in Alcott's household, "Mr. A aids me in general principles, though nobody can aid me in the detail."

Books like Alcott's *Conversations with Children on the Gospels* (1836) flooded forth during these years and appealed greatly to isolated and underemployed women. Many adopted the advertised **cult of domesticity** completely. Turning inward, these women centered their lives on their homes and children. In doing so, they believed they were performing an important duty for God and country and fulfilling their most important, perhaps their only, natural calling.

Other genteel women agreed with the general tone of the domestic message but widened the woman's supposedly natural sphere outward, beyond the nursery, to encompass the whole world. They banded together with like-minded women to get out into the world in order to reform it, involving themselves in a variety of reform movements, such as founding Sunday schools or opposing alcohol abuse. These causes let them use their nurturing and purifying talents to improve what appeared to be an increasingly chaotic and immoral society.

---

infant depravity   The idea that children are naturally sinful because they share in the original sin of the human race but have not learned the discipline to control their evil instincts.

cult of domesticity   The belief that women's proper role lies in domestic pursuits.

A New Empire in the West

While life in the cotton South and manufacturing Northeast underwent radical change, the American West too was experiencing wholesale transformation. Enterprising capitalists often led the way in systematic exploration, looking for furs, gold, and other sources of quick profit. But it did not take long before a wide variety of others followed. Whether they expected a wasteland, a paradise, or something in between, what all of these newcomers to the West did find was a natural and cultural world that was much more complex than anything they had imagined.

**Moving
Westward**

The image of the solitary trapper braving a hostile environment and even more hostile Indians is the stuff of American adventure novels and movies. Although characters such as Christopher "Kit" Carson and Jeremiah "Crow Killer" Johnson really did exist, these men were merely advance agents for an **extractive industry** geared to the efficient removal of animal pelts.

What drew men like Carson and Johnson into the Far West in the 1830s and 1840s was an innovation in the fur business instigated by long-time entrepreneur William Henry Ashley. Taking advantage of the large numbers of underemployed young men seeking fortune and adventure in the West, Ashley broke the long

The mountain fur trade is a colorful part of the nation's history and folklore. While millionaire fur entrepreneurs like John Jacob Astor lived in luxury in eastern cities, trappers like Joe Meek (pictured here) occupied the wild and lawless territory of the upper Missouri River. Like many of his contemporaries, Meek survived his wilderness experiences to become an economic and political leader in the Far West when the fur business finally wound down in the 1840s.

Image from the Yale Collection of Americana. Beinecke Rare Book and Manuscript Library.

extractive industry   An industry, such as fur trapping, logging, or mining, that removes natural resources from the environment.

tradition of depending exclusively on Indian labor for collecting furs. In 1825 he set up the highly successful rendezvous system. Under this arrangement, individual trappers—white adventurers like Carson and Johnson, African Americans such as James Beckwourth, and a large number of Indians—combed the upper Missouri, trapping, curing, and packing furs. Once each year Ashley conducted a fur rendezvous in the mountains, where the trappers brought their furs and exchanged them for goods. Pioneer missionary Pierre Jean de Smet called these gatherings "one of the most picturesque features of early frontier life in the Far West."

Often the first people to join the former fur trappers in settling the West were not rugged yeoman farmers but highly organized and well-financed land speculators and developers. From the earliest days of the republic, federal public land policy favored those who could afford large purchases and pay in cash. Liberalization of the land laws during the first half of the nineteenth century put smaller tracts—for less money and on credit terms—within reach of more citizens, but speculators continued to play a role in land distribution by often offering even smaller tracts and more liberal credit (see Chapter 10). This was particularly true as states granted rights-of-way, first to canal companies and then, increasingly, to railroad developers as a way of financing internal improvements. Land along transportation routes was especially valuable, and developers could often turn an outright grant into enormous profits.

A third group of expectant fortune hunters was lured into the Far West by the same magnet that had drawn the Spanish to the American Southwest: gold. Since colonial times, Americans had persistently hunted precious metals, usually without much success. The promise of gold continued to draw people westward, however, onto Winnebago lands in 1827 and into Cherokee territory in 1829. But the most impressive case of gold fever would not strike until 1848, when a group of laborers digging a millrace in northern California found flakes and then chunks of gold. Despite efforts to suppress the news, by September, news reached the East that the light work of panning for gold in California could yield $50 a day, two months' wages for an average northern workingman. In 1849 more than a hundred thousand **forty-niners** took up residence in California.

As in earlier gold rushes, most of these fortune hunters did not discover gold, but many of them stayed to establish trading businesses, banks, and farms. Others moved on, still seeking their fortunes. But eventually they too settled down to become shopkeepers, farmers, and entrepreneurs.

Distinct waves of Americans pushed westward into the areas opened by gold seekers, fur trappers, and land speculators. All of these migrants were responding to promises of abundant land in America's interior. But different groups were reacting to very different conditions in the East, and those differences gave shape to their migrations and to the settlements they eventually created.

"To make money was their chief object," one young pioneer woman in Texas commented; "all things else were subsidiary to it." Like her family, many settlers went west to improve their fortunes. Many, too, were pushed by economic forces. Throughout New England, for example, people faced a choice between moving into cities or migrating westward. Others, however, saw the unsettled West as a refuge

forty-niners Prospectors who streamed into California in 1849 after the discovery of gold in the Sierra foothills in 1848.

for establishing or expanding particular religious or social practices. Many Protestant sects sent battalions of settlers and missionaries to carve out new "Plymouth Colonies" in the West. The most notable of these religious pioneer groups was the Mormons, who came to dominate the Great Basin Region.

This movement was founded in upstate New York in 1830 by **Joseph Smith Jr.** Announcing that he had experienced a revelation that called for him to establish a community in the wilderness, Smith led his congregation out of New York in 1831 to settle in the northeastern Ohio village of Kirtland. There the Mormons thrived for a while, stressing notions of community, faith, and hard work. But religious persecution eventually convinced Smith to lead his followers farther west into Missouri and then to the Illinois frontier, where they founded the city of Nauvoo in 1839. Continuing conversions to the new faith brought a flood of Mormons to Smith's Zion in Illinois. In 1844 Nauvoo, with a population of fifteen thousand Mormons, dwarfed every other Illinois city.

Despite their growth in numbers and prosperity, Smith's community in Nauvoo continued to be victims of religious and economic persecution. On June 27, 1844, Smith was murdered by a mob in neighboring Carthage, Illinois. The remaining church leaders concluded that the Mormons would never be safe until they moved far from mainstream American civilization. **Brigham Young**, Smith's successor, decided to search for a safe refuge beyond the Rocky Mountains and led sixteen hundred Mormons to the valley of the **Great Salt Lake**.

Whether they were hopeful cotton planters from the South, Yankee farmers from New England, or religious refugees in the **Great Basin**, most people went west not as the stalwart individualists immortalized by Western movies, but as part of a larger community. Beginning with early parties going to Ohio or Texas in the 1820s, most traveled in small-to-medium-size groups. Even those few who arrived alone seldom stayed that way. "Those of us who have no families of our own, reside with some of the families in the settlement," one young migrant observed. "We remain here notwithstanding the scarcity of provisions, to assist in protecting the settlement."

During the 1830s and 1840s, migrating parties became larger and more organized. It took six months to cross the more than 2,000 miles separating the settled part of the nation from the **Oregon Country**. Describing an Oregon-bound wagon train in the 1840s, one young woman reported that "Probably there were sixty-five or seventy, or possibly more than that, wagons in our train, and hundreds of loose cattle and horses." "We were not allowed to travel across the plains in any haphazard manner," she continued. "No family or individual was permitted to go off alone from the company." Among such groups on the **Oregon Trail**, life remained much as it had been at home. "Everybody was supposed to rise at daylight, and while the women were preparing breakfast, the men rounded up the cattle, took down the tents, yoked the oxen to the wagons and made everything ready for an immediate start after the morning meal was finished." Even social customs remained the same. "Life on the plains was a primitive edition of life in town or village," the same pioneer woman remarked.

One other thing most pioneers had in common was that hard cash was always in short supply. Frontier farmers in every region of the West lived on a shoestring, barely making ends meet when conditions were good and falling into debt when weather or other hazards interrupted farming. Still, those who were lucky and

Benjamin Franklin Reinhart, "An Evening Halt–Emigrants Moving to the West in 1840", 1867, oil on canvas, 40 × 70 inches. The Corcoran Gallery of Art, Washington, D.C. Gift of Mr. and Mrs. Lansdell K. Christie, 59.21.

Though highly idealized, this painting of an emigrant wagon train settling down for the night on the Oregon Trail does capture many accurate details. Notice, for example, the division of labor: women are washing, cooking, and tending to small children while men are drawing water, herding animals, and preparing to hunt for food. Diaries kept by actual emigrants confirm this was the way life was on the trail.

exercised careful management were able to carve out excellent livings. Strongly centralized authority and a deeply felt sense of community helped the Mormons, for example, to overcome even bad luck and deficient skills. Many in other communities, however, had to sell out to satisfy creditors or saw their land repossessed for debts. Pulling up stakes again, they often moved to new lands exhausted of furs and opened to settlement by merchant-adventurers and Indian agents.

Many pioneers had no legal claim to their lands. People bankrupted by unscrupulous speculators or by their own misfortune or mismanagement often settled wherever they could find a spread that seemed unoccupied. Thousands of squatters living on unsold federal lands were a problem for the national government when the time came to sell off the public domain. Always with an eye to winning votes, western politicians frequently advocated "squatter rights," as Thomas Hart Benton had done in 1830. Western congressmen finally maneuvered the passage of a **preemption bill** in 1841, allowing squatters to purchase the lands they occupied. Of course, this right did not guarantee that they would have the money or that they would make profitable use of the land. Thus shoestring farming, perpetual debt, and an uncertain future continued to challenge frontier farmers.

Pioneer Life in the New Cotton Country

Migrants to cotton country in the Mississippi Valley and beyond brought a particular lifestyle with them. Often starting out as landless herders, migrating families carved out claims beyond the **frontier line** and survived on a mixture of raised and gathered food until they could put the land into agricultural production. The Indians who preceded them in the Mississippi Valley unintentionally simplified life for these families, having already cleared large expanses of land for agriculture. Removal of the Indians to the Far West and the continuing devastation of Indian populations by disease meant that southern frontiersmen could plant corn and cotton quickly and reap early profits with minimal labor.

Although some areas were cleared and extremely fertile, others were swampy, rocky, and unproductive. In these less desirable locales, settlers were allowed to survey their own claims. The result was the re-creation of the southern class system in the new lands: those fortunate enough to get profitable lands might become great planters; those not so fortunate had to settle for lesser prosperity and lower status.

During the pioneer phase of southern frontier life, all the members of migrating families devoted most of their time to the various tasks necessary to keep the family alive. Even their social and recreational lives tended to center on practical tasks. House building, planting, and harvesting were often done in cooperation with neighbors. On such occasions participants consumed plenty of food and homemade whiskey, and at day's end, music and dancing often lasted long into the night. Women gathered together separately for large-scale projects such as group quilting. Another community event for southwestern settlers was the periodic religious revival, which brought people from miles around to revival meetings that might last for days. Here they could make new acquaintances, court sweethearts, and discuss the common failings in their souls and on their farms.

Life among Westering Yankees
For migrants to areas such as Michigan and Oregon, the overall frontier experience differed in many respects from that in the Mississippi Valley. In the Old Northwest, Indians had also cleared the land for planting; pioneers snatched up the Indians' deserted farms. Here, however, professional surveyors had already carved the land into neat rectangular lots. These surveys generally included provision for a township, where settlers quickly established villages similar to those left behind in New England. Here they recreated the social institutions they already knew and respected—first and foremost, law courts, churches, and schools.

Conditions in the Oregon Country resembled those farther east in most respects, but some significant differences did exist. Most important, the Indians in the Oregon Country had never practiced agriculture—their environment was so rich in fish, meat, and wild vegetables that farming was unnecessary—and they still occupied their traditional homelands and outnumbered whites significantly. Although both of these facts might have had a profound impact on life in Oregon, early pioneers were bothered by neither. Large open prairies flanking the Columbia, Willamette, and other rivers provided abundant fertile farmland. And the Indians helped rather than hindered the pioneers.

---

frontier line   The outer limit of agricultural settlement bordering on areas still under Indian control or unoccupied.

Like their southwestern counterparts, pioneers in both the Old and the Pacific Northwest cooperated in house building, annual planting and harvesting, and other big jobs, but a more sober air prevailed at these gatherings among the descendants of New England Puritans. Religious life was also more solemn. Religious revivals swept through Yankee settlements during the 1830s and 1840s, but the revival meetings tended to be held in churches at the center of communities rather than in outlying campgrounds. As a result, they were usually briefer and less emotional than their counterparts on the cotton frontier and strongly reinforced the Yankee notion of village solidarity.

The Hispanic Southwest   In addition to a physical environment very different from that in the Pacific Northwest, the Southwest bore the lasting cultural imprint of Spain's and then Mexico's control of the region.

Although Spain could assert a claim extending back to the mid-1500s, systematic Spanish exploration into most of the American Southwest did not begin until the eighteenth century. In California, for example, Russian expansion into the Oregon region prompted the Spanish to begin moving northward; garrisons were established at San Diego and Monterey in 1769 and 1770. **Junípero Serra**, a Franciscan friar, accompanied this expedition and established a mission, San Diego de Alcalá, near the present city of San Diego. Eventually Serra and his successors established twenty-one missions extending from San Diego to the town of Sonoma, north of San Francisco.

The mission system provided a framework for Spanish settlement in California. Established in terrain that resembled the hills of Spain, the missions were soon surrounded by groves, vineyards, and lush farms. California Indians provided the labor needed to create this new landscape, but not willingly: the missionaries often forced them into the missions, where they became virtual slaves. The death rate from disease and harsh treatment among the mission Indians was terrible, but their labor turned California's coastal plain into a vast and productive garden.

The Franciscans continued to control the most fertile and valuable lands in California until after Mexico won independence from Spain. Between 1834 and 1840, however, the Mexican government seized the mission lands in California and sold them off to private citizens living in the region. An elite class of Spanish-speaking **Californios** snatched up the rich lands.

At first, the Californios welcomed outsiders as neighbors and trading partners. Ships from the United States called at California ports regularly, picking up cargoes of beef **tallow**, cow hides, and other commodities to be shipped around the world, and settlers who promised to open new lands and businesses were given generous grants and assistance. **John Sutter**, for example, received an outright grant of land extending from the Sierra foothills southwest to the Sacramento

---

tallow   Hard fat obtained from the bodies of cattle and other animals and used to make candles and soap.

With two wives and several children to help share the burden of work, this Mormon settler was in a good position to do well, even in the harsh conditions that prevailed in the near-desert environment of Utah. Sensitive to disapproval from more traditional Christians, families like this tended to associate exclusively with other Mormons and pressured outsiders to leave as quickly as possible.

Valley, where in 1839 he established a colony called New Helvetia, eventually a thriving cosmopolitan center.

A similar pattern of cosmopolitan cooperation existed in other Spanish North American provinces. In 1821 trader William Becknell began selling and trading goods along the Santa Fe Trail from St. Louis to New Mexico. By 1824, the business had become so profitable that people from all over the frontier moved in to create a permanent Santa Fe trade. As had taken place in St. Louis, an elite class emerged in Santa Fe from the intermingled fortunes and intermarriages among Indian, European, and American populations, and a strong kinship system developed. Thus, based on kinship, the Hispanic leaders of New Mexico consistently worked across cultural lines, whether to fight off Texan aggression or eventually to lobby for **annexation** to the United States.

Intercultural cooperation also characterized the early history of Texas settlement. Spanish and then Mexican officials aided the empresarios, hoping that the aggressive Americans would form a frontier line between southern Plains Indians and prosperous silver-mining communities south of the **Rio Bravo**. Tensions rose, however, as population increased. Despite the best efforts of the Mexican government to encourage Hispanics to settle in Texas, fully four-fifths of the thirty-five

annexation   The incorporation of a territory into an existing political unit such as a neighboring country.

hundred land titles perfected by the empresarios went to non-Hispanics. Cultural insensitivity and misunderstanding created disharmony between **Texians** and **Tejanos** and each tended to cling to their own ways.

The Mormon   Physical conditions in the Great Basin led to a completely
Community   different social and cultural order in that area. Utah is a high-
                        desert plateau where water is scarce and survival depends on
careful management. The tightly ordered community of Mormons was perfectly suited to succeed in such an inhospitable place.

Mormons followed a simple principle: "Land belongs to the Lord, and his Saints are to use so much as they can work profitably." The church measured off plots of various sizes, up to 40 acres, and assigned them to settlers on the basis of need. Thus a man with several wives, a large number of children, and enough wealth to hire help might receive a grant of 40 acres, but a man with one wife, few children, and little capital might receive only 10. The size of a land grant determined the extent to which the recipient was obligated to support community efforts. When the church ordered the construction of irrigation systems or other public works, a man who had been granted 40 acres had to provide four times the amount of labor as one who had been granted 10 acres. Like settlers elsewhere, the Mormons in Utah joined in community work parties, but cooperation among them was more rigidly controlled and formal.

Mormons had their own peculiar religious and social culture, and because of their bad experiences in Missouri and Illinois, they were unaccepting of strangers. The General Authorities of the church made every effort to keep Utah an exclusively Mormon society, welcoming all who would embrace the new religion and its practices but making it difficult for non-Mormons to stay in the region. The one exception was the American Indian population. Because Indians—defined by the Book of Mormon as descendants of the Lamanites, a lost tribe of Israel—occupied a central place in Mormon sacred literature, the Mormons practiced an accepting and gentle Indian policy. Like other missionaries, Mormons insisted that Indians convert to their religion and lifestyle, but the Mormon hierarchy used its enormous power in Utah to prevent private violence against Indians whenever possible.

Tying the West   Rapid expansion created an increased demand for reliable
to the Nation   transportation and communications between the new regions
                        in the West and the rest of the nation. An early first step in
meeting this demand was building the so-called National Road, which between 1815 and 1820 snaked its way across the Cumberland Gap in the Appalachian Mountains and wound from the Atlantic shore to the Ohio River at Wheeling, Virginia. By 1838 this state-of-the-art highway—with its evenly graded surface, gravel pavement, and stone bridges—had been pushed all the way to Vandalia,

Texians Non-Hispanic settlers in Texas in the nineteenth century.
Tejanos Mexican settlers in Texas in the nineteenth century.

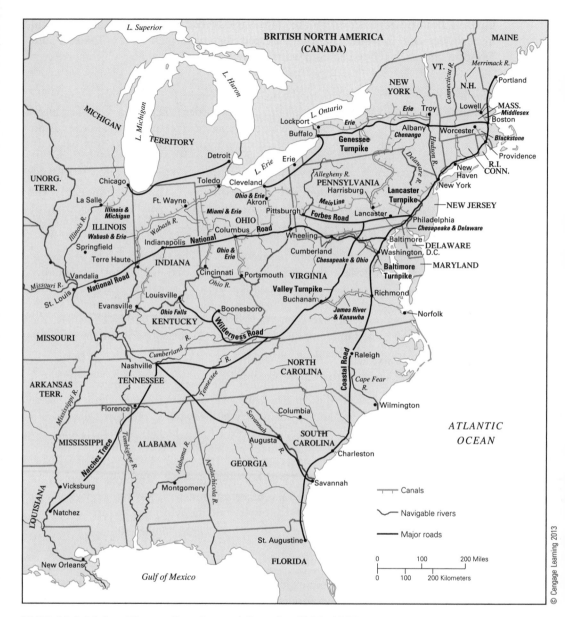

MAP 11.1 Major Rivers, Roads, and Canals, 1825–1860

Railroads and canals increasingly tied the economy of the Midwest to that of the Northeast.

Illinois. Within a few more years, it reached St. Louis, the great jumping-off point for the Far West.

At the same time, a series of other roads was beginning to merge into a trans-portation network. The so-called Military Road connecting Nashville to New

Orleans also earned federal funding, as did the Nashville Road that, in turn, connected Nashville to Knoxville, where a traveler could pick up the Great Valley Road to Lynchburg, Virginia, and from there the Valley Turnpike, which connected with the Cumberland Road. Eventually towns from Portland, Maine, to Saint Augustine, Florida, and from Natchez, Mississippi, to New Haven, Connecticut, were linked by intersecting highways. Increasing numbers of people used these new roads to head west looking for new opportunities. Farmers, craftsmen, fur hunters, and others already settled in the West used them too, moving small loads of goods to the nearby towns and small cities that always sprang up along the unfolding transportation routes. But the new roads did little to advance large-scale commerce. Heavy and bulky products were too expensive to move: at a minimum, hauling a ton of freight along the nation's roads cost 15 cents a mile. At that rate, the cost of shipping a ton of oats from Buffalo to New York City amounted to twelve times the value of the cargo.

But the new roads also linked rural America to an ever-expanding network of waterways that made relatively inexpensive long-distance hauling possible. Completed in 1825, the Erie Canal revolutionized shipping: the cost of transporting a ton of oats from Buffalo to Albany fell from $100 to $15, and the transit time dropped from twenty days to just eight. All of New York State celebrated. The spectacular success of the Erie Canal prompted businessmen, farmers, and politicians throughout the country to promote canal building. State governments offered exclusive charters to canal-building companies, giving them direct financial grants, guaranteeing their credit, and easing their way in every possible manner. The result was an explosion in canal building that lasted through the 1830s.

This new mobility did not come cheaply. Canals cost as much as $20,000 to $30,000 a mile to build, and financing was always a problem. Hoping for large profits, entrepreneurs such as John Jacob Astor invested heavily in canal building. Before 1836, careful investors could make a 15 to 20 percent return on capital in canal building, but after that, most canal companies faced bankruptcy, as did the states that had helped finance them.

Steam power took canal building's impact on inland transportation a revolutionary step further. After Shreve's pioneer voyage in 1816, the cost of shipping a ton of goods down American rivers fell annually. By 1840, the price had declined from an average of 1¼ cents a mile to less than half a cent, and the cost of upstream transport from over 10 cents a mile to less than a cent. In addition, steamboats could carry bulky and heavy objects that could not be hauled upstream for any price by any other means. The impact of steam technology on the economies of the South and West was staggering. The presence of dependable transportation on the Mississippi drew cotton cultivation farther into the nation's interior, western farmers flooded into the Ohio Valley, and fur trappers and traders pressed up the Missouri River.

Steam technology also began to have applications for towns lacking water routes to the interior. As they began losing inland trade revenue to canal towns such as Albany and Philadelphia, entrepreneurs in places like Baltimore looked for other ways to move cargo. Demands from Baltimore merchants spurred Maryland to take the lead in developing a new transportation technology: the steam railroad. In 1828 the state chartered the **Baltimore and Ohio Railroad** (B&O). The B&O

soon demonstrated its potential when inventor Peter Cooper's steam locomotive *Tom Thumb* sped 13 miles along B&O track. Seeking publicity and increased funding, Cooper staged a race between his steam-drawn train and a horse-drawn car. The horse won, and the embarrassed B&O abandoned steam power.

Despite Cooper's failure, South Carolina chose to invest in steam technology and chartered a 136-mile rail line from Charleston to Hamburg. Here, the first full-size American-built locomotive, the *Best Friend of Charleston,* successfully pulled cars until the engine exploded, taking much of the train and many of its passengers with it. The Charleston and Hamburg Railroad, however, had the engine rebuilt and began experimenting with making trains safer. Massachusetts followed this practice as well as it tried to siphon off trade from New York by building a railroad from Boston to Albany.

Although rail transport enjoyed some success during this early period, it could not rival water-based transportation systems. By 1850 individual companies had laid approximately 9,000 miles of track, but not in any coherent network. Rails were laid with little or no standardization of track size, and as a result, railcars could not be transferred from one company's line to another's. Other problems plagued the fledgling industry. Boiler explosions, fires, and derailments were common because pressure regulators, spark arresters, and brakes were inadequate. And in state capitals, investors who hoped to profit from canals, roads, and steam shipping lobbied to prevent legislatures from supporting rail expansion.

Distance impaired not only American commerce but also the conduct of the republic itself. Since the nation's founding, American leaders had expressed the fear that the continent's sheer size would make true federal democracy impractical. Voting returns, economic data, and other information crucial to running a republic seemed to take an impossibly long time to circulate, and the problem promised to get worse as the nation grew. During the 1790s, for example, it took a week for news to travel from Virginia to New York City and three weeks for a letter to get from Cincinnati to the Atlantic coast. The transportation revolution, however, made quite a difference in how quickly news got around. After the Erie Canal opened, letters posted in Buffalo could reach New York City within six days and might get to New Orleans within two weeks.

As the nation expanded, and as economics and social life became more complicated, Americans felt growing pressure to keep up with news from across the nation and its new territories. Transportation improvements helped them do so by moving printed matter faster and more cheaply. At the same time, revolutions in printing technology and paper production significantly lowered the cost of printing and speeded up production. Organizations such as the American Bible Society and the American Tract Society joined newspaper and magazine publishers in producing a flood of printed material. In 1790 the 92 newspapers being published in America had a total **circulation** of around 4 million. By 1835 the number of periodicals had risen to 1,258, and circulation had surpassed 90 million.

The explosion in the volume and velocity of communications was enhanced by an even greater revolution in information technology that was in its starting

---

circulation   The number of copies of a publication sold or distributed.

phases. In the mid-1830s, Samuel F. B. Morse began experimenting with the world's first form of electronic communication: the **electric telegraph**. Morse developed a code consisting of dots (short pulses) and dashes (longer pulses) that represented letters of the alphabet. With this device, a skilled operator could quickly key out long messages and send them at nearly the speed of light. Over the next several years, Morse worked on improvements to extend the distance that the impulses would travel along the wires. Finally, in 1843, Congress agreed to finance an experimental telegraph line from Washington, D.C., to Baltimore. Morse sent his first message on the experimental line on May 24, 1844. His message, "What hath God wrought!" was a fitting opening line for the telecommunications revolution.

STUDY TOOLS

SUMMARY

Although seemingly the most old-fashioned region of the country, the South that emerged during the years leading up to 1840 was a profoundly different place from what it had been before the War of 1812. As an industrial revolution overturned the economies in Great Britain and the American Northeast, economic options for southerners also changed radically. Although elite southerners clothed their new society in romanticized medieval garb, they were creating an altogether new kind of economy and society. The efficient production of cotton by the newly reorganized South was an essential aspect of the emerging national market economy and a powerful force in the Great Transformation.

Change in the North was more obvious, as factories replaced craft shops and cities replaced towns. The new economy and new technology created wonderful new opportunities but also imposed serious constraints. A revamped social structure replaced the traditional order as unskilled and semiskilled workers, a new class of clerks, and the genteel elite carved out new lives. As in the South, the outcome was a remarkable transformation in the lives of everyone in the region.

Meanwhile, the westward movement of Americans steadily gained momentum. Some successful entrepreneurs such as William Henry Ashley made enormous profits from their fur-trading empires. Land speculators and gold seekers, too, helped open areas to settlement. Such pioneers were usually followed by distinct waves of migrants who went west in search of land and opportunity. In Texas, Oregon, California, Utah, and elsewhere in the West, communities sprang up like weeds. Here they interacted—and often clashed—with one another, with those who had prior claims to the land, and with the land itself. As a result, a variety of cultures and economies developed in the expansive section of the country.

Tying the regions together, a new network of roads, waterways, and communications systems accelerated the process of change. After 1840, it was possible to ship goods from any one section of the country to any other, and people in all sections were learning more about conditions in far distant parts of the growing nation. Often this new information promised prosperity, but it also made more and more people aware of the enormity of the transformation taking place and the glaring differences between regions. The twin outcomes would be greater integration in the national economy and increasing tension between mutually dependent participants in the new marketplace.

CHRONOLOGY

THE DAWN OF MODERNIZATION

1821	William Becknell opens Santa Fe Trail to American traders
1822	John H. Hall perfects interchangeable parts for gun manufacturing
1828	Baltimore and Ohio Railroad commissioned
1830	Church of Latter-day Saints (Mormons) founded in New York
1830–1840	Ten-year immigration figure for United States exceeds 500,000
1835	Number of U.S. periodicals exceeds 1,250, with combined circulation of 90 million
1836	Samuel F. B. Morse invents electric telegraph Bronson Alcott's *Conversations with Children on the Gospels*
1838	National Road completed to Vandalia, Illinois First mass-produced brass clock
1839	John Sutter founds New Helvetia Mormons build Nauvoo, Illinois
1841	Congress passes preemption bill
1844	Murder of Joseph Smith
1847	Mormons arrive in Utah
1848	Gold discovered in California

FOCUS QUESTIONS

If you have mastered this chapter, you should be able to answer these questions and explain the terms that follow the questions.

1. Why did living conditions for southerners—black and white—change after 1820?
2. How did elite white southerners respond to the change? How did their response affect slaves, free blacks, and poor whites?
3. How did manufacturing and the nature of work change in the United States after 1820?
4. In what ways did the American system of manufacturing change the traditional pattern of U.S. foreign trade?
5. How did the developing factory system affect the lives of artisans, factory owners, and middle-class Americans?
6. How did most Americans imagine "the West"? To what extent were their imaginings accurate?
7. Who generally were the first pioneers to move into the West? How did they and those who followed actually move westward and establish communities there?

KEY TERMS

Cotton Belt (*p.* 287)

slave codes (*p.* 290)

putting-out system (*p.* 293)

interchangeable parts (*p.* 294)

Joseph Smith Jr. (*p.* 304)

Brigham Young (*p.* 304)

Great Salt Lake (*p.* 304)

Great Basin (*p.* 304)

Oregon Country (*p.* 304)

Oregon Trail (*p.* 304)

preemption bill (*p.* 305)

Junípero Serra (*p.* 307)

Californios (*p.* 307)

John Sutter (*p.* 307)

Rio Bravo (*p.* 308)

Baltimore and Ohio Railroad (*p.* 311)

electric telegraph (*p.* 313)

12

RESPONSES TO THE
GREAT TRANSFORMATION,
1828–1848

REACTIONS TO CHANGING CONDITIONS

As industrialization and urbanization mushroomed in the Northeast, cotton cultivation and its peculiar cultural and labor systems expanded across the South, and hundreds of communities grew up in the West. At the same time, however, increasing economic interdependence between regions and revolutionary transportation and communications systems pulled the geographically expansive nation closer together. These opposing forces helped define not only the social and political tendencies throughout the country but also the trends that would shape a distinctive American culture.

Romanticism and Genteel Culture   Underlying the new mood in American culture was an artistic and philosophical attitude that swept across the Atlantic and found a fertile new home in North America. **Romanticism**, the European rebellion against Enlightenment reason, stressed the heart over the mind, the wild over the controlled, the mystical over the rational. The United States, with its millions of acres of wilderness, was the perfect setting for romanticism to flower. Many of the era's leading intellectuals emphasized the positive aspects of life in the United States, celebrating it in new forms of religious thought, literary presentation, and artistic expression that won broad recognition among the genteel and middle classes.

This new influence had its earliest impact in the religious realm. Reeling under the shock of social change that was affecting every aspect of life, many young

The Spread of Mass Literacy

During the colonial and early national eras, literacy beyond basics like signing your name was reserved to a small number of elite people in American society. Books were expensive, and newspapers were few in number; there was little opportunity for most people to read and little incentive for them to do so. During the early nineteenth century, however, the spread of public education, creation of literary and self-improvement societies, and mass publication of books and magazines caused an upsurge in both the availability and demand for literacy. Many saw in universal literacy a device that would ensure continuation of the American democratic republic, and writers saw in it a burgeoning marketplace for making personal fortunes. For their part, young men and women saw in literacy an opportunity to break away from traditional roles in a traditional political and economic system to forge new lives in a new society. From this era onward, Americans took widespread literacy among all classes for granted as part of our national life.

- What developments arose during the early nineteenth century that helped to produce mass literacy in the United States?
- How would American society today be different if only a wealthy elite minority could read? How would your life be different in such a society?

people sought a religious anchor to engender some stability. Many, especially in the rising cities in the Northeast, found a voice in New Englander **Ralph Waldo Emerson.**

Pastor of the prestigious Second Unitarian Church in Boston, Emerson experienced a religious crisis in 1831 when his young wife, Ellen Louisa, died. Looking for new inspiration, he traveled to Europe where he met the famous Romantic writers William Wordsworth and Thomas Carlyle, who influenced him to seek truth in nature and spirit rather than in rationality and order. Emerson combined this Romantic influence with his already strong Unitarian leaning, creating a new philosophical creed called **transcendentalism.** Recovered from his grief, he returned to the United States to begin a new career as an essayist and lecturer, spreading the transcendentalist message.

"Historical Christianity has fallen into the error that corrupts all attempts to communicate religion," Emerson told the students at the Harvard Divinity School in 1838. "Men have come to speak of revelation as somewhat long ago given and done, as if God were dead." But for Emerson, God was "everywhere active, in each ray of the star, in each wavelet of the pool." Only through direct contact with the transcendent power in the universe could men and women know the truth.

Emerson's writings were in tune with the cultural and economic currents of his day. In celebrating the individual, Emerson validated the surging individualism of

Jacksonian America. In addition, because each person had to find his or her own path to knowledge, Emerson could extol many of the disturbing aspects of modernizing America as potentially liberating forces. Rather than condemning the money grubbing that many said characterized Jacksonian America, Emerson stated that money represented the "prose of life" and was, "in its effects and laws, as beautiful as roses."

Emerson not only set the tone for American philosophical inquiry but also suggested a bold new direction for American literature. His 1837 address at Harvard University entitled "The American Scholar" was a declaration of literary independence from European models. Young American writers responded enthusiastically. During the twenty years following this speech, Henry David Thoreau, Walt Whitman, Henry Wadsworth Longfellow, and other writers and poets elaborated the nationalistic and transcendentalist gospels, emphasizing the uniqueness of the individual and the role of literature as a vehicle for self-discovery and national expression. "I celebrate myself, and sing myself," Whitman wrote. They also carried the Romantic message, celebrating the primitive and the common. Longfellow sang the praise of the village blacksmith, and in "I Hear America Singing," Whitman conveyed the poetry present in the everyday speech of America's common folk.

Perhaps the most radical of the transcendentalists was Emerson's good friend and frequent houseguest **Henry David Thoreau.** Emerson and his other followers made the case for self-reliance, but Thoreau embodied it, camping on the shore of Walden Pond near Concord, Massachusetts, where he did his best to live independent of the rapidly modernizing market economy. "I went to the woods because I wished to live deliberately," Thoreau wrote, "and not, when I came to die, discover that I had not lived."

Among women who were seeking meaning through their writing, Margaret Fuller was the leading transcendentalist. After demonstrating her own equality by editing the transcendentalist magazine *The Dial* as well as serving as chief literary critic for the *New York Tribune,* Fuller advocated for women's rights in her *Woman in the Nineteenth Century* (1845).

But the most popular women writers of the day were those who were most successful at communicating the sentimentalized role for the new genteel woman. Lydia Sigourney was one of the first American women to carve out an independent living as a writer, focusing on themes that were popular among women of the elite and emerging middling classes. Catharine Beecher was another writer who enjoyed enormous success for her practical advice guides aimed at making women more effective homemakers. The novels of women writers E. D. E. N. Southworth and Susan Warner were among the most popular books published in the first half of the nineteenth century.

Other authors joined Sigourney, Southworth, and Warner in pushing American literature in Romantic directions. James Fenimore Cooper and Nathaniel Hawthorne each helped to popularize American themes and scenes in their writing. Even before Emerson's "American Scholar," Cooper had launched a new sort of American novel and American hero. Cooper's *The Pioneers* (1823) was the first of five novels featuring Natty Bumppo, a frontiersman whose rough-hewn virtues were beloved by Romantics and popularly associated with the American frontier.

Nathaniel Hawthorne explored different American literary themes. In *Twice-Told Tales* (1837), Hawthorne presented readers with a collection of moral **allegories** stressing the evils of pride, selfishness, and secret guilt among puritanical New Englanders. He brought these themes to fruition in his novel *The Scarlet Letter* (1850), in which adulteress Hester Prynne overcomes shame to gain redemption, while her secret lover, Puritan minister Arthur Dimmesdale, is destroyed by his hidden sins.

George Bancroft did for American history what novelists like Cooper did for American literature. Bancroft set out in 1834 to capture the history of the United States from its first settlement, a story that eventually filled ten volumes when he completed it in 1874. Focusing on strong leaders who carried out God's design by bringing liberty into the world, Bancroft made clear that the middle-class qualities of individualism, self-sufficiency, and a passionate love of liberty were the essence of the American experience and the American character. Bancroft's history became the definitive work of its kind, influencing generations of American students and scholars in their interpretations of the nation's past.

The drive to celebrate American scenes and the young nation's uniqueness also influenced the visual arts during this period. Neoclassicism, a style influenced by Enlightenment rationalism that emphasized the simple, logical lines found in Greek and Roman art, dominated the art scene at first. Artists often used classical imagery in their portrayals of contemporary figures and events. Horatio Greenough's statue of George Washington, for example, presented the nation's first president wrapped in a toga, looking like a Roman statesman. After 1825, however, classical scenes were gradually being replaced by American ones. Englishman Thomas Cole came to the United States in 1818 hoping to find a romantic paradise. Cole was disappointed by the neoclassical art scene in Philadelphia, but eventually found the paradise he was seeking in the Hudson River valley. There he began painting romantically exaggerated renderings of the landscape. The refreshing naturalness and Americanness of Cole's paintings attracted a large following, and other artists took up the style. This group of landscapists is known as the **Hudson River school**, after the area where most of them painted.

The paintings of George Caleb Bingham exemplify another movement in American art that reflected the temper of the time. Bingham was born in Virginia and educated for a time in Pennsylvania before he went west to Missouri. There he painted realistic pictures of common people engaged in everyday activities. The flatboat men, marketplace-dwellers, and electioneering politicians in Bingham's paintings were artistic testimony to the emerging democratic style of America in the Jacksonian period.

Culture among Workers and Slaves

Most genteel people in the antebellum era would have denied that working people, whether wage-earning immigrants in northern cities or slaves in the South, had a "culture." But each of these groups crafted viable cultures that suited their living

---

allegory   A story in which characters and events stand for abstract ideas and suggest a deep, symbolic meaning.

and working conditions and were distinct from the genteel culture of their owners or supervisors.

Wretched living conditions and dispiriting poverty encouraged working-class people in northern cities to choose social and cultural outlets that were very different from those of upper- and middle-class Americans. Offering temporary relief from unpleasant conditions, drinking was the social distraction of choice. Whiskey and gin were cheap and available during the 1820s and 1830s as western farmers used the new roads and canals to ship distilled spirits to urban markets. In the 1830s, consumers could purchase a gallon of whiskey for 25 cents.

Even activities that did not center on drinking tended to involve it. While genteel and middle-class people remained in their private homes reading Sigourney or Hawthorne, working people attended popular theaters cheering entertainments designed to appeal to their less polished tastes. **Minstrel shows** featured fast-paced music and raucous comedy. Plays, such as Benjamin Baker's *A Glance at New York in 1848,* presented caricatures of working-class "Bowery B'hoys" and "G'hals" and of the well-off Broadway "pumpkins" they poked fun at. To put the audience in the proper mood, theater owners sold cheap drinks in the lobby or in basement pubs. Alcohol was also sold at sporting events that drew large working-class audiences—bare-knuckle boxing contests, for instance, where the fighting was seldom confined to the boxing ring.

Stinging from their low status in the urbanizing and industrializing society, angry about living in hovels, and freed from inhibitions by hours of drinking, otherwise rational workingmen often pummeled one another to let off steam. And in working-class neighborhoods, where police forces were small, fist-fights often turned into brawls and then into riots pitting Protestants against Catholics, immigrants against the native-born, and whites against blacks.

Working-class women experienced the same dull but dangerous working conditions and dismal living circumstances as working-class men, but their lives were even harder. Single women were particularly bad off. They were paid significantly less than men but had to pay as much and sometimes more for living quarters, food, and clothing. Marriage could reduce a woman's personal expenses—but at a cost. While men congregated in the barbershop or candy store drinking and socializing during their leisure hours, married women were stuck in tiny apartments caring for children and doing household chores.

Like their northern counterparts, slaves fashioned for themselves a culture that helped them to survive and to maintain their humanity under dehumanizing conditions. Traces of an enduring African heritage were visible in slaves' clothing, entertainment, and folkways. Often the plain garments that masters provided were upgraded with colorful headscarves and other decorations similar to ornaments worn in Africa. Hairstyles often resembled those characteristic of African tribes. Music, dancing, and other forms of public entertainment and celebration also showed strong African roots. Musical instruments were copies of traditional ones, modified only by the use of New World materials. And stories that were told around the stoves at night were

minstrel show   A variety show in which white actors made up as blacks presented jokes, songs, dances, and comic skits.

a New World adaptation of African **trickster tales.** Other links to Africa abounded. Healers among the slaves used African ceremonies, Christian rituals, and both imported and native herbs to effect cures. Taken together, these survivals and adaptations of African traditions provided a strong base underlying a solid African American culture.

Abiding family ties helped to make this cultural continuity possible. Slave families endured despite kinship ties made fragile by their highly precarious life. Children could be taken away from their parents, husbands separated from wives at the whim of masters. And anyone might be sold at any time. In this precarious environment, another African legacy, the concept of fictive kinship contributed to family stability by turning the whole community of slaves into a vast network of aunts and uncles.

Within families, the separation of work along age and gender lines followed traditional patterns. Slave women, when not laboring at the assigned tasks of plantation work, generally performed domestic duties and tended children, while the men hunted, fished, did carpentry, and performed other "manly" tasks. Children were likely to help out by tending family gardens and doing other light work until they were old enough to join their parents in the fields or learn skilled trades.

Slaves' religion, like family structure, was another means for preserving unique African American traits. Though slaves often were designated as Baptists or Methodists, the Christianity they practiced differed in significant ways from that of their white neighbors. Slave preachers untrained in white theology often merged Christian and African religious figures, creating unique African American religious symbols. Ceremonies too combined African practices such as group dancing with Christian prayer. The merging of African musical forms with Christian lyrics gave rise to a new form of Christian music: the **"Negro spiritual."**

Radical Attempts to Regain Community

To many of all classes, society seemed to be spinning out of control as modernization rearranged basic lifestyles. Some religious groups and social thinkers tried to ward off the excesses of Jacksonian individualism by forming **utopian** communities that experimented with various living arrangements and ideological commitments.

A wealthy Welsh industrialist, Robert Owen, began one of the earliest experiments along these lines. In 1825 he purchased a tract of land in Indiana called **New Harmony.** Believing that the solution to poverty in modern society was to collect the unemployed into self-contained and self-supporting villages, Owen opened a textile factory in which ownership was held communally by the workers and

---

trickster tales   Stories that feature as a central character a clever figure who uses his wits and instincts to adapt to changing times; a survivor, the trickster is used by traditional societies, including African cultures, to teach important cultural lessons.

utopian   Ideal; refers to the reformist belief that a perfect society can be created on Earth and that a particular group or leader has the knowledge to actually create such a society.

decisions were made by group consensus. Even though the community instituted innovations like an eight-hour workday, cultural activities for workers, and the nation's first school offering equal education to boys and girls, New Harmony did not succeed. Owen and his son, Robert Dale Owen, were outspoken critics of organized religion and joined their close associate **Frances (Fanny) Wright** in advocating radical causes. These leanings made the Owenites unpopular with more traditional Americans, and when their mill experienced economic hardship in 1827, New Harmony collapsed.

A more famous experiment, **Brook Farm**, had its origin in the transcendentalist movement. The brainchild of George Ripley, Brook Farm was designed to "prepare a society of liberal, intelligent and cultivated persons, whose relations with each other would permit a more wholesome and simple life than can be led amidst the pressure of our competitive institutions." To carry out this enterprise Ripley set up a joint-stock company. Most of the stockholders were transcendentalist celebrities such as Nathaniel Hawthorne and Ralph Waldo Emerson, but they disappointed Ripley by failing to invest their time and labor, merely dropping in from time to time. In 1844 Ripley adopted a new constitution based on **socialism**. Drawing on French utopian socialist **Charles Fourier** for inspiration, Ripley emphasized community self-sufficiency, the equal sharing of earnings among members of the community, and the periodic redistribution of tasks and status to prevent boredom and elitism. With this new disciplined ideology in place, Brook Farm began to appeal to serious artisans and farmers, but a disastrous fire in 1845 cut the experiment short. Other Fourierist communities were also founded during this period—nearly a hundred such organizations sprang up from Massachusetts to Michigan and southward into Texas.

Unlike Fourierist communities, some communal experiments were grounded in religious beliefs. The **Oneida Community**, established in central New York in 1848, for example, reflected the notions of its founder, John Humphrey Noyes. Though educated in theology at Andover and Yale, Noyes could find no church willing to ordain him because of his strange belief that his followers could escape sin through faith in God, communal living, and group marriage. Unlike Brook Farm and New Harmony, the Oneida Community was very successful financially, establishing thriving logging, farming, and manufacturing businesses. It was finally dissolved as the result of local pressures directed at the "free love" practiced by its members.

Economically successful communes were also operated by the **Shakers**. Free love never disturbed their settlements: Shakers practiced absolute celibacy. Founded in Britain in 1770 and then transported to America in 1774, the sect grew slowly at first, but in the excitement of the early nineteenth century, it expanded at a more vigorous rate. By 1826 eighteen Shaker communities had been planted in eight states and were home to as many as six thousand followers. The Shaker communities succeeded by pursuing farming activities and the

---

socialism   The public ownership of manufacturing, farming, and other forms of production so that they benefit society rather than produce individual or corporate profits.

manufacture and sale of furniture and handcrafts admired for their design and workmanship. But like the Oneida Community, the Shakers' ideas about marriage and family stirred up controversy. In a number of cases, converts deserted husbands or wives to join the organization, often bringing their children with them. This led to several highly publicized lawsuits. Like most such experiments, the Shaker movement went into decline after 1860, though vestiges of it remain operative today.

A Second Great Awakening   While some were drawn to transcendentalism and a handful chose to follow radical communitarian leaders, others sought solace within existing, mainstream denominations. Beginning in the 1790s both theologians and popular preachers sought to create a new Protestant creed that would maintain the notion of Christian community in an atmosphere of increasing individualism and competition. Disturbed by perceptions of rising secularism and declining church memberships, Protestant activists like **Joseph Tracy** crafted a new evangelical movement that they hoped would launch a Second Great Awakening.

Mirroring tendencies in the political and economic realms, Protestant thinking during the opening decades of the nineteenth century emphasized the role of the individual. Under the leadership of Jonathan Edwards's grandson, Timothy Dwight, Yale College became a hotbed of liberalizing Protestant theology. One young Yale theologian, Nathaniel Taylor, created a new theology that was entirely consistent with the prevailing secular creed of individualism. According to this new doctrine, God offers salvation to all, but it is the individual's responsibility to seek it. Thus the individual has "free will" to choose or not choose salvation. Taylor's ideas struck a responsive chord in a restless and expanding America. Hundreds of ordained ministers, licensed preachers, and **lay exhorters** carried the message of individual empowerment to an anxious populace.

Unlike Calvinist Puritanism, which characterized women as the weaker sex, the new evangelicalism stressed women's spiritual equality with—and even spiritual superiority to—men. Not surprisingly, young women generally were the first to respond to the new message. The most effective preachers of the day turned women into agents spreading the word to their husbands, brothers, and children. **Charles Grandison Finney** stood out among a new generation of preachers. A former schoolteacher and lawyer, Finney experienced a soul-shattering religious conversion in 1821. Declaring that "the Lord Jesus Christ" had retained him "to plead his cause," Finney performed on the pulpit as a spirited attorney might argue a case in court. Seating those most likely to be converted on a special "anxious bench," Finney focused on them as a lawyer might a jury. The result was likely to be dramatic. Many of the targeted people fainted, jerked, or cried out in hysteria. Such drama brought Finney enormous publicity, which he and an army of imitators used to gain access to communities all over

---

lay exhorter   A church member who preaches but is not an ordained minister.

Revival meetings were remarkable affairs. Often lasting several days, they drew huge crowds who might listen to as many as forty preachers in around-the-clock sessions. The impact on the audience frequently was dramatic: one attendee at a New York revival commented that there were "loud ejaculations of prayer ... some struck with terror ... others, trembling weeping and crying out ... fainting and swooning away."

the West and Northeast. The result was a nearly continuous season of religious revival. The **Second Great Awakening** spread from rural community to rural community like a wildfire until, in the late 1830s, Finney carried the fire into Boston and New York City.

The new revivals led to the breakdown of traditional church organizations and the creation of various Christian denominations. Congregationalists, Presbyterians, Baptists, and Methodists split into groups who supported the new theology and those who clung to more traditional notions. Church splits also occurred for reasons that now seem petty. One Baptist congregation, for example, split over the hypothetical question of whether it would be a sin to lie to marauding Indians to protect hidden family members. Those who said lying to protect one's family was no sin formed a separate congregation of "Lying Baptists." Those who said lying was sinful under any circumstances gathered as "Truth-Telling Baptists."

In the face of such fragmentation—and competition—all denominations became concerned about state/church relations. In fact, those most fervent in their

Christian beliefs joined deists and other Enlightenment-influenced thinkers in arguing steadfastly for even more stringent separation of church and state. Under such pressure, in 1838 Massachusetts became the last state to abolish its legally established church. Disestablishment, in turn, added to the spirit of competition as individual congregations vied for voluntary contributions to keep their churches alive.

Even though religious conversion had become an individual matter and competition over parishioners a genuine concern, revivalists did not ignore the idea of community. "I know this is all algebra to those who have never felt it," Finney said. "But to those who have experienced the agony of wrestling, prevailing prayer, for the conversion of a soul, you may depend on it, that soul ... appears as dear as a child is to the mother who brought it forth with pain." This intimate connection forged bonds of mutual responsibility, giving a generation of isolated individuals a common starting point for joint action.

The Middle Class and Moral Reform   The missionary activism that accompanied the Second Great Awakening dovetailed with a reforming inclination among genteel and middle-class Americans. The **Christian benevolence movement** gave rise to hundreds of voluntary societies ranging from maternal associations designed to improve child rearing to political lobby groups aiming at outlawing alcohol, Sunday mail delivery, and other perceived evils. Such activism drew reformers together in common causes and led to deep friendships and a shared sense of commitment—antidotes to the alienation and loneliness common in the competitive world of the early nineteenth century.

The new theology reinforced the reforming impulse by emphasizing that even the most depraved might be saved if proper means were applied. This idea had immediate application in the realm of crime and punishment. Reformers characterized criminals not as evil but as lost and in need of divine guidance. In Auburn, New York, an experimental prison system put prisoners to work during the day, condemned them to absolute silence during mealtimes, and locked them away in solitary confinement at night. Reformers believed that this combination of hard work, discipline, and solitude would put criminals on the path to productive lives and spiritual renewal.

Mental illness underwent a similar change in definition. Rather than viewing the mentally ill as possessed agents of evil, reformers now spoke of them as lost souls in need of help. **Dorothea Dix**, a young, compassionate, reform-minded teacher, advocated publicly funded asylums for the insane. For the balance of the century, Dix toured the country pleading the cause of the mentally ill, succeeding in winning both private and public support for mental health systems.

A hundred other targets for reform joined prisons and asylums on the agenda of middle-class Christian activists. Embracing the Puritan tradition of strict observance of the Sabbath, newly awakened Christians insisted on stopping mail delivery and demanded that canals be closed on Sundays. Some joined Bible and tract societies that distributed Christian literature; others founded Sunday schools or operated domestic missions devoted to winning either the **irreligious** or the wrongly religious (as Roman Catholics were perceived to be) to the new covenant of the Second Great Awakening.

Many white-collar reformers acted in earnest and were genuinely interested in forging new social welfare systems. A number of their programs, however, seemed more like social control because they tried to force people to conform to a middle-class standard of behavior. Immigrants who chose to cling to familiar ways were suspected of disloyalty. This aspect of benevolent reform was particularly prominent in two important movements: public education and the **temperance movement**.

Before the War of 1812, most Americans believed that education was the family's or the church's responsibility and did not require children to attend school. But as the complexity of economic, political, and cultural life increased during the opening decades of the nineteenth century, **Horace Mann** and other champions of education pushed states to introduce formal public schooling. Like his contemporary Charles G. Finney, Mann was trained as a lawyer, but unlike Finney, he believed that ignorance, not sin, lay at the heart of the nation's problems. When Massachusetts made Mann the superintendent of a state-wide board of education, he immediately extended the school year to a minimum of six months and gradually replaced the traditional curriculum, rooted in the classics of ancient Roman and Greek learning, with courses like arithmetic, practical geography, and physical science.

But Mann and other reformers were interested in more than "knowledge"; they were equally concerned that new immigrants and the children of the urban poor be trained in Protestant values and middle-class habits. Thus the books used in public schools emphasized virtues such as promptness, discipline, and obedience to authority. In Philadelphia and other cities where Roman Catholic immigrants concentrated, Catholic parents resisted such cultural pressure on their children. They supported the establishment of **parochial schools**—a development that aggravated the strain between native-born Protestants and immigrant Catholics.

Another source of such tension was a Protestant crusade against alcohol. Drinking alcohol had always been common in America but before the early nineteenth century was not broadly perceived as a social problem. During the 1820s and 1830s, however, three factors contributed to a new, more ominous perception. One was the increasing visibility of drinking and drunkenness, as populations became more concentrated in cities. In Rochester, New York, a fast-growing Erie Canal port town, the number of drinking establishments multiplied rapidly as the population grew. Anyone with a few cents could get a glass of whiskey at grocery stores, either of two candy stores, barbershops, or even private homes—all within a few steps of wherever a person might be. By 1829 this proliferation of public

---

irreligious   Hostile or indifferent to religion.

parochial school   A school supported by a church parish; in the United States, the term usually refers to a Catholic school.

drinking led the county grand jury to conclude that strong drink was "the cause of almost all of the crime and almost all of the misery that flesh is heir to."

The second factor was alcohol's economic impact in a new and more complex world of work. Factory owners and managers recognized that workers who drank often and heavily threatened the quantity and quality of production (and profits). Owners and supervisors alike thus rallied around the temperance movement. By promoting temperance, these reformers believed they could clean up the worst aspects of city life and turn the raucous lower classes into clean-living, self-controlled, peaceful workers.

The third factor was theological. Drunkenness earned special condemnation from reawakened Protestants, who believed that people were responsible not only for their sins but also for their own salvation. A person whose reason was besotted by alcohol simply could not rise to the demand. Christian reformers, therefore, believed that temperance was necessary not only to preserve the nation but also to win people's souls.

The institution of slavery also became a hot topic among the nation's reborn Christians. Although some people had always had doubts about the morality of slavery, little organized opposition to it appeared before the American Revolution. By the end of the Revolution, only Georgia and South Carolina continued to allow the importation of slaves, while Massachusetts specifically prohibited slavery altogether and Pennsylvania had begun to phase it out. By the mid-1780s, most states, including those in the South, had active antislavery societies. In 1807, when Congress voted to outlaw permanently the importation of slaves in the following year, little was said in defense of slavery as an institution.

Public feeling about slavery during these years is reflected in the rise of the **American Colonization Society**, founded in 1817. This society was rooted in economic pragmatism, humanitarian concern for slaves' well-being, and white supremacy. Such ideas prompted the organization to propose that if slave owners emancipated their slaves, or if funds could be raised to purchase their freedom, the freed slaves should immediately be shipped to Africa.

Most preachers active in the Second Great Awakening supported the idea of colonization, but a few individuals pressed for more radical reforms. The most vocal leader among the antislavery forces during the early nineteenth century was **William Lloyd Garrison**. In 1831 he founded the nation's first prominent abolitionist newspaper, *The Liberator*. In it he advocated immediate emancipation for African Americans, with no compensation for slaveholders. In the following year, Garrison founded the New England Anti-Slavery Society and then, in 1833, the national American Anti-Slavery Society.

At first, Garrison stood alone. Some Christian reformers joined his cause, but the majority held back. In eastern cities, workers lived in dread of either enslaved or free blacks flooding in, lowering wages, and destroying job security. In western states, farmers feared that competition could arise from a slaveholding aristocracy. In both regions, white supremacists argued that the extension of slavery beyond the Mississippi River and north of the **Mason-Dixon Line** would eventually lead to blacks mixing with the white population, a possibility they found extremely distasteful. Thus most whites detested the notion of immediate emancipation, and radical abolitionists at this early date were almost universally ignored or, worse,

Though they were often in the majority in the various reform movements that arose during the 1830s and 1840s, women were consistently denied leadership roles and forbidden to express their views in public. In 1848, a number of women led by reformers Lucretia Mott and Elizabeth Cady Stanton (pictured here) brought attention to their unequal status by holding a Women's Rights Convention in Seneca Falls, New York. This marked the beginning of a self-conscious movement designed to win full equality for women in the United States, an objective for which women continue to struggle today.

© Bettmann/Corbis

attacked when they denounced slavery. Still, support for the movement gradually grew. In 1836 petitions flooded into Congress demanding an end to the slave trade in Washington, D.C. Not ready to engage in an action quite so controversial, Congress passed a **gag rule** that automatically **tabled** any petition to Congress that addressed the abolition of slavery. The rule remained in effect for nearly a decade. Many state assemblies followed suit, but not all governments remained closed to the discussion of slavery. In these state battles, a new group often led the fight against slavery: women.

Having assumed the burden of eliminating sin from the world back in the 1830s, many evangelical women became active in the antislavery cause. Moved by their activism, in 1840 Garrison proposed that a woman be elected to the executive committee of the American Anti-Slavery Society. And later that year women were members of Garrison's delegation to the first World Anti-Slavery Convention in London, but British antislavery advocates considered the presence of women inappropriate and refused to seat them.

gag rule   A rule that limits or prevents debate on an issue.
table   Action by a legislative body (Congress, for example) to postpone debate on an issue until a positive vote removes the topic from the table.

One prominent female abolitionist, Angelina Grimké, gave voice to her contemporaries' frustration at such treatment: "Are we aliens, because we are women? ... Have women no country—no interests staked in public weal [welfare]—no liabilities in the common peril—no partnership in a nation's guilt and shame?" In that same year, her sister Sarah went further, writing a powerful indictment against the treatment of women in America and a call for equality. In *Letters on the Equality of the Sexes and the Condition of Woman,* Sarah proclaimed, "The page of history teems with woman's wrongs ... and it is wet with woman's tears." Women must, she said, "arise in all the majesty of moral power ... and plant themselves, side by side, on the platform of human rights, with man, to whom they were designed to be companions, equals and helpers in every good word and work."

Like Sarah Grimké, many other women backed away from male-dominated causes and began advancing their own cause. In 1848 two women who had been excluded from the World Anti-Slavery Convention, **Lucretia Mott** and **Elizabeth Cady Stanton**, called concerned women to a convention at Seneca Falls, New York, to discuss their common problems. At Seneca Falls, they presented a Declaration of Sentiments that cited "the history of repeated injuries and usurpations on the part of man toward woman, having in direct object the establishment of an absolute tyranny over her." The convention adopted eleven resolutions relating to equality under the law, rights to control property, and other prominent gender issues. A twelfth resolution, calling for the right to vote, failed to receive unanimous endorsement.

Free and Slave Labor Protests

Like the predominantly white and middle-class women who were founding female protest movements in America, some northern workers and southern slaves began to perceive their miseries as the product of their exploitation by others. In view of their grim working and living conditions, it is not surprising that some manufacturing workers and slave laborers protested their situations and embraced increasingly active strategies for dealing with them.

The first organized labor strike in America took place in 1806, when a group of journeymen shoemakers stopped work to protest the hiring of unskilled workers to perform some tasks that higher-paid journeymen and apprentices had been doing. The strike failed when a New York court declared the shoemakers' actions illegal, but in the years to come many other journeymen's groups would try the same tactic. Industrialization robbed them of their status as independent contractors, forcing many to become wage laborers, and they bemoaned their loss of power in having to accept owner-dictated hours, conditions, and wages for the work they performed.

Unlike the British Luddites, journeymen simply asked for decent wages and working conditions and some role in decision making. Throughout the industrializing cities of the Northeast and the smaller manufacturing centers of the West, journeymen banded together in **trade unions**: assemblies of skilled workers grouped by

---

trade union   A labor organization whose members work in a specific trade or craft.

specific occupation. During the 1830s, trade unions from neighboring towns merged with one another to form the beginnings of a national trade union movement. In this way, house carpenters, shoemakers, and other craft workers established national unions through which they attempted to enforce uniform wage standards in their industries. In 1834 journeymen's organizations from a number of industries joined to form the **National Trades' Union,** the first labor organization in the nation's history to represent many different crafts.

Not surprisingly, factory owners, bankers, and others who had a vested interest in keeping labor cheap used every device available to prevent unions from succeeding. Employers formed manufacturing associations to resist union activity and used the courts to keep organized labor from disrupting business. Despite such efforts, a number of strikes affected American industries during the 1830s. In 1834 and again in 1836, women working in the textile mills in Lowell, Massachusetts, closed down production in the face of wage reductions and rising boarding house rates. Such demonstrations of power by workers frightened manufacturers, and gradually employers replaced native-born women in the factories with immigrants, who were less liable to organize successfully and, more important, less likely to win approval from sympathetic judges or consumers.

Still, workers won some small victories in the battle to organize. A significant breakthrough finally came in 1842 when the Massachusetts Supreme Court decided in the case of **Commonwealth v. Hunt** that Boston's journeymen boot makers were within their rights to organize "in such manner as best to subserve their own interests" and to call strikes. By that time, however, economic changes had so undermined labor's ability to withstand the rigors of strikes and court cases that legal protection became somewhat meaningless.

Though never as violent as those of the Luddites, not all labor protests were peaceful. In 1828, for example, immigrant weavers protested the pitiful wages paid by Alexander Knox, New York City's leading textile employer. Storming Knox's home to demand higher pay, the weavers invaded and vandalized his house and beat Knox's son and a cordon of police guards. The rioters then marched to the garret and basement homes of weavers who had refused to join the protest and destroyed their looms.

Unlike workers in the North, who at least had some legal protections and civil rights, slaves had nothing but their own wits to protect them against a society that classed them as disposable personal property. Slaves were skilled at the use of **passive resistance.** The importance of passive resistance was evident in the folk tales and songs that circulated among slaves. Perhaps the best-known example is the stories of Br'er Rabbit, a classic trickster figure. In one particularly revealing tale, Br'er Rabbit is caught by Br'er Fox, who threatens Rabbit with all sorts of horrible tortures. Rabbit begs Br'er Fox to do anything but throw him into the nearby briar patch. Seizing on Rabbit's apparent fear, Fox unties Br'er Rabbit and pitches him deep into the middle of the briar patch, expecting to see the rabbit struggle and die amid the thorns. Br'er Rabbit, however, scampers away through the briars, calling back over his shoulder that he was born and bred in a briar patch and laughing

passive resistance   Resistance by nonviolent methods.

at Br'er Fox's gullibility. Such stories taught slaves how to deal cleverly with powerful adversaries.

Not all slave resistance was passive. Perhaps the most common form of active resistance was running away. The number of slaves who escaped may never be known, though some estimate that an average of about a thousand made their way to freedom each year. But running away was always a dangerous gamble. One former slave recalled, "No man who has never been placed in such a situation can comprehend the thousand obstacles thrown in the way of the flying slave."

The most frightening form of slave resistance was open and armed revolt. Despite slaveholders' best efforts, slaves planned an unknown number of rebellions during the antebellum period, and many of them were actually carried out. The most serious and violent of these uprisings was the work of a black preacher, Nat Turner. After years of planning and organization, in 1831 Turner led a force of about seventy slaves in a predawn raid against the slaveholding households in Southampton County, Virginia. It took four days for white forces to stop the uprising; Turner and sixteen of his followers were finally captured and executed.

In the wake of Nat Turner's Rebellion, fear of slave revolts reached paranoid levels in the South, especially in areas where slaves greatly outnumbered whites. After seeing a play depicting a slave insurrection, Mary Boykin Chesnut gave expression to the fear that plagued whites in the slave South: "What a thrill of terror ran through me as those yellow and black brutes came jumping over the parapets! Their faces were like so many of the same sort at home.... How long would they resist the seductive and irresistible call: 'Rise, kill, and be free!'"

Frightened and often outnumbered, whites felt justified in imposing stringent restrictions and using harsh methods to enforce them. In most areas, free African Americans were denied the right to own guns, buy liquor, hold public assemblies, testify in court, and vote. Slaves were forbidden to own any private property, to attend unsupervised worship services, and to learn reading and writing.

THE WHIG ALTERNATIVE TO JACKSONIAN DEMOCRACY

The fundamental structural changes that led to social and cultural transformations had an enormous impact on politics as well. Although Andrew Jackson was quite possibly the most popular president since George Washington, not all Americans agreed with his philosophy, policies, or political style. Men like Henry Clay and Daniel Webster, who inherited the crumbling structure of Jefferson's Republican Party, continually opposed Jackson in and out of Congress but seemed unable to overcome sectional differences to challenge Jackson's and Van Buren's cohesive Democratic Party. Gradually, however, anger over Jackson's policies and anxiety about change forged cooperation among the disenchanted, who coalesced into a new national party.

The End of the Old Party Structure   The last full year of Jackson's first term in office, 1832, was a landmark year in the nation's political history. In the course of that single year, the Seminoles declared war on the United States, Jackson declared war on the Second Bank, South Carolina declared war on the binding power of the Constitution, and the

Cherokees waged a continuing war in the courts to hold on to their lands. The presidential election that year reflected the air of political crisis.

Henry Clay had started the Bank War to rally Jackson's opponents. The problem was that Jackson's enemies were deeply divided among themselves. Clay opposed Jackson because the president refused to support the American System and used every tool at his disposal to attack Clay's economic policies. Southern politicians like Calhoun, however, feared and hated Clay's nationalistic policies as much as they did Jackson's assertions of federal power. And political outsiders like the Antimasons distrusted all political organizations. The 1832 election campaign underscored these divisions.

The Antimasons kicked off the anti-Jackson free-for-all in September 1831 when they held the nation's first nominating convention in Baltimore. Party co-founder Thurlow Weed's skillful political manipulation had pulled in a wide range of people who were disgusted with what Jefferson had called "political party tricks," and the convention drew a broad constituency. Using all his charm and influence, Weed cajoled the convention into nominating William Wirt, a respected lawyer from Maryland, as its presidential candidate.

Antimasons fully expected that when the Republicans met in convention later in the year, they would rubber-stamp the Antimasonic nomination and present a united front against Jackson. But the Republicans, fearful of the Antimasons' odd combination of **machine politics** and antiparty paranoia, nominated Clay as their standard-bearer. The Republicans then issued the country's first formal **party platform**, a ringing document supporting Clay's economic ideas and attacking Jackson's use of the **spoils system**.

Even having two anti-Jackson parties in the running did not satisfy some. Distrustful of the Anti-masons and put off by Clay's nationalist philosophy, southerners in both parties refused to support any of the candidates. They finally backed nullification advocate John Floyd of Virginia.

Lack of unity contributed to disaster for Jackson's opponents. Wirt and Floyd received votes that might have gone to Clay. But even if Clay had gotten those votes, Jackson's popularity and the political machinery that he and Van Buren controlled would have given him the victory. The president was reelected with a total of 219 electoral votes to Clay's 49, Wirt's 7, and Floyd's 11. Jackson's party lost five seats in the Senate but gained six in the House of Representatives. Despite unsettling changes in the land and continuing political chaos, the people still wanted the hero of New Orleans as their leader.

The New Political Coalition   If one lesson emerged clearly from the election of 1832, it was that Jackson's opponents needed to pull together if they expected to challenge the growing power of "King Andrew."

machine politics   The aggressive use of influence, favors, and tradeoffs by a political organization, or "machine," to mobilize support among its followers.

party platform   A formal statement of the principles, policies, and promises on which a political party bases its appeal to the public.

spoils system   System associated with American politics in which a political party, after winning an election, gives government jobs to its supporters as a reward for working toward victory.

Calling themselves Whigs after the English political party that opposed royal authority, Henry Clay, John C. Calhoun, and Daniel Webster joined forces to oppose what they characterized as Andrew Jackson's kingly use of power. This lithograph from 1834 depicting Jackson in royal dress stepping on the Constitution expresses their view quite vividly.

BORN TO COMMAND.

OF VETO MEMORY.

HAD I BEEN CONSULTED.

KING ANDREW THE FIRST.

© Collection of the New-York Historical Society

Imitating names used by political organizations in Great Britain, Clay and his associates began calling Jackson supporters Tories—supporters of the king—and calling themselves Whigs. The antimonarchical label stuck, and the new party formed in 1834 was called the **Whig Party**.

The Whigs eventually absorbed all the major factions that opposed Jackson. At the heart of the party were Clay supporters: advocates of strong government and the American System in economics. The nullifiers in the South, however, quickly came around when Clay and Calhoun found themselves on the same side in defeating Jackson's appointment of Van Buren as American minister to England. This successful campaign, combined with Calhoun's growing awareness that Jackson was perhaps more dangerous to his constituents' interests than was Clay, led the southerner and his associates into the Whig camp. The Antimasons joined because their disgust at Jackson's use of patronage and back-alley politics—not to mention the fact that he was a Mason—overcame their distrust of Clay's party philosophy. A final major group to rally to the Whigs were evangelicals who disapproved of Jackson's personal lifestyle, his views on slavery, his Indian policy, and his refusal to involve government in their moral causes. The orderly and sober society that Clay and the Whigs envisioned appealed to such people.

The congressional elections in 1834 provided the first test for the new coalition. In this first electoral contest, the Whigs won nearly 40 percent of the seats in the

House of Representatives and more than 48 percent in the Senate. Clearly cooperation was paying off.

Van Buren in the White House   Jackson had seemed to be a tower of strength when he was first elected to the presidency in 1828, but by the end of his second term, he was nearly 70 years old and plagued by various ailments. Old Hickory decided to follow Washington's example and not run for a third term. Instead, Jackson used all the power and patronage at his command to ensure that Martin Van Buren, his most consistent loyalist, would win the presidential nomination at the Democratic Party convention.

Van Buren was a skilled organizer whose ability to create unlikely political alliances had earned him the nickname "the Little Magician." Throughout Jackson's first term, Van Buren had headed the Kitchen Cabinet and increasingly became Jackson's chief political henchman. In 1832 Jackson had repaid his loyalty by making him vice president, with the intention of launching him into the presidency.

Meanwhile, Clay and his Whig associates were hatching a plot to deny the election to the Democrats. Instead of holding a convention and thrashing out a platform, the Whigs let each region's party organization nominate its own candidates. Whig leaders hoped a large number of candidates would confuse voters and throw the election into the House of Representatives, where skillful political management and Van Buren's unpopularity might unseat the Democrats. As a result, four **favorite sons** ran on the Whig ticket. Daniel Webster of Massachusetts represented the Northeast. Hugh Lawson White, a Tennessean and former Jackson supporter, ran for the Southwest. South Carolina nullifier W. P. Mangum represented the South. William Henry Harrison, former governor of Indiana Territory and victor at the Battle of Tippecanoe in 1811, was tapped to represent the Northwest.

Weed underestimated the Democrats' hold on the minds of the voters. Van Buren captured 765,483 popular votes—more than Jackson had won in the previous election—but his performance in the Electoral College was significantly weaker than Jackson's had been. Van Buren squeaked by with a winning margin of less than 1 percent, but it was a victory, and the presidential election did not go to the House of Representatives.

It became clear from the beginning that Van Buren's presidency would be a troubled one. As soon as he assumed office, the nation was hit by another terrible financial crisis. The **Panic of 1837** was a direct outcome of the Bank War and Jackson's money policies, but it was Van Buren who would take the blame. The crisis had begun with Nicholas Biddle's manipulation of credit and interest rates in an effort to discredit Jackson and have the Second Bank rechartered in spite of the president's veto. Jackson had added to the problem by removing paper money and credit from the economy in an effort to win support from hard-money advocates. Arguing that he wanted to end "the monopoly of the public

---

favorite son   A candidate nominated for office by delegates from his or her own region or state.

lands in the hands of speculators and capitalists," Jackson had issued the **Specie Circular** on August 15, 1836. From that day forward payment for public land had to be made in specie.

The contraction in credit and currency had the same impact in 1836 as it had in 1819: the national economy collapsed. By May 1837, New York banks were no longer accepting any paper currency, and soon all banks had adopted the policy of accepting specie only. Unable to pay back or collect loans, buy raw materials, or conduct any other sort of commerce, hundreds of businesses, plantations, farms, factories, canals, and other enterprises spiraled into bankruptcy. More than a third of the population was thrown out of work, and people who were fortunate enough to keep their jobs found their pay reduced by as much as 50 percent. Fledgling industries and labor organizations were cast into disarray, and the nation sank into both an economic and an emotional depression.

As credit continued to collapse through 1838 and 1839, President Van Buren tried to address the problems. First, he extended Jackson's hard-money policy, which caused the economy to contract further. Next, in an effort to keep the government solvent, Van Buren cut federal spending to the bone, shrinking the money supply even more. Then, to replace the stabilizing influence lost when the Second Bank was destroyed, he created a national treasury system endowed with many of the powers formerly wielded by the bank. The new regional treasury offices accepted only specie in payment for federal lands and other obligations and used that specie to pay federal expenses and debts. As a result, specie was sucked out of local banks and local economies. While fiscally sound by the wisdom of the day, Van Buren's decisions only made matters worse for the average person and drove the last nail into his political coffin.

The Log Cabin and Hard Cider Campaign of 1840

The Whigs had learned their lesson in the election of 1836: only a unified party could possibly destroy the political machine built by Jackson and Van Buren. As the nation sank into depression, the Whigs determined to use whatever means were necessary to break the Democrats' grip on the voters and were prepared to line up behind a single candidate.

Once again, Henry Clay hoped to be the party's nominee, but Thurlow Weed convinced the party that William Henry Harrison would have a better chance in the election. For Harrison's running mate, the party chose **John Tyler**, a Virginia senator who had bolted from Jackson's Democratic Party during the Bank War. Weed clearly hoped that the Virginian would draw votes from the planter South while Harrison carried the West and North.

Although the economy was in bad shape, the Whig campaign avoided addressing any serious issues. Instead, the Whigs launched a smear campaign against Van Buren. Although he was the son of a lowly tavern keeper, the Whig press portrayed him as an aristocrat whose expensive tastes were signs of dangerous excess during an economic depression. Harrison really was an aristocrat, but the Whigs played on the Romantic themes so popular among their genteel and middle-class constituents by characterizing him as a simple frontiersman—a Natty Bumppo—who had risen to greatness through his own efforts. Whig claims were so extravagant that the Democratic press soon satirized Harrison in political cartoons showing a rustic hick swilling hard cider. The satire backfired. Whig newspapers and speechmakers seized on the image and sold Harrison, the longtime political insider, as a simple man of the people.

Van Buren had little with which to retaliate. Harrison had a distinguished political and military career behind him. Tyler, too, was well respected. And Van Buren had simply not done a good job of addressing the nation's pressing economic needs. Voters cried out for change and Van Buren could not offer them one. The combination of political dissatisfaction and campaign hype brought the biggest voter turnout to that time in American history: nearly twice as many voters came to the polls in 1840 as had voted in 1836. And while Harrison won only 53 percent of the popular vote, Weed's successful political manipulations earned the Whigs nearly 80 percent of the electoral votes, sweeping the Democrats out of the White House.

THE TRIUMPH OF MANIFEST DESTINY

The key to Harrison's success was the Whig Party's skillful manipulation of the former general's reputation as a frontiersman and popular advocate for westward expansion. With politics bogged down in debates over tariffs, states' rights, public finance, and dozens of other practical, if boring policy matters, the nationalistic appeal of seizing and occupying the West brought an air of excitement to public discourse. It was this allure that helped to draw out the thousands of new voters in 1840 and would provide a new basis for political cooperation and contention in the years to come.

The Rise of Manifest Destiny

The new spirit that came to life in American politics and rhetoric in the years after 1840 found expression in a single phrase: manifest destiny. To some extent, manifest destiny can be traced back to the sense of mission that had motivated colonial Puritans. Like John Winthrop and his Massachusetts Bay associates, many early nineteenth-century Americans believed they had a duty to go into new lands. During the antebellum period, romantic nationalism, land hunger, and the evangelicalism of the Second Great Awakening shaped this sense of divine mission into a new and powerful commitment to westward expansion. As the American Board of Commissioners for Foreign Missions noted in its annual report for 1827, "The tide of emigration is rolling westward so rapidly, that it must speedily surmount every barrier, till it reaches every habitable part of this continent." The power of this force led many to conclude that the westward movement was not just an economic process but was part of a divine plan for North America and the world.

Not surprisingly, the earliest and most aggressive proponents of expansion were Christian missionary organizations, whose many magazines, newsletters, and reports were the first to give it formal voice. Politicians, however, were not far behind. Democratic warhorse and expansion advocate Thomas Hart Benton of Missouri borrowed both the tone and content of missionary rhetoric in his speeches promoting generous land policies, territorial acquisition, and even overseas expansion. In 1825, for example, Benton argued in favor of American colonization of the Pacific coast and eventually of Asia, bringing "great and wonderful benefits" to the western Indians and allowing "science, liberal principles in government, and true religion [to] cast their lights across the intervening sea."

Expansion to the North and West   One major complication standing in the way of the nation's perceived manifest destiny was that other countries already owned large parts of the continent. The continued presence of the British, for example, proved to be a constant source of irritation. During the War of 1812, the War Hawks had advocated conquering Canada and pushing the British from the continent altogether. Although events thwarted this ambition, many continued to push for that objective by either legal or extralegal means.

One source of dispute between the United States and Great Britain was the **Oregon Question**. The vast Oregon tract had been claimed at one time or another by Spain, Russia, France, England, and the United States. By the 1820s, only England and the United States continued to contest for its ownership. At the close of the War of 1812, the two countries had been unable to settle their claims, and in 1818 they had agreed to joint occupation of Oregon for ten years. They extended this arrangement indefinitely in 1827, with the **proviso** that either country could end it with one year's notice.

Oregon's status as neither British nor American presented its occupants with an unstable situation. One early incident occurred in 1841 when a wealthy pioneer died and because the Oregon Country had no laws, no guidelines existed on who was entitled to inherit his property. Settlers finally created a **probate court**, instructing it to follow the statutes of the state of New York, and appointed a committee to frame a constitution and draft a basic code of laws. Opposition from the British put an end to this early effort at self-rule, but the movement continued. Two years later, Americans began agitating again, this time because of wolves preying on their livestock. They held a series of "Wolf Meetings" in 1843 to discuss joint protection and resolved to create a civil government. Although the British tried to prevent it, the assembly passed the **First Organic Laws of Oregon** on July 5, 1843, making Oregon an independent republic in all but name. Independence, however, was not the settlers' long-term goal. The document's preamble announced that the code of laws would continue in force "until such time as the United States of America extend their jurisdiction over us."

proviso   A clause making a qualification, condition, or restriction in a document.

probate court   A court that establishes the validity of wills and administers the estates of people who have died.

Revolution
in Texas

Similar problems faced American settlers who had taken up residence in Spain's, then Mexico's territories in the Southwest. Although the Spanish and then the Mexican government had invited Anglo-Americans to settle in the region, these pioneers generally ignored Mexican customs and disregarded Mexican law. This was particularly the case after 1829, when Mexico began attaching duties to trade items moving between the region and the neighboring United States. Mexico also abolished importing slaves. Bad feelings grew over the years, but the distant and politically unstable Mexican government could do little to enforce laws and customs. In addition, despite the friction between cultures in Texas, many Tejanos were disturbed by the corruption and political instability in Mexico City and were as eager as their Texian counterparts to participate in the United States' thriving cotton market.

Assuming responsibility for forging a peaceful settlement to the problems between settlers in Texas and the Mexican government, Stephen F. Austin went to Mexico City in 1833. While Austin was there, **Antonio López de Santa Anna** seized power. Although he had supported Mexico's republican constitution, adopted in 1824, Santa Anna had since come to the conclusion that Mexico was not ready for democracy. Upon assuming power, he suspended the constitution, dismissed Congress, and set himself up as the self-declared "Napoleon of the West."

Throughout Mexico, former revolutionaries and common citizens who had anticipated democracy were outraged by Santa Anna's actions. To the south, in Yucatán and elsewhere, provinces openly rebelled. The same potential existed along the northern frontier as well. Trying to avoid an open break, Austin met with Santa Anna in 1834 and presented several petitions advocating reforms and greater self-government in Texas, but Santa Anna made it clear that he intended to exert his authority over the region. On his arrival back in Texas in 1835, Austin declared, "War is our only recourse." He was immediately made chairman of a committee to call for a "Consultation" of delegates from all over Texas.

Mexican officials, viewing the unrest in Texas as rebellion against their authority, issued arrest warrants for all the Texas troublemakers they could identify and **deployed** troops to San Antonio. Austin's committee immediately sent out word for Texans to arm themselves. The **Texas Revolution** started quickly thereafter when the little town of Gonzales refused to surrender a cannon to Mexican officials on September 29, 1835.

Angered by the rebellion, Santa Anna personally led the Mexican army into Texas, arriving in San Antonio on February 23, 1836. Knowing that Santa Anna was on his way, Texas militia commander William Travis moved his troops into the **Alamo**. On March 6 Santa Anna ordered an all-out assault and despite staggering casualties was able to capture the former mission. Most of the post's defenders were killed in the assault, and Santa Anna executed those who survived

---

deploy To position military resources (troops, artillery, equipment) in preparation for action.

the battle, including former American congressman and frontier celebrity Davy Crockett. While Travis, Crockett, and others struggled at the Alamo, General **Sam Houston** was busy rounding up troops for a more general war against the invading Santa Anna.

Despite the loss at the Alamo, Texans continued to underestimate Santa Anna's strength and his resolve to put down the rebellion. After a series of defeats, however, the Texans scored a stunning victory on April 21 at the San Jacinto River and captured Santa Anna. In exchange for his release, in May 1836 Santa Anna signed the **Treaty of Velasco**, officially recognizing Texas's independence and acknowledging the Rio Grande as the border between Texas and Mexico.

As in Oregon, many leaders in Texas hoped their actions would lead to swift annexation by the United States. In 1838 Houston, by then president of the Republic of Texas, invited the United States to annex Texas. Because all of Texas lay below the Missouri Compromise line, John Quincy Adams, now a Whig member of the House of Representatives, **filibustered** for three weeks against the acquisition of such a massive block of potential slave territory. Seeking to avoid national controversy, Congress refused to ratify the annexation treaty.

The Politics of Manifest Destiny

Although Adams was typical of one wing of the Whig coalition, he certainly did not speak for the majority of Whigs on the topic of national expansion. The party of manufacturing, revivalism, and social reform inclined naturally toward the blending of political, economic, and religious evangelicalism that was manifest destiny. William Henry Harrison himself, the united party's first national candidate, was a colorful figure in American westward expansion, and his political campaign in 1840 celebrated the simple virtues of frontier life. When Harrison died soon after taking office in 1841, his vice president, John Tyler, picked up the torch of American expansionism.

Tyler was a less typical Whig than even Adams. A Virginian and a states' rights advocate, he had been a staunch Democrat until the nullification crisis, when he bolted the party to protest Jackson's strong assertion of federal power. As president, Tyler seemed still to be more Democrat than Whig. Although he had objected to Jackson's use of presidential power, like Old Hickory, Tyler as president was unyielding where ideology was concerned. He vetoed high protective tariffs, internal improvement bills, and attempts to revive the Second Bank of the United States. Tyler's refusal to promote Whig economic policies led to a general crisis in government in 1843, when his entire cabinet resigned over his veto of a bank bill.

Tyler did share his party's desire for expansion, however. He assigned his secretary of state, Daniel Webster, to negotiate a treaty with Britain to settle disputes over the Canadian border. The resulting **Webster-Ashburton Treaty** (1842) gave a large chunk of Lower Canada to the United States and finalized the nation's

---

filibuster To use obstructionist tactics, especially prolonged speechmaking, to delay legislative action.

northeastern border. In that same year, Tyler also adopted an aggressive stance on the Oregon Question by appointing Elijah White, one of the organizers of the Wolf Meetings, as the federal Indian agent for the region, undercutting British authority.

Tyler also pushed a forceful policy toward Texas. In 1842 Sam Houston repeated his invitation for the United States to annex Texas, only to be rebuffed by Secretary of State Webster, a New Englander who shared Adams's views. When Webster resigned with the other cabinet officers in 1843, however, Tyler replaced him with fellow Virginian Abel P. Upshur, who immediately reopened the matter of Texas annexation.

Negotiations between Houston's representatives and Tyler's secretary of state— Upshur at first, then, after Upshur's death, John C. Calhoun—led to a treaty of annexation on April 11, 1844. In line with the Treaty of Velasco, the annexation document named the Rio Grande as the southern boundary of Texas. Annexation remained a major arguing point between proslavery and antislavery forces, however, and the treaty failed ratification in the Senate. The issue of Texas annexation then joined the Oregon Question as a major campaign issue in the presidential election of 1844.

Expansion and the Election of 1844   As the Whigs and the Democrats geared up for a national election, it became clear that expansion would be the key issue. This put the two leading political figures of the day, Democrat Martin Van Buren and Whig Henry Clay, in an uncomfortable position. Van Buren was on record as opposing the extension of slavery and was therefore against the annexation of Texas. Clay, the architect of the American System, was opposed to any form of uncontrolled expansion, especially if it meant fanning sectional tensions, and he too opposed immediate annexation of Texas. Approaching the election, both issued statements to the effect that they would back annexation only with Mexico's consent.

Clay's somewhat ambiguous stance on expansion contrasted sharply with Tyler's efforts to advance the cause of manifest destiny. However, President Tyler's constant refusal to support the larger Whig political agenda led the party to nominate Clay anyway. Van Buren was not so lucky. The strong southern wing of the Democratic Party was so put off by Van Buren's position on slavery that it blocked him, securing the nomination of Tennessee congressman **James K. Polk**.

The Democrats based their platform on the issues surrounding Oregon and Texas. They implied that the regions rightfully belonged to the United States, stating "that the *re-occupation* of Oregon and the *reannexation* of Texas at the earliest practicable period are great American measures." Polk vowed to stand up to the British by claiming the entire Oregon Country up to 54°40′ north latitude and to defend the territorial claims of Texas. For his part, Clay continued to waffle on expansionism, emphasizing economic policies instead.

The election demonstrated the people's commitment to manifest destiny. Clay was a national figure, well respected and regarded as one of the nation's leading statesmen, whereas Polk was barely known outside Tennessee. Still, Polk polled

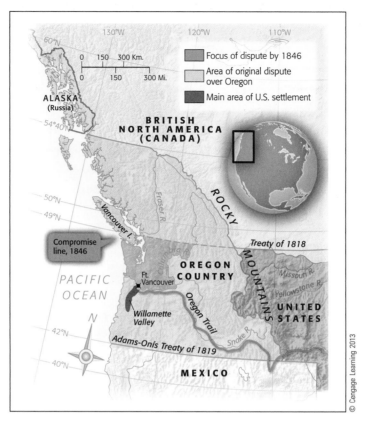

MAP 12.1 Oregon Boundary Dispute

Although demanding that Britain cede the entire Oregon Territory south of 54°40', the United States settled for a compromise at the forty-ninth parallel.

40,000 more popular votes than Clay and garnered 65 more electoral votes. Seeing the election as a political barometer, outgoing president Tyler prepared a special message to Congress in December 1844 proposing a **joint resolution** annexing Texas. Many congressmen who had opposed annexation could not ignore the clear mandate given to manifest destiny in the presidential election, and the bill to annex Texas passed in February 1845.

Holding to the position he had taken prior to the election, in his annual message for 1845 Polk asked Congress to end the joint occupation of Oregon. Referring to the largely forgotten Monroe Doctrine, the president insisted that no nation other than the United States should be permitted to occupy any part of

joint resolution   A formal statement adopted by both houses of Congress and subject to approval by the president; if approved, it has the force of law.

Collection of David J. and Janet L. Frent

This campaign banner celebrating the Democratic candidacy of James K. Polk and George M. Dallas subtly conveys the party's platform. Surrounding Polk's picture are twenty-five stars, one for each state in the Union. Outside the corner box, a twenty-sixth star stands for Texas, which Polk promised to annex.

North America and urged Congress to assert exclusive control over the Oregon Country even if doing so meant war.

Neither the United States nor Britain intended to go to war over Oregon. The only issue—where the border would be—was a matter for the bargaining table, not the battlefield. Recalling the rhetoric that had gotten him elected, Polk insisted on 54°40′. The British lobbied for the Columbia River as the boundary, but their position softened quickly. The fur trade along the Columbia was in rapid decline and had become unprofitable by the early 1840s. As a result, in the spring of 1846, the British foreign secretary offered Polk a compromise boundary at the 49th parallel. The Senate recommended that Polk accept the offer, and a treaty settling the Oregon Question was ratified on June 15, 1846.

STUDY TOOLS

SUMMARY

Americans responded in many different ways to the many unsettling changes that had been taking place as part of the Great Transformation. Different economic classes responded by creating their own cultures and by adopting specific strategies for dealing with anxiety. Some chose violent protest, some passive resistance. Some looked to heaven for solutions and others to earthly utopias. And out of this complex swirl, something entirely new and unexpected emerged: a new

America, on its way to being socially, politically, intellectually, and culturally modern.

A new generation emerged that grasped greedily at the new opportunities offered by new economic and cultural arrangements. Literacy grew as never before in the nation's history and with it a thirst for new knowledge. Book publishers, magazine editors, and charitable societies competed to meet this new demand for information and entertainment. And this group of young readers sought to express itself not only in literature, but in politics as well. As expanding media made more people aware of issues taking place nationwide, they were drawn into politics as never before. In the presidential election of 1840 almost two and a half million men cast ballots, more than a million more than had voted four years earlier.

In that election, William Henry Harrison, a man who had become a national figure by fighting against Indian sovereignty and for westward expansion, swept a new sentiment into national politics. Increasingly Americans came to believe that the West would provide the solutions to the problems ushered in during the Great Transformation. In the short term, this notion led to an exciting race by Americans toward the Pacific. But different visions about how the West would solve the nation's problems soon added to the ever-growing air of crisis.

CHRONOLOGY

MODERNIZATION AND RISING STRESS

1821	Charles G. Finney experiences a religious conversion
1823	James Fenimore Cooper's *The Pioneers*
1825	Thomas Cole begins Hudson River school of painting Robert Owen establishes community at New Harmony, Indiana
1826	Shakers have eighteen communities in the United States
1831	Nat Turner's Rebellion William Lloyd Garrison begins publishing *The Liberator*
1832	Jackson reelected
1833	Lydia Sigourney publishes bestsellers *Letters to Young Ladies* and *How to Be Happy* George Bancroft publishes volume 1 of his American history Formation of National Trades' Union Formation of Whig Party
1835	Texas Revolution begins
1836	Congress passes the gag rule Martin Van Buren elected president
1837	Horace Mann heads first public board of education Panic of 1837 Ralph Waldo Emerson's "American Scholar" speech Senate rejects annexation of Texas

1838 Emerson articulates transcendentalism
Sarah Grimké publishes *Letters on the Equality of the Sexes and the Condition of Women*

1840 Log cabin campaign
William Henry Harrison elected president

1841 Brook Farm established
Death of President Harrison; John Tyler becomes president

1842 *Commonwealth v. Hunt*

1843 Dorothea Dix advocates state-funded insane asylums
Oregon adopts First Organic Laws

1844 James K. Polk elected president

1845 United States annexes Texas
Term "manifest destiny" coined

1846 Oregon boundary established

Focus Questions

If you have mastered this chapter, you should be able to answer these questions and explain the terms that follow the questions.

1. How did developments in American arts and letters reflect the spirit of change during the Jacksonian era?
2. To what extent did international forces influence American cultural expressions?
3. What did Jackson's opponents hope to accomplish when they built their coalition to oppose the Democrats? How successful were they?
4. What forces in American life contributed to the concept of manifest destiny?
5. To what extent did the actions taken by American settlers in Oregon and Texas reflect the ideal of manifest destiny?

Key Terms

romanticism (*p.* 316)

Ralph Waldo Emerson (*p.* 317)

transcendentalism (*p.* 317)

Henry David Thoreau (*p.* 318)

Hudson River school (*p.* 319)

"Negro spiritual" (*p.* 321)

New Harmony (*p.* 321)

Frances (Fanny) Wright (*p.* 322)

Brook Farm (*p.* 322)

Charles Fourier (*p.* 322)

Oneida Community (*p.* 322)

Shakers (*p.* 322)

Joseph Tracy (*p.* 323)

Charles Grandison Finney (*p.* 323)

Second Great Awakening (*p.* 324)

Christian benevolence movement (*p.* 325)

Dorothea Dix (*p.* 325)

temperance movement (*p.* 326)

Horace Mann (*p.* 326)

American Colonization Society (*p.* 327)

William Lloyd Garrison (*p.* 327)

Mason-Dixon Line (*p.* 327)

13

SECTIONAL CONFLICT AND
SHATTERED UNION, 1848–1860

CHAPTER OUTLINE

• New Political Options • Toward a House Divided • The Divided
Nation • The Nation Dissolved • Study Tools

NEW POLITICAL OPTIONS

The presidential elections in 1840 and 1844 had put American expansion at the heart of political debate. While all could affirm the existence of manifest destiny, there was significant disagreement about exactly what form it should take. The political system held together during these years, but the successes enjoyed by third-party challenges were evidence that significant problems churned under the surface. It was clear to many that the nation's political system was not meeting their economic and ideological needs, and they began looking for new options.

Opting for War with Mexico

With the Oregon agreement and the annexation of Texas in place, the nation's border issues were now settled from Congress's point of view, but Mexico had a completely different outlook. Many Mexicans pointed out that the Treaty of Velasco ending the Texas Revolution had been signed under duress, and Mexico's popular press demanded renegotiation. The Mexican government agreed, threatening war. President Polk added to the tension and seemed to confirm Mexican fears by declaring that the entire Southwest should be annexed.

Late in 1845, the president dispatched John Slidell to Mexico City to negotiate the boundary dispute. He also authorized Slidell to purchase New Mexico and California if possible. At the same time, Polk dispatched American troops to Louisiana, ready to strike if Mexico resisted Slidell's offers. He also notified Americans in California that if war broke out the Pacific fleet would seize California ports and support an insurrection against Mexican authority.

Nervous but bristling over what seemed to be preparations for war, the Mexican government refused to receive Slidell; in January 1846 he sent word to the president that his mission was a failure. Polk then ordered **Zachary Taylor** to lead troops from New Orleans toward the Rio Grande. Shortly thereafter, an American military party led by **John C. Frémont** entered California's Salinas Valley. Reaching an end to its patience, on April 22 Mexico proclaimed that its territory had been violated and declared war. Two days later, Mexican troops engaged a detachment of Taylor's army at Matamoros on the Rio Grande, killing

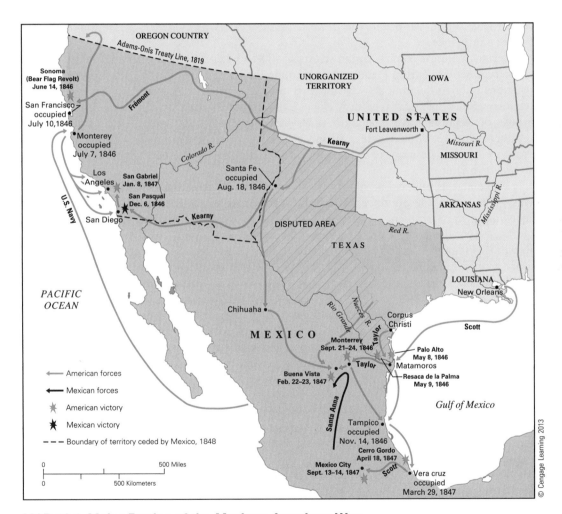

MAP 13.1 Major Battles of the Mexican-American War

The Mexican War's decisive campaign began with General Winfield Scott's capture of Vera cruz and ended with his conquest of Mexico City.

eleven and capturing the rest. When news of the battle reached Washington, Polk immediately called for war. Although the nation was far from united on the issue, Congress agreed on May 13, 1846.

The outbreak of war disturbed many Americans. In New England, for example, protest ran high. Henry David Thoreau chose to be jailed rather than pay taxes that would support the war. It was not expansion as such that troubled Thoreau, but the potential that annexing so much land south of the Missouri Compromise line would expand slavery and embolden southern political agendas. Since the Missouri Compromise, some northerners had come to believe that a slaveholding **oligarchy** controlled life and politics in the South. Abolitionists warned that this "Slave Power" sought to expand its reach until it controlled every aspect of American life. Many viewed Congress's adoption of the gag rule in 1836 and the drive to annex Texas as evidence of the Slave Power's influence.

Serious political combat began in August 1846 when David Wilmot, a Democratic representative from Pennsylvania, proposed an amendment to the war appropriations bill that "neither slavery nor involuntary servitude shall ever exist" in any territory gained in the War with Mexico. The **Wilmot Proviso** twice passed in the House of Representatives but both times failed in the Senate, where equal state representation gave the South a stronger position. The House finally decided in April to appropriate money for the war without stipulating whether or not slavery would be permitted.

While all this political infighting was going on in Washington, D.C., a real war was going on in the Southwest. In California, American settlers rallied in open rebellion in the Sacramento Valley and declared independence in June 1846. They crafted a flag depicting a grizzly bear and announced the birth of the Bear Flag Republic. Frémont's force rushed to join the Bear Flag rebels, and when the little army arrived in Monterey on July 19, they found that the Pacific fleet had already acted on Polk's orders and seized the city. The Mexican forces were in full flight southward.

To round out the greater southwestern strategy, Polk ordered Colonel Stephen Kearny to invade New Mexico on May 15. After leading his men across 800 miles of desert to Santa Fe, Kearny found a less-than-hostile enemy. Members of the interracial upper class of Santa Fe had already expressed interest in joining the United States and given the opportunity, they surrendered without firing a shot.

Within a short time, all of the New Mexico region and California were securely in the hands of U.S. forces. In Texas, however, Zachary Taylor faced more serious opposition. Marching across the Rio Grande, Taylor headed for the regional capital of Monterrey, capturing the city in September 1846. Because of his military successes, Taylor became a political threat to Polk within the party. In an attempt to undermine Taylor's political appeal, Polk turned the war effort

oligarchy   A small group of people or families who hold power.

over to **Winfield Scott**, ordering him to gather an army, drawing men from Taylor's and other forces, and sail to Veracruz. From there the army was to move inland to take Mexico City.

Planning to crush Taylor's remaining force and then wheel around to attack Scott, General Santa Anna and his numerically superior army encountered Taylor at Buena Vista in February 1847. Tired and dispirited from a forced march across the desert, the Mexican army was in no shape to fight, but Santa Anna ordered an attack anyway. Tactically speaking, the **Battle of Buena Vista** was a draw, but it was a strategic victory for the Americans: Taylor's fresher troops stalled Santa Anna's forces, permitting Scott's army to capture Veracruz on March 9. Marching and fighting their way to Mexico City, Scott's force captured it on September 13, 1847.

With Mexico City, all of Texas, New Mexico, and California in American hands, the direction of treaty talks should have been fairly predictable. Scott's enormous success, however, caused the Mexican government's collapse, leaving no one to negotiate with American peace commissioner Nicholas Trist. The Mexican government eventually elected a new president, and finally, on February 2, 1848, Trist and the Mexican delegation signed the **Treaty of Guadalupe Hidalgo**, granting the United States all the territory between the Nueces River and the Rio Grande and between there and the Pacific. In exchange, Trist agreed that the United States would pay Mexico $15 million and would pay any **war reparations** owed to Americans.

Polk was very angry when he heard the terms of the treaty, believing that the sweeping American victory justified annexing all of Mexico. In Congress, however, many antislavery voices protested bringing so much potential slave territory into the Union. Others opposed the annexation because they feared that Mexico's largely Roman Catholic population might be a threat to Protestant institutions in the United States. Still others, many of whom had opposed the war to begin with, had moral objections to taking any territory by force. Perhaps more convincing than any of these arguments, however, was that the war had cost a lot of money, and congressmen were unwilling to allocate more if peace was within reach. With these considerations in mind, the Senate approved the treaty by a vote of 38 to 14.

Politicizing Slavery: The Election of 1848

The American victory in the War with Mexico was an enormous shot in the arm for American nationalism and manifest destiny, but it also brought the divisive issue of slavery back into mainstream politics to a degree unknown since the Missouri Compromise. Of course, being opposed to the expansion of slavery was not the same thing as opposing the institution itself, and antislavery sentiments were still not widespread among the American people during the 1840s. However, as the debates over the Mexican War indicate, abolitionist voices were getting more politically insistent. Despite strong and

---

war reparations Payments made to settle damage and injury claims resulting from a war; usually paid by the losing side.

sometimes violent opposition, the abolition movement had continued to grow, especially among the privileged and educated classes in the Northeast. Throughout the 1830s, evangelicals increasingly stressed the sinful nature of slavery, urging the immediate, uncompensated liberation of slaves.

But the leading voice among the abolitionists, William Lloyd Garrison, consistently alienated his followers. Calling the Constitution "a covenant with death and an agreement with hell," Garrison burned a copy of it, telling his followers, "so perish all compromises with tyranny," and he urged them to have no dealings with a government that permitted so great an evil as slavery. Citing the reluctance of most organized churches to condemn slavery outright, Garrison urged his followers to break with them as well. He also offended many of his white evangelical supporters by associating with and supporting free black advocates of abolition.

During the 1830s, even moderates within the abolition movement had celebrated **Frederick Douglass** (a former Baltimore slave who disguised himself as a merchant sailor and escaped to New York City, now an influential lecturer in the antislavery cause), **Sojourner Truth,** and other African American abolitionists, welcoming them as members of the American Anti-Slavery Society. But more insistent black voices frightened white abolitionists. African American abolitionist David Walker cried, "The whites want slaves, and want us for their slaves, but some of them will curse the day they ever saw us." Walker advocated that African Americans should "kill or be killed." Another black spokesman, Henry Highland Garnet, proclaimed, "Strike for your lives and liberties. Now is the day and hour. Let every slave in the land do this and the days of slavery are numbered. Rather die freemen than live to be slaves."

Garrison's sentiments mobilized some, but most of his followers were more conservative. In 1840 this and other controversial issues caused many of those moderates to bolt from Garrison's American Anti-Slavery Society to form the more temperate American and Foreign Anti-Slavery Society. This new group forged strong ties with mainstream politicians and church leaders who, while opposed to any extension of slavery and sympathetic to moderate abolitionist proposals, had been relatively silent because of Garrison's reputation for radicalism.

Efforts by moderate antislavery supporters to bring limited abolitionism into the political mainstream meshed with the political aspirations of both those who opposed slavery's expansion primarily for political and economic reasons and those who were motivated by purely ethical concerns. Moderates in 1840 challenged both Whig and Democrat ambivalence by forming the **Liberty Party**.

Specifically disavowing Garrison's radical aims, Liberty Party leaders argued that slavery would eventually die on its own if it could be confined geographically. In addition, the Liberty Party called for the abolition of slavery in Washington, D.C., and in all the territories where it already existed. Though certainly more popular than Garrison's radical appeals, this moderate message drew little open political support: in 1840 Liberty Party presidential candidate James G. Birney garnered only about 7,000 votes. But in 1844, when he again ran on the Liberty Party ticket,

Sojourner Truth was a remarkable woman for her time, or for any time. One anecdote claims that a white policeman in New York state demanded that she identify herself. Using her cane to thrust herself upright to her full six feet of height, she boomed out the same words that God used to identify himself to Moses: "I am that I am." The policeman was unnerved and scurried away. Showing such bravery and pride in both her race and sex, it is little wonder that she commanded great respect in both antislavery and women's rights circles throughout her lifetime.

Sophia Smith Collection, Smith College

he won 62,000 popular votes. Clearly a moderate antislavery position was becoming more acceptable.

Even in the face of such evidence, both major parties continued to practice the politics of avoidance. Suffering ill health, Polk chose not to run for a second term in 1848, leaving the Democrats scrambling for a candidate. They chose Lewis Cass of Michigan—a longtime moderate on slavery issues—as their presidential candidate and balanced the ticket with General William Butler of Kentucky. The Whigs hoped to ride a wave of nationalism following the War with Mexico by running military hero Zachary Taylor, a Louisianan and a slaveholder, for president and moderate New Yorker Millard Fillmore for vice president. Not satisfied with either party's candidates, a number of anti-slavery advocates banded together to launch yet another third party, the **Free-Soil Party**, and promoted Martin Van Buren as its candidate. Adopting the slogan "free soil, free speech, free labor, and free men," this new coalition avoided taking a radical stand on the issue of slavery itself but was firm about excluding slavery from the territories. When all the votes were counted, Taylor came out the winner with Cass a very close second, but the Free-Soilers netted nearly 10 percent of all votes cast.

Disaffected Voices and Political Dissent

It did not take long after the election of 1848 for cracks in the system to become more prominent. In an effort to compete with Democrats in northeastern cities, the Whigs had tried to win Catholic and immigrant voters away from the rival party. The strategy backfired. Not only did the

Whigs not attract large numbers of immigrants, they also alienated two core groups among their existing supporters. One such group was artisans, who saw immigrants as the main source of their economic and social woes. The other was Protestant evangelicals, to whom Roman Catholic Irish and German immigrants symbolized all that was threatening to the American republic. Whig leaders could do little to address these voters' immediate concerns, and increasing numbers left the Whig Party to form state and local coalitions more in tune with their hopes and fears.

One of the most prominent of these locally oriented groups was the anti-Catholic, anti-immigrant group that sprung up in New York but soon spread nationally. Bearing close ties, in terms of both leadership and attitudes, with the Antimasons, this loosely knit political network grafted **xenophobic** views onto strong antiparty sentiments, alleging wholesale voter fraud and government corruption by both major parties. They insisted that issues of slavery and sectionalism dominating national political debate were nothing but devices being used by political insiders and the established parties to divert ordinary Americans from real issues of concern and that immigration, loss of job security, urban crowding and violence, and political corruption were the true threats to American liberties. Behind it all was a perceived Catholic plot to overthrow democracy in the United States. Seeking to protect their members from this conspiracy, leaders told them to say "I know nothing" if they were questioned about the organization or its political intrigues, hence their name: the **Know-Nothings**. Increasingly after 1848, these secretive groups became more public and more vocal, promoting a twenty-one-year naturalization period, a ban against naturalized citizens holding public office, and the use of the Protestant Bible in public schools. As future president Rutherford B. Hayes noted, these people were expressing a "general disgust with the powers that be."

Many Know-Nothings had deep ties with the evangelical Protestant movement and indeed represented one dimension of Christian dissent, but not all Protestant dissenters shared their single-mindedness. In addition to Catholicism and immigration, many evangelicals pointed to slavery, alcohol, and religious heresy as threats to the nation's moral fiber. In their efforts to create moral government and to direct national destiny, these reformers advocated social reform through both religious and political action. Overall, however, progress seemed slow, and like Know-Nothings and others, Christian reform advocates became increasingly impatient with the traditional political parties.

The Politics of Compromise   While dissidents of various types attacked the political parties from outside, problems raised by national expansion were continuing to erode party unity from within. Immediately after Zachary Taylor's election in 1848, California's future became a new divisive issue.

---

xenophobic   Fearful of or hateful toward foreigners or those seen as being different.

California presented a peculiar political problem. Once word reached the rest of the nation that California was rich with gold, politicians immediately began grasping for control over the newly acquired territory. Although large parts of the area lay below the 36°30′ line that the Missouri Compromise had set for slavery expansion, that legislation had applied only to territory acquired in the Louisiana Purchase, and the failure of Congress to pass Wilmot's Proviso left the question of slavery in the new territories wide open.

Having been primarily responsible for crafting the earlier compromise, Henry Clay took it upon himself to find a solution. Clay was convinced that any successful agreement would have to address all sides of the issue. He thus proposed a complex **omnibus bill** to the Senate on January 20, 1850. California would enter the Union as a free state, but the slavery question would be left to **popular sovereignty** in all other territories acquired through the Treaty of Guadalupe Hidalgo. The bill also directed Texas to drop a continuing border dispute with New Mexico in exchange for federal assumption of Texas's public debt. Then, to appease abolitionists, Clay called for an end to the slave trade in Washington, D.C., and balanced that with a clause popular with southerners: a new, more effective **fugitive slave law**.

Though Clay was trying to please all sectional interests, the omnibus bill satisfied no one; Congress debated it without resolution for seven months. Finally, in July 1850, Clay's proposals were defeated. The 73-year-old political veteran left the capital tired and dispirited, but **Stephen A. Douglas** of Illinois set himself to the task of reviving the compromise. Using practical economic arguments and backroom political arm twisting, Douglas proposed each component of Clay's omnibus package as a separate bill, steering it forward toward a comprehensive compromise. Finally, in September, Congress passed the **Compromise of 1850**.

The Compromise of 1850 did little to relieve underlying regional differences and only aggravated political dissent. That slaveowners could pursue runaway slaves into northern states and return them into bondage brought slavery too close to home for many northerners. Many joined both antislavery and evangelical Whigs in chafing at this provision and increasingly joined forces with African Americans to seek solutions outside the political realm. Throughout the 1850s, both white and African American activists helped slaves escape from the South through a covert network of hiding places called the **Underground Railroad**. Individuals like **Harriet Tubman** conducted slaves along routes through American territory made hostile by the fugitive slave law and on to safety in Canada. Nor did southerners find any reason to celebrate: admission of another nonslave state further drained their power in Congress and slavery had gained no positive protection, either in the territories or at home. Still, the compromise created a brief respite from the slavery-extension question at a time when the nation's attention increasingly needed to focus on other major changes in national life.

---

omnibus bill   A piece of legislation with many parts.

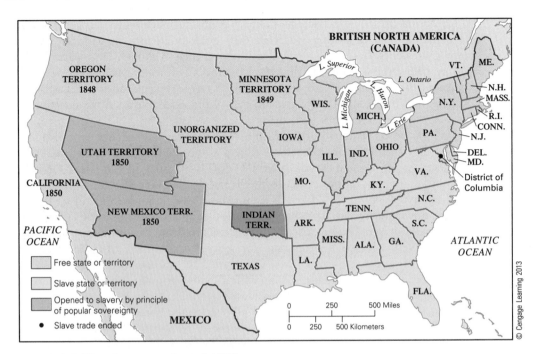

MAP 13.2 The Compromise of 1850

The Compromise of 1850 admitted California as a free state. Utah and New Mexico were left open to slavery or freedom on the principle of popular sovereignty.

A Changing Political Economy

In the years following the Compromise of 1850, American economic and territorial growth continued to play a destabilizing role in both national and regional development. Most notably, during the 1850s industrial growth accelerated, further altering the nation's economic structure. By 1860 less than half of all northern workers made a living from agriculture as northern industry became more concentrated. Steam began to replace water as the primary power source, and factories were no longer limited to locations along rivers and streams. The use of interchangeable parts became more sophisticated and intricate. In 1851, for example, Isaac Singer devised an assembly line using this technology and began mass-producing sewing machines, fostering a boom in ready-made clothing. As industry expanded, the North became more reliant on the West and South for raw materials and for the food consumed by those working in northeastern factories.

Railroad development stimulated economic and industrial growth. Between 1850 and 1860, the number of miles of railroad track in the United States increased from nine thousand to more than thirty thousand. In 1852 the

AN EXPRESS FREIGHT SHIPMENT OF 30 COACHES, APRIL 15, 1868
BY ABBOT, DOWNING & CO., CONCORD, N.H. TO WELLS, FARGO CO., OMAHA, NEB.

New Hampshire Historical Society, Concord

The expansion of railroads improved transportation in a number of ways. Not only could western farmers get their produce to market and buy bulky manufactured goods delivered by train, but other modes of transportation were made easier. This illustration shows thirty stagecoaches built by a New Hampshire firm being hauled in a single load to the Wells Fargo Company in Omaha, Nebraska, which, in turn, used them to haul passengers and small freight to places where the trains did not go.

Michigan Southern Railroad completed the first line into Chicago from the East, and by 1855 that city had become a key transportation hub linking regions farther west with the eastern seaboard. Developing this transportation system was difficult. A lack of bridges and of a standard **rail gauge**—at least twelve different measurements were used—meant that cargos frequently had to be transferred from one rail line to another. Despite these problems, railroads quickly became an integral part of the expanding American economy. Western farmers who had previously shipped their products downriver to New Orleans now sent them much more rapidly by rail to eastern industrial centers. The availability of reliable transportation induced farmers to cultivate more land, and enterprising individuals started up related businesses such as warehouses and **grain elevators,** simplifying storage and loading along railroad lines. Mining boomed, particularly the iron industry; the railroads not only transported ore but also became a prime consumer.

rail gauge   The distance between train tracks.

grain elevator   A building equipped with mechanical lifting devices and used for storing grain.

Building a railroad required huge sums of money. In populous areas, where passenger and freight traffic was heavy, the promise of a quick and profitable return on investment allowed railroads to raise sufficient capital by selling company stock. In sparsely settled regions, however, where investment returns were much slower, state and local governments loaned money directly to rail companies, financed them indirectly by purchasing stock, or extended state tax exemptions. The most crucial aid to railroads, however, was federal land grants.

The federal government, which owned vast amounts of unsettled territory, gave land to railroad developers who then leased or sold plots along the proposed route to finance construction. In 1850 one such federal proposal made by Illinois senator Stephen A. Douglas resulted in a 2.6-million-acre land grant to Illinois, Mississippi, and Alabama for a railroad between Chicago and Mobile. Congress also invested heavily in plans for a transcontinental railroad and on March 4, 1853, appropriated $150,000 to survey potential routes across the continent.

While Americans were enjoying the rail boom, crop failures throughout Europe were creating new markets for American produce. During the 1850s, the price of grain rose sharply in world markets. Railroads allowed western farmers to ship directly to eastern seaports and on to Europe. Meanwhile, technological advances in farming equipment enabled American farmers to harvest enough grain to meet world demand. Using the steel plow devised in 1837 by **John Deere**, farmers could cultivate more acres with greater ease. The mechanical reaper invented in 1831 by **Cyrus McCormick** allowed a single operator to harvest as much as fourteen field hands could. The combination of greater production potential and speedy transportation prompted westerners to increase farm size and concentrate on cash crops. The outcome of these developments was a vast increase in the economic and political power of the West.

Western grain markets provided the foodstuffs for American industrialization, and Europe provided much of the labor. Factories employed unskilled workers for the most part, and immigrants made up the majority of that labor pool as food shortages, poverty, and political upheaval drove millions from Europe, especially from Ireland and Germany. The flow increased when, in 1848, revolutions spread throughout much of continental Europe, followed by the outbreak of several wars. Total immigration to the United States exceeded 100,000 for the first time in 1848, and in 1851, 221,000 people migrated to the United States from Ireland alone. In 1852 the number of German immigrants reached 145,000. Many of these newcomers were not trained in skilled crafts and wound up settling in the industrial urban centers of the Northeast, where they could find work in the factories.

This combination of changes set the stage for political crisis. Liberalized suffrage rules transformed naturalized immigrants into voters, and both parties courted them, adding their interests to the political pot. Meanwhile, a mechanized textile industry, hungry for southern fiber, lent vitality to the continued growth of the cotton kingdom and the slave labor system that gave it life. Northern political leaders visualized an industrial nation based on free labor, but that view ran counter to the southern elites' ideals of **agrarian capitalism** based on slavery. In the West, most continued to believe in the Jeffersonian ideal of an agricultural nation of small and medium-size farms and could not accept either industrial or cotton capitalism as positive developments.

| Political Instability and the Election of 1852 | Dynamic economic progress improved material life throughout the nation, but it also raised serious questions about what course progress should take. As one clear-sighted northern minister pointed out in 1852, the debate was not about whether America should pursue progress but |

about "different kinds and methods of progress." Contradictory visions of national destiny were about to cause the breakdown of the existing party system.

Slavery seemed to loom behind every debate, but most Americans, even southerners, had no personal investment in the institution. Two-thirds of southerners owned no slaves, tolerating the institution but having only fleeting contact with the great plantations and their peculiar labor system. Northerners, too, were largely indifferent. Men like young Illinois state congressman **Abraham Lincoln** believed the institution was wrong but were not inclined to do anything about it. What mattered to these people was not slavery but autonomy—control over local affairs and over their own lives.

The slavery question challenged notions of autonomy in both the North and the South. In their widely disseminated rhetoric, abolitionists expanded the specter of the Slave Power conspiracy, especially in the aftermath of the Compromise of 1850. Growing numbers perceived this conspiracy as intent on imposing southern ways and installing southern elites or their sympathizers in seats of power in every section of the nation. Whether farmers in Illinois or artisans in Pennsylvania, common people stood ready to resist a southern takeover of local institutions. Likewise, common people in the South feared interference from outsiders in view of the ever more vigorous antisouthern crusade by northern radicals.

After the Compromise of 1850 momentarily eased regional fears, sectional tensions flamed anew in 1852 with the publication of *Uncle Tom's Cabin* by **Harriet Beecher Stowe**. Stowe portrayed the darkest inhumanities of southern slavery in the first American novel to include African Americans as central characters. *Uncle Tom's Cabin* sold 300,000 copies in its first year. Adapted for the stage, it became one of the most popular plays of the period. The book stirred public opinion and breathed new life into antislavery sentiments, leading Free-Soilers and so-called **conscience Whigs** to renew their efforts to limit or

---

agrarian capitalism   A system of agriculture based on the efficient, specialized production of crops intended to generate profits rather than subsistence.

end slavery. When these activists saw that the Whig Party was incapable of addressing the slavery question in any effective way, they began to look for other political options.

Superficially, the Whigs seemed well organized and surprisingly unified as a new presidential election approached in 1852. Zachary Taylor had died in office in July 1850, and they nominated General Winfield Scott, Taylor's rival for fame in the War with Mexico. The Democrats remained divided through forty-nine ballots, unable to decide among Lewis Cass of Michigan, Stephen A. Douglas of Illinois, and **James Buchanan** of Pennsylvania. They finally settled on the virtually unknown **Franklin Pierce** of New Hampshire, who pledged to uphold the Compromise of 1850 and keep slavery out of politics. This promise was enough to bring Martin Van Buren back to the Democrats, and he brought many Free-Soilers back with him. Many others, though, abandoned Van Buren and joined forces with conscience Whigs.

Scott was a national figure and a distinguished military hero, but Pierce gathered 254 electoral votes to Scott's 42, exposing the disarray in the Whig Party. Splits between "cotton" and "conscience" groups splintered Whig unity, and regional tension escalated as Free-Soil rhetoric clashed with calls for extending slavery. Confrontations between Catholics and Protestants and between native-born and immigrant laborers caused bitter animosity. In the North, where immigration, industrialization, and antislavery sentiment were most prevalent and economic friction most pronounced, massive numbers of voters, believing the Whigs incapable of addressing current problems, deserted the party.

Harriet Beecher Stowe's Uncle Tom's Cabin *was the first American novel that featured African American characters in prominent roles. It was issued in various editions with many different covers, but most of them featured the lead character, Uncle Tom— another first in American publishing. This particular cover, from an early "Young Folks' Edition" of the book, depicts the stooped old man with his owner's young, sympathetic daughter.*

Increasing
Tension
under Pierce
The Democratic Party and Franklin Pierce also felt the pressures of a changing electorate. Pierce was part of the **Young America Movement**, which, as a whole, tried to ignore the slavery issue, advocating romantic and aggressive nationalism, manifest destiny, and republican revolutions throughout the Americas. In line with the Young America agenda, Pierce emphasized expansion; choosing a route for a transcontinental railroad became the keystone in his agenda for the nation.

Southerners knew that a railroad based in the South would channel the flow of gold from California through their region and would also allow new settlement and cotton agriculture to spread beyond the waterways that had proved necessary for expansion so far. Eventually the new territories would become states, increasing the South's national political power.

That model of development was totally unacceptable to several groups: to northern evangelicals, who viewed slavery as a moral blight on the nation; to Free-Soil advocates, who believed the spread of slavery would degrade white workers; and to northern manufacturers, who wanted to maintain dominance in Congress to ensure continued economic protection. In May 1853, only two months after assuming office, Pierce inflamed all of these groups by sending James Gadsden, a southern railroad developer, to Mexico to purchase a strip of land lying below the southern border of the New Mexico Territory. Any rail line built westward from a southern city to California would have to cross that land, and Pierce and his southern supporters wanted to make sure it was part of the United States. The **Gadsden Purchase**, signed on December 30, 1853, added 29,640 square miles of land to the United States for a cost of $10 million. It also finalized the southwestern border of the United States.

The Gadsden Purchase prompted proponents of a southern route for the transcontinental railroad, led by Secretary of War **Jefferson Davis**, to push for government sponsorship of the project. Having invested his own money in more northerly rail development, Illinois senator Stephen A. Douglas blocked Davis's efforts and pushed for a route westward from his home town of Chicago. But this route would have to pass through Indian Territory that was not open to rail development. To rectify this problem, Douglas introduced a bill on January 4, 1854, incorporating the entire northern half of Indian Territory into a new federal entity called Nebraska.

Douglas knew that he would need both northern and southern support to get his bill through Congress, and he sought to silence possible opposition by proposing that the slavery question in the territory be left to popular sovereignty—let the voters of Nebraska decide. When southerners pointed out that the proposed territory was above the Missouri Compromise line and that Congress might prohibit popular sovereignty from functioning, Douglas responded that the Compromise of 1850 superseded the 1820 Missouri Compromise. But to calm southerners he finally supported an amendment to his original bill dividing the territory in half—Nebraska in the north and Kansas in the south. The amended legislation—called the **Kansas-Nebraska Act**—

rested on the assumption that popular sovereignty would lead to slavery in Kansas and free labor in Nebraska.

TOWARD A HOUSE DIVIDED

Once again slavery threatened national political stability. In the North, opponents of the bill formed local coalitions to defeat it. On January 24, 1854, a group of Democrats including Salmon P. Chase, Gerrit Smith, Joshua Giddings, and **Charles Sumner** published "The Appeal of the Independent Democrats in Congress, to the People of the United States." They called the bill an "atrocious plot" to make Nebraska a "dreary region of despotism, inhabited by masters and slaves." On February 28, opponents of the Kansas-Nebraska bill met in Ripon, Wisconsin, and recommended the formation of a new political party. Similar meetings took place in several northern states as opposition to the bill grew. In the wake of these meetings, the existing party system collapsed and a new one arose to replace it.

A Shattered Compromise   Despite this strong opposition, Douglas and Pierce rallied support for the Kansas-Nebraska Act. On May 26, 1854, after gaining approval in the House of Representatives, the bill passed the Senate, and Pierce soon signed it into law. Passage of the act crystallized northern antislavery sentiment. To protest, many northerners threatened **noncompliance** with the fugitive slave law of 1850. As Senator William Seward of New York vowed, "We will engage in competition for the virgin soil of Kansas, and God give the victory to the side which is stronger in numbers as it is in right."

Antislavery forces, however, remained divided into at least three major groups. The Free-Soil contingent opposed any extension of slavery but did not necessarily favor abolishing the institution. The other two groups—Garrisonians and evangelicals—wanted immediate abolition but disagreed on many particulars. William Lloyd Garrison and his followers believed that slavery was the primary evil facing the nation, while evangelicals agreed that slavery was evil, but believed it was one among many vices undermining the virtuous republic. All three groups constantly agitated against slavery and what they perceived as southern control of national politics. They weakened the Democratic Party's strength in the North but could not bring themselves to align behind a single opposition party.

Actions perceived as further evidence of the Slave Power conspiracy also undermined Democratic unity. Private armies, led by adventurers like **William Walker**, invaded territories in Latin America and the Caribbean, which many in

---

noncompliance   Failure or refusal to obey a law or request.

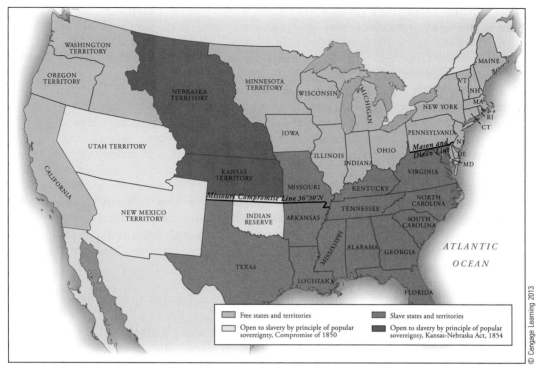

MAP 13.3 Kansas-Nebraska and Slavery

The Kansas Territory, adjacent to slaveholding Missouri but well north of the Missouri Compromise line, stood as a place both slaveholders and Free-Soilers felt they could claim as their own.

the North concluded were Slave Power efforts. In this atmosphere, President Pierce unintentionally undermined the party by pushing for the purchase of Cuba from Spain. When the Spanish refused, three of Pierce's European ministers met in Ostend, Belgium, in October 1854, and secretly drafted a justification for taking Cuba by force. When the so-called **Ostend Manifesto** became public in 1855, many northerners were convinced that Pierce and the Democratic Party approved of Walker-like adventurism to expand slavery. These perceptions stirred antislavery anxieties and fueled the growth of the newly formed anti-Democratic coalitions.

Bleeding Kansas   Meanwhile, political friction was about to ignite Kansas. In April 1854, abolitionist Eli Thayer of Worcester, Massachusetts, organized the New England Emigrant Aid Society to encourage antislavery supporters to move to Kansas. They reasoned that flooding a region subject to popular sovereignty with right-minded residents could effectively "save" it from slavery. This group eventually sent two thousand armed settlers to Kansas, founding Lawrence and other communities. With similar designs, proslavery southerners, particularly those in Missouri, also encouraged settlement in the territory. Like their northern counterparts, these southerners came armed and ready to fight for their cause.

President Pierce appointed governors in both Kansas and Nebraska and instructed them to organize elections for territorial legislatures. As proslavery and antislavery settlers vied for control of Kansas, the region became a testing ground for popular sovereignty. When the vote came on March 30, 1855, a large contingent of armed slavery supporters from Missouri—so-called border ruffians—crossed into Kansas and cast ballots for proslavery candidates. According to later Senate investigations, 60 percent of the votes cast were illegal. These unlawful ballots gave proslavery supporters a large majority in the Kansas legislature. They promptly expelled all abolitionist legislators and enacted the Kansas Code—a group of laws meant to drive all antislavery forces out of the territory. Antislavery advocates responded by organizing their own free-state government and drawing up an alternative constitution, which they submitted to the voters.

Bloodshed soon followed. Attempting to bring the conflict to conclusion, proslavery territorial judge Samuel LeCompte called a grand jury of slavery supporters that indicted members of the free-state government for treason and sent a **posse** of about eight hundred men to Lawrence. There they "arrested" the antislavery forces and sacked the town, burning buildings and plundering shops and homes. The violence did not end there. Hearing news of the "Sack of Lawrence," **John Brown**, an antislavery zealot, murdered five proslavery men living along the Pottawatomie River south of Lawrence. This "Pottawatomie Massacre" triggered a series of episodes in which more than two hundred men were killed. Much of the violence was the work of border ruffians and zealots like Brown, but to many people in both the North and the South, the events symbolized the "righteousness" of their cause.

The Kansas issue also led to violence in Congress. During the debates over the admission of the territory, Massachusetts senator Charles Sumner made insulting remarks about South Carolina and its 60-year-old senator Andrew Butler. Butler was out of town, but Butler's nephew, Representative Preston Brooks, accosted Sumner and beat him nearly to death with a cane. Though **censured** by the House of Representatives, Brooks was overwhelmingly reelected by his home district and openly praised for his actions—he received canes as gifts from admirers all over the South.

Meanwhile the presidential election of 1856 was approaching. The Pierce administration's actions, southern expansionism, and the Kansas-Nebraska controversy swelled the ranks of dissenters like those who had convened in

---

posse   A group of citizens deputized by a court or peace officer to assist in law enforcement.

censure   To issue an official rebuke, as by a legislature to one of its members.

Ripon. Now formally calling themselves the **Republican Party**, these northern and western groups began actively seeking support. Immigration also remained a major issue, but the Know-Nothings, despite their success at the local and state levels, split over slavery at their initial national convention in 1855; many then joined Republican coalitions, though some loyalists proceeded to nominate Millard Fillmore. John C. Frémont, a moderate abolitionist who had achieved fame as the "liberator of California," won the Republican nomination. For their part, the Democrats rejected both Pierce and Douglas and nominated James Buchanan from Pennsylvania, selecting John C. Breckinridge of Kentucky as Buchanan's running mate to balance the ticket between the North and the South.

The election became a contest for party survival rather than a national referendum on slavery. Buchanan received 45 percent of the popular vote and 163 electoral votes. Frémont finished second with 33 percent of the popular vote and 114 electoral votes. Fillmore received 21 percent of the popular vote but only 8 electoral votes. Frémont's surprisingly narrow margin of defeat demonstrated the appeal of the newly formed Republican coalition to northern voters. The Know-Nothings disappeared and never again attempted a national organization.

Bringing Slavery Home to the North

On March 4, 1857, James Buchanan became president of the United States. The 65-year-old Pennsylvanian had begun his political career in Congress in 1821 and owed much of his success to southern support. His election came at a time when the nation needed strong leadership, but Buchanan seemed unable to provide it. Despite his campaign promise to emphasize national unity, he proved incapable of achieving a unifying compromise. His attempt to preserve the politics of avoidance only strengthened radicalism in both the North and the South. **Regionalism** colored all political issues, and every debate became a contest between competing social, political, and economic ideologies.

Though Buchanan's shortcomings contributed to the rising crisis, an event occurred within days of his inauguration that sent shock waves through the already troubled nation. **Dred Scott**, a slave once owned by army surgeon John Emerson, sued for his freedom. Scott's attorney argued that between 1831 and 1833, Emerson had taken Scott with him during various military postings to areas where the Missouri Compromise banned slavery, making Scott a free man. When, after nearly six years in the Missouri courts, the state supreme court rejected this argument in 1852, Scott, with the help of abolitionist lawyers, appealed to the United States Supreme Court. In a 7-to-2 decision, the Court ruled against Scott. Chief Justice Roger B. Taney, formerly a member of Andrew Jackson's Kitchen Cabinet and a stalwart Democrat, argued that in the eyes of

regionalism Loyalty to the interests of a particular region of the country.

It Matters Today

The Dred Scott *Case*

As Frederick Douglass and other former slaves inevitably discovered, freedom for African Americans did not also mean equality. This was reinforced by one of the most important cases ever to reach the Supreme Court. Denying once and for all that freedom and equality for people of African heritage were identical, the Court's decision in *Dred Scott v. Sanford* declared that because no state at the time that the Constitution was ratified had included African Americans as citizens, then no one of African descent could become a citizen of the United States. Ever! It would take the Thirteenth, Fourteenth, and Fifteenth Amendments to the Constitution to remove the legal justification behind the Court's opinion, but even these did not reverse the racism underlying the decision. The *Dred Scott* case and the amendments designed to correct the constitutional defects that led to it still play a key role in dozens of cases in the nation's courts each year as men and women of many backgrounds seek to make real the tie between freedom and equality that Dred Scott and Frederick Douglass only dreamed of.

- To what extent do you think that the *Dred Scott* case made Civil War in the United States inevitable? Explain.

- Choose a post–Civil War court case dealing with racial equality issues (the American Civil Liberties Union and other organizations as well as the federal government maintain catalogues of important cases). In what ways does the case you have chosen reflect the *Dred Scott* case and the constitutional amendments passed in response? Assess the continuing legacy of this case in American life and justice.

the law slaves were not people but property; as such, they could not be citizens of the United States and had no right to petition the Court. Taney then ignited a political powder keg by ruling that Congress had no constitutional authority to limit slavery in a federal territory, thereby declaring the Missouri Compromise unconstitutional.

While southerners generally celebrated the decision, antislavery forces and northern evangelical leaders called the *Dred Scott* decision a mockery of justice and a crime against a "higher law." Some radical abolitionists argued that the North should separate from the Union. Others suggested impeaching the Supreme Court. Already incensed by events in Kansas, antislavery leaders predicted that the next move by the Slave Power conspiracy would be to get the Supreme Court to strike down antislavery laws in northern states.

Meanwhile, the Kansas issue still burned. That very few slaveholders actually moved into the territory did nothing to deter proslavery leaders, who met in Lecompton, Kansas, in June 1857 to draft a state constitution favoring slavery. When the **Lecompton constitution** was submitted for voters' approval, antislavery forces protested by refusing to vote, so it was easily ratified. But when it was revealed that more than two thousand nonresidents had voted illegally, both Republicans and northern Democrats in Congress roundly denounced it. The Buchanan administration joined southerners in support of admitting Kansas to the Union as a slave state and managed to push the statehood bill through the Senate, but the House of Representatives rejected it. Congress then returned the Lecompton constitution to Kansas for another vote. This time Free-Soilers participated in the election and defeated the proposed constitution. Kansas remained a territory.

As this cartoon makes clear, the Dred Scott case set the agenda for the presidential election of 1860. Here Scott provides the music as each of the four presidential candidates dances with a partner who symbolizes his perceived political orientation. John C. Breckinridge (upper left) dances with fellow southern Democrat James Buchanan, illustrating his alignment with southern proslavery hard-liners. John H. Bell (lower right) dances with a Native American, symbolizing his nativist Know-Nothing affiliations, suggesting avoidance of the slavery issue. Meanwhile, Stephen A. Douglas (lower left) escorts a disheveled Irishman, suggesting his alignment with northeastern urban interests including immigrants and other "undesirables." Finally, Abraham Lincoln (upper right) is seen with an African American woman, an obvious reference to his party's perceived abolitionist leanings.

Growing Friction and Expanding Violence

The *Dred Scott* decision dangerously accelerated the ever-expanding debate between North and South. Both the Kansas controversy and Dred Scott undermined the Democratic commitment to popular sovereignty. Entertaining presidential ambitions, party leader Stephen Douglas sought a solution that might win him both northern and southern support in a run for that office in 1860. His immediate goal, however, was reelection to the Senate.

Illinois Republicans selected Abraham Lincoln to run against Douglas for the Senate in 1858. Born on the Kentucky frontier in 1809, Lincoln had accompanied his family from one failed farm to another, picking up schooling in Indiana and Illinois as opportunities arose. As a young man he worked odd jobs—farm worker, ferryman, flatboatman, surveyor, and store clerk. He was eventually elected to the Illinois legislature and began a serious study of law. A strong Whig, Lincoln followed Henry Clay's economic philosophy and steered a middle course between the "cotton" and "conscience" wings of the Whig Party. Lincoln acknowledged that slavery was evil but contended that it was the unavoidable consequence of black racial inferiority. The only way to get rid of the evil, he believed, was to prevent the expansion of slavery into the territories, forcing it to die out naturally.

Lincoln was decidedly the underdog in the contest with Douglas and sought to improve his chances by challenging the senator to a series of debates. Douglas agreed. During the debate at Freeport, Lincoln asked Douglas to explain how the people of a territory could exclude slavery in light of the *Dred Scott* ruling. Douglas's reply became known as the **Freeport Doctrine**. Slavery, he said, needed the protection of "local police regulations." In any territory, citizens opposed to slavery could elect representatives who would "by unfriendly legislation" prevent the introduction of slavery. Lincoln did not win Douglas's Senate seat, but the debate drew national attention to the Illinois race, and Lincoln won recognition as an up-and-coming Republican figure.

Southerners bristled at claims by Lincoln and others that slavery was immoral. Charles C. Jones and other southern evangelical leaders, for example, offered a religious defense of slavery, arguing that whites had a moral responsibility to care for blacks and instruct them in the Christian faith. However, many southerners, like some of their Republican opponents, were less interested in the slaves than in how slavery affected white society and white labor. Southern apologists contended that whites in the South enjoyed a greater degree of freedom than northern whites because slaves did all the demeaning work, freeing whites for more noble pursuits. Moreover, southern lawyer George Fitzhugh argued, both the North and the South relied equally on a subjugated work force. The only meaningful difference between northern **wage slaves** and southern slaves, Fitzhugh concluded, was that northerners accepted no responsibility for housing

wage slaves   Workers who, though legally free, are underpaid, trapped in debt, and living in extreme poverty.

and feeding their work force, condemning laborers to suffer at below-subsistence conditions.

Northern radicals increasingly called for a violent response to the Slave Power movement, and in 1857 Kansas zealot John Brown came to the East to oblige them. He convinced several prominent antislavery leaders to finance a daring plan to raise an army of slaves in an all-out insurrection against their masters. Brown and a small party of followers attacked the federal arsenal at **Harpers Ferry**, Virginia, on October 16, 1859, attempting to seize weapons. The arsenal proved an easy target, but no slaves joined the uprising. Local citizens surrounded the arsenal, firing on Brown and his followers until federal troops commanded by Colonel **Robert E. Lee** arrived. On October 18, Lee's forces battered down the barricaded entrance and arrested Brown. He was tried, convicted of treason, and hanged on December 2, 1859.

Brown's raid on Harpers Ferry captured the imagination of radical abolitionists. Republican leaders denounced it, but other northerners proclaimed Brown a martyr. Church bells tolled in many northern cities on the day of his execution. In New England, Ralph Waldo Emerson proclaimed Brown "that new saint." Such reactions caused many appalled southerners—even very moderate ones—to seriously consider **secession**. In Alabama, Mississippi, and Florida, state legislatures resolved that a Republican victory in the upcoming presidential election would provide sufficient justification for such action.

THE DIVIDED NATION

The Republicans were a new phenomenon on the American political scene: a purely regional political party. Rather than making any attempt to forge a national coalition, the party drew its strength and ideas almost entirely from the North. The Republican platform—"Free Soil, Free Labor, and Free Men"— stressed the defilement of white labor by slavery and contended that the Slave Power conspiracy was eroding the rights of free whites everywhere. By taking up a cry against "Rum, Romanism, and Slavery," the Republicans drew former Know-Nothings and temperance advocates into their ranks. The Democrats hoped to maintain a national coalition, but as the nation approached a new presidential election, their hopes began to fade.

The Dominance of Regionalism During the Buchanan administration, Democrats found it increasingly difficult to achieve national party unity. Facing Republican pressure in their own states, northern Democrats realized that any concession to southern Democratic demands for extending or protecting slavery would cost them votes at home. In April 1860, as the party convened in Charleston, South Carolina, each side was ready to do battle for its political life.

The fight began when northern supporters of Stephen A. Douglas championed a popular sovereignty position. Southern radicals demanded a plank calling for the legal protection of slavery in the territories. After heated debates, neither side would compromise. When the delegates finally voted, the Douglas forces carried the day. Disgusted delegates from eight southern states walked out of the convention. Shocked, the remaining delegates adjourned; they would reconvene in Baltimore in June. Most southern delegates boycotted the Baltimore proceedings, and Douglas easily won the Democratic presidential nomination with moderate southerner Herschel V. Johnson of Georgia as his running mate. Hoping to attract moderate voters from both the North and the South, the party's final platform supported popular sovereignty and emphasized allegiance to the Union.

The southern Democratic contingent met one week later, also in Baltimore, and nominated Vice President John C. Breckinridge of Kentucky as its presidential candidate and Joseph Lane of Oregon as his running mate. The southern Democrats' platform vowed support for the Union but called for federal protection of the right to own slaves in the territories and for the preservation of slavery where it already existed.

In May 1860, a group of former Whigs and Know-Nothings along with some disaffected Democrats convened in Baltimore and formed the **Constitutional Union Party**. They nominated John Bell, a former southern Know-Nothing and wealthy slaveholder from Tennessee, and Edward Everett of Massachusetts, a former Whig leader, as his running mate. Hoping to resurrect the politics of compromise, the party resolved to take no stand on the sectional controversy and pledged to uphold the Constitution and the Union and to enforce the laws of the nation.

Having lost most of its moderates to the Constitutional Union coalition and having virtually no southerners in its ranks to start with, the Republican convention faced few ideological divisions, but personality conflicts were rife. The front-runner for the Republican nomination appeared to be William Seward of New York. A former Whig and longtime New York politician, Seward had actively opposed any extension of slavery during the early 1850s but had switched to the popular-sovereignty position during the Kansas controversy. Several other Republican favorites—Salmon P. Chase of Ohio, Simon Cameron of Pennsylvania, and Edward Bates of Missouri—agreed with Seward's position but sought the nomination for themselves. Eventually, however, Abraham Lincoln emerged as Seward's major competition. Many delegates considered Seward too radical and his campaign manager, Thurlow Weed, was perceived by many as a corrupt opportunist. Lincoln, in contrast, had a reputation for integrity and had not seriously alienated any of the Republican factions. He won the nomination on the third ballot.

The Election of 1860

The 1860 presidential campaign began as several separate contests. Lincoln and Douglas competed for northern votes; the Republicans were not even on the ballot in the

Deep South. Douglas proclaimed himself the only national candidate but received most of his support from northerners who feared the consequences of a Republican victory. By the same token, Breckinridge and the southern Democrats expected no support in the North. Bell and the Constitutional Unionists attempted to campaign in both regions but attracted mostly southern voters anxious to stave off disunion.

Slavery and sectionalism were the key issues. Even when a congressional investigation revealed evidence of graft, bribery, and shady dealings in the Buchanan administration, Republicans linked these charges to the supposed Slave Power conspiracy. The slaveholding elite, they contended, not only had attempted to subvert liberty but had used fraudulent means to keep the Democrats in power. "Honest Abe Lincoln," the man of the people, would lead the fight against the forces of slavery and corruption. This argument drew in many northern voters, including a lot of former Know-Nothings. Sensing that Lincoln would win the North, Douglas launched a last-ditch effort to win the election and hold the Union together by pushing his campaign into the South. As the election drew near, the likelihood of a Republican victory deeply alarmed southerners. Even moderate southerners started to believe that the Republicans intended to crush their way of life and to enslave southern whites economically while freeing southern blacks. Northern qualms were aroused as well when the pro-Democrat *New York Herald* contended that the election of Lincoln would bring "hundreds of thousands" of slaves north to compete with whites for jobs, resulting in "African amalgamation with the fair daughters of the Anglo-Saxon, Celtic, and Teutonic races."

Seeking to counter such scare tactics, national Republican leaders forged a platform that advocated limits on slavery's expansion but contained no planks seeking an end to slavery in areas where it already existed. They also called for higher tariffs (to appeal to northern industrialists) and for internal improvements and public lands legislation (to appeal to westerners). Particularly in the Midwest, party leaders worked hard to portray themselves as "the white man's party." In line with the position Lincoln had taken in his 1858 debates with Douglas, Republicans argued that excluding slavery meant excluding blacks from competition with whites. These tactics alienated a few abolitionists but persuaded many northerners and westerners to support the party.

On November 6, 1860, Abraham Lincoln was elected president of the United States with 180 electoral votes—a clear majority—but only 40 percent of the popular vote. Lincoln carried all the northern states, California, and Oregon. Douglas finished second with 29 percent of the popular vote but just 12 electoral votes. He won only Missouri. Bell won the 39 electoral votes of Virginia, Kentucky, and Tennessee. Breckinridge, as expected, carried the Deep South but tallied only 72 electoral votes and 18 percent of the popular vote nationwide. For the first time

---

Deep South   The region of the South farthest from the North, usually said to include the states of Alabama, Florida, Georgia, Louisiana, Mississippi, and South Carolina.

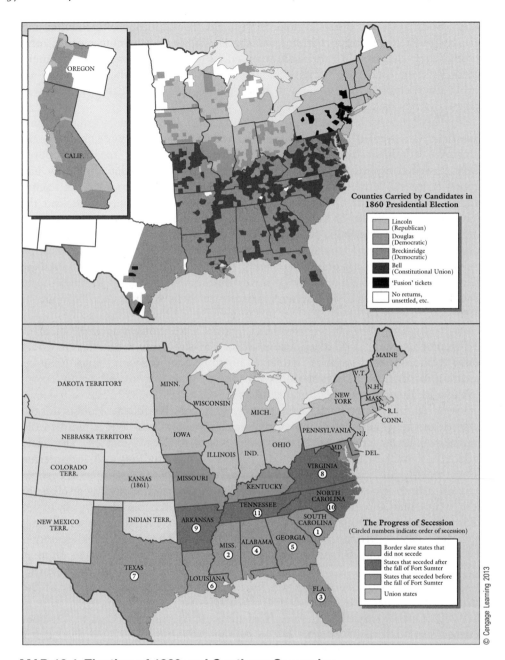

MAP 13.4 Election of 1860 and Southern Secession

Note the similarity of the geographical voting patterns in the upper map to the 1856 election. Another striking pattern shows the correlation between the vote for Breckinridge (upper map) and the first seven states to secede (lower map).

in American history, a purely regional party held the presidency. The Republicans, who had made no effort to win votes in the South, also swept congressional races in the North and secured a large majority in the House of Representatives for the upcoming term.

The First Wave of Secession   After the Republican victory, southern sentiment for secession snowballed, especially in the Deep South. The Republicans were a "party founded on a single sentiment," stated the *Richmond Examiner:* "hatred of African slavery." The *New Orleans Delta* agreed, calling the Republicans "essentially a revolutionary party." But this party now controlled the national government. To a growing number of southerners, the Republican victory was proof that secession was the only alternative to political domination. Most Republicans did not believe that the South would actually leave the Union: Seward had ridiculed threats of secession and Lincoln believed that the "people of the South" had "too much sense" to launch an "attempt to ruin the government." During the campaign, he had promised "no interference by the government, with slaves or slavery within the states," and he continued to urge moderation.

In a last-ditch attempt at compromise, **John J. Crittenden** proposed a block of constitutional amendments that could never be repealed on December 18, 1860. These called for extending the Missouri Compromise line westward across the continent, forbidding slavery north of the line, and protecting slavery to the south; maintaining the interstate slave trade; and requiring federal compensation to slaveowners who were unable to recover fugitive slaves from northern states. Surprisingly, this plan appealed to some northerners, especially businessmen who feared that secession would cause a major depression. Lincoln warned, however, that such a plan would "lose us everything we gained by the election." The Senate defeated Crittenden's proposal by a vote of 25 to 23.

Meanwhile, on December 20, 1860, delegates in South Carolina met to consider seceding from the Union. South Carolina had long been a hotbed of resistance to federal authority, and state officials determined to take action to protect slavery before the newly elected Republican administration came to power. Amid general jubilation, South Carolina delegates voted unanimously to dissolve their ties with the United States. Just as the radicals hoped, other southern states followed. During January 1861, delegates convened in Mississippi, Florida, Alabama, Georgia, and Louisiana and voted to secede.

On February 4, 1861, delegates from the six seceding states and from several states still considering secession met in Montgomery, Alabama, and formed the **Confederate States of America**. During the several weeks that followed, the provisional congress drafted a constitution, and the six Confederate states ratified it on March 11, 1861.

The Confederate constitution emphasized the "sovereign and independent character" of the states and guaranteed the protection of slavery in any new territories acquired. It allowed tariffs solely for the purpose of raising government revenue and prohibited government funding of internal improvements. It also limited the president and vice president to a single six-year term. A cabinet composed of six executive department heads rounded out the executive branch. In all other respects, the Confederate government was identical to that in the United States. In fact, the U.S. Constitution was acknowledged as the supreme law in the Confederacy except in those particulars where it conflicted with provisions in the Confederate Constitution.

While this process was under way, the Confederate cause got a significant boost when Texas, which had been holding back, declared itself part of the new nation. Despite unionist pleas from Governor Sam Houston, the heavily populated cotton-growing region in the eastern part of the state opted to join neighboring Louisiana in rebellion, and the rest of the state followed suit. The Confederacy now numbered seven states.

Responses to Disunion   Even as late as March 1861, a significant number of southerners did not favor secession. John Bell and Stephen Douglas together had received more than 50 percent of southern votes in 1860, winning support from southerners who desired compromise. These "plain folk" joined together with some large planters, who stood to suffer economic loss from disunion, in calls for moderation and compromise. And the border states, which were less invested in cotton and had numerous ties with the North, were not strongly inclined toward secession. In February, Virginia had called for a peace conference to meet in Washington in an effort to forestall hostilities, but this attempt, like Crittenden's effort, also failed to hold the Union together.

The division in southern sentiments was a major stumbling block to the election of a Confederate president. Many moderate delegates to the constitutional convention refused to support radical secessionists, believing them to be equally responsible with the Republicans for initiating the crisis. The convention remained deadlocked until two pro-secession Virginia attendees nominated Mississippi moderate Jefferson Davis as a compromise candidate.

Davis appeared to be the ideal choice. Austere and dignified, he had not sought the job but seemed extremely capable of handling it. A West Point graduate, he served during the War with Mexico, was elected to the Senate soon afterward, then left the Senate in 1851 to run unsuccessfully for governor in Mississippi. After serving as secretary of war under Franklin Pierce, he returned to the Senate in 1857. Although Davis had long championed southern interests and owned many slaves, he was no romantic, fire-eating secessionist. Before 1860 he had been a strong **Unionist**, arguing only that the South be allowed to maintain its own economy, culture, and institutions, including slavery. He had supported the Compromise of 1850. When he had fought for a southern route for a transcontinental railroad as secretary of war, he believed that it would benefit the South economically,

Unionist Loyal to the United States of America.

but he also felt that it would tie the whole nation more firmly together. Like many of his contemporaries, however, Davis had become increasingly alarmed by the prospect of declining southern political power. Immediately after Mississippi's declaration of secession, Davis resigned his Senate seat and threw in with the Confederacy.

To moderates like Davis, the presidential election of 1860 was simply a forceful demonstration that unless the South took a strong stand against outside interference, the region would no longer be able to control its own internal affairs. The initial northward tilt in the Senate created by California's admission in 1850 had been aggravated in 1858 by the admission of Minnesota and by Oregon's statehood in 1859. Southerners, Davis believed, needed to act in concert to convince northerners to either leave the South alone or face the region's withdrawal from the nation. "To rally the men of the North, who would preserve the government as our fathers found it," Davis proclaimed, "we ... should offer no doubtful or divided front."

Elected provisional president of the Confederate States of America unanimously on February 9, 1861, Davis addressed the cheering crowds in Montgomery a week later and set forth the Confederate position: "The time for compromise has now passed," he said. "The South is determined to maintain her position, and make all who oppose her smell Southern powder and feel Southern steel." In his inaugural address several days later, he stressed a desire for peace but reiterated that the "courage and patriotism of the Confederate States" would be "found equal to any measure of defense which honor and security may require."

Northern Democrats and Republicans alike watched developments in the South with dismay. President Buchanan argued that secession had no constitutional validity and that any state leaving the Union did so unlawfully, but he also asserted that the federal government had no constitutional power to "coerce a State" to remain in the Union. He blamed the crisis on "incessant and violent agitation on the slavery question," chiding northerners for disregarding fugitive slave laws and calling for a constitutional amendment protecting slavery.

Waiting to assume the office he had just won, Lincoln wrestled with the twin problems of what he would do about secession and slavery. On one hand, he directly opposed Buchanan's position, stating that "My opinion is that no state can, in any way, lawfully get out of the Union, without the consent of the others." But he was more moderate where slavery was concerned, writing to reassure southerners that "a republican administration" would not "directly or indirectly, interfere with their slaves, or with them, about their slaves."

Before he could do anything else, Lincoln first had to unite his party. In an attempt to appease all the Republican factions, he chose his cabinet with great care. His vice president, Hannibal Hamlin of Maine, had supported Lincoln but was also a friend of William Seward and had been chosen to balance the ticket factionally. Lincoln continued this balancing act with cabinet appointments for his four main rivals for nomination. Seward received the job of secretary of state. Edward Bates of Missouri became attorney general and Simon Cameron of Pennsylvania secretary of war. Salmon P. Chase of Ohio became secretary of the Treasury. Despite Lincoln's evenhandedness, his political balancing act was not easy to maintain. Chase and Seward, for instance, had a long history of political infighting and hated each other. That Lincoln would appoint Chase to any position so angered Seward that he threatened to resign, and Lincoln had to persuade him to remain.

THE NATION DISSOLVED

Abraham Lincoln was inaugurated on March 4, 1861. In his inaugural address he repeated themes that he had been stressing since the election: no interference with slavery in states where it existed, no extension of slavery into the territories, and no tolerance of secession. Lincoln believed that the nation remained unbroken, and he pledged to see "that the laws of the Union be faithfully executed in all the States." This policy, he continued, necessitated "no bloodshed or violence, and there shall be none, unless it is forced upon the national authority." If war came, he argued, it would be over secession, not slavery, for the federal government had a duty to maintain the Union by any means, including force.

Lincoln, Sumter, and War   Lincoln's first presidential address drew mixed reactions. Most Republicans found it firm and reasonable, applauding its tone. Union advocates in both the North and the South thought the speech held promise for the future. Even former rival Stephen Douglas stated, "I am with him." Moderate southerners commended Lincoln's "temperance and conservatism" and believed the speech was all "any reasonable Southern man" could have expected. Confederates and their sympathizers, however, branded the speech a "Declaration of War."

But war was brewing even before Lincoln assumed office. In December 1860, South Carolina officials ordered the state militia to seize two federal forts—Fort Moultrie and Castle Pinckney—and the federal arsenal at Charleston. In response, Major Robert Anderson moved all federal troops from Charleston to **Fort Sumter**, an island stronghold in Charleston Harbor. The Confederate congress demanded that President Buchanan remove all federal troops from the sovereign territory of the Confederacy. Despite his sympathy for the southern cause, Buchanan announced that Fort Sumter would be defended "against all hostile attacks, from whatever quarter." On January 9, 1861, a Charleston Harbor **battery** fired on a supply ship as it attempted to reach the fort. Buchanan denounced the action but did nothing.

---

battery   An army artillery unit, usually supplied with heavy guns.

Immediately after taking office in March, Lincoln received a report from Fort Sumter that supplies were running low. Under great pressure from northern public opinion to do something, he responded cleverly. He informed South Carolina governor Francis Pickens of his peaceful intention to send unarmed boats carrying food and supplies to the besieged fort. Lincoln thus placed the Confederacy in a no-win position: allow the fort to be resupplied or fire on an unarmed ship, which would be sufficiently dishonorable to justify stronger federal action. After studying the situation, Confederate officials determined to beat Lincoln to the punch. President Davis ordered the Confederate commander at

In this vivid engraving, South Carolina shore batteries under the command of P. G. T. Beauregard shell Fort Sumter, the last federal stronghold in Charleston Harbor, on the night of April 12, 1861. Curious and excited civilians look on from their rooftops, never suspecting the horrors that would be the outcome of this rash action.

Charleston, General P. G. T. Beauregard, to demand the evacuation of Sumter and, if the federals refused, to "proceed, in such a manner as you may determine, to reduce it." On April 11, while the supply ships were still on their way, Beauregard called on Anderson to surrender. When Anderson rejected the ultimatum, shore batteries opened fire. After a thirty-four-hour artillery battle, Anderson surrendered. Neither side had inflicted casualties on the other, but civil war had officially begun.

Across the North, newspapers contrasted the president's resolute but restrained policy with the violent aggression of the Confederates, and the public rallied behind the Union cause. In New York City, where southern sympathizers had once vehemently criticized abolitionist actions, a million people attended a Union rally. Even northern Democrats rallied behind the Republican president, hearkening to Stephen Douglas's statement that "there can be no neutrals in this war, only patriots—or traitors." Spurred by the public outcry and confident of support, Lincoln called for seventy-five thousand militiamen to be mobilized "to maintain the honor, the integrity, and the existence of our National Union, and the perpetuity of popular government." Northern states responded immediately and enthusiastically. Across the Upper South and the border regions, however, the call to arms meant that a decision had to be made: whether to continue in the Union or join the Confederacy.

Choosing Sides in Virginia   The need for southern unity in the face of what he saw as northern aggression pushed Jefferson Davis to employ a combination of political finesse and force to create a solid southern alignment. He selected his cabinet with this in mind, choosing one cabinet member from each state except his own Mississippi and appointing men of varying degrees of radicalism. But unity among the seven seceding states was only one of Davis's worries. A more pressing concern was alignment among the eight slave states that remained in the Union. These states were critical, for they contained more than half of the entire southern population (two-thirds of its white population), possessed most of the South's industrial capacity, produced most of its food, and raised more than half of its horses. In addition, many experienced and able military leaders lived in these states. If the Confederacy was to have any chance of survival, the human and physical resources of the whole South were essential.

It was not Davis's appeal for solidarity but Lincoln's call to mobilize the militia that won most of the other slave states for the Confederate cause. In Virginia, Governor John Letcher refused to honor Lincoln's demand for troops, and on April 17 a special convention declared for secession. Voters in Virginia overwhelmingly ratified this decision in a popular referendum on May 23. By then Letcher had offered **Richmond** as a site for the new nation's capital. The Confederate congress accepted the offer in order to strengthen ties with Virginia.

Not all Virginians were flattered at becoming the seat for the Confederacy. Residents of the western portion of the state had strong Union ties and longstanding political differences with their neighbors east of the Allegheny Mountains. Forty-six counties called mass Unionist meetings to protest the state's secession, and in a June convention at Wheeling, they elected their own governor, Francis H. Pierpoint, and drew up a constitution. In May 1862 the West Virginia legislature convened and requested admission to the United States.

For many individuals in the Upper South, the decision to support the Confederacy was not an easy one. Virginian Robert E. Lee, for example, was deeply devoted to the Union. A West Point graduate and career officer in the U.S. Army, he had a distinguished record in the war with Mexico and as superintendent of West Point. General Winfield Scott, commander of the Union forces, called Lee "the best soldier I ever saw in the field." Recognizing his military skill, Lincoln offered Lee field command of the Union armies, but the Virginian refused, deciding that he should serve his native state instead. Lee agonized over the decision but told a friend, "I cannot raise my hand against my birthplace, my home, my children." He resigned his U.S. Army commission in April 1861. When he informed Scott, a personal friend and fellow Virginian, of his decision, Scott replied, "You have made the greatest mistake of your life, but I feared it would be so." Scott chose to remain loyal to the Union.

A Second Wave of Secession   Influenced by Virginia and by Lee's decision, three other states joined the Confederacy. Arkansas had voted against secession in March, hoping that bloodshed might be averted, but when Lincoln called for militia units, Governor Henry M. Rector answered, "None will be furnished. The demand is only adding insult to injury." The state then called a second convention and on May 6 seceded from the Union. North Carolinians had also hoped for compromise, but moderates turned secessionist when Secretary of War Simon Cameron **requisitioned** "two regiments of militia for immediate service" against the Confederacy. Governor John W. Ellis replied, "I regard the levy of troops made by this administration for the purpose of subjugating the states of the South [to be] in violation of the Constitution and a gross usurpation of power." North Carolina seceded on May 20.

Tennessee, the eleventh and final state to join the Confederacy, was the home of many moderates, including John Bell, the Constitutional Union candidate in 1860. Eastern residents favored the Union, and those in the west favored the Confederacy. The state's voters at first rejected disunion overwhelmingly, but after the fighting began, Governor Isham C. Harris and the state legislature initiated military ties with the Confederacy, forcing another vote on the issue. Western voters carried the election, approving the agreement and seceding from the Union on June 8. East

---

requisition To demand for military use.

Tennesseans, who remained loyal Unionists, tried to divide the state much as West Virginians had done, but Davis ordered Confederate troops to occupy the region, thwarting the effort.

Trouble in the Border States   Four slave states remained in the Union, and the start of hostilities brought political and military confrontation in three of the four. Delaware quietly stayed in the Union. Voters there had favored Breckinridge in 1860, but the majority of voters disapproved of secession, and few of the state's citizens owned slaves. Maryland, Missouri, and Kentucky, however, each contained large, vocal secessionist factions and appeared poised to bolt to the Confederacy.

Maryland was particularly vital to the Union, for it enclosed Washington, D.C., on the three sides not bordered by Virginia. Maryland's significance became apparent on April 6, 1861, when a Massachusetts regiment responding to Lincoln's call for troops passed through Baltimore on the way to the capital. A mob confronted the soldiers, attacking them with bricks, bottles, and pistols. The soldiers returned fire. When the violence subsided, twelve Baltimore residents and four soldiers lay dead, and dozens more were wounded. Secessionists reacted violently, destroying railroad bridges to keep additional northern troops out of the state. In effect, Washington, D.C., was cut off from the North.

Lincoln and General Scott ordered the military occupation of Baltimore and declared **martial law**, much as Davis had dispatched Confederate troops to occupy eastern Tennessee. The state legislature finally met and voted to remain neutral. Lincoln then instructed the army to arrest suspected southern sympathizers and hold them without formal hearings or charges. With southern sympathizers suppressed, new state elections were held. The new legislature, overwhelmingly Unionist, voted against secession.

Kentucky had important economic ties to the South but was strongly nationalistic. The governor refused to honor Lincoln's call for troops, but the state legislature voted to remain neutral. Both the North and the South honored that neutrality. Kentucky's own militia, however, split into two factions, and the state became a leading example of bloody fighting among members of the same family.

In Missouri, Governor Claiborne F. Jackson, a former proslavery border ruffian, pushed for secession, arguing that Missourians were bound together "in one brotherhood with the States of the South." When Unionists frustrated the secession movement, Jackson's forces seized the federal arsenal at Liberty and wrote to Jefferson Davis requesting artillery to support an assault on the

---

martial law Temporary rule by military authorities, imposed on a civilian population in time of war or when civil authority has broken down.

arsenal at St. Louis. Union sympathizers, however, fielded their own forces and fought Jackson at every turn. Rioting broke out in St. Louis as civilians clashed with soldiers, and mob violence marred the nights. Jackson's secessionist movement sent representatives to the Confederate congress in Richmond, but Union forces maintained nominal control of the state and drove prosouthern leaders into exile.

STUDY TOOLS

SUMMARY

The war with Mexico that began in 1846 raised, and then the Compromise of 1850 failed to alleviate, regional tension and debates. Slavery dominated the political agenda. The Whig Party, strained by fragmentation among its factions, disintegrated, and two completely new groups—the Know-Nothings and the Republicans—competed to replace it. A series of events—including the Kansas-Nebraska Act and the *Dred Scott* decision—intensified regional polarization, and radicals on both sides fanned the flames of sectional rivalry. Even the Democratic Party could not hold together, splitting into northern and southern wings. By 1859, the young Republican Party, committed to restricting slavery's expansion, seemed poised to gain control of the federal government. Fearing that the loss of political power would doom their way of life, southerners recoiled in terror. Neither side felt it could afford to back down.

With the election of Abraham Lincoln in 1860, six southern states withdrew from the Union. Last-minute efforts at compromise failed, and on April 12, 1861, five weeks after Lincoln's inauguration, Confederate forces fired on federal troops at Fort Sumter in Charleston Harbor. Lincoln believed that he had to call the nation to arms, and this move forced wavering states to choose sides. Internal divisions in Virginia, Tennessee, Maryland, Kentucky, and Missouri brought further violence and military action. Before summer, a second wave of secession finally solidified the lineup and established the boundary lines between the two competing societies. The stakes were set, the division was complete: the nation was poised for the bloodiest war in its history.

CHRONOLOGY

TOWARD A SHATTERED UNION

1846	War with Mexico begins
1848	Treaty of Guadalupe Hidalgo Zachary Taylor elected president Immigration to United States exceeds 100,000
1850	Compromise of 1850 Zacharay Taylor dies; Millard Fillmore becomes president

1852	First railroad line completed to Chicago
	Harriet Beecher Stowe's *Uncle Tom's Cabin*
	Franklin Pierce elected president
	Whig Party collapses
	Know-Nothing Party emerges
1853	Gadsden Purchase
1854	Republican Party formed
	Kansas-Nebraska Act
	Ostend Manifesto
1855	Proslavery posse sacks Lawrence, Kansas
1856	James Buchanan elected president
1857	*Dred Scott* decision
1858	Lincoln-Douglas debates
1859	John Brown's raid on Harpers Ferry
1860	Abraham Lincoln elected president
	Crittenden compromise fails
1861	Confederate States of America formed
	Fort Sumter shelled

Focus Questions

If you have mastered this chapter, you should be able to answer these questions and explain the terms that follow the questions.

1. How did the war with Mexico and its outcomes influence politics over the following decade?
2. What new political options affected the political system during the 1850s? In what ways?
3. How did various political coalitions react to the Kansas-Nebraska Act?
4. What was the effect on the national political climate?
5. In what ways was the presidential election in 1860 an outcome of the realignment of the party system during the 1850s?
6. Why did the election results have the political effects that they did?
7. What problems confronted Abraham Lincoln and Jefferson Davis in March 1861?
8. How did their actions contribute to the escalating national crisis?

Key Terms

Zachary Taylor (*p.* 347)

John C. Frémont (*p.* 347)

Wilmot Proviso (*p.* 348)

Winfield Scott (*p.* 349)

Battle of Buena Vista (*p.* 349)

Treaty of Guadalupe Hidalgo (*p.* 349)

Frederick Douglass (*p.* 350)

Sojourner Truth (*p.* 350)

14

A VIOLENT CHOICE: CIVIL WAR, 1861–1865

THE POLITICS OF WAR

Running the war posed complex problems for both Abraham Lincoln and Jefferson Davis. At the outset, neither side had the experience, soldiers, or supplies to wage an effective war, and foreign diplomacy and international trade were vital to both. But perhaps the biggest challenge confronting both Davis and Lincoln was internal politics. Lincoln had to contend not only with northern Democrats and southern sympathizers but also with divisions in his own party. Not all Republicans agreed with the president's war aims. Davis also faced internal political problems. The Confederate constitution guaranteed a great deal of autonomy to the Confederate states, and each state had a different opinion about war strategy and national objectives.

Union Policies and Objectives Abraham Lincoln took the oath of office in March 1861, but Congress did not convene until July. In effect, Lincoln ruled by executive proclamation for three months, vastly expanding the wartime powers of the presidency. Lincoln called for seventy-five thousand militiamen from the states to put down the rebellion. And ignoring specific constitutional provisions, he suspended the civil rights of citizens in Maryland when it appeared likely that the border state would join the Confederacy. At various times during the war, Lincoln would resort to similar invasions of civil liberties when he felt that dissent threatened either domestic security or the Union cause.

Having assumed nearly absolute authority, Lincoln faced the need to rebuild an army in disarray. When hostilities broke out, the Union had only sixteen thousand men in uniform, and nearly one-third of the officers resigned to support the Confederacy. What military leadership remained was aged: seven of the eight heads of army bureaus had been in the service since the War of 1812, including General in Chief Winfield Scott, who was 74 years old. Only two Union officers had ever commanded a **brigade**, and both were in their seventies. Weapons were old, and supplies were low. On May 3, Lincoln again exceeded his constitutional authority by calling for regular army recruits to meet the crisis. "Whether strictly legal or not," he asserted, such actions were based on "a popular demand, and a public necessity," and he expected "that Congress would readily ratify them."

Lincoln had also ordered a naval blockade of the Confederate states, which became an integral part of the Union strategy devised by the aged Winfield Scott. Scott ordered that the blockade of southern ports be combined with a strong Union thrust down the Mississippi River, the primary artery in the South's transportation system. This strategy would break the southern economy and split the Confederacy into two isolated parts. Like many northerners, Scott believed that economic pressure would bring southern moderates forward to negotiate a settlement and perhaps return to the Union. A war-fevered northern press ridiculed what it called the **anaconda plan**.

When Congress finally convened on July 4, 1861, Lincoln explained his actions and reminded congressmen that he had neither the constitutional authority to abolish slavery nor any intention of doing so. Rebellion, not slavery, had caused the crisis, he said, and the seceding states must be brought back into the Union, regardless of the cost. "Our popular government has been called an experiment," he argued, and the point to be settled now was "its successful maintenance against a formidable internal attempt to overthrow it." On July 22 and 25, 1861, both houses of Congress passed resolutions validating Lincoln's actions.

This seemingly unified front lasted only a short time. Viewing vengeance as the correct objective, **Radical Republicans** pressured Congress to create a special committee to oversee the conduct of the war. Radical leader Thaddeus Stevens of Pennsylvania growled, "If their whole country must be laid waste, and made a desert, in order to save this union, so let it be." Stevens and the Radicals pressed for and passed a series of confiscation acts that inflicted severe penalties against individuals in rebellion. Treason was punishable by death, and anyone aiding the Confederacy was to be punished with imprisonment, attachment of property, and confiscation of slaves. All persons living in the eleven seceding states, whether loyal to the Union or not, were declared enemies of the Union and subject to the provisions of the law.

---

brigade   A military unit consisting of two or more regiments and composed of between 1,500 and 3,500 men.

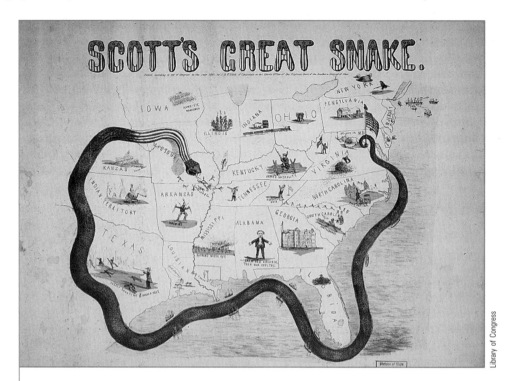

Though many northerners thought it was too passive, General Winfield Scott's "anaconda plan" was actually very well conceived. As this 1861 lithograph shows, Scott called for a naval blockade of the South and seizure of the Mississippi River, shutting down transportation routes to ruin the Confederate economy. Scott retired at the end of the war's first year, but his plan continued to shape the Union's overall strategy.

The Radicals splintered any consensus Lincoln might have achieved in his own party, and northern Democrats railed against his accumulation of power. To keep an unruly Congress from undermining his efforts, Lincoln shaped early Union strategy to appease all factions and used military appointments to smooth political feathers. His attitudes frequently enraged radical abolitionists, but Lincoln maintained his calm in the face of their criticism and merely reinforced his intentions. "What I do about slavery and the colored race," he stated in 1862, "I do because it helps to save the Union; and what I forbear, I forbear because I do not believe it would help to save the Union."

Nevertheless, Lincoln had far greater physical and human resources at his command than did the Confederates (see Table 14.1). The Union was home to more than twice as many people as the Confederacy, had vastly superior manufacturing and transportation systems, and enjoyed almost a monopoly in banking and foreign exchange. Lincoln also had a well-established government structure and formal diplomatic relations with other nations of the world. Still, these advantages could not help the war effort unless properly harnessed.

TABLE 14.1 | COMPARISON OF UNION AND CONFEDERATE RESOURCES

	Union (23 States)	Confederacy (11 States)
Total population	20,700,000	9,105,000[a]
Manufacturing establishments	110,000	18,000
Manufacturing workers	1,300,000	110,000
Miles of railroad	21,973	9,283
Troop strength (est.)	2,100,000	850,000

[a]Includes 3,654,000 blacks, most of them slaves and not available for military duty.

Source: Data from *Battles and Leaders of the Civil War* (1884–1888; reprinted ed., 1956).

Confederate Policies and Objectives

At the start of the war, the Confederacy had no army, no navy, no war supplies, no government structure, no foreign alliances, and a political situation as ragged as the Union's. Each Confederate state had its own ideas about the best way to conduct the war. After the attack on Fort Sumter, amassing supplies, troops, ships, and war materials was the main task for Davis and his cabinet. Politics, however, influenced southern choices about where to field armies and who would direct them, how to run a war without offending state leaders, and how to pursue foreign diplomacy.

The Union naval blockade posed an immediate problem. The Confederacy had no navy and no capacity to build naval ships. But it did have the extremely resourceful Stephen Mallory as secretary of the navy. Under Mallory's direction, southern coastal defenders converted river steamboats, tugboats, and **revenue cutters** into harbor patrol gunboats, and they developed and placed explosive mines at the entrances to southern harbors.

Confederates pinned their main hope of winning the war on the army. Fighting for honor was praiseworthy behavior in the South, and southerners strongly believed they could "lick the Yankees" despite their disadvantage in manpower and resources. Thousands volunteered before the Confederate war department was even organized. By the time Lincoln issued his call for seventy-five thousand militiamen, the Confederates already had sixty thousand men in uniform.

Despite this rush of fighting men, the South faced major handicaps. Even with the addition of the four Upper South states (Virginia, North Carolina, Tennessee, and Arkansas), as of 1860, the South built only 4 percent of all locomotives and only 3 percent of all firearms manufactured in the United States. The North

revenue cutter A small, lightly armed boat used by government customs agents to apprehend merchant ships violating customs laws.

produced almost all of the country's cloth, **pig iron**, boots, and shoes. Early in the war, the South could produce enough food but lacked the means to transport it where it was needed.

The miracle worker in charge of supplying southern troops with weapons and ammunition was Josiah Gorgas, who became chief of **ordnance** in April 1861. Gorgas purchased arms from Europe while his ordnance officers bought or stole copper pots and tubing to make **percussion caps**, bronze church bells to make cannon, and lead weights to make bullets. He built factories and foundries to manufacture small arms. But despite his extraordinary skill, he could not supply all of the Confederate troops. When the Confederate congress authorized the enlistment of four hundred thousand additional volunteers in 1861, the war department had to turn away more than half of the enlistees because it lacked equipment for them.

Internal politics also plagued the Davis administration. First, he alienated his high-spirited populace by advocating a defensive war in the belief the Union would give up if the war was made too costly. As one southern editor put it, the "idea of waiting for blows, instead of inflicting them is altogether unsuited to the genius of our people." But even a defensive posture proved hard to maintain. Despite the shortage of arms, state governors hoarded weapons seized from federal arsenals for their own state militias and demanded that their states' borders be protected, spreading troops dangerously thin.

The Diplomatic Front   Perhaps the biggest challenge facing the Confederacy was gaining international recognition and foreign aid. The primary focus of Confederate foreign policy was Great Britain. For years, the South had been exporting huge amounts of cotton to Britain, and many southerners felt that formal recognition of Confederate independence would immediately follow secession. Political and economic realities as well as ethical issues doomed them to disappointment. After all, the Union was still an important player in international affairs, and the British were not going to risk offending the emerging industrial power without good cause. Also, many English voters were morally opposed to slavery and would have objected to an open alliance with the slaveholding Confederacy. On May 13, 1861, Queen Victoria proclaimed official neutrality but granted **belligerent status** to the South.

---

pig iron   Crude iron, direct from a blast furnace, that is cast into rectangular molds called pigs in preparation for conversion into steel, cast iron, or wrought iron.

ordnance   Weapons, ammunition, and other military equipment.

percussion cap   A thin metal cap containing an explosive compound, needed to fire the guns used in the Civil War.

belligerent status   Recognition that a participant in a conflict is a nation engaged in warfare rather than a rebel against a legally constituted government; full diplomatic recognition is one possible outcome.

The British pronouncement set the tone for other European responses and was much less than southerners had hoped for. But Britain's rejection of Lincoln's position that the conflict was a rebellion against duly authorized government was also a blow to the North. Lincoln could do little but accept British neutrality. In November 1861, however, an incident at sea nearly scuttled British-American relations. James Murray Mason, the newly appointed Confederate emissary to London, and John Slidell, the Confederate minister to France, were traveling to their posts aboard the *Trent,* a British merchant ship bound for London. After the *Trent* left Havana, the U.S. warship *San Jacinto* stopped the British ship. Mason, Slidell, and their staffs were removed from the *Trent* and taken to Boston as prisoners of war.

Northerners celebrated the action, but the British viewed the *Trent* affair as aggression against a neutral government, a violation of international law, and an affront to their national honor. Lincoln ordered the release of the prisoners and apologized to the British, handling the incident so adroitly that the public outcry was largely forgotten when Mason and Slidell arrived in London.

The Union's First Attack

Like most southerners, northerners were confident that military action would bring the war to a quick end. General Irvin McDowell made the first move when his troops crossed into Virginia. McDowell's troops, though high-spirited, were poorly trained and undisciplined. They ambled along as if they were on a country outing, allowing P. G. T. Beauregard enough time to position his troops in defense of a vital rail center near Manassas Junction along a creek called **Bull Run.**

McDowell attacked on Sunday, July 21, and maintained the offensive most of the day. He seemed poised to overrun the Confederates until southern reinforcements under **Thomas J. Jackson** stalled the Union advance. Jackson's unflinching stand at Bull Run earned him the nickname "Stonewall," and under intense cannon fire, Union troops panicked and began fleeing into a throng of northern spectators who had brought picnic lunches and settled in to watch the battle. Thoroughly

TABLE 14.2 | BATTLE OF BULL RUN, JULY 22, 1861

	Union Army	Confederate Army
Commanders	Irvin McDowell	P. G. T. Beauregard
Troop strength	17,676	18,053
Killed	460	387
Wounded	1,124	1,582
Captured	1,312	13
Total losses	2,896	1,982

Source: Data from *Battles and Leaders of the Civil War* (1884–1888; reprinted ed., 1956).

humiliated before a hometown crowd, Union soldiers retreated toward Washington. Jefferson Davis immediately ordered the invasion of the Union capital, but the Confederates were also in disarray and made no attempt to pursue the fleeing Union forces.

This battle profoundly affected both sides. In the South, the victory stirred confidence that the war would be short and victory complete. Northerners, disillusioned and embarrassed, pledged that no similar retreats would occur. Under fire for the loss, Lincoln removed McDowell and appointed **George B. McClellan**. McClellan was to create the **Army of the Potomac** to defend the capital from Confederate attack and spearhead any offensives into Virginia. Lincoln also replaced Secretary of War Simon Cameron with Edwin Stanton, a politician and lawyer from Pennsylvania.

General McClellan's strengths were in organization and discipline. Both were sorely needed. Before Bull Run, Union officers had lounged around Washington while largely unsupervised raw recruits in army camps received no military instruction. Under McClellan, months of training turned the 185,000-man army into a well-drilled and efficient unit. Calls to attack Richmond began anew, but McClellan, seemingly in no hurry for battle, continued to drill the troops and remained in the capital. Finally on January 27, 1862, Lincoln called for a broad offensive, but his general in chief ignored the order and continued to delay.

FROM BULL RUN TO ANTIETAM

Reorganizing the military and forming the Army of the Potomac did not accomplish Lincoln's goal of toppling the Confederacy quickly and bringing the rebellious South back into the Union. In the second year of the war, frustration followed frustration as Confederate forces continued to outwit and outfight numerically superior and better-equipped federal troops. After Bull Run it was clear that the war would be neither short nor glorious. Military, political, and diplomatic strategies became increasingly entangled as both North and South struggled for the major victories that would end the war.

The War in the West   While the war in the East slid into inactivity, events in the West seemed almost as futile for the Union forces. In the border state of Missouri, the conflict rapidly degenerated into guerrilla warfare. Confederate William Quantrill's Raiders matched atrocities committed by Unionist guerrilla units called Jayhawkers. Union officials seemed unable to stop the ambushes, arson, theft, and murder, and Missouri remained a lawless battleground throughout the war.

Both the United States and the Confederacy coveted the western territories nearly as much as they did the border states. In 1861 Confederate Henry Hopkins Sibley recruited thirty-seven hundred Texans and marched into New Mexico, defeating a Union force at Valverde, but his losses were high. Needing provisions to continue the operation, he sent units to raid abandoned Union storehouses at Albuquerque and Santa Fe, but withdrawing federal troops had burned whatever supplies they could not carry. The small Confederate force at Santa Fe encountered a much larger federal force and won a miraculous victory, but the effort left the Confederates destitute of supplies. Under constant attack, the starving Confederate detachment evaded Union troops and retreated back into Texas.

Confederate leaders sought alliances with several Indian tribes in the newly set-tled Indian Territory south of Kansas. Many of the residents there had endured the Trail of Tears and had no particular love for the Union. If these Indian tribes aligned with the Confederacy, they not only could supply troops but might also form a buffer between Union forces in Kansas and the thinly spread Confederate defenses west of the Mississippi River. President Davis appointed General Albert Pike, an Arkansas lawyer who had represented the Creeks in their battle against removal in the 1830s, as special commissioner for the Indian Territory in March 1861. Pike negotiated with several tribes and on October 7 signed a treaty with members of the Cherokee, Choctaw, Creek, Chickasaw, and Seminole tribes that granted the Indians more nearly equal status—at least on paper—than any previous federal treaty, and it guaranteed that Indians would be asked to fight only to defend their own territory. One Cherokee leader, Stand Watie, became a Confederate general and distinguished himself in battle.

| **Struggle for the Mississippi** | Union efforts in the west were dictated largely by Scott's anaconda plan as **Ulysses S. Grant** moved against southern strongholds in the Mississippi Valley in 1862. On February 6, |

he took Fort Henry along the Tennessee River and ten days later captured Fort Donelson on the Cumberland River near Nashville, Tennessee. In this one swift stroke, Grant successfully penetrated Confederate western defenses and brought Kentucky and most of Tennessee under federal control.

Confederate general Albert Sidney Johnston finally reorganized the retreating southern troops while Grant was waiting for reinforcements. Early on April 6, to Grant's surprise, Johnston attacked at Pittsburg Landing, Tennessee, near a small country meetinghouse called Shiloh Church (see Table 14.3). Some Union forces under General **William Tecumseh Sherman** were driven back, but the Confederate attack soon lost momentum as Union defenses stiffened. The **Battle of Shiloh** raged until midafternoon. When Johnston was mortally wounded, General Beauregard took command and by day's end believed the enemy defeated. But Union reinforcements arrived during the night, and the next morning Grant counterattacked, push-ing the Confederates back.

The losses on both sides were staggering. The Battle of Shiloh made the reality of war apparent to everyone but made a particularly strong impression on the com-mon soldier. After Shiloh, one Confederate wrote: "Death in every awful form, if it really be death, is a pleasant sight in comparison to the fearfully and mortally wounded." Few people foresaw that the horrible carnage at Shiloh was but a taste of what was to come.

Farther south, Admiral David G. Farragut led a fleet of U.S. Navy gunboats against New Orleans, the commercial and banking center of the South, and on

TABLE 14.3 | BATTLE OF SHILOH, APRIL 6–7, 1862

	Union Army	Confederate Army
Commanders	William Tecumseh Sherman	Albert Sidney Johnston (killed)
	Ulysses S. Grant	P. G. T. Beauregard
Troop strength	75,000	44,000
Killed	1,754	1,723
Wounded	8,408	8,012
Captured, missing	2,885	959
Total losses	13,047	10,694

Source: Data from *Battles and Leaders of the Civil War* (1884–1888; reprinted ed., 1956).

April 25 forced the city's surrender. Farragut then sailed up the Mississippi, hoping to take the well-fortified city of **Vicksburg**, Mississippi. He scored several victories, but at Port Hudson, Louisiana, the combination of Confederate defenses and shallow water forced him to halt. Meanwhile, on June 6, Union gunboats destroyed a Confederate fleet at Memphis, Tennessee, and brought the upper Mississippi under Union control. Vicksburg remained the only major obstacle to Union control over the entire river.

Lee's Aggressive Defense of Virginia   The anaconda plan was well on its way to cutting the Confederacy in two, but the general public in the North thought that the path to real victory led to Richmond, capital of the Confederacy. Confederates, too, realized that Richmond would be an important prize for the North and took dramatic steps to keep their capital city out of enemy hands.

In an effort to skirt Confederate defenses, when McClellan finally acted on Lincoln's insistence for action, he executed a surprise move by transporting the entire Army of the Potomac by ship to Fort Monroe, Virginia, to attack Richmond from the south. Initiating what would be called the **Peninsular Campaign**, the army marched up the peninsula between the York and James Rivers. In typical fashion, McClellan proceeded cautiously. The outnumbered Confederate forces took advantage of his indecision and twice slipped away, retreating toward Richmond while McClellan followed. Hoping to overcome the odds by surprising his opponent, General Joseph E. Johnston, commander of the Confederate Army of Northern Virginia, wheeled about and attacked at Seven Pines on May 31. Though the battle was indecisive—both sides claimed victory—it halted McClellan's progress and disabled Johnston, who was seriously wounded.

With McClellan stalled, Confederate stalwart Stonewall Jackson staged a brilliant diversionary thrust down the Shenandoah Valley toward Washington. Jackson, who had grown up in the region, seemed to be everywhere at once. In

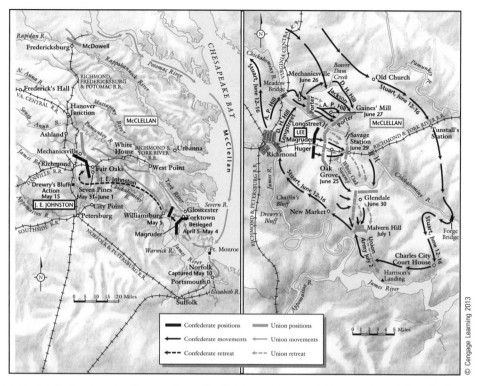

MAP 14.1 Peninsula Campaign, April–May 1862 and Seven Days' Battles, June 25–July 1, 1862

General McClellan used Union naval control of the York and James Rivers to protect his flanks in his advance up the peninsula formed by these rivers (left map). When Robert E. Lee's Army of Northern Virginia counterattacked in the Seven Days' Battles (right map), McClellan was forced back to the James River at Harrison's Landing.

thirty days, he and his "foot cavalry" marched 350 miles, defeated three Union armies in five battles, captured and sent back to Richmond a fortune in provisions and equipment, inflicted twice as many casualties as they received, and confused and immobilized Union forces in the region.

Meanwhile, McClellan was marking time near Richmond while waiting for reinforcements. With Johnston wounded, Davis had been forced to replace him, choosing Robert E. Lee. Daring, bold, and tactically aggressive, Lee enjoyed combat, pushed his troops to the maximum, and was well liked by those serving under him. He had an uncanny ability to read the character of his opponents, predict their maneuvers, and exploit their mistakes. It now fell to Lee to deal with the invading Yankees. In a move that became typical of his generalship, Lee split his forces and attacked from all sides over a seven-day period in August, forcing McClellan into a defensive position. The Peninsular Campaign was over. The self-promoting Union general had been beaten in part by his own indecisiveness.

Fed up with McClellan, Lincoln ordered the Army of the Potomac back to Washington and gave command to General John Pope, who soon encountered Lee's army again at the Manassas rail line on August 30. The Confederates pretended to retreat, and when Pope followed, Lee soundly defeated Lincoln's new general in the **Second Battle of Bull Run**. Thoroughly disappointed with Pope's performance, but lacking any other viable replacement, Lincoln once again named McClellan commander of the Army of the Potomac.

Lee's Invasion of Maryland   Feeling confident after the second victory at Bull Run, Lee devised a bold offensive against Maryland. On September 4, he crossed the Potomac, formulating an intricate offensive by dividing his army into three separate attack wings. But someone was careless— Union soldiers found a copy of Lee's detailed instructions wrapped around some cigars at an abandoned Confederate campsite. If McClellan had acted swiftly on this intelligence, he could have crushed Lee's army piece by piece, but he waited sixteen hours before advancing. By then, Lee had learned of the missing orders and quickly withdrew. Lee reunited some of his forces at Sharpsburg, Maryland, around **Antietam Creek**. There, on September 17, the Army of the Potomac and the Army of Northern Virginia engaged in the bloodiest single-day battle of the Civil War.

The casualties in this one battle were more than double those suffered in the War of 1812 and the War with Mexico combined. "The air was full of the hiss of bullets and the hurtle of grapeshot," one Union soldier said, and "the whole landscape turned red." The bitter fighting exhausted both armies. After a day of rest, Lee retreated across the Potomac. Stonewall Jackson, covering Lee's retreat, soundly thrashed a force that McClellan sent in pursuit. But for the first time, General Lee experienced defeat.

Although Lee's offensive had been thwarted, Lincoln was not pleased with the performance of his army and its leadership. He felt that McClellan could have destroyed Lee's forces if he had attacked earlier or, failing that, had pursued the fleeing Confederate army. He fired McClellan again, this time for good, and placed Ambrose E. Burnside in command.

Burnside moved his forces to the east bank of the Rappahannock River overlooking **Fredericksburg**, Virginia, where he delayed for almost three weeks. Lee used the time to fortify the heights west of the city with men and artillery. On December 13, in one of the worst mistakes of the war, Burnside ordered a daylong frontal assault. The results were devastating. Federal troops, mowed down from the heights, suffered tremendous casualties, and once again the Army of the Potomac retreated to Washington.

Diplomacy and the Politics of Emancipation   The first full year of the war ended with mixed results for both sides. Union forces in the West had scored major victories, breaking down Confederate defenses and taking Memphis and New Orleans. But the failure of the Army of the Potomac under three different generals seemed to outweigh those successes. Lee's victories, however, carried heavy casualties, and the South's ability to supply and deploy troops was rapidly diminishing. A long, drawn-out conflict favored the Union unless Jefferson Davis could secure help for the Confederacy from abroad.

The Confederacy still expected British aid, but nothing seemed to shake Britain's commitment to neutrality. To some extent, this resistance was due to the efforts of Charles Francis Adams, Lincoln's ambassador in London, who demonstrated his diplomatic skill repeatedly during the war. Also, Britain possessed a surplus of cotton and did not need southern supplies, neutralizing the South's only economic lever and frustrating Davis's diplomatic goals.

Radical Republicans were also frustrated. No aspect of the war was going as they had expected. They had hoped that the Union army would defeat the South in short order. Instead the war effort was dragging on. More important from the Radicals' point of view, nothing was being done about slavery. They pressed Lincoln to take a stand against slavery, and they pushed Congress for legislation to prohibit slavery in federal territories.

Politically astute as always, Lincoln acted to appease the Radical Republicans, foster popular support in the North for the war effort, and increase favorable sentiment for the Union cause abroad. During the summer of 1862, he drafted a proclamation freeing the slaves in the Confederacy and submitted it to his cabinet. Cabinet members advised that he postpone announcing the policy until after the Union had achieved a military victory. On September 22, five days after the Battle of Antietam, Lincoln unveiled the **Emancipation Proclamation**, which would abolish slavery in the states "in rebellion" on January 1, 1863.

Although the Emancipation Proclamation was a major step toward ending slavery, it actually freed no slaves. The proclamation applied only to slavery in areas controlled by the Confederacy, not in any area controlled by the Union. Some found this exception troubling, but the president's reasoning was sound. He could not afford to alienate the four slave states that had remained in the Union, nor could he commit any manpower to enforce emancipation in the areas that had been captured from the Confederacy. Lincoln made emancipation entirely conditional on a Union military victory, a gambit designed to force critics of the war, whether in the United States or Great Britain, to rally behind his cause.

Whether or not it was successful as a humanitarian action, issuing the Emancipation Proclamation at the time he did and in the form he did was a profoundly successful political step for Lincoln. Although a handful of northern Democrats and a few Union military leaders called it an "absurd proclamation of a political coward," more joined Frederick Douglass in proclaiming, "We shout for joy that we live to record this righteous decree." Meanwhile, some in Britain pointed to the paradox of the proclamation: it declared an end to slavery in areas where Lincoln could not enforce it, while having no effect on slavery in areas where he could. But even there, most applauded the document and rallied against recognition of the Confederacy.

Still, Lincoln's new general in chief, Henry Halleck, was chilled by the document. As he explained to Grant, the "character of the war has very much changed within the last year. There is now no possible hope of reconciliation." The war was now about slavery as well as secession, and the Emancipation Proclamation committed the Union to conquering the enemy. As Lincoln told one member of his cabinet, the war would now be "one of subjugation."

THE HUMAN DIMENSIONS OF THE WAR

The Civil War imposed tremendous stress on American society. As the men marched off to battle, women faced the task of caring for families and property alone. As casualties increased, the number of voluntary enlistments decreased, and both sides searched for ways to find replacements for dead and wounded soldiers. The armies constantly demanded not only weapons and ammunition but also food, clothing, and hardware. Government spending was enormous, and inflation soared as both governments printed paper money to pay their debts. Society in both North and South changed to meet an array of hardships as individuals facing unfamiliar conditions attempted to carry on their lives amid the war's devastation.

Instituting the Draft   By the end of 1862, heavy casualties, massive desertion, and declining enlistments had depleted both armies. Although the North had a much larger population to draw from, its enlistments sagged with its military fortunes during 1862. More than a hundred thousand Union soldiers were absent without official leave. Most volunteers had enlisted in 1861 for limited terms, which would soon expire. Calling on state militias netted few replacements because the Democrats, who made tremendous political gains at the state level in 1862, at times refused to cooperate. To bypass state officials and ensure enough manpower Congress passed the **Conscription Act** in March 1863. In effect, the law made all single men between the ages of 20 and 45 and married men between 20 and 35 eligible for service. Government agents collected names in a house-to-house survey, and draftees were selected by lottery.

The conscription law did offer "escape routes." Drafted men could avoid military service by providing—that is, hiring—an "acceptable substitute" or by paying a $300 fee to purchase exemption. The burden of service thus fell on farmers and urban workers who were already suffering from high taxation and inflation caused by the war. Added to that was workers' fear that multitudes of former slaves freed by the Emancipation Proclamation would pour into the already crowded job market, further lowering the value of their labor. Overall, the urban poor felt a sense of alienation, which exploded in the summer of 1863.

The trouble started on July 13 in New York City. Armed demonstrators protesting unfair draft laws engaged in a spree of violence, venting their frustration over the troubles plaguing working people. During three nights of rioting, white workingmen beat many African Americans and lynched six. The Colored Orphan Asylum and several homes owned by blacks were burned. Mobs ransacked businesses owned by African Americans and by people who employed them. Irish men and women and members of other groups that seemed to threaten job security also

Angered by the fact that rich men were virtually exempt from the draft, frightened by the prospect of job competition from freed southern slaves, and frustrated by the lack of resolution on the battlefield, workingmen took to the streets in New York City during the summer of 1863 to protest against the war. Well-dressed men, African Americans, and leading war advocates were the main targets of mob violence during three nights of uncontrolled rioting. As this illustration shows, federal troops finally put down the rioting in a series of battles around the city. An unknown number of people were killed and injured.

felt the fury as mobs attacked their churches, businesses, and homes. The rioters also expressed their frustration against Republican spokesmen and officials. Republican journalist **Horace Greeley** was **hanged in effigy**, and the homes of other prominent Republicans and abolitionists were vandalized. Protesting draft exemptions for the rich, rioters also set upon well-dressed strangers on the streets. After four days of chaos, federal troops put down the riot. Fearful of future violence, the city council of New York City voted to pay the $300 exemption fee for all poor draftees who chose not to serve in the army.

The Confederacy also instituted a draft after the first wave of enlistments dried up. Conscription in the South, as in the North, met with considerable resentment and resistance. Believing that plantations were necessary to the war effort and that slaves would not work unless directly overseen by masters, in 1862 Confederate officials passed the **Twenty Negro Law**, which exempted planters owning twenty or more slaves from military service. Like the exemptions in the North, the southern policy fostered the feeling that the poor were going off to fight while the rich stayed safely at home. The law was modified in 1863, requiring exempted planters to pay $500, and in 1864, the number of slaves required to earn an exemption was lowered to fifteen. Nevertheless, resentment continued to smolder.

hang in effigy To hang, as if on a gallows, a crude likeness or dummy—an effigy—representing a hated person.

Wartime Economy in the North and South   In his 1864 message to Congress, Abraham Lincoln stated that the war had not depleted northern resources. Although the president exaggerated a bit, the statement contained some truth. Northern industry and population did grow during the Civil War. Operating in cooperation with government, manufacturing experienced a boom. Manufacturers of war supplies benefited from government contracts. Textiles and shoemaking boomed as new labor-saving devices improved efficiency and increased production. Congress stimulated economic growth by means of subsidies and land grants to support a transcontinental railroad, higher tariffs to aid manufacturing, and land grants that states could use to finance higher education. In 1862 Congress passed the **Homestead Act** to make land available to more farmers. The law granted 160 acres of the public domain in the West to any citizen or would-be citizen who lived on, and improved, the land for five years.

Of course, the economic picture was not entirely positive. The Union found itself resorting to financial tricks to keep the economy afloat. Facing a cash-flow emergency in 1862, Congress passed the Legal Tender Act, authorizing Treasury Secretary Salmon Chase to issue $431 million in paper money, known as **greenbacks**, that was backed not by gold but only by the government's commitment to redeem the bills. Financial support also came through selling bonds. In the fall of 1862, Philadelphia banker Jay Cooke started a bond drive. More than $2 billion worth of government bonds were sold, and most of them were paid for in greenbacks. These emergency measures helped the Union survive the financial pressures created by the war, but the combination of bond issues and unbacked currency set up a highly unstable situation that came back to haunt Republicans after the war.

The South, an agrarian society, began the war without an industrial base. In addition to lacking transportation, raw materials, and machines, the South lacked managers and skilled industrial workers. The Confederate government intervened more directly in the economy than did its Union counterpart, offering generous loans to new or existing companies that would produce war materials. Josiah Gorgas started government-owned production plants in Alabama, Georgia, and South Carolina. These innovative programs, however, could not compensate for inadequate prewar industrialization.

The supply of money was also a severe problem in the South. Like the North, the South tried to ease cash-flow problems by printing paper money, eventually issuing more than $1 billion in unbacked currency. The outcome was runaway inflation. By the time the war ended, southerners were paying more than $400 for a barrel of flour and $10 a pound for bacon.

Southern industrial shortcomings severely handicapped the army. Many Confederate soldiers were barefoot because shoes were in such short supply. Ordnance was always in demand. Northern plants could produce more than five thousand muskets a day; Confederate production never exceeded three hundred. The most serious shortage, however, was food. Although the South was an agricultural region, most of its productive acreage was devoted to cotton, tobacco, and other crops that were essential to its overall economy but not edible. Corn and rice were the primary food products, but supplies were continually reduced by military campaigns and Union occupation of farmlands. Hog production suffered from the same disruptions, and while Southern cattle were abundant, most were range stock grown for hides and tallow rather than for food. Hunger became a miserable part of daily life for the Confederate armies.

Civilians in the South suffered from the same shortages as the army. Because of prewar shipping patterns, the few rail lines that crossed the Confederacy ran north and south. Distribution of goods became almost impossible as invading Union forces cut rail lines and disrupted production. The flow of cattle, horses, and food from the West diminished when Union forces gained control of the Mississippi. Imported goods had to evade the Union naval blockade. Southern society, cut off from the outside world, consumed its existing resources and found no way to obtain more.

Women in Two Nations at War   Because the South had fewer men than the North to send to war, a larger proportion of southern families were left in the care of women. Some women successfully supported their families. Others struggled in complete poverty amid the ravages of war. One woman wrote to the Confederacy's secretary of war, pleading that he "discharge" her husband so that "he might do his children some good" rather than leaving them "to suffer." Some disregarded the authorities. "Desert again, Jake," one shouted to her husband, who was being drafted for the second time. Most southern women, however, supported the war effort. Women became responsible for much of the South's agricultural and industrial production, overseeing crops and laboring in the fields, working in factories, managing estates, and operating businesses while, in most cases, also running the household—and waiting for the dreaded message that a husband or child would not return from the front. As one southern soldier wrote, women bore "the greatest burden of this horrid war."

Women in the North served in much the same capacity as their southern counterparts. They maintained families and homes alone, working to provide income and raise children. Although they did not face the shortages and ravages of battle that made life so hard for southern women, they did work in factories, run family businesses, teach school, and supply soldiers. Many served in managerial capacities or as writers and civil servants. Even before the war ended, northern women were going south to educate former slaves and help them find a place in American society. Women thus assumed new roles that helped prepare them for greater involvement in social and political life after the war.

Women from both South and North actively participated in the war itself. Many women on both sides served as scouts, couriers, and spies; and more than four hundred disguised themselves as men and served as active soldiers until they were discovered. General William S. Rosecrans expressed dismay when one of his sergeants was delivered of "a bouncing baby boy," which was, the general complained, "in violation of all military regulations." Army camps frequently included officers' wives, female employees, camp followers, and women who came to help in whatever way they could. Susie King Taylor, a former slave who had attended an illegal school for slave children in Savannah, Georgia, served the 33rd U.S. Colored

Women served in many different capacities during the Civil War. An unknown number of them actually dressed as men to join the fighting. Frances Clayton was one of the few documented cases of such Civil War gender-bending.

Troops for four years and three months without pay, teaching the men to read and write and binding up their wounds.

Free Blacks, Slaves, and War   The Civil War marked a revolution for African Americans, but radical changes were not always for the better. At first, many free blacks attempted to enlist in the Union army but were turned away. In 1861 General Benjamin F. Butler began using runaway slaves, called contrabands, as laborers. Several other northern commanders quickly adopted the practice. As the number of contrabands increased, however, the Union grappled with problems of housing and feeding them.

In the summer of 1862, Congress authorized the acceptance of "persons of African descent" into the armed forces, but enlistment remained low. After the Emancipation Proclamation, Union officials actively recruited former slaves, raising troops from among the freedmen and forming them into regiments known as the U.S. Colored Troops. Some northern state governments sought free blacks to fill state draft quotas; agents offered generous bonuses to those who signed up. By the end of the war, about 180,000 African Americans had enlisted in northern armies; by 1865, almost two-thirds of Union troops in the Mississippi Valley were black.

At first, African American regiments were used as laborers rather than being allowed to fight. But several black regiments, when finally allowed into battle, performed so well that they won grudging respect. These men fought in 449 battles in every theater of the war and had a casualty rate 35 percent higher than white soldiers. Still, discrimination was the rule, not the exception. Army officials discriminated against African American soldiers in a variety of ways. Units were segregated, and until 1864, blacks were paid less than whites. All black regiments had white commanders; only one hundred African Americans were commissioned as officers, and none ever received a commission higher than major. And Confederates violently resented the Union's use of these troops: African American soldiers suffered atrocities because some Confederate leaders refused to take black prisoners. At Fort Pillow, Tennessee, for example, Confederate soldiers massacred more than a hundred African American soldiers who were trying to surrender. In all, about sixty-eight thousand black Union soldiers were killed or wounded in battle, and twenty-one were awarded the Congressional Medal of Honor.

The war effort in the South relied heavily on the slave population, mostly as producers of food and as military laborers. Slaves constituted more than half of the work force in armament plants and military hospitals. Though crucial to the southern war effort, slaves suffered more than other southerners in the face of food shortages and other privations. And after Lincoln issued the Emancipation Proclamation, fears of slave revolts prompted whites to institute harsh security procedures. Hungry and even less free than usual, slaves became the greatest unsung casualties of the war.

| Life and Death at the Front | Many volunteers on both sides in the Civil War had romantic notions about military service. Most were disappointed. Life as a common soldier was anything but glorious. Letters and |

diaries written by soldiers tell of long periods of doing nothing in overcrowded camps, interrupted only by furious spells of dangerous action.

Though life in camp was tedious, it could be nearly as dangerous as time spent on the battlefield. Problems with supplying safe drinking water and disposing of waste constantly plagued military leaders. Diseases such as dysentery and **typhoid fever** frequently swept through unsanitary camps. And in the overcrowded conditions that often prevailed, smallpox and other contagious diseases passed rapidly from person to person. At times, as many as a quarter of the uninjured people in camps were disabled by one or another of these ailments.

---

typhoid fever   An infectious disease transmitted through contact with contaminated water, milk, or food; causes severe intestinal distress and high fever.

Lacking in resources, organization, and expertise, the South did little to upgrade camp conditions. In the North, however, women drew on the organizational skills they had gained as antebellum reformers and created voluntary organizations to address the problem. At the local level, women like Mary Livermore and Jane Hoge created small relief societies designed to aid soldiers and their families. Gradually these merged into regional organizations that would take the lead in raising money and implementing large-scale public health efforts, both in the army camps and at home. Mental health advocate and reformer Dorothea Dix was also one of these crusaders. In June 1861, President Lincoln responded to their concerns by creating the **United States Sanitary Commission,** a government agency responsible for advising the military on public health issues and investigating sanitary problems. "The Sanitary," as it was called, put hundreds of nurses into the field, providing much-needed relief for overburdened military doctors.

Nurses on both sides showed bravery and devotion. Often working under fire at the front and with almost no medical supplies, these volunteers nursed sick and wounded soldiers, watched as they died not only from their wounds but also from infection and disease, and offered as much comfort and help as they could. **Clara Barton,** known as the "Angel of the Battlefield," recalled "speaking to and feeding with my own hands each soldier" as she attempted to nurse them back to health. Hospitals were unsanitary, overflowing, and underfunded.

The numbers of wounded who filled the hospital tents was unprecedented, largely because of technological innovations in weaponry that had taken place during the antebellum period. New **rifled** muskets had many times the range of the old smooth-bore weapons used during earlier wars—the effective range of the Springfield rifle used by many Union soldiers was 400 yards, and a stray bullet could still kill a man at 1,000 yards. Waterproof cartridges, perfected by gunsmith Samuel Colt, made these weapons much less prone to misfire and much easier to reload. And at closer range, the revolver, also perfected by Colt, could fire six shots without any reloading. Rifled artillery also added to the casualty count, as did exploding artillery shells, which sent deadly shrapnel ripping through lines of men.

Many surgeons at the front lines could do little more than amputate limbs to save lives. Hospitals, understaffed and lacking supplies and medicines, frequently became breeding grounds for disease. The war exacted a tremendous emotional toll on everyone, even on those who escaped physical injury. As one veteran put it, soldiers had seen "so many new forms of death" and "so many frightful and novel kinds of mutilation."

Conditions were even worse in prison camps. Throughout much of the war, an agreement provided for prisoner exchanges, but that did not prevent overcrowding and unsanitary conditions. And as the war dragged on, the exchange system

---

rifled   Having a series of spiral grooves inside the barrel of a gun that cause the projectile to spin, giving it greater range and accuracy.

© Mary Evans Picture Library/The Image Works

In 1862, photographer Mathew Brady put on a public display of battlefield scenes in his New York gallery that brought the war home to civilians as nothing had before. The New York Times *proclaimed: "Mr. Brady has done something to bring home to us the terrible reality and earnestness of war. If he has not brought bodies and laid them on our dooryard and along the streets, he has done something very like it."*

stopped working effectively. In part the program collapsed because of the enormity of the task: moving and accounting for the large numbers of prisoners presented a serious organizational problem. Another contributing factor, though, was the refusal by Confederate officials to exchange African American prisoners of war—those who were not slaughtered like the men at Fort Pillow were enslaved. Also, late in the war, Union commanders suspended all prisoner exchanges in hopes of depriving the South of much-needed replacement soldiers.

The most notorious of the Civil War prison camps was **Andersonville**, in northern Georgia, where thousands of Union captives languished in an open stockade with only a small creek for water and virtually no sanitary facilities. Without enough food to feed its own armies and civilian population, the Confederacy could allocate little food for its overcrowded prison camps. Designed to house 10,000 men,

Andersonville held more than 33,000 prisoners during the summer of 1864. As many as 100 men died of disease and malnutrition within its walls each day; estimates put the death toll at that one prison at nearly 14,000 over the course of the war.

Even death itself came to be redefined, as 8 percent of the white male population in the United States between the ages of 13 and 43 died in such a short time and in such grisly ways. People at the front reported being numbed by the horror. One army surgeon reported, "I pass over the putrefying bodies of the dead ... and feel as ... unconcerned as though they were two hundred pigs." Nor was distance any insulation from the horrors of death. The new art of photography brought graphic images of the gruesome carnage directly into the nation's parlors. "Death does not seem half so terrible as it did long ago," one Texas woman reported. "We have grown used to it."

WAGING TOTAL WAR

As northerners anticipated the presidential election of 1864, Lincoln faced severe challenges on several fronts. The losses to Lee and Jackson in Virginia and the failure to catch Lee at Antietam had eroded public support. Many northerners resented the war, conscription, and abolitionism. Others feared Lincoln's powerful central government.

Northern Democrats advocated a peace platform and turned to George B. McClellan, Lincoln's ousted general, as a potential presidential candidate. Lincoln also faced a challenge from within his own party. Radical Republicans, who felt he was too soft on the South and unfit to run the war, began planning a campaign to win power. They championed the candidacy of John C. Frémont, who had become an ardent advocate of the complete abolition of slavery.

Lincoln's Generals and Southern Successes   The surest way for Lincoln to stop his political opponents was through military success. After Burnside's disaster at Fredericksburg, Lincoln demoted him and elevated General Joseph Hooker. Despite Hooker's reputation for bravery in battle—his nickname was "Fighting Joe"—Lee soundly defeated his forces at **Chancellorsville** in May 1863 (see Table 14.4). After Hooker had maneuvered Lee into a corner, Stonewall Jackson unleashed a vicious attack, and Fighting Joe simply "lost his nerve," according to one of his subordinates. Hooker resigned, and Lincoln replaced him with General George E. Meade.

Chancellorsville was a devastating loss for the North, but it was perhaps more devastating for the Confederates. After he led the charge that unnerved Hooker, Jackson's own men mistakenly shot him as he rode back toward his camp in the darkness. Doctors amputated Jackson's arm in an attempt to save his life. "He has lost his left arm," moaned Lee, "but I have lost my right." Eight days later, Jackson died of pneumonia.

TABLE 14.4 | BATTLE OF CHANCELLORSVILLE, MAY 1–4, 1863

	Union Army	Confederate Army
Commanders	Joseph Hooker	Robert E. Lee
Troop strength	75,000	50,000
Killed	1,606	1,665
Wounded	9,762	9,081
Captured, missing	5,919	2,018
Total losses	17,287	12,764

Source: Data from *Battles and Leaders of the Civil War* (1884–1888; reprinted ed., 1956).

Despite that loss, at a meeting of Confederate leaders in Richmond, Lee proposed another major invasion of the North, arguing that such a maneuver would allow the Confederates to gather supplies and might encourage the northern peace movement, revitalize the prospects of foreign recognition, and perhaps capture the Union capital. Confederate leaders agreed and approved Lee's plan.

The Army of Northern Virginia met only weak opposition as it crossed the Potomac River and marched into Union territory. In Maryland and Pennsylvania the troops seized livestock, supplies, food, clothing, and shoes. Learning that a Union contingent was in the area of **Gettysburg**, Pennsylvania, and believing them to be weaker than they were, on June 29 Lee moved to engage the Federals. Meade, whose Army of the Potomac had been trailing Lee's army as it marched north from Chancellorsville, immediately dispatched a detachment to reinforce Gettysburg. On the following day, the two armies began a furious three-day battle.

Arriving in force on July 1, Meade took up an almost impregnable defensive position on the hills along Cemetery Ridge. The Confederates hammered both ends of the Union line but could gain no ground. On the third day, Lee ordered a major assault on the middle of the Union position. Eleven brigades, more than thirteen thousand men, led by fresh troops under Major General George E. Pickett, tried to cross open ground and take the hills held by Meade, while Major J. E. B. "Jeb" Stuart's cavalry attacked from the east. Lee made few strategic mistakes during the war, but Pickett's charge was foolhardy. Meade's forces drove off the attack. The whole field was "dotted with our soldiers," wrote one Confederate officer. Lee met his retreating troops with the words "It's all my fault, my fault." Losses on both sides were high (see Table 14.5), but Confederate casualties exceeded twenty-eight thousand men, more than half of Lee's army. Lee retreated, his invasion of the North a failure.

On the heels of this major victory for the North came news from Mississippi that Vicksburg had fallen to Grant's siege on July 4. Sherman had been beating back Confederate forces in central Mississippi, and Union guns had been

TABLE 14.5 | BATTLE OF GETTYSBURG, JULY 1–3, 1863

	Union Army	Confederate Army
Commanders	George E. Meade	Robert E. Lee
Troop strength	75,000	50,000
Killed	3,155	3,903
Wounded	14,529	18,735
Captured, missing	5,365	5,425
Total losses	23,049	28,063

Source: Data from *Battles and Leaders of the Civil War* (1884–1888; reprinted ed., 1956).

shelling the city continuously for nearly seven weeks, driving residents into caves and barricaded shelters. But it was starvation and disease that finally subdued the defenders. Then on July 9, after receiving news of Vicksburg's fate, Port Hudson, the last Confederate garrison on the Mississippi River, also surrendered. The "Father of Waters," said Lincoln, "again goes unvexed to the sea."

Despite jubilation over the recent victories, Lincoln and the North remained frustrated. After Gettysburg, Lincoln waited for word of Lee's capture, believing it would signal the end of the rebellion. But like McClellan, Meade failed to pursue the retreating Confederates. When the president learned of Lee's escape, he said in disbelief, "Our Army held the war in the hollow of their hand and they would not close it."

Disappointment in Tennessee also soon marred the celebration over Gettysburg and Vicksburg. Union general William S. Rosecrans had taken the rail center of Chattanooga, but on September 18, Braxton Bragg's forces attacked Rosecrans at Chickamauga Creek. Rosecrans scurried back to refuge in Chattanooga, leaving troops in place to cover his retreat. This force, under the command of George H. Thomas, delayed the Confederate offensive and, in the words of one veteran, "saved the army from defeat and rout." Bragg nonetheless was able to follow and laid siege to Chattanooga from the heights of Missionary Ridge and Lookout Mountain, overlooking the city.

With Lee and his army intact and Rosecrans pinned down in Tennessee, the war, which in July had appeared to be so nearly over, was, in Lincoln's words, "prolonged indefinitely." Lincoln needed a new kind of general.

Grant, Sherman, and the Invention of Total War   Among the available choices, Grant had shown the kind of persistence and boldness Lincoln thought necessary. Lincoln placed him in charge of all Union forces in the West on October 16. Grant immediately replaced Rosecrans with the more intrepid and decisive Thomas. Sherman's troops joined Thomas under

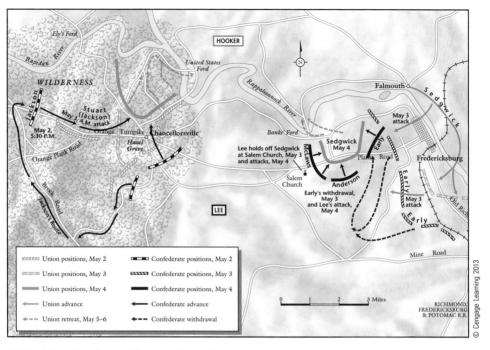

MAP 14.2 Battle of Chancellorsville, May 2–6, 1863

This map demonstrates the advantage of holding "interior lines," which enabled General Lee to shift troops back and forth to and from the Chancellorsville and Fredericksburg fronts over the course of three days while the two parts of the Union army remained separated.

Grant's command on November 14. This united force rid the mountains above Chattanooga of Confederate strongholds and drove Bragg's forces out of southern Tennessee. Confederate forces also withdrew from Knoxville in December, leaving the state under Union control.

While fighting raged in Tennessee, Lincoln took a break from his duties in the White House to participate in the dedication of a national cemetery at the site where, just months before, the Battle of Gettysburg had taken the lives of thousands. In the speech he delivered on November 19, 1863, Lincoln dedicated not only the cemetery but the war effort itself to the fallen soldiers, and also to a principle. "Fourscore and seven years ago," Lincoln said, "our fathers brought forth on this continent a new nation, conceived in liberty and dedicated to the proposition that all men are created equal." Though delivered in a low voice that most of the crowd could not hear, the **Gettysburg Address** was circulated in the media and galvanized many Americans who had come to doubt the war's purpose.

Delighted with Grant's successes in Tennessee, Lincoln promoted him again on March 10, 1864, this time to general in chief. Grant immediately left his command

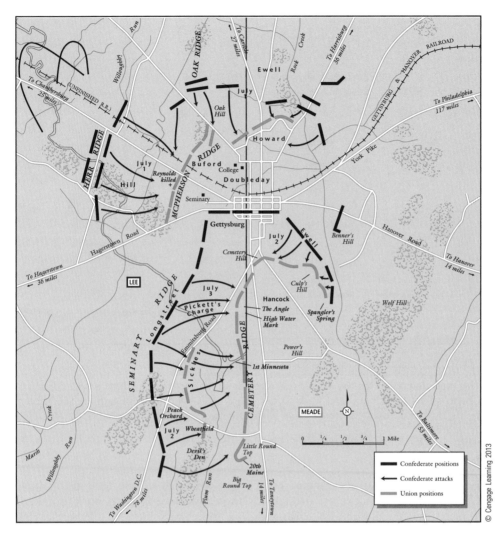

MAP 14.3 Battle of Gettysburg, July 1–3, 1863

On July 2 and 3, the Union army had the advantage of interior lines at Gettysburg, which enabled General Meade to shift reinforcements from his right on Culp's Hill to his left near Little Round Top over a much shorter distance than Confederate reinforcements from one flank to the other would have to travel.

in the West to prepare an all-out attack on Lee and Virginia, authorizing Sherman to pursue a campaign into Georgia.

In Grant and Sherman, Lincoln had found what he needed. On the surface, neither seemed a likely candidate for a major role in the Union army. Both were West Point graduates but left the army after the War with Mexico to seek their fortunes. Neither had succeeded in civilian life: Grant was a binge drinker who had accomplished little, and Sherman had failed as a banker and a lawyer. Both were

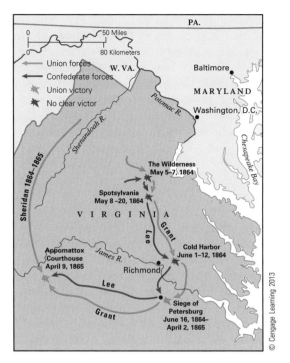

MAP 14.4 The Final Virginia Campaign, 1864–1865

Refusing to abandon his campaign in the face of enormous casualties, Grant finally pushed Lee into defensive fortifications around Petersburg, whose fall doomed Richmond. When Lee tried to escape to the west, Grant cut him off and forced his surrender.

"political generals," owing their Civil War commissions to the influence of friends or relatives. Despite their checkered pasts, these two men invented a new type of warfare that eventually brought the South to its knees. Grant and Sherman were willing to wage **total war** to destroy the South's will.

One of Grant's first acts was to cut the supply of Confederate soldiers by suspending prisoner of war exchanges. He understood that one outcome of this policy would be slow death by starvation for Union prisoners, but he reasoned that victory was his primary goal and that suffering and death were unavoidable in war. Throughout the remainder of the war, this single-mindedness pushed Grant to make decisions that cost tens of thousands of lives on both sides.

On May 4, Grant and Meade moved toward Richmond and Robert E. Lee. The next day, Union and Confederate armies collided in a tangle of woods called The Wilderness, near Chancellorsville. Two days of bloody fighting followed. Grant decided to skirt Lee's troops and head for Richmond, but Lee anticipated the maneuver and blocked Grant's route at Spotsylvania. Twelve days of fighting

total war   War waged with little regard for the welfare of troops on either side or for enemy civilians; the objective is to destroy both the human and the economic resources of the enemy.

ensued. Grant again attempted to move around Lee, and again Lee anticipated him. On June 1, the two armies met at **Cold Harbor**, Virginia. After each side had consolidated its position, Grant ordered a series of frontal attacks against the entrenched Confederates on June 3. Lee's veteran troops waited patiently in perhaps the best position they had ever defended, while Union soldiers expecting to die marched toward them. The assault failed amid unspeakable slaughter.

One southerner described Grant's assaults as "inexplicable and incredible butchery." Many of the young federal attackers at Cold Harbor had pinned their names on their shirts in the hope that their shattered bodies might be identified after the battle. Casualties on both sides at Spotsylvania and Cold Harbor were staggering, but Union losses were unimaginably horrible. As one Confederate officer put it, "We have met a man, this time, who either does not know when he is whipped, or who cares not if he loses his whole army." During the three encounters, Grant lost a total of sixty thousand troops, more than Lee's entire army. Said Lee, "This is not war, this is murder." But Grant's seeming wantonness was calculated, for the Confederates lost more than twenty-five thousand troops. And Grant knew, as did Lee, that the Union could afford the losses but the Confederacy could not.

After Cold Harbor, Grant steered the Union army toward Petersburg, south of Richmond, to try to take the vital rail center and cut off the southern capital. But Lee rapidly shifted the **vanguard** of his troops, beat back Grant's advance, and occupied Petersburg. Grant bitterly regretted this failure, feeling that he could have ended the war. Instead, the campaign settled into a siege that neither side wanted.

The Election of 1864 and Sherman's March to the Sea

Lincoln was under fire from two directions. On May 31, 1864, the Republicans met in Cleveland and dumped him from the ticket, officially nominating John C. Frémont as their presidential candidate. Lincoln supporters, who began calling themselves the Union Party, held their nominating convention in June and renominated Lincoln. To attract Democrats who still favored fighting for a clear victory, Union Party delegates dumped Republican Vice President Hannibal Hamlin and chose **Andrew Johnson**, a southern Democrat, as Lincoln's running mate. Then, in August, the Democratic National Convention met at Chicago. The Democrats pulled together many **Copperheads** and other northerners who were so upset by the heavy casualties that they were determined to stop the war, even at the cost of allowing slavery to continue. The Democrats selected McClellan as their presidential candidate and included a peace plank in their platform. Thus Lincoln sat squarely in the middle between one group that castigated him for pursuing the war and another group that rebuked him for failing to punish the South vigorously enough.

Jefferson Davis's administration also faced serious criticism as deprivation and military losses mounted. In an effort to solve their mutual problems, Lincoln and

vanguard   The foremost unit in any army advancing into battle.

Confederate vice president Alexander H. Stephens had conversations about negotiating a settlement. Lincoln stated his terms: reunion, abolition, and amnesty for Confederates. Stephens balked, pointing out that "amnesty" applied to criminals and that the South had "committed no crime." The only possible outcomes of the war for the South, he concluded, were independence or extermination, even if it meant enduring the sight of "every Southern plantation sacked and every Southern city in flames." The words proved prophetic.

Grant had instructed Sherman "to get into the interior of the enemy's country as far as you can, inflicting all the damage you can against their war resources." Sherman responded with a vengeance. Slowly and skillfully his army advanced southward from Tennessee toward Atlanta, one of the South's few remaining industrial centers. Confederate general Joseph E. Johnston repeatedly retreated to keep Sherman from annihilating his army. President Davis then replaced Johnston with John Bell Hood, who vowed to take the offensive. Hood attacked, but Sherman inflicted such serious casualties that Hood had to retreat to Atlanta.

For days Sherman shelled Atlanta and wrought havoc in the surrounding countryside. When a last-ditch southern attack failed, Hood evacuated the city on September 1. Sherman's victory caused tremendous despair among Confederates but gave great momentum to Lincoln's reelection campaign. Also boosting Lincoln's reelection efforts was General Philip Sheridan's campaign in the Shenandoah Valley, an important source of food for Lee's army. Adopting the same sort of devastating tactics that Sherman used so successfully, Sheridan's men lived off the land and destroyed both military and civilian supplies whenever possible. Accepting high casualties, Sheridan drove Confederate forces from the region in October, laying waste to much of Lee's food supply in the process.

These victories proved the decisive factor in the election of 1864. Sherman's and Sheridan's successes defused McClellan's argument that Lincoln was not competent to direct the Union's military fortunes and quelled much antiwar sentiment in the North. Equally discredited, the Radical Republican platform and the Frémont candidacy disappeared before election day. When the votes were counted, Lincoln learned that he had defeated McClellan—by half a million popular votes and by a landslide margin of 212 to 21 in the Electoral College.

The southern peace movement had viewed a Democratic victory as the last chance to reach a settlement. Without it, all hope of negotiation appeared lost. Amid the bleak prospects, animosity toward Jefferson Davis increased in the South. But with Lee's forces still in Petersburg and Hood's in Georgia, southern hopes were dimmed but not extinguished.

Sherman soon grew bored with the occupation of Atlanta and posed a bold plan to Grant. He wanted to ignore Hood and go on the offensive, cutting "a swath through to the sea." "I can make Georgia howl," he promised. Despite some misgivings, Grant agreed and convinced Lincoln.

A week after the election, Sherman began preparing for his 300-mile **March to the Sea**. His intentions were clear. "We are not only fighting hostile armies, but a hostile people," he stated. By devastating the countryside and destroying the South's ability to conduct war, he intended to break down southerners' will to resist. "We cannot change the hearts of those people of the South," he concluded,

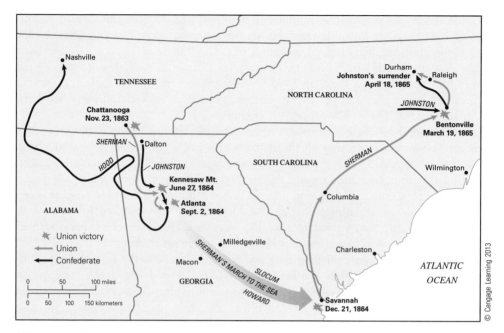

MAP 14.5 Sherman's March to the Sea

The Deep South proved a decisive theater at the end of the war. From Chattanooga, Union forces drove into Georgia, capturing Atlanta. Following the fall of Atlanta, General Sherman embarked on his march of destruction through Georgia to the coast and then northward through the Carolinas.

but we can "make them so sick of war that generations would pass away before they would again appeal to it." With that, he burned most of Atlanta and then set out on his march to the coastal town of Savannah. His troops plundered and looted farms and towns on the way, foraging for food and supplies and destroying everything in their path. Sherman entered Savannah unopposed on December 21.

The March to the Sea completed, Sherman turned north. In South Carolina, the first state to secede and fire shots, Sherman's troops took special delight in ravaging the countryside. When they reached Columbia, flames engulfed the city. With the state capital in flames, Confederate forces in South Carolina abandoned their posts, moving north to join with Joseph E. Johnston's army in an effort to stop Sherman from crossing North Carolina and joining Grant in Virginia. Union forces quickly moved into abandoned southern strongholds, including Charleston, where Major Robert Anderson, who had commanded Fort Sumter in April 1861, returned to raise the Union flag over the fort that he had surrendered four years earlier.

The End of Lee and Lincoln   Under increasing pressure from Sherman, the Confederacy's military situation was deteriorating rapidly. In a last-ditch effort to keep the Confederacy alive, Lee advised Davis to

The Gettysburg Address

When the Civil War began, Lincoln made it clear that defending the Constitution was his only objective. But when he spoke on the Gettysburg battlefield two years later, commemorating the deaths of the thousands who fell there, he gave voice to a broader vision and a more noble goal. In that speech, Lincoln referenced the Declaration of Independence, *not* the Constitution, transforming Thomas Jefferson's stirring announcement of the Enlightenment principle that "all men are created equal" into the central element in the great American struggle. We seldom take political speeches very seriously these days, but this one changed the conception of the Constitution itself. After Lincoln's death, Congress enacted the Fourteenth Amendment, transforming Jefferson's—and Lincoln's—statement of principle into the law of the land. To this day—well more than "fourscore and seven years" since Lincoln's famous speech—"we hold this truth to be self-evident" in principle and in law through the Constitution Lincoln envisioned in that speech.

- What does the Gettysburg Address reflect about popular attitudes toward the war following the Battle of Gettysburg? Given what you know about the era, what do you think explains the speech's impact?
- In what significant ways did the principles stated by Lincoln at Gettysburg modify the nation's understanding of the Constitution? How has this understanding manifested itself in legislation and landmark legal cases in recent years?

evacuate Richmond—the army intended to withdraw from besieged Petersburg and abandon the capital, moving west as rapidly as possible toward Lynchburg. From there Lee hoped to use surviving rail lines to move his troops south to join with Johnston's force in North Carolina. The unified armies might then halt Sherman's advance and wheel around to deal with Grant.

Suffering none of his predecessors' indecisiveness, Grant ordered an immediate assault as Lee's forces retreated from Petersburg. Lee had little ammunition, almost no food, and only thirty-five thousand men. As they retreated westward, hundreds of southern soldiers collapsed from hunger and exhaustion. On April 9, Sheridan's Army of the Shenandoah arrived, cutting off Lee's retreat. Union forces now surrounded Lee's broken army. Saying, "There is nothing left for me to do but go and see General Grant," Lee sent a note offering surrender.

The two generals met at a private home in the little village of Appomattox Courthouse, Virginia. Grant offered generous terms, allowing Confederate officers and men to go home "so long as they observe their paroles and the laws in force where they reside." This guaranteed them immunity from prosecution for treason and became the model for surrender. Grant sent the starving Confederates rations and let them keep their horses.

Determined to "make Georgia howl," William Tecumseh Sherman and his band of
"bummers" slashed their way through the South during the winter of 1864, destroying
military and civilian property along the way. Having abandoned traditional lines of
supply, Sherman's men raided farms for pork, grain, and other necessities, leaving ruin
in their wake.

On the following day, Lincoln addressed a crowd outside the White House about his hopes and plans for rebuilding the nation. He talked about the need for flexibility in pulling the nation back together after the long and bitter conflict. He had already taken steps to bring southerners back into the Union. In December 1863, he had issued a Proclamation of Amnesty and Reconstruction offering pardons to any Confederates who would take a loyalty oath. After his reelection in 1864, Lincoln had begun to plan for the Confederacy's eventual surrender, and he pushed for a constitutional ban on slavery, which passed on January 31, 1865.

With victory at hand and a peace plan in place, on April 14, after an exhausting day in conference with his cabinet and with General Grant, Lincoln chose to relax by attending a play at Ford's Theater in Washington. At about ten o'clock, **John Wilkes Booth**, an actor and a southern sympathizer, entered the president's box and shot him behind the ear. Meanwhile, one of Booth's accomplices entered the home of Secretary of State Seward, who was bedridden as a result of a carriage accident, and stabbed him several times before being driven out by

Seward's son and a male nurse. Another accomplice was supposed to assassinate Vice President Johnson but apparently lost his nerve. Although the conspiracy had failed, one of its main objectives succeeded: the following morning, Lincoln died of his wound.

Even though Lincoln was dead and Lee had fallen, the war continued. Joseph E. Johnston, whose forces succeeded in preventing Sherman from joining Grant, did not surrender until April 18. And although most of his forces had been defeated, Jefferson Davis remained in hiding and called for guerrilla warfare and continued resistance. But one by one, the Confederate officers surrendered to their Union opponents. On May 10, Davis was captured near Irwinville, Georgia. Andrew Johnson, who had assumed the presidency upon Lincoln's death, issued a statement to the American people that armed rebellion against legitimate authority could be considered "virtually at an end." The last Confederate general to lay down his arms was Cherokee leader Stand Watie, who surrendered on June 23, 1865.

The price of victory was high for both the winner and the loser. More than 350,000 Union soldiers had been killed in action. No exact figures exist for the Confederacy, but southern casualties probably equaled or exceeded those of the Union. The war had wrecked the economy of the South. Union military campaigns had wiped out most southern rail lines, destroyed the South's manufacturing capacity, and severely reduced agricultural productivity. Both sides had faced rising inflation during the war, but the Confederacy's actions to supply troops and keep the war effort going had bled the South of most of its resources and money. Secession had been defeated, but reunion remained a distant and difficult objective.

STUDY TOOLS

SUMMARY

Both the Union and the Confederacy entered the war in 1861 with glowing hopes. Jefferson Davis pursued a defensive strategy, certain that northerners would soon tire of war and let the South withdraw from the Union. Abraham Lincoln countered by using the superior human, economic, and natural resources of the North to strangle the South into submission. But both leaders became increasingly frustrated during the first year of the war.

For Lincoln, the greatest frustration was military leadership. Beginning with the first Battle of Bull Run, Union forces seemed unable to win any major battles. Although Union forces under Ulysses S. Grant's command scored victories in the Mississippi Valley, the Federals were stalemated. Robert E. Lee and Thomas "Stonewall" Jackson seemed able to defeat any Union general that Lincoln sent to oppose them.

The war's nature and direction changed after the fall of 1862, however. Lee invaded Maryland and was defeated at Antietam. Despite this crushing loss, Union generals still failed to capture Lee or to subdue Confederate forces in Virginia. Still angered by military blundering, political attacks, and popular unrest, Lincoln issued the Emancipation Proclamation in an effort to undermine southern efforts and unify northern ones. After the proclamation, the only option for either side was total victory or total defeat.

After further reversals in the spring of 1863, Union forces turned the tide in the war by defeating Lee's army at Gettysburg and taking Vicksburg to gain full control of the Mississippi. With an election drawing near, Lincoln spurred his generals to deal the death blow to the Confederacy, and two in particular rose to the occasion. During the last half of 1864, William Tecumseh Sherman wreaked havoc, making Georgia "howl." And Grant, in a wanton display of disregard for human life, drove Lee into a defensive corner. In November, buoyed by Sherman's victories in Georgia, Lincoln was reelected.

Suffering was not confined to those at the front. Governments in both the North and the South had to dig deep into depleting economic resources to keep the war effort going. Inflation plagued both nations, and common people faced hunger, disease, and lawlessness. Riots broke out in major cities, including New York. But throughout the country many people responded heroically to their own privations and to suffering at the front. Women such as Clara Barton and others faced up to epidemics, enemy gunfire, and gender bias to institute public health standards and bring solace to suffering civilians and soldiers alike.

As hope dwindled for the South in the spring of 1865, Lee made a final desperate effort to keep the flagging Confederacy alive, racing to unify the last surviving remnants of the once-proud southern army. But Grant closed a net of steel around Lee's troops, forcing surrender. Lincoln immediately promoted a gentle policy for reunion, but his assassination ended this effort. The saintly American hero was gone, leaving a southern Democrat—Andrew Johnson—as president and a nation reeling in shock. The war was over, but the issues were still unresolved.

CHRONOLOGY

WAR BETWEEN THE STATES

1861 Lincoln takes office and runs Union by executive authority until July
Fort Sumter falls
Battle of Bull Run
McClellan organizes the Union army

1862 Grant's victories in Mississippi Valley
Battle of Shiloh
U.S. Navy captures New Orleans
Peninsular Campaign
Battle of Antietam
African Americans permitted in Union army

1863 Emancipation Proclamation takes effect
Union enacts conscription
Battle of Chancellorsville and death of Stonewall Jackson
Union victories at Gettysburg and Vicksburg
Draft riots in New York City

1864   Grant invades Virginia
Sherman captures Atlanta
Lincoln reelected
Sherman's March to the Sea

1865   Lee abandons Petersburg and Richmond
Lee surrenders at Appomattox Courthouse
Lincoln proposes a gentle reconstruction policy
Lincoln assassinated

Focus Questions

If you have mastered this chapter, you should be able to answer these questions and explain the terms that follow the questions.

1. What problems did Abraham Lincoln and Jefferson Davis face as they led their respective nations into war?
2. How did each chief executive deal with those problems?
3. How did military action during the opening years of the war affect the people's perceptions of the war in the North and South?
4. Why did Lincoln issue the Emancipation Proclamation when and in the way he did? What sorts of responses did it elicit?
5. How did the burdens of war affect society in the North and the South?
6. How did individuals and governments in both regions respond to those burdens?
7. What factors contributed to the Union's adoption of a total war strategy after 1863?
8. Was total war justifiable in light of the human and property damage it inflicted and the overall consequences it achieved? Why or why not?

Key Terms

anaconda plan (*p.* 383)

Radical Republicans (*p.* 383)

Bull Run (*p.* 387)

Thomas J. Jackson (*p.* 387)

George B. McClellan (*p.* 388)

Army of the Potomac (*p.* 388)

Ulysses S. Grant (*p.* 389)

William Tecumseh Sherman (*p.* 389)

Battle of Shiloh (*p.* 389)

Vicksburg (*p.* 390)

Peninsular Campaign (*p.* 390)

Second Battle of Bull Run (*p.* 392)

Antietam Creek (*p.* 392)

Fredericksburg (*p.* 392)

Emancipation Proclamation (*p.* 393)

Conscription Act (*p.* 394)

Horace Greeley (*p.* 395)

Twenty Negro Law (*p.* 395)

Homestead Act (*p.* 396)

greenbacks (*p.* 396)

15

RECONSTRUCTION:
HIGH HOPES AND SHATTERED DREAMS,
1865–1877

CHAPTER OUTLINE

- Presidential Reconstruction • Freedom and the Legacy of Slavery
- Congressional Reconstruction • Black Reconstruction • The End of
Reconstruction • Study Tools

The years following the Civil War were a time of physical rebuilding throughout the South, but the term **"Reconstruction"** refers primarily to the rebuilding of the federal union and to the political, economic, and social changes that came to the South as it was restored to the nation. Reconstruction involved some of the most momentous questions in American history: How was the defeated South to be treated? What was to be the future of the 4 million former slaves? Should key decisions be made by the federal government or in state capitols and county courthouses throughout the South? Which branch of the government was to establish policies?

PRESIDENTIAL RECONSTRUCTION

On New Year's Day, 1863, the Emancipation Proclamation took effect. More than four years earlier, President **Abraham Lincoln** had insisted that "this government cannot endure permanently half slave and half free.... It will become all one thing, or all the other." With the Emancipation Proclamation, President Lincoln began to make the nation all free. At the time, however, the proclamation did not affect any slave because it abolished slavery only in territory under Confederate control, where it was unenforceable. But every advance of a Union army after January 1, 1863, brought emancipation, the release from slavery, to the slaves of the Confederacy.

Republican
War Aims

For Lincoln and the Republican Party, freedom for the slaves became a central concern partly because **abolitionists** were influential within the party. The Republican Party had promised only to prohibit slavery in the territories during its 1860 electoral campaign, and Lincoln initially defined the war as one to maintain the Union. Some leading Republicans, however, favored abolition of slavery everywhere. As Union troops moved into the South, some slaves simply walked away from their owners. Many sought safety with the Union army. Soon former slaves became Union soldiers as well. Abolitionists throughout the North—including **Frederick Douglass,** an escaped slave and an important leader of the abolition movement—began to argue that emancipation would be meaningless unless the government guaranteed the civil and political rights of the former slaves. Thus some Republicans expanded their definition of war objectives to include abolishing slavery, extending citizenship for the former slaves, and guaranteeing the equality of all citizens before the law. At the time, these were extreme views on abolition and equal rights, and the people who held them were called **Radical Republicans,** or simply Radicals.

Thaddeus Stevens, 73 years old in 1865, was the leading Radical in the House of Representatives. He had made a successful career as a Pennsylvania lawyer and iron manufacturer before winning election to Congress in 1858. Born with a clubfoot, he identified with those outside the social mainstream. He became a compelling spokesman for abolition and an uncompromising advocate of equal rights for African Americans. A masterful parliamentarian, he was known for his honesty and sarcastic wit. From the beginning of the war, Stevens urged that the slaves be not only freed but also armed to fight the Confederacy. By the end of the war, some 180,000 African Americans, the great majority of them freedmen, had served in the Union army and a few thousand in the Union navy. Many more worked for the army as laborers.

Charles Sumner of Massachusetts, a prominent Radical in the Senate, had argued for **racial integration** of Massachusetts schools in 1849 and won election to the U.S. Senate in 1851. The Senate's foremost champion of abolition, he suffered a severe beating in 1856 because of an antislavery speech. After emancipation, Sumner, like Stevens, fought for full political and civil rights for the freed people.

Stevens, Sumner, and other Radicals opposed slavery not only on moral grounds but also because they believed free labor was more productive. Slaves worked to escape punishment, they argued, but free workers worked to benefit themselves. Eliminating slavery and instituting a free-labor system in its place, they claimed, would benefit everyone by increasing the nation's productivity. Free labor not only contributed centrally to the dynamism of the North's economy, they argued, but was crucial to democracy itself. "The middling classes who own the soil, and work it with their own hands," Stevens once proclaimed, "are the main support of every free government." Not all Republicans agreed with the Radicals. All Republicans objected to slavery, but not all Republicans were abolitionists.

---

abolitionist   An individual who condemns slavery as morally wrong and seeks to abolish (eliminate) slavery.

racial integration   Equal opportunities to participate in a society or organization by people of different racial groups; the absence of race-based barriers to full and equal participation.

Similarly, not all Republicans wanted to extend full citizenship rights to the former slaves. Some favored rapid restoration of the South to the Union so that the federal government could concentrate on stimulating the nation's economy and developing the West. Such Republicans are usually referred to as **moderates**.

Lincoln's Approach to Reconstruction: "With Malice Toward None"
After the Emancipation Proclamation, President Lincoln and the congressional Radicals agreed that abolition of slavery had to be a condition for the return of the South to the Union. Major differences soon appeared, however, over other terms for reunion and the roles of the president and Congress in establishing those terms. In his second inaugural address, a month before his death, Lincoln defined the task facing the nation:

> With malice toward none; with charity for all; with firmness in the right, as God gives us to see the right, let us strive on to finish the work we are in: to bind up the nation's wounds; to care for him who shall have borne the battle, and for his widow and orphan, to do all which may achieve and cherish a just and lasting peace among ourselves, and with all nations.

Lincoln began to rebuild the Union on the basis of these principles. As soon as Union armies occupied portions of southern states, he appointed temporary military governors for those regions and tried to restore civil government as quickly as possible.

Drawing on the president's constitutional power to issue **pardons** (Article II, Section 2), Lincoln issued a Proclamation of **Amnesty** and Reconstruction in December 1863. Often called the "Ten Percent Plan," it promised a full pardon and restoration of rights to those who swore their loyalty to the Union and accepted the abolition of slavery. Only high-ranking Confederate leaders were not eligible. Once those who had taken the oath in a state amounted to 10 percent of the votes cast by that state in the 1860 election, the pardoned voters were to write a new state constitution that abolished slavery, elect state officials, and resume self-government. Some Radicals considered Lincoln's approach too lenient. When they tried to set more stringent standards, Lincoln blocked them, fearing their plan would slow restoration of civil government and perhaps lengthen the war.

Under Lincoln's Ten Percent Plan, new state governments were established in Arkansas, Louisiana, and Tennessee during 1864 and early 1865. In Louisiana, the new government denied voting rights to men who were one-quarter or more black. Radicals complained, but Lincoln urged patience, suggesting the reconstructed government in Louisiana was "as the egg to the fowl, and we shall sooner have the fowl by hatching the egg than by smashing it." Radicals, however, concluded that freed people were unlikely to receive equitable treatment

moderates People whose views are midway between two extreme positions; in this case, Republicans who favored some reforms but not all the Radicals' proposals.

pardon A governmental directive canceling punishment for a person or people who have committed a crime.

amnesty A general pardon granted by a government, especially for political offenses.

from state governments formed under the Ten Percent Plan. Some moderates agreed and moved toward the Radicals' position that only **suffrage** could protect the freedmen's rights and that only federal action could guarantee black suffrage.

Abolishing Slavery Forever: The Thirteenth Amendment
Amid questions about the rights of freed people, congressional Republicans prepared the final destruction of slavery. The Emancipation Proclamation had been a wartime measure, justified partly by military necessity. It never applied in Union states. State legislatures or conventions abolished slavery in West Virginia, Maryland, Missouri, and the reconstructed

These white southerners are shown taking the oath of allegiance to the United States in 1865, as part of the process of restoring civil government in the South. Union soldiers and officers are administering the oath.

Library of Congress

suffrage   The right to vote.

state of Tennessee. In early 1865, however, slavery remained legal in Delaware and Kentucky, and prewar state laws—which might or might not be valid—permitted slavery in the states that had seceded. To destroy slavery forever, Congress in January 1865 approved the **Thirteenth Amendment**, which read simply, "Neither slavery nor involuntary servitude, except as a punishment for crime whereof the party shall have been duly convicted, shall exist within the United States, or any place subject to their jurisdiction."

The Constitution requires any amendment to be ratified by three-fourths of the states—then 27 of 36. By December 1865, only 19 of the 25 Union states had ratified the amendment. The measure passed, however, when 8 of the reconstructed southern states approved it. In the end, therefore, the abolition of slavery hinged on action by reconstructed state governments in the South.

Andrew Johnson and Reconstruction   In April 1865, shortly after the surrender of the main Confederate army, Lincoln was assassinated by a supporter of the Confederacy. Vice President **Andrew Johnson** became president. Johnson never had the opportunity to attend school and spent his early life in a continual struggle against poverty. As a young man in Tennessee, he worked as a tailor, then turned to politics. His wife, Eliza McCardle Johnson, tutored him in reading, writing, and arithmetic. A Democrat, Johnson was elected to Congress and later was governor before winning election to the U.S. Senate in 1857. His political support came primarily from small-scale farmers and working people. The state's elite of plantation owners usually opposed him. Johnson, in turn, resented their wealth and power, and blamed them for secession and the Civil War.

Johnson was the only southern senator who rejected the Confederacy. Early in the war, Union forces captured Nashville, the capital of Tennessee, and Lincoln appointed Johnson as military governor. Johnson dealt harshly with Tennessee secessionists, especially wealthy planters. Radical Republicans approved. Johnson was elected vice president in 1864, receiving the nomination in part because Lincoln wanted to appeal to Democrats and Unionists in border states.

When Johnson became president, Radicals hoped he would join their efforts to transform the South. Johnson, however, was strongly committed to **states' rights** and opposed the Radicals' objective of a powerful federal government. "White men alone must manage the South," Johnson announced, although he recommended limited political roles for the freedmen. Self-righteous and uncompromising, Johnson saw the major task of Reconstruction as **empowering** the region's white middle class and excluding wealthy planters from power.

states' rights   A political position favoring limitation of the federal government's power and the greatest possible self-government by the individual states.

empower   To increase the power or authority of some person or group.

Johnson's approach to Reconstruction differed little from Lincoln's. Like Lincoln, he relied on the president's constitutional power to grant pardons. He wanted a quick restoration of the southern states to the Union, and he granted amnesty to most former Confederates who pledged loyalty to the Union and support for emancipation. In one of his last actions as president, he granted full pardon and amnesty to all southern rebels, although the Fourteenth Amendment prevented him from restoring their right to hold office.

Johnson appointed **provisional** civilian governors for the southern states not already reconstructed. He instructed them to reconstitute state government and to call constitutional conventions of delegates elected by pardoned voters. Some provisional governors, however, appointed former Confederates to state and local offices, outraging those who expected Reconstruction to bring to power loyal Unionists committed to a new southern society.

The Southern Response: Minimal Compliance   Johnson expected the state constitutional conventions to abolish slavery within each state, ratify the Thirteenth Amendment, renounce secession, and **repudiate** their state's war debts. The states were then to hold elections and resume their places in the Union. State conventions during the summer of 1865 usually complied with these requirements, some grudgingly. Every state, however, rejected black suffrage.

By April 1866, a year after the close of the war, all the southern states had fulfilled Johnson's requirements for rejoining the Union and had elected legislators, governors, and members of Congress. Johnson had hoped for the emergence of new political leaders in the South, but was dismayed at the number of rich planters and former Confederate officials who won state contests.

Most white southerners, however, viewed Johnson as their protector, standing between them and the Radicals. His support for states' rights and his opposition to federal determination of voting rights led white southerners to expect that they would shape the transition from slavery to freedom—that they, and not Congress, would define the status of the former slaves.

FREEDOM AND THE LEGACY OF SLAVERY

As state conventions wrote new constitutions and politicians argued in Washington, African Americans throughout the South set about creating new, free lives for themselves. In the antebellum South, all slaves and most free African Americans had led lives tightly constrained by law and custom. They were permitted few social organizations of their own. Not surprisingly, the central theme of the black response to emancipation was a desire for freedom from white control, for **autonomy** as

---

provisional Temporary.

repudiate The act of rejecting the validity or authority of something; to refuse to pay.

autonomy Control of one's own affairs.

individuals and as a community. The prospect of autonomy touched every aspect of life—family, churches, schools, newspapers, and a host of other social institutions. From this ferment of freedom came new, independent black institutions that provided the basis for southern African American communities. At the same time, the economic life of the South had been shattered by the Civil War and was being transformed by emancipation. Thus white southerners also faced drastic economic and social change.

| Defining the Meaning of Freedom | At the most basic level, freedom came every time an individual slave stopped working for a master and claimed the right to be free. Thus freedom did not come to all slaves at the same time or in the same way. |

For some, freedom came before the Emancipation Proclamation when they walked away from their owners, crossed into Union-held territory, and asserted their liberty. Toward the end of the war, as civil authority broke down throughout much of the South, many slaves declared their freedom and left the lands they had worked when they were in bondage. Some left for good, but many remained nearby, though with a new understanding of their relationship to their former masters. For some, freedom did not come until ratification of the Thirteenth Amendment.

Across the South, the approach of Yankee troops set off a joyous celebration—called a Jubilee—among those who knew that their enslavement was ending. As one Virginia woman remembered, "Such rejoicing and shouting you never heard in your life." Once the celebrating was over, however, the freed people had to decide how best to use their freedom.

The freed people expressed their new status in many ways. Some chose new names to symbolize their new beginning. Many freed people changed their style of dress, discarding the cheap clothing provided to slaves. Some acquired guns. A significant benefit of freedom was the ability to travel without a pass and without being checked by the **patrollers** who had enforced the **pass system**.

Many freed people took advantage of this new opportunity to travel. Indeed, some felt they had to leave the site of their enslavement to experience full freedom. One freed man later recalled that he refused to work for his last owner, not because he had anything against him but because he wanted "to take my freedom." A freed woman said, "If I stay here I'll never know I'm free." Most traveled only short distances, to find work or land to farm, to seek family members separated from them by slavery, or for other well-defined reasons.

The towns and cities of the South attracted some freed people. The presence of Union troops and federal officials promised protection from the random violence against freed people that occurred in rural areas. In March 1865, Congress created the **Freedmen's Bureau** to assist the freed people in their transition to

patrollers   During the era of slavery, white guards who made the rounds of rural roads to make certain that slaves were not moving about the countryside without written permission from their masters.

pass system   Laws that forbade slaves to travel without written authorization from their owners.

freedom. In cities and towns, this agency offered assistance with finding work and necessities. Cities and towns also held black churches, newly established schools, and other social institutions, some begun by free blacks before the war. Some African Americans came to towns and cities looking for work. Little housing was available, however, so freed people often crowded into hastily built shanties. Sanitation was poor and disease a common scourge. Such conditions improved only very slowly.

Creating Communities   During Reconstruction, African Americans created their own communities with their own social institutions, beginning with family ties. Joyful families were sometimes reunited after years of separation caused by the sale of a spouse or children. Other people spent years searching for lost family members.

The new freedom to conduct religious services without white supervision was especially important. Churches quickly became the most prominent social organizations in African American communities. Churches were, in fact, among the very first social institutions that African Americans fully controlled. During Reconstruction, black denominations, including the African Methodist Episcopal, African Methodist Episcopal Zion, and several Baptist groups (all founded before the Civil War), grew rapidly in the South. Black ministers helped congregation members adjust to the changes that freedom brought, and ministers often became key leaders within developing African American communities.

Throughout the cities and towns of the South, African Americans—especially ministers and church members—created schools. Setting up a school, said one, was "the first proof" of independence. Many new schools were for both children and adults, whose literacy and learning had been restricted by laws prohibiting education for slaves. The desire to learn was widespread and intense. One freedman in Georgia wrote to a friend: "The Lord has sent books and teachers. We must not hesitate a moment, but go on and learn all we can."

Before the war, free public education had been limited in much of the South and was absent in many places. When African Americans set up schools, they faced severe shortages of teachers, books, and schoolrooms—everything but students. As abolitionists and northern reformers tried to assist the transition from slavery to freedom, many of them also focused first on education.

The Freedmen's Bureau played an important role in organizing and equipping schools. Freedmen's Aid Societies sprang up in most northern cities and, along with northern churches, collected funds and supplies for the freed people. Teachers—mostly white women, often from New England, and often acting on religious impulses—came from the North. Northern aid societies and church organizations, together with the Freedmen's Bureau, established schools to train black teachers. Some of those schools evolved into black colleges. By 1870, the Freedmen's Bureau supervised more than 4,000 schools, with more than 9,000 teachers and 247,000 students. Still, in 1870, only one-tenth of school-age black children were in school.

Churches were the first institutions to be completely controlled by African Americans, and ministers were influential figures in the African American communities that emerged during Reconstruction. This photograph of the Colored Methodist Episcopal mission church in Hot Springs, Arkansas, was first published in 1898 in The History of the Colored Methodist Episcopal Church in America.

Schomburg Center/Art Resource, New York

African Americans created other social institutions in addition to churches and schools, including **fraternal orders**, **benevolent societies**, and newspapers. By 1866, the South had ten black newspapers, led by the *New Orleans Tribune,* and black newspapers played important roles in shaping African American communities.

In politics, African Americans' first objective was recognition of their equal rights as citizens. Frederick Douglass insisted, "Slavery is not abolished until the black man has the ballot." In 1865, political conventions of African Americans attracted hundreds of leaders of the emerging black communities. They called for equality and voting rights, and pointed to black contributions in the American Revolution and the Civil War as evidence of patriotism and devotion. They also appealed to the nation's republican traditions, in particular the Declaration of Independence and its dictum that "all men are created equal."

Land and Labor   Former slaveowners reacted to emancipation in many ways. Some tried to keep their slaves from learning of their

fraternal order A men's organization, often with a ceremonial initiation, that typically provided rudimentary life insurance; many fraternal orders had auxiliaries for female relatives of members.

benevolent society An organization dedicated to some charitable purpose.

freedom. Very few white southerners welcomed the end of slavery, and few former slave owners provided financial assistance to their former slaves.

Many freed people looked to Union troops for assistance. When General William T. Sherman led his victorious army through Georgia in the closing months of the war, thousands of African American men, women, and children claimed their freedom and followed in the Yankees' wake. Their leaders told Sherman that they wanted to "reap the fruit of our own labor." In January 1865, Sherman issued Special Field Order No. 15, setting aside the Sea Islands and land along the South Carolina coast for freed families. Each family, he specified, was to receive 40 acres and the loan of an army mule. By June, the area had filled with forty thousand freed people settled on 400,000 acres of "Sherman land."

Sherman's action encouraged African Americans to expect that the federal government would redistribute land throughout the South. "Forty acres and a mule" became a rallying cry. Only land, Thaddeus Stevens proclaimed, would give freed people control of their own labor. "If we do not furnish them with homesteads," Stevens said, "we had better left them in bondage."

By the end of the war, the Freedmen's Bureau controlled some 850,000 acres of land abandoned by former owners or confiscated from Confederate leaders. In July 1865, General Oliver O. Howard, head of the bureau, directed that this land be divided into 40-acre plots to be given to freed people. However, President Johnson ordered Howard to halt **land redistribution** and to reclaim land already handed over and return it to its former owners. Johnson's order displaced thousands of African Americans who had already taken their 40 acres. Those who had expected land of their own felt betrayed. One later recalled that they had expected "a heap from freedom dey didn't git."

The congressional act that created the Freedmen's Bureau authorized it to assist white refugees. In a few places, white recipients of aid outnumbered the freed blacks. A large majority of southern whites had never owned slaves, and some had opposed secession. The outcome of the war, however, meant that some lost their livelihood, and many feared they would have to compete with the freed people for farmland or wage labor. Like the freed people, many southern whites lacked the means to farm on their own. When the Confederate government collapsed, Confederate money became worthless. This sudden reduction in the amount of money in circulation, together with the failure of southern banks and the devastation of the southern economy, meant that the entire region was short of **capital**.

Sharecropping slowly emerged across much of the South, derived from the central realities of southern agriculture. Much of the land was in large holdings,

---

land redistribution   The division of land held by large landowners into smaller plots that are turned over to landless people.

capital   Money, especially the money invested in a commercial enterprise.

sharecropping   A system for renting farmland in which tenant farmers give landlords a share of their crops, rather than cash, as rent.

but the landowners had no one to work it. Capital was scarce. Many landowners lacked cash to hire farm workers. Many families, both black and white, wanted to raise their own crops with their own labor but had no land, no supplies, and no money. Under sharecropping, an individual—usually a family head—signed a contract with a landowner to rent land as home and farm. The tenant—the sharecropper—was to pay, as rent, a share of the harvest. The share might amount to half or more of the crop if the landlord provided mules, tools, seed, and fertilizer as well as land. Many landowners thought that sharecropping encouraged tenants to be productive, to get as much value as possible from their shares of the crop.

Southern farmers—black or white, sharecroppers or owners of small plots—often found themselves in debt to a local merchant who advanced supplies on credit. In return for credit, the merchant required a lien (a legal claim) on the growing crop. Many landlords ran stores that they required their tenants to patronize. Often the share paid as rent and the debt owed the store exceeded the value of the entire harvest. Furthermore, many rental contracts and **crop liens** were automatically renewed if all debts were not paid at the end of a year. Thus, in spite of their efforts to achieve greater control over their lives and labor, many southern farm families, black and white alike, found themselves trapped by sharecropping and debt. Still, sharecropping gave freed people more control over their daily lives than had slavery.

Landlords could exercise political as well as economic power over their tenants. Until the 1890s, casting a ballot was an open process, and any observer could see how an individual voted. Thus, when a landlord or merchant advocated a particular candidate, the unspoken message was often an implicit threat to cut off credit at the store or to evict a sharecropper if he did not vote accordingly. Such forms of economic **coercion** could undercut voting rights.

The White South: Confronting Change   The Civil War and the end of slavery transformed the lives of white southerners as well as black southerners. For some, the changes were nearly as profound as for the freed people. Savings vanished. Some homes and other buildings were destroyed. Thousands left the South.

Before the war, few white southerners had owned slaves, and very few owned large numbers. Distrust or even hostility had always existed between the privileged planter families and the many whites who farmed small plots. Some regions populated by small-scale farmers had resisted secession, and some welcomed the Union victory and supported the Republicans during Reconstruction. Some southerners

crop lien A legal claim to a farmer's crop, similar to a mortgage, based on the use of crops as collateral for extension of credit by a merchant.

coercion Use of threats or force to compel action.

also welcomed the prospect of the economic transformation that northern capital might bring.

Most white southerners, however, shared what one North Carolinian described in 1866 as "the bitterest hatred toward the North." Even people with no attachment to slavery detested the Yankees who so profoundly changed their lives. For many white southerners, the "lost cause" of the Confederacy came to symbolize their defense of their prewar lives, not an attempt to break up the nation or protect slavery. During the early phases of Reconstruction, most white southerners apparently expected that, except for slavery, things would soon be put back much as they had been before the war.

In late 1865 and 1866, the newly organized state legislatures passed **black codes** defining the new legal status of African Americans. These regulations varied from state to state, but every state placed significant restrictions on black people. Various black codes required African Americans to have an annual employment contract, limited them to agricultural work, forbade them from moving about the countryside without permission, restricted their ownership of land, and provided for forced labor by those guilty of **vagrancy**—which usually meant anyone without a job. Taken together, the black codes represented an effort by white southerners to define a legally subordinate place for African Americans and to put significant restrictions on their newly found freedom.

Some white southerners used violence to coerce freed people into accepting a subordinate status within the new southern society. Violence and terror became closely associated with the **Ku Klux Klan**, a secret organization formed in 1866 and led by a former Confederate general. The turn to terror suggests that Klan members felt themselves largely powerless through normal politics, and used terror to create a climate of fear among their opponents. Most Klan members were small-scale farmers and workers, but the leaders were often prominent within their own communities—one Freedmen's Bureau agent observed, "The most respectable citizens are engaged in it." Klan groups existed throughout the South, but operated with little central control. Their major goals were to restore **white supremacy** and to destroy the Republican Party. Other, similar organizations also formed and adopted similar tactics.

Klan members were called ghouls. Officers included cyclops, night-hawks, and grand dragons, and the national leader was called the grand wizard. Klan members covered their faces with hoods, wore white robes, and rode horses draped in white as they set out to intimidate black Republicans and their white allies. Klan members also attacked less politically prominent people, whipping African Americans accused of not showing sufficient deference to whites. Nightriders also burned black

---

black codes   Laws passed by the southern states after the Civil War restricting freed people; in general, the black codes limited the civil rights of freed people and defined their status as subordinate to whites.

vagrancy   The legal condition of having no fixed place of residence or means of support.

white supremacy   The racist belief that whites are inherently superior to other races and are therefore entitled to rule over them.

churches and schools. By such tactics, the Klan devastated Republican organizations in many communities.

CONGRESSIONAL RECONSTRUCTION

The black codes, violence against freed people, and the failure of southern authorities to stem the violence turned northern opinion against President Johnson's lenient approach to Reconstruction. Increasing numbers of moderate Republicans accepted the Radicals' arguments that the freed people required greater federal protection, and congressional Republicans moved to take control of Reconstruction. When stubborn and uncompromising Andrew Johnson ran up against stubborn and uncompromising Thaddeus Stevens, the nation faced a constitutional crisis.

Challenging Presidential Reconstruction: The Civil Rights Act of 1866   In December 1865, the Thirty-ninth Congress (elected in 1864) met for the first time. Republicans outnumbered Democrats by more than three to one. President Johnson proclaimed Reconstruction complete and the Union restored, but few Republicans agreed. Events in the South had convinced most moderate Republicans of the need to protect free labor in the South and establish basic rights for freed people. Most also agreed that Congress could withhold representation from the South until reconstructed state governments met these conditions.

On the first day of the Thirty-ninth Congress, moderate Republicans joined Radicals to exclude newly elected congressmen from the South. Citing Article I, Section 5, of the Constitution (which makes each house of Congress the judge of the qualifications of its members), Republicans set up a Joint Committee on Reconstruction to evaluate the qualifications of the excluded southerners and to determine whether the southern states were entitled to representation. In the meantime, the former Confederate states had no representation in Congress.

Congressional Republicans also moved to provide more assistance to the freed people. Moderates and Radicals approved a bill extending the Freedmen's Bureau and giving it more authority against racial discrimination. When Johnson vetoed it, Congress drafted a slightly revised version. Republicans also produced a **civil rights** bill, a far-reaching measure that extended citizenship to African Americans and defined some of the rights guaranteed to all citizens. Johnson vetoed both the civil rights bill and the revised Freedmen's Bureau bill, but Congress passed both over his veto. With creation of the Joint Committee on Reconstruction and passage of the Civil Rights and Freedmen's Bureau acts, Congress took control of Reconstruction.

The Civil Rights Act of 1866 defined all persons born in the United States (except Indians not taxed) as citizens and listed certain rights of all citizens,

civil rights   The rights, privileges, and protections that are a part of citizenship.

including the right to testify in court, own property, make contracts, bring law-suits, and enjoy "full and equal benefit of all laws and proceedings for the security of person and property." This was the first effort to define in law some of the rights of American citizenship. It placed significant restrictions on state actions on the grounds that the rights of national citizenship took precedence over the powers of state governments. The law expanded federal powers in unprecedented ways and challenged traditional concepts of states' rights. Though the law applied to all citizens, its most immediate consequence was to benefit African Americans.

Debate in Congress focused on the freed people. Some supporters saw the Civil Rights Act as a way to secure freed people's basic rights. For other Republicans, the bill carried broader implications because it empowered the federal government to force states to abide by the principle of equality before the law. They applauded its redefinition of federal–state relations. Senator Lot Morrill of Maine described it as "absolutely revolutionary" but added, "Are we not in the midst of a revolution?"

When President Johnson vetoed the bill, he argued that it violated states' rights. By defending states' rights and confronting the Radicals, Johnson may have hoped to generate enough political support to elect a conservative Congress in 1866 and to win the presidency in 1868. He probably expected his veto to turn voters against the Radicals. Instead, the veto led most moderate Republicans to abandon hope of cooperating with him. In April 1866, when Congress passed the Civil Rights Act over Johnson's veto, it was the first time ever that Congress had overridden a presidential veto of major legislation.

Defining Citizenship: The Fourteenth Amendment

Leading Republicans worried that the Civil Rights Act could be amended or repealed by a later Congress or declared unconstitutional by the Supreme Court. Only a constitutional amendment, they concluded, could permanently safeguard the freed people's rights as citizens.

The **Fourteenth Amendment** began as a Radical proposal for a constitutional guarantee of equality before the law. However, the final wording—the longest of any amendment—resulted from many compromises. Section 1 of the amendment defined American citizenship in much the same way as the Civil Rights Act of 1866, then specified that

> No State shall make or enforce any law which shall abridge the privileges or immunities of citizens of the United States; nor shall any State deprive any person of life, liberty, or property, without due process of law; nor deny to any person within its jurisdiction the equal protection of the laws.

The Constitution and Bill of Rights prohibit federal interference with basic civil rights. The Fourteenth Amendment extends this protection against action by state governments.

The amendment was vague on some points. For example, it penalized states that did not **enfranchise** African Americans by reducing their congressional and electoral representation, but it did not specifically guarantee to African Americans the right to vote.

Not everyone approved of the final wording. Charles Sumner condemned the provision that permitted a state to deny suffrage to male citizens if it accepted a penalty in congressional representation. Woman suffrage advocates, led by **Elizabeth Cady Stanton** and **Susan B. Anthony**, complained that the amendment, for the first time, introduced the word *male* into the Constitution in connection with voting rights.

Despite such concerns, Congress approved the Fourteenth Amendment by a straight party vote and sent it to the states for ratification. Tennessee promptly ratified the amendment, became the first reconstructed state government to be recognized by Congress, and was exempted from most later Reconstruction legislation.

Although Congress adjourned in the summer of 1866, the nation's attention remained fixed on Reconstruction. In May and July, in Memphis and New Orleans, bloody riots aimed at African Americans turned more moderates against Johnson's Reconstruction policies. Some interpreted congressional elections that fall as a referendum on Reconstruction and the Fourteenth Amendment, pitting Johnson against the Radicals. Republicans swept the 1866 elections, outnumbering Democrats 143 to 49 in the new House of Representatives, and 42 to 11 in the Senate. Lyman Trumbull, senator from Illinois and a leading moderate, voiced the consensus of congressional Republicans: Congress should now "hurl from power the disloyal element" in the South.

Radicals in Control   As congressional Radicals struggled with President Johnson over control of Reconstruction, it became clear that the Fourteenth Amendment might fall short of ratification. Rejection by ten states could prevent its acceptance. By March 1867, the amendment had been rejected by twelve states—Delaware, Kentucky, and all the former Confederate states except Tennessee. Moderate Republicans who had expected the Fourteenth Amendment to be the final Reconstruction measure now became receptive to other proposals that the Radicals put forth.

On March 2, 1867, Congress overrode Johnson's veto of the Military Reconstruction Act, which divided the Confederate states (except Tennessee) into five military districts. Each district was to be governed by a military commander authorized by Congress to use military force to protect life and property. These ten states were to elect delegates and hold constitutional conventions, and all adult male citizens were to vote, except former Confederates who were barred from office under a provision of the proposed Fourteenth Amendment. The constitutional conventions were then to create new state governments that permitted black suffrage, and the new

---

enfranchise   To grant the right to vote to an individual or group.

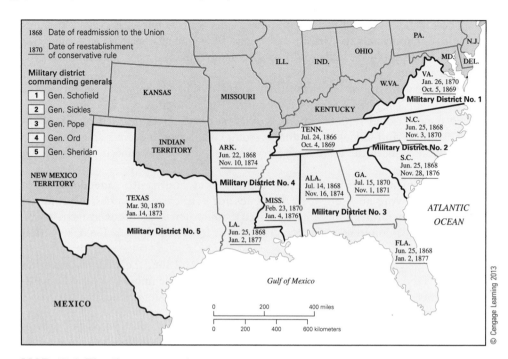

MAP 15.1 The Reconstruction

This map shows the five military districts established when Congress passed the Reconstruction Act of 1867. As the dates within each state indicate, conservative Democratic forces quickly regained control of government in four southern states. So-called Radical Reconstruction was curtailed in most of the others as factions within the weakened Republican Party began to cooperate with conservative Democrats.

governments were to ratify the Fourteenth Amendment. Congress would then evaluate whether those state governments were ready to regain representation in Congress.

Congress had wrested a major degree of control over Reconstruction from the president, but it was not finished. The Command of the Army Act specified that the president could issue military orders only through the General of the Army—Ulysses S. Grant, considered an ally of Congress—and that the General of the Army could not be removed without Senate permission. Congress thereby blocked Johnson from direct communication with military commanders in the South. The Tenure of Office Act specified that officials appointed with the Senate's consent were to remain in office until the Senate approved a successor, thereby preventing Johnson from removing federal officials who opposed his policies. Johnson understood both measures as invasions of presidential authority.

Early in 1867, some Radicals began to consider impeaching President Johnson. The Constitution (Article I, Sections 2 and 3) gives the House of Representatives exclusive power to **impeach** the president—that is, to charge the chief

---

impeach   To charge a public official with improper, usually criminal, conduct.

The Fourteenth Amendment

The Fourteenth Amendment is one of the most important sources of Americans' civil rights, next to the Bill of Rights (the first ten amendments). One key provision in the Fourteenth Amendment is the definition of American citizenship. Previously, the Constitution did not address that question. The Fourteenth Amendment cleared up any confusion about who was, and who was not, a citizen.

The amendment also specifies that no state could abridge the liberties of a citizen "without due process of law." Until this time, the Constitution and the Bill of Rights restricted action by the *federal* government to restrict individual liberties. The Supreme Court has interpreted the Fourteenth Amendment to mean that the restrictions placed on the federal government by the First Amendment also limit state governments—that no *state* government may abridge freedom of speech, press, assembly, and religion.

The Supreme Court continues to interpret the Fourteenth Amendment when it is presented with new cases involving state restrictions on the rights of citizens. For example, in *Roe v. Wade* (1973), the Supreme Court cited the due process clause among other provisions of the Constitution to conclude that state laws may not prevent women from having abortions. In *Lawrence v. Texas* (2003), the Court cited the Fourteenth Amendment to conclude that states may not punish adults for engaging in consensual sexual activities. Current arguments over same-sex marriage often focus on the equal-protection clause of the Fourteenth Amendment.

- Look up the Fourteenth Amendment in the back of this book. How does the Fourteenth Amendment define citizenship? Using an online newspaper, can you find recent proposals to change the definition of American citizenship?
- What current political issues may lead to court cases in which the Fourteenth Amendment is likely to be invoked?

executive with misconduct. The Constitution specifies that the Senate shall hold a trial on those charges, with the chief justice of the Supreme Court presiding. If found guilty by a two-thirds vote of the Senate, the president is removed from office.

When Johnson directly challenged Congress over the Tenure of Office Act by removing Edwin Stanton as secretary of war, Johnson's opponents now claimed he had violated the law. When the House Judiciary Committee failed to bring impeachment charges, the Joint Committee on Reconstruction, led by Thaddeus Stevens, took over. On February 24, 1868, the House adopted eleven articles, or charges, nearly all based on the Stanton affair. The actual reasons the Radicals wanted Johnson removed were clear to all: they disliked him and his actions.

Collection of David J. and Janice L. Frent

Tickets such as these were in high demand, for they permitted the holder to watch the proceedings as the Radical leaders presented their evidence to justify removing Andrew Johnson from the presidency.

To convict Johnson and remove him from the presidency required a two-thirds vote by the Senate. Johnson's defenders argued he had done nothing to warrant impeachment. The Radicals' legal case was weak, but they urged senators to vote on whether they wished Johnson to remain as president. Republican unity unraveled when some moderates, fearing the precedent of removing a president for such flimsy reasons, joined with Democrats to defeat the Radicals. The vote was 35 in favor of conviction and 19 against, one vote short of the required two-thirds. By this tiny margin, Congress endorsed the principle that it should not remove the president from office simply because members of Congress disagree with or dislike the president.

Political Terrorism and the Election of 1868

The Radicals' failure to unseat Johnson left him with less than a year remaining in office. As the election approached, the Republicans nominated Ulysses S. Grant for president. A war hero, popular throughout the North, Grant committed himself to the congressional view of Reconstruction. The Democrats nominated Horatio Seymour, a former governor of New York, and denounced Reconstruction.

In the South, the campaign stirred up fierce activity by the Ku Klux Klan and similar groups. **Terrorists** assassinated an Arkansas congressman, three members of the South Carolina legislature, and several other Republican leaders. Throughout the South, mobs attacked Republican offices and meetings, and sometimes

---

terrorists Those who use threats and violence to achieve ideological or political goals.

attacked any black person they could find. Such coercion had its intended effect at the ballot box.

Despite such violence, many Americans may have anticipated a calmer political future. In June 1868 Congress had readmitted seven southern states that met the requirements of congressional Reconstruction. In July, the secretary of state declared the Fourteenth Amendment ratified. In November, Grant easily won the presidency, carrying twenty-six of the thirty-four states and 53 percent of the vote.

Voting Rights and Civil Rights   With Grant in the White House, Radical Republicans moved to secure voting rights for all African Americans. The states still defined voting rights. Congress had required southern states to enfranchise black males as the price of readmission to the Union, but only seven northern states had taken that step. Further, any state that had enfranchised African Americans could change its law at any time. In addition to the principled arguments of Douglass and other Radicals, many Republicans concluded that they needed to guarantee black suffrage in the South if they were to continue to win presidential elections and enjoy majorities in Congress.

To secure suffrage rights for all African Americans, Congress approved the **Fifteenth Amendment** in February 1869. The amendment prohibited both federal and state governments from restricting a person's right to vote because of "race, color, or previous condition of servitude." Like the Fourteenth Amendment, the Fifteenth marked a compromise between moderates and Radicals. Some African American leaders argued for language guaranteeing voting rights to all male citizens, because prohibiting some grounds for **disfranchisement** might imply the legitimacy of other grounds. Some Radicals tried, unsuccessfully, to add "**nativity**, property, education, or religious beliefs" to the prohibited grounds. Democrats condemned the Fifteenth Amendment as a "revolutionary" attack on states' authority to define voting rights.

Elizabeth Cady Stanton, Susan B. Anthony, and other advocates of woman suffrage opposed the amendment because it ignored restrictions based on sex. For nearly twenty years, the cause of women's rights and the cause of black rights had marched together. Once black male suffrage came under discussion, however, this alliance began to fracture. The break between the women's movement and the black movement was eventually papered over, but the wounds never completely healed.

Despite such opposition, within thirteen months the proposed amendment received the approval of enough states to take effect. Success came in part because Republicans, who might otherwise have been reluctant to impose black suffrage in

disfranchisement The taking away of an individual's or group's right to vote.
nativity Place of birth.

This engraving appeared on the cover of Harper's Weekly in November 1867. It shows black men lined up to cast their ballots. The artist has shown first an older workingman, with his tools in his pocket; and next a well-dressed, younger man, probably a city-dweller and perhaps a leader in the emerging black community; and next a Union soldier. Voting was open. Voters received a ballot (a "party ticket") from a party campaigner and deposited that ballot in a ballot box, in full sight of all. Voting was not secret until much later.

The Granger Collection, New York

the North, concluded that the future success of their party required black suffrage in the South.

The Fifteenth Amendment did nothing to reduce the violence—especially at election time—that had become almost routine in the South after 1865. When Klan activity escalated in the elections of 1870, southern Republicans looked to Washington for support. In 1870 and 1871, Congress adopted several Enforcement Acts—often called the Ku Klux Klan Acts—to enforce the Fourteenth and Fifteenth Amendments.

Despite many obstacles, the prosecution of Klansmen began in 1871. Across the South hundreds were indicted, and many were convicted. In South Carolina, President Grant declared martial law. By 1872, federal intervention had broken much of the strength of the Klan. (The Klan that appeared in the 1920s, covered in Chapter 21, was a new organization that borrowed the regalia and tactics of the earlier organization.)

Congress passed one final Reconstruction measure. Charles Sumner introduced a bill prohibiting **discrimination** in 1870 and in each subsequent session of Congress until his death in 1874. On his deathbed, Sumner urged his visitors to "take care of the civil-rights bill," begging them, "Don't let it fail." Approved after Sumner's death, the **Civil Rights Act of 1875** prohibited racial discrimination in the selection of juries and in public transportation and **public accommodations**.

BLACK RECONSTRUCTION

Congressional Reconstruction set the stage for new developments at state and local levels throughout the South. African Americans never completely controlled any state government but did form a significant element in the governments of several states. The years when African Americans participated prominently in state and local politics are usually called **Black Reconstruction**. It began with efforts by African Americans to take part in politics as early as 1865 and lasted for more than a decade. A few African Americans continued to hold elective office in the South after 1877, but by then they could do little to bring about significant political change.

The Republican Party in the South   Nearly all African Americans who participated actively in politics did so as Republicans, and they formed the large majority of the Republican Party in the South. Nearly all black Republicans were new to politics, and they often braved considerable personal danger by participating in a party that many white southerners equated with the conquering Yankees.

Suffrage made politics a centrally important activity for African American communities. The state constitutional conventions that met in 1868 included 265 black delegates. Only in Louisiana and South Carolina were half or more of the delegates black. With suffrage established, southern Republicans began to elect African Americans to public office. Between 1869 and 1877, fourteen black men served in the national House of Representatives, and Mississippi sent two African Americans to the U.S. Senate.

Across the South, six African Americans served as lieutenant governors, and one of them, P. B. S. Pinchback, succeeded to the governorship of Louisiana. More than six hundred black men served in southern state legislatures during Reconstruction, but only in South Carolina did African Americans have a majority in the state legislature. Elsewhere they formed part of a Republican majority but rarely held key legislative positions. Only in South Carolina and Mississippi did legislatures elect black presiding officers.

discrimination   Denial of equal treatment based on prejudice or bias.

public accommodations   Hotels, bars and restaurants, theaters, and other places set up to do business with anyone who can pay the price of admission.

Although politically inexperienced, most African Americans who held office during Reconstruction had some education. Of the eighteen who served in state-wide offices, all but three are known to have been born free. P. B. S. Pinchback, for example, was educated in Ohio and served in the army as a captain before entering politics in Louisiana. Most black politicians first achieved prominence through service with the army, the Freedmen's Bureau, the new schools, or the religious and civic organizations of black communities.

Throughout the South, Republicans gained power only by securing support from some white voters. These white Republicans are usually remembered by the names fastened on them by their political opponents: "carpetbaggers" and "scalawags." Both groups included idealists who hoped to create a new southern society, but both also included opportunists expecting to exploit politics for personal gain.

Southern Democrats applied the term **carpetbagger** to northern Republicans who came to the South after the war, regarding them as second-rate schemers—outsiders with their belongings packed in a cheap carpet bag. In fact, most northerners who came south were well-educated men and women from middle-class backgrounds. Most men had served in the Union army and moved south before blacks could vote. Some were lawyers, businessmen, or newspaper editors. Whether as investors in agricultural land, teachers in the new schools, or agents of the Freedmen's Bureau, most hoped to transform the South by creating new institutions based on northern models, especially free labor and free public schools. Few in number, transplanted northerners nonetheless took leading roles in state constitutional conventions and state legislatures. Some were also prominent advocates of economic modernization.

Southern Democrats reserved their greatest contempt for those they called **scalawags**, slang for someone unscrupulous and worthless. Scalawags were white southerners who became Republicans. They included many southern Unionists, who had opposed secession, and others who thought the Republicans offered the best hope for economic recovery. Scalawags included merchants, artisans, and professionals who favored a modernized South. Others were small-scale farmers who saw Reconstruction as a way to end political domination by the plantation owners.

The freedmen, carpetbaggers, and scalawags who made up the Republican Party in the South hoped to inject new ideas into that region. They tried to modernize state and local governments and make the postwar South more like the North. They repealed outdated laws and established or expanded schools, hospitals, orphanages, and penitentiaries.

---

carpetbagger   Derogatory term for the northerners who came to the South after the Civil War to take part in Reconstruction.

scalawag   Derogatory term for white southerners who aligned themselves with the Republican Party during Reconstruction.

Creating Public Education, Fighting Discrimination, and Building Railroads

Free public education was perhaps the most enduring legacy of Black Reconstruction. Reconstruction constitutions throughout the South required tax-supported public schools. Implementation, however, was expensive and proceeded slowly. By the mid-1870s, only half of southern children attended public schools.

In creating public schools, Reconstruction state governments faced a central question: would white and black children attend the same schools? Many African Americans favored racially integrated schools. Southern white leaders, including many southern white Republicans, argued that integration would destroy the fledgling public school system by driving whites away. In consequence, no state required school integration. Similarly, southern states set up separate black normal schools (to train schoolteachers) and colleges.

On balance, most blacks probably agreed with Frederick Douglass that separate schools were "infinitely superior" to no public education at all. Some found other reasons to accept segregated schools—separate black schools gave a larger role to black parents, and they hired black teachers.

Creating and operating two educational systems, one white and one black, was costly, and funds were always limited. Black schools almost always received fewer dollars per student than white schools. Despite their accomplishments, the segregated schools institutionalized discrimination.

Reconstruction state governments moved toward protection of equal rights in other areas. Southern Republicans often wrote into their new state constitutions prohibitions against discrimination and protections for civil rights. Some Reconstruction state governments enacted laws guaranteeing **equal access** to public transportation and public accommodations. Elsewhere, efforts to pass equal access laws foundered on the opposition of southern white Republicans, who often joined Democrats to favor **segregation**. Such conflicts pointed up the internal divisions within the southern Republican Party. Even when equal access laws were passed, they were often not enforced.

Republicans everywhere sought to use government to encourage economic growth and development. Promoting economic development—North, South, and West—often meant encouraging railroad construction. In the South, as elsewhere, some state governments granted land to railroads, or lent them money, or committed the state's credit to **underwrite** bonds for construction. Sometimes they promoted railroads without planning adequately or determining whether companies were financially sound. Some railroad projects failed as companies squandered funds without building rail lines. During the

equal access The right of any person to make use of a public facility, such as streetcars, as freely as any other person.

segregation Separation on account of race or class from the rest of society, such as the separation of blacks from whites in most southern school systems.

underwrite To assume financial responsibility for; here, to guarantee the purchase of bonds so that a project can go forward.

1870s, only seven thousand miles of new track were laid in the South, compared with forty-five thousand miles elsewhere in the nation. Even that was a considerable accomplishment for the South, given its dismal economic situation.

Railroad companies sometimes sought favorable treatment by bribing public officials. All too many officeholders—South, North, and West—accepted their offers. Given the excessive favoritism that most public officials showed to railroads, revelations and allegations of corruption became common from New York City to Mississippi to California.

Southern politics proved especially ripe for corruption as government responsibilities expanded rapidly and created new opportunities for scoundrels. Too many Reconstruction officials—white and black—saw politics as a way to improve their own finances. One South Carolina legislator bluntly described his attitude toward electing a U.S. senator: "I was pretty hard up, and I did not care who the candidate was if I got two hundred dollars." Corruption was usually nonpartisan, but it seemed more prominent among Republicans because they held the most important offices.

THE END OF RECONSTRUCTION

From the beginning, most white southerners resisted the new order that the conquering Yankees imposed on them. Initially, resistance took the form of black codes and the Klan. Later, some southern opponents of Reconstruction developed new strategies, but terror remained an important instrument of resistance.

The "New Departure" and the 1872 Presidential Election   By 1869, some leading southern Democrats had abandoned their resistance to change, deciding instead to accept some Reconstruction measures and African American suffrage. At the same time, they also tried to secure restoration of political rights for former Confederates. Behind this **New Departure** for southern Democrats lay the belief that continued resistance would only cause more regional turmoil and prolong federal intervention.

Sometimes southern Democrats supported conservative Republicans for state and local offices instead of members of their own party, hoping to defuse concern in Washington and dilute Radical influence in state government. This strategy appeared first in Virginia, where William Mahone, a former Confederate general, railroad promoter, and leading Democrat, forged a broad political **coalition** that accepted black suffrage. In 1869 Mahone's organization elected

---

coalition   An alliance, especially a temporary one of different people or groups.

as governor a northern-born banker and moderate Republican. Mahone got state support for his railroad plans, and Virginia avoided Radical Republican rule.

Coalitions of Democrats and moderate Republicans won in Tennessee in 1869 and in Missouri in 1870. Elsewhere leading Democrats also accepted black suffrage but attacked Republicans for raising taxes, increasing state spending, and corruption. Such campaigns brought a positive response from many taxpayers because southern tax rates had risen significantly to support the new schools, railroad subsidies, and other modernizing programs. The victories of several so-called **Redeemers** and New Departure Democrats in the early 1870s also coincided with renewed terrorist activity aimed at Republicans. The worst single incident occurred in 1873. A group of armed freedmen fortified the town of Colfax, Louisiana, to hold off Democrats who were planning to seize the county government. After a three-week siege, well-armed whites overcame the black defenders and killed 280 African Americans. Leading Democrats rarely endorsed such bloodshed, but they reaped political advantages from it.

The New Departure movement coincided with a nationwide division within the Republican Party. The Liberal Republican movement attracted moderates, concerned that the Radicals had gone too far. Others opposed Grant on issues unrelated to Reconstruction, especially growing evidence of corruption.

Horace Greeley, editor of the *New York Daily Tribune,* won the Liberal nomination for president in 1872. An opponent of slavery before the Civil War, Greeley had given strong support to the Fourteenth and Fifteenth Amendments. But he had sometimes taken puzzling positions, including a willingness to let the South secede. His unkempt appearance and whining voice conveyed little of a presidential image. One political observer described him as "honest, but ... conceited, fussy, and foolish." Greeley had long ripped the Democrats in his newspaper columns, but the Democrats nonetheless nominated him in an effort to defeat Grant. Grant won convincingly, carrying 56 percent of the vote and winning every northern state and ten of the sixteen southern and border states.

The Politics of Terror: The "Mississippi Plan"

By 1872, nearly all southern whites had abandoned the Republicans, and Black Reconstruction had ended in several states. African Americans, however, maintained their Republican loyalties. As Democrats worked to unite all southern whites behind their banner of white supremacy, the South polarized politically along racial lines. Elections in 1874 proved disastrous for Republicans: Democrats won more than two-thirds of the South's seats in the House of Representatives and "redeemed" several more states.

Terrorism against black Republicans and their remaining white allies played a role in some Democratic victories in 1874. Where the Klan had worn disguises and ridden at night, by 1874 Democrats often formed rifle companies, put on red-flannel shirts, and marched and drilled in public. In some areas, armed whites prevented African Americans from voting or terrorized prominent Republicans, especially African American Republicans.

Republicans in 1874 also lost support in the North because of scandals within the Grant administration and because a major economic **depression** that had begun in 1873 was producing high unemployment. In the 1874 elections, Democrats won control of the House of Representatives for the first time since the 1850s and could block any new Reconstruction proposals.

During 1875 in Mississippi, political violence reached such levels that the use of terror to overthrow Reconstruction became known as the **Mississippi Plan**. Democratic rifle clubs broke up Republican meetings and attacked Republican leaders. One black Mississippian described the election as "the most violent time we have ever seen." When Mississippi's carpetbagger governor, Adelbert Ames, requested federal help, President Grant declined. Grant feared that the southern Reconstruction governments had become so discredited that further federal military intervention might endanger the election prospects of Republican candidates in the North.

The Democrats swept the Mississippi elections, winning four-fifths of the state legislature. When the legislature convened, it impeached and removed from office Alexander Davis, the black Republican lieutenant governor, on grounds no more serious than those brought against Andrew Johnson. Facing similar action, Governor Ames resigned and left the state. Ames had foreseen the result during the campaign when he wrote, "A revolution has taken place— by force of arms."

The Troubled Presidential Election of 1876   In 1876, on the centennial of American independence, the nation stumbled through a deeply troubled—and potentially dangerous—presidential election. As revelations of corruption in the Grant administration multiplied, both parties sought candidates known for their integrity. The Democrats nominated Samuel J. Tilden, governor of New York, who had fought political corruption in New York City. The Republicans selected **Rutherford B. Hayes**, a Civil War general and governor of Ohio, who was virtually unknown outside his home state. During the campaign in the South, intimidation of Republicans, both black and white, continued in many places.

The first election reports indicated a victory for Tilden. In addition to the border states and South, he also carried New York, New Jersey, and Indiana. Tilden received 51 percent of the popular vote versus 48 percent for Hayes.

State Republican officials still controlled the counting and reporting of ballots in South Carolina, Florida, and Louisiana, and those three states could change

---

depression   A period of economic contraction, characterized by decreasing business activity, falling prices, and high unemployment.

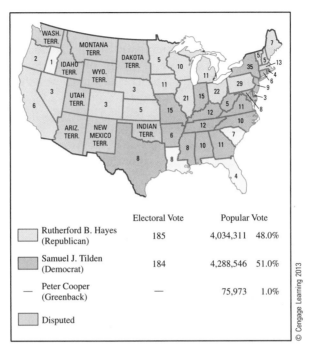

	Electoral Vote	Popular Vote	
Rutherford B. Hayes (Republican)	185	4,034,311	48.0%
Samuel J. Tilden (Democrat)	184	4,288,546	51.0%
Peter Cooper (Greenback)	—	75,973	1.0%
Disputed			

MAP 15.2 The Disputed Election of 1876

Congress resolved the contested electoral vote of 1876 in favor of Republican Rutherford B. Hayes.

the Electoral College majority from Tilden to Hayes. Charging voting fraud, Republican election boards in those states rejected enough ballots so that the official count gave Hayes narrow majorities and thus a one-vote margin of victory in the Electoral College. Crying fraud in return, Democratic officials in those states submitted their own versions of the vote count. Angry Democrats vowed to see Tilden inaugurated, by force if necessary. Some Democratic newspapers ran headlines that read "Tilden or War."

For the first time, Congress faced the problem of disputed electoral votes that could decide the outcome of an election. To resolve the challenges, Congress created a commission of five senators, five representatives, and five Supreme Court justices. The Republicans had a one-vote majority on the commission.

As commission hearings droned on through January and into February 1877, informal discussions took place among leading Republicans and Democrats. The result has often been called the **Compromise of 1877**.

Southern Democrats demanded an end to federal intervention in southern politics but insisted on federal subsidies for railroad construction and waterways in the South. And they wanted one of their own as postmaster general because that office held the key to most federal patronage. In return, southern Democrats seemed willing to abandon Tilden's claim to the White House. The

Compromise of 1877, however, was never set down in one place or agreed to by all parties.

By a straight party vote, the commission confirmed the election of Hayes. Soon after his inauguration, the new president ordered the last of the federal troops withdrawn from the South. The era of a powerful federal government pledged to protect "equality before the law" for all citizens was over. The last three Republican state governments fell in 1877, giving the Democrats, the self-described party of white supremacy, control in every southern state. One Radical journal bitterly concluded that African Americans had been forced "to relinquish the artificial right to vote for the natural right to live." In parts of the South thereafter, election fraud and violence became routine. A Mississippi judge acknowledged in 1890 that "since 1875 ... we have been preserving the ascendancy of the white people by ... stuffing ballot boxes, committing perjury and here and there in the state carrying the elections by fraud and violence."

Reconstruction was over. The Civil War was more than ten years in the past. Many moderate Republicans had hoped that the Fourteenth and Fifteenth Amendments and the Civil Rights Act would guarantee black rights without a continuing federal presence in the South. Southern Democrats persistently argued—on paltry evidence—that carpetbaggers and scalawags were all corrupt, that they manipulated black voters, that African American officeholders were ignorant and illiterate, and that southern Democrats wanted only honest self-government. The truth of the situation made little difference.

Northern Democrats had always opposed Reconstruction and readily adopted the southern Democrats' version of reality. Such portrayals found growing acceptance among other northerners too, for many had shown their own racial bias when they resisted black suffrage and kept their public schools segregated. In 1875, when Grant refused to use federal troops to protect black rights, he declared that "the whole public are tired out with these ... outbreaks in the South." He was quoted widely and with approval throughout the North. In addition, a major depression in the mid-1870s, unemployment and labor disputes, the growth of industry, the emergence of big business, and the development of the West focused the attention of many Americans, including many members of Congress, on economic issues.

Some Republicans, to be certain, kept the faith of their abolitionist and Radical forebears and hoped the federal government might again protect black rights. After 1877, however, though Republicans routinely condemned violations of black rights, few Republicans showed much interest in using federal power to prevent such outrages.

After Reconstruction   After 1877, southern Democrats moved to establish new systems of politics and race relations. Most Redeemers worked to reduce taxes, dismantle Reconstruction legislation and agencies, and eliminate meaningful black participation in politics. They also began the process of turning the South into a one-party region, a situation that reached its fullest development around 1900 and persisted until the 1950s and in some areas later.

Voting and officeholding by African Americans did not cease in 1877, but without federal enforcement of black rights, the threat of violence and the potential for economic retaliation by landlords and merchants sharply reduced meaningful political involvement by African Americans. Efforts to mobilize black voters posed dangers to candidates and voters, and many black political leaders concluded that their political survival depended on favors from influential white Republicans or even from Democratic leaders. The public schools survived, segregated and underfunded, but presenting an important opportunity. Many Reconstruction-era laws remained on the books. Until about 1890, many theaters, bars, restaurants, hotels, streetcars, and railroads continued to serve African Americans without discrimination. White supremacy had been established by force of arms, however, and blacks exercised their rights at the sufferance of the dominant whites.

After 1877, Reconstruction was held up as a failure. Although far from accurate, the southern whites' version of Reconstruction—that conniving carpetbaggers and scalawags had manipulated ignorant freedmen—appealed to many white Americans throughout the nation, and it gained widespread acceptance among many novelists, journalists, and historians. William A. Dunning endorsed that interpretation in his history of Reconstruction, published in 1907. Thomas Dixon's popular novel *The Clansman* (1905) inspired the highly influential film *The Birth of a Nation* (1915). Historically inaccurate and luridly racist, the book and the movie portrayed Ku Klux Klan members as heroes who rescued the white South, and especially white southern women, from domination and debauchery at the hands of depraved freedmen and carpetbaggers.

Against this pattern stood some of the first black historians, notably George Washington Williams, a Union army veteran whose two-volume history of African Americans appeared in 1882. *Black Reconstruction in America,* by W. E. B. Du Bois, appeared in 1935. Both presented fully the role of African Americans in Reconstruction and pointed to the accomplishments of the Reconstruction state governments and black leaders. Not until the 1950s and 1960s, however, did large numbers of American historians begin to reconsider their interpretations of Reconstruction. Historians today recognize that Reconstruction was not the failure that had earlier been claimed. The creation of public schools was the most important of the changes in southern life produced by the Reconstruction state governments. At a federal level, the Fourteenth and Fifteenth Amendments eventually provided the constitutional leverage to restore the principle of equality before the law that so concerned the Radicals. Historians also recognize that Reconstruction collapsed partly because of internal flaws, partly because of divisions within the Republican Party, and partly because of the political terrorism unleashed in the South and the refusal of the North to commit the force required to protect the constitutional rights of African Americans.

STUDY TOOLS

SUMMARY

At the end of the Civil War, the nation faced difficult choices regarding the restoration of the defeated South and the future of the freed people. Committed to ending slavery, President Lincoln nevertheless chose a lenient approach to restoring states to the Union, partly to persuade southerners to abandon the Confederacy and accept emancipation. When Johnson became president, he continued Lincoln's approach.

The end of slavery brought new opportunities for African Americans, whether or not they had been slaves. Taking advantage of the opportunities that freedom opened, they tried to create independent lives for themselves, and they developed social institutions that helped to define black communities. Because few managed to acquire land of their own, most became either sharecroppers or wage laborers. White southerners also experienced economic dislocation, and many also became sharecroppers. Most white southerners expected to keep African Americans in a subordinate role and initially used black codes and violence toward that end.

In reaction against the black codes and violence, Congress took control of Reconstruction and passed the Civil Rights Act of 1866, the Fourteenth Amendment, and the Reconstruction Acts of 1867. An attempt to remove Johnson from the presidency was unsuccessful. Additional federal Reconstruction measures included the Fifteenth Amendment, laws against the Ku Klux Klan, and the Civil Rights Act of 1875. Several of these measures strengthened the federal government at the expense of the states.

Enfranchised freedmen, white and black northerners who moved to the South, and some southern whites created a southern Republican Party that governed most southern states for a time. The most lasting contribution of these state governments was the creation of public school systems. Like government officials elsewhere, however, some southern politicians fell prey to corruption.

In the late 1860s, many southern Democrats chose a "New Departure": they grudgingly accepted some features of Reconstruction and sought to recapture control of state governments. By the mid-1870s, however, southern politics turned almost solely on race. The 1876 presidential election was very close and hotly disputed. In the end, Hayes took office and ended Reconstruction. Without federal protection for their civil rights, African Americans faced terrorism, violence, and even death if they challenged their subordinate role. With the end of Reconstruction, the South entered an era of white supremacy in politics and government, the economy, and social relations.

CHRONOLOGY

RECONSTRUCTION	
1863	Emancipation Proclamation
1864	Lincoln reelected
1865	Freedmen's Bureau created
	Civil War ends

	Andrew Johnson becomes president Thirteenth Amendment (abolishing slavery) ratified
1866	Ku Klux Klan formed Congress takes control over Reconstruction
1867	Military Reconstruction Act
1868	Impeachment and acquittal of President Johnson Fourteenth Amendment (defining citizenship) ratified Grant elected president
1869–1870	Victories of "New Departure" Democrats in some southern states
1870	Fifteenth Amendment (guaranteeing voting rights) ratified
1870–1871	Ku Klux Klan Acts
1872	Grant reelected
1875	Civil Rights Act of 1875 Mississippi Plan ends Reconstruction in Mississippi
1876	Disputed presidential election
1877	Compromise of 1877; Hayes becomes president End of Reconstruction

Focus Questions

If you have mastered this chapter, you should be able to answer these questions and explain the terms that follow the questions.

1. What did Presidents Lincoln and Johnson seek to accomplish for the South? How did white southerners respond to those efforts?
2. What seem to have been the leading objectives among freed people as they explored their new opportunities?
3. How do the differing responses of freed people and southern whites show different understandings of the significance of emancipation?
4. Why did congressional Republicans take control over Reconstruction policy? How successful were they?
5. How did the Fourteenth and Fifteenth Amendments change the nature of the federal union?
6. What major groups made up the Republican Party in the South during Reconstruction? Compare their reasons for being Republicans, their relative size, and their objectives.
7. What were the most lasting results of the Republican state administrations?
8. What major factors brought about the end of Reconstruction? Evaluate their relative significance.
9. Many historians began to reevaluate their understanding of Reconstruction during the 1950s and 1960s. Why do you suppose that happened?

KEY TERMS

Reconstruction (*p.* 417)

Abraham Lincoln (*p.* 417)

Frederick Douglass (*p.* 418)

Radical Republicans (*p.* 418)

Thirteenth Amendment (*p.* 421)

Andrew Johnson (*p.* 421)

Freedmen's Bureau (*p.* 423)

Ku Klux Klan (*p.* 428)

Fourteenth Amendment (*p.* 430)

Elizabeth Cady Stanton (*p.* 431)

Susan B. Anthony (*p.* 431)

Fifteenth Amendment (*p.* 435)

Civil Rights Act of 1875 (*p.* 437)

Black Reconstruction (*p.* 437)

New Departure (*p.* 440)

Redeemers (*p.* 441)

Mississippi Plan (*p.* 442)

Rutherford B. Hayes (*p.* 442)

Compromise of 1877 (*p.* 443)

16

THE NATION INDUSTRIALIZES, 1865–1900

FOUNDATION FOR INDUSTRIALIZATION

By 1865, conditions in the United States were ripe for rapid industrialization. A wealth of natural resources, a capable work force, an agricultural base that produced enough food for a large urban population, and favorable governmental policies combined to lay the foundation.

Resources, Skills, Capital, and New Federal Policies   At the end of the Civil War, **entrepreneurs** could draw on vast and virtually untapped natural resources. Americans had long since plowed the fertile farmland of the Midwest (where corn and wheat dominated) and the South (where cotton was king). They had just begun to farm the rich soils of Minnesota, Nebraska, Kansas, Iowa, and the Dakotas, as well as the productive valleys of California and Oregon. Through the central part of the nation stretched vast grasslands that received too little rain for most farming but were well suited for grazing. The Pacific Northwest, the western Great Lakes region, and the South all held extensive forests untouched by the lumberman's saw.

entrepreneur   A person who takes on the risks of creating, organizing, and managing a business enterprise.

449

The nation was also rich in mineral resources. Before the Civil War, the iron **industry** had developed in Pennsylvania as a result of easy access to iron ore and coal. Pennsylvania was also the site of early efforts to tap underground pools of crude oil. The California gold rush, beginning in 1848, had drawn many people west, and some of them found great riches. At the end of the war, other minerals lay unused or undiscovered across the country, including iron ore, coal, oil, gold and silver, and copper. Many of these natural resources were far from population centers, and their use awaited adequate transportation facilities. Exploitation of some of these resources also required new technologies.

A skilled and experienced work force was also essential for economic growth. In the 1790s and early nineteenth century, New Englanders had developed manufacturing systems based on **interchangeable parts** (first used for guns and clocks) and factories for cotton cloth. These accomplishments gave them a reputation for "Yankee ingenuity"—a talent for devising new tools and inventive methods. Such skills and problem-solving abilities were not limited to New England—they were key ingredients in nearly all large-scale manufacturing because early factories usually relied on skilled **artisans** to supervise less-skilled workers in assembling products. Some of the early artisans and factory owners came from Great Britain, the world's first industrial nation.

Another crucial element for industrialization was capital. Before the Civil War, capital became centered in the seaport cities of the Northeast—Boston, New York, and Philadelphia, especially—where prosperous merchants invested their profits in banks and factories. Banks were important instruments for mobilizing capital. Before the war, some bankers had begun to specialize in arranging financing for large-scale enterprises, and some had opened offices in Britain to tap sources of capital there. **Stock exchanges** had also developed long before the Civil War as important institutions for raising capital for new ventures.

Still another important element for rapid economic development was favorable governmental policies. When Republicans took command of the federal government in 1861, they were immediately faced with the need to wage war against the Confederacy. At the same time, however, they forged new policies to stimulate economic growth, beginning with a new **protective tariff** in 1861. The tariff increased the price of imports to equal or exceed the price of American-made goods, thereby protecting domestic products from foreign competition and

---

industry A basic unit of business activity in which the various participants do similar activities; for example, the railroad industry consists of railroad companies and the firms and factories that supply their equipment.

interchangeable parts Identical mechanical parts that can be substituted for one another.

artisan A skilled worker, whether self-employed or working for wages.

stock exchange A place where people buy and sell stocks (shares in the ownership of companies); stockholders may participate in election of the company's directors and share in the company's profits.

protective tariff A tax placed on imported goods for the purpose of raising the price of imports as high as or higher than the prices of the same item produced within the nation.

encouraging investment in manufacturing. Tariff rates changed periodically, but the protective tariff remained central to federal economic policy for more than a half-century.

New federal land policies also stimulated economic growth. At the beginning of the Civil War, the federal government claimed a billion acres of land as federal property—the **public domain**—half of the land area of the nation. Republicans used the public domain to encourage economic development in several ways. The **Homestead Act** (1862) provided that any person could receive free as much as 160 acres (a quarter of a square mile) of government land by building a house, living on the land for five years, and farming it. The **Land-Grant College Act** (1862)—often called the Morrill Act for its sponsor, Senator Justin Morrill of Vermont—gave land to each state to fund a public university, which was required to provide education in engineering and agriculture and to train military officers. Also in 1862, Congress approved land grants for the first transcontinental railroad, and more land grants to railroads followed.

The Transformation of Agriculture

The expanding economy rested on a highly productive agricultural base. Improved transportation—canals early in the nineteenth century and railroads later—speeded the expansion of agriculture by making it possible to move agricultural produce over long distances. Up to the Civil War, farmers had developed 407 million acres into productive farmland. During the next forty years, this figure more than doubled, to 841 million acres.

The federal government contributed to the rapid settlement of Kansas, Nebraska, the Dakotas, and Minnesota through the Homestead Act. Between 1862 and 1890, 48 million acres passed from government ownership to private hands in this way. Other federally owned land could be purchased for as little as $1.25 per acre, and much more was obtained at this bargain price than was acquired free under the Homestead Act.

Production of leading commercial crops increased especially rapidly. When the total number of acres in farmland doubled, the number of acres planted in corn, wheat, and cotton more than tripled. New farming methods increased harvests even more—corn by 264 percent, wheat by 252 percent, and cotton by 383 percent. Through these years, farm output grew more than twice as much as the population.

As production of major crops rose, prices for them fell. Figure 16.1 shows the prices for wheat, corn, and cotton—the most significant commercial crops. Though several factors contributed to this decline in farm prices, the most obvious was that supply outpaced demand. Production increased more rapidly than the population (which determined the demand within the nation) and the demand from other countries. When American farmers received less for their crops, they often raised

public domain Land claimed by the federal government.

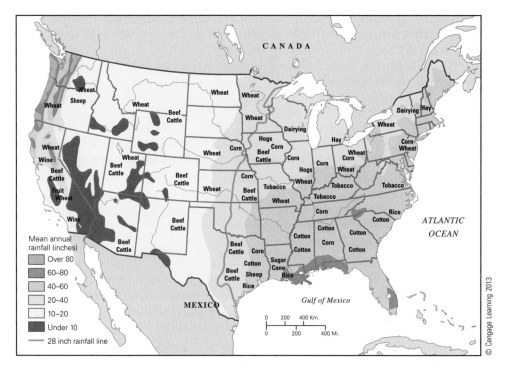

MAP 16.1 Agricultural Regions of the United States, 1890

In the Pacific Northwest and east of the twenty-eight-inch-rainfall line, farmers could grow a greater variety of crops. Territory west of the line was either too mountainous or too arid to support agriculture without irrigation. The grasslands that once fed buffalo herds could now feed beef cattle.

more in an effort to maintain the same level of income. To increase their harvests, they bought fertilizers and elaborate machinery. Between 1870 and 1890, the amount of fertilizer consumed in the nation more than quadrupled. And the more the farmers raised, the lower prices fell—and with them, the economic well-being of many farmers.

New machinery greatly increased the amount of land one person could farm. A single farmer with a hand-held scythe and cradle could harvest 2 acres of wheat in a day. Using the McCormick reaper (first produced in 1849), a single farmer and a team of horses could harvest 2 acres in an hour. For other crops too, a person with modern machinery could farm two or three times as much land as a farmer fifty years before.

Agricultural expansion also stimulated the farm equipment industry and, in turn, the iron and steel industry. Agricultural exports—cotton, tobacco, wheat, meat—spurred oceanic shipping and shipbuilding, and increased shipbuilding meant a greater demand for iron and steel. Railroads played a crucial role in the expansion and commercialization of agriculture by carrying farm products to

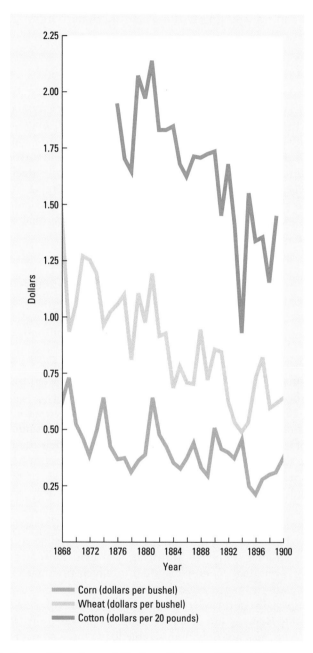

FIGURE 16.1 Corn, Wheat, and Cotton Prices, 1868–1900

From the late 1860s through the end of the century, prices for major crops fell. This graph shows the year-to-year fluctuations in prices and the general downward trend in prices for major crops.

Source: U.S. Department of Commerce, Bureau of the Census, *Historical Statistics of the United States, Colonial Times to 1970*, Bicentennial edition, 2 vols. (Washington: Government Printing Office, 1975), I: 510–512, 517–518.

distant markets and transporting fertilizer and machinery from factories to farming regions.

THE DAWN OF BIG BUSINESS

To many Americans of the late nineteenth century, nothing symbolized economic growth so effectively as a locomotive—a huge, powerful, noisy, smoke-belching machine barreling forward. Railroads set much of the pace for economic expansion after the Civil War. Growth of the rail network stimulated industries that supplied materials for railroad construction and operation—especially steel and coal—and industries that relied on railroads to connect them to the emerging national economy. Railroad companies also came to symbolize "big business"—companies of great size, employing thousands of workers, operating over large geographic areas—and some Americans began to fear their power.

Railroads: The First Big Business

Before the Civil War, much of the nation's commerce moved on water—on rivers, canals, and coastal waterways. At the end of the Civil War, the nation still lacked a comprehensive national transportation network. Railroads clearly had that potential, but railway companies operated on tracks of varying **gauges**, which made the transfer of railcars from one line to another impossible. Few railway bridges crossed major rivers. Until 1869, no railroad connected the eastern half of the country to the booming Pacific Coast region.

By the mid-1880s, all the elements were in place for a national rail network. The first transcontinental rail line was completed in 1869, connecting California to Omaha, Nebraska, and ultimately to eastern cities. Within the next twenty-five years, four more rail lines linked the Pacific Coast to the eastern half of the nation. Between 1865 and 1890, railroads grew from 35,000 miles of track to 167,000 miles. By the mid-1880s, major rivers had been bridged. Companies had replaced iron rails with steel ones, allowing them to haul heavier loads. New inventions increased the speed, carrying capacity, and efficiency of trains. In 1886 the last major lines converted to a standard gauge, making it possible to transfer railcars from one line to another simply by throwing a switch. Entrepreneurs could now think in terms of a national economic system in which raw materials and finished products moved easily from one region to another.

Railroads, especially in the West, expanded with generous governmental assistance. In the **Pacific Railway Act** of 1862, Congress provided the Union Pacific and Central Pacific companies not only with sizable loans but also with 10 square miles of the public domain for every mile of track laid—an amount doubled in 1864. By 1871, Congress had authorized some seventy railroad land grants, involving 128 million acres—more than one-tenth of the public domain, approximately equal

---

gauge   In this usage, the distance between the two rails making up railroad tracks.

to Colorado and Wyoming together—though not all companies qualified to claim their entire grants. Most railroads sold their land to raise capital for railroad operations. By encouraging farmers, businesses, or organizations to develop the land, railroad companies tried to build up the economies along their tracks and thereby to boost the demand for their freight trains to haul supplies to new settlers and carry settlers' products (wheat, cattle, lumber, ore) to market.

The expansion of railroads created the potential for a nationwide market, stimulated the economic development of the West, and created a demand for iron, steel, locomotives, and similar products. Railroad companies also provided an organizational model for newly developing industrial enterprises.

Because they spanned such great distances and managed so many employees and so much equipment, railroads encountered problems of scale that few companies had faced before but that other industrial entrepreneurs soon had to address. Railroad companies also required a much higher degree of coordination and long-range planning than most previous businesses. Earlier companies typically operated at a single location, but railroads functioned over long distances and at multiple sites. They had to keep up numerous maintenance and repair facilities and maintain many stations to receive and discharge freight and passengers. Financial transactions carried on over hundreds of miles by scores of employees required a centralized accounting office. One result was development of a company bureaucracy of clerks, accountants, managers, and agents. Railroads became training grounds for administrators, some of whom later entered other industries. Indeed, the experience of the railroads was central in defining the subject of business administration when it began to be taught in colleges at the turn of the century.

Railroads faced higher **fixed costs** than most previous companies. These costs included payments on debts and the expense of maintaining and protecting far-flung equipment and property. To pay their fixed costs and keep profits high, railroad companies tried to operate at full capacity whenever possible. Doing so, however, often proved difficult. Where two or more lines competed for the same traffic, one might choose to cut rates in an effort to lure business from the other. But if the other company responded with cuts in its rates, neither stood to gain significantly more business, and both took in less income. Competition between railroad companies sometimes became so intense that no line could show a profit.

Some railroad operators chose to defuse intense competition by forming a **pool**. In a pool, the railroads agreed to divide the existing business among themselves and not to compete on rates. The most famous was the Iowa Pool, made up of railroads running between Chicago and Omaha, across Iowa. Formed in 1870, the

fixed costs Costs that a company must pay even if it closes down all its operations—for example, interest on loans, debt payments, and property taxes.

pool An agreement among businesses in the same industry to divide up the market and charge equal prices instead of competing; another name for a cartel.

Iowa Pool operated until 1874, and some pooling continued until the mid-1880s. Few pools lasted very long. Often one or more pool members tired of a restricted market share and broke the pool arrangement in an effort to expand, thereby setting off a new price war. When a pooling arrangement became known, it brought loud complaints from customers, who concluded that they paid higher rates because of the pool.

To compete more effectively, railroads adjusted their rates to attract companies that did a great deal of shipping. Such favored customers sometimes received a rebate. Large shipments sent over long distances cost the railroad companies less per mile than small shipments sent over short distances, so companies developed different rate structures for long hauls and short hauls. Thus the largest shippers, with the power to secure rebates and low rates, could often ship more cheaply than small businesses and individual farmers. Railroad companies defended the differences on the basis of differences in costs, but small shippers who paid high prices saw themselves as victims of rate discrimination.

Railroads viewed state and federal governments as sources of valuable subsidies. At the same time, they constantly guarded against efforts by their customers to use government to restrict or regulate their enterprises—by outlawing rate discrimination, for example. Companies sometimes campaigned openly to secure the election of friendly representatives and senators and to defeat unfriendly candidates. They maintained well-organized operations to **lobby** public officials in Washington, D.C., and in state capitals. Most railroad companies issued free passes to public officials—a practice that reformers attacked as bribery. Some railroads won reputations as the most influential political power in entire states—the Southern Pacific in California, for example, or the Santa Fe in Kansas.

Stories of railroad officials bribing politicians became commonplace after the Civil War. The Crédit Mobilier scandal (discussed in Chapter 18) touched some of the most influential members of Congress in the 1870s. A decade later, Collis P. Huntington of the Southern Pacific Railroad candidly explained his expectations regarding public officials: "If you have to pay money to have the right thing done, it is only just and fair to do it." For Huntington, "the right thing" meant favorable treatment for his company.

Politically powerful or not, railroads produced significant change. Between 1850 and 1880, railroads transformed Chicago from a town of 30,000 residents to the nation's fourth-largest city, with a half-million people. By 1890, it was second only to New York in population, and in 1900 it claimed 1.7 million people. Thanks in part to local promoters and in part to geography, Chicago emerged as the rail center not just of the Midwest but of much of the nation. By 1880, more than twenty railroad lines and 15,000 miles of tracks connected Chicago with nearly all of the United States and much of Canada. The boom in railroad construction during the 1880s only reinforced the city's prominence. Entrepreneurs in manufacturing and commerce soon developed new enterprises based on Chicago's unrivaled location at the hub of a great transportation network.

lobby   To try to influence the thinking of public officials for or against a specific cause.

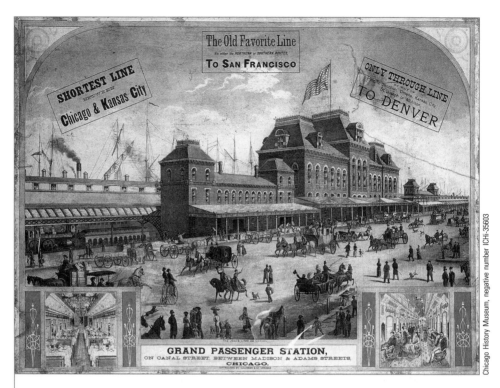

The Old Favorite Line
Via either the NORTHERN or SOUTHERN ROUTES.
TO SAN FRANCISCO

SHORTEST LINE
BETWEEN
Chicago & Kansas City

ONLY THROUGH LINE
TO DENVER

GRAND PASSENGER STATION,
ON CANAL STREET, BETWEEN MADISON & ADAMS STREETS,
CHICAGO.

Chicago was perhaps the most important single center for the nation's rail traffic in the late nineteenth century. This lithograph shows Chicago's Grand Passenger Station in 1880 and advertises some of the many rail connections possible through this station—to Kansas City, Denver, and San Francisco. Note also the many forms of street transportation in front of the station, including a coach, several varieties of carriages, and bicycles.

Chicago's rail connections made it the logical center for the new business of **mail-order sales.** Central location and rail connections also made Chicago a major manufacturing center. By the 1880s, Chicago's factories produced more farm equipment than those of any other city, and its iron and steel production rivaled that of Pittsburgh. Other leading Chicago industries produced railway cars and equipment, metal products, a wide variety of machinery, and clothing. The city also claimed the title of the world's largest grain market.

Location and rail lines made Chicago the nation's largest center for **meatpacking.** Livestock from across the Midwest and from as far as southern Texas was unloaded in Chicago's Union Stockyards—over 400 acres of railroad sidings, chutes, and pens filled with cattle, hogs, and sheep. Huge slaughterhouses flanking the stockyards

meatpacking   The business of slaughtering animals and preparing their meat for sale as food.

received a steady stream of live animals and disgorged an equally steady stream of fresh, canned, and processed meat. The development in the 1870s of refrigeration for railroad cars and ships permitted fresh meat to be sent throughout the nation and to Europe.

Railroads, Investment Bankers, and "Morganization"

Railroads expanded significantly in the 1880s, but some lines earned little profit. Some traversed sparsely populated areas of the West. Others spread into areas already saturated by rail service. In the 1880s, a few ambitious, talented, and occasionally unscrupulous railway executives maneuvered to produce great regional railway systems. The Santa Fe and the Southern Pacific, for example, came to dominate the Southwest, and the Great Northern and the Northern Pacific held sway in the Northwest. The Pennsylvania and the New York Central controlled much of the shipping in the Northeast. By consolidating lines within a region, railway executives tried to create more efficient systems with less duplication, fewer price wars, and more dependable profits.

Railroads required far more capital than most manufacturing concerns. Even railroads that received government subsidies required large amounts of private capital. The railroads' huge appetite for capital made them the first American businesses to seek investors on a nationwide and international scale. Those who invested their money could choose to buy either stocks or **bonds**. Sales of railroad stocks provided the major activity for the New York Stock Exchange through the second half of the nineteenth century.

To raise the enormous amount of capital necessary for construction and consolidation, railroad executives turned increasingly to **investment banks**. By the late 1880s, **John Pierpont Morgan** had emerged as the nation's leading investment banker. Born in Connecticut in 1837, he was the son of a successful merchant who turned to banking. After schooling in Switzerland and Germany, young Morgan began working in his father's bank in London. In 1857 he moved to New York, where his father had arranged a banking position for him.

Morgan's experience and growing stature in banking gave him access to capital within the United States and abroad, in London and Paris. His investors wanted to put their money where it would be safe and give them a reliable **return**. Morgan therefore tried to stabilize the railroad business, especially the cutthroat rate competition that often resulted when several companies served one market.

---

bonds   A certificate of debt issued by a government or corporation guaranteeing payment of the original investment plus interest at a specified future date.

investment bank   An institution that acts as an agent for corporations issuing stocks and bonds.

return   The yield on money that has been invested in an enterprise. Today, companies typically pay a dividend (a proportionate share of the profits) to their stockholders each quarter.

Railroad companies that turned to Morgan for help in raising capital found that Morgan wanted a say in their management. He insisted that companies seeking his help reorganize to simplify corporate structures and to combine small lines into larger, centrally controlled systems. He often demanded a seat on the board of directors as well, to guard against risky decisions in the future. Some began to refer to this process as "Morganization," and "Morganized" lines soon included some of the largest in the country. A few other investment bankers followed similar patterns.

Andrew Carnegie and the Age of Steel   The new, industrial economy rode on a network of steel rails, propelled by locomotives made of steel. Steel plows broke the tough sod of the western prairies. Skyscrapers, which first appeared in Chicago in 1885, relied on steel frames as they boldly shaped urban skylines. Steel, a relative latecomer to the industrial revolution, defined the age.

Made by combining carbon and molten iron and then burning out impurities, steel has greater strength, resilience, and durability than iron. This superior metal was difficult and expensive to make until the 1850s, when Henry Bessemer in England and William Kelly in Kentucky independently discovered ways to make steel in large quantities at a reasonable cost. Even so, the first Bessemer or Kelly process plants did not begin production in the United States until 1864. In that year, the entire nation produced only 10,000 tons of steel.

In 1875, just south of Pittsburgh, Pennsylvania, **Andrew Carnegie** drew upon a loan from J. P. Morgan's father's bank to construct the nation's largest steel plant, employing 1,500 workers. From then until 1901 (when the plant had grown to more than eight thousand workers), Carnegie held the central place in the steel industry. Born in Scotland in 1835, Carnegie and his penniless parents came to the United States in 1848. Young Andrew worked first in a textile mill, then as a messenger in a telegraph office. He soon became a telegraph operator, then the personal telegrapher for a high official of the Pennsylvania Railroad. Carnegie rose rapidly within that company and became a superintendent (a high management position) at the age of 25. At the end of the Civil War, he devoted his full attention to the iron and steel industry, in which he had previously invested money. He quickly applied to his own companies the management lessons he had learned with the railroad.

Carnegie's basic rule was "Cut the prices; scoop the market; run the mills full." An aggressive competitor, he repeatedly cut costs so that he might show a profit while charging less than his rivals. He usually chose to undersell competitors rather than cooperate with them. In 1864, steel rails sold for $126 per ton; by 1875, Carnegie was selling them for $69 per ton. Driven by improved technology and Carnegie's competitiveness, steel prices fell to $29 a ton in 1885 and less than $20 a ton in the late 1890s. Carnegie was the largest steel manufacturer in the United States, though his company accounted for only a quarter of the nation's production. By 1900, the nation produced nearly 10 million tons of steel each year, more than any other nation.

Carnegie's company was larger and more complex than any manufacturing enterprise in pre–Civil War America. In its own day, however, other companies operated plants that were as complex, and several challenged it in size. By 1880, five steel companies had more than 1,500 employees, as did several textile mills and a locomotive factory. The size of such operations continued to grow. In 1900 the three largest steel plants each employed 8,000 to 10,000 workers, and seventy other factories employed more than 2,000, producing everything from watches to locomotives, from cotton cloth to processed meat.

Carnegie and other entrepreneurs transformed the organizational structure of manufacturing. They often joined a range of operations formerly conducted by separate businesses—acquisition of raw materials, processing, distribution of finished goods—into one company, achieving **vertical integration**. Companies usually developed vertical integration to ensure steady operations and to gain a competitive advantage. Control over the sources and transportation of raw materials, for example, guaranteed a reliable flow of crucial supplies at predictable prices. Such control may also have denied materials to a competitor.

Steel plants stood at one end of a long chain of operations that Carnegie owned or controlled: iron ore mines in Minnesota, a fleet of ships that transported iron ore across the Great Lakes, hundreds of miles of railway lines, tens of thousands of acres of coal lands, ovens to produce coke (coal treated to burn at high temperatures), and plants for turning iron ore into bars of crude iron. Carnegie Steel was vertically integrated from the point where the raw materials came out of the ground through the delivery of steel rails and beams.

Survival of the Fittest?

The concentration of power and wealth during the late nineteenth century generated extensive comment and concern. One prominent view on the subject was known as **Social Darwinism,** reflecting its roots in Charles Darwin's work on evolution. In his book *On the Origin of Species* (published in 1859), Darwin concluded that creatures compete with one another for survival in an often inhospitable environment, and those that survive are those that have, through mutation and inheritance, developed the traits best adapted to their surroundings. Such adaptation, he suggested, leads to the evolution of different species, each uniquely suited to a particular ecological niche.

Two philosophers, Herbert Spencer, writing in England in the 1870s and after, and William Graham Sumner, writing in the United States in the 1880s and after, put their own interpretations on Darwin's reasoning and applied it to the human situation, producing Social Darwinism (a philosophical perspective that bore little relation to Darwin's original work). Social Darwinists

---

vertical integration   The process of bringing together into a single company several of the activities involved in creating a manufactured product, such as acquiring raw materials, manufacturing products, and marketing, selling, and distributing finished goods.

contended that competition among people, and by extension among powerful entrepreneurs, produced "progress" through "survival of the fittest" and that unrestrained competition provided the best route for improving humankind and advancing civilization. Further, they argued that efforts to ease the harsh impact of competition only protected the unfit and thereby worked to the long-term disadvantage of all. When applied to government, this notion became a form of **laissez faire**.

The wealthiest entrepreneurs, though, could be inconsistent. Carnegie, for example, embraced Spencer's arguments but also preached what he called the **Gospel of Wealth**: the idea that the wealthy should return their riches to the community. Carnegie spent his final eighteen years giving away his fortune. He funded 3,000 public library buildings and 4,100 church organs all across the nation, gave gifts to universities, built Carnegie Hall in New York City, and created several foundations. Like Carnegie, other great entrepreneurs of that time gave away vast sums to promote learning and research—even as some of them also built ostentatious mansions, threw extravagant parties, and otherwise flaunted their wealth.

Although many Americans subscribed to the vision of Social Darwinism propounded by Spencer and Sumner, many others did not. Entrepreneurs themselves sometimes welcomed some forms of government intervention in the economy— from railroad land grants to the protective tariff to suppression of strikes—although most agreed with the Social Darwinists that government should not assist the poor and destitute.

Other Americans disagreed with the Social Darwinists' equating of laissez faire with progress. Henry George, a San Francisco journalist, pointed out in *Progress and Poverty* (1879) that "amid the greatest accumulations of wealth, men die of starvation," and concluded that "material progress does not merely fail to relieve poverty—it actually produces it." Lester Frank Ward, a sociologist, in 1886 posed a carefully reasoned refutation of Social Darwinism, suggesting that biological competition produced bare survival, not civilization. Civilization, he argued, derived not from "aimless competition" but from rationality and cooperation.

Expansion of the Industrial Economy

Innovative technologies and the integrated railway network began to change the ways that Americans shopped for goods from clothing to food to home lighting products. John D. Rockefeller took the lead in bringing vertical and horizontal integration to the production of kerosene and other petroleum products, and other entrepreneurs created similar corporate structures in other consumer-goods industries.

---

laissez faire   The principle that the government should not interfere in the workings of the economy.

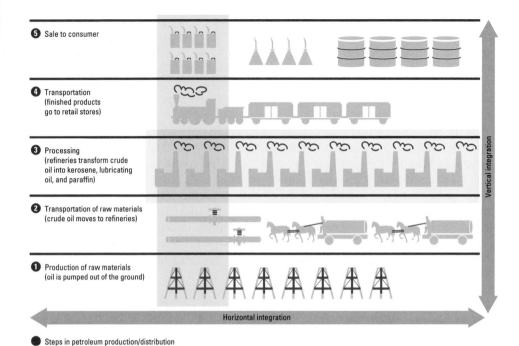

❺ Sale to consumer

❹ Transportation
(finished products
go to retail stores)

❸ Processing
(refineries transform crude
oil into kerosene, lubricating
oil, and paraffin)

❷ Transportation of raw materials
(crude oil moves to refineries)

❶ Production of raw materials
(oil is pumped out of the ground)

Vertical integration

Horizontal integration

● Steps in petroleum production/distribution

FIGURE 16.2 Vertical and Horizontal Integration of the Petroleum Industry

This diagram represents the petroleum industry before Standard Oil achieved its dominance. The symbols represent different specialized companies, each engaged in different steps in the production of kerosene. Rockefeller entered the industry by investing in a refinery, and first expanded *horizontally* by absorbing several other refineries (indicated by the light blue band). His Standard Oil Company then practiced *vertical integration* (indicated by the darker blue band) by acquiring oil leases, oil wells, pipelines, advantageous contracts with railroads, and eventually even retail stores. For a time, Standard Oil controlled nearly 90 percent of the industry.

**Standard Oil:
Model for
Monopoly**
Just as Carnegie provided a model for other steel companies and for heavy industry in general, John D. Rockefeller revolutionized the petroleum industry and provided a model for other consumer-goods industries. The major product of oil refining was kerosene, which transformed home lighting as kerosene lamps replaced candles and oil lamps. Rockefeller, in 1863, invested his wartime profits in a **refinery**. After the war, he bought control of more refineries and incorporated them as Standard Oil in 1870.

The refining business was relatively easy to enter and highly competitive. Aggressive competition became a distinctive Standard Oil characteristic. Recognizing that technology could bring a competitive advantage, Rockefeller recruited experts to

refinery   An industrial plant that transforms raw materials into finished products; a petroleum refinery processes crude oil to produce a variety of products for use by consumers.

IT MATTERS TODAY

Vertical Integration

Since Rockefeller's day, vertical integration has been a central feature in the corporate structure of American manufacturing. Many manufacturing companies have sought a competitive advantage by controlling raw materials and other components of manufacturing (like Carnegie), or distribution and marketing of finished products (like automobile makers in the 1920s), or both (like Rockefeller).

American Apparel proudly calls itself a vertically integrated and sweatshop-free company that designs, produces, and distributes clothing; does its own advertising without professional models, often using its own employees in its ads; and operates some 250 retail stores worldwide. Through vertical integration, American Apparel argues that it is able to convert a design to a product ready for distribution within a week. All design and production is done in Los Angeles.

- Use an online newspaper to research a recent corporate acquisition that provides vertical integration, for example, SBC's acquisition of AT&T. What advantages were presented to justify the acquisition? How does the acquisition affect those who work for the two companies?
- Why might vertical integration be disadvantageous in the computer industry?

make Standard the most efficient refiner. He secured favorable treatment from railroads by offering a heavy volume of traffic on a predictable basis. He usually sought to persuade his competitors to join the cartel he was creating. If they refused, he sometimes tried to drive them out of business.

By 1881, following a strategy of **horizontal integration**, Rockefeller and his associates controlled some forty refineries, with about 90 percent of the nation's refining capacity. Standard also moved toward vertical integration by gaining control of oil fields, building transportation facilities (including pipelines and oceangoing tanker ships), and creating retail marketing operations (see Figure 16.2). By the early 1890s, Standard Oil had achieved almost complete vertical and horizontal integration of the American petroleum industry—a virtual **monopoly** over an entire industry.

Between 1879 and 1881, Rockefeller and his associates centralized decision making among all their companies by creating the Standard Oil Trust. The **trust** was a new organizational form designed to get around state laws that

horizontal integration Merging one or more companies doing the same or similar activities as a way of limiting competition or enhancing stability and planning.

monopoly Exclusive control by an individual or company of the production or sale of a product.

trust A legal arrangement in which an individual (the trustor) gives control of property to a person or institution (the trustee); in the late nineteenth century, a legal device to get around state laws prohibiting a company chartered in one state from operating in another state, and often synonymous in common use with *monopoly;* first used by John D. Rockefeller to consolidate Standard Oil.

prohibited one company from owning stock in another. To create the Standard Oil Trust, Rockefeller and others who held shares in the individual companies exchanged their stock for trust certificates issued by Standard Oil. Standard Oil thus controlled all the individual companies, though technically it did not own them. Eventually, new laws in New Jersey made it legal for corporations chartered in New Jersey to own stock in other companies. So Rockefeller set up Standard Oil of New Jersey as a **holding company** for the companies in the trust.

Once Standard Oil achieved its near-monopoly, it consolidated its operations by closing older refineries and building larger plants that incorporated the newest technology. Such innovations reduced the cost of producing petroleum products by more than two-thirds, leading to a decline by more than half in the price paid by consumers of fuel and home lighting products. Standard also took a leading role in the world market, producing nearly all American petroleum products sold in Asia, Africa, and Latin America during the 1880s. Rockefeller retired from active participation in business in the mid-1890s.

Standard's monopoly was short-lived, because of the discovery of new, rich oil fields in Texas and elsewhere at the turn of the century. New companies tapped those fields and quickly followed their own paths to vertical integration. Nonetheless, the "Rockefeller interests" (companies dominated by Rockefeller or his managers) steadily gained in power. They included the National City Bank of New York (an investment bank second only to the House of Morgan), railroads, mining, real estate, steel plants, steamship lines, and other industries.

Thomas Edison and the Power of Innovation   By the late nineteenth century, most American entrepreneurs had joined Rockefeller and Carnegie in viewing technology as a powerful competitive device. Railroads wanted more powerful locomotives, roomier freight cars, and stronger rails so they could carry more freight at a lower cost. Steel companies demanded larger and more efficient furnaces to make more steel more cheaply. Ordinary citizens as well as famous entrepreneurs seemed infatuated with technology. One invention followed another: an ice-making machine in 1865, the vacuum cleaner in 1869, the telephone in 1876, the phonograph in 1878, the electric light bulb in 1879, an electric welding machine in 1886, and the first American-made gasoline-engine automobile in 1895, to name only a few. By 1900, many Americans had come to expect a steady flow of ever more astounding creations, especially those that could be purchased by the middle and upper classes.

Many new inventions relied on electricity, and in the field of electricity one person stood out: **Thomas A. Edison**. Born in 1847, he secured the first of his thousand-plus **patents** at age 22. In 1876 Edison set up the first modern research laboratory, and he opened a new and improved facility in 1887. Edison promised

---

holding company   A company that exists to own other companies, usually through holding a controlling interest in their stocks.

patent   A government statement that gives the creator of an invention the sole right to produce, use, or sell that invention for a set period of time.

This photograph from 1893 shows Thomas A. Edison in his laboratory, the world's leading research facility when it opened in 1876. By creating research teams, the Edison laboratories could pursue several projects at once. They developed a dazzling stream of new products, most based on electrical power.

"a minor invention every ten days and a big thing every six months," and he backed up his words with results. His laboratories invented or significantly improved electrical lighting, electrical motors, the storage battery, the electric locomotive, the phonograph, the microphone, and many other products. Research and development by Edison's laboratories and others soon translated into production and sales. Nationwide, sales of electrical equipment were insignificant in 1870 but reached nearly $2 million ten years later and nearly $22 million in 1890.

Such sales meant that generating and distribution systems had to be constructed, and wires to carry electrical current had to be installed along city streets and in homes. The pace of this work picked up appreciably after Nikola Tesla demonstrated the superiority of alternating current (AC) to direct current (DC) for transmitting power over long distances. Edison's distribution networks had relied on DC, which had limited their range.

Early developers of electrical devices and electrical distribution systems needed major financial assistance, and investment bankers came to play an important role in public utilities industries. General Electric, for example, developed out of Edison's company through a series of **mergers** arranged by J. P. Morgan.

merger   The joining together of two or more organizations.

Selling to
the Nation

The expansion of manufacturing in the 1880s accelerated earlier trends toward new and more affordable consumer goods. Large, vertically integrated manufacturers of consumer products often competed to sell items that differed little from one another and that cost virtually the same to produce. Such companies frequently competed not on the basis of price but through advertising.

By the late nineteenth century, advertisements in newspapers and magazines had become large and complex as manufacturers relied on large-scale advertising to promote a host of mass-produced consumer goods, including **patent medicines**, clothing, books, packaged foods, soap, and petroleum products. In some cases—notably cigarettes—advertising greatly expanded the market for the product. After the federal Patent Office registered the first **trademark** in 1870, companies rushed to develop brands and logos that they hoped would distinguish their products from nearly identical rivals.

Along with advertising came new ways of selling. Previously, most people expected to purchase goods directly from artisans who made items on order (shoes, clothes, furniture), or from door-to-door peddlers (pots and pans), or in small specialty stores (hardware, dry goods) or general stores. In urban areas following the Civil War, the first American **department stores** appeared and flourished, offering a wide range of choices in ready-made products—fashionable clothing, household furnishings, shoes, and much more. Department stores' products, unlike the wares in most previous retail outlets, not only had clearly marked prices but also could be returned or exchanged if the customer were dissatisfied. R. H. Macy's in New York City, Jordan Marsh in Boston, Marshall Field in Chicago, and similar stores relied heavily on newspaper advertising to attract large numbers of customers, especially women, from throughout the city and its suburbs. They targeted middle- and upper-class women, but the stores also appealed to young, single women who worked for wages and had an eye for the fashions that were now within their financial reach. Young, single women also often found white-collar jobs as clerks in the new department stores.

The variety presented by department stores paled when compared with the vast array of goods available through the new mail-order catalogs. Led by two Chicago companies, Montgomery Ward (which issued its first catalog in 1872) and Sears, Roebuck and Co. (whose first general catalogs appeared in 1893), mail-order houses aimed at rural America. They offered a wider range of choices than most rural-dwellers had ever before seen—everything from hams to hammers, handkerchiefs to harnesses.

Department stores and mail-order houses became feasible because manufacturers had begun to produce many types of consumer goods in huge volumes. Mail-order houses also depended on railroads and the U.S. mail to deliver their

patent medicine   A medical preparation that is advertised by brand name and available without a physician's prescription.

trademark   A name or symbol that identifies a product and is officially registered and legally restricted for use by the owner or manufacturer.

catalogs and products across great distances, and department stores relied on railroads to bring goods from distant factories. Together, advertising, mail-order catalogs (in rural areas), and the new department stores (in urban areas) began to change not only Americans' buying habits but also their thinking about what they expected to buy ready-made.

Economic	Carnegie, Rockefeller, Edison, Morgan, and a few others
Concentration in	redefined the expectations of American entrepreneurs and
Consumer-Goods	provided models for their activities. In a number of consumer-
Industries	goods industries, massive, complex companies—vertically

integrated, sometimes horizontally integrated, often employing extensive advertising—appeared relatively suddenly in the 1880s.

The American Sugar Refining Company, created in 1887, imitated Rockefeller's organization to control three-quarters of the nation's sugar-refining capacity by the early 1890s. In the 1880s, James B. Duke used efficient machinery, extensive advertising, and vertical integration to become the largest manufacturer of cigarettes. In 1890 he merged with his four largest competitors to create the American Tobacco Company, which dominated the cigarette industry. Gustavus Swift in the early 1880s began to ship fresh meat from his slaughterhouse in Chicago to markets in the East, using his own refrigerated railcars. He eventually added refrigerated storage plants in several cities, along with a sales and delivery staff. Other meatpacking companies followed Swift's lead. By 1890, half a dozen firms dominated meatpacking. Such a market, in which a small number of firms dominate an industry, is called an **oligopoly**. Oligopolies were (and are) more typical than monopolies.

Some of the new manufacturing companies did not sell stock or use investment bankers to raise capital. Standard Oil, like Carnegie Steel, never "went public"—that is, Rockefeller never used the stock exchange to raise capital. Instead, he expanded either through mergers or by making purchases capitalized by his profits. Rockefeller and his associates, like Carnegie and his partners, concentrated ownership and control in their own hands. So did many others among the new manufacturing companies. As late as 1896, the New York Stock Exchange sold stock in only twenty manufacturing concerns.

Gradually, however, with the passing of the first generation of industrial empire builders, ownership grew apart from management. Many new business executives were professional managers. Ownership rested among hundreds or thousands of stockholders, all of whom wanted a reliable return on their investment, even though the vast majority remained uninvolved with business operations. The huge size of the new companies also meant that most managers rarely saw or talked with most

---

oligopoly   A market or industry dominated by a few firms (from Greek words meaning "few sellers"); more common than a *monopoly* (from Greek words meaning "one seller").

of their employees. Careful **cost analysis**, the desire for efficiency, and the need to pay shareholders regular **dividends** led many companies to treat most of their employees as expenses to be increased or cut as necessary, with little regard to the effect on individuals.

Laying the Economic Basis for a New South   The term **New South** usually refers to efforts by some southerners to modernize their region during the years after Reconstruction. Some advocates of the New South promoted a more diverse economic base, with more manufacturing and less reliance on a few staple agricultural crops, as a way to strengthen the southern economy and integrate it more thoroughly into the national economy.

Foremost among proponents of the New South was **Henry Grady**, who built the *Atlanta Constitution* into a powerful regional newspaper in the 1880s. Like Chicago, Atlanta grew as a railroad center. Though destroyed by Sherman's troops in 1864, Atlanta rebuilt quickly. It became the capital of Georgia in 1877. Thanks in part to Grady's skillful journalism, the city emerged as a symbol of the New South—a center for transportation, industry, and finance.

The importance of railroads in spurring Atlanta's growth was no coincidence. After the Civil War, inadequate transportation, especially railroads, posed a critical limit on the South's economic growth. During the 1880s, however, southern railroads more than doubled their miles of track. In the 1890s, J. P. Morgan led in reorganizing southern railroads into three large systems, dominated by the Southern Railway. With the emergence of better rail transportation, some entrepreneurs began to consider introducing new industries.

Some southerners had long advocated that their cotton be manufactured into cloth in the South, rather than in the New England textile mills that had been using southern cotton since early in the century. The southern cotton textile industry finally boomed during the 1880s and 1890s. The South counted 161 textile mills in 1880 and 400 in 1900. The new mills had more modern equipment and were larger and more productive than the mills of New England. They also had cheaper labor costs, partly because they relied on child labor. Similar patterns characterized the emergence of cigarette manufacturing as another new southern industry. In the end, these enterprises did little to improve the lives of many southerners. Most of the new companies paid low wages, and some located in the South specifically to take advantage of its cheap, unskilled, nonunion labor.

Other southerners tried to diversify the region's agriculture and to reduce its dependence on cotton and tobacco. Such efforts, however, ran up against the cotton textile and cigarette industries, both of which built factories in the South to be near their raw materials. Thus southern agriculture changed little: owners and sharecroppers farmed small plots, obligated by their rental contracts or crop liens

---

cost analysis   Study of the cost of producing manufactured goods to find ways to cut expenses.

dividend   A share of a company's profits received by a stockholder.

to raise cotton or tobacco. In parts of the South, farmers became even more dependent on cotton than they had been before the Civil War. Parts of Georgia, for example, produced almost 200 percent more cotton in 1880 than in 1860.

Of greater potential to transform part of the South was the iron and steel industry that emerged in northern Alabama. Dominated by the Tennessee Coal, Iron, and Railroad Company, the industry drew on coal from Tennessee and Alabama mines and iron ore from northern Alabama. By the late 1890s, Birmingham, Alabama, had become one of the world's largest producers of pig iron. In 1897, the first southern steel mill opened in Ensley, Alabama, and soon established itself as a serious rival to those of the North. In 1907, J. P. Morgan arranged the merger of the Tennessee Company into his United States Steel Corporation.

The turn of the century also saw the beginning of a southern oil industry near Beaumont, Texas, with the tapping of the Spindletop Pool—so productive the press labeled it "the world's greatest oil well." The center of petroleum production now shifted from the Midwest to Texas, Oklahoma, and Louisiana, where important discoveries also came in 1901. In addition to attracting attention from Standard Oil, the new discoveries prompted the growth or creation of new companies, notably Gulf and Texaco.

INCORPORATING THE WEST INTO THE NATIONAL ECONOMY

As Rockefeller was monopolizing the petroleum industry and Edison was perfecting the light bulb, the U.S. Army was subduing the last Indian resistance in the West. Before the Civil War, the issue of slavery had blocked efforts at the economic development of the West. The secession of the southern states permitted the Republicans who took over the federal government to open the West to economic development, through such measures as the Pacific Railway Act and the Homestead Act. The end result was the incorporation of the West into the emerging national industrial economy.

War for the West   When Congress decided to use the public domain—western land—to encourage economic development, most white Americans considered the West to be largely vacant. In fact, American Indians lived throughout most of the West. The most tragic outcome of the development of the West was the upheaval in the lives of the Native Americans who lived there.

At the end of the Civil War, as many white Americans began to move west, the acquisition of horses and guns had long since transformed the lives of western Native Americans. The transformation was most dramatic among tribes living on or near the **Great Plains**. This vast, relatively flat, and treeless region was the

---

Great Plains High grassland of western North America, stretching north to south across the center of the nation; it is generally level, treeless, and fairly dry.

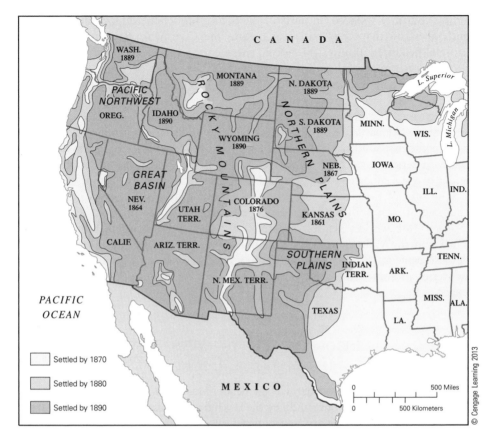

MAP 16.2 The Settlement of the Trans-Mississippi West, 1860–1890

The West was not settled by a movement of peoples gradually creeping westward from the East. Rather, settlers first occupied California and the Midwest and then filled up the nation's vast interior.

rangeland of huge herds of buffalo. Horses found their way onto the Great Plains slowly, trickling northward from Spanish settlements in what is now New Mexico and reaching the upper plains in the mid-eighteenth century. By that time, French and English traders working northeast of the plains had begun to provide guns to the Indians in return for furs. Together, horses and guns transformed the culture of some Plains tribes.

Although the possession of horses might confer status, among most of the Plains Indians a person achieved high social standing not by accumulating possessions but by sharing. Francis La Flesche, son of an Omaha leader, learned from his father that "the persecution of the poor, the sneer at their poverty is a wrong for which no punishment is too severe." His mother reinforced the lesson: "When you see a boy barefooted and lame, take off your moccasins and give them to him. When you see a boy hungry, bring him to your home and give him food."

The Native American peoples of the plains included both farmers and nomadic hunters. The farmers lived most of the year in large permanent villages. Among this group were the Arikaras, Pawnees, and Wichitas (parts of the Caddoan language family) and the Mandans, Hidatsas, Omahas, Otos, and Osages (who spoke Siouan languages). Women raised corn, squash, pumpkins, and beans, and gathered wild fruit and vegetables. Men hunted and fished near their villages and cultivated tobacco. Before the arrival of horses, twice a year entire villages went, on foot, on extended hunting trips for buffalo. During these hunts, the people lived in **tipis**, cone-shaped tents of buffalo hide that were easy to move. Acquisition of horses changed the culture of these Indians only slightly.

The horse revolutionized the lives of other Plains Indians. Because a hunter on horseback could kill twice as many buffalo as one on foot, the horse substantially increased the number of people the plains could support. The horse also increased mobility, permitting a band to follow the buffalo as they moved across the grasslands. Some groups abandoned farming and became nomadic, living in tipis year-round and following the buffalo herds. By the early nineteenth century, the **horse culture** existed throughout the Great Plains. The largest groups practicing this lifestyle included—from north to south—the Blackfeet, Crows, Lakotas, Cheyennes, Arapahos, Kiowas, and Comanches.

The **Lakotas**, largest of all the groups, were the westernmost members of a group of Native American peoples often called Sioux—a name applied to them by the French. Their name for themselves can be translated as *allies,* reflecting their organization as a **confederacy**. The Lakotas shared a common language, but the northern Cheyenne were generally considered members of the Lakota confederacy by the mid-nineteenth century.

Before 1851, federal policymakers had considered the region west of Arkansas, Missouri, Iowa, and Minnesota and east of the Rocky Mountains to be a permanent Indian country. But farmers bound for Oregon and gold seekers on their way to California carved trails across the central plains, and in 1851 Congress approved a new policy, designed in part to open the central plains as a railroad route to the Pacific. The new policy promised each tribe a definite territory "of limited extent and well-defined boundaries," within which the tribe was to live. The government was to supply whatever needs the tribes could not meet themselves. Federal officials first planned large reservations taking up much of the Great Plains.

As more easterners thronged westward, conflicts erupted along the trails. In April 1868, many members of the northern Plains tribes met at Fort Laramie and signed treaties creating a Great Sioux Reservation on the northern plains. They believed that they retained "unceded lands" for hunting in the Powder River

---

tipis   Conical tents made from buffalo hide and used as a portable dwelling by Indians on the Great Plains.

confederacy   An organization of separate groups who have allied for mutual support or joint action.

country—present-day northeastern Wyoming and southeastern Montana. In return, the army abandoned its posts along the Bozeman Trail, a victory for the Lakotas and Cheyennes.

The creation of the new reservation was part of a larger plan. With the end of the Civil War in 1865, railroad construction crews prepared to build westward. Federal policymakers tried to head off hostilities by carving out a few great western reservations. The remainder of the West was to be opened for development—railroad building, mining, and farming. Native Americans on the reservations were to receive food and shelter, and agents were to teach them how to farm and raise cattle.

Other treaties were negotiated in 1867 and 1868 in fulfillment of the new policy. In 1867 a conference at Medicine Lodge Creek produced treaties by which the major southern Plains tribes accepted reservations in what is now western Oklahoma. In May 1868 the Crows agreed to a reservation in Montana. In June 1868 the Navajos accepted a large reservation in the Southwest. Given the fluid structure of authority among most Indian peoples, however, those who signed the treaties did not necessarily obligate those who did not.

As some federal officials were negotiating these treaties, other federal officials were permitting and even encouraging white hunters to kill the buffalo—for sport, for meat, and for hides purchased by **tanneries** in the East. In the mid-1870s more than 10 million buffalo were killed and stripped of their hides, which sold for a dollar or so. The southern herd was wiped out by 1878, the northern herd by 1883. Only two thousand survived, the remnant of a species whose numbers once seemed as vast as the stars. Given the importance of the buffalo in the lives of the Plains Indians, their way of life was doomed once the slaughter began.

Some members of the southern Plains tribes refused to accept the terms of the Medicine Lodge Creek treaties and continued to live in their traditional territory. Resisting efforts to move them onto the reservations, they occasionally attacked stagecoach stations, ranches, travelers, and military units. After a group of southern Cheyennes inflicted heavy losses on an army unit, General William Tecumseh Sherman, the Civil War general and now head of the army, decreed that all Native Americans not on reservations "are hostile and will remain so till killed off."

Sherman's response was the usual reaction of a conventional military force to **guerrilla warfare**: concentrate the friendly population in defined areas (in this case, reservations) and then open fire on anyone outside those areas. In the winter of 1868–1869, the army launched a southern campaign under the command of General Philip Sheridan, another Union army veteran, who directed his men to "destroy their villages and ponies, to kill and hang all warriors, and bring back all

---

tannery   An establishment where animal skins and hides are made into leather.

guerrilla warfare   A method of warfare in which small bands of fighters in occupied territory harass and attack their enemies.

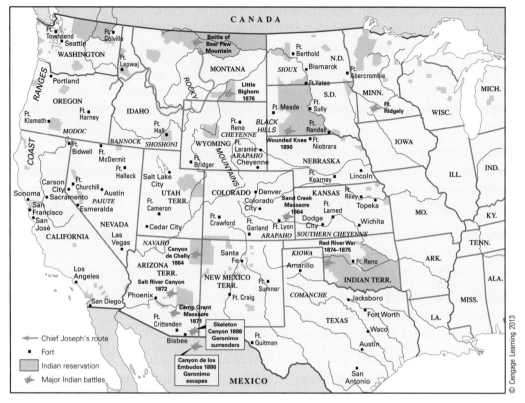

MAP 16.3 Major Indian Battles in the West

Although they were never recognized as such in the popular press, the battles between the Native Americans and the U.S. Army on the Great Plains amounted to an undeclared war.

women and children." The brutality that ensued convinced most southern Plains tribes to abandon further resistance.

In the early 1870s, however, sizable buffalo herds still roamed west and south of Indian Territory, in the Red River region of Texas. Though this was not reservation land, the Medicine Lodge Creek treaties permitted Indians to hunt there. When white buffalo hunters began work there in 1874, young men from the Kiowa, Comanche, and southern Cheyenne tribes attacked them. Sheridan responded with another **war of attrition**, destroying tipis, food, and animals. When winter came, the cold and hungry Indians surrendered to avoid starvation. War leaders were imprisoned in Florida, far from their families. Buffalo hunters then quickly exterminated the remaining buffalo on the southern plains.

war of attrition   A form of warfare based on deprivation of food, shelter, and other necessities; if successful, it drives opponents to surrender out of hunger or exposure.

On the northern plains, many Lakotas and some northern Cheyennes, led by **Crazy Horse** and **Sitting Bull**, lived on unceded hunting lands in the Powder River region. Complicating matters further, gold was discovered in the Black Hills, in the heart of the Great Sioux Reservation, in 1874, touching off an invasion of Indian land by miners. As the Northern Pacific Railroad prepared to lay track in southern Montana, federal authorities determined to force all Lakota and Cheyenne people onto the reservation, triggering a conflict sometimes called the **Great Sioux War**.

Military operations in the Powder River region began in the spring of 1876. Sheridan ordered troops to enter the area from three directions and converge on the Lakotas and Cheyennes. The offensive went dreadfully wrong when Lieutenant Colonel George A. Custer, without waiting for the other units, sent his Seventh Cavalry against a major village that his scouts had located. The encampment, on the **Little Big Horn River**, proved to be one of the largest ever on the northern plains. Custer unwisely divided his force, and more than two hundred men, including Custer, met their deaths.

That winter, U.S. soldiers unleashed another campaign of attrition on the northern plains. Troops defeated some Indian bands. Hunger and cold drove others to surrender. Crazy Horse and his band held out until spring and surrendered only when told that they could live in the Powder River region. A few months later, Crazy Horse was killed when he resisted being put into an army jail. Sitting Bull and his band escaped to Canada and remained there until 1881, when he finally surrendered. The government cut up the Great Sioux Reservation into several smaller units and took away the Powder River region, the Black Hills (which the Lakotas considered sacred), and other lands. After the Great Sioux War, no Native American group could muster the capacity for sustained resistance. Small groups occasionally left their reservations but were promptly tracked down by troops. In 1877 an effort to move the Nez Perces to a new reservation in western Idaho led to a battle in which a small group of Nez Perces defeated a larger group of U.S. troops and local civilian volunteers. Led by **Chief Joseph**, the Nez Perces then attempted to flee to Canada. Between July and early October, they evaded the army as they traveled east and north. More than two hundred members of the band died along the way. In the end, Joseph surrendered on the condition that the Nez Perces be permitted to return to their previous home. Federal officials sent the Nez Perces to faraway Indian Territory, where, in an unfamiliar climate, many died of disease.

The last sizable group to resist confinement was Geronimo's band of Chiricahua Apaches, who long managed to elude the army in the mountains of the Southwest. They finally gave up in 1886, and the men were sent to prison in Florida.

The last major confrontation between the army and Native Americans came in 1890, in South Dakota. Some Lakotas had taken up a new religion, the **Ghost Dance**, which promised to restore the buffalo and sweep away the whites. Fearing an uprising, federal authorities ordered the Lakotas to stop the ritual and, concerned that Sitting Bull might encourage defiance, ordered his arrest. He was killed when some of his followers resisted. A small band of

Lakotas, led by Big Foot, fled but was surrounded by the Seventh Cavalry near **Wounded Knee Creek**. When one Lakota refused to surrender his gun, both Indians and soldiers fired their weapons. The soldiers, with their vastly greater firepower, quickly prevailed. As many as 250 Native Americans died, as did 25 soldiers.

The events at Wounded Knee marked the symbolic end of armed conflict on the Great Plains. Once the federal government began to encourage rapid economic development in the West, displacement of the Indians was probably inevitable. From the beginning, the Indians faced overwhelming odds—they had a superior knowledge of the terrain, superior horsemanship and mobility, and great courage, but the U.S. Army had superior numbers and superior technology. The army was also often able to find allies among Native American groups who were traditional enemies of the defiant tribes.

Transforming the West: Railroads, Cattle, and Mining

Long before the last battles between the army and the Indians, the incorporation of the West into the national economy was well under way. Railroad construction played a major role. In the eastern United States, railroad construction usually meant connecting established population centers. Eastern railroads moved through areas with developed economies, connected major cities, and hauled freight to and from the many towns along their lines. At the end of the Civil War, this situation existed almost nowhere in the West.

Most western railroads were built first to connect the Pacific Coast to the eastern half of the country. Only slowly did they begin to find business along their routes. Railroad promoters understood that a transcontinental line was unlikely at first to carry enough freight to justify the high cost of construction. Thus they turned to the federal government for assistance. The Pacific Railway Act of 1862 provided loans and 10 square miles (later increased to 20) of the public domain for every mile of track laid. In this way, federal lawmakers sought to tie California and Nevada, with their rich deposits of gold and silver, to the Union and to stimulate the rapid economic development of other parts of the West.

Two companies received this federal support: the Union Pacific, which began laying tracks westward from Omaha, Nebraska, and the Central Pacific, which began building eastward from Sacramento, California. Construction began slowly, partly because crucial supplies—rails and locomotives—had to be brought to each starting point from the eastern United States, either by ship around South America to California or by riverboat to Omaha. Both lines experienced labor shortages. The Union Pacific solved its labor shortages only after the end of the Civil War, when former soldiers and construction workers flooded west. Many were Irish immigrants. The Central Pacific filled its work gangs earlier by recruiting Chinese immigrants. By 1868, Central Pacific construction crews totaled six thousand workers, Union Pacific crews five thousand.

The sheer cliffs and rocky ravines of the Sierra Nevadas slowed construction of the Central Pacific. Chinese laborers sometimes dangled from ropes to create a roadbed by chiseling away the solid rock face of a mountain. Because the companies earned their federal subsidies by laying track, construction became a race in which each company tried to build faster than the other. In 1869, with the Sierras far behind, the Central Pacific boasted of laying 10 miles of track in a single day. The tracks of the two companies finally met at Promontory Summit, north of Salt Lake City, on May 10, 1869. Other lines followed during the next twenty years, bringing most of the West into the national market system.

Westerners greeted the arrival of a railroad in their communities with joyful celebrations, but some soon wondered if they had traded isolation for dependence on a greedy monopoly. The Southern Pacific, successor to the Central Pacific, became known as the "Octopus" because of its efforts to establish a monopoly over transportation throughout California. It had a reputation for charging the most that a customer could afford. James J. Hill of the Great Northern, in contrast, was called the "Empire Builder" for his efforts to build up the economy and prosperity of the region alongside his rails, which ran west from Minneapolis to Puget Sound. Whether "Octopus" or "Empire Builder," railroads provided the crucial transportation network for the economic development of the West. In their wake, cattle raising, mining, farming, and lumbering all expanded rapidly.

Millions of cattle roamed the ranges of south Texas. Cattle had first been brought into south Texas—then part of New Spain (Mexico)—in the eighteenth century. The environment encouraged the herds to multiply, and Mexican ranchers developed an **open-range** system. The cattle grazed on unfenced grasslands and *vaqueros* (cowboys) hearded the half-wild longhorns from horseback. Many practices that developed in south Texas were subsequently transferred to the range-cattle industry, including **roundups** and **branding**.

At the end of the Civil War, 5 million cattle ranged across Texas. And in the slaughterhouses of Chicago, cattle brought ten times their price in Texas or more. To get cattle from south Texas to markets in the Midwest, Texans herded cattle north from Texas through Indian Territory (now Oklahoma) to the railroads being built westward. Half a dozen cowboys, a cook, and a foreman (the trail boss) could drive one or two thousand cattle. Between 1866 and 1880, some 4 million cattle plodded north from Texas.

As railroad construction crews pushed westward, cattle towns sprang up—notably Abilene and Dodge City, Kansas. In cattle towns, the trail boss sold his herd and paid off his cowboys, most of whom quickly headed for the saloons, brothels, and gambling houses. Eastern journalists and writers of **dime novels**

open range Unfenced grazing lands on which cattle ran freely and cattle ownership was established through branding.

roundup A spring event in which cowboys gathered together the cattle herds, branded newborn calves, and castrated most of the new young males.

branding Burning a distinctive mark into an animal's hide using a hot iron as a way to establish ownership.

dime novel A cheaply produced novel of the mid-to-late nineteenth century, often featuring the dramatized exploits of western gunfighters.

When the Central Pacific and Union Pacific companies raced to build their part of the first transcontinental railroad, Chinese laborers were responsible for some of the most dangerous construction on the Central Pacific route through the Sierra Nevadas. This photograph was apparently taken by a photographer for the Union Pacific when the two lines joined near Promontory Summit, in Utah Territory.

discovered and embroidered the exploits of town marshals like James B. "Wild Bill" Hickok and Wyatt Earp, giving them national reputations—deserved or not—as "town-tamers" of heroic dimensions. In fact, the most important changes in any cattle town came when middle-class residents—especially women—organized churches and schools, and were determined to create law-abiding communities like those from which they had come.

Most Texas cattle were loaded on eastbound trains, but some continued north to where cattlemen had virtually free access to vast lands still in the public domain. One result of these "long drives" was the extension of open-range cattle raising from Texas into the northern Great Plains. By the early 1870s, the profits in cattle raising on the northern plains attracted attention in the East, England, and elsewhere among investors eager to make a fortune. Some brought in new breeds of cattle, which they bred with Texas longhorns, producing hardy range cattle that yielded more meat.

By the early 1880s so many cattle ranches were operating that beef prices began to fall. Then, in the severe winter of 1886–1887, uncounted thousands of cattle froze or starved to death on the northern plains. Many investors went bankrupt.

Cattle raising lost some of its romantic aura and afterward became more of a business than an adventure. Surviving ranchers fenced their ranges and made certain that they could feed their herds during the winter.

Another important change, both on the northern plains and in the Southwest, was the rise of sheep raising. By 1900, Montana had more sheep than any other state, and the western states accounted for more than half of the sheep raised in the nation.

As the cattle industry grew, the cowboy became a popular **icon**. Fiction after the 1870s, and motion pictures later, created the cowboy image: a brave, white, clean-cut hero who spent his time outwitting rustlers and rescuing fair-haired white women from snarling villains. In fact, most real cowboys were young and unschooled; many were African Americans or of Mexican descent, and others were former Confederate soldiers. On a cattle drive, they worked long hours (up to twenty a day), faced serious danger if a herd stampeded, slept on the ground, and ate biscuits and beans. They earned about a dollar a day and spent much of their working time in the saddle with no human companionship.

Just as railroads made possible the cattle drives, so too did railroad construction advance the expansion of mining. Discoveries of precious metals and valuable

At some time in the 1870s, these cowboys put on good clothes and sat for a photographer before a painted background. They probably worked together and were friends. Most cowboys were young African Americans, Mexican Americans, or poor southern whites.

Collection of William Gladstone

icon A symbol, usually one with virtues considered worthy of imitating.

minerals in the mountainous regions of the West inevitably prompted the construction of rail lines to the sites of discovery, and the rail lines in turn permitted rapid exploitation of the mineral resources by bringing in supplies and heavy equipment. The mining industry changed rapidly. Solitary prospectors panning for gold in mountain streams gave way to corporations and wage workers. Mining operations quickly became vertically integrated, including mines, ore-crushing mills, railroads, and companies that supplied fuel and water for mining.

In most parts of the West, the exhaustion of surface deposits led to construction of underground shafts and tunnels. Such operations required elaborate machinery to move men and equipment thousands of feet into the earth and to keep the tunnels cool, dry, and safe. By the mid-1870s, some Nevada silver mines boasted the most advanced mining equipment in the world. There, temperatures soared to 120 degrees in shafts more than 2,200 feet deep. Mighty air pumps circulated air from the surface to the depths, and ice was used to reduce temperatures. Massive water pumps kept the shafts dry. Powerful drills speeded the removal of ore, and enormous ore-crushing machines operated day and night on the surface. In Butte, Montana, a gold discovery in 1864 led to discoveries of copper, silver, and zinc in what has been called the richest hill on earth. Mine shafts there reached depths of a mile and required 2,700 miles of tunnels.

Western miners organized too, forming strong unions. Beginning in Butte and spreading throughout the major mining regions of the West, miners' unions secured wages five to ten times higher than what miners in Britain or Germany earned.

Transforming the West: Farming and Lumbering

Railroad construction also facilitated the expansion of western farming. After the Civil War, the land most easily available for new farms stretched southward from Canada through the current state of Oklahoma. Mapmakers in the early nineteenth century had labeled this region the Great American Desert. It was not a desert—some parts were very fertile—but west of the line of **aridity**, roughly the 98th or 100th **meridian**, sparse rainfall limited farming. Farmers who followed traditional farming practices risked not only failing but also damaging a surprisingly fragile **ecosystem**.

After the Civil War, farmers pressed steadily westward, spurred by the offer of 160 acres of free land under the Homestead Act or lured by railroad advertising that promised fertile and productive land at little cost. Those who came to farm were as diverse as the nation itself. Thousands of African Americans left the

aridity   Dryness; lack of enough rainfall to support trees or woody plants.

meridian   One of the imaginary lines representing degrees of longitude that pass through the North and South Poles and encircle the Earth.

ecosystem   A community of animals, plants, and microorganisms, considered together with the environment in which they live.

South, seeking farms of their own. Immigrants from Europe—especially Scandinavia, Germany, **Bohemia**, and Russia—also flooded in. Most homesteaders, however, moved from areas a short distance to the east, where farmland had become too expensive for them to buy.

Single women could and did claim their own land. Sometimes the wife of a male homesteader did the same, claiming 160 acres in her own name next to the claim of her husband. By one estimate, one-third of all homestead claims in Dakota Territory were held by women in 1886. Some single women seem to have seen home-steading as a speculative venture, intending to sell the land and use the money for such purposes as starting a business, paying college tuition, or creating a nest egg for marriage.

The Homestead Act had clear limits, however. The 160 acres that it provided were sufficient for a farm only east of the line of aridity. West of that line, it was often possible to raise wheat, but most land required irrigation for other crops or was suitable only for cattle raising, which required much more than 160 acres.

Federal officials were sometimes lax in enforcing the Homestead Act's require-ments. Some cattle ranchers manipulated the law by having their cowboys file claims and then transfer the land to the rancher after they received title to it. Or ranchers claimed the land along both sides of streams, knowing that surrounding land was worthless without access to water, and thus they could control the whole watershed without establishing ownership.

Those who complied with the requirement to build a house and farm the land often faced an unfamiliar environment. The plains were virtually barren of trees. The new plains settlers, therefore, scavenged for substitutes for the construction material and fuel that eastern pioneers obtained without cost from the trees on their land. Initially, many families carved homes out of the land itself. Some tun-neled into the side of a low hill to make a cavelike dugout. Others cut the tough prairie **sod** into blocks and laid them like bricks to make the walls of a house. Many combined dugout and sod construction. "Soddies" became common throughout the plains but seldom made satisfactory dwellings. For fuel to use in cooking or heating, women burned dried cow dung or sunflower stalks.

Plains families looked to technology to meet many of their needs. Barbed wire, first patented in 1874, provided a cheap and easy alternative to wooden fences. The barbs effectively kept ranchers' cattle off farmland. Ranchers eventually used it, too, to keep their herds from straying. Much of the plains had abundant groundwater, but the **water table** was deeper than in the East, so settlers used windmills to pump the water. Because the sod was so tough, special plows were developed to make the

Bohemia   A region of central Europe now part of the Czech Republic.

sod   A piece of earth on which grass is growing; the dense sod of the plains was tough and fibrous with roots, dead grass from previous growing seasons, and hard-packed soil.

water table   The level at which the ground is completely saturated with water.

first cut through it. These plows were so expensive that most farmers hired a specialist (a "sodbuster") to break their sod.

The most serious problem for pioneers on the Great Plains was a much-reduced level of rainfall compared with eastern farming areas. During the late 1870s and into the 1880s, when the central plains were farmed for the first time, the area received unusually heavy rainfall. Then, in the late 1880s, rainfall fell below normal, and crop failures drove many homesteaders off the plains. By one estimate, half of the population of western Kansas left between 1888 and 1892. Only after farmers learned better techniques of dry farming, secured improved strains of wheat (some brought by **Russian-German** immigrants), and began to practice irrigation did agriculture become viable. Even so, farming practices in some western areas failed to protect soil that had formerly been covered by natural vegetation. This exposed soil became subject to severe wind erosion in years of low rainfall.

Throughout the Northeast and Middle West, the family farm was the typical agricultural unit. In the South after the Civil War, family-operated farms, whether run by owners or by sharecroppers, also became typical. Very large farming operations in those areas tended to be exceptions. In California and some other parts of the West, however, agriculture sometimes involved huge areas, the intensive use of heavy equipment, and wage labor. Today agriculture on such a large scale is known as **agribusiness**.

Wheat was the first major crop for which farming could be entirely mechanized. By 1880, in the Red River Valley of what is now North Dakota and in the San Joaquin Valley in central California, wheat farms were as large as 100 square miles. Such farming businesses required major capital investments in land, equipment, and livestock. One Dakota farm required 150 workers during spring planting and 250 or more at harvest time. By the late 1880s, some California wheat growers were using huge steam-powered tractors and **combines**.

Most of the great Dakota wheat farms had been broken into smaller units by the 1890s, but in some parts of California agriculture flourished on a scale unknown in most parts of the country. One California company, Miller and Lux, held more than a million acres, scattered throughout three states. Though California wheat raising declined in significance by 1900, large-scale agriculture employing many seasonal laborers became established for several other crops.

Growers of fruits and similar crops tended to operate small farms, but they still required a large work force at harvest time to pick the crops quickly so that they could be shipped to distant markets while still fresh. Fruit raising spread rapidly as

---

Russian-German Refers to people of German ancestry living in Russia; most had come to Russia in the eighteenth century at the invitation of the government to develop agricultural areas.

agribusiness A large-scale farming operation typically involving considerable land-holdings, hired labor, and extensive use of machinery; may also involve processing and distribution as well as growing.

combine A large harvesting machine that both cuts and threshes grain.

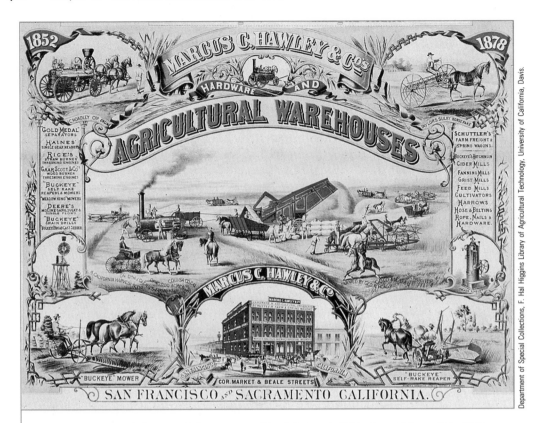

Mechanization greatly increased the amount of land that an individual could farm. This 1878 lithograph depicts a California crew setting a world's record for the amount of wheat harvested in a single day.

California growers took advantage of refrigerated railroad cars and ships. By 1892, fresh fruit from California was for sale in London.

The coastal areas of the Pacific Northwest are very different from other parts of the West. There, heavy winter rains and cool, damp, summer fogs nurture thick stands of evergreens, especially tall Douglas firs and coastal redwoods. The growth of California cities and towns required lumber, and it came first from the coastal redwoods of central and northern California. When the most accessible stands of timber had been cut, attention shifted north to Oregon and Washington. Seattle developed as a lumber town from the late 1850s onward, as companies in San Francisco helped to finance an industry geared to providing lumber for California cities. By the late nineteenth century, some companies had become vertically integrated, owning **lumber mills** along the northwest coast, a fleet of schooners that hauled rough lumber down the coast to California, and lumberyards in the San Francisco Bay area.

---

lumber mill   A factory or place where logs are sawed into rough boards.

As railroads extended into the Pacific Northwest, they promoted the development of the lumber industry by offering cheap rates to ship logs. Lumber production in Oregon and Washington boomed, leaving behind treeless hillsides subject to severe erosion during heavy winter rains. Westerners committed to rapid economic development seldom thought about ecological damage, for the long-term cost of such practices was not immediately apparent.

Water and Western Development

It has been said that, in the West, "whiskey is for drinking, water is for fighting over." Throughout much of the West, water was scarce but crucial to economic development. Mining used large amounts of water for cooling the mines and separating valuable ore from worthless rock. On the Great Plains, a cattle rancher claimed grazing land by controlling a stream. In the West, competition for water sometimes produced conflict—usually in the form of courtroom battles.

In many parts of the West, irrigation was vital to the success of farming. As early as 1899, irrigated land in the eleven westernmost states produced $84 million in crops. Although individual entrepreneurs and companies undertook significant irrigation projects, the magnitude of the task led many westerners to look for federal assistance, just as they had sought federal assistance for railroad development. "When Uncle Sam," wrote one irrigation proponent, "waves his hand toward the desert and says, 'Let there be water!' we know that the stream will obey his commands." The National Irrigation Association, created in 1899, organized lobbying efforts, producing the **Reclamation Act** in 1902. Under that law, the Reclamation Service became a major power in the West as it moved the region's water to areas where it could be used for irrigation. Reclamation projects sometimes drew criticism, however, for disproportionately benefiting large landowners.

Lack of water potentially posed stringent limits on western urban growth. Beginning in 1901, San Francisco sought federal permission to create a resevoir by damming the Hetch Hetchy Valley, on federal land adjacent to Yosemite National Park in the Sierra Nevadas. Opposition came from the **Sierra Club**, formed in 1892 and dedicated to preserving Sierra Nevada wilderness. Congress finally approved the project in 1913, and the enormous construction task took more than twenty years to complete. Los Angeles resolved its water problems in a similar way, by diverting the water of the Owens River to its use—even though Owens Valley residents tried to dynamite the **aqueduct** in resistance.

Despite potential water worries, between the end of the Civil War and 1900, San Francisco emerged as the **metropolis** of the West and was long unchallenged as the commercial, financial, and manufacturing center for much of the region west of the Rockies. Building on the city's role as the major port on the Pacific

aqueduct   A pipe or channel designed to transport water from a remote source, usually by gravity.

metropolis   An urban center, especially one that is dominant within a region.

Coast, San Francisco bankers played key roles in development in the West, channeling profits from gold and silver mining into railroad and steamboat lines and manufacturing enterprises. By the 1880s, San Francisco was home to foundries that produced locomotives, technologically advanced mining equipment, agricultural implements for large-scale farming, and ships. Not until 1900 did a few other western cities—Denver, Salt Lake City, Seattle, Portland, and especially Los Angeles—seriously challenge the economic dominance of San Francisco.

BOOM AND BUST: THE ECONOMY FROM THE CIVIL WAR TO WORLD WAR I

The nation grew dramatically in the late nineteenth and early twentieth centuries. Between 1865 and 1920, the population increased by nearly 200 percent, from 36 million to 106 million. During the same years, railroad mileage increased by more than 1,000 percent. The output of manufacturing increased by a similar margin. Agricultural production grew far faster than the population. Perhaps most significantly, the total domestic product, per capita, in constant dollars, nearly tripled. (Figure 16.3 presents some of these patterns.)

Cycles of Growth and Depression in the 1870s and 1880s

Much of this growth was sporadic. Economic historians think of the economy as developing through a cycle in which periods of **expansion** (growth) alternate with times of **contraction** (**recession** or **depression**, characterized by high unemployment and low productivity). Though this alternation between expansion and contraction is predictable, there is no predictability or regularity to the duration of any given up or down period. During the late nineteenth century, contractions were sometimes severe, producing widespread unemployment and distress. After 1865, a postwar recession lasted until late 1867, reflecting sharp dislocations as the economy shifted from wartime production to other ventures. This was followed by several short expansions and contractions. A major depression began in October 1873 and lasted until March 1879. The period from 1879 to 1893 was generally one of expansion (105 months of growth), spurred in particular by railroad construction, but growth was interrupted three times by contractions (totaling 61 months), two of them quite short.

expansion   In the economic cycle, a time when the economy is growing, characterized by increased production of goods and services and usually by low rates of unemployment.

contraction   In the economic cycle, a time when the economy has ceased to grow, characterized by decreased production of goods and services and often by high rates of unemployment.

recession/depression   A recession is an economic contraction of relatively short duration; a depression is an economic contraction of longer duration.

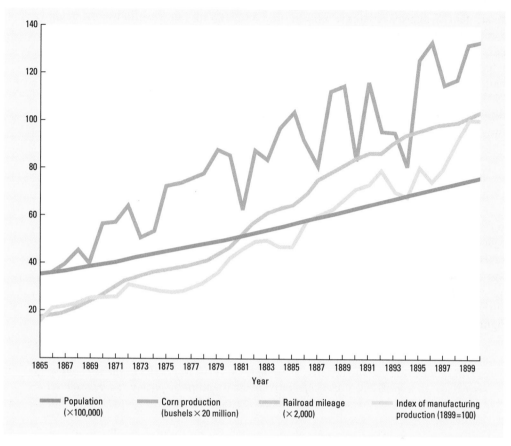

FIGURE 16.3 Measures of Growth, 1865–1900

Though many measures of economic productivity are related to population size, this graph shows how several measures of economic productivity grew more rapidly than did the population.

Source: U.S. Department of Commerce, Bureau of the Census, *Historical Statistics of the United States, Colonial Times to 1970*, Bicentennial edition, 2 vols. (Washington: Government Printing Office, 1975), I: 8, 510–512; 2: 667, 727–731.

During boom periods, companies advertised for workers and ran their operations at full capacity. When the demand for manufactured goods fell, companies reduced production, cutting hours of work or dismissing employees as they waited for business to pick up. Some businesses shut down temporarily; others closed permanently.

Thus Americans living in the late nineteenth and early twentieth centuries came to expect that hard times were likely in the future, regardless of how prosperous life seemed at the moment. Until the early twentieth century, federal intervention in the economy was limited largely to stimulating growth through the protective tariff and land distribution programs, but state and federal governments provided no unemployment benefits. Unemployed workers had little to fall back on besides their savings or the earnings of other family members, though some churches and private charity organizations gave out food. Families who failed to find work might go hungry or even become homeless. In a depression, jobs of any sort were scarce, and competition for every opening was intense. Most adult Americans therefore understood the wisdom of saving up for hard times, whether or not they were able to do so.

The depression that began in 1873 was both severe and long-lasting. Between 1873 and 1879, 355 banks closed down, a number equivalent to one bank in nine that existed in 1873. State and federal governments did nothing to save failing banks. Given the crucial role of banks as a source of credit for industry and agriculture, bank failures led to a credit contraction that, in turn, significantly delayed recovery. Nearly 54,000 businesses failed—equivalent to one in nine operating in 1873.

No reliable unemployment data exist, but evidence indicates that the contraction hit urban wage earners especially hard. Many lost their jobs or suffered a reduced workweek. Workers who kept their jobs saw their daily wages fall 17–18 percent from 1873 to 1878 or 1879. One Massachusetts worker described the consequences for his family in 1875:

> I have six children.... Last year three of my children were promoted [to the next grade in school], and I was notified to furnish different books. [Schoolchildren then were responsible for providing their own textbooks.] I wrote a note to the school committee, stating that I was not able to do so.... I then received a note stating that, unless I furnished the books called for, I must keep my children at home. I then had to reduce the bread for my children and family, in order to get the required books to keep them at school. Every cent of my earnings is consumed in my family; and yet I have not been able to have a piece of meat on my table twice a month for the last eight months.

Thus, though long-term economic trends reflect dramatic growth, the short-run boom-and-bust nature of the economy repeatedly claimed its victims.

Economic Collapse and Depression in the 1890s   Another major depression began in January 1893 and lasted (despite a brief upswing) until June 1897. It began when the Reading Railroad declared bankruptcy. A **financial panic** quickly set in. One business journal reported in August that "never before has there been such a sudden and striking cessation of industrial activity." Everywhere, industrial plants shut down in large numbers. More than fifteen thousand businesses failed in 1893, more proportionately than in any year since the depression of the 1870s.

At the time, no one understood why the economy collapsed so suddenly and completely. In retrospect, two important underlying weaknesses seem to have contributed: the slowing of both agricultural expansion and railroad construction.

---

financial panic Widespread anxiety about financial and commercial matters; in a panic, investors often sold large amounts of stock to cut their own losses, which drove prices much lower. Banks often called in their loans, forcing investors to sell assets at reduced prices, further driving down stock prices.

Railroad building drove the industrial economy in the 1880s, but slowed and then fell by half between 1893 and 1895. The decline in railroad construction initiated a domino effect, toppling industries that supplied the railroads, especially steel. Production of steel rails fell by more than a third, and thirty-two steel companies closed their doors. (Figure 16.3 shows the drop in manufacturing in the mid-1890s.) Some railway companies found they lacked sufficient traffic to pay their fixed costs, especially their obligations to bondholders, requiring them to declare bankruptcy. By 1894, almost one-fifth of the nation's railroad mileage had fallen into bankruptcy. Banks with investments in railroads and steel companies collapsed. One bank out of every ten failed between 1893 and 1897. Bank failures further contracted credit, limiting the possibilities for new investments that would spur expansion.

No agency kept careful national records on unemployment, but a third or more of the workers in manufacturing may have been out of work. During the winter of 1893–1894, Chicago counted one hundred thousand unemployed—roughly two workers out of five. Many who kept their jobs received smaller paychecks as employers cut wages and hours.

The depression produced widespread suffering. Many who lost their jobs had little to fall back on except charity. Newspapers told of people who chose suicide when faced with the dire options of starving to death or stealing food. Many men and some women left home desperate to find work, hoping to send money to their families as soon as they could. Some walked the roads, and others hopped on freight trains, riding in **boxcars**.

The "Merger Movement"   As the economy finally revived in the late 1890s, Americans witnessed an astonishing number of mergers in manufacturing and mining—a "merger movement" that lasted from 1898 until 1902. The high point came in 1899, with 1,208 mergers involving $2.3 billion in capital. The merger movement resulted partly from economic weaknesses revealed by the railroad companies. The threat of vicious competition among reviving manufacturing companies prompted reorganization there too.

The most prominent of the new corporations was United States Steel. As the economy edged out of the depression, J. P. Morgan began combining separate steel-related companies to create a vertically integrated operation. Andrew Carnegie had never carried vertical integration to the point of manufacturing final steel products such as wire, barrels, or tubes. By vertically integrating to include that last step, Morgan threatened to close off a significant part of Carnegie's market. Faced with the formidable prospect of having to build his own manufacturing plants for finished products, Carnegie sold all his holdings to Morgan for $480 million. In 1901 Morgan combined Carnegie's company with his own to create

boxcars An enclosed railroad car with sliding side doors, used to transport freight.

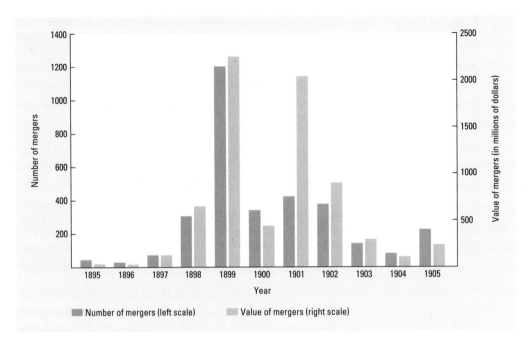

FIGURE 16.4 Recorded Mergers in Mining and Manufacturing, 1895–1905

The last few years of the 1890s and early 1900s witnessed the "merger movement," a restructuring of significant parts of corporate America. Note how the creation of United States Steel, the first "billion-dollar corporation," affects the bar for value for 1901.

United States Steel, the first corporation capitalized at over a billion dollars (see Figure 16.4).

As with railroad reorganization in the 1880s, investment bankers usually sought two objectives in reorganizing an industry: first, to make the industry stable so that investments would yield predictable dividends, and second, to make the industry efficient and productive so that dividends would be high. Toward that end, investment bankers not only drove the mergers but also placed their representatives on the boards of directors of the newly created companies, to guarantee that those two objectives were top priority. By 1912, the three leading New York banking firms together occupied 341 directorships in 112 major companies. Investment bankers argued that benefits from their activities extended far beyond the dividends that shareholders received. One of Morgan's associates predicted in 1901 that as a result of mergers and restructuring, "production would become more regular, labor would be more steadily employed at better wages, and panics caused by overproduction would become a thing of the past."

In fact, the new industrial combinations failed to produce long-term economic stability. The economy continued to alternate between expansion and contraction. After the severe depression of 1893–1897, for example, a period of general expansion was interrupted by downturns in 1903, 1907–1908, 1910–1911, and

1913–1914. Morgan's hopes for stability through centralized control failed to be realized, but his activities and those of his contemporaries created many of the characteristics of modern business. Many industries were oligopolistic, dominated by a few vertically integrated companies, and the stock market had moved beyond the sale of railroad securities to play an important role in raising capital for industry.

STUDY TOOLS

SUMMARY

After 1865, large-scale manufacturing developed quickly in the United States, built on a foundation of abundant natural resources, a pool of skilled workers, expanding harvests, and favorable government policies. The outcome was the transformation of the U.S. economy.

Entrepreneurs improved and extended railway lines, creating a national transportation network. Manufacturers and merchants now began to think in terms of a national market for raw materials and finished goods. Railroads were the first businesses to grapple with the many problems related to size, and they made choices that other businesses imitated. Investment bankers, notably J. P. Morgan, led in combining separate rail companies into larger and more profitable systems. Steel was the crucial building material for much of industrial America, and Andrew Carnegie revolutionized the steel industry. He became one of the best known of many entrepreneurs who developed manufacturing operations of unprecedented size and complexity.

What Carnegie did in steel, John D. Rockefeller did in oil. Others followed their lead, producing oligopoly and vertical integration in many industries. Technology and advertising emerged as important competitive devices. One important result was the introduction of both a wide range of new consumer goods and new ways for consumers to purchase. Some southerners promoted the creation of a New South through industrialization and a more diversified agricultural base. The outcome was mixed—the South did acquire significant industry, but the region's poverty was little reduced.

Federal policymakers hoped for the rapid development of the West and often used the public domain to accomplish that purpose. Native Americans, especially those of the Great Plains, seemed to pose an obstacle to industrial development, but most were defeated by the army and relegated to reservations. Throughout the West, railroad construction overcame the vast distances, making possible cattle raising on the western Great Plains, farming in the central part of the nation, extensive mining, and lumbering. In California especially, landowners transformed western agriculture into a large-scale commercial undertaking. Water posed a significant constraint on economic development in many parts of the West, prompting efforts to reroute natural water sources.

Throughout the late nineteenth century, the economy moved through cycles of expansion and contraction, with especially severe depressions in the 1870s and

1890s. At the end of the 1890s, a large number of mergers in mining and manufacturing were seen as having the potential to stabilize the economy, but ultimately failed to do so.

CHRONOLOGY

RECONSTRUCTION	
1850s	Development of Bessemer and Kelly steel-making processes
1861	Protective tariff
1862	Land-Grant College Act, Homestead Act, Pacific Railroad Act
1865	Civil War ends
1866–1880	Cattle drives north from Texas
1867–1868	Treaties establish major western reservations
1869	First transcontinental railroad completed
1870	Standard Oil incorporated
1870s–1880s	Extension of farming to Great Plains
1872	Montgomery Ward opens first U.S. mail-order business
1873–1879	Depression
1874	American Indian resistance ends on southern plains
1875	Andrew Carnegie opens nation's largest steel plant
1876	Alexander Graham Bell invents the telephone Indian victory in Battle of Little Big Horn
1879	Invention of the incandescent light bulb
1880s	Railroad expansion and consolidation Standard Oil Trust organized
1882–1885	Recession
1883	Northern Pacific Railroad completed to Portland
1887	American Sugar Refining Company formed
1890	Conflict at Wounded Knee Creek
1902	Reclamation Act

FOCUS QUESTIONS

If you have mastered this chapter, you should be able to answer these questions and explain the terms that follow the questions.

1. What factors encouraged economic growth and industrial development after the Civil War?
2. What was the significance of the railroad and steel industries in the new industrial economy that emerged after the Civil War?

3. How did investment bankers such as J. P. Morgan contribute to the new industrial economy?
4. How and why did companies expand their operations and control within an industry?
5. In what ways was the economy of the South distinctive?
6. What were the causes and outcomes of the Indian wars of the late nineteenth century? Could they have been avoided?
7. What were the major ways in which the West was incorporated into the national economy?
8. What were the major changes in the U.S. economy from the Civil War to World War I?

KEY TERMS

Homestead Act (*p.* 451)

Land-Grant College Act (*p.* 451)

Pacific Railway Act (*p.* 454)

mail-order sales (*p.* 457)

John Pierpont Morgan (*p.* 458)

Andrew Carnegie (*p.* 459)

Social Darwinism (*p.* 460)

Gospel of Wealth (*p.* 461)

Thomas A. Edison (*p.* 464)

department stores (*p.* 466)

New South (*p.* 468)

Henry Grady (*p.* 468)

horse culture (*p.* 471)

Lakota (*p.* 471)

Crazy Horse (*p.* 474)

Sitting Bull (*p.* 474)

Great Sioux War (*p.* 474)

Little Big Horn River (*p.* 474)

Chief Joseph (*p.* 474)

Ghost Dance (*p.* 474)

Wounded Knee Creek (*p.* 475)

Reclamation Act (*p.* 483)

Sierra Club (*p.* 483)

17

LIFE IN THE GILDED AGE, 1865–1900

CHAPTER OUTLINE

• The New Urban America • New South, Old Problems • Ethnicity and Race in the Gilded Age • Workers Organize • Study Tools

---

THE NEW URBAN AMERICA

During the late nineteenth century, American cities boomed in size. Chicago doubled to take second rank, behind New York. In just ten years, Brooklyn grew by more than 40 percent, St. Louis by nearly 30 percent, and San Francisco by almost as much. Cities not only added more people but also expanded upward and outward, and became more complex, both socially and economically. The burgeoning cities presented new vistas of opportunity for some, especially the middle class. In the new urban environments, some women questioned traditionally defined gender roles, as did gays and lesbians. But as cities grew, so did the population of their most disadvantaged residents.

The New Face of the City Many Americans were fascinated by their burgeoning cities. Cities boasted technological innovations that many equated with progress, but the lure of the city stemmed from more than telephones, streetcars, and technological gadgetry. Samuel Lane Loomis in 1887 listed the many activities to be found in cities: "The churches and the schools, the theatres and concerts, the lectures, fairs, exhibitions, and galleries … and the mighty streams of human beings that forever flow up and down the thoroughfares." Not every urban vista was so appealing. Some visitors were shocked and repulsed by the poverty, crime, and filth that cluttered the urban landscape.

Filled with glamour and destitution, cities grew rapidly. Cities with more than 50,000 people grew almost twice as fast as rural areas (see Figure 17.1). The nation

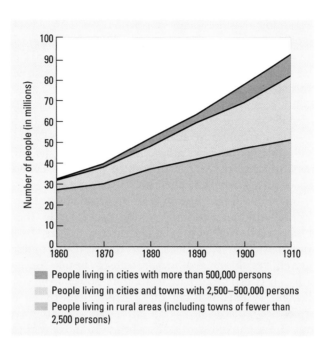

FIGURE 17.1 Urban and Rural Population of the United States, 1860–1910

Although much of the population increase between 1860 and 1910 came in urban areas, the number of people living in rural areas increased as well. Notice, too, that the largest increase was in towns and cities that had between 2,500 and 500,000 people.

Source: U.S. Bureau of the Census, Department of Commerce, *Historical Statistics of the United States*, 2 vols. (Washington, D.C.: U.S. Government Printing Office, 1975), Series A-58, A-59, A-69, A-119.

had twenty-five cities that large in 1870, with a total population of 5 million. By 1890, fifty-eight cities had reached that size and held nearly 12 million people. Nearly all these cities were in the Northeast and near the Great Lakes. The mechanization of American agriculture meant that farming required fewer workers, so America's farmlands contributed significantly to the growth of the cities, along with immigration from outside the United States, especially Europe.

The growth of manufacturing went hand in hand with urban expansion. By the late nineteenth century, the nation had developed a manufacturing belt. This region, which included nearly all the largest cities as well as the bulk of the nation's manufacturing and finance, may be thought of as constituting the nation's urban-industrial "core." Some of the cities in this region—notably Boston, New York, Baltimore, Buffalo, and St. Louis—had long been among the busiest ports in the nation. Now manufacturing also flourished there. Other cities developed as industrial centers from their beginnings. Some cities became known for a particular product—iron and steel in Pittsburgh, clothing in New York City, meatpacking in Chicago, flour milling in Minneapolis. A few cities, especially New York, stood out as major centers for finance.

As the urban population swelled and the urban economy grew more complex, cities expanded upward and outward. In the early 1800s, most cities measured only a few miles across, and most residents got around on foot. Historians call such places "**walking cities**." Buildings were rarely higher than four stories. Small factories existed here and there among warehouses and commercial offices near the docks. In the late nineteenth century, new technologies for construction and transportation transformed the cities.

Until the 1880s, construction techniques restricted building height because the lower walls carried the structure's full weight. William LeBaron Jenney designed the first skyscraper—ten stories high, erected in Chicago in 1885. Chicago architects also took the lead in designing other tall buildings, adapting Jenney's approach by using a steel frame to carry the weight instead of the walls. Economical and efficient, skyscrapers created unique city skylines.

Just as steel-frame buildings allowed cities to grow upward, so new transportation technologies permitted cities to expand outward. In the 1850s, horses pulled the first streetcars over iron rails laid in city streets. By the 1870s and 1880s, some cities boasted streetcar lines powered by underground moving cables. Electricity, however, revolutionized urban transit. Frank Sprague designed a streetcar driven by an electric motor that drew its power from an overhead wire and first installed his system in Richmond, Virginia, in 1888. Within a dozen years, electric streetcars replaced nearly all horse cars and cable cars. In the early 1900s, some large cities, choked with traffic, began to move their electrical streetcars above or below street level, thereby creating elevated trains and subways. Thus elaborate networks of rails came to connect **suburbs** to central business districts. Middle-class women wearing white gloves and stylish hats rode on streetcars to well-stocked downtown department stores. Skilled workers took other streetcar lines to and from their jobs. Streetcars also carried the typists, bookkeepers, and corporate executives who filled the banks and offices in the city's center.

New construction technologies also launched bridges spanning rivers and bays that had once limited urban growth. When the Brooklyn Bridge was completed in 1883, it was hailed as a new wonder of the world. Other great bridges soon followed.

As bridges and streetcar lines pushed outward from the city center, cities annexed suburban areas. In 1860 Chicago had occupied 17 square miles; forty years later, it took in 190 square miles. Boston grew from 5 square miles to 39, and St. Louis from 14 square miles to 61. As streetcars expanded the city, suburban railroad lines began to bring more distant villages within commuting distance of urban centers. Wealthier residents who could afford the passenger fare now left the city at the end of the workday. As early as 1873, nearly a hundred suburban communities sent between five and six thousand commuters into Chicago each day, and by 1890 seventy thousand suburbanites were pouring

---

walking city   Term describing cities before changes in urban transportation permitted cities to expand beyond the distance that a person could easily cover on foot.

suburb   A residential area lying outside the central city; many residents of suburbs work and shop in the central city though living outside it.

in daily. At about the same time, commuter lines brought more than a hundred thousand workers daily into New York City just from its northern suburbs.

New suburbs ranged outward from the city center in order of wealth. Those who could afford to travel the farthest could also afford the most expensive homes. Those too poor to ride the new transportation lines lived in densely populated and deteriorating neighborhoods in the center of the city or clustered around industrial plants. Much of the burgeoning urban middle class lived between the two extremes, far enough from the central business district that many residents rode streetcars downtown to work or shop.

Caught up in headlong growth, cities and their **infrastructure** developed with only minimal planning. Local governments did little to regulate expansion or create building standards, leaving individual landowners, developers, and builders to make most decisions about land use and construction practices. Everywhere, builders and owners hoped to produce the most space for the least cost. Such profit calculations rarely left room for amenities such as varied designs or open space. Most of the great urban parks that exist today, including Central Park in New York City, Prospect Park in Brooklyn, and Golden Gate Park in San Francisco, were established on the outskirts of their cities, before the surrounding areas were developed.

Given the rapid and largely unplanned nature of most urban growth, city governments usually had difficulty meeting all the demands for expanded municipal utilities and services—fire and police protection, schools, sewage disposal, street maintenance, water supply.

The quality and quantity of the water supply varied greatly from city to city. Some cities spent enormous sums to transport water over long distances, but water quality remained a problem in most locales. As city officials began to understand that germs caused diseases, some cities introduced filtration and **chlorination** of their water. Even so, by the early twentieth century, only 6 percent of urban residents received filtered water.

City residents also faced major obstacles in disposing of sewage, cleaning streets (especially given the ever-present horses), and removing garbage. Even when cities built sewer lines, they usually dumped the untreated sewage into some nearby body of water. The disgusted mayor of Cleveland in 1881 called the Cuyahoga River "an open sewer through the center of the city"; similar situations existed in most large cities.

Few city streets were paved, and most became mud holes in the rain, threw up clouds of dust in dry weather, and froze into deep ruts in the winter. Chicago in 1890 included 2,048 miles of streets, but only 629 miles were paved, typically with wooden blocks—and Chicago was not unusual. Only in the late nineteenth century did cities begin using asphalt paving. Sometimes it was easier to pave streets than to maintain them: after clearing garbage from a street in the 1890s, one Chicagoan discovered pavement buried under 18 inches of trash.

infrastructure   Basic facilities that a society needs to function, such as transportation systems, water and power lines, and public institutions such as schools, post offices, and prisons.

chlorination   The treatment of water with the chemical chlorine to kill germs.

City utilities and services, including gas, public transit, sometimes water, and later electricity and telephone service, were typically provided by private companies operating under **franchises** from the city. Entrepreneurs eagerly competed for such franchises, sometimes bribing city officials to secure them. As a result, new residential areas sometimes had gas lines before sewers, and streetcars before paved streets.

At first, urban growth seemed to outstrip the abilities of city officials and residents to provide for its consequences. Nonetheless, most city utilities and services improved significantly between 1870 and 1900. New York City created the first uniformed police force in 1845, and other cities followed. By 1871, major cities had switched from volunteer fire companies to paid, professional firefighters. The new system proved inadequate, however, in the Great Chicago Fire of 1871, which devastated 3 square miles, including much of the downtown, killed more than 250 people, and left 18,000 homeless. Such disasters spurred efforts to improve fire protection by better training and equipping firefighters and by regulating construction so that buildings were more fire-resistant. By 1900, most American cities had impressive firefighting forces. Chicago had more firefighters and fire engines than London, a city three times its size.

The New Urban Middle Class   The Gilded Age brought significant changes to the lives of many middle-class Americans, especially those who made up the army of accountants, lawyers, secretaries, agents, and managers who staffed developing corporate headquarters and professional offices in the rising central business districts. Streetcar lines allowed this growing middle class to live in expanding suburbs distinct from both the neighborhoods of the industrial working class and the enclaves of the wealthy.

Single-family houses set amid carefully tended lawns were common in many new middle-class neighborhoods or suburbs in the late nineteenth century. Such developments accelerated the tendency of American urban and suburban areas to sprawl for miles and have population densities much lower than those of European cities of the same time. Owning property had long been central to the American dream. In the late nineteenth century, the single-family house became the realization of that dream for many middle-class families. Many members of the middle class found it especially attractive to acquire that house in a suburb connected to the city by streetcar or commuter rail. Such suburbs allowed the urban middle class to avoid the congestion of the slums, the violence of labor conflicts, and the higher property taxes that funded city governments.

In the new middle-class suburbs and urban neighborhoods, many middle-class families employed a domestic servant to assist with household chores, and middle-class women often participated in social organizations outside the home. Unlike many working-class families, middle-class parents rarely expected their children to contribute to the family's finances.

---

franchise   Government authorization allowing a company to provide a public service in a certain area.

Middle-class families provided the major market for an expansion of daily newspapers, which began to include sections designed to appeal to women—household hints, fashion advice, and news of women's organizations—along with sports sections aimed at men, and comics for the children. Urban middle-class households were also likely to subscribe to family magazines such as the *Ladies' Home Journal* and the *Saturday Evening Post*. Much of the advertising in such publications was aimed at the middle class, fostering the emergence of what historians have called a **consumer culture** among middle-class women, who became responsible for nearly all their family's shopping.

Middle-class parents' concern for their children's education combined with other factors to produce important changes in American education. Between 1870 and 1900, most northern and western states and territories established school attendance laws, requiring children between certain ages (usually 8 to 14) to attend school for a minimum number of weeks each year, typically twelve to sixteen. The largest increase in school attendance was at the secondary level. There were fewer than 800 high schools in the entire nation in 1878, but 5,500 by 1898. The proportion of high school graduates in the population tripled in the late nineteenth century. By 1890, four-year, public high schools were to be found in urban areas throughout most of the country, except for the South (as discussed later in this chapter). The high school curriculum also changed, adding courses in the sciences, civics, business, home economics, and skills needed by industry, such as drafting, woodworking, and the mechanical trades. From 1870 onward, women outnumbered men among high school graduates. The growth of high schools, however, was largely an urban, middle-class phenomenon. In rural areas, few students continued beyond the eighth grade, and urban working-class youth often started working full-time at about the same age.

College enrollments also grew, with the largest gains in the new state universities created under the Land-Grant College Act of 1862. Even so, college students came disproportionately from middle-class and upper-class families and rarely from farms. The college curriculum changed from courses required of all students (Latin, Greek, mathematics, rhetoric, and religion) to a system in which students focused on a major. Land-grant universities were required to provide instruction in engineering and agriculture. Other new college subjects included economics, political science, modern languages, laboratory sciences, business administration, and teacher preparation. In 1870 the curricula in most colleges still resembled those of a century before. By 1900, curricula looked much like those today.

Despite the growing female majority through the high school level, far fewer women than men marched in college graduation processions. Only one college graduate in seven was a woman in 1870, and this ratio improved to only one in four by 1900 (see Figure 17.2). In 1879 fewer than half of the nation's colleges admitted women, although most public universities did so. Twenty years later, four-fifths of all colleges, universities, and professional schools enrolled women.

---

consumer culture   A consumer buys products for personal use; a consumer culture emphasizes the values and attitudes that derive from the participants' roles as consumers.

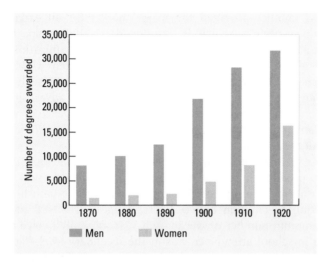

FIGURE 17.2 Number of First Degrees Awarded by Colleges and Universities, 1870–1920

This figure shows the change in the number of people receiving B.A., B.S., or other first college degrees, at ten-year intervals from 1870 to 1920. Notice that after 1890, the number of women increased more rapidly than the number of men.

Source: U.S. Department of Commerce, Bureau of the Census, *Historical Statistics of the United States, Colonial Times to 1970*, Bicentennial edition, 2 vols. (Washington, D.C.: Government Printing Office, 1975), 1: 385–386.

Regardless of such impressive gains for coeducation, some colleges remained all-male enclaves, especially prestigious private institutions such as Harvard and Yale. Colleges exclusively for women began to appear after the Civil War, partly because so many colleges still refused to admit women and partly in keeping with the notion that men and women should occupy "separate spheres." Such institutions also provided opportunities for women as faculty members. The initial faculty of Vassar College, chartered in 1861, consisted of eight men and twenty-two women, including Maria Mitchell, a leading astronomer and the first female member of the American Academy of Arts and Sciences.

Redefining Gender Roles   Greater educational opportunities for women marked one part of a major reconstruction of gender roles. Throughout the nineteenth century, most Americans defined women's roles as those of wife and mother and guardian of the family, responsible for its moral, spiritual, and physical well-being. This emphasis on **domesticity** also permitted women to take important roles in the church and the school. Business and politics, however, with their competition and potential for corruption, were thought to endanger women's roles as their families' spiritual guardians.

domesticity The notion common throughout much of the nineteenth century that women should focus on the home, nurture of children, church, and school.

Domesticity, some argued, required women to occupy a so-called **separate sphere**, immune from such dangers. Widely touted from the pulpits and in the journals of the day, the concepts of domesticity and separate spheres applied mostly to white middle- and upper-class women in towns and cities. Farm women and working-class women (including most women of color) witnessed too much of the world to fit easily into the patterns of dainty innocence prescribed by advocates of separate spheres.

The concepts of domesticity and, especially, separate spheres came under increasing fire in the late nineteenth century. One challenge came through education. As more and more women finished college, some entered the professions. In 1849 Elizabeth Blackwell became the first woman to complete medical school, and she helped to open a medical school for women in 1868. By the 1880s, some twenty-five hundred women held medical degrees. After 1900, however, medical schools imposed admission practices that sharply reduced the number of female medical students. In 1869, Arabella Mansfield became the first woman admitted to practice law, but the entire nation counted only sixty practicing women attorneys ten years later. Most law schools refused to admit women until the 1890s. Other professions also yielded very slowly to women seeking admission.

Professional careers attracted a few women, but many middle- and upper-class women in towns and cities became involved in other women's activities, especially women's clubs, which claimed 100,000 members nationwide by the 1890s. Ida Wells-Barnett, a crusader for black civil rights, actively promoted the development of black women's clubs. Such clubs often began within the separate women's sphere as forums for discussing literature or art, but they sometimes led women into reform activities in the public sphere. (Of course, women had publicly participated in reform before, especially in the movement to abolish slavery.)

The **Woman's Christian Temperance Union** (WCTU) was organized in 1874 by women who regarded alcohol as the chief reason for men's neglect and abuse of their families. WCTU members committed themselves to total abstinence from all alcohol and sought to protect the home and family by converting others to abstinence and the legal prohibition of alcohol. The organization typically operated through old-stock Protestant churches—especially the Methodists, Presbyterians, Congregationalists, and Baptists. From 1879 until her death in 1898, Frances Willard was the driving force in the organization. Her personal motto was "Do everything," and she was untiring in her work for temperance. By the early 1890s, the WCTU claimed 150,000 members, making it the largest women's organization in the nation. Yet for Willard the organization remained very much devoted to the ideals of domesticity. She once offered a simple statement of purpose for the WCTU: "to make the whole world homelike."

Women's church organizations, clubs, and reform societies all provided experience in working together toward a common cause and sometimes in seeking changes in public policy. Through them, women cultivated leadership skills. These experiences and contacts contributed to the growing effectiveness of women's efforts to establish their right to vote. In 1882 the WCTU

The WCTU developed out of activities by women in various locations in the early 1870s. These early temperance advocates gathered outside saloons, sang hymns, and urged men to come out or to not go in. This group of temperance workers was photographed in Mount Vernon, Ohio, around 1873 or 1874.

endorsed woman suffrage, the first support for that cause from a major women's organization other than those formed specifically to advocate woman suffrage.

Just as women's gender roles were undergoing reconstruction in the late nineteenth century, so too were those of men. In the early nineteenth century, manliness was defined largely in terms of "character," which included courage, honor, independence, duty, and loyalty (including loyalty to a political party), along with providing a good home for a family. With the growth of the urban industrial society, fewer men were self-employed (and thus no longer "independent"), and fewer men had the opportunity to demonstrate courage or boldness. The rise of big-city political organizations dominated by saloonkeepers and working-class immigrants caused some middle- and upper-class males to question older notions of party loyalty.

In response, some middle-class men turned to activities that emphasized male bonding or masculinity. Fraternal organizations modeled on the **Masons** multiplied in the late nineteenth century, usually providing both a ritualistic retreat to a preindustrial era and meager insurance benefits for widows and orphans. Professional athletics, including baseball and boxing, began to attract male spectators of all classes. The Young Men's Christian Association (YMCA) spread rapidly in American cities after the Civil War, emphasizing Christian values, physical fitness, and service. Wilderness camping and hunting—necessities for many Americans in earlier times—became a middle- and upper-class male sport, a demonstration of masculinity. Theodore Roosevelt claimed that hunting big game promoted the manly virtues of "nerve control" and "cool-headedness."

Emergence of a Gay and Lesbian Subculture   Urbanization and economic change contributed to the social redefinition of gender roles for middle-class women and men, but a quite different redefinition occurred at the same time, as burgeoning cities provided a setting for the development of gay and lesbian subcultures.

Homosexual behavior was illegal everywhere. At the same time, however, men and women engaged in a wide variety of socially acceptable same-sex relationships. The concept of separate spheres and the tendency for most schools and workplaces to be segregated by sex meant that many men and women spent much of their time with others of their own sex. Many occupations involved working closely with a partner, sometimes over long periods of time. Such partners—both male or both female—could speak of each other with deep affection without violating prevailing social norms. Same-sex relationships may not have involved physical contact, although kisses and hugs—and sleeping in the same bed—were common expressions of affection among young women. Participants in such same-sex relationships did not consider themselves to be committing what the laws called "an unnatural act," and most married partners of the opposite sex.

Same-sex relationships that involved genital contact violated the law and the expectations of society. In rural communities, where most people knew one another, people physically attracted to those of their own sex apparently suppressed those desires or exercised them discreetly. The record of convictions for **sodomy** indicates that some failed to conceal their activities. A few men and somewhat more women changed their dress and behavior, passed for a member of the other sex, and married someone of their own sex.

In the late nineteenth century, in parts of the United States and Europe, burgeoning cities permitted an anonymity not possible in rural societies. Homosexuals and lesbians gravitated toward the largest cities and began to create distinctive **subcultures**. By the 1890s, one researcher reported that "perverts of

sodomy Varieties of sexual intercourse prohibited by law in the nineteenth century, typically including intercourse between two males.

subculture A group whose members differ from the dominant culture in some values or interests but who share most values and interests with the dominant culture.

both sexes maintained a sort of social set-up in New York City, had their places of meeting, and [the] advantage of police protection." Reports of regular homosexual meeting places—clubs, restaurants, steam baths, parks, streets—also issued from Boston, Chicago, New Orleans, St. Louis, and San Francisco. Although most participants in these subcultures were secretive, some flaunted their sexuality.

In the 1880s, physicians began to study members of these emerging subcultures and created medical names for them, including "homosexual," "lesbian," "invert," and "pervert." Earlier, law and religion had defined particular *actions* as illegal or immoral. The new, clinical definitions emphasized not the actions but instead the *persons* taking the actions. As medical and legal definitions shifted from actions to persons, the nature of same-sex relationships also changed. Once-acceptable behavior, including expressions of affection between heterosexuals of the same sex, became less common as individuals tried to avoid any suggestion that they were anything but heterosexual.

"How the Other Half Lives"   In 1890 Jacob Riis shocked many Americans with the revelations in *How the Other Half Lives*. Of New York City's million and a half inhabitants, Riis claimed, half a million (136,000 families) had begged for food at some time over the preceding eight years. Of these, more than half were unemployed, but only 6 percent were physically unable to work. Most of Riis's book described the appalling conditions of **tenements**—home, he claimed, to three-quarters of the city's population.

Strictly speaking, a tenement is a building occupied by three or more families, but the term came to imply overcrowded and badly maintained housing that was hazardous to the health and safety of its residents. Riis described the typical, cramped New York tenement of his day as

> a brick building from four to six stories high on the street, frequently with a store on the first floor.... Four families occupy each floor, and a set of rooms consists of one or two dark closets, used as bedrooms, with a living room twelve feet by ten. The staircase is too often a dark well in the center of the house ... no direct through ventilation is possible.

Such buildings, Riis insisted, "are the hotbeds of the epidemics that carry death to rich and poor alike; the nurseries of pauperism and crime that fill our jails and police courts.... Above all, they touch the family life with deadly moral contagion." He especially deplored the harmful influence of poverty and miserable housing conditions on children and families.

Crowded conditions in working-class sections of large cities developed in part because so many of the poor needed to live within walking distance of sources of employment for various family members. By dividing buildings into small rental units, landlords packed in more tenants and collected more rent. To pay the rent,

tenement A multifamily apartment building, often unsafe, unsanitary, and overcrowded.

many tenants took in lodgers. Such practices produced shockingly high population densities in lower-income urban neighborhoods.

No other city was as densely populated as New York, but nearly all urban, working-class neighborhoods were crowded. Most Chicago stockyard workers, for example, lived in small row houses near the slaughterhouses. Many owned their own homes. A survey in 1911 revealed that three-quarters of the houses were subdivided into two or more living units, typically of four rooms each, and that a small shanty often sat in the backyard. More than half of all families took in lodgers, and lodgers who worked different shifts at the stockyards sometimes took turns sleeping in the same bed.

Few agreed on the causes of urban poverty, still fewer on its cure. Riis divided the blame among greedy landlords, corrupt officials, and the poor themselves. Henry George, a San Francisco journalist, in *Progress and Poverty*, pointed to the increase in the value of real estate due to urbanization and industrialization, which made it difficult or impossible for many to afford a home of their own. In contrast, the Charity Organization Society (COS), with chapters in a hundred cities by 1895, claimed that, in most cases, individual character defects produced poverty and that assistance for such people only rewarded immorality or laziness. Public or private help should be given only after careful investigation, the COS insisted, and only until the person secured work. Moreover, COS officials expected the recipients of aid to be moral, thrifty, and hardworking.

NEW SOUTH, OLD PROBLEMS

The booming cities of the Gilded Age were located mostly in New England, the Middle Atlantic States, and the east North Central states. As discussed in Chapter 16, some southerners worked to promote a more diverse economic base, with more manufacturing and less reliance on a few staple agricultural crops; they and their neighbors—white and black alike—grappled, too, with the legacy of slavery, Civil War, Reconstruction, and poverty. In the end, white southerners created a racially segregated social structure that persisted with little change for more than a half-century.

Social Patterns in the New South
Of the nation's twenty-five largest cities in 1890, only New Orleans was located in the South, and no other southern city came close to its 242,000 people. Atlanta, which prided itself as the center of the New South and had nearly doubled in size between 1880 and 1890, counted nearly 81,000 people in 1890 but ranked only forty-first among the nation's cities. Birmingham, center of the developing southern iron and steel industry, grew by ten times between 1880 and 1900, but still ranked only one hundredth in the nation in size as late as 1900. Thus, while an urban middle class did develop and grow in the South, it was proportionately smaller than its counterpart to the north—and was sharply divided by the lines of race.

Education lagged throughout much of the South, especially in rural areas. Compared with much of the rest of the nation, fewer children attended school in the South, where the school term was often limited to a few months, and school facilities were often inadequate. Few southern states had compulsory school attendance laws. Southerners were slow to create public high schools—as late as 1903, the entire state of Georgia had only four four-year, public high schools. Instead, most public schools stopped at the eighth grade, and private academies educated the children of the upper class. Some of the industries of the New South, especially textiles and cigarettes, were built on child labor, so many children worked instead of attending school. Seventy percent of southern cotton-mill workers were younger than 21, and most were under 14. Mostly girls, they worked 70-hour weeks and earned 10 to 20 cents a day. Not surprisingly, illiteracy remained much higher in the South than elsewhere in the nation. As late as 1900, 10 percent of the southern white population was illiterate, compared with fewer than 4 percent in the rest of the country. Illiteracy among African Americans was significantly higher—35 percent in the South, and 19 percent in the rest of the country.

Despite repeated backing for the idea of a New South by some southern leaders, and despite growth of some industry in the South, the late nineteenth century was also the time when the myths of the **Old South** and the **Lost Cause** reached into nearly every aspect of white southern life. Popular fiction and song, North and South, romanticized the pre–Civil War "Old South" as a place of gentility and gallantry, where "kindly" plantation owners cared for "loyal" slaves. The "Lost Cause" myth portrayed the Confederacy as a heroic, even noble, effort to retain the life and values of the Old South. Leading southerners—especially Democratic Party leaders—promoted the Lost Cause myth. Hundreds of statues of Confederate soldiers appeared on courthouse lawns, and gala commemorative events and organizations reflected devotion to the myth among many white southerners. One of the few dissenting voices was that of Samuel Clemens (Mark Twain).

The Second Mississippi Plan and the Atlanta Compromise   Although Reconstruction ended in 1877, the Civil Rights Act of 1875 should have protected African Americans against discrimination in public places. Some state laws required racial separation—for example, many states prohibited racial intermarriage. State or local law, or sometimes local practice, had produced racially separate school systems, churches, hospitals, cemeteries, and other voluntary organizations. Segregation existed throughout the South, driven by local custom and the ever-present threat of violence against any African American

---

Old South Term for a romanticized view of the pre–Civil War South as a place of gentility and gallantry.

Lost Cause Term for a romanticized view of the Confederate struggle in the Civil War as a noble but doomed effort to preserve a way of life.

who dared to challenge it. Restrictions on black political participation were also extralegal, enforced through coercion or intimidation.

Then, in the **Civil Rights Cases** of 1883, the U.S. Supreme Court ruled the Civil Rights Act of 1875 unconstitutional. The Court said that the "equal protection" promised by the Fourteenth Amendment applied only to state governments, not to individuals or companies. Though state governments were obligated to treat all citizens as equal before the law, private businesses need not do the same. Southern lawmakers soon began to require businesses to practice segregation. In 1887 the Florida legislature ordered separate accommodations on railroad trains. Mississippi passed a similar law the next year, and other southern states soon followed.

Mississippi whites took a more brazen step in 1890, holding a state constitutional convention to eliminate African Americans' participation in politics. The new provisions did not mention the word *race*. Instead, they imposed a **poll tax**, a literacy test, and other requirements for voting. Everyone understood, though, that these measures were designed to **disfranchise** black voters. Men who failed the literacy test could vote if they could understand a section of the state constitution or law when a local (white) official read it to them. The typical result was that the only illiterates who could vote were white. Most of the South watched this so-called Second Mississippi Plan unfold with great interest.

In 1895 a black educator signaled his apparent willingness to accept disfranchisement and segregation for the moment. Born into slavery in 1856, **Booker T. Washington** worked as a janitor while studying at Hampton Normal and Agricultural Institute in Virginia, a school that combined preparation for elementary school teaching with vocational education in agriculture and industrial work. Washington then taught at Hampton. In 1881 the Alabama legislature authorized a black **normal school** at Tuskegee. Washington became its principal, and he made Tuskegee Normal and Industrial Institute into a leading black educational institution.

In 1895 Atlanta hosted the Cotton States and International Exposition. The exposition directors invited Washington to speak at the opening ceremonies, hoping he could reach out to southern whites, southern blacks, and northern whites. Washington did not disappoint the directors. In his speech, he seemed to accept an inferior status for blacks for the present: "No race can prosper till it learns that there is as much dignity in tilling a field as in writing a poem. It is at the bottom of life we must begin, and not at the top." While implying that equal rights had to be earned, Washington also seemed to condone segregation: "In all things that are purely social, we can be as separate as the fingers, yet one as the hand in all things essential to mutual progress."

poll tax   Annual tax imposed on each citizen; used in some southern states to disfranchise black voters, as the only penalty for not paying was loss of voting rights.

disfranchise   To take away the right to vote.

normal school   Two-year school for training teachers for grades 1–8.

Booker T. Washington posed for this formal portrait around the time of his Atlanta address.

Library of Congress

The speech—soon dubbed the **Atlanta Compromise**—won great acclaim. Southern whites were pleased to hear a black educator urge his race to accept segregation and disfranchisement. Northern whites too were receptive to the notion that the South would work out its race relations by itself. Until his death in 1915, Washington was the most prominent black leader in the nation, at least among white Americans.

Among African Americans, Washington's message found a mixed reception. Some accepted his approach as best for the moment. Others criticized him for sacrificing black rights. Henry M. Turner, a bishop of the African Methodist Episcopal Church in Atlanta, declared that Washington "will have to live a long time to undo the harm he has done our race." Privately, however, Washington never accepted disfranchisement and segregation as permanent fixtures in southern life.

Even as African Americans debated Washington's Atlanta speech, southern lawmakers were redefining the legal status of African Americans. State after state followed the lead of Mississippi and disfranchised black voters. Louisiana, in

1898, added the infamous **grandfather clause**, specifying that men who failed to meet new requirements could vote if their fathers or grandfathers had been eligible to vote in 1867 (before the Fourteenth Amendment extended the suffrage to African Americans). Thus, poor or illiterate whites could vote. Methods varied, but each southern state set up barriers to voting and then carved holes through which only whites could pass. Southern Democrats, who had long defined themselves as the "white man's party" or the party of white supremacy, also restricted their primaries and conventions to whites only. South Carolina took this step first, in 1896, and other states followed.

Southern lawmakers also began to extend segregation by law, especially after the U.S. Supreme Court's decision in **Plessy v. Ferguson** (1896), involving a Louisiana law requiring segregated railroad cars. When the Court ruled that "separate but equal" facilities did not violate the equal protection clause of the Four-teenth Amendment, southern legislators applied that reasoning elsewhere, requiring segregation of almost everything—and especially public places such as parks and restaurants.

Violence against African Americans accompanied the new laws, providing an unmistakable lesson in the consequences of resistance. From 1885 to 1900, when the South was redefining relations between the races, the region witnessed more than twenty-five hundred deaths by lynching—about one every two days. The vic-tims were almost all African Americans, and the largest numbers were in the states with the most black residents.

ETHNICITY AND RACE IN THE GILDED AGE

By 1890, immigrants made up more than 40 percent of the population of New York, San Francisco, and Chicago, and more than a third of the population in sev-eral other major cities. The United States has always attracted large numbers of immigrants, but never before experienced a flood of immigrants like that between the Civil War and World War I. Nearly all these immigrants came from Europe, and many settled in cities. Significant numbers of immigrants also came from Asia, nearly all of whom settled in the West. At the same time, American Indians and Latinos in the Southwest, like African Americans in the South, faced new con-straints on their choices and opportunities.

A Flood of Immigrants from Europe   The numbers of immigrants varied from year to year—higher in prosperous years, lower in depression years—but the trend was constantly upward. Nearly a quarter of a million arrived in 1865, two-thirds of a million in 1881, and a million in

---

grandfather clause Louisiana rule that permitted a man to vote if his father or grandfather was eligible in 1867, allowing white men to circumvent rules disfranchising blacks; now refers to any law that exempts some people from current regulations based on past practice.

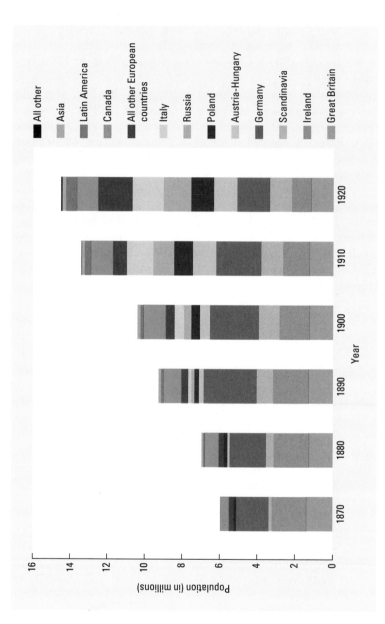

FIGURE 17.3 Foreign-Born Population of the United States, 1870–1920

This graph shows the largest foreign-born groups living in the United States at the time of the census every ten years. The number of foreign-born increased dramatically during these fifty years, and the foreign-born were increasingly diverse by country of origin.

Source: U.S. Department of Commerce, Bureau of the Census, *Historical Statistics of the United States, Colonial Times to 1970*, Bicentennial edition, 2 vols. (Washington, D.C.: Government Printing Office, 1975), 1: 116–117.

1905. In the 1870s and 1880s, most immigrants came from Great Britain, Ireland, **Scandinavia**, Germany, and Canada, but after about 1890 increasing numbers arrived from southern and eastern Europe. By 1910, immigrants and their children made up more than 35 percent of the total population. Figure 17.3 shows the place of birth of the foreign-born population for the census years from 1870 through 1920. Note especially how the foreign-born population became increasingly diverse after 1890.

Immigrants left their former homes for a variety of reasons. In Ireland, for example, a fourfold population increase between 1750 and 1850 combined with changes in agriculture to push people off the land. Repeated failure of potato crops after 1845 produced widespread **famine** and starvation, greatly increasing migration. Similar population pressures in other parts of Europe, though without famine, produced significant population movements—from rural areas to cities, to other parts of Europe, to other parts of the world, including Canada, Argentina, and Australia.

The United States attracted the largest number and the greatest diversity of European immigrants. Some came because of the reputation of the United States for democracy and toleration of religious difference. But nearly all came because America was the "land of opportunity." They came, as one bluntly said, for "jobs" and, as another declared, "for money." In fact, the reasons for immigrating to America varied from person to person, country to country, and year to year.

Irish immigrants, many desperately poor, arrived in greatest numbers before the Civil War, but Irish immigration continued at high levels until the 1890s. Many Irish settled in the cities of the Northeast, comprising a quarter of the population in New York City and Boston as early as 1860. Many immigrants who came in the 1870s and 1880s found that good farmland was available in the north-central states at reasonable prices or even free under the Homestead Act. One woman recalled that, in rural Nebraska in the 1880s, her family could attend Sunday church services in Norwegian, Danish, Swedish, French, Czech, or German, as well as English. Scandinavians, Dutch, Swiss, Czechs, and Germans were most likely to be farmers, but all those groups were also to be found in cities, especially in the Midwest. Many immigrants lived in the urban-industrial core region, or **manufacturing belt**, especially in urban areas, but immigrant communities were not limited to cities or industrial areas.

Patterns of immigrant settlement reflect the expectations immigrants had about America, as well as opportunities they found when they arrived. After 1890, farmland was more difficult to obtain. The 1890s also marked a shift in the sources of immigration, with proportionately more coming from southern and eastern Europe and arriving with little or no capital. Newcomers after 1890 were more likely to find work in the rapidly expanding industries, especially mining, transportation,

Scandinavia   The region of northern Europe consisting of Norway, Sweden, Denmark, and Iceland.

famine   A serious and widespread shortage of food.

manufacturing belt   The region that included most factories and, in the late nineteenth century, also included most of the nation's large cities and railroad lines and much of its mining.

and manufacturing. Of course, there were many individual variations on these patterns. Some immigrants coming after 1890 intended to become farmers and succeeded. Many who came before 1890 became industrial workers or took other urban jobs.

In the nineteenth century, most old-stock Americans assumed that immigrants should quickly learn English, become citizens, and restructure their lives and values to resemble those of long-time residents. Most immigrants, however, resisted rapid **assimilation**. For the majority, assimilation took place over a lifetime or even over generations. Most retained elements of their own cultures even as they embraced their new lives in America. Their sense of identity drew on two elements—where they had come from and where they lived now—and they often came to think of themselves as hyphenated Americans: German-Americans, Irish-Americans, Norwegian-Americans.

On arriving in America, with its strange language and customs, many immigrants sought others who shared their cultural values, practiced their religion, and especially, spoke their language. Ethnic communities emerged wherever there were large numbers of immigrants. These communities played a significant role in newcomers' transition from the old country to America. They gave new immigrants a chance to learn about their new home with assistance from those who had come earlier. At the same time, newcomers could, without apology or embarrassment, retain cultural values and behaviors from their homelands. Foreign-language newspapers helped to connect the old country to the new, for they provided news from the old country as well as from other similar communities in the United States.

For members of nearly every **ethnic group**, religious institutions provided important building blocks of ethnic group identity. Protestant immigrant groups created new church organizations based on both theology and language. Catholic parishes in immigrant neighborhoods often took on the ethnic characteristics of the community, with services in the immigrants' language and special observances transplanted from the old country. Jewish congregations, too, often differed according to the ethnic background of their members.

Nativism   Though most immigrants changed their behavior, many old-stock Americans (including some only a generation removed from immigrant forebears themselves) expected immigrants to lay aside their previous identities and blend into prevailing cultural patterns. But many old-stock Americans fretted over the multiplication of German and Italian newspapers, feared to go into communities where they rarely heard an English sentence, and shuddered at the sprouting of Catholic schools. Such fears and

---

assimilation   Among culturally distinct groups, the process of adopting the behaviors and values of the dominant society and its culture.

ethnic group   A group that shares a racial, religious, linguistic, cultural, or national heritage.

misgivings fostered the growth of **nativism**: the view that old-stock values and social patterns were preferable to those of immigrants. Nativists argued that only their values and institutions were genuinely American, and they feared that immigrants threatened those traditions.

Nativism was often linked to anti-Catholicism. Irish and German immigrant groups, and later Italian and Polish groups, included large numbers of Catholics, and many old-stock Americans came to identify the Catholic Church as an immigrant church. The **American Protective Association** (APA), founded in 1887, loudly proclaimed itself the voice of anti-Catholicism. Its members pledged not to hire Catholics, not to vote for them, and not to strike with them. A half-million strong by 1894, APA members often tried to dominate the Republican Party—and succeeded in parts of the Midwest—before they died out by the late 1890s.

Jews, too, faced religious antagonism. In the 1870s, increasing numbers of organizations and businesses began to discriminate against Jews. Some employers refused to hire Jews. After 1900, such discrimination intensified. Many social organizations barred Jews from membership, and **restrictive covenants** kept them from buying homes in certain neighborhoods.

During the 1890s, a diverse political coalition emerged aimed at reducing immigration. Labor organizations began to look at immigrants as potential threats to jobs and wage levels. Some employers began to connect immigrants with unions and radicalism and to charge that unions represented foreign, un-American influences. Foreign-born radicals and **anarchists** were a special target, as newspapers claimed that "there is no such thing as an American anarchist." In 1901 Leon Czolgosz, an American-born anarchist with a foreign-sounding name, assassinated President William McKinley, and Congress promptly passed a bill barring anarchists from immigrating to the United States.

During the 1890s, nativism grew as the sources of European immigration began to shift from northwestern Europe to southern and eastern Europe, bringing larger numbers of Italians, Poles and other Slavs, and eastern European Jews. Anti-Catholicism and anti-Semitism combined to create a sense that these "**new immigrants**" were less desirable than "**old immigrants**" from northwestern Europe.

The arrival of many "new immigrants" after 1890 coincided with a growing tendency to glorify Anglo-Saxons (ancestors of the English) and accomplishments

---

nativism   The view that old-stock values and social patterns were preferable to those of immigrants.

restrictive covenant   Provision in a property title restricting subsequent sale or use of the property, often specifying sale only to a white Christian.

anarchist   A person who believes that all forms of government are oppressive and should be abolished.

"new immigrants"   Newcomers from southern and eastern Europe who began to arrive in the United States in significant numbers during the 1890s and after.

"old immigrants"   Newcomers from northern and western Europe who made up much of the immigration to the United States before the 1890s.

by the English and English Americans. Proponents of Anglo-Saxonism became alarmed by statistics showing old-stock Americans having fewer children than immigrants. Some voiced fears of "race suicide" in which Anglo-Saxons allowed themselves to be bred out of existence. With such anxieties feeding their prejudices, some nativists became blatant racists. By the 1890s, these economic, political, religious, and racist strains converged in demands that the federal government restrict immigration from Europe.

Immigrants to the Golden Mountain   The West has long had greater ethnic diversity than the rest of the nation (as illustrated in Figure 17.4). In 1900 the western half of the United States included more than 80 percent of all Native Americans, Mexican Americans, and Asian Americans. Between 1854 and 1882, some 300,000 Chinese immigrants entered the United States. Most came from southern China, which in the 1840s and 1850s suffered from political instability, economic distress, and famine. Among early Chinese immigrants who came as part of the California gold rush, California became known as *gam saan*, or "gold mountain." Many Chinese worked in mining or construction, especially western railroad building. Others worked as agricultural laborers and farmers, notably in California. Some made important contributions to crop development, especially fruit growing.

In San Francisco and elsewhere in the West, Chinese immigrants established **Chinatowns**—relatively autonomous and largely self-contained Chinese communities. In San Francisco's Chinatown, immigrants formed kinship organizations and district associations (whose members had come from the same part of China) to assist and protect each other. A confederation of such associations, the Chinese Consolidated Benevolent Association (often called the "Six Companies"), eventually dominated the social and economic life of Chinese communities in much of the West. Such communities were largely male, partly because immigration officials permitted only a few Chinese women to enter the country, apparently to prevent an American-born generation. As was true in many largely male communities, gambling and prostitution flourished, giving Chinatowns reputations as centers for vice.

Almost from the beginning, Chinese immigrants encountered discrimination and violence. During the Gold Rush, a California state tax on foreign-born miners posed a significant burden on Chinese (and also Latino) gold seekers. During the 1870s, many white workers blamed the Chinese for driving wages down and unemployment up. In fact, different economic factors depressed wage levels and brought unemployment, but white workers seeking a scapegoat instigated anti-Chinese riots in Los Angeles in 1871 and in San Francisco in 1877. In these riots, the message was usually the same: "The Chinese Must Go."

In 1882 Congress responded to repeated pressures from Pacific Coast unions by passing the **Chinese Exclusion Act**, prohibiting entry to all Chinese people

Chinatown   A section of a city inhabited chiefly by people of Chinese birth or ancestry.

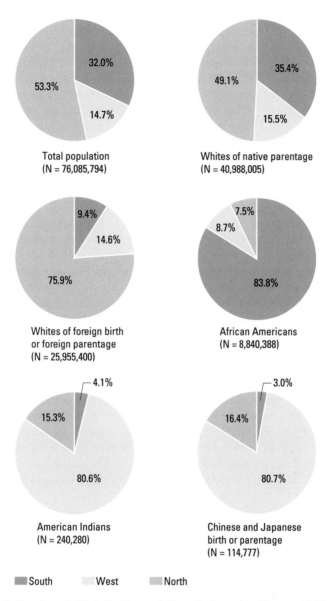

Total population
(N = 76,085,794)

Whites of native parentage
(N = 40,988,005)

Whites of foreign birth
or foreign parentage
(N = 25,955,400)

African Americans
(N = 8,840,388)

American Indians
(N = 240,280)

Chinese and Japanese
birth or parentage
(N = 114,777)

■ South   West   ■ North

FIGURE 17.4 Regional Distribution of Population, by Race, 1900

These pie charts indicate the distinctiveness of the West with respect to race and ethnicity. Note that the West held about 15 percent of the nation's total population and about the same proportion of the nation's white population (including whites who were foreign-born or of foreign parentage) but included more than four-fifths of American Indians and those of Chinese and Japanese birth or parentage.

Source: Data from *Twelfth Census of the United States: 1900* (Washington, D.C., 1901), Population Reports, vol. 1, p. 483, Table 9.

except teachers, students, merchants, tourists, and officials. This was the first significant restriction on immigration. The law reaffirmed that Asian immigrants were not eligible to become naturalized citizens. Soon after, in 1885 anti-Chinese riots swept through much of the West. In Rock Springs, Wyoming Territory, white coal miners burned the Chinatown and killed twenty-eight Chinese. In response, many Chinese retreated to the largest Chinatowns, and some returned to China.

In some parts of the West, the Chinese were subjected to segregation similar to that imposed on African Americans in the South, including residential and occupational segregation rooted in local custom rather than law. In 1871 the San Francisco school board barred Chinese students from that city's public schools. The ban lasted until 1885, when the parents of Mamie Tape convinced the courts to order the city to provide education for their daughter. The city then opened a segregated Chinese school. Segregated schools for Chinese American children were set up in a few other places in the West, but that school segregation began to break down in the 1910s and 1920s.

Organizations based on kinship, region, or occupation sometimes succeeded in fighting anti-Chinese legislation through the courts. When a San Francisco law restricted Chinese laundry owners, they brought a court challenge. In *Yick Wo v. Hopkins* (1886), the U.S. Supreme Court for the first time declared a licensing law unconstitutional because local authorities had used it to discriminate on the basis of race. The decision also extended the Fourteenth Amendment to cover immigrants who were not citizens.

When other immigrants began to arrive from Asia, they too concentrated in the West. Japanese immigrants started coming in significant numbers after 1890. From 1891 through 1907, nearly 150,000 arrived, most through Pacific Coast ports. Whites in the West, especially organized labor, viewed Japanese immigrants in much the same way as they had earlier immigrants from China—with hostility and scorn. Pushed by western labor organizations, President Theodore Roosevelt in 1907 negotiated an agreement with Japan to halt immigration of Japanese laborers.

Forced Assimilation   As headlines about the Great Sioux War, the Nez Perces, and Geronimo faded from the nation's newspapers, many Americans began to describe American Indians as a "vanishing race." But Indian people did not vanish. With the end of armed conflict, relations between Native Americans and the rest of the nation entered a new phase.

Well before the end of the Indian wars, federal policymakers began to implement plans to assimilate Native Americans into white society. Leading scholars, notably Lewis Henry Morgan of the Smithsonian Institution, viewed culture as an evolutionary process. They analyzed groups as being at one of three stages of development: savagery (hunters and gatherers), barbarism (those who farmed and made pottery), and civilization (those with a written language). All peoples, they thought, were evolving toward "higher" cultural types. Most white Americans probably agreed that western Europeans and their descendants around the world had reached the highest level of development. Not until the 1890s did this perspective come under serious challenge, notably from Franz Boas, an anthropologist who held that every culture develops and should be understood on its own, rather than as part of an evolutionary chain.

Public support for changes in federal policy grew in response to speaking tours by American Indians and white reformers and to publication of several exposés, notably Helen Hunt Jackson's *A Century of Dishonor* (1881) and *Ramona* (a novel, 1884). Federal policy-makers accepted reformers' arguments for speeding up the evolutionary process for Native Americans. Apparently no reformers or federal policymakers understood that American Indians had complex cultures that were very different from—but not inferior to—the culture of Americans of European descent.

Education was an important element in the reformers' plans for "civilizing" the Indians. Federal officials worked with churches and philanthropic organizations to establish schools distant from the reservations, where many Native American children were sent to live and study. Intending to assimilate their students into white society, teachers forbade Indian students to speak their languages, practice their religion, or otherwise follow their own cultural patterns. Other educational programs aimed to train adult Indian men to be farmers or mechanics. Federal officials also tried to prohibit some religious observances and traditional practices on reservations.

The **Dawes Severalty Act** (1887) was an important tool in the "civilizing" effort. Its objective was to make the Indians into self-sufficient, property-conscious, profit-oriented, individual farmers—model citizens of nineteenth-century white America. The law created a governmental policy of severalty—that is, individual ownership of land by Native Americans. Reservations were to be divided into individual family farms of 160 acres. Once each family received its allotment, surplus reservation land was to be sold by the government and the proceeds used for Indian education. This policy found enthusiastic support among both reformers urging rapid assimilation and westerners who coveted Indian lands.

Individual landownership, however, violated traditional Native American views that land was for the use of all and that sharing was a major obligation. Though some Indian leaders favored the Dawes Act, others urged Congress to defeat it. Delegates from the Cherokee, Creek, and Choctaw Nations bluntly told Congress, "Our people have not asked for or authorized this.... Our own laws regulate a system of land tenure suited to our condition."

Nonetheless, Congress approved the Dawes Act. The result bore out the warning of Senator Henry Teller of Colorado, who called it "a bill to despoil the Indians of their land." Once allotments to Indian families were made, about 70 percent remained of the reservation lands, much of which were sold. In the end, the Dawes Act did not end the reservation system, nor did it reduce the Indians' dependence on the federal government. It did separate the Indians from a good deal of their land.

Native Americans responded to their situation in various ways. Some tried to cooperate with the assimilation programs. Susan La Flesche, for example, daughter

Luther Standing Bear was called Ota K'te when he was born in 1868, son of a chief who fought against Custer at the Battle of the Little Big Horn. Standing Bear attended the Carlisle Indian School in Pennsylvania, toured with a Wild West Show, became an actor, and belonged to the Actors' Guild (a union). He was also a hereditary chief of the Oglala Lakota. This photo, probably taken in Hollywood in the 1920s, shows him wearing a traditional Lakota headdress.

Denver Public Library, Western History Collection

of an Omaha leader, graduated from medical college in 1889 at the head of her class. But she disappointed her teachers, who wanted her to abandon Indian culture, when she set up her medical practice near the Omaha Reservation, treated both white and Omaha patients, took part in tribal affairs, and managed her land allotment and those of other family members. She also participated in the local white community through the temperance movement and sometimes by preaching in the local Presbyterian church.

Dr. La Flesche seems to have moved easily between two cultures. Some Native Americans preferred the old ways, keeping their children out of school and secretly practicing traditional religious ceremonies. Native American peoples' cultural patterns changed, but not always in the way federal officials anticipated. In Oklahoma, where groups with different traditional cultures lived in close proximity, people began to borrow cultural practices from others. In some places, Indians became part of the wage-earning work force near their reservations, sometimes against the wishes of reservation officials. In the late nineteenth century, the **peyote cult**, based on the hallucinogenic properties of the peyote cactus, emerged as an alternative

peyote cult A religion that included ceremonial use of the hallucinogenic peyote cactus, native to Mexico and the Southwest.

Denver Public Library, Western History Collection

Throughout the Southwest during the late nineteenth and early twentieth centuries, many Mexican American men found work as railway maintenance workers, called section hands. These Mexican American section hands were photographed in Arizona in 1904, traveling on a hand-truck to repair track.

religion. It evolved into the Native American Church, combining elements of traditional Indian culture, Christianity, and peyote use.

Mexican Americans in the Southwest   The United States annexed Texas in 1845 and soon after acquired vast territories from Mexico at the end of the Mexican War. There large numbers of people lived who spoke Spanish, many of them **mestizos**—people of mixed Spanish and Native American ancestry. The treaties by which the United States acquired those territories specified that Mexican citizens living there automatically became American citizens.

Throughout the Southwest during the late nineteenth century, many Mexican Americans lost their land as the region attracted English-speaking whites (often called **Anglos** by those whose first language was Spanish). The Treaty of Guadalupe Hidalgo, which ended the war with Mexico, guaranteed Mexican Americans'

mestizo   A person of mixed Spanish and Indian ancestry.

Anglos   A term applied in the Southwest to English-speaking whites.

landholdings, but the vagueness of Spanish and Mexican land grants encouraged legal challenges. Sometimes Mexican Americans were cheated out of their land through fraud.

The California gold rush, beginning in 1849, attracted fortune seekers from around the world, most from the eastern United States and Europe. In northern California, a hundred thousand gold seekers inundated the few thousand Mexican Americans. People from Latin America who came to California as gold seekers were often driven from the mines by racist harassment and a tax on foreign miners. In southern California, however, there were fewer Anglos until late in the nineteenth century. There, **Californios** won election to local and state office, including Romualdo Pacheco, who served as state treasurer and lieutenant governor and succeeded to the governorship in 1875.

By the 1870s, many of the pueblos (towns created under Mexican or Spanish governments) had become **barrios**—some rural, some in inner cities. Such barrios somewhat resembled the ethnic neighborhoods created by European immigrants. Both had mutual benefit societies, political associations, and newspapers published in the language of the community, and the cornerstone of both was often a church. There was an important difference, however. European immigrants had come to a new land where they anticipated making changes in their own lives to adjust. Barrio residents, in contrast, lived in regions that had been home to Mexicans for generations but now found themselves surrounded by English-speaking Americans who hired them for cheap wages, sometimes scorned their culture, and pressured them to assimilate.

In Texas, as in California, some **Tejanos** had welcomed the break with Mexico. Lorenzo de Zavala, for example, served briefly as the first vice president of the Texas Republic. By 1900, though, much of the land in south Texas had passed out of the hands of Tejano families—sometimes legally, sometimes fraudulently—but the new Anglo ranch owners usually maintained the social patterns characteristic of Tejano ranchers.

A large section of south Texas remained culturally Mexican, home to Tejanos and two-thirds of all Mexican immigrants who came to the United States before 1900. In the 1890s, one journalist described the area as "an overlapping of Mexico into the United States." During the 1860s and 1870s, conflict sometimes broke out as Mexican Americans challenged the political and economic power of Anglo newcomers. In social relations and in politics, all but a few wealthy Tejanos came to be subordinate to the Anglos, who dominated the regional economy and the professions.

In New Mexico Territory, **Hispanos** were clearly the majority throughout the nineteenth century. They consistently made up a majority in the territorial legislature and were frequently elected as territorial delegates to Congress (the only

Californios   The Spanish-speaking settlers of California and their descendants.

barrio   A Spanish-speaking community, often a part of a larger city.

Tejanos   Spanish-speaking people born in Texas.

Hispanos   The Spanish-speaking settlers of New Mexico and their descendants.

territorial position elected by voters). Anglos began to arrive in significant numbers with the first railroad in 1879. Although Hispanos were the majority, many lost their small landholdings in ways similar to patterns in California and Texas—except that some who enriched themselves in New Mexico were wealthy Hispanos.

Until 1910, the Latino population in the Southwest grew more slowly than the Anglo population. After 1910, however, that situation reversed itself as political and social upheavals in Mexico prompted massive migration to the United States. Probably a million people—equivalent to one-tenth of the entire population of Mexico in 1910—arrived over the next twenty years. More than half stayed in Texas, but significant numbers settled in southern California and elsewhere in the Southwest. Inevitably, this new stream of immigrants changed some of the patterns of ethnic relations that had characterized the region since the mid-nineteenth century.

WORKERS ORGANIZE

The rapid expansion of railroads, mining, and manufacturing created a demand for labor to lay the rails, dig the ore, tend the furnaces, and carry out a thousand other tasks. America's new workers—men, women, and children from many ethnic groups—came from across the nation and around the world. Despite hopes for a rags-to-riches triumph such as Andrew Carnegie's, very few rose from shop floor to manager's office.

Workers for Industry

The labor force grew rapidly after the Civil War, almost doubling by 1890. The largest increases occurred in industries undergoing the greatest changes (see Figure 17.5). Agriculture continued to employ the largest share of the labor force, ranging downward from more than half in 1870 to two-fifths in 1900, but the agricultural work force grew the least, proportionately, of all major categories of workers.

Some workers for the rapidly expanding economy came from within the nation, especially from rural areas. At the same time that mechanization was reducing the number of farm workers needed, farm birth rates remained high. Thus, throughout rural parts of New England and the Middle Atlantic states, many people found it difficult to make a living from agriculture and moved to urban or industrial areas.

The expanding economy, however, needed many more workers than the nation itself could supply. The large-scale immigration of the time contributed many adult males to the work force—especially in mining, manufacturing, and transportation. The expanding economy also pulled women and children into the industrial work force. A study in 1875 showed that the average male factory worker in Lawrence, Massachusetts, earned $500 per year. The study also showed that the average family in Lawrence required a minimum annual income of $600 to provide sufficient food, clothing, and shelter. Since Lawrence was fairly typical of much of the new

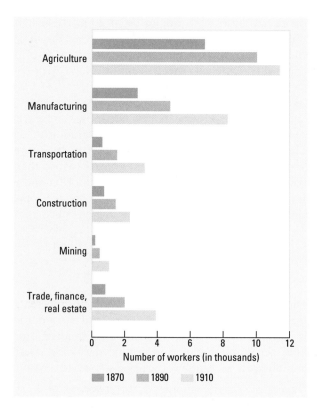

FIGURE 17.5 Industrial Distribution of the Work Force, 1870, 1890, 1910

The number of workers in every industry grew significantly after the Civil War. Though agriculture continued to employ more workers than any other industry, other industries were growing more rapidly than agriculture.

industrial economy, this study and others in other cities indicate that workers' families often required two or more incomes.

By 1880, a million children (under the age of 16) worked for wages, the largest number in agriculture. Children worked in the fields and mills of the South, operated sewing machines in New York, and sorted vegetables in Delaware canneries. Others worked as newsboys, bootblacks, or domestic servants, and still others worked at home, alongside their parents who brought home **piecework**. Nationwide, most working children turned over their wages to their parents.

Most women who worked outside the home were unmarried. In 1890, 40 percent of all single women worked for wages, along with 30 percent of

piecework Work for which someone is paid for the number of items turned out, rather than by the hour.

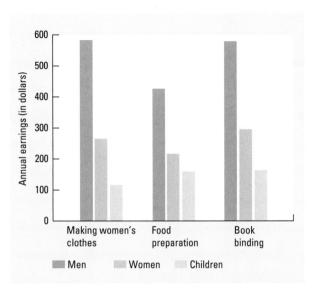

FIGURE 17.6 Average Annual Earnings for Men, Women, and Children, in Selected Industries, 1890

widowed or divorced women. Among married women, only 5 percent did so. Black women were employed at much higher rates in all categories. Some occupations came to be filled mainly by women. By 1900, females—adults and children—made up more than 70 percent of the work force in clothing factories, knitting mills, and other textile operations. Women also dominated certain types of office work, including more than 70 percent of the nation's secretaries and typists and 80 percent of telephone operators. However, as women moved into office work, displacing men, wage levels fell, along with the likelihood of promotion from clerical worker to managerial status. For women, office work usually paid less than factory work but was considered safer and of higher status.

Women and children workers almost always earned less than their male counterparts. In most industries, work was separated by age and gender, and adult males usually held the more skilled jobs commanding the best pay. Even when men and women did the same work, they rarely received the same pay (see Figure 17.6). This wage differential was often explained by the argument that a man had to support a family, whereas a woman worked to supplement the income of her husband or father.

Not all women earned money through working for wages. Some women were self-employed, for example, in making and selling women's hats or dresses. In urban working-class neighborhoods, married or widowed women often rented a room to a boarder or charged to do other people's laundry or sewing. In rural areas, married women often kept chickens and sold eggs to supplement their family's income.

It Matters Today

Workplace Safety

The high rate of workplace fatalities in the early twentieth century has been reduced substantially by the combined efforts of employers, unions, individual workers, academic researchers, and government at all levels. In 1907, the worst year on record, 3,242 men and boys died in coal mining accidents, leading to establishment of the Federal Bureau of Mines to study and improve mine safety. Mining has remained among the most dangerous jobs throughout the twentieth century and since. The Federal Coal Mine Health and Safety Act of 1969 set federal mine safety standards and was followed by a 50 percent reduction in deaths over the next five years. Similarly, a 33 percent reduction in mining deaths followed further legislation, the Federal Mine Safety and Health Act of 1977. Still, an average of more than thirty miners have died each year in recent years.

- Laws regulating workplace safety remain politically controversial. Use online newspapers to research contention over the Occupational Safety and Health Act of 1970. What arguments are made by those who seek to modify such laws?

- Research the origins of workers' compensation laws. Why were they first developed? Why do they remain politically controversial today?

Because so many of the new industrial workers had been born into a rural society, either in the United States or in Europe, they found industrial work quite different from their previous work. Farm families might toil from sunrise to sunset, but they did so at their own speed, taking a break when they felt the need and adjusting the pace of their work to avoid exhaustion. Self-employed blacksmiths, carpenters, dressmakers, and other skilled workers also controlled the speed and intensity of their work, although, like the farmer, they might work long hours. Some considered this autonomy to be part of the dignity of labor. In many early factories, the skilled workers often set the pace of work around them. They also earned more than other workers and were difficult to replace.

In the late nineteenth century, the workday in most industries averaged ten or twelve hours, six days a week. People expected to work long hours but found that industrial work controlled them, rather than the other way around. In many factories, the speed of the machines set the pace of the work, and machine speeds were often centrally controlled. If managers ordered a **speed-up**, workers worked faster. The job of the foreman was typically to demand faster and faster work. Ten- or twelve-hour days at a constant, rapid pace drained the workers. A woman textile worker in 1882 said, "I get so exhausted that I can scarcely drag myself home when night comes."

---

speed-up   An effort to make employees produce more goods in the same time or for the same pay.

The pace of the work, together with inadequate safety precautions, contributed to a high rate of industrial accidents, injuries, and deaths. The first thorough study of workplace fatalities was not conducted until 1913, when the Bureau of Labor Statistics found 23,000 industrial deaths among a work force of 38 million, equivalent to 61 deaths per 100,000 workers. (Today there are about 4 deaths per 100,000 workers.) Injuries and disabilities were even more numerous. Those disabled by industrial accidents received no benefits from the federal government and rarely received anything from state or local government or from their employers. On the contrary, many businesses considered an on-the-job injury to be due to carelessness by the employee and grounds for firing.

Despite rags-to-riches success stories, extreme mobility was highly unusual. Nearly all successful business leaders, in fact, came from middle- or upper-class families. Few workers moved more than a step or so up the economic scale. An unskilled laborer might become a semiskilled worker, or a skilled worker might become a foreman, but few wage earners moved into the middle class. If they did, it was usually as the owner of a small and often struggling business.

The Origins of Unions and Labor Conflict in the 1870s

Just as the entrepreneurs of the late nineteenth century faced choices between competition and cooperation, so too did their employees. Some workers reacted to the far-reaching changes in the nature of work by joining with other workers in efforts to maintain or regain control over their working conditions.

Skilled workers remained indispensable in many fields. Only a skilled iron molder could set up the molds and know exactly when and how to pour molten iron into them. Only an experienced carpenter could build stairs or hang doors properly. Only a skilled typesetter could quickly transform handwritten copy into lines of lead type. Such workers took pride in the quality of their work and knew that their skill was crucial to their employer's success. One union leader was referring to such workers when he said, "The manager's brains are under the workman's cap."

Skilled workers formed the first unions, called **craft unions** or **trade unions** because membership was limited to skilled workers in a particular craft or trade. Before the Civil War, workers in most American cities created local trade unions in attempts to regulate the quality of work, wages, hours, and working conditions within their craft. Local unions eventually formed national trade organizations—twenty-six of them by 1873, thirty-nine by 1880. They sometimes called themselves brotherhoods—for example, the United Brotherhood of Carpenters and Joiners, formed in 1881—and they drew on their craft traditions to forge bonds of unity.

craft union, trade union Labor union that organizes skilled workers engaged in a specific craft or trade.

The skills that defined craft unions' membership also provided the basis for their success. Skills that sometimes took years to develop made craft workers valuable to their employers and difficult to replace. Such unions often limited their membership not just to workers with particular skills but to white males with those skills. If most craft workers within a city belonged to the local union, a strike could badly disrupt or shut down the affected businesses. The strike, therefore, was a powerful weapon for skilled workers. Strikes most often succeeded in times of prosperity, when employers wanted to continue operating and were able financially to make concessions to workers. When the economy turned down and employers reduced work hours or laid off workers, craft unions usually disintegrated because they could not use the strike effectively. Only after the 1880s did local and national unions develop strategies that permitted them to survive depressions.

Unskilled or semiskilled workers—the majority of employees in many emerging industries—lacked the skills that gave the craft unions their bargaining power. Without such skills, they could be replaced easily if they chose to strike. The most effective unions, therefore, were groups of skilled workers—sometimes called the "aristocracy of labor."

Shortly after the Civil War, in 1866, craft unionists representing a variety of local and national organizations joined with reformers to create the **National Labor Union** (NLU), headed by William Sylvis of the Iron Molders until his death in 1869. The NLU also included representatives of women's organizations and, after vigorous debate, decided to encourage the organization of black workers. The most important of the NLU objectives was to establish eight hours as the proper length for a day's work. In 1870 the NLU divided itself into a labor organization and a political party, the National Labor Reform Party. In 1872 the political party nominated candidates for president and vice president, but the campaign was so unsuccessful and divisive that neither the NLU nor the party met again.

In 1877, for the first time, the nation witnessed widespread labor strife. After the onset of depression in 1873, railroad companies reduced costs by repeatedly cutting wages. Railroad workers' pay fell by more than a third from 1873 to 1877. Union leaders talked of striking but failed to bring it off. Railway workers took matters into their own hands when companies announced additional pay cuts. On July 16, 1877, some firemen and brakemen on the Baltimore & Ohio Railroad stopped work in Maryland. The next day, nearby in West Virginia, a group of railway workers refused to work until the company restored their wages. Members of the local community supported the strikers. The governor of West Virginia sent in the state **militia**, but the strikers prevented the trains from running. The governor then requested federal troops, and President Rutherford B. Hayes sent them.

Federal troops restored service on the Baltimore & Ohio, but the strike spread to other lines. Strikers shut down trains in Pittsburgh. When the local militia

---

militia   A volunteer military force, organized by state governments, consisting of civilians who agree to be mobilized in times of emergency; now superseded by the National Guard.

Library of Congress

This engraving depicts striking railroad workers in Martinsburg, West Virginia, as they stopped a freight train on July 17, 1877, in the opening days of the Great Railway Strike. Engravings such as this, showing strikers as heavily armed, may not have been accurate depictions of events. The technology of the day could not reproduce photographs in newspapers, so the public's understanding of events such as the 1877 strike was formed largely through artists' depictions.

refused to act against the strikers, the governor of Pennsylvania sent militia units from Philadelphia. When the militia killed twenty-six people, strikers and their sympathizers attacked the militia, forced the troops to retreat, and burned and looted railroad property throughout Pittsburgh.

Strikes erupted across Pennsylvania and New York and throughout the Midwest. Everywhere, the strikers drew support from their local communities. In various places, coal miners, factory workers, small business owners, farmers, black workers, and women demonstrated their solidarity with the workers. In St. Louis, local unions declared a **general strike** to secure the eight-hour workday and to end child labor. State militia, federal troops, and local police eventually broke up the strikes, but not before hundreds had lost their lives. By the strikes' end, railroad companies had suffered property damage worth $10 million, half of the losses in Pittsburgh.

The **Great Railway Strike of 1877** revealed widespread dislike for the railroad companies and significant community support for striking workers.

general strike A strike by members of all unions in a particular region.

However, the strike alarmed many other Americans. Some considered the use of troops only a temporary expedient and, like President Hayes, hoped for "education of the strikers," "judicious control of the capitalists," and some way to "remove the distress which afflicts laborers." Others saw in the strike a forecast of future labor unrest, and they called for better means to enforce law and order.

Competing Labor Organizations in the 1880s   The Great Railway Strike of 1877 suggested that working people could unite across lines of occupation, race, and gender, but no organization drew on that potential until the early 1880s, when the **Knights of Labor** emerged as an alternative to craft unions.

The Knights grew out of an organization of Philadelphia garment workers formed in 1869. Abandoning their craft union origins, they proclaimed that labor was "the only creator of values or capital," and they recruited members from what they considered "the producing class"—those who, by their labor, produced value. Anyone joining the Knights was required to have worked for wages at some time, but the organization specifically excluded only professional gamblers, stockbrokers, lawyers, bankers, and liquor dealers.

The Knights accepted African Americans as members, and some sixty thousand joined by 1886. After an organizer formed a local organization of women in 1881, the Knights officially opened their ranks to women and enrolled about fifty thousand by 1886. Some women and African Americans held local and regional leadership positions, and the Knights briefly appointed a woman as a national organizer. Through their activities, the Knights provided both women and African Americans with experience in organizing.

Terence V. Powderly, a machinist, directed the Knights from 1879 to 1893. Under his leadership, they focused on organization, education, and cooperation as their chief objectives. The Knights favored political action to accomplish such labor reforms as health and safety regulations, the eight-hour workday, prohibition of child labor, equal pay for equal work regardless of gender, and the graduated income tax. They also endorsed government ownership of the telephone, telegraph, and railroad systems. In 1878, 1880, and 1882, Powderly won election as mayor of Scranton, Pennsylvania, as the candidate of a labor party. Local labor parties often appeared in other cities where the Knights were strong.

A major objective of the Knights was "to secure to the workers the full enjoyment of the wealth they create." They committed themselves in 1878 to promote producers' and consumers' **cooperatives**, which they hoped would "supersede the wage-system." They established some 135 cooperatives by the mid-1880s, but few lasted very long. Most failed because of lack of capital, opposition from rival businesses, or poor organization.

---

cooperative A business enterprise in which workers and consumers share in ownership and take part in management.

Before the problems with their cooperatives became apparent, the Knights of Labor became the largest labor organization in the country, expanding from 9,000 members in 1879 to 703,000 in 1886. This meteoric growth suggested that many working people were seeking ways to respond to the emerging corporate behemoths or to regain some control over their own working lives. Though the rise of the Knights of Labor seemed to signal a growing sense of common purpose among many working people, labor organizations soon found themselves on the defensive and divided.

On May 1, 1886, some eighty thousand Chicagoans marched through the streets in support of an eight-hour workday, a cause that united many unions and radical groups. Three days later, Chicago police killed several strikers at the McCormick Harvester Works. Hoping to build on the May Day unity, a group of anarchists called a protest meeting for the next day at Haymarket Square. When police tried to break up the rally, someone threw a bomb at the officers. The police then opened fire on the crowd, and some protesters fired back. Eight policemen died, along with an unknown number of demonstrators, and a hundred people suffered injuries.

The Haymarket bombing sparked public anxiety and antiunion feelings. Employers who had previously opposed unions now tried to discredit them by playing on fears of terrorism. Some people who had supported union goals of better wages and working conditions now shrank back in horror. In Chicago, amid widespread furor over the violence, eight leading anarchists stood trial for inciting the bombing and, on flimsy evidence, were convicted. Four were hanged, one committed suicide, and three remained in jail until a sympathetic governor, John Peter Altgeld, released them in 1893.

Two weeks after the Haymarket bombing, trade union leaders met in Philadelphia to discuss the inroads that the Knights of Labor were making among their members. They proposed an agreement with the Knights: trade unions would recruit skilled workers, and the Knights would limit themselves to unskilled workers. The Knights refused, so the trade unions organized the **American Federation of Labor** (AFL). Membership in the AFL was limited to national trade unions. The combined membership of the thirteen founding unions amounted to about 140,000—only one-fifth of the number claimed by the Knights at the time.

Samuel Gompers became the AFL's first president. Born in London in 1850 to Dutch Jewish parents, he learned the cigarmaker's trade before coming to the United States in 1863. He joined the Cigarmakers' Union and became its president in 1877. Except for one year, Gompers continued as president of the AFL until his death in 1924. As AFL president, Gompers opposed labor involvement with radicalism or politics, and favored what he called "pure and simple" unionism: higher wages, shorter hours, and improved working conditions for union members, achieved not through politics but through the power of their organizations in relation to their employers. Though most AFL unions did not challenge capitalism, they repeatedly used strikes and sometimes engaged in long and bitter struggles with employers.

After the 1880s, the AFL suffered little competition from the Knights of Labor. The decline of the Knights came swiftly: 703,000 members in 1886;

260,000 in 1888; 100,000 in 1890. The failure of several strikes involving the Knights in the late 1880s cost them many supporters. Some who left were probably disappointed when a "cooperative commonwealth" was not quickly achieved. Some units of the Knights were organized like trade unions, and these groups often preferred the more practical AFL. The United Mine Workers of America switched from the Knights to the AFL in 1890 but retained some central principles of the Knights, including commitments to include both whites and African Americans and to organize all workers in coal mining, rather than only the most skilled.

Labor on the Defensive in the 1890s   In the 1890s, workers often found that even the largest unions could not withstand the power of the new industrial companies. A major demonstration of this power came in 1892 in Homestead, Pennsylvania, at the giant Carnegie Steel plant managed by Henry Clay Frick, Carnegie's partner. There a union had a contract with Carnegie Steel. When Frick proposed major wage cuts and the union balked, Frick locked out the union members and prepared to bring in replacements.

Frick had the Pinkerton National Detective Agency send three hundred guards to protect strikebreakers. They arrived by riverboat, but ten thousand strikers and community supporters resisted when the private army tried to land. Shots rang out. In the ensuing battle, seven Pinkertons and nine strikers were killed, and sixty people were injured. The Pinkertons surrendered, leaving the strikers in control. Soon after, however, the governor of Pennsylvania sent in the state militia to patrol the city and protect the strikebreakers. The union never recovered. This crushing defeat suggested that no union could stand up to America's industrial giants, especially when they could call on the government for assistance.

A similar fate befell the most ambitious organizing drive of the 1890s. In 1893, under the leadership of **Eugene V. Debs**, railway workers launched the American Railway Union (ARU). Born in Indiana in 1855, Debs had served as an officer of the locomotive firemen's union. Railway workers had organized separate unions for engineers, firemen, switchmen, and conductors, but Debs hoped to bring all railway workers, skilled and unskilled, together into one union, thereby creating an **industrial union**. Success came quickly. Within a year, the ARU claimed 150,000 members and became the largest single union in the nation.

The twenty-four railway companies whose lines entered Chicago had formed the General Managers Association (GMA) to address common problems. Alarmed at the rise of the ARU, they found an opportunity to challenge the new union in 1894. Striking workers at the Pullman Palace Car Company, which manufactured luxury railway cars, asked the ARU to boycott Pullman cars—to disconnect them from trains and proceed without them. When the ARU agreed, the managers promised to fire any worker who observed the boycott. Their real purpose, as expressed by the GMA chairman, was to eliminate the ARU and "to wipe him [Debs] out."

Within a short time, all 150,000 ARU members were on strike in support of members who were fired for boycotting Pullman cars. Rail traffic in and out of Chicago ground to a halt, affecting railways from the Pacific Coast to New York. The companies found an ally in U.S. Attorney General Richard Olney, a former railroad lawyer. Olney obtained an **injunction** against the strikers on the grounds that the strike prevented delivery of the mail and also violated the Sherman Anti-Trust Act (discussed in the next chapter). President Cleveland then assigned thousands of **U.S. marshals** and federal troops to protect trains operated by strikebreakers. In response, mobs attacked railroad property, especially in Chicago, burning trains and buildings. ARU leaders condemned the violence, but a dozen people died before the strike finally ended. Union leaders, including Debs, were jailed, and the ARU was destroyed.

The depression that began in 1893 further weakened the unions. In 1894 Gompers acknowledged that nearly all AFL affiliates "had their resources greatly diminished and their efforts largely crippled" through lost strikes and unemployment. Nevertheless, the AFL hung on. By 1897, the organization claimed fifty-eight national unions with a combined membership of nearly 270,000.

Study Tools

Summary

In the Gilded Age, as industrialization transformed the economy, immigration and urbanization challenged many established social patterns. As rural Americans and European immigrants sought better lives in the cities, urban America changed dramatically. New technologies in construction, transportation, and communication produced a new urban geography with residential neighborhoods defined by economic status. Urban growth brought a new urban middle class. Education underwent far-reaching changes. Socially defined gender roles began to change as some women chose professional careers and took active roles in reform. Some men responded by redefining masculinity through organizations and athletics. Urbanization offered new choices to gay men and lesbians by making possible the development of distinctive urban subcultures. In response, medical specialists tried to define homosexuality and lesbianism.

The South shared in some of the changes of the Gilded Age, but lagged in others, notably education. The myths of the Old South and the Lost Cause obscured for some southerners the real source of their difficulties. Changes in state laws disfranchised black voters and other new laws legalized and extended racial segregation.

Many Europeans immigrated to the United States because of economic and political conditions in their homelands and their expectations of better opportunities in America. Immigrants often formed distinct communities, frequently

injunction   A court order requiring an individual or a group to do something or to refrain from doing something.

U.S. marshal   A federal law-enforcement official.

centered on a church. The flood of immigrants spawned nativist reactions among some old-stock Americans. The West included immigrants from Asia, American Indians, and Latino peoples in substantial numbers. White westerners used politics and sometimes violence to exclude and segregate Asian immigrants. Federal policy toward American Indians proceeded from the expectation that they could and should be rapidly assimilated and must shed their separate cultural identities, but such policies largely failed. Latinos—descendants of those living in the Southwest before it became part of the United States and those who came later from Mexico or elsewhere in Latin America—often found their lives and culture under challenge.

Industrial workers had little control over the pace or hours of their work and often faced unpleasant or dangerous working conditions. Even so, people in both the United States and other parts of the world chose to migrate to expanding industrial centers from rural areas. The new work force included not only adult males but also women and children. Some workers formed labor organizations to seek higher wages, shorter hours, and better conditions. Trade unions, based on craft skills, were the earliest and most successful of such organizations. The Great Railway Strike of 1877 was the first indication of what widespread industrial strife could do to the nation's new transportation network based on railroads, and public officials resorted to federal troops to suppress the strike. Espousing cooperatives and reform, the Knights of Labor opened its membership to the unskilled, to African Americans, and to women—groups usually not admitted to craft unions. The Knights died out after 1890. The American Federation of Labor was formed by craft unions, and its leaders rejected radicalism and sought instead to work within capitalism to improve wages, hours, and conditions for its members. Organized labor suffered two dramatic defeats in the 1890s, one at the Homestead steel plant in 1892 and the other over the Pullman car boycott in 1894.

CHRONOLOGY

1862	Land-Grant College Act
1865	Civil War ends
1866	National Labor Union organized
1870	Populations in 25 cities exceed 50,000
1871–1885	Anti-Chinese riots across the West
1871	Great Chicago Fire
1872	Montgomery Ward opens first U.S. mail-order business
1873–1879	Depression
1874	Women's Christian Temperance Union founded
1877	Great Railway Strike

1881	669,431 immigrants enter United States
	Publication of Helen Hunt Jackson's *A Century of Dishonor*
1886	Knights of Labor reaches peak membership
	Haymarket Square bombing
	American Federation of Labor founded
1887	American Protective Association founded
	Dawes Severalty Act
1888	First electric streetcar system
1890	Populations in 58 cities exceed 50,000
	Second Mississippi Plan
1892	Homestead strike
1893–1897	Depression
1894	Pullman strike
1895	Booker T. Washington delivers Atlanta Compromise
1896	*Plessy v. Ferguson*

Focus Questions

If you have mastered this chapter, you should be able to answer these questions and explain the terms that follow the questions.

1. What were the key factors in the transformation of American cities in the late nineteenth century?
2. What important new social patterns emerged in urban areas in the late nineteenth century?
3. What new social patterns appeared in the South after the end of Reconstruction?
4. How did southern racial relations develop after the end of Reconstruction?
5. How did the expectations of European immigrants differ from their actual experiences?
6. Compare experiences of Chinese Americans, American Indians, Mexican Americans, and African Americans in the Gilded Age.
7. How did industrialization affect those who worked in the new industries?
8. How did the various labor organizations define their membership and purpose? Does this help to explain their successes and shortcomings?

Key Terms

separate sphere (*p.* 499)

Woman's Christian Temperance Union (*p.* 499)

Masons (*p.* 501)

Civil Rights Cases (*p.* 505)

Booker T. Washington (*p.* 505)

Atlanta Compromise (*p.* 506)

Plessy v. Ferguson (*p.* 507)

American Protective Association (*p.* 511)

Chinese Exclusion Act (*p.* 512)

Dawes Severalty Act (*p.* 515)

National Labor Union (*p.* 524)

Great Railway Strike of 1877 (*p.* 525)

Knights of Labor (*p.* 526)

Terence V. Powderly (*p.* 526)

American Federation of Labor (*p.* 527)

Samuel Gompers (*p.* 527)

Eugene V. Debs (*p.* 528)

industrial union (*p.* 528)

18

POLITICS AND FOREIGN RELATIONS
IN A RAPIDLY CHANGING NATION,
1865–1902

CHAPTER OUTLINE

• Parties, Spoils, Scandals, and Stalemate, 1865–1880 • Challenges to
Politics as Usual • Political Upheaval in the 1890s • Standing Aside from
World Affairs, 1865–1889 • Stepping into World Affairs: Harrison and
Cleveland, 1889–1897 • Striding Boldly in World Affairs: McKinley, War,
and Imperialism, 1898–1902 • Study Tools

PARTIES, SPOILS, SCANDALS, AND STALEMATE, 1865–1880

Political parties were central to politics and government throughout most of the
nineteenth century, but they were organized and behaved very differently from
their counterparts today. Before looking at national politics, therefore, it is important to look first at political parties.

**Parties,
Conventions,
and Patronage**

After the 1830s, nominations for political offices came from
party conventions. The process of selecting convention
delegates began when neighborhood voters gathered in
party **caucuses** to choose delegates to local conventions.

---

party convention Party meeting to nominate candidates for elective offices and adopt a platform.

caucus A meeting of people with a common political interest—for example, to choose delegates to
a party convention.

Conventions took place at county, state, and national levels and for congressional districts and various state districts. At most conventions, the delegates listened to long-winded speakers glorifying their party and denouncing the opposition. They nominated candidates for elective offices or chose delegates to another convention further up the federal ladder. And they adopted a **platform**. Party leaders worked to negotiate compromises among major groups within their party, on both candidates and platform language, and such deal-making sometimes occurred in informal settings—perhaps hotel rooms thick with cigar smoke and cluttered with whiskey bottles. Such behind-the-scenes deal making reinforced the notion of political parties as all-male bastions into which no self-respecting women would venture.

After choosing their candidates, the parties launched their campaigns. Campaigns focused on party identity. Newspapers were the major source of news, and nearly every newspaper identified closely with a political party. The parties subsidized sympathetic newspapers, and the newspapers delivered both effusive support for their party and scathing attacks on the opposition. Before an election, local party organizations whipped up enthusiasm among party loyalists and tried to recruit new or undecided voters through parades, barbecues, and rallies capped by hours of speechmaking.

On election day, each party tried to mobilize all its supporters and make certain that they voted. This produced very high levels of voter participation—more than 80 percent of eligible voters cast their ballots in 1876. At polling places, party workers distributed lists, or "tickets," of their party's candidates, which voters used as ballots. Voting was not secret until the 1890s. Before then, everyone could see which party's ticket a voter turned in. The voting process discouraged voters from crossing party lines.

Once the votes were counted, newly elected presidents or governors or mayors began appointing their loyal supporters to government jobs, which were widely considered appropriate rewards for hard work during a winning campaign. Those appointed to such jobs were also expected to return part of their salaries to the party. This was called the **patronage system** or spoils system, after a statement by Senator William Marcy in 1831: "To the victor belong the spoils." Its defenders were labeled **spoilsmen**.

Party loyalists inevitably outnumbered the available jobs, so competition for appointments was fierce. When James A. Garfield became president in 1881, he was so overwhelmed with demands for jobs that he exclaimed in disgust, "My God! What is there in this place that a man should ever want to get into it?" Jobs in highest demand often involved purchasing or government contracts, which became another form of spoils, awarded to businessmen who supported the party. This system invited corruption. One Post Office official, for example, pressured **postmasters** across the country to buy clocks from one of his political

platform   A written statement of the principles, policies, and promises on which a political party appeals to voters.

spoilsmen   Derogatory term for defenders of the patronage or spoils system.

postmaster   An official appointed to manage a local post office.

associates. Such opportunities were limited only by the imagination of the spoilsmen.

Some critics, including Carl Schurz, argued that, by concentrating so much on patronage, politics ignored principles and issues and revolved instead around greed for office. The spoils system had many defenders, however. George W. Plunkitt, a longtime participant in New York City politics, explained, "You can't keep an organization together without patronage. Men ain't in politics for nothin'." Plunkitt described the reality: given the many party workers needed to identify supporters and mobilize voters, politics required some rewards.

In 1905, a newspaper reporter published a series of conversations with Plunkitt. His observations provide insights into the nature of urban politics and its relation to urban poverty. Born in a poor Irish neighborhood of New York City, Plunkitt left school early, entered politics, and eventually became a district leader of **Tammany Hall**, a political organization that dominated the city's Democratic Party. Between 1868 and 1904, he served in several elected positions in state and city government. Plunkitt explained how he kept the loyalty of his neighborhood voters:

> Go right down among the poor families and help them in the different ways they need help.... It's philanthropy, but it's politics, too—mighty good politics.... The poor are the most grateful people in the world, and, let me tell you, they have more friends in their neighborhoods than the rich have in theirs.... The consequence is that the poor look up to George W. Plunkitt as a father, come to him in trouble—and don't forget him on election day.

Plunkitt typified many big-city politicians across the country. Throughout the late nineteenth century, urban politicians cultivated lower-income voters by addressing their needs directly and personally. They tried to build a personal rapport with the voters, and responded to the needs of the urban poor by providing an occasional basket of food or a job in some city department. In return, they wanted political loyalty. Such urban political organizations flourished during the years 1870–1910, and some survived long after that. Similar organizations—sometimes Republican but more often Democratic—emerged in nearly all large cities, based among lower-income voters, usually led by men of recent immigrant backgrounds. Where they amassed great power, their rivals denounced the leader as a boss and the organization as a **machine**.

In every city, opponents of the machine charged corruption. Some bosses accumulated sizable fortunes—sometimes through gifts or retainers from companies seeking franchises or city contracts (their critics called these bribes), sometimes through advance knowledge of city planning. Richard Croker, the boss of Tammany in the 1890s, accumulated an immense personal fortune, but he always insisted that he had never taken a dishonest dollar.

---

machine   When applied to urban political organizations, a derogatory term implying that the organization concentrated on patronage and graft to the exclusion of issues and principles.

Above all, the bosses centralized political decision making. "There's got to be in every ward somebody that any bloke can come to," a Boston politician insisted, "to get help." If a pushcart vender needed a permit to sell tinware, or a railroad president needed permission to build a bridge, or a saloonkeeper wanted to stay open on Sunday in violation of the law, the machine could help them all—if they showed the proper gratitude in return.

Republicans and Democrats   Beneath the hoopla and interminable speeches, important differences characterized the major parties. Republicans pointed to their defense of the Union during the Civil War and claimed a monopoly on patriotism, arguing that Democrats—especially southern Democrats—had proven themselves disloyal. "Every man that shot a Union soldier," one Republican orator proclaimed, "was a Democrat." Such rhetoric was often called "waving the bloody shirt." Republicans in Congress voted generous pensions to disabled Union army veterans and the widows and orphans of those who died, and Republican leaders cultivated the Grand Army of the Republic (GAR), the organization of Union veterans, attending their meetings and urging them to "vote as you shot." Republican presidential candidates were usually Union veterans, as were many state and local officials throughout the North.

Republicans proudly claimed responsibility for prosperity, insisting that postwar economic growth resulted from their policies, especially the protective tariff. Republicans boasted that they were the party of decency and morality, and portrayed as typical Democrats "the old slave-owner and slave-driver, the saloon-keeper, the ballot-box-stuffer, the Kuklux [Klan], the criminal class of the great cities, the men who cannot read or write."

Where Republicans defined themselves in terms of what their party did and who they were, Democrats typically focused on what they opposed. Most leading Democrats stood firm against "governmental interference" in the economy, especially the protective tariff and land grants, equating government activism with privileges for a favored few. The protective tariff, they charged, protected manufacturers from international competition at the expense of consumers who paid higher prices. The public domain, they argued, should provide farms for citizens, not subsidies for railroad corporations. In general, Democrats favored a strictly limited role for the government in the economy.

Just as the Democrats opposed governmental interference in the economy, so too did they oppose governmental interference in social relations and behavior. In the North, especially in Irish and German communities, they condemned **prohibition**, which they called a violation of personal liberty. In the South, Democrats rejected federal enforcement of equal rights for African Americans, which they denounced as a violation of states' rights. There, Democrats stood for white supremacy.

---

prohibition A legal ban on the manufacture, sale, and use of alcoholic beverages.

Thomas Nast, the most influential cartoonist of the 1870s and most talented cartoonist of his age, began using an elephant to symbolize the Republicans and a donkey for the Democrats. At the time, however, Republicans often preferred an eagle, and Democrats usually chose a rooster.

Most voters developed strong loyalties to one party or the other, often on the basis of ethnicity, race, or religion. Nearly all Catholics and many Irish, German, and other immigrants supported the Democrats. Most southern whites supported the Democrats as the party of white supremacy. The Democrats' opposition to the protective tariff attracted entrepreneurs with interests in international commerce. The Democrats, all in all, comprised a diverse coalition, holding together primarily because their various components opposed government action on social or economic matters.

Outside the South, most old-stock Protestants voted Republican, as did most Scandinavian and British immigrants. Nearly all African Americans supported the Republicans as the party of emancipation, as did most veterans of the abolition movement. So many Union veterans supported the Republicans that someone suggested GAR stood for "generally all Republicans." Republicans usually carried New England, Pennsylvania, and much of the Midwest.

Republicans comprised the more coherent political organization, united around a set of policies that involved action by the federal government to foster economic growth and protect blacks' rights. The protective tariff and use of the public domain to encourage rapid economic development both involved positive governmental action. During Reconstruction, the dominant Republicans had changed the very nature of the federal government, redefining citizenship and relations between the federal government and the states. As one leading Republican put it, "The Republican party does things, the Democratic party criticizes." Neither party, however, proposed to regulate, restrict, or tax the new industrial corporations.

Grant's Troubled Presidency: Spoils and Scandals Despite success as a general, Ulysses S. Grant seemed unprepared when he won the presidency in 1868. During his two terms in office (1869–1877), he usually deferred to Congress for domestic policymaking. Too often he appointed friends or acquaintances to posts for which they possessed few qualifications, and he proved too willing to believe their denials of wrongdoing. He failed to form a competent cabinet and faced constant turnover among his executive advisers. He did choose a highly capable secretary of state, Hamilton Fish, and eventually found in Benjamin Bristow a secretary of the treasury who vigorously combated corruption.

Congress supplied its full share of scandal. Visiting Washington in 1869, Henry Adams was surprised to hear a cabinet member bellow, "You can't use tact with a Congressman! A Congressman is a hog! You must take a stick and hit him on the snout!" Too many members of Congress behaved in ways that confirmed such cynical views. In 1868, before Grant became president, several congressional leaders became stockholders in the **Crédit Mobilier**, a company that the chief shareholders in the Union Pacific Railroad created and then gave a generous contract to build the railroad. Thus the company's leaders paid themselves handsomely to construct their own railroad. To prevent congressional scrutiny, the company sold shares at cut-rate prices to key congressmen. Revelation of these arrangements in 1872–1873 scandalized the nation. No sooner did that furor pass than Congress voted itself a 50 percent pay raise and made the increase two years retroactive. Only after widespread public protest did Congress repeal its "salary grab."

Public disgrace was not limited to the federal government or to Republicans. In New York City, the **Tweed Ring** scandal involved city and state officials accused of using bribery, **kickbacks**, and padded accounts to steal money from New York City and the state. At the center was **William Marcy Tweed**, whose name became synonymous with urban political corruption. Tweed entered New York City politics in the 1850s and became head of Tammany Hall in 1863. Labeled "Boss Tweed" by opponents, he and his associates built public support by spending tax funds on charities and giving to the poor from their own pockets—pockets filled with ill-gotten gains.

Under Tweed's direction, city government launched major construction projects: public buildings, streets, parks, and sewers. Much of the construction was riddled with corruption. Between 1868 and 1871, the Tweed Ring may have plundered $200 million from the city, mostly by giving bloated construction contracts to businesses that returned a kickback to the ring. In 1871 evidence of corruption led to Tweed's indictment and ultimately his conviction and imprisonment.

Grant easily won reelection in 1872, but the midterm elections of 1874 were a different story. The congressional scandals alienated some voters. Moreover, the depression that began in 1873 undercut Republicans' claim to have produced prosperity. Throughout the South, political terrorism suppressed the Republican vote. As a result, Democrats took control of the House of Representatives. For twenty years, from 1874 until 1894, Democrats usually kept their majority in the House of Representatives. Though Republicans usually won the presidency, Democratic control of the House made it difficult or impossible for the Republicans to enact major legislation.

More scandals were to come. In 1875 Treasury Secretary Bristow revealed that a **Whiskey Ring** of federal officials and distillers, centered in St. Louis, had defrauded the government of millions of dollars in whiskey taxes. The 230 men indicted included several of Grant's appointees and even his private secretary. The next year, William Belknap, Grant's secretary of war, resigned shortly before he was impeached for accepting bribes.

The Politics of Stalemate, 1876–1889

From the mid-1870s through the 1880s, as the nation's economy and social patterns changed with astonishing speed, American politics seemed frozen in place. From the end of the Civil War to the mid-1870s, politics had revolved largely around issues of war and Reconstruction. By the late 1870s, other issues emerged as crucial, notably the economy and political corruption. After the mid-1870s, however, voters divided almost evenly between the two major political

---

kickback   An illegal payment by a contractor to the official who awarded the contract.

parties, beginning a long political **stalemate** during which neither party could enact its proposals.

Republican Rutherford B. Hayes became president after the closely contested election of 1876 (discussed in Chapter 15). His personal integrity and principled stand on issues helped restore his party's reputation after the embarrassments of the Grant administration. However, he faced a Democratic majority in the House of Representatives and significant opposition within his own party. Roscoe Conkling, a flamboyant senator and boss of New York's powerful and patronage-hungry Republican organization, became Hayes's harshest Republican critic after Hayes refused Conkling's demands regarding patronage. Hayes also estranged reformers by not seeking a full-scale revision of the spoils system. He did not seek reelection in 1880.

In 1880, the Republican nominating convention deadlocked between the supporters of James G. Blaine of Maine, a spellbinding orator who attracted loyal supporters and bitter enemies, and Conkling and his followers, who called themselves **Stalwarts** and wanted to nominate former president Grant. Eventually the deadlock produced a compromise, James A. Garfield, a congressman from Ohio. Born in a log cabin, Garfield had grown up in poverty. A minister, college president, and lawyer before the Civil War, he became the Union's youngest major general. For vice president, the delegates tried to placate the Stalwarts by nominating Conkling's chief lieutenant, Chester A. Arthur.

Garfield won the popular vote by half a percentage point but won the electoral vote convincingly. He brought to the presidency a solid understanding of Congress and a studious approach to issues. Though he appointed Blaine as secretary of state, the most prestigious cabinet position, Garfield also hoped to work cooperatively with the Stalwarts. When Conkling arrogantly demanded his supporters be appointed to key federal positions, Garfield proved to be politically shrewder than any president since Lincoln. Humiliated, Conkling resigned from the Senate, and Garfield scored a victory for a stronger presidency.

On July 2, 1881, four months after taking office, Garfield was shot while walking through a Washington railroad station. His assassin, Charles Guiteau, a mentally unstable religious fanatic and disappointed office-seeker, claimed he had acted to save the Republican Party. Two months later, Garfield died of the wound—or of incompetent medical care.

Chester A. Arthur now became president. Probably best known as a member of the Conkling organization and a dapper dresser, Arthur soon showed, as one of his former associates said, that "He isn't 'Chet' Arthur any more; he's the President." In 1882 doctors diagnosed him as suffering from Bright's disease, a kidney condition that produced fatigue, depression, and eventually death. Arthur kept the news secret from all but his family and closest friends. Despite political liabilities and his own physical limitations, Arthur proved more capable than anyone might have predicted.

---

stalemate In chess, a situation where neither player can move, and therefore neither can win. Thus, any situation where neither side can gain an advantage.

In 1884, Blaine—charming and quick-witted—finally secured the Republican nomination. The Democrats chose Grover Cleveland, the governor of New York, who had earned a reputation for integrity and political courage by attacking Tammany Hall. Many Irish voters—a large component in Tammany—seemed attracted to Blaine. Seeking to tarnish Cleveland's image of integrity, Republicans trumpeted that Cleveland had fathered a child outside marriage by chanting, "Ma! Ma! Where's my pa?" The election hinged on New York State, where Blaine hoped to cut into the usually Democratic Irish vote. A few days before the election, however, Blaine was present when a preacher in New York City called the Democrats the party of "rum, Romanism [Catholicism], and rebellion." Blaine failed to respond quickly to this insult to his Irish Catholic supporters. Cleveland won New York by a tiny margin, and New York's electoral votes gave him victory.

Cleveland enjoyed support from many who opposed the spoils system, and he insisted on demonstrated ability in those he appointed to office. Staunchly committed to minimal government and cutting federal spending, Cleveland vetoed 414 bills—most granting pensions to individual Union veterans—twice as many vetoes as all previous presidents *combined*. Cleveland deferred to Congress regarding policymaking and approved several important measures produced by the Democratic House and Republican Senate, including the Dawes Severalty Act (discussed in Chapter 17) and the Interstate Commerce Act.

The Interstate Commerce Act grew out of political pressure from farmers and small businesses. In the early 1870s, several midwestern states passed laws regulating railroad freight rates (usually called Granger laws, discussed later in this chapter). In 1886, however, the Supreme Court limited states' power to regulate railroad rates. In response, and amid protests over railroad rate discrimination, Congress passed the Interstate Commerce Act in 1887. The new law created the **Interstate Commerce Commission (ICC),** the first federal regulatory commission. Though the law prohibited pools and rebates and required that rates be "reasonable and just," the ICC had little real regulatory power until the Hepburn Act strengthened it in 1906.

Cleveland considered the nation's greatest problem to be the federal budget surplus. After the Civil War, the tariff usually generated more income than the country needed (see Figure 18.1). Worried that the surplus encouraged wasteful spending and that tariffs reduced competition among the developing industrial corporations, Cleveland demanded in 1887 that Congress cut tariff rates. His action divided Democrats, but Cleveland provided little leadership. The House and Senate deadlocked, each writing a quite different version of tariff reform, and Congress then adjourned without taking any action. Cleveland's call for tariff reform came to nothing.

In the 1888 presidential election, Democrats renominated Cleveland, but he backed off from the tariff issue and did little campaigning. Republicans nominated Benjamin Harrison, senator from Indiana and a former Civil War general. Thoughtful and cautious, Harrison impressed many as cool and distant. Republicans campaigned vigorously in defense of the protective tariff, raising unprecedented amounts of campaign money from business leaders and issuing record amounts of

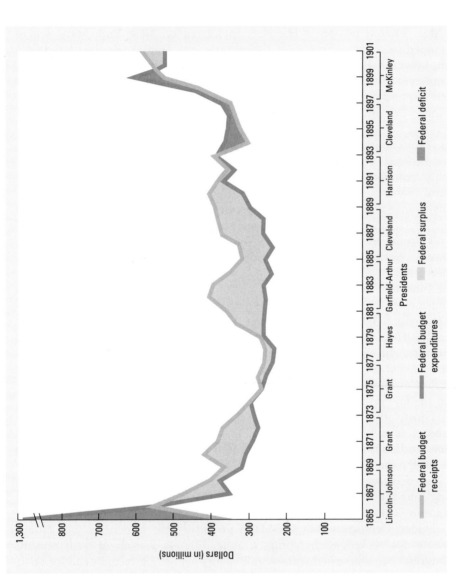

FIGURE 18.1 Federal Receipts and Expenditures, 1865–1901

The federal surplus usually shrank during economic downturns (mid-1870s and mid-1890s) and grew in more prosperous periods (1880s). During the Harrison administration, however, the surplus virtually disappeared, reflecting efforts to reduce income and increase expenditures.

Source: U.S. Department of Commerce, Bureau of the Census, *Historical Statistics of the United States, Colonial Times to 1970,* Bicentennial edition, 2 vols. (Washington, D.C.: U.S. Government Printing Office, 1975), 1: 1104.

campaign materials. Harrison received fewer votes than Cleveland (47.9 percent to Cleveland's 48.7 percent) but won in the Electoral College. As important for the Republicans as their narrow presidential victory, however, were the majorities they secured in the House and Senate.

Harrison and the Fifty-First Congress   With Harrison in the White House and Republican majorities in Congress, the Republicans set out to do a lot and to do it quickly. When the fifty-first session of Congress opened late in 1889, Harrison worked more closely with congressional leaders of his own party than any other president in recent memory. Democrats in the House of Representatives tried to delay, but Speaker Thomas B. Reed—an enormous man renowned for his wit—imposed new rules designed to speed up House business.

The Republicans first turned to tariff revision, to cut the troublesome federal surplus without reducing protection. Led by **William McKinley** of Ohio, the **House Ways and Means Committee** drafted a bill that moved some items to the free list (notably sugar, a major source of tariff revenue) but raised tariff rates on other items, sometimes so high as to be prohibitive. The House passed the **McKinley Tariff** in May 1890 and sent it on to the Senate.

The House also approved a federal elections bill, intended to protect the voting rights of African Americans in the South. Sponsored by Representative Henry Cabot Lodge of Massachusetts, the bill proposed federal supervision over congressional elections to prevent disfranchisement, fraud, or violence. Its Democratic opponents called it a "force bill," evoking memories of Reconstruction. After passing the House, the measure went to the Senate, where approval by the Republican majority seemed likely.

Harrison wanted the two bills passed as a party package, but Republicans feared that a Democratic **filibuster** against the elections bill would prevent passage of both measures. Despite protests by Lodge and others, a compromise emerged—Republicans would table the elections bill, and Democrats would not delay the tariff bill. Thus, Republicans sacrificed African Americans' voting rights to gain the revised tariff. Harrison signed the McKinley Tariff on October 1, 1890, and the revised tariff soon produced the intended result: it reduced the surplus by cutting tariff income.

The Senate, meanwhile, had been laboring over two measures named for Senator John Sherman of Ohio: the Sherman Silver Purchase Act (discussed shortly) and the **Sherman Anti-Trust Act**. The Anti-Trust Act, drafted by several Republican senators working with Harrison, was Republicans' response to concerns about monopolies. Approved overwhelmingly, the law declared that "every contract, combination in the form of trust or otherwise, or conspiracy, in restraint of trade or commerce among the several states, or with foreign nations, is hereby

filibuster A speech by a bill's opponents to delay legislative action; usually applies to extended speeches in the U.S. Senate, which has no time limit on speeches and where a minority may therefore "talk a bill to death" by holding up all other business.

IT MATTERS TODAY

The Defeat of the Lodge Bill

The failure of the Fifty-first Congress to approve the Lodge bill marked a long-term retreat from federal enforcement of voting rights, and southern states systematically disfranchised African Americans. Many African Americans and a few white allies continued to challenge this situation, but their efforts did not succeed until the 1960s.

Serious federal enforcement of voting rights came only with the Voting Rights Act of 1965, which included features similar to those in the Lodge bill. The 1965 act has since been amended, interpreted by the courts, and periodically extended. In 2006, the Republican leadership in Congress pushed through a twenty-five-year renewal of the Voting Rights Act a year ahead of schedule.

- Go online and read newspapers from 1965 when the original Voting Rights Act was being discussed in Congress. How is the Voting Rights Act similar to the Lodge bill? What were the arguments against the Voting Rights Act?
- Go online and read the newspapers from 2006 when the Voting Rights Act was most recently renewed. What were the arguments for early renewal, and how were they related to the possibility that the Democrats might take control of Congress in elections later that year? What opposition was there to renewal? How does the opposition in 2006 compare with the opposition to the Lodge bill? To the original act in 1965? How was the law amended in 2006?

declared to be illegal." The law made the United States the first industrial nation to attempt to prevent monopolies, but it proved difficult to interpret and had little initial effect.

In ten months the Republicans passed what one Democrat called "a raging sea of ravenous legislation." In addition to the McKinley Tariff, the Sherman Anti-Trust Act, and the Silver Purchase Act, the record number of new laws included appropriations that laid the basis for a modern navy, a major increase in pension eligibility for disabled Union veterans and their dependents, statehood for North and South Dakota, Montana, Washington, Idaho, and Wyoming, and creation of territorial government in Oklahoma. Republicans hoped they had finally broken the political logjam that had clogged politics since 1875.

CHALLENGES TO POLITICS AS USUAL

Though political change seemed to move at a glacial pace in the Gilded Age, several groups challenged mainstream politics and sought new policies and new ways of making political decisions. Given the number of Americans still engaged in agriculture, it should not be surprising that farmers were prominent in several significant movements.

Grangers,
Greenbackers,
and Silverites

Crop prices fell steadily after the Civil War as production of wheat, corn, and cotton grew much faster than the population (see Figure 16.1). Some farmers, however, denied that prices were falling solely because of overproduction, pointing to the hungry and ragged residents of urban slums. Farmers condemned the monopolistic practices of **commodity markets** in Chicago and New York that determined crop prices. They knew that the bushel of corn they sold for 10 or 20 cents in October brought three or four times that amount in New York in December. When they brought their crops to market, however, farmers accepted the price that was offered because they needed cash to pay their debts and could not store their crops for later sale at a higher price.

Many farmers borrowed heavily to establish new farms after the Civil War. Falling prices magnified their indebtedness. Because crop prices sank lower and lower, farmers raised more and more just to pay their mortgages and buy necessities. Given the relation between supply and demand, the more they raised, the lower prices fell. They must have felt as if they were running faster and faster just to stay in the same place, and many found they could not keep up.

In addition, the railroads seemed to be greedy monopolies that charged as much as possible to deliver supplies to rural America and carry farm crops to market. It sometimes cost four times as much to ship freight in the West or South as in the East. Farmers also protested that the railroads dominated politics in many western and southern states and distributed free passes to politicians in return for favorable treatment.

Soon organizations began to address the scourges of falling prices and high railroad freight rates. The first was formed by Oliver H. Kelley in 1867. Officially called the Patrons of Husbandry, it was usually known as the **Grange** and extended full participation to women as well as men. Kelley saw the Grange as a social outlet for farm families and a way to educate them in new farming methods.

The Grange grew rapidly, especially in the Midwest and central South. In the 1870s, it became a leading proponent for cooperative buying and selling. Many local Granges set up cooperative stores (consumers' cooperatives), where members did their shopping and divided any profits among themselves. Some formed producers' cooperatives, in which farmers agreed to hold their crops back from market and jointly negotiate over prices. Two state Granges began manufacturing farm machinery, and Grangers planned for cooperative factories producing everything from wagons to sewing machines. Some Grangers formed mutual insurance companies, and a few experimented with cooperative banks.

The Grange defined itself as nonpartisan. However, as Grange membership boomed in the 1870s, its midwestern and western members moved toward political action. New political parties emerged in eleven states, usually called "Granger

---

commodity market   Financial market in which brokers buy and sell agricultural products in large quantities, thus determining the prices paid to farmers for their harvests.

Parties." They demanded state legislation to prohibit railroad rate discrimination. Other groups, especially merchants, also sought such laws, but the Grangers were so prominent that the resulting state laws, most dating to 1872–1874, were usually called **Granger laws**. When the constitutionality of such regulation was challenged, the Supreme Court ruled, in *Munn v. Illinois* (1877), that businesses with "a public interest," including warehouses and railroads, "must submit to be controlled by the public for the common good."

The Grange reached its zenith in the mid-1870s. Hastily organized cooperatives soon encountered financial problems that were compounded by the national depression. As cooperatives collapsed, they often pulled down Grange organizations. Political activity brought some successes but also generated bitter internal disputes. The organization lost many members, and surviving Granges generally avoided both cooperatives and politics.

With the decline of the Grange, some farmers looked to **monetary policy** for relief. After the Civil War, most prices fell (a situation called **deflation**) because of increased production, more efficient techniques in agriculture and manufacturing, and the failure of the money supply to grow as rapidly as the economy. Deflation has always injured debtors because it means that the money to pay off a loan has greater purchasing power (and so is harder to come by) than the money of the original loan. The Greenback Party argued that increasing the supply of money by printing more **greenbacks**, the paper money issued during the Civil War, would stabilize prices. They found a receptive audience among farmers in debt.

In the congressional elections of 1878, the Greenback Party received nearly a million votes and elected fourteen congressmen. In the 1880 presidential election, Greenbackers tried to attract urban workers by supporting the eight-hour workday, legislation to protect workers, and the abolition of child labor. They also called for regulation of transportation and communication, a **graduated income tax** (which they considered the fairest form of taxation), and woman suffrage. For president, they nominated James B. Weaver of Iowa, a Greenback congressman and former Union army general. He got only 3.3 percent of the vote. In 1884, the Greenbackers fared even worse.

The prevalent currency deflation also motivated those who wanted the government to resume issuing silver dollars. In 1873 Congress dropped the silver dollar

---

monetary policy Now, the regulation of the money supply and interest rates by the Federal Reserve. Before 1913, federal monetary policy was largely limited to defining the medium of the currency (gold, silver, or paper) and the relations between the types of currency.

deflation Falling prices, a situation in which the purchasing power of the dollar increases; the opposite of deflation is inflation, when prices go up and the purchasing power of the dollar declines.

greenbacks Paper money, not backed by gold, that the federal government issued during the Civil War.

graduated income tax Tax based on income, such that the percentage of income paid as tax increases with income level, so that those with the lowest income pay the lowest percentage and those with higher incomes pay a larger percentage.

In this illlustration, the Grange tries to awaken the public to the approaching locomotive (a symbol of monopoly power) that is bringing consolidation (mergers), extortion (high prices), bribery, and other evils. Railroad ties (the wooden pieces on which the rails rested) were sometimes called sleepers.

from the list of approved coins, following the lead of Britain, Germany, and other European nations, which had specified that only gold was to serve as money. Some Americans believed that adhering to this **gold standard** was essential if American businesses were to compete effectively in international markets for capital and goods.

Given major silver discoveries in the West, resuming silver coinage seemed a way to counteract deflation without resorting to greenbacks. Silver coinage quickly found support not just among farmers but also among silver mining interests. Members of this farming-mining coalition were soon called "silverites." In 1878, over Hayes's veto, Congress passed the **Bland-Allison Act** authorizing a limited amount of silver dollars. The act failed to counteract deflation, and satisfied neither silverites nor gold supporters. The **Sherman Silver Purchase Act** of 1890 increased the

gold standard   A monetary system based on gold, under which legal contracts typically called for the payment of all debts in gold, and paper money could be redeemed in gold at a bank.

amount of silver to be coined, but both silverites and advocates of the gold standard still found it unsatisfactory.

Reforming the Spoils System   A very different set of reformers challenged the spoils system. Known as **Mugwumps** to their contemporaries and centered in Boston and New York, most were Republicans of high social status. Like Carl Schurz, they blamed many of the defects of politics on the spoils system, argued that eliminating patronage would drive out the machines and opportunists, and advocated a merit system based on a job seeker's ability to pass a comprehensive examination. As they did with others who broke with their party, party politicians sometimes questioned the Mugwumps' manhood.

The assassination of President Garfield by a disappointed office seeker spurred efforts to reform the patronage system. Sponsored by Senator George Pendleton (an Ohio Democrat), the **Pendleton Act** of 1883 created a merit system for filling federal positions. The new law designated certain federal positions, about 15 percent of the total, as "classified" and required these **classified civil service** positions to be filled only through competitive examinations. The law authorized the president to add positions to the classified list. Within twenty years, the law applied to 44 percent of federal employees. Most state and local governments eventually adopted merit systems as well.

Challenging the Male Bastion: Woman Suffrage   In the masculine political world of the Gilded Age, men were expected to display strong loyalty to a political party, but men considered women—who could not vote—to stand outside the party system. The concepts of domesticity and separate spheres dictated that women avoid politics, especially party politics. Some women nonetheless involved themselves in reform efforts, and a few even took part in party activities. In the late nineteenth century, some women also pushed for full political participation through the right to vote.

The struggle for woman suffrage was of long standing. In 1848 Elizabeth Cady Stanton and four other women organized the world's first Women's Rights Convention, held at Seneca Falls, New York. Their Declaration of Principles announced, in part, "It is the duty of the women of this country to secure to themselves their sacred right to the elective franchise." Stanton and Susan B. Anthony became the most prominent advocates for women's rights, especially voting rights, through the turn of the century. They convinced lawmakers to modify some laws that discriminated against women but failed to secure voting rights. During the nineteenth century, however, women increasingly participated in public affairs: in movements to abolish slavery, mobilize support for the Union, improve educational opportunities, end child labor, and more.

classified civil service   Federal jobs filled through the merit system instead of by patronage.

In 1866 Stanton and Anthony unsuccessfully opposed inclusion of the word *male* in the Fourteenth Amendment. In 1869 they formed the **National Woman Suffrage Association (NWSA)**, with membership open only to women, and sought an amendment to the federal Constitution as the only sure route to woman suffrage. The NWSA built alliances with other reform and radical organizations and worked to improve women's status, promoting women's trade unions and lobbying for easier divorce laws and access to birth-control information. In contrast, the **American Woman Suffrage Association (AWSA)**, organized by Lucy Stone and other suffrage advocates, also in 1869, concentrated strictly on winning the vote and avoided other issues. The two organizations merged in 1890 to become the National American Woman Suffrage Association.

The first victories for suffrage came in the West. In 1869, in Wyoming Territory, the territorial legislature extended the franchise to women. Wyoming women had forged a well-organized suffrage movement and persuaded some male legislators to support their cause. Some legislators also hoped that woman suffrage would attract more women to Wyoming, which at the time had about seven thousand men but only two thousand women. Thereafter, women in Wyoming Territory voted, served on juries, and held elective office. In 1889, when Wyoming asked for statehood, some congressmen balked at admitting a state with woman suffrage. Wyoming legislators, however, bluntly stated, "We will remain out of the Union a hundred years rather than come in without the women." Congress finally voted to approve Wyoming statehood—with woman suffrage—in 1890.

Utah Territory adopted woman suffrage in 1870. Mormon men formed the majority of Utah's voters, and Mormon women far outnumbered the relatively few non-Mormon women. By enfranchising women, Mormons strengthened their voting majority and may have hoped, at the same time, to silence those who claimed that **polygamy** degraded women. However, in an act aimed at the Mormons, Congress outlawed polygamy in 1887 and simultaneously disfranchised Utah women. Not until Utah became a state, in 1896, did its women regain the vote. In 1893, Colorado voters (all male) approved woman suffrage, making Colorado the first state to adopt woman suffrage through a popular vote. In addition to a well-organized campaign by Colorado women, their cause was assisted by support from the new Populist Party (discussed in the next section). In Idaho, where both Mormon and Populist influences were strong, male voters approved woman suffrage in 1896. These western states were among the first places in the world to grant women equal voting rights with men.

Several states also began to extend limited voting rights to women, especially for school board elections and school bond issues. These concessions perhaps reflected the widespread assumption that women's gender roles included child

---

polygamy   The practice of a man having more than one wife; Mormons practiced polygamy, which they referred to as plural marriage, until 1890.

rearing. By 1890, women could vote in school elections in nineteen states and on bond and tax issues in three.

Structural Change and Policy Change   Grangers, Greenbackers, local labor parties, the WCTU, Mugwumps, and advocates of woman suffrage all challenged basic features of the party-bound political system of the Gilded Age. They and other groups sought political changes that the major parties ignored: abolition of the spoils system, woman suffrage, prohibition, the secret ballot, regulation of business, an end to child labor, changes in monetary policy, and more.

Most of these groups called themselves reformers, meaning that they wanted to change the *form* of politics. Most reforms fall into one of two categories—structural change and policy change. Structural reform modifies the *structure* of political decision making, for example, the way in which public officials are selected or eligibility for voting. Advocates of woman suffrage and those seeking to eliminate the spoils system were seeking to change the *structure* of politics.

Policy issues, in contrast, have to do with the way that government uses its powers to accomplish particular objectives. The debate over federal economic policy in the Gilded Age provides an array of contrasting positions. Many Democrats favored a policy of laissez faire, believing that federal interference in the economy created a privileged class. Republicans used land grants and the protective tariff to encourage economic growth. Grangers wanted the government to regulate economic activity by prohibiting pools and rebates and setting railroad rates. Greenbackers wanted monetary policy to benefit debtors—or, as they would have put it, to stop benefiting lenders.

Groups seeking change may find they have little in common or may seek to cooperate with other groups. Frances Willard of the WCTU embraced a wide range of reforms. One key distinction between the National Woman Suffrage Association and the American Woman Suffrage Association was that the NWSA welcomed political alliances with groups who supported suffrage for all citizens. The AWSA feared such alliances might lose more support than they gained and focused narrowly on suffrage.

Some groups combined structural and policy proposals. The tiny Prohibition Party wanted government to eliminate alcohol but also favored woman suffrage because they assumed that women voters would oppose alcohol. Thus, they promoted a structural reform, woman suffrage, in part to accomplish a policy reform, prohibition of alcohol. Advocates of woman suffrage also argued that enfranchising women would lead to a new approach to politics and to new policies.

One important structural change received widespread support from many political groups, and many states adopted it soon after its first appearance.

---

policy   A course of action adopted by a government, usually pursued over a period of time and potentially involving several laws and agencies.

The **Australian ballot**—printed and distributed by the government, not by political parties, listing all candidates of all parties, and marked in a private voting booth—was first adopted by Massachusetts in 1888. The idea quickly spread to all states and carried important implications for political parties. Now voters could easily cross party lines. No longer could party activists see which party's ballot a voter dropped into the ballot box. The switch to the Australian ballot and the Pendleton Act marked significant efforts to limit parties' power and influence.

POLITICAL UPHEAVAL IN THE 1890S

In 1890–1891, farmers who felt hard-pressed by debts, low prices for their crops, and the monopoly power of the railroads formed the People's Party, or **Populists**, and won elections in several states. The Depression that began in 1893 set the stage for more political change, culminating in the 1896 presidential election, which made the Republicans the majority party for a generation.

The People's Party   Populism grew out of the economic problems of farmers, especially falling prices for crops, the economic power of the railroads, and currency issues. The Grange, the Greenback Party, and the silver movement in the late 1870s had expressed farmers' grievances, but those movements faded during the relatively prosperous 1880s. By 1890, however, falling crop prices and widespread indebtedness brought renewed concern among farmers.

In the 1880s, three new organizations emerged, all called **Farmers' Alliances**. One was centered in the north-central states. Another, the Southern Alliance, began in Texas in the late 1870s and spread eastward across the South. The Southern Alliance limited its membership to white farmers, but a third group, the Colored Farmers' Alliance, recruited southern black farmers. Like the Grange and Knights of Labor, the Alliances defined themselves as organizations of the "producing classes" and looked to cooperatives as a partial solution to their problems. Alliance stores were most common. The Texas Alliance also experimented with cooperative cotton selling, and some midwestern local Alliances tried cooperative grain storage and selling.

Local Alliance meetings featured social and educational activities. By the late 1880s, a host of weekly newspapers across the South and West presented Alliance views. One Kansas woman described the result: "People commenced to think who had never thought before, and people talked who had seldom spoken.... Thoughts and theories sprouted like weeds after a May shower."

The Alliances defined themselves as nonpartisan and expected their members to work within the major parties. This was especially important in the South, where any white person who challenged the Democratic Party risked being condemned as a traitor to both race and region. Many Midwestern Alliance leaders, however, came out of the Granger Party tradition, and some had been Greenbackers. During the winter of 1889–1890, corn prices had fallen so low that some farmers found it cheaper to burn their corn than to sell it and buy fuel. More and more Alliance members talked of political action.

Through the hot summer of 1890, Alliance members in Kansas, Nebraska, the Dakotas, Minnesota, and surrounding states formed new political parties to contest state and local elections. One explained that the political battle they waged was "between the insatiable greed of organized wealth and the rights of the great plain people." Women took a prominent part in Populist campaigning, especially in Kansas and Nebraska. Mary Elizabeth Lease was among the most effective.

Populists emphasized three elements in their campaigns: **antimonopolism**, government action on behalf of farmers and workers, and increased popular control of government. Their antimonopolism drew on their unhappy experiences with railroads, grain buyers, and manufacturing companies. It also derived from a long American tradition of opposition to concentrated economic power. Populists quoted Thomas Jefferson on the importance of equal rights for all, and they compared themselves to Andrew Jackson in his fight against the Bank of the United States.

"We believe the time has come," Populists proclaimed in 1892, "when the railroad companies will either own the people or the people must own the railroads." Their solution to the dangers of monopoly was government action on behalf of farmers and workers, including federal ownership of the railroads and the telegraph and telephone systems, and government alternatives to private banks. Currency inflation, through greenbacks, silver, or both, formed an important part of the Populists' platform, along with a graduated income tax. Through such measures, they hoped, in the words of their 1892 platform, that "oppression, injustice, and poverty shall eventually cease in the land." They hoped to gain support among urban and industrial workers by calling for the eight-hour workday and opposing companies' use of private armies in labor disputes.

Finally, the People's Party favored structural changes to make government more responsive to the people, including expansion of the merit system for government employees, election of U.S. senators by the voters instead of state legislatures, a one-term limit for the president, and the secret ballot. Many also favored woman suffrage. In the South, Populists posed a serious challenge to the prevailing patterns of politics by seeking to forge a political alliance of the disadvantaged of both races. Populists usually opposed disfranchisement of black voters.

Thus Populists wanted to use government to control, even to own, the corporate behemoths that had evolved in their lifetimes. They also deeply distrusted the old parties and wanted to increase the influence of the individual voter in political decision making.

---

antimonopolism   Opposition to great concentrations of economic power such as large corporations, as well as to actual monopolies.

The Elections of
1890 and 1892

Despite Republicans' hopes for breaking the political logjam during the Fifty-first Congress, they immediately found themselves on the defensive. The issues in the 1890 elections for members of the House of Representatives and for state and local offices varied by region. In the West, the Populists stood at the center of the campaign, lambasting both major parties for ignoring the needs of the people. In the South, Democrats held up Lodge's "force bill" as a warning of the potential dangers if southern whites should bolt the party of white supremacy. There, members of the Southern Alliance worked within the Democratic Party to secure candidates committed to the farmers' cause. In the Northeast, Democrats attacked the McKinley Tariff for producing higher prices for consumers. In the Rocky Mountain region, nearly all candidates pledged their support for unlimited silver coinage.

The new Populist Party scored several victories, marking it as the most successful new party since the Republicans in the 1850s. Kansas Republican Senator John J. Ingalls had dismissed Populists as "a sort of turnip crusade," but Populists won control of the Kansas legislature and elected a Populist to replace him in the Senate. Elsewhere Populists elected state legislators, members of Congress, and one other U.S. senator. All across the South, the Alliance claimed that successful candidates owed their victories to Alliance voters.

Everywhere Republicans suffered defeat, losing nearly half their seats in the House of Representatives. Many Republican candidates for state and local offices also lost. The losses bred dissension within the party, and President Harrison could not maintain party unity.

For the 1892 presidential election, the Republicans renominated Harrison though he aroused little enthusiasm among many party leaders. The Democrats again chose Grover Cleveland. Southern Alliance activists joined western Populists to form a national People's Party and nominated James Weaver, the Greenback presidential candidate in 1880. Democrats and Populists scored the most impressive victories. Cleveland became the only president in American history to win two nonconsecutive terms. Democrats kept control of the House of Representatives and won a majority in the Senate. Populists displayed particular strength in the West and South. The Democrats now found themselves where the Republicans had stood four years before: in control of the presidency and Congress.

Failure of
the Divided
Democrats

When Congress met in 1893, Democrats faced several controversial issues, especially silver coinage and the tariff. The depression that had begun earlier that year (discussed in Chapter 16) and rising unemployment also demanded attention. President Cleveland, holding to his party's traditional commitment to minimal government and laissez faire, opposed any federal assistance to those in need. In the midst of financial crisis, Cleveland suffered a personal crisis—doctors detected cancer in his mouth. Fearing this news might lead to further financial panic, the president kept his surgery and recuperation secret.

Many business leaders argued that the Sherman Silver Purchase Act of 1890 had caused the gold drain that set off the depression, but many western and southern Democrats supported it as better than no silver coinage at all. Convinced that silver coinage had contributed to the economic collapse, Cleveland asked Congress to repeal the Silver Purchase Act. In the House of Representatives, most Republicans voted for repeal, but more than a third of the Democrats were opposed. In the Senate, Republicans supported Cleveland by 2 to 1, but Democrats divided almost evenly. Cleveland won but divided his own party, pitting the Northeast against the West and much of the South.

The Democrats also had to grapple with the tariff. After their harsh condemnation of the McKinley Tariff during the 1892 elections, they now had to do better. The tariff bill produced by the House reduced duties, tried to balance sectional interests, and created an income tax to replace lost federal revenue. Senate Democrats, however, loaded on many amendments. Cleveland characterized the result as "party dishonor" and refused to sign it. It became law without his signature in 1894. (The Supreme Court soon declared the income tax unconstitutional.)

By 1894, many Americans were becoming concerned by growing signs of social disorder. Early that year, Jacob S. Coxey, an Ohio Populist, announced a march on Washington to promote public works programs to provide jobs to the unemployed. The response electrified the nation—by April, six thousand people were camped outside Washington. Soon after, the Pullman Strike shut down many of the nation's railroads until Cleveland deployed U.S troops and marshals against the strikers.

Voters recorded their disgust with the disorganized Democrats in the 1894 elections. Democrats lost everywhere but in the Deep South, giving up 113 seats in the House of Representatives. Populists made few gains and suffered some losses. Republicans scored their biggest gains ever, adding 117 House seats, and looked forward eagerly to the 1896 presidential election.

The 1896 Election and the New Republican Majority   Republicans confidently anticipated victory in the presidential election of 1896. They nominated William McKinley, a Union veteran who had risen to the rank of major. McKinley had served fourteen years in Congress (where he had specialized in the tariff) and two terms as governor of Ohio. Known as calm and competent, McKinley billed himself as the "Advance Agent of Prosperity." The Republican platform supported the gold standard and opposed silver, but McKinley preferred to focus on the tariff. When the convention voted against silver, several western Republicans walked out of the convention and out of the party.

When the Democratic convention met, silverites held the majority but were split among several candidates. Then the platform committee chose **William Jennings Bryan** of Nebraska to speak in a debate on silver. Blessed with a commanding voice, Bryan had won election to the House of Representatives in 1890 and 1892 and gained national attention for his eloquent defense of silver. His speech was masterful. Defining the issue as a conflict between "the producing masses" and "the idle holders of idle capital," he argued that the first priority of federal policy should be "to make the masses prosperous," rather than to benefit the rich in the hope that "their prosperity will leak through on those below." His closing rang defiant: "We will answer their demand for a gold standard by saying to them: You shall not press down upon the brow of labor this crown of thorns. You shall not crucify mankind upon a cross of gold." The speech provoked an enthusiastic half-hour demonstration in support of silver—and Bryan. Only 36 years old, Bryan soon won the presidential nomination.

The Populists and defecting Republicans, who were quickly dubbed Silver Republicans, held nominating conventions next, amid frustration that the Democrats had stolen their thunder. Bryan favored silver, the income tax, and other reforms that Populists favored, and had worked closely with Populists. Populists gave him their nomination too, and Silver Republicans did the same. Subsequently, a group of Cleveland supporters nominated a Gold Democratic candidate.

Bryan and McKinley fought all-out campaigns but used sharply contrasting tactics. Bryan, vigorous and young, used his speaking voice as his greatest campaign tool. He spoke directly to the voters in four grueling train journeys through twenty-six states and more than 250 cities. Speaking to perhaps 5 million people in all, he stressed over and over that silver was the most important issue and that other reforms would follow once it was settled. Large crowds of excited and enthusiastic supporters greeted him nearly everywhere.

While McKinley himself campaigned from his home in Canton, Ohio, the Republicans flooded the country with speakers, pamphlets, and campaign paraphernalia, and also chartered trains and brought thousands of supporters to hear McKinley speak. Many business leaders feared that Bryan and silver coinage would bring financial collapse and opposed Bryan's other proposals, especially the income tax and lower tariff rates. McKinley's campaign played on such fears to secure a fund more than double any previous effort and many times what Bryan could raise.

McKinley won by the largest margin since 1872. Bryan carried the South and most of the West. McKinley prevailed in the urban, industrial Northeast, and he carried nearly every major city. The crucial battleground was the Midwest, where McKinley carried not only the urban industrial regions but also many farming areas.

Bryan's defeat spelled the end of the Populist Party. Some Populists moved into Bryan's Democratic Party, but others tried to hold together the tattered remnants of Populism. A few joined the Socialist Party, some returned to the Republican Party, and a few simply ignored politics. The issues they had raised—control of huge corporations, the extension of democratic processes, a fair monetary system—lived on in politics. Their influence remained especially prominent in Bryan's wing of the Democratic Party.

Bryan had appealed most to debt-ridden farmers, western miners, and traditional Democrats in the South and big cities. McKinley forged a broader appeal by emphasizing the gold standard and protective tariff as keys to economic recovery. For many urban residents—workers and the middle class alike—silver seemed to promise only higher prices, but the protective tariff meant manufacturing jobs. McKinley also won, in part, by restraining his party's nativist tendencies and denouncing the anti-Catholic American Protective Association, thereby gaining support among some immigrants who approved of his stand on gold and the tariff.

McKinley's victory ushered in a new generation of Republican dominance of national politics. Republicans had majorities in the House of Representatives for twenty-eight of the thirty-six years after 1894, and in the Senate for thirty of those thirty-six years. Republicans won seven of the nine presidential elections between 1896 and 1932, and similar patterns of Republican dominance appeared in state and local government.

Bryan led the Democrats over much of the next sixteen years, and he and his allies moved the party away from its traditional commitment to minimal government. While retaining Democrats' opposition to monopoly and to government favoritism toward business, Bryan and other new Democratic leaders agreed that the solution to the problems of economic concentration lay in a more active government. "A private monopoly," Bryan never tired of repeating, "is indefensible and intolerable." Democrats nonetheless clung to their version of states' rights, which permitted southern Democrats to perpetuate white-supremacist regimes. And most northern Democrats continued to oppose nativism and such moral reforms as prohibition.

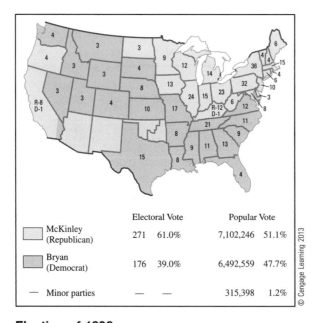

		Electoral Vote		Popular Vote	
☐	McKinley (Republican)	271	61.0%	7,102,246	51.1%
☐	Bryan (Democrat)	176	39.0%	6,492,559	47.7%
—	Minor parties	—	—	315,398	1.2%

© Cengage Learning 2013

MAP 18.1 The Election of 1896

Republicans won the election by carrying the urban vote.

McKinley provided strong executive leadership and worked closely with congressional leaders of his party to develop new policies. In 1897 a revised protective tariff fulfilled one Republican campaign promise, driving tariff rates sharply higher and reducing tariff-free imports. The surplus disappeared as an issue partly because of large naval expenditures. In 1900 the **Gold Standard Act** wrote another Republican pledge into law.

Whether Republican or Democrat, many voters now held their party commitments less intensely than before. For most voters before 1890, ethnicity and party went hand in hand. Now voters sometimes felt pulled toward one party by their economic situation and toward the other party by their ethnicity. Such voters sometimes supported Republicans for some offices and Democrats for others, choices now much easier because of the Australian ballot.

The political role of newspapers also changed. In the 1890s, William Randolph Hearst and Joseph Pulitzer took the lead in transforming urban newspapers into mass circulation dailies, competing for readership through eye-catching headlines and sensational stories. As they focused on increasing their circulation and advertising, they also played down their ties to political parties. Some journalists began to develop the idea of providing balanced political coverage.

American politics in 1888 looked much like American politics in 1876 or even 1844. But in the 1890s, American politics changed. In the early 1900s, the continued decline of political parties and partisan loyalties among voters combined with the emergence of organized interest groups to create even more change, producing the major structural features of American politics in the twentieth century.

STANDING ASIDE FROM WORLD AFFAIRS, 1865–1889

The years when domestic politics seemed deadlocked saw little change in the nation's relations with the rest of the world. The nation's role in world affairs was slight, and most Americans expected their nation to follow George Washington's advice to "steer clear of permanent alliances with any portion of the foreign world." The effect of America's economic transformation on its foreign relations, as on its domestic politics, was slow in appearing.

Alaska, Canada, and the *Alabama* Claims   **William H. Seward**, one of the Gilded Age's most capable secretaries of state, often voiced his belief in America's destiny to expand across the North American continent. When he learned in 1866 that Tsar Alexander II might sell Russian holdings in North America if the price were right, Seward made an offer, and in 1867, for slightly over $7 million, Alaska was in U.S. hands.

The Alaska treaty differed from earlier agreements acquiring territory in one significant way. Like previous treaties, it extended immediate citizenship to all inhabitants of the territory (except Indians), but unlike previous treaties, it carried no promise that the acquired territory would eventually become a state. This half-step away from earlier patterns of territorial expansion foreshadowed later patterns of colonial acquisition.

Some journalists derided Alaska as a frozen wasteland and branded it "Seward's Folly." Charles Sumner, chairman of the **Senate Foreign Relations Committee**, voiced more enthusiasm, looking on the purchase of Alaska as a first step toward acquiring Canada. Sumner thought a second step might lie in claims against Great Britain arising out of the Civil War. Confederate warships, notably the *Alabama* and *Florida*, built in British shipyards and given refuge and repairs in British ports, had badly disrupted northern shipping. The United States claimed that Britain owed compensation for the damage done by the Confederate cruisers, and Sumner unrealistically suggested that Britain could meet this obligation by ceding all its North American possessions, including Canada, to the United States. Ultimately, however, the two countries agreed to **arbitration**, and the 1872 arbitration decision set $15.5 million as damages to be paid to the United States.

The United States and Latin America

After the Civil War, American diplomats took new interest in Latin America, partly because European powers were starting to exert influence there and partly because some Americans wanted a more prominent role there. In 1823 President James Monroe had announced that the United States would consider any attempt by a European power to colonize in North and South America to be a threat to the United States, but that the United States would neither interfere with existing colonies nor involve itself in European politics. Though later a linchpin of American policy, the **Monroe Doctrine** was rarely mentioned by presidents until the 1890s.

In 1861, as the United States lurched into civil war, France, Spain, and Britain sent a joint force to Mexico to collect debts that Mexico could not pay. Spain and Britain withdrew, but French troops remained despite resistance led by **Benito Juarez**, president of Mexico. Some of Juarez's political opponents cooperated with the French emperor, Napoleon III, to name Archduke **Maximilian** of Austria as emperor of Mexico. Maximilian, a young idealist, apparently believed that the Mexican people genuinely wanted him as their leader. He antagonized some conservative supporters with talk of reform but failed to win other support. In reality, Maximilian held power only because of the French troops.

Involved in its own civil war, the U.S. government recognized Juarez as president but could do little else. When the Civil War ended, however, Seward demanded that Napoleon III withdraw his troops, and underscored his demand by sending fifty thousand battle-hardened troops to the Mexican border. Napoleon III

Senate Foreign Relations Committee   A standing committees of the Senate; its chairman often wields considerable influence over foreign policy.

arbitration   Process by which parties to a dispute submit their case to the judgment of an impartial person or group (the arbiter) and agree to accept the arbiter's decision.

soon brought the French soldiers home. Maximilian unwisely remained behind, where he was defeated in battle by Juarez and then executed. Seward did not cite the Monroe Doctrine, but the withdrawal of French troops in the face of American military force renewed respect in Europe for the role of the United States in Latin America.

Eastern Asia and the Pacific   Americans had long-standing commercial interests in eastern Asia. The China trade dated to 1784, and the first treaty between China and the United States, in 1844, included a provision granting **most-favored-nation status** to the United States. Goods from Asia and the Pacific accounted for 8 percent of U.S. imports after the Civil War. Exports were disappointing, however, and some Americans dreamed of selling to the millions of Chinese. American missionaries began to preach in China in 1830. Although they gained few converts, their lectures in the United States stimulated public interest in eastern Asia.

Japan and Korea had also refused to engage in trade, their way of deflecting Western influences and avoiding European power rivalries. In 1854 an American naval force convinced the Japanese government to open its ports to foreign trade. A similar navy action opened Korea in 1882.

Growing trade between eastern Asia and the United States fueled American interest in the Pacific. American commercial ships needed ports in the Pacific for supplies and repairs, and interest focused especially on Hawai'i. Hawai'i had attracted Christian missionaries from New England as early as 1819, shortly after King Kamehameha united the islands into one nation. The missionaries were first concerned with preaching the Gospel and convincing the unabashed Hawaiians to wear clothes, but later some missionaries and their descendants came to exercise great influence over several Hawaiian monarchs.

Ideally located for resupply of ships traveling the Pacific, after 1848 Hawai'i became a routine stop for ships sailing from New York around South America to San Francisco. As early as 1842, President John Tyler announced that the United States would not allow the islands to pass under the control of another power, but Britain and France continued to take a keen interest in them.

David Kalakaua became king of Hawai'i in 1874. During his reign, relations with the United States became much closer. Kalakaua became the first reigning monarch ever to visit the United States, in 1874. In 1875 he approved a treaty that gave Hawaiian sugar free access to the United States. The Hawaiian sugar industry then expanded rapidly as descendants of missionaries joined American companies in developing huge plantations. Soon Hawaiian sugar spawned a vertically integrated industry that included American-owned plantations, ships to carry raw sugar to the mainland, and sugar refineries in California—and the economies of the two nations became closely linked.

---

most-favored-nation status In a treaty between nation A and nation B, the provision that commercial privileges extended by A to other nations automatically become available to B.

Despite these economic ties, relations between Kalakaua and the **haole** community of Hawai'i were never comfortable. Kalakaua wanted to preserve political power for **indigenous** Hawaiians, but *haole*s charged that he was ignoring the needs of business and the sugar plantations. In 1887 the news broke that Kalakaua had profited from bribery related to opium. Leaders of the *haole* community used that excuse to force a constitution on him, reducing his power. *Haoles* soon dominated much of the government. That same year, Kalakaua approved an extension of the treaty of 1875, with an additional provision giving the U.S. Navy exclusive rights to use Pearl Harbor. Among some members of the royal family, resentment festered over the new constitution, the Pearl Harbor provision, and especially the extent of *haole* control. Those resentments boiled over after Kalakaua's death in 1891.

STEPPING INTO WORLD AFFAIRS: HARRISON AND CLEVELAND, 1889–1897

During the 1890s, America's involvement in world affairs changed in important ways. One element revolved around a new role for the U.S. Navy and the commissioning of modern ships able to carry it out. Another related to the emergence and acceptance of new concepts of America's global status and foreign policy.

Building a Modern Navy Most presidents of the Gilded Age paid little attention to the army and navy. After the last Indian wars, the army was limited to a few garrisons, most near Indian reservations. Most federal decision-makers understood the role of the navy as limited to protecting American coasts. The navy's wooden sailing vessels deteriorated so badly that some ridiculed them as fit only for firewood. Not until 1882 did Congress authorize construction of two steam-powered cruisers—the first new ships in almost twenty years—and four more ships in 1883. Still, Secretary of the Navy William C. Whitney announced in 1885 that "we have nothing which deserves to be called a navy," and persuaded Congress to fund several more cruisers and the first two modern battleships.

Alfred Thayer Mahan played a key role in developing a modern navy. President of the Naval War College, Mahan exerted a powerful influence through lectures to navy officers, a book, *The Influence of Sea Power upon History* (1890), and articles in the press. Mahan argued that sea power had been the determining factor in European power struggles for the previous 150 years and explored the significance of geography, population, and government for establishing sea power. He advocated a large, modern navy centered on huge battleships capable of carrying American power to distant seas. He also

haole   Hawaiian word for persons not of native Hawaiian ancestry, especially whites.
indigenous   Original to an area.

stressed the need to establish and control a canal through Central America, command the Caribbean, dominate strategic locations in the Pacific, and create naval bases at key points.

In 1889, with Harrison in the White House and Republican majorities in both houses of Congress, Secretary of the Navy Benjamin F. Tracy urged Congress to modernize and significantly expand the navy. Tracy's ambitious proposal might have eliminated the federal budget surplus all by itself! Congress did not give him all he wanted but did vote funds for a modern navy centered on battleships. With construction under way on three battleships, Tracy happily announced that "we shall rule [the sea] as certainly as the sun doth rise!"

A New American Mission?   Mahan's strategic arguments and Tracy's battleship launchings came as some Americans began, in Mahan's phrase, to "look outward." Advocacy came from many sources: Protestant ministers, scholars, business figures, historians, politicians. Together they redefined the way many Americans, and American policymakers, viewed the nation's role in world affairs. Josiah Strong offered the perspective of a Protestant missionary, arguing that expansion of American Protestant ideals to the world constituted a Christian duty. "The world is to be Christianized and civilized," he predicted, adding that "commerce follows the missionary."

Social Darwinism and the notion of "progress" merged with a belief in the superiority of the Anglo-Saxons—the people of England and their descendants. In the 1880s, popular books claimed that Anglo-Saxons had demonstrated a unique capacity for civilization and had a duty to enlighten and uplift other peoples. Albert Beveridge, Republican senator from Indiana, blended some of these ideas with American nationalism when he proclaimed, "[God] has made us the master organizers of the world to establish system where chaos reigns." Rudyard Kipling, an English poet, in 1899 urged the United States to "take up the white man's burden," a phrase that came to describe a self-imposed obligation to go into distant lands, bring the supposed blessings of Anglo-Saxon civilization to their peoples, Christianize them, and sell them manufactured goods.

Today historians understand Anglo-Saxonism and the "white man's burden" as imbued with racism. Such views assumed that some people, by virtue of race, possessed a superior capability for self-government and cultural accomplishment. This thinking elevated only one cultural pattern as "civilization," dismissing all others as inferior and ignoring their cultural accomplishments.

Revolution in Hawai'i   New views on the strategic significance of the Pacific focused the attention of many Americans on Hawai'i when a revolution broke out there early in 1893. The revolution stemmed in part from changes in American tariff rates on sugar. In 1890, the McKinley Tariff provided that all sugar could enter the United States without paying a tariff. Previously only Hawaiian sugar had this privilege. Now it faced new competition, notably from Cuban sugar. Facing economic disaster, many Hawaiian planters began to discuss annexation to the United States.

This painting of Queen Lili'uokalani dates to 1892. Lili'uokalani was a gifted musician and wrote the song "Aloha 'Oe," which is still performed today.

The Granger Collection, New York

In 1891 King Kalakaua died and was succeeded by his sister, **Lili'uokalani**, who hoped to restore Hawai'i to the indigenous Hawaiians and return political power to the monarchy. Some *haole* entrepreneurs feared that they might lose their political clout and economic holdings. On January 17, 1893, a group of plotters proclaimed a republic and announced they would seek annexation by the United States. John L. Stevens, the U.S. minister to Hawai'i, promptly ordered the landing of 150 U.S. Marines. Lili'uokalani surrendered, as she put it, "to the superior force of the United States." Stevens immediately recognized the new republic, declared it a **protectorate** of the United States, and raised the American flag.

The Harrison administration **repudiated** Stevens's overzealous deeds but opened negotiations with representatives of the new republic. The Senate received a treaty of annexation shortly before Cleveland became president. Cleveland was

protectorate   A country partially controlled by a stronger power and dependent on that power for protection from foreign threats.

repudiate   To reject as invalid or unauthorized.

willing to consider annexing Hawai'i if the Hawaiian people requested it. However, he withdrew the annexation treaty temporarily, then learned the revolution would have failed had the marines not intervened. He asked the new officials to restore the queen. They refused, and Hawai'i continued as an independent republic, dominated by its *haole* business and planter community.

Crises in Latin America   Harrison and Cleveland disagreed regarding Hawai'i, but both presidents extended American involvement in Latin America.

In 1891 a mob in Chile set upon several American sailors on shore leave and beat them, injuring several and killing two. When the Chilean government gave no sign of apologizing, Harrison threatened "such action as may be necessary." When the Chilean government would not back down, Harrison responded with plans for a naval war. Chile then gave in, apologized, and promised to pay damages.

In 1895 and 1896, Cleveland also took the nation to the edge of war. At issue was an old boundary dispute between Venezuela and British Guiana. Venezuela proposed arbitration, which Cleveland also favored, but Britain refused. In July 1895, Secretary of State Richard Olney cited the Monroe Doctrine, demanded Britain submit to arbitration, and bombastically declared the United States preeminent throughout the Western Hemisphere. Britain still refused. Cleveland then asked Congress for authority to determine the boundary and enforce it. Britain now faced the possibility of conflict with the United States—at a time when the British were increasingly concerned about the rising power of Germany and facing possible war in South Africa. Britain agreed to arbitration.

Both presidents behaved more forcefully than their predecessors since Seward stood up to Napoleon III in Mexico. However, where Seward's action had restored Mexican control over its own affairs, Harrison's heavy-handed threats toward Chile discouraged closer relations with Latin America. Cleveland, however, may have had some effect in persuading European imperial powers that the Western Hemisphere was off-limits in the ongoing scramble for colonies.

Cuba presented a very different situation. Cuba and Puerto Rico were all that remained of the once-mighty Spanish empire in the Americas, and Cubans had repeatedly rebelled against Spain. In the early 1890s, when the McKinley Tariff permitted Cuban sugar to enter the United States without charge, the Cuban sugar industry boomed. In 1894, though, the new tariff law restored a duty on Cuban sugar and depressed the island's economy. Fueled by economic distress, a new insurrection erupted against Spanish rule. Advocates of *Cuba libre* ("free Cuba") received support from sympathizers in the United States. In 1896, in response to the **insurgents'** guerrilla warfare, the Spanish commander, General Valeriano

---

insurgent Rebel or revolutionary; one involved in an insurrection or rebellion against constituted authority.

Weyler, established a **reconcentration** policy. The civilian population was ordered into fortified towns or camps. Everyone outside these fortified areas was considered an insurgent, subject to military action. Disease and starvation swept through the camps, killing many Cubans.

American newspapers—especially **Joseph Pulitzer's** *New York World* and **William Randolph Hearst's** *New York Journal*—presented Spanish atrocities in screaming headlines, sometimes exaggerating and sensationalizing their reporters' stories (a practice called **yellow journalism**). In response, many Americans began clamoring to rescue the Cubans.

Intent on avoiding American involvement, Cleveland proclaimed U.S. neutrality and warned Americans not to support the insurrection. When members of Congress pushed Cleveland to seek Cuban independence, he only urged Spain to grant concessions to the insurgents. Just as he had earlier opposed annexation of Hawai'i, Cleveland now resisted intervention in Cuba, fearing it might lead to annexation regardless of the will of the Cuban people. Nonetheless, by the time he left the presidency in early 1897, he suggested possible American intervention.

STRIDING BOLDLY IN WORLD AFFAIRS: MCKINLEY, WAR, AND IMPERIALISM, 1898–1902

In 1898 the United States went to war with Spain over Cuba. John Hay, the American ambassador to Great Britain, celebrated the conflict as "a splendid little war," and the description stuck. Some envisioned a quick war to save the suffering Cubans and establish a Cuban republic. Others saw war with Spain as an opportunity to seize territory and acquire an American colonial empire.

McKinley and War   William McKinley became president amid increasing demands for action regarding Cuba. He moved cautiously, gradually stepping up diplomatic efforts to resolve the crisis. In response, Spain softened the reconcentration policy and offered limited self-government but not independence. In February 1898, however, events scuttled progress toward a negotiated solution.

First, Cuban insurgents stole a letter from **Enrique Dupuy de Lôme**, the Spanish minister to the United States, and released it to the *New York Journal*. In it, de Lôme criticized President McKinley as "weak and a bidder for the admiration of the crowd." The letter also implied that the Spanish government's commitment to reform in Cuba was not serious. Although de Lôme

reconcentration Spanish policy in Cuba in 1896 that ordered the civilian population into fortified areas so as to isolate and annihilate the revolutionaries who remained outside.

yellow journalism The use of sensational exposés, embellished reporting, and attention-grabbing headlines to sell newspapers.

On February 15, 1898, an explosion destroyed the USS Maine at Havana, Cuba. Many Americans blamed the Spanish government, although there was no evidence to suggest who was responsible.

immediately resigned, the letter aroused intense anti-Spanish feeling among many Americans.

A few days later, on February 15, an explosion ripped open the **USS _Maine_**, anchored in Havana Harbor. The battleship sank, killing more than 260 Americans. The yellow press accused Spain of sabotage but without evidence. An official inquiry blamed a submarine mine but could not determine its source. Years later, an investigation indicated that the blast was probably of internal origin, resulting from a fire. Regardless of how the explosion occurred, those advocating intervention now had a rallying cry: "Remember the _Maine!_"

McKinley extended his demands: an immediate end to the fighting, an end to reconcentration, measures to relieve the suffering, and **mediation** by McKinley himself. He specified that one possible outcome of mediation might be Cuban independence. In reply, the Spanish government promised reforms, agreed to end reconcentration, and consented to cease fighting if the insurgents asked for

mediation   An attempt to bring about the peaceful settlement of a dispute through the intervention of a neutral party.

an **armistice**—but said nothing about mediation by McKinley or independence for Cuba.

On April 11, McKinley sent a message to Congress stating that "the war in Cuba must stop" and asking for authority to act. Congress answered on April 19 with four resolutions: (1) declaring that Cuba was and should be independent, (2) demanding that Spain withdraw "at once," (3) authorizing the president to use force to accomplish Spanish withdrawal, and (4) disavowing any intention to annex the island. The first three resolutions amounted to a declaration of war. The fourth is usually called the **Teller Amendment** for its sponsor, Senator Henry M. Teller, a Silver Republican from Colorado. In response, Spain declared war.

Most Americans wholeheartedly approved what they understood to be a war undertaken to bring independence and aid to the long-suffering Cubans. Some, however, distrusted the McKinley administration's motives. The Teller Amendment reflected this concern that the McKinley administration might try to make Cuba an American possession rather than granting it independence.

The "Splendid Little War"   Americans' attention had been riveted on Cuba. Many were surprised that the first engagement in the war occurred in the **Philippine Islands**—nearly halfway around the world from Cuba. The Philippines had been a Spanish colony for three hundred years, but had rebelled repeatedly, most recently in 1896.

Some Americans understood the islands' strategic location with regard to eastern Asia—including Assistant Secretary of the Navy **Theodore Roosevelt**. In February 1898, six weeks before McKinley's war message to Congress, Roosevelt drew upon planning exercises by the Naval War College when he cabled George Dewey, the American naval commander in the Pacific, to crush the Spanish fleet at Manila Bay if war broke out.

At sunrise on Sunday, May 1, Dewey's squadron of four cruisers, two gunboats, and three support vessels steamed into the harbor and quickly destroyed or captured seven Spanish cruisers and four gunboats. The Spanish lost 161 men and 210 were wounded. The Americans lost one, a victim of heat prostration, and nine were wounded. Dewey instantly became a national hero.

Dewey's victory at Manila focused public attention on the western Pacific, raising the prospect of a permanent American presence there. This possibility, in turn, revived interest in the Hawaiian Islands as a base halfway to the Philippines. Anti-imperialist sentiment in the Senate made approval of an annexation treaty unlikely, so McKinley revived the joint-resolution precedent by which Texas had been annexed in 1844. Only a majority vote in both houses of Congress was required to adopt a joint resolution, rather than the two-thirds vote of the Senate needed to approve a treaty. Annexation of Hawai'i was accomplished on July 7.

armistice   An agreement to halt fighting.

Dewey's victory clearly demonstrated American naval superiority. In contrast, the Spanish army in Cuba outnumbered the entire American army by five to one and had years of experience fighting on the island. When McKinley called for volunteers, nearly a million men responded—five times as many as the army needed. Next the army began to train and supply the new recruits.

Sent to training camps in the South, the new soldiers found chaos and confusion. Food, uniforms, and equipment arrived at one location while the intended recipients stood hungry and idle at another. Uniforms were often of heavy wool, unsuited for the Cuban climate. Disease raged through some camps, killing many men. Others died from tainted food, called "embalmed beef" by the troops. Some African American soldiers refused to comply with racial segregation, and many white southerners objected to the presence in their communities of uniformed and armed black men. Congress declared war in late April, but not until June did the first troop transports head for Cuba.

When they finally arrived in Cuba, American forces tried to capture the port city of Santiago, where the Spanish fleet had taken refuge. Inexperienced, poorly equipped, and unfamiliar with the terrain, the Americans landed some distance from Santiago and assaulted the fortified hills surrounding the city.

Theodore Roosevelt had resigned as assistant secretary of the navy to organize a cavalry unit known as the Rough Riders. At Kettle Hill, he led a successful charge of Rough Riders and regular army units, including parts of the Ninth and Tenth Cavalry, made up of African Americans. All but Roosevelt were on foot because their horses had not yet arrived. Driving the Spanish from the crest of Kettle Hill cleared a serious impediment to the assault on nearby San Juan Heights and San Juan Hill. Journalists loved Roosevelt—and newspapers all over the country declared him the hero of the Battle of San Juan Hill.

Nearly 10 percent of U.S. troops were killed or wounded during the first few days of the attack on Santiago. Worsening the situation, the surgeon in charge of medical facilities refused assistance from Red Cross nurses because he thought field hospitals were not appropriate places for women. He was later overruled. Red Cross nurses also helped care for injured Cuban insurgents and civilians.

Once American troops gained control of the high ground around Santiago harbor, the Spanish fleet tried to escape. A larger American fleet met them and duplicated Dewey's rout at Manila—every Spanish ship was sunk or run aground. The Spanish suffered 323 deaths, the Americans one.

Their fleet destroyed, surrounded by American troops, the Spanish in Santiago surrendered on July 17. A week later American forces occupied Puerto Rico. Spanish land forces in the Philippines surrendered when the first American troops arrived in mid-August. The "splendid little war" lasted only sixteen weeks. More than 306,000 men served in the American forces. Only 385 of them died in battle, but more than 5,000 died of disease and other causes.

| The Treaty of Paris | On August 12, the United States and Spain agreed to stop fighting and hold a peace conference in Paris. The major question for the conference centered on the Philippines. |

Finley Peter Dunne, a popular humorist, parodied the national debate in a discussion between his fictional characters, Mr. Dooley (a Chicago saloonkeeper) and a customer named Hennessy. Hennessy insists that McKinley should take the islands. Dooley retorts that "it's not more than two months since you learned whether they were islands or canned goods," then confesses his own indecision: "I can't annex them because I don't know where they are. I can't let go of them because someone else will take them.... It would break my heart to think of giving people I've never seen or heard tell of back to other people I don't know.... I don't know what to do about the Philippines. And I'm all alone in the world. Everybody else has made up his mind."

McKinley voiced almost as many doubts as Mr. Dooley. At first, he seemed to favor only a naval base, leaving Spain in control elsewhere. However, Spanish authority collapsed by mid-August as Filipino insurgents took charge throughout the islands. Britain, Japan, and Germany watched carefully, and one or another seemed likely to step in if the United States withdrew. McKinley and his advisers decided that a naval base on Manila Bay would require control of the entire island group. No one seriously considered the Filipinos' desire for independence.

McKinley was well aware of the political and strategic importance of the Philippines for eastern Asia. He invoked other reasons, however, when he explained his decision to a group of visiting Methodists. He repeatedly prayed for guidance on the Philippine question, he told them. Late one night, he said, it came to him that "there was nothing left for us to do but to take them all, and to educate the Filipinos, and uplift and civilize and Christianize them and by God's grace do the very best we could by them." In fact, most Filipinos had been Catholics for centuries, but no one ever expressed more clearly the concept of the "white man's burden."

Spain resisted giving up the Philippines, but McKinley was adamant. The Treaty of Paris, signed in December 1898, required Spain to surrender Cuba, cede Puerto Rico and Guam to the United States, and sell the Philippines for $20 million. For the first time in American history, a treaty acquiring new territory failed to confer U.S. citizenship on the residents. Nor did the treaty mention future statehood. Thus these acquisitions represented a new kind of expansion—America had become a colonial power.

The **Treaty of Paris** dismayed Democrats, Populists, and some conservative Republicans, sparking a public debate over acquisition of the Philippines in particular and **imperialism** in general. An anti-imperialist movement quickly formed, with William Jennings Bryan, Andrew Carnegie, Grover Cleveland, Carl Schurz, and Mark Twain among its outspoken proponents. The treaty, they argued, denied self-government for the newly acquired territories. For the United States to hold colonies, they claimed, threatened the very concept of democracy. "The Declaration of Independence," warned Carnegie, "will make every Filipino a thoroughly dissatisfied subject." Others voiced racist arguments,

imperialism   The practice by which a nation acquires and holds colonies and other possessions, denies them self-government, and usually exploits them economically.

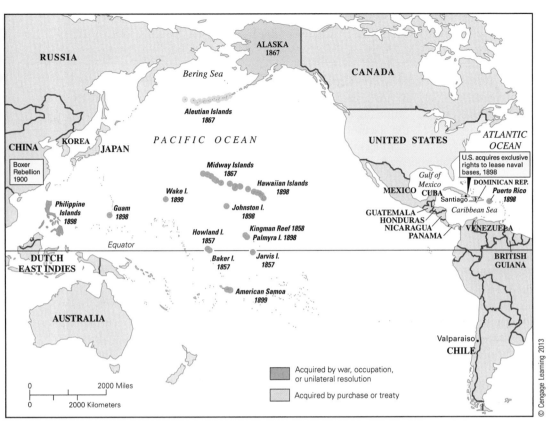

MAP 18.2 U.S. Territorial Expansion in the Late Nineteenth Century

The major U.S. territorial expansion abroad came in a short burst of activity in the late 1890s, when newspapers and some politicians urged Americans to acquire strategic ports and coaling stations abroad.

claiming that Filipinos were incapable of self-government and that the United States would be corrupted by ruling such people. Union leaders, fearing Filipino migration to the United States, repeated arguments once used to secure Chinese exclusion.

Those who defended acquisition of the Philippines echoed McKinley's lofty pronouncements about America's duty. Albert Beveridge, senator from Indiana, among others, also cited economic benefits: "We are raising more than we can consume, making more than we can use. Therefore we must find new markets for our produce." Such "new markets" were not limited to the new possessions. A strong naval and military presence in the Philippines would make the United States a leading power in eastern Asia, thereby supporting access for American business to markets in China.

William Jennings Bryan urged senators to approve the treaty. That way, he reasoned, the United States alone could determine the future of the Philippines. Once the treaty was approved, he argued, the United States should immediately grant them independence. By a narrow margin, the Senate approved the treaty on February 6, 1899. Soon after, senators rejected a proposal for Philippine independence.

The New American Empire

Bryan hoped to make independence for the Philippines the central issue in the 1900 presidential election. He easily won the Democratic nomination for a second time, and the Democrats' platform condemned the McKinley administration for its "imperialism." Bryan found, however, that many conservative anti-imperialists would not support his candidacy because he still insisted on silver coinage and attacked big business.

The Republicans renominated McKinley. For vice president, they chose Theodore Roosevelt, "hero of San Juan Hill." McKinley's reelection seemed unstoppable. Republican campaigners pointed proudly to a short and highly successful war, legislation on the tariff and gold standard, and the return of prosperity. Bryan repeatedly attacked imperialism. McKinley and Roosevelt never used the term at all and instead took pride in expansion. McKinley easily won a second term with 52 percent of the vote.

Now the United States had to organize its new empire. The Teller Amendment specified that the United States would not annex Cuba, but the McKinley administration refused to recognize the insurgents as the legitimate government. Instead, the U.S. Army took control. Among other tasks, the army undertook sanitation projects to reduce disease, especially yellow fever. After two years of army rule, the McKinley administration permitted Cuban voters to hold a constitutional convention.

The convention met in 1900 and drafted a constitution modeled on that of the United States. Nowhere did it define relations between Cuba and the United States. In response, the McKinley administration drafted, and Congress adopted, terms for Cuba to adopt before the army would withdraw. Called the **Platt Amendment**, the terms specified that (1) Cuba was not to make any agreement with a foreign power that impaired the island's independence, (2) the United States could intervene in Cuba to preserve Cuban independence and maintain law and order, and (3) Cuba was to lease facilities to the United States for naval bases and coaling stations. Cubans reluctantly agreed, changed their constitution, and signed a treaty with the United States stating the Platt conditions. In 1902 Cuba thereby became a protectorate of the United States.

The Teller Amendment did not apply to Puerto Rico. There, the army provided a military government until 1900, when Congress approved the **Foraker Act**. That act made Puerto Ricans citizens of Puerto Rico but not citizens of the United States. Puerto Rican voters could elect a legislature, but final authority rested with a governor and council appointed by the president of the United States. In 1901, in the **Insular Cases**, the U.S. Supreme Court confirmed the colonial status of Puerto Rico and, by implication, the other new possessions. The Court ruled that they were not equivalent to earlier territorial acquisitions and that their people did not possess the constitutional rights of citizens.

Establishment of civil government in the Philippines took longer. Between Dewey's victory and arrival of the first American soldiers three months later, a Philippine independence movement led by **Emilio Aguinaldo** established a provisional government and took control everywhere but Manila, which remained in Spanish hands until American troops arrived. Aguinaldo and his government wanted independence. When the United States determined to keep the islands, the Filipinos resisted.

Quelling what American authorities called the "Philippine insurrection" required three years (1899–1902), took the lives of 4,196 American soldiers, and perhaps 700,000 or more Filipinos (most through disease and other noncombat causes), and cost $400 million (twenty times the price of the islands). When some Filipinos resorted to guerrilla warfare, U.S. troops adopted practices similar to those Spain had used in Cuba. Both sides committed atrocities, and anti-imperialists pointed to brutal behavior by American troops as proof that a colonial policy was corrupting American values. American troops captured Aguinaldo in 1901, but resistance continued into mid-1902.

Congress set up a government for the Philippines similar to that of Puerto Rico. Filipinos became citizens of the Philippine Islands, but not of the United States. The president of the United States appointed the governor. Filipino voters elected one house in the two-house legislature, and the governor appointed the other. Both the governor and the U.S. Congress could veto laws passed by the legislature. **William Howard Taft**, governor from 1901 to 1904, tried to build local support for American control, secured limited land reforms, and started to build public schools, hospitals, and sanitary facilities. However, when the first Philippine legislature met, in 1907, more than half of its members favored independence.

The Open Door and the Boxer Rebellion in China

Late in 1899, Britain, Germany, and the United States signed the Treaty of Berlin, which divided **Samoa** between Germany and the United States. The new Pacific acquisitions of the United States—Hawai'i, the Philippines, Guam, and Samoa—all contained excellent sites for naval bases. Combined with the modernized navy, these acquisitions greatly strengthened American ability to assert power in the region and protect Americans' commercial access to eastern Asia. The United States now began to seek full participation in the East Asian **balance of power**.

Weakened by war with Japan in 1894–1895, the Chinese government could not resist European nations' demands for territory. Britain, Germany, Russia, and France had carved out **spheres of influence**—areas where they claimed special

balance of power   In international politics, the notion that nations may restrict one another's actions because of the relative equality of their naval or military forces, either individually or through alliance systems.

sphere of influence   A region where a foreign nation exerts significant authority.

rights, usually a monopoly over trade, and sought to exclude other powers. The United States argued instead for the "Open Door"—the principle that citizens of all nations should have equal status in seeking trade. American diplomats, however, began to fear the breakup of China into separate European colonies and the exclusion of American commerce.

In 1899 Secretary of State John Hay circulated a letter to Germany, Russia, Britain, France, Italy, and Japan, asking them to preserve Chinese sovereignty within their spheres of influence and not to discriminate against citizens of other nations engaged in commerce within their spheres. Hay wanted both to prevent the dismemberment of China and to maintain commercial access for American business throughout China. Some replies proved less than fully supportive, but Hay announced in a second letter that all had agreed to his "Open Door" principles. Hay's letters have usually been called the **Open Door notes**.

In 1900, a Chinese secret society tried to expel all foreigners from China. Because the rebels used a clenched fist as their symbol, westerners called them Boxers. The Boxers laid siege to the section of Beijing, the Chinese capital, that housed foreign **legations**. Hay feared that other powers might use the rebellion as a pretext to take control and divide China permanently. To block such a move, the United States took full part in an international military expedition to rescue the besieged foreign diplomats and to crush the **Boxer Rebellion**.

Although China did not lose territory, the intervening nations required it to pay an **indemnity**. After compensating U.S. citizens for their losses, the U.S. government returned the remainder of its indemnity to China. To show its appreciation, the Chinese government used the money to send Chinese students to study in the United States.

STUDY TOOLS

SUMMARY

In the late nineteenth century, political parties dominated politics. All elected public officials were nominated by party conventions and elected through party campaigns. Nearly all government jobs came through the spoils system. Republicans used government to promote rapid economic development, but Democrats argued for minimal government. Voters divided between the major parties largely along the lines of region, ethnicity, and race.

The presidency of Ulysses S. Grant was plagued by scandals. Thereafter, the closely balanced strengths of the two parties contributed to a long-term political stalemate. In 1889–1890, however, Republicans wrote most of their campaign promises into law.

---

legation   Diplomatic officials representing their nation to another nation, and their offices and residences.

indemnity   Payment for damage, loss, or injury.

Grangers, Greenbackers, and silverites challenged the major parties, appealing most to debt-ridden farmers. Mugwumps argued for the merit system in the civil service, accomplished through the Pendleton Act of 1883. By the late nineteenth century, a well-organized woman suffrage movement had emerged. A wide range of reform groups sought both structural changes and policy changes.

The 1890s saw major, long-lasting changes in American politics. A political upheaval began when western and southern farmers joined the Farmers' Alliances, then launched a new political party, the Populist Party. Elected in 1892, President Grover Cleveland failed to meet the political challenges of the depression that began in 1893; his party, the Democrats, lost badly in the 1894 congressional elections. In 1896 the Democrats nominated for president William Jennings Bryan, a supporter of silver coinage. The Republicans chose William McKinley, who favored the protective tariff. McKinley won, beginning a period of Republican dominance in national politics that lasted until 1930. Under Bryan's leadership, the Democratic Party promoted government action against monopolies and other powerful economic interests.

From 1865 to 1889, few Americans expected their nation to be significantly involved in world affairs outside North America. The United States did acquire Alaska, pressured the French to withdraw from Mexico, and took actions to encourage trade with eastern Asia. The kingdom of Hawai'i became closely integrated with the American economy. During the early 1890s, the United States moved toward a new role in world affairs. Presidents Harrison and Cleveland asserted American power in Latin America.

A revolution in Cuba led the United States into a one-sided war with Spain in 1898, resulting in acquisition of the Philippines, Guam, and Puerto Rico. Congress annexed Hawai'i in the midst of the war, and the United States acquired part of Samoa in 1899. Filipinos resisted American authority, leading to a three-year war. With the Philippines and an improved navy, the United States gained new prominence in eastern Asia, especially in China, where the United States promoted the Open Door and American troops helped suppress the Boxer Rebellion.

CHRONOLOGY

POLITICS AND FOREIGN RELATIONS

1867	French troops leave Mexico United States purchases Alaska
1868	Ulysses S. Grant elected president
1869	National Woman Suffrage Association and American Woman Suffrage Association formed Wyoming Territory adopts woman suffrage
1872	Crédit Mobilier scandal Grant reelected
1872–1874	Granger laws
1873–1879	Depression

1877	Rutherford B. Hayes becomes president
1878	Greenback Party peaks
1880	James A. Garfield elected president
1881	Garfield assassinated
	Chester A. Arthur becomes president
1883	Pendleton Act
1884	Grover Cleveland elected president
1887	Interstate Commerce Act
1888	Benjamin Harrison elected president
1890	Sherman Anti-Trust Act
	Sherman Silver Purchase Act
	McKinley Tariff
	Significant increase in naval appropriation
	Lodge federal elections bill defeated
	Populist movement begins
1892	Cleveland elected president again
1893	*Haole* planters and businessmen proclaim Hawaiian republic
1893–1897	Depression
1895–1896	Venezuelan boundary crisis
1896	William Jennings Bryan's "Cross of Gold" speech
	William McKinley elected president
1898	War with Spain
	United States annexes Hawai'i
1899	Treaty of Paris ratified
	Open Door notes
1899–1902	Philippine insurrection
1900	McKinley reelected
1902	Civil government in the Philippines
	Cuba becomes a protectorate

Focus Questions

If you have mastered this chapter, you should be able to answer these questions and explain the terms that follow the questions.

1. What was the significance of political parties in the late nineteenth century?
2. Compare the presidencies from Grant through Cleveland. Which do you consider successful? Why?
3. What were the major goals of the various reform groups?
4. Why were some reformers more successful than others?
5. Which groups and issues led to the formation of the Populist Party?
6. What were the issues in the 1896 presidential election, and what were the short-term and long-term results?

7. How did American policymakers define the role of the United States in North America and other parts of the world during the period 1865–1889?
8. How and why did some Americans' attitudes about the U.S. role in world affairs begin to change between 1889 and 1897?
9. What led the United States into war with Spain?
10. What new attitudes about America's role in world affairs appeared in the debate over acquiring new possessions?

KEY TERMS

patronage system (*p. 534*)

Tammany Hall (*p. 535*)

Crédit Mobilier (*p. 538*)

Tweed Ring (*p. 539*)

William Marcy Tweed (*p. 539*)

Whiskey Ring (*p. 539*)

Stalwarts (*p. 540*)

Interstate Commerce Commission (ICC) (*p. 541*)

William McKinley (*p. 543*)

House Ways and Means Committee (*p. 543*)

McKinley Tariff (*p. 543*)

Sherman Anti-Trust Act (*p. 543*)

Grange (*p. 545*)

Granger laws (*p. 546*)

Bland-Allison Act (*p. 547*)

Sherman Silver Purchase Act (*p. 547*)

Mugwumps (*p. 548*)

Pendleton Act (*p. 548*)

National Woman Suffrage Association (NWSA) (*p. 549*)

American Woman Suffrage Association (AWSA) (*p. 549*)

Australian ballot (*p. 551*)

Populists (*p. 551*)

Farmers' Alliances (*p. 551*)

William Jennings Bryan (*p. 554*)

Gold Standard Act (*p. 557*)

William H. Seward (*p. 557*)

Monroe Doctrine (*p. 558*)

Benito Juarez (*p. 558*)

Maximilian (*p. 558*)

Alfred Thayer Mahan (*p. 560*)

Liliʻuokalani (*p. 562*)

Joseph Pulitzer's (*p. 564*)

William Randolph Hearst's (*p. 564*)

Enrique Dupuy de Lôme (*p. 564*)

USS *Maine* (*p. 565*)

Teller Amendment (*p. 566*)

Philippine Islands (*p. 566*)

Theodore Roosevelt (*p. 566*)

Treaty of Paris (*p. 568*)

Platt Amendment (*p. 570*)

Foraker Act (*p. 570*)

Insular Cases (*p. 570*)

Emilio Aguinaldo (*p. 571*)

William Howard Taft (*p. 571*)

Samoa (*p. 571*)

Open Door notes (*p. 572*)

Boxer Rebellion (*p. 572*)

19

THE PROGRESSIVE ERA, 1900–1917

ORGANIZING FOR CHANGE

During the early twentieth century, politics expanded to embrace wide-ranging concerns raised by a complex assortment of groups and individuals. In the swirl of proponents and proposals, politics more than ever before came to reflect the interaction of organized interest groups.

The Changing Face of Politics   As Americans entered the twentieth century, their lives were changing in important ways. The railroad, telegraph, and telephone transformed concepts of time and space and fostered formation of new organizations. Executives of new industrial corporations now thought in terms of regional or national markets. Union members allied with others of their trade in distant cities. Farmers in Kansas and Montana studied grain prices in Chicago and Liverpool. Physicians organized nationwide to establish higher standards for medical schools.

Manufacturers, farmers, merchants, carpenters, teachers, lawyers, physicians, and many others established or reorganized national associations to advance their economic or professional interests. Sometimes that meant seeking governmental assistance. As early as the 1870s, for example, associations of merchants, farmers, and oil producers had pushed for laws to regulate railroad freight rates.

Some graduates emerged from the recently transformed universities with the conviction that their knowledge and skills could improve society, and they formed

576

professional associations to advance those objectives. Long-established church organizations sometimes fostered the emergence of new associations devoted to moral reform, especially prohibition. Some people formed groups with humanitarian goals such as ending child labor. Members of ethnic and racial groups set up societies to further their groups' interests. Reformers organized to limit the power of corporations or to defeat party bosses. Overlapping with many of these new associations were the organizational activities of women, including middle-class women, new college graduates, and factory and clerical workers.

Sooner or later, many of the new associations sought changes in laws to help them reach their objectives. Increasing numbers of citizens related to politics through such organized **interest groups**, even as the traditional political parties found they could no longer count on the voter loyalty typical of the Gilded Age.

Many of these new groups optimistically believed that responsible citizens, acting together, assisted by technical know-how, and sometimes drawing on the power of government, could achieve social progress—improvement of the human situation. As early as the 1890s, some had begun to call themselves "progressive citizens." By 1910, many were simply calling themselves "progressives."

Historians use the term *progressivism* to signify three related developments during the early twentieth century: (1) the emergence of new concepts of the purposes and functions of government, (2) changes in government policies and institutions, and (3) the political agitation that produced those changes. A progressive, then, was a person involved in one or more of these activities. Many individuals and groups promoted their own visions of change, making progressivism a complex phenomenon. There was no single progressive movement. To be sure, an organized **Progressive Party** emerged in 1912, sputtered for a brief time after, but failed to capture the allegiance of all who called themselves progressives. Nonetheless, many aspects of progressivism reflected concerns of the urban middle class, especially urban middle-class women.

Progressivism appeared at every level of government—local, state, and federal. And progressives promoted a wide range of new government activities: regulation of business, moral revival, consumer protection, conservation of natural resources, educational improvement, tax reform, and more. Through all these avenues, they brought government more directly into the economy and more directly into the lives of most Americans.

"Spearheads for Reform": The Settlement Houses   During the 1890s, in several large cities, young college-educated men and women began to provide assistance for the poor. The **settlement house** idea originated in England in 1884, at Toynbee Hall, in London's slums, where idealistic university graduates lived among the poor and tried to help them. In 1886, young male college graduates opened a similar settlement house in New York City. In 1889 several women, graduates of Smith College (a women's college), opened another settlement house in New York.

settlement house   Community center operated by resident social reformers in a poor urban neighborhood.

Also in 1889, Jane Addams and Ellen Gates Starr opened **Hull House,** the first settlement house in Chicago. For many Americans, Jane Addams became synonymous with the settlement house movement and with reform more generally. Born in 1860 in a small town in Illinois, youngest daughter of a bank president, Addams attended college, then traveled in Europe. There she and Ellen Gates Starr, a friend from college, visited Toynbee Hall and learned about its work with the poor. Inspired by that example, the two set up Hull House in a working-class, immigrant neighborhood in Chicago. They lived at Hull House for most of their lives, attracting impressive associates and making Hull House the best known example of settlement work. Hull House eventually offered a variety of services to the families of its neighborhood: a nursery, childcare, classes for mothers, a playground, a gymnasium, and adult education classes. Hull House activists also challenged the power of city bosses and lobbied state legislators, seeking cleaner streets, the abolition of child labor, health and safety regulations for factories, compulsory school attendance, and more. Their efforts brought national recognition and helped to establish the reputation of the settlement houses as what one historian called "spearheads for reform."

Other settlement house workers across the country provided similar assistance to poor urban families: cooking and sewing classes, public baths, English lessons, and housing for unmarried working women. Some settlement houses were church

Jane Addams, co-founder of Hull House, had become the most prominent settlement house worker in the country by the time she posed for this portrait, around 1900.

Swarthmore College Peace Collection

sponsored. Nearly all tried to minimize class conflict because they agreed with Addams that "the dependence of classes on each other is reciprocal." Some historians have suggested that settlement house workers tried to bridge the gap between urban economic classes by imparting middle-class values to the poor and persuading the wealthy to help mitigate poverty. Such a view suggests that their efforts reflected urban middle-class anxieties over growing extremes of wealth and poverty. Other historians have noted that some settlement house workers drew on the bonds of gender solidarity to appeal to upper- and middle-class women for funds to assist working-class and poor women and children. Like Addams, many settlement house workers became forces for urban reform, promoting better schools, improved public health and sanitation, and honest government.

Settlement houses spread rapidly, with some four hundred operating by 1910. Three-quarters of settlement house workers were women, and settlement houses became the first institutions created and staffed primarily by college-educated women. They led to a new profession—social work. When universities began to offer study in social work (first at Columbia, in 1902), women tended to dominate that field, too. Women college graduates thus created a new and uniquely urban profession at a time when many careers remained closed to them.

Church-affiliated settlement houses often reflected the influence of the **Social Gospel**, a movement popularized by Protestant ministers concerned about urban social and economic problems. Washington Gladden, of Columbus, Ohio, called for "Applied Christianity," by which he meant the application to business of Christ's injunctions to love one another and to treat others as you would have them treat you. A similar strain of social activism appeared among Catholics, especially those inspired by Pope Leo XIII's 1891 *Rerum Novarium* ("Of New Things"), an **encyclical** urging greater attention to the problems of the industrial working class.

Women and Reform	The settlement houses are among many women's organizations that burst onto politics during the Progressive Era. By 1900 or so, a new ideal for women had emerged from the

women's clubs, women's colleges, and settlement houses, and from discussions on national lecture circuits and in the press. The "New Woman" stood for self-determination rather than unthinking acceptance of roles prescribed by the concepts of domesticity and separate spheres. By 1910, this attitude, sometimes called **feminism**, was accelerating the transition from the nineteenth-century movement for suffrage to the twentieth-century struggle for equality and individualism.

Women's increasing control over one aspect of their lives is evident in the birth rate, which fell steadily throughout the nineteenth and early twentieth centuries as

---

encyclical   A letter from the pope to Roman Catholic bishops, intended to guide them in their relations with the churches under their jurisdiction.

feminism   The conviction that women are and should be the social, political, and economic equals of men.

couples (or perhaps women alone) chose to have fewer children. Abortion was illegal, and state and federal laws banned distribution of information about contraception. In 1915 a group of women formed the National Birth Control League to seek repeal of laws prohibiting contraceptive information. In 1916 **Margaret Sanger**, a nurse practicing among the poor, attracted wide attention when she went to jail for informing women about birth control.

Other women formed organizations to advance specific causes. The National Consumers' League (founded in 1890) and the Women's Trade Union League (1903) tried to improve the lives of working women. Such efforts received a tragic boost in 1911 when fire roared through the Triangle Shirtwaist Company's clothing factory in New York City, killing 146 workers—nearly all young women—who were trapped in a building with no outside fire escapes and locked exit doors. The public outcry produced a state investigation and, in 1914, a new state factory safety law.

Some states passed laws to protect working women. In *Muller v. Oregon* (1908), the Supreme Court approved the constitutionality of one such law, limiting women's hours of work. Louis Brandeis, a lawyer working with the Consumers' League, defended the law by arguing that women needed special protection because of their social roles as mothers. Such arguments ran contrary to the New Woman's rejection of separate spheres and ultimately raised questions for women's drive for equality. At the time, however, the decision was widely hailed as a vital and necessary protection for women wage earners. By 1917, laws in thirty-nine states restricted women's working hours.

Though prominent in reform politics, most women could neither vote nor hold office. Support for suffrage grew, however, as more women recognized the need for political action to bring social change. By 1896, four western states had extended the vote to women. No other state did so until 1910, when Washington approved female suffrage. Seven more western states soon followed. In 1916 **Jeannette Rankin** of Montana—born on a ranch, educated as a social worker, experienced as a suffrage campaigner—became the first woman elected to the U.S. House of Representatives. Suffrage scored few victories outside the West, however.

Convinced that only a federal constitutional amendment would gain the vote for all women, the **National American Woman Suffrage Association** (NAWSA), led by Carrie Chapman Catt and Anna Howard Shaw, developed a national organization geared to lobbying in Washington, D.C. Alice Paul advocated public demonstrations and civil disobedience, tactics she learned from suffragists in England, where she had been a settlement house worker. In 1913 Paul formed the Congressional Union to pursue militant strategies. Some white suffragists tried to build an interracial movement for suffrage—NAWSA, for example, condemned lynching in 1917—but most feared that attention to other issues would weaken their position.

Although its leaders were predominantly white and middle-class, the suffrage cause became a mass movement during the 1910s, mobilizing women of all ages and socioeconomic classes. Their opponents argued that voting would bring women into the male sphere, expose them to corrupting influences, and render them unsuitable as guardians of the moral order. Suffrage advocates turned that argument on its head, however, claiming that women would make politics more moral and family oriented. Others, especially feminists, argued that women should vote because they deserved full equality with men.

Moral Reform   Other causes also stirred women to action. Moral reformers focused especially on banning alcohol—Demon Rum. The temperance movement dated to 1820s, but early temperance advocates worked to persuade individuals to give up strong drink. By the late nineteenth century, they looked to government to prohibit production, sale, or consumption of alcoholic beverages. Many saw prohibition as a progressive reform and expected government to safeguard what they saw as the public interest.

The drive against alcohol developed a broad base during the Progressive Era. Some old-stock Protestant churches—notably the Methodists—termed alcohol one of the most significant obstacles to a better society. Most adherents of the Social Gospel urged that prohibition could save the victims of industrialization and urbanization. Others emphasized protecting the family and home from the destructive influence of alcohol. Sociologists demonstrated links between liquor and prostitution, sexually transmitted diseases, poverty, crime, and broken families. Other evidence pointed to alcohol as contributing to industrial accidents, absenteeism, and inefficiency on the job.

By the late 1890s, the **Anti-Saloon League** became the model for successful interest-group politics. Proudly describing itself as "the Church in action against the saloon," the Anti-Saloon League usually operated through old-stock Protestant churches and focused on the saloon as corrupting not only individuals—men who neglected their families—but politics as well. Saloons, where political cronies struck deals and mingled with voters, had long been identified with big-city political machines.

The League endorsed only politicians who opposed Demon Rum, regardless of party or their stands on other issues. As the prohibition cause demonstrated growing political clout, more politicians lined up against the saloon. Between 1900 and 1917, voters adopted prohibition in nearly half of the states, including nearly all of the West and the South. Elsewhere, many towns and rural areas voted themselves "dry" under **local option laws.**

Opposition to prohibition came especially from immigrants, and their American-born descendants, from Ireland, Germany, and southern and eastern Europe who did not regard alcohol as inherently sinful. For them, beer or wine was an accepted part of social life. Companies that produced alcohol, especially beer-brewers, also organized to fight the prohibitionists. "Personal liberty" became the slogan for these "wets."

The drive against alcohol, ultimately successful at the national level, was not the only target for moral reformers. Reformers—including many women—tried to eliminate prostitution through state and federal legislation. Other moral

---

local option laws   A state law that permitted the residents of a town or city to decide, by an election, whether to ban liquor sales in their community.

reform efforts—to ban gambling or make divorces more difficult, for example—also represented attempts to use government power to regulate individual behavior.

Organizing against Racism

During the Progressive Era, racial issues generally drew less attention than other causes. Only a few white progressives actively opposed disfranchisement and segregation in the South. Indeed, southern white progressives often took the lead in enacting discriminatory laws. Ray Stannard Baker was one of the few white progressives to examine the situation of African Americans. In his book *Following the Color Line* (1908), Baker asked, "Does democracy really include Negroes as well as white men?" For most white Americans, the answer appeared to be no.

Lynchings and violence continued as facts of life for African Americans. Between 1900 and World War I, lynchings claimed more than eleven hundred victims, most in the South. During the same years, race riots wracked several cities. In 1906 Atlanta erupted into a riot as whites randomly attacked African Americans, killing four, injuring many more, and vandalizing property. In 1908, in Springfield, Illinois (where Abraham Lincoln had made his home), a mob of

A brilliant young intellectual, W. E. B. Du Bois had to choose between leading the life of a quiet college professor or challenging Booker T. Washington's claim to speak on behalf of African Americans.

Schomburg Center/Art Resource, New York

whites lynched two black men, injured others, and destroyed black-owned businesses.

During the Progressive Era, some African Americans challenged the accommodationist leadership of Booker T. Washington. **W. E. B. Du Bois**, the first African American to receive a Ph.D. degree from Harvard, wrote some of the first scholarly studies of African Americans. He emphasized the contributions of black men and women, disproved racial stereotypes, and used his book *Souls of Black Folk* (1903) to criticize Washington and exhort African Americans to struggle for their rights "unceasingly." "The hands of none of us are clean," he argued, speaking to both whites and blacks, "if we bend not our energies to a righting of these great wrongs."

African American leaders organized in support of black rights. In 1905 Du Bois and others met in Canada, near Niagara Falls, and drafted demands for racial equality. In 1910 black and white delegates formed the **National Association for the Advancement of Colored People** (NAACP), which provided important leadership in the fight for racial equality. Du Bois became the NAACP's director of publicity and research.

An unknown photographer captured this lynching on film and preserved its brutality and depravity. Although there are many photographic records of lynch mobs, local authorities nearly always claimed that they were unable to determine the identity of those responsible for the murder.

R. P. Kingston/Photolibrary

Ida B. Wells provided important leadership for the struggle against lynching. Born in Mississippi in 1862, she attended a school set up by the Freedmen's Bureau and worked as a rural teacher. Then, in Memphis, Tennessee, she began to write for a black newspaper and attacked lynching, arguing that several local victims had been targeted to eliminate successful black businessmen. When a mob destroyed the newspaper office, she moved north. During the 1890s and early 1900s, Wells attacked lynching on speaking tours and in print. Eventually she persuaded some white northerners to recognize and condemn the horror of lynching. She lived in Chicago during the Progressive Era, where she promoted black women's clubs and a black settlement house. Initially a supporter of the NAACP, she came to regard it as too cautious.

Challenging Capitalism: Socialists and Wobblies   Many progressive organizations reflected middle- and upper-class concerns, such as businesslike government and greater reliance on experts. Not so the **Socialist Party of America** (SPA), formed in 1901. Proclaiming themselves the political arm of workers and farmers, the Socialists argued that industrial capitalism had produced "an economic slavery which renders intellectual and political tyranny inevitable." They rejected most progressive proposals as inadequate and called instead for workers to control the means of production. Most looked to the political process to accomplish this transformation.

The Socialists' best-known national leader was Eugene V. Debs, leader of the Pullman strike and virtually the only person able to unite the many socialist factions. Strong among immigrants, some of whom had become socialists in their native lands, the SPA attracted some trade unionists, municipal reformers, and intellectuals, including W. E. B. Du Bois, Margaret Sanger, and Upton Sinclair. The party also had some support among farmers, especially in Oklahoma and Kansas, where they attracted some former Populists.

Hundreds of cities and towns—ranging from Reading, Pennsylvania, to Milwaukee, Wisconsin, to Berkeley, California—elected Socialist mayors or council members. Socialists won election to state legislatures in several states. Districts in New York City and Milwaukee sent Socialists to the U.S. House of Representatives. Most Americans, however, had no interest in eliminating private property. Most progressive reformers looked askance at the Socialists and sometimes tried to undercut their appeal with reforms that addressed some of their concerns but stopped short of challenging capitalism.

In 1905 a group of unionists and radicals organized the **Industrial Workers of the World** (IWW, or "Wobblies"). IWW organizers boldly proclaimed, "We have been naught, we shall be all," as they set out to organize the most exploited unskilled and semiskilled workers. They aimed their message at **sweatshop** workers in eastern cities, **migrant** farm workers who harvested western crops,

---

sweatshop A shop or factory in which employees work long hours at low wages under poor conditions.

migrant Traveling from one area to another.

southern sharecroppers, women workers, African Americans, and immigrants from southern and eastern Europe. Such workers were usually ignored by the American Federation of Labor, which emphasized skilled workers, most of them white males. The Wobblies' objective was simple: when most workers had joined the IWW, they would call a general strike, labor would refuse to work, and capitalism would collapse.

The IWW did organize a few dramatic strikes and demonstrations and scored a handful of significant victories but made few lasting gains. More often, the IWW met brutal suppression by local authorities.

THE REFORM OF POLITICS, THE POLITICS OF REFORM

Progressivism emerged at all levels of government as cities elected reform-minded mayors and states swore in progressive governors. In their quest for change, reformers sometimes came up against the entrenched leaders of political parties and therefore sought to limit the power of those parties.

Exposing Corruption: The Muckrakers

Journalists prepared the ground for reform. By the early 1900s, magazine publishers discovered that their sales boomed when they presented dramatic exposés of political corruption, corporate wrongdoing, and other scandalous offenses. Such journalists acquired the name **muckrakers** in 1906 when President Theodore Roosevelt compared them to "the Man with the Muck-rake," a character in John Bunyan's classic allegory *Pilgrim's Progress*. Roosevelt intended the comparison as a criticism, but journalists proudly claimed the label.

McClure's Magazine led the surge in muckraking, especially after October 1902, when the magazine began a series by Lincoln Steffens on corruption in city governments. By early 1903, *McClure's* added a series by Ida Tarbell on Standard Oil and a piece revealing corruption and violence in labor unions. Sales of *McClure's* soared, and other journals—including *Collier's* and *Cosmopolitan*—copied its style, publishing exposés on patent medicines, fraud by insurance companies, child labor, and more.

Muckraking soon extended from periodicals to books. Many muckraking books were investigations into social problems. The most famous muckraking book, however, was a novel: *The Jungle,* by **Upton Sinclair** (1906). In following the experiences of fictional immigrant laborers in Chicago, Sinclair exposed the disgusting failings of the meatpacking industry. He described in chilling detail the afflictions of packinghouse workers—severed fingers, tuberculosis, blood poisoning. The nation was shocked to read of men who "fell into the vats" and "would be overlooked for days, till all but the bones of them had gone out to the world as Durham's Pure Leaf Lard!" Sinclair, a Socialist, hoped readers would recognize that the offenses he portrayed were the results of industrial capitalism.

The Jungle horrified many Americans. President Roosevelt appointed a commission to investigate its allegations, and the report confirmed Sinclair's charges. Congress responded with the **Pure Food and Drug Act**, banning impure and mislabeled food and drugs, and the **Meat Inspection Act**, requiring federal inspection of meatpacking—something the industry itself welcomed to reassure nauseated consumers. Sinclair, however, was disappointed because his revelations produced only regulation rather than converting readers to socialism. "I aimed at the public's heart," Sinclair later complained, "and by accident I hit it in the stomach."

Reforming City Government   By the time of Lincoln Steffens's first article (1902) on corruption in city government, advocates of **municipal reform** had already won office and brought changes to some cities, and municipal reformers soon appeared elsewhere.

Municipal reformers argued that eliminating corruption and inefficiency required changes in the structure of city government. City councils usually consisted of members elected from **wards** corresponding roughly to neighborhoods. Middle- and working-class wards usually dominated city councils. Reformers condemned the ward system as producing city council members unable to see beyond their own neighborhoods. Reformers also recognized that poor immigrant neighborhoods supported political bosses and machines despite their corruption. They argued that citywide elections, in which all city voters chose from one list of candidates, would produce city council members who could better address the problems of the city as a whole—men with citywide business interests, for example—and would undercut the influence of ward bosses and machines.

James Phelan of San Francisco was an early structural reformer. Son of a pioneer banker, he attacked corruption in city government and won election as mayor in 1896. He then spearheaded adoption of a new charter that strengthened the office of mayor and required citywide election of supervisors (equivalent to city council members).

Some municipal reformers proposed more fundamental changes in the structure of city government, notably the **commission system** and the **city manager plan**, which reflected many progressives' distrust of political parties and desire for expertise and efficiency. The commission system was first tried in Galveston, Texas, after a devastating hurricane and tidal wave in 1900. Typically, in commission systems, the city's voters elected a few commissioners, each of whom managed a specific city function. The city manager plan—an adaptation of the structure of the corporation—featured a professional city manager (similar to a corporate executive) appointed by an elected city council (similar to a corporate board of

---

municipal reform   Political activity intended to bring about changes in the structure or function of city government.

ward   A division of a city or town, especially an electoral district, for administrative or representative purposes.

commission system   System of city government in which executive and legislative powers are vested in a small elective board, each member of which supervises some aspect of city government.

city manager plan   System of city government in which the city council hires a city manager who exercises broad executive authority.

In 1909, John D. Rockefeller, Sr. contributed $1 million to create the Rockefeller Sanitary Commission for the Eradication of Hookworm Disease. The commission launched a public-health campaign in eleven southern states, including education and medical dispensaries to provide treatment. This photograph shows the dispensary and some of the patients in Greenbrier, Tennessee, in May 1914.

directors) to handle most municipal administration. In 1913 a serious flood prompted the citizens of Dayton, Ohio, to adopt a city manager plan, and other cities then followed.

A few reformers went beyond structural reform to advocate social reforms. Hazen Pingree, a successful businessman, attracted national attention as mayor of Detroit. Elected in 1889, he soon took on the city's gas, electric, and streetcar companies for overcharging customers and providing poor service. He responded to the depression of 1893 with community vegetable gardens and work projects for the unemployed. Samuel "Golden Rule" Jones, a prosperous manufacturer, won election as mayor of Toledo, Ohio, in 1897. He promoted free concerts, free public baths, childcare for working mothers, and the eight-hour workday for city employees. Phelan, Pingree, Jones, and a few others also advocated city ownership of utilities—the gas, water, electricity, and streetcar systems.

The Progressive Era also saw early efforts at city planning, as city officials began to designate separate zones for residential, commercial, and industrial use (first in Los Angeles, in 1904–1908). By 1910, a few cities had created city planning commissions. The emergence of **city planning** represents an important transition in thinking about government and the economy, for it emphasized expertise and presumed greater government control over use of private property.

The emergence of public health, mental health, social work, and other new professions led to efforts to use local government to solve the problems of an urban industrial society. Their objective was to use scientific and social scientific knowledge to control social forces and thereby to shape the future. New medical knowledge presented an opportunity to reduce disease on a significant scale. Public health emerged as a new medical field, combining the knowledge of the medical doctor with the insight of the social scientist and the skills of the corporate manager. New public health programs sought to wipe out **hookworm** in the South, **tuberculosis** in the slums, and sexually transmitted diseases. Social workers often found themselves allied with public health professionals in efforts to use local government to improve urban health and safety.

The public schools also attracted reformers. As university programs began graduating teachers and school administrators, these new professionals sought greater control over education. Professional educators often pushed for greater centralization and professionalization in school administration by reducing the role of local, usually elected, **school boards** and by replacing elected school superintendents with appointed professionals. Professional educators also began to use recently developed intelligence tests to identify children unable to perform at average levels, and then to isolate them in special classes.

Reforming State Government   As reformers launched changes in many cities and as new professionals considered ways to improve society, **Robert M. La Follette** pushed Wisconsin to the forefront of reform. A Republican, he entered politics soon after graduating from the University of Wisconsin. He served three terms in Congress in the 1880s but found his political career blocked by the leader of the state Republican organization. He was firmly convinced of the need for reform when he finally won election as governor in 1900.

Conservative legislators, mostly Republicans, defeated La Follette's proposals to regulate railroad rates and to reduce the power of party bosses by replacing nominating conventions with the **direct primary**. La Follette threw himself into

---

city planning   The policy of planning urban development by regulating land use.

hookworm   A parasite, formerly common in the South, that causes loss of strength.

tuberculosis   An infectious disease that attacks the lungs; spread by unsanitary conditions and practices, such as spitting in public, it was common and often fatal in the nineteenth and early twentieth centuries and is reappearing today.

school board   Policymakers who oversee the public schools of a local political unit.

direct primary   Election in which voters who identify with a specific party choose that party's candidates to run later in the general election.

an energetic campaign to elect reformers to the state legislature. He earned the nickname "Fighting Bob" as he traveled the state and propounded his views. Most of his candidates won, and La Follette built a strong following among Wisconsin's farmers and urban wage earners, who reelected him in 1902 and 1904.

La Follette secured legislation to regulate corporations and political parties. Acclaimed as a "laboratory of democracy," Wisconsin adopted the direct primary, set up a commission to regulate railroads, increased taxes on corporations, enacted a merit system for state employees, and restricted lobbyists. In many of his efforts, La Follette drew on the expertise of faculty members at the University of Wisconsin. These reforms, along with reliance on experts, came to be called the **Wisconsin Idea**. La Follette won election to the U.S. Senate in 1905 and remained a leading progressive voice there until his death in 1925.

La Follette's success prompted imitation elsewhere. In 1901 Iowans elected Albert B. Cummins governor, and Cummins launched a campaign against railroad corporations similar to La Follette's. He too went on to the Senate. Reformers won office in other states as well, but only a few matched La Follette's legislative and political success.

Progressivism came to California relatively late. Reformers accused the Southern Pacific Railroad of running a political machine that controlled the state by dominating the Republican Party. In 1910, **Hiram Johnson** ran for governor as a reformer and won. California progressives produced a volume of reform that rivaled that of Wisconsin—regulation of railroads and public utilities, restrictions on political parties, protection for labor, conservation, and woman suffrage. Johnson appointed union leaders to state positions and promoted measures to benefit working people. California progressives in both parties, however, condemned Asian immigrants and Asian Americans, and progressive Republicans in 1913 pushed through a law that prohibited Asian immigrants from owning land in California.

Like La Follette, Johnson moved on to national politics. In 1912 he was the vice-presidential candidate of the new Progressive Party. Reelected governor in 1914, he won election to the U.S. Senate in 1916 and served there until his death in 1945.

Southern progressivism took up concerns similar to those that motivated reformers elsewhere and blended them with that region's racial politics. Often inspired by northern models of reform and by northern reform organizations or philanthropists, southern progressives promoted school and public health reforms, limits on child labor, prohibition, and woman suffrage. Southern progressives could point to success in some states, especially on railroad regulation, prohibition, improved schools, and child labor laws. However, some southern reformers ran up against a long-standing insistence on local control. Given the South's one-party politics, the Democratic Party sometimes became the battleground between progressives and conservatives. Some southern reformers were also among the most demagogic advocates of white supremacy, pushing both corporate regulation and racist policies.

The Weakening of Parties and Rise of Organized Interest Groups   Like Wisconsin and California, other states moved to restrict political parties. Reformers charged that bosses and machines manipulated nominating conventions and public officials, and that bosses, in return for payoffs, used their influence on behalf of corporate interests. Articles by muckrakers and some highly publicized bribery trials convinced many voters that the reformers were correct. The mighty party organizations that had dominated politics during the nineteenth century came under attack along a broad front.

Progressives nearly everywhere proposed measures to enhance the power of individual voters and reduce the power of party organizations. State after state adopted the direct primary, and many reformers sought to replace state patronage systems with the merit system. In many states, judgeships, school board seats, and educational offices were made nonpartisan.

A number of cities and states also adopted the **initiative** and **referendum**. The initiative permitted voters to adopt a new law directly: if enough voters signed a petition, the proposed law would be voted on at the next election; if approved by the voters, it became law. The referendum permitted voters, through a petition, to reject a law adopted by the legislature. Oregon voters approved these reforms in 1902, and Oregon reformers used the initiative to create new laws, giving the initiative and referendum so much national attention that they were sometimes called the Oregon System. Some states also adopted the **recall**, permitting voters, through petitions, to initiate a special election to remove an elected official from office. The direct primary, initiative and referendum, and recall are known collectively as **direct democracy** because they remove intermediate steps between the voter and final political decisions.

With the switch to direct primaries and the weakening of party organizations, campaigns focused more on individual candidates and less on parties. Candidates now appealed directly to voters rather than to party leaders and convention delegates. Individual candidates' personal organizations and advertising supplanted the armies of party retainers who had mobilized voters in the nineteenth century. At the same time, new voter registration laws and procedures disqualified some voters, especially transient workers. Voter turnout fell. Ironically, the emergence of new channels for political participation created the illusion of a vast outpouring of public involvement in politics—but proportionally fewer voters actually cast ballots.

---

initiative   Procedure allowing voters to petition to have a new law placed on the ballot to be voted up or down, bypassing the legislature.

referendum   Procedure whereby voters petition to have a legislative act submitted to the voters, who can overturn it.

recall   Provision that permits voters, through petition, to hold a special election to remove an elected official from office.

direct democracy   Provisions that permit voters to make political decisions directly, including the direct primary, initiative, referendum, and recall.

New avenues of political participation opened not only through direct democracy but also through organized interest groups who used politics to advance their agendas. Groups could cooperate when their political objectives coincided, as when merchants and farmers both favored regulation of railroad rates. Other times, they found themselves in conflict, perhaps over tariff policy. Within the many groups that advocated change, participants sometimes fought among themselves over which reform goals were most important and how to achieve them. Many groups adopted the tactics of the Anti-Saloon League—they ignored parties, pressured candidates to accept their group's position, and urged their members to vote only for approved candidates. In 1904, for example, the National Association of Manufacturers (NAM) targeted and defeated two pro-labor members of Congress, one in the House and one in the Senate. The American Federation of Labor (AFL) responded in 1906 with a similar strategy and elected six union members to the House of Representatives.

Organized interest groups often focused on the legislative process. They retained full-time representatives, or **lobbyists**, who urged legislators to support their group's position on pending legislation, reminded lawmakers of their group's electoral clout, and arranged campaign backing for those who supported their cause. Thus, as political parties became weaker, organized interest groups gained strength. Pushed one way by the AFL and the other by the NAM, under opposing pressure from the Anti-Saloon League and liquor interests, some elected officials came to see themselves less as loyal members of a political party and more as mediators among competing interest groups.

ROOSEVELT, TAFT, AND REPUBLICAN PROGRESSIVISM

When Theodore Roosevelt became president upon the death of William McKinley, he fascinated Americans—one visitor reported that the most exciting things he saw in the United States were "Niagara Falls and the President ... both great wonders of nature!" "TR" quickly became recognizable everywhere, as cartoonists delighted in sketching his bristling mustache, thick glasses, and toothy grin.

Roosevelt later wrote, "I cannot say that I entered the Presidency with any deliberately planned and far-reaching scheme of social betterment." Nonetheless, Americans soon saw Roosevelt as the embodiment of progressivism. In seven years, he changed the nation's domestic policies more than any president since Lincoln—and made himself a legend.

Roosevelt: Asserting the Power of the Presidency

Roosevelt was unlike most politicians of his day. He had inherited wealth and added to it from the many books he wrote. He saw politics as a duty to the nation rather than an opportunity for personal advancement, and he defined his politics in terms of character, morality, hard work, and patriotism. Uncertain whether to call himself a "radical conservative" or a "conservative radical," he considered politics the tool for forging an ethical and stable society. Confident in his own personal principles,

lobbyist   A person who tries to influence the opinions of legislators or other public officials for or against a specific cause.

Roosevelt did not hesitate to wield all the powers of the presidency. He especially liked to use the office as what he called a "bully pulpit" to publicize his concerns.

In his first message to Congress, in December 1901, Roosevelt sounded a theme that he repeated again and again: the growth of powerful corporations was "natural," but some exhibited "grave evils" that required correction. As Roosevelt later explained, "When I became President, the question as to the method by which the United States Government was to control the corporations was not yet important. The absolutely vital question was whether the Government had power to control them at all." He determined to establish that power.

The chief obstacle to regulating corporations was a Supreme Court decision, *United States v. E. C. Knight* (1895), preventing the Sherman Anti-Trust Act from being used against manufacturers. Roosevelt looked for an opportunity to challenge the *Knight* decision. In 1901, some of the nation's most prominent business leaders had joined forces to create the Northern Securities Company, creating a railroad monopoly in the Northwest. The *Knight* case involved manufacturing; the Northern Securities Company provided interstate transportation. If any industry could satisfy the Supreme Court that it fit the constitutional language authorizing Congress to regulate interstate commerce, Roosevelt believed, the railroads could.

Roosevelt's attorney general, Philander C. Knox, filed suit against the Northern Securities Company for violating the Sherman Act. Wall Street leaders condemned Roosevelt's action, but most Americans applauded to see the federal government finally challenge a powerful corporation. In 1904 the Supreme Court agreed that the Sherman Act could be applied to the Northern Securities Company and ordered it dissolved.

Bolstered by this confirmation of federal power, Roosevelt launched additional antitrust suits, but he used **trustbusting** selectively. Large corporations, he thought, were potentially beneficial. He thought regulation was preferable to breaking them up. Companies that met Roosevelt's standards of character and public service—and that acknowledged the power of the presidency—had no reason to fear antitrust action.

Roosevelt's willingness to act boldly was not limited to trustbusting. In time of crisis, he felt, the president should "do whatever the needs of the people demand, unless the Constitution or the laws explicitly forbid him to do it." In 1902, coal miners went on strike in Pennsylvania, seeking higher wages, an eight-hour workday, and union recognition from the mine owners. Roosevelt was not required to intervene, but he called both sides to Washington and urged them to submit to arbitration. The mine owners refused, insisting that the army be used against the miners. Roosevelt instead considered using the army to dispossess the mine owners and reopen the mines. He sent his secretary of war to discuss this possibility with J. P. Morgan, who then convinced the companies to accept arbitration. The arbitration board granted the miners higher wages and a nine-hour workday but denied their other objectives. The companies were permitted to raise their prices to cover their additional costs. As he illustrated in asserting new presidential powers to deal with the coal miners' strike, Roosevelt intended to produce what he called a **Square Deal**, fair treatment for all parties.

---

trustbusting   Use of antitrust laws to prosecute and dissolve big businesses ("trusts").

The Square Deal in Action: Creating the Regulatory State

Roosevelt's trustbusting and handling of the coal strike brought him great popularity. In 1903 Congress approved several measures he requested or endorsed: an act to speed up prosecution of antitrust suits; creation of a cabinet-level Department of Commerce and Labor, including a bureau to investigate corporate activities; and the Elkins Act, which penalized railroads that paid rebates.

When Roosevelt sought election in 1904, he won by one of the largest margins up to that time—more than 56 percent of the popular vote. Elected in his own right, with a powerful demonstration of public approval, Roosevelt set out to secure meaningful regulation of the railroads, largest of the nation's big businesses.

Roosevelt and reformers in Congress wanted to regulate railroads' prices for both freight and passengers. In Roosevelt's year-end message to Congress in 1905, he asked for legislation to regulate railroad rates, open the financial records of railroads to government inspection, and increase federal authority in strikes involving interstate commerce. At the same time, the attorney general filed suits against some of the nation's largest corporations. Muckrakers (some of them Roosevelt's friends) fired off scathing exposés of railroads and attacks on Senate conservatives.

Although Roosevelt compromised on some issues, he got most of what he wanted. On June 29, 1906, Congress passed the **Hepburn Act**, allowing the Interstate Commerce Commission (ICC) to establish maximum railroad rates and to regulate other forms of transportation. The act also limited railroads' ability to issue free passes, a practice that reformers had long considered bribery. The next day, on June 30, Congress approved the Pure Food and Drug Act and the Meat Inspection Act, the aftermath to Sinclair's stomach-turning revelations. Taken together, these three measures can be considered the beginning of the federal regulatory state.

Regulating Natural Resources

An advocate for strenuous outdoor activities, Roosevelt took great pride in establishing five national parks and more than fifty wildlife preserves to save what he called "beautiful and wonderful wild creatures whose existence was threatened by greed and wantonness." **Preservationists**, such as John Muir of the Sierra Club, applauded these actions and urged that such wilderness areas be kept forever safe from developers. Parks and wildlife refuges, however, were only part of Roosevelt's **conservation** agenda.

Roosevelt and **Gifford Pinchot**, the president's chief adviser on natural resources, believed conservation required not only preservation of wild and beautiful lands but also carefully planned use of resources. Trained in scientific forestry in Europe, Pinchot combined scientific expertise with a managerial outlook. He and Roosevelt withdrew large tracts of federal timber and grazing land from

preservationist One who advocates reserving natural areas so as to protect them against human disturbance.

conservation The careful management of natural resources so that they yield the greatest benefit to present generations while maintaining their potential to meet the needs of future generations.

public sale or use. By careful management of these lands, they hoped to provide for the needs of both the present and the future. Roosevelt removed nearly 230 million acres from public sale, more than quadrupling the land under federal protection.

Roosevelt strongly supported the Reclamation Act of 1902, which set aside proceeds from federal land sales in sixteen western states to finance irrigation projects. The act established a commitment later greatly expanded: the federal government would construct western dams, canals, and other facilities to support agriculture in areas of scant rainfall. Thus water, perhaps the most important natural resource in the West, came to be managed. Far from preserving the western landscape, federal water projects profoundly transformed it, vividly illustrating the vast difference between the preservation of wilderness that Muir advocated and the careful management of resources that Pinchot sought.

Taft's Troubles   Soon after Roosevelt won the election of 1904, he announced that he would not seek reelection in 1908. He remained immensely popular, however, and virtually named his successor. Republicans nominated William Howard Taft. A graduate of Yale and former federal judge, Taft had served as governor of the Philippines before joining Roosevelt's cabinet as secretary of war in 1904.

William Jennings Bryan, leader of the progressive wing of the Democratic Party, won his party's nomination for the third time. Roosevelt's popularity and strong endorsement of Taft carried the day. Taft won just under 52 percent of the vote, and Republicans kept control of the Senate and the House. Roosevelt turned over the presidency to Taft, then set off to hunt big game in Africa.

Taft's legalistic approach often appeared timid when compared with Roosevelt's boldness. But Taft's attorney general initiated some ninety antitrust suits in four years, twice as many as during Roosevelt's seven years. And Taft approved legislation to strengthen regulatory agencies.

During the Taft administration, progressives amended the Constitution twice. Reformers had long considered an income tax to be the fairest means of raising federal revenues. With support from Taft, enough states ratified the **Sixteenth Amendment** (permitting a federal income tax) for it to take effect in 1913. In contrast, Taft took no position on the **Seventeenth Amendment**, proposed in 1912 and ratified shortly after he left office in 1913. It changed the method of electing U.S. senators from election by state legislatures to election by voters, another long-time goal of reformers, who claimed that corporate influence and outright bribery had swayed state legislatures and shaped the Senate.

Roosevelt had left Taft a Republican Party divided between progressives and conservatives. Those divisions grew, and Taft increasingly sided with the conservatives. In 1909, he called on Congress to reform the tariff. The resulting Payne-Aldrich Tariff retained high rates on most imports, but Taft signed it. When Republican progressives protested, Taft became defensive, alienating them further by calling it "the best bill that the Republican party ever passed."

Republican progressives also attacked the high-handed exercise of power by Joseph Cannon, the conservative Speaker of the House of Representatives. Taft first favored the progressives, then backed off and made his peace with Cannon. Republican progressives then joined Democrats in a "revolt against Cannonism" that reduced the Speaker's powers.

A dispute over conservation further damaged Republican unity. Taft had kept Gifford Pinchot as head of the Forest Service, but Pinchot charged that Taft's secretary of the interior, Richard A. Ballinger, had weakened the conservation program. Taft concluded that Ballinger had done nothing improper. When Pinchot persisted, Taft fired him. By 1912, when Taft faced reelection, the Republican Party was in serious disarray, and he faced opposition from most progressive Republicans.

"CARRY A BIG STICK": ROOSEVELT, TAFT, AND WORLD AFFAIRS

Theodore Roosevelt not only remolded the presidency and established new federal regulatory authority, he also significantly expanded America's role in world affairs. Few presidents have had so great an influence. He once expressed his fondness for what he called a West African proverb: "Speak softly and carry a big stick; you will go far." As president, however, Roosevelt seldom spoke softly. Well read in history and current events, Roosevelt entered the presidency with definite ideas on the place of the United States in the world. As he advised Congress in 1902, "The increasing interdependence and complexity of international political and economic relations render it incumbent on all civilized and orderly powers to insist on the proper policing of the world." The United States, Roosevelt made clear, stood ready to do its share of "proper policing."

Taking Panama

While McKinley was still president, American diplomats began efforts to create a canal through Central America. Many people had long shared the dream of such a passage between the Atlantic and Pacific Oceans. A French company actually began construction in the late 1870s, but abandoned the project when the task proved too great.

During the Spanish-American War, the battleship *Oregon* took well over two months to steam from the West Coast around South America to join the rest of the fleet off Cuba. A canal would have cut the time to three weeks or less. McKinley pronounced an American-controlled canal "indispensable."

Experts identified two possible locations for a canal, Nicaragua and Panama (then part of Colombia). The Panama route was shorter, and the French company had completed some work there. **Philippe Bunau-Varilla**—formerly chief project engineer for the French effort, now a major stockholder—did his utmost to sell the French company's interests to the United States. Building through Panama, however, meant overcoming formidable mountains and fever-ridden swamps. Previous studies had preferred Nicaragua. Its geography posed fewer natural obstacles, and much of the route lay through Lake Nicaragua.

In 1902, shortly before Congress was to vote on the two routes, Bunau-Varilla distributed to senators a Nicaraguan postage stamp showing a smoldering volcano looming over a lake. Bunau-Varilla's lobbying—and his stamps—reinforced efforts by prominent Republican senators. The Senate approved the route through the Colombian state of Panama.

Negotiations with Colombia bogged down, then the Colombian government offered to accept limitations on its sovereignty in return for more money. Outraged, Roosevelt called the offer "pure bandit morality." Bunau-Varilla and his associates then encouraged and financed a revolution in Panama. Roosevelt ordered U.S. warships to the area to prevent Colombian troops from crushing the uprising. The revolution quickly succeeded. Panama declared its independence on November 3, 1903, and the United States immediately extended diplomatic recognition. Bunau-Varilla became Panama's minister to the United States and promptly signed a treaty that gave the United States much the same arrangement earlier rejected by Colombia.

The **Hay–Bunau-Varilla Treaty** (1903) granted the United States perpetual control over the Canal Zone, a strip of Panamanian territory 10 miles wide, for a price of $10 million and annual rent of $250,000; it also made Panama the second American protectorate (Cuba was the first). The United States purchased the assets of the French company and began construction. Roosevelt considered the canal his crowning deed in foreign affairs. "When nobody else could or would exercise efficient authority, I exercised it," he wrote in his *Autobiography* (1913). He always denied any part in instigating the revolution but he once bluntly claimed, "I took the canal zone."

Construction proved difficult. Just over 40 miles long, the canal took ten years to build and cost nearly $400 million. Completed in 1914, just as World War I began, it was considered one of the world's great engineering feats.

Making the Caribbean an American Lake   With canal construction under way, American policy-makers considered how to protect it. Roosevelt determined to establish American dominance in the Caribbean and Central America, where the many harbors might permit a foreign power to prepare for a strike against the canal or even the Gulf Coast of the United States. Acquisition of Puerto Rico, protectorates over Cuba and Panama, and naval facilities in all three locations as well as on the Gulf Coast made the United States a powerful presence.

The Caribbean and the area around it contained twelve independent nations. Britain, France, Denmark, and the Netherlands held nearly all the smaller islands, and Britain had a coastal colony (British Honduras, now Belize). Several Caribbean nations had borrowed large amounts of money from European bankers, raising the prospect of intervention to secure loan payments. In 1902, Britain and Germany declared a blockade of Venezuela over such debts. In 1904, when several European nations hinted that they might intervene in the Dominican Republic, Roosevelt presented what became known as the **Roosevelt Corollary** to the Monroe Doctrine. He warned European nations against any intervention in the Western Hemisphere. If intervention by what he termed "some civilized nation" became necessary in the Caribbean or Central America to correct "chronic wrongdoing," Roosevelt insisted that the United States would handle it, acting as "an international police power."

Theodore Roosevelt, in his 1904 Corollary to the Monroe Doctrine, asserted that the United States was dominant in the Caribbean. Here a cartoonist capitalized on Roosevelt's boyish nature, depicting the Caribbean as Roosevelt's pond.

Roosevelt acted forcefully to establish his new policy. In 1905 the Dominican Republic agreed to permit the United States to collect customs (taxes on imports, the major source of governmental revenue) and supervise government expenditures, including debt repayment, thereby becoming the third U.S. protectorate.

Roosevelt's successors, William Howard Taft and Woodrow Wilson, continued and expanded American domination in the Caribbean. The Taft administration encouraged American investments there, hoping that American investments would block investment by other nations and also stabilize and develop the Caribbean economies. Taft supported such **"dollar diplomacy"** (as his critics called it) throughout the region, especially in Nicaragua.

In 1912 Taft sent U.S. Marines to Nicaragua to suppress a rebellion against President Adolfo Díaz. They remained after the turmoil settled, ostensibly to guard the American legation but actually to prop up the Díaz government—making Nicaragua the fourth U.S. protectorate. A treaty was drafted giving the United States responsibility for collecting customs, but the Senate rejected it. At that point, the State Department, several American banks, and Nicaragua set up a **customs receivership** through the banks.

Roosevelt and Eastern Asia   In eastern Asia, Roosevelt built on the Open Door notes and American participation in the international force that suppressed the Boxer Rebellion. He was both concerned and optimistic about the rise of Japan as a major industrial and imperial power. Aware of Alfred Thayer Mahan's warnings that Japan posed a potential danger to the United States in the Pacific, Roosevelt hoped that Japan might exercise an international police power in its vicinity similar to that which the United States claimed under the Roosevelt Corollary.

In 1904 Russia and Japan went to war over **Manchuria**, part of northeastern China. Russia had pressured China to grant so many concessions in Manchuria that it seemed to be turning into a Russian colony. Russia seemed also to have designs on Korea, nominally an independent kingdom. Japan saw Russian expansion as a threat to its own interests and responded with force. The Japanese scored smashing naval and military victories over the Russians but had too few resources to sustain a long-term war.

Roosevelt concluded that American interests were best served by reducing Russian influence in the region so as to maintain a balance of power. Such a balance, he thought, would be most likely to preserve nominal Chinese sovereignty in Manchuria. Early in the war, he indicated some support for Japan. As its resources ran low, Japan asked Roosevelt to act as mediator. The president agreed, concerned that a Japanese victory might be as dangerous as Russian expansion. The peace conference took place in Portsmouth, New Hampshire. The **Treaty of Portsmouth** (1905) recognized Japan's dominance in Korea and gave Japan the southern half of Sakhalin Island and Russian concessions in southern Manchuria. Russia kept its railroad in northern Manchuria. China remained responsible for civil authority in Manchuria. For his mediation, Roosevelt received the 1906 Nobel Peace Prize.

In 1906–1907, Roosevelt mediated another dispute. The San Francisco school board ordered students of Japanese parentage to attend the city's segregated Chinese school. The Japanese government protested what it considered an insult, and Japanese newspapers even hinted at war. Roosevelt convinced the school officials to withdraw the order, in return for restrictions on Japanese immigration, and he negotiated a so-called **gentlemen's agreement** by which Japan agreed to limit the departure of laborers to the United States.

In 1908 the American and Japanese governments further agreed to respect each other's territorial possessions (the Philippines and Hawai'i for the United States;

customs receivership   An agreement whereby one nation takes over the collection of another nation's customs and exercises some control over that nation's expenditures of customs receipts, thus limiting the autonomy of the nation in receivership.

Manchuria   A region of northeastern China.

gentlemen's agreement   An agreement rather than a formal treaty; in this case, Japan agreed in 1907 to limit Japanese emigration to the United States.

Korea, Formosa, and southern Manchuria for Japan) and to honor as well "the independence and integrity of China" and the Open Door.

The United States and World Affairs, 1901–1913

Before the 1890s, the United States had few clear or consistent foreign-policy commitments or objectives. By 1905, the Philippines, Guam, Hawai'i, Puerto Rico, eastern Samoa, and the Canal Zone were highly visible evidence of a dramatic change in America's role in world affairs.

Central to that concept was a large, modern navy, without which every other commitment was merely a moral pronouncement. Roosevelt was so proud of the navy that in 1907 he dispatched sixteen battleships—painted white to signal their peaceful intent—on an around-the-world tour. Though Roosevelt claimed that he sent the Great White Fleet "to impress the American people," he was clearly interested in impressing other nations, especially Japan, and in demonstrating that the American navy was fully capable of moving quickly to distant parts of the globe.

The need to protect the canal led the United States to dominate the Caribbean and Central America, but the new American role also focused on the Pacific. As Mahan and others pointed out, the Pacific Ocean was a likely theater of twentieth-century conflict. Thus considerations of commercial enterprise, such as the China trade, coincided with naval strategy and led the United States to acquire possessions at key locations in the Pacific.

American policymakers' new vision of the world seemed to divide nations into broad categories. In one class were the "civilized" nations. In the other were those nations that Theodore Roosevelt described, at various times, as "barbarous," "impotent," or simply unable to meet their obligations. When dealing with "civilized" countries—the European powers, Japan, the large, stable nations of Latin America, Canada, Australia, New Zealand—American diplomats focused on finding ways to realize mutual objectives, especially arbitration of disputes. In eastern Asia, McKinley, Roosevelt, and Taft looked to a balance of power among the contending "civilized" powers as most likely to realize the American objective of maintaining the "open door" in China.

The conviction that arbitration was the appropriate means to settle disputes among "civilized" countries was widespread. An international conference in 1899 created a **Permanent Court of Arbitration** in the Netherlands, which provided neutral arbitrators for international disputes. Roosevelt and Taft tried to negotiate arbitration treaties with major powers, but the Senate refused for fear that arbitration might diminish the Senate's role in foreign relations.

The United States and Great Britain repeatedly used arbitration to settle their disputes. Throughout the late nineteenth and early twentieth centuries, American relations with Britain improved steadily, mostly due to British initiatives. The more Germany expanded its army and navy, the more British policymakers worked to improve relations with the United States, the only nation besides Britain with a navy comparable to Germany's. During America's war with Spain, Britain alone among the major European powers sided with the United States. By reducing its naval forces in the Caribbean, Britain delivered a clear signal—it not only accepted

American dominance there but now depended on the United States to protect its holdings in the region.

WILSON AND DEMOCRATIC PROGRESSIVISM

The presidential election of 1912 marks a moment when Americans actively and seriously debated their future. All three nominees were well educated and highly literate. Roosevelt and Wilson had written respected books on American history and politics. They approached politics with a sense of destiny and purpose, and they talked frankly to the American people about their ideas for the future.

Debating the Future: The Election of 1912   As Taft watched the Republican Party unravel, Theodore Roosevelt was hunting in Africa and then hobnobbing with European leaders. When he returned in 1910, he undertook a speaking tour and proposed a broad program of reform he labeled the **New Nationalism**. In the 1910 congressional elections, Republicans fared badly, plagued by divisions within their party and an economic downturn. For the first time since 1892, Democrats won a majority in the House of Representatives. Democrats, including Woodrow Wilson in New Jersey, also won a number of governorships. Many Republican progressives now looked to Robert La Follette to wrest the Republican nomination from Taft in 1912. Roosevelt had lost confidence in Taft, but he considered La Follette too radical and irresponsible. Finally, in February 1912, Roosevelt announced he would oppose Taft for the Republican presidential nomination.

In the thirteen states with direct primaries, Roosevelt won 278 delegates to the national nominating convention to 48 for Taft and 36 for La Follette. However, Taft had all the advantages of an incumbent president in control of the party machinery. At the Republican convention, many states sent rival delegations, one pledged to Taft and one to Roosevelt. Taft's supporters controlled the **credentials committee** and gave most contested seats to Taft delegates. Roosevelt's supporters stormed out, complaining that Taft was stealing the nomination. The remaining delegates nominated Taft on the first ballot.

Roosevelt refused to accept defeat. "We stand at Armageddon," he thundered, invoking the biblical prophecy of a final battle between good and evil. "And," he continued, "we battle for the Lord." His supporters quickly formed the Progressive Party, nicknamed the **Bull Moose Party** after Roosevelt's boast that he was "as fit as a bull moose." At their convention, they sang "Onward, Christian Soldiers" and issued a platform based on the New Nationalism, including tariff reduction, regulation of corporations, a minimum wage, an end to child labor, woman suffrage, and the initiative, referendum, and recall. Women were prominent at the Progressive convention and helped draft the platform—especially the sections dealing with

---

credentials committee Party convention committee that settles disputes arising when rival delegations from the same state demand to be seated.

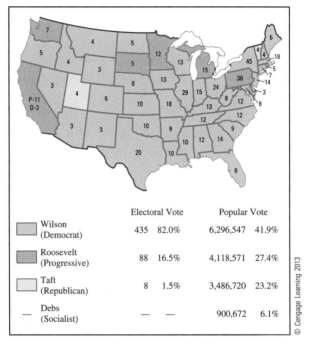

	Electoral Vote		Popular Vote	
Wilson (Democrat)	435	82.0%	6,296,547	41.9%
Roosevelt (Progressive)	88	16.5%	4,118,571	27.4%
Taft (Republican)	8	1.5%	3,486,720	23.2%
Debs (Socialist)	—	—	900,672	6.1%

© Cengage Learning 2013

MAP 19.1 The Election of 1912

labor. Jane Addams addressed the convention to second the nomination of Roosevelt.

Democrats were overjoyed, certain that the Republican split gave them their best chance at the presidency in twenty years. Their nomination was hotly contested, requiring forty-six ballots to nominate Woodrow Wilson. Their platform attacked monopolies, favored limits on campaign contributions by corporations, and called for tariff reductions. Wilson labeled his program the **New Freedom**. Afterward, Wilson met with **Louis Brandeis**, a Boston attorney and leading critic of corporate consolidation, who convinced him to center his campaign on the issue of big business.

Much of the campaign focused on Roosevelt and Wilson. Roosevelt argued that the behavior of corporations was the problem, not their size, and that regulation was the solution. Wilson followed Brandeis's lead and depicted monopoly itself as the problem. Breaking up monopolies and restoring competition, he argued, would benefit consumers because competition would yield better products and lower prices. Wilson also pointed to what he considered the most serious flaw in regulation: as long as monopolies faced regulation, they would seek to control the regulator—the federal government. Only antitrust actions, Wilson argued, could protect democracy from this threat. Taft was the most conservative of the candidates. Eugene V. Debs, the Socialist candidate, rejected both regulation and antitrust actions and argued for government ownership of monopolies.

The real contest was between Roosevelt and Wilson. In the end, Wilson received nearly all the usual Democratic vote and won with 42 percent of the total. Democrats also won sizable majorities in both houses of Congress. Roosevelt and Taft split the traditional Republican vote, 27 percent for Roosevelt and 23 percent for Taft. Debs, with only 6 percent, placed first in a few counties and city precincts.

Wilson and Reform, 1913–1916   Born in Virginia in 1856, Woodrow Wilson grew up in the South during the Civil War and Reconstruction. His father, a Presbyterian minister, impressed on him lessons in morality and responsibility that remained with him his entire life. Wilson earned a Ph.D. in political science from Johns Hopkins University, and his first book, *Congressional Government,* analyzed federal lawmaking. A professor at Princeton University after 1890, he became president of Princeton in 1902.

In 1910, conservatives who controlled the New Jersey Democratic Party picked Wilson to run for governor because of his reputation as a conservative and a good public speaker. He won the election but shocked his party's leaders by embracing reform. As governor, he led the legislature to adopt several progressive measures, and his record won support from many Democratic progressives when he sought the 1912 presidential nomination.

Wilson firmly believed in party government and an active role for the president in policymaking. He wanted to work closely with Democrats in Congress and succeeded to such an extent that, like Roosevelt, he changed the nature of the presidency itself. Confident in his oratorical skills, he became the first president since John Adams to address Congress in person.

Wilson first tackled tariff reform, arguing that high tariff rates helped breed monopolies by reducing competition. Despite opposition from manufacturers, Congress passed the **Underwood Tariff** in October 1913, establishing the most significant reductions since the Civil War. To offset federal revenue losses, the Underwood Act implemented the income tax recently authorized by the Sixteenth Amendment.

Wilson and the Democrats next took up banking. The national banking system dated to 1863, and periodic economic problems—most recently, a panic in 1907— had demonstrated the system's major shortcomings: it had no real center to provide direction and no way to adjust the money supply (the amount of money available in the economy as cash and in bank accounts). A congressional investigation also revealed the concentration of great power in the hands of a few investment bankers. Conservatives, led by Carter Glass of Virginia, joined with bankers in proposing a more centralized system with minimal federal regulation. Progressive Democrats, especially William Jennings Bryan (now Wilson's secretary of state) and Louis Brandeis, favored strong federal regulation.

The debate ended in compromise. In December 1913, Wilson approved the **Federal Reserve Act**, establishing twelve regional Federal Reserve Banks. These were "bankers' banks," institutions where commercial banks kept their reserves. All national banks were required to belong to the Federal Reserve System. The

The Federal Reserve Act

The Federal Reserve Act stands as the most important domestic act of the Wilson administration, for it still provides the basic framework for the nation's banking and monetary system. Though the original act of 1913 has been amended many times, the Federal Reserve System remains an independent entity within the federal government, having both public purposes and private aspects.

Congress has charged the Federal Reserve to carry out the nation's monetary policy, including regulating the money supply and interest rates to accomplish the goals of maximum employment, stable prices, and moderate long-term interest rates. The Federal Reserve also supervises and regulates banks and financial institutions to ensure their safety and soundness. (Chapter 22's It Matters Today feature discusses the Fed's role in recent economic events.)

- Look at a basic macroeconomics textbook for its description of the role of the Federal Reserve. How does that text present its functions? How does "the Fed" seek to control inflation?
- Look at an online newspaper and find the most recent story about the Federal Reserve Board or the chairman of "the Fed." What does the story imply about the significance of the Federal Reserve for American business?

participating banks owned all the stock in their regional Federal Reserve Bank and named two-thirds of its board of directors; the president named the other third. The regional banks were to be regulated and supervised by the Federal Reserve Board, a new federal agency with members chosen by the president. Economists agree that creation of the Federal Reserve system was the most important single measure to come out of the Wilson administration.

In 1913, Congress also fulfilled a Democratic campaign promise by creating a separate cabinet-level Department of Labor, and in 1914 Congress passed the **Clayton Antitrust Act**, which prohibited specified business practices, including **interlocking directorates** among large companies that could be proven to inhibit competition. It exempted farmers' organizations and unions from antitrust prosecution under the Sherman Act. The antitrust sections in the final version of the Clayton Act, however, did little to break up big corporations. Instead of breaking up big business, Wilson now moved closer to Roosevelt's position favoring regulation. Wilson also supported passage of the **Federal Trade Commission Act** (1914), a regulatory measure intended to prevent unfair methods of competition.

During his first year in office, Wilson drew sharp criticism from some northern social reformers when his appointees (especially southern Democrats) initiated racial

interlocking directorates Situation in which the same individuals sit on the boards of directors of various companies in one industry.

segregation in several federal agencies. As a southerner himself, Wilson undoubtedly believed in segregation even though he resisted his party's most extreme racists. Wilson was surprised at the swell of protest, not just from African Americans but also from some white progressives in the North and Midwest. He never designated a change in policy, but the process of segregating federal facilities slowed significantly.

Though many progressives applauded Wilson for tariff reform, the Federal Reserve Act, and the Clayton Act, some progressives criticized his appointees to the Federal Trade Commission and the Federal Reserve Board as being too sympathetic to business and banking. Moreover, Wilson considered federal action to outlaw child labor to be unconstitutional, and he questioned the need to amend the Constitution for woman suffrage. The approach of the 1916 presidential election seems to have spurred Wilson to reconsider. In 1912 he had received less than half of the popular vote and had won the White House only because the Republicans split. As the 1916 election approached, Wilson joined progressives in pushing measures intended to secure his claim as the true voice of progressivism and to capture progressive voters.

In January 1916, Wilson nominated Louis Brandeis for the Supreme Court. Brandeis's reputation as a staunch progressive and critic of business aroused intense opposition from conservatives, but he was confirmed in June 1916. Wilson followed up with support for several reform measures—credit facilities for farmers, workers' compensation for federal employees, and the elimination of child labor. Under threat of a railroad strike, Congress passed and Wilson signed the Adamson Act, securing an eight-hour workday for railroad employees.

The presidential election of 1916 was conducted against the background of war in Europe (covered in the next chapter). Wilson's shift toward social reform helped solidify his support among progressives. His support for organized labor earned him strong backing among unionists, and labor's votes probably ensured his victory in a few states, especially California. In states where women could vote, many of them seem to have preferred Wilson, probably because he backed issues of interest to women, such as outlawing child labor and keeping the nation out of war. In a very close election, Wilson won with 49 percent of the popular vote to 46 percent for Charles Evans Hughes, a progressive Republican.

NEW PATTERNS IN CULTURAL EXPRESSION

The changes sweeping American society also affected cultural expression. Shortly after 1900, the director of the nation's most prominent art museum, the Metropolitan Museum of New York, observed "a state of unrest" in art, literature, music, painting, and sculpture. Unrest meant change, and Americans at that time witnessed dramatic changes in art, literature, and music—many of them directly influenced by the new urban industrial society, and some of them reflecting the concerns of the Progressive Era.

Realism, Impressionism, and Ragtime   At the turn of the century, American novelists increasingly turned to a realistic—and sometimes critical—portrayal of life. The towering figure of the era remained **Mark Twain** (pen name of Samuel L. Clemens), whose novel *The Adventures* *of Huckleberry Finn* (1885) may be read at many levels, from a nostalgic account of boyhood to profound social satire. In this masterpiece, Twain reproduced the everyday speech of unschooled whites and blacks, poked fun at social pretensions, scorned the Old South myth, and challenged racially biased attitudes toward African Americans. Twain continued as an important social commentator until his death in 1910. The novels of William Dean Howells and Henry James, in contrast, presented restrained, realistic portrayals of upper-class men and women, and Kate Chopin sounded feminist themes in *The Awakening* (1899), dealing with repression of a woman's desires. Stephen Crane, Theodore Dreiser, and Frank Norris showed the influence of Émile Zola, a prominent French novelist, as they sharpened the critical edge of fiction. In Crane's *Maggie: A Girl of the Streets* (1893), urban squalor, alcohol, and callous men drive a young woman to prostitution. Norris's *The Octopus* (1901) portrayed the abusive power of a railroad over farmers.

As American literature moved toward realism and social criticism during these years, many American painters looked for inspiration to French **impressionism**, which emphasized less an exact reproduction of the world and more the artist's impression of it. Mary Cassatt was the only American—and one of only two women—to rank among the leaders of impressionism, but she lived and painted mostly in France. Among prominent impressionists working in the United States was Childe Hassam, who often depicted urban scenes. Attention to the city was also characteristic of work by Robert Henri, John Sloan, and others labeled the **Ash Can School** because of their preoccupation with everyday urban life and people. Their work has been considered the artistic counterpart to critical realism in literature.

In 1913 the most widely publicized art exhibit of the era permitted Americans to view works by the most innovative European painters. Known as the Armory Show for its opening in New York's National Guard Armory (it was later displayed in Chicago and Boston), the exhibit presented works by Pablo Picasso, Henri Matisse, Marcel Duchamp, Wassily Kandinsky, and others. Sophisticated critics and popular newspapers alike dismissed them as either insane or anarchists. One reviewer scornfully suggested that Duchamp's cubist painting *Nude Descending a Staircase* be retitled "explosion in a shingle factory." The abstract, modernist style, however, became firmly established by the 1920s.

As with painting, many aspects of American music derived from European models. John Philip Sousa, who produced well over a hundred works between the 1870s and his death in 1932, was the most popular American composer of the day, best known for his stirring patriotic marches. Perhaps more significant in the long run was the African American composer Scott Joplin. Born in Texas, Joplin had formal instruction in the piano, then traveled through black communities from New Orleans to Chicago where he encountered **ragtime** music. He soon began to

impressionism A style of painting that developed in France in the 1870s and emphasized the artist's impression of a subject; American impressionism was prominent from the 1880s through the 1910s.

ragtime Style of popular music characterized by a syncopated rhythm and a regularly accented beat; considered the immediate precursor of jazz.

write his own. In 1899 he published "Maple Leaf Rag" and quickly soared to fame as the leading ragtime composer in the country. Though condemned by some as vulgar, ragtime contributed significantly to the later development of jazz (discussed in Chapter 21).

Mass Entertainment in the Early Twentieth Century   By 1900, changes in transportation (the railroads) and communication (telegraph and telephone) combined with increased leisure time among the middle class and some skilled workers to foster new forms of entertainment.

Traveling dramatic and musical troupes had long entertained some Americans, but now booking agencies could schedule such groups into nearly every corner of the country. Traveling actors, singers, and other performers offered everything from Shakespeare to **slapstick**, from opera to **melodrama.**

Other traveling spectacles also took advantage of improved transportation and communication to establish regular circuits, including circuses and Wild West shows. A less sensational traveling show but one of the most popular was the **Chautauqua**, a blend of inspirational oratory, educational lectures, and entertainment.

During the late nineteenth century, a quite different form of mass entertainment appeared—professional baseball. Teams traveled by train from city to city, and urban rivalries built loyalty among fans. In 1876 team owners formed the National League as a cartel to dominate the industry by excluding rival clubs from their territories and controlling the movement of players from team to team. Because African Americans were barred from the National League, separate black clubs and Negro leagues emerged. In the 1880s and 1890s, the National League warded off challenges from rival leagues and defeated a players' union. Not until 1901 did another league—the American League—successfully organize. In 1903 the two leagues merged into a new, stronger cartel and staged the first World Series—in which the Boston Red Sox beat the Pittsburgh Pirates. As other professional spectator sports developed, they often imitated the organization, labor relations, and racial discrimination first established in baseball.

Celebrating the New Age   In 1893, when the World's Columbian Exposition opened in Chicago, Hamlin Garland, a writer living there, wrote to his parents in South Dakota, "Sell the cook stove if necessary and come.... You must see this fair." Between 1876 and World War I, Americans repeatedly held great expositions, beginning with one in Philadelphia in 1876 that

---

slapstick   A rowdy form of comedy marked by crude practical jokes and physical humor, such as falls.

melodrama   A sensational or romantic stage play with exaggerated conflicts and stereotyped characters.

Chautauqua   A traveling show offering educational, religious, and recreational activities, part of a nationwide movement of adult education that began in the town of Chautauqua, New York.

commemorated the centennial of independence and concluding with one in San Francisco in 1915 that celebrated the opening of the Panama Canal. Others took place in Atlanta, Buffalo, Omaha, Portland (Oregon), San Diego, and St. Louis. The most impressive and influential was the Columbian Exposition in Chicago, marking the four hundredth anniversary of Columbus's voyage to the New World.

These expositions typically featured vast exhibition halls where companies demonstrated their latest technological marvels, artists displayed their creations, and farmers presented their most impressive produce. In other halls, states and foreign nations showcased their accomplishments. The exhibits nearly always expressed the conviction that technology and industry would inevitably improve the lives of all. After 1898, most also included demeaning exhibits of "savage" or "barbarian" people from the nation's new overseas possessions.

Behind the gleaming machines in the imitation marble palaces, however, lurked troubling questions that never appeared in the exhibits glorifying "Progress." What should be the working conditions of those whose labor created such technological marvels? Were democratic institutions compatible with the concentration of power and control in industry and finance or with the acquisition of colonies?

PROGRESSIVISM IN PERSPECTIVE

The Progressive Era began with efforts at municipal reform in the 1890s and sputtered to a close during World War I. Some politicians who called themselves progressives remained in prominent positions afterward, and progressive concepts of efficiency and expertise continued to guide government decision making. But American entry into the war in 1917 diverted attention from reform, and by the end of the war political concerns had changed. By the mid-1920s, many of the major leaders of progressivism had passed from the political stage.

The changes of the Progressive Era transformed American politics and government. Before the Hepburn Act and the Federal Reserve Act, the federal government's role in the economy consisted largely of distributing land grants and setting protective tariffs. After the Progressive Era, the federal government became a significant and permanent player in the economy, regulating a wide range of economic activity and enforcing laws to protect consumers and some workers. The income tax quickly became the most significant source of federal funds. Without the income tax, it is impossible to imagine the many activities that the federal government has assumed since then—from vast military expenditures to social welfare to support for the arts. Since the 1930s, the income tax has sometimes been an instrument of social policy, by which the federal government has redistributed income.

During the Progressive Era, political parties declined in significance, and political campaigns focused increasingly on personality and advertising. These patterns accelerated in the second half of the twentieth century under the influence of television and public opinion polling. Organized pressure groups have proliferated and become ever more important. Women's participation in politics has continued to increase, especially in the last third of the twentieth century and the first decade of the twenty-first.

The assertion of presidential authority by Theodore Roosevelt and Woodrow Wilson reappeared in the presidency of Franklin D. Roosevelt (1933–1945). The two Roosevelts and Wilson transformed Americans' expectations regarding the office of the presidency itself. Throughout the nineteenth century, Congress had dominated the making of domestic policy. During the twentieth century, Americans came to expect domestic policy to flow from forceful executive leadership in the White House.

Finley Peter Dunne, the political humorist, realized that change is an integral part of American politics. He quoted this conversation between a woman who ran a boarding house and one of her lodgers:

> "I don't know what to do," says she. "I'm worn out, and it seems impossible to keep this house clean. What is the trouble with it?"
> "Madam," says my friend Gallagher, … "the trouble with this house is that it is occupied entirely by human beings. If it was a vacant house, it could easily be kept clean."

Thus, Dunne concluded about progressive reform, "The noise you hear is not the first gun of a revolution. It's only the people of the United States beating a carpet." In fact, however, the most important changes of the Progressive Era were more than just housekeeping—they may not have been revolutionary, but they laid the basis for many aspects of our modern politics and government.

STUDY TOOLS

SUMMARY

Progressivism, a phenomenon of the late nineteenth and early twentieth centuries, refers to new concepts of government, to changes in government based on those concepts, and to the political process by which change occurred. Those years marked a time of political transformation brought about by many groups and individuals who approached politics with often contradictory objectives. Organized interest groups became an important part of this process. Women broke through long-standing constraints to take a more prominent role in politics. The Anti-Saloon League was the most successful of several organizations that appealed to government to enforce morality. Some African Americans fought segregation and disfranchisement, notably W. E. B. Du Bois and the NAACP. Socialists and the Industrial Workers of the World saw capitalism as the source of many problems, but few Americans embraced their radical solutions.

Political reform took place at every level, from cities to states to the federal government. Muckraking journalists exposed wrongdoing and suffering. Municipal reformers introduced modern methods of city government in a quest for efficiency and effectiveness. Some tried to use government to remedy social problems by employing the expertise of new professions such as public health and social work. Reformers attacked the power of party bosses and machines by reducing the role of political parties.

At the federal level, Theodore Roosevelt set the pace for progressive reform. Relishing his reputation as a trustbuster, he challenged judicial constraints on federal authority over big business and promoted other forms of economic regulation, thereby increasing government's role in the economy. He also regulated the use of natural resources. His successor, William Howard Taft, failed to maintain Republican Party unity and eventually sided with conservatives against progressives.

Roosevelt played an important role in defining America's status as a world power, as he secured rights to build a U.S. controlled canal through Panama and established Panama as an American protectorate. The Roosevelt Corollary declared that the United States was the dominant power in the Caribbean and Central America. In eastern Asia, Roosevelt tried to bolster the Open Door policy by maintaining a balance of power. Roosevelt and others sought arbitration treaties with leading nations but failed because of Senate opposition. Faced with the rise of German military and naval power, Great Britain improved relations with the United States.

In 1912 Roosevelt led a new political party, the Progressives, making that year's presidential election a three-way contest. Roosevelt called for regulation of big business, but Wilson, the Democrat, favored breaking up monopolies through antitrust action. Wilson won the election but soon preferred regulation over antitrust actions. He helped to create the Federal Reserve System to regulate banking nationwide. As the 1916 election approached, Wilson also pushed for social reforms in an effort to unify all progressives behind his leadership.

The new urban, industrial, multiethnic society contributed to critical realism in literature, new patterns in painting, and ragtime music, although many creative artists continued to look to Europe for inspiration. Urbanization and changes in transportation and communication also fostered the emergence of a mass entertainment industry.

Progressive reforms made a profound impression on later American politics. In many ways, progressivism marked the origin of modern American politics and government.

CHRONOLOGY

THE PROGRESSIVE ERA

1885	Mark Twain's *The Adventures of Huckleberry Finn*
1890	National American Woman Suffrage Association formed
1893	World's Columbian Exposition, Chicago
1895	Anti-Saloon League formed
	United States v. E. C. Knight
1898	War with Spain
1899	Permanent Court of Arbitration (the Hague Court) created
	Scott Joplin's "Maple Leaf Rag"

1900   Robert M. La Follette elected governor of Wisconsin
President William McKinley reelected

1901   Socialist Party of America formed
McKinley assassinated; Theodore Roosevelt becomes president

1902   Muckraking journalism begins
Antitrust action against Northern Securities Company
Roosevelt intervenes in coal strike
Reclamation Act

1903   W. E. B. Du Bois's *Souls of Black Folk*
Panama becomes a protectorate
Hay–Bunau-Varilla Treaty; work begins on Panama Canal

1904   Roosevelt Corollary
Roosevelt elected president

1905   Industrial Workers of the World organized
Roosevelt mediates Russo-Japanese War
Dominican Republic becomes third U.S. protectorate

1906   Upton Sinclair's *The Jungle*
Hepburn Act
Meat Inspection Act
Pure Food and Drug Act

1908   *Muller v. Oregon*
Race riot in Springfield, Illinois
William Howard Taft elected president

1910   National Association for the Advancement of Colored People formed
Hiram W. Johnson elected governor of California

1911   Fire at Triangle Shirtwaist factory

1912   Progressive ("Bull Moose") Party formed
Wilson elected president
Nicaragua becomes a protectorate

1913   Sixteenth Amendment (federal income tax) ratified
Seventeenth Amendment (direct election of U.S. senators) ratified
Federal Reserve Act
Armory Show

1914   Clayton Antitrust Act
Federal Trade Commission Act
Panama Canal completed

1915   National Birth Control League formed

1916   Louis Brandeis appointed to the Supreme Court
Jeannette Rankin of Montana becomes first woman elected to U.S.
House of Representatives
Wilson reelected

1917   United States enters World War I

Focus Questions

If you have mastered this chapter, you should be able to answer these questions and explain the terms that follow the questions.

1. What important changes transformed American politics in the early twentieth century?
2. What did women and African Americans seek to accomplish by creating new organizations devoted to political change?
3. What did the muckrakers contribute to reform?
4. What characterized reforms of city and state government and what role did organized interest groups play?
5. What did Theodore Roosevelt mean by a "Square Deal"? Do his accomplishments fit this description?
6. How did Roosevelt's presidency change the federal role in the economy and alter the presidency itself?
7. What were Roosevelt's objectives for the United States in world affairs?
8. How did Roosevelt reshape American foreign policy?
9. What choices confronted American voters in the presidential election of 1912?
10. How did Wilson's views on reform evolve from 1912 through 1916 and how did his administration change the federal government's role in the economy?
11. Did developments in cultural expression draw more from American sources or European sources?
12. How did social and technological changes contribute to new patterns in mass entertainment?
13. Was progressivism successful? How do you define success?
14. How did progressivism affect modern American politics?

Key Terms

interest groups (*p. 577*)

Progressive Party (*p. 577*)

Hull House (*p. 578*)

Social Gospel (*p. 579*)

Margaret Sanger (*p. 580*)

Muller v. Oregon (*p. 580*)

Jeannette Rankin (*p. 580*)

National American Woman Suffrage Association (*p. 580*)

Anti-Saloon League (*p. 581*)

W. E. B. Du Bois (*p. 583*)

National Association for the Advancement of Colored People (*p. 583*)

Ida B. Wells (*p. 584*)

Socialist Party of America (*p. 584*)

Industrial Workers of the World (*p. 584*)

muckrakers (*p. 585*)

Upton Sinclair (*p. 585*)

Pure Food and Drug Act (*p. 585*)

Meat Inspection Act (*p. 586*)

Robert M. La Follette (*p. 588*)

Wisconsin Idea (*p. 589*)

Hiram Johnson (*p. 589*)

Square Deal (*p. 592*)

Hepburn Act (*p. 593*)

Gifford Pinchot (*p. 593*)

Sixteenth Amendment (*p. 594*)
Seventeenth Amendment (*p. 594*)
Philippe Bunau-Varilla (*p. 595*)
Hay–Bunau-Varilla Treaty (*p. 596*)
Roosevelt Corollary (*p. 596*)
dollar diplomacy (*p. 597*)
Treaty of Portsmouth (*p. 598*)
Permanent Court of Arbitration (*p. 599*)
New Nationalism (*p. 600*)

Bull Moose Party (*p. 600*)
New Freedom (*p. 601*)
Louis Brandeis (*p. 601*)
Underwood Tariff (*p. 602*)
Federal Reserve Act (*p. 602*)
Clayton Antitrust Act (*p. 603*)
Federal Trade Commission Act (*p. 603*)
Mark Twain (*p. 604*)
Ash Can School (*p. 605*)

20

THE UNITED STATES IN A WORLD AT WAR, 1913–1920

> **CHAPTER OUTLINE**
>
> • Inherited Commitments and New Directions • The United States and the Great War, 1914–1917 • The Home Front • Planning for Peace in the Midst of War • The Peace Conference and the Treaty • America in the Aftermath of War, November 1918–November 1920 • Study Tools

On June 28, 1914, a Serbian terrorist killed Archduke Franz Ferdinand, heir to the throne of Austria-Hungary, and his wife, Sophie. The royal couple was visiting Sarajevo, in Bosnia-Herzegovina, which Austria had recently annexed against the wishes of the neighboring kingdom of Serbia. In response to the assassinations, Austria first consulted with its ally Germany and then made stringent demands on Serbia. Serbia sought help from Russia, which was allied with France. Tense diplomats invoked elaborate, interlocking alliances. Huge armies began to move. By August 4, most of Europe was at war.

By this point, the United States was no minor player on the international scene. Between 1898 and 1908, America acquired the Philippines and the Panama Canal, came to dominate the Caribbean and Central America, and actively participated in the balance of power in eastern Asia. The three presidents of the Progressive Era—Roosevelt, William Howard Taft, and Woodrow Wilson—agreed wholeheartedly that the United States should exercise a major role in world affairs.

INHERITED COMMITMENTS AND NEW DIRECTIONS

When Woodrow Wilson entered the White House in 1913, he expected to spend most of his time dealing with domestic issues. Although well read on international affairs, he had neither significant international experience nor set foreign policies. For secretary of state he chose William Jennings Bryan, who also had devoted his political career to domestic matters and had little experience in foreign relations.

Both men were devout Presbyterians, sharing a confidence that God had a plan for humankind and specifically for the United States. Both hoped—perhaps naively—that they might make the United States a model among nations for peaceful settlement of international disputes. Initially, Wilson fixed his attention on the three regions of greatest American involvement: Latin America, the Pacific, and eastern Asia. There, he tried to balance the anti-imperialist principles of his Democratic Party against the expansionist practices of his Republican predecessors. He marked out some new directions but in the end extended many previous commitments.

Anti-Imperialism, Intervention, and Arbitration   Wilson's Democratic Party had opposed many of the foreign policies of McKinley, Roosevelt, and Taft, especially imperialism. Secretary of State Bryan was a leading anti-imperialist who had criticized Roosevelt's "Big Stick" in foreign affairs. During the Wilson administration, the Democrats wrote into law a limited version of their opposition to imperialism. In 1916 Congress established a bill of rights for residents of the Philippines, provided more autonomy, and promised eventual independence. The next year, Congress made Puerto Rico an American territory and extended American citizenship to its residents.

Democrats had criticized Roosevelt's actions in the Caribbean, but Wilson eventually intervened more in Central America and the Caribbean than any previous administration. In Nicaragua, where Taft had used marines to prop up the rule of President Adolfo Diaz, Wilson sought more authority for the United States. Senate Democrats rejected his efforts, reminding him of their party's opposition to further protectorates. Even so, Bryan negotiated a treaty in 1914 that gave the United States significant concessions, including the right to build a canal through Nicaragua.

Haiti owed a staggering debt to foreign bankers, and its government was extremely unstable. When a mob killed the president in 1915, Wilson sent in the marines. A treaty followed, making Haiti a protectorate in which American forces controlled most aspects of government until 1933. Wilson sent marines into the Dominican Republic in 1916, and U.S. naval officers exercised control there until 1924. In 1917, the United States bought the Virgin Islands from Denmark for $25 million. Thus, Wilson made few changes in previous policies regarding American dominance of the Caribbean.

Wilson and Bryan did, however, bring a new approach to the arbitration of international disputes. Roosevelt's and Taft's secretaries of state had sought arbitration treaties, but the Senate had refused to accept them. Bryan drafted a model treaty and first obtained approval from the Senate Foreign Relations Committee. The Senate ultimately ratified treaties with twenty-two nations. All featured a "cooling-off" period for disputes, typically a year, during which the nations agreed to seek arbitration instead of going to war. These treaties marked the beginning of efforts by Wilson to redefine international relations, substituting rational negotiations for raw power.

Wilson and the Mexican Revolution   In Mexico, Wilson attempted to influence internal politics but eventually found himself on the verge of war. **Porfirio Díaz** had ruled Mexico for a third of a century, supported by great landholders, the church, and the military. During his rule, many

American companies invested in Mexico. However, discontent was growing among peasants, workers, and intellectuals. Rebellion broke out, and Díaz resigned in 1911. Francisco Madero, a leading advocate of reform, assumed the presidency but failed to unite the country. Conservatives feared Madero as a reformer, but radicals dismissed him as too timid. In some places, peasant armies demanding *tierra y libertad* ("land and liberty") attacked the mansions of great landowners. In February 1913, conservatives joined with the commander of the army, General **Victoriano Huerta**, to overthrow Madero. Huerta took control of the government and had Madero executed.

Most European governments extended diplomatic recognition to Huerta because his government clearly held power in Mexico City. Wilson faced that decision soon after his inauguration. American companies with investments in Mexico urged recognition because they considered Huerta likely to protect their holdings. Wilson, however, considered Huerta a murderer and privately vowed "not to recognize a government of butchers." In public, Wilson announced he withheld recognition because Huerta's regime did not rest on the consent of the governed.

Wilson's addition of an ethical dimension to diplomatic recognition constituted something new in foreign policy. Previous American presidents had automatically extended diplomatic recognition to governments in power. Wilson's approach, sometimes labeled "missionary diplomacy," implied that the United States would discriminate between virtuous and corrupt governments. Telling one visitor, "I am going to teach the South American republics to elect good men," Wilson waited for an opportunity to act against Huerta. In the meantime, anti-Huerta forces led by **Venustiano Carranza** made significant gains.

In April 1914, Mexican officials in Tampico arrested some American sailors. The city's army commander immediately released them and apologized, but Wilson used the incident to justify ordering the U.S. Navy to occupy **Veracruz**, the leading Mexican port. Veracruz was the major source of the Huerta government's revenue (from customs) and the landing point for most government military supplies. The occupation cut these off. However, it cost more than a hundred Mexican lives and turned many Mexicans against Wilson for violating their sovereignty. Without munitions and revenue, Huerta fled the country in mid-July. Wilson withdrew the last American forces from Veracruz in November.

Carranza succeeded Huerta as president, and Wilson officially recognized his government. Carranza faced armed opposition, however, from **Francisco "Pancho" Villa** in northern Mexico and Emiliano Zapata in the south. When Villa suffered setbacks, he apparently set out to involve Carranza in a war with the United States. Villa's men murdered several Americans in Mexico and then, in March 1916, raided across the border and killed several Americans in New Mexico. With Carranza's reluctant approval, Wilson sent an expedition of nearly seven thousand men, commanded by General John J. Pershing, into Mexico to punish Villa. Villa evaded the American troops, but drew them ever deeper into Mexico, alarming Carranza.

When a clash between Mexican government forces and American soldiers produced deaths on both sides, Carranza asked Wilson to withdraw the American troops. Wilson refused. Only in early 1917, when Wilson recognized that America might soon go to war with Germany, did he pull back the troops, leaving behind deep resentment and suspicion toward the United States.

THE UNITED STATES AND THE GREAT WAR, 1914–1917

At first, Americans paid little attention to the assassinations at Sarajevo. When Europe plunged into war, however, Wilson and all Americans faced difficult choices.

The Great
War in Europe
Throughout much of the nineteenth and early twentieth centuries, most European governments had encouraged their citizens to identify strongly with their nation, thereby cultivating the intense patriotism known as nationalism. Within the ethnically diverse empires of Austria-Hungary, Russia, and Turkey, a different sort of nationalism fueled hopes for independence based on language and culture. Ethnic antagonisms and aspirations were especially powerful in the **Balkan Peninsula**, where the Ottoman (Turkish) Empire had lost territory as several groups had established their independence. Some of the new Balkan states were weak, however, attracting the neighboring Austrian and Russian empires. As Austria-Hungary sought to annex new territories, Russia claimed the role of protector of other **Slavic** peoples.

During the same years, competition for world markets and territory spawned an unprecedented arms buildup. By the 1870s, Germany had the most powerful army in Europe and had set out to make its navy as powerful as Britain's. By 1900, most European powers had a professional officer corps and **universal military service**. Technology produced new and powerful weapons, including the machine gun, and designers quickly adapted automobiles and airplanes for combat. The major powers of Europe had avoided war with one another since 1871, when Germany had humiliated France. But they continued to prepare for war. Eventually European diplomats constructed two major alliance systems: the Triple Entente (Britain, France, and Russia) and the Triple Alliance (Germany, Austria-Hungary, and Italy). Britain was also allied with Japan.

Called the "powder keg of Europe," the Balkans lived up to their explosive nickname in 1914. The assassinations at Sarajevo grew out of a territorial conflict between Austria-Hungary and Serbia. Russia, alarmed over Austrian expansion into the Balkans, presented itself as the protector of Serbia. Austria first assured itself of Germany's backing, then declared war on Serbia. Russia confirmed France's support, then **mobilized** its army in support of Serbia. Germany declared war on Russia on August 1 and on France soon after. German strategists planned to bypass French defenses along their border by invading **neutral** Belgium. Britain entered the war in defense of Belgium. By August 4, much of Europe was at war. Eventually Germany and Austria-Hungary combined with Bulgaria and the Ottoman Empire to form the **Central Powers**. Italy abandoned its Triple Alliance partners and joined Britain, France, Russia, Romania, and Japan as the **Allies**.

Slavic   Ethnic and linguistic groups, mainly in eastern and central Europe; includes Bulgarians, Croats, Czechs, Poles, Russians, Serbs, Slovaks, Ukrainians, and others.

universal military service   Governmental policy requiring all adult males (or, rarely, all adults) to serve in the military for some period of time.

mobilize   To make ready for combat or other forms of action.

neutral   A nation not aligned with either side in a war; traditionally, neutral nations could engage in certain types of trade with nations at war.

At first, Secretary of State Bryan tried to take a hopeful view of events in Europe. "It may be," he suggested, "that the world needed one more awful object lesson to prove conclusively the fallacy of the doctrine that preparedness for war can give assurance for peace." Sir Edward Grey, Britain's foreign minister, was less optimistic as he mourned to a friend, "The lamps are going out all over Europe. We shall not see them lit again in our lifetime." Grey proved a more accurate prophet than Bryan.

The Germans expected to roll through Belgium, small and militarily weak, and quickly defeat France. The Belgians resisted long enough for French and British troops to block the Germans. The opposing armies then settled into defensive lines across 475 miles of Belgian and French countryside, extending from the English Channel to the Alps. By the end of 1914, the **western front** consisted of elaborate networks of trenches on both sides, separated by a desolate no man's land filled with coils of barbed wire, where any movement brought a burst of machine-gun fire. As the war progressed, terrible new weapons—poison gas, aerial bombings, tanks—took thousands of lives but failed to break the deadlock.

American Neutrality   Wilson's initial reaction to the European conflagration revealed his own deep religious beliefs—he wrote privately of his confidence that "Providence has deeper plans than we could possibly have laid for ourselves." On August 4, he announced that the United States was neutral. Later, on August 19, he urged Americans to be "neutral in fact as well as in name … impartial in thought as well as in action."

Wilson hoped not only that America would remain neutral but also that he might serve as peacemaker. Such hopes proved unrealistic. The warring nations wanted to gain territory, and only a decisive victory could accomplish that. The longer they fought, the more territory they wanted. So long as they saw a chance of winning, they had no interest in the appeals of any would-be peacemakers.

Wilson's hope that Americans could remain impartial was also unrealistic. Though few Americans wanted to go to war, most probably sided with the Allies. England had cultivated American friendship for decades, and trade and finance united many of their business leaders. French assistance during the American Revolution helped to fuel support for France. And the martyrdom of Belgium aroused American sympathy. Allied **propagandists** worked hard to generate anti-German sentiment in America, publicizing—and exaggerating—German atrocities and portraying the war as a conflict between civilized peoples and barbarian **Huns**.

Not all Americans sympathized with the Allies. Nearly 8 million of the 97 million people in the United States had one or both parents from Germany or Austria. Not surprisingly, many of them objected to depictions of their cousins as bloodthirsty barbarians. Many of the 5 million Irish Americans disliked England for ruling their ancestral homeland.

---

propagandist   One who provides information in support of a cause, especially one-sided or exaggerated information.

Hun   Disparaging term applied to Germans during World War I, derived from warlike people who invaded Europe in the fourth and fifth centuries.

THE ROAD TO WAR, SUMMER 1914

1. June 28
Assassination at Sarajevo

2. July 28
Austria-Hungary declares war on Serbia

3. July 30
Russia begins mobilization

4. August 1
Germany declares war on Russia

5. August 3
Germany declares war on France

6. August 4
Great Britain declares war on Germany

7. August 6
Russia and Austria-Hungary at war

8. August 12
Great Britain declares war on Austria-Hungary

© Cengage Learning 2013

MAP 20.1 Europe Goes to War

In the First World War, Great Britain, France, and Russia squared off against Germany, Austria-Hungary, and the Ottoman Empire. Most of the fighting occurred in Europe along the western front in France (solid line) or the eastern front in Russia (dashed line). This map also shows Britain's blockade of German ports. British armies based in Egypt (then a British colony) clashed with Ottoman armies in Arabia and other parts of the Ottoman Empire.

Neutral Rights and German U-Boats

Wilson and Bryan agreed that the United States should remain neutral but took different approaches to that goal. Bryan proved willing to sacrifice traditional neutral rights if insistence on those rights seemed likely to pull the United

States into the conflict. Wilson, in contrast, stood firm on maintaining traditional neutral rights, a posture that actually favored the Allies.

Bryan initially opposed loans to **belligerent** nations as incompatible with neutrality. Wilson agreed at first, then realized that the ban hurt the Allies more. He then agreed to permit buying goods on credit. Eventually, he dropped the ban on loans, partly because neutrals had always been permitted to lend to belligerents and partly, perhaps, because the freeze endangered the stability of the American economy.

Traditional neutral rights included freedom of the seas: neutrals could trade with all belligerents. When both sides turned to naval warfare to break the deadlock on the western front, Wilson found himself defending the rights of neutral shipping to both Britain and Germany.

Britain commanded the seas and tried to redefine neutral rights by blockading German ports and neutral ports from which goods could reach Germany, and by expanding definitions of **contraband** to include anything that might indirectly aid Germany—even cotton and food. Britain extended the right of belligerent nations to stop and search neutral ships for contraband by insisting that large, modern ships could not be searched at sea and must be escorted to port, thus imposing costly delays.

Germany also challenged neutral rights, declaring a blockade of the British Isles, to be enforced by its submarines, called **U-boats**. Because U-boats were relatively fragile, a lightly armed merchant ship might sink one that surfaced and ordered the merchant ship to stop in the traditional manner. Consequently, submarines struck from below without warning. Britain began disguising its ships by flying the flags of neutral countries, so Germany declared that neutral flags no longer guaranteed protection.

Wilson had issued token protests over Britain's practices but strongly denounced those of Germany. Because Germany's violations of neutrality produced loss of life, he considered them to be significantly different from Britain's, which caused only financial hardship. On February 10, 1915, Wilson warned that the United States would hold Germany to "strict accountability" for its actions and would do everything necessary to "safeguard American lives and property" and maintain American rights on the high seas. On May 7, 1915, a German U-boat torpedoed the British passenger ship *Lusitania*. More than a thousand people died, including 128 Americans. Americans reacted with shock and horror. Upon learning that *Lusitania* carried ammunition and other contraband, Bryan urged restraint in protesting to Germany. Wilson, however, sent a strong message that stopped just short of demanding an end to submarine attacks on merchant ships. The German response was noncommittal. When Wilson composed an even stronger protest, Bryan feared it would lead to war. He resigned as secretary of state rather than sign it.

belligerent   A nation formally at war.

contraband   Goods prohibited from being imported or exported; in time of war, contraband included materials of war.

U-boat   A German submarine (in German, *Unterseeboot*).

Robert Lansing, Bryan's successor, strongly favored the Allies. Where Bryan had counseled restraint, Lansing urged a show of strength. U-boat attacks continued. Wilson sent more protests but knew most Americans opposed going to war over that issue. Then a U-boat sank the unarmed French ship *Sussex* in March 1916, injuring several Americans. Wilson warned Germany that if unrestricted submarine warfare did not stop, the United States would sever diplomatic relations—the last step before declaring war. Germany responded with the **Sussex pledge:** U-boats would no longer strike noncombatant vessels without warning, provided the United States convinced the Allies to obey "international law." Wilson accepted the pledge but did little to persuade the British to change tactics.

The war strengthened America's economic ties to the Allies. Exports to Britain and France soared from $756 million in 1914 to $2.7 billion in 1916. American companies exported $6 million worth of explosives in 1914 and $467 million in 1916. Even more significant was the transformation of the United States from a debtor to a **creditor nation.** By April 1917, American bankers had loaned more than $2 billion to the Allied governments. However, the British blockade stifled Americans' trade with the Central Powers, which fell from around $170 million in 1914 to almost nothing two years later.

Wilson concluded that the best way to maintain American neutrality was to end the war. He sent his closest confidant, Edward M. House, to London and Berlin early in 1916 to present proposals for peace and for a league of nations to maintain peace in the future. House received no encouragement from either side and concluded that they were not interested in negotiations.

Some Americans had begun to demand "preparedness"—a military buildup. In response, in the summer of 1916, Congress appropriated the largest naval expenditures in peacetime history and approved the National Defense Act, which doubled the size of the army. Wilson accepted both measures.

The Election of 1916   By embracing preparedness, Wilson defused an issue that might otherwise have helped the Republicans in the 1916 presidential campaign. The Democrats nominated Wilson for a second term, and they campaigned on their domestic reforms and preparedness programs, frequently repeating the slogan "He kept us out of war."

Republicans nominated Charles Evans Hughes, a Supreme Court justice and former governor of New York with a reputation as a progressive. Hughes avoided taking a clear position on preparedness and neutrality, hoping for support both from German Americans upset with Wilson's harshness toward Germany and from those who wanted maximum assistance for the Allies. As a result, he failed to present a compelling alternative to Wilson.

The vote was very close. Most voters identified themselves as Republicans, and Wilson needed support from some of them. He won by uniting the always-Democratic South with the West, much of which was progressive. Wilson also

---

creditor nation   A nation whose citizens or government have loaned more money to the citizens or governments of other nations than the total amount that they have borrowed from the citizens or governments of other nations.

received significant backing from unions, socialists, and women in states where women could vote. In the end, Wilson received 49 percent of the vote to 46 percent for Hughes.

The Decision
for War

After the election, events moved very quickly. In January 1917, Wilson spoke to the Senate on the need to achieve and preserve peace. The galleries were packed as he eloquently called for an international organization to keep peace in the future. He urged that the only lasting peace would be a "peace without victory" in which neither side exacted gains from the other. He called for government by consent of the governed, freedom of the seas, and reductions in armaments. Wilson acknowledged privately that he had aimed his speech toward "the people of the countries now at war," hoping to build public pressure on those governments to seek peace. He won praise from **left-wing** opposition parties in several countries, but the British, French, and German governments had no interest in "peace without victory."

At the same time, the German government decided to resume unrestricted submarine warfare. They expected this would bring the United States into the war but gambled on being able to defeat the British and French before American troops could make a difference. When Germany announced it was resuming unrestricted submarine warfare, Wilson broke off diplomatic relations. German U-boats began immediately to devastate Atlantic shipping.

A few weeks later, on March 1, Wilson released a decoded message from the German state secretary for foreign affairs, **Arthur Zimmermann,** to the German minister in Mexico. Zimmermann proposed that, if the United States went to war with Germany, Mexico should join with Germany and attack the United States. Zimmermann promised that if Germany and Mexico won, Mexico would recover its "lost provinces" of Texas, Arizona, and New Mexico. Zimmermann also proposed that Mexico should encourage Japan to enter the war against the United States. The British intercepted the message and gave it to Wilson.

Zimmermann's suggestions outraged Americans, increasing public support for a proposal to arm American merchant ships for protection against U-boats. A few senators, mostly progressives, blocked the measure, arguing that it was safer to bar merchant ships from the war zone. Wilson then acted on his own and authorized merchant ships to be armed.

By March 21, German U-boats had sunk six American ships. Wilson could avoid war only by backing down from his insistence on "strict accountability." He did not retreat. Wilson's major objective in going to war was not to protect American commerce with the Allies, but to defeat German autocracy and militarism and to put the United States, and himself, in a position to determine the terms of peace. On April 2, 1917, Wilson asked Congress to declare war on Germany and tried to unite Americans in a righteous, progressive crusade.

---

left-wing   Not conservative; usually implies socialist or other radical leanings.

Condemning German U-boat attacks as "warfare against mankind," he proclaimed, "The world must be made safe for democracy." He promised that the United States would fight for self-government, "the rights and liberties of small nations," and a league of nations to "bring peace and safety to all nations and make the world itself at last free."

Not all members of Congress agreed that war was necessary; nor were all ready to join Wilson's campaign to transform the world. During the debate, Senator George W. Norris, a progressive Republican from Nebraska, best voiced the opposing arguments. The nation, he argued, was going to war "upon the command of gold" to "preserve the commercial right of American citizens to deliver munitions of war to belligerent nations." In the Senate, Norris, Robert La Follette, and four others voted no, but eighty-two senators voted for war. Jeannette Rankin of Montana, the first woman in the House of Representatives, was among those who said no when the House voted 373 to 50 for war. In December, Congress also declared war against Austria-Hungary.

THE HOME FRONT

Historians call World War I the first "total war" because it was the first war to demand mobilization of an entire society and economy. The war altered nearly every aspect of the economy as the progressive emphasis on expertise and efficiency produced unprecedented centralization of economic decision making. Mobilization extended beyond war production to the people themselves and especially to shaping their attitudes toward involvement in the war.

Mobilizing the Economy   The ability to wage war effectively depended on a fully engaged industrial economy. Thus warring nations sought to direct economic activities toward supplying their war machines. In the United States, railway transportation delays, shortages of supplies, and the sluggish pace of some manufacturing led to increased federal direction over transportation, food and fuel production, and manufacturing. This was not unusual among the nations at war and in fact was probably less extreme than in other nations. Even so, the extent of direct federal control over so much of the economy has never been matched since World War I.

Though unprecedented, much of the government intervention was also voluntary. Business enlisted as a partner with government and supplied its cooperation and expertise. Some prominent entrepreneurs volunteered their services for a dollar a year. Much of the wartime centralization of economic decision making came through new agencies composed of government officials, business leaders, and prominent citizens.

The **War Industries Board** supervised production of war materials. At first, it had only limited success in increasing productivity. Then, in early 1918, Wilson appointed Bernard Baruch, a Wall Street financier, to head the board. By pleading, bargaining, and sometimes threatening, Baruch usually persuaded companies to meet production quotas, allocate raw materials, develop new industries, and streamline operations. Though Baruch once threatened steel company executives with a government takeover, he accomplished most goals without coercion. And industrial production increased by 20 percent.

Efforts to conserve fuel included the first use of **daylight saving time**. To improve rail transportation, the federal government consolidated the country's railroads and ran them for the duration of the war. The government also took over the telegraph and telephone system and launched a huge shipbuilding program to expand the merchant marine.

The **National War Labor Board** (NWLB), created in 1918, endorsed **collective bargaining** to facilitate production by resolving labor disputes. The board also helped to settle labor disputes. Never before had a federal agency interceded this way. The board gave some support for an eight-hour workday in return for a no-strike pledge from unions.

Most unions promised not to strike for the duration of the war, and many of them secured contracts with significant wage increases. Union membership boomed from 2.7 million in 1916 to more than 4 million by 1919. Most union leaders fully supported the war. Samuel Gompers, president of the AFL, called it "the most wonderful crusade ever entered upon in the whole history of the world." Nevertheless, many workers felt that their purchasing power was not keeping pace with increases in prices.

Demands for increased production at a time when millions of men were marching off to war opened many opportunities for women. Employment of women in factory, office, and retail jobs had increased before the war, and the war accelerated those trends. Some of the new, wartime union members were women. At the war's end, many women's wartime jobs returned to male hands, but in office work and some retail positions women continued to predominate after the war.

One crucial American contribution to the Allies was food, for the war severely disrupted European agriculture. Wilson appointed as food administrator **Herbert Hoover**, who had already won wide praise for directing the relief program in Belgium when America was still neutral. Now he both promoted increased food production and also urged families to conserve food through Meatless Mondays and Wheatless Wednesdays and by planting "war gardens" to raise vegetables. Farmers brought large areas under cultivation for the first time. Food shipments to the Allies tripled.

Some progressives urged that the Wilson administration pay for the war by taxing the wartime profits and earnings of corporations. That did not happen, but taxes—especially the new income tax—did account for almost half of the $33 billion the United States spent on the war between April 1917 and June 1920. The government borrowed the rest, much of it through **Liberty Loan** drives. Rallies, parades, and posters pushed all Americans to buy "Liberty Bonds." Groups such

daylight saving time Setting of clocks ahead by one hour to provide more daylight at the end of the day during late spring, summer, and early fall.

collective bargaining Negotiation between the representatives of organized workers and their employer to determine wages, hours, and working conditions.

Labor shortages attracted new people into the labor market and opened up some jobs to women and members of racial minorities. In May 1918, these women worked in the Union Pacific Railroad freight yard in Cheyenne, Wyoming.

as the Red Cross and the YMCA urged people to donate time and energy in support of American soldiers.

Mobilizing Public Opinion   Not all Americans supported the war. Some German Americans were reluctant to send their sons to war against their cousins. Some Irish Americans became even more hostile to Britain after English troops brutally suppressed an attempt at Irish independence in 1916. The Socialist Party openly opposed the war, and Socialist candidates dramatically increased their share of the vote in several places in 1917— to 22 percent in New York City and 34 percent in Chicago—suggesting that their antiwar stance attracted many voters.

To mobilize public opinion in support of the war, Wilson created the Committee on Public Information, headed by George Creel. Creel set out to sell the war to all Americans. The **Creel Committee** eventually counted 150,000 lecturers, writers, artists, actors, and scholars championing the war and whipping up hatred of the "Huns." Social clubs, movie theaters, and churches all joined what Creel called

James Montgomery Flagg created this poster in 1918, showing Columbia, a traditional symbol for America, sowing grain as a way of appealing to American women to contribute to victory by raising and preserving food for their families. Columbia was usually garbed in an American flag, wearing a red liberty cap, a traditional symbol of freedom.

"the world's greatest adventure in advertising." "Four-Minute Men"—volunteers ready to make a short patriotic speech any time and place a crowd gathered—made 755,190 speeches.

Wilson's war message had stressed that "We have no quarrel with the German people," but wartime propaganda quickly moved toward demonizing all things German, and wartime patriotism sparked extreme measures against those considered "slackers" or pro-German. "Woe to the man or group of men that seeks to stand in our way," warned Wilson. "He who is not with us, absolutely and without reserve of any kind," echoed former president Theodore Roosevelt, "is against us, and should be treated as an alien enemy."

"Americanization" drives promoted rapid assimilation among immigrants. Some states prohibited the use of foreign languages in public. Officials removed German books from libraries and sometimes publicly burned them. Some communities banned music by Bach and Beethoven and dropped German classes from their schools. Even words became objectionable: sauerkraut became "liberty cabbage."

Sometimes mobs hounded people with German names and occasionally attacked or even lynched people suspected of antiwar sentiments.

Civil Liberties in Time of War   Not only German Americans but also pacifists, socialists, and other radicals became targets for government repression and **vigilante** action. Congress passed the **Espionage Act** in 1917 and the **Sedition Act** in 1918, prohibiting interference with the draft and outlawing criticism of the government, the armed forces, or the war effort. Violators faced large fines and long prison terms. Officials arrested fifteen hundred people for violating these acts, including Eugene V. Debs, leader of the Socialist Party. The Espionage Act authorized the postmaster general to bar objectionable publications from the mail. By the war's end, he had denied mailing privileges to some four hundred periodicals, including, at least temporarily, the *New York Times* and other mainstream publications.

When opponents of the war challenged the Espionage Act as unconstitutional, the Supreme Court ruled that freedom of speech was never absolute. Just as no one has the right to falsely shout "Fire!" in a theater and create panic, said Justice Oliver Wendell Holmes, Jr., so in time of war no one has a constitutional right to say anything that might endanger the security of the nation. The Court also upheld the Sedition Act.

The Industrial Workers of the World (IWW) made no public pronouncement against the war, but most Wobblies probably opposed it. IWW members and leaders quickly came under attack from employers, government officials, and vigilantes, most of whom had disliked the IWW before the war. In September 1917, Justice Department agents raided IWW offices nationwide and arrested IWW leaders, who were sentenced to jail for up to twenty-five years and fined millions of dollars. Deprived of most leaders and virtually bankrupted, the IWW never recovered.

A few Americans protested the abridgment of civil liberties. One group formed the Civil Liberties Bureau—forerunner of the American Civil Liberties Union. Most Americans, however, did not object to the repression, and many who did kept silent.

The Great Migration and White Reactions   In 1910, about 90 percent of all African Americans lived in the South, 75 percent in rural areas. By 1920, as many as a half-million had moved north in what has been called the **Great Migration**. Many went to the industrial cities of the Midwest. Gary, Indiana, showed one of the greatest gains—1,284 percent between 1910 and 1920. New York City, Philadelphia, and Los Angeles also attracted many blacks. Several factors produced this migration, but the most important were the brutality and hardships of southern life and the economic opportunities in the cities of the North. "Every time a lynching takes place in a community down South," said

---

vigilante   A person who takes law enforcement into his or her own hands, usually on the grounds that normal law enforcement has broken down.

T. Arnold Hill of Chicago's Urban League, "colored people will arrive in Chicago within two weeks."

Perhaps the most significant factor in the Great Migration was American industry's desperate need for workers. The labor needs of northern cities attracted hundreds of thousands of African Americans seeking better jobs and higher pay. In the North, one could earn almost as much in a day as in a week in the South. While they found better wages, they also found racial discrimination in housing and in access to many jobs. New black neighborhoods developed in some cities where African Americans were able to find housing.

Racial conflicts erupted in several cities at the northern end of the Great Migration trail, as whites attacked individual African Americans or tried to burn their neighborhoods. One of America's worst race riots swept through the industrial city of East St. Louis, Illinois, on July 2, 1917. Thousands of black laborers, most from the South, had settled there during the previous two years. Thirty-nine African Americans perished in the riot, and six thousand lost their homes. Incensed that such brutality could occur just weeks after the nation's moralistic entrance into the war, W. E. B. Du Bois charged, "No land that loves to lynch [black people] can lead the hosts of Almighty God," and the NAACP led a silent protest parade of ten thousand people through **Harlem**.

PLANNING FOR PEACE IN THE MIDST OF WAR

Some who supported the war expected that the United States would send only supplies and not soldiers, but it quickly became clear that the United States needed to mobilize troops. The army, however, was tiny compared with the armies contesting in Europe. Millions of men and thousands of women had to be inducted, trained, and transported to Europe.

Mobilizing for Battle   The navy was large and powerful after nearly three decades of shipbuilding, and preparedness measures in 1916 further strengthened it. The American and British navies' convoy technique, in which several cargo or passenger ships traveled together under the protection of destroyers, helped to cut shipping losses in half by late 1917. By spring 1918, U-boats ceased to pose a significant danger.

In April 1917, the combined strength of the U.S. Army and National Guard stood at only 372,000 men. Many men volunteered but not enough. In May, Congress passed the **Selective Service Act**, requiring men aged 21 to 30 (later extended to 18 to 45) to register with local boards to determine who would be drafted (that is, called to duty). The law exempted those who opposed war on religious grounds, but such **conscientious objectors** were sometimes badly treated.

Harlem   A section of New York City in the northern part of Manhattan; it became one of the largest black communities in the United States.

conscientious objector   Person who refuses to bear arms or participate in military service because of religious beliefs or moral principles.

About 10,000 American Indians served in the army during World War I, including John Miller (left) and Charlie Wolf, members of the Omaha tribe. Some Indians who went to war first underwent tribal ceremonies, long unpracticed, that prepared warriors for battle, thus helping preserve traditional customs. Indians' participation in the war led to increased demands for full citizenship and enfranchisement for all American Indians.

Nebraska State Historical Society

Few people demonstrated against the draft, and most seemed to accept it as efficient and fair. Twenty-four million men registered, and 2.8 million were drafted—about 72 percent of the entire army. By the end of the war, the combined army, navy, and Marine Corps counted 4.8 million members.

No women were drafted, but almost 13,000 served in the navy and marines, most in clerical capacities. For the first time, women held naval and marine rank and status. The army, however, refused to enlist women, considering it too "radical." Nearly 18,000 women served as army nurses, but without army rank, pay, or benefits. At least 5,000 civilian women also served in France, the largest number through the Red Cross, which helped to staff hospitals and rest facilities.

Nearly 400,000 African Americans served during World War I. Almost 200,000 served overseas, but most were assigned to menial tasks. Nonetheless, nearly 30,000 fought on the front lines. Emmett J. Scott, an African American and former secretary to Booker T. Washington, became special assistant to the secretary of war, responsible for African Americans. Nevertheless, black soldiers were often treated as second-class citizens. They served in segregated units in the army, were limited to food service in the navy, and were excluded altogether from the marines. More than six hundred African Americans earned commissions as officers, but the army refused to put a black officer in authority over white officers. White officers commanded most black troops.

Americans "Over There"   Shortly after the United States entered the war, a new song by George M. Cohan rocketed to national popularity:

> *Over there, over there,*
> *Send the word, send the word over there,*
> *The Yanks are coming, the Yanks are coming,*
> *And we won't come back 'til it's over over there.*

A few Yanks—troops in the **American Expeditionary Force** (AEF)—arrived in France in June 1917, commanded by General John J. Pershing, recently returned from Mexico. Most American troops, however, were still to be inducted, supplied, trained, and transported across the Atlantic.

Throughout the war, Wilson held the United States apart from the Allies, referring to the United States as an Associated Power, rather than one of the Allies. He also insisted that American troops have their own sector of the western front. This distinction stemmed from his distrust of Allied war aims and his wish to make the American contribution to victory as prominent as possible so as to maximize American influence at the peace conference.

As American troops trickled into France in mid-1917, the Allies were stretched thin. French and British offensives in spring and summer 1917 had failed, and the Italians suffered a major defeat late in the year. After disastrous losses, Russia withdrew from the war late in 1917, permitting German commanders to shift troops to the western front. Hoping to win the war before Americans could make a difference, the Germans planned a massive offensive for spring 1918.

The German thrust came in Picardy with sixty-four divisions smashing into the French and British lines and attempting to advance along the Marne River. By late May, the Germans were within 50 miles of Paris. As French officials considered evacuating the capital, all available troops, including AEF units, were rushed to the front. At Château-Thierry and at Belleau Wood, AEF troops took 8,000 casualties during a month-long battle over a single square mile of wheat fields and woods. Of 310,000 AEF troops who fought in the Marne region, 67,000 were killed or wounded. The German advance failed.

The Allies then launched a counteroffensive in July as American troops poured into France, topping a million. In September Pershing launched a successful offensive against the St. Mihiel **salient**. AEF forces then joined a larger Allied offensive in the Meuse River–Argonne Forest region, the last major assault of the war and one of the fiercest battles in American military history.

---

salient   In military usage, a portion of one's front line that projects into enemy territory. In this instance, it was a German salient that projected into the Allied front line.

On October 8, Corporal Alvin York, a skilled sharpshooter from the Tennessee mountains, was in the Argonne Forest. His unit came under fire and most were wounded or killed. York, however, coolly practiced his mountaineer sharpshooting, single-handedly killing twenty-five enemy soldiers and silencing thirty-five machine guns. He and the six surviving members of his unit took 132 prisoners. York received the Congressional Medal of Honor, the Croix de Guerre (France's highest decoration), and similar awards from other nations. York's courage and coolness were not unique among the Americans in the Meuse–Argonne campaign—Harry J. Adams, with only an empty pistol, captured 300 prisoners; Hercules Korgia, captured by the Germans, persuaded his captors to become his prisoners; and Samuel Woodfill single-handedly took out five machine guns.

By late October, German military leaders were urging an armistice. Fighting ended at 11:00 A.M., November 11, 1918. By then, nearly 9 million combatants had died: Germany lost 1.8 million, Russia 1.7 million, France 1.4 million, Austria-Hungary 1.1 million, the British Empire 1.1 million. Of the 4.5 million who served in the French army, 31 percent were killed and 44 percent were wounded. American losses were small in comparison—365,000 **casualties**, including 126,000 deaths. Some 800,000 civilians from the Central Powers died of famine resulting from the British blockade. Millions of other civilians, worldwide, died from war-related causes, including starvation and disease. A global **influenza** epidemic in 1918 and 1919 killed 20–40 million people or perhaps more, more than died in the war, including 500,000 Americans.

Some white Americans, including some military officers, worried that experiences in France might cause African American soldiers to resist segregation at home. In August 1918, AEF headquarters secretly requested that the French not prominently commend black units. The French, however, awarded the **Croix de Guerre** to several all-black units that had distinguished themselves in combat and presented awards to individual soldiers for acts of bravery and heroism. When the Allies staged a grand victory parade down Paris's Champs Élysées, the British and French contingents included all races and ethnicities, but American commanders directed that no African American troops take part.

Bolshevism, the Secret Treaties, and the Fourteen Points

In March 1917, before the United States entered the war, war-weary and hungry Russians deposed their **tsar** and created a provisional government. In November, a group of radical socialists, the **Bolsheviks**, seized power. Soon renamed Communists, the Bolsheviks condemned capitalism and imperialism and sought to destroy them. **Vladimir Lenin**,

---

casualty A member of the military lost through death, wounds, injury, sickness, or capture.

influenza Contagious viral infection characterized by fever, chills, congestion, and muscular pain, nicknamed "the flu"; an unusually deadly strain of the H1N1 subtype, usually called "Spanish flu," swept across the world in 1918 and 1919.

Croix de Guerre French military decoration for bravery in combat; in English, "the Cross of War."

tsar The monarch of the Russian Empire; also spelled *czar*.

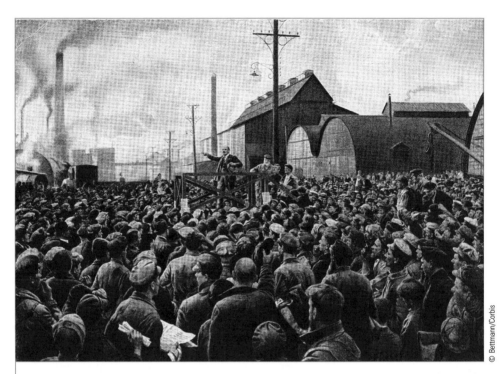

This painting by Isaac I. Brodsky depicts Vladimir Lenin addressing workers at the Putilov Works in Petrograd (now St. Petersburg) in 1917. Workers from this factory gave crucial support to the Russian revolutions of 1917. The Communists saw art as a major tool for building public support, and Brodsky became a leader in the rise of Socialist Realism after Joseph Stalin came to power in the late 1920s.

the Bolshevik leader, initiated peace negotiations with the Germans. The **Treaty of Brest-Litovsk**, in March 1918, was harsh and humiliating, requiring Russia to surrender vast territories—Finland, its Baltic provinces, parts of Poland and Ukraine—a third of its population, half of its industries, its most fertile agricultural land, and a quarter of its territory in Europe.

The Bolsheviks condemned the war as a scramble for imperial spoils, and in December 1917, before their treaty with Germany, they published the secret treaties by which the European Allies had agreed to divide colonies and territories of the defeated Central Powers among themselves. These exposés strengthened Wilson's intent to keep American war aims separate and to impose his war objectives on the Allies.

On January 8, 1918, Wilson spoke to Congress. He denounced both the secret treaties and the harsh terms the Germans were demanding from Russia. American war goals, he proclaimed, derived from "the principle of justice to all peoples and nationalities, and their right to live on equal terms of liberty and safety with one another, whether they be strong or weak." Seeking to seize the initiative, he presented fourteen objectives, soon called the **Fourteen Points**. Points one through five provided a general context for lasting peace:

no secret treaties, freedom of the seas, reduction of barriers to trade, reduction of armaments, and adjustment of colonial claims based partly on the interests of colonial peoples. Point six called for other nations to withdraw from Russian territory and to welcome Russia "into the society of free nations." Points seven through thirteen addressed particular situations: return of territories France had lost to Germany in 1871 and self-determination in Central Europe and the Middle East. The fourteenth point called for "a general association of nations" that could afford "mutual guarantees of political independence and territorial integrity to great and small states alike."

Showing little enthusiasm, the Allies accepted Wilson's Fourteen Points as starting points for discussion. When the Germans asked for an end to the fighting, however, they made clear that their request was based on the Fourteen Points.

THE PEACE CONFERENCE AND THE TREATY

With the war over, Wilson hoped that the peace process would not sow the seeds of future wars. He hoped, too, to create an international organization to keep the peace. Most of the Allies, however, were more interested in grabbing territory and punishing Germany.

The World in 1919   In December 1918, Wilson sailed for France—the first American president to go to Europe while in office and the first president to negotiate directly with other world leaders. Wilson brought along reports from some 150 experts on European history, culture, **ethnology**, and geography who had been working since the fall of 1917 on plans for the postwar era. In France, Italy, and Britain, huge welcoming crowds cheered the great "peacemaker from America."

Delegates to the peace conference assembled amid the collapse of ancient empires and the birth of new republics. The Austro-Hungarian Empire had crumbled, producing the new nations of Poland and Czechoslovakia and the republics of Austria and Hungary. The German monarch, Kaiser Wilhelm, had **abdicated**, and a republic was forming. In January 1919, communists tried unsuccessfully to seize power in Berlin. Throughout the ruins of the Russian Empire, ethnic groups were proclaiming independent republics (most eventually incorporated into the Soviet Union, often by the Bolsheviks' **Red Army**). The Ottoman Empire was collapsing, too, as Arabs, with aid from Britain and France, overthrew Turkish rule in many areas.

Throughout Europe and the Middle East, national **self-determination** and sometimes government by the consent of the governed—part of Wilson's design for the postwar world—seemed to be lurching into reality. Nor were the British

---

ethnology The study of ethno-cultural groups.

abdicate To relinquish a high office; usually said only of monarchs.

self-determination The freedom of a given people to determine their own political status.

and French colonial empires immune, for both faced growing independence movements among their many possessions.

In Russia, civil war raged between the Bolsheviks and their opponents. When the Bolsheviks left the world war, the Allies pushed Wilson to join them in intervening in Russia, ostensibly to protect war supplies from falling into German hands. In mid-1918, Wilson sent American troops as part of Allied expeditions to northern Russia and eastern Siberia. In Siberia, his intent was primarily to head off a Japanese grab of Russian territory. Lenin had initially accepted the intervention in northern Russia as necessary, but the purpose of the Allied intervention soon changed to support for the foes of the Bolsheviks. By late 1918, Wilson was expressing concern over what he called "mass terrorism" directed by the Bolsheviks toward "peaceable Russian citizens." Before the last American troops withdrew from northern Russia in May 1919 and from eastern Siberia in early 1920, they had engaged in conflict with units of the Red Army.

Wilson at Versailles	The peace conference opened on January 18, 1919, just outside Paris, at the glittering Palace of Versailles, once home to French kings. Representatives attended from all

nations that had declared war against the Central Powers, but major decisions were made by the Big Four: Wilson, David Lloyd George of Britain, Georges Clemenceau of France, and Vittorio Orlando of Italy. Germany was excluded. Terms of peace were to be imposed, not negotiated. Russia, too, was absent, on the grounds that it had withdrawn from the war and made a separate peace with Germany. Although Russia was barred from Versailles, anxiety about Bolshevism hung over the proceedings, especially affecting decisions about central and eastern Europe.

Wilson quickly realized that European leaders were more interested in their own national interests than in his Fourteen Points. Clemenceau, nicknamed "the Tiger," remembered Germany's humiliating defeat of France in 1871 and hoped to disable Germany so thoroughly that it could never again threaten his nation. Lloyd George agreed with many of Wilson's goals but felt he carried orders from British voters to exact heavy **reparations** from Germany. Orlando insisted on the territorial gains promised when Italy joined the Allies in 1915. Various Allies were also expecting to gain territories promised in the secret treaties. In addition, the European Allies feared the spread of Bolshevism and intended to create buffers to keep it at bay.

Facing the insistent and acquisitive Allies, Wilson had to compromise. He did secure a **League of Nations**, a world organization created to promote peace and international cooperation. Instead of "peace without victory," however, the **Treaty of Versailles** imposed harsh victors' terms, requiring Germany to accept the blame for starting the war, pay reparations to the Allies (the exact amount to be determined later), and surrender all its colonies along with Alsace-Lorraine (which Germany had taken from France in 1871) and other European territories. The

---

reparations Payments as compensation for damages.

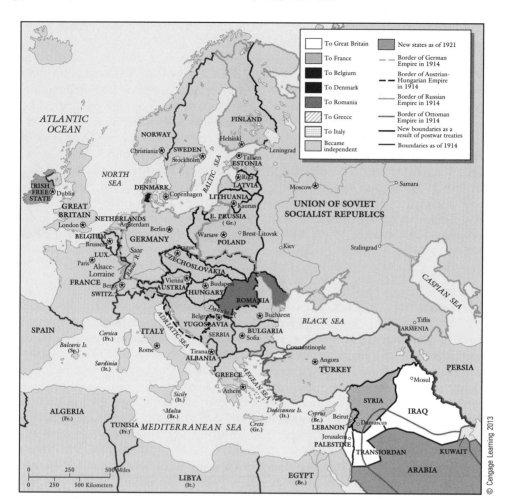

☐ To Great Britain	▨ New states as of 1921
▨ To France	– – Border of German Empire in 1914
■ To Belgium	– ▪ – Border of Austrian-Hungarian Empire in 1914
■ To Denmark	
▨ To Romania	— Border of Russian Empire in 1914
▨ To Greece	— Border of Ottoman Empire in 1914
▨ To Italy	— New boundaries as a result of postwar treaties
▨ Became independent	— Boundaries as of 1914

MAP 20.2 Europe and the Near East after the First World War

The First World War and the Treaty of Versailles changed the geography of Europe and the Near East. Nine nations in Europe, stretching from Yugoslavia in the south to Finland in the north, were created (or re-formed) out of the defeated Austro-Hungarian and Ottoman Empires. In the Near East, meanwhile, Syria, Lebanon, Palestine, Transjordan, and Iraq were carved out of the Ottoman Empire, placed under British or French control, and promised eventual independence.

treaty deprived Germany of its navy and merchant marine and limited its army to 100,000 men. German representatives signed on June 28, 1919.

Wilson reluctantly agreed to the massive reparations but insisted that colonies taken from Germany and territories taken from the Ottoman Empire should not go permanently to the Allies. Called **mandates**, they were to be

mandate A territory that the League of Nations authorized a member nation to administer and move toward independence.

Redrawing the Map of the Middle East

Several current nations in the Middle East arose from mandates created through the League of Nations. During the war, Britain assisted Arabs to revolt against the Ottoman Empire and encouraged their desires for self-determination. However, Britain and France secretly agreed to divide much of the Ottoman Empire between them. At stake, the British knew, was oil.

Britain and France largely drew the boundaries of Iraq, Syria, Lebanon, Palestine, and Transjordan (now Jordan), but not based on Wilson's goal of self-determination. Britain received the League mandate for Iraq, which Britain created by combining parts of the Ottoman Empire that included known oilfields.

In 1932, Iraq achieved independence under a king chosen by the British, who continued to wield influence. The new nation experienced conflict between Sunni and Shia, and Kurds in the north resisted their inclusion in Iraq. The government was unstable from 1920 until Saddam Hussein consolidated his power in the 1970s.

- How do decisions made at Versailles influence world affairs today?

- Do more research on Iraq from 1920 onward. In 2003, would you have assumed that removing Saddam Hussein would produce a stable, democratic government? Why or why not?

administered by one of the Allies on behalf of the League of Nations and were to move toward independence. In nearly every case, however, the mandate went to the nation slated to receive the territory under the secret treaties. Wilson blocked Italy's most extreme territorial demands but gave in on others. The peace conference recognized new republics in Central Europe, thereby creating a so-called quarantine zone between Russian Bolshevism and Western Europe. The treaty ignored those people—from Ireland to Vietnam—seeking the right of self-determination in colonies held by one of the victorious Allies. Japan failed to secure a statement supporting racial equality.

Though Wilson compromised on most of his Fourteen Points, every compromise intensified his commitment to the League of Nations. The League, he hoped, would not only resolve future controversies without war but also solve problems created by the compromises. Even so, Wilson had to threaten a separate peace with Germany before the Allies agreed to incorporate the **League Covenant**, the constitution of the League of Nations, into the treaty. Wilson was especially committed to Article 10 of the League Covenant—he called it the League's "heart." It specified that League members agreed to protect one another's independence and territory against external attacks and take joint action against aggressors.

The Senate and the Treaty

While Wilson was in Paris, opposition to his plans was brewing at home. The Senate, controlled by Republicans since the 1918 elections, had to approve any treaty.

Presented with the treaty, the Senate split into three groups. **Henry Cabot Lodge**, chairman of the Senate Foreign Relations Committee, led the largest faction, called reservationists after the reservations, or amendments, to the treaty that Lodge developed. Article 10 of the League Covenant especially bothered Lodge, for he feared it might commit American troops to war without congressional approval. A small group called irreconcilables, mostly Republicans, opposed any American involvement in European affairs. A third Senate group, nearly all Democrats, supported the president and his treaty.

Wilson decided to appeal directly to the American people. In September 1919, he undertook an arduous speaking tour—9,500 miles with speeches in twenty-nine cities. The effort proved too demanding for his fragile health. Soon after, he suffered a serious stroke. Half-paralyzed and weak, Wilson could fulfill few duties. His wife, Edith Bolling Wilson, exercised what she later called a "stewardship," strictly limiting her ailing husband's contact with the outside world.

Lodge proposed that the Senate accept the treaty with reservations. Some of his amendments were minor, but others would have permitted Congress to block action under Article 10. Wilson refused any compromise. On November 19, 1919, the Senate defeated the treaty with the Lodge reservations by votes of 39 to 55 and 41 to 50, with the irreconcilables joining the president's supporters in opposition. Then the Senate defeated the original version of the treaty by 38 to 53, with the irreconcilables joining the reservationists in voting no.

The treaty came to a vote again in March 1920. By then, some treaty supporters had concluded that the League could never be approved without Lodge's reservations, so they joined the reservationists to produce a vote of 49 in favor to 35 opposed—still short of the two-thirds majority required. Enough Wilson loyalists—following their stubborn leader's order not to compromise—joined the irreconcilables to defeat the treaty once again. The United States did not join the League of Nations.

Legacies of the Great War

Wilson had appealed to progressives' optimism and confidence in claiming that the United States was going to make the world "safe for democracy." One of his supporters even spoke of the "war to end war." Just as progressives defined their domestic policies in terms of progress, democracy, and social justice, so Wilson tried to invest his foreign policy with enlightened values. In doing so, however, he fostered unrealistic expectations that world politics might be transformed overnight.

Many Americans became disillusioned by the Allies' cynical opportunism. The war to make the world "safe for democracy" turned out to be a chance for Italy to annex Austrian territory and for Japan to seize German concessions in China. And the "war to end war" spun off several wars in its wake: Romania invaded Hungary in 1919, Poland invaded Russia in 1920, the Russian civil war continued until late 1920, and Greece and Turkey battled until 1923.

The peace conference left unresolved many problems. Wilson's promotion of self-government and self-determination encouraged aspirations for independence throughout the Allies' colonies and among the new League mandates. Some of the new nations of Central Europe, supposedly based on ethnic self-determination, actually included different and sometimes antagonistic ethnic groups. Above all, the war and the treaty contributed to economic and political instability in much of Europe, making it a breeding ground for totalitarian and nationalistic movements that eventually generated another world war.

AMERICA IN THE AFTERMATH OF WAR, NOVEMBER 1918–NOVEMBER 1920

Almost as soon as French church bells pealed for the armistice, the United States began to demobilize. By November 1919, nearly 4 million men and women were out of uniform. Industrial demobilization occurred even more quickly, as officials canceled war contracts. The year 1919 saw both the return of American troops from Europe and also raging inflation, massive strikes, bloody race riots, widespread fear of radical **subversion**, violations of civil liberties—and two new constitutional amendments that embodied important elements of progressivism, prohibition, and woman suffrage.

"HCL" and Strikes

Inflation—described in newspapers as "HCL" for "High Cost of Living"—was the most pressing single problem Americans faced after the war. Between 1913 and 1919, prices almost doubled. When the armistice ended unions' no-strike pledge, unions made wage demands to match the soaring cost of living. In 1919, however, employers were ready for a fight.

Many companies wanted to return labor relations to prewar patterns. They blamed wage increases for inflation, and some linked unions to "dangerous foreign ideas" from Bolshevik Russia. In February 1919, Seattle's Central Labor Council called out the city's unions in a five-day general strike to support shipyard workers. Seattle's mayor branded the strike a Bolshevik plot. Boston's police struck in September 1919 after the police commissioner fired nineteen policemen for joining a union. The governor of Massachusetts, Calvin Coolidge, called out the national guard to maintain order and break the union. "There is no right to strike against the public safety by anybody, anywhere, anytime," he proclaimed. By mid-1919, many unionists concluded that conservative politicians were joining business leaders to block union organizing and roll back wartime gains.

The largest and most dramatic strike came against United States Steel. Few steelworkers were represented by unions after the 1892 Homestead strike. Steel

subversion Efforts to undermine or overthrow an established government.

companies often hired recent immigrants, keeping steelworkers divided by language. Most steelworkers put in twelve-hour workdays. Wages had not increased as fast as inflation—or as fast as company profits. In 1919 the AFL launched an ambitious unionization drive in the steel industry, and many steelworkers responded eagerly.

Steel industry leaders refused to deal with the new organization. The workers went on strike in late September, demanding union recognition, collective bargaining, the eight-hour workday, and higher wages. The company blamed the strike on radicals and mobilized public opinion against the strikers. Company guards protected strikebreakers, and U.S. military forces moved into Gary, Indiana, to help round up "the Red element." By January 1920, after eighteen workers had been killed and hundreds beaten, the strike was over and the unions were ousted.

Red Scare   The steel industry's charges of Bolshevism to discredit strikers came as many government and corporate leaders were declaiming against the dangers of Bolshevism at home and abroad. A few anarchist bombers contributed to stirring up a widespread frenzy aimed at rooting out subversive radicals. In late April 1919, thirty-four bombs addressed to prominent Americans—including J. P. Morgan, John D. Rockefeller, and Supreme Court Justice Oliver Wendell Holmes—were discovered in various post offices after the explosion of two others addressed to a senator and Seattle's mayor. In June, bombs in several cities damaged buildings and killed two people. Probably the work of a few anarchists, the bombs fueled fears of a nationwide conspiracy against the government.

Attorney General A. Mitchell Palmer organized an anti-Red campaign, hoping that success might bring him the 1920 presidential nomination. "Like a prairie fire," Palmer claimed, "the blaze of revolution was sweeping over every American institution." He appointed **J. Edgar Hoover**, a young lawyer, to head an antiradical unit in the Justice Department's Bureau of Investigation, the predecessor of the Federal Bureau of Investigation. In November 1919, Palmer launched the first of what were soon called the **Palmer raids** to arrest suspected radicals. Authorities rounded up some five thousand people by January 1920. Although officials found few firearms and no explosives, the raids led to the **deportation** of several hundred aliens with some tie to radicalism. The rest were released.

State legislatures produced their own antiradical measures, including criminal syndicalism laws—measures criminalizing the advocacy of Bolshevik, IWW, or anarchist ideologies. In January 1920, the assembly of the New York state legislature expelled five members elected as Socialists, solely because they were Socialists.

---

deportation Expulsion of an undesirable alien from a country.

After a wide range of respected public figures denounced the legislature's action as undemocratic, public opinion regarding the **Red Scare** began to shift. With the approach of May 1, a day of celebration for radicals, Palmer issued dramatic warnings about a general strike and bombings. When nothing happened, many concluded that the radical threat might have been overstated.

As the Red Scare sputtered to an end, in May 1920, police in Massachusetts arrested **Nicola Sacco** and **Bartolomeo Vanzetti**, Italian-born anarchists, and charged them with robbery and murder. Despite inconclusive evidence and the men's protestations of innocence, a jury found them guilty, and they were sentenced to death. Many argued that they had been convicted because of their political beliefs and Italian origins, and that they had not received a fair trial because nativism and antiradicalism had infected the judge and jury. Over loud protests at home and abroad, both men were executed in 1927. Historians continue to debate the evidence, many arguing that Sacco was probably guilty and Vanzetti innocent, and others insisting both were innocent and that the state police concealed evidence.

Race Riots and Lynchings

The racial tensions of the war years continued into the postwar period. Black soldiers encountered more acceptance and less discrimination in Europe than they had ever known at home. In May 1919, the NAACP journal *Crisis* expressed what the more militant returning soldiers felt:

> We return. We return from fighting. We return fighting. Make way for Democracy! We saved it in France, and by the Great Jehovah, we will save it in the U.S.A., or know the reason why.

Some whites, however, greeted returning black troops with furious violence intended to restore prewar race relations. Southern mobs lynched ten black soldiers, some still in uniform. In all, rioters lynched more than seventy blacks in the first year after the war and burned eleven victims alive.

Rioting also struck outside the South. In July 1919, violence reached the nation's capital, where white mobs, including many soldiers and sailors, attacked blacks throughout the city for three days, killing several. The city's African Americans organized their own defense, sometimes arming themselves. In Chicago in late July, war raged between white and black mobs for nearly two weeks, despite efforts by the national guard. The rioting caused thirty-eight deaths (fifteen white, twenty-three black). A thousand families—nearly all black—were burned out of their homes. In Omaha in September, a mob tried to hang the mayor when he bravely stood between them and a black prisoner accused of rape. Police saved the mayor but not the prisoner.

By the end of 1919, race riots had flared in more than two dozen places. The year saw not only rampant lynchings but also the appearance of a new Ku Klux Klan (discussed in the next chapter). Despite violence and coercion directed at African Americans, some things had changed. As W. E. B. Du Bois observed, black veterans "would never be the same again. You cannot ask them to go back to what they were before. They cannot, for they are not the same men."

**Amending
the Constitution:
Prohibition
and Woman
Suffrage**

At the end of the war, two of the great campaigns of the Progressive Era finally realized their goals. Both had roots in the nineteenth century, both attracted numerous supporters during the Progressive Era, and both received a boost by the war. Prohibition was adopted as the **Eighteenth Amendment** to the Constitution, and woman suffrage as the Nineteenth Amendment.

Pushed by the Anti-Saloon League, Congress passed a temporary prohibition measure in 1917. A more important victory came when Congress adopted and sent to the states the Eighteenth Amendment, prohibiting the manufacture, sale, or transportation of alcoholic beverages. Intense and single-minded lobbying persuaded three-fourths of the state legislatures to ratify the amendment in 1919. It took effect in January 1920.

The cause of woman suffrage also received a boost from the war, as suffrage advocates added women's contributions to the war effort to their previous arguments (discussed in Chapters 17–19). In June 1919, by a narrow margin, Congress proposed the **Nineteenth Amendment**, to enfranchise women, and sent it to the states for ratification. After a grueling, state-by-state battle, ratification came in August 1920. Though many women by then already exercised the franchise, especially in western states, ratification meant that the electorate for the 1920 elections was significantly expanded.

**The Election
of 1920**

Republicans confidently expected to regain the White House in 1920. The Democrats had lost their congressional majorities in the 1918 elections, and postwar misgivings and disillusionment often focused on Wilson. One reporter described the stricken president as the "sacrificial whipping boy for the present bitterness."

Any competent Republican nominee was practically guaranteed election. Several candidates attracted significant support, notably former army chief of staff General Leonard Wood, Illinois governor Frank Lowden, and California senator Hiram Johnson. However, no candidate counted a majority in the convention. Months earlier, Harry Daugherty, campaign manager for Ohio senator Warren G. Harding, had foreseen a deadlock and had predicted that it would be broken by a compromise candidate, chosen at about "eleven minutes after two o'clock" in the morning, when "fifteen or twenty men, bleary-eyed and perspiring profusely from the heat" chose a compromise candidate. And so it was. A small group of party leaders met late at night in a smoke-filled hotel room and picked Harding. Even some of his supporters were unenthusiastic—one called him "the best of the second-raters." For vice president, the Republicans nominated Calvin Coolidge, the governor who had broken the Boston police strike.

The Democrats also suffered severe divisions. After forty-four ballots, they chose James Cox, governor of Ohio, as their presidential candidate. For vice president, they nominated Franklin D. Roosevelt, Wilson's assistant secretary of the navy and a remote cousin of Theodore Roosevelt.

Usually described as good-natured and likable—and sometimes as bumbling—Harding had published a small-town newspaper in Ohio until his wife, Florence, and some of his friends pushed him into politics. Eventually winning election to the Senate, unhappy with his marriage, Harding apparently took pleasure from a series of mistresses. The press knew of Harding's liaisons but never reported them.

During the campaign, an uproar arose over a claim that Harding's ancestry included African Americans. The story spread rapidly, and a reporter asked Harding, "Do you have any Negro blood?" Harding replied mildly, "How do I know, Jim? One of my ancestors may have jumped the fence." The allegation, and Harding's response to it, apparently did not hurt his cause. Most of Harding's campaign reflected his promise to "return to normalcy."

After the stress of the war and the postwar years, voters enthusiastically endorsed returning to "normalcy." Harding took thirty-seven of the forty-eight states and 60 percent of the popular vote—the largest popular majority up to that time. Wilson had hoped for a "solemn referendum" on the League of Nations, but the election proved more a reaction against the war launched with lofty ideals that turned sour at Versailles, the high cost of living, and the strikes and riots of 1919. Americans, it seemed, had had enough of idealism and sacrifice for a while.

STUDY TOOLS

SUMMARY

Woodrow Wilson took office expecting to focus on domestic policy, not world affairs. He fulfilled some Democratic Party commitments to anti-imperialism but intervened extensively in the Caribbean. He also intervened in Mexico but failed to accomplish all his objectives there.

When war broke out in Europe in 1914, Wilson declared the United States to be neutral, and most Americans agreed. German submarine warfare and British restrictions on commerce, however, threatened traditional definitions of neutrality. Wilson secured a German pledge to refrain from unrestricted submarine warfare. He was reelected in 1916 on the argument that "he kept us out of war." Shortly after he won reelection, the Germans violated their pledge, and in April 1917 Wilson asked for war against Germany.

The war changed most aspects of America's economic and social life. The federal government developed a high degree of centralized economic planning, and tried to mold public opinion and restrict dissent. When the federal government backed collective bargaining, unions registered important gains. In response to labor shortages, more women and African Americans entered the industrial work force, and many African Americans moved to northern and midwestern industrial cities.

Germany launched an offensive in 1918, hoping to achieve victory before Americans could make a difference. However, the AEF helped to break the German advance, and the Germans surrendered. In his Fourteen Points, Wilson expressed his goals for peace.

Facing opposition from the Allies, Wilson compromised at the Versailles peace conference but hoped that the League of Nations would maintain the peace. Fearing obligations that League membership might place on the United States, enough senators opposed the treaty to defeat it. Thus the United States did not become a member of the League.

The end of the war brought disillusionment and high prices, many strikes, a Red Scare, and race riots and lynchings. In 1920 the nation returned to its previous Republican majority when it elected Warren G. Harding, a mediocre conservative, to the White House.

CHRONOLOGY

THE UNITED STATES AND WORLD AFFAIRS, 1913–1920

1912	Woodrow Wilson elected president
1913	Victoriano Huerta takes power in Mexico; Wilson denies recognition
1914	U.S. Navy occupies Veracruz War in Europe, United States declares neutrality Stalemate on the western front
1915	German U-boat sinks the *Lusitania* United States occupies Haiti
1915–1920	Great Migration
1916	U.S. troops pursue Pancho Villa into Mexico Wilson reelected
1917	Wilson calls for "peace without victory" Germany resumes submarine warfare Overthrow of tsar of Russia United States declares war on Germany Race riot in East St. Louis Bolsheviks seize power in Russia, publish secret treaties, withdraw Russia from the war Railroads placed under federal control
1918	Wilson presents Fourteen Points to Congress Germans launch offensive but fail; Allies launch successful counteroffensive U.S. troops sent to northern Russia and Siberia Armistice in Europe
1918–1919	Worldwide influenza epidemic
1919	Signing of Treaty of Versailles Eighteenth Amendment (prohibition) approved Race riots Major strikes
1919–1920	Red Scare, Palmer raids
1920	Senate defeats Versailles for second and final time Nineteenth Amendment (woman suffrage) approved Warren G. Harding elected president

Focus Questions

If you have mastered this chapter, you should be able to answer these questions and explain the terms that follow the questions.

1. In what new directions did Wilson steer U.S. foreign policy before the coming of war in Europe?
2. Why did Wilson proclaim American neutrality? How did Americans respond?
3. What made neutrality difficult?
4. How did Wilson justify going to war?
5. How successful was the federal government in mobilizing the economy and society to support the war?
6. How did the war affect Americans, especially women, African Americans, and opponents of war?
7. What role did American ships and troops play in the war?
8. How and why did Wilson keep America's participation in the war separate from the Allies?
9. How successful was Wilson at the peace conference?
10. What caused the defeat of the treaty?
11. How did Americans react to the outcome of the war and the events of 1919?
12. How did the events of 1917–1920 affect the 1920 presidential election?

Key Terms

Porfirio Díaz (*p.* 614)

Victoriano Huerta (*p.* 615)

Venustiano Carranza (*p.* 615)

Veracruz (*p.* 615)

Francisco "Pancho" Villa (*p.* 615)

Balkan Peninsula (*p.* 616)

Central Powers (*p.* 616)

Allies (*p.* 616)

western front (*p.* 617)

Lusitania (*p.* 619)

Sussex pledge (*p.* 620)

Arthur Zimmermann (*p.* 621)

War Industries Board (*p.* 622)

National War Labor Board (*p.* 623)

Herbert Hoover (*p.* 623)

Liberty Loan (*p.* 623)

Creel Committee (*p.* 624)

Espionage Act (*p.* 626)

Sedition Act (*p.* 626)

Great Migration (*p.* 626)

Selective Service Act (*p.* 627)

American Expeditionary Force (*p.* 629)

Bolsheviks (*p.* 630)

Vladimir Lenin (*p.* 630)

Treaty of Brest-Litovsk (*p.* 631)

Fourteen Points (*p.* 631)

Red Army (*p.* 632)

League of Nations (*p.* 633)

Treaty of Versailles (*p.* 633)

League Covenant (*p.* 635)

21

PROSPERITY DECADE, 1920–1928

CHAPTER OUTLINE

• The Bullish Decade • The "Roaring Twenties" • Traditional America Roars Back • New Social Patterns in the 1920s • The Politics of Prosperity • The Diplomacy of Prosperity • Study Tools

---

THE BULLISH DECADE

By 1920, the American economy had been thoroughly industrialized, with most industry controlled by large corporations run by professional managers. During the 1920s, the rise and growth of the automobile industry dramatized the new prominence of industries producing **consumer goods**. This significant change in direction carried implications for advertising, banking, and even the stock market.

The Economics of Prosperity With the end of the war in 1918, the government cancelled most orders for war supplies, from ships to uniforms. Large numbers of recently discharged military and naval personnel swelled the ranks of job seekers. However, no immediate economic collapse ensued. Given wartime shortages and overtime pay, many Americans had been earning more than they could spend. At the end of the war, their spending helped to delay the postwar slump until 1920 and 1921. The gross national product (GNP) dropped by only 4.3 percent between 1919 and 1920, then fell by 8.6 percent between 1920 and 1921. During the war, unemployment affected only about 1 percent of the work force. The jobless rate increased to 5 percent in 1920 and 12 percent in 1921. Some employers also cut hours and wages. Figure 21.1 presents earnings for three groups of Americans and indicates the impact of recession in the early 1920s. In the end, reduced earnings, unemployment, and declining demand halted the rampaging inflation of 1918 and 1919.

---

consumer goods Products such as clothing, food, automobiles, and radios, intended for purchase and use by individuals or households, as opposed to products such as steel beams, locomotives, and electrical generators.

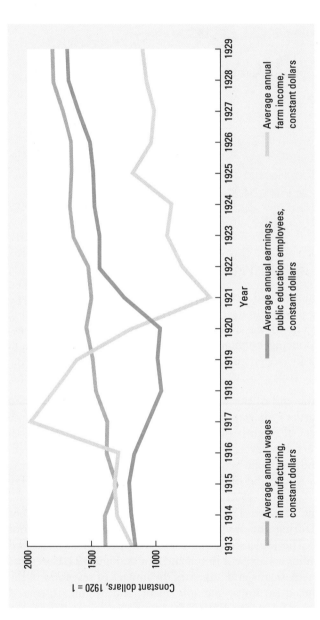

FIGURE 21.1 Patterns of Annual Income for Three Groups of Americans, 1913–1929

This graph depicts the patterns of annual income for three different groups of Americans. Income has been converted to constant dollars; that is, the dollar amounts are adjusted for changes in the purchasing power of the dollar. The year 1920 is used as the base year for calculating the value of the dollar. Wages for manufacturing workers rose during the war years, leveled during the recession of the early 1920s, then rose again. For public education employees—mostly teachers—real earnings fell dramatically with the inflation of the war years and the postwar recession, then rose to parallel those of manufacturing workers. Farmers had a boom in income during the war, then saw their real earnings plunge at the end of the war, with only a modest recovery after the recession of the early 1920s.

Source: U.S. Department of Commerce, Bureau of Census, *Historical Statistics of the United States, Colonial Times to 1970*, Bicentennial Edition, 2 vols. (Washington, D.C.: Government Printing Office, 1975), I: 167, 170, 483.

The economy quickly rebounded. Gross domestic product increased by 15 percent between 1921 and 1922, a bigger jump than during the booming war years. Unemployment remained at 2–5 percent from 1923 through 1929, and prices for most manufactured goods remained relatively stable. Thus many Americans seemed slightly better off by 1929 than in 1920.

Targeting Consumers   By the 1920s, many business leaders understood that persuading Americans to buy their products was crucial to keeping the economy healthy. In 1921 General Foods Company invented Betty Crocker to give its baking products a womanly, domestic image. In 1924 General Mills first advertised Wheaties as the "Breakfast of Champions," tying breakfast cereal to star athletes. Americans responded by buying those products and many others, all with their own creative pitches. "We grew up founding our dreams on the infinite promises of American advertising," Zelda Sayre Fitzgerald later wrote.

The marketing of Listerine provided a model for others. Listerine had been devised as a general antiseptic, but in 1921 Gerard Lambert developed a more persuasive—and profitable—approach when he plucked the obscure term *halitosis* (bad breath) from a medical journal. Through aggressive advertising, he fostered anxieties about the effect of halitosis on popularity and made millions by selling Listerine to combat the condition. Until then, few Americans had been concerned about freshening their breath. Now other entrepreneurs rushed to sell products by defining needs that consumers had not previously identified.

Changes in fashion encouraged increased consumption. Short hairstyles for women led to development of hair salons and stimulated sales of the recently invented **bobby pin**. Cigarette advertisers began to target women, as when the American Tobacco Company urged women to "Reach for a Lucky instead of a sweet" to attain a fashionably slim figure. Disposable products promoted regular, recurring consumer buying. Technological advances in the processing of wood cellulose fiber led in 1921 to the marketing of Kotex, the first manufactured disposable sanitary napkin, and in 1924 to the first disposable handkerchiefs, later known as Kleenex tissues.

Technological advances also contributed to the growth of consumer-oriented manufacturing. In 1920 about one-third of all residences had electricity. By the end of the decade, electrical power had reached nearly all urban homes but fewer than 10 percent of farm homes. As the number of residences with electricity increased, advertisers stressed that housewives could save time and labor by using electric washing machines, irons, vacuum cleaners, and toasters. Between 1919 and 1929, consumer expenditures for household appliances grew by more than 120 percent.

Increased consumption encouraged changes in spending habits. Before the war, most families saved their money until they could pay cash for what they needed. In the 1920s many retailers encouraged buyers to "Buy now, pay

bobby pin   Small metal hair clip with ends pressed tightly together, designed for holding short or "bobbed" hair in place.

later." Many consumers did so, taking home a new radio and worrying about paying for it tomorrow. By the late 1920s, about 15 percent of all retail purchases were made through the **installment plan**, especially furniture, phonographs, washing machines, and refrigerators. Charge accounts in department stores also became popular, and **finance companies** (which made loans) grew rapidly.

The Automobile: Driving the Economy   The automobile epitomized the consumer-oriented economy of the 1920s. Early automobiles were luxuries, but **Henry Ford** developed a mass-production system that drove down production costs.

Ford, a former mechanic, built his success on the **Model T**, introduced in 1908. As early as 1918, the Model T dominated the market. By 1927, Ford had produced more than 15 million of them. "Get the prices down to the buying power," Ford ordered, and his dictatorial management style combined with technological advances and high worker productivity to bring the price of a new Model T as low as $290 by 1927 (equivalent to $3,400 today). It was a dream come true for many Americans. Families came to love their ungraceful but reliable "Tin Lizzies," so named because of their lightweight metal bodies. The Model T sacrificed style and comfort for durability, ease of maintenance, and the ability to handle almost any road. It made Henry Ford a folk hero—a wealthy one. By 1925, Ford Motor Company showed a daily profit of some $25,000.

Ford's company provides an example of efforts by American entrepreneurs to reduce labor costs by improving efficiency. In the process, work on Ford's assembly line became a thoroughly dehumanizing experience. Ford workers were prohibited from talking, sitting, smoking, singing, or even whistling while working. As one critic put it, workers were to "put nut 14 on bolt 132, repeating, repeating, repeating until their hands shook and their legs quivered."

Still, Ford paid his workers well, and they could increase their pay by completing Americanization classes. Ford workers earned enough to buy their own Model T. Ford's high wages pushed other automakers to increase pay for their workers, to keep them from defecting to Ford. Auto workers thus came to enjoy some of the consumer buying previously restricted to middle- and upper-income groups.

Competition helped to keep auto prices low. Other automobile companies challenged Ford's predominance, notably General Motors (GM), founded by William Durant in 1908, and Chrysler, created by Walter Chrysler in 1925. GM and Chrysler adopted many of Ford's production techniques, but their cars also offered more comfort and style than the Model T. Ford ended production of the Model T in 1927, when Chevrolet passed Ford in sales. The next year, Ford

---

installment plan   A way of paying for a purchase over time, so that the price of the product is spread over several payments, typically due monthly.

finance company   Business that makes loans to clients based on some form of collateral, such as a new car, thus allowing a form of installment buying when sellers do not extend credit.

introduced the Model A, which incorporated some features promoted by his competitors.

Advertising made the automobile the symbol not only of the ability of Americans to acquire material goods but also of technology, progress, and the freedom of the open road. American consumers were receptive. By the late 1920s, about 80 percent of the world's registered vehicles were in the United States. By then, America's roadways sported nearly one automobile for every five people.

The automobile industry often led the way in devising new sales techniques. By 1927 two-thirds of all American automobiles were sold on credit. GM began introducing new models every year, encouraging owners to keep up with changes in design, color, and optional features. Small automakers soon found they could not compete with Chrysler, Ford, and GM—the Big Three. By 1929, the Big Three were making 83 percent of all cars manufactured in the country. The industry had become an oligopoly.

Changes in Banking and Business

Just as Henry Ford brought automobiles within reach of most Americans, so **A. P. Giannini** did something similar for banking. The son of Italian immigrants, Giannini founded the Bank of Italy in 1904 as a bank for shopkeepers and workers in San Francisco's Italian neighborhood. Until then, most banks had only one location, in the center of a city, and limited their services to businesses and substantial citizens. Giannini brought his bank to ordinary people by opening branches near people's homes and workplaces. Called the greatest innovator in twentieth-century American banking, Giannini broadened the base of banking by encouraging working people to open small checking and savings accounts and to borrow for such purposes as car purchases. In the process, his bank—renamed the Bank of America—became the third largest in the nation by 1927.

Giannini's bank and Ford's auto factory survived as relics of family management in a new world of modern corporations with large bureaucracies. Ownership and control continued to grow apart, as salaried managers came to run most big businesses.

Even though the number of corporations increased steadily throughout the 1920s, corporate mergers also accelerated, continuing earlier patterns toward greater economic concentration. By 1930, 5 percent of American corporations were receiving 85 percent of all net corporate income, up from 78 percent in 1921.

Ford and Giannini were not the only entrepreneurs to emerge as popular and respected public figures. Perhaps the ultimate glorification of the entrepreneur came in 1925, in a book entitled *The Man Nobody Knows*. The author, Bruce Barton, founder of a leading advertising agency, suggested that Jesus Christ could best be understood as a business executive who "had picked up twelve men from the bottom ranks of business and forged them into an organization that conquered the world." Portraying Jesus' parables as "the most powerful advertisements of all time," Barton's book led the nonfiction bestseller lists for two years.

"Get Rich Quick" —Speculative Mania   During the 1920s, the stock market captured people's imagination as the fast track to riches. Stock market speculation—buying a stock with the expectation of selling it at a higher price—ran rampant. Articles in popular magazines proclaimed that everyone could participate and get rich quickly. By 1929, 4 million Americans owned stock, equivalent to about 10 percent of American households.

Just as Americans purchased cars and radios on the installment plan, some also bought stock on credit. One could purchase stock listed at $100 a share with as little as $10 down and the other $90 "on margin"—owed to the stockbroker. If the stock price advanced to $150, the investor could sell, pay off the broker, and gain a profit of $50 (500 percent!) on the $10 investment. Unfortunately, if the stock price fell to $50, the investor would still owe $90 to the broker. In fact, fewer than 1 percent of stock buyers purchased on margin, and the margin rarely exceeded 50 percent. More people borrowed money to buy stocks, but buying stocks with borrowed money carried the same potential for disaster as buying on margin.

Driven partly by real economic growth and partly by speculation, stock prices rose higher and higher (see Figure 21.2). Common stock prices tripled between 1920 and 1929. As long as the market stayed **bullish** and stock prices kept climbing, prosperity seemed endless.

The ever-rising stock prices and corporate dividends of the 1920s encouraged creation of holding companies. Samuel Insull created a vast empire of electrical utilities companies. Much of his enterprise—and others like it—consisted of holding companies, which existed solely to own the stock of another company, some of which existed primarily to own the stock of yet another company. The entire structure rested on the dividends produced by the underlying **operating companies**. Those dividends enabled the holding companies to pay dividends on their bonds. Any interruption in the dividends from the operating companies could bring the collapse of the entire pyramid, swallowing up the investments of speculators.

Although the stock market held the nation's attention as the most popular path to instant riches, other speculative opportunities abounded. A land boom developed when people poured into Florida, especially Miami, attracted by the climate, the beaches, and the ease of travel from the cities of the chilly Northeast. Speculators bought land—almost any land—expecting its value would soar. Stories circulated of land that increased 1,500 percent in value over ten years. Like stocks, land was bought with borrowed money. Early in 1926, the population influx slowed. The boom began to falter, then collapsed when a hurricane slammed into Miami. By 1927, many Florida land speculators were facing bankruptcy.

---

bullish   Optimistic or confident; regarding stocks, stock prices go up in a bull market and down in a bear market.

operating company   A company that directly sells goods or services, as opposed to a holding company that exists to own other companies.

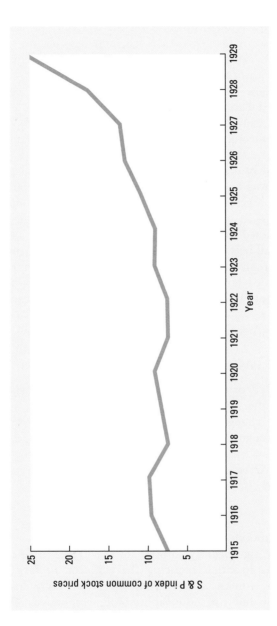

FIGURE 21.2 Stock Prices, 1915–1929

This graph shows the Standard & Poor index of common stock prices, with 1941–1942 as the base years (the index = 10 for those years). Figures for other years show stock prices in comparison to the base year. The Great Bull Market began in late 1924/early 1925 and roared upward until late 1929.

Source: U.S. Department of Commerce, Bureau of Census, *Historical Statistics of the United States, Colonial Times to 1970,* Bicentennial Edition, 2 vols. (Washington, D.C.: Government Printing Office, 1975), II: 10–4.

Agriculture: Depression in the Midst of Prosperity Prosperity never extended to most farmers, and farmers made up nearly 30 percent of the work force in 1920. During the war, many farmers expanded operations in response to government demands for more food, and exports of farm products nearly quadrupled. After the war, European farmers resumed production, exports of farm products fell, and agricultural prices dropped. Throughout the 1920s, American farmers consistently produced more than the domestic market could absorb, causing prices to fall.

The average farm's net income for the years 1917 to 1920 ranged between $1,196 and $1,395 (in current dollars) per year. Farm income fell to a dreadful $517 in 1921, then slowly rose, but never reached 1917–1920 levels until World War II. Although farmers' net income fell in the immediate postwar years and never recovered to prewar levels, their mortgage payments more than doubled over prewar levels, partly because of debts incurred to expand wartime production. Tax increases, purchases of tractors and trucks—now necessities on most farms—and the cost of fertilizer and other supplies bit further into farmers' meager earnings.

As the farm economy continued to hemorrhage, the average value of an acre of farmland fell by more than half between 1920 and 1928. The average farm was actually less valuable in 1928 than in 1912. Thousands of people left farming each year, and the proportion of farmers in the work force fell from nearly 30 percent to less than 20 percent. The 1920s were not the prosperity decade for rural America.

THE "ROARING TWENTIES"

"The world broke in two in 1922 or thereabouts," wrote novelist Willa Cather, and she didn't like what came after. F. Scott Fitzgerald, another novelist, agreed with the date but embraced the change. He believed 1922 marked "the peak of the younger generation," who brought about an "age of miracles"—that, he admitted, became an "age of excess." Evidence of sudden and dramatic social change was easy to see, from automobiles, radios, and movies to a new youth culture and an impressive cultural outpouring by African Americans.

Putting a People on Wheels: The Automobile and American Life The automobile profoundly changed Americans' lives. Highways significantly shortened the travel time from rural areas to cities, reducing the isolation of farm life. One farm woman, when asked why her family had an automobile but no indoor plumbing, responded, "Why, you can't go to town in a bathtub." Trucks allowed farmers to take more products to market more quickly and conveniently than before. Tractors expanded the amount of land that one family could cultivate. By reducing the need for human labor, gasoline-powered farm vehicles stimulated migration to urban areas.

The automobile changed city life even more profoundly. The 1920 census, for the first time, recorded more Americans living in urban areas (places having 2,500 people or more) than in rural ones. As the automobile freed suburbanites from their dependence on commuter rail lines, new suburbs mushroomed, with most of the growth in single-family houses. From 1922 through 1928, construction began on an average of 883,000 new homes each year. New home construction rivaled the auto industry as a major driving force behind economic growth.

The automobile soon demonstrated its ability to strangle urban traffic. One response was the development of traffic lights. Various versions were tried, but the four-directional, three-color traffic light first appeared in Detroit in 1920. Traffic lights spread rapidly to other large cities, but traffic congestion nonetheless worsened. By 1926, cars in the evening rush hour in Manhattan crawled along at less than 3 miles per hour—slower than a person could walk—and many commuters had returned to trains and subways.

Los Angeles: Automobile Metropolis

Manhattan was not designed to handle automobile traffic, but the fastest-growing major city of the early twentieth century—Los Angeles—was. The population of Los Angeles increased tenfold between 1900 and 1920, then more than doubled by 1930, reaching 2.2 million. Expansion of citrus-fruit raising, major oil discoveries, and the development of the motion-picture industry laid an economic foundation for rapid population growth in southern California. Manufacturing also expanded—during the 1920s, the city moved from twenty-eighth to ninth place among American cities based on manufacturing.

Lack of sufficient water threatened to limit growth until city officials diverted the Owens River to Los Angeles through a 233-mile-long aqueduct, opened in 1913. Throughout the 1920s, southern California promoters attracted hundreds of thousands of people by presenting an image of perpetual summer, tall palm trees lining wide boulevards filled with automobiles, fountains gushing water into the sunshine, and broad sandy beaches.

Los Angeles boomed as the automobile industry was promoting the notion of a car for every family and real-estate developers were pushing the ideal of the single-family home. By 1930, 94 percent of all residences in Los Angeles were single-family homes, an unprecedented level for a major city, and Los Angeles had the lowest urban population density of any major city in the nation.

Life in Los Angeles came to be organized around the automobile. The first modern supermarket, offering "one-stop shopping," appeared there, and the "Miracle Mile" along Wilshire Boulevard was the first large shopping district designed for the automobile. Such innovations set the pace for new urban development everywhere. The *Los Angeles Times* put it this way in 1926: "Our forefathers in their immortal independence creed set forth 'the pursuit of happiness' as an inalienable right of mankind. And how can one pursue happiness by any swifter and surer means ... than by the use of the automobile?" By then, Los Angeles had one automobile for every three residents, twice the national average.

A Homogenized Culture Searches for Heroes Los Angeles was the capital of the movie industry. By the mid-1920s, most towns of any size boasted at least one movie theater, and movie attendance increased rapidly from a weekly average of 40 million people in 1922 to 80 million in 1929—the equivalent of two-thirds of the total population. As Americans all across the country laughed or wept at the same movie, this new medium helped to **homogenize** the culture, that is, to make it more uniform by breaking down differences based on region or ethnicity.

Radio also contributed to greater homogeneity. The first commercial radio station began broadcasting in 1920. Within six years, 681 were operating. By 1930, 40 percent of all families had radios, including half of urban families. Other important factors in promoting more homogeneity included the automobile, which cut travel time, and new laws that sharply reduced immigration.

Radio and film joined newspapers and magazines in creating and publicizing national trends and fashions as Americans pursued one fad after another. In 1924, crossword puzzles captured the attention of many Americans, and contract bridge,

Charles Lindbergh chose photo settings in which he appeared to be alone with his plane, thereby emphasizing the individual nature of his flight. This photo was taken before his historic solo flight across the Atlantic.

Culver Pictures, Inc.

homogenize To make something uniform throughout.

a card game, became the rage in 1926. Such fads created markets for new consumer goods, from crossword dictionaries to folding card tables.

The media also helped to make spectator sports an obsession. Baseball had long been the preeminent national sport, and radio began to broadcast baseball games nationwide. Other sports now vied with baseball for fans' attention—and dollars. Most Americans in the 1920s were familiar with the exploits of Lou Gehrig and Babe Ruth on the baseball diamond, Jack Dempsey and Gene Tunney in boxing, and Bobby Jones, a golfer. Gertrude Ederle won national acclaim in 1926 when she became the first woman to swim the English Channel and did so two hours faster than any previous man. The rapid spread of movie theaters created a new category of fame—the movie star. Charlie Chaplin, Buster Keaton, Harold Lloyd, and others brought laughter to the screen. Tom Mix was the best known movie cowboy. Actress Clara Bow became the original "It" Girl by starring in the movie *It* (where "It" stood for sex appeal), sex also made a star of Theda Bara, the **vamp**, and Rudolph Valentino soared to fame as a male sex symbol, with his most famous film, *The Sheik,* set in a fanciful Arabian desert.

The greatest popular hero of the 1920s, however, was neither athlete nor actor but a small-town airmail pilot—**Charles Lindbergh**. At the time, aviation was barely out of its infancy. A few transatlantic flights had been logged by 1926, but the longest nonstop flight before 1927 was from San Diego to New York—2,500 miles.

Lindbergh, in 1927, set his sights on the $25,000 offered by a New York hotel owner to the pilot of the first successful nonstop flight between New York and Paris—3,500 miles. His plane, *The Spirit of St. Louis,* was a stripped-down, one-engine craft. In a sleepless, 33½-hour flight, Lindbergh earned both the $25,000 and the adoration of crowds on both sides of the Atlantic. In an age devoted to materialism and dominated by a corporate mentality, Lindbergh's accomplishment suggested that old-fashioned individualism, courage, and self-reliance could still triumph over odds and adversity.

Alienated Intellectuals   Other Americans, too, went to Paris and other European cities in the 1920s, but for different reasons than Lindbergh. These **expatriates** left the United States to escape what they considered America's intellectual shallowness, dull materialism, and spreading uniformity. As Malcolm Cowley put it in *Exile's Return* (1934), his memoir of life in France, "by expatriating himself, ... the artist can break the puritan shackles, drink, live freely, and be wholly creative." Paris in the 1920s, he added, "was a great machine for stimulating the nerves and sharpening the senses."

Sinclair Lewis and H. L. Mencken did not move to Paris but became leading critics of middle-class materialism and uniformity. Lewis, in *Main Street*

---

vamp   A woman who uses her sexuality to entrap and exploit men.

expatriate   A person who takes up long-term residence in a foreign country.

(1920), presented small-town, middle-class existence as not just boring but stifling. In *Babbitt* (1922), Lewis presented a suburban businessman (George Babbitt) as narrow-minded and complacent, speaking in clichés and buying every gadget on the market. H. L. Mencken, editor of *The American Mercury,* relentlessly pilloried the "booboisie," jeered at all politicians, and celebrated only writers who shared his disdain for most of American life.

Others added to the critique of modern life. In *The Waste Land* (1922), T. S. Eliot, an American poet who fled to England, presented modernity as sterile and futile. F. Scott Fitzgerald, in *The Great Gatsby* (1925), portrayed the pointless lives of wealthy pleasure seekers and their careless disregard for life and values. Ernest Hemingway, in *The Sun Also Rises* (1926), depicted disillusioned and jaded expatriates.

Renaissance among African Americans   For the most part, despair and disillusionment troubled white writers and intellectuals. Such sentiments were rarely apparent in the striking outpouring of literature, music, and art by African Americans in the 1920s.

African Americans continued to move from the South to northern cities in the 1920s. Harlem, the largest black neighborhood in New York City, came to symbolize the new urban life of African Americans. The term **Harlem Renaissance**, or Negro Renaissance, refers to a literary and artistic movement in which black artists and writers insisted on the value of black culture and drew upon African and African American traditions in their writing, painting, and sculpture. Black actors, notably Paul Robeson, now appeared in serious theaters and earned acclaim for their abilities. Earlier black writers, especially Alain Locke, James Weldon Johnson, and Claude McKay, encouraged and guided the novelists and poets of the Harlem Renaissance.

Among the movement's poets, Langston Hughes became the best known. Born in Joplin, Missouri, in 1902, Hughes began to write poetry in high school, briefly attended college, then worked and traveled in Africa and Europe. By 1925, he was a significant figure in the Harlem Renaissance, sometimes reading his poetry to the musical accompaniment of jazz.

Other important writers included Zora Neale Hurston, who came from a poor southern family, won a scholarship to Barnard College, and began her long writing career with several short stories in the 1920s. Jean Toomer's novel *Cane* (1923), dealing with African Americans in rural Georgia and Washington, D.C., has been praised as "the most impressive product of the Negro Renaissance."

The 1920s have been called the Jazz Age. African American musicians in southern cities, especially New Orleans, developed **jazz** in the early twentieth century, drawing from several strains in African American music, particularly the blues and ragtime. Jazz moved north, began to attract white audiences in the 1910s, and influenced white composers, notably George Gershwin, whose *Rhapsody in Blue* (1924) brought jazz into the symphony halls. Some attacked the new sound, claiming it encouraged people to abandon self-restraint, especially with regard to sex. Despite—or perhaps because of—such condemnation, the wail of the saxophone became as much a part of the 1920s as the roar of the roadster and the flicker of the movie projector.

The great black jazz musicians of the 1920s—Louis "Satchmo" Armstrong, Bessie Smith, Fletcher Henderson, Ferdinand "Jelly Roll" Morton, and others—drew white audiences into black neighborhoods to hear them. Harlem came to be associated with exotic nightlife and glittering jazz clubs. Edward "Duke" Ellington came to lead the Cotton Club band in 1927 and began to develop the works that made him one of America's most respected composers.

Few African Americans experienced the glitter of the Cotton Club, but one Harlem black leader affected black people throughout the country and beyond. **Marcus Garvey**, born in Jamaica, advocated a form of **black separatism**. His organization, the Universal Negro Improvement Association (UNIA), founded in 1914, stressed racial pride, the importance of Africa, and racial solidarity across national boundaries. Garvey supporters urged blacks around the world to help Africans overthrow colonial rule and build a strong Africa. Garvey's message of racial pride and solidarity attracted wide support among African Americans, especially in the cities. However, black integrationist leaders, especially W. E. B. Du Bois of the NAACP, opposed Garvey's separatism and argued that the first task facing blacks was integration and equality in the United States. Garvey and Du Bois each labeled the other a traitor to his race. Garvey was convicted of mail fraud in 1923 due to irregularities in his fundraising. After two years in jail, he was deported to his native Jamaica.

"Flaming Youth"   African Americans created jazz, but those who danced to it, in the popular imagination of the 1920s, were white—a male college student, clad in a stylish raccoon-skin coat with a hip flask of illegal liquor in his pocket, and his female counterpart, the uninhibited flapper, with bobbed hair and a daringly short skirt. This stereotype of "flaming youth"—the title of a popular novel—reflected far-reaching changes among many white, college-age youths of middle- or upper-class background.

In the 1920s adolescence emerged as a separate subculture. The booming economy allowed more middle-class families to send their children to college. Before World War I, just over 3 percent of people aged 18 to 24 were in college. By 1930, that proportion had more than doubled, with larger increases among women, and women were receiving 40 percent of all bachelor's degrees. Students reshaped colleges into youth centers, where football games and dances assumed as much significance as examinations and term papers.

Young women who captured public attention with their clothes and behavior were called **flappers** because of the flapping sound made by their fashionably unfastened galoshes. They scandalized their elders with skirts that stopped at the knee, stockings rolled below the knee, short hair often dyed black, and generous amounts of rouge and lipstick. Many observers assumed that their outrageous look reflected outrageous behavior—that young women were aban-doning their parents' moral values. In fact, women's sexual activity outside marriage began to increase before the war, especially among working-class women and radicals. "Dating," too, owed its origins to prewar working-class young people. In the 1920s, these behaviors appeared among college and high school students from middle-class families. About half of the women who came of age during the 1920s had intercourse before marriage, a marked increase from prewar patterns.

Such changes in behavior were often linked to the automobile. It brought greater freedom to young people, for there they had no chaperone and could go where they wanted. Sometimes they went to a **speakeasy** (where illegal alcohol was sold). Before Prohibition, few women entered saloons, but men and women alike went to speakeasies to drink, smoke, and dance to jazz. While some adults criticized the frivolities of the young, others emulated them, launching the first American youth culture. F. Scott Fitzgerald later called the years after 1922 "a children's party taken over by elders."

Traditional America Roars Back

Most Americans embraced cars, movies, and radios, but many felt threatened by the pace of change and the upheaval in social values that seemed centered in the cities. In nearly every case, though, efforts to stop the tide of change appeared in both cities and rural areas, and many of those efforts dated to the prewar era. In the 1920s, several movements seeking to restore elements of an older America came to fruition at the same time as Fitzgerald's "age of excess."

Prohibition   The **Eighteenth Amendment** (Prohibition) came to symbolize many of the efforts to preserve white, old-stock, Protestant values. Prohibition did reduce drinking somewhat, but many Americans simply ignored it, and it grew less popular the longer it lasted. By 1926, a poll indicated that only 19 percent of Americans supported Prohibition, 50 percent wanted the amendment modified, and 31 percent favored outright **repeal**. Prohibition, however, remained the law, if not the reality, from 1920 until 1933, when the Twenty-first Amendment finally did repeal it.

Prohibition was never well enforced anywhere, partly because of the immensity of the task and partly because Congress never provided enough money for serious federal enforcement. In 1923 a federal agent visited major cities to see how long it

---

speakeasy A place that illegally sells liquor and sometimes offers entertainment.

repeal The act of canceling a law or regulation; repeal of a constitutional amendment requires a new amendment.

On the 150th anniversary of the Declaration of Independence, Life presented this cover parodying the famous painting The Spirit of '76 by depicting "The Spirit of '26"—an uninhibited flapper with a jazz saxophonist and drummer, and banners with the snappy sayings of the day. The caption reads: "1776–1926: One Hundred and Forty-three Years of LIBERTY and Seven Years of PROHIBITION."

Collection of Picture Research Consultants and Archives

took to find an illegal drink: 35 seconds in New Orleans, 3 minutes in Detroit, and 3 minutes and 10 seconds in New York City.

Previously, neighborhood saloons had often attracted working-class and lower-middle-class men, but the new speakeasies were often more glamorous, drawing an upper- and middle-class clientele, women as well as men. **Bootlegging**—production and sale of illegal beverages—flourished. Some bootleggers brewed only small amounts of beer and sold it to their neighbors. In the cities, bootlegging provided criminals with a fresh and lucrative source of income, part of which they used to buy influence in city politics and protection from police.

In Chicago, **Al Capone**'s gang counted nearly a thousand members and, in 1927, took in more than $100 million (equivalent to $1.2 billion today)—$60 million of it from bootlegged liquor. Capone faced competition from other gangs, and gang warfare raged across Chicago throughout the 1920s, producing some five hundred slayings. In 1931 federal officials finally managed to convict Capone—of income-tax evasion—and sent him to prison.

bootlegging   Illegal production, distribution, or sale of liquor.

Elsewhere, other gangsters—many of recent immigrant background, including Italians, Irish, Germans, and Jews—also found riches in bootlegging, gambling, prostitution, and **racketeering**. Through racketeering they gained power in some labor unions. The gangs, killings, and corruption confirmed other Americans' long-standing distrust of cities and immigrants, and they clung to the vision of a dry America as the best hope for renewing traditional values.

Fundamentalism and the Campaign against Evolution

Fundamentalism, a movement within Protestant Christianity, represented another effort to maintain traditional values. Where Christian modernists tried to reconcile their religious beliefs with modern science, fundamentalists rejected anything—including science—they considered incompatible with the Scriptures. Every word of the Bible, they argued, is the revealed word of God. The fundamentalist movement grew throughout the first quarter of the twentieth century, led by figures such as Billy Sunday, a baseball player turned evangelist.

In the early 1920s, some fundamentalists focused on **evolution** as contrary to the Bible. Biologists cite evolution to explain how living things developed over millions of years. The Bible, however, states that God created the world and all living things in six days. Fundamentalists saw in evolution not just a challenge to the Bible's account of creation but also a challenge to religion itself.

William Jennings Bryan, former Democratic presidential candidate and secretary of state, fixed on the evolution controversy after 1920. His energy, eloquence, and enormous following guaranteed that the issue received wide attention. "It is better," Bryan wrote, "to trust in the Rock of Ages than to know the age of rocks." Bryan played a central role in the most famous dispute over evolution—the Scopes trial.

In March 1925, the Tennessee legislature made it illegal for public school teachers to teach evolution. When the American Civil Liberties Union (ACLU) offered to defend a teacher willing to challenge the law, John T. Scopes, who taught biology in Dayton, accepted. Bryan volunteered to assist the local prosecutors, who faced an ACLU defense team that included the famous attorney **Clarence Darrow**. Bryan claimed that the only issue was the right of the people to regulate public education as they saw fit, but Darrow insisted he was

racketeering   Crimes such as extortion, loansharking, and bribery, sometimes behind the front of a seemingly legitimate business or union.

fundamentalism   Originally an early twentieth-century Protestant Christian religious movement that emphasized the literal truth of the Bible and opposed efforts to reconcile the Bible with scientific knowledge; applied today to any religious movement based on uncompromising adherence to a set of principles.

evolution   The central organizing principle of the biological sciences, which holds that genetic change in organisms over generations can produce new species; it includes the concept that humans evolved from nonhuman ancestors.

there to prevent "ignoramuses from controlling the education of the United States."

The court proceedings were carried nationwide via radio. Toward the end of the trial, in a surprising move, Darrow called Bryan to the witness stand as an authority on the Bible. Under Darrow's withering questioning, Bryan revealed that he knew little about findings in archaeology, geology, and linguistics that cast doubt on Biblical accounts, and he also admitted, to the dismay of many fundamentalists, that he did not always interpret the words of the Bible literally. "Darrow never spared him," one reporter wrote. "It was masterful, but it was pitiful." Bryan died a few days later. Scopes was found guilty, but the Tennessee Supreme Court threw out his sentence on a technicality, preventing appeal.

Nativism, Immigration Restriction, and Eugenics
Throughout the 1920s, nativism and discrimination were widespread. **Restrictive covenants** attached to real-estate titles prohibited future sale to particular groups, typically African Americans and Jews. Exclusive colleges placed quotas on the number of Jews admitted each year, and some companies refused to hire Jews. In 1920 Henry Ford accused Jewish bankers of controlling the American economy, then suggested an international Jewish conspiracy to control virtually everything from baseball to bolshevism. After Aaron Sapiro, an attorney, sued Ford for defamation and challenged him to prove his claims, Ford retracted his charges and apologized in 1927. Ethnic hostility sometimes turned violent, as when rioting towns-people beat and stoned Italians in West Frankfort, Illinois, in 1920.

Laws to restrict immigration resulted in significant part from nativist anxieties that immigrants, especially those from southern and eastern Europe, were transforming the United States. Advocates of restriction redoubled their efforts in response to an upsurge in immigration after the war—430,000 in 1920 and 805,000 in 1921, with more than half from southern and eastern Europe. Efforts to cut off immigration were not new. However, the presence of many German Americans during the war with Germany, the Red Scare and fear of foreign radicalism, and the continued influx of poor immigrants at a time of growing unemployment came together with nativism after the war. Congress reacted, limiting immigration with a temporary measure in 1921, then in 1924 passing a permanent law, the **National Origins Act**, which restricted total immigration to 150,000 per year. Quotas for each country were set at 2 percent of the number of Americans whose ancestors came from that country, but all Asians were excluded. In attempting to freeze the ethnic composition of the nation, the law reflected the arguments of those nativists who contended that immigrants from southern and eastern Europe and Asia made less desirable citizens than people from northern and

restrictive covenant Provision in a property title that prohibits subsequent sale to specified groups, especially people of color and Jews.

IT MATTERS TODAY

Teaching Evolution in Public Schools

Other state legislatures followed Tennessee and prohibited the teaching of evolution. Textbook publishers diluted or omitted treatment of evolution. Not until the 1950s, when national science education standards were developed, did a thorough treatment of evolution return to most high school textbooks.

In 1968, the U.S. Supreme Court overturned a 1928 Arkansas law prohibiting the teaching of evolution because it reflected the views of a particular religious group that considered evolution to be in conflict with the Bible, and therefore violated the First Amendment, which prohibits Congress from adopting any law that privileges one religious group, and the Fourteenth Amendment, which applies the First Amendment to state governments.

Opponents of evolution then secured laws requiring teaching "creationism."

This the U.S. Supreme Court struck down in 1987, in a case involving a Louisiana law. Since then, opponents of evolution have often used the term "intelligent design." In 2005, President George W. Bush endorsed teaching both intelligent design and evolution in high school biology classes, and that issue continues to be hotly debated in several states.

- Search online newspapers to find examples of recent controversies over the teaching of evolution. What are the arguments?
- William Jennings Bryan argued, in part, that in a democracy elected officials should control the content of courses in the public schools. Should course content be determined by elected officials or by specialists in each discipline?

western Europe. However, the law permitted unrestricted immigration from Canada and Latin America.

In its transparent effort to restrict immigration from southern and eastern Europe while admitting larger numbers from northern and western Europe, the National Origins Act also reflects the concerns of one group of **eugenics** advocates. The eugenics movement developed in the late nineteenth and early twentieth century; its proponents hoped to use genetics to improve the human race by selective breeding. Some eugenicists argued that most southern and eastern Europeans showed undesirable genetic traits, and therefore favored barring them from immigration. Other eugenicists focused on mental ability or mental illness to argue that those with "undesirable" traits should not be permitted to marry or should be sterilized. In 1927, the U.S. Supreme Court approved a Virginia law permitting the state to sterilize those considered mentally retarded; such state laws were widespread by the 1920s, and most continued in force until the 1960s.

---

eugenics The notion that information about genetics should be used to improve the human race.

The Ku Klux Klan   Nativism, anti-Catholicism, anti-Semitism, and fear of radicalism all contributed to the spectacular growth of the Ku Klux Klan in the early 1920s. The original Klan, created during Reconstruction to intimidate former slaves, had long since died out. But D. W. Griffith's hugely popular film *The Birth of a Nation,* released in 1915, glorified the old Klan.

The new Klan claimed to be devoted to traditional American values, old-fashioned Protestant Christianity, and white supremacy; it opposed Catholics, Jews, immigrants, and blacks, along with bootleggers, corrupt politicians, and gamblers. Growth came slowly at first but surged to 5 million members nationwide by 1925.

The Klan was strong in the South, Midwest, West, and Southwest, and in towns and cities as well as rural areas. Klan members participated actively in local politics, and Klan leaders exerted powerful political influence in some communities and state governments, notably Texas, Oklahoma, Kansas, Oregon, and Indiana. In Oklahoma, the Klan led a successful impeachment campaign against a governor who tried to restrict it. In Oregon, the Klan claimed responsibility for a 1922 law aimed at eliminating Catholic schools. (The Supreme Court ruled the law unconstitutional.) Many local and state elections in 1924 divided along pro- and anti-Klan lines.

Extensive corruption underlay the Klan's self-righteous rhetoric. Some Klan leaders joined primarily for personal gain, both legal (from recruiting) and illegal (mostly from political payoffs). Some shamelessly violated the morality they preached. In 1925, D. C. Stephenson, Grand Dragon of Indiana and a nationally prominent Klan leader, was convicted of second-degree murder after the death of a woman who had accused him of raping her. When the governor refused to pardon him, Stephenson produced records proving the corruption of the governor, a member of Congress, the mayor of Indianapolis, and other officials. Klan membership fell sharply amid factional disputes and further evidence of fraud and corruption.

NEW SOCIAL PATTERNS IN THE 1920s

The Harlem Renaissance and Klan nightriders represent polar extremes of racial relations in the 1920s. For most people of color, the realities of daily life fell somewhere in between. For working people, the 1920s represented what one historian has termed "the lean years" when earlier gains were lost and unions remained on the defensive. For women, the 1920s opened with the political victory of suffrage, but the unity mustered in support of that measure soon broke down.

Ethnicity and Race: North, South, and West   Discrimination against Jews, violence against Italians, and the Klan's appeal to white Protestants all point to the continuing significance of ethnicity in American life during the 1920s. Throughout the decade, racial relations remained deeply troubled at best, violent at worst.

The Harlem Renaissance helped produce greater appreciation for black music and other accomplishments, but racial discrimination still confronted most African Americans, no matter where they lived. A few gained better jobs by moving north, but many found work only in low-paying service occupations. In nearly every city, social pressures and restrictive covenants limited access to desirable housing. Those who did succeed sometimes became targets for racial hostility, like the black physician whose home was attacked by a white mob when he moved into a white Detroit neighborhood in 1925. A race riot devastated Tulsa, Oklahoma, in 1921, leaving nearly 40 confirmed dead (with blacks outnumbering whites by more than two to one), hundreds injured, and 1,400 black businesses and homes burned. Rumors circulated of hundreds more buried in mass graves.

The NAACP continued to lobby for a federal antilynching law, but southern legislators defeated each attempt, arguing against any federal interference in the police power of the states. In its efforts to combat lynching, the NAACP worked to educate the public by publicizing violence against blacks.

In the eastern United States, North, and South, race relations usually meant black-white relations. In the West, race relations were always more complex, and

African Americans intensified their efforts to end lynching. This protest was held in Washington, D.C., in 1922. The NAACP's efforts to secure a federal anti-lynching law were repeatedly defeated by southerners in Congress.

became more so in the years around World War I, when Filipinos began to arrive in Hawai`i and on the West Coast. Most of them worked in agriculture and aboard ships. Sikhs from India also entered the West Coast work force, mainly as agricultural laborers.

California had long led the way among western states with laws discriminating against Asian Americans. By the 1920s, other western states had copied California laws forbidding Asian immigrants to own or lease land.Westerners, especially Californians, also had a lengthy record of violence against Asians. In 1930, for example, a white mob killed a Filipino farm worker in Watsonville, California.

Some Asian immigrants and Asian Americans fought discrimination through the courts, but with little success. In the early 1920s, the U.S. Supreme Court affirmed that only white persons and persons of African descent could become naturalized citizens, denying citizenship to persons born in Asia. The U.S. Supreme Court also ruled that Mississippi could require a Chinese American schoolchild to attend a segregated school established for African Americans.

Beginnings of Change in Federal Indian Policy

During the 1920s, several events began to converge in support of changes in federal policy toward American Indians. In the early 1920s, Interior Secretary Albert Fall tried to lease parts of reservations to white developers and to extinguish Pueblo Indians' title to lands along the Rio Grande. Fall's proposals, especially the Pueblo land issue, led directly to organization by John Collier of the **American Indian Defense Association** (AIDA), in 1923.

Collier, a social worker, and the AIDA soon emerged as leading voices for changes in federal Indian policy. They sought better health and educational services on reservations, creation of tribal governments, tolerance of Indian religious ceremonies and other customs, and an end to land allotments—all in all, changes away from the policy of forced assimilation toward a policy of recognizing Indian cultures and values. Political pressure by AIDA and similar groups, along with political efforts by Indians themselves, secured several new laws favorable to Indians, including full citizenship for all Native Americans. These efforts laid the basis for a significant shift in federal policy in the 1930s.

Mexican Americans

California and the Southwest have been home to many Mexican and Mexican American families since the region was part of Mexico. Those states attracted growing numbers of Mexican immigrants after 1910. Many Mexicans went north, most to Texas and California, to escape the revolution and civil war that devastated their nation from 1910 into the 1920s. Nearly 700,000 Mexicans legally entered the United States between 1910 and 1930, and probably the same number came illegally.

The agricultural economies of the Southwest were changing. By 1925, the Southwest was relying on irrigation to produce 40 percent of the nation's fruits and vegetables, crops that were highly labor-intensive. By the late 1920s, Mexicans made up 80 to 85 percent of farm laborers in that region. At the same time, the southwestern states also experienced large increases in their Anglo populations. These changes in population and economy reshaped relations between Anglos and Mexicans.

In south Texas, many Anglo newcomers looked on Mexicans as what one Anglo called a "partly colored race," and white newcomers tried to import elements of southern black-white relations, including disfranchisement and segregation. Disfranchisement was unsuccessful, but some schools were segregated despite Mexican opposition. The League of United Latin American Citizens (LULAC) could sometimes halt discrimination by businesses—but only occasionally.

In California, Mexican workers' efforts to organize and strike for better pay and working conditions were often broken quickly and brutally by local authorities or growers' private guards. Leaders were likely to be deported. Nevertheless, Mexican labor had become vital to agriculture, and growers opposed any restrictions on immigration from Mexico—the National Origins Act of 1924 permitted unlimited immigration from the Western Hemisphere.

Not all immigrants from Mexico stayed in the Southwest. As the doors to European immigration closed with the new immigration law, midwestern manufacturers began to recruit Mexican workers to work in steel mills, meatpacking plants, and auto factories. By 1930, significant numbers of Mexican Americans were to be found in such industrial cities as Chicago, Detroit, and Gary.

Labor on the Defensive   Difficulties in establishing unions among Mexican workers mirrored a larger failure of unions in the 1920s. When unions tried to recover lost purchasing power by calling strikes in 1919 and 1920, nearly all failed. After 1921, employers increasingly challenged Progressive Era legislation benefiting workers. The Supreme Court responded by limiting workers' rights, voiding laws that eliminated child labor, and striking down minimum-wage laws for women and children.

Many companies undertook anti-union drives. Arguing that unions were unnecessary and either corrupt or radical, some employers used the term **American Plan** to describe their refusal to deal with unions. At the same time, some companies began to provide workers with programs such as insurance, retirement pensions, cafeterias, paid vacations, and stock purchase plans, an approach sometimes called **welfare capitalism**. Such innovations stemmed from both genuine concern about workers' well-being and the expectation that such improvements would increase productivity and discourage unionization.

The 1920s marked the first period of prosperity since the 1830s when union membership declined, falling from 5 million in 1920 to 3.6 million in 1929, a 28 percent decline at a time when the total work force increased by 15 percent. AFL leaders, insisting on separate unions for each skill group, made no serious effort to organize the great mass-production industries. Some unions suffered from internal battles—the International Ladies' Garment Workers' Union lost two-thirds of its members during power struggles between Socialists and Communists.

The Communists sought power within other unions, but the membership of the **Communist Party of the United States** (CP) never approached the numbers claimed by the Socialist Party before World War I. In 1929 the CP counted only 9,300 members. Always closely tied to the leadership of the Soviet Union, the CP labored strenuously to organize workers throughout the 1920s but had little success.

Changes in Women's Lives The attention given to the flapper should not detract from important changes in women's gender roles during these years. Significant changes occurred in two arenas: family and politics.

Marriage among white middle-class women and men came increasingly to be valued as companionship between two partners. Although the ideal of marriage was often expressed in terms of man and woman taking equal responsibility for a relationship, the actual responsibility for the smooth functioning of the family typically fell on the woman.

Many women in the 1920s seem to have increased their control over decisions about childbearing. Usually in American history, prosperity brings increases in the birth rate. In the 1920s, however, changing social values together with more options for birth control resulted in fewer births. Women who came of childbearing age in the 1910s and 1920s are distinctive in three ways when compared with women of both earlier and later periods: (1) they had fewer children on average, (2) more of them had no children at all, and (3) far fewer had very large families (see Figure 21.3).

This declining birth rate reflected, in part, some success for earlier efforts to secure wider availability of birth-control information and devices, for example, diaphragms, but it is also typical that the birth rate falls as a society becomes more urban. The birth-control movement also gained the backing of some male physicians and became a more respectable, middle-class reform movement. By 1925, the American Medical Association had declared its support for birth control, and the Rockefeller Foundation began to fund medical research into contraception methods. Nevertheless, until 1936, federal law restricted public distribution of information about contraception, and many women continued to rely on illegal abortions to terminate unwanted pregnancies. In Clara Bow's Hollywood, abortions became almost routine as a way for actresses to meet their contractual obligations to perform in films and to avoid public scandal.

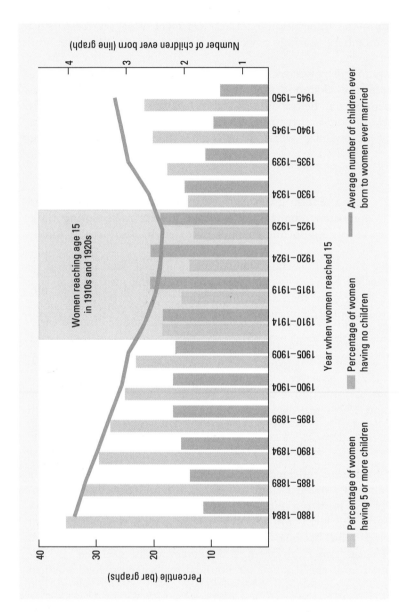

FIGURE 21.3 Changing Patterns of Childbearing among Women

This figure depicts three different choices regarding family size: (1) the number of children born to women ever married, (2) the percentage of women ever married having large families, and (3) the percentage of women ever married having no children at all. Childbearing ages are considered to be between 15 and 45.

Sources: Series B42–48, U.S. Bureau of the Census, *Historical Statistics of the United States, Colonial Times to 1970, Bicentennial Edition,* 2 vols. (Washington, D.C.: U.S. Government Printing Office, 1975), I: 53; Table 270, U.S. Bureau of the Census, *1980 Census of Population* (Washington, D.C.: U.S. Government Printing Office, 1984), 1–103.

Throughout the 1920s, working-class women still struggled to stretch their finances to cover their families' needs. As before, some women and children worked outside the home because the family needed additional income. The proportion of women working for wages remained quite stable during the 1920s, at about one in four. The proportion of married women working for wages increased, though, from 23 percent of the female labor force in 1920 to 29 percent in 1930.

After the implementation of the Nineteenth Amendment (woman suffrage) in 1920, the unity of the suffrage movement disintegrated in disputes over the proper role for women voters. Both major political parties welcomed women as voters and modified the structure of their national committees to provide that each state be represented by both a national committeeman and a national committeewoman. Some suffrage activists joined the League of Women Voters, a nonpartisan group committed to social and political reform. The Congressional Union, led by Alice Paul, converted itself into the National Woman's Party and, after 1923, focused its efforts on securing an **Equal Rights Amendment** to the Constitution. The League of Women Voters disagreed, arguing that such an amendment would endanger laws providing protection for women.

Development of Gay and Lesbian Subcultures   In the 1920s, gay and lesbian subcultures became more established and relatively open in several cities. *The Captive,* a play about lesbians, opened in New York in 1926, and some movies included unmistakable homosexual references. Novels with gay and lesbian characters were published in the late 1920s and early 1930s. In Chicago, the Society for Human Rights was organized to advocate equal treatment. A relatively open gay and lesbian community emerged in Harlem, where some prominent figures of the Renaissance were gay or bisexual. The annual Hamilton Lodge drag ball in Harlem attracted as many as seven thousand revelers and spectators of all races.

At the same time, however, more and more psychiatrists and psychologists were labeling homosexuality a **perversion**. By the 1920s, the work of **Sigmund Freud** had become well known, and most psychiatrists and psychologists labeled homosexuality a sexual disorder that required a cure, though no "cure" ever proved viable. Thus Freud's theories may have been liberating for heterosexual relations, but they proved harmful for same-sex relations.

The new medical definitions were slow to work their way into the larger society. The armed forces, for example, continued previous practices, making little effort to prevent homosexuals from enlisting and taking disciplinary action only against behavior that clearly violated the law.

The late 1920s and early 1930s brought increased suppression of gays and lesbians. New state laws gave police greater authority to prosecute open expressions of homosexuality. In 1929 Adam Clayton Powell, a leading Harlem minister, launched a highly publicized campaign against gays. Motion-picture studios

perversion Sexual practice considered abnormal or deviant.

instituted a morality code that, among its wide-ranging provisions, prohibited any depiction of homosexuality. The end of Prohibition after 1933 brought increased regulation of businesses selling liquor, and local authorities often used this power to close establishments with gay or lesbian customers. Thus, by the 1930s, many gays and lesbians were becoming more secretive about their sexual identities.

THE POLITICS OF PROSPERITY

Sooner or later, nearly all the social and economic developments of the 1920s found their way into politics, from highway construction to prohibition, from immigration restriction to the teaching of evolution, from farm prices to lynching. After 1918, the Republicans resumed the majority role they had exercised from the mid-1890s to 1912, and they continued as the unquestioned majority throughout the 1920s. Progressivism largely disappeared, although some veteran progressives, led by Robert La Follette and George Norris, persisted in seeking to limit corporate power. The Republican administrations of the 1920s shared a faith in the ability of business to establish prosperity and benefit the American people and considered government the partner of business, not its regulator.

Harding's Failed Presidency   Elected in 1920, Warren G. Harding looked presidential—handsome, gray-haired, dignified, warm, outgoing—but had little intellectual depth. For some of his appointments, he chose the most respected leaders of his party, including Charles Evans Hughes for secretary of state, Andrew Mellon for secretary of the Treasury, and Herbert Hoover for secretary of commerce. Harding, however, was most comfortable playing poker with his friends, and he gave hundreds of government jobs to his cronies and political supporters. They turned his administration into one of the most corrupt in American history. As their misdeeds began to come to light, Harding put off taking action until after a trip to Alaska. During his return, on August 2, 1923, he died when a blood vessel burst in his brain.

The full extent of corruption became clear after Harding's death. Albert Fall, secretary of the interior, had accepted huge bribes from oil companies for leases on federal oil reserves at Elk Hills, California, and Teapot Dome, Wyoming. Attorney General Harry Daugherty and others pocketed payoffs to approve the sale of government-held property for less than its value. Daugherty may also have protected bootleggers. The head of the Veterans Bureau swindled the government out of more than $200 million. In all, three cabinet members resigned, four officials went to jail, and five men committed suicide. As if the financial dishonesty were not enough, in 1927 Nan Britton published a book claiming that she had been Harding's mistress, had borne his child, and had carried on trysts with him in the White House.

In the midst of these scandals, hard-pressed and debt-ridden farmers turned to the federal government for help. In 1921 farm organizations worked with senators and representatives to form a bipartisan **Farm Bloc,** which promoted legislation to assist farmers. The bloc enjoyed a substantial boost in the 1922 elections, when distraught farmers across the Midwest turned out conservatives and elected candidates attuned to farmers' problems. Congress passed a few assistance measures in the early 1920s, but none addressed the central problems of overproduction and low prices. By 1922, some farm organizations joined with unions, especially unions of railroad workers, to form the Conference for Progressive Political Action and agitate for a new Progressive Party.

The Three-Candidate Presidential Election of 1924   When Harding died, Vice President Calvin Coolidge became president. Fortunately for the Republican Party, the new president exemplified honesty, virtue, and sobriety. In 1924 Republicans quickly chose Coolidge as their candidate for president.

The Democratic convention, however, sank into a long and bitter deadlock. Since the Civil War, the party had divided between southerners (mostly Protestant and committed to white supremacy) and northerners (often city-dwellers and of recent immigrant descent, including many Catholics). In 1924 the Klan was approaching its peak membership and exercised significant influence among many Democratic delegates from the South and parts of the Midwest.

Many northern Democrats wanted to nominate **Al Smith** for president. Highly popular as governor of New York, Smith epitomized urban, immigrant America. Catholic and the son of immigrants, he was everything the Klan—and most of the southern convention delegates—opposed. After nine hot days of stalemate and 103 ballots, the exhausted Democrats turned to a virtually unknown compromise candidate, John W. Davis, who had served in the Wilson administration, then became a corporate lawyer. All in all, the convention seemed to confirm the observation by the contemporary humorist Will Rogers: "I belong to no organized political party. I am a Democrat."

Surviving progressives welcomed the independent candidacy of Senator Robert M. La Follette, nominated by a new Progressive Party formed by farmers, unions, and reformers. The La Follette Progressives attacked big business and promoted collective bargaining, reform of politics, public ownership of railroads and water power, and a public referendum on questions of war and peace. La Follette was the first presidential candidate to be endorsed by the American Federation of Labor.

Republican campaigners largely ignored Davis and focused on portraying La Follette as a dangerous radical. Coolidge claimed the key issue was "whether America will allow itself to be degraded into a communistic or socialistic state" or "remain American." Coolidge won with nearly 16 million votes and 54 percent of the total. Davis held on to most traditional Democratic voters, especially in the South, receiving 8 million votes and 29 percent. La Follette carried only his home state of Wisconsin but garnered almost 5 million votes, 17 percent, and did well both in urban working-class neighborhoods and in parts of the rural Midwest and Northwest.

The Politics of Business

Committed to limited government and content to let problems work themselves out, Coolidge tried to reduce the significance of the presidency—and succeeded. He announced that "the business of America is business" and believed that the free market would best sustain economic prosperity for all. As president, he set out to prevent government from interfering with business.

Coolidge had little sympathy for efforts to secure federal help for the faltering farm economy. Congress tried to address low prices for farm products and persistent agricultural surpluses with the **McNary-Haugen bill**, which would have created federal price supports and authorized the government to buy farm surpluses and sell them abroad. The Farm Bloc pushed the bill through Congress in 1927, but Coolidge vetoed it. The same thing happened in 1928. In contrast, the **Railway Labor Act of 1926** drew on wartime experiences to establish collective

This cartoon depicts Coolidge playing praise of big business. Big business, dressed like a flapper, wildly dances the Charleston and sings, "Yes Sir, He's My Baby."

Library of Congress

bargaining for railroad employees. Passed by overwhelming margins in Congress, the new law met most of the railway unions' demands and effectively removed them from politics.

Andrew Mellon, one of the wealthiest men in the nation, served as secretary of the Treasury throughout the 1920s. Acclaimed by Republicans and business leaders as the greatest secretary of the Treasury since Alexander Hamilton, Mellon argued that high taxes on the wealthy stifled the economy. He secured tax breaks for the affluent, arguing that they would benefit everyone through "productive investments" of the tax savings. Herbert Hoover, secretary of commerce under Harding and Coolidge, urged Coolidge to regulate the increasingly wild use of credit, which contributed to rampant stock market speculation, but Coolidge refused.

Coolidge cut federal spending and staffed federal agencies with people who shared his distaste for too much government. Unlike Harding, Coolidge found honest and competent appointees. Like Harding, he named probusiness figures to regulatory commissions and put conservative, probusiness judges in the courts. The *Wall Street Journal* described the outcome: "Never before, here or anywhere else, has a government been so completely fused with business."

The 1928 Campaign and the Election of Hoover	In August 1927, President Coolidge told reporters, "I do not choose to run in 1928," stunning the country and his party. Secretary of Commerce Herbert Hoover immediately declared his candidacy, and Republicans found him an ideal candidate, representing what most Americans

believed was best about the United States: individual effort and honestly earned success.

Son of a Quaker blacksmith from Iowa, Hoover was orphaned at 10 and grew up believing that hard work was the only way to success. Graduating from Stanford University, he traveled the world as a mining engineer and became a millionaire. When World War I broke out, he turned to public service, organizing relief for Belgium. "This man is not to be stopped anywhere under any circumstance," the Germans noted on his passport. When the United States entered the war, President Wilson named Hoover to head the U.S. Food Administration. By the end of the war, Hoover emerged as an international hero. As secretary of commerce under Harding and Coolidge, he attracted wide support in the business community for his efforts to encourage economic growth through associationalism—voluntary cooperation among otherwise competing groups.

In launching his campaign before thousands of supporters gathered in the Stanford football stadium, Hoover sounded the theme of his candidacy: "We in America today are nearer to the final triumph over poverty than ever before."

The Democrats nominated Al Smith—like Hoover, a self-made man. Unlike Hoover, who had gone to Stanford, Smith's education came on the streets of New York City and as part of Tammany Hall, the Democratic machine that ran the city.

As a reform-minded, progressive governor of New York, Smith streamlined state government, improved its efficiency, and supported legislation to set a minimum wage and maximum hours of work and to establish state ownership of hydroelectric plants.

In many places, Smith became the main issue in the campaign. Opponents attacked his Catholic religion, his big-city background, his opposition to Prohibition, his Tammany connections, and even his New York accent. Anti-Catholic sentiment burned hotly in parts of the country, often fanned by remnants of the Klan. Evangelist Billy Sunday called Smith supporters "damnable whiskey politicians, bootleggers, crooks, pimps and businessmen who deal with them." Thus, for many voters, the choice seemed to be between a candidate who represented hard work and the pious values of small town, old-stock, Protestant America and a candidate who represented Catholics, foreigners, machine politics, and the ugly problems of the cities.

Hoover won easily, with 58 percent of the popular vote. Prosperity and the nation's long-term Republican majority probably would have spelled victory for any competent Republican. Smith's religion and anti-Prohibition stance cost him in the South, where Hoover carried areas that had not voted Republican since Reconstruction. Smith brought Democratic gains in northern cities, partly by drawing to the polls Catholic voters, especially women who had not previously voted.

The first president born west of the Mississippi River, Hoover came to the presidency with definite ideas about both domestic and foreign policy. He set out to be an active president. The role of government, he believed, was to promote cooperation. He warned that once government, especially the federal government, stepped in to solve problems directly, the people gave up some of their freedom, and government became part of the problem. Hoover recognized that the federal government had a responsibility to help find solutions to social and economic problems, but the key word was *help:* Hoover looked to the government to help but not to solve problems by itself.

THE DIPLOMACY OF PROSPERITY

Two realities shaped American foreign policy in the 1920s: rejection of Woodrow Wilson's internationalism and a continuing quest for economic expansion by American business. As president, Harding dismissed any American role in the League of Nations and refused to accept the Treaty of Versailles. Undamaged by the war, American firms outproduced and outtraded the rest of the world. U.S. trade amounted to 30 percent of the world's total, and American firms produced more than 70 percent of the world's oil and almost 50 percent of the world's coal and steel. American bankers loaned billions of dollars to other nations, expanding the global economy.

Harding and Coolidge had neither expertise nor interest in foreign affairs, so they left most foreign policy decisions to their secretaries of state, Charles Evans Hughes and Frank Kellogg. Both were capable men interested in developing American business and influence abroad through what historians have called "independent internationalism." Independent (or **unilateral**) internationalism had two central thrusts: avoidance of **multilateral** commitments—sometimes called **isolationism**—and expansion of economic opportunities overseas. The Commerce and State Departments promoted American business activities worldwide and encouraged private investments in Japan and China. American officials worked to allow U.S. oil companies to drill in Iran, Iraq, the Persian Gulf region, and Saudi Arabia. Their efforts to expand Americans' economic position in Latin America and Europe were quite successful. As president, Hoover and his secretary of state, Henry L. Stimson, followed a similar approach.

The United States and Latin America
When Harding took office in 1921, the United States had troops stationed in Cuba, Panama, Haiti, the Dominican Republic, and Nicaragua. During the presidential campaign, Harding had criticized Wilson's "bayonet rule" in Haiti and the Dominican Republic and expressed his intention to end those occupations. To maintain American dominance in the Caribbean, however, U.S. officials wanted stable and friendly local governments. Therefore, American administrators kept some control over national finances and trained each nation's national guard to act as its police force. American troops left Cuba in 1922, the Dominican Republic in 1924, Nicaragua in 1932, and Haiti in 1934. In the Dominican Republic and in Haiti, however, the United States kept control of the customhouse—and tariff revenues—until the 1940s.

When American troops withdrew from the Dominican Republic and Haiti, they left better roads, improved sanitation systems, governments favorable to the United States, and well-equipped national guards. But the years of occupation had not advanced the educational systems, the national economies, or most residents' standard of living. Nor did the United States do much to promote democracy, favoring stability instead—even if it meant accepting dictators such as Rafael Trujillo, who seized power in the Dominican Republic in 1930 and ruled brutally until his death in 1961.

In Nicaragua, American forces left in 1925 but returned in mid-1926 to protect the pro-American government when civil war broke out. Coolidge sent Henry L. Stimson to negotiate a peace agreement that ended most fighting in 1927. However, the guerilla leader **Augusto Sandino**, who wanted to rid Nicaragua of American influence, rejected the peace agreement and continued guerrilla warfare.

Elsewhere in Latin America, American involvement was not military, but commercial. Throughout Central America, American firms such as the United Fruit Company purchased thousands of acres for plantations to produce,

unilateral An action taken by a country by itself, as opposed to actions taken jointly with other nations.

multilateral Involving more than two nations (when two nations are involved, the term is *bilateral*).

isolationism The notion that the United States should avoid political, diplomatic, and military entanglements with other nations.

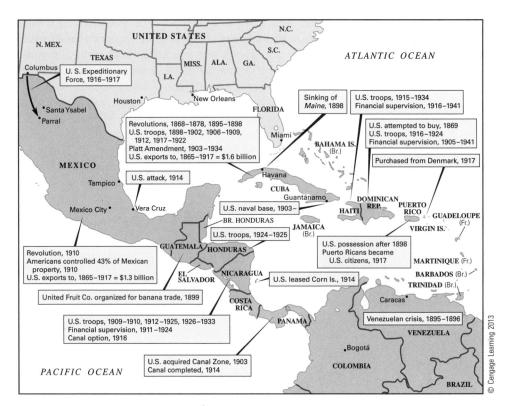

MAP 21.1 Hegemony in the Caribbean and Latin America

Through many interventions, territorial acquisitions, and robust economic expansion, the United States became the predominant power in Latin America in the early twentieth century. The United States often backed up the Roosevelt Corollary's declaration of a "police power" by dispatching troops to Caribbean nations, where they met nationalist opposition.

especially bananas and coffee, for the American and European market. United Fruit came to exercise a powerful influence in several Central American countries. In Venezuela and Colombia, American oil companies, with State Department help, negotiated contracts for drilling rights, outmaneuvering European oil companies. U.S. investments in Latin America rose from nearly $2 billion in 1919 to over $3.5 billion in 1929.

Oil played a key role in relations with Mexico. The Mexican constitution of 1917 limited foreign ownership, and Mexico moved to **nationalize** its subsurface resources, including oil. American businessmen strongly objected. By 1925, American oilmen and some members of the Coolidge administration called for

---

nationalize   To convert an industry or enterprise from private to government ownership and control.

military action to protect American oil interests in Mexico, But Coolidge sent Dwight W. Morrow—a college friend—as ambassador to Mexico with instructions "to keep us out of war with Mexico." Morrow understood Mexican nationalism and pride, knew some Spanish, and cultivated a personal relationship with Mexican president Plutarco Calles. He succeeded in reducing tensions and delayed nationalization of oil until 1938. Following the election of 1928, president-elect Hoover undertook a goodwill tour of eleven Latin American countries, seeking better relations.

America and the European Economy

World War I shattered much of Europe physically and economically. The American economy soared to unprecedented heights, however, and the United States became the world's leading creditor nation. After the war, Republican leaders joined with business figures to expand exports and restrict imports. In 1922 the **Fordney-McCumber Tariff** set the highest rates ever for most imported industrial goods. The tariff not only limited European imports but also made it difficult for Europeans to acquire the dollars needed to repay their war debts to the United States.

While Harding and Coolidge sought debt repayment, Secretary of State Hughes and Secretary of Commerce Hoover worked to expand American economic interests in Europe, especially Germany. They believed that if Germany recovered economically and paid its $33 billion war reparations, other European nations would also recover and repay their debts. With government encouragement, over $4 billion in American investments flowed into Europe, doubling American investments there. General Motors purchased Opel, a German automobile firm. Ford built the largest automobile factory outside the United States, in England, and constructed a tractor factory in the Soviet Union.

Even so, Germany could not make its reparation payments, defaulting in 1923 to France and Belgium. France responded by sending troops to occupy Germany's **Ruhr Valley**, a key economic region, igniting an international crisis. Hughes sent Charles G. Dawes, a Chicago banker and prominent Republican, to resolve the situation. Under the **Dawes Plan**, American bankers loaned $2.5 billion to Germany for economic development, and the Germans promised to pay $2 billion in reparations to the European Allies, who, in turn, were to pay $2.5 billion in war debts to the United States. This circular flow of capital was the subject of jokes at the time but worked fairly well until 1929, when the Depression ended nearly all loans and payments.

Encouraging International Cooperation

Committed to independent internationalism, Republican policymakers of the 1920s also understood that some international cooperation was necessary to achieve policy goals and solve international problems. On such issues, they were willing to cooperate with other nations and enter into international agreements, but only with the understanding that the United States was not

Ruhr Valley   Region surrounding the Ruhr River in northwestern Germany, containing major industrial cities and valuable coal mines.

entering an alliance or otherwise agreeing to commit resources or troops in defense of another nation.

Disarmament was such an issue. The destruction caused by World War I had spurred pacifism and calls for disarmament. In the United States, support for arms cuts was widespread and vocal. In early 1921, Senator William E. Borah of Idaho suggested an international conference to reduce the size of the world's navies. Fearing that naval expenditures would prevent tax cuts, Treasury Secretary Mellon and many members of Congress joined the disarmament chorus.

American policymakers had other reasons for promoting disarmament, notably concerns about Japan. The United States and Britain had the largest navies, roughly equal in strength, and had no interest in further naval construction. Japan, the next largest naval power, wanted to expand its navy. Americans worried that Japanese pressures on China could endanger Chinese territory and the Open Door policy. Harding and Hughes therefore agreed to host international discussions on limiting the size of navies and ensuring the status quo in China. In November 1921, Harding invited the major naval powers to Washington to discuss reducing "the crushing burdens of military and naval establishments."

When the delegates assembled for the **Washington Naval Conference**, Hughes shocked them with a radical proposal: scrap nearly 2 million tons of warships, mostly battleships. He also called for a ten-year ban on naval construction and limits on the size of navies that would keep the Japanese well behind the British and Americans. Hughes suggested a ratio of 5 to 5 to 3 for the United States, Britain, and Japan, with Italy and France allocated 1.7 each. Hughes's plan gained immediate support among the American public and most of the nations attending—but not Japan. The Japanese called it an insult and demanded equality. Discussions dragged on for two months, but the Japanese finally agreed. U.S. intelligence had broken the Japanese diplomatic code, so Hughes knew that the Japanese delegates had orders to concede if he held firm.

In February 1922, the United States, Britain, Japan, France, and Italy agreed to build no more **capital ships** for ten years and to abide by the 5:5:3:1.7:1.7 ratio for future shipbuilding. A British observer commented that Hughes had sunk more British ships in one speech "than all the admirals of the world." The powers also agreed to prohibit the use of poison gas and not to attack one another's Asian possessions. The **Nine-Power Pact**, which included China, the Netherlands, Portugal, and Belgium, affirmed the sovereignty and territorial boundaries of China and guaranteed equal commercial access to China, thereby maintaining the Open Door.

Hughes considered the meetings successful, though critics complained that there were no enforcement provisions and no mention of smaller ships, including submarines. Other attempts to reduce armaments had mixed outcomes. In 1930, Britain, the United States, and Japan established ratios for cruisers and destroyers similar to those of the Washington Conference. By the mid-1930s, however, Japan's demands for naval equality ended British and American cooperation and spurred new naval construction by all three.

capital ships   A navy's largest, most heavily armed ships; at the Washington Naval Conference, capital ships were those over 10,000 tons and carrying guns with at least an 8-inch bore.

Many Americans and Europeans applauded the achievements of the Washington Naval Conference but wanted to go further. In 1923 Senator Borah introduced a resolution in the Senate to outlaw war. In 1924 La Follette campaigned for a national referendum as a requirement for declaring war. In 1927 the French foreign minister, Aristide Briand, suggested a pact formally outlawing war between the France and the United States, privately hoping such an agreement would commit the United States to aid France if attacked. Secretary of State Kellogg instead suggested a multinational statement opposing war, thereby removing any hint of an American commitment to any nation. On August 27, 1928, the United States and fourteen other nations, including Britain, France, Germany, Italy, and Japan, signed the Pact of Paris, or **Kellogg-Briand Pact**, renouncing war "as an instrument of national policy" and agreeing to settle disputes peacefully. Eventually sixty-four nations signed, but the pact included no enforcement provisions, and nearly every **signatory** reserved its right to self-defense.

Thus, late in 1928, American independent internationalism seemed a success. Investments and loans by American businesses were fueling an expansive world economy and contributing to American prosperity. Avoiding entangling alliances, the United States had protected its Asian and Pacific interests against Japan, while protecting China and promoting disarmament and world peace. In Latin America, the United States had withdrawn some troops from the Caribbean, avoided intervention in Mexico, and tried to broker a peace in Nicaragua. Foreign policies based on economic expansion and noncoercive diplomacy appeared to be establishing a promising era of cooperation and peace in world affairs.

STUDY TOOLS

SUMMARY

The 1920s were a decade of prosperity. Unemployment was low, productivity grew steadily, and many Americans fared well. Sophisticated advertising campaigns created bright expectations, and installment buying freed consumers from paying cash. Many consumers bought more and bought on credit—stimulating manufacturing and expanding personal debt. Expectations of continuing prosperity also encouraged speculation. The stock market boomed, but agriculture did not share in this prosperity.

During the Roaring Twenties, Americans experienced significant social change. The automobile, radio, and movies, abetted by immigration restriction, produced a more homogeneous culture. Many American intellectuals, however, rejected the consumer-oriented culture. During the 1920s, African Americans produced an outpouring of significant art, literature, and music. Some young people rejected traditional constraints, and one result was the emergence of a youth culture.

---

signatory   One who has signed a treaty or other document.

Not all Americans embraced change. Some tried instead to maintain or restore earlier cultural values. The outcomes were mixed. Prohibition was largely unsuccessful. Fundamentalism grew and prompted a campaign against the teaching of evolution. Nativism helped produce significant new restrictions on immigration. The Ku Klux Klan, committed to nativism, traditional values, and white supremacy, experienced nationwide growth until 1925, but membership declined sharply thereafter.

Discrimination and occasional violence continued to affect the lives of people of color. Federal Indian policy had long stressed assimilation and allotment, but some groups successfully promoted different policies based on respect for Indian cultural values. Immigrants from Mexico came especially to California, Texas, and the Southwest. Some Mexicans working in agriculture tried, in vain, to organize unions. Nearly all unions faced strong opposition from employers. Some older gender roles for women broke down as women gained the right to vote and exercised more control over having children. A gay and lesbian subculture became more visible, especially in cities.

The politics of the era were marked by greater conservatism than before World War I. Warren G. Harding was a poor judge of character, and some of his appointees accepted bribes and disgraced their chief. Harding and his successor, Calvin Coolidge, expected government to act as a partner with business, and their economic policies minimized regulation and encouraged speculation. With some exceptions, progressive reform disappeared from politics, and efforts to secure federal assistance for farmers failed. The federal government was strongly conservative, staunchly probusiness, and unwilling to regulate economic activity. Herbert Hoover defeated Al Smith in the 1928 presidential election, in which the values of an older, rural America seemed to be pitted against those of the new, urban, immigrant society.

During the 1920s, the United States followed a policy of independent internationalism that stressed voluntary cooperation among nations, while at the same time enhancing opportunities for American business around the world. Relations with Latin America improved somewhat, and the Washington Naval Conference held out the hope for preventing a naval arms race.

CHRONOLOGY

AMERICA IN THE 1920s	
1908	Henry Ford introduces Model T General Motors formed
1914	Universal Negro Improvement Association founded
1914–1918	War in Europe
1920	Eighteenth Amendment (Prohibition) takes effect Nineteenth Amendment (women suffrage) takes effect Warren G. Harding elected president
1920–1921	Nationwide recession

1921	Farm Bloc formed
1921–1922	Washington Naval Conference
1922	Fordney-McCumber Tariff Sinclair Lewis's *Babbitt*
1923	Harding dies; Calvin Coolidge becomes president Jean Toomer's *Cane* American Indian Defense Association formed France occupies Ruhr Valley
1923–1927	Harding administration scandals revealed
1924	National Origins Act Coolidge elected Full citizenship for American Indians Dawes Plan U.S. forces withdraw from Dominican Republic
1924–1929	Great Bull Market
1925	Scopes trial F. Scott Fitzgerald's *The Great Gatsby* Ku Klux Klan claims 5 million members
1926	Florida real-estate boom collapses Railway Labor Act of 1926
1927	Charles Lindbergh's transatlantic flight Duke Ellington conducts jazz at Cotton Club
1928	Ford introduces Model A Kellogg-Briand Pact Herbert Hoover elected
1929	Great Depression begins

FOCUS QUESTIONS

If you have mastered this chapter, you should be able to answer these questions and explain the terms that follow the questions.

1. What was the basis for the economic expansion of the 1920s?
2. What weaknesses existed within the economy?
3. What groups most challenged traditional social patterns during the 1920s?
4. What role did technology play in social change during the 1920s?
5. Why and how did some Americans try to restore traditional social values during the 1920s?
6. What continuities and changes characterized racial and ethnic relations during the 1920s?
7. Is it appropriate to describe the 1920s as "the lean years" for working people?
8. How did gender roles and definitions change in the 1920s?
9. Compare the attitude of the Harding and Coolidge administrations toward the economy with the attitude of the Roosevelt and Wilson administrations.

10. How did the third-party candidacy of La Follette in 1924 resemble that of Roosevelt in 1912 and the Populists in 1892?
11. What role did the United States play in world affairs during the 1920s?
12. How successful was Hughes at the Washington Naval Conference?

KEY TERMS

Henry Ford (*p. 648*)

Model T (*p. 648*)

A. P. Giannini (*p. 649*)

Charles Lindbergh (*p. 655*)

Sinclair Lewis (*p. 655*)

Harlem Renaissance (*p. 656*)

jazz (*p. 656*)

Marcus Garvey (*p. 657*)

black separatism (*p. 657*)

flappers (*p. 657*)

Eighteenth Amendment (*p. 658*)

Al Capone (*p. 659*)

Clarence Darrow (*p. 660*)

National Origins Act (*p. 661*)

American Indian Defense Association (*p. 665*)

American Plan (*p. 666*)

welfare capitalism (*p. 666*)

Communist Party of the United States (*p. 667*)

Equal Rights Amendment (*p. 669*)

Sigmund Freud (*p. 669*)

Farm Bloc (*p. 671*)

Al Smith (*p. 671*)

McNary-Haugen bill (*p. 672*)

Railway Labor Act of 1926 (*p. 672*)

Augusto Sandino (*p. 675*)

Fordney-McCumber Tariff (*p. 677*)

Dawes Plan (*p. 677*)

Washington Naval Conference (*p. 678*)

Nine-Power Pact (*p. 678*)

Kellogg-Briand Pact (*p. 679*)

22

THE GREAT DEPRESSION AND THE NEW DEAL, 1929–1939

CHAPTER OUTLINE

• The Economic Crisis and Hoover's Response • The Election of 1932 and the Early New Deal • The Later New Deal, 1935–1939 • Americans Face the Depression • The Great Depression and New Deal in Perspective • Study Tools

---

THE ECONOMIC CRISIS AND HOOVER'S RESPONSE

Campaigning for the presidency in 1928, Herbert Hoover had promised a "New Day" for America, but his sweeping victory was more a vote for the status quo. The United States had experienced almost a decade of economic growth, and people voted for Hoover expecting that trend to continue. The outcome was much different, as the nation was soon tested by economic and social trauma.

The Crash and the Great Depression

Hoover took office as president in the midst of rising stock prices, shiny new cars, and rapidly expanding suburbs that seemed to verify his observation about "the final triumph over poverty." But behind the rush for homes, radios, and vacuum cleaners were serious economic weaknesses, some of which were already becoming visible. Less than eight months later, on "Black Thursday," October 24, 1929, the stock market crashed. The value of stocks plummeted, and across the country frenzied brokers rushed to place sell orders. Few places were untouched. In the mid-Atlantic, on board the passenger liner *Berengaria*, Helena Rubenstein watched stock prices fall and finally sold 50,000 shares of Westinghouse Company. She had lost more than a million dollars in a few hours. The market rebounded a bit on Friday but crashed again on Monday. The next day—"Black Tuesday"—prices plunged and continued to fall throughout the year. Within the first week of the crash, stocks fell by a total of $30 billion. Thousands who had speculated on an ever rising market were ruined. Stories circulated of New York hotel clerks asking guests whether they wanted rooms for sleeping or jumping. In fact, nationwide, the suicide rate increased by almost 50 percent in 1929, as compared to the previous eight years. The Dow Jones Industrial Averages measure the stock market performance of selected major stocks. From a high point of 381.17 on September 3, 1929, the Dow fell to a low of 41.22 on July 8, 1932. Similar losses occurred in stock markets around the world. The Dow did not recover to pre-1929 levels until the 1950s.

The crash was a starting point for the **Great Depression**, but it was a catalyst, not the cause. The Depression resulted from uneven economic growth, overproduction, a poor distribution of income, excessive credit buying, and a **credit crunch** resulting from serious weaknesses in the banking system. The prosperity of the 1920s had in part rested on expanding industries—especially construction, automobiles, movies, and electronics—that pushed the rest of the economy forward. By 1927, most of those industries were slowing down. Construction starts, for example, fell from 11 billion to 9 billion units between 1926 and 1929, causing producers of household merchandise to reduce production. The expansion of the 1920s had been uneven. Older industries, including railroads, textiles, and iron and steel had barely made a profit, while mining suffered steady losses. Workers in those industries saw little increase in wages or standards of living. The postwar economic expansion completely bypassed agriculture, and farmers watched their incomes and property values slip to about half of their wartime highs. Compounding these problems, credit had virtually dried up in rural America, as five thousand banks, many in rural areas, closed between 1921 and 1928. By the end of 1928, thousands of people had left their farms, and agriculture was approaching an economic crisis.

Another weakness of the economy lay in the distribution of wealth. Economists estimate that, in 1929, the richest 5 percent of Americans received about one-third of all income, much of which was in the form of interest, dividends, and rent. Given the amount of wealth in the hands of those few, reductions in spending or investment by the wealthiest could have a disproportionate effect on the entire economy. Much of the $30 billion loss in stock values represented losses for the wealthiest. The distribution of wealth affected consumer spending in other ways as well. In the late 1920s, the Brookings Institution judged that an annual salary of $2,500 provided an American family a comfortable standard of living. It also found that 70 percent of American families earned less than that amount. When Hoover took office, many people were buying on credit, especially through installment buying (discussed in the preceding chapter). Americans had spent about $100 million buying on credit in 1919, but ten years later that amount had soared over $7 billion. Still, few worried as long as the economy seemed stable, unemployment remained low,

---

credit crunch (or credit crisis)   A significant reduction in the availability of credit, caused by changes in banks' lending policies.

and Americans had confidence in the economy. All that changed with the stock market crash.

The stock market crash undermined economic confidence and highlighted the weaknesses of the economy. A soaring stock market was a symbol of a vigorous economy, but the market's continued fall made investors and business leaders wary. Reduced demand led manufacturers to cut production and lay off workers or reduce hours. As more and more people found themselves out of work or with smaller paychecks, they cut back consumer purchases and stopped buying on credit, thereby further reducing demand. They often found that they could not make their installment payments, so they lost their car or radio.

As the economy spiraled downward, the banking system appeared to be collapsing. Too many banks had made risky loans and now found that they could not collect on them. As rumors circulated of a bank's instability, customers lined up at teller windows to empty their accounts. As such "runs" on banks intensified, more and more banks were unable to meet their obligations, declared bankruptcy, and closed their doors. Many thousands of depositors lost their savings, jarring the well-being of many upper- and middle-class families.

As some banks closed their doors and others struggled to remain open, the nation entered a credit crunch. Unable to collect on many of their current loans, bankers became highly cautious about making new loans—and credit dried up. In the midst of this, the Federal Reserve *raised* interest rates, which further discouraged borrowing. Many Americans dumped their stocks for whatever they could get and refused to invest in the stock market so long as it kept falling. Because economic growth and expansion require access to both credit from banks and funds from the sale of stocks, the entire economy lurched toward paralysis.

By 1933, American exports were at their lowest level since 1905, nearly ninety thousand businesses had failed, and corporate profits were down 60 percent. Unemployment rose from 3 percent in 1929 to 9 percent in 1930 and to 25 percent by 1933, with much higher rates in manufacturing areas. American industry, according to *Fortune,* suffered 46 percent unemployment, but in many areas it was much worse. In Gary, Indiana, nearly the entire working class was out of a job by 1932. Nine thousand banks had closed, with depositors losing $2.5 billion. The drastic decline in the value of stocks, the closing of banks, and actions by the Federal Reserve all contributed to a serious shrinkage in the money supply, causing deflation. Average annual income dropped 35 percent— from $2,300 to $1,500—by 1933. Prices for most products began to fall, reducing income to both merchants and producers, but the decline in income and uncertainties about the overall economy meant that people were unable or unwilling to buy even at reduced prices. Automobile purchases dropped by 75 percent.

Other industrial nations also experienced economic contraction and significant unemployment. During the last half of the 1920s, the European economy was recovering from the devastation of the Great War, greatly aided by over $5.1 billion dollars borrowed from American sources. However, by the end of 1928, American investors were already reducing their loans to Europe.

The onset of the Depression in the United States made the international credit contraction much worse. As the Depression spread, many nations, including the United States, raised tariffs to protect their industries from foreign goods. The 1930 Smoot-Hawley Tariff set the highest tariff rates in U.S. history. While these actions may have protected domestic markets, they also undermined world trade—including American exports. World trade slowed to a crawl by 1931.

Hoover's Response to Economic Crisis   At first, the most common response to the plunge in stock prices was that voiced by Secretary of the Treasury Andrew Mellon, who stated that the economy remained strong, that the market plunge was temporary, and that it would actually strengthen the economy. Though many experts argued that the free-market sysem would eventually heal itself, Hoover disagreed. He summoned the nation's economic leaders, asking them to help absorb the economic shock by reducing profits rather than cutting jobs and wages. At the same time, he urged Congress, states, and cities to increase spending on **public works projects**, including government buildings and highways, to stimulate the economy. He called on local groups to raise money to help the unemployed. The Agricultural Marketing Act (1929) tried to address farmers' problems with the creation of a Farm Board to help support agricultural prices. Despite some initial successes, these efforts did little to counteract the credit crunch and produced no sustained recovery. As profits declined, businesses cut production, reduced wages, and laid off workers. Agricultural prices continued to collapse, and state, local, and private efforts to aid the growing number of unemployed were overwhelmed (see Figure 22.1).

With the country slipping further into the Depression, Hoover took new steps in 1931, some of which finally addressed the credit crunch. He asked Congress for banking reforms, financial support for home mortgages, the creation of the **Reconstruction Finance Corporation** (RFC), and higher taxes to pay for it all. Congress responded in 1932 with the **Glass-Steagall Act**, which encouraged lending, and the **Federal Home Loan Bank Act**, which allowed homeowners to remortgage their homes at lower rates and payments. Hoover intended the RFC to be the major tool to fight the Depression by pumping money into the economy. Created in 1932—several years after the beginning of the credit crunch that was producing economic paralysis—the RFC used federal funds to provide loans to banks, railroads, and large corporations to prevent their collapse and expand their operations. Hoover and his advisers hoped the benefits of this expansion would "trickle down" to workers and the unemployed through higher wages and new jobs. But the RFC came years too late and, even then, was slow to begin operations. It did loan over $805 million within its first five months, but with

---

public works projects   Construction projects financed by public funds and carried out by federal, state, or local governments.

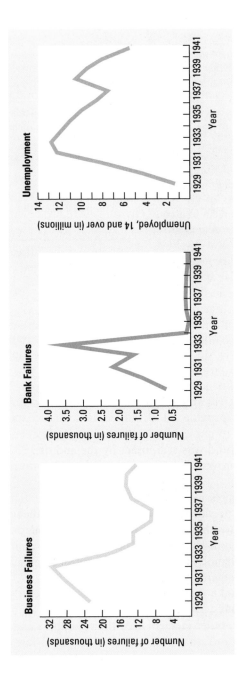

FIGURE 22.1 Charting the Economics of the Depression

Between 1929 and 1933, the number of people unemployed and of bank and the number of business failures steadily increased. As the New Deal began, not only did the statistics improve, but for many a sense of hope also emerged.

IT MATTERS TODAY

Preventing Another Great Depression

In September 2008, major financial institutions faced bankruptcy owing to unwise loans. Panic swept through financial markets. Fifteen banks failed, and the stock market crashed throughout the month of October, recording some of the greatest losses ever.

Ben Bernanke was chairman of the Federal Reserve System. A former economics professor, Bernanke had previously researched the causes of the Great Depression. The key factor, he had concluded, had been the failure of the Federal Reserve to stop bank failures. In 2008, when banks began to fail and the stock market crashed, Bernanke moved quickly

and worked closely with Henry Paulson, secretary of the treasury, to prevent some bank failures and to secure approval of hundreds of billions of dollars of federal loans to and investments in key financial institutions to keep them stable and discourage a credit crunch that could lead to another Great Depression.

- Do newspaper accounts from September and October 2008 draw comparisons to the events of 1929?
- Can you find other examples when historical analysis, such as that of Bernanke, has affected recent governmental policies?

little apparent effect on the economy. Critics branded the program "welfare for the rich" and insisted Hoover do more for the poor and unemployed. Hoover opposed federal relief to the poor, however, believing that it was too expensive and eroded the work ethic. But as unemployment reached nearly 25 percent and pressure mounted from Congress and the public, he accepted an Emergency Relief Division within the RFC to provide $300 million in loans to states to pay for relief. Yet few states wanted to put themselves more deeply in debt by borrowing, and 90 percent of the relief fund was still intact by the end of 1932. Whether for recovery or relief, the RFC proved to be too little and too late to resolve the economic crisis.

The onslaught of the Depression changed Hoover's and the nation's fortunes. Many Americans blamed the president and the Republicans for the worsening economy and for callousness toward the hardships besetting the country. As people who lost their homes began to live in shantytowns on the outskirts of many cities, the head of publicity for the Democratic National Committee sarcastically dubbed them "**Hoovervilles**," and the name stuck.

Some farmers began to take matters into their own hands. In October 1931, when an Iowa bank **foreclosed** on a mortgage and held an auction sale of the farmer's land and equipment, other farmers used their numbers and threats of violence to force a "penny auction" that returned the foreclosed farm to its owners

foreclose To confiscate property when mortgage payments are delinquent; in the 1930s, it was typical to auction off all foreclosed assets.

for a fraction of its value. Penny auctions quickly spread across the Midwest. In Ohio, for example, one farmer, backed by a crowd of angry neighbors, regained his farm for a high bid of $1.90 to settle a mortgage of $800. In the summer of 1932, some midwestern farmers joined the **Farmers' Holiday Association,** led by Milo Reno. Reno called on farmers to "stay home, buy nothing, sell nothing," to push up prices by destroying their crops rather than selling them. Many farmers responded not just by withholding their own produce from market but also by setting up roadblocks to prevent other farmers from selling theirs. By 1932, Communist Party organizers were signing up members among desperate farmers. Farmers were not alone. Across the nation, strikes, protest rallies, "bread marches," and rent riots took place as citizens demanded more jobs, higher wages, and relief payments. Overall, the Communist Party signed up nearly 20,000 new members between 1931 and 1932, though most dropped out after a short time.

A major protest took place in the spring and summer of 1932 when thousands of World War I veterans, usually called the **Bonus Army,** converged on Washington, D.C., to demonstrate support for the "bonus bill," which promised early payment of veteran's bonuses originally scheduled for 1945. The marchers, some with their families, set up a Hooverville across from Congress at Anacosta Flats. When the bill failed, most left, but nearly ten thousand stayed behind. In late July, Hoover ordered the army to remove them. Led by Army Chief of Staff General Douglas MacArthur, troops armed with cavalry sabers, rifles, tear gas, and fixed bayonets evicted the veterans and their families and burned their shelters. Over one hundred veterans were injured and two were killed, but rumors quickly swelled those numbers and intensified the public's angry reaction. Upon hearing of the army's action, the governor of New York, Franklin D. Roosevelt, exclaimed, "This will elect me."

THE ELECTION OF 1932 AND THE EARLY NEW DEAL

Like the elections of 1860 and 1896, the election of 1932 was one of the great turning points in American political history. Since 1860, Republicans had usually been able to win the White House and set the agenda for national politics. After 1932, however, the Democrats, under the leadership of Franklin D. Roosevelt, created bold new policies and established themselves as the majority party for a generation.

The Roosevelt Landslide   Nearly any Democratic candidate could have defeated Hoover in 1932, but the Democrats nominated an exceptional politician in Franklin D. Roosevelt, born into wealth and educated at the exclusive Groton School and Harvard College. After graduation, with a recognizable name, Roosevelt entered New York politics. Tall, handsome, charming, and a good speaker, he became assistant secretary of the navy (a position his distant cousin Theodore had once held) in the Wilson administration, then won the Democratic nomination for vice president in 1920.

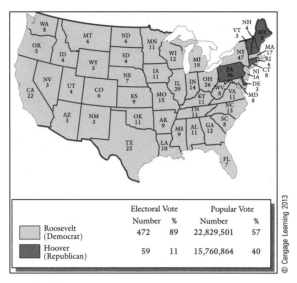

	Electoral Vote		Popular Vote	
	Number	%	Number	%
Roosevelt (Democrat)	472	89	22,829,501	57
Hoover (Republican)	59	11	15,760,864	40

© Cengage Learning 2013

MAP 22.1 Presidential Election, 1932

The trauma of the Great Depression can be gauged by the shifting fortunes of President Herbert Hoover. In 1928, he had won 444 electoral votes and carried all but eight states. In 1932, by contrast, he won only 59 electoral votes and carried only seven states. His Democratic opponent, Franklin D. Roosevelt, was the big winner.

Though he and presidential candidate James Cox lost, his political future looked bright. Then, in 1921, he was stricken with polio and paralyzed from the waist down. Greatly aided by his wife, Eleanor, he kept his political career alive and in 1928 won the governorship of New York. Roosevelt was one of the few governors to mobilize his state's limited resources to help the unemployed and poor. Although the results were modest, his efforts suggested a caring and energetic leader—a champion of the "forgotten man." The opposite image stuck to Hoover, who seemed to have little concern for the 11 million unemployed Americans.

When nominated for president in 1932, Roosevelt broke with all precedents and flew to Chicago to give his acceptance speech to the convention. Establishing a theme for the coming campaign, Roosevelt emphatically announced that he and the Democratic Party had no fear of breaking with "all foolish traditions" and closed by promising a "new deal for the American people." The media quickly picked up the term, and Roosevelt's campaign acquired a memorable slogan: the **New Deal**. Although his speech offered no concrete solutions to the nation's problems, it promised hope and instilled the belief that Roosevelt would move the nation along new paths.

During the campaign, Roosevelt tried to avoid any commitments and policy proposals that might offend voters. He supported direct federal relief while promising to balance the budget, but mostly he stressed hope and the prospect of change.

After his bout with polio in 1921, Roosevelt could walk using braces and supports but usually used a wheelchair—yet few pictures exist of him in a wheelchair because news photographers generally respected his wish not to be photographed that way. Here he relaxes at his family estate at Hyde Park in New York State.

AP Photo/M.L/Suckley/FDR Libraries

Hoover claimed that the campaign was "more than a contest between two men," that it was "a contest between two philosophies of government." The electorate chose the philosophy of Roosevelt and the Democratic Party. Across the nation, people voted for Democrats at every level, from local to national. Roosevelt won in a landslide, with 57 percent of the vote to 40 percent for Hoover, who carried only six states.

1933—The First Hundred Days   In the four months between the election and Inauguration Day, Americans eagerly waited for the New Deal to start even as the economy worsened. Many expected that Roosevelt and his advisers, labeled by the press as the Brain Trust because the group included several college professors, were developing a plan to restore prosperity. In fact, Roosevelt's advisers were frequently at odds about which path to follow. Some, like Rexford Tugwell and Raymond Moley, supported a collective approach, working with business through joint economic planning. Others, like Harry Hopkins, Eleanor Roosevelt, and Frances Perkins, advocated social programs. All agreed, however, that the worst path was doing nothing.

Roosevelt took office on March 4, as many of the country's banks seemed in danger of closing. Millions listened to the radio and heard the president reassure Americans that they had "nothing to fear but fear itself" and promise that the economy would revive. "We must act quickly," he specified, adding that he would call Congress into emergency session to deal with the banking crisis. On March 6, Roosevelt—soon widely referred to as FDR—declared a national **Bank Holiday,** closing all the country's banks. Three days later, as freshmen congressmen were still finding their seats, the president presented Congress with the **Emergency Banking Bill.** Without even seeing a written version of the bill, Democrats and Republicans gave Roosevelt what he wanted in less than four hours. The new law required a federal inspection before banks could reopen, thus reassuring depositors that those that reopened were safe, and it allowed the Federal Reserve and the Reconstruction Finance Corporation (held over from the Hoover administration) to prop up the nation's banking system by providing funds and buying stocks of some banks. On Sunday evening, March 12, Roosevelt took to the radio in the first of his **fireside chats.** He told the nation that the federal government was solving the banking crisis and banks would be safe again, adding that "It is safer to keep your money in a reopened bank than under the mattress." Over 60 million Americans listened to the speech, and most believed him. On the following day in Atlanta, for example, deposits outnumbered withdrawals by over 3 to 1. Within a month, nearly 75 percent of the nation's banks were operating again.

The New Deal had begun. Riding a wave of popular support and great expectations, Roosevelt faced a unique political climate of almost total **bipartisanship.** Some Republicans even enthusiastically embraced aspects of the New Deal. Within its **First Hundred Days,** the Roosevelt administration and Congress created a long list of new federal agencies and programs. A few carried out traditional Democratic Party goals, such as the repeal of Prohibition, but most were aimed at relief, recovery, and reform.

Among the first bills Roosevelt offered Congress was the **Agricultural Adjustment Act** (AAA), intended to bring the recovery of agriculture. Passed by Congress on May 12, the act created the Agricultural Adjustment Administration (AAA), which paid farmers to reduce production as a way of cutting the surpluses that drove down prices for farm produce. Focusing on wheat, cotton, corn, rice, tobacco, hogs, and dairy products, a planning board determined the amount to be removed from production. The program was to be funded by a special tax on industrial food processors. Some critics argued that the AAA gave too much power to the government. Others complained that it did nothing to help small farmers, sharecroppers, and tenant farmers, or to make surplus food available for the needy.

The AAA addressed the problems of agriculture, and the Roosevelt administration next turned to industrial recovery. The **National Industrial Recovery Act** (NIRA) was approved in June, with Roosevelt calling it the "most

---

bipartisanship   In American politics, when the two major parties work together cooperatively to resolve issues.

important and far reaching legislation passed by the American Congress." The act, a compromise among Roosevelt's advisers who had advocated two quite different approaches, incorporated both approaches by creating two new agencies, the **National Recovery Administration** (NRA) and the **Public Works Administration** (PWA).

The NRA, led by Hugh Johnson, a former army general, sought to stimulate the economy through national economic planning by establishing, industry by industry, codes that set prices, production levels, and wages. Business supported the NRA because it allowed **price fixing** that raised both prices and profits. Labor was attracted by Section 7a, which gave workers the right to organize unions and bargain collectively, outlawed child labor, and established minimum wages and maximum hours of work. By early 1935, some 700 industries with 2.5 million workers were displaying a poster with a blue eagle that meant they were covered by NRA codes.

The PWA took a different approach, stimulating recovery by putting federal funds into major construction projects, thereby providing jobs directly for construction workers and more jobs in the industries that supplied construction materials. These jobs would then stimulate demand for consumer products and create still more jobs. The PWA was, by far, the largest federal public works program up to that time and still ranks as one of the largest ever. Administered by the Department of the Interior, the PWA was slow to begin operations, partly because the projects required significant planning and partly because the secretary of the interior, "Honest Harold" Ickes, was scrupulous about preventing any waste or graft. Nonetheless, over six years PWA spent some $6 billion (equivalent to almost $100 billion today), usually in cooperation with state and local governments, funding some 34,000 projects, including roads, bridges, giant electricity-generating dams, 70 percent of all new school buildings, one-third of all new hospital buildings, two aircraft carriers, and much more.

One of the most innovative programs of the First Hundred Days was the **Tennessee Valley Authority** (TVA). The goal was to develop a regional approach to planning and development for a rural and impoverished region of 40,000 square miles including parts of seven states. The most immediate benefit was to provide jobs repairing and building dams and improving flood controls. But the TVA did much more. The TVA improved the navigability of hundreds of miles of rivers and lakes and reduced soil erosion. TVA dams provided electricity through federally owned and operated hydroelectric systems, making possible the introduction of electricity to many rural areas. The TVA also provided a model for other federal dam-building projects, especially in the West, that provided water and electricity for economic development. Critics of the New Deal opposed such government-owned agencies as socialist.

Recovery was one thrust of Roosevelt's offensive against the Depression. He had campaigned on the slogan of helping the "forgotten man," and in March

---

price fixing   The artificial setting of commodity prices.

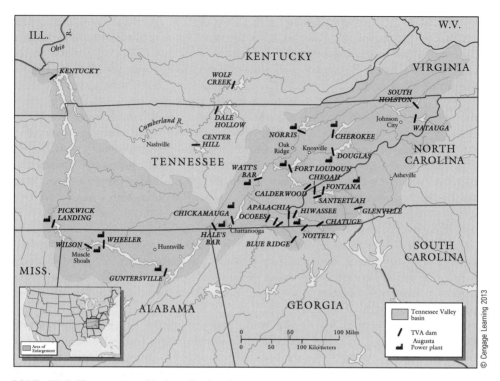

MAP 22.2 Tennessee Valley Authority

This map shows the vast scale of the TVA and pinpoints the locations of 29 dams and 13 power plants that emerged from this project.

1933 unemployment was at a historic high—25 percent of the work force. In industrial states such as New York, Ohio, Pennsylvania, and Illinois, unemployment pushed toward 33 percent and was even higher in some manufacturing centers. Recognizing that state and private relief sources could not cope with people's needs, Roosevelt proposed and Congress enacted federal relief programs. Though all were temporary measures, they established a new role for the federal government. By the end of the decade, about 46 million people had received some form of relief support.

The first relief program was the **Civilian Conservation Corps** (CCC), passed on March 31, 1933. It established several thousand army-style camps to house, employ, and provide a healthy, moral environment for unemployed urban males aged 18 to 25. Within months it had enrolled over 300,000 men, paying them $30 a month, $25 of which had to be sent to their parents. By 1941, more than 3 million men had received employment through the CCC camps. The "Conservation Army" built and improved national park facilities, constructed roads and firebreaks, worked to control erosion, dug irrigation ditches, fought forest fires, and planted trees. In the camps, 35,000 men were taught to read.

The CCC reached only a small percentage of those needing relief. To widen the range of assistance, the Roosevelt administration created the **Federal Emergency Relief Administration** (FERA). FERA provided states with money for their relief needs. In some cases it bypassed state and local governments and instituted federally administered programs. One such FERA program opened special centers to provide housing, meals, and medical care for many of the homeless roaming the nation. In the program's first year of operation, it cared for as many as 5 million people. One man who had been riding the rails was pulled off a train in Omaha and taken to a transient camp where he was deloused and given a bath, a bed, and food. "We ate a great meal," he recalled years later. "We thought we'd gone to heaven." In other programs, half a million people attended literacy classes and 1 million received vaccinations and immunizations.

The **Civil Works Administration** (CWA) was a temporary measure to help the unemployed through the winter of 1933–34 by hiring 4 million jobless people for federal, state, and local work projects. Though critics argued that the CWA sometimes created meaningless jobs, the goal of the program was to provide work to as many unemployed people as possible, and CWA projects did result in many permanent public works.

The list of new programs approved during the "hundred days" did not end there. The **Home Owners' Loan Corporation** (HOLC), established in May 1933, permitted homeowners to refinance their mortgages at lower interest rates through the federal government. Before it stopped making loans in 1936, the HOLC had refinanced 1 million homes, including 20 percent of all mortgaged urban homes. To correct problems within the banking industries, the Banking Act of 1933 gave more power to the Federal Reserve System and created the **Federal Deposit Insurance Corporation** (FDIC), which provided federal insurance for those who deposited money in member banks. In less than six months, 97 percent of all commercial banks had joined the system.

The special session and first session of the Seventy-third Congress met for 102 days, but this period quickly became known as the Hundred Days. Never before had such a long list of major legislation been passed in so short a time. Since 1933, journalists have popularized the notion that a new president should be judged on the basis of his accomplishments during his first hundred days in office, and an activist president is always compared to FDR. However, such comparisons rarely take into account the seriousness of the crisis facing the president and Congress in 1933 or the unusual degree of bipartisanship that characterized much of the hundred days.

1934—Year of Turmoil

The New Deal started with almost total support in Congress and among the people. However, as the economy began to improve, opposition emerged. By mid-1933, most Republicans and some conservative Democrats opposed relief programs, federal spending, and increased governmental controls over business. A few new policies were approved in 1934, notably creation of the **Securities and Exchange**

Commission (SEC), to regulate stock markets, and the National Housing Act, which set up the **Federal Housing Administration** (FHA) to make home loans more available. But in that year conservative Democrats, including Al Smith, the 1928 presidential candidate, joined with representatives of several major corporations to establish the **American Liberty League**, which opposed New Deal policies through an extensive media campaign funded mostly by the Du Pont family and leaders of other powerful corporations. Many vocal conservatives fumed that Roosevelt threatened free enterprise, if not capitalism. The Hearst newspaper chain instructed its editors to tell the public that the New Deal was a "raw deal" and that Roosevelt was leading the nation into socialism. The Communist Party, meanwhile, stridently attacked the New Deal as a tool of big business that was pushing the nation toward fascism. By late 1934, Communists claimed 25,000 members and 6,000 youth members; half of the members were unemployed, but the Communists also claimed an additional 50,000 followers in Communist-controlled unions and organizations of the unemployed.

A major target of anti-New Dealers was the NRA, which ran into trouble almost from the beginning. As implementation proceeded, support for NRA programs waned, and critics soon dubbed it the "National Run Around." Workers complained that NRA codes set wages too low and hours too long, and that employers resisted unionization. One woman textile worker wrote to the president that her husband was "laid off, for no other reason than they got a union hear [*sic*] and My Husband became president of it." Consumers grumbled that the NRA caused prices to rise without creating any noticeable growth in wages or jobs. Farmers griped that NRA-generated price increases ate up any AAA benefits they received. Some businesses resisted the restrictions and regulations in NRA codes and questioned the government's right to impose such controls.

The NRA's Section 7a had raised workers' expectations by ensuring their right to organize, but they were disappointed in the actual support for their unions. As union membership grew, many thousands of workers in 1934 walked picket lines in nearly two thousand strikes in almost every city. Thirty thousand cab drivers shut down New York City's taxis in late January and most of February. Between January and early May, more than 80,000 coal miners walked out in a half-dozen separate strikes in nine states. Nearly 40,000 auto workers struck, sometimes only for a day, at nine plants in four states. Several hundred thousand textile workers walked out in six states, the largest of all the strikes in 1934, but were unsuccessful in gaining union recognition. Nearly 22,000 longshore and maritime workers were more successful after tying up shipping on the entire Pacific Coast for three months. A strike by Minneapolis Teamsters eventually gained union recognition and led to the first organization of over-the-road drivers (truckers driving between cities). Communists or other Marxists were prominent in some of those strikes.

The organizing drives and strikes often met stubborn resistance from employers and local officials. Between July 1 and the end of 1933 alone, before the biggest wave of strikes even began, the American Civil Liberties Union counted fifteen strikers killed, two hundred injured, and hundreds arrested and a half-dozen deployments of National Guard troops. Further, the ACLU claimed, the NRA lacked "the will or the power to overcome the defiance of employers." "Labor's rights to meet, organize and strike have been widely violated," the ACLU concluded. Further violence came in 1934, and in some places, notably San Francisco and Minneapolis, there were brief general strikes when all those cities' unions stopped work to protest the killing of strikers.

By 1934, too, several figures began to attract significant attention by arguing that the New Deal had not gone far enough. At three o'clock every Sunday afternoon, **Father Charles Coughlin**, a Roman Catholic priest, used the radio to preach to nearly 30 million Americans. Formerly a strong supporter of Roosevelt, the "radio priest" now turned against the New Deal and advocated a guaranteed annual income, the redistribution of wealth, tougher antimonopoly laws, and the nationalization of banking. His attacks on Roosevelt also began to carry anti-Semitic overtones. His organization, the National Union for Social Justice, soon claimed 5 million members. **Huey Long**, a flamboyant senator from Louisiana, proposed a dramatic **"Share Our Wealth"** plan: every family would receive an annual check for $2,000, a home, a car, a radio, and a college education for each child, all to be funded by taxing the rich, including confiscating all income over $1 million. Share Our Wealth societies quickly signed up over 4 million members throughout the country. Dr. Francis Townsend advocated an old-age pension plan to provide every American aged 60 and older with a monthly pension check for $200. To qualify, individuals could not work and had to spend the money within a month. Thousands of Townsend clubs sprang up with an estimated membership of several million, including sixty members of Congress.

Upton Sinclair, the socialist who had exposed the unsanitary conditions in meatpacking with his novel, *The Jungle* (1905), won the Democratic nomination for governor of California in 1934, arguing for a program he called "End Poverty in California," or EPIC, which proposed to take over idle factories and farmland for use by the unemployed. When Sinclair lost the election, he broadened his EPIC program to "End Poverty in Civilization" and sought to build a national movement.

Amid the attacks on the New Deal and the problems with the NRA, the first real measure of voter sentiment came in the 1934 state and congressional elections. Democrats had a one-vote majority in the House of Representatives after the 1930 elections, and Roosevelt's landslide victory in 1932 boosted them to a 313–117 majority. Most politicians and journalists expected the 1934 congressional elections to follow the usual off-year pattern in which the president's party lost seats. In 1934, however, Democrats made further gains, now outnumbering Republicans by 320 to 103 in the house and 60–35 in the Senate. Roosevelt, it seemed, had become immensely popular despite all the criticism from the right and left.

THE LATER NEW DEAL, 1935–1939

Roosevelt was encouraged by the strong endorsement of the New Deal apparent in the 1934 election results, looked forward to expanding the New Deal, and became less willing to cooperate with the conservatives and business leaders who had moved into the opposition. At the same time, he was also concerned that recovery was not progressing as rapidly as desired and that the New Deal had not provided sufficient help to the unemployed.

1935—The Second Hundred Days   Despite the huge Democratic majorities in Congress, the early months of 1935 registered little new legislation, and FDR himself provided scant leadership. He did launch one new initiative when he asked Congress to provide more **work relief**. Months later, Congress responded by allocating nearly $5 billion for relief and creating a new agency, the **Works Progress Administration** (WPA). **Harry Hopkins,** the former social worker whom FDR put in charge of the WPA, set out to put the unemployed to work. (WPA programs are discussed later in this chapter.)

Beyond the WPA, Roosevelt seemed uncertain where to turn next. He anxiously watched both Huey Long and the Supreme Court. He considered Long dangerous because of his contempt for democracy in Louisiana, where he completely controlled state politics, and his demagogic appeals for national support. If Long were to run as a third-party candidate in 1936 and unite the supporters of Coughlin, Townsend, and Sinclair, he might be able to win the presidency or, at the least, throw the election to a Republican. The Supreme Court was also a source of anxiety because many New Deal programs were coming under challenge for their constitutionality. Then, on May 27, 1935, in *Schechter Poultry Corporation v. the United States*, the Supreme Court ruled that the NRA was unconstitutional because it improperly delegated legislative authority to the executive branch and exceeded congressional authority to regulate only interstate commerce. Roosevelt furiously exclaimed that the Court still had a "horse and buggy" mentality.

Roosevelt now seized the initiative, calling on Congress a few days later to pass several pieces of legislation. Members of Congress had been planning to go home and avoid the steamy Washington summer but now stayed in session and, over the next three months, passed some of the most significant legislation of the twentieth century.

The establishment of a federal old-age and survivor insurance program set the tone of the **Second Hundred Days** and significantly modified the government's role in society. Frances Perkins, the secretary of labor and the first woman to serve in a president's cabinet, was the driving force behind the **Social Security Act** (1935). She had been working on the bill since early 1933, and now that Roosevelt gave it his full support it moved toward passage. The act's most controversial element was a pension plan for retirees 65 or older. The program was to begin in 1937, and initial benefits would vary depending on how much an individual paid into the system.

Compared to Perkins's original plan or to many existing European systems, the Social Security system was limited and conservative. It failed to cover domestic and agricultural laborers and provided no health insurance. Roosevelt insisted

---

work relief   Government programs to provide paid work for the unemployed.

Michigan artist Alfred Castagne sketching Works Progress Administration (WPA) construction workers, 1939. The WPA provided a wide variety of jobs, from those requiring little or no previous training to jobs for artists and classical musicians.

that workers should pay for their old-age pensions, saying, "We put those payroll contributions there so as to give the contributors a legal, moral, and political right to collect their pensions and unemployment benefits. With those taxes in there, no damn politician can ever scrap my social security program." For Americans, the new Social Security program provided not only old-age pensions but also federal aid to families with dependent children and to the disabled, and it helped fund state-run systems of unemployment compensation. Within two years, every state was part of the unemployment compensation system, paying between $15 and $18 a week in unemployment compensation and supplying support to over 28 million people. Passage of the Social Security Act established a major new function for the federal government and is one of the most durable legacies of the New Deal. Since its inception, amendments have changed the method of payments, instituted cost-of-living increases, and added medical coverage. Millions of Americans have benefited from the system. Though controversial for years after its passage, no one has seriously argued for dismantling the program for many decades.

The next bill that Roosevelt called on Congress to approve was the National Labor Relations Act (NLRA). Largely the work of Senator Robert Wagner of New York and called the **Wagner Act**, it strengthened unions by putting the power of government behind workers' right to organize and to bargain collectively with their employers over the terms and conditions of their employment. It created the National Labor Relations Board as a new regulatory agency to oversee labor relations and ensure workers' rights, including their right to conduct elections to determine union representation and to prevent unfair labor practices, such as firing or **blacklisting** workers for union activities. The act excluded workers in agriculture and service industries. Nonetheless, the Wagner Act altered the relationships among business, labor, and the government and, in a very real way, redistributed economic power from employers to unions.

The final bill that Roosevelt pushed was a revision of income tax rates for those making over $50,000 a year. Often called the "Wealth Tax Act," it was intended to increase federal revenues to pay for such new programs as the WPA. Taken together with WPA, the Wealth Tax Act provides the first significant example of a federal redistributive policy—taxing the wealthy to provide work relief for the unemployed. Social Security also had some modestly redistributive features. Since 1935, a modest level of redistribution has been a continuing feature of federal economic policy.

The New Deal in Action   By 1935 and 1936, the New Deal had touched the lives of a large majority of Americans and changed the United States in important ways (see Table 22.1). The activities of New Deal agencies were so widespread and various that it is possible to describe only some of the most prominent.

In the West, several huge dam construction projects significantly changed the course of rivers. Boulder Dam, on the Colorado River, later renamed Hoover Dam, was begun during the Hoover administration to generate electricity and to provide water to southern California. In Washington and Oregon, the PWA funded the massive Grand Coulee Dam on the Columbia River, the largest electrical power facility in the United States, providing the foundation for economic development in that region. The Fort Peck Dam in Montana, a PWA project on the Missouri River, was the largest earthen dam in the world when it was completed in 1939. The Central Valley Project in central California began with WPA funding and built dams, reservoirs, and irrigation canals.

The WPA employed over 2.1 million people a year between 1935 and 1938. Many did manual labor, building roads, schools, and other public facilities in partnership with local governments. The WPA sought to pay wages higher than relief payments but lower than local wages. Wages for nonwhites and women were the exception, generally exceeding the local rate. The WPA did not duplicate the PWA. Its projects usually spent less on materials than the PWA, and often created less durable structures.

The WPA was more than construction—it also created jobs for professionals, writers, artists, actors and actresses, and musicians. Unemployed historians, writers, and teachers conducted oral interviews, including sessions with nearly every living ex-slave, and wrote state and local histories and guidebooks. Theater groups and orchestras toured towns and cities, performing Shakespeare and Beethoven. By 1939 an estimated 30 million people had watched a WPA production. Unemployed artists created works for public buildings. Some Americans objected to actors, artists, and writers receiving aid, arguing that their labor was not real work. But Hopkins bluntly responded, "Hell, they got to eat just like other people."

---

blacklisting   Practice in which businesses share information to deny employment to workers known to belong to unions.

TABLE 22.1 | SELECTED MAJOR LEGISLATION OF THE NEW DEAL

Year	New Deal Programs	Purpose
1933	March 9–June 16: The "First Hundred Days"	
	Emergency Banking Relief Act	Stabilize banking
	Civilian Conservation Corps	Put young men to work on conservation projects
	Federal Emergency Relief Act	Supplement state and local relief efforts
	Agricultural Adjustment Act	Bring agricultural recovery through limiting production
	Tennessee Valley Authority	Plan economic development of Tennessee River Valley
	Home Owners Refinancing Act	Assist homeowners to prevent foreclosures
	Banking Act of 1933	Establish FDIC to insure bank deposits and stabilize banking
	National Industrial Recovery Act, Title I: National Recovery Administration	Create industry-wide codes of fair competition to plan recovery of industries
	National Industrial Recovery Act, Title II: Public Works Administration	Stimulate economy through public works projects
1934	Securities and Exchange Act	Regulate issuance of corporate stocks and bonds
	Indian Reorganization Act	Restore tribal government, halt some forced assimilation programs
1935	Emergency Relief Appropriations Act (ERAA)	Establish Works Progress Administration to work with state and local governments to provide jobs to the unemployed
	June–August: the "Second Hundred Days"	
	National Labor Relations Act (Wagner Act)	Regulate labor relations and collective bargaining
	Social Security Act	Provide old-age pensions, unemployment compensation, support for the disabled
	Revenue Act of 1935 ("Wealth Tax Act")	Increase taxes on upper incomes to pay for relief and recovery programs

The WPA also made special efforts to help women, members of racial and ethnic minority groups, students, and young adults. Prodded by Eleanor Roosevelt, the WPA employed between 300,000 and 400,000 women a year. Some were hired as teachers and nurses, but the majority, especially in rural areas, worked on sewing and canning projects. Efforts to ensure African American employment met with success in the northeastern states but were less successful in the South. The **National Youth Administration** (NYA), created in 1935 and directed by Aubrey Williams, developed a successful program to aid college and high school students and young people not in school. **Mary McLeod Bethune**, an African American educator, directed the NYA's Division of Negro Affairs. Through determination and constant, skillfully applied pressure, she obtained support for black schools and colleges and increased the number of African Americans enrolled in vocational and recreational programs.

While the WPA was intended primarily for relief, the Wagner Act was a major reform. It came at a time when organized labor was at a crossroads. The unions that made up the American Federation of Labor (discussed in Chapter 17) had organized many skilled workers but not those of the major mass-production industries—steel, automobiles, rubber, textiles—and had generally avoided unskilled or less skilled workers. Some AFL unions limited their membership to whites or males. John L. Lewis of the United Mine Workers (coal miners), an industrial union that originated in the Knights of Labor, had insisted on the inclusion of Section 7a in the NRA and had used it to launch a successful organizing drive among coal miners. He argued that the AFL should organize the large mass-production industries on an industrial model, with one union for all workers in the industry, regardless of skill. That approach violated the long-standing AFL policy of separate unions for each skill group. When the AFL leaders turned Lewis down, in 1935, he formed the Committee on Industrial Organization (CIO) within the AFL. Composed of several AFL affiliates committed to the industrial model, the CIO launched organizing drives in the automobile, steel, rubber, electrical equipment, and textile industries. The Wagner Act gave their efforts important federal support. Most AFL craft unions opposed Lewis's efforts, and after marking important victories in the automobile and steel industries in 1937, Lewis led the CIO unions out of the AFL in 1938. They formed the **Congress of Industrial Organizations** and began to charter new industrial unions. Some of the AFL unions, notably the Carpenters, Machinists, and Teamsters, launched their own organizing drives, sometimes on an industrial model. Under the Wagner Act, unions nearly doubled their membership in five years, and the percentage of the **private-sector** work force in unions eventually reached an all-time high of 39 percent in 1958.

Like industrial workers, many farmers put their trust in Roosevelt and the New Deal. By 1935, the AAA appeared to be working as farm prices climbed and the purchasing power of farmers increased (see Figure 22.2). But there was a cost. Tenant farmers and sharecroppers usually received no share of the AAA payments paid to their landlords and sometimes found themselves evicted from

private sector Businesses owned by shareholders or individuals.

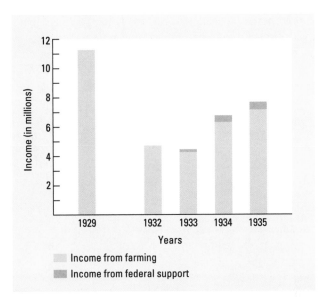

FIGURE 22.2 Farm Income, 1929–1935

Prices for farm products fell rapidly as the Depression set in, but by 1933, with support from New Deal programs, some farm incomes were rising. Some of the increase was a direct result of government payments.

Source: U.S. Department of Commerce, *Historical Statistics of the United States, Colonial Times to 1970,* Bicentennial Edition, 2 vols. (Washington, D.C.: U.S. Government Printing Office, 1975), 1: 483–484.

their farms—a million by the end of 1935—so that landlords could obtain payment for taking the land out of production. In 1936, the New Deal plan for agriculture collapsed when the Supreme Court ruled that the AAA's production quotas and special tax on processing companies were unconstitutional in **United States v. Butler**. Quickly, the administration turned to other programs, including the **Soil Conservation and Domestic Allocation Act**, to reduce production.

In 1938, Congress approved a second Agricultural Adjustment Act that reestablished the principle of federal quotas on production, acreage reduction, and subsidies. By 1939, farm income had more than doubled since 1932, with the government providing over $4.5 billion in aid to farmers. Initially intended as a short-term measure, federal farm subsidies have continued and significantly changed the relationship between agricultural producers and the federal government.

Nature also helped take land out of production as drought devastated a five-state region in the southern Great Plains. Above-average rainfall previously had encouraged the extension of wheat farming, but in the early 1930s reduced rainfall led to crop failure. The drought continued for several years, becoming the worst in U.S. history. Then high winds swept across the drought-plagued land, generating gigantic dust storms that could stretch more than 200 miles across and over 7,000 feet high. A reporter labeled the region the **Dust Bowl**. Millions of tons of topsoil

MAP 22.3 The Dust Bowl

From the Dakotas southward to the Mexican border, farmers in the Great Plains suffered from a lack of rainfall and severe soil erosion in the 1930s, worsening the hardships of the Great Depression.

blew away, much of it all the way to the Atlantic Ocean. Beginning in 1937, New Deal programs planted trees in shelterbelts across the drought-ravaged region and taught farmers new farming techniques, reducing erosion by two-thirds within a short time.

By the mid-1930s, thousands of farm families displaced by drought, technology, Depression, or the AAA headed for California, hoping to start over. Many of them found work as seasonal agricultural workers, following the crops, picking peaches and peas, grapes and plums. Few Californians greeted them warmly. The Los Angeles police chief sent police units to the state border to encourage them to turn back. Usually denigrated as Okies regardless of the state from which they came, they encountered miserable living conditions. Most migratory labor camps lacked even rudimentary sanitation, and most migratory labor families could not afford proper diets or health care. A survey of a thousand migratory children in the San Joaquin valley during 1936–37 found 831 with medical problems, most caused by malnutrition or poor hygiene.

California's migratory farm workers were among those who benefited from the work of the Resettlement Administration (RA), created by executive order in 1935. The RA sought to address rural poverty everywhere in the country—western migrant farm workers, southern sharecroppers, and other impoverished farm families—by helping them to establish new working lives in planned communities or, in a few cases, communal farms. The Resettlement Administration only touched a small percentage of those in need before it was absorbed by a new agency, the Farm Security Administration (FSA), in 1937, which continued its work. In California, the RA began to construct migrant labor camps with adequate sanitation and housing, and the FSA continued that work.

Rural Americans everywhere benefited from the **Rural Electrification Administration** (REA), created in 1935. Utility companies had refused to extend electrical service to much of rural America, arguing that rural areas could not be profitable. In 1935, only 10.5 percent of farms had electricity. The REA bypassed private utility companies by aiding in the formation of rural electrical cooperatives. Within just five years, the REA had extended electrical service to a million more farms, 25 percent of the total. By 1950, 90 percent of farms were electrified. The electrification of rural America helped integrate those areas into modern culture. Electricity improved education, health, and sanitation, and encouraged the diversification of agriculture and the introduction of new industries. It lessened the drudgery of farm life, giving families running water and access to a variety of electrical appliances. Within eight months of receiving electricity, new consumers bought an average of $180 in appliances—with the two most common an electric iron and a radio.

The Election of 1936 and the Waning of the New Deal

By the end of 1935, Roosevelt had effectively reasserted his leadership and popularity. The chances of a successful Republican or third-party challenge to the president were remote. In a less than enthusiastic convention, Republicans nominated **Alfred Landon** of Kansas, one of the few Republican governors reelected in 1934. As governor, he had accepted and used most New Deal programs, but in keeping with party wishes he attacked Roosevelt and the New Deal as destroying the values of America. After the death of Huey Long in 1935, Townsend and Coughlin formed a third party, the Union Party, but posed no threat to Roosevelt's reelection. Roosevelt followed a wise path, reminding voters of the New Deal's achievements and denouncing big business as greedy. Roosevelt won with the largest percentage of the vote up to that time. Landon carried Maine and Vermont.

The Democratic victory demonstrated not only the personal appeal of Roosevelt but also an acceptance of an activist government that could provide social and economic benefits. Roosevelt's second inaugural address, sometimes referred to as the "one-third speech," raised expectations of a Third Hundred Days. "I see millions of families trying to live on incomes so meager that the pall of family disaster hangs over them day by day," he announced. "I see one-third of a nation ill-housed, ill-clad, ill-nourished." The words seemed to promise new legislation aimed at helping the poor and the working class.

A Third Hundred Days failed to materialize. Instead of promoting new social legislation, Roosevelt first pitched his popularity against the Supreme Court.

The president's anger at the Court had been growing since the Court had invalidated the NRA and the AAA. As 1937 began, legal challenges to the TVA, the Wagner Act, and the Social Security Act were on their way to the Court. Further, there had been not a single vacancy on the Court during Roosevelt's first term, a highly unusual occurrence. Fearing the Court was determined to undo the New Deal, Roosevelt proposed to enlarge the Court. His rationale was that the Court's elderly judges were unable to keep up with their work, and he asked Congress for authority to add a new justice for every one over age 70 who had served on the Court more than ten years. His real objective was obvious to all—he wanted to be able to add enough justices to protect the New Deal from the Court's conservative majority.

The **court-packing plan** proved a major political miscalculation. Several conservative Democrats, especially those in the South, saw an opportunity to break with the president and led opposition in the Senate. Roosevelt's effort was further weakened when enough justices changed sides that the Court upheld a state's minimum-wage law, the Wagner Act, and the Social Security system, something since called the **Judicial Revolution of 1937**. After Justice Willis Van Devanter, a conservative, announced his retirement, Roosevelt dropped his proposal and happily appointed Hugo Black, a New Deal senator from Alabama, to the Court. Before he left office, Roosevelt had appointed every member of the Court but one.

Another setback that snagged the Roosevelt agenda was a recession, dubbed **Roosevelt's recession** by critics. As the economy stabilized by 1937, industrial outputs reached their 1929 levels, and unemployment fell to 14 percent. Secretary of the Treasury Henry Morgenthau urged Roosevelt to reduce government spending and move toward a more balanced budget. Roosevelt agreed and cut back relief programs, releasing nearly 1.5 million workers from the WPA. But the economy was not strong enough to cope with reduced government spending and thousands of people seeking jobs. At the same time, the new Social Security payments somewhat reduced the paychecks of most employed people, causing some people to cut back purchases. Unemployment soared to 19 percent. The recovery collapsed, and in April 1938 Roosevelt restored spending. The WPA and other agencies rehired those released, but Roosevelt's image of being able to manage recovery was tarnished.

It was not just the court-packing plan and the recession that weakened the New Deal. Some Americans also opposed the higher taxes on the wealthy approved in 1935. Labor strife was increasing concern about unions and their relation to the New Deal. The United Automobile Workers, one of the new CIO unions, had occupied factories as part of a strike, and such "sit-down" strikes alienated many who considered them violations of property rights. The public's mood had changed. The American people, Hopkins observed, were now "bored with the poor, the unemployed, and the insecure."

Despite waning support, the administration managed to pass two more significant pieces of legislation. In 1938, a second Agricultural Adjustment Act reestablished the principle of federally set quotas on specific commodities, acreage reduction, and subsidy payments. The **Fair Labor Standards Act**, also passed in 1938, addressed issues that Frances Perkins had long championed. It established forty-four hours as the standard workweek, set a minimum wage (25 cents an hour), and outlawed child labor (under age 16). With its minimum-wage provision, the act was especially beneficial to unskilled and nonunion workers and to workers from racial and ethnic minority groups. It was also the last piece of New Deal legislation.

In the November 1938 congressional elections, Roosevelt failed to get New Deal supporters elected, and Republicans increased their numbers and influence in Congress. Now conservative Democrats, mostly from the South, increasingly joined Republicans in a **conservative coalition** that could derail new liberal programs. Roosevelt recognized political reality and asked for no new domestic programs. The legislative New Deal was over, but the changes it generated remained part of the American social, economic, and political culture. By 1939, the economy was recovering, with some economic indicators reaching the point where they had been in 1929 and 1937, before the Roosevelt recession. But unemployment and under-employment persisted. Eight million were still unemployed, and there was no effort to provide more relief jobs or programs. Jobs and full "recovery" did not appear until 1942, when the United States mobilized for a second world war. Wartime spending finally propelled the American economy out of the Depression and to new levels of prosperity.

AMERICANS FACE THE DEPRESSION

One reason the New Deal was able to establish new patterns of government respon-sibility was that the Depression touched every segment of American life. Poverty and hardship were no longer reserved for those viewed as unworthy or relegated to remote areas and inner cities. Now poverty included blue- and white-collar workers, and even some of the once-rich. Most Americans worried about their futures and economic insecurity—that the next day might bring a reduction in wages, the loss of a job, or the closing of a business.

"Making Do"   To help those facing economic insecurity, magazines and newspapers provided useful hints and "Depression recipes" that stretched budgets and included information about nutrition. According to home economists, a careful shopper could feed a family of five on as little as $8 (equivalent to $132 today) a week. This was comforting news for those with that much to spend, but for many families and for relief agencies $8 a week for food was beyond possibility. Before the New Deal, New York City provided only $2.39 a week for each family on relief. Things were bad, comedian Groucho Marx joked, when "pigeons started feeding people in Central Park."

Like New York, most towns and cities by 1933 had little ability to provide more than the smallest amount of relief and struggled unsuccessfully to

conservative coalition An informal cooperative relationship between conservative Democrats, mostly from the South, and Republicans, which often controlled Congress during the three or four decades following 1937.

maintain basic city services. Experiencing a shrinking tax base, local, county, and state governments not only cut back or eliminated relief but were sometimes forced to lay off teachers, policemen, and other workers. A city spokesman in Birmingham, Alabama, presented the choices: "I am as much in favor of relief … as anyone, but I am unwilling to continue this relief at the expense of bankrupting … Birmingham." Because state and local governments depended on property taxes, the New Deal indirectly provided assistance for local and state governments as the HOLC and the FHA saved homes, stimulated some new construction, and restored property tax bases. Federal agencies, especially the PWA and the WPA, not only provided many local civic improvements—schools, post offices, hospitals, other government buildings, roads, and bridges—but also reduced local relief responsibilities. Other federal programs also helped to lessen the burdens of local and state governments. In North Dakota, for example, it was estimated that two-thirds of the people drew some form of federal assistance. Thus, the New Deal drastically altered the relationship between local and national government. Increasingly people saw the national government as having an obligation to support families and communities against economic adversity.

"Use it up, wear it out, make it do, or do without" became the motto of most American families. In many working-class and middle-class neighborhoods, "making do" meant that many homes sprouted signs announcing a variety of services—household beauty parlors, kitchen bakeries, rooms for boarders. A Milwaukee woman recalled, "I did baking at home to supplement our income. I got 9 cents for a loaf of bread and 25 cents for an apple cake.… I cleared about $65 a month." A sewing machine salesman commented that he was selling more and more machines to people who would not previously have done their own sewing. For farm families, feed sacks had long provided fabric for sewing, and companies now competed by printing attractive designs on their sacks. One woman remembered her mother making a pretty new school dress out of a sack that had "a sky-blue background with gorgeous mallard ducks on it."

Still, even with "making do," many families—especially in the working class—failed, first losing jobs, and then homes. Some families moved in with relatives. One man remembered that during the Depression most households were like his, "where father, mother, children, aunts, uncles and grandma lived together." Approximately one-sixth of America's urban families "doubled up." Millions of others took to the road. Over 3 million loaded their meager possessions on their jalopies and traveled across the country looking for a better life. Many found their families and lives torn apart. Some rode the rails, hitching rides in boxcars, living in Hoovervilles, begging and scrounging for food and supplies along the road. Records show increased numbers of suicides, admissions to state mental hospitals, and children placed in orphanages. Some worried about the psychological problems created as women and children replaced husbands and fathers as breadwinners. A social worker remembered, "I used to see men cry because they didn't have a job."

Despite the hardships and migrations, American society did not collapse, as some had predicted. The vast majority of Americans clung tightly to traditional social norms and even expanded family togetherness. Economic necessity kept families at home. They played cards and board games, read books and magazines, and tended vegetable and flower gardens. The game of Monopoly, which allowed players to fantasize about becoming millionaires and bankrupting the other players, zoomed to popularity in the mid-1930s. Church attendance rose, and the number of divorces declined. Fewer people got married, and the birth rate fell.

Discrimination and Depression   The Depression and the New Deal provided mixed experiences for women, African Americans, Asian Americans, Latinos, and American Indians. For the large majority of American males, their self-image included the responsibility of providing for their families. As unemployment rose, public opinion polls found that most people, including women, believed that men should have jobs. Some companies dismissed or refused to hire married women. The number of women in the professions declined from 14.2 to 12.3 percent. Teachers were particularly vulnerable. One survey found that, of 1,500 school districts, 77 percent did not hire married women, and 63 percent had fired women when they married. By 1932, 2 million women were out of work, and an estimated 145,000 women were homeless, wandering across America. But employment patterns were uneven. Women in low-paying and low-status jobs were less likely to be laid off and more likely to find employment. White women also took jobs traditionally held by African Americans, especially in domestic service.

Few working women, however, found that bringing home a paycheck changed their status or role within the family. Most husbands still expected to be the head of the household—to maintain authority and dominance within the home, even if unemployed. Few husbands helped with work around the house, as such work challenged their notions of masculinity. One husband agreed to help with the laundry but refused to hang the wash outside for fear that neighbors might see him. At home women renewed and reaffirmed traditional roles: they sewed, baked bread, and canned fruits and vegetables. At the same time, a woman's traditional role as mother continued to change somewhat—the birth rate continued to fall, as did family size, thus extending the patterns first seen in the 1920s of married couples having fewer children or even no children (as indicated in Figure 21.3). While some of the change was probably due to couples agreeing that they could not afford children at the time, in other cases it was undoubtedly due to decisions made by women. The declining size of families also resulted from the postponement of marriage because of finances—the older a couple is when they marry, the fewer children they are likely to have. Through it all, women were often praised as pillars of stability in a changing and perilous society. One woman remembered, "I did what I had to do. I seemed to always find a way to make things work."

The Depression's economic impact intensified economic and social difficulties for African Americans, Latinos, and Asians, who faced increased racial hostility and demands that they give up their jobs to whites. In Tucson,

Arizona, "Mexicans" were accused of "taking the bread out of our white children's mouths." Low-paying, frequently temporary jobs and high unemployment made life in Latino communities difficult. On farms in California, Mexican American workers were being replaced by Anglos, including those fleeing the Dust Bowl. Those managing to find work in the fields earned only $289 a year—about a third of what the government estimated it took to maintain a subsistence budget.

In the early 1930s, especially, the Immigration and Naturalization Service (INS) worked with local authorities to facilitate **repatriation** of Mexican nationals to Mexico. Some local and state agencies gave free transportation to the border for those willing to leave. In one Indiana town, Mexicans and Mexican Americans were denied relief and encouraged to board a special train to Mexico. "They weren't forcing you to leave," recalled one *repatriado*; "they gave you a choice, starve or go back to Mexico." In several cities, the INS conducted sweeps of Mexican American communities to scare Mexicans into leaving and to round up illegal immigrants for deportation. In Los Angeles such sweeps resulted in nearly ten thousand Mexicans and Mexican Americans boarding special trains bound for Mexico. Nationally, more than half a million had left by 1937.

There was no comparable effort to repatriate Asians living on the West Coast, but Asian immigrants and Asian Americans remained isolated and often received inadequate relief. In San Francisco, where nearly one-sixth of the Asian population picked up benefits, they received from 10 to 20 percent less than whites, probably because relief agencies subscribed to the stereotype that Asians could subsist on a less expensive diet. Hoping to remove economic and social barriers, some Asians intensified ongoing efforts to assimilate, becoming "200 percent Americans." The Japanese American Citizens League was organized in 1929 to overcome discrimination and oppose anti-Asian legislation, but by 1940 the group had made little headway.

Before 1929, African Americans working as sharecroppers, farm hands, and tenant farmers in the South were already experiencing depression conditions, earning only about $200 a year. Their lives worsened as farm prices continued to fall and as hard times and the AAA increased evictions during the Depression. Many migrated to urban areas, seeking more economic security. Cities, however, provided few opportunities because whites were taking jobs that, like domestic service jobs, were previously held by African Americans. In most cases, joblessness among African Americans in urban areas averaged 20 to 50 percent higher than for whites. Compounding the high unemployment, across the nation blacks faced increased racial hostility, violence, and intimidation. In 1931 the attention of the nation was drawn to Scottsboro, Alabama, where nine black men had been arrested and charged with raping two white prostitutes.

---

repatriation   The return of people to their nation of birth or citizenship; repatriation of Mexicans from the United States during the Depression was at its height from 1929 to 1931.

Although no physical evidence linked the men to the crime, a jury of white males did not question the testimony of the women and quickly found the so-called **Scottsboro Nine** guilty. Eight were sentenced to death; the ninth, a minor, escaped the death penalty. Through appeals, intervention by the Supreme Court, retrials, parole, and escape, all those convicted were free by 1950.

A New Deal for All?   Like the Depression, the New Deal affected women and members of racial and ethnic minority groups in different ways, but generally it inspired a belief that the Roosevelt government cared and was trying to improve their lives. Eleanor Roosevelt was at the center of this image of compassion. She frequently acted as the social conscience of the administration and prodded her husband and other New Dealers not to forget women and people of color. "I'm the agitator," she once said. "He's the politician." She crossed the country meeting and listening to people. She received thousands of letters that described people's hardships and asked for help. Although she was rarely able to provide direct assistance, her replies emphasized hope and pointed to the changes being made by the New Deal.

Within the White House, she helped convene a special White House conference on the needs of women in 1933 and, with the help of Frances Perkins and other women in the administration, worked to ensure that women received more than just token consideration from New Deal agencies. Ellen Woodward, who served as assistant director of the FERA and the WPA, was successful in promoting a few women's programs—headed by women. Still, New Deal agencies frequently paid women less than men, and fewer women were enrolled in relief programs. Women made up only about 10 percent of the WPA's work force, and the largest number were in programs focused on traditional women's skills, such as sewing. Large numbers of female wage-earners were left outside the Social Security Act and the Fair Labor Standards Act because both excluded domestic workers and similar service occupations with large proportions of women. Yet, despite these shortcomings, the New Deal provided women with more programs and positions in government than at any previous time in American history.

For African Americans and Latinos, the Roosevelts and the New Deal provided a large amount of hope and a lesser amount of change. More African Americans than ever before were appointed to government positions. Mary Bethune in 1936 organized African Americans in the administration into a **"Black Cabinet"** that met in her home and acted as a semiofficial advisory commission on racial relations. "We must think in terms of a 'whole' for the greatest service of our people," she said. Among the most pressing needs, the Black Cabinet concluded, was access to relief and jobs. The New Deal provided both, but never to the extent needed. Some New Deal administrators, notably Interior Secretary Harold Ickes and Hopkins, took steps to ensure that the PWA, WPA, and other New Deal agencies included members of racial and ethnic minority groups,

Library of Congress

Some WPA projects sought to teach new skills to the unemployed. This WPA project at Costilla, New Mexico, taught local women, many of them of Mexican ancestry, how to make rag rugs using a loom. This woman is running a shuttle through a warp.

especially African Americans. In northern cities, the WPA and the PWA nearly eliminated discrimination from their programs, but they had less success in other parts of the nation, where skilled African American workers were often given menial minimum-wage jobs. Other agencies were less supportive. The Civilian Conservation Corps and the Tennessee Valley Authority practiced racial segregation and wage discrimination. Still, by 1938, nearly 30 percent of African Americans were receiving some federal relief, with the WPA alone supporting almost a million African American families. But even in the best of cases, it was not enough. In Cleveland, 40 percent of PWA jobs were reserved for African Americans, but there, as across the nation, black unemployment and poverty remained higher than for whites.

FDR also refused to support civil rights legislation. When confronted by black leaders for his refusal to promote an antilynching law, Roosevelt explained, "If I come out for the anti-lynching bill now, they [powerful southern Democrats] will block every bill I ask Congress to pass.... I just can't take that risk." Eleanor Roosevelt was willing to take more risks and visibly supported equality for racial and ethnic minority groups. In 1939, when the Daughters of the American Revolution refused to allow renowned black opera singer Marian Anderson to sing at their concert hall in Washington, the First Lady resigned her membership and, with assistance from Ickes, arranged a public concert on the steps of the Lincoln Memorial. Anderson's performance before Lincoln's statue attracted more than seventy-five thousand people.

Latinos benefited from the New Deal in much the same way as African Americans. In New Mexico and other western states, the Depression curtailed much of the migratory farm work for Mexican American workers, devastating local economies. New Deal agencies such as the CCC, PWA, and WPA provided welcome jobs and income. A worker in a CCC camp in northern New Mexico remembered, "I had plenty to eat, ... I had brand new clothes when I went to the CCC camps." Throughout the Southwest, federal agencies not only included Mexican Americans but also sometimes paid wages that exceeded what they received in the private sector. The WPA paid $8.54 a week for unskilled labor, whereas a comparable job in the private sector would have yielded an average of $6.02 or less. Discrimination, however, was still practiced, often enhanced by language differences.

New Deal legislation helped union organizers trying to assist Latino workers throughout the West. San Antonio's Mexican American pecan shellers, mostly women, were among the lowest-paid workers in the country, earning less than 4 cents per pound of shelled pecans, which amounted to an annual wage of less than $180. In 1934, 1935, and again in 1938, union organizers, including local activist "Red" Emma Tenayuca, led the pecan shellers in strikes, finally gaining higher wages and union recognition in 1938, under the auspices of the recently chartered United Cannery, Agricultural, Packing, and Allied Workers of America (UCAPAWA), the CIO's industrial union for farm workers and food processing workers. The UCAPAWA, which included a number of Communists among its organizers, also organized Mexican women working in California canneries. Efforts to organize field workers, however, came up against strong opposition from local growers, organized in California as the Associated Farmers and backed by some of the most powerful corporations in the West.

Despite its limitations, the New Deal provided hope and support for many women and members of racial and ethnic minority groups, who in turn praised Roosevelt. "The WPA came along, and Roosevelt came to be a god," said one African American. "You worked, you got a paycheck, and you had some dignity." Politically, such sentiments were more than praise because, where they could vote, many women and members of racial and ethnic minority groups began to vote for Roosevelt and the Democratic Party. Blacks bolted the Republican Party and enlisted in extraordinary numbers in the Democratic Party. In the 1936 presidential election, Roosevelt carried every black ward in Cleveland and, nationally, received nearly 90 percent of the black vote. By 1939, the Democratic Party was providing a political vehicle for the aspirations of industrial workers, people of color, and farmers.

Native Americans directly benefited from the New Deal. They had two strong supporters in Secretary of the Interior Ickes and Commissioner of Indian Affairs John Collier. Both opposed existing Indian policies that since 1887 had sought to destroy the reservation system and eradicate Indian cultures. At Collier's urging, Congress passed the **Indian Reorganization Act** in 1934. Designed to restore tribal sovereignty under federal authority, the act returned land and community control to tribal organizations, permitted Indian self-rule on a reservation if reservation residents so decided, and ended the process of allocating reservation lands in severalty (discussed in Chapter 17). Each tribe had to ratify the act to participate, and not all tribes did so. Seventy-seven rejected the changes, including the Navajos, the nation's largest tribe, although some of those who initially rejected the act later changed their decision.

To improve the squalid conditions on most reservations and to provide jobs, Collier organized a CCC-type agency for Indians and ensured that other New Deal agencies played a part in improving Indian lands and providing jobs. He also promoted Native American culture. Working with tribal leaders, Collier took measures to protect, preserve, and encourage Indian customs, languages, religions, and folkways. Reservation school curricula incorporated Indian languages and customs, and Native Americans could once more openly and freely exercise their religions. While a positive effort, the so-called Indian New Deal did little to improve the standard of living for most American Indians. Funds were too few, and the problems created by years of poverty and government neglect were too great. Some tribal leaders complained that Collier's programs had been drafted with little or no participation by Indians themselves. At best, the programs slowed a long-standing economic decline and allowed Native Americans to regain some control over their cultures and societies.

Cultural Expression in the Midst of Depression   The homogenization of culture that began in the 1920s due to the movies and radio continued in the 1930s. At the same time, however, there were significant changes in cultural expression. During the 1920s, many American writers and artists had rejected their consumer-oriented society, producing novels depicting hedonism or escapism (discussed in the previous chapter). Many leading writers of the 1930s changed that focus, portraying instead working people and their problems or looking for inspiration to figures in American history. Many artists turned to a more realistic style.

A generation of painters, some of whom produced works of social criticism during the 1930s, were influenced by Diego Rivera, a great Mexican muralist whose work in Rockefeller Center in New York City was destroyed in 1934 because of its Marxist politics. Other Depression-era artists, particularly those in the Federal Arts Project (FAP) of the WPA, depicted the lives of ordinary people or themes from American history, especially scenes of hardy white pioneers. By one count, FAP artists produced some 200,000 individual works of art—murals, paintings, and sculptures—nearly all intended for public display.

Novels during the 1930s were frequently critical of American society and politics. Some leading authors depicted inequities caused by capitalism, racism, and class differences. John Steinbeck defined the social protest novel of the 1930s. Among his early works, *Tortilla Flat* (1933) portrayed the lives of Mexican Californians and *In Dubious Battle* (1936) presented an apple-pickers' strike through the eyes of an idealistic young Communist. *The Grapes of Wrath* (1939), which won the Pulitzer Prize for the best novel of the year, presented the Joad family, who lost their farm in Oklahoma and migrated to California where their family disintegrated under the strain of life as migratory farm workers. Similar social criticism appeared in Erskine Caldwell's *Tobacco Road* (1932), about Georgia sharecroppers, and Richard Wright's *Native Son* (1940), a critique of racism that became the first Book of the Month Club selection by an African American author. Ernest Hemingway's *For Whom the Bell Tolls* (1940) depicted an American fighting fascism in the Spanish Civil War (discussed in the next chapter), a sharp contrast to the hedonism of his *The Sun Also Rises* (1926, discussed in the previous chapter).

Dorothea Lange began photographing the victims of the Depression in the early 1930s and continued that work with the Resettlement Administration and FSA. Lange was among the leading figures in creating the new genre of documentary photography. Her 1936 photograph of a migratory farm worker and her children, later entitled "Migrant Mother," emerged as the most famous and perhaps the most moving photograph of the era. Margaret Bourke-White joined Lange as a pioneer in documentary photography with dramatic photographs of the Fort Peck Dam and moving shots of the victims of the Depression.

As in the 1920s, movies remained popular, providing a welcome break from the woes of the Depression for many people. On a national average, 60 percent of the people saw a movie a week. In the 1920s, some films had glorified gangsters or reveled in the sexuality of such stars as Clara Bow. To head off pressure for federal regulation to prevent such films, the major studios in 1930 created the Motion Picture Production Code, which specified, among other things, that "the sympathy of the audience should never be thrown to the side of crime, wrongdoing, evil or sin." In the context of the Depression, many studio heads insisted that the public needed escapist entertainment to distract them from the Depression. Musical extravaganzas like *Forty-Second Street* (1933) and *Gold Diggers of 1933* (1933) fit the bill, as did the slapstick comedy of the Marx Brothers, whose *Duck Soup* (1933) is ranked among the best films of all time. Some disdain for the wealthy could be found in popular comedies that contrasted members of a snobby and selfish upper class with the honesty and common sense of ordinary people. Some westerns and gangster films were equally escapist, but others probed more deeply into the human condition. *Stagecoach* (1939), directed by John Ford, so defined the western genre that it inspired imitators for years after. Frank Capra directed several films that sympathized with the problems of ordinary people; *Mr. Smith Goes to Washington* (1939) showed a naïve but honest ordinary citizen battling political corruption. Hollywood occasionally produced films of social criticism, notably an adaptation of *The Grapes of Wrath* (1940), starring Henry Fonda. Charlie Chaplin's leftist politics were apparent in two important works, *Modern Times* (1936), portraying the dehumanizing tendencies of technology, and *The Great Dictator* (1940), which mocked and criticized Adolph Hitler.

Like movies, radio provided an escape from the concerns of the Depression. Nearly 90 percent of American households included a radio, suggesting that listening to the radio was nearly universal. "Gloom chasers"—that is, comedians, including Jack Benny and the comedy teams of George Burns and Gracie Allen and of

Margaret Bourke-White was making a strong social statement in this 1937 photograph of flood victims in Louisville, Kentucky, waiting in line for food.

Fibber McGee and Molly—filled the radio airways. Crime fighters were popular on the radio, and also in newspaper comic strips and comic books, where Dick Tracy (1931), Superman (1938), and Batman (1939) protected innocent victims from harm and oppression.

THE GREAT DEPRESSION AND NEW DEAL IN PERSPECTIVE

A depression—a contraction of the economy causing significant unemployment and lasting several years—was nothing new. Americans had experienced serious depressions every thirty to forty years since the 1830s. For generations, mothers had advised daughters always to save up for "hard times." The Great Depression confirmed that wisdom, and left its mark on a generation. For those who lived through the 1930s, "making do" became not just a way of surviving the depression, but a way of life that many continued long after the economy revived.

The New Deal also left its mark on a generation. Some spent the rest of their lives criticizing Roosevelt for destroying free enterprise. Others proudly voted Democratic because their families had survived financially only because of the New Deal. Democrats had been the minority from the election of Lincoln in 1860 until the election of Roosevelt in 1932. Thereafter, Democrats usually won the presidency until 1968, and usually controlled Congress until 1994. But the New Deal Democratic coalition was inherently unstable, including union members and small-scale farmers, southern white supremacists and African Americans in the cities of the north and west, and former socialists and states-rights conservatives.

The New Deal also left the permanent legacy of a more activist federal government—increased regulation of business, Social Security, the Wagner Act, the Fair Labor Standards Act, and more. Virtually no one at the beginning of the twenty-first century questions the appropriateness of a federal program benefiting the elderly or of a federally defined minimum wage. Similarly, Americans now expect that the federal government should take prompt action to prevent any future depression, reduce unemployment, and assist those most in need. Since Roosevelt, Americans have expected presidents, rather than Congress, to be the chief policymakers. In all these ways and more, the Great Depression and New Deal changed how Americans think about themselves and what they expect from their government.

STUDY TOOLS

SUMMARY

The Great Depression brought about significant changes in American life, altering expectations of government, society, and the economy. When Hoover assumed the presidency, most believed that the economy and quality of life would continue to improve. The Depression changed that. Flaws in the economy were suddenly exposed as the stock market crashed, legions of banks and businesses closed, unemployment soared, and people lost their homes and their hopes for the future.

More than previous presidents, Hoover expanded the role of the federal government to meet the economic and social crises. However, Hoover's measures, including the Reconstruction Finance Corporation, failed to stimulate a worsening economy.

Losing faith in Hoover, most Americans put their trust in Roosevelt and his promise of a New Deal. Roosevelt easily won the 1932 presidential election and took office amid widespread expectations for a major shift in the role of government. The First Hundred Days witnessed a barrage of legislation, most dealing with the immediate problems of unemployment and economic collapse. The Agricultural Adjustment Administration (AAA) and the National Recovery Administration (NRA) were designed to bring economic recovery, while programs such as the Civilian Conservation Corps (CCC) and Public Works Administration (PWA) were intended both to relieve unemployment and to stimulate the economy.

In 1935, assailed by both liberals and conservatives, Roosevelt responded with a second burst of legislation that focused more on putting people to work, economic redistribution, and social legislation, especially Social Security. New Deal programs touched the lives of many Americans, from unemployed laborers to unemployed artists, from struggling farmers to industrial workers. The overwhelming Democratic victory in 1936 confirmed Roosevelt's popularity. But FDR's ill-conceived court-packing plan, an economic downturn, labor unrest, and growing conservatism generated opposition to new legislation, and the New Deal wound down after 1938.

The Depression affected all Americans, as they had to adjust their values and lifestyles to meet the economic and psychological crisis. Lives were disrupted, homes and businesses lost, but most people learned to cope with the Great Depression and hoped for better times. Gender roles were affected by the depression as men lost their jobs. Members of racial and ethnic minority groups carried the extra burdens of discrimination, sometimes by New Deal agencies. During the 1930s, for the first time the federal government provided significant support to artists, writers, and musicians. While movies and radio often provided escape from daily worries, other forms of cultural expression focused on the problems faced by ordinary people.

The New Deal never fully restored the economy, but it engineered a profound shift in the nature of government and in society's expectations about the federal government's role in people's lives.

Chronology

Depression and New Deal	
1928	Herbert Hoover elected president
1929	Stock market crash
	Mexican repatriation begins
	Depression deepens
1929–1933	Thousands of banks and businesses fail
	Unemployment rises from 9 to 25 percent
1931	Scottsboro Nine convicted
1932	Reconstruction Finance Corporation
	Bonus Army marches to Washington
	Franklin D. Roosevelt elected president
1933	Drought and wind create the Dust Bowl
	Franklin D. Roosevelt inaugurated
	New Deal begins
	National Bank Holiday
	First fireside chat
	First Hundred Days (March 9–June 16): CCC, AAA, TVA, HOLC, NRA, and PWA, repeal of Prohibition, Bank Act
1934	Huey Long's Share Our Wealth plan
	Indian Reorganization Act
	Securities and Exchange Commission (SEC) created
	American Liberty League established
	Dr. Francis Townsend's movement begins
	Federal Housing Administration

1935	Works Progress Administration created
	NRA ruled unconstitutional in *Schechter* case
	Second Hundred Days: Social Security, Wagner Act,
	Wealth Tax Act
	Rural Electrification Administration (REA) formed
	Long assassinated
	Committee on Industrial Organization (CIO) established
1936	AAA ruled unconstitutional in *Butler* case
	Roosevelt reelected
	"Black Cabinet" organized
1937	Court-packing plan
	"Roosevelt's recession"
1938	Fair Labor Standards Act
	Second AAA
	Congress of Industrial Organizations formed
1939	Marian Anderson's concert at Lincoln Memorial
	John Steinbeck's *The Grapes of Wrath*
1940	Richard Wright's *Native Son*

FOCUS QUESTIONS

If you have mastered this chapter, you should be able to answer these questions and explain the terms that follow the questions.

1. What was the effect of the stock market crash on the American economy, and what major economic weaknesses contributed to the crash and the Great Depression?
2. How did Hoover try to deal with the Depression? How successful were his efforts?
3. How did the New Deal's "First Hundred Days" represent a change in the role of the federal government?
4. What were the initial responses to New Deal measures?
5. What new reforms came during the Second Hundred Days, and how did they differ from those of the First Hundred Days?
6. What happened to restrict expansion of the New Deal after 1936?
7. How did Americans cope with the many challenges presented by the Great Depression?
8. What opportunities opened for women, African Americans, Latinos, Asian Americans, and Native Americans, and what challenges faced these groups during the 1930s?
9. How did the Depression and New Deal affect cultural expression?
10. How did the Great Depression and New Deal affect Americans over the long run?

KEY TERMS

Great Depression (*p.* 684)

Reconstruction Finance Corporation (*p.* 686)

Glass-Steagall Act (*p.* 686)

Federal Home Loan Bank Act (*p.* 686)

Hoovervilles (*p.* 688)

Farmers' Holiday Association (*p.* 689)

Bonus Army (*p.* 689)

New Deal (*p.* 690)

Bank Holiday (*p.* 692)

Emergency Banking Bill (*p.* 692)

fireside chats (*p.* 692)

First Hundred Days (*p.* 692)

Agricultural Adjustment Act (*p.* 692)

National Industrial Recovery Act (*p.* 692)

National Recovery Administration (*p.* 693)

Public Works Administration (*p.* 693)

Tennessee Valley Authority (*p.* 693)

Civilian Conservation Corps (*p.* 694)

Federal Emergency Relief Administration (*p.* 695)

Civil Works Administration (*p.* 695)

Home Owners' Loan Corporation (*p.* 695)

Federal Deposit Insurance Corporation (*p.* 695)

Securities and Exchange Commission (*p.* 695)

Federal Housing Administration (*p.* 696)

American Liberty League (*p.* 696)

Father Charles Coughlin (*p.* 697)

Huey Long (*p.* 697)

Share Our Wealth (*p.* 697)

Works Progress Administration (*p.* 698)

Harry Hopkins (*p.* 698)

Second Hundred Days (*p.* 698)

Social Security Act (*p.* 698)

Wagner Act (*p.* 699)

National Youth Administration (*p.* 702)

Mary McLeod Bethune (*p.* 702)

Congress of Industrial Organizations (*p.* 702)

United States v. Butler (*p.* 703)

Soil Conservation and Domestic Allocation Act (*p.* 703)

Dust Bowl (*p.* 703)

Rural Electrification Administration (*p.* 705)

Alfred Landon (*p.* 705)

court-packing plan (*p.* 706)

Judicial Revolution of 1937 (*p.* 706)

Roosevelt's recession (*p.* 706)

Fair Labor Standards Act (*p.* 706)

Scottsboro Nine (*p.* 711)

Black Cabinet (*p.* 711)

Indian Reorganization Act (*p.* 713)

23

AMERICA'S RISE TO WORLD LEADERSHIP, 1929–1945

THE ROAD TO WAR

When Herbert Hoover became president in 1929, the world appeared stable and increasingly prosperous. He saw no reason to change foreign policy. The United States remained aloof from the world's political and diplomatic bickering. The onslaught of the Depression only strengthened most Americans' resolve to stay out of world affairs and attend to business at home. However, as the global depression deepened and governments changed, some nations sought solutions to their internal problems abroad. Japan was the first as it seized Manchuria in 1931.

Japan's economy rested in part on international commerce, and with the collapse of world trade many Japanese nationalists pursued other means to ensure economic vitality and power. They turned to Manchuria, a province of China situated north and west of Japanese-controlled Korea. It was rich in iron and coal, accounted for 95 percent of Japanese overseas investment, and supplied large amounts of foodstuffs. Equally important, Japan maintained an army in Manchuria to protect its interests. In September 1931, Japanese officers used the army to seize the province. The world, including the League of Nations, condemned Japan's aggression, but did little else as Japan created a new puppet nation, Manchukuo, under its control. Hoover instituted a policy of **non-recognition** of the new state. Humorist Will Rogers sarcastically noted that the world's diplomats would run out of stationery writing protests before Japan ran out of soldiers. Rogers was right. Japan's success strengthened its leaders' idea of a Japanese-dominated

non-recognition A policy of not acknowledging changes in government or territory to show displeasure with the changes. In this way, the United States refused to accept the creation of Manchukuo.

Greater East Asian Co-Prosperity Sphere and further increased tensions with China. Roosevelt maintained Hoover's policy of non-recognition, but dealing with an expansionist Japan would test Roosevelt's abilities to protect American interests.

Diplomacy in a
Dangerous
World

Roosevelt also continued Hoover's Latin American policy. Announcing a "Good Neighbor" policy, he affirmed that the United States had no right to militarily intervene in regional affairs. But events in Cuba and Mexico put nonintervention to the test. In 1933, political unrest weakened Cuba's oppressive president, Gerardo "the Butcher" Machado. Roosevelt sent special envoy Sumner Wells to convince Machado to resign. He grudgingly resigned, but Wells considered his successor, Ramón Grau San Martín, too radical and asked Roosevelt for armed intervention to remove him. Roosevelt refused but applied the non-recognition policy to the new regime. In Cuba, Wells turned to **Colonel Fulgencio Batista** and convinced him to oust Grau and establish a new government. Batista's regime was immediately recognized by the United States and received a favorable trade agreement.

Mexico in 1938 nationalized its foreign-owned oil properties. American oil interests argued that Mexico had no right to seize their properties, demanded their return, and asked that Roosevelt intervene, with military force if necessary. Roosevelt rejected the request. Instead, he accepted the principle of nationalization and sought a fair monetary settlement for the American companies. Not until 1941 did Mexico and the United States agree on the amount of compensation, but throughout, American relations with Mexico remained cordial. The American **Good Neighbor policy**, stressing economic ties and nonintervention toward Latin America, was also enhanced when Roosevelt visited the Caribbean and South America, Congress repealed the Platt Amendment in 1934, and the United States affirmed at the 1938 Pan-American Conference that there were no acceptable reasons for armed intervention.

Roosevelt and
Isolationism

While Roosevelt upheld nonintervention and American interests in Latin America, maintaining American interests around the world was becoming difficult. As tensions rose regarding Japan, in Europe **fascist** Germany and Italy were seeking to expand their influence and power. Adolf Hitler took office in 1933, promising to improve the economy and Germany's role in the world. Benito Mussolini, ruling Italy since 1921, argued that Italy needed to expand its influence abroad. As global tensions increased, U.S. isolationists were in full cry. In 1934, a congressional investigation chaired by Senator Gerald P. Nye of North Dakota alleged that America's entry into World War I had been engineered by arms manufacturers, bankers, and war profiteers—"the merchants of death." At the same time, public opinion polls revealed that a large majority of Americans believed that the

fascist   Refers to a political system led by a dictator having total control over society and the economy; facism places the needs of the nation above those of the individual and is often characterized by racism and organized violence against opposition.

nation's intervention in the war was a mistake and that the country should avoid any actions that might draw it into another conflict. Congress responded in August 1935 by enacting the **Neutrality Act of 1935**. It prohibited the sale of arms and munitions to any nation at war, whether aggressor or victim. It also permitted the president to warn Americans traveling on ships of belligerent nations that they sailed at their own risk. Roosevelt would have preferred **discriminatory neutrality** but, anxious to see the Second Hundred Days through Congress, he accepted political reality. When Italian troops invaded the poorly armed African nation of Ethiopia in October, Roosevelt immediately announced American neutrality, denying the sale of war supplies to either side. Moving beyond strict neutrality, he also asked, to no avail, that Americans implement a "moral embargo" against Italy to reduce the sale of nonwar goods, like coal and oil. Italy formally annexed Ethiopia in May 1936.

International tensions continued to heighten in 1936 when Japan stepped up construction of new warships, German troops violated the Treaty of Versailles by occupying the **Rhineland**, and civil war broke out between Nationalists led by Francisco Franco and the Republican government of Spain. With isolationism still strong, Congress modified the neutrality legislation (the Second Neutrality Act) to forbid U.S. involvement in civil wars and making loans to countries at war—whether victim or aggressor.

With the peace seemingly slipping away, both political parties championed neutrality in the 1936 presidential elections. Roosevelt told an audience at Chautauqua, New York, that he hated war and that if it came to "the choice of profits over peace, the nation will answer—must answer—'We choose peace.'" The Republican candidate, Alfred Landon, was equally adamant that the Republicans were the best party to keep the nation out of war. Roosevelt easily defeated Landon. In 1937, the new Congress, with strong public support, passed another neutrality act. It required warring nations to pay cash for all "nonwar" goods and to carry them away on their own ships, and it barred Americans from sailing on belligerents' ships. Roosevelt would have liked more flexibility but appreciated that the law allowed the president to determine which nations were at war and which goods were nonwar goods.

Roosevelt used that provision in July 1937, following a Japanese invasion of northern China. Ignoring reality and disregarding protests, he refused to recognize that China and Japan were at war and allowed unrestricted American trade to continue with both nations. Hoping that isolationist views had softened, on October 5 Roosevelt suggested that the United States and other peace-loving nations should quarantine "bandit nations" that were contributing to "the epidemic of world lawlessness." The "quarantine speech" was applauded in many foreign capitals, but not in Berlin, Rome, or Tokyo, and not at home. The *Wall Street Journal* argued that Roosevelt should "stop ... meddling: America Wants

discriminatory neutrality Withholding aid and trade from one nation at war while providing them to another.

Rhineland Region of western Germany along the Rhine River, which under the terms of the Versailles Treaty was to remain free of troops and military fortifications.

Peace." As Japan continued to gobble up Chinese territory, on December 12, 1937, Japanese aircraft strafed, bombed, and sank the American gunboat *Panay*. Two Americans died, and over thirty were wounded. Outraged, Roosevelt favored retaliatory action. The *Christian Science Monitor*, expressing public and congressional opinion, pointed out that the *Panay* was not the *Maine*. Realizing he had no support for initiating any action against Japan, Roosevelt accepted Japan's apology and payment of over $2 million in damages for the *Panay* attack.

As fighting raged on in China and Spain in 1938, Hitler pronounced his intentions to unify all German-speaking lands and create a new German empire, or *Reich*. He first annexed Austria and then incorporated the Sudeten region of western Czechoslovakia into the German Reich. With a respectable military force and defense treaties with France and the Soviet Union, the Czechoslovakian government was prepared to resist. However, France, the Soviet Union, and Britain wanted no confrontation with Hitler. Choosing a policy of **appeasement**, in late September Britain's prime minister, Neville Chamberlain, met with Hitler in Munich and accepted Germany's annexation of the Sudetenland. France concurred. Chamberlain returned to England promising the **Munich Agreement** had secured "peace for our time." Within Germany, Hitler stepped up the persecution of the country's nearly half-million Jews. In government-sponsored violence, synagogues and Jewish businesses and homes were looted and destroyed. Detention centers—concentration camps—at Dachau and Buchenwald soon confined over fifty thousand Jews. Thousands of German and Austrian Jews fled to other countries. Many applied to enter the United States, but most were turned away. Public opinion polls found American anti-Semitism strong. One survey found that 85 percent of Protestants, 84 percent of Catholics, and even 25.8 percent of Jews in the United States opposed more Jewish refugees entering the country. The State Department, citing immigration requirements against admitting anyone who would become "a public charge," routinely denied entry to Jews whose property and assets had been seized by the German government. Roosevelt expressed concern, but Congress rejected efforts to change immigration restrictions. In all, only about sixty thousand Jewish refugees entered the United States between 1933 and 1938—many of them scientists, academics, and musicians.

Discussing world affairs in his 1939 State of the Union address, Roosevelt bolstered his own words by echoing Abraham Lincoln: "Events abroad have made it increasingly clear to the American people that the dangers within are less to be feared than dangers without.... This generation will nobly save or meanly lose the last best hope of earth." He then asked Congress to increase military spending for the construction of aircraft and to repeal the arms **embargo** section of the 1937 Neutrality Act. Congress rejected changing the neutrality law

appeasement Granting concessions to potential enemies to maintain peace. Since the Munich agreement did not stop Hitler's aggression, appeasement has become a policy that most nations avoid.

embargo A ban on trade with a country or countries, covering all goods or certain items, usually ordered and enforced by a government.

MAP 23.1 German Expansion at Its Height

This map shows the expansion of German power from 1938 through 1942. Which countries fell to German control? Why might Americans have differed over whether these moves by Germany represented a strategic threat to the United States?

but approved money for aircraft construction, some of which Roosevelt loaned to aircraft companies through the Reconstruction Finance Corporation. Boeing and Beechcraft, for example, received over $11 million to build long-range bombers in Wichita, Kansas.

In quick succession, events seemed to verify Roosevelt's prediction. Hitler ominously concluded a military alliance with Italy and a **German-Soviet Nonaggression Pact** with Stalin. He seized what remained of Czechoslovakia and demanded that Poland turn over to Germany the Polish Corridor, which connected Poland to the Baltic Sea. When Warsaw refused, Hitler invaded Poland on September 1, 1939.

In September 1939, Germany introduced the world to a new word and type of warfare,
Blitzkrieg—lightning war. Combining the use of tanks, aircraft, and infantry, German forces
quickly overran first Poland, then most of Western Europe. This picture shows a German
victory parade in Warsaw, Poland.

Two days later, Britain and France declared war on Germany. Within a matter of
days, German troops overran nearly all of Poland. On September 17, Soviet
forces entered the eastern parts of Poland as they had secretly agreed to do in the
Nonaggression Pact.

War and American Neutrality   As war began in Europe, isolationism remained strong in
the United States, with polls showing that sizeable
majorities of Americans in every part of the country
wanted the United States to stay out of the conflict. Roosevelt proclaimed
neutrality, but was determined to do everything possible, short of war, to help
the nations opposing Hitler. He called Congress into special session and asked
that the cash-and-carry policy of the Neutrality Act of 1937 be modified to allow
the sale of any goods, including arms, to any nation, provided the goods were
paid for in cash and carried away on ships belonging to the purchasing country.
A "peace bloc" argued that the request was a ruse to aid France and Britain and
would drag America into the war, but Congress yielded to the president and
passed the **Neutrality Act of 1939** in November. With this act, any nation could
now buy weapons from the United States. Roosevelt also worked with Latin
American countries to establish a 300-mile neutrality zone around the Western
Hemisphere, excluding Canada and other British and French possessions. Within
the zone, patrolled by the U.S. Navy, warships of warring nations were
forbidden.

Although neutral in appearance, both acts were designed to help France and
England. While any nation could now buy weapons from the United States,

German ships would be denied access to American ports by the British navy. The neutrality zone had to allow French and British warships to reach their possessions in the Western Hemisphere; therefore, it was only German warships that would be stopped by the U.S. Navy. If the navy happened to sink any German submarines, Roosevelt joked to his cabinet, he would apologize like "the Japs do, 'So sorry. Never do it again.' Tomorrow we sink two."

As 1940 began most people did not expect Roosevelt to run for a third term, nor did Roosevelt seem anxious to run. Yet he was worried about the direction of American foreign policy under someone else. He told the secretary of treasury: "I do not want to run unless ... things get very worse in Europe." Things got worse quickly. In April Hitler unleashed his forces on Denmark and Norway, which quickly fell. On May 10 the German offensive against France began with an invasion of Belgium and the Netherlands. On May 26 Belgian forces surrendered, while French and British troops began their remarkable evacuation to England from the French port of Dunkirk. On June 10, Mussolini entered the war and invaded France from the southeast. Twelve days later, France surrendered, leaving Germany and Italy, called the **Axis powers**, controlling most of western and central Europe. Britain now faced the seemingly invincible German army and air force alone. England's new prime minister, Winston Churchill, pledged never to surrender until the Nazi threat was destroyed and pleaded with Roosevelt for immediate help. He needed ships, aircraft, weapons, and steel and other raw materials. Roosevelt made two decisions: to aid England and to run for a third term. In June, Republicans nominated Wendell Willkie, an ex-Democrat from Indiana. Roosevelt became the official Democratic candidate in July.

Between the convention and election day, events in Europe shaped much of the political debate. To prepare for the invasion of England, Hitler ordered the navy to block supplies coming to Britain and the air force to bomb targets throughout England. As Britain's Royal Air Force rose to fight the *Luftwaffe*, Churchill repeated his requests to Roosevelt for warships and aircraft. Across the United States, opinion polls showed public confusion about what course the country should take. A large majority favored the United States staying out of the war, but a slightly smaller majority approved giving Britain aid, and support for preparedness was increasingly bipartisan. Roosevelt, determined to aid Britain, promised help and asked Congress to increase the military budget. He supported a bipartisan bill to create the first peacetime military draft in American history. Isolationists opposed both actions, especially the draft. Senator Nye expressed the view of many, saying, "If we get into this war it will not be because the President tried to keep us out." But Nye and other isolationists were unable to prevent Congress from approving the draft and over $37 billion for military spending, more than the total cost of World War I.

In September, Roosevelt signed the **Burke-Wadsworth Act**, and the government began drafting men into the military in October. He also, by executive order, exchanged fifty old destroyers for ninety-nine-year leases on British military bases in Newfoundland, the Caribbean, and British Guiana. The public responded favorably, contributing to a 10 percent Roosevelt lead in the political race. With Willkie trailing in the polls, Republican leaders convinced him to attack Roosevelt for pushing the nation toward war. If Roosevelt was elected, he told a Baltimore audience, "you may expect war by April." Willkie's popularity surged. Roosevelt countered with a promise to American mothers: "Your boys are not going to be sent into any foreign wars." Roosevelt won easily, but his victory did not sweep other Democrats into office; Republicans gained seats in both the Senate and House of Representatives.

The Battle for the Atlantic   While Roosevelt relaxed in the Caribbean after the election, he received an urgent message from Churchill. Britain was out of money to pay for American goods, as required by the 1939 Neutrality Act, and needed credit to pay for supplies. He also asked Roosevelt to allow American ships to carry goods to England and for American help to protect merchant ships from German submarines. Roosevelt agreed, but knowing that the requests faced tough congressional and public opposition, he turned to his powers of persuasion. In his December fireside chat, he told his audience that if England fell, Hitler would surely attack the United States next. He urged the people to make the nation the "arsenal of democracy" and to supply Britain with all the material help it needed to defeat Hitler. He then presented Congress with a bill allowing the president to lend, lease, or in any way provide goods to any country considered vital to American security. The request drew the expected fire from isolationists. Senator Burton K. Wheeler from Montana called it a military Agricultural Adjustment Act that would "plow under every fourth American boy." Supporters countered with "Send guns, not sons." On March 11, 1941, the 60-year-old president breathed a sigh of relief when the **Lend-Lease Act** passed easily.

By the summer of 1941, the U.S. Navy's patrols of the neutrality zone overlapped Hitler's Atlantic war zone. It was only a matter of time until American and German ships confronted each other. Having called off the invasion of Britain, Hitler directed German forces into Yugoslavia, Greece, and North Africa. He also planned to crush the Soviets with the largest military force ever assembled on a single front. On June 22, 1941, German forces, supported by allied Finnish, Hungarian, Italian, and Romanian armies, opened the eastern front. Claiming he would join even the devil to defeat Hitler, Churchill made an ally of Stalin, while Roosevelt extended credits and lend-lease goods to the Soviet Union. Despite initial crushing victories in which German soldiers advanced within miles of Moscow, by November it was becoming clear that the Soviets were not going to collapse.

With the battle for the Atlantic reaching a tipping point and Germany rolling through Russia, Roosevelt and Churchill met secretly off the coast of Newfoundland (the Argentia Conference, August 9–12, 1941). Churchill pleaded for an American declaration of war, but Roosevelt's main concern was more political than strategic. He urged Churchill to subscribe to an **Atlantic Charter** that would highlight the distinctions between the open, cooperative world of the democracies and the closed, self-serving world of fascist expansion. Championing self-determination, freedom of trade and the seas, and the establishment of a "permanent system of general security" in the form of a new world organization, Roosevelt explained, would help Americans support entry into the war. Churchill agreed but reminded Roosevelt that Britain could not fully accept the goals of self-determination and free trade within its Commonwealth and the British Empire. Returning to London, Churchill told his ministers that Roosevelt meant to "wage war, but not declare it, and that he would become more and more provocative ... to force an incident ... which would justify him in opening hostilities."

On September 4, 1941, the United States moved a step closer to ending its neutrality. In the North Atlantic, near Iceland, the American destroyer *Greer* skirmished with a German U-boat. Neither ship was damaged, but Roosevelt used the skirmish to get Congress to amend the neutrality laws to permit armed U.S. merchant ships to sail into combat zones. In October, following an attack on the U.S.S. *Kearney* and the sinking of the U.S.S. *Reuben James,* Congress rescinded all neutrality laws and public opinion seemed to accept the prospect of war. Throughout the country, FBI agents instructed local officials in how to best deal with problems of a nation at war, including espionage and sabotage, air raids and blackouts, and even gas contamination. Roosevelt accepted the War Department's "Victory Program," which concluded that the United States would have to fight a two-front war against Germany and against Japan. It also stated that Hitler needed to be defeated before the Japanese, and that July 1943 was about the earliest date that American troops could be ready for any large-scale operation.

Pearl Harbor   Since 1937, Japanese troops had seized more and more of China, while the United States did little but protest. By 1940, popular sentiment favored not only beefing up American defenses in the Pacific but also using economic pressure to slow Japanese aggression. In July 1940, Roosevelt began placing restrictions on Japanese-American trade, forbidding the sale and shipment of aviation fuel, steel, and scrap iron. Many Americans believed the action was too limited and pointed out that Japan was still allowed to buy millions of gallons of American oil, which it was using to "extinguish the lamps of China."

The situation in East Asia soon worsened when Japanese troops entered French Indochina, and Japan signed a defense treaty with Germany and Italy. America promptly strengthened its forces in the Philippines and tightened trade restrictions on Japan. Within the Japanese government some still hoped for an agreement with the United States and sought to negotiate. The subsequent discussions between Secretary of State Cordell Hull and Admiral Kichisaburo Nomura, Japan's ambassador to the United States, were confused and nonproductive. The lack of progress in the negotiations convinced many in the Japanese government that war was unavoidable to break the "circle of force" that denied Japan its interests. High on the list of interests was control over Malaysia and the Dutch East Indies (Indonesia), sources of vital raw materials, including oil. Seizing those regions, they concluded, would probably involve fighting the United States.

For Minister of War Hideki Tojo, the choice was simple: either submit to American demands, giving up the achievements of the past ten years and accepting a world order defined by the United States, or safeguard the nation's honor and achievements by initiating a war. In his mind, war could be averted only if the United States released frozen Japanese assets, suspended aid to China, capped its military presence in the Pacific, and resumed full trade with Japan. Without these concessions, Japan would begin military operations in the first week of December. Negotiations remained stalled until November 26, when Hull made it clear that the United States would make no concessions and insisted that Japan withdraw from China.

On November 26, Admiral Isoroku Yamamoto dispatched part of the Japanese fleet, including six aircraft carriers, toward Hawai`i. American observers, however, focused on the activity of a larger part of the Japanese fleet, which joined troop ships in sailing on December 5 toward the South China Sea and the Gulf of Siam. At 7:49 A.M. December 7 (Hawaiian time), before Japan's declaration of war had been received in Washington, Japanese planes struck the American fleet anchored at Pearl Harbor. By 8:12, seven battleships of the American Pacific fleet lined up along Battleship Row were aflame, sinking, or badly damaged. Eleven other ships had been hit, nearly two hundred American aircraft had been destroyed, and twenty-five hundred Americans had lost their lives.

The attack on Pearl Harbor, however, was only a small part of Japan's strategy. Elsewhere that day Japanese planes struck Singapore, Guam, the Philippines, and Hong Kong. Everywhere, British and American positions in the Pacific and East Asia were being overwhelmed. Roosevelt declared that the unprovoked, sneak attack on Pearl Harbor made December 7 "a day which will live in infamy" and asked Congress for a declaration of war against Japan. Only Representative Jeannette Rankin of Montana, a pacifist, kept the December 8 declaration of war from being unanimous. Three days later, Germany and Italy declared war on the United States. In England Churchill "slept the sleep of the saved and thankful." He knew that with the economic and human resources of the United States finally committed to war, the Axis would be "ground to powder."

AMERICA RESPONDS TO WAR

Americans were angry and full of fight, and the attack on Pearl Harbor unified the nation as no other event had done. It was almost impossible to find an American isolationist as thousands of young men rushed to enlist. On December 8, 1,200 applicants besieged the navy recruiting station in New York City, some having waited outside the doors all night. Eventually over 16.4 million Americans would serve in the armed forces during World War II.

The shock of Japan's attack on Pearl Harbor raised fears of further attacks, especially along the Pacific Coast. On the night of December 7 and throughout the next week, West Coast cities reported enemy planes overhead and practiced blackouts. Phantom Japanese planes were spotted above San Francisco and Los

It Matters Today

Internment

Does war or national crisis allow for the reduction and elimination of a person's rights, of a citizen's rights? During the war the government interned 110,000 people of Japanese ancestry because they were regarded as potential threats to American security. With the memory of Pearl Harbor still fresh, fears of spying and sabotage played a role; race, too was a factor. Many argued that the culture and values of Japan made the conflict a "race war" and that all Japanese, even those who were citizens, could not be trusted: "Once a Jap always a Jap!" The dissenting Justices in the *Korematsu* case believed internment was clearly a result of racism that violated the American concept of democracy and that the decision was the "legalization of racism." How a society acts in time of war often provides insights into not only the strengths of the nation but its weaknesses as well.

- Since the Al Qaeda attacks on September 11, 2001, the United States has fought a war on international terrorism and defined radical Islamic fundamentalism as a source of that terrorism. These actions have raised the issues of race, religion, and culture, and have led to comparisons to the treatment of the Nisei and the Issei during World War II. Are these comparisons valid? Why or why not?

Angeles. The Rose Bowl game between Oregon State and Duke was moved from the bowl's home in Pasadena to Duke's stadium in Durham, North Carolina. Stores everywhere removed "made in Japan" goods from shelves. Alarm and anger were focused especially on Japanese Americans. Rumors circulated wildly that they intended to sabotage factories and military installations, paving the way for the invasion of the West Coast. Within a week, the FBI had arrested 2,541 citizens of Axis countries: 1,370 Japanese, 1,002 Germans, and 169 Italians.

Japanese Amer-ican Internment   There were nearly 125,000 Japanese Americans in the country, about three-fourths of whom were **Nisei**— Japanese Americans who had been born in the United States. The remaining fourth were Japanese immigrants, or **Issei**—officially citizens of Japan, although nearly all had lived in the United States prior to 1924 when Asians were barred from the country. Reflecting a popular view, General John L. De Witt, commanding general of the Western Defense District, stated, "We must worry about the Japanese all the time until he is wiped off the map." Echoing long-standing anti-Japanese sentiment, the West Coast moved to "protect" itself. Japanese Americans were fired from state jobs, and their law and medical licenses were revoked. Banks froze Japanese American assets, stores refused service, and loyal citizens vandalized Nisei and Issei homes and businesses. The few voices that came forward to speak on behalf of Japanese Americans were shouted down by those demanding their removal from the West

Coast. On February 19, 1942, Roosevelt signed **Executive Order #9066**, which allowed the military to remove anyone deemed a threat from official military areas. When the entire West Coast was declared a military area, the eviction of those of Japanese ancestry from the region began. By the summer of 1942, over 110,000 Nisei and Issei had been transported to ten **internment camps**. When tested in court, the executive order was upheld by the Supreme Court in *Korematsu v. the United States* in 1944.

The orders to relocate allowed almost no time to prepare. Families could pack only a few personal possessions and had to store or sell the rest of their property, including homes and businesses. Finding storage facilities was nearly impossible, and most families had to liquidate their possessions at ridiculously low prices. "It is difficult to describe the feeling of despair and humiliation experienced," one man recalled, "as we watched the Caucasians coming to look over all our possessions and offering such nominal amounts knowing we had no recourse but to accept." In the relocation it is estimated that Japanese American families lost from $810 million to $2 billion in property and goods.

Having disposed of a lifetime of possessions, Japanese Americans began the process of internment. Tags with numbers were issued to every family to tie to luggage and coats—no names, only numbers. "From then on," wrote one woman, "we were known as family #10710." In the camps, the Nisei and Issei were surrounded by barbed wire and watched over by guards. The internees were assigned to 20-by-25-foot apartments in long barracks of plywood covered with tarpaper, and each camp was expected to create a community complete with farms, shops, and small factories. Within a remarkably short time, they did. Making the desert bloom, by 1944 the internees at Manzanar, east of the Sierra in California's Owens Valley, were producing more than $2 million worth of agricultural products.

Some internees were able to leave the camps by working outside, supplying much-needed labor, especially farm work. By the fall of 1942, one-fifth of all males had left the camps to work. Others left for college or volunteered for military service. Japanese American units served in both the Pacific and European theaters, the most famous being the four-thousand-man 442nd Regimental Combat Team, which saw action in Italy, France, and Germany. The men of the 442nd would be among the most decorated in the army. Years later, in 2000, the federal government, citing racial bias during the war for the delay, awarded the Medal of Honor to twenty-one Asian Americans—most belonging to the 442nd Regiment. Included in the group was Daniel Ken Inouye, who was elected to the U.S. Senate from Hawai`i in 1960.

Aware of rabidly anti-Japanese public opinion, Roosevelt waited until after the off-year 1943 elections to allow internees who passed a loyalty review to go home. A year later, most of the camps were empty, each internee having been given train fare home and $25. Returning home, the Japanese Americans discovered that nearly everything they once owned was gone. Stored belongings had been stolen. Land, homes, and businesses had been confiscated by the government for unpaid taxes. Denied even an apology from the government, Japanese Americans nevertheless began to reestablish their homes and businesses. Decades later, in 1988, and after several lawsuits on behalf of victims, a semi-apologetic federal government paid $20,000 in compensation to each of the surviving sixty thousand internees.

Mobilizing the Nation for War   When President Roosevelt gave his first fireside chat following Pearl Harbor, "Dr. New Deal" became "Dr. Win the War." To produce the goods necessary for victory factories were to run twenty-four hours a day, seven days a week. Gone was the antibusiness attitude that had characterized much New Deal rhetoric, and in its place was the realization that only big business could produce the vast amount of armaments and supplies needed. Secretary of War Henry L. Stimson noted: "You have to let business make money out of the process or business won't work." Overall, the United States paid over $240 billion in defense contracts, with 82 percent of them going to the nation's top one hundred corporations. At the same time more than half a million small businesses collapsed. Every part of the nation benefited from defense-based prosperity, but the South and the coastal West saw huge economic gains. The South experienced a remarkable 40 percent increase in its industrial capacity, and the West did even better.

Since 1929, the Depression and New Deal governmental programs had provided the West with important resources such as electricity, experience in large-scale production projects, and a growing population. Now, billions of dollars of government contracts flowed into the region, with California receiving nearly 40 percent of the total. Wrote one observer, "It was [as] if someone had tilted the country: people, money, and soldiers all spilled west."

Among the contractors, few outdid Henry J. Kaiser, "Sir Launchalot." He transformed the shipbuilding industry by constructing massive shipyards in California. By using **prefabricated** sections, he cut the time it took to build a merchant ship from about three hundred days to an average of eighty days in 1942. Nationally, by the end of 1942, one-third of all production was geared to the war, and the government had allocated millions of dollars to improve productivity by upgrading factories and generating new industries. When the war cut off some supplies of raw rubber, government and business cooperated to develop and produce synthetic rubber. By the end of the war, the United States had pumped more than $320 billion into the American economy, and the final production amounts exceeded almost everyone's expectations: U.S. manufacturers had built more than 300,000 aircraft, 88,140 tanks, and 86,000 warships. Neither Germany nor Japan could come close to matching the output of American products.

Millions of dollars were also spent on research and development (R&D) to create and improve a variety of goods from weapons to medicines. In "science cities" constructed by the government across the country, researchers and technicians of the **Manhattan Project** harnessed atomic energy and built an atomic bomb. Hundreds of colleges and universities and private laboratories, such as Bell Labs, received research and development grants. Improved radar and sonar allowed

---

prefabricated   Parts of an item that are manufactured in advance, usually in standardized sections for easy shipment and quick assembly.

American forces to detect and destroy enemy planes and ships. New medical techniques and new, more effective medicines, including penicillin, saved millions of lives. Potent pesticides fought insects that carried typhus, malaria, and other diseases at home and overseas.

As the economy retooled to provide the machines of war, Roosevelt acted to provide government direction and planning. An array of governmental agencies and boards arose to regulate prices and production. The size of the federal bureaucracy grew 400 percent. The War Production Board (WPB) and the War Labor Board (WLB), both created in January 1942, sought to coordinate and plan production, establish the allotment of materials, and ensure harmonious labor relations. An Office of Price Administration (OPA), established in 1941, tried to limit inflation and equalize consumption by setting prices and issuing ration books with coupons needed to buy a wide range of commodities, such as shoes, coffee, meat, and sugar. When the agencies failed to resolve problems and create a smoothly working economy, Roosevelt and Congress expanded the agencies' scope and created new ones. Seeking to improve coordination, in 1942 and 1943 Roosevelt added two new umbrella agencies, the Office of Economic Stabilization (OES) and the **Office of War Mobilization**. To direct both agencies, he appointed former Supreme Court justice James F. Byrnes. Armed with extensive powers and the president's trust, Byrnes became known as the "Assistant President." By the fall of 1943, production was booming, jobs were plentiful, wages and family incomes were rising, and inflation was under control. Even farmers were climbing out of debt as farm income had tripled since 1939.

The war provided full employment and new opportunities for labor organizations. Union leaders, in exchange for their agreements not to strike, expected industry to agree to union recognition, collective bargaining, **closed shops**, and increased wages. Others, however, argued that unions should be forbidden to strike or otherwise hinder war production and should accept the open shop. In 1941, even before the United States entered the war, four thousand strikes had stopped work on defense production and had forced the government on one occasion—a strike at North American Aviation—to seize the plant and threaten the strikers with induction into the military if they did not return to work. Roosevelt hoped his war production agencies could find a middle ground between union advocates and opponents. In 1942 OPA, the WLB, and other agencies hammered out a compromise promoting union membership and accepting the closed shop and collective bargaining, while getting pledges from unions to control wages and oppose strikes.

While most workers and employers accepted the guidelines, others did not. Every year nearly 3 million workers went on strike or conducted work slowdowns. Most lasted only a brief time and did not jeopardize production, but several strikes were more serious, generating the wrath of the president, Congress, and the public and prompting government intervention. The most serious strike occurred in 1943 when CIO president and head of the United Mine Workers John L. Lewis

---

closed shop A business or factory whose workers are required to be union members.

demanded higher wages and safer working conditions. An angry president threatened to take over the mines. Congress wanted Lewis jailed as a traitor and pushed through, over the president's veto, the **Smith-Connally War Labor Disputes Act**. It gave the president the power to seize and operate any strikebound industries considered vital for war production. Eventually, the parties in the mine strike compromised, giving higher wages to the miners. By the end of the war, American workers had produced a massive amount of material and were receiving higher wages than ever before. Unions represented 35 percent of the labor force and had gained unprecedented influence.

Taxes were also up, reflecting Roosevelt's desire to fund the war through taxation. The 1942 and 1943 Revenue Acts increased the number of people paying taxes and raised rates. In 1939, 4 million Americans paid income taxes; by the end of the war, more than 40 million did so. Individuals making $500,000 or more a year paid 88 percent in taxes. Corporate taxes averaged 40 percent, with a 90 percent tax on excess profits.

These tax changes moderately altered the basic distribution of income by reducing the proportion held by the upper two-fifths of the population—but tax revenues paid for only about half of the cost of the war. The government borrowed the rest. The national debt jumped from $40 billion in 1940 to near $260 billion by 1945 (see Figure 23.1). The most publicized borrowing effort encouraged the purchase of war bonds. Movie stars and other celebrities asked Americans to "do their part" and buy bonds. The public responded by purchasing more than $40 billion in individual bonds, but the majority of bonds—$95 billion—were bought by corporations and financial institutions.

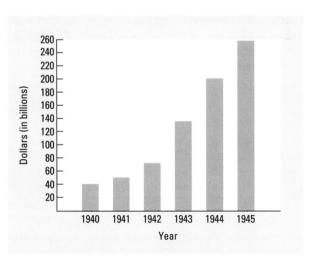

FIGURE 23.1 The National Debt, 1940–1945

As the United States fought to defeat the Axis nations, its national debt soared. Rather than further raise taxes, the government chose to borrow about 60 percent of the cost. By the end of the war the debt had reached near $260 billion.

Wartime Politics   As Roosevelt mobilized the nation for war, Republicans and conservative Democrats moved to bury what was left of the New Deal. People secure in their jobs were no longer as concerned about social welfare programs. They griped about higher taxes, rents, and prices, the scarcity of some goods, and government inefficiency. Congressional elections in November 1942 continued the trend started in 1937 and returned more Republicans to Congress. A more conservative Congress axed the Civilian Conservation Corps (CCC), the Works Progress Administration (WPA), and the National Youth Administration (NYA) and slashed the budgets of other government agencies.

Roosevelt, seeking an unprecedented fourth term in 1944, hoped to recapture some social activism and called for the passage of an economic bill of rights that included government support for higher-wage jobs, home construction, and medical care, but his plea fell on deaf ears. Instead, Congress passed a smaller version that would reward veterans of the war. In June the **G.I. Bill** became law. It guaranteed a year's unemployment compensation for veterans while they looked for "good" jobs, provided economic support if they chose to go to school, and offered low-interest home loans.

Roosevelt brushed aside concerns about his age and health, but responding to conservatives in the party, he agreed to drop his liberal vice president, Henry Wallace, and replace him with a more conservative running mate. The choice was Senator **Harry S Truman** from Missouri. Roosevelt campaigned on a strong wartime economy, his record of leadership, and by November 1944, a successful war effort.

As their candidate, Republicans nominated Governor Thomas Dewey of New York, who attacked government inefficiency and waste, and argued that his youth, 42, made him a better candidate than Roosevelt. A Republican-inspired "whispering campaign" hinted that at 62 Roosevelt was ill and close to death. Voters ignored the rumors and reelected Roosevelt, whose winning totals, although not as large as in 1940, were still greater than pollsters had predicted and proved that Roosevelt still generated widespread support.

A People at   America's entry into the war changed nearly everything
Work and War   about everyday life. Government agencies set prices and
                        froze wages and rents. Cotton, silk, gasoline, and items made of metal, including hair clips and safety pins, became increasingly scarce. By the end of 1942, most Americans had a ration book containing an array of different-colored coupons of various values that limited their purchases of such staples as meat, sugar, and gasoline. Explaining why most Americans received only 3 gallons of gasoline a week, Roosevelt noted that a bomber required nearly 1,100 gallons of fuel to bomb Naples, Italy, the equivalent of about 375 gasoline ration tickets. Speeding was unpatriotic as it wasted gas and rubber. Also, the War Production Board changed fashion to conserve fabrics. In men's suits, lapels were narrowed, and vests and pant cuffs were eliminated. The amount of fabric in women's skirts was also reduced, and the two-piece bathing suit was introduced as "patriotic chic." Families collected scrap metal, paper, and rubber to be recycled for the war

effort and growing a **victory garden** became a symbol of patriotism. When some people complained about shortages and inconveniences, more would challenge, "Don't you know there's a war on?"

Even with rationing, most Americans were experiencing a higher-than-ever standard of living. Consumer spending rose by 12 percent, and Americans were spending more than ever on entertainment, from books to movies to horse racing. Included in those discovering prosperity were women, African Americans, Latinos, and Indians who by 1943 were being hired because of severe labor shortages. As noted, even the Nisei were allowed to leave their relocation camps when their labor was needed. To gain access to new jobs, 15 million Americans relocated between 1941 and 1945. Two hundred thousand people, many from the rural South, headed for Detroit, but more went west, where defense industries beckoned. Shipbuilding and the aircraft industry sparked boomtowns that could not keep pace with the growing need for local services and facilities. San Diego, California, once a small retirement community with a quiet naval base, mushroomed into a major military and defense industrial city almost overnight. Nearly fifty-five thousand people flocked there each year of the war, with thousands living in small travel trailers leased by the federal government for $7 a month. Mobile, Alabama; Norfolk, Virginia; Seattle, Washington; Denver, Colorado—all experienced similar rapid growth.

With the expanding populations, industrial war cities experienced massive problems providing homes, water, electricity, and sanitation. Crime flourished. Marriage, divorce, family violence, and juvenile delinquency rates soared. Contributing to the social problems of the booming cities were those posed by many unsupervised teenage children. Juvenile crime increased dramatically during the war, much of it blamed on lockout and latchkey children whose working mothers left them alone during their job shifts. In Mobile, authorities speculated that two thousand children a day skipped school, some going to movies but most just hanging out looking for something to do.

Particularly worrisome to authorities were those nicknamed "V-girls." Victory girls were young teens, sometimes called "khaki-wacky teens," who hung around gathering spots like bus depots and drugstores to flirt with GIs and ask for dates. Wearing hair ribbons, bobby sox, and saddle shoes, their young faces thick with makeup and bright red lipstick, V-girls traded sex for movies, dances, and drinks. Seventeen-year-old Elvira Taylor of Norfolk took a different approach—she became an "Allotment Annie." She simply married the soldiers and collected their monthly **allotment checks.** Eventually, two American soldiers at an English pub showing off pictures of their wives discovered they had both married Elvira! It turned out she had wed six servicemen.

New Opportunities and Old Constraints   Mobilization forced the restructuring and redirecting of economic and human resources. Families had to adjust to new challenges. Men and women confronted new roles and

---

allotment checks   Checks that a soldier's wife received from the government, amounting to a percentage of her husband's pay.

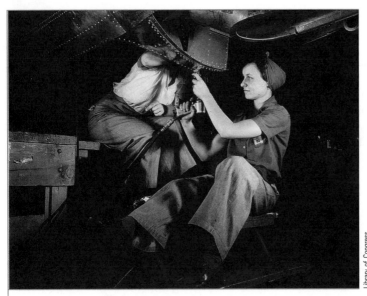

Library of Congress

As during World War I, the Second World War opened up new job opportunities for women. In this picture, a real-life "Rosie the Riveter" works on the fuselage of a bomber.

accepted new responsibilities, both on the home front and in the military. Like men, many women were anxious to serve in the military. But at first the armed forces did not employ women except as nurses. To expand women's roles, Congresswoman Edith Norse Rogers prodded Congress and the Army to create the Women's Auxiliary Army Corps (WAAC) in March 1942, which became the Women's Army Corps (WAC) a year later. Other services followed suit by creating the navy's Women Appointed for Volunteer Emergency Service (WAVES) and the Marines' Women's Reserve. Relegated to noncombat roles, most women served as nurses and clerical workers. But those in the Women's Airforce Service Pilots (WASPS) tested planes, ferried planes across the United States and Canada, and trained male pilots. At the marine flight-training center at Cherry Point, North Carolina, all the flight instructors were women. By war's end, over 350,000 women had donned uniforms, earned equal pay with men who held the same rank, and provided a new female image.

Women serving in the military were not the only break with tradition. With over 10 million men marching off to war, employers increasingly turned to women. The federal government supported the move with training and a campaign stressing that women could shorten the war if they joined the workforce. The image of **Rosie the Riveter** became the symbol of the patriotic woman doing her part. As more jobs opened, women filled them. A Billings, Montana newspaper noted, "petticoat troops are making forced landings in businesses and industry, and the situation is in hand." Increasingly women filled those jobs once held by men. In Detroit, women made up 56 percent of the labor force, while in Boeing's Seattle plant women filled 47 percent of the payroll. Women went to work for many reasons—some because of patriotism, but most because they wanted both the job and the wages. Leaving home, Peggy Terry

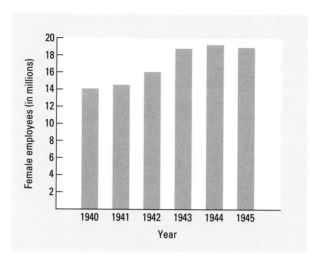

FIGURE 23.2 Women in the Workforce, 1940–1945

As men went to war, the nation turned increasingly to women to fill vital jobs. With government's encouragement, the number of women in the workforce swelled from 14 million to nearly 20 million. With the war's end, however, many women left the workplace and returned to the home.

worked in a munitions plant and considered it "an absolute miracle.... We made the fabulous sum of $32 a week.... Before, we made nothing." Other women left menial jobs for better-paying positions with industries and the federal government. By 1944, 37 percent of all adult women were working, almost 19.4 million (see Figure 23.2). Of these, the majority (72.2 percent) were married, and over half were 35 or older.

New opportunities did not diminish familiar constraints. Professional and supervisory positions remained dominated by men, and not all was rosy at work. Despite the labor shortage, male workers frequently resented and harassed women. "The hardest thing about the job," remembered one woman cab driver, "was the hostility of men toward women driving." Similar complaints echoed across the country even as management and the media praised women's work ethics and abilities. Edsel Ford commented that women did the hardest welding and the most delicate jobs "superbly," while a Yellow Cab manager pointed out that women drivers had more "tact" and a "very, very low" accident rate. Keeping with tradition, women were generally paid less than men, even though the WLB promoted the idea of the same pay for the same job. Women with children faced the problem of daycare. Although the 1942 Lanham Act provided communities with federal funds for child care, there were never enough money, centers, or programs to meet the needs of working families. Many women who found it too difficult to balance family needs and work left their jobs. Finally, women worked under the reminder that despite their wishes, employers and most men expected them to return to their traditional roles at home when the war ended.

Those expectations proved correct. By the summer of 1945, many of the women found themselves among the unemployed. Shipyards and the aircraft plants dismissed nearly three-fourths of their women employees. In Detroit, the automobile industry executed a similar cut in women workers, from 25 to 7.5 percent. Those who managed to remain at work were frequently transferred to less attractive, poorly paying jobs. Thus, for most women, the war experience was mixed, with new choices cut short by changing circumstances.

The war also provided new opportunities for African Americans, but they were accompanied by racial and ethnic tensions and the knowledge that when the war ended, the opportunities were likely to vanish. Initially, many companies resisted hiring nonwhite workers. North American Aviation Company spoke for the aircraft industry when, in early 1942, it announced that it would not hire blacks "regardless of their training."

The antiblack bias began to change by mid-1942 for a variety of reasons. One was that African Americans were unwilling to be denied job opportunities. Even before the war, in early 1941, **A. Philip Randolph**, leader of the powerful Brotherhood of Sleeping Car Porters union, proposed that African Americans march on Washington to demand equality in jobs and the armed forces. To avoid such an embarrassing demonstration, Roosevelt issued Executive Order #8802 in June 1941, creating the **Fair Employment Practices Commission (FEPC)**, and forbidding racial job discrimination by the government and companies holding government contracts. Bending under federal pressure and recognizing worsening labor shortages, businesses began to integrate their workforces.

In California, these pressures dissolved the color line by the end of 1942. West Coast shipyards were the first to integrate. When Lockheed Aircraft broke the color barrier in August, even North American Aviation grudgingly complied. Word soon spread to the South that blacks could find work in California, and between the spring of 1942 and 1945, more than 340,000 African Americans moved to Los Angeles. Overall, nearly 400,000 African Americans abandoned the South for the West. Thousands of others went north to cities such as Chicago and Detroit.

The FEPC and increased access to jobs did not mean that segregation and discrimination ended. Black wages rose from an average of $457 to $1,976 a year but remained only about 65 percent of white wages. To continue their quest for equality, blacks advocated the "Double V" campaign: victory over racist Germany and victory over racism at home. Membership of the NAACP and Urban League increased as both turned to public opinion, the courts, and Congress to attack segregation, lynching, the poll tax, and discrimination. In 1942 the newly formed **Congress of Racial Equality (CORE)** adopted the **sit-in** tactic to attempt to integrate public facilities. Led by black civil rights activist **James Farmer**, CORE integrated some public facilities in Chicago and Washington, although it failed in the South, where many CORE workers were badly beaten.

---

sit-in The act of occupying seats or an area; a tactic used, for example, to protest segregation or strengthen the effect of a labor strike.

In many places across the nation, racial tensions increased as the population of African Americans grew. In Detroit, white workers went on strike when three black workers were promoted. A Justice Department examination reported, "White Detroit seems to be a particularly hospitable climate for native fascist-type movements." On a hot summer Sunday, June 20, 1943, the tensions in Detroit erupted into a major race riot. Before federal troops arrived on June 21 and restored order, twenty-five blacks and nine whites were dead.

The opportunities and difficulties of African Americans in uniform paralleled those of black civilians. Prior to 1940, blacks served at the lowest ranks and in the most menial jobs in a segregated army and navy. The Army Air Corps and the Marines Corps refused to accept blacks at all. Compounding the problem, most in the military openly agreed with Secretary of War Henry L. Stimson when he asserted, "Leadership is not embedded in the Negro race." The manpower needs of war changed the role of the black soldier, opening up new ranks and occupations. In April 1942, Secretary of the Navy James Forrestal permitted black **non-commissioned officers** in the U.S. Navy, although blacks would wait until 1944 before becoming upper-rank officers. With only a small number of African American officers, in 1940 the army began to encourage the recruitment of black officers and promoted Benjamin O. Davis, Sr. from colonel to brigadier general. His son, **Benjamin O. Davis, Jr.,** was quickly promoted to lieutenant colonel and given command of the 99th Pursuit Squadron–the Tuskegee Airmen. Eventually six hundred African Americans were commissioned as pilots. The army also organized other African American units that fought in both the European and Pacific theaters of operations, such as the 371st Tank Battalion, which battled its way across France and into Germany and liberated the concentration camps of Dachau and Buchenwald.

Higher ranks and better jobs for a few still did not disguise that for most blacks, even officers, military life was often demeaning and brutal, and almost always segregated. In Indiana, more than a hundred black officers were arrested for trying to integrate an officers' club. Across the country, blacks objected to the Red Cross practice of segregating its blood supply. German prisoners of war held in Salina, Kansas, could eat at any local lunch counter and go to any movie theater, but their black guards could not. One dismayed soldier wrote, "The people of Salina would serve these enemy soldiers and turn away black American GIs.... If we were ... in Germany, they would break our bones. As 'colored' men in Salina, they only break our hearts." In truth, many black soldiers had their bones broken, and their lives taken, on the home front. As in the civilian world, blacks in the military resisted discrimination and called on Roosevelt and the government for help. But their requests accomplished little.

Latinos, too, found new opportunities during the war while encountering continued segregation and hostility. Like other Americans, Latinos, almost invariably called "Mexicans" by their fellow soldiers, rushed to enlist as the war started. More than 300,000 Latinos served—the highest percentage of any

noncommissioned officer Enlisted member of the armed forces who has been promoted to a rank such as corporal or sergeant, conferring leadership over others.

About 700,000 African Americans served in segregated units in all branches of the military, facing discrimination at all levels. Among those units were the four squadrons of the Tuskegee Airmen commanded by General Benjamin O. Davis. "We fought two wars," commented Airman Louis Parnell, "one with the enemy and the other back home."

National Archives

ethnic community—and seventeen won the nation's highest award for valor, the Medal of Honor. Although they faced some institutional and individual prejudices in the military, Latinos, unlike African Americans and most Nisei, served in integrated units and generally faced less discrimination in the military than in society.

For those remaining at home, more jobs were available, but still Latinos almost always worked as common laborers and agricultural workers. In the Southwest, it was not until 1943 that the FEPC attempted to open semiskilled and skilled positions to Mexican Americans. Jobs drew Mexican Americans, like others, to cities, creating serious social tensions as well as significant shortages of farm workers across the Southwest. As Los Angeles' already large Latino population expanded, social tensions became especially acute between Anglos and young Mexican Americans, known as **pachucos**, who expressed their rejection of Anglo culture by wearing **zoot suits**. Newspapers fanned racial tensions with articles highlighting a Mexican crime wave and depicting the "zooters" as dope addicts and draft dodgers. In June 1943, Anglo mobs,

pachucos A Spanish term originally meaning "bandits," it became associated with juvenile delinquents of Mexican American heritage.

zoot suit A long jacket with wide lapels and padded shoulders, worn over pleated trousers pegged and cuffed at the ankle.

including several hundred servicemen, descended on East Los Angeles for three successive nights. They dragged zoot suiters out of movies, stores, even houses, beating them and tearing apart their clothes. When the police acted, it was to arrest the victims—over six hundred Mexican American youths were taken into "preventive custody." The riot lasted a week. Afterward, the Los Angeles city council outlawed the wearing of zoot suits.

To relieve the need for agricultural workers, Washington turned to Mexico. Together they negotiated the *bracero* (Spanish for "helping arms") program. The agreement stipulated that the **braceros**, or Mexican nationals, receive fair wages and adequate housing, transportation, food, and medical care. But guarantees mattered little. Most ranchers and farmers paid low wages and provided substandard facilities. The average Mexican American family earned about $800 a year, well below the U.S. government's established $1,130 annual minimum standard for a family of five.

Jobs and higher wages were available to many American Indians during the war and lured more than forty thousand of them away from their reservations, many of whom never returned following the war. In addition, over twenty-five thousand Indians served in the military. Among the most famous were about four hundred Navajos who served as **code talkers** for the Marine Corps, using their native language as a secure means of communication. Although often called "chief," American Indians met little discrimination in the military. Whether in the armed forces or in the domestic workforce, those who left the reservations saw their families' average incomes rise from $400 a year in 1941 to $1,200 in 1945, and many chose to assimilate into American culture, abandoning their old patterns of life.

Nearly invisible in society, homosexuals also served in the military. The official policy was not to enlist them, but the screening process was ineffective, merely asking if a person was a homosexual and looking only for effeminate behavior. Once enlisted, many gays and lesbians discovered that the military generally tolerated them unless they were caught in a sexual act. In a circular letter sent to military commanders, the surgeon general's office asked that homosexual relationships be overlooked as long as they did not disrupt the unit. During the war, gays' war records were much like those of other soldiers. "I was super patriotic," said one gay combat veteran.

WAGING WORLD WAR

In the days following Pearl Harbor, many Americans wanted the defeat of Japan to be the country's first priority. To Churchill's and Stalin's relief, however, Roosevelt remained committed to victory first in Europe. But what was the best strategy to defeat Hitler? The Soviets, fighting against 3.3 million Germans, called for a second front in northern Europe as soon as possible. The British considered an invasion across the English Channel into France too risky and promoted an easier and safer landing in western North Africa, Operation Torch, in 1942. Believing the people needed a victory anywhere, Roosevelt ignored opposition from his chiefs of staff and approved the operation.

As planning began for the invasion, the course of the war darkened for the Allies. German forces were advancing toward Egypt and penetrating deeper into the Soviet Union. In the Atlantic, German U-boats were sinking ships at an appalling rate. April and May 1942 saw the surrender of most American forces in the Philippines, and Japanese successes continued elsewhere in the Pacific. General Patrick Hurley admitted, "We were out-shipped, out-planed, out-manned, and out-gunned by the Japanese."

Halting the Japanese Advance   Despite the commitment to defeating Germany, the nation's first victory came in the Pacific on May 8, 1942, at the **Battle of the Coral Sea**. Having deciphered secret Japanese codes, American military planners successfully deployed carrier forces to intercept and halt a Japanese invasion fleet aimed at New Guinea. Soon after the Coral Sea success, again reading top-secret Japanese messages, the United States learned of a Japanese thrust spearheaded by an aircraft carrier group aimed at **Midway Island**.

The Battle of Midway, June 4–6, 1942, helped change the course of the war in the Pacific. The air-to-sea battle was several hours old when a flight of American dive-bombers attacked the Japanese carriers in the middle of rearming and refueling their planes. Their decks cluttered with planes, fuel, and bombs, the Japanese carriers suffered staggering casualties and damage. Three immediately sank, and a fourth went down later in the battle. Although the Americans lost the U.S.S. *Yorktown*, they had destroyed the carrier-based air superiority of the Japanese. In the war of machines, the United States quickly replaced the *Yorktown* and by the end of the war had constructed fourteen additional large carriers—Japan was able to build only six.

The next step in the Pacific was to begin an island-hopping campaign intended, eventually, to close in on Japan. **General Douglas MacArthur** and the army would advance toward the Philippines from the south. The navy, under the direction of Admiral Chester Nimitz, would seize selected islands and atolls in the Solomon, Marshall, Gilbert, and Mariana island groups, approaching the Philippines from the east. Both forces would join for the final attack on Japan. On August 7, 1942, soldiers of the 1st Marine Division waded ashore on **Guadalcanal Island** in the Solomons. Japan, considering the invasion to be "the fork in the road that leads to victory for them or for us," furiously defended the island. Both sides suffered significant losses in the horrendous face-to-face combat that characterized the war in the Pacific. After heavy losses, the Japanese withdrew in early February.

Roads to Berlin   While American marines sweated in the jungles of Guadalcanal, British and American armies closed in on German forces in North Africa. With the British driving the Germans from Egypt westward, American troops landed in Morocco in November 1943 and pushed eastward. In early May 1943, the Americans linked up with the British, forcing 300,000 German troops to surrender.

German losses in North Africa were light compared with those in Russia, where Soviet and German forces were locked in a titanic struggle. Through the summer and fall of 1942, German armies advanced steadily, but during the winter the Soviet army drove them from the Caucasus oil fields and trapped them at Stalingrad. On February 2, 1943, after a three-month Soviet counteroffensive in

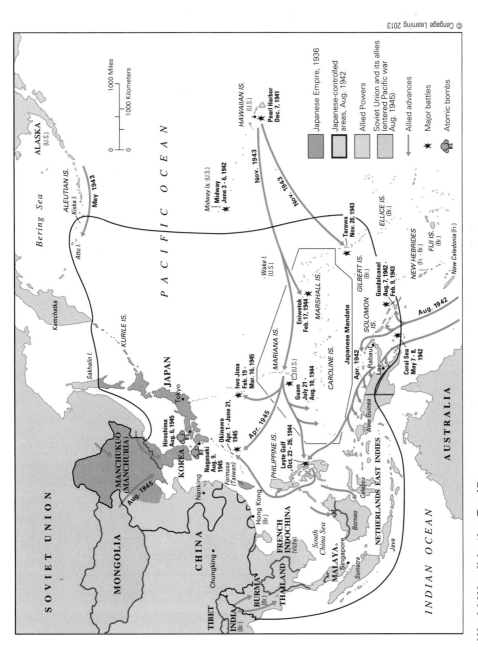

© Cengage Learning 2013

MAP 23.2 World War II in the Pacific

American ships and planes stemmed the Japanese offensive at the Battles of the Coral Sea and Midway Island. Thereafter, the Japanese were on the defensive against American amphibious assaults and air strikes.

the dead of winter, 300,000 German soldiers surrendered, their 6th Army having lost more than 140,000 men.

Although it was hard to predict in February, the tide of the war had turned in Europe. Soviet forces would continue to grind down the German army all the way to Berlin. But in February, Stalin knew only that the **Battle of Stalingrad** had cost the Russians dearly and that German strength was still formidable. He again demanded a second front in Western Europe. Again, he would be disappointed. Meeting with Churchill at Casablanca (January 1943), Roosevelt agreed with the British leader to invade Sicily and Italy, targets that Churchill called the "soft

MAP 23.3 World War II in Europe and Africa

The momentous German defeat at Stalingrad in early 1943 marked the turning point in the war against the Axis. By 1945, Allied conquest of Hitler's "thousand-year" Reich was imminent.

underbelly of the Axis." General Albert Wedemeyer expressed the U.S. military reaction to the Casablanca deal: "We lost our shirts ... we came, we listened, and we were conquered."

The invasion of Sicily—Operation Husky—took place in early July 1943, and within a month the Allies controlled the island. In response, the Italians overthrew Mussolini and opened negotiations with Britain and the United States to change sides. Italy surrendered unconditionally on September 8. Immediately, German forces assumed the defense of Italy and halted the Allied advance just north of Salerno. Not until late May 1944 did Allied forces finally break through the German defenses in southern Italy. On June 4, U.S. forces under General Mark Clark entered Rome. Two days later, the world's attention turned toward Normandy along the west coast of France. The second front demanded by Stalin had, at long last, begun.

In November 1943 the leaders of the **Grand Alliance**, Roosevelt, Churchill, and Stalin, had met in the Iranian capital of Tehran to discuss strategy and to consider the process of establishing a postwar settlement. The **Tehran Conference** was a productive meeting. The Allies made plans to coordinate a Soviet offensive with the Allied landings at Normandy and to work together to create a positive peace. Roosevelt was especially pleased because Stalin had agreed to support a new world organization and to enter the Japanese war once the battle with Hitler was over.

The invasion of Normandy, France—**Operation Overlord**—was the grandest **amphibious** assault ever assembled: 6,483 ships, 1,500 tanks, and 200,000 men. Opposing the Allies were thousands of German troops behind the Atlantic Wall they had constructed along the coast to stop such an invasion. On D-Day, June 6, 1944, American forces landed on Utah and Omaha Beaches, while British and Canadian forces hit Sword, Gold, and Juno Beaches. At the landing sites, German resistance varied: the fiercest fighting was at Omaha Beach. One soldier from Arizona wrote:

> *Let the thunder roll,*
> *Smoke and flame, will show th' way.*
> *I am the Beach at Omaha.*
> *The gates of hell are open wide,*
> *For all who come to play.*
> *The stakes are high,*
> *The game is death,*
> *No winners here today.*

After a week of attacks and counterattacks, the five beaches were linked, and the Allied forces coiled to break through the German positions blocking the roads to the rest of France. On July 25, American soldiers pierced the stubbornly held German defensive lines at Saint-Lô. Paris was liberated on August 25, and in October, the Allies reached the west side of the Rhine River. From November 1944 to March 1945, American forces readied themselves to attack across the

---

amphibious   In historical context, a military operation that coordinates air, land, and sea military forces to land on a hostile shore.

Rhine. At the same time, Allied bombers and fighter-bombers continued to bomb German-held Europe night and day. They destroyed vital industries and transportation systems as well as German cities. In one of the worst raids, during the night of February 13, 1945, three flights of British and American bombers set Dresden aflame, creating a firestorm that killed more than 135,000 civilians. Nearly 600,000 German civilians would die in Allied air raids, with another 800,000 injured.

With his cities being destroyed from the air and his forces crumbling in the east, Hitler approved a last-ditch attempt to halt the Allied advance in the west. Taking advantage of bad weather that grounded Allied aircraft, on December 16 German forces launched an attack through the Ardennes Forest designed to split American forces. It created a 50-mile "bulge" in the Allied lines. At Bastogne, a critical crossroads, American soldiers hung on until a relief column reached the city. When asked to surrender, General A. C. McAuliffe simply told the Germans, "Nuts." After ten days, the weather improved, and the German offensive slowed and was driven back. The Battle of the Bulge was the last major Axis counteroffensive on the western front. In March 1945, British and American forces crossed the Rhine and battled eastward. At the same time, Soviet forces began the bloody, house-to-house conquest of Berlin. On April 25, American and Soviet infantrymen shook hands at the Elbe River 60 miles south of Berlin. Inside the city, Hitler committed suicide on April 30 and had aides burn his body. On May 8, 1945, German officials surrendered. The war in Europe was over.

Stresses in the
Grand Alliance   As the Soviets pushed toward Berlin, they liberated parts of Poland, Romania, Bulgaria, Hungary, and Czechoslovakia. Following the Red Army were Soviet officials and Eastern European Communists who had lived in exile in the Soviet Union before and during the war. The Soviet goal was to establish new Eastern European governments that would be "friendly" to the Soviet Union. A Communist Lublin government (named after the town where the government was installed) was established in Poland, while in Romania and Bulgaria "**popular front**" governments, heavily influenced by local and returning Communist Party members, took command. Only Czechoslovakia and Hungary managed to establish non-Communist-dominated governments as the German occupation collapsed.

On February 4, 1945, the Big Three met at the Black Sea resort of **Yalta** amid growing Western apprehension about Soviet goals in Eastern Europe. Confident that he could work with Stalin, Roosevelt wanted to ensure that the Soviet Union would enter the war against Japan and maintain its support for a new United Nations. He also wanted the Soviets to show some willingness to modify their controls over Eastern Europe. Stalin's goals were Western acceptance of a Soviet sphere of influence in Eastern Europe, the weakening of

---

popular front   An organization or government composed of a wide spectrum of political groups; popular fronts were used by the Soviet Union in forming allegedly non-Communist governments in Eastern Europe.

Germany, and the economic restoration of the Soviet Union. Central to Allied differences over Eastern Europe was the nature of the Polish government. Roosevelt and Churchill considered the Lublin regime to be undemocratic and a puppet of the Soviet Union and instead supported a London-based government in exile. Stalin labeled the London-based government hostile to the Soviet Union and demanded a friendly government in Poland. After considerable acidic haggling, the powers compromised in language so vague that Admiral William Leahy, one of Roosevelt's primary advisers, ruefully noted it could be "stretched from Yalta to Washington" without breaking. Roosevelt reluctantly allowed the Lublin government to remain the center of a larger coalition government, with free elections to be held after the war. Poland's borders were shifted to the West, leaving the Soviets in control of those lands seized during their invasion of Poland in 1939. The agreement hardly applied the ideals of the Atlantic Charter, but Roosevelt concluded that it was the best he could do for Poland at the moment. Still Roosevelt had achieved two of his major goals: Stalin

National Archives

As Allied armies fought their way closer to Berlin, Stalin, Roosevelt, and Churchill met at the Black Sea resort of Yalta in February 1945 to discuss military strategy and postwar concerns. Two months later, Roosevelt died and Harry S Truman assumed the presidency.

agreed to maintain Soviet support in defeating Japan and engage in a new world organization. Although disappointed over the continued Soviet domination of Eastern Europe, Roosevelt realized that little could be done to prevent the Soviet Union from keeping what it already had, or could easily take. He hoped that his goodwill would encourage Stalin to respond in kind, maintaining at least a semblance of representative government in Eastern Europe and continuing to cooperate with the United States.

Roosevelt returned from Yalta exhausted with rapidly failing health. Relaxing at Warm Springs, Georgia, the 63-year-old president suffered a cerebral hemorrhage on April 12, 1944, and died. Long-time political opponent Senator Robert Taft spoke for the nation: "He dies a hero of the war, for he literally worked himself to death in the service of the American people." Truman, a man few knew much about, was now president and determined to continue Roosevelt's road to victory.

The Holocaust   As Allied forces advanced into Germany, they and the world came to realize the full horror of the **Holocaust**. In 1941 the Nazi political leadership had ordered what it called the **Final Solution** to rid German-occupied Europe of Jews. In concentration camps, Jews, along

YIVO Institute for Jewish Research./Courtesy of the United States Holocaust Memorial Museum.

Hitler ordered the "Final Solution"—the extermination of Europe's Jews—soon after the United States entered the war. In this picture, German troops arrest residents of the Warsaw ghetto for deportation to concentration camps. Few would survive the camps, where over 6 million Jews died.

with homosexuals, gypsies, and the mentally ill, were brutalized, starved, worked as slave labor, and systematically exterminated. At Auschwitz, Nazis used gas chambers—disguised as showers—to execute 12,000 victims a day.

Reports of German brutalization of Jews in the concentration camps had circulated even before the war, but the Western governments and the press did little to expose or prevent the atrocities. Roosevelt, like other leaders, did not see a personal, political, diplomatic, or military need to make Holocaust information widely known; and he did not give the plight of the Jews or other refugees a high priority. Only in January 1944 did Roosevelt establish a **War Refugee Board.**

As British, American, and Soviet troops liberated the camps, reporters and photographers recorded the reality of the sweeping horrors found there. Among the American units freeing Jewish survivors at Buchenwald and Dachau were the African American 761st Tank Battalion and the Japanese American 522nd Field Artillery Battalion. One survivor at first thought that the Japanese had won the war, until realizing the soldiers were Americans. "I had never seen black men or Japanese," another recalled. "They were riding in these tanks and jeeps; they were like angels who came down from heaven to save our lives." While thousands were saved, over 6 million Jews, nearly two-thirds of prewar Europe's Jewish population, were slaughtered in the death camps.

Closing the Circle on Japan   On May 8, 1945, V-E Day—celebrating victory in Europe—touched off parades and rejoicing in the United States. But Japan still had to be defeated. Japan's defensive strategy was simple: force the United States to invade a seemingly endless number of Pacific islands before it could launch an invasion against Japan, with each speck of land costing the Americans dearly in lives and materials. The American military, however, realized that it had to seize only the most strategic islands. With carriers providing mobile air superiority, the Americans could bypass and isolate others.

Throughout 1943, U.S. forces continued to advance toward the Philippines from the south. At the same time, far to the northeast, the U.S. Navy and the Marines Corps were establishing footholds in the Gilbert and Marshall Islands. Exemplifying the bitter fighting was "bloody Tarawa," where marines fought their way ashore on November 21, 1943. Overcoming five thousand well-entrenched Japanese troops, nearly all of whom fought to the death, American marines suffered nearly three thousand casualties. The Mariana Islands were next. In the battle for Saipan, the Japanese lost 243 planes and three more aircraft carriers, while nearly thirty-two thousand Japanese defenders fought to the death. Shocking American troops, nearly two-thirds of the island's Japanese civilians, mostly women and children, committed suicide. Marines next seized the nearby islands of Tinian and Guam. By late summer of 1944, the southern and eastern approaches to the Philippines were in American hands.

Island bases added support facilities for bombing military and domestic targets in Japan, which began in February 1944. Long-range bombers, the B-29s, made devastating raids against Japanese cities, with the intention of weakening the Japanese will to resist. Although the estimated number of Japanese civilians killed in the bombing far exceeded the number of Japanese soldiers killed in combat, the raids did little to reduce Japanese citizens' support for the war or the government.

In October 1944, American forces landed on Leyte in the center of the Philippine archipelago. General MacArthur, who had evacuated the Philippines in March 1942, had fulfilled his promise to return. The Japanese navy moved to halt the invasion, and in the largest naval battle in history, the **Battle of Leyte Gulf** (October 23–25, 1944), American forces shattered what remained of Japanese air and sea power.

After the Battle of Leyte Gulf, the full brunt of the American Pacific offensive bore down on Iwo Jima and Okinawa, only 750 miles from Tokyo. To defend the islands, Japan made large-scale use of the *kamikaze* attack—in which pilots made suicide crashes on targets in explosive-laden airplanes. The American assault on Iwo Jima began on February 19, 1945, and before it ended on March 17, virtually all of the 21,000 Japanese defenders had fought to the death, and American losses approached one-third of the landing force: 6,821 dead and 20,000 wounded.

On Okinawa, from April through June, the carnage was even worse. While American forces took heavy losses along Japanese defensive lines, Japanese planes and *kamikazes* rained terror and destruction on the American fleet. But the Japanese air onslaughts became weaker each month as Japan ran out of planes and pilots. By the end of June, Okinawa was in American hands, but at a fearful price: 12,000 Americans, 110,000 Japanese soldiers, and 160,000 Okinawan and Japanese civilians dead.

Entering the Nuclear Age   The experience of Okinawa suggested to most American planners that any invasion of Japan would result in large numbers of American casualties. But by the summer of 1945, the United States had a possible alternative to invasion: a new and untried weapon—the atomic bomb. The A-bomb was the product of years of British-American research and development in the Manhattan Project. From the beginning of the conflict, science had developed and improved the tools of combat, providing, in addition to radar and sonar, flamethrowers, rockets, and a variety of other useful and frequently deadly products. But the most fearsome and secret of the projects was the drive started in 1941 to construct a nuclear weapon. Between then and 1945, the Manhattan Project scientists, led by physicists J. Robert Oppenheimer and Edward Teller, controlled a chain reaction involving uranium and plutonium to create the atomic bomb. By the time Germany surrendered, the project had consumed more than $2 billion, but the bomb was born. When it was tested at Alamogordo, New Mexico, on July 16, 1945, the results were spectacular. In the words of Brigadier General Leslie R. Groves, the U.S. Army engineer who headed the project: "The effect could well be called unprecedented, magnificent, beautiful, stupendous and terrifying.... The whole country was lighted by a searing light.... Thirty seconds after the explosion came ... the air blast ... followed almost immediately by the strong, sustained, awesome roar which warned of doomsday and made us feel that we puny things were blasphemous to dare tamper with the forces heretofore reserved to The Almighty." Word of the successful test was quickly relayed to Truman, who at the time was meeting with Churchill and Stalin at Potsdam, outside Berlin.

Before leaving for Potsdam, Truman had decided not to tell Stalin any details about the atomic bomb and to use it as soon as possible against Japan. Using the atomic bomb, he hoped, would serve two purposes. It would force Japan to surrender without an invasion, and it would impress the Soviets and, just maybe, make them more amenable to American views on the postwar world order.

Soon after his arrival for the Potsdam Conference (July–August, 1945), Truman obtained confirmation from Stalin that the Soviet Union would enter the Japanese war in mid-August, and he informed Stalin about a new and powerful weapon to use against Japan. Stalin, who knew from spies that it was an atomic bomb, appeared unimpressed and told Truman to go ahead and use it. Working with Prime Minister Clement Attlee of Britain (who was told of the atomic bomb), Truman released the **Potsdam Declaration**, which called on Japan to surrender by August or face total destruction. The declaration reflected two developments—one Japan knew about, and the other it was soon to learn. Japanese officials had asked the "neutral" Soviets to try to persuade the Americans to consider negotiating a Japanese surrender. Stalin, Attlee, and Truman agreed instead to insist on unconditional surrender. In the Potsdam Declaration, the Japanese could read the rejection of their overture, but they had no way of knowing that the utter destruction referred to in the declaration meant the A-bomb. On July 25, Truman ordered the use of the atomic bomb as soon after August 3 as possible, provided the Japanese did not surrender.

On the island of Tinian, B-29s were readied to carry the two available bombs to targets in Japan; a third was waiting to be assembled. A B-29 bomber named the *Enola Gay* dropped the first bomb over **Hiroshima** at 9:15 A.M. on August 6, 1945. Japan's eighth-largest city, Hiroshima had a population of over 250,000 and to that point had not suffered heavy bombing. In the atomic blast and fireball, almost 100,000 Japanese were killed or terribly maimed. Another 100,000 would eventually die from the effects of radiation. The United States announced that unless the Japanese surrendered immediately, they could "expect a rain of ruin from the air, the like of which has never been seen on this earth."

As Tokyo contemplated surrender, on August 8 the Soviets declared war and advanced into Japanese-held Manchuria. The next day a second atomic bomb destroyed **Nagasaki**. Nearly 60,000 people were killed. Although some within the Japanese army argued for continuing the fight, Emperor Hirohito, watching the Red Army slice through Japanese forces and afraid of losing more cities to atomic attacks, made the final decision. Japan must "bear the unbearable," he said, and

COUNTRY	DEAD
Soviet Union	8.6 million
China	1.3 million
Poland	130 thousand
Germany	3.6 million
Japan	1.75 million
Britain and Commonwealth	384 thousand
United States	292 thousand

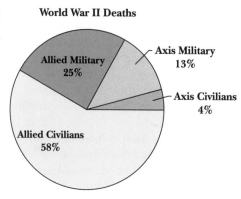

World War II Deaths

Allied Military 25%
Axis Military 13%
Axis Civilians 4%
Allied Civilians 58%

FIGURE 23.3 Military War Dead

surrender. On August 14, 1945, Japan officially surrendered, and the United States agreed to leave the position of emperor intact.

World War II was over, but much of the world lay in ruins. Some 50 million people, military and civilian, had been killed (see Figure 23.3). The United States was spared most of the destruction. It had suffered almost no civilian casualties, and its cities and industrial centers stood unharmed. In many ways, in fact, the war had been good to the United States. It had decisively ended the Depression, and although some economists predicted an immediate postwar recession, the overall economic picture was bright. Government regulation and planning for the economy that had their beginnings in the New Deal took root and flourished during the war. As the war ended, only a few wanted a return to the laissez-faire-style government that had characterized the 1920s. Big government was here to stay, and at the center of big government was a powerful presidency ready to direct and guide the nation.

STUDY TOOLS

SUMMARY

In 1929 Hoover believed that he would preside over a world at peace. But he and Roosevelt faced the collapse of the international system as Japan, Italy, and Germany increased their territories, influence, and power. Japan seized Manchuria and later invaded China, while Mussolini conquered Ethiopia, and Hitler created a new German empire. In the lengthening shadow of world conflict, the majority of Americans maintained isolationism, and Congress passed neutrality laws designed to keep the nation from involvement in the faraway conflicts. Even as Germany invaded Poland in 1939, most Americans were still anxious to remain outside the conflict. Roosevelt, however, chose to help those fighting Germany, linking the United States' economic might first to England and then to the Soviet Union.

Roosevelt also used economic and diplomatic pressures to halt Japan's expansion. But the pressure only heightened the crisis, convincing many in the Japanese government that the best choice was to attack the United States before it grew in strength. Japan's attack on Pearl Harbor on December 7, 1941, brought a fully committed American public and government into World War II.

Mobilizing the nation for war ended the Depression and increased government intervention in the economy. Another outcome of the war was a range of new choices for Americans in the military and the workplace. Japanese Americans, however, suffered a loss of freedom and property as the government placed them in internment camps.

Fighting a two-front war, American planners gave first priority to defeating Hitler. The effort began in North Africa in 1942, expanded to Italy in 1943, and to France in 1944. By the beginning of 1945, Allied armies were threatening Nazi Germany from the west and the east, and on May 8, 1945, Germany surrendered. In the Pacific theater, the victory at Midway in mid-1942 checked Japan's offensive and allowed the use of aircraft carriers to begin tightening the noose around the enemy. To bring the war to a close without a U.S. invasion, Truman elected to use the atomic bomb. Following the destruction of Hiroshima and Nagasaki, Japan surrendered on August 14, 1945, ending the war and for many Americans ushering in the beginning of "America's century."

CHRONOLOGY

A WORLD AT WAR

1929 Herbert Hoover becomes president

1931 Japan seizes Manchuria

1933 Franklin D. Roosevelt becomes president
Hitler and Nazi Party take power in Germany

1934 Fulgencio Batista assumes power in Cuba

1935 First Neutrality Act
Italy invades Ethiopia

1936 Germany reoccupies the Rhineland
Italy annexes Ethiopia
Spanish Civil War begins
Second Neutrality Act

1937 Third Neutrality Act
Roosevelt's quarantine speech
Sino-Japanese War begins

1938 Germany annexes Austria and Sudetenland
Munich Conference

1939 German-Soviet Nonaggression Pact
Germany invades Poland; Britain and France declare war on Germany
Neutrality Act of 1939

1940　Germany occupies most of Western Europe
　　　　U.S. economic sanctions against Japan
　　　　Burke-Wadsworth Act
　　　　Destroyers-for-bases agreement
　　　　Roosevelt reelected

1941　Lend-Lease Act
　　　　Fair Employment Practices Commission created
　　　　Germany invades Soviet Union
　　　　Atlantic Charter
　　　　U-boats attack U.S. warships
　　　　Japan attacks Pearl Harbor; United States enters World War II

1942　War Production Board created
　　　　Japanese conquer Philippines
　　　　Japanese Americans interned
　　　　Battles of Coral Sea and Midway
　　　　Congress of Racial Equality founded
　　　　U.S. troops invade North Africa

1943　U.S. forces capture Guadalcanal
　　　　Soviets defeat Germans at Stalingrad
　　　　Smith-Connally War Labor Disputes Act
　　　　Detroit race riot
　　　　U.S. and British forces invade Sicily and Italy;
　　　　Italy surrenders
　　　　Tehran Conference

1944　Operation Overlord—June 6 invasion of Normandy
　　　　G.I. Bill becomes law
　　　　U.S. forces invade the Philippines
　　　　Roosevelt reelected
　　　　Soviet forces liberate Eastern Europe
　　　　Battle of the Bulge

1945　Yalta Conference
　　　　Roosevelt dies; Harry S Truman becomes president
　　　　United Nations created
　　　　Germany surrenders; Potsdam Conference
　　　　United States drops atomic bombs on Hiroshima and Nagasaki
　　　　Japan surrenders

Focus Questions

If you have mastered this chapter, you should be able to answer these questions and explain the terms that follow the questions.

1. How were Roosevelt's policies toward Latin America a continuation of Hoover's?
2. What obstacles did Roosevelt face in trying to implement a more assertive foreign policy from 1935 to 1939?

3. Following the outbreak of World War II in 1939, how did Roosevelt reshape American neutrality?
4. What actions did Roosevelt take to mobilize the nation for war and how did they affect the relationship between business and government?
5. What new social and economic choices did Americans confront during the war? How were different groups affected?
6. What factors did Roosevelt consider in shaping America's strategy for global conflict?
7. Why did Truman and his advisers choose to use the atomic bomb?

KEY TERMS

Greater East Asian Co-Prosperity Sphere (*p.* 722)

Colonel Fulgencio Batista (*p.* 722)

Good Neighbor policy (*p.* 722)

Neutrality Act of 1935 (*p.* 723)

Munich Agreement (*p.* 724)

German-Soviet Nonaggression Pact (*p.* 725)

Neutrality Act of 1939 (*p.* 726)

Axis powers (*p.* 727)

Burke-Wadsworth Act (*p.* 727)

Lend-Lease Act (*p.* 728)

Atlantic Charter (*p.* 728)

Nisei (*p.* 731)

Issei (*p.* 731)

Executive Order #9066 (*p.* 732)

internment camps (*p.* 732)

Manhattan Project (*p.* 733)

Office of War Mobilization (*p.* 734)

Smith-Connally War Labor Disputes Act (*p.* 735)

G.I. Bill (*p.* 736)

Harry S Truman (*p.* 736)

victory garden (*p.* 737)

Rosie the Riveter (*p.* 738)

A. Philip Randolph (*p.* 740)

Fair Employment Practices Commission (FEPC) (*p.* 740)

Congress of Racial Equality (CORE) (*p.* 740)

James Farmer (*p.* 740)

Benjamin O. Davis, Jr. (*p.* 741)

braceros (*p.* 743)

code talkers (*p.* 743)

Battle of the Coral Sea (*p.* 744)

Midway Island (*p.* 744)

General Douglas MacArthur (*p.* 744)

Guadalcanal Island (*p.* 744)

Battle of Stalingrad (*p.* 746)

Grand Alliance (*p.* 747)

Tehran Conference (*p.* 747)

Operation Overlord (*p.* 747)

Yalta (*p.* 748)

Holocaust (*p.* 750)

Final Solution (*p.* 750)

War Refugee Board (*p.* 751)

Battle of Leyte Gulf (*p.* 752)

Potsdam Declaration (*p.* 753)

Hiroshima (*p.* 753)

Nagasaki (*p.* 753)

24

$$\blacktriangledown$$

TRUMAN AND COLD WAR AMERICA, 1945–1952

THE COLD WAR BEGINS

Around the globe people hoped an enduring peace would follow the defeat of the Axis powers. But could the cooperative relationship of the Allies continue into the postwar era without a common enemy to unite them? Suspicion and distrust already had surfaced when Britain and the United States objected to the establishment of pro-Soviet governments in Eastern Europe, and President Harry S Truman appeared less willing than Roosevelt to place much trust in the Soviets. "The Soviet Union needs us more than we need them," Truman told a colleague. Although he was new to conducting foreign and domestic policies, Truman believed in the idea that at critical times individuals were called to rise to positions of leadership and to shape history. He was now in that situation. "The buck stops here," read a plaque in his office.

Truman and Paths to Peace   Truman and other American leaders identified two overlapping paths to peace: international cooperation and **deterrence** based on military strength. In 1944, as a means to achieve global cooperation and economic development, the International Monetary Fund and the World Bank were created, and at the Dumbarton Oaks conference delegates from the United States, China, Britain, and the Soviet Union mapped the basic structure of the **United Nations** (UN). Building on a series of high-level discussions in April 1945, a conference in San Francisco

deterrence Measures that a state takes to discourage attacks by other states, often including a military buildup.

finished the task. It wrote the charter of the United Nations, an organization of six distinct bodies, the most important of which are the **General Assembly** and the **Security Council**. Composed of all member nations, the General Assembly was the weaker body with authority only to discuss issues, whereas resolving issues was the responsibility of the Security Council, composed of eleven nations. Six nations were elected by the General Assembly, but the real power was held by five permanent members: the United States, the Soviet Union, the United Kingdom, China, and France. To give the United Nations authority, the Security Council could apply economic and military pressures against other nations, but to protect their interests, each of the five permanent nations could veto Security Council decisions. When it was decided to house the headquarters of the UN in New York City, Truman noted that the center of Western civilization had shifted from Europe to the United States.

Still, Truman and most Americans chose not to rely solely on international cooperation for national security or maintaining peace. They concluded that the United States must continue to field a strong military force with bases around the globe, maintain its atomic monopoly, and take the lead in creating the conditions for an enduring peace. Drawing on lessons learned from World War II, most Americans believed aggressors should be halted, democratic governments supported, and a prosperous world economy created. These were the ideals of the Atlantic Charter, and most Americans saw them as fundamental values on which to construct peace.

In looking at international affairs, many Americans, including most in the Truman administration, saw the Soviet Union as a potential threat to world peace. It seemed that Moscow was ignoring the principles of the Atlantic Charter and following an "ominous course" in Eastern Europe that violated the Yalta agreements by creating undemocratic **puppet governments** and closing the region to free trade. By the end of 1945, Truman concluded that he was "tired of babying the Soviets." In February 1946, the State Department asked its Russia expert, George Kennan, to evaluate Soviet policy to determine its motivations and goals.

Kennan's "Long Telegram" described Soviet totalitarianism as internally weak. Soviet leaders, he said, held Communist ideology secondary to remaining in power, needing Western capitalism to serve as an enemy. But, he argued, Soviet leaders were not fanatics and would retreat when met with opposition. He recommended a policy of **containment**, meeting head-on any attempted expansion of Soviet power. His report immediately drew high praise from Washington's official circles. Soon thereafter, Truman adopted a policy designed to "set will against will, force against force, idea against idea ... until Soviet expansion is finally worn down."

The Soviets had prewar and wartime experiences different from those of the United States and as a result had different postwar concerns and objectives. They wanted to be treated as a major power, to have Germany reduced in power, and to establish a "zone of security" with "friendly" governments in neighboring states. While accepting the United Nations, the Soviets preferred to work bilaterally and to

puppet governments Governments imposed, supported, and directed by an outside force, usually a foreign power.

Novikov Telegram

The foreign policy of the United States ... reflects the imperialist tendencies of American monopolistic capital ... striving for world supremacy. This is the real meaning of the many statements by President Truman and other representatives of American ruling circles; that the United States has the right to lead the world. All the forces of American diplomacy—the army, the air force, the navy, industry, and science—are enlisted in the service of this foreign policy. For this purpose ... plans for expansion have been developed and are being implemented through diplomacy and the establishment of a system of naval and air bases stretching far beyond the boundaries of the United States, through the arms race, and through the creation of ever newer types of weapons ... [they are] indications of the U.S. effort to establish world dominance ... [and they] constitute a political and military demonstration against the Soviet Union.

rely on their own resources. As 1946 began, Soviet officials warned of "capitalist encirclement" and accused the Truman administration of being less friendly than Roosevelt's. Moscow interpreted several American actions and policies as threatening and ideologically motivated. In September 1946, the Soviet ambassador in Washington, Nikolai Novikov, depicted the United States as globally aggressive, seeking to establish military bases around the world and to maintain a monopoly over atomic technology. He believed the United States was using its economic power to further its capitalistic goals while forcing other countries to adopt American interests, and he praised the Soviet Union for resisting the power and demands of the United States (see the Novikov Telegram above).

By the spring of 1946, fear of Soviet intentions was becoming a rising concern as Democrats and Republicans tried to educate the public about the Soviet threat to world stability. One of the most dramatic warnings, however, came from Winston Churchill on March 5, 1946, at Westminster College in Fulton, Missouri. With President Truman sitting beside him, the former prime minister of Britain decried Soviet expansionism and stated that an **"iron curtain"** had fallen across Europe, establishing a military, political, and ideological barrier between the Soviet Bloc and Western Europe. Churchill called for a "fraternal association of the English-speaking peoples" to halt the Russians. Truman thought it was a wonderfully eloquent speech and would do "nothing but good." Churchill, *Time* magazine pronounced, had spoken with the voice of a "lion."

As Churchill spoke, it appeared that an "American lion" was needed in Iran. During World War II, the Big Three had stationed troops in Iran to ensure the safety of lend-lease materials going to the Soviet Union. The troops were to be withdrawn by March 1946, but as that date neared, Soviet troops remained in northern Iran. Suddenly, on March 2, reports flashed from northern Iran that Soviet tanks were moving toward Tehran, the Iranian capital, as well as toward Iraq and Turkey. Some believed that war was imminent. Britain and the United States sent

Joseph Stalin controlled the Soviet Union from 1926 until his death in 1953. His popular image was "Uncle Joe" during World War II, but by the time of the Truman Doctrine in March 1947, Stalin's image resembled Hitler's. Truman's first impression of the Soviet dictator, at Potsdam in July 1945, was that he was "dishonest but smart as hell" and they could work together. One of Truman's closest advisers bluntly stated that Stalin was "a liar and a crook."

Private Collection/Archives Charmet/The Bridgeman Art Library International

harshly worded telegrams to Moscow and petitioned the United Nations to consider an Iranian complaint against the Soviet Union. War did not break out, and Soviet forces soon evacuated Iran. The crisis was over, but it convinced many Americans that war with the Soviets was possible. "Red Fascism" had replaced Nazi fascism, and for the sake of civilization there could be no more appeasement.

The Division of Europe   As the crisis in Iran receded, events in Europe assumed priority. A deepening economic crisis across Europe appeared to favor leftist parties and their assertion that state controls and state planning led to quicker economic recovery. But the most immediate trouble spots were in Greece and Turkey. The Soviets were pressuring Turkey to permit them some control over the Dardanelles, the straits linking the Black Sea to the Mediterranean. In Greece, a civil war raged between Communist-backed rebels and the British-supported conservative government. In February 1947, Britain informed Washington that it was no longer able to provide economic or military aid to the two nations and asked the United States to assume its role in the region to prevent Communist expansion. Truman eagerly assumed the responsibility of "world leadership with all of its burdens and all of its glory."

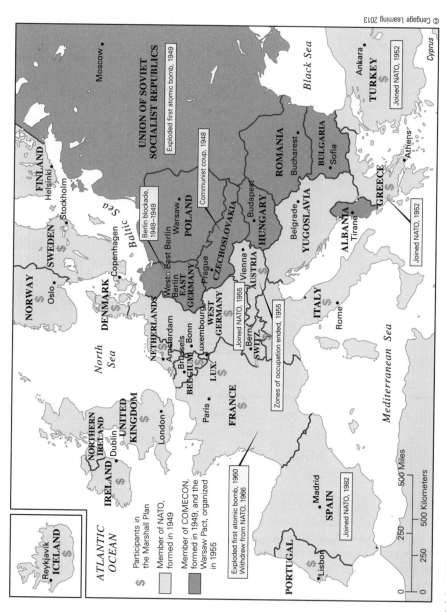

© Cengage Learning 2013

MAP 24.1 Divided Europe

After the Second World War, Europe broke into two competing camps. When the United States launched the Marshall Plan in 1948, the Soviet Union countered with its own economic plan the following year. When the United States created NATO in 1949, the Soviet Union answered with the Warsaw Pact in 1955. On the whole, these two camps held firm until the late 1980s.

To convince Congress and gain public support for $400 million to support Greece and Turkey, Truman overstated the "crisis," presenting an image of the world under attack from the forces of evil. On March 12, 1947, he set forth the **Truman Doctrine**, offering an ideological, black-and-white view of world politics. He said it was the duty of the United States "to support free people" who resisted subjugation "by armed minorities or by outside pressure." Congress agreed and provided aid for Greece and Turkey. Bolstered by American support, Turkey resisted Soviet pressure and retained control over the straits, and the Greek government was able to defeat the Communist rebels in 1949.

Although the Truman administration asked Congress only to support Greece and Turkey, officials admitted among themselves that the request was just the beginning. "It happens that we are having a little trouble with Greece and Turkey at the present time," stated a War Department official, "but they are just one of the keys on the keyboard of this world piano."

On June 5, 1947, in a commencement address at Harvard, Secretary of State George Marshall uncovered more of the keyboard. He offered Europe a program of economic aid to restore stability and prosperity—the **Marshall Plan**. For the Truman administration, the difficult question was whether to include the Soviets and Eastern Europeans in the invitation. To allow the Soviets and their satellites to participate seemed contrary to the intent of the Truman Doctrine. Would a Congress that had just spent $400 million to keep Greece and Turkey out of Soviet hands be willing to provide millions of American dollars to the Soviet Union? But if the Soviets were excluded, the United States might seem to be encouraging the division of Europe, an image the State Department wanted to avoid. Chaired by Kennan, the State Department planning staff recommended that the United States take "a hell of a big gamble" and offer economic aid to all Europeans. Kennan believed the Soviets would reject the offer because it involved economic and political cooperation with capitalists. Thus, when Marshall spoke at Harvard, he invited all Europeans to work together and write a program "designed to place Europe on its feet economically."

The gamble worked. At a June 26, 1947, meeting in Paris of potential Marshall Plan participants, Soviet foreign minister Molotov rejected a British and French written proposal for an economically integrated Europe, joint economic planning, and a requirement to purchase mostly American goods. At first the Marshall Plan looked like a "tasty mushroom," commented one Soviet official, but on closer examination it turned out to be a "poisonous toadstool." The Soviets and the Eastern Europeans left the conference, and over the next ten months the Soviet Union took steps to solidify its control over its satellite states. In July 1947, Moscow announced the Molotov Plan, which further incorporated Eastern European economies into the Soviet system. Throughout the region non-Communist elements were expelled from governments, an effort that culminated in the February 1948 Soviet-engineered **coup** that toppled the Czechoslovakian government. "We are faced with exactly the same situation with which Britain and France were faced in 1938 and 1939 with Hitler," Truman announced. The

---

coup   Sudden overthrow of a government by a group of people, usually with military support.

IT MATTERS TODAY

Appeasement

Some say that history provides lessons for the present. This may be true, but too often it is used as an analogy, oversimplifying the complex problems of security, war, and peace into something like a "sound bite." The image of Munich and appeasement, a "lesson" learned from World War II, is one such example. "No more Munichs!" is a phrase and image that has been used by nearly every administration since 1945 to explain choices to use force or coercion rather than diplomacy. This analogy suggests that negotiations with a stubborn opponent are nonproductive and should not be tried, and more forceful policies need to be implemented.

- Diplomacy involves give and take to reach mutually suitable conclusions. Under what circumstances might diplomacy be considered appeasement and other choices needed? When might appeasement be an effective policy?

- Examine decisions and statements made by recent policymakers regarding Iran and Iraq, North Korea, and terrorists to determine if the imagery of appeasement, Munich, and Hitler has been applied.

Czech coup helped convince Congress to approve $12.5 billion in Marshall Plan aid to Western Europe.

In March 1948, the United States announced that the western zones of Germany were eligible for Marshall Plan aid, would hold elections to select delegates to a constitutional convention, and would adopt a standard currency. The meaning of these actions seemed clear: a West German state was being formed. Faced with the prospect of a pro-Western, industrialized, and potentially remilitarized Germany, Stalin reacted. On June 24, the Russians blockaded all land traffic to and from Berlin, which had been divided into British-, French-, Soviet-, and U.S.-controlled zones after the war. With West Berlin isolated 120 miles inside the Soviet zone of Germany, the Soviet goal was to force the West either to abandon the creation of West Germany or to face the loss of Berlin. Americans viewed the blockade as proof of Soviet hostility and were determined not to back down. Churchill affirmed the West's stand. We want peace, he stated, "but we should by now have learned that there is no safety in yielding to dictators, whether Nazi or Communist." "We are very close to war," Truman wrote in his diary.

American strategists confronted the dilemma of how to stay in Berlin and supply 2.4 million people without starting a shooting war. Although some recommended fighting across the Soviet zone to the city, Truman chose another option, one that would not violate Soviet-occupied territory or any international agreements. Marshaling a massive effort of men, provisions, and aircraft, British and Americans flew supply planes to three Berlin airports on an average of one flight every three minutes, month after month. To drive home to the Soviets the depth of American resolve, Truman ordered a wing of B-29 bombers, the "atomic bombers," to Britain. These planes carried no atomic weapons, but the general impression was that their presence lessened the likelihood of Soviet aggression.

The **Berlin airlift** was a victory for the United States in the Cold War. The increasing flow of supplies into West Berlin testified to America's resolve to stand firm against the Soviets and protect Western Europe. In May 1949, Stalin, finding no gains from the blockade, without explanation ended it and allowed land traffic to cross the Soviet zone to Berlin. The crisis swept away most congressional opposition to the Marshall Plan and the creation of West Germany and silenced those who had protested a permanent American military commitment to Western Europe. In June 1949, Congress approved American entry into the **North Atlantic Treaty Organization** (NATO), a mutual defense alliance formed in 1949 to contain communism, ensuring that American forces would remain in the newly created West Germany. The Mutual Defense Assistance Act passed in 1949 provided $1.5 billion in arms and equipment for NATO member nations. By 1952, 80 percent of American assistance to Europe was military aid.

A Global Presence   To facilitate fighting a global Cold War, Congress passed the National Security Act in 1947. It created the Air Force as a separate service and unified command of the military with a new cabinet position, the Department of Defense. To improve coordination between the State Department and the Department of Defense, the **National Security Council** (NSC) was formed to provide policy recommendations to the president. The act also established the Central Intelligence Agency to collect and analyze foreign intelligence information and to carry out covert actions believed necessary for American national security. By mid-1948, covert operations were increasing in scope and number, including efforts to influence Italian elections (a success) and to topple the communist Albanian government (a failure).

While the Truman administration's primary foreign-policy concern was Europe, it could not ignore the rest of the world. In Latin America, the administration encouraged private firms to develop the region and in 1947 helped organize the **Rio Pact**. It established the concept of collective security for Latin America and created a regional organization—the **Organization of American States** (OAS)—to coordinate common defense, economic, and social concerns.

In the Middle East, fear of future oil shortages led the United States to promote the expansion of American petroleum interests in Saudi Arabia, Kuwait, and Iran. At the same time, the United States became a powerful supporter of a new Jewish state to be created in Palestine. The area of Palestine had been administered by the British since the end of World War I and had experienced increasing tensions between the indigenous Arab population, the Palestinians, and a growing number of Jews, largely immigrants from Europe. As World War II ended, Britain faced growing pressure to create a new Jewish state in Palestine. Truman asked in August 1945 that at least 100,000 displaced European Jews be allowed to migrate to Palestine. Considering the Nazi terror against Jews, he believed that the Jews should have their own nation—a view strongly supported by a well-organized, pro-Jewish lobbying effort across the United States.

In May 1947, Britain turned the problem over to the United Nations, which voted to **partition** Palestine into Arab and Jewish states on May 14, 1948. Truman recognized the nation of Israel within fifteen minutes. War quickly broke out between Israel and the surrounding Arab nations—who refused to recognize the partition. Although outnumbered, the better-equipped Israeli army drove back the invading armies, and in January 1949 UN mediator **Ralph Bunche** arranged a cease-fire. When the fighting stopped, Israel had added 50 percent more territory to its emerging nation. No Palestinian state was created, and more than 700,000 Arabs left Israeli-controlled territory, many living as refugees in the Gaza Strip, Lebanon, Jordan, and Egypt. Bitter at the loss of what they regarded as their homeland, the majority of Palestinians and other Arabs were determined to destroy the Jewish state.

If Americans were pleased with events in Latin America and the Middle East, Asia provided several disappointments. Under American occupation, Japan's government was reshaped into a democratic system and placed safely within the American orbit, but diplomatic setbacks occurred in China and Korea. During World War II, the **Nationalist Chinese government** of Jiang Jieshi (Chiang Kai-shek) and the Chinese Communists under Mao Zedong (Mao Tse-tung) had collaborated to fight the Japanese. But when the war ended, old animosities quickly resurfaced, and civil war followed in February 1946. American supporters of Jiang, led by the "China Lobby," recommended that the United States increase its economic and military support for the Nationalist government, arguing that Soviet power threatened China and the rest of Asia as much as it did Europe. Truman and Marshall (who was now secretary of state) dreaded Communist success in China but questioned whether the corrupt and inefficient Nationalist government could ever effectively rule the vast country. While willing to continue some political, economic, and military support, neither wanted to commit American resources to an Asian war. Increasing U.S. aid would be like "throwing money down a rat hole," Truman told his cabinet.

Overmatched by an efficient and popular opponent and denied additional American support, Jiang's forces soon disintegrated, and in 1949 the Nationalist government fled to the island of Taiwan. Conservative Democrats and Republicans labeled the rout of Jiang a humiliating American defeat and complained that the Truman administration was too soft on communism. To quiet critics and to protect Jiang, Truman refused to recognize the People's Republic of China on the mainland and ordered the U.S. 7th Fleet to the waters near Taiwan.

Pressure to expand the containment policy beyond Europe intensified in late August 1949, when the Soviets detonated their own atomic bomb, shattering the American nuclear monopoly. A joint Pentagon–State Department committee, headed by Paul Nitze, concluded that the Soviets were driven by "a new fanatic faith, antithetical to our own," whose objective was to dominate the world, and might be able to launch a nuclear attack on the United States as early as 1954. The committee's report, **NSC Memorandum #68**, called for global containment and a massive buildup of American military force, amounting to an almost

---

partition To divide a country into separate, autonomous nations.

400 percent increase in military spending for the next fiscal year, which would have raised military expenditures to nearly $50 billion. A separate report concluded that the projected mobilization of industry for the Cold War would reduce automobile construction by nearly 60 percent and cut production of radios and television sets to zero. Truman, worried about such an impact on the manufacture of domestic goods, eventually agreed to a "moderate" $12.3 billion military budget for 1950 that included building the **hydrogen bomb**. Proponents of NSC 68 won the final argument on June 25, 1950, when North Korean troops stormed across the 38th parallel.

THE KOREAN WAR

When World War II ended, Soviet forces occupied Korea north of the 38th parallel and American forces remained south of it, and by mid-1946, two Koreas existed. In the south was an American-supported Republic of Korea (ROK), led by Syngman Rhee, while in the north a Communist-backed Democratic People's Republic of Korea, headed by Kim Il Sung. In 1949 the Soviet and American forces withdrew, leaving behind two hostile regimes. Both claimed to be Korea's rightful government and launched raids across the border. The raids accomplished little except to kill more than 100,000 Koreans and to expand each side's military capabilities.

Having received approval from the Soviets, on June 25, 1950, Kim Il Sung launched a full-scale invasion of the south. Overwhelmed, South Korean forces rapidly retreated. Truman concluded that South Korea's survival required American intervention, but he feared that a congressional declaration of war against North Korea might trigger a Chinese and Soviet response. Instead, he asked the UN Security Council to intervene. The Security Council complied and called for a cease-fire, asking member nations to provide assistance to South Korea.

Halting Communist Aggression
American forces led by General Douglas MacArthur, officially under United Nations control, arrived in Korea in July but were unable to halt the North Korean advance. By the end of July, North Korean forces occupied most of South Korea. United Nations forces, including nearly 122,000 Americans and the whole South Korean army, held only the southeastern corner of the peninsula—the Pusan perimeter. In September the tide turned as seventy thousand American troops landed at Inchon, near Seoul, while UN forces advanced north from Pusan. The North Koreans fled back across the 38th parallel. Seoul was liberated on September 27. The **police action** (the official U.S. term for its role in the conflict) had achieved its purpose: the South Korean government was saved, and the 38th parallel was again a real border.

Seeking to Liberate North Korea
Now, however, the South Korean leadership, MacArthur, Truman, and most Americans wanted to unify the peninsula under South Korean rule. Bending under American pressure,

---

hydrogen bomb Nuclear weapon of much greater destructive power than the atomic bomb.

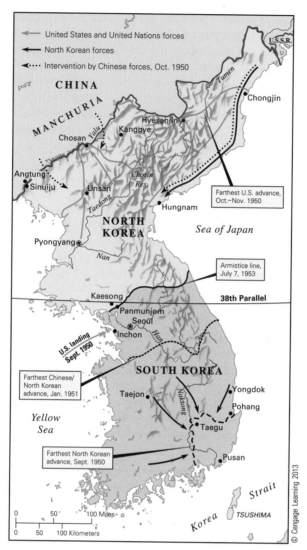

MAP 24.2 The Korean War, 1950–1953

The experience of fighting an undeclared war for the limited objective of containing communism confused the generation of Americans who had just fought an all-out war for the total defeat of the Axis. General MacArthur spoke for the many who were frustrated by the Korean conflict's mounting costs in blood and dollars: "There is no substitute for victory."

the United Nations on October 7 approved a new goal, to "liberate" North Korea from Communist rule. In mid-October UN forces pushed northward toward the Korean-Chinese border at the Yalu River. The Chinese threatened intervention if the invaders approached the border. Nevertheless, General MacArthur was supremely confident. Intelligence estimates said that any intervening Chinese forces would number less than 50,000 and easily be defeated. When American, British, and Korean forces advanced within a few miles of the Yalu River, nearly 300,000 Chinese soldiers entered the Korean Conflict.

Blowing their bugles, the Chinese attacked in waves, hurling grenades, taking massive casualties, and nearly trapping several American and South Korean units in the most brutal fighting of the war. UN forces fell back in bitter combat. The U.S. 1st Marine Division was nearly surrounded at the Chosin Reservoir. When asked about the marines retreating, General O. P. "Slam" Smith responded, "Gentlemen, we are not retreating. We are merely advancing in another direction." Within three weeks, the North Koreans and Chinese had shoved the UN forces back to the 38th parallel. American casualties exceeded twelve thousand, but the Chinese had lost three times as many.

Truman now abandoned the goal of a unified pro-Western Korea and sought a negotiated settlement, even if it left two Koreas. The decision was not popular. Americans wanted victory. Encouraged by public opinion polls and Truman's Republican critics, General MacArthur publicly objected to the limitations his commander-in-chief had placed on him. He put it simply: there was "no substitute for victory." Already displeased by MacArthur's arrogance, Truman replaced him with General Matthew Ridgeway.

The decision unleashed a storm of protest. Some called for Truman's impeachment, and Congress opened hearings to investigate the conduct of the war. MacArthur testified that expanding the war could achieve victory, while the administration argued that it might lead to a global nuclear war. The face-off between MacArthur and Truman produced no winner. Polls showed Truman's approval rating falling to a dismal 24 percent by late 1951. At the same time, MacArthur's hopes for a presidential candidacy collapsed because most Americans feared his aggressive policies might indeed result in World War III. By the beginning of 1952, the vast majority of Americans were simply tired of the "useless" conflict and wanted it to end.

The Korean front, meanwhile, stabilized along the 38th parallel as four-power peace talks among the United States, South Korea, China, and North Korea began on July 10, 1951. The negotiations did not go smoothly. While the powers postured and argued about prisoners, cease-fire lines, and a multitude of lesser issues, soldiers fought and died over scraps of territory. When the Eisenhower administration finally concluded the cease-fire on July 26, 1953, the Korean conflict had cost more than $20 billion and thirty-three thousand American lives, but it had left South Korea intact.

The "hot war" in Korea had far-reaching military and diplomatic results for the United States. The expansion of military spending envisioned by NSC 68 had occurred. In Europe, Truman moved forward to rearm West Germany and Italy. Throughout Asia and the Pacific, a large American presence was made permanent. In 1951 the United States concluded a settlement with Japan that kept American forces in Japan and Okinawa. The Australia–New Zealand–United States (ANZUS) treaty of 1951 promised American military protection to those countries. At the same time, the United States was increasing its military aid and commitments to Nationalist China and French **Indochina**. The containment policy had been expanded—formally and financially—to cover East Asia and the Pacific.

Postwar Politics

When Roosevelt died, many wondered if Truman would continue the Roosevelt–New Deal approach to domestic policies. Would he work to protect the social and economic gains that labor, women, and minorities had earned during the war? Conservatives and some of Truman's friends predicted that the new president was "going to be quite a shock to those who followed Roosevelt–that the New Deal is as good as dead ... and that the 'Roosevelt nonsense' was over." But Truman had no intention of extinguishing the New Deal.

Truman and Liberalism   In September 1945, Truman presented to Congress what one Republican critic called an effort to "out–New Deal the New Deal." Truman set forth an ambitious program designed to ease the transition to a peacetime economy and reenergize the New Deal. To prevent inflation and a recession, he wanted Congress to continue wartime economic agencies to help control wages and prices. He also asked that the Fair Employment Practices Commission be renewed. Furthering the New Deal, he recommended an expansion of Social Security coverage and benefits, an increase in the minimum wage, the development of additional housing programs, and a national health system.

Opposing Truman's proposals was a conservative coalition of southern Democrats and Republicans who had successfully blocked extensions of the New Deal since 1937. They embarked on a campaign to persuade the American public of the dangers of Truman's "socialistic" program, which involved too much government, threatened private enterprise, and endangered existing class and social relations. "Public sentiment is everything," wrote an officer of Standard Oil. "He who molds public sentiment goes deeper than he who enacts statutes or pronounces decisions." A Truman official sadly agreed: "The consuming fear of communism fostered a widespread belief that change was subversive and that those who supported change were Communists or **fellow-travelers**."

Congress rejected or severely scaled back nearly all of Truman's proposals. Wartime economic controls and the Fair Employment Practices Commission quickly faded away. Congress spurned any idea of a national health program and substituted a program to build hospitals. While Congress and Truman disagreed over the domestic agenda, the country experienced economic and social dislocations caused by the conversion to a peacetime economy. Inflation quickly emerged as a principal issue, with prices rising 25 percent within 18 months after the defeat of

---

Indochina   French colony in Southeast Asia, including present-day Vietnam, Laos, and Cambodia; it began fighting for its independence in the mid-twentieth century.

fellow-traveler   Individual who sympathizes with or supports the beliefs of the Communist Party without being a member.

As the nation moved from a wartime to peacetime economy, workers initiated more than five thousand strikes. Pictured here are strikers in Detroit in 1945.

Germany. Inflation, cuts in hours, and layoffs cut into many workers' purchasing power, reducing it for some by as much as 30 percent. The economic changes led to nearly 4.5 million workers staging more than five thousand strikes. United Automobile Workers (UAW) strikers wanted a 30 percent increase in wages and a guarantee that car prices would not rise—they got neither.

Unions hoped their strikes would save wages and expand their power, but the opposite occurred. Congress and state and local governments responded with antilabor measures designed to weaken unions and end work stoppages. **Right-to-work laws** banned compulsory union membership (the closed shop) and in some cases provided legal and police protection for workers crossing picket lines. In the spring of 1946, Truman joined the attack. In April, he squared off against John L. Lewis and 400,000 striking United Mine Workers. Taking drastic action, the president seized the mines and ordered miners back to work. As miners returned to work, Truman pressured mine owners to meet most of the union's demands. When locomotive engineers walked off the job in May, Truman asked Congress for power to draft the strikers. The railroad strike was settled before Congress responded, but momentum mounted in Congress to take legislative action to control strikes and weaken unions.

Amid strikes, soaring inflation, divisions within Democratic ranks, and widespread dissatisfaction with Truman's leadership—"to err is Truman" was a common quip—Republicans asked the public, "Had enough?" Voters responded affirmatively in 1946, filling both houses of the Eightieth Congress with more Republicans and anti–New Deal Democrats. Refusing to retreat, Truman opened 1947 by presenting Congress with a restatement of many of the programs he had offered in 1945. The political battle between the president and Congress fired up again. Congress rejected Truman's proposals, Truman vetoed 250 bills, and Congress overrode 12 of Truman's vetoes. Among the most critical vetoes cast by Truman and overridden by Congress was the **Taft-Hartley Act**. The Taft-Hartley Act, passed in June 1947, was a clear victory for management over labor. It banned the closed shop, prevented industry-wide collective bargaining, and legalized state-sponsored right-to-work laws that hindered union organizing. It also required that union officials sign **affidavits** that they were not Communists. Echoing Truman's actions in the coal strike, the law also empowered the president to use a court injunction to force striking workers back to work for an eighty-day cooling-off period. Privately, Truman supported much of the bill and cast his veto knowing it would be overridden. He also knew his veto would help "hold labor support" for his 1948 run for the presidency.

Truman's veto of Taft-Hartley was an easy political decision. In contrast, the issue of civil rights was extremely complex and politically dangerous. Democrats were clearly divided. Southern Democrats opposed any mention of civil rights, while African Americans and liberals, including Eleanor Roosevelt, demanded that Truman "speak" to the issue. Truman was cautious but supportive of civil rights and aware of Soviet criticism of American segregation. Confessing that he did not know how bad conditions were for African Americans and that "the top dog in a world ... ought to clean his own house," Truman agreed in December 1946 to create a committee on civil rights to examine race relations in the country. The December 1947 report *To Secure These Rights* described the racial inequalities in American society and called on the government to take steps to correct the imbalance. Among its recommendations were the establishment of a permanent commission on civil rights, the enactment of anti-lynching laws, and the abolition of the poll tax. The committee also called for integration of the U.S. armed forces and support for integrating housing programs and education. Truman asked Congress in February 1948 to act on the recommendations, but provided no direction or legislation. After black labor leader A. Philip Randolph again threatened a march on Washington, in July 1948, Truman issued executive orders desegregating the armed forces and the federal workforce. The navy and air force complied, but the army resisted until high casualties in Korea during the summer of 1950 forced the integration of black replacements into white combat units. Despite his caution, Truman had done more in the area of civil rights than any president since Lincoln, a record that ensured African American and liberal support for his 1948 bid to be elected president in his own right.

The 1948 Election

Republicans' hopes were high in 1948. They had done well in congressional elections in 1946 and 1947. To take on Truman they chose New York governor Thomas E. Dewey.

---

affidavit A formal, written legal document made under oath; those signing the document state that the facts in the document are true.

He had lost to Roosevelt in 1944, but had earned a respectable 46 percent of the popular vote, and Truman was not Roosevelt. The Democrats were also mired in bitter infighting over the direction of domestic policy. Many Democratic liberals and minorities wished that Truman had pushed harder to sell his New Deal–type programs to the public and Congress. Truman worried that some liberals might switch their votes to Henry A. Wallace, the former vice president, who was running as a Progressive Party candidate. Southern Democrats, meanwhile, opposed any efforts to support organized labor or civil rights and walked out of the convention when a civil rights plank was inserted into the party's platform. Unwilling to support a Republican, they met in Birmingham and organized the States' Rights Democratic Party, better known as the **Dixiecrat Party**, nominating South Carolina governor J. Strom Thurmond for president.

Confounding the pollsters, Truman defeated Dewey. His victory was a triumph for Roosevelt's New Deal coalition. Despite the Dixiecrats, most southerners did not abandon the Democratic Party. Thurmond carried only four southern states; Wallace carried none. Democrats also won majorities in Congress, and Truman hoped that in 1949 he would succeed with his domestic program, which he called the **Fair Deal**.

In his inaugural address, Truman asked for increases in Social Security, public housing, and the minimum wage, the repeal of the Taft-Hartley Act, and the creation of a national health program. He also gave civil rights and federal aid to education a place on the national agenda. Rewarding farmers for their role in his victory, Truman submitted the Brannan Plan, which included federal benefits for

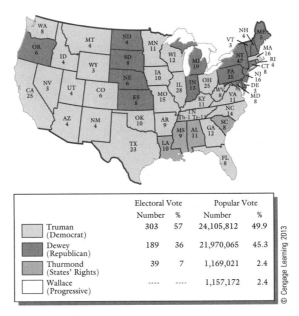

		Electoral Vote		Popular Vote	
		Number	%	Number	%
	Truman (Democrat)	303	57	24,105,812	49.9
	Dewey (Republican)	189	36	21,970,065	45.3
	Thurmond (States' Rights)	39	7	1,169,021	2.4
	Wallace (Progressive)	----	----	1,157,172	2.4

© Cengage Learning 2013

MAP 24.3 Presidential Election, 1948

This electoral map helps show how, in this close election, Truman won the presidency with less than 50 percent of the popular vote.

Many considered Harry S Truman's 1948 victory over Thomas E. Dewey a major political upset— nearly all of the major polls had named the Republican an easy winner. Here Truman holds up the Chicago Tribune's *incorrect headline announcing Dewey's triumph.*

© Bettmann/Corbis

small farmers. Congress responded favorably to Truman's programs in areas already well established by the New Deal: a 65-cent minimum hourly wage, funds for low- and moderate-income housing, and increases in Social Security coverage and payments. Proposals going beyond the scope of the New Deal encountered effective opposition from a coalition of southern Democrats and Republicans. A national health system and government intervention in education was communistic, said opponents, while civil rights efforts were part of a Communist conspiracy to undermine American unity. Adding their voices to the chorus, agribusiness leaders attacked the Brannan Plan as socialistic and class oriented.

COLD WAR POLITICS

Attacks on liberal programs as being socialistic or communistic were not new. But the developing Cold War intensified fears that Communists and their supporters were undermining American values and stability, leading to a second Red Scare. Some of the growing concerns were valid. The Soviets had a well-developed espionage system operating in the country, including within the atomic bomb program. Other concerns, though, arose from political opportunism and antiliberalism. Tobacco giant R. J. Reynolds characterized unionism as a step toward socialism in its multimillion-dollar public ad campaign to defeat the CIO's "Operation Dixie" effort to organize southern workers. In Pittsburgh, Pennsylvania, a local paper labeled those trying to integrate a public swimming pool "Commies." Across the country, neighborhoods and communities organized "watch groups," which screened books, movies, and public speakers and questioned teachers and public officials, seeking to ban or dismiss those considered suspect.

The Red Scare   Responding to increasing accusations, including those of the **House Un-American Activities Committee** (HUAC), that his administration tolerated Communist subversion, Truman moved to beef up the existing loyalty program by issuing Executive Order #9835, establishing the Federal Employee Loyalty Program. Attorney General Tom Clark provided a list of subversive organizations, and government administrators screened their employees for membership. But the program went beyond membership in one of the listed groups. If "reasonable grounds" existed for believing a federal employee was disloyal in belief or action, the employee could, after a hearing, be fired. Soon supervisors and workers began to accuse one another of "un-American" thoughts and activities. Between 1947 and 1951, the government discharged more than three thousand federal employees because of their supposed disloyalty. In almost every case, the accused had no right to confront the accusers or to refute the evidence. While the Soviets used American citizens to conduct espionage, few of those forced to leave government service were Communists.

Truman's loyalty program intensified rather than calmed fears, especially when Federal Bureau of Investigation (FBI) director J. Edgar Hoover proclaimed that there was one American Communist for every 1,814 loyal citizens, and Attorney General Clark warned that Communists were everywhere, "in factories, offices, butcher shops, on street corners, in private businesses," carrying "the germs of death for society." Grabbing headlines in 1947, HUAC targeted Hollywood, intent on removing people with liberal, leftist viewpoints from the entertainment industry and ensuring that the mass media promoted American capitalism and traditional American values. Just as World War II had mobilized the film industry, committee supporters believed, the Cold War necessitated that movies promote the "right" images. With much fanfare, HUAC called Hollywood notables to testify about Communist influence in the industry. Many of those called used the opportunity to prove their patriotism and to denounce communism. Actor Ronald Reagan, president of the Screen Actors Guild, denounced Communist methods that "sucked" people into carrying out "Red policy without knowing what they are doing" and testified that the Conference of Studio Unions was full of Reds.

Not all witnesses were cooperative. Some, including the **"Hollywood Ten,"** a group of screenwriters and producers, took the Fifth Amendment and lashed out at the activities of the committee. Labeled "Fifth Amendment Communists," the ten were jailed for contempt of Congress and blacklisted by the industry. Eric Johnson, president of the Motion Picture Association, announced that Hollywood would produce no more films like *The Grapes of Wrath*, featuring the hardships of poor Americans or "the seamy side of American life." Moviemakers soon issued a new code—*A Screen Guide for Americans*—that demanded, "Don't Smear the Free Enterprise System"; "Don't Show That Poverty Is a Virtue."

Just before the election of 1948, HUAC zeroed in on spies within the government, bringing forth a number of informants who had been Soviet agents and were now willing to name others who allegedly had sold out the United States. The most sensational revelation came from a repentant ex-Communist named Whittaker Chambers. He accused **Alger Hiss**, a New Deal liberal and one-time State Department official, of being a Communist. At first Hiss denied knowing Chambers, but under interrogation by HUAC members, especially Congressman **Richard M. Nixon** of California, Hiss admitted an acquaintance with Chambers in the 1930s but denied he was or had been a Communist. When Hiss sued Chambers for libel, Chambers escalated the charges. He stated that Hiss had passed State Department secrets to him in the 1930s, and he produced rolls of microfilm that he said Hiss had delivered to him. In a controversial and sensationalized trial, in 1949 Hiss was found guilty of **perjury** (the statute of limitations on espionage had expired) and sentenced to five years in prison.

As the nation followed the Hiss case, news of the Communist victory in China and the Soviet explosion of an atomic bomb heightened American fears. Many people believed that such Communist successes could have occurred only with help from American traitors. Congressman Harold Velde of Illinois proclaimed, "Our government from the White House down has been sympathetic toward the views of Communists and fellow-travelers, with the result that it has been infiltrated by a network of spies." Congress responded in 1950 by passing, over Truman's veto, the **McCarran Internal Security Act**. The law required all Communists to register with the attorney general and made it a crime to conspire to establish a totalitarian government in the United States. The following year the Supreme Court upheld the **Smith Act** (passed in June 1940), ruling that membership in the Communist Party was equivalent to conspiring to overthrow the American government and that no specific act of treason was necessary for conviction.

Congressman Velde's observation about spies seemed vindicated in February 1950, when **Julius and Ethel Rosenberg** were accused of being part of a Soviet atomic spy ring. At trial in 1951, the prosecution alleged that the information the Rosenbergs passed to the Soviets was largely responsible for the successful Soviet atomic bomb. The Rosenbergs professed innocence but were convicted of espionage. (Soviet documents indicate that Julius Rosenberg was engaged in espionage but that Ethel was probably guilty only of being loyal to him. Documents concerning Hiss are inconclusive, continuing a spirited debate about his innocence.)

Joseph McCarthy and the Politics of Loyalty

Feeding on the furor over the enemy within, Republican senator **Joseph McCarthy** of Wisconsin emerged at the forefront of the anti-Communist movement. Running for the Senate in 1946, he invented a glorious war record for himself that included the nickname "Tail-gunner Joe" and several wounds—he even walked with a fake limp—to help himself win the election. In February 1950, he announced to a Republican women's group in Wheeling, West Virginia, that the United States was losing the Cold War because of traitors within the government. He claimed to know of 205 Communists working in the State Department.

His charges were examined by a Senate committee and shown to be at best inaccurate. When the chair of the committee, Democrat Millard Tydings of Maryland, pronounced McCarthy a hoax and a fraud, the Wisconsin senator

---

perjury   The deliberate giving of false testimony under oath.

At the heart of the Red Scare was Senator Joseph McCarthy. Using inquisition–style tactics to attack his opponents, he became one of the most powerful politicians in the nation by 1952. In this picture from the 1952 presidential campaign, McCarthy waves a report on Democratic candidate Adlai Stevenson showing that he endorsed policies favoring the Soviets.

countered by accusing Tydings of questionable loyalty. During Tydings's 1950 reelection campaign, McCarthy worked for his defeat, spreading false stories and even a faked photograph of the Democrat talking to Earl Browder, head of the American Communist Party. When Tydings lost by forty thousand votes, McCarthy's stature soared. The outbreak of the Korean War and the reversals at the hands of the Chinese only increased the senator's popularity. Few dared to oppose him and many supported his allegations. The Senate's most powerful Republican, Robert Taft of Ohio, slapped McCarthy on the back saying, "Keep it up, Joe."

By 1952, with the Korean Conflict stalemated, Truman's popularity was almost nonexistent, and Republicans were having a field day attacking "cowardly containment" and calling for victory in Korea. When Truman lost the opening presidential primary in New Hampshire, he withdrew from the race, leaving no clear choice for a Democratic candidate. Again, Republicans were sure voters would elect a Republican president—someone who, in Thomas Dewey's opinion, would "save the country from going to Hades in the hand basket of paternalism-socialism-dictatorship."

HOMECOMING AND SOCIAL ADJUSTMENTS

With World War II over, Americans were eager to return home and resume normal lives. Organized "Bring Daddy Back" clubs flooded Washington with letters demanding a speedy return of husbands and fathers. By November 1945, 1.25 million GIs were returning home each month. For Americans entering the postwar world, the homecoming was buoyed with expectations and fraught with anxieties. The nation had experienced dramatic economic growth, but remembering the Depression, Americans wondered if the postwar economy would remain strong. Still, most were optimistic that any recession would be short-lived and they would be able to spend savings, find jobs, and enjoy the American dream. "Consumption is the frontier of the future," chirped one economic forecast.

Rising
Expectations
Owning a home was for many the symbol of the American dream. Before 1945 the housing industry had focused on building custom homes or multifamily dwellings. But the postwar demand changed the housing industry. To meet the demand, William Levitt and other developers supplied mass-produced, prefabricated houses—the suburban **tract homes**. Using building techniques developed during the war, timber from his forests, and nonunion workers, Levitt boasted that he could construct an affordable house on an existing concrete slab in sixteen minutes. Standardized, with few frills, the house had two stories with four and a half rooms. Built on generous 60-by-100-foot lots, complete with a tree or two, Levitt homes cost slightly less than $8,000 and still provided Levitt with a $1,000 profit per house. The first Levittown sprang up in Hempstead, Long Island, and was a planned community with more than seventeen thousand homes, seven village greens, fourteen playgrounds, and nine swimming pools. Hundreds of look-alike suburban neighborhoods were soon built across the nation, contributing to a growing migration from rural and urban America to the suburbs.

Nowhere were tract homes more prominent than in southern California. During and after the war, networks of roads extended out from southern California cities, developing "satellite" economic centers, pulling businesses, homes, and industries away from the central cities. In Los Angeles this resulted in a 50 percent loss in sales and tax revenues, the reduction of public transportation, a loss of jobs, and a growing urban poverty rate. This pattern of development became increasingly common across the country as suburbs multiplied.

Although part of the American dream, suburbs were not for everyone. Widespread discrimination kept some out by design. Whether it was the official policy of developers like Levitt, neighborhood covenants written to exclude minorities, or lack of home loans, almost every suburb in the nation was predominately white and Christian. Even though the Supreme Court ruled in *Shelly v. Kraemer* (1948) that

---

tract homes   Numerous houses of similar design built on small plots of land.

restrictive housing covenants could not be enforced by lower courts, the decision failed to have much effect. Neither did the Court's decision to prevent banks and the FHA from rejecting home loan applications from minorities trying to buy houses in white neighborhoods. Real-estate agents continued to abide by the Realtors' Code of Ethics, which called it unethical to permit the "infiltration of inharmonious elements" into a neighborhood. Across the nation, fewer than 5 percent of suburban neighborhoods provided nonwhites access to the American dream house.

For many veterans a cozy home was only part of the postwar dream—so too was going to college. Armed with economic support through the G.I. Bill in September 1946, nearly 1 million veterans enrolled in college. New Jersey's Rutgers University saw its enrollment climb from seven thousand to sixteen thousand. At Lehigh University in Pennsylvania, 940 veteran students outnumbered the 396 "civilians" and refused to don the traditional freshman beanie. Faculty and administrators soon discovered that veterans made exceptional students and rarely needed disciplinary action. Schools, responding to the influx of students, not only hired more faculty and built more facilities but also began providing special housing, daycare centers, and expanded health clinics for married students. By the time the G.I. Bill expired in 1952, over 2 million veterans, including sixty-four thousand women, had earned their degrees under its umbrella.

Veterans expected jobs, too, and most figured that "wartime" workers would relinquish their jobs and return to traditional roles. At first jobs were scarce. The cancellation of wartime contracts and the nationwide switch to domestic production resulted in 2.7 million workers being dismissed from their jobs within a month of Japan's surrender. Fortunately for veterans, the G.I. Bill provided unemployment compensation for a year until a job was found. And within a year, jobs were becoming more and more available. By 1947, 60 million people were working, 7 million more than at the peak of wartime production. But the workforce had changed, with noticeably fewer women and minorities as industries and businesses resumed their prewar hiring habits.

From Industrial Worker to Homemaker   "Last hired, first fired" fit the workplace as the war ended. Across the nation women, African Americans, and Latinos were told that they were no longer needed in the industrial workplace. In the aircraft and shipbuilding industries, companies drastically trimmed their workforces as wartime orders ended, dismissing most of the women and African Americans who had provided much-needed labor during the war. Mirroring the rest of the nation, in Seattle and Baltimore two-thirds of aircraft workers and one-third of the shipbuilding workers lost their jobs within one month after Japan's surrender. In the aircraft industry women had made up 40 percent of the workforce, but by 1948 they numbered a mere 12 percent. For most women the loss of jobs was expected. "We will work as long as they need us," stated a woman employee at Boeing, "and when we're through we will go back to our meals and dishes and children."

Indeed, most of society assumed that women would want to go back to domesticity. A *Fortune* poll in the fall of 1945 revealed that 57 percent of women and 63 percent of men believed that married women should not work outside the home. Other polls, however, found that a sizable majority of women, especially single women, wanted and needed to keep their jobs. One single woman asked simply: "What are we to do? I need a job badly." While the vast majority of women wanting to continue work hoped to stay in the same field, it was clear that employers had different expectations, and as rapidly as it had changed after 1942, the postwar workplace became highly gender oriented again. Those women finding or keeping work took lower-paying "female" jobs. Rosie the Riveter had become Fran the File Clerk, as wages declined from about $50 to $35 a week.

While some women struggled to find or keep jobs, society stressed a renewed social emphasis on femininity, family, and a woman's proper role. Psychiatrists and marriage counselors argued that men wanted their wives to be feminine and submissive, not fellow workers. Fashion designers, such as Christian Dior in his "New Look," lengthened skirts and accented waists and breasts to emphasize femininity. Marriage was more popular than ever: by 1950, two-thirds of the population was married and having children. Factors contributing to the rush to the altar were fears of "male scarcity" caused by war losses and a new attitude that viewed marriage as the ideal state for young people. Many women's magazines and marriage experts championed the idea that men should marry at around age 20 and women at age 18 or 19. With veterans returning home, with society celebrating family, and with prosperity increasing came the **"baby boom"** that would last for nearly twenty years. From a Depression level of under 19 births per 1,000 women per year, the birth rate rose to more than 25 births per 1,000 women by 1948 (see Figure 24.1).

Not all women accepted the role of contented, submissive wives and homemakers—the war experience had changed relationships. When one veteran informed his wife that she could no longer handle the finances because it was not "woman's work," she indignantly reminded him that she had successfully balanced the checkbook for four years and that his return had not made her suddenly stupid. Reflecting such tensions and too many hasty wartime marriages, the divorce rate rose dramatically. Twenty-five percent of all wartime marriages were ending in divorce in 1946, and by 1950 over a million GI marriages had dissolved. As the number of female heads of household rose, so also did the poverty and social stigma attached to single parenthood. Following her divorce, one suburban resident recalled that her neighbors "avoided" her and made remarks like "Why don't you get a job instead of taking tax monies?" She also noted that her children were singled out at school because they did not have a father at home.

Restrained Expectations   For Latinos the war years had brought many positive changes. Many experienced a higher degree of equality than before and, especially among Mexican Americans, there was more of a sense of being part of the United States, "American-ness."

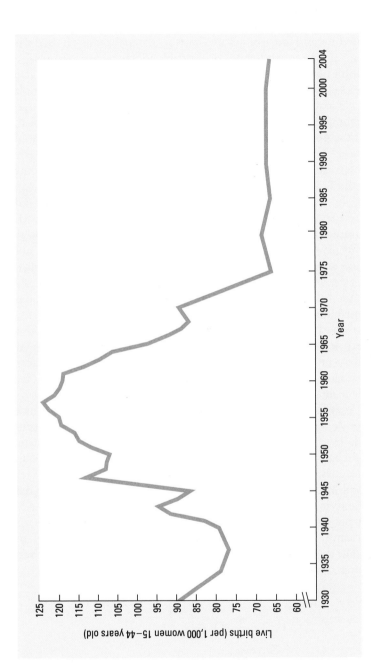

FIGURE 24.1 Birth Rate, 1930–2004

Between 1946 and 1964, rebounding from the low birth rate of the Depression, families chose to have more children. This increase is often called the "baby boom." In the 1960s, the birth rate slowed, and since the mid-1970s, it has remained fairly constant.

A wounded veteran and resident of El Paso, Texas, Moises Flores recalled: "I am proud to be an American. Sometimes I even call myself gringo, which I'm not. I'm still Mexican, but I'm an American first." The war also saw in many an increasing unwillingness to return to traditional roles. Antonio Campo, for one, had experienced a segregated life in Houston before the war. After the war he used the G.I. Bill to go to college and later ran for political office. When told in response to his activism, "If you don't like it, why don't you go back to Mexico?" he shot back: "I was born here in Texas. I went overseas and put my life on the line so you people can make decisions." He lost the election but, like many other Latinos, drew from the same desire for change that energized the League of United Latin American Citizens (LULAC) and the **American GI Forum** to attack discrimination throughout the West and Southwest. The American GI Forum, organized in Texas in early 1948 by Mexican American veterans, worked to secure for Latino veterans the benefits provided by the G.I. Bill and to develop leadership within the Mexican American population. In California and Texas, LULAC and the American GI Forum successfully used federal courts to correct school systems that segregated Latino from white children. In *Mendez v. Westminster* (1946) and in *Delgado v. Bastrop School District* (1948), federal courts ruled that school systems could not educate Mexican Americans separately from Anglos. Despite these rulings, throughout the Southwest and West, Latino students remained in predominantly "Mexican" schools and classrooms, which perpetuated inferior educational opportunities and contributed to high dropout rates.

African Americans had experiences similar to those of Latinos and also exhibited a heightened degree of resistance to returning to old norms. Even as African Americans lost industrial and other higher-paying jobs as the war ended, some positive changes occurred. In the South, African American voter registration increased, primarily in the Upper South and in urban areas. In several northern cities, African Americans displayed their growing political voice by electing black representatives to local and state office and, in 1945, sent Adam Clayton Powell, Jr., to Congress from New York. That same year, Jackie Robinson, a gifted baseball athlete, gained national recognition when he began playing in the minor leagues. In 1947 he became the first African American player in major league baseball since the 1890s with the Brooklyn Dodgers, and entered the Baseball Hall of Fame in 1962.

While the postwar period generally saw significant loss of income and status for women, African Americans, and Latinos, their experiences had energized many to pursue their own vision of the American dream, one that included not only improved prosperity but an unfettered role in society and an unmuzzled voice in politics.

STUDY TOOLS

SUMMARY

People hoped that the end of World War II would usher in a period of international cooperation and peace. This expectation vanished with the start of the Cold War. To protect the country and the world from Soviet expansion, the United States implemented a containment policy that was first applied to Western Europe but eventually included Asia as well. By the end of Truman's presidency, the United States viewed its national security in global terms and vowed to use its resources to combat the spread of Communist power.

At home Truman sought to expand on the New Deal but found success difficult. While existing New Deal programs such as Social Security, farm supports, and a minimum wage were extended, a conservative Congress blocked new programs. Linking liberal ideas and programs with communism, moderates and conservatives, with the House Un-American Activities Committee and Joseph McCarthy leading the way, promoted their own political, social, and economic interests.

Most Americans expected to enjoy an expanding postwar economy that would bring increased prosperity and more consumer goods. For many the vision of the suburbs with its stable family structure and new-model car in every garage seemed obtainable. Women were encouraged to return to "domestic" life and raise a family. Postwar America saw a rise in marriages and the start of a baby boom. But alongside these trends were an increasing number of divorces and women dissatisfied with their traditional roles.

While white families seemed poised to achieve the American dream, African Americans and Latinos found that discrimination undid many of the economic and social gains they had made during the war. Though forced into lesser jobs and still living in a socially segregated society, many saw changes that they hoped would bring economic and educational improvement as well as full political and civil rights.

CHRONOLOGY

FROM WORLD WAR TO COLD WAR

1945 United Nations formed
Potsdam Conference

1946 Kennan's "Long Telegram"
Churchill's "iron curtain" speech
Iran crisis
Construction begins on first Levittown
Vietnamese war for independence begins

1947 Truman Doctrine
Truman's Federal Employee Loyalty Program
Taft-Hartley Act
HUAC begins to investigate Hollywood
Jackie Robinson joins Brooklyn Dodgers
To Secure These Rights issued
Rio Pact organized

1948 Communist coup in Czechoslovakia
State of Israel founded
Congress approves Marshall Plan
Shelly v. Kraemer
Truman defeats Dewey

1949	North Atlantic Treaty Organization created
	Berlin blockade broken by Allied airlift
	Soviet Union explodes atomic bomb
	Communist forces win civil war in China
	Alger Hiss convicted of perjury
1950	U.S. hydrogen bomb project announced
	McCarthy claims Communists riddle the State Department
	NSC 68
	Korean War begins
	McCarran Internal Security Act
1951	General MacArthur relieved of command
	Rosenbergs convicted of espionage
1953	Korean War armistice signed

Focus Questions

If you have mastered this chapter, you should be able to answer these questions and explain the terms that follow the questions.

1. What views and actions chosen by the Soviet Union and United States contributed to the Cold War?
2. How did the Truman administration seek to promote American global interests between 1947 and 1951 and why was the outcome in Asia less than satisfactory?
3. What events contributed to NSC 68 and how did it represent a change in strategy?
4. As the North Koreans invaded South Korea, why did Truman decide to refer the issue to the United Nations?
5. What were Truman's and MacArthur's goals in Korea? What was the consequence of China's entry into the war?
6. In what ways did Truman attempt to maintain and expand the New Deal? How did the fear of communism strengthen conservative opposition to his programs?
7. Why did Truman win the 1948 election?
8. What fears and events heightened society's worries about internal subversion, and how did politicians respond to the public's concerns?
9. Why and how did Joseph McCarthy become so powerful by 1952?
10. How did suburban America reflect the social and economic expectations of many Americans?
11. What adjustments did women and minorities have to make in postwar America?

KEY TERMS

United Nations (*p. 758*)
General Assembly (*p. 759*)
Security Council (*p. 759*)
containment (*p. 759*)
iron curtain (*p. 760*)
Truman Doctrine (*p. 763*)
Marshall Plan (*p. 763*)
Berlin airlift (*p. 765*)
North Atlantic Treaty Organization (*p. 765*)
National Security Council (*p. 765*)
Rio Pact (*p. 765*)
Organization of American States (*p. 765*)
Ralph Bunche (*p. 766*)
Nationalist Chinese government (*p. 766*)
NSC Memorandum #68 (*p. 766*)
police action (*p. 767*)
Right-to-work laws (*p. 771*)
Taft-Hartley Act (*p. 772*)

To Secure These Rights (*p. 772*)
Dixiecrat Party (*p. 773*)
Fair Deal (*p. 773*)
House Un-American Activities Committee (*p. 775*)
Hollywood Ten (*p. 775*)
Alger Hiss (*p. 775*)
Richard M. Nixon (*p. 775*)
McCarran Internal Security Act (*p. 776*)
Smith Act (*p. 776*)
Julius and Ethel Rosenberg (*p. 776*)
Joseph McCarthy (*p. 776*)
Shelly v. Kraemer (*p. 778*)
baby boom (*p. 780*)
American GI Forum (*p. 782*)
Mendez v. Westminster and *Delgado v. Bastrop School District* (*p. 782*)

25

QUEST FOR CONSENSUS, 1952–1960

CHAPTER OUTLINE

• Politics of Consensus • Eisenhower and World Affairs • The Best of Times • Outside Suburbia • Study Tools

---

POLITICS OF CONSENSUS

"Time for a change," cried Republicans in 1952. Politically wounded by the lingering war in Korea and the soft-on-communism label, the Democrats' twenty-year hold on the White House seemed in jeopardy. Bypassing would-be presidential candidate Senator Robert Taft, moderate Republicans turned to General Dwight David Eisenhower. Although politically inexperienced, "Ike" was well known, revered as a war hero, and carried the image of an honest man thrust into public service. Skillfully gaining the nomination at the Republican convention, Eisenhower chose Richard M. Nixon of California as his vice-presidential running mate. Nixon was young and had risen rapidly in the party because of his outspoken anticommunism, made visible in the Hiss investigation. The Democrats nominated Adlai E. Stevenson, a liberal New Dealer and governor of Illinois.

Eisenhower Takes Command The Republican campaign took two paths. One concentrated on the popular image of Eisenhower. Republicans introduced "spot commercials" on television that stressed his honesty, integrity, and "Americanness." Eisenhower crusaded for high standards and good government and posed as another George Washington. A war-weary nation applauded his promise to go to Korea "in the cause of peace." McCarthy, Nixon, and others took the second path, brutally attacking the Democrats' Cold War and New Deal records, blasting the Democrats as representing "plunder at home and blunder abroad." They boasted of "no

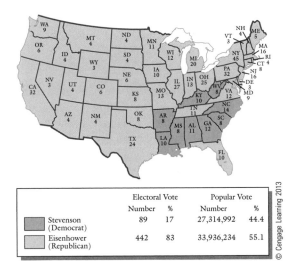

	Electoral Vote		Popular Vote	
	Number	%	Number	%
Stevenson (Democrat)	89	17	27,314,992	44.4
Eisenhower (Republican)	442	83	33,936,234	55.1

© Cengage Learning 2013

MAP 25.1 Presidential Election, 1952

An overwhelming victory for Eisenhower, this election saw Stevenson carrying a handful of states. Note that the so-called "Solid South," though, remained largely Democratic. The nation's political configuration, especially for presidential elections, would change substantially over the next two decades.

Communists in the Republican Party," promised to roll back communism, and vowed to dismantle the New Deal. Stevenson's effort to "talk sense" to the voters stood little chance.

The campaign's only tense moment came with an allegation that Nixon had accepted gifts and money from business friends. To counter the accusations and stay on the ticket, Nixon used television. In the "Checkers speech," the teary-eyed candidate denied the fund existed and claimed that the only gift his family had ever received was a puppy, Checkers. His daughter loved the puppy, Nixon stated, and he would not make her give it back, no matter what it did to his career. It was an overly sentimental speech, but the public and Eisenhower rallied behind Nixon. Eisenhower buried Stevenson in popular and electoral votes, and his broad political coattails also swept Republican majorities into Congress. Four years later, the 1956 presidential election was a repeat of 1952, with Eisenhower receiving 457 electoral votes and again swamping Stevenson, who carried only seven southern states. But in 1956, the Republican victory was Eisenhower's alone, as Democrats maintained the majorities in both houses of Congress they had won in the 1954 midterm races.

During both of his administrations, Eisenhower was "Ike" to the public, a warm, friendly, grandfather figure who projected middle-class values and habits. Critics complained that he seemed almost an absentee president, often leaving the government in the hands of Congress and his cabinet while he played golf or bridge. But to those who knew and worked with him, he was far from bumbling or neglectful. In military fashion, Eisenhower relied on his staff to provide a full discussion of any issue. We had a "good growl," he would say after especially heated cabinet talks, but he made the final decisions, and he expected them to be carried out.

Dynamic Conservatism

Eisenhower wanted to follow a "middle course" that was "conservative when it comes to money and liberal when it comes to human beings." He believed that government should be run efficiently, like a successful business, and he staffed his cabinet with a majority of businessmen, most of whom were millionaires. Among the president's key priorities was to reduce spending and the presence of the federal government. Yet, like Truman, Eisenhower recognized the politics of the practical and understood that many New Deal agencies and functions could and should not be attacked. He told his brother that any political party that tried "to abolish Social Security, unemployment insurance, and eliminate labor laws and farm programs" would not be heard of again. He meant to pick and choose his domestic battles, staying to the right but still in the "vital center."

To balance the budget, Eisenhower used a "meat ax" on Truman's projected budgets. He dismissed 200,000 government workers, cut domestic spending by 10 percent, and slashed the military budget. His budget cutting gave Eisenhower a vehicle for reducing New Deal programs and returning control of some to local and state governance. Eisenhower thought he could eliminate or curtail the federal government's role in the areas of energy, the environment, and trusteeship over Indian reservations. Advocating private ownership and state responsibility, he signed legislation allowing private ownership of nuclear power plants and reducing federal control over the industry. Congress also approved legislation placing much of the nation's offshore oil sources under state authority and opening federal lands to lumber and mining companies.

Citing costs and expanding opportunities for Native Americans, Congress in 1954 passed a resolution establishing a termination program, which began to withdraw federal services and economic support to tribes, encouraged Indians to leave the reservations, and liquidated tribal lands and resources. The Klamath tribe in Oregon, for example, sold much of their ponderosa pine lands to lumber companies. Before the policy was reversed in the 1960s, sixty-one tribes were involved. Some experienced short-term economic gains with the sale of valuable lands and resources, but long-term benefits failed to materialize. Reservations were poorer, and the nearly half of reservation Indians who had abandoned their reservations and moved to urban areas found that few jobs or opportunities were available.

Recognizing political reality, Eisenhower stood by as Congress increased agricultural subsidies, the minimum wage (to $1.00 an hour), funds for urban development, and Social Security benefits. But he also expanded the role of government in new directions. In 1953, he created the Department of Health, Education and Welfare, directed by Oveta Culp Hobby, who had commanded the Women's Army Corps during World War II. Still, even public health was something Eisenhower felt was best left to states and communities. In 1955, Jonas Salk developed a vaccine for polio, and many called for a nationwide federal program to inoculate children against the disease, which in 1952 had infected 52,000 people, mostly children. However, Eisenhower, Secretary Hobby, and the American Medical Association rejected such a program, calling it socialistic. State and local vaccination programs did reduce the number of polio cases to less than one thousand annually by the 1960s.

There were also two new major government spending programs: the St. Lawrence Seaway Act (1954) and the **Federal Highway Act** (1956). The first funded joint U.S.-Canadian construction of an inland waterway connecting the Great Lakes with the Atlantic. The second provided funds to construct an interstate highway system; the military, Eisenhower maintained, needed such a nationwide transportation network, which would also meet the needs of an automobile-driven nation.

In 1957, Eisenhower again extended federal spending after the Soviet Union launched **Sputnik I** and **Sputnik II**, the first artificial satellites, into space. Not only did the nation seem vulnerable to Soviet missiles, but it appeared that the American education system was not putting enough effort into teaching mathematics and science. Eisenhower promptly asked Congress to provide money for public education and to create a new agency to coordinate the country's space program.

The **National Defense Education Act** of 1958 provided funds for public education to improve the teaching of math, languages, and science and set aside $295 million in **National Defense Student Loans** for college students. To improve the space program, Congress created the National Aeronautics and Space Administration (NASA), which unveiled Project Mercury with the goal of sending astronauts into space.

The Problem with McCarthy	With the Democrats defeated, Eisenhower and most Republicans thought McCarthy would end his crusade against Communists.

But he continued to criticize the administration's foreign policy as soft on communism and to search for subversives. To weaken McCarthy's rhetoric, the administration, claiming loyalty issues, dismissed more than two thousand federal employees in 1953. None were proven to be Communists, but nearly all were Roosevelt and Truman appointees. When, in 1954, McCarthy claimed favoritism toward known Communists in the army, anti-McCarthy forces in Congress, quietly supported by Eisenhower, moved to defang the senator and established a committee to examine the senator's claims.

The American Broadcasting Company's telecast of the 1954 **Army-McCarthy hearings** allowed more than 20 million viewers to see McCarthy's ruthless bullying firsthand. When the army's lawyer, Joseph Welch, asked the brooding McCarthy, "Have you no sense of decency?" the nation burst into applause. McCarthy's power ebbed and several months later the Senate voted 67 to 22 to censure McCarthy's "unbecoming conduct." Drinking heavily, shunned by his colleagues, and ignored by the media, McCarthy died in 1957.

EISENHOWER AND WORLD AFFAIRS

During the 1952 campaign, part of Eisenhower's popularity reflected the view that Republicans would conduct a more forceful foreign policy. Republican spokesmen promised the rollback of communism and the liberation of peoples under communist control. After his election Eisenhower kept his campaign promise to go to Korea. He went—for three days. Many expected him to find a means to win the conflict, but after visiting the front lines, he was convinced that a negotiated peace was the only solution. The problem was how to persuade the North Koreans and Chinese that a settlement would be in their best interests. Eisenhower, wary of being too assertive and too simplistic in approaching international problems, approached foreign policy as a realist. Despite the campaign rhetoric of liberation and rollback, he embraced the principle of containment and sought to modify it to match what he believed to be the nation's capabilities and needs. His new policy was called the **New Look**.

The New Look   The core of the New Look was nuclear deterrence—an enhanced arsenal of nuclear weapons and delivery systems—and the threat of **massive retaliation**. In explaining the shift to more atomic weapons, Vice President Nixon stated, "Rather than let the Communists nibble us to death all over the world in little wars, we will rely ... on massive mobile retaliation." Secretary of Defense Charles E. Wilson, noting that the nuclear strategy was cheaper than conventional forces, quipped that the policy ensured "more bang for the buck." Demonstrating the country's nuclear might, the United States exploded its first hydrogen bomb in November 1952 (the Soviets tested theirs in August 1953), expanded its arsenal of strategic nuclear weapons to six thousand, and developed tactical nuclear weapons of a lower destructive power that could be used on the battlefield.

The New Look was sold to the public as more positive than Truman's defensive containment policy, but insiders recognized that it had flaws. The central problem was where the United States should draw the massive-retaliation line: "What if the enemy calls our bluff? How do you convince the American people and the U.S. Congress to declare war?" asked one planner. The answer was to convince potential aggressors that the United States would strike back, raining nuclear destruction not only on the attackers but also on the Soviets and Chinese so that the bluff would never be called. This policy was called **brinkmanship**, because it required the administration to take the nation to the brink of war, trusting that the opposition would back down. Thus Secretary of State John Foster Dulles and Eisenhower

---

brinkmanship   Practice of seeking to win disputes in international politics by creating the impression of being willing to push a highly dangerous situation to the limit.

To protect themselves from the effect of a nuclear explosion, the government recommended that once the flash was seen or the warning signal was given, students should "duck and cover," assuming the fetal position and covering the head with their hands. Burt the Turtle became a popular mascot for the exercises that were practiced from 1951 to the mid-1980s. In this picture elementary school children in Ohio successfully practice "duck and cover."

indulged in dramatic speeches explaining that nuclear weapons were as usable as conventional ones. It was necessary "to remove the taboo" from using nuclear weapons, Dulles informed the press.

To prod the North Koreans and Chinese to sign a Korean truce agreement, Eisenhower used public and private channels to suggest that the United States might use atomic weapons. By July 1953, the strategy apparently had worked. A truce signed at Panmunjom ended the fighting and brought home almost all the troops but left Korea divided by a **demilitarized zone**. Had the nuclear threat, "atomic diplomacy," worked? Some thought it had, but others pointed to Stalin's death in March 1953 and the resolution of central issues as more important. Still, Americans praised Eisenhower's new approach.

To strengthen the idea of "going nuclear" and make the possibility of World War III less frightening, the administration stressed that nuclear war was survivable. Public and private underground **fallout shelters**—well stocked with food, water, and medical supplies—could, it was claimed, provide safety against an attack. A 32-inch-thick slab of concrete, *U.S. News & World Report* related, could protect people from an atomic blast "as close as 1,000 feet away." Across the nation, civil defense drills were established for factories, offices, and businesses. "Duck-and-cover" drills were held in schools: when their teachers shouted "Drop!" students immediately got into a kneeling or prone position and placed their hands behind their necks.

While people were being convinced that they could survive a nuclear war, movies and novels showed the horror of nuclear death and destruction. Nevil Shute portrayed the extinction of humankind in his novel *On the Beach* (1957). In *Them!* (1954) and dozens of other **B movies**, giant ants and other hideous creatures mutated by atomic fallout threatened the world.

As with Korea, Eisenhower recognized the limits of American power—areas under Communist control could not be liberated, and a thermonuclear war would yield no winners. Consequently, the administration sought other ways to promote American power and influence, including alliances and **covert operations**. Alliances would identify areas protected by the American nuclear umbrella and would protect the United States from being drawn into limited "brushfire" wars. When small conflicts erupted, the ground forces of regional allies, perhaps supported with American naval and air strength, would snuff them out.

In Asia, Eisenhower concluded **bilateral** defense pacts with South Korea (1953) and Taiwan (1955) and a **multilateral** agreement, the Southeast Asia Treaty Organization (SEATO, 1954), that linked the United States, Australia, Thailand, the Philippines, Pakistan, New Zealand, France, and Britain. In the Middle East, the United States officially joined Britain, Iran, Pakistan, Turkey, and Iraq in the **Baghdad Pact** in 1957, later called the Central Treaty Organization (CENTO) after Iraq withdrew in 1959. In Europe, the United States approved the rearming of West Germany in 1954 and welcomed it into NATO in 1958. In all, the

demilitarized zone　An area in which military forces, operations, and installations are prohibited.

fallout shelters　Underground shelters stocked with food and supplies that were intended to provide safety in case of atomic attack; *fallout* refers to the irradiated particles falling through the atmosphere after a nuclear attack.

B movies　Poorer quality, more cheaply made films that were shown in addition to the main movies.

covert operation　A program or event carried out in secret.

bilateral　Involving two parties.

multilateral　Involving more than two parties.

Eisenhower administration signed forty-three pacts to help defend regions or individual countries from Communist aggression. In 1955, the Soviet Union created its own military alliance, the **Warsaw Pact**.

The Third World   In 1946, fifty-one nations, most located in Europe and the Western Hemisphere, signed the United Nations' charter. Over the next ten years, twenty-five more nations entered, about a third of them having achieved independence from European nations through revolution and political and social protests. By 1960, thirty-seven new nations existed in Africa, Asia, and the Middle East. For many of the emerging nations, independence did not bring prosperity or stability, and the so-called **third world**, which claimed to be independent of either the Western capitalist or Communist blocs, became part of the Cold War. Both sides competed for the "hearts and minds" of the emerging nations. Commenting on nationalistic movements in Latin America, Secretary of State Dulles said: "In the old days we used to be able to let South America go through the wringer of bad times ... but the trouble is, now, when you put it through the wringer, it comes out red."

One solution to the problem was to use economic and military aid, political pressure, and the **Central Intelligence Agency** (CIA) to support those governments that were anti-Communist and provided stability, even if that stability was achieved through ruthless and undemocratic means. It seemed a never-ending and largely thankless task. "While we are busy rescuing Guatemala or assisting Korea and Indochina," Eisenhower observed, the Communists "make great inroads in Burma, Afghanistan, and Egypt." To meet the growing need, the CIA expanded by 500 percent and shifted its resources to covert activities—80 percent by 1957. In its conduct of activities, the CIA, headed by Allen Dulles, operated with almost no congressional oversight or restrictions.

Turmoil in the   In the Middle East, Arab nationalism, fired by anti-Israeli
Middle East   and anti-Western attitudes, posed a serious threat to American interests. Iran and Egypt offered the greatest challenges. In Iran, Prime Minister Mohammed Mossadegh had nationalized British-owned oil properties and seemed likely to sell oil to the Soviets. Eisenhower considered him to be "neurotic and periodically unstable" and gave the CIA the green light to overthrow the Iranian leader and replace him with a pro-Western government. On August 18, 1953, Mossadegh was forced from office and was replaced by **Shah Mohammad Reza Pahlavi**, who awarded the United States 40 percent of Iranian oil production.

Egyptian leader Gamal Abdel Nasser, who assumed power in 1954, posed a similar problem. At first the United States hoped that Nasser would act as a stabilizing influence in the region and offered money and help to build the Aswan Dam on the Nile. But the U.S. attitude changed when Nasser's relations with Israel deteriorated and he denounced the Baghdad Pact and purchased arms from the Soviet bloc. Calling him an "evil influence," Eisenhower canceled the Aswan Dam project

(July 1956). Days later, claiming the need to finance the dam, Nasser nationalized the Anglo-French–owned Suez Canal.

Israel, France, and Britain responded with military action to regain control of the canal. Eisenhower was furious. He disliked Nasser but could not approve armed aggression. Fearful that the Soviets were ready "to take any wild adventure" and intervene, Eisenhower moved rapidly to sponsor a UN General Assembly resolution (November 2, 1956) calling for an end to the fighting, the removal of foreign troops from Egyptian soil, and the assignment of a UN peacekeeping force there. Faced with worldwide opposition and intense pressure from the United States—including a threat to withhold oil shipments—France, Britain, and Israel withdrew their forces. Nasser regained control of the canal and, as Eisenhower had feared, emerged a major leader in the Arab world willing to accept Soviet support.

The outcome of the Suez War and the growth of Soviet influence in the Middle East forced Eisenhower to expand American interests in the region. To protect Arab friends from Communist-nationalist revolutions, he asked Congress for permission to commit American forces, if requested, to resist "armed attack from any country controlled by internationalism" (by *internationalism* Eisenhower meant the forces of communism). Congress agreed in March 1957, establishing the so-called **Eisenhower Doctrine** and providing $200 million in military and economic aid to improve military defenses in the nations of the Middle East.

It did not take long for the Eisenhower Doctrine to be applied. When an internal revolt threatened Jordan's King Hussein in 1957, the White House announced Jordan was "vital" to American interests, moved the U.S. 6th Fleet into the eastern Mediterranean, and supplied more than $10 million in aid. King Hussein put down the revolt, dismissed parliament and all political parties, and instituted authoritarian rule. A year later, when Lebanon's Christian president Camile Chamoun faced an uprising of Muslim nationalistic and anti-West elements, Eisenhower committed nearly fifteen thousand troops to protect the pro-American government. Within three months Washington, without firing a shot, oversaw the formation of a new government and withdrew American forces.

A Protective Neighbor   During the 1952 presidential campaign, Eisenhower charged Truman with following a "Poor Neighbor policy" toward Latin America, allowing the development of economic problems and popular uprisings that had been "skillfully exploited by the Communists." He was most concerned about Guatemala, disapproving of the reformist president, Jacobo Arbenz, who had instituted agrarian reforms by nationalizing thousands of acres of land, much of it owned by the American-based United Fruit Company. These actions led to a CIA effort to remove Arbenz. A CIA-organized and supplied rebel army led by Colonel Carlos Castillo Armas invaded Guatemala on June 18, 1954. Within weeks a new, pro-American government was installed in Guatemala City. But the effort failed to reduce social and economic inequalities or foster goodwill toward the United States. The next crisis was closer to home when a rebellion led by Fidel Castro toppled the Cuban government of Fulgencio Batista, who had controlled the island since the 1940s.

The corrupt and dictatorial Batista had become an embarrassment to the United States, and many Americans believed that Castro could be a pro-American reformist leader. By 1959, rebel forces had control of the island, but by midyear many of Castro's economic and social reforms were endangering American investments and interests, which dominated Cuba's economy. Concerned about Castro's political leanings, Washington tried to push Cuba in the right direction by applying economic pressure. In February 1960, Castro reacted to the American arm twisting by signing an economic pact with the Soviet Union. Eisenhower seethed: Castro was a "madman ... going wild and harming the whole American structure." In March, Eisenhower approved a CIA plan to prepare an attack against Castro. Actual implementation of the plot to overthrow the Cuban leader, however, was left to Eisenhower's successor.

The New Look in Asia Korea was not the only problem in Asia that Eisenhower faced when he took office. Chinese threats continued toward Taiwan and its offshore islands, and a "war of national liberation" raged in French Indochina. In both cases, he continued Truman's policies—supporting the Nationalist Chinese and the French. By 1954, the struggle between France and the **Viet Minh**, the Vietnamese army made up of Communist and other nationalist groups led by Ho Chi Minh, was not going well for Paris. Watching the French military position worsen, Eisenhower announced the **domino theory**, warning that if Indochina fell to communism, the loss "of Burma, of Thailand, of the [Malay] Peninsula, and Indonesia" would certainly follow, endangering Australia and New Zealand. To many it meant that the United States needed to take a more direct role in the conflict.

As Viet Minh forces launched murderous attacks on the beleaguered French fortifications at Dienbienphu, the French—and some members of the Eisenhower administration—wanted American intervention to save the garrison. Eisenhower rejected the idea, saying that "no military victory" was "possible in that kind of theater." The surrender of Dienbienphu on May 7, 1954, left the French and Eisenhower no option but to try to salvage a partial victory at an international conference in Geneva.

But the West could piece together no victory at Geneva either. The **Geneva Agreement** "temporarily" partitioned Vietnam along the 17th parallel and created the neutral states of Cambodia and Laos. Within two years, the two Vietnams were to hold elections to unify the nation, and neither was to enter into military alliances or allow foreign bases on its territory. American strategists called the settlement a "disaster"—half of Vietnam was lost to communism. Showing its displeasure, the United States refused to sign the agreement. Eisenhower immediately moved to support South Vietnam's new government and prime minister, Ngo Dinh Diem. With American blessings, Diem ignored the Geneva-mandated unification elections, quashed his political opposition, and in October 1955 staged a **plebiscite** that created the Republic of Vietnam and elected him president.

---

plebiscite Special election that allows people to either approve or reject a particular proposal.

The Soviets and Cold War Politics   To strengthen the New Look deterrent capability, the Eisenhower administration developed a three-way system to deliver a nuclear attack on the Soviet Union and China. Efforts were intensified to develop an intercontinental and intermediate-range ballistic missile system that could be fired from land bases and from submarines. At the same time, the nation's bomber fleet was improved, introducing the jet-powered B-47. While deterrence was critical, Stalin's death in 1953 offered an opportunity to improve American-Soviet relations. When the Russian premier, Georgii Malenkov, called for "peaceful coexistence," Dulles dismissed the suggestion, but Eisenhower said they should assume that "Malenkov was a reasonable man … and talk accordingly." He called on the Soviets to demonstrate their willingness to cooperate with the West. Malenkov responded positively and some headway followed when the Soviets removed their controls and troops from Austria, but overall, deep-seeded suspicions remained.

In 1955, as both nations continued to test their hydrogen bombs, Eisenhower agreed to a summit meeting in Geneva with the new Soviet leadership team of Nikolai Bulganin and **Nikita Khrushchev**, who had replaced Malenkov. Eisenhower expected no resolution of the two major issues—disarmament and Berlin—but saw the meeting as good public relations. He would make a bold disarmament initiative—the Open Skies proposal—that would earn broad international support. In a dramatic presentation, highlighted by a sudden thunderstorm that momentarily blacked out the conference room, Eisenhower asked the Soviets to share information about military installations and permit aerial reconnaissance to verify the information while work began on general disarmament. Bulganin voiced official interest, but Khrushchev considered the proposal a "very transparent espionage device." In the end, the Geneva Summit ended as most expected, with each side agreeing to disagree, although publicly both Eisenhower and the Soviets said the "spirit of Geneva" reduced East-West tensions.

The spirit of Geneva vanished when Soviet forces invaded Hungary in November 1956 to quell an anti-Soviet revolt. Many Americans favored supporting the Hungarian freedom fighters, but facing the Suez crisis and seeing no way to send aid to the Hungarians without risking all-out war, the administration only watched as the Soviets crushed the revolt. Soviet-American relations cooled, and Eisenhower and Khrushchev jousted with each other over nuclear testing, disarmament, and Germany and Berlin. First one leader and then the other, with little belief in success, offered to end testing and reduce nuclear weapons if certain provisions were met. When in 1958 NATO agreed to include West Germany, the simmering issue of Berlin erupted. When the Soviets stated that Berlin was to be unified under East German control, Eisenhower, joined by the British and French, declared that their forces would remain in West Berlin.

Faced with unflinching Western determination, Khrushchev backed down and suggested that he and Eisenhower exchange visits and hold a summit meeting. East-West relations seemed to improve as Khrushchev took a twelve-day tour of the United States in September 1959, and the two leaders met at a summit in Paris in May of 1960. But a "thaw" in the Cold War failed to materialize. Just

In this cartoon, an American suburban family sits contentedly next to their cozy home with little concern about the delicate Cold War balance between peace and destruction. By 1953, both the United States and the Soviet Union had tested hydrogen bombs and seemed willing to use the A-bomb to protect national interests.

as the summit began, the Soviets shot down an American U-2 spy plane over the Soviet Union and captured its pilot. At first, the United States claimed the U-2 was a stray weather plane, but the Soviets' display of the captured pilot and pictures of the plane's wreckage clearly proved otherwise. In Paris, Eisenhower took full responsibility but refused to apologize for such flights, which he contended were necessary to prevent a "nuclear Pearl Harbor." Khrushchev withdrew from the summit, and Eisenhower canceled his forthcoming trip to the Soviet Union.

Eisenhower remained popular, but the loss of the U-2, Soviet advances in missile technology and nuclear weaponry, and a Communist Cuba only 90 miles from Florida provided the Democrats with strong claims that the Republican administration had been deficient in meeting Soviet threats. In 1960, turning the Republicans' tactics of 1952 against them, Democrats cheerfully accused their opponents of endangering the United States by being too soft on communism.

THE BEST OF TIMES

According to the popular magazine *Reader's Digest,* in 1954 the average American male stood 5 feet 9 inches tall and weighed 158 pounds. He liked brunettes, baseball, bowling, and steak and French fries. In seeking a wife, he could not decide if brains or beauty was more important, but he definitely wanted a wife who could run a home efficiently. The average female was 5 feet 4 inches tall and weighed 132 pounds. She preferred marriage to career, but she wanted to remove the word *obey* from her marriage vows. Both man and woman were enjoying life to the fullest, according to the *Digest,* and buying more of just about everything. The economy appeared to be bursting at the seams, providing jobs, good wages, a multitude of products, and profits.

**The Web
of Prosperity**
The expanding economy was a result of big government, big business, and an expanding population. World War II and the Cold War had created military-industrial-governmental linkages that primed the economy through government spending, what some have labeled "military **Keynesianism**," after the economic theories of Lord John Maynard Keynes. National security needs by 1955 accounted for half of the U.S. budget—equaling about 17 percent of the gross national product—and exceeded the total net incomes of all American corporations.

The connection between government and business went beyond direct spending: millions of research and development dollars flowed into colleges and industries. The electronics industry drew 70 percent of its research money from the government, producing not only new scientific and military technology but marketable consumer goods like the transistor radio and televisions.

In addition, a revolving door seemed to connect government and business positions. Few saw any real conflict of interest even when those from businesses to be regulated staffed regulatory agencies and cabinet positions. Secretary of Defense Wilson, the ex-president of General Motors, later voiced the common view: "What was good for our country was good for General Motors and vice versa." It was an era of "new economics" where, according to a 1952 ad in the *New York Times,* industry's "efforts are not in the selfish interest" but "for the good of many." The Advertising Council called the economic system "people's capitalism" and said it was creating "the highest standard of living ever known by any people ... at any time." Not all agreed that the connections between government and business were without risk. In his farewell address, President

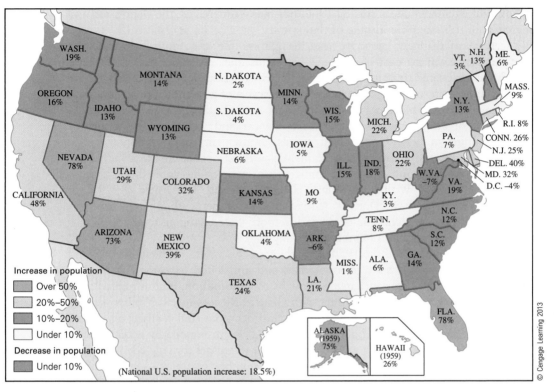

MAP 25.2 Rise of the Sunbelt, 1950–1960

The years after the Second World War saw a continuation of the migration of Americans to the Sunbelt states of the Southwest and the West Coast.

Eisenhower warned of the power of the "military-industrial complex" and its potential threat to the "democratic process."

However, few Americans worried about military-industrial connections when corporate profits doubled between 1948 and 1958 and industrial wages steadily rose from about $55 to $80 a week over the decade. Nor was there much concern that corporations were getting bigger. Many companies were either closing their doors or merging into larger industries to create **conglomerates**. Expanding giant International Telephone and Telegraph, for example, was acquiring construction and insurance firms, food companies, hotels, and other companies not associated with communications.

The outcome of all this explosive business activity was that the GNP reached $500 billion in 1960, double its level in 1940. Exports also doubled, giving the

conglomerates The combination of two or more firms engaging in entirely different businesses.

nation a $5 billion trade surplus by 1960. For many Americans, the Depression and scarcities of the war were a thing of the past.

Central to the new economy was the automobile and those industries and jobs that made the car part of the American landscape. The more than $32 billion Eisenhower allocated to build an interstate highway system represented only a fraction of funds spent on road construction by all levels of government. New and better highways led to more cars, and more cars needed still more roads. By 1960, 75 percent of all Americans had at least one car and were driving millions of miles, stopping at newly constructed motels, amusement parks, shopping malls, drive-in theaters, and fast-food restaurants. Disneyland opened in 1955, with acres of parking lots to accommodate the family cars of people who entered the "Happiest Place on Earth." Within six months a million people had visited the "Magic Kingdom." Meanwhile, McDonald's "drive-to" restaurants, with take-out windows and an assembly-line technique of preparing food, were changing the nation's eating habits, serving a million hamburgers a day by 1963.

The new economics of the 1950s also changed the nature of the workforce and organized labor. In the wake of lost strikes and anti-union legislation in the late 1940s and facing workplace changes wrought by **automation**, unions altered their tactics. Beginning with a new contract with General Motors in 1950, union leaders dropped efforts to gain control over managerial decisions and focused on getting better wages and benefits. GM and other corporations responded by accepting collective bargaining and creating an economic/social safety net that included pensions and health care. Yet despite higher wages, the number of union workers in the workforce fell to 31 percent by 1960. Much of the decline was a consequence of there being fewer industrial workers as the economy shifted to public- and service-sector jobs. By 1956, white-collar workers outnumbered blue-collar workers. Neither the AFL nor the CIO, which merged in 1956, responded well to the shift, showing little interest in recruiting workers from the service sector.

Suburban and Family Culture The suburban housing boom continued to spark the economy and, like the automobile, to shape the American landscape. "We were thrilled to death," recalled one newly arrived suburbanite. "Everyone was arriving with a sense of forward momentum. Everyone was taking courage from the sight of another orange moving van pulling in next door, a family just like us, unloading pole lamps and cribs and Formica dining tables like our own...." Many of the families were moving into a new "ranch" or California-style home, designed to match the most modern family's needs. It was a single-story rectangular or L-shaped house with a simple floor plan, an attached garage, and a family room—sometimes complete with a television, now the focus of the house. Near the family room was the "modern" kitchen with its new appliances that made life easier for the stay-at-home housewife.

At the heart of the home was the American nuclear family. Families were the strength of the nation, and the number of families continued to grow, with

---

automation   A process or system designed so that equipment functions automatically, often replacing workers with machines.

the baby boom peaking at 4.3 million births in 1957. Within the family there were clearly defined roles. Husbands were the breadwinners and directed weekend events. Wives managed the home, cared for the children, and deferred to their husbands' decisions. "There was this pressure to be the perfect housekeeper," remembered one suburban wife. For guidance on how to raise babies and children, millions of Americans turned to Dr. Benjamin Spock's popular book *Baby and Child Care* (1946). A mother's love and positive parental guidance were keys to healthy and well-adjusted children. Strict rules and corporal punishment were to be avoided. To ensure proper gender identity, boys should participate in sports and outdoor activities, whereas girls should concentrate on their appearance and domestic skills. Toy guns and doctor bags were for boys; dolls, tea sets, and nurse kits were for girls. Conforming—being part of the group—was as important for parents as for children. Those not fulfilling those roles were suspected of being homosexual, immature, or simply irresponsible.

Television helped define suburban life. Developed in the 1930s, televisions were not widely available until after the war, and then they were very expensive. But as prices fell the number of homes with a television rocketed from about 9 percent in 1950 to nearly 90 percent by the end of the decade. At the same time, programming developed audience-oriented time slots with cartoons and westerns for children on weekend mornings and sports for dad on Saturday and Sunday afternoons. The most watched time-slot, however, was after dinner and designed for family viewing. By 1960 most people watched television five hours a day.

Among the most popular shows during the family time slot were situation comedies ("sitcoms") like *Father Knows Best* (1953) and *Leave It to Beaver* (1957). They depicted "normal" middle-class families that were white with hardworking fathers and attractive, stay-at-home mothers. The children, usually numbering between two and four, did well in school, rarely worried about the future, and provided humorous dilemmas for Mom to untangle with common sense and sensitivity. After the dislocations of the Depression and the war, stable households seemed to represent the strength and future of the country.

Part of the family's strength and stability, many argued, came from religious faith. "The family that prays together stays together," announced the Advertising Council. Church attendance reached a historic high of 59.5 percent in 1953, and that did not include those who attended religious revivals or listened to religious radio and television programs. Religious leaders like the **Reverend Norman Vincent Peale** and Billy Graham were commonly rated as the most important members of society. Peale's message of Christian positive thinking as a means to improve both the individual and society found a wide audience. More conservative evangelists like Graham questioned society's materialism and stressed a higher level of personal morality, and they drew huge audiences in packed stadiums. While their views on religion and the problems facing America differed, religious leaders were unanimous on the need to promote faith to prevent the spread of Communism. In keeping with the spirit of the times, Congress added "under God" to the Pledge of Allegiance in 1954 and "In God We Trust" to the American currency in 1955.

Consumerism   Another dimension of suburbia was consumerism. Radio and television bombarded their audiences with images of products Americans supposedly needed. The average television watcher saw over five hours a week of ads enticing viewers to indulge themselves by buying goods that would improve their lives. New goods were a sign of success and a matter of status, and Americans were in a shopping mood. "Our old car just didn't cut it," remarked one new home owner. "A car was a real status symbol and who didn't want to impress the neighbors?"

To sell cars and other products, advertisers used images of youth, glamour, sex appeal, and sophistication. When market research showed that it was mostly the middle and upper classes who bought new cars, automobile makers closed the gap in size, equipment, and style between luxury and nonluxury cars. Their ads emphasized "modern" styles with fins and linked the car to the idealized family that saw the "USA in their Chevrolet." The public responded, and a record 8 million new cars were sold by Detroit in 1955.

Increasingly, to pay for cars, televisions, washing machines, toys, and "Mom's night out," Americans were turning to credit, and a new form of credit was available—the all-purpose credit card. The Diner's Club credit card made its debut in 1950, followed by American Express and a host of other plastic cards. By 1958, credit purchases reached $44 billion, more than five times the amount bought on credit in 1946.

Another View of Suburbia   Unlike that of the families shown on television, life in the suburbs was not always idyllic or equal to expectations. "Togetherness" was more often seen on televisions than in real life. Studies found that of eighteen common household chores, men were willing to do three—lock up at night, do yard work, and make repairs—and that more than one-fifth of suburban wives were unhappy with their marriages and lives. Many women complained of the drudgery and boredom of housework and the lack of understanding and affection from their husbands.

Responding to personal motives or economic needs, more married middle-class women were working outside the home, even those with young children (see Figure 25.1). While some sought self-fulfillment in careers, others worked to safeguard their family's existing **standard of living**. Most found part-time jobs or sales-clerk or clerical positions that paid low wages and provided few benefits. *Look* magazine, in a 1956 article, pointed out that about a third of the workforce were women, most of whom were seeking to fill their "hope chest" or to buy "a new home freezer," and happily conceded "the top job rungs to men." Whether they conceded gracefully or not, in the banking sector, women made up 46 percent of the workforce but held only 15 percent of upper-level positions.

The suburbs were also more sexually active than people wanted to admit. **Alfred Kinsey** raised eyebrows when his book *Sexual Behavior in the Human Female* (1953) indicated that a majority of American women had sexual intercourse

---

standard of living   Level of material comfort as measured by the goods, services, and luxuries currently available and affordable.

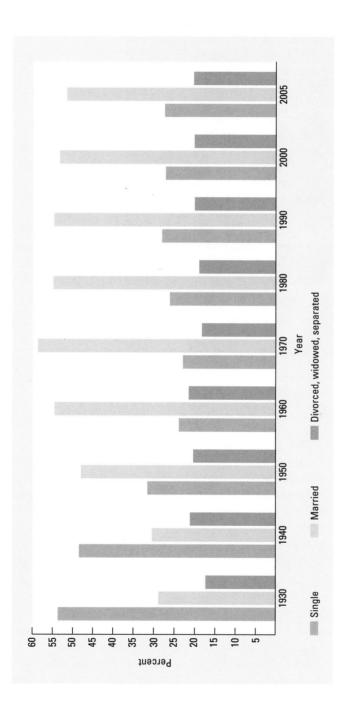

FIGURE 25.1 Marital Status of Women in the Workforce, 1930–2005

This figure shows the percentage of women in the workforce from the Great Depression through 2005. While the number of women who fell into the category of divorced, widowed, and separated remained fairly constant, a significant shift occurred in the number of single and married women in the workforce, with the number of single women declining as the number of married women increased.

Source: U.S. Department of Commerce, *Historical Statistics of the United States, Colonial Times to 1970*, Vol. I (Washington, D.C.: U.S. Government Printing Office, 1970), pp. 20–21, 131–132; and U.S. Department of Commerce, *Statistics of the United States, 1993* (Washington, D.C.: U.S. Government Printing Office, 1993), pp. 74, 399; U.S. Department of Commerce, *Statistical Abstract of the United States: 2003* (Washington, D.C.: U.S. Government Printing Office, 2003), pp. 390–391; Richard Smith and Susan Carlan, eds., *Historical Statistics of the United States: Earliest Times to the Present*, Vol. 2 (New York, Cambridge University Press, 2006), pp. 131–133.

Paul Schutzer/Time Life Pictures/Getty Images

Hosted by Dick Clark, American Bandstand *first aired nationally in 1957, showing teens dancing to the latest top-forty records and helping to create the youth culture. Not all stations agreed that the program was "wholesome," and some refused to air it.*

before marriage and that 25 percent were having extramarital affairs. The steamier side of life was popularized in Grace Metalious's best-selling novel *Peyton Place* (1956), which set America buzzing over the licentious escapades of the residents of a quiet town in New England.

The Trouble with Kids   Nor did children always match the image of the ideal family, and juvenile delinquency became a serious concern for parents and society. Juvenile crime among gangs operating in cities was not new, but as the 1950s progressed, many in the middle-class suburbs were alarmed about the behavior of their own teens who seemed to flout traditional values and behavior. At the center of the problem, many believed, was the public high school, where middle-class kids mixed with children of the "other America." The children of working-class whites, Latinos, and African Americans were attending high school in larger numbers and were thought to be a bad influence. Their clothing choices—T-shirts, jeans, leather jackets—their disrespect for authority, and their music conflicted with middle-class norms. Adding to the problem, experts said, was the availability of the car. It not only allowed teens to escape adult controls but provided "a private lounge for drinking and for petting or sex episodes."

It came down to the values and discipline that the proper family should have. In the film *Rebel Without a Cause* (1955), which starred teen idol James Dean, the rebellious characters came from atypical suburban homes where gender roles were reversed. Audiences saw dominating mothers and fathers who cooked and assumed many traditional housewifely duties. Viewers took home the message that an "improper" family environment bred juvenile delinquents.

The problem with kids also seemed connected to "rock 'n' roll," a term Cleveland disc jockey Alan Freed coined in 1951. He noticed that white teens were buying rhythm and blues (R&B) records popular among African Americans. But he knew that few white households would listen to a radio program playing "black music." Freed decided to play the least sexually suggestive of the R&B records and call the music rock 'n' roll. His radio program, *Moondog's Rock 'n' Roll Party*, was a smash hit. Quickly the barriers between "black music" and "white music" blurred as white singers copied and modified R&B songs to produce **cover records.**

Cover artists like Pat Boone sold millions of records that avoided suggestive lyrics and were heard on hundreds of radio stations that refused to play the original versions by black artists. By mid-decade, African American artists like Chuck Berry, Little Richard, and Ray Charles were successfully "crossing over" and being heard on "white" radio stations. At the same time, white artists, including the 1950s' most dynamic star, **Elvis Presley**, were making their own contributions. Beginning with "Heartbreak Hotel" in 1956, Presley recorded fourteen gold records within two years. In concerts, he drove his audiences into frenzies with sexually suggestive movements that earned him the nickname "Elvis the Pelvis."

Critics argued that rock 'n' roll was responsible for a decline in morals, if not civilization, and called for action. A Catholic Youth Center newspaper asked readers to "smash" rock 'n' roll records because they promoted "a pagan concept of life." But such opponents were waging a losing battle. Rock 'n' roll continued to surge in popularity, and by the end of the decade Dick Clark's *American Bandstand,* a weekly television show featuring teens dancing to rock 'n' roll, was one of the nation's most watched and most accepted programs.

Rejecting Consensus   Rock 'n' roll became tolerated and then accepted by the end of the decade, but homosexuality was another matter.

Kinsey's studies of sexuality found that a sizeable number of gays and lesbians lived "closeted" lives throughout the United States and that an increasingly open gay subculture was centered in major cities. In a society that emphasized the traditional family and feared internal subversion, homosexuals represented deviant behavior that could not be condoned. Some argued homosexuality was a psychological illness, but most considered it a crime subject

---

cover records   A version of a song already recorded by an original artist.

to legal prosecution. **Vice squads** frequently raided gay and lesbian bars, and newspapers often listed the names, addresses, and employers of those arrested. McCarthy targeted gays and lesbians, and a Senate investigating committee concluded that because of sexual perversions and lack of moral fiber, one homosexual could "pollute a Government office." Responding to such views, the Eisenhower administration barred homosexuals from most government jobs. In response to the attacks, many took extra efforts to hide their homosexuality, but some organized to confront the prejudice. In Los Angeles, Henry Hay formed the Mattachine Society in 1951 to fight for homosexual rights, and in San Francisco in 1955 Del Martin and Phyllis Lyon organized a similar organization for lesbians, the Daughters of Bilitis.

Also viewed as extreme were the **Beats**, or "beatniks," a group that rejected the morality and lifestyles of mainstream American culture. Allen Ginsberg in his poem *Howl* (1956) and Jack Kerouac in his novel *On the Road* (1957) denounced American materialism and sexual repression, and glorified a freer, natural life. In an interview in the New York alternative newsweekly, *The Village Voice,* Ginsberg praised the few "hipsters" who were battling "an America gone mad with materialism, a police-state America, a sexless and soulless America." A minority, especially among young college students, found the beatnik critique of "square America" meaningful, but most Americans easily rejected the Beats' message and lifestyles.

Americans could justify the suppression of beatniks and homosexuals because they appeared to mock traditional values of family and community. Other critics of American society, however, were more difficult to dismiss. Several respected writers and intellectuals claimed that the suburban and consumer culture was destructive— stifling diversity and individuality in favor of conformity. Mass-produced homes, meals, toys, fashions, and the other trappings of suburban life, they said, created a gray sameness about Americans. Sociologist David Riesman argued in *The Lonely Crowd* (1950) that postwar Americans, unlike earlier generations, were "outerdirected"—less sure of their values and morals and overly concerned about fitting into a group. Peer pressure, he suggested, had replaced individual thinking. William H. Whyte's controversial *Organization Man* (1956) echoed Riesman's concerns and found that working as a team had surpassed self-reliance as a trait of American workers. Both urged readers to resist being packaged like cake mixes and to reassert their own identities. In another vein, Holden Caulfield, the hero of J. D. Salinger's *The Catcher in the Rye* (1951), unable to find his place in society, merely concluded that the major features of American life were all phony.

OUTSIDE SUBURBIA

The average American depicted by *Reader's Digest* was a white, middle-class suburbanite. This portrait excluded a huge part of the population, especially minorities and the poor. Although the percentage of those living below the poverty line—set during the 1950s at around $3,000 a year—was declining, it was still

---

vice squads   Police units charged with the enforcement of laws dealing with vice—that is, immoral practices such as gambling and prostitution.

over 22 percent and included large percentages of the elderly, minorities, and women heads of households. Even with Social Security payments, as 1959 ended nearly 31 percent of those over 65 lived below the poverty line, with 8 million receiving less than $1,000 a year. Women heads of household contributed another 23 percent of those living in poverty, while throughout rural America, especially among small farmers and farm workers, poverty was common, with most earning $1,000 below the national average of about $3,500. In rural Mississippi, the annual per capita income was less than $900.

Poverty also increased in major cities as blacks and Latinos continued to migrate there. By 1960 half of all African Americans and nearly 80 percent of Latinos lived in urban centers. New York's Puerto Rican community, for example, increased more than 1,000 percent. In some cities, including Atlanta and Washington, D.C., African Americans became the majority, but they rarely exercised any political power proportionate to their numbers. No matter what the city, there was little economic opportunity; nonwhite unemployment commonly reached 40 percent.

At the same time, cities were less able or willing to provide services. Cities lost tax revenues and deteriorated at an accelerating rate as white middle- and working-class families moved into the suburbs and were followed by shopping centers and businesses. When funds were available for urban renewal and development, many city governments, like Miami and Los Angeles, used those funds to relocate and isolate minorities in specific neighborhoods away from developing entertainment, administrative, and shopping areas and upscale apartments. Cities also chose to build wider roads connecting the city to the suburbs rather than invest in mass transit within the city. In South and East Central Los Angeles, freeway interchanges gobbled up 10 percent of the housing space and divided neighborhoods and families. For nearly all minorities, discrimination and **de facto** segregation put upward mobility and escaping poverty even further out of reach.

Integrating Schools

For many African Americans, poverty was just one facet of life. They also faced a legally sanctioned segregated society.

Legal, or **de jure**, segregation existed not only in the South but also in the District of Columbia and several western and midwestern states. Changes had occurred, but most African Americans regarded them as minor victories, indicating no real shift in white America's racial views. By 1952 the NAACP had won cases permitting African American law and graduate students to attend white colleges and universities, even though the separate-but-equal ruling established in 1896 by the Supreme Court in *Plessy v. Ferguson* remained intact.

A step toward more significant change came in 1954 when the Supreme Court considered the case of **Brown v. Board of Education**, *Topeka, Kansas*. The *Brown* case had started four years earlier, when Oliver Brown sued to allow his daughter to attend a nearby white school. The Kansas courts had rejected his suit, pointing out that the availability of a school for African Americans fulfilled the Supreme

---

de facto   Existing in practice, though not officially established by law.

de jure   According to, or brought about by, law, such as "Jim Crow" laws that separated the races throughout the South until passage of the 1964 Civil Rights Act.

Court's separate-but-equal ruling. The NAACP appealed. In addressing the Supreme Court, NAACP lawyer **Thurgood Marshall** argued that the concept of "separate but equal" was inherently self-contradictory. He used statistics to show that black schools were *un*equal in financial resources and the quality and number of teachers. He also used a psychological study indicating that black children educated in a segregated environment suffered from low self-esteem. Marshall stressed that segregated educational facilities, even if physically similar, could never yield equal results.

In 1952 a divided Court was unable to make a decision, but two years later the Court heard the case again. Now sitting as chief justice was **Earl Warren**, the Republican former governor of California who had been appointed to the Court by Eisenhower in 1953. To the dismay of many who had considered Warren a legal conservative, the chief justice moved the Court down new judicial paths. Rejecting social and political consensus, the activist Supreme Court promoted new visions of society as it deliberated racial issues and individual rights. Reflecting the opinion of a unanimous Court, the *Brown* decision stated that "separate educational facilities are inherently unequal." While governor of California in 1947, Warren, following a federal court decision in *Mendez v. Westminister*, had signed legislation ending segregation in education in the state's public schools. In 1955, in addressing how to implement *Brown*, the Court gave primary responsibility to local school boards. Not expecting integration overnight, the Court ordered school districts to proceed with "all deliberate speed." The justices instructed lower federal courts to monitor progress according to this vague guideline.

Reactions to the case were predictable. African Americans and liberals hailed the decision and hoped that segregated schools would soon be an institution of the past. Southern whites vowed to resist integration by all possible means. Virginia passed a law closing any integrated school. Southern congressional representatives issued the **Southern Manifesto**, in which they proudly pledged to oppose the *Brown* ruling. Eisenhower, who believed the Court had erred, refused to support the decision publicly.

While both political parties carefully danced around school integration and other civil rights issues, the school district in Little Rock, Arkansas, moved forward with "all deliberate speed." Central High School was scheduled to integrate in 1957. Opposing integration were the parents of the school's students and Governor Orval Faubus, who ordered National Guard troops to surround the school and prevent desegregation. When Elizabeth Eckford, one of the nine integrating students, walked toward Central High, National Guardsmen blocked her path as a hostile mob roared, "Lynch her! Lynch her!" Spat on by the jeering crowd, she retreated to her bus stop. Central High remained segregated.

For three weeks the National Guard prevented the black students from enrolling. Then on September 20 a federal judge ordered the integration of Central High School. Faubus complied and withdrew the National Guard. But segregationists remained determined to block integration and were waiting for the black students on Monday, September 23, 1957. When they discovered that the nine had slipped into the school unnoticed, the mob rushed the police lines and battered the school doors open. Inside the school, integrating student Melba Patella Beaus thought,

As Elizabeth Eckford approached Little Rock's Central High School, the crowd began to hurl curses, and a National Guardsman blocked her entrance into the school with his rifle. Terrified, she retreated down the street away from the threatening mob. Weeks later, this photograph was taken when Eckford, with army troops protecting her, finally attended—and integrated—Central High School.

Francis Miller/Time Life Pictures/Getty Images

"We were trapped. I'm going to die here, in school." Hurriedly, the students were loaded into cars and warned to duck their heads. School officials ordered the drivers to "start driving, do not stop.... If you hit somebody, you keep rolling, 'cause [if you stop] the kids are dead."

Integration had lasted almost three hours and was followed by rioting throughout the city, forcing the mayor to ask for federal troops to restore order. Faced with insurrection, Eisenhower, on September 24, nationalized the Arkansas National Guard and dispatched a thousand troops of the 101st Airborne Division to Little Rock. Speaking to the nation, the president emphasized that he had sent the federal troops not to integrate the schools but to uphold the law and to restore order. The distinction was lost on most white southerners, who fumed as soldiers protected the nine black students for the rest of the school year.

The following school year (1957–1958), the city closed its high schools rather than integrate them. To prevent such actions, the Supreme Court ruled in **Cooper v. Aaron** (1959) that an African American's right to attend school could not "be nullified openly" or "by evasive schemes for segregation." Little Rock's high schools reopened, and integration slowly spread to the lower grades. But in Little Rock, as in other communities, many white families fled the integrated public schools and enrolled their children in private schools that were beyond the reach of the federal courts. With no endorsement from the White House and entrenched southern opposition, "all deliberate speed" amounted to a snail's pace. By 1965, less than 2 percent of all southern schools were integrated.

IT MATTERS TODAY

The Brown *Decision*

The *Brown v. Board of Education* decision by the Supreme Court remains a milestone in American history. "It is doubtful that any child may reasonably be expected to succeed in life if he is denied the opportunity of an education. Such an opportunity," the Court wrote, "is a right which must be made available to all in equal terms." It raised expectations, it desegregated public schools, but it also fell short of its expectations and has not provided effective integration or equality of education. Other cases have since tested the definitions of equality and the methods used to achieve racial diversity. Until the late 1970s, the Court's decisions upheld the view that race could be used as a determining factor to achieve racial diversity. However, since then, several of the Court's decisions have

indicated that the use of race has discriminated against Caucasians—a reverse discrimination. Is there a way, one Justice recently asked, to decide when the "use of race to achieve diversity" is benign or discriminatory?

- Some argue that the Supreme Court should apply "color-blind" criteria when deciding if institutions and business can use race to create racial diversity. How does this view reflect the view of the original *Brown* decision?
- Research the issues behind the December 2006 Supreme Court cases involving the Seattle, Washington, and Louisville, Missouri, school districts. Compare the issues to the decisions made by the Court on the issue in June 2007.

The Montgomery Bus Boycott While the nation responded to the *Brown* decision, other events involving civil rights grabbed national headlines, including the death of Emmett Till and the Montgomery bus boycott. In 1955, Till, an African American teenager from Chicago, visited relatives in Mississippi and was brutally tortured and murdered for speaking to a white woman—saying "Bye, baby"—without her permission. In the trial that followed, the two confessed murderers were acquitted. It was not an unexpected verdict in Mississippi, but it and the brutality of the murder shocked much of the nation.

Later in 1955, on December 1 in Montgomery, Alabama, **Rosa Parks** refused to give up her seat on a city bus so that a white man could sit. At 42, Mrs. Parks earned $23 a week as a seamstress, and she had not boarded the bus with the intention of disobeying the seating law, although she strongly opposed it. But that afternoon, her fatigue and humiliation were suddenly too much. She refused to move and was arrested.

Hearing of her arrest, local African American community leaders saw an opportunity to contest segregation. When the city and the bus company refused to consider a petition for more equitable bus seating, black leaders called for a boycott of the bus line.

On December 5, 1955, the night before the boycott began, nearly four thousand people filled and surrounded Holt Street Baptist Church to hear

Martin Luther King, Jr., the newly selected leader of the boycott movement—now called the Montgomery Improvement Association. The 26-year-old King firmly believed that the church had a social justice mission and that violence and hatred, even when considered justified, brought only ruin. In shaping that evening's speech, he wrestled with the problem of how to balance disobedience with peace, confrontation with civility, and rebellion with tradition—and his words overcame the contradictions, electrifying the crowd: "We are here this evening to say to those who have mistreated us so long that we are tired of being segregated and humiliated, tired of being kicked about by the brutal feet of oppression." King asked the crowd to boycott the buses, to protest "courageously, and yet with dignity and Christian love," and when confronted with violence, to "bless them that curse you."

On December 6, Rosa Parks was tried, found guilty, and fined $10, plus $4 for court costs. She appealed, and the boycott, 90 percent effective, stretched into days, weeks, and finally months. Police issued basketfuls of traffic tickets to drivers taking part in the car pools that provided transportation for boycotters. Insurance companies canceled their automobile coverage, and acid was poured on their cars. On January 30, 1956, someone threw a stick of dynamite that destroyed King's front porch, almost injuring King's wife and a friend. King remained calm, reminding supporters to avoid violence and persevere. Finally, as the boycott approached its first anniversary, the Supreme Court ruled in *Gayle et al. v. Browser* (1956) that the city's and bus company's policy of segregation was unconstitutional. "Praise the Lord. God has spoken from Washington, D.C.," cried one boycotter.

The Montgomery bus boycott shattered the traditional white view that African Americans accepted segregation, and it marked the beginning of a pattern of nonviolent resistance. Across the South thousands of African Americans were eager to take to the streets and to use the federal courts to achieve equality. Building on the energy generated by the boycott, in 1956, King and other black leaders formed a new civil rights organization, the **Southern Christian Leadership Conference** (SCLC).

Ike and Civil Rights

As the Montgomery boycott steamrolled into the headlines month after month, from the White House came either silence or carefully selected platitudes. When asked, Eisenhower gave elusive replies: "I believe we should not stagnate.... I plead for understanding, for really sympathetic consideration of a problem.... I am for moderation, but I am for progress; that is exactly what I am for in this thing." Personally, Eisenhower believed that government, especially the executive branch, had little role in integration. Max Rabb, the president's adviser on minority affairs, thought the "Negroes were being too aggressive." On a political level, cabinet members and Eisenhower were disappointed in the low number of blacks who had voted Republican in 1952 and 1956.

But not all within the administration were unsympathetic toward civil rights. Attorney General Herbert Brownell drafted the first civil rights legislation since Reconstruction. The **Civil Rights Act of 1957** passed Congress after a year of political maneuvering, having gained the support of Democratic majority leader

Lyndon B. Johnson of Texas. A moderate law, it provided for the formation of a Commission on Civil Rights and opened the possibility of using federal lawsuits to ensure voter rights. A second act passed Congress in 1960 that strengthened efforts to use the courts to gain voting rights, but like its predecessor, it was too weak to counter white opposition and violence in the South. Still, Congress had acted and many African Americans hoped that a new president might provide the needed leadership to achieve equal rights.

STUDY TOOLS

SUMMARY

Had enough?" Republicans asked voters in 1952. Voters responded by electing Eisenhower. Though promising change, Eisenhower in practice chose foreign and domestic policies that continued the basic patterns established by Truman. Republicans were able to cut domestic programs, but public acceptance of existing federal responsibilities prevented any large-scale dismantling of the New Deal. In foreign policy, the New Look relied on new tactics, but Eisenhower continued containment, expanding American influence in southern Asia and the Middle East. Although the Soviets spoke of peaceful coexistence, relations with the Soviet Union deteriorated over the decade, and Moscow seemed to score victories with *Sputnik* and in Cuba.

Reflecting the image of Ike in the White House, the 1950s spawned comforting, if not entirely accurate, images of America centered on affluent suburbs and a growing consumer culture. The postwar trend continued with white working-class and middle-class Americans fulfilling their expectations in a society shaped by cars, expanded purchasing power, and middle-class values. Critics argued that America's middle-class culture bred a social grayness and stifled individualism. Yet life in suburbia did not necessarily fit either the popular or the critics' image. Many people behaved contrary to the supposed norms of family and suburban culture. Teens and young adults, especially, turned to forms of expression that seemed to reject established norms and values.

Outside the suburbs another America existed, where economic realities, social prejudices, and entrenched politics blocked equality and upward mobility. Although declining, poverty persisted, especially in rural America and among minorities living in urban areas. While poverty remained largely ignored, it became increasingly difficult to ignore the actions taken by African Americans to overturn decades of segregation. By the end of the decade, civil rights had emerged as an issue that neither political party nor white, suburban America could avoid.

CHRONOLOGY

THE FIFTIES

1950	Korean War begins
1951	Mattachine Society formed
	Alan Freed's *Moondog's Rock 'n' Roll Party*

1952   Dwight David Eisenhower elected president
United States tests hydrogen bomb

1953   Korean armistice at Panmunjom
CIA helps overthrow Mohammed Mossadegh in Iran
Termination programs for American Indians implemented
Earl Warren appointed chief justice of Supreme Court
Father Knows Best debuts on television
Department of Health, Education, and Welfare created

1954   *Brown v. Board of Education*
Army-McCarthy hearings
CIA helps overthrow Jacobo Arbenz in Guatemala
Geneva Agreement (Vietnam)
SEATO founded

1955   Montgomery bus boycott
AFL-CIO merger
Geneva Summit
Montgomery, Alabama, bus boycott begins

1956   Federal Highway Act
Southern Christian Leadership Conference formed
Eisenhower reelected
Suez crisis
Soviets invade Hungary
Elvis Presley records "Heartbreak Hotel"

1957   Little Rock crisis
Civil Rights Act
Eisenhower Doctrine
United States joins Baghdad Pact
Soviets launch *Sputnik*
Baby boom peaks at 4.3 million births

1958   Berlin crisis
United States sends troops to Lebanon
National Defense Education Act
NASA established

1959   Fidel Castro takes control in Cuba
Nikita Khrushchev visits the United States
Cooper v. Aaron

1960   Soviets shoot down U-2 and capture pilot
Paris Summit

FOCUS QUESTIONS

If you have mastered this chapter, you should be able to answer these questions and explain the terms that follow the questions.

1. What were the popular images of Eisenhower, and how did they compare with reality?

2. What constraints did Eisenhower face in trying to roll back New Deal programs?
3. How did Eisenhower alter the federal government?
4. What were the weaknesses of the New Look and how did Eisenhower address them?
5. What tactics did the Eisenhower administration pursue in the "third world," especially in the Middle East and Latin America, to protect American interests?
6. What new economic factors contributed to prosperity in the 1950s?
7. What stresses and contradictions were at work beneath the placid surface of suburbia? Who voiced criticism and how did they express it?
8. Why were rock 'n' roll and rebellious teens seen as threats to social norms?
9. How did African Americans attack de jure segregation in American society during the 1950s?
10. What role did the federal government play in promoting civil rights?

KEY TERMS

Federal Highway Act (*p. 789*)

Sputnik I (*p. 789*)

Sputnik II (*p. 789*)

National Defense Education Act (*p. 789*)

National Defense Student Loans (*p. 789*)

Army-McCarthy hearings (*p. 789*)

New Look (*p. 790*)

massive retaliation (*p. 790*)

Baghdad Pact (*p. 792*)

Warsaw Pact (*p. 793*)

third world (*p. 793*)

Central Intelligence Agency (*p. 793*)

Shah Mohammad Reza Pahlavi (*p. 793*)

Eisenhower Doctrine (*p. 794*)

Viet Minh (*p. 795*)

domino theory (*p. 795*)

Geneva Agreement (*p. 795*)

Nikita Khrushchev (*p. 796*)

Keynesianism (*p. 798*)

Reverend Norman Vincent Peale (*p. 801*)

Alfred Kinsey (*p. 802*)

Elvis Presley (*p. 805*)

Beats (*p. 806*)

Brown v. Board of Education (*p. 807*)

Thurgood Marshall (*p. 808*)

Earl Warren (*p. 808*)

Southern Manifesto (*p. 808*)

Cooper v. Aaron (*p. 809*)

Rosa Parks (*p. 810*)

Martin Luther King, Jr. (*p. 811*)

Southern Christian Leadership Conference (*p. 811*)

Civil Rights Act of 1957 (*p. 811*)

26

GREAT PROMISES, BITTER DISAPPOINTMENTS, 1960–1968

CHAPTER OUTLINE

• The Politics of Action • Flexible Response • Defining a New
Presidency • New Voices • Study Tools

THE POLITICS OF ACTION

Republicans had every reason to worry as the 1960 presidential campaign neared. The last years of the 1950s were not kind to the Republican Party. Neither the president nor Republicans nor Congress appeared able to deal with the problems of the country—civil rights agitation, a slowing economy, and a soaring national debt that had reached $488 billion. Cold War victories seemed equally illusive as the Soviets launched *Sputnik* and gained a foothold in Cuba. Vice President Richard Nixon calculated the Republican candidate would have to get practically all Republican votes, more than half of the independents—and, in addition, the votes of 5 to 6 million Democrats to become president.

The 1960 Campaign   On the Democratic side stood John Fitzgerald Kennedy, a youthful, vigorous senator from Massachusetts. A Harvard graduate, Kennedy came from a wealthy Catholic family. Some worried about his young age (43) and lack of experience. Others worried about his religion—no Catholic had ever been elected president. To offset these possible liabilities, Kennedy astutely added the politically savvy Senate majority leader Lyndon Johnson of Texas to the ticket, called for a new generation of leadership, and suggested that those who were making religion an issue were bigots. He challenged the nation to enter a **New Frontier** to improve the overall quality of life of all Americans, and to stand fast against the Communist threat. He offered action, and empowerment to the government, people, and institutions.

The 1960 presidential race was, at the time, the closest in recent history, with many people believing that the outcome hinged on the public's perception of the candidates during their nationally televised debates. The majority of viewers believed that Kennedy (on page) won the debates and looked more in control and presidential than Nixon (next page).

© Bettmann/Corbis

Facing Kennedy was Nixon. To distance himself from the image of Eisenhower's leadership, he promised a forceful, energetic presidency, vowing to improve the quality of life and support civil rights. To distinguish himself from Kennedy, he emphasized his executive experience and history of anticommunism. Several political commentators called the candidates "two peas in a pod" and speculated that the election would probably hinge on appearances more than on issues.

Trailing in the opinion polls and hoping to give his campaign a boost, Nixon agreed to televised debates. Kennedy seized the opportunity, recognizing that the candidate who appeared more calm and knowledgeable—more "presidential"—would "win" each debate. Before the camera's eye, in the war of images, Kennedy appeared fresh and confident and spoke directly to the camera. Nixon appeared tired and haggard and looked at Kennedy rather than the camera. The contrasts were critical. Unable to see Nixon, the radio audience believed he won the debates, but to the 70 million television viewers, the winner was the self-assured Kennedy. The televised debates helped Kennedy, but victory depended on his holding the Democratic coalition together, maintaining southern Democratic support while wooing African American and liberal voters. The Texan Johnson used his political clout to keep the South largely loyal while Kennedy blasted the lack of Republican leadership on civil rights. Every vote was critical but when the ballots were counted, Kennedy had secured popular and electoral victories, although Nixon carried more states, 25 to 21.

© Bettmann/Corbis

The New
Frontier

The weather in Washington was frigid when Kennedy gave his inaugural address, but his speech fired the imagination of the nation. He pledged to march against "the common enemies of man: tyranny, poverty, disease, and war itself." He then invited all Americans to participate, exhorting them to "ask not what your country can do for you; ask what you can do for your country." Believing that most of the nation's problems were "technical" and could be solved by experts, Kennedy selected advisers with know-how who were willing to take action. He chose from the ranks of Rhodes scholars, Harvard professors, and successful businessmen, including Ford Motor Company President Robert McNamara, who was tapped for secretary of defense. In a more controversial move, Kennedy named his brother Robert as attorney general. Many hailed Kennedy's choices as representing "the best and the brightest." But not everyone thought so. Referring to their lack of political background, Speaker of the House Sam Rayburn, a Democrat, remarked that he would "feel a whole lot better ... if just one of them had run for sheriff once."

Kennedy asked Congress for a wide range of domestic programs, including a national health system and increased federal aid to education, but, like Truman, he received only modest results. By 1963, Congress had approved small increases in Social Security, the minimum wage (to $1.25 an hour), and

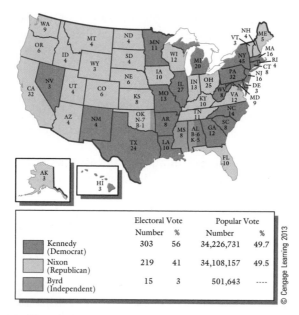

	Electoral Vote		Popular Vote	
	Number	%	Number	%
Kennedy (Democrat)	303	56	34,226,731	49.7
Nixon (Republican)	219	41	34,108,157	49.5
Byrd (Independent)	15	3	501,643	----

© Cengage Learning 2013

MAP 26.1 Presidential Election, 1960

In one of the closest elections in American history in terms of the popular vote, Kennedy only narrowly outpolled Nixon. Kennedy's more commanding victory in the electoral vote generated some discussion about the consequences of the Electoral College one day producing a president who had failed to carry the popular vote, a situation that the election of 2000 did create.

a housing and **urban renewal** bill. He had better luck with the economy, which grew by 13 percent.

To spur the economy out of a recession that began in 1960, Kennedy turned to the "**new economics**" advocated by Walter Heller, his chairman of the Council of Economic Advisers. Heller recommended an aggressive Keynesian use of monetary and **fiscal policies** including tax cuts to stimulate the economy. While the new economics helped, it was the nearly 10 percent increase in defense spending that energized the economy. The Soviets were still leading the missile race, and Soviet cosmonaut Yuri Gagarin had recently orbited the earth. Congress also approved more money for NASA and the Apollo program to send a man to the moon and back. In 1969, after the expenditure of nearly $33 billion, Neil Armstrong would become the first human to step on the surface of the moon.

Kennedy and Civil Rights   When Kennedy was elected African Americans showed a guarded confidence that the new administration would take a more active role in aiding the civil rights movement.

urban renewal   Effort to revitalize run-down areas of cities by providing federal funding for the construction of apartment houses, office buildings, and public facilities.

fiscal policy   The use of government spending to stimulate or slow down the economy.

At the same time, most realized that the movement should not wait quietly for Kennedy to act. Civil rights activists continued to build on momentum created by the **sit-in** movement, which had begun in February 1960 when four black freshmen at North Carolina Agricultural and Technical College in Greensboro, North Carolina, decided to integrate the public lunch counter at the local F. W. Woolworth store. They entered the store, sat down at the lunch counter, and ordered a meal. Refused service, but not arrested, they sat until the store closed. The next day twenty black A&T students sat at the lunch counter demanding service.

The movement quickly spread to more than 140 cities, including some outside the South, in Nevada, Illinois, and Ohio. In some cities, including Greensboro, integration was achieved with a minimum of resistance. But elsewhere, particularly in the Deep South, thousands of participants in sit-ins were beaten and jailed. Most of those taking part were young and initially unorganized, but as the movement grew, civil rights groups moved to incorporate the new tactic and its practitioners. In April 1960, SCLC official Ella Baker helped form the **Student Nonviolent Coordinating Committee** (SNCC, pronounced "snick"), a new civil rights organization built around the sit-in movement. Although its statement of purpose emphasized nonviolence, SNCC members were more militant than other civil rights activists. As one stated, "We do not intend to wait placidly for those rights which are already legally and morally ours."

Despite the sit-ins, with southern Democrats entrenched in Congress, Kennedy saw little reason to "raise hell" and waste legislative efforts on civil rights. Instead, he relied on limited executive action, appointing African Americans to federal positions (more than any previous president), including NAACP lawyer Thurgood Marshall to the U.S. Court of Appeals. Civil rights activists applauded, but pointed out that Kennedy also appointed segregationists and was not rushing to fulfill his campaign pledge to ban segregation in federal housing. (Kennedy signed the order in November 1962.)

To prod executive action, James Farmer of the Congress of Racial Equality (CORE) announced a series of **"freedom rides"** to force integration in southern bus stations. In December 1960, the Supreme Court had ruled in *Boynton v. Virginia* that all interstate buses, trains, and terminals were to be desegregated, and Farmer intended to make that decision a reality. The buses of riders left Washington, D.C., in May 1961, headed toward Alabama and Mississippi. Trouble was anticipated, and in Anniston, Alabama, angry whites attacked the buses, setting them on fire and severely beating several freedom riders. "[I]t was going to be the end of me," one freedom rider recalled thinking when his bus caught fire. Some buses continued on to Birmingham where the savagery continued. As Farmer hoped, the violence forced the attorney general to place federal agents on the buses. Robert Kennedy also negotiated state and local protection for the riders through Alabama. When the buses arrived in Montgomery, Alabama, however, the police and National Guard escorts vanished, and a large mob attacked the riders and federal agents. Furious, the attorney general deputized local federal officials as marshals and ordered them to escort the freedom riders to the state line, where Mississippi forces would take over. Battered and bloodied, the riders continued to the state capital, Jackson. There they were

MAP 26.2 Shifts in African American Population Patterns, 1940–1960

During and after the Second World War, large numbers of African Americans left the rural South and migrated to new locations. Which states had the largest percentage of outmigration? Which saw the greatest percentage of population increase? How might this migration have affected American life?

peacefully arrested for violating Mississippi's recently passed **public order laws**. The jails quickly filled as more freedom riders arrived and were arrested—328 by the end of the summer. The freedom rides ended in September 1961 when the administration declared that the Interstate Commerce Commission would uphold the Supreme Court decision prohibiting segregation. Faced with direct federal involvement, most state and local authorities desegregated bus and train terminals.

Robert Kennedy hoped similar direct involvement would ease the integration of the University of Mississippi by **James Meredith** in September 1962. A hundred

public order laws   Laws passed by many southern communities to discourage civil rights protests; the laws allowed the police to arrest anyone suspected of intending to disrupt public order.

federal marshals arrived to guard Meredith, but thousands of white students and nonstudents attacked Meredith and the marshals. Two people were killed, and nearly all the marshals were injured before five thousand army troops arrived and restored order. Protected by federal forces, Meredith finished the year. In May 1963, the University of Mississippi had its first African American graduate.

As Meredith prepared to graduate, Martin Luther King Jr. organized a series of protest marches to overturn segregation in Birmingham. King expected a violent white reaction, which would force federal intervention and raise national awareness and support. On Good Friday, 1963, King led the first march. He was quickly arrested and, from his cell, wrote a nineteen-page "letter" defending his confrontational tactics. The "Letter from a Birmingham Jail" called for immediate and continuous peaceful civil disobedience. Freedom was "never given voluntarily by the oppressor," King asserted, but "must be demanded by the oppressed." Smuggled out of jail, read aloud in churches, and printed in newspapers across the nation, the letter rallied support for King's efforts.

In Birmingham the marches continued, and on May 3 young and old alike filled the city's streets. Sheriff "Bull" Connor's police attacked the marchers with nightsticks, attack dogs, and high-pressure fire hoses. Television caught it all, including the arrest of more than thirteen hundred battered and bruised children. Connor's brutality not only horrified much of the American public but also caused many Birmingham blacks to reject the tactic of nonviolence. The following day, some clashed with the police, and fearing more violence, King and Birmingham's business element met on May 10. To ease tensions, business owners agreed to hire black salespeople. But neither the agreement nor King's pleading halted the violence, and two days later President Kennedy ordered three thousand troops to Birmingham to maintain order and to uphold the integration agreement. "The sound of the explosion in Birmingham," King observed, "reached all the way to Washington."

Birmingham encouraged Kennedy to make civil rights a priority. In June 1963, he announced that America could not be truly free "until all its citizens were free" and sent Congress civil rights legislation that would mandate integration in public places. To pressure Congress to act on the bill, King and other civil rights leaders organized a **March on Washington**. During the August 28 march, King gave an address that electrified the throng. He warned about a "whirlwind of revolt" if black rights were denied. "I have a dream," he offered, "that my four little children will one day live ... where they will not be judged by the color of their skin but by the content of their character ... that even Mississippi could become an oasis of freedom and justice" and that "all of God's children, black men and white men, Jews and Gentiles, Protestants and Catholics, will be able to join hands and sing ... 'Free at last! Free at last! Thank God almighty, we are free at last!'" It was a stirring speech, but it did not move Congress to act. The civil rights bill stalled in committee, while in the South whites vowed to maintain segregation, and racial violence continued. In Birmingham, within weeks of King's speech, a church bombing killed four young black girls attending Sunday school.

"Letter from a Birmingham Jail"

In 1963, Martin Luther King Jr. wrote and smuggled out of a Birmingham jail a lengthy letter calling for support for his civil rights struggle. The letter was in response to those, especially within the clergy, who argued that his confrontational approach of disobedience generated too much backlash and that negotiation was a better course. He sought not only to address that issue of disobedience to "unjust laws," but to point out that he was a centrist in responding to segregation and discrimination. Working from an assumption that "[o]ppressed people cannot remain oppressed forever," King asserted that his path was the only way out of a "frightening racial nightmare." He rejected both "the do-nothingism" of those worn out and "drained of self-respect" by racism, and the angry voices of black nationalists, who had "lost faith in America [and] ... concluded that the white man is an incurable 'devil.'" He offered choices—choices that are relevant today.

- How does one determine what laws are just and unjust? Can unjust laws be constitutionally correct?
- What issues in today's society and world present similar choices that King mentions in the letter? What alternatives really exist?

FLEXIBLE RESPONSE

From day one, President Kennedy favored foreign over domestic policy. In his inaugural address, he dropped most of the material on domestic policy and concentrated on foreign policy, generating the powerful lines: "We shall pay any price, bear any burden, meet any hardship, ... to assure the survival and success of liberty." Advised by his close circle of "action intellectuals," Kennedy was anxious to meet whatever challenges the United States faced.

To back up his foreign policies, Kennedy instituted a new defense strategy called **flexible response** and significantly expanded military spending to pay for it. Flexible response involved continuing support for NATO and other multilateral alliances, plus further development of nuclear capabilities and **intercontinental ballistic missiles** (ICBMs). Flexible response also centered on conventional, nonnuclear warfare. With increased budgets, each branch of the service sought new weapons and equipment.

The world's developing and third world nations were a special concern. Khrushchev had just announced Moscow's support for "wars of national liberation" as a means to expand communism, and Kennedy meant to thwart that threat. To strengthen pro-Western governments with advisers and to combat revolutionaries, special counterinsurgency forces, such as the Green Berets, were

intercontinental ballistic missiles (ICBMs) Missiles whose path cannot be changed once launched; their range can be from a few miles to intercontinental. In 2003 an estimated thirty-five nations had ballistic missiles.

developed. The military commitment, though, was second to wider economic strategies that provided direct government aid and private investment to "friendly" nations. This effort also included the personal involvement of American volunteers participating in the **Peace Corps**. Beginning in March 1961, more than ten thousand idealistic young Americans enrolled for two years to help win the "hearts and minds" of what Kennedy called "the rising peoples" around the world, staffing schools, constructing homes, building roads, and making other improvements.

Confronting Castro and the Soviets   Castro's success in Cuba reinforced the idea that developing nations of Latin America and the Caribbean were important battlegrounds in the struggle against communism. Seeking a new approach to Latin America, in 1961, Kennedy introduced the **Alliance for Progress**, a foreign-aid package promising more than $20 billion. In return, Latin American governments were to introduce land and tax reforms and commit themselves to improving education and their people's standard of living. Kennedy believed this plan could "successfully counter the Communists in the Americas." Results fell short of expectations. The United States granted far less aid than proposed, and Latin American governments implemented few reforms and frequently squandered the aid. Throughout the 1960s in Latin America, the gap between rich and poor widened, and the number of military dictatorships increased.

The Alliance for Progress, however, did not address the problem of Castro. Determined to remove the Cuban dictator, Kennedy implemented the Eisenhower administration's covert plan to topple him. In 1960, the Central Intelligence Agency (CIA) had begun training Cuban exiles and mercenaries for an invasion of Cuba, and Kennedy gave the green light to launch the mission in April 1961. On April 17, more than fourteen hundred "liberators" landed at the *Bahía de Cochinos*, the **Bay of Pigs**. Within three days Castro's forces had captured or killed most of the invaders. Kennedy took responsibility for the fiasco but indicated no regrets and vowed to continue the "relentless struggle" against Castro and communism. Responding to Kennedy's orders, U.S. planners devised **Operation Mongoose** and other operations that sponsored about thirty attempts to assassinate Castro and CIA-backed raids that destroyed roads, bridges, factories, and crops.

After the Bay of Pigs disaster, in early June 1961, Kennedy met with Soviet leader Nikita Khrushchev in Vienna. With both men eager to show their toughness, the issue of Berlin was especially worrisome, because Khrushchev was threatening to sign a peace treaty with East Germany that would give the East Germans full control of all four zones of the city.

Returning home, Kennedy asked for massive increases in military spending, tripled the draft, and called fifty-one thousand reservists to active duty. Back in Moscow, Khrushchev renewed atmospheric nuclear weapons testing and reaffirmed his determination to oust the Allies from Berlin. Kennedy responded by beginning American nuclear testing and voicing his strong support for West Berlin. Some within the administration advocated the use of force if the East

Germans or the Soviets interfered with West Berlin. With both sides posturing, many feared armed confrontation.

In August 1961, the tension finally broke. The Soviets and East Germans suddenly erected a wall between East and West Berlin to block refugees fleeing East Germany and Eastern Europe. Although the **Berlin Wall** challenged Western ideals of freedom, it did not directly threaten the West's presence in West Berlin.

The Berlin crisis paled beside the possibility of nuclear confrontation over Cuba in October 1962. On October 14, an American U-2 spy plane discovered that medium-range nuclear missile sites were being built on the island. Launched from Cuba, such missiles would drastically reduce the time for mobilizing a U.S. counterattack on the Soviet Union. Kennedy promptly decided on a showdown with the Soviets and mustered a small crisis staff.

The military offered a series of recommendations ranging from a military invasion to a "surgical" air strike to destroy the missiles. These were rejected as too dangerous, possibly inviting a Soviet attack on West Berlin or on American nuclear missile sites in Turkey. President Kennedy, supported by his brother, the attorney general, decided to impose a naval blockade around Cuba until Khrushchev met the U.S. demand to remove the missiles. On Monday, October 22, Kennedy went on television and radio to inform the public of the missile sightings and his decision to quarantine Cuba. As 180 American warships got into position to stop Soviet ships carrying supplies for the missiles, army units converged on Florida. The **Strategic Air Command** (SAC) kept a fleet of nuclear-armed B-52 bombers in the air at all times. On Wednesday, October 24, confrontation and perhaps war seemed imminent as two Soviet freighters and a Russian submarine approached the quarantine line. Robert Kennedy recalled, "We were on the edge of a precipice with no way off." Voices around the world echoed his anxiety.

The Soviet vessels, however, stopped short of the blockade. Khrushchev had decided not to test Kennedy's will. After a series of diplomatic maneuvers, the two sides reached an agreement based on an October 26 message from Khrushchev: if the United States agreed not to invade Cuba, the Soviets would remove their missiles. Khrushchev sent another letter the following day that called for the United States to remove existing American missiles in Turkey. Kennedy ignored the second message, and the Soviets agreed to remove their missiles without a public link to missiles in Turkey. Keeping its unpublicized promise to the Soviets, the United States withdrew all of its missiles in Turkey and Italy by April 1963. The world breathed a collective sigh of relief. Kennedy basked in what many viewed as a victory in the **Cuban missile crisis**, but he recognized how near the world had come to nuclear war and concluded that it was time to improve Soviet-American relations. A "hot line" telephone link was established between Moscow and Washington to allow direct talks in case of another East-West crisis.

In a major foreign-policy speech in June 1963, Kennedy suggested an end to the Cold War and offered that the United States, as a first step toward improving relations, would halt its nuclear testing. By July, American-Soviet negotiations had produced the **Limited Test Ban Treaty**, which forbade those who signed to conduct nuclear tests in the atmosphere, in space, and under the seas. Underground testing was still allowed. By October 1963, one hundred nations had signed the treaty, although the two newest atomic powers, France and China, refused to participate and continued to test in the atmosphere.

Vietnam

South Vietnam represented one of the most challenging issues Kennedy faced. Like Eisenhower, Kennedy saw it as a place where the United States' flexible response could stem communism and develop a stable, democratic nation. But by 1961, President **Ngo Dinh Diem** was losing control of his nation. South Vietnamese Communist rebels, the **Viet Cong**, controlled a large portion of the countryside, having battled Diem's troops, the Army of the Republic of Vietnam (ARVN), to a standstill. Military advisers argued that American troops were necessary to turn the tide. Kennedy was more cautious. "The troops will march in, the bands will play," he said privately, "the crowds will cheer; and in four days everyone will have forgotten. Then we will be told we have to send in more troops. It's like taking a drink. The effect wears off and you have to take another." The South Vietnamese forces would have to continue to do the fighting, but the president agreed to send more "advisers." By November 1963, the United States had sent $185 million in military aid and had committed sixteen thousand advisers to Vietnam—compared with only a few hundred in 1961.

The Viet Cong were only part of the problem. Diem's administration was unpopular, out of touch with the people, and unwilling to heed Washington's pleas for political and social reforms. Some were even concerned that Diem might seek an accord with North Vietnam, and by autumn of 1963, Diem and his inner circle seemed more a liability than an asset. American officials in Saigon secretly informed several Vietnamese generals that Washington would support a change of government. The army acted on November 1, killing Diem and installing a new military government. The change of government, however, brought neither political stability nor improvement in the ARVN's capacity to fight the Viet Cong.

Death in Dallas

With his civil rights and tax-cut legislation in limbo in Congress, Kennedy in late 1963 watched his popularity rating drop below 60 percent. He decided to visit Texas in November to try to heal divisions within the Texas Democratic Party. He was assassinated there on November 22, 1963. The police quickly captured the reputed assassin, Lee Harvey Oswald. Two days later a local nightclub owner and gambler, Jack Ruby, shot Oswald to death in the basement of the police station.

Many wondered whether Kennedy's assassination was the work of Oswald alone or part of a larger conspiracy. To dispel rumors, the government hastily formed a commission headed by Chief Justice Earl Warren to investigate the assassination and determine if others were involved. The commission hurriedly examined most, but not all available evidence and announced that Oswald was a psychologically disturbed individual who had acted alone. No other gunmen were involved, nor was there any conspiracy. While many Americans accepted the conclusions of the Warren Commission, others continued to find errors in the report and to suggest additional theories about the assassination.

Kennedy's assassination traumatized the nation. Many people idealized the fallen president as a brilliant, innovative chief executive who combined vitality, youth, and good looks with forceful leadership and good judgment. Lyndon B. Johnson, sworn in as president as he flew back to Washington on the plane carrying Kennedy's body, did not appear to be cut from the same cloth. Kennedy had attended the best eastern schools, enjoyed the cultural and social life associated with wealth, and surrounded himself with intellectuals. Johnson, a product of public schools and a state teachers college, distrusted intellectuals. Raised in the hill country of Texas, his passion was politics. By 1960, his congressional experiences were unrivaled: he had served in the House of Representatives and in the Senate, where he had become Senate majority leader. Johnson knew how to wield political power and get things done in Washington.

Defining a New Presidency

As president, Johnson described himself as a New Dealer and told one adviser that Kennedy was "a little too conservative to suit my taste." Johnson wanted to build a better society, "where progress is the servant of the neediest." Recognizing the political opening generated by the assassination, Johnson immediately committed himself to Kennedy's agenda, and in January 1964 he expanded on it by announcing an "unconditional war on poverty."

Old and New Agendas   Throughout 1964, Johnson transformed Kennedy's quest for action into his own quest for social reform. Wielding his considerable political skill, he moved Kennedy's tax cut and civil rights bill out of committee and toward passage. The Keynesian tax cut (the Tax Reduction Act) became law in February but the civil rights bill moved more slowly, especially in the Senate, where it faced a stubborn southern **filibuster**. Johnson traded political favors for Republican backing to silence the fifty-seven-day filibuster, and the **Civil Rights Act of 1964** became law on July 2. The act made it illegal to discriminate for reasons of race, religion, or gender in places and businesses that served the public. Putting force behind the law, Congress established a federal Fair Employment Practices Committee (FEPC) and

---

filibuster   Using obstructionist tactics, especially prolonged speechmaking, to delay legislative action.

empowered the executive branch to withhold federal funds from institutions that violated the act's provisions.

By August 1964, the War on Poverty had begun, aimed at benefiting the 20 percent of the population who were classified as poor. In 1962, social critic Michael Harrington had alerted the public to widespread poverty in America with his book *The Other America*. Subsequently, the U.S. government, which defined the poverty line as $3,130 for an urban household of four and $1,925 for a rural family, found that almost 40 percent of the poor (15.6 million) were under the age of 18.

The **War on Poverty** was to be fought on two fronts: expanding economic opportunities and improving the social environment. The August 1964 Economic Opportunity Act established an Office of Economic Opportunity to coordinate a variety of programs that Johnson stated would "help more Americans, especially young Americans, to escape from squalor and misery." The cornerstones were education and job training. The Job Corps program enrolled unemployed teens and young adults (16 to 21) lacking skills, while Head Start reached out to disadvantaged pre-kindergarten children to provide important thinking and social skills. Another program, called Volunteers in Service to America (VISTA), sent service-minded Americans to help improve life in regions of poverty. Among the most ambitious programs was the Community Action Program (CAP), which allowed disadvantaged community organizations to target local needs by giving them direct access to federal funds. The program never met expectations, but it helped generate local activism and led to services like legal aid and community health clinics.

As the 1964 presidential election neared, Johnson was confident. He could claim credit for tax cuts, a civil rights bill, and starting a war on poverty. Public opinion polls showed significant support for the president in all parts of the nation, except the South.

Opposing Johnson's liberal programs were conservatives and Republicans energized by the emerging **New Right**. Intellectually led by William F. Buckley and the *National Review*, conservatives cried that liberalism was destroying vital traditional American values of localism, self-help, and individualism. They opposed government activism, the growth of the welfare state, and the decisions of the Warren Court. From the mid-1950s through the 1960s, the Warren Court was at the forefront of liberalism, altering the obligations of the government and expanding the rights of citizens over the states's authority. Its decisions in the 1950s contributed to the legal base for the 1964 Civil Rights Act and began to reverse earlier decisions about the rights of those accused of crimes. Between 1961 and 1969, the Court issued over two hundred criminal justice decisions that, according to critics, hampered law enforcement. Among the most important were *Gideon v. Wainwright* (1963), *Escobedo v. Illinois* (1964), and *Miranda v. Arizona* (1966). In those rulings the Court declared that all defendants have a right to an attorney, even if the state must provide one, and that those arrested must be informed of their right to remain silent and to have an attorney present during questioning (the *Miranda* warning).

Further angering conservatives was a series of decisions that expanded freedom of expression, separated church and state, and redrew voting districts. Especially

President Johnson's Great Society greatly expanded the role of society in the lives of Americans through passage of civil rights, welfare, and education legislation. In this picture, President Johnson signs legislation establishing Medicare. His wife, Lady Bird, and Vice President Hubert Humphrey watch in the background.

onerous were two decisions in which the Warren Court applied the First Amendment—separation of church and state—to state and local actions that allowed prayer and Bible reading in public schools. Both decisions produced outcries of protest across the nation and from Democrats and Republicans in Congress. As Governor George Wallace of Alabama put it, "We find the court ruling against God." Congress introduced over 150 resolutions demanding that reading the Bible and praying aloud be permitted in schools. Still, the Court's decisions remained law, and communities and classrooms complied.

The New Right also complained that the Court's actions not only undermined the tradition of religion but condoned and promoted immorality. The Court weakened "community standards" in favor of broader ones regarding "obscene" and sexually explicit materials in *Jacobvellis v. Ohio* (1963). In the 1964 *Griswold v. Connecticut* decision, the Court attacked the state's responsibility to establish moral standards; it overturned Connecticut's laws that forbade the sale of contraceptives, arguing that individuals have a right to privacy that the state cannot abridge.

Leading the Republican assault against the values of liberalism was Senator **Barry Goldwater** of Arizona. Plainspoken and direct, Goldwater opposed the 1964 Civil Rights Act, "Big Government," and New Deal–style programs. Riding a wave of conservative and New Right support, Goldwater seized the nomination for the presidency, launching an attack on liberalism and vowing to implement an anti-Communist crusade. When he appeared willing not only to commit American troops in Vietnam but also to use nuclear weapons against Communist nations, including Cuba and North Vietnam, Democrats quickly painted him as a dangerous radical. Johnson, meanwhile, promoted his Great Society and promised that "American boys" would not "do the fighting for Asian boys." Johnson won easily in a lopsided election.

Implementing the Great Society

Not only did Goldwater lose, but so too did many Republicans—moderates and conservatives—as more than forty new Democrats entered Congress. Armed with a seeming mandate for action, Johnson pushed forward legislation to enact his **Great Society**. He told aides that they must hurry before the natural opposition of politics returned. Between 1964 and 1968, more than sixty Great Society programs were put in place (see Table 26.1). Most sought to provide better economic and social opportunities by removing barriers thrown up by health, education, region, and race.

One of Johnson's goals was to further equality for African Americans. Within months of his election, he signed an executive order that, like the old Fair Employment Practices Commission, required government contractors to practice nondiscrimination in hiring and on the job. He also appointed the

TABLE 26.1 | WAR ON POVERTY AND GREAT SOCIETY PROGRAMS, 1964–1966

1964	1965	1966
Tax Reduction Act	Elementary and Secondary Education Act	Demonstration Cities and Metropolitan Development Act
Civil Rights Act	Voting Rights Act	Motor Vehicle Safety Act
Economic Opportunity Act	Medical Care Act (Medicare and Medicaid)	Truth in Packaging Act
Equal Employment Opportunity Commission	Head Start (Office of Economic Opportunity)	Model Cities Act
Twenty-fourth Amendment	Upward Bound (Office of Economic Opportunity)	Clean Water Restoration Act
Job Corps (Office of Economic Opportunity)	Water Quality Act and Air Quality Act	Department of Transportation
Legal services for the poor	Department of Housing and Urban Development	
VISTA	National Endowment for the Arts and Humanities	
Wilderness Act	Immigration and Nationality Act	

first African American to the cabinet, Secretary of Housing and Urban Development Robert Weaver; the first African American woman to the federal courts, Judge Constance Baker Motley; and the first African American to the Supreme Court, Justice Thurgood Marshall.

Blacks applauded the president's actions but realized that appointments and the civil rights act did not end discrimination or poverty and that large pockets of active opposition to civil rights remained—especially in Alabama and Mississippi. A major goal was to expand black voting in the South. For nearly one hundred years, most southern whites had viewed voting as an activity for whites only and, through the poll tax and their control of the ballot, had maintained their political power and a segregated society. The ratification of the Twenty-fourth Amendment (banning the poll tax) in January 1964 was a major step toward dismantling that system, and by mid-1964 plans were under way to increase black voter registration. Bob Moses of SNCC organized a **Freedom Summer** in Mississippi. Whites and blacks opened "Freedom Schools" to teach literacy and black history, stress black pride and achievements, and help residents register to vote. In Mississippi, as in several other southern states, a voter literacy test required that all questions be answered to the satisfaction of a white registrar. Thus a question calling for "a reasonable interpretation" of an obscure section of the state constitution could be used to block blacks from registering.

In the face of white hostility, voter registration was dangerous work. "You talk about fear," an organizer told recruits. "It's like the heat down there, it's continually oppressive. You think they're rational. But, you know, you suddenly realize, they want to kill you." Indeed, from June through August of 1964, more than thirty-five shooting incidents rocked Mississippi, and thirty buildings, many of them churches, were bombed. Hundreds were beaten and arrested, and three Freedom Summer workers were murdered. But the crusade drew national support and registered nearly sixty thousand new African American voters.

Keeping up the pressure, King announced a voter registration drive in Selma, Alabama, where only 2.1 percent of eligible black voters were registered. As expected, the police, led by Sheriff Jim Clark, confronted protesters, arresting nearly two thousand. King then called for a **freedom march** from Selma to Montgomery. On March 7, 1965, as scores of reporters watched, hundreds of freedom marchers faced fifty Alabama state troopers and Clark's mounted forces at Pettus Bridge. Firing tear gas and brandishing clubs, Clark's men chased the marchers down. Television coverage of the assault stirred nationwide condemnation of Clark's tactics and support for King and the marchers. When Alabama's staunch segregationist governor, George Wallace, told President Johnson that he could not provide protection for the marchers, Johnson ordered the National Guard, two army battalions, and 250 federal marshals to escort the protesters. The march resumed on March 21 with about 3,200 marchers. When it arrived in Montgomery on March 27, more than 25,000 had joined.

Johnson used the violence in Selma to pressure Congress to pass the **Voting Rights Act** in August 1965. It banned a variety of methods that states had been using to deny the right to vote, including Mississippi's literacy test, and had immediate effect. Across the South, the percentage of African Americans registered to vote rose an average of 30 percent between 1965 and 1968.

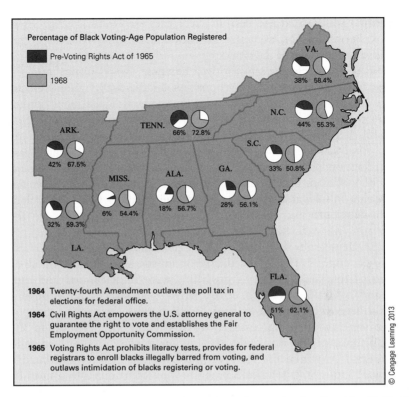

Percentage of Black Voting-Age Population Registered

■ Pre-Voting Rights Act of 1965

▢ 1968

VA. 38% 58.4%
N.C. 44% 55.3%
TENN. 66% 72.8%
ARK. 42% 67.5%
S.C. 33% 50.8%
MISS. 6% 54.4%
ALA. 18% 56.7%
GA. 28% 56.1%
LA. 32% 59.3%
FLA. 51% 62.1%

1964 Twenty-fourth Amendment outlaws the poll tax in elections for federal office.

1964 Civil Rights Act empowers the U.S. attorney general to guarantee the right to vote and establishes the Fair Employment Opportunity Commission.

1965 Voting Rights Act prohibits literacy tests, provides for federal registrars to enroll blacks illegally barred from voting, and outlaws intimidation of blacks registering or voting.

© Cengage Learning 2013

MAP 26.3 Voter Registration of African Americans in the South, 1960–1968

As blacks overwhelmingly registered to vote as Democrats, some former segregationist politicians, among them George Wallace, started to court the black vote, and many southern whites began to cast their ballots for Republicans, inaugurating an era of real two-party competition in the South.

In Mississippi, it went from 7 to 59 percent, and in Selma, more than 60 percent of qualified African Americans voted in 1968, stopping Sheriff Clark's bid for reelection.

But civil rights legislation was only one of many facets of the Great Society. Several acts, like the Appalachian Regional Development Act (1965) and the Model Cities Act (1966), focused on developing economic growth in long-depressed regional and urban areas and on providing funds for housing and mass transit systems. In a related move, a cabinet-level Department of Housing and Urban Development was created in 1965.

Responding to rising environmental concerns, Johnson signed the Water Quality and Air Quality Acts in October 1965. Over the next three years, he would guide through Congress acts to expand wilderness areas, regulate waste removal, and remove billboards from federal highways.

Johnson also signed a major overhaul of the nation's immigration laws. The Immigration and Nationality Act of 1965 dropped the racial and ethnic discrimination in immigration policies that had been in effect since the 1920s. The act set a uniform yearly limit on immigration from any one nation, allowing for increased immigration from non-European parts of the world.

At the top of Johnson's priorities, however, were health and education. Above all, he wanted those two "coonskins on the wall." The Elementary and Secondary Education Act (1965) was the first general educational funding act by the federal government. It granted more than a billion dollars to public and parochial schools for textbooks, library materials, and special education programs. Poor and rural school districts were supposed to receive the highest percentage of federal support. But, as with many Great Society programs, implementation fell short of intention, and much of the money went to affluent suburban school districts. Johnson's biggest "coonskin" was the Medical Care Act (1965), which established **Medicare** and **Medicaid** to help pay healthcare costs for the elderly and individuals on welfare.

In 1966 Democrats were calling the Eighty-ninth Congress "the Congress of accomplished hopes." They were overly optimistic. Despite the flood of legislation, most of the Great Society's programs were underfunded and diminishing in popularity. Republicans and conservative Democrats had enough votes in Congress to effectively oppose further "welfare state" proposals. Supporting the opposition were the growing cost and dissatisfaction with the war in Vietnam, a backlash against urban riots and feminist militancy, and an expanding view that the federal government's efforts to wage war on poverty and build a "Great Society" were futile. Still, Johnson's programs had contributed to a near 10 percent decrease in the number of people living in poverty and a one-third drop in infant mortality. For African Americans statistics were also good: unemployment dropped over four years to 42 percent while average family income rose 53 percent.

New Voices

By the end of 1965, legislation had ended de jure segregation and voting restrictions. Equality, however, depended on more than laws. Neither the Civil Rights Act nor the Voting Rights Act guaranteed justice, removed oppressive poverty, provided jobs, or ensured a higher standard of living. De facto discrimination and prejudice remained, and African American frustrations—born of raised expectations—soon changed the nature of civil rights protest and ignited northern cities. During the 1960s, more than a million mostly poor and unskilled African Americans left the South each year. Most sought a better life in northern and western cities, but they found soaring unemployment and cities unable or unwilling to provide adequate social services. Economics, not segregation, was the key issue: "I'd eat at your lunch counter—if only I had a job," spelled out the problem for many urban blacks. By the mid-1960s, the nation's cities were primed for racial trouble. Minor race riots occurred in Harlem and Rochester, New York, during the summer of 1964, but it was the Watts riot and militant new voices that shook the nation.

Urban Riots and Black Power   Within Los Angeles, the area of **Watts** had a largely African American population. Although Watts was a community having many well-maintained single-family homes and duplexes, its 250,000-plus residents gave it a population density more than four times higher than the rest of the city. Schools were overcrowded, and male unemployment hovered at 34 percent. Patrolling Watts was the nearly all-white L.A. police force, which had a reputation for racism and brutality.

In this climate, on August 11, 1965, an arrest of an African American for drunk driving led to an altercation that mushroomed into a riot. For thirty-six hours, rioters looted and set fire to stores, overturned and set ablaze cars, and attacked firefighters and police, who were unable to put out the flames or restore order. The costs of the riot were high: thirty-four dead, including twenty-eight African Americans, more than nine hundred injured, and $45 million in property destroyed. It also shattered the complacency of many whites who thought civil rights was just a southern problem.

For African Americans, Watts demonstrated a rejection of hopeful nonviolence and a demand for concrete changes. In 1964 Martin Luther King Jr. had received the Nobel Peace Prize, but in 1965, when he spoke in Watts after the rioting, he was shouted down and jeered. "Hell, we don't need no damn dreams," one skeptic remarked. "We want jobs."

Competing with King were new voices like that of **Stokely Carmichael** who called on blacks to seek power through solidarity, independence, and, if necessary, violence. "I'm not going to beg the white man for anything I deserve," Carmichael announced in 1966. "I'm going to take it." SNCC and CORE quickly changed from biracial, nonviolent organizations to **Black Power** resistance movements that stressed Black Nationalism. The insistence on independence from white allies and the violent rhetoric widened the gap between moderates and radicals.

Joining the emergence of Black Power was the growing popularity and visibility of the Nation of Islam, or **Black Muslims**. Founded by Elijah Muhammad in the 1930s, the movement attracted mostly young males and demanded adherence to a strict moral code that prohibited the use of drugs and alcohol. Black Muslims preached black superiority and separatism from an evil white world. By the early 1960s, there were nearly a hundred thousand Black Muslims, including **Malcolm X**, who by 1952 had become one of the Black Muslims' most powerful and respected leaders. A mesmerizing speaker, he rejected integration with a white society that, he said, emasculated blacks by denying them power and personal identity. "Our enemy is the white man!" he roared. But in 1964 he reevaluated his policy. Though still a Black Nationalist, he admitted that to achieve their goals Black Muslims needed to cooperate with other civil rights groups and with some whites. He broke with Elijah Muhammad, and the defection cost him his life. On February 21, 1965, three Black Muslims assassinated him in Harlem.

Carmichael and Malcolm X represented only two of the strident African American voices advocating direct—and, if necessary, violent—action. The new leader of SNCC, H. Rap Brown, told followers to grab their guns and, if necessary, "shoot the honky." Brown's rhetoric was repeated in 1966 when Huey P. Newton, Eldridge Cleaver, and Bobby Seale organized the **Black Panthers** in Oakland, California. Although they pursued community action, such as developing school lunch programs, they were more noticeable for being well armed and willing to use their weapons. FBI director J. Edgar Hoover called them "the most dangerous ... of all extremist groups."

The spread of militant Black Nationalism paralleled a growing number of race riots that shook more than three hundred cities between 1965 and 1968. The summer of 1967 saw over seventy-five riots. The deadliest, in Detroit, killed forty-three people and destroyed millions of dollars in property. The next year, following the assassination of Martin Luther King Jr. 350 American cities went up in flames of racial unrest. Stressing the need for social and economic justice, King had gone to Memphis to support striking sanitation workers. There, on April 4, 1968, he was killed by James Earl Ray.

The 1968 riots came as the Kerner Commission was releasing its report on the causes of urban unrest and making its recommendations for a solution. In 1967, Johnson had asked Governor Otto Kerner of Illinois to chair this commission, and the commission's report put the primary blame for unrest on the racist attitudes of white America. The study described two Americas, one white and one black, and concluded, "Pervasive discrimination and segregation in employment, education, and housing have resulted in the continuing exclusion of great numbers of Negroes from the benefits of economic progress." The study recommended more government programs and spending to improve the lives of African Americans. But it fell on deaf ears. The urban violence and militant rhetoric had created a white backlash against civil rights and Great Society efforts. Governors Ronald Reagan (California) and Spiro Agnew (Maryland) blamed "mad dogs," "lawbreakers," and activists for the riots, and applauded FBI and police efforts to crack down on militants, especially members of the Black Panther Party, many of whom were arrested or killed in battles with authorities.

The civil rights movement had begun in the 1950s, but by the 1960s, African Americans were not alone in confronting the existing political and social norms. An increasing number of women were seeking to alter the status quo. And young adults, many of whom had been energized by the civil rights movement, now voiced demands for a more liberated society.

Rejecting the Feminine Mystique

By the end of the 1950s, the image of women as stay-at-home wives and mothers no longer matched the reality. Increasingly, women were entering the work force, graduating from college, getting divorces, and becoming heads of households. They also recognized that like African Americans they were frequently treated as second-class citizens and faced discrimination based on gender. The 1963 report of the Presidential Commission on the Status of Women confirmed that women worked for less pay than white males (on average 40 percent less), were more likely to be fired or laid off, and rarely reached top

An avid supporter of women's rights, Bella Abzug (1920–1998) was elected to the House of Representatives in 1970 and a year later co-founded the National Women's Political Caucus.

career positions. It also indicated that throughout the country divorce, credit, and property laws generally favored men, and in several states women were not even allowed to serve on juries. The president's commission provided statistics, but it was **Betty Friedan's** 1963 bestseller *The Feminine Mystique* that many regard as the beginning of the women's movement. After reviewing the responsibilities of the housewife (making beds, grocery shopping, driving children everywhere, preparing meals and snacks, and pleasing her husband), Friedan asked: "Is this all?" She concluded that women needed to overcome the "feminine mystique" that promised them fulfillment in the domestic arts. She called on women to set their own goals and seek careers outside the home. Her book, combined with the presidential report, contributed to a renewed women's movement.

In 1963, Congress began to address women's issues when it passed the **Equal Pay Act**, forbidding different wages for equal work based on gender. Also engendering more activism was the passage of the 1964 Civil Rights Act with the inclusion of **Title VII**. The original version of the bill made no mention of discrimination on account of sex, but Representative Martha Griffins (D.–Michigan) joined with conservative Democrat Howard Smith of Virginia to add the word *sex* to the Civil Rights Act. As finally approved, Title VII prohibited discrimination on the basis of race, religion, creed, national origin, or sex.

Despite Title VII, the Equal Employment Opportunity Commission and the Johnson administration showed little interest in dealing with gender discrimination, leading women to form organizations to promote their interests and to persuade the government to enforce Title VII. The most prominent was the **National Organization for Women** (NOW), formed in 1966. With Betty Friedan as president, NOW launched an aggressive campaign to draw attention to sex discrimination and redress wrongs. It demanded an Equal Rights Amendment to the Constitution to ensure gender equality and pushed for easier access to birth-control devices and the right to have an abortion. NOW grew rapidly from about 300 members in 1966 to 175,000 in 1968. But the women's movement was larger than NOW and represented a variety of voices.

Rejecting   Some of those seeking change went beyond economics and
Gender Roles   politics in their critique of American society, taking aim at
                       existing norms of sex and gender roles. Radical feminists,
for example, called for a redefinition of sexuality and repudiated the moral rightness of family, marriage, and male domination in American society. "We identify the agents of our oppression as men.... We are exploited as sex objects, breeders, domestic servants and cheap labor," declared the Redstocking Manifesto in 1969. The New York group that issued the manifesto was among the first to use **"consciousness-raising"** groups to educate women about the oppression they faced because of the sex-gender system. Author Rita Mae Brown went further, advocating lesbian rights. Her acclaimed first novel, *Rubyfruit Jungle* (1973), presented lesbianism in a positive light and provided a literary basis for discussion of lesbian life and attitudes.

Brown joined a growing chorus of voices asking society to reconsider its views toward sexuality. Since the 1950s, gay and lesbian organizations had worked quietly to promote new attitudes toward same-sex orientation and to overturn laws that punished homosexual activities. But most gays remained in the closet, fearful of reprisals by the straight community and its institutions. The Stonewall Riot in 1969, however, brought increased visibility and renewed activism to the gay community.

The police raided the Stonewall Inn in New York City because it catered to a gay clientele. The raid resulted in an unexpected riot as gay patrons fought the police and were joined by other members of the community. After the riot, a Gay Manifesto called for homosexuals and lesbians to raise their consciousness and rid their minds of "garbage" poured into them by old values. "Liberation ... is defining for ourselves how and with whom we live.... We are only at the beginning."

Success came slowly, though. Polls in the early 1970s indicated that the majority of Americans still considered homosexuality immoral and even a disease. But by the mid-1970s, new polling showed a shift as a slight majority of Americans opposed job discrimination based on sexual orientation and appeared to show more tolerance of gay lifestyles. Responding to gay rights pressure in 1973, the

consciousness-raising Achieving greater awareness of the nature of political or social issues through group interaction.

American Psychiatric Association ended its classification of homosexuality as a mental disorder.

The Youth Movement Within the 1960s movements for change, young adults in college were among the most active participants. By 1965, the baby boomers were heading off to college in record numbers. More than 40 percent of the nation's high school graduates were attending college, a leap of 13 percent from 1955. Graduate and professional schools were churning out unprecedented numbers of advanced degrees. Although the majority of young adults remained quite traditional, an expanding number began to question the goals of education. Students complained that higher education seemed sterile, an assembly line producing standardized products, not a crucible of ideas creating independent, thinking individuals. Many demanded more concern for the individual, more freedom of expression, and a more flexible curriculum.

Marches and sit-ins proliferated on campus to protest restrictions on student behavior and living arrangements, to seek a reduction in required courses, and to promote campuses as havens for free thought and a marshaling ground for efforts to change society. By the end of the decade, many colleges had given up the role of guardian for student behavior and decision making. They relaxed or eliminated dress codes, lifted dorm curfews and visitation restrictions, reduced the number of required courses, and introduced programs in nontraditional fields such as African American, Native American, and women's studies.

Across the country, campuses also served as venues for social and political debate and staging grounds for activism. At the University of Michigan in 1960, Tom Hayden and Al Haber organized **Students for a Democratic Society** (SDS). SDS members insisted Americans recognize that their affluent nation was also a land of poverty and want and that business and government chose to ignore social inequalities. In 1962 SDS issued its **Port Huron Statement**, which maintained that the country should reallocate its resources according to social need and strive to build "an environment for people to live in with dignity and creativeness." Accusing society of being "plastic" in its materialism, SDS and other youth activists represented an emerging **New Left** movement that maintained the threat to democracy came from liberals who had sold out to corporate America. "Corporate liberals" dominated the government, making just enough reforms to promote stability and profits while rejecting efforts to achieve social and economic equality. The liberal establishment could send thousands to kill in Vietnam, one New Left leader said, but would not "send 100 voter registrars ... into Mississippi."

In 1964, at the University of California at Berkeley, administration efforts to limit political activity on and near campus sparked a **Free Speech Movement** with confrontation and protest. When student protesters seized the administration building, the police were called to remove the students. Barbara Zahn recalled: "I'm tired, dirty, scared, but most of all proud ... we sit and we sing." She was also arrested, but the students succeeded. In January 1965 Berkeley allowed political activities on campus for the first time since the 1930s.

The Counterculture   Another, very visible, aspect of the youth movement was the emergence of a "counterculture." Rejecting the values of traditional society, by the mid-1960s **"hippies"** were replacing the "beats," adopting a lifestyle that emphasized personal freedom and a culture of opposition to "plastic" America. Some used drugs, especially marijuana, which they claimed reinforced ideals of peace, serenity, and self-awareness, and LSD or "acid," a dangerous and unpredictable hallucinogenic drug that alters perception. Many turned to religion to achieve a higher level of understanding, peace, and love. Non-Western mystic and religious practices like Zen Buddhism were widely adopted, while some found the "real" Jesus, whose original message, they argued, was altered by established religious institutions. Northern California became a center of the counterculture, especially in the Haight-Ashbury neighborhood of San Francisco. There, "beats" like Alan Ginsberg helped shape alternative lifestyles and culture. Elsewhere, groups abandoned the "old-fashioned" nuclear family and lived together as extended families on communes. In their communes and across the nation, those in the counterculture expressed nonconformity in their appearance, favoring long, unkempt hair and blue jeans or long flowered dresses, in their advocacy of sexual freedom, and in their music.

After the Supreme Court's 1964 decision in *Griswold v. Connecticut,* the availability of birth control, especially in the form of "the pill," contributed to a sexual revolution that spread far beyond the counterculture's advocacy of "free love." With fewer concerns of pregnancy, many women and men were willing to adopt less traditional relationships. Marriage was still popular, but living together emerged as an alternative, and for many women there was the image of the "single girl" popularized by Helen Gurley Brown's *Sex and the Single Girl* (1962) and articles aimed at the single market in the pages of *Cosmopolitan.*

Whether Bob Dylan's lyrics or those of the Jefferson Airplane's "White Rabbit," whose pills could "make you larger" or "small," music provided a unifying medium not only for the counterculture but for the 1960s movements in general. Across the spectrum, musicians aimed their songs at large social and cultural issues like race, alienation, war, and love. Some musicians, including Bob Dylan and Joan Baez, challenged society with protest and antiwar songs rooted in folk music, but for the majority the evolving "rock" remained dominant. In 1964, the Beatles, an English group, exploded on the American music scene. They and their music mirrored the irreverence and values of the youth movement. They soon shared the stage with other British imports such as the Rolling Stones, whose behavior and songs depicted alienation and lack of social restraints. "Music," said one writer, was a liberating and revolutionary force that could "change the world." LSD advocate Timothy Leary merely proclaimed the Beatles "evolutionary agents sent by God."

In many ways the counterculture peaked in the summer of 1969, when musicians and an army of young adults converged on **Woodstock**, New York, for the largest free rock concert in history. For three days, through summer rains and deepening mud, more than 400,000 came together in a temporary open-air community, where many of the most popular rock 'n' roll bands performed day and night. Touted as three days of peace and love, sex, drugs, and rock 'n' roll, Woodstock symbolized the power of counterculture values to promote cooperation and happiness.

The spirit of Woodstock was fleeting. For most people, at home and on campus, the communal ideal was impractical, if not unworkable. Nor did the vast majority of young people who took up some counterculture notions completely reject their parents' society. Most stayed in school and continued to participate in the society they were criticizing. But parts of the youth movement and counterculture infiltrated into mainstream society and had a lasting impact.

STUDY TOOLS

SUMMARY

John F. Kennedy's election generated a wave of optimism that individual, institutional, and governmental activism could combine to solve the nation's and the world's problems. This spirit fueled the New Frontier, the War on Poverty, and the Great Society. Many African Americans, in particular, looked to Kennedy and Johnson for legislation to end segregation and discrimination. Kennedy's domestic goals included a comprehensive civil rights bill and education and tax legislation, but the measures became mired in congressional politics and were never passed. Kennedy had to settle for modest legislative successes that merely expanded existing programs and entitlements (government programs and benefits provided to particular groups, such as the elderly, farmers, the disabled, and the poor).

Less constrained in his foreign policy, Kennedy implemented a more comprehensive, flexible strategy to confront communism. Confrontations over Berlin and Cuba, escalating arms and space races, and expanding commitments to Vietnam were accepted as part of the United States' global role and passed intact to Johnson.

President Johnson expanded Kennedy's domestic agenda. Announcing a War on Poverty and the formation of a Great Society, Johnson expanded New Deal liberalism into new areas of public policy. Between 1964 and 1966, Johnson pushed through Congress legislation that tackled poverty and discrimination, expanded educational opportunities, and created a national system of health insurance for the poor and elderly.

The decade's emphasis on activism encouraged more Americans to push their own agendas. As the civil rights movement focused more on economic and social issues, some African Americans rejected assimilation and more militantly demanded basic institutional changes. Drawing from the civil rights movement, a women's movement arose, demanding social, legal, and economic equality and questioning gender roles in a male-dominated society. Across the nation, young adults, especially those of college age, challenged traditional societal values and championed a more tolerant society.

CHRONOLOGY

NEW FRONTIERS

1960	Sit-ins begin SNCC formed Students for a Democratic Society formed John F. Kennedy elected president
1961	Peace Corps formed Alliance for Progress Bay of Pigs invasion Freedom rides begin Vienna summit Berlin Wall erected
1962	SDS's *Port Huron Statement* James Meredith enrolls at the University of Mississippi Cuban missile crisis
1963	Report on the status of women Betty Friedan's *The Feminine Mystique* Equal Pay Act Martin Luther King's "Letter from a Birmingham Jail" March on Washington Diem assassinated Kennedy assassinated; Lyndon Baines Johnson becomes president
1964	War on Poverty begins Freedom Summer Civil Rights Act Johnson elected president
1965	Malcolm X assassinated Selma freedom march Medicaid and Medicare Voting Rights Act Watts riot Water Quality and Air Quality Acts
1966	Black Panther Party formed National Organization for Women founded
1967	Urban riots in over 75 cities
1968	Martin Luther King Jr. assassinated
1969	Woodstock Stonewall Riot Neil Armstrong sets foot on moon

Focus Questions

If you have mastered this chapter, you should be able to answer these questions and explain the terms that follow the questions.

1. How successful was the Kennedy administration in achieving its domestic agenda?
2. What form of African American activism pushed the civil rights movement forward, and how did Kennedy respond to those efforts?
3. How did Kennedy modify the strategy and tactics of Eisenhower's foreign policy?
4. What actions did Kennedy take in Latin America and Vietnam to promote American interests?
5. In what ways did the legislation associated with Johnson's Great Society differ from New Deal programs?
6. How did Johnson's War on Poverty and Great Society further the civil rights movement?
7. How did "new voices" conflict with traditional social norms, and what new organizations and agendas arose to provide a platform for those voices?
8. How did the urban riots and the emergence of the Black Power movement reflect a new agenda for the civil rights movement?

Key Terms

New Frontier (*p. 815*)

new economics (*p. 818*)

sit-in (*p. 819*)

Student Nonviolent Coordinating Committee (*p. 819*)

freedom rides (*p. 819*)

James Meredith (*p. 820*)

March on Washington (*p. 821*)

flexible response (*p. 822*)

Peace Corps (*p. 823*)

Alliance for Progress (*p. 823*)

Bay of Pigs (*p. 823*)

Operation Mongoose (*p. 823*)

Berlin Wall (*p. 824*)

Strategic Air Command (*p. 824*)

Cuban missile crisis (*p. 824*)

Limited Test Ban Treaty (*p. 825*)

Ngo Dinh Diem (*p. 825*)

Viet Cong (*p. 825*)

Civil Rights Act of 1964 (*p. 826*)

War on Poverty (*p. 827*)

New Right (*p. 827*)

Gideon, Escobedo, and *Miranda* (*p. 827*)

Barry Goldwater (*p. 828*)

Great Society (*p. 829*)

Freedom Summer (*p. 830*)

freedom march (*p. 830*)

Voting Rights Act (*p. 830*)

Medicare (*p. 832*)

Medicaid (*p. 832*)

Watts (*p. 833*)

Stokely Carmichael (*p. 833*)

Black Power (*p. 833*)

Black Muslims (*p. 833*)

Malcolm X (*p. 833*)

Black Panthers (*p. 834*)

Betty Friedan's (*p. 835*)

Equal Pay Act (*p. 835*)

Title VII (*p. 835*)

National Organization for Women (*p. 836*)

Students for a Democratic Society (*p. 837*)

Port Huron Statement (*p. 837*)

New Left (*p. 837*)

Free Speech Movement (*p. 837*)

hippies (*p. 838*)

Woodstock (*p. 839*)

27

AMERICA UNDER STRESS, 1967–1976

JOHNSON AND THE WAR

As president, Lyndon Johnson inherited two foreign policy problems from Kennedy: Latin America and Vietnam. While not experienced in foreign affairs, Johnson was sure of one thing—he was not going to allow further erosion of American power.

In the Western Hemisphere, Castro's determination to export revolution appeared the biggest problem. Johnson continued Kennedy's economic boycott of Cuba and the CIA's efforts to destabilize the Castro regime. But he refocused Kennedy's Alliance for Progress. Stability became more important than reform. This new approach, labeled the **Mann Doctrine**, increased American military equipment and advisers in Latin America to help various regimes suppress disruptive elements they labeled "Communist." In 1965 the new policy led to direct military intervention in the Dominican Republic. There, supporters of deposed, democratically elected president Juan Bosch rebelled against a repressive, pro-American regime. Deciding that the pro-Bosch coalition was dominated by Communists and asserting the right to protect the Dominican people from an "international conspiracy," Johnson sent in twenty-two thousand American troops. They restored order; monitored elections that put a pro-American president, Joaquín Balaguer, in power; and left the island in mid-1966. Johnson claimed to have saved the Dominicans from communism, but many Latin Americans saw the American intervention only as an example of Yankee arrogance and intrusiveness.

Americanization of the Vietnam War   As Johnson took office, his advisers told him that the South Vietnamese government remained unstable, its army ineffective, and that the Viet Cong, supported by North Vietnam, appeared to be winning the conflict. There would be no improvement, they said, without a large and direct American involvement. Johnson felt trapped: "I don't think it is worth fighting for," he told an adviser, "and I don't think we can get out." "I am not going to be the president who saw Southeast Asia go the way China went," he asserted. In formulating policy, Johnson concluded that a gradual **escalation** of American force against North Vietnam and the Viet Cong would be the most effective course. It would pressure the North Vietnamese to halt their support of the Viet Cong while limiting domestic opposition. He also wanted to wait until a Communist action justified U.S. retaliation before asking Congress for permission to use whatever force was necessary to defend South Vietnam.

The chance came off the coast of North Vietnam. On August 2, 1964, North Vietnamese torpedo boats skirmished with the American destroyer *Maddox* in the Gulf of Tonkin. On August 4, experiencing rough seas and poor visibility, radar operators on the *Maddox* and another destroyer, the *C. Turner Joy*, concluded that the patrol boats were making another attack. Confusion followed. Both ships fired at targets visible only on radar screens. Johnson immediately ordered retaliatory air strikes on North Vietnam and prepared a resolution for Congress. Although within hours he learned that the second incident probably had not occurred, Johnson told the public and Congress that Communist attacks against "peaceful villages" in South Vietnam had been "joined by open aggression on the high seas against the United States of America." On August 7, Congress approved the **Gulf of Tonkin Resolution,** allowing the United States "to take all necessary measures to repel" attacks against American forces in Vietnam and "to prevent further aggression." It was, in Johnson's terms, "like Grandma's nightgown, it covered everything." Public opinion polls showed strong support for the president, and only two senators opposed the resolution: Wayne Morse of Oregon and Ernest Gruening of Alaska.

Although the resolution gave Johnson freedom of action, he chose to wait until a Communist incident occurred before escalating and to begin with air attacks on targets in North Vietnam. The air offensive, Operation Rolling Thunder, began on March 2, 1965, with the 3rd Marine Division arriving a week later. By July, American planes were flying more than nine hundred missions a week, and a hundred thousand American ground forces had reached Vietnam. Near their bases, American forces patrolled aggressively, searching out the enemy. Johnson's strategy soon showed its flaws. Instead of reducing its support for the Viet Cong, North Vietnam committed units of the North Vietnamese army (NVA) to the fight. The U.S. commanding general in Vietnam, **William Westmoreland,** asked for more American soldiers to carry out larger land offensives. Reluctantly, Johnson gave the green light. Vietnam had become an American war.

Westmoreland intended to use overwhelming numbers and firepower to destroy the enemy and planned a large-scale sweep of the Ia Drang Valley in November

---

escalation   An increase in something; the term became associated with the steady increase in U.S. forces and the intensity of U.S. military activity in Vietnam.

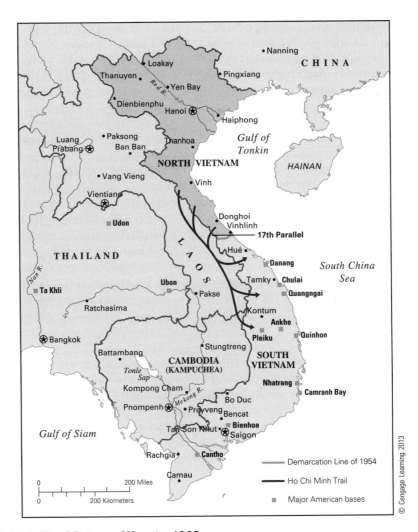

MAP 27.1 The Vietnam War, to 1968

Wishing to guarantee an independent, noncommunist government in South Vietnam, Lyndon Johnson remarked in 1965, "We fight because we must fight if we are to live in a world where every country can shape its own destiny. To withdraw from one battlefield means only to prepare for the next."

1965. Ten miles from the Cambodian border, the Ia Drang Valley contained no villages and was a longtime sanctuary for Communist forces. Airlifted into the valley to search out and destroy the enemy, air cavalry units soon came under fierce attack from North Vietnamese troops. The North Vietnamese commander Nguyen Huu remembered: "There was very vicious fighting ... soldiers fought valiantly. They had no choice, you were dead if not." Both sides claimed victory and drew different lessons from the engagement. Examining the losses, 305 Americans versus

3,561 Vietnamese, American officials embraced the strategy of **search and destroy**—
the enemy would be ground down. *Time* magazine named Westmoreland "Man of
the Year" for 1965. Hanoi concluded its "peasant army" had withstood America's
best firepower and had fought U.S. troops to a draw. The North Vietnamese were
confident: the costs would be great, but they would wear down the Americans.
Both sides, believing victory was possible, committed more troops and prepared
for a lengthy war.

The war's intensity spiraled upward in 1966 and 1967. The United States
and the North Vietnamese committed more troops, while American aircraft
rained more bombs on North Vietnam and on supply routes, especially the
Ho Chi Minh Trail. The bombing of North Vietnam produced great results—
on paper. Nearly every target in North Vietnam had been demolished by
1968, but the North Vietnamese continued the struggle. China and the Soviet
Union increased their support, while much of North Vietnamese industrial production moved underground. By mid-1966, it appeared to some in Washington
that the war had reached a stalemate, with neither side able to win nor willing
to lose. Some speculated that any victory would be a matter of will and feared
that growing opposition to the war in the United States might be a deciding
factor.

The Antiwar   Throughout 1964, support at home for an American role
Movement   in Vietnam was widespread. As the war escalated in 1965
                         a largely college-based opposition arose—with Students for
a Democratic Society (SDS) the prime instigators. The University of Michigan held
the first Vietnam "teach-in" to mobilize opposition to American policy on March
24, 1965. In April, SDS organized a protest march of nearly twenty thousand past
the White House, and by October its membership had increased 400 percent. But
by mid-1966, SDS was only one of many groups and individuals demonstrating
against the expanding war.

Those opposing the war fell into two major types who rarely agreed on anything other than that the war should be ended. Pacifists and radical liberals on the
political left opposed the war for moral and ideological reasons. Others, as the
American military commitment grew and the military draft claimed more young
men, opposed the war for more pragmatic reasons: the draft, the loss of lives and
money, and the inability of the United States either to defeat the enemy or to create
a stable, democratic South Vietnam. A University of Michigan student complained
that if he were drafted and spent two years in the army, he would lose more than
$16,000 in income. "I know I sound selfish," he explained, "but ... I paid $10,000
to get this education."

search and destroy   Military strategy for ground operations in Vietnam during the Johnson administration; using mobility and superior fire power U.S. forces would attack the enemy in their territory
with the goal of destroying as many as possible; the term "body count" became a means to explain
the outcome of the operation.

Yet college students and graduates were not the most likely to be drafted or go to Vietnam. Far more often, minorities and the poor served in Vietnam, especially in combat roles. African Americans constituted about 12 percent of the population but in Vietnam they made up nearly 50 percent of frontline units and accounted for about 25 percent of combat deaths. Stokely Carmichael and SNCC had opposed the war as early as 1965, but it was Martin Luther King Jr.'s denunciation of the war in 1967 that made international headlines and shook the administration. King called the war immoral and said it was wrong to send young blacks to defend democracy in Vietnam when they were denied it in Georgia.

Johnson publicly dismissed critics, labeling King a "crackpot." But as the antiwar movement grew and public opinion polls registered increasing disapproval of the war effort, the administration responded with more direct action. **COINTELPRO**, an FBI program, and **Operation Chaos**, a CIA operation, were implemented to infiltrate, spy on, discredit, and disrupt antiwar groups. Nevertheless, opposition to the war swelled. During "Stop-the-Draft Week" in October 1967 more than 10,000 demonstrators blocked the entrance of an induction center in Oakland, California, and over 200,000 people staged a massive protest march in Washington against "Lyndon's War."

Like the country, the administration was experiencing increasing disagreement about the course of the war. Hawks supported General Westmoreland's assertions that the war was being won but that more troops were needed to complete the job. Others, including Secretary of Defense Robert McNamara, were taking a different view. In November 1967, McNamara recommended a sharp reduction in the war effort, including a permanent end to the bombing of North Vietnam. Johnson rejected the idea, and McNamara left the administration. Still, Johnson decided to consider a "withdrawal strategy" that would reduce American support while the South Vietnamese assumed a larger role. But first it was necessary to commit more troops, intensify the bombing, and put more pressure on the South Vietnamese to make domestic reforms. "The clock is ticking," Johnson said.

TET AND THE 1968 PRESIDENTIAL CAMPAIGN

Johnson was correct: the clock was ticking—not only for the United States but also for North Vietnam. As Westmoreland reported success, North Vietnamese leaders planned an immense campaign to capture South Vietnamese cities during **Tet**, the Vietnamese lunar New Year holiday.

The Tet Offensive   Catching American intelligence agencies and forces totally off guard, in January 1968, the Viet Cong struck forty-one cities throughout South Vietnam, including the capital, Saigon. In some of the bloodiest fighting of the war, American and South Vietnamese forces recaptured the lost cities and villages. It took twenty-four days to oust the Viet Cong from the old imperial city of Hue, leaving the city in ruins and costing more than 10,000 civilian, 5,000 Communist, 384 South Vietnamese, and 216 American lives. The Tet offensive was a military defeat for North Vietnam and the Viet Cong. It provoked no popular uprising against the South Vietnamese government, the Communists held no cities or provincial capitals, and they suffered staggering losses. Tet was, nevertheless, a "victory" for the North Vietnamese, for it seriously weakened American support for the war. Amid official pronouncements of "victory just around the corner," Tet destroyed the Johnson administration's credibility and inflamed a growing antiwar movement. The highly respected CBS news anchor Walter Cronkite had supported the war, but Tet changed his mind. He announced on the air that there would be no victory in Vietnam and that the United States should make peace. "If I have lost Walter Cronkite, then it's over. I have lost Mr. Average Citizen," Johnson lamented.

By March 1968, Johnson and most of his advisers had concluded that the war was not going to be won. In the words of the new secretary of defense, Clark Clifford, four years of "enormous casualties" and "massive destruction from our bombing" had not weakened "the will of the enemy" and a new strategy was needed. Johnson decided to send fewer troops than Westmoreland had asked for, seek a diplomatic end to the war, and place more responsibility on the South Vietnamese.

Unlike previous wars, Vietnam was a war without fixed frontlines. In this picture, marines work their way through the jungle south of the demilitarized zone (DMZ), trying to cut off North Vietnamese supplies and reinforcements moving into South Vietnam.

Larry Burrows/Time Magazine/Time Life Pictures/Getty Images

Changing of the Guard
Two months after Tet came the first presidential primary in New Hampshire. There, Minnesota senator **Eugene McCarthy** was campaigning primarily on Johnson's record and conduct of the war. At the heart of his New Hampshire effort were hundreds of student volunteers who, deciding to "go clean for Gene," cut their long hair and shaved their beards. They knocked on doors and distributed bales of flyers and pamphlets touting their candidate and condemning the war. As McCarthy's antiwar candidacy strengthened, Johnson's advisers organized a **write-in campaign** for the president, who had not entered the primary. Johnson won by 6 percent of the votes, but political commentators named McCarthy the real winner. The results in New Hampshire prompted New York senator **Robert Kennedy** to announce his candidacy in mid-March. Watching his popularity decline and that of his opponents surge, Johnson decided not to run for the presidency.

On March 31, 1968, a haggard-looking president delivered a major televised speech announcing changes in his Vietnam policy. The United States would seek a political settlement through negotiations in Paris with the Viet Cong and North Vietnamese. The escalation of the ground war was over, and the South Vietnamese would take a larger role in the war. The bombing of northern North Vietnam would end, and a complete halt of the air war would follow the start of negotiations. At the end of his speech, Johnson calmly announced: "I shall not seek, and I will not accept, the nomination of my party for another term as president." Listeners were shocked. Although he later claimed that his fear of having a heart attack while in office was the primary reason for his decision not to run, nearly everyone agreed that the Vietnam War had ended Johnson's political career and undermined his Great Society.

The Election of 1968
There were now three Democratic candidates. McCarthy campaigned against the war and the "imperial presidency." Kennedy opposed the war, but not executive and federal power, and he called on the government to better meet the needs of the poor and minorities. Vice President Hubert H. Humphrey, running in the shadow of Johnson, stood behind the president's foreign and domestic programs.

By June, Kennedy was winning the primary race, drawing heavily from minorities and urban Democratic voters. But his candidacy abruptly ended when, after celebrating his victory in the California primary, Kennedy was shot by Sirhan Sirhan, a Jordanian immigrant. He died the next day. His death stunned the nation and ensured Humphrey's nomination. McCarthy continued his campaign but generated little support among party regulars. By the time of the national convention in Chicago in August, Humphrey had enough pledged votes to guarantee his

write-in campaign An attempt to elect a candidate in which voters are urged to write the name of an unregistered candidate directly on the ballot.

nomination. Nevertheless, the convention was dramatic. Inside and outside the convention center, antiwar and anti-establishment groups demonstrated for McCarthy, peace in Vietnam, and social justice. By August 24, the second day of the convention, clashes between the police and protesters started and grew more belligerent every day. Protesters threw eggs, bottles, rocks, and balloons filled with water, ink, and urine at the police, who responded with tear gas and nightsticks. On August 28, the police indiscriminately attacked protesters and bystanders alike as television cameras recorded the scene. The violence in Chicago's streets overshadowed Humphrey's nomination.

The 1968 presidential campaign soon became a three-party race. Drawing on growing dissatisfaction with liberal social policies within Democratic ranks, Governor **George Wallace** of Alabama left the Democratic Party and ran for president as the American Independent Party's candidate. He aimed his campaign at southern whites, blue-collar workers, and low-income white Americans, all of whom deplored the social unrest and "loss" of traditional American values. On the campaign trail, Wallace called for victory in Vietnam and gleefully attacked the counterculture and the "rich-kid" war protesters who avoided serving in Vietnam while the sons of working-class Americans died there. He also opposed federal civil rights and welfare legislation. Two months before the election, Wallace commanded 21 percent of the vote, according to national opinion polls. "On November 5," he confidently predicted, "they're going to find out there are a lot of rednecks in this country."

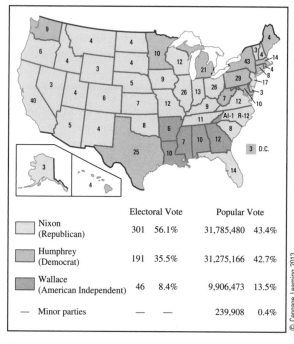

	Electoral Vote		Popular Vote	
Nixon (Republican)	301	56.1%	31,785,480	43.4%
Humphrey (Democrat)	191	35.5%	31,275,166	42.7%
Wallace (American Independent)	46	8.4%	9,906,473	13.5%
— Minor parties	—	—	239,908	0.4%

© Cengage Learning 2013

MAP 27.2 The Election of 1968

Richard Nixon was the Republican candidate, having easily won his party's nomination. He focused his campaign on the need for effective international leadership, law and order, and the restoration of values. He denounced the four "Ps": pot, pornography, protesters, and permissiveness. On the critical issue of Vietnam, he offered no specifics but promised to "end the war and win the peace." Nixon won with a comfortable margin in the Electoral College, although he received only 43 percent of the popular vote. Together, Nixon and Wallace attracted almost 56 percent of the popular vote, which conservatives interpreted as wide public support for an end to liberal programs, a return to traditional values, and a major political realignment that emphasized the suburbs and the **Sunbelt**.

DEFINING THE AMERICAN DREAM

By 1968, there seemed little agreement on the nature of the American dream and the role of government in helping to achieve that end. From King to Carmichael, African Americans had confronted the old order with increasing militancy. But they were not alone. Like blacks, Latinos and American Indians remained near society's lowest levels of income and education. As the 1960s progressed, they too organized grassroots movements and confronted the status quo, demanding change.

The Emergence of *La Causa* Initially enthusiastic about Kennedy, many Latino leaders were disappointed in his presidential actions. Few Hispanics were appointed to government positions, nor did there seem much interest in listening to Latino voices or promoting their civil rights. Federal agencies appeared to defer those issues to local and state governments, which frequently resisted Latino activism, especially by Mexican Americans, who despite being the largest minority in the western states, were still, according to one Mexican American leader, the "invisible minority."

Among the most invisible and poorest were those working in the fields. Trapped at the bottom of the occupational ladder, not covered by Social Security or minimum-wage and labor laws, unskilled and uneducated farm laborers—nearly one-third of all Mexican Americans—toiled long hours for low wages under often deplorable conditions. In 1962, drawing from a traditional base of farm worker organizations, **César Chávez** and **Dolores Huerta** organized farm workers in central California, creating the National Farm Workers Association (NFWA). The union gained national recognition three years later when it struck against the grape growers. The union demanded a wage of $1.40 an hour and asked the public to buy only union-picked grapes. After five years, the strike and the nationwide boycott forced most of the major growers to accept unionization and to improve

Sunbelt   A region stretching from Florida in a westward arc across the South and Southwest.

wages and working conditions. Eventually, California and other states passed legislation to recognize farm workers' unions and to improve the wages and conditions of work for field workers, but agricultural workers, especially migrants, remain among the lowest-paid workers in the nation.

Chávez was central in promoting *La Causa* (Spanish for "the cause"), but he was not alone. Similar grassroot movements focusing on jobs, wages, and education were forming throughout the West and Southwest. Latino leaders like Rodolfo "Corky" Gonzales argued that discrimination and segregation barred their children from a decent education and that school districts needed to offer programs to meet the special needs of Hispanic students, including bilingual education.

In Los Angeles, Raul Ruiz told Mexican American students: "If you are a student you should be angry! You should demand! You should protest! You should organize for a better education!" He called for students to walk out of their classes if schools did not meet their demands. In 1967, "walkouts" spread in California and Texas. In the small South Texas school district of Edcouch-Elsa, Mexican American students walked out of the high school in November 1968. They demanded dignity, respect, and an end to "blatant discrimination," including corporal punishment—paddling—for speaking Spanish. The school board blamed "outside agitators" and suspended more than 150 students. But as in other school districts, the protests brought results. The Edcouch-Elsa school district implemented Mexican American studies and bilingual programs, hired Mexican American teachers, and created programs for migrant farm worker children, who moved from one school to another during picking season. Prominent in the growing grassroots militancy among Mexican Americans were young adults, who called themselves **Chicanos**. They stressed pride in their heritage and Latino culture and called for resistance to the dictates of Anglo society—"We're not in the melting pot.... Chicanos don't melt."

It was not only in the West that Latinos were becoming more visible. In the urban Northeast, the Puerto Rican population had increased to about a million while economic opportunities declined as manufacturing jobs, especially in the garment industry, relocated to the Sunbelt or overseas. The Puerto Rican Forum attempted to coordinate federal grants and to find jobs, while the more militant Young Lords organized younger Puerto Ricans in Chicago and New York with an emphasis on their island culture and Hispanic heritage. "Brown Power" had joined Black Power, soon to be joined by "Red Power."

American Indian Activism   American Indians, responding to poverty, federal and state termination policies, and efforts by state government to seize land for development, organized and asserted their rights with new vigor in the 1960s. In 1961, reservation and nonreservation Indians met in Chicago to discuss problems and consider plans of action. They produced the "Declaration of Indian Purpose" that called for the end of the termination policies and for improved education, economic, and health opportunities. "What we ask of America is not charity, not paternalism" but that "our situation be recognized and be made a basis ... of action." Presidents Kennedy and Johnson responded positively, ensuring that Indians benefited from New Frontier and Great Society programs. Johnson, in 1968, declared that Native Americans should have the same "standard of living" as the rest of the nation and signed the Indian Civil Rights Act. It officially ended the termination program and gave more power to tribal organizations.

Kennedy's and Johnson's support was a good beginning, but many activists wanted to redress old wrongs. The National Indian Youth Council called for "Red Power"—for Indians to use all means possible to resist further loss of their lands, rights, and traditions. They began "fish-ins" in 1964 when the Washington state government, in violation of treaty rights, barred Indians from fishing in certain areas. Protests, arrests, and violence continued until 1975, when the state complied with a federal court decision (*United States v. Washington*) upholding treaty rights. Indian leaders also demanded the protection and restoration of their water and timber rights and ancient burial grounds. Museums were asked to return for proper burial the remains and grave goods of Indians on display. But for most, the crucial issue was self-determination, which would allow Indians control over their lands and over federal programs that served the reservations.

In 1969 a group of San Francisco Indian activists, led by **Russell Means**, gained national attention by seizing **Alcatraz Island** and holding it until 1971 when, without bloodshed, federal authorities regained control. Two years later, in a more violent confrontation, **American Indian Movement** (AIM) leaders Means and Dennis Banks led an armed occupation of Wounded Knee, South Dakota, the site of the 1890 massacre of the Lakotas by the army. AIM controlled the town for seventy-one days before surrendering to federal authorities. Two Indians were killed, and over 230 activists arrested, in the "Second Battle of Wounded Knee."

President Nixon opposed AIM's actions at Wounded Knee but agreed that tribal and individual lives needed to be improved. He doubled funding for the Bureau of Indian Affairs, promoted tribal economies, and signed bills that returned 40 million acres of Alaskan land to Eskimos and other native peoples. In 1974 Congress passed the **Indian Self-Determination and Education Assistance Act**, giving tribes control and operation of many federal programs on their reservations. Tribal and pan-Indian movements sparked cultural pride and awareness. "We're a giant that's been asleep because we've been fed through our veins by the federal government," stated a Navajo leader. "But now that's ending, and we're waking up and flexing muscles we never knew we had. And no one knows what we're capable of."

As federal courts asserted Indian treaty rights and tribes gained more control over their resources, some experienced economic growth and cultural revivals. Indian languages were revived and on many reservations disease and

---

Alcatraz Island   Rocky island, formerly a federal prison, in San Francisco Bay occupied by Native American activists who demanded that it be made available to them as a cultural center.

mortality rates declined, leading to population growth. Economically, some Indian tribes greatly benefitted from the Indian Gaming Regulatory Act in 1988 that allowed reservations to open gaming casinos. By 2006 over 228 tribes had casinos earning over $23 billion. But profits are not equally distributed. Casinos near urban areas, like Mohegan Sun casino in Connecticut, do well while those in rural areas often struggle to break even. Consequently, few tribes see substantial economic gains and overall Indians remain the nation's most impoverished peoples.

NIXON AND THE WORLD

In 1969 Nixon achieved the dream denied him in 1960—he was the president. Determined to be the center of decision making, he relied primarily on his own judgment and on a few close and loyal advisers. For domestic affairs, he looked to John Mitchell, his attorney general, and longtime associates H. R. "Bob" Haldeman and John Ehrlichman. In foreign affairs, he tapped Harvard professor **Henry Kissinger** as his national security adviser and later made him secretary of state. In both domestic and foreign affairs, Nixon wanted to institute policies that would consolidate his presidency and strengthen the Republican Party.

Vietnamization   Vietnam was the foremost issue; it influenced nearly all others—the budget, public and congressional opinion, foreign policy, and domestic stability. Nixon needed a solution before he could move ahead on other fronts. The central question was not whether American troops should be withdrawn, but how best to do it while ensuring that the government of Nguyen Van Thieu remained intact and maintaining America's international and his own credibility. If the United States left Vietnam too abruptly, it would harm American relations. "A nation cannot remain great," Nixon said, "if it betrays its allies and lets down its friends."

The outcome was **Vietnamization**. Better-trained and better equipped South Vietnamese units would assume the bulk of the fighting as American troops left (see Figure 27.1). Changing the "color of bodies" and bringing American soldiers home, Nixon believed, would rebuild public support and diminish the crowds of protesters. Expanding the theme of limiting American involvement, in July, the president announced the **Nixon Doctrine**: countries warding off communism would have to shoulder most of the military burden, with the United States providing political and economic aid and limited naval and air support.

Nixon publicly announced Vietnamization in the spring of 1969, telling the public that 25,000 American soldiers were coming home. Against a backdrop of some of the largest antiwar rallies in fall of 1969, Nixon worked to discredit protestors and called upon the Silent Majority to rally behind Vietnamization. "North Vietnam cannot defeat or humiliate" us, Nixon stated, "[o]nly Americans can do that." Nixon's approval rating soared after the speech and he was able to convince much of the media to alter their coverage of the war, downplaying

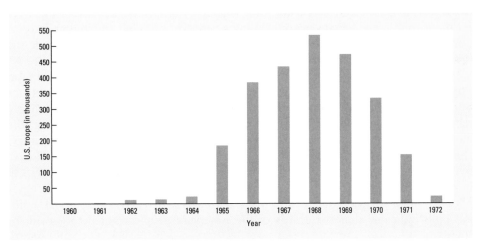

FIGURE 27.1 Troop Levels by Year, 1960–1972

For America, the Vietnam War went through two major phases: Americanization from 1960 to 1968 and Vietnamization from 1969 to 1972.

the fighting and emphasizing "themes and stories under the general heading: We are on our way out of Vietnam." By the end of the year, American forces in Vietnam had declined by over 110,000, public opinion polls indicated support for Nixon's policy, and it appeared that the antiwar movement was losing momentum.

While Nixon's public Vietnam policy appeared to find approval at home, he and Kissinger quietly worked to improve relations with the Soviets and Chinese and to encourage them to reduce their support for North Vietnam. At the same time, Nixon ordered an expansion of the air war to support Vietnamization. Bombing of North Vietnam resumed and secret air attacks (Operation Menu) expanded the war by targeting enemy bases inside Cambodia and Laos. The air assault was part of a "madman strategy" that Nixon designed to convince the North Vietnamese to negotiate. Nixon said he wanted Hanoi "to believe that I've reached the point where I might do anything to stop the war." "We'll just slip the word," Nixon told his advisers, "that 'for God's sake, you know Nixon.... We can't restrain him when he's angry—and he has his hand on the nuclear button.'"

The strategy did not work. The North Vietnamese believed that victory was only a matter of waiting until America was fed up with the war. Nixon remained committed to his strategy and in April 1970 ordered American troops to cross the border into Cambodia and destroy Communist bases and supply areas. The mission successfully demolished enemy bases and large amounts of supplies, but it also created a firestorm of protest in the United States.

A new wave of antiwar protests occurred around the country. Demonstrations against the war at the universities of Kent State (Ohio) and Jackson State

(Mississippi) resulted in six dead students; eighty thousand protesters marched on the Capitol. The Senate overwhelmingly repealed the Gulf of Tonkin Resolution, which had provided the legislative foundation for the war, and forbade the further use of American troops in Laos or Cambodia.

Adding to broadening opposition to the war, the release of the **Pentagon Papers** showed that American administrations from Truman to Nixon had not told the truth about Vietnam. Stories about drug use, **fragging**, and seemingly mindless slaughter strengthened the belief that the war was unraveling the morality of American soldiers. The court martial of Lieutenant William Calley, charged with murder, was a case in point. Calley's platoon had killed over five hundred men, women, and children in and around the village of **My Lai** in 1968. "This is not what the American soldier does," explained a helicopter pilot who had rescued some of the My Lai villagers. By early 1972, public opinion polls indicated that two-thirds of the American people wanted to get out of Vietnam.

Aware of declining support for the war in the United States and the weakness of South Vietnamese forces, North Vietnam in March 1972 launched its "Easter Offensive." Pushing aside Army of South Vietnam (ARVN) troops, Communist forces advanced toward Saigon. Nixon ordered massive bombing raids against North Vietnam and Communist forces in South Vietnam that enabled ARVN forces to regroup and drive back the North Vietnamese and encouraged the North Vietnamese to renew peace talks in Paris. In October, Kissinger announced "Peace is at hand," just in time for the 1972 presidential election.

South Vietnamese president Nguyen Van Thieu, however, rejected the plan. Reluctantly, Nixon supported Thieu, and he ordered the Christmas bombing of Hanoi and North Vietnam to convince Thieu that the United States would use its power to protect South Vietnam. After eleven days the bombing stopped. When talks resumed, Washington advised Thieu to accept the next peace settlement or fend for himself. On January 27, 1973, Thieu accepted a peace settlement that did not differ significantly from the one offered in October. Nixon proclaimed peace with honor. The peace settlement imposed a cease-fire, removed the twenty-four thousand remaining American troops, and promised the return of American prisoners of war. The peace terms permitted the United States to end its role in the war. Because the settlement left North Vietnamese troops in South Vietnam, it did little to ensure the existence of Thieu's government or nation. When Haldeman asked Kissinger how long the South Vietnamese government could last, Kissinger answered bluntly, "If they're lucky, they can hold out for a year and a half."

Pentagon Papers   Classified government documents on policy decisions leaked to the press by Daniel Ellsberg and printed by the *New York Times* in 1971.

fragging   An effort to kill fellow soldiers, frequently officers, by using a grenade. It may have accounted for over a thousand American deaths in Vietnam.

© Bettmann/Corbis

As North Vietnamese forces entered Saigon in April 1975, the last American evacuees left by helicopter. Here, they scramble to the roof of the Pittman apartments in Saigon; others left from the roof of the American embassy. Henry Kissinger asked the nation "to put Vietnam behind us."

To reassert congressional power to limit the president's war-making abilities, in November 1973, Congress passed over Nixon's veto the **War Powers Act**. The law requires the president to inform Congress within forty-eight hours of the deployment of troops overseas and to withdraw those troops within sixty days if Congress fails to authorize the action. As expected, North Vietnam continued to funnel men and supplies to the south, and in March 1975, they renewed the war. Congress refused to supply military aid and a month later, North Vietnamese troops entered Saigon. The Vietnam War ended as it had started, with Vietnamese fighting Vietnamese (see Table 27.1)

Modifying the Cold War

Ending the Vietnam War was a necessity in Nixon's grand plan to reshape the Cold War. An "era of confrontation" must give way to an "era of negotiation," Nixon said as he pursued **détente**, a policy that reduced tensions with the two Communist

détente   Relaxing of tensions between the superpowers in the early 1970s, which led to increased diplomatic, commercial, and cultural contact.

TABLE 27.1 | THE VIETNAM GENERATION, 1964–1975

	Men	Women
Total in military service	8,700,000	250,000
Served in Vietnam	2,700,000	6,431
Killed in Vietnam	58,219	8
Wounded	303,000*	
Missing in action	2,330	1
Draft resisters (estimate)	570,000	—
Accused	210,000	—
Convicted	8,750	—

*Combined men and women

Source: Department of Defense and Veterans Administration.

superpowers. China was the key to the strategy. The United States did not recognize the Beijing government and there had been no diplomatic contact since the end of the Chinese civil war in 1949. Establishing diplomatic connections with Communist China would provide new trade opportunities and would, in Nixon's and Kissinger's view, encourage the Soviets to improve their relations with the United States. The Soviets and Chinese had engaged in several bloody clashes along their border, and the Chinese hoped that better relations with the United States would help deter Soviet aggression. They also wanted access to American technology. Sending a signal to China, Nixon lowered restrictions on trade. The Chinese responded by inviting an American ping-pong team to tour China in April 1971. Three months later, Kissinger secretly met with Premier Zhou Enlai in Beijing. On Kissinger's return, Nixon stunned the world when he announced he would meet with Communist Party chairman Mao Zedong and Zhou in Beijing in February 1972. The first step in moving toward détente was in place. The second occurred in May when Nixon met Soviet President **Leonid Brezhnev**, saying their two nations should "live together and work together." The meeting was a success. Brezhnev obtained increased trade with the United States, especially much needed grain. The two superpower leaders also announced the **Strategic Arms Limitation Talks agreement** (SALT I), which restricted antimissile sites and established a maximum number of intercontinental ballistic missiles (ICBMs) and submarine-launched ballistic missiles (SLBMs) for each side.

Nixon pursued détente with China and the Soviet Union, but in other areas of the world it was business as usual. In Latin America, he continued efforts to isolate Cuba and sought to remove the democratically elected socialist-Marxist government of **Salvador Allende** in Chile. Kissinger thought they should not "let a country go Marxist just because its people are irresponsible." From 1970 to 1973, the United States openly and covertly worked to destabilize the

Allende government and support his opponents until, in September 1973, the Chilean military stormed the presidential palace, killing Allende. The Nixon administration denied any direct American role in the coup but quickly recognized the repressive military government of General Augusto Pinochet, who promptly reinstated a free-market economy. Other Latin American dictators and the repressive governments of Iran and South Africa also received economic and military aid.

NIXON AND THE DOMESTIC AGENDA

Like Kennedy, Nixon favored foreign over domestic affairs. He had a grand scheme for changing foreign policy, but no similar plan for domestic affairs. And he was the first president since 1858 to take office without his own party controlling either house of Congress, which clearly complicated implementing traditional Republican agendas. Consequently, Nixon adopted a complex and pragmatic approach that balanced his desire to expand the Republican Party with an unexpectedly progressive social agenda.

Nixon as Pragmatist   Shocking many conservative Republicans, between 1969 and 1971, Nixon's administration adopted a surprisingly liberal agenda. It increased welfare support and approved legislation that enhanced the regulatory powers of the federal government. Food stamps became more accessible, and Social Security, Medicare, and Medicaid payments were increased. By 1972, for the first time since 1942, the government was spending more on social programs than on defense. Nixon's approaches to affirmative action and welfare were innovative and many considered them to be more liberal than conservative. Pat Buchanan, Nixon's speechwriter, considered Nixon "a fellow traveler of the right" but not a true conservative.

The "Philadelphia Plan," Nixon's affirmative action plan, paralleled earlier Democratic efforts. It required companies receiving federal contracts to file plans for hiring minority and women workers within 120 days of receiving the contract. It also required unions to open membership to more minorities. His effort to keep his campaign promise to fix the "welfare mess" was a pragmatic effort to replace "millions on welfare rolls" with "millions on payrolls," keep the nuclear family intact, and eliminate many existing welfare agencies. The Family Assistance Plan that emerged in 1969 provided low-income families a direct monetary payment from the government, along with food stamps, as long as recipients worked or enrolled in job training programs. It was defeated by a coalition of conservatives and liberals in Congress in 1969 and again in 1971. Nixon blamed Congress, conservatives, and "damn social workers."

Like his predecessors, Nixon, too, expanded the federal government, creating the Occupational Safety and Health Administration (OSHA) and the **Environmental Protection Agency** (EPA). The modern environmental movement was gaining

Banning DDT

In 1972, the United States banned the use of the pesticide DDT. Widely used in agriculture to protect crops from insects, it entered the food chain, creating medical problems in animals and humans. Momentum for the ban began with Rachel Carson's publication of *Silent Spring* (1962), which examined the effects of the chemical on nature and questioned societies' blind faith in technological progress. Since 1972, many other nations have stopped the use of DDT, and in 2008 the United Nations announced its goal to halt its worldwide use by 2020. Carson's views and the banning of DDT were, and continue to be, strongly criticized. Some have claimed that following her logic would mean returning to the "Dark Ages" when "insects and diseases ... would ... again inherit the earth" and that she is responsible for more deaths than Hitler.

- Should developed nations be able to dictate the ban of chemicals like DDT to countries that might benefit economically from using such toxic chemicals?
- The reference to Carson's killing of millions of people refers to deaths from malaria—a disease linked to mosquitoes—because DDT has been banned. Research the spread of malaria and the use of DDT since 1972 to determine if this accusation is valid.

momentum when Nixon took office. Rachel Carson alerted the nation to the dangers of DDT in her book *Silent Spring* (1962) and touched off a wave of environmental concerns. By 1969, it was hard to ignore reports on urban air pollution, the ecological death of Lake Erie, and growing mountains of garbage everywhere. A national response came in April 1970, when communities and thousands of schools and colleges hosted Earth Day activities. It was the largest single-day demonstration in American history and showed a public deeply concerned about a worsening environment.

Nixon was not an environmentalist and thought the movement was "overrated." But he recognized an emerging political issue. In July, he proposed the creation of the EPA to monitor and implement pollution standards. Congress approved it in December. Between 1970 and 1974, Congress and Nixon also approved a wide variety of environment legislation, including a Clean Air Act, Safe Drinking Water Act, and an Endangered Species Act. Watching the actions of OSHA, the EPA, and other regulatory agencies, many conservatives, including Nixon's economic adviser, complained that he was imposing the most "regulation on the economy ... since the New Deal."

Nixon also proved flexible in economic matters. When he took office, he faced a budget deficit of nearly $25 billion and a climbing rate of inflation. Nixon cut spending, increased interest rates, and balanced the budget in 1969. But economic recovery failed to follow, and inflation rose as economic growth slowed—giving

On January 29, 1969, six miles off the coast of Santa Barbara, California, a Union Oil Co. platform oil spill occurred that in more than eleven days released over 200,000 gallons. The oil spill spread over 800 square miles and washed ashore along the California coast. In this picture, workers and volunteers work to clean up the oil-soaked beaches, and others sought to save oil-coated wildlife. President Nixon said the spill at Santa Barbara "touched the conscience of the American people."

rise to a new phenomenon, **stagflation**. By 1971, the economy was in its first serious recession since 1958. Unemployment and bankruptcies increased, but inflation still climbed, approaching 5.3 percent. Fearing that economic woes would erode his support, Nixon shifted his approach and asked for increased federal spending to boost recovery and for a wage and price freeze to stall inflation. Shocked conservatives complained bitterly at the betrayal of their values. But the economy responded positively as inflation and unemployment declined. Nonetheless, Nixon's battle with inflation was a losing one. Wages and prices climbed when Nixon lifted the wage and price freeze, and they soared in 1973 when Arab nations raised oil prices and limited oil sales to the United States (discussed later in this chapter).

stagflation   Persistent inflation combined with stagnant consumer demand and relatively high unemployment.

Building the   While pursuing his pragmatic approach, Nixon was deter-
Silent Majority   mined to expand and strengthen the Republican Party. To do
                          this he looked at two regions, the Sunbelt and the South.
He adopted a "**southern strategy**" to shatter the once solid Democratic South. In
the rest of the Sunbelt, he hoped that Republican policies opposing liberal
activism and supporting state authority would attract voters to the Republican
Party. By opposing forced school integration and supporting neighborhood
schools Nixon believed he could attract white southerners and many urban
northern blue-collar workers to the Republican Party. He told Haldeman to "go
for the Poles, Italians, Irish" but not "Jews or Blacks." In response to a 1969
request from Mississippi to postpone court-ordered integration of several school
systems, Attorney General John Mitchell petitioned the Supreme Court for a
delay. At the same time, the administration lobbied Congress for a revision of the
1965 Voting Rights Act that would have weakened southern compliance. Neither
effort was successful. In October 1969, the Supreme Court unanimously decreed
in *Alexander v. Holmes* that it was "the obligation of every school district to
terminate dual school systems at once." The White House's support for de facto
segregated neighborhood schools suffered another loss in 1971 when the Burger
Court reaffirmed the use of busing to achieve integration in a North Carolina
case, *Swann v. Charlotte-Mecklenburg*. The Nixon administration criticized the
decisions but agreed to "carry out the law." By 1973, most African American
children in the South were attending integrated public schools. Nixon was unable
to slow the process of integration, but he won increasing political support among
white southerners.

Another part of Nixon's political strategy was to stress his administration's
support for law and order with the passage of anticrime legislation that would
strengthen the criminal justice system and alter the liberal composition of the
federal court system. He intended to appoint judges and justices who would be
tougher on criminals and more narrowly interpret the Constitution. In 1969, Chief
Justice Earl Warren retired, and Nixon nominated Warren Burger, a respected, conservative federal judge, who was easily confirmed by the Senate. Within months,
another resignation gave Nixon a second chance to alter the Court. Merging his
desire for a conservative judge with his southern strategy, Nixon first chose South
Carolinian Clement Haynesworth and then G. Harrold Carswell of Florida for
the position. The Senate rejected both nominees because of their lack of support
for integration. On his third try, Nixon abandoned his southern strategy and
chose Harry Blackmun, a conservative from Minnesota. Blackmun was confirmed easily. In 1971 Nixon appointed two more justices, Lewis Powell of
Virginia and William Rehnquist of Arizona, creating a more conservative Burger
Supreme Court.

An Embattled   By the end of Nixon's first term, nearly 60 percent of
President   respondents in national opinion polls approved of the
                          president's record. The South was no longer solidly

Democratic, and Sunbelt and blue-collar worker voters seemed to be supporting Republican issues and candidates. The economy, while still a worry, seemed under control. Diplomatically, Nixon had scored major successes with China and the Soviets, and a peace agreement in Paris seemed possible. Nixon projected that he would easily win reelection in 1972.

Meanwhile, Democrats were in disarray. Their most enthusiastic members appeared to be migrating to either the liberal Senator **George McGovern** or the conservative George Wallace. The newest category of voter, ages 18–21, voting for the first time as a result of the Twenty-sixth Amendment (ratified in 1971), seemed to be in McGovern's camp. When Senator McGovern won the nomination, George Wallace—confined to a wheelchair following an assassination attempt that left him paralyzed—again bolted the party to run as a third-party candidate on the American Independent ticket.

Despite almost certain victory, Nixon obsessed about enemies surrounding him. This preoccupation was not new but one that lay beneath the surface throughout his political career. Repeatedly, as president, he spoke about "screwing" his domestic enemies before they got him and how the press hated him. He warned his cabinet and staff that the press would "run lies about you ... and the cartoonists will depict you as ogres." To combat his foes, Nixon kept an "enemies list," used illegal wiretaps and infiltration to spy on anti-administration organizations and people, and instructed the FBI, the Internal Revenue Service, and other governmental organizations to intimidate and punish his opponents. As the 1972 campaign began, Nixon and his campaign coordinators longed to humiliate their enemies and smash the Democrats. To achieve this, Nixon's staff and the **Committee to Re-elect the President** (CREEP), directed by John Mitchell, stepped outside the normal bounds of election behavior. A Special Investigations Unit, known informally as the "Plumbers," conducted "dirty tricks" to disrupt the Democrats' activities. Seeking inside information on the opposition, CREEP approved a burglary of the Democratic National Committee headquarters in the **Watergate** building in Washington, D.C., to copy documents and tap phones.

On June 17, 1972, a Watergate security guard detected the burglars and notified the police. Five men were arrested carrying "bugging" equipment and two others were apprehended across the street. The burglars were soon linked to CREEP. Although the committee denied any connection to the burglary, both CREEP and the White House tried to disrupt any investigations and paid the suspects to help in the cover-up. "I want you all to stonewall it," Nixon told Mitchell. "Cover it up." The furor passed, and in November, Nixon buried McGovern in an avalanche of electoral votes, winning every state except Massachusetts.

Despite Democrats still holding majorities in Congress, Nixon was overjoyed. "Seventy-three can be and should be the best year yet," he informed his cabinet. But his optimism faded as the cover-up unraveled. The burglars were convicted in January 1973. By then, *Washington Post* reporters Bob Woodward and Carl Bernstein, helped by "Deep Throat," a secret source inside the FBI, had uncovered

Despite his efforts to keep his role in the Watergate break-in hidden, the Watergate tapes and other testimony clearly indicated Nixon's direct role in the affair. When it became evident that he would be removed from office through the process of impeachment, he chose to resign from the presidency. In this picture taken on August 9, 1974, in the East Room of the White House, surrounded by his family, President Nixon informs his staff and others of his resignation.

Keystone/Hulton Archive/Getty Images

a trail of "hush money" leading to CREEP and the White House. By May three separate investigations of the Watergate affair were under way. The most public was by a Special Committee of the Senate chaired by a Democrat, Senator Sam Ervin, Jr., of North Carolina, but the federal grand jury investigation led by Judge John Sirica and a Justice Department investigation conducted by Archibald Cox could result in criminal prosecutions.

Throughout the spring and summer, testimony linked the break-in and cover-up to CREEP and the executive branch. Trying to limit the damage, Nixon accepted the resignations of Haldeman, Ehrlichman, and others on his staff. "Until March, I remained convinced," he announced, that "the charges of involvement by ... the White House staff were false." Nixon continued to deny he was involved, but his statements were less and less credible as the testimony unfolded, especially after **John Dean** said he had discussed the break-in with Nixon as early as mid-1972.

In July 1973, the nature of the investigations changed when it was revealed that Nixon had secretly recorded meetings in the Oval Office, including those with Dean. Claiming executive privilege, Nixon refused demands for the tapes from Cox, Sirica, and Ervin. When Cox refused to drop his subpoena, Nixon ordered him fired. A firestorm of protest erupted, and the House Judiciary Committee started to gather evidence for impeachment proceedings. Adding to Nixon's woes in October, Vice President **Spiro Agnew** was forced to resign for accepting bribes while governor of Maryland. In keeping with the Twenty-fifth Amendment, Nixon appointed Agnew's successor, choosing Representative Gerald R. Ford of Michigan. Ford would be confirmed by Congress in December.

In March 1974, the Sirica grand jury investigating the Watergate break-in **indicted** Mitchell, Haldeman, and Ehrlichman and named Nixon as an "unindicted coconspirator." Nixon, under tremendous pressure, released transcripts of selected tapes. The outcome was devastating. The transcripts contradicted some official testimony, and Nixon's apparent callousness, lack of decency, and profane language shocked the nation. In July, the Supreme Court rejected Nixon's executive privilege position and ordered him to hand over all the tapes. Having ample evidence, the House Judiciary Committee charged Nixon with three impeachable crimes: obstructing justice, abuse of power, and defying subpoenas. Nixon's choices were to either resign or be impeached and removed from office. He resigned on August 9, 1974. Eventually, twenty-nine people connected to the White House were convicted of crimes related to Watergate and the 1972 campaign.

An Interim President	The nation's first unelected president, Gerald Ford, got off to a positive start. He was liked by members of both parties and considered an honest administrator by the public. But that

quickly changed when he pardoned Nixon for any crimes he might have committed as president and seemed unable to deal with the problems facing the nation. The economy continued to slump, its decline quickened by the sharp rise in oil prices following the **Organization of Petroleum Exporting Countries'** (OPEC) embargo on the sale of oil to the United States in response to continuing American support for Israel in the ongoing conflict that had erupted into the **Yom Kippur War** in 1973. When Democrats, who won a record number of congressional seats in the 1974 elections, sponsored a bill to create jobs and increase spending, Ford resorted to the veto—which he would use to block thirty-seven bills. The result was political stalemate.

Despite relying heavily on Henry Kissinger, who was now national security adviser and secretary of state, Ford scored few foreign policy successes. Kissinger's efforts to negotiate a peace settlement in the Yom Kippur War and to reduce tensions in the Middle East earned him high praise. But little rubbed off on Ford, who

---

indict To make a formal charge of wrongdoing against a person or party.

could provide no help to Saigon as the North Vietnamese finished their conquest of South Vietnam, and whose handling of the Soviets alienated many within his own party. Trying to maintain the Nixon-Kissinger effort at détente with Moscow, he met with Soviet leader Brezhnev at Vladivostok in Siberia and in Helsinki, Finland. At the summits he made progress toward strategic arms limitation and improved East-West relations, but he received little credit at home, where his actions drew fire from those who wanted a tougher, more traditional Cold War policy toward the Soviet Union.

Among the most forceful Republican critics was presidential hopeful Ronald Reagan, who sought the Republican nomination in 1976. Representing the conservative wing of the party, he attacked détente as well as Ford's political ineffectiveness. Ford managed to eke out a victory at the convention, embracing a conservative agenda that called for smaller government and tougher policies toward communism.

STUDY TOOLS

SUMMARY

Following Kennedy's policies, President Johnson expanded American efforts to oppose communism around the world. In South Vietnam he implemented a series of planned escalations that Americanized the war. North Vietnam kept pace and showed no slackening of resolve or resources. Within the United States, however, as the American commitment grew, a significant antiwar movement developed. The combination of the Tet offensive and presidential politics divided the Democratic Party and compounded the divisions in American society.

By 1968, the country seemed aflame with urban riots and protests. Hispanics and Native Americans joined their voices with other groups demanding more recognition of their needs and calling upon the federal government for support. Those advocating social change, however, faced a resurgence of conservatism that helped elect Nixon. Seeking a strategy for withdrawing from Vietnam, Nixon implemented a policy of Vietnamization. To restructure the Cold War, he worked to improve relations with the Soviet Union and China. At home, Nixon charted a pragmatic course, switching between government activism and more traditional Republican policies, hoping to cement the Sunbelt and the South to the Republican Party.

Despite Nixon's domestic and foreign-policy successes, his desire to crush his enemies led to the Watergate scandal and his resignation. President Ford tried to restore confidence in government but faced too many obstacles. As the 1976 bicentennial election approached, the nation seemed mired in a slowing economy and public cynicism toward government and politics. Many wondered if the optimism that began the 1960s would ever return.

Chronology

1962 César Chávez and Dolores Huerta form National Farm Workers Association

1963 Lyndon B. Johnson becomes president

1964 Gulf of Tonkin Resolution
Johnson elected president

1965 U.S. air strikes against North Vietnam begin
American combat troops arrive in South Vietnam
Anti-Vietnam "teach-ins" begin
Dominican Republic intervention

1967 Antiwar march on Washington

1968 Tet offensive
My Lai massacre
Johnson withdraws from presidential race
Robert Kennedy assassinated
Mexican American student walkouts
American Indian Movement founded
Richard Nixon elected president

1969 Secret bombing of Cambodia
First American troop withdrawals from Vietnam
American Indians occupy Alcatraz

1970 U.S. troops invade Cambodia
Kent State and Jackson State killings
First Earth Day observed
Environmental Protection Agency created

1972 Nixon visits China and Soviet Union
Attempted assassination of George Wallace
Watergate break-in
Nixon reelected
SALT I treaty

1973 Vietnam peace settlement
"Second Battle of Wounded Knee"
Watergate hearings
Salvador Allende overthrown in Chile
War Powers Act
Arab oil boycott

1974 Nixon resigns
Gerald Ford becomes president

1975 South Vietnam government falls to North Vietnamese

Focus Questions

If you have mastered this chapter, you should be able to answer these questions and explain the terms that follow the questions.

1. How did Johnson modify Kennedy's policies toward Latin America and Southeast Asia?
2. What considerations led Johnson to expand America's role in Vietnam and how did the North Vietnamese respond to the changes?
3. What were the political, social, and military outcomes of the Tet offensive?
4. What key issues shaped the 1968 campaign? What strategy did Richard Nixon use to win?
5. How did Latinos and Native Americans seek to address the problems they faced in American society?
6. How did the federal government respond to their efforts?
7. How did Richard Nixon plan to achieve an "honorable" peace in Vietnam?
8. How did Nixon's Cold War policies differ from those favored by earlier administrations?
9. How did Nixon's policies dealing with the economy, welfare, and the environment reflect his pragmatic approach? What did he do to increase the base of the Republican Party?
10. What actions led to the Watergate investigation and Nixon's resignation?

Key Terms

Mann Doctrine (*p.* 843)

Gulf of Tonkin Resolution (*p.* 844)

William Westmoreland (*p.* 844)

Ho Chi Minh Trail (*p.* 846)

COINTELPRO (*p.* 847)

Operation Chaos (*p.* 847)

Tet (*p.* 847)

Eugene McCarthy (*p.* 849)

Robert Kennedy (*p.* 849)

George Wallace (*p.* 850)

César Chávez (*p.* 851)

Dolores Huerta (*p.* 851)

Chicano (*p.* 852)

Russell Means (*p.* 853)

American Indian Movement (*p.* 853)

Indian Self-Determination and Education Assistance Act (*p.* 853)

Henry Kissinger (*p.* 854)

Vietnamization (*p.* 854)

Nixon Doctrine (*p.* 854)

My Lai (*p.* 856)

War Powers Act (*p.* 857)

Leonid Brezhnev (*p.* 858)

Strategic Arms Limitation Talks agreement (*p.* 858)

Salvador Allende (*p.* 858)

Environmental Protection Agency (*p.* 859)

southern strategy (*p.* 862)

George McGovern (*p.* 863)

Committee to Re-elect the President
(*p.* 863)
Watergate (*p.* 863)
John Dean (*p.* 864)

Spiro Agnew (*p.* 865)
Organization of Petroleum Exporting
Countries (*p.* 865)
Yom Kippur War (*p.* 865)

28

NEW ECONOMIC AND POLITICAL ALIGNMENTS, 1976–1992

CHAPTER OUTLINE

• The Carter Presidency • Resurgent Conservatism • A Society and Economy in Transition • Asserting World Power • In Reagan's Shadow • Study Tools

---

THE CARTER PRESIDENCY

In 1976 the United States celebrated the two-hundredth anniversary of its independence. Amid the festivities and praise for its institutions and accomplishments, however, lurked a deepening sense of cynicism and uncertainty. President Ford's efforts to restore faith in government had not succeeded and the public's lack of trust and confidence only increased when the economy slowed. For the first time since the Depression, many parents worried that their children would not enjoy a higher standard of living. The optimism that had characterized the 1960s had faded into frustration and apathy.

The political forecast did not look especially promising as the two presidential contenders began their race for the White House. Polls showed that people liked Gerald Ford but considered him ineffective, while his Democratic opponent, James Earl Carter, who preferred to be called "Jimmy," boasted about his lack of political experience—aside from being a one-time governor of Georgia. Carter's nonpolitical, folksy background was refreshing, but some wondered whether he had the experience to lead Congress and the nation. Both men seemed full of good intentions but vague on the issues. Neither ignited the nation politically; even the televised debates were dull. In a very close election where only 54.4 percent of eligible voters cast ballots, Ford won more states but lost the electoral count to Carter by 56 votes. Giving one reason for the low voter turn-out, a Californian explained he did not want "to force a second-class decision on my neighbors."

Jimmy Carter arrived in the nation's capital in January 1977 brimming with enthusiasm. He stressed he was free of Washington politics and the lures of special interests. He pledged honesty and hard work and said he was determined to take different and more moral approaches in tackling foreign and domestic problems. With majorities in Congress, Democratic congressional leaders also were eager to assert their leadership. The problem was that Carter had little intention of playing politics as usual, which meant he would frequently ignore Congress. Democratic congressional leaders, in turn, announced that Congress had no intention of "rolling over and playing dead." The results were repeated conflicts between Congress and the president that left few satisfied.

Domestic Priorities   Carter faced an economic recession in 1977, and nearly everyone agreed that fixing the economy was a priority, but the question was how and at what expense to other issues. Fiscally conservative, Carter chose to attack the recession by raising interest rates, cutting taxes, and trimming federal spending, including budgets for social programs. He announced that liberalism had its limits and government could not "eliminate poverty or provide a bountiful economy." When he argued that improving regulatory agencies and better enforcing existing regulations and laws would produce better social results than costly expanded or new programs, many liberals and congressional Democrats disagreed and thought he was sacrificing social needs for the cause of **fiscal stringency**. Already unhappy with his approach and attitude, Democrats in Congress rebelled when Carter proposed a twenty-cent raise in the minimum wage, passing an increase of ninety-five cents instead.

The disagreement over the minimum wage was just one example. Ted Kennedy and liberal Democrats sought to push Carter forward on a variety of social fronts, including **affirmative action**. Since the mid-1960s, in an effort to provide more opportunities, many businesses and colleges had established affirmative action slots for minorities. But by the 1970s, a growing number of Americans believed these programs constituted preferential treatment for minorities that limited their own opportunities. In 1974 **Alan Bakke** sued the University of California at Davis Medical School for reverse discrimination. He claimed that he had been denied admission because he was white, and that in his place the medical school had accepted less-qualified African American students. When the case was heard by the Supreme Court in 1978, supporters of affirmative action pleaded with Carter to have the Justice Department back the university. The Justice Department did petition the Court to uphold the university's admissions program, but Carter's public statements that he hated "to endorse the proposition of quotas" seemed to

fiscal stringency   The need because of real or perceived economic conditions to restrict, cut, or eliminate funding for programs.

affirmative action   Policy that seeks to redress past discrimination through active measures to ensure equal opportunity, especially in education and employment.

undermine the administration's support for affirmative action. Bakke won his case in a 5-to-4 decision with the Court ruling that the university's admissions program created a quota system, which violated the Constitution. Bakke was admitted to the medical school and graduated in 1982.

Like those wanting Carter to fight harder for affirmative action, many women found his support for women's issues, including the ERA and freedom of choice regarding abortion, uneven and not strong enough. In 1972, Congress had proposed an **Equal Rights Amendment** (ERA) and sent it to the states for ratification. In two years, thirty-three of the needed thirty-eight states had approved the amendment and supporters were confident of its passage. But opposition stiffened under the leadership of conservative **Phyllis Schlafly**, who claimed the amendment diminished the rights and status of women and altered the "role of the American woman as wife and mother." Schlafly organized a "Stop-ERA" movement, drawing from white middle-class women who identified themselves as regular churchgoers. They pressured state legislatures to vote no on the ERA, and by 1974, ratification had been defeated in seventeen state legislatures. With passage stalled and the deadline for ratification (1979) approaching, pro-ERA groups asked Carter to endorse the amendment and an extension for ratification. Carter endorsed both and Congress extended the ratification process by thirty-nine months, but in the end, the amendment fell three states short of ratification. Many of its supporters complained that Carter might have taken a more active part in ensuring the amendment was ratified.

Conservative women had found a voice, and they quickly linked the ERA to abortion and other issues, creating a wider "pro-family" movement. In 1973, the Supreme Court in a 5-to-2 decision, *Roe v. Wade*, invalidated a Texas law that prohibited abortion. Justice Harry Blackmun, writing for the majority, held that "the right to privacy" gave women the freedom to choose to have an abortion during the first three months of pregnancy. The controversial ruling struck down laws in forty-six states that had made abortions nearly impossible to obtain legally except in cases of rape or to save the life of the mother.

Although most public opinion polls indicated that a majority of Americans favored giving women the right to choose an abortion, at least under some circumstances, many religious organizations worked with conservative groups to organize a **Right to Life movement** "opposing abortion rights on moral and legal grounds." It found common cause with the pro-family and anti-ERA movements in voicing a multifaceted critique of American society, feminism, and liberalism. Pointing out that the Great Society's Medicaid program paid out more than $45 million for abortion services in 1973, anti-abortion forces demanded that Congress pass the Hyde Amendment (1976), which prohibited the use of federal Medicaid funds to pay for abortions. When Carter refused to oppose the Hyde Amendment, some within the NOW camp argued that their organization should support anyone but Carter in the forthcoming 1980 election.

For Carter the critical issue was not affirmative action or social legislation, but finding ways to stimulate economic growth. His approaches, as in the case of domestic issues, generated opposition from both Democrats and Republicans. Still, there was nearly unanimous agreement that it was important to reduce dependence on foreign oil, which supplied about 60 percent of the country's oil needs.

Consequently, Carter's announcement that solving the **energy crisis** was the "moral equivalent of war" drew widespread applause. When Carter began to lay out his solutions, however, much of the applause quieted. Rather than stress more production of American-based gas and oil, he called for developing **alternative fuels** and for conservation, asking the nation to use less energy. Proponents of oil and gas production argued that alternative fuels were too expensive and could not meet the nation's demands. Nuclear energy, however, appeared a viable alternative—until March 1979, when a serious accident at the nuclear power plant site **Three Mile Island** in central Pennsylvania released a cloud of radioactive gas and nearly caused a **meltdown**. No one was injured in the accident, but nuclear power now appeared a less attractive energy source, and more than thirty energy companies canceled their nuclear energy projects.

Overall, Carter offered Congress more than a hundred energy proposals, but Congress approved only fragments of them, including the formation of a cabinet-level Department of Energy. His pleas to the public to reduce their energy consumption by wearing sweaters, lowering their thermostats in winter, and using public transportation also found few takers. When Iran sparked another oil crisis in 1978, it was clear that the United States was still dependent on foreign oil and that the country had no real energy program. Nor had the economy improved, with inflation in 1980 at 14 percent—the highest rate since 1947—and unemployment reaching nearly 7.6 percent.

New Directions in Foreign Policy

Carter arrived at the White House wanting to reshape American foreign policy. Believing the nation's policies focused too much on Europe, the Cold War, and an "inordinate fear of communism," he wanted to provide a new path for the United States to lead by example and not through dominance. The "soul of our foreign policy," he said, should be **human rights**. But, it was easier to announce a new approach than to implement one. Carter never succeeded in developing a "thought-out and planned" approach to foreign policy and frequently received conflicting advice from his main foreign policy advisers, Secretary of State Cyrus Vance and National Security Adviser Zbigniew Brzezinski, who had decidedly different views on the conduct of foreign policy.

Despite highlighting human rights, Carter chose to denounce, apply sanctions, and reduce aid only to some governments that abused their citizenry but not all.

energy crisis Vulnerability to dwindling oil supplies, wasteful energy consumption, and potential embargoes by oil-producing countries.

alternative fuels Sources of energy other than coal, oil, and natural gas, such as solar, wind, geothermal, hydroelectric, and nuclear energy.

meltdown Severe overheating of a nuclear reactor core, resulting in the melting of the core and the escape of life-threatening radiation.

human rights Basic rights and freedoms to which all human beings are entitled, such as the right to life and liberty, to freedom of thought and expression, and to equality before the law.

One of President Carter's greatest triumphs was the signing of the 1978 peace accords between Egyptian President Anwar Sadat and Israeli Prime Minister Menachem Begin. Sadat and Begin received the Nobel Peace Prize for their efforts.

Governments of El Salvador, Guatemala, Chile, Nicaragua, Uganda, the Soviet Union, and the minority white governments in southern Africa were among those targeted. But for repressive governments like those of the Philippines, Iran, and the People's Republic of China, it was business as usual, with Carter restoring full diplomatic relations with China in January 1979.

Seeking to reduce the tensions of the Cold War, Carter continued efforts to conclude a second arms limitation treaty and in June 1979, he and Brezhnev signed the second Strategic Arms Limitation Treaty (SALT II). It placed limits on the numbers of long-range bombers, missiles, and nuclear warheads each nation could deploy. But the treaty faced strong bipartisan opposition in the Senate, and when the Soviets invaded Afghanistan in December, Carter withdrew the treaty from consideration. Reverting to more traditional Cold War rhetoric, he labeled the invasion the "gravest threat to peace since 1945," imposed **economic sanctions** on the Soviets, and announced the United States would boycott the 1980 Moscow Olympic Games. Fearful that the Soviets would use Afghanistan as a "stepping stone" to

economic sanctions   Trade restrictions imposed on a country that has violated international law.

Middle Eastern oil, Carter proclaimed the "**Carter Doctrine,**" vowing "to repel by any means necessary, including the use of force" any attempt to take control of the Persian Gulf region. He also approved aid to the **mujahedeen,** Afghan rebels who were fighting the Soviets.

SALT II failed, but Carter notched two successes with the Panama Canal treaty and a peace agreement between Israel and Egypt. Both agreements charted new paths and matched Carter's goal of leading by example. For decades, Panamanians had argued and protested to gain control over the canal that split their nation. During the 1976 campaign, Carter had supported a treaty, even though the majority of Americans thought the Panama Canal should remain in American hands. Carter overcame bipartisan opposition, and in 1978 the Senate approved treaties giving Panama complete sovereignty over the canal in 2000.

Carter's persistence also was instrumental in working toward a peace agreement between Israel and its Arab neighbors. He invited Egyptian president Anwar Sadat and Israeli prime minister Menachem Begin to join him for peace talks at the presidential retreat at Camp David in Maryland. Surprisingly, both accepted, and at a series of meetings in September 1978, Carter shuttled between the two leaders, smoothing relations and stressing his personal commitment to both nations. The outcome was a set of carefully crafted agreements by which Egypt recognized Israel's right to exist and Israel returned the Israeli-occupied Sinai Peninsula to Egypt. It took several months to finalize the **Camp David Accords,** but on March 26, 1979, Carter looked on as Begin and Sadat signed the first peace treaty between an Arab state and Israel.

The Soviet intervention in Afghanistan and the Carter Doctrine were responses to more than just events in Afghanistan. Both the Americans and the Soviets were reacting to the revolution in Iran, which had toppled the pro-American ruler, Mohammad Reza Shah Pahlavi, in early 1979. The shah, restored to power by the United States in 1953, was America's staunchest ally in the Persian Gulf region. But his authoritarian rule had generated widespread opposition led by Iran's religious leaders, especially the **Ayatollah Ruhollah Khomeini,** who assumed power during the revolution and established an Islamic fundamentalist state.

Tensions between Iran and the United States increased as the anti-Western revolutionary government called the United States the main source of evil in the world. On November 4, after the exiled shah entered a New York hospital for cancer treatment, an angry mob stormed the American embassy in Tehran taking sixty-six American hostages.

As the world watched televised pictures of the hostages, Carter received conflicting options from Vance and Brzezinski. Brzezinski recommended using military force to free the hostages, but Carter agreed with Vance and opted for negotiations. For a while it seemed the right choice; thirteen hostages, mostly women and African Americans, were released. But when further discussions failed, with his popularity falling to nearly 30 percent, Carter ordered a military rescue mission. It failed, losing three helicopters in a violent dust storm in Iran. In late 1980, Canadian and Algerian diplomatic efforts obtained the release of the remaining hostages, who were set free on January 20, 1981, the day Carter left the presidency, ending 444 days of captivity.

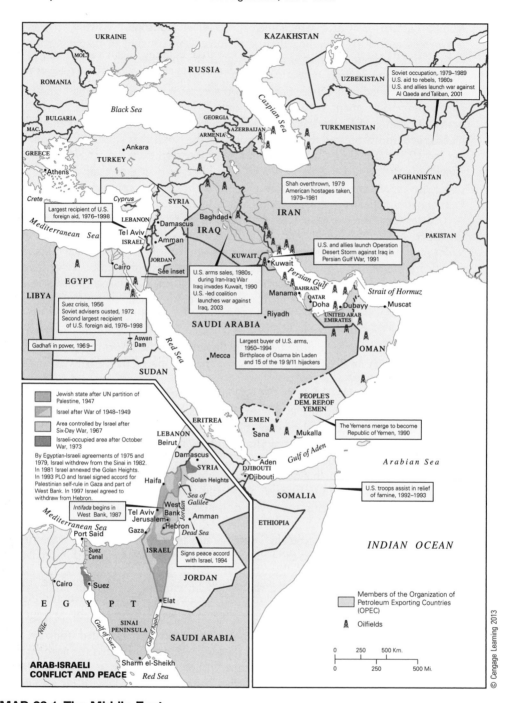

The following labels and annotations appear on the map:

UKRAINE
MOL.
ROMANIA
RUSSIA
KAZAKHSTAN
UZBEKISTAN
Soviet occupation, 1979–1989
U.S. aid to rebels, 1980s
U.S. and allies launch war against
Al Qaeda and Taliban, 2001
BULGARIA
Black Sea
MAC.
GEORGIA
TURKMENISTAN
Caspian Sea
GREECE
Ankara
AZERBAIJAN
ARMENIA
AFGHANISTAN
Athens
TURKEY
Crete
Cyprus
SYRIA
Largest recipient of U.S.
foreign aid, 1976–1998
LEBANON
Damascus
Baghdad
IRAN
Shah overthrown, 1979
American hostages taken,
1979–1981
PAKISTAN
Mediterranean Sea
Tel Aviv
ISRAEL
Amman
IRAQ
KUWAIT
Kuwait
U.S. and allies launch Operation
Desert Storm against Iraq in
Persian Gulf War, 1991
JORDAN
Cairo
See inset
U.S. arms sales, 1980s,
during Iran-Iraq War
Iraq invades Kuwait, 1990
U.S.-led coalition
launches war against
Iraq, 2003
Persian Gulf
BAHRAIN
Manama
QATAR
Doha
UNITED ARAB
EMIRATES
Dubayy
Strait of Hormuz
Muscat
EGYPT
LIBYA
Suez crisis, 1956
Soviet advisers ousted, 1972
Second largest recipient
of U.S. foreign aid, 1976–1998
Gadhafi in power, 1969–
Aswan
Dam
Riyadh
OMAN
SAUDI ARABIA
Largest buyer of U.S. arms,
1950–1994
Birthplace of Osama bin Laden
and 15 of the 19 9/11 hijackers
Red Sea
Mecca
SUDAN
Jewish state after UN partition of
Palestine, 1947
Israel after War of 1948–1949
Area controlled by Israel after
Six-Day War, 1967
Israeli-occupied area after October
War, 1973
PEOPLE'S
DEM. REP.OF
YEMEN
ERITREA
YEMEN
Sana
Mukalla
The Yemens merge to become
Republic of Yemen, 1990
By Egyptian-Israeli agreements of 1975 and
1979, Israel withdrew from the Sinai in 1982.
In 1981 Israel annexed the Golan Heights.
In 1993 PLO and Israel signed accord for
Palestinian self-rule in Gaza and part of
West Bank. In 1997 Israel agreed to
withdraw from Hebron.
LEBANON
Beirut
Damascus
SYRIA
Golan Heights
Haifa
Sea of
Galilee
Aden
DJIBOUTI
Djibouti
Gulf of Aden
Arabian Sea
SOMALIA
U.S. troops assist in relief
of famine, 1992–1993
Intifada begins in
West Bank, 1987
Mediterranean Sea
Port Said
Tel Aviv
Jerusalem
West
Bank
Amman
ETHIOPIA
Gaza
Hebron
Dead Sea
INDIAN OCEAN
Suez
Canal
ISRAEL
Signs peace accord
with Israel, 1994
Cairo
Suez
E G Y P T
Elat
JORDAN
Members of the Organization of
Petroleum Exporting Countries
(OPEC)
Oilfields
SINAI
PENINSULA
Gulf of Suez
Gulf of Aqaba
SAUDI ARABIA
0   250   500 Km.
0   250   500 Mi.
ARAB-ISRAELI
CONFLICT AND PEACE
Sharm el-Sheikh
Red Sea
Nile

© Cengage Learning 2013

MAP 28.1 The Middle East

Extremely volatile and often at war, the nations of the Middle East maintained precarious relations with the United States. To protect its interests, the United States extended large amounts
of economic and military aid, and sold huge quantities of weapons to the area. At times,
Washington ordered U.S. troops to the region. The Arab-Israeli dispute particularly upended
order, although the peace process moved forward intermittently.

RESURGENT CONSERVATISM

While liberals disagreed with Carter's view that liberalism had its limits, growing numbers of people were going even farther and agreeing with the ex-governor of California, Ronald Reagan, that the central "problem" facing the nation was liberalism. Reagan said the federal government was too big, too inefficient, and too expensive, and that liberal programs actually harmed those who worked hard, saved their money, and paid their taxes. But there was also a new, sharper edge to the criticisms voiced by an emerging New Right that placed its emphasis on social and moral issues.

The New Right   The New Right emerged as a coalition of conservative grassroots movements that believed the social and governmental liberal activism of the 1960s had weakened the national identity, contributed to a moral breakdown, and threatened "to destroy everything that is good and moral here in America." To save America, advocates of the New Right proclaimed the 1980 election needed to be a triumph of conservatism. Seeking to tap into the discontent voiced by many blue-collar and suburban voters, the New Right challenged the liberal use of government to induce social equality. It passionately claimed that liberalism sought to alter the foundation of the American family by promoting abortion rights, feminism, the ERA, and homosexuality.

Highly visible among New Right groups were evangelical Christian sects, many of whose ministers were **televangelists**—preachers who used radio and television to spread the gospel. Receiving donations that exceeded a billion dollars a year, they did not hesitate to mix religion and politics. Jerry Falwell's **Moral Majority** promoted New Right views on more than five hundred television and radio stations. Reaching millions of Americans, Falwell called on listeners to wage political war against liberal government officials whose views on the Bible, homosexuality, prayer in school, abortion, and communism were too liberal. Falwell told his listeners to get people "saved, baptized, and registered."

The New Right generated new levels of political activism, and its message found a growing audience among many working-class and young Americans who believed that their taxes were too high and were not being efficiently or correctly used. Throughout the 1970s, state and local taxes had risen while at the federal level Social Security taxes, now including Medicare, grew by 30 percent and income taxes, pushed by an inflation-fueled "**bracket creep**," increased by as much as 20 percent. Taxes and government spending, especially for social programs, were rapidly becoming broad-based issues. In California, Republicans and Democrats joined forces and used a referendum in 1978 to pass **Proposition 13**, which placed

televangelist Protestant evangelist minister who conducts televised worship services; many such ministers used their broadcasts as a forum for promoting conservative values.

bracket creep Inflation of salaries pushing individuals into higher tax brackets.

limits on property taxes and state spending. It "isn't just a tax revolt," observed a Carter official, "it is a revolution against government."

Promising to restore America by reducing government involvement and embracing the social positions of the New Right, Ronald Reagan benefited from the conservative resurgence. He attacked Carter's domestic and foreign policy record and offered to restore the nation's economy, power, and pride. Embracing the image of the "citizen politician, speaking out for the … common sense of everyday Americans," Reagan quipped, "A recession is when your neighbor loses his job. A depression is when you lose yours. A recovery is when Jimmy Carter loses his."

Reagan's message not only energized traditional Republicans and the New Right, but also resonated with many Democrats and independents, especially those living in the Sunbelt. By 1980, the Sunbelt's population not only exceeded that of the industrial North and East but it had taken the lead in opposing the cost and intrusive power of the federal government. As the November election approached, the central question was not if Reagan would win, but what the size of his majority would be and how many Republicans his **political coattails** would carry into office. When the votes were counted, Reagan had received an impressive 51 percent of the popular vote and an even more impressive 91 percent of the electoral count. The coattails had worked as well, with Republicans keeping their majority in the Senate and substantially narrowing the Democratic majority in the House of Representatives.

Reaganism   Called the "Great Communicator" by the press, Reagan brought to the White House an unusual ability to convey his views and agenda to the American public. The New Right and conservatives were expectant as he took office. He had campaigned not just on restoring prosperity and cutting intrusive government, but also on promoting traditional American values and strengthening the family. In office, however, Reagan disappointed the New Right by choosing to concentrate on the economy and foreign policy. The administration's economic plan was simple: cut the number and cost of social programs, increase military spending, and reduce taxes and government restrictions. "If we can do that, the rest will take care of itself," Reagan's chief of staff, James A. Baker, III, argued.

Calling the formula for restoring economic vitality **supply-side economics**, the Reagan administration fought inflation by keeping interest rates high—they spiked at 18 percent, the highest in the twentieth century—and promoted economic growth by reducing federal regulations, taxes, and social programs. In implementing **Reaganomics**, over $25 billion was slashed from federal spending on social programs, including programs like food stamps and **Aid to Families with Dependent Children**. Federal controls over business were reduced in a flurry of

---

political coattails   Term referring to the ability of a presidential candidate to attract voters to other office seekers from the same political party.

A former radio sports announcer, movie star, and host of television shows, Ronald Reagan used television and radio very effectively to outline his visions of American domestic and foreign policies. Because of his communication style, he was called "the Great Communicator."

© Bettmann/Corbis

deregulation that affected industries like oil and gas, banking, and communications. To further stimulate growth, Secretary of the Interior James Watt opened federally controlled land, coastal waters, and wetlands to mining, lumber, oil, and gas companies—a policy strongly advocated by many in the West. At the same time, to help business growth, the Environmental Protection Agency relaxed enforcement of federal guidelines for reducing air and water pollution. Finally, the 1981 **Economic Recovery Tax Act** lowered income taxes and most business taxes by an average of 25 percent.

Reagan's economic policies were not immediately effective; indeed, the economy worsened, as unemployment climbed to over 12 percent, the **trade deficit** soared, and bankruptcies for small businesses and farmers increased. Also growing at an alarming rate was the **federal deficit**, pushed by declining tax revenues and

trade deficit Amount by which the value of a nation's imports exceeds the value of its exports.
federal deficit The total amount of debt owed by the national government during a fiscal year.

increases in military spending and entitlement programs like social security. Reagan called for patience, assuring the public that his economic programs eventually would work.

As Reagan predicted, in 1983, the economy recovered. Inflation dropped to 4 percent and unemployment fell to 7.5 percent. Many, especially corporate leaders, loudly cheered Reaganomics, applauding deregulation. Deregulating of financial institutions was seen as especially positive because it spurred investment, which drove the stock market upward—the Great Bull Market. "I think we hit the jack-pot," Reagan announced when in 1982 he signed the Garn–St. Germain Act, which expanded the types of loans that the **savings and loan industry** (S&Ls) could make beyond those for single-family homes.

The recession ended just in time for the 1984 election. Using the theme "Morning in America," Reagan's campaign projected continued economic growth and affirmed his commitment to a strong America abroad. Democrats nominated Carter's vice president and traditional liberal Walter Mondale, whom Republicans immediately defined as a "tax and spend" liberal. Hoping to energize voters, Mondale selected New York Representative Geraldine Ferraro as the nation's first female vice presidential nominee. His choice made political history but had no effect on the election. President Reagan scored an overwhelming victory, taking 59 percent of the popular vote and carrying every state except Mondale's Minnesota.

Reagan continued to push Reaganomics during his second term, but the results were mixed, and by 1987 the economy was showing important weaknesses. Concerns grew about the size of the federal deficit and a **national debt** that had reached new records, requiring 14 percent of the annual budget to pay the interest. Others feared that the recently deregulated savings and loan industry, because of its aggressive and risky investment and loan policies, was tottering on the verge of collapse. The warnings proved true when in 1989 many S&Ls, especially in the southwest, faced bankruptcy and asked the federal government to provide more than $500 billion to cover the losses. Adding to the economic problems, in 1989 the stock market, which had been climbing since 1983, suddenly fell, losing 23 percent of its value on October 19. Not since Black Thursday, in the 1929 crash preceding the Great Depression, had such panic struck the market.

A SOCIETY AND ECONOMY IN TRANSITION

More than Reagonomics shaped the economy. Since the Johnson administration, the American public and politicians had struggled with an economy that seemed

savings and loan industry (S&Ls) Network of financial institutions originally founded to provide home mortgage loans; deregulation allowed S&Ls to provide loans for office buildings, shopping malls, and other commercial properties.

national debt The total amount of money owed by the United States to domestic and foreign creditors.

Part of globalization made possible by advanced telecommunications is the establishment of customer service centers in India that provide 24/7 answering and information services for American and British companies. In this picture dozens of Indians answer toll-free calls from English-speaking customers for a variety of American companies.

to resist conventional solutions. In the first decades after 1946, the nation had experienced its longest era of consistent economic growth in its history, with the gross national product rising at an average annual rate slightly higher than 2.5 percent. This growth translated into higher-paying jobs, more home ownership, accessible college educations, and overall an expanding consumer society with rising expectations. But by the early 1970s, economic growth had slowed, dipping to slightly over 1 percent, while the cost of living increased over 200 percent. In personal terms, this slowdown meant higher prices, fewer jobs, and for many, shattered expectations.

Many of the problems had roots in the shift from a manufacturing base to a service-based economy and in increasing **globalization**. Since the late 1960s, the expanding economies of West Germany, Japan, Korea, and Taiwan had

globalization   Interaction among countries worldwide in the free flow of trade, capital, ideas and information, and people.

begun to successfully compete for American domestic and foreign markets. Japanese goods were beginning to dominate the electronics industry and cut deeply into the American automobile market. American companies that in 1946 had produced two-thirds of the world's steel by 1980 made only 15 percent. Aggravating the problem were higher oil prices and a growing national dependence on foreign oil.

To maintain profitability and survive in the global and what some called **postindustrial economy**, corporations devised new strategies. Many rid themselves of less profitable manufacturing operations and invested more heavily in service industries. General Electric, for example, once one of the largest American manufacturing firms, sold off most of its manufacturing divisions and moved its resources into the service sector by buying the entertainment giant RCA as well as a number of investment and insurance firms. Other companies closed less-productive plants and shifted their production to locales with lower operating costs. Many moved to southern and western states, but an increasing number of companies relocated overseas.

Across the country, but especially in the northeast, as American companies lost money, shed workers, and closed plants, an expanding **"Rust Belt"** formed. Philadelphia, from 1969 to 1981, lost 14 percent of its population and 42 percent of its factory jobs. Pittsburgh, Cleveland, Detroit, and other Rust Belt cities also faced staggering economic losses as plants closed. But changes were felt everywhere. Suburban Lakewood, California, which had seen economic success for three decades after World War II, experienced economic decline when nearby defense-related and other industries relocated and downsized and stores like Walmart replaced higher-end department stores like Macy's.

With higher-paying manufacturing jobs on the decline, many Americans found new jobs in the service industry—which paid about one-third less and used more part-time help. Suddenly, McDonald's was one of the largest employers in the nation. Between 1980 and 1992, the average hourly wage of the American worker declined from $10.59 to $9.87. But the shift away from industry brought new opportunities for some, especially those able to participate in the expanding sector linked to advances in technology.

Technological developments by the mid-1970s were opening new fields and business opportunities, especially in communications and electronics. In part a by-product of military research and development, advances in miniaturization led to development in satellite transmissions, handheld calculators, videocassette recorders (VCRs), computers, and computer networks. With Apple and IBM leading the way, office and personal computers restructured the process of handling information and communications, spawning a new wave of "tech" companies and a new crop of millionaires such as Bill Gates. A Harvard dropout, Gates developed computer software, founded Microsoft in 1975, and became America's youngest billionaire.

---

postindustrial economy   An economy whose base is no longer driven by manufacturing but by service and information industries.

Gates was not alone. It seemed that thousands of people were riding the now expanding economy to wealth and power, from inventors to financial "wizards" who brokered mergers. Stories of economic success filled the news media and the plots of television shows and movies, creating a money culture. "Buy high, sell higher," *Fortune* magazine proclaimed. The pursuit of wealth and the goods that it could buy became a lifestyle sought after by many young Americans, particularly the baby boomers, who were reaching their peak earning and spending years. Income-conscious college graduates hoping to become highly paid, aggressive professionals eagerly applied to law, business, and other postgraduate schools. Consequently, the number of doctors, lawyers, and MBAs (those with degrees as master's of business administration) swelled, while in the business world, many executive salaries broke $40 million. The 1980s were called by some the "Me Decade," and *Newsweek* declared 1984 the "Year of the **Yuppie**"—the young, upwardly mobile urban professional who was on the leading edge of the new economic vitality.

But for every Gates or successful yuppie, there seemed to be many more Americans whose economic realities were going in the other direction. Society seemed to be settling into a two-tiered structure with a widening gap separating rich and poor. Between 1980 and 1990, the percentage of the nation's wealth held by the richest 1 percent of American families climbed, but the other 99 percent of families saw their share of the nation's wealth decline. Put simply, the rich got richer and everyone else, on average, got poorer. The ranks of those in economic and social distress grew. Across the country, the number of homeless increased, placing more pressure on social programs even as their budgets were being reduced. The employed were not immune. With 15 percent blue-collar unemployment in Los Angeles, Juan Sanchez was happy to have a good job at a furniture factory, although he and his wife and three children were unable to afford a home and had to live in his brother-in-law's garage. Contributing to stresses on the two-tiered society was a new wave of immigrants who entered the United States following the passage of the 1965 Immigration and Nationality Act.

New Immigrants   The 1965 Immigration Act ended the national quota system established in the 1920s for immigration. A steady increase in the rate of immigration followed (see Figure 28.1). The 1965 act also set new criteria for immigration that favored those with family members in the United States and those having desired job skills and education. It set general annual immigration totals by nation (20,000 per nation) and hemispheric limits that for the first time set a ceiling on immigrants from the Western Hemisphere. The most immediate result was a change in the place of origin of those coming to the United States. Before the 1965 act, three of every four immigrants came from Europe, but within two decades, more than half of all immigrants arrived from the Caribbean and Latin America, with Asians immigrants becoming the second largest group, surpassing those arriving from Europe. Most came for the traditional reasons: jobs and security. Because the new immigration law favored those with education and skills, many filled the ranks of professionals and technicians, found well-paying jobs, and merged into American society. This

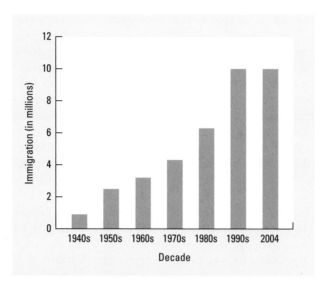

FIGURE 28.1 Immigration to the United States Since 1940

Since the 1940s, the number of immigrants coming to the United States has grown steadily. Changes in immigration laws in 1965 and 1990 not only allowed more immigrants to enter the country but also changed the point of departure for most of those immigrants from Europe to Latin America and Asia.

appeared to be especially true of those from Japan, China, Korea, and India. But other Asians, especially those coming as refugees from Vietnam, Laos, and Cambodia, along with many from Latin America, arrived with little education or skills. They added to the tier of society that worked at low-paying, part-time jobs in the service and agriculture sectors. Mired in poverty, many had difficulty assimilating into American society and faced growing intolerance and hostility.

By the mid-1980s, some critics of immigration, especially conservatives, voiced fears about the expanding cultural diversity that threatened their vision of an America centered on European culture. They pushed for Protestant Christian prayer in school and adoption of English as the official language of the United States. Other critics called for increased efforts to stop illegal immigration, especially from Latin America. The 1965 act's limit on immigrants from the Western Hemisphere led to an increased number entering the United States illegally. Most crossed over the border with Mexico and spread out across the country seeking jobs. They found employment as migrant farm workers, laborers, and workers in the service industry. By the mid-1980s, citing competition for jobs and increased social and welfare costs, many Americans called upon Congress to reduce the flow of illegals. Congress responded with the **Immigration Reform and Control Act**, which strengthened the U.S. Border Patrol and established stiffer punishments for employing illegal immigrants. But rather than deportation, the act offered amnesty and possible citizenship to illegal immigrants who had arrived in the United States before 1982.

IT MATTERS TODAY

Migrant Workers

For most of the twentieth century, farmers have relied on migrant workers to harvest crops. The life of migrant workers is one of long hours, low wages, and little respect. Working conditions are not much different from those described by John Steinbeck in *The Grapes of Wrath*. A majority of migrant families live near or below the poverty line and face more health risks and shorter life expectancy than any other occupational group in the country.

Since the 1970s, the number of illegal immigrants working as migrants has increased steadily. Today, it is estimated that over 90 percent of migrants are foreign born and more than 65 percent are illegal immigrants. Those hiring these workers argue that not enough Americans are willing to do hard agricultural work. Some claim that the growers prefer foreign-born workers, including illegal immigrants, because they can pay lower wages and provide few benefits to workers who are not likely to complain about abusive treatment for fear of arrest and deportation.

- California has the highest percentage of foreign-born residents, causing a state senator to say: "We have the best benefit package ... for illegal immigrants, so they come here." Do you think illegal immigrants should receive federal and state benefits like access to education, health care, and welfare?

© Bob Daemmrich Photography, Inc.

Latinos, Asians, and people from the Caribbean make up the majority of immigrants arriving in the United States today. Critics of immigration worry that these groups will not assimilate easily and want to limit further immigration. Supporters argue that assimilation is taking place and point to increased rates of nationalization and citizenship. Here, a Vietnamese family participates in the all-American sport of baseball (T-ball).

Except for those who thereby became American citizens, few found much merit in the act, and as illegal immigration continued, so too did the calls for more assertive actions to prevent it.

ASSERTING WORLD POWER

Reagan's victories in 1980 and 1984 resulted not only from the popularity of his domestic agenda but also from public support for his views on the role of the United States in world affairs. Throughout the 1980 presidential campaign, the Republicans had hammered at Carter's ineffective foreign policy and at slipping American prestige in the world. Reagan promised to restore American power and influence. Although he had little expertise in foreign policy, Reagan held firm beliefs about America's role in the world and the importance of working from positions of military strength. The Soviets were the "focus of evil" in the world, an "evil empire," but he understood that the Soviet Union was weaker than the United States and that, when faced with strength, some in the Kremlin would be smart enough to negotiate. The United States "could outspend them forever," he explained, and when "we turn our full industrial might into an arms race, they cannot keep pace." The problem was how best to get to that point.

Cold War Renewed   The first step was to reverse Carter's policies that Reagan and his supporters thought made America look vulnerable. One way was to increase the offensive military's capabilities. A second was to develop and deploy a system of defense against Soviet missiles: the **Strategic Defense Initiative** (SDI). A compliant Congress quickly funded Reagan's military budget, adding more than $100 billion a year in appropriations. Congress also funded SDI research—more than $17 billion between 1983 and 1990—even as many scientists argued that the project was conceptually and technologically flawed and could not provide full protection against Soviet missiles.

To add more pressure on Soviet capabilities while projecting American strength, Reagan was determined to confront the Soviets and their minions around the globe. His program was labeled the "Reagan Doctrine," and he explained that as part of its "self-defense" and "mission," the United States would support "freedom fighters" and governments confronting communism, especially in the third world. In these "battles," Reagan supplied increasing amounts of economic and military aid, including covert operations in Afghanistan, Angola, Ethiopia, El Salvador, and Nicaragua. In the Caribbean, Reagan went further and approved a military strike against the island nation of **Grenada**. There, Reagan and his advisers believed, Soviet-Cuban influence was behind the building of an extended airport runway that could be used as a staging area for enemy aircraft. When the government, "a brutal gang of leftist thugs," seemed to threaten the freedom of nearly five hundred American students attending medical school on the island, Reagan ordered an invasion. On October 25, 1983, more than two thousand American soldiers quickly overcame minimal opposition, brought home the American students, and installed a pro-American government on the island. The administration basked in public approval.

Concern was growing, however, over Washington's efforts to fight Communist elements in Central America. Many in the administration believed that the Marxist Sandinista Nicaraguan government was part of a Soviet-Cuban effort to take over Central America and was exporting revolution to El Salvador, which was a key to the rest of the region. It was, they stated, a "textbook case of indirect armed aggression by Communists." Consequently, the Reagan administration increased its economic and military aid to the non-Communist government of El Salvador and discounted reports of human rights violations by "death squads" linked to the Salvadoran military. Concerns about abuses in El Salvador were linked to increasing opposition to Reagan's covert activities in Nicaragua.

Hoping to duplicate Eisenhower's success in toppling the Guatemalan government in 1954, Reagan supported organizing an army, the **Contras**, in neighboring Honduras that would overthrow the Sandinista government in Nicaragua. But public and congressional opposition arose in 1984 when the press uncovered large-scale American covert aid to the Contras, including the CIA's mining of Nicaraguan harbors. Many worried that Reagan's efforts in Central America would escalate, creating another Vietnam-like scenario. In response, Congress passed the **Boland Amendment**, which prohibited the CIA and other U.S. intelligence agencies from "directly or indirectly" supporting any military operations in Nicaragua. Reagan and CIA director William Casey ignored the intent of the amendment and found alternative ways to continue arming the Contras. One plan involved improving relations with Iran, which they hoped might have the added benefit of helping to reduce a spreading wave of terrorism throughout the Middle East.

Terrorism   Since the Iranians had seized American hostages, the problem of terrorism had gotten worse. Initially, it was primarily connected to the struggle between Israel and the **Palestine Liberation Organization** (PLO) and its Arab supporters. By the late 1970s, pro-Palestinian organizations were being supported by the ayatollah in Iran and **Muammar Qaddafi**, the ruler of Libya.

Throughout the Mediterranean region, terrorists kidnapped and killed Americans and Europeans, hijacked planes and ships, and attacked airports and other public places. Americans in Lebanon became direct targets on two occasions in 1983. In April Muslim terrorists attacked the American embassy in Beirut, killing 63 people, and six months later, a suicide bombing at the Marine barracks at the Beirut airport killed 241 Marines who were part of a United Nations (UN) peacekeeping force. Reagan vehemently denounced the terrorist attacks but found no solution to the problem except to remove American troops from Lebanon in January 1984.

The administration found a more satisfying response two years later when it bombed targets in Libya. Muammar Qaddafi was regarded as a major supporter

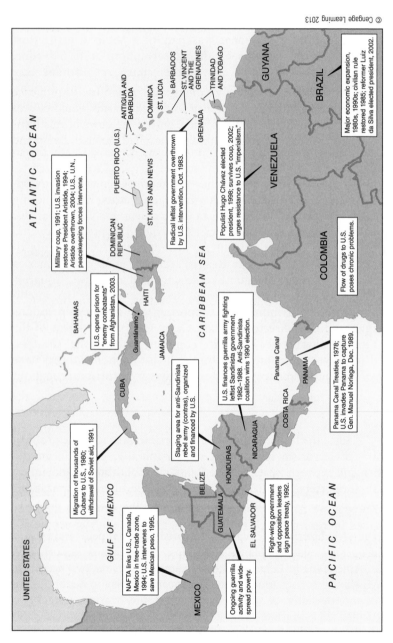

© Cengage Learning 2013

UNITED STATES

ATLANTIC OCEAN

GULF OF MEXICO

Migration of thousands of Cubans to U.S., 1980; withdrawal of Soviet aid, 1991.

NAFTA links U.S., Canada, Mexico in free-trade zone, 1994; U.S. intervenes to save Mexican peso, 1995.

MEXICO

BAHAMAS

CUBA

Guantánamo

U.S. opens prison for "enemy combatants" from Afghanistan, 2003.

JAMAICA

HAITI

DOMINICAN REPUBLIC

Military coup, 1991; U.S. invasion restores President Aristide, 1994; Aristide overthrown, 2004; U.S., U.N., peacekeeping forces intervene.

PUERTO RICO (U.S.)

ST. KITTS AND NEVIS

ANTIGUA AND BARBUDA

DOMINICA

ST. LUCIA

BARBADOS

ST. VINCENT AND THE GRENADINES

TRINIDAD AND TOBAGO

GRENADA

Radical leftist government overthrown by U.S. intervention, Oct. 1983.

CARIBBEAN SEA

GUYANA

BRAZIL

Major economic expansion, 1980s, 1990s; civilian rule restored 1985; reformer Luiz da Silva elected president, 2002.

VENEZUELA

Populist Hugo Chávez elected president, 1998; survives coup, 2002; urges resistance to U.S. "imperialism."

COLOMBIA

Flow of drugs to U.S. poses chronic problems.

Staging area for anti-Sandinista rebel army (contras), organized and financed by U.S.

U.S. finances guerrilla army fighting leftist Sandinista government, 1982–1988. Anti-Sandinista coalition wins 1990 election.

BELIZE

HONDURAS

NICARAGUA

COSTA RICA

Panama Canal

PANAMA

Panama Canal Treaties, 1978; U.S. invades Panama to capture Gen. Manuel Noriega, Dec. 1989.

GUATEMALA

EL SALVADOR

Ongoing guerrilla activity and widespread poverty.

Right-wing government and opposition leaders sign peace treaty, 1992.

PACIFIC OCEAN

MAP 28.2 The United States in Central America and the Caribbean, 1978–2006

Plagued by poverty, population pressures, repressive regimes, and drug trafficking, this region has experienced turmoil and conflict—but also some hopeful developments—in recent decades.

of international terrorism, and when intelligence sources linked him to a bombing in West Berlin that killed two American soldiers, Reagan ordered the raid on Libya. "You can run but you can't hide," he told terrorists. Neither the bombing nor Reagan's declaration deterred the terrorists, who continued their activities, especially in Lebanon. There, it was thought, one of the most active terrorist groups, Hezbollah, received direct support from Iran.

Trying to merge two problems, in 1985, American agents sought to gain the release of American hostages held in Lebanon by wooing Iran with the sale, through Israel, of weapons. In return for the weapons, Iran would use its influence to gain the release of the hostages, while the money paid for the arms would be sent to a Swiss bank account that could be used by the Contras. As news of this **Iran-Contra Affair** increased, it was clear that the administration had violated the Boland Amendment. Responding to growing public concern, Reagan appointed a special investigating commission, while Congress began its own investigation. By mid-1987, both investigations agreed that members of the CIA and the National Security Council (NSC) had acted independently, without the knowledge or approval of Congress, and had lied to Congress to hide their operation. Eventually, fourteen people were charged with committing crimes, and eleven—including several top-level advisers to Reagan—were convicted of violating a variety of federal laws and were sentenced to prison terms. Investigators found no direct proof of Reagan's involvement in the affair but concluded that he had encouraged such illegal activities by ordering continued support for the Contras. Reagan's protest, "I just didn't know," made it appear that he was out of touch with and not in control of what his aides were doing.

Reagan and Gorbachev
Until 1985, Reagan's foreign policy had focused on combating the power of the Soviet Union around the globe. Then, unexpectedly, the president executed a reversal of policy. Reagan and his advisers saw in the new Soviet leader **Mikhail Gorbachev** a true reformer committed to making fundamental changes in the Soviet Union and improving relations with the United States. Gorbachev released political prisoners, and with his policy of **perestroika** ("restructuring"), he began to restructure an economy that was stagnating under the weight of military spending and state planning. His policy of **glasnost** ("openness") initiated reforms that provided increased political and civil rights to the Soviet people. To demonstrate to the West that he was a new type of Soviet leader, Gorbachev unilaterally stopped nuclear testing and deployment of missiles in Eastern Europe and informed Reagan that he wanted to work "vigorously" to improve relations with the United States.

perestroika   Organizational restructuring of the Soviet economy and bureaucracy that began in the mid-1980s.

glasnost   Official policy of the Soviet government under Gorbachev emphasizing freedom of thought and candid discussion of social problems.

Reagan, too, wanted to improve relations, and he met with Gorbachev seven times between 1985 and 1989, with arms control the central issue. When the two leaders met in Reykjavik, Iceland, in October 1986, differences over SDI prevented an agreement to reduce strategic weapons. Both left the summit disappointed, but they agreed to keep working on arms limitations and in December 1987, they signed the **Intermediate Nuclear Force Treaty**, which removed their intermediate-range missiles from Europe. Soviet-American relations continued to improve as Gorbachev withdrew Soviet forces from Afghanistan and Reagan visited Moscow. Assessing the changes, Secretary of State George Shultz noted that the Cold War "was all over but the shouting."

IN REAGAN'S SHADOW

Despite some concerns over the economy and the Iran-Contra revelations, most Republicans believed that the Reagan years had cemented a conservative ascendency and that Vice President George Herbert Walker Bush would be able to defeat any Democratic candidate. Although some in the New Right worried that he was not conservative enough, most Republicans believed that Bush had earned the nomination. He had served the party faithfully, holding important posts under Presidents Nixon and Ford, including chair of the Republican National Committee, ambassador to China, and director of the Central Intelligence Agency. He was expected to continue the Reagan revolution and defeat the Democratic candidate, Governor Michael Dukakis of Massachusetts.

Bush Assumes Office   The 1988 campaign followed a familiar pattern. Republicans labeled Dukakis too liberal, especially on fighting crime and drugs, while Bush emphasized his foreign policy experience and promised not to raise taxes: "Read my lips ... no new taxes." Dukakis had no effective answer to the Republican attacks and Bush sailed to an easy victory. With 79.2 percent of the electoral vote and 54 percent of the popular vote, he became the first sitting vice president to be elected president since Martin Van Buren in 1836. Although Bush trounced Dukakis, the victory was not as sweet as he had hoped. Democrats maintained large majorities in the House and the Senate.

During the campaign, Bush had rested largely on Reagan's policies, saying that changes and "new directions" were not needed. As president, he kept many of Reagan's advisers and announced his goal was not "to remake society" but to "see that government doesn't get in the way." It was a realistic goal, given that he faced a Congress in which Democrats had a ten-vote majority in the Senate and an eighty-nine-vote majority in the House. By the end of his first year in office, Bush and his advisers believed they were managing well. Bush had used the veto extensively to block or modify Democratic-sponsored legislation, while also promoting a "kinder and gentler nation." His veto had blocked a Democratic effort to raise the minimum wage to $4.65 an hour and had forced Congress to accept his proposal of $4.25 an hour. Bush also supported passage of the **Americans with Disabilities Act** of 1990, giving it his administration's highest priority, despite opposition from many business groups and the high cost of the bill. He also credited his administration for protecting the environment and wilderness areas. The Clean Air Act of 1990 significantly reduced smokestack and auto emissions and created standards for a wide variety of pollutants in the air.

If Bush was pleased about his limited domestic agenda, he was concerned about the nation's economic condition. Facing a huge budget deficit, a recession, and an expensive bailout of the federal savings and loan system, Bush agreed that an increase in tax revenue was necessary—violating his election pledge not to raise taxes. His decision brought immediate condemnation from many Republicans and some Democrats. As the battle over the budget raged, Bush reluctantly agreed to the Omnibus Budget Reconciliation Act, which included a significant increase in the income tax, along with smaller increases on other taxes, like the gasoline tax. Bush's popularity dropped 25 percent and in the 1990 congressional elections, Democrats gained ten more Senate seats and twenty-five more seats in the House. Political gridlock followed.

While Bush's popularity recovered as he oversaw successes in foreign policy, the economy did not. Between 1990 and 1993 more than 1.9 million people lost their jobs, and 63 percent of American corporations cut their staffs. Families watched as average levels of income dropped below 1980 levels, to $37,300 from a 1980 high of $38,900. Consumers—caught between rising unemployment, falling wages, and nagging inflation—saw their savings shrink, and their confidence in the economy followed suit. "I don't see the United States regaining a substantial percentage of the jobs lost for five to ten years," said one chief executive.

Bush and a New International Order   Bush's own preferences and international events dictated that foreign affairs would consume most of his attention. The world was changing rapidly, and Bush considered the management of international relations as one of his strengths. As he assumed office, Gorbachev's reforms touched off a series of political changes that rocked the Soviet Union and its Eastern European satellites. Nationalism and the rejection of Communist rule resulted in new democratic governments in Poland, Hungary, and Czechoslovakia, as well as the unification of Germany and the fragmentation of Yugoslavia. By 1989, the **Berlin Wall** was torn down, and Gorbachev and Bush, meeting on the island of Malta in the Mediterranean Sea, had declared that the Cold War was over. In 1990, the Soviet Union began to disintegrate when the Baltic States—Latvia, Estonia, and Lithuania—declared their independence. Fearful that Gorbachev would allow the further fragmentation of the Soviet Union, in August 1991 conservatives staged a coup to replace him. The poorly planned coup failed

---

Berlin Wall   Barrier that the Communist East German government built in 1961 to divide East and West Berlin; it was torn down in November 1989 as the Cold War was ending.

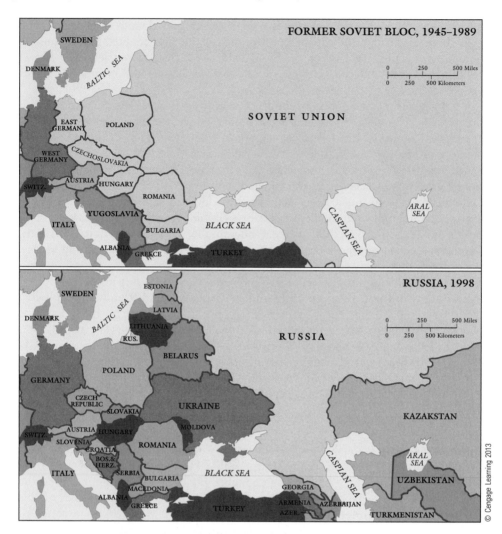

MAP 28.3 Collapse of the Soviet Bloc

These contrasting maps show the Soviet Union and the countries it dominated before and after the fall of communist governments. What countries in Eastern Europe escaped Russian control after 1989? What new countries emerged out of the old Soviet Union?

when **Boris Yeltsin**, the president of the Russian Republic, called for a popular uprising against it. As Yeltsin emerged as the new leader of the reform movement, Gorbachev resigned, and by Christmas the Soviet Union ceased to exist. In its place was the **Commonwealth of Independent States** (CIS), a weak federation of once-Soviet republics, led by Yeltsin.

Central and Eastern Europe were not the only sites of democratic reform. In South Africa, the one-time apartheid (white supremacist) government freed

Lionel Cironneau/AP Images

With the collapse of the Soviet Union and communism across Eastern Europe, the symbol of the iron curtain and the Cold War came tumbling down in Berlin. Jubilant Berliners sit atop the Berlin Wall, which had divided the city from 1962 to November 1989.

opposition leader Nelson Mandela after twenty-seven years in prison, and in a 1992 election white voters officially ended apartheid and moved to allow nonwhites to vote. The political changes in South Africa and much of Eastern Europe were relatively peaceful, but in parts of Yugoslavia religious and ethnic differences led to horrific violence.

In Yugoslavia, ethnic separatist movements demanded the dismantling of Yugoslavia and called for independence for the regions of Slovenia, Croatia, Bosnia-Herzegovina, and Macedonia. Representing a united Yugoslavia, Serbia fought to maintain its control, but by 1992 all but Bosnia-Herzegovina had achieved independence. In Bosnia-Herzegovina a religious and ethnic civil war continued until 1995 as Serb forces instituted a policy of "ethnic cleansing" to remove the Muslim population (as discussed further in the next chapter).

Democratic reformers were not always successful. In several Communist countries, like Cuba, Romania, and the People's Republic of China, the existing leadership maintained control. In China, thousands of people filled the massive expanse of Tiananmen Square in 1989 calling for political, social, and economic reforms, only to be attacked by Chinese troops who killed hundreds of protesters as the world watched on television. Bush condemned the attacks, but stuck to his policy of nonintervention and verbal support for the growth of democracy.

While some argued that the collapse of the Soviet Union created a "peace dividend," allowing the United States to reduce its global role and military budget, Bush insisted that the world was still a dangerous place and American power was still needed to promote national interests and world stability. His position seemed prudent when in 1990 American military force was needed to end an Iraqi invasion of neighboring Kuwait.

In August 1990, Iraq's forces overran the oil-rich sheikdom of Kuwait. Concerned that Iraqi leader Saddam Hussein intended to dominate the Persian Gulf and gain control over more than 40 percent of the world's oil supply, Bush decided to intervene. Within hours of the Iraqi invasion, the president organized a UN response. A multinational force of more than 500,000, including 200,000 Americans, went to Saudi Arabia in Operation Desert Shield to protect Saudi borders and oil. To pressure Iraq to withdraw from Kuwait, Bush and coalition leaders set January 15, 1991, as a deadline. If Iraq still occupied Kuwait by that date, the coalition would use force. On January 12, after three days of debate and a five-vote margin in the Senate, Congress approved the use of American soldiers in offensive operations against Iraq.

Eighteen hours after the deadline expired, with Iraq making no move to pull out, the UN coalition began devastating air attacks on Iraqi positions in Kuwait and on Iraq itself, beginning what many called the **Persian Gulf War**. On February 23, American General Norman Schwarzkopf loosed coalition ground forces against Iraqi positions in what Saddam had said would be the "mother of all battles."

Within a hundred hours, the war against Iraq, called by U.S. forces Operation Desert Storm, was over. Coalition forces liberated Kuwait, capturing thousands of demoralized Iraqi soldiers. It was the "mother of all victories," quipped many Americans. As the architect of the coalition, President Bush saw his approval rating soar above 90 percent. Some, less euphoric, speculated that the offensive had ended too soon and should have continued until all, or nearly all, of the Iraqi army had been destroyed and Hussein ousted from power.

Bush also gained applause for his policies in Central America, where he helped end the violence in Nicaragua and El Salvador. Reversing Reagan's policy, he ended support for the Contras and worked to get Gorbachev's help in convincing Sandinista government leader Daniel Ortega to hold free elections, which took place in 1990 and resulted in the defeat of the Ortega government. In neighboring El Salvador, American-supported peace negotiations helped end the civil war. Bush relied on diplomacy to reduce conflict in Nicaragua and El Salvador, but Panama required a different approach. The problem centered on Manuel Noriega, who ruled the country with an iron hand. Once useful to the United States as a supporter of the Contras, Noriega had become increasingly dictatorial and an embarrassment to Washington. When he ignored American pressure to step down and was implicated in the torture and murder of political opponents and in facilitating shipments of drugs to the United States, Bush ordered American troops into Panama to arrest Noriega on drug-related charges. On December 20, 1989, in Operation Just Cause, American forces invaded Panama and within seventy-two hours, Noriega was in custody. In 1992, a Miami court found him guilty of drug-related offenses and sentenced him to prison.

The Election of 1992   As the presidential election season approached, the Democrats' strategy of "depending on Bush's screwing up and the economy going to hell in a handbasket" finally seemed to be paying off. While Bush could point to a success in Operation Desert Storm, the economy was still a problem—and to compound Bush's difficulty, he faced a conservative revolt in his own party, led by journalist and political commentator Patrick Buchanan. Although Buchanan failed to derail Bush's nomination, conservative Republicans were able to ensure that the party platform forcefully adopted their social agenda. It attacked permissiveness in American society, opposed abortion and alternative lifestyles, advocated less government, and stressed the "traditional American values" that emphasized family and religion. Buchanan roused the convention by calling for a "**cultural war** ... for the soul of the nation." Bush accepted the platform, but chose to emphasize his experience and foreign policy victories.

The Democratic nominee, Governor William (Bill) Clinton of Arkansas, was an unknown to many Americans. A 46-year-old baby boomer, he had gained support throughout his primary campaign and easily won the nomination. Joining Clinton in the race to defeat Bush was a third presidential candidate, the millionaire **H. Ross Perot**. Perot's messages were simple: politicians had messed up the nation, Congress was ineffective, the deficit needed to be reduced, and his election would return control to the people. By June, Perot led in the polls but as the election neared Bush and Clinton passed Perot in the polling. For Clinton and his advisers there was one basic message, the economy. James Carvell, Clinton's chief political adviser, tacked reminders over his own desk reading, "It's the Economy, Stupid." Republicans had no answer to the economic issues and instead focused on their cultural agenda and Clinton's character. Bush had served gallantly in World War II, while Clinton had avoided the draft during the war in Vietnam. Bush had experience and family values. Clinton had used drugs and was a known womanizer.

The campaign culminated in the third televised debate, watched by an estimated 88 million people. Both Bush and Perot gained in the polls following the

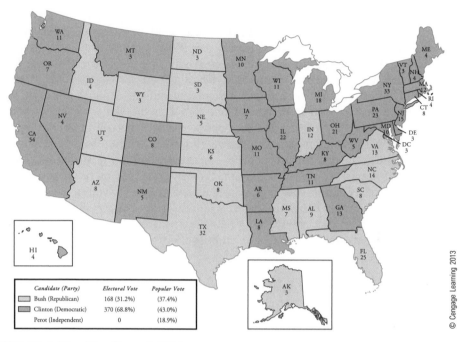

Candidate (Party)	Electoral Vote	Popular Vote
Bush (Republican)	168 (31.2%)	(37.4%)
Clinton (Democratic)	370 (68.8%)	(43.0%)
Perot (Independent)	0	(18.9%)

© Cengage Learning 2013

MAP 28.4 The Election of 1992

This map shows the ability of Bill Clinton to capitalize on the discontent with George Bush and the Republicans and carve out a landslide electoral victory. Because Clinton received only 43 percent of the vote, however, Republicans soon questioned his legitimacy as president.

head-to-head encounter, but they could not overtake the front-running Clinton. In a three-way race, Clinton earned 43 percent of the popular vote, compared with Bush's 37 percent and Perot's 19 percent. Clinton swept to victory with 370 votes in the Electoral College, 100 more than he needed to win. While Democrats still held the majority in Congress, Republicans had gained nine seats in the House of Representatives. In both parties, a record number of women and minorities were elected to Congress.

STUDY TOOLS

SUMMARY

The years between Carter's inauguration and Clinton's election witnessed changing expectations based in part on the health of the American economy. The economic growth that had characterized the postwar period was slowing, making the American dream harder to attain. During Carter's presidency the nation seemed beset by blows to its domestic prosperity and international status that neither Carter nor Congress seemed able to solve. These problems contributed to a conservative resurgence that blamed liberal policies for most of the nation's troubles.

During the 1980 campaign Reagan rejected Carter's view that the nation faced limits and argued that American greatness was constrained only by the government's excessive regulation and interference in society. He promised to reassert American power and renew the offensive in the Cold War. It was a popular message that elevated Reagan to the presidency. As president, Reagan fulfilled many conservative expectations by reducing support for some social programs, easing and eliminating some government regulations, and exerting American power around the world—altering the structure of Soviet-American relations. Supporters claimed that Reagan's choices had restored prosperity and pride and that the administration had worked to "change a nation, and instead ... changed a world."

Bush used Reagan's legacy to ensure his election in 1988 but found that unlike Reagan, he was unable to project an image of strong and visionary leadership. Although he gained public approval for his handling of world affairs, those successes seemed only to highlight his inability to overcome a nagging recession that sapped the public's confidence in Republican leadership and the economy. Confident that his good intentions and foreign policy successes would propel him to another term, Bush lost to Clinton when the Democrat stressed the need for change, especially in the way the Republicans dealt with the economy.

CHRONOLOGY

NEW DIRECTIONS, NEW LIMITS

1976	Jimmy Carter elected president
1977	Department of Energy created
	Panama Canal treaties
1978	Camp David Accords
1979	Ayatollah Khomeini assumes power in Iran
	United States recognizes People's Republic of China
	Nuclear accident at Three Mile Island, Pennsylvania
	Egyptian-Israeli peace treaty signed in Washington, D.C.
	Hostages seized in Iran
	Soviet Union invades Afghanistan
1980	Carter applies sanctions against Soviet Union
	Carter Doctrine
	Ronald Reagan elected president
1981	Iran releases American hostages
	Economic Recovery Tax Act
1983	Congress funds Strategic Defense Initiative
	United States invades Grenada
1984	Withdrawal of U.S. forces from Lebanon
	Boland Amendment
	Reagan reelected
	Newsweek's "Year of the Yuppie"

1985	Mikhail Gorbachev assumes power in Soviet Union
	Secret arms sales to Iran to obtain funds for the Contras
1986	U.S. bombing raid on Libya
	Gorbachev-Reagan summit in Reykjavik, Iceland
1987	Iran-Contra hearings
	Stock market crash
	Intermediate Nuclear Force Treaty
1988	George Bush elected president
1989	Berlin Wall pulled down
	United States invades Panama
1990	Recession begins
	Clean Air Act
	Iraq invades Kuwait
	Americans with Disabilities Act
1991	Breakup of the Soviet Union
	Gorbachev resigns
	First Iraqi War
1992	Clinton elected

Focus Questions

If you have mastered this chapter you should be able to answer these questions and explain the terms that follow the questions.

1. What problems did Carter face in implementing his domestic policies, and why were many Democrats unhappy with his approach?
2. What new directions in foreign policy did Carter take, especially in Central America and the Middle East?
3. What issues contributed to the emergence of the New Right, and how did the New Right help shape the 1980 election?
4. What is "Reaganomics," and what were the consequences of Reagan's economic policies?
5. How was the changing U.S. economy affecting Americans?
6. Who were the "new immigrants," and how were they received?
7. What did the Reagan administration view as the main issue in world affairs, and how did it try to implement a more assertive foreign policy?
8. How and why did Reagan shift U.S.-Soviet policy during his second term?
9. What constraints hampered Bush in developing a domestic agenda?
10. What foreign-policy choices did Bush face in protecting American global interests?

KEY TERMS

Alan Bakke (*p.* 871)

Equal Rights Amendment (*p.* 872)

Phyllis Schlafly (*p.* 872)

Roe v. Wade (*p.* 872)

Right to Life movement (*p.* 872)

Three Mile Island (*p.* 873)

Carter Doctrine (*p.* 875)

mujahedeen (*p.* 875)

Camp David Accords (*p.* 875)

Ayatollah Ruhollah Khomeini (*p.* 875)

Moral Majority (*p.* 877)

Proposition 13 (*p.* 877)

supply-side economics (*p.* 878)

Reaganomics (*p.* 878)

Aid to Families with Dependent Children (*p.* 878)

Economic Recovery Tax Act (*p.* 879)

Rust Belt (*p.* 882)

Yuppie (*p.* 883)

Immigration Reform and Control Act (*p.* 884)

Strategic Defense Initiative (*p.* 886)

Grenada (*p.* 886)

Contras (*p.* 887)

Boland Amendment (*p.* 887)

Palestine Liberation Organization (PLO) (*p.* 887)

Muammar Qaddafi (*p.* 887)

Iran-Contra Affair (*p.* 889)

Mikhail Gorbachev (*p.* 889)

Intermediate Nuclear Force Treaty (*p.* 890)

Americans with Disabilities Act (*p.* 890)

Boris Yeltsin (*p.* 892)

Commonwealth of Independent States (*p.* 892)

Persian Gulf War (*p.* 894)

cultural war (*p.* 895)

H. Ross Perot (*p.* 895)

29

ENTERING A NEW CENTURY, 1992–2010

CHAPTER OUTLINE

• Economy and Society in the 1990s • The Clinton Years • The Testing of
President Bush • War and Politics • Study Tools

ECONOMY AND SOCIETY IN THE 1990S

According to Clinton's supporters, Reaganomics and Republican policies had
benefited the upper class and polarized the nation, but Clinton's election, they
said, would allow for the restoration of economic and social opportunities for
all Americans, especially those in the middle class. Although both parties
stressed their traditional slogans, there were significant changes taking place in
the economy that opened the door to new opportunities for some and closed it
for others.

Since the 1980s, laptop computers, cell phones, and "wi-fi" have made communications and acquisition of information nearly global and instantaneous. Here, two of the most recent additions to the global network of "connectivity" are highlighted as a man snaps a picture of the "new" iPad with his iPhone.

© David Brabyn/Corbis

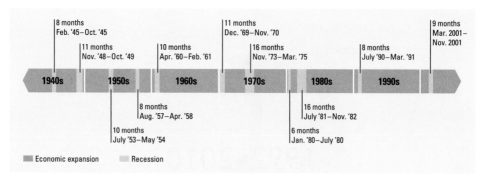

FIGURE 29.1 Expansion and Recession, 1940–2010

Economists define a recession as a contraction in the economy that is characterized by rising unemployment and decreasing production. Since the end of World War II, the average recession has lasted about ten months. As this figure shows, the period of economic expansion that ended in March 2001 was the longest period of growth since the end of World War II. Not shown on this figure is the recession that began in December 2007 and as of the summer of 2010 has not been declared over by the National Bureau of Economic Research, making its duration of over 31 months the longest U.S. economic decline since the Great Depression of 1929.

A Revitalized Economy

The economy started to climb out of the recession in 1992 (see Figure 29.1). It would continue to improve for almost a decade, averaging about 3 percent growth a year, before slowing again in 2001, one of the longest periods of sustained economic growth in the nation's history. The revitalized economy was an outcome of several developments. In 1993, Clinton initiated an economic plan that led to lower inflation and interest rates, increased trade, and a reduced deficit, which encouraged businesses to invest; business investment led to a drop in unemployment and increased consumer spending. But the improving economy was also in large part the result of the rapid growth in the **information technology** industries and the continued expansion of the service sector of the economy (see Figure 29.2). The new computer industry's stocks pushed upward, especially those listed on the **Nasdaq** index, which tracked the stocks in many new high-tech industries. Suddenly, the ranks of the rich included "dot-com" millionaires, men and women who owned or invested in companies associated with the new technologies and telecommunications industries, like Microsoft and the Internet. Northern California's Silicon Valley emerged as a center of the microprocessing industry and boasted the greatest concentration of new wealth in the nation.

information technology   A broad range of businesses concerned with managing and processing information, especially with the use of computers and other forms of telecommunications.

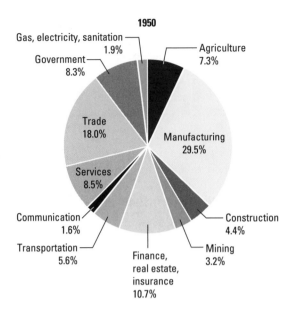

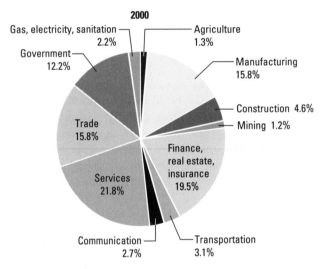

FIGURE 29.2 Main Sectors of U.S. Economy

A comparison of the 1950 and 2000 graphs shows that many of the economic sectors that deal with the production and marketing of goods—such as manufacturing, agriculture, transportation, and trade—have declined, while those sectors that mainly provide services have increased, especially government, services, and finance.

The explosion of information technology in the 1990s was only a beginning. As the nation entered the twenty-first century, the industry continued its innovations and tumultuous growth, spreading around the globe. Computer and digital communications devices have grown smaller, faster, more powerful, and cheaper with each passing year. The outcome has been a revolution affecting everything from social chit-chat and politics to the foods we eat, medical breakthroughs that save countless lives, and how we learn about events across the globe. New words like "googling," "smart phones," "iPhone," "apps," and "tweeting" have become universally used jargon.

Rich, Poor, and in Between   The surging stock market seemed to be reflected in increasing prosperity and wages. In 1996, national prosperity matched that of the peak year of 1989 and continued upward as take-home pay mushroomed. Average wages for men grew at about 4 percent beginning in 1997, with low-income workers' incomes growing by 6 percent between 1993 and 1998. The median household income in 2000 was $42,151, with Hispanic and black incomes reaching new highs ($33,455 and $30,436, respectively). Unemployment shrank, reaching 4.1 percent in 1999, the lowest figure since 1968. Minority unemployment rates also recorded new lows, 7.2 percent for Hispanics and 8.9 percent for African Americans. With more jobs and higher wages, the number of Americans living in poverty (incomes below $17,029 for a family of four) fell to 11.8 percent, the lowest rate since 1979.

Hidden within the statistics were grim realities. As the economy developed through the 1990s, the continued loss of industrial jobs and lack of technological skills forced many people into service industry jobs where wages were low and benefits scarce. African American and Hispanic poverty rates still averaged above 20 percent. Many Americans, especially those living in rural areas and urban centers, remained poor, and the income gap between the poor and the upper class continued to widen. Between 1979 and 1995, the wealthiest 20 percent of the population increased their wealth by 26 percent, with many company executives receiving 209 times more income than a factory worker.

Immigrants continued to contribute to the nation's diversity, and while some with education and skills quickly joined the ranks of the middle class, many fell into the poorest sections of society, with unemployment, crime, and dropout rates surpassing the national level. By the turn of the century, 6 percent of immigrants ended up on the welfare rolls—double the percentage of those born in the United States.

Prosperity was also uncertain for the middle class. During the 1990s, middle-class incomes, when adjusted for inflation, stayed the same or declined slightly. Adding to the concerns of middle- and working-class families were rising medical and fuel costs and fears about retirement security. As baby boomers were getting older and approaching retirement age, fewer and fewer younger workers were paying into the Social Security system. Many worried that without a major overhaul, both Social Security and Medicare would go broke as early as 2040, just as the last of the boomer generation should be starting to benefit from them.

Even more worrisome, medical expenses were among the country's fastest rising costs. In 1989, federal healthcare costs amounted to nearly 12 percent of the federal budget, but by 1998 the percentage had soared to 40 percent. For working

Americans, too, the costs of healthcare were rushing upward. In 1990, Americans spent $714 billion on healthcare, only to watch costs mushroom to over $2.2 trillion in 2007, an average $7,421 per person that represented 16.2 percent of the nation's gross domestic product. Over the same period, an increasing number of Americans found their coverage reduced or had no health insurance at all. By 2007 an estimated 15 percent of the population, led by Hispanics (32 percent) and African Americans (19.5 percent), had no health insurance.

Women, Family, and the Culture War   Women faced particular challenges through the 1990s. Dramatic changes were taking place in the structure of the family. By 2000 only 53 percent of families matched the traditional model of a husband and wife raising children, and more than half of all children were being born to unwed mothers. More marriages were ending in divorce, even as changes in divorce laws eliminated or reduced alimony. Child support payments frequently went unpaid. Concern was growing about the feminization of poverty and an increase in the percentage of children living in poverty—26.3 percent in 1993.

Other problems faced by nearly all women revolved around the workplace and lifestyles. More than three-fourths of all women worked outside the home, and according to one 1997 poll, 40 percent of women preferred a full-time job to raising a family. Many of those women, however, found employment in the service industries, where wages and opportunities frequently did not match those available to men. In many companies, women were not promoted to management positions or paid the same as men for comparable jobs. In California, a woman manager discovered that she made less than half the salary of one of the male assistant managers. When she confronted the company, a spokesman stated that the assistant manager had a wife and two children. She responded that she was a single mother with one child to support. At higher corporate levels, women holding managerial and executive positions also experienced a **"glass ceiling"** and various forms of **sexual harassment**. Women also argued that more needed to be done to adjust the workplace to fit the needs of women with families. Programs such as **flextime** and **flexplace**, job sharing, family leave, and more accessible daycare needed to be more widely adopted.

glass ceiling An intangible barrier within the hierarchy of a company that prevents women or minorities from rising to upper-level positions.

sexual harassment Unwanted sexual advances, sexually derogatory remarks, gender-related discrimination, or the existence of a sexually hostile work environment.

flextime Policy allowing an employee to select the hours of work, usually within specified limits set by the employer; options include a condensed workweek or varying hours during a regular workweek. In 2001 approximately 30 percent of the national work force was using some type of flextime.

flexplace Allows employees to work at the office or from an alternate work site during part of their scheduled hours; working at home is the most common alternative.

Failing to resolve such inequalities, women and groups like the National Organization for Women initiated individual and class action lawsuits for sexual discrimination against a variety of companies, including the Publix chain of super-markets and Wal-Mart. In 1993, the Supreme Court, in *Harris v. Forklift Systems*, found that sexual harassment involved not only "verbal and physical conduct" but also the creation of a "hostile environment."

The changing family and expanding roles of women also continued to fuel the culture wars. Conservatives and groups like Concerned Women of America claimed that liberalism and feminism endangered the traditional American family. They argued that even "mommy-friendly" workplaces were not a replacement for full-time mothers and an environment that respected moral values. As one antifeminist explained: "It all comes down to values. Traditional values work because they are the guidelines most consistent with human nature."

For many Americans, abortion remained one of the most divisive issues in the culture wars. Conservatives applauded the Supreme Court's 1992 decision in *Planned Parenthood of Southeastern Pennsylvania v. Casey,* which said that, in some cases, states could modify the right to an abortion. But many opponents of abortion were increasingly impatient with Congress's and the court's inability to reverse *Roe v. Wade.* Some within the Right to Life movement opted to take more direct and forceful tactics, targeting abortion clinic doctors, staff, and patients. By 1994, more than half of all abortion clinics reported varied cases of intimidation and violence, and a hundred clinics had been targets of arson or bombings. In response to these occurrences, in 1994 the Clinton adminis-tration supported the Freedom of Access to Clinic Entrances Act. It restricted the tactics of intimidation that pro-life supporters such as **Operation Rescue** could use.

THE CLINTON YEARS

Like many presidents entering office, Bill Clinton had an ambitious domestic agenda. "I want to get something done," he told a press conference. On his list of "to-dos" were parts of a liberal agenda, including providing national healthcare, signing the **Family and Medical Leave Act**, which had previously been vetoed by Bush, and supporting gay rights. But the economy was his first priority. As he assumed office, it appeared that the economy was beginning to recover, but Clinton understood that solving the problem of the deficit and putting the government on a firm financial foundation was a vital necessity. He told his economic team, "if we don't do this, we can't do anything else."

Clinton, the Economy, and Congress   The previous two administrations had quadrupled the national debt and piled up more debt in twelve years than the nation had in the previous two hundred. Clinton understood that he needed to take a bold step and implement a system that established fiscal discipline, supported critical social programs, and opened foreign markets to American producers. His economic plan crossed party lines and drew intense criticism from both Democrats and Republicans. Democrats protested his reduced spending, while Republicans vehemently opposed his increased taxes, which they claimed would harm the economy. The outcome was an August budget that passed the House by two votes and passed the Senate only when Vice President Al Gore cast the tie-breaking vote. For the first time since World War II, a bill had passed Congress when all members of the opposition party opposed it.

In an effort to improve the economy by increasing international trade, Clinton asked Congress to approve the **North American Free Trade Agreement** (NAFTA) and the **General Agreement on Tariffs and Trade** (GATT). Both initiatives were started by Bush but had encountered strong opposition, especially NAFTA, from many Democrats and from organized labor. Opponents claimed that both measures harmed the American economy by encouraging U.S. factories to relocate to nations with lower costs and standards. Unable to convince many Democrats to support the bills, Clinton was forced to rely on Republican votes for their passage.

The Family and Medical Leave Act was less contentious, with several Republican supporters, and was signed by Clinton in February 1993. It allowed workers to take up to 12 months' unpaid leave because of illness or family needs and guaranteed they would be able to return to the same job. Clinton's efforts to expand gay rights by asking Congress to lift the ban against homosexuals in the military met irresistible opposition from both political parties, the military, and the public. Faced with such opposition, Clinton accepted a compromise that did not lift the ban but instead required the military not to ask recruits about their sexual preferences and expected gays and lesbians in the service to refrain from homosexual activities. The compromise, "Don't Ask, Don't Tell, Don't Pursue," failed to please either side but remains in force in the military. The future of the policy appeared in jeopardy when in 2010, the House of Representatives, with White House support, repealed the law and pressure mounted on the Senate to also vote to repeal the policy.

Clinton's efforts reflected growing support for efforts by gay-rights activists to gain antidiscriminatory sexual preference laws that would protect jobs, provide work-related benefits for partners, and allow same-sex marriages. By the end of 2007, they could count some major victories as 19 states and the District of Columbia and over 140 cities and counties had passed legislation banning employment discrimination based on sexual orientation, and the Supreme Court in *Lawrence v. Texas* (2003) declared sodomy laws unconstitutional.

On a related issue, Clinton and Congress supported more funds to fight the AIDS epidemic. AIDS, or **acquired immune deficiency syndrome** (AIDS), began to be noticed in American cities in the early 1980s. Because the disease infected mostly

---

acquired immune deficiency syndrome (AIDS)   Gradual and eventually fatal breakdown of the immune system caused by the human immunodeficiency virus (HIV); HIV/AIDS is transmitted by the exchange of body fluids through such means as sexual intercourse or needle sharing.

In 1987, the San Francisco-based Names Project started to make quilts in memory of those who had died of AIDS in the United States. In 1992, the quilts were displayed on the Mall in Washington, D.C., displaying the names of twenty-six thousand people.

Robert Giroux/AFP/Getty Images

gay men and drug users, and seemed confined to the inner cities, official and public response was at first largely apathetic. Linking AIDS to the "morality battle," some, like Pat Buchanan and Senator Jesse Helms (R.–North Carolina), even suggested that those with the disease were being punished for their unnatural perversions. Responding to conservative pressure, the Reagan administration did little to fight AIDS. However, as the number of victims climbed and the disease spread to the heterosexual population, the public's fear of AIDS grew rapidly, and in the 1990s federal support became available for education and prevention programs and research. By 2007 AIDS had claimed more than half a million American lives and had killed over 20 million people worldwide. While significant advances have been made in research toward controlling AIDS, throughout many African countries AIDS remains at an epidemic stage.

In addition to the budget, Clinton recorded several other political victories during his first two years in office, including the Brady Handgun Violence Prevention

Act, which required federal background checks on those purchasing firearms and prohibited some individuals, like felons, from having handguns. But Clinton also suffered a glaring defeat in attempting to implement a national healthcare system. He had made it a campaign priority and after assuming office, he announced a task force, chaired by First Lady Hillary Rodham Clinton, to draft legislation. In September 1993, President Clinton asked Congress to write a "new chapter in the American story" and pass an extremely complicated plan—called Godzilla by one Democratic congressional leader. Republicans attacked the bill with gusto as an example of big government and bigger spending, saying that healthcare was too important to leave to the federal government. After a year of heated public and congressional hearings and debate, President Clinton admitted defeat and abandoned the effort.

The bitter fights over the budget, healthcare, and gays in the military, combined with allegations of various wrongdoings by the Clintons, boosted Republican popularity. In 1994, Republicans led by Newt Gingrich, a conservative representative from Georgia, seized the political initiative with a political agenda called the "**Contract with America.**" It called for supporting family values, large cuts in federal spending, and a balanced budget by 2002. The public responded by giving the Republicans majorities in both houses of Congress for the first time in forty years. The new conservative majority was "going to change the world," predicted Gingrich, now the Republican Speaker of the House.

Judicial Restraint and the Rehnquist Court   Part of the Republican plan for a conservative restructuring of government and society rested with the Supreme Court under Chief Justice William Rehnquist. Reagan and Bush had appointed six justices who practiced **judicial restraint** and deferred to Congress, the president, and the consensus of the people, creating a narrow, but not always stable, conservative majority. Conservatives hoped the Court would reverse previous positions taken on desegregation and affirmative action programs while supporting gun-owners' rights and anti-abortion efforts.

But the results of the Rehnquist Court's decisions were mixed. Conservatives were disappointed when the Court upheld the right to an abortion, the ban on prayer in school, and the *Miranda* decision. But they hoped that Rehnquist's view that the Court had erred by "reflecting society's changing and expanding values" would produce desired decisions, and they applauded the Court's ruling in the *DeKalb County, Georgia* case (1992) that busing could not be used to integrate schools segregated by de facto housing patterns. Conservatives also approved the Court's position regarding affirmative action when, on several occasions, it ruled that government could not "set aside" positions for minorities and that age and disability discrimination did not always violate equal protection under the law. In addition, the Court earned Republican praise for its support of laws passed in California, Washington, and Florida that forbid special consideration for race, gender, or both in state hiring and in admissions to state colleges and universities.

The Rehnquist Court also chipped away at the federal government's power to make state and local governments comply with its directives. In several cases throughout the 1990s, the Court upheld state sovereignty by deciding that states and municipalities could resist implementing executive and congressional directives. In *Printz v. United States* (1997), the Court declared unconstitutional certain provisions in the so-called Brady Bill that required state police to do a background search of anyone wanting to buy a handgun. Continuing the pattern, in 2000 a divided Court invalidated provisions in the Violence Against Women Act that permitted suits in federal courts by victims of gender-motivated crimes. In writing for the majority, Chief Justice Rehnquist announced that distinctions must be made between "what is truly national and what is truly local."

| Clinton's Comeback | The conservative resurgence in the 1994 election encouraged congressional Republicans to assume the political offensive and to reject compromises with the White House. They |

Clinton's Comeback   The conservative resurgence in the 1994 election encouraged congressional Republicans to assume the political offensive and to reject compromises with the White House. They focused on the 1995 budget as a way to roll back social programs and worked on an economic plan that slashed spending on education, welfare, Medicare, Medicaid, and the environment. "You cannot sustain the old welfare state" with a balanced budget, Gingrich proclaimed.

Although he agreed that balancing the budget was the first priority, Clinton called the Republican cuts too extreme. He vowed to protect spending for education, Medicare, Social Security, and the environment. As the battle for the budget began, Clinton reasserted his leadership when, on April 19, 1995, an act of domestic terrorism destroyed the Murrah Federal Building in Oklahoma City, killing 168 people, including 19 children. The bombing was the work of Timothy McVeigh, an American extremist who believed that the federal government threatened the freedom of the American people. To many, his views and actions not only symbolized the dangers of extremism but also reflected what seemed deepening social and political divisions in the nation. Consequently, when Clinton asked that people reject such extremism and stressed national unity, public opinion responded positively to the president's position.

Continuing to emphasize his centrism and to present Republicans as too extreme, Clinton gave a series of "common ground" speeches that committed his administration to passing anticrime legislation, finding methods to limit sex and violence on television, reforming welfare, and fixing affirmative action. This approach not only undercut Republican positions but, as in the case of welfare reform, made them appear hard-hearted. Conservatives argued that welfare programs created a class of welfare-dependent people—"welfare mothers" with little integrity and no work ethic who represented "spiritual and moral poverty." Clinton called such statements mean spirited and blind to the reality of those on welfare—especially considering the number of children on welfare. To replace relief with jobs, he said, it was vital to increase funds for daycare, job training, and educational programs.

When Republicans passed their budget bill, Clinton rejected it and sent it back to Congress. Overconfident, Republicans then refused to pass a temporary measure to keep the government operating unless their budget was accepted. Unmoved,

Clinton shut down all nonessential functions of the government—first for six days in November, then for twenty-one days from December 16 to January 6, 1996. With the public blaming Republicans for the budget impasse, Clinton and Congress reached an agreement. Clinton accepted some Republican cuts, while congressional Republicans accepted most of the president's requests, including those for education, Medicare, and Medicaid. Having won the battle of the budget, Clinton committed himself to balancing the budget by 2002.

As the 1996 presidential election approached, Republicans chose to emphasize two issues: the culture war and Clinton's budget. They argued that the president's spending cuts were inadequate and that his "big spending" had "sucked the life out of the economy and eaten up the American workers' pay." The problem with the Republicans' rhetoric was that the economy was beginning to achieve the highs described in the first section of the chapter, allowing Clinton to boast that his administration had created 10 million new jobs and had reduced poverty.

Clinton's Second Term   Despite the improving economy and Clinton's shrewd political manuevering, Republicans remained confident they would regain the presidency in the 1996 election. Conservative Republicans dominated the convention, once again attacking Clinton's liberalism and personality. Amid battle cries of the "cultural war" they nominated conservative Kansas Senator Robert Dole. Their expectations quickly faded as public opinion polls showed that over 60 percent of Americans gave Clinton's record good marks, even though 54 percent thought he was not necessarily "honest" or "trustworthy." Facing Clinton's popularity and a rebounding economy, Dole's campaign lacked energy. In an election marked by low voter turnout, Clinton became the first Democratic president to be reelected since Franklin D. Roosevelt. He captured 379 electoral votes and 49 percent of the popular vote.

In his 1997 State of the Union address, Clinton set a centrist agenda for his second term. The balanced budget, he stated, marked "an end to decades of deficits that have shackled our economy, paralyzed our policies, and held our people back." To undermine Republican calls for tax cuts, Clinton stressed that any surplus should be set aside to ensure the viability of Social Security. "Let's save Social Security first," he told Congress. Calling for an end to "bickering and extreme partisanship," he asked Congress to approve programs to improve education, daycare, Medicare, and Medicaid. Finding some common ground, Republicans and Democrats managed to approve the budget, pass the Balanced Budget Act of 1997, provide a small cut in taxes (the Taxpayer Relief Act of 1997), and make minor reforms to the healthcare system that helped limit growing costs. Beyond those agreements, however, Republicans and Democrats marched to different agendas and expressed bitter partisanship.

In January 1998, Republicans seized on Clinton's sexual involvement with a White House intern, **Monica Lewinsky**, to try to remove him from office. At first Clinton denied the allegations, but an investigation confirmed the affair

On August 5, 1997, Bill Clinton signed the Balanced Budget Act. Applauding the president are Vice President Al Gore (left) *and House Speaker Newt Gingrich* (right). *In the fall of 1998, Clinton announced a federal budget surplus of $70 billion, the first surplus since 1969.*

had gone on between 1995 and 1997. Clinton then admitted that he had had "inappropriate relations" with Lewinsky and had "misled" Congress and the public. His supporters argued that the affair was a private matter and in no way affected his running of the government. Even though the public seemed to agree with this assessment, Republicans—in a purely partisan action—cited two offenses, perjury and obstruction of justice, and in December 1997 voted to impeach Clinton. Clinton became the second president to face trial in the Senate to remove him from office (the first, Andrew Johnson, was acquitted in 1868, covered in Chapter 15).

The Republicans had a 55-to-45 majority in the Senate but needed a two-thirds majority for conviction. The trial lasted five weeks and confirmed to many that Republicans were more interested in destroying Clinton politically than in governing. On February 19, 1998, the Senate voted. On the issue of perjury, 10 Republicans voted with the Democrats to defeat the charge, 55 to 44. The vote on obstruction of justice was tied, 50 to 50, but nowhere near a

Alexander Zemlianichenko/AP Images

American forces played a key role in the United Nations (UN) and North Atlantic Treaty Organization (NATO) peacekeeping effort in Bosnia and Kosovo. In this picture, an American patrol greets Albanian children from a Kosovo village.

two-thirds majority. The drama of impeachment was over. Clinton expressed his sorrow for the burden he had placed on the nation and the government returned to business.

Clinton's Foreign Policy   In foreign policy, Clinton proceeded cautiously and followed the general outline set by President Bush to expand trade. He oversaw passage of the NAFTA and GATT agreements, supported global economic efforts by the **G-8 nations** and the formation of the **World Trade Organization** (WTO), and improved trade with China. To promote global economic stability, the Clinton administration provided loans and encouraged the **International Monetary Fund** to do so to support the economies of several countries, including Mexico, Russia, and Indonesia.

Moving beyond economics, Clinton applied both direct diplomatic and military intervention to promote peace and resolve international issues. He actively supported

G-8 Nations The leading industrial nations (Canada, China, France, Germany, Italy, Japan, the United Kingdom, and the United States), which meet annually to discuss economic and other global issues facing their countries and the international community.

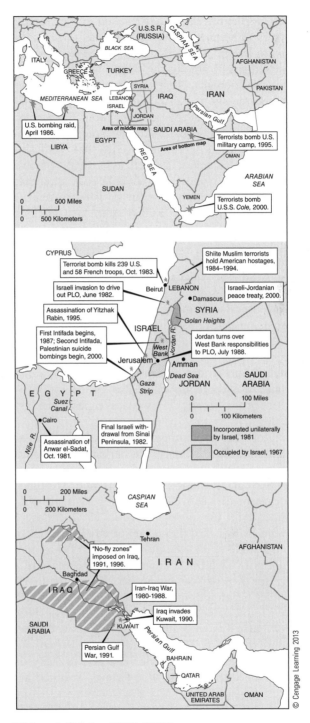

MAP 29.1 The Mideast Crisis, 1980–2000

With terrorist attacks, the Iran-Iraq War, the Persian Gulf War, and the ongoing struggle between Israel and the Palestinians, the Middle East was the site of almost unending violence and conflict in these years.

the peace process in Northern Ireland that resulted in the Good Friday Agreements and ended thirty years of sectarian violence. Anxious to promote a solution to the "troubles" in Northern Ireland, Clinton in 1995 asked ex-Senator George J. Mitchell to help negotiate a settlement among the opposing political/religious factions and the Irish and British governments. After three years of negotiations and continued violence, Mitchell, with the aid of last-minute direct telephone calls from Clinton to those negotiating a settlement, was able to bring about a peace accord.

To help stabilize the Middle East, Clinton sought to ease tensions between Israel and the Palestinians by brokering an accord that established Palestinian self-rule in some Israeli-occupied areas, as well as a treaty of cooperation between Jordan and Israel. In Haiti, following the failure of diplomatic and economic efforts, Clinton obtained UN support for an invasion to remove a military junta from power and restore democracy. Rather than face an invasion, in October 1994 the junta opened discussions that restored the presidency of Jean-Bertrand Aristide, who had been overthrown in a 1991 military coup, and established a time frame for free elections.

In the Balkan nation of Bosnia, Clinton faced a more difficult problem. Warring elements within Bosnia—Serbs, Christian and Muslim Bosnians, and Croats—fought each other with increasing intensity and brutality. Initially supporting UN peacekeeping and relief efforts there, Clinton sent American forces to join with the United Nations to establish and protect "safe areas" for refugees displaced by the fighting. In the fall of 1995, the United States sponsored peace talks resulting in the **Dayton Agreement**, which partitioned the country into a Bosnian-Croat federation and a Serb republic. It also called for UN forces, including twenty thousand Americans, to remain as peacekeepers. The last American forces were removed in 2004.

Clinton's commitment to promoting stablity in the Balkans was tested again in 1998 when President Slobodan Milosevic of Serbia sought to crush dissident and insurgent forces in the Serbian province of Kosovo. The conflict involved ancient hostilities between Serbian Orthodox Christians and Muslim ethnic Albanians, who made up 90 percent of Kosovo's population. When the Kosovo Liberation Army (KLA) began to fight for independence in 1998, Milosevic responded with force—instituting what many called a program of **ethnic cleansing** that targeted the Muslim population. Unable to halt the bloodshed, NATO leaders and Secretary of State Madeleine Albright called for "humanitarian intervention" and the establishment of autonomy for Kosovo within Serbia. Unwilling to use ground forces, NATO and U.S. forces began a bombing campaign in March 1999. When bombs fell on the Serbian capital of Belgrade, Milosevic, in June 1999, agreed to withdraw his troops, recognize Kosovo's autonomy, and allow UN peacekeeping forces into the area to ensure the peace. The war had cost the lives of more than ten thousand ethnic Albanian civilians. Milosevic, charged in May 1999 with crimes against humanity by the International War Crimes Tribunal at The Hague, was

---

ethnic cleansing   An effort to eradicate an ethnic or religious group from a country or region, often through mass killings.

Islamic Fundamentalism

When the shah of Iran was overthrown, most Americans were introduced to Islamic fundamentalism for the first time. It appeared to many Americans that Islamic fundamentalism was anti-American, antidemocratic, and militant, advocating violence, even the use of terrorism, to accomplish its goals. Since 1979, that belief has been hardened by terrorist attacks against the United States, including those against the World Trade Center and Pentagon. Some argue that fundamentalists' "objective is nothing less than the total destruction of the West" and there can be "no peaceful coexistence." Others respond that the extremists within the Islamic fundamentalist movement are a small minority and that most Muslims are neither anti-democratic nor anti-Western. Whether it is benign or hostile, it is clear that Islamic fundamentalism has become a powerful force in international politics and American politics.

- More Americans than ever before have negative views toward Islam and believe that it promotes violence more than other religions. Are these views based on their perceptions of terrorism, of fundamentalism, or of Islam?
- With Islam the fastest growing religion in the United States, should schools and institutions recognize Muslim religious holidays and dress codes?

overthrown in October 2000 in a popular uprising and in 2001 stood trial for his war crimes. He died in prison before the trial could be completed.

To explain his decisions to intervene, Clinton argued in what is called the Clinton Doctrine that the United States should act "where our values and our interests are at stake, and where we can make a difference" and that genocide necessitated a response. But Clinton did not apply his view evenly. In eastern Africa in 1994, he and most of the world ignored genocide in Rwanda; while in Somalia, after eighteen American UN peacekeeping troops were killed, Clinton withdrew American forces that President Bush had sent to the civil-war-torn nation in 1992 to provide humanitarian aid and keep the peace.

In other areas Clinton continued the previous administration's policies in supporting international efforts to control and eliminate biological and chemical weapons. In Iraq, he maintained Bush's efforts to pressure Saddam Hussein to allow UN inspection teams access to sites where he was suspected of manufacturing or stockpiling such weapons. Clinton, with the help of key Republican senators, also approved a Chemical Weapons Convention treaty that provided stronger sanctions against countries continuing to maintain and develop chemical weapons. The following year, however, without Republican support, Clinton failed to get Senate approval for the **Kyoto Protocol** to reduce global air pollution.

THE TESTING OF PRESIDENT BUSH

Americans welcomed the twenty-first century with celebrations and optimism. With the economy expanding, it was an upbeat and popular President Clinton who told the American people: "We have restored the vital center, replacing outdated ideologies with a new vision anchored in basic enduring values: opportunity for all, responsibility from all, and a community for all Americans." Looking forward to the new year of 2000 and the upcoming presidential election, he called for a political agenda that included improving Social Security, healthcare, and the quality of education. It was an agenda that Vice President Al Gore could embrace as the expected Democratic candidate for the presidency. Republicans labeled the agenda as typically liberal and focused on the dangers of big government, "tax-and-spend" Democrats, and the need to cut taxes. They also stressed the need to restore integrity to the White House.

The 2000 Election

Leading the Republican hopefuls was George W. Bush, governor of Texas and son of the former president, who quickly outdistanced his rivals and won the nomination. Running for the presidency, Bush announced a policy of "compassionate

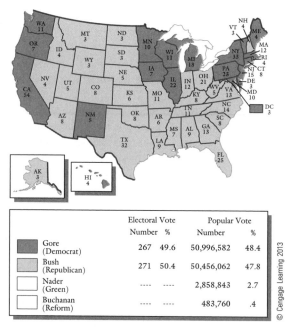

	Electoral Vote		Popular Vote	
	Number	%	Number	%
Gore (Democrat)	267	49.6	50,996,582	48.4
Bush (Republican)	271	50.4	50,456,062	47.8
Nader (Green)	----	----	2,858,843	2.7
Buchanan (Reform)	----	----	483,760	.4

© Cengage Learning 2013

MAP 29.2 Presidential Election, 2000

Although Gore won the popular vote, Bush won the electoral vote after a bitter fight over disputed ballots in Florida.

conservatism" that avoided the militancy of the cultural war and stressed the use of private sector initiatives to improve education, Social Security, and healthcare. At the heart of this campaign, however, was a promise to reduce taxes and restore dignity to the White House.

The campaign generated a lot of spending and almost no excitement, or heated rhetoric, or sharp debates. On the issues, the candidates' differences were largely matters of "how to," reflecting party ideologies. To improve education, Bush supported state initiatives and more stringent testing, whereas Gore wanted federal funds to hire more teachers and repair school facilities. On how to spend the budget surplus, Bush advocated a tax cut to give money back to the people. Gore called the tax cut dangerous and unfair—it favored the rich, he insisted—and said he would use the surplus to reduce the national debt and fund government programs.

The two candidates ran a dead heat, but the geography of support told a different story—of a confrontation between two Americas. Bush ran strong in the less populated states and was particularly popular with white males, who voted for him 5 to 3. Gore's strength was in urban areas (he received over 70 percent of the vote in large metropolitan areas), in the Northeast and Pacific Coast, and among Latinos and African Americans. On election day Gore received a minuscule majority of popular votes—half a million more out of the 10.5 million votes cast—but Bush won the Electoral College vote with 271 votes to 267, one vote more than necessary to win.

But there was a question over Florida's twenty-five electoral votes. Bush carried Florida by less than 1,000 popular votes and Florida law required a recount. As the recount proceeded, Gore supporters claimed voting irregularities and asked the Florida Supreme Court to set aside certification of the vote until hand counts were completed in several largely Democratic counties. When the court agreed, Bush supporters protested that Gore was trying to "steal" the election and filed their own suit in federal court. Ultimately, on December 4, a special session of the U.S. Supreme Court decided, 5 to 4, that the outcome favoring Bush should be certified. Bush had won Florida's electoral votes and the presidential election. Gore conceded, and an hour later President-elect Bush stated, "Whether you voted for me or not, I will do my best to serve your interest, and I will work to earn your respect."

Establishing the Bush Agenda   Despite his contested election, George Walker Bush entered the presidency determined to implement his campaign promises as if he had received a clear mandate from the voters. He had a Republican majority in the House of Representatives and a 50-50 tie in the Senate (which, if necessary, could be broken by the vote of the vice president). Among Bush's highest priorities were tax cuts and education reform. Bush's tax cut, $1.6 trillion over a six-year period, had two objectives: to stimulate the economy and to force a reduction in government spending. Most Democrats rejected the projected tax cut, arguing that it was too large and favored the rich. But others found it difficult to oppose a tax cut in a period of government surplus and in June voted with the Republicans to approve a slightly smaller $1.35 trillion tax cut.

Next, Bush pushed forward on his education bill, which included a controversial voucher system that many Republicans thought would restructure the American education system. Vouchers, drawn from local, state, or federal education funds, would provide a way for people to take their children out of "failing" public schools and enroll them in private and alternative schools. Democrats objected that vouchers would undermine the public school system and called for more federal spending for additional teachers and improved public schools. As the debate on education intensified, in June, Vermont senator James Jeffords shocked his party by leaving the Republican fold and becoming an Independent. His switch gave the Democrats a one-vote majority in the Senate and, equally important, leadership in the Senate and all its committees. Congressional gridlock followed. Caught in the gridlock were proposals for education, campaign financing reform, energy, and healthcare.

Adding to the partisanship in Congress was the economy. Led by heavy losses in high-tech stocks on the Nasdaq—highlighted by the rapid devaluation of dot-com stocks—the stock market plummeted in March 2001. An abrupt slowdown in sales in the service and technology sectors of the economy, combined with higher oil prices, produced widespread layoffs, climbing unemployment, and a loss of investor and consumer confidence. Democrats blamed Bush's handling of the economy and his tax cut for the recession. Republicans fought back, saying that the Bush administration was more fiscally responsible than the tax-and-spend Democrats. Speaking to a crowd in California, President Bush echoed his father's promise of no new taxes: "Not over my dead body will they raise your taxes." Some chuckled about the president's verbal misstatement, but no one misunderstood what he meant.

Charting New Foreign Policies   As with domestic policy, the Bush administration had fundamental differences with Clinton's foreign policy. Many Republicans believed that Clinton had been too interested in international cooperation, which had undermined the nation's power and failed to promote national interests. As president, Bush appointed a recognized advocate of international cooperation, General Colin Powell, as secretary of state, but he listened to aides like National Security Adviser Condoleezza Rice, Secretary of Defense Donald Rumsfeld, and Vice President Dick Cheney who favored a more unilateral approach. Almost immediately, Bush reversed Clinton's policies on **global warming** and international controls on

---

global warming   The gradual warming of the surface of the Earth; most scientists argue that over the past twenty years the Earth's temperature has risen at an unnaturally rapid rate because of industrial emission of gases that trap heat; the consequence of continued emissions, they argue, could be major ecological changes.

biological and chemical weapons. Bush stated that the Kyoto Protocol, with its goal to reduce carbon dioxide emissions, would harm the economy. He also broke off discussions regarding nuclear nonproliferation and wanted to reenergize Reagan's antiballistic missile defense system. Many, including the Russians, feared that Bush's decision would destabilize the international system of arms reduction and control and start a new arms race with Russia and China. European newspapers denounced American foreign policy, calling the president "Bully Bush" and the "Toxic Texan."

An Assault against a Nation   It was an event that no one thought possible that shaped Bush's foreign policy and altered his presidency. On the morning of September 11, 2001, four hijacked airplanes became flying bombs aimed at symbols of American financial and military power. At 8:48 A.M., a group of five terrorists led by Mohammed Atta crashed American Airlines Flight 11 into the North Tower of the World Trade Center. As New York fire and police departments responded, a second airliner struck the South Tower of the World Trade Center at 9:06 A.M. The second crash confirmed that the United States was being attacked by terrorists. The scope of the attack expanded when a third hijacked plane slammed into the Pentagon, just outside Washington, D.C., at 9:45 A.M. A fourth plane crashed into a field southeast of Pittsburgh, Pennsylvania. On that flight, passengers, learning about the other hijackings by cell phone, attempted to regain control of the aircraft, causing the plane to crash short of its Washington, D.C., target. In New York City the tragedy was soon magnified when the twin towers of the World Trade Center, the tallest structures in the city, collapsed, engulfing and killing thousands, including many of the firefighters and police officers who had rushed into the towers to provide help. Over three thousand people died that morning. President Bush, speaking to a stunned nation, declared that Americans had witnessed "evil, the very worst of human nature" and vowed to track down those responsible and bring them to justice. Patriotism and support for the president swept across the country. American flags flew from homes and car antennas.

But there was also a feeling of vulnerability. Sales of guns and gas masks increased. Assaults and threats targeted Arab Americans and those who looked Middle Eastern. In Congress, battles over education, Social Security, missile defense, and the budget were set aside. "The war we have now is against terrorism," said Democrat John Breaux of Louisiana. Congress quickly appropriated $40 billion for disaster relief and support for the effort to fight terrorism. Lawmakers passed the **USA Patriot Act** in October. It provided law-enforcement agencies wider discretion in dealing with those suspected of terrorism. It loosened restrictions on the use of searches, wiretaps, and monitoring the Internet. The attorney general's office was given the power to detain and deport noncitizens thought to be a security risk. While some criticized the Patriot Act for restricting civil liberties, most Americans supported actions that might prevent further acts of terrorism, including the Justice Department's detention of over 1,200 people, mostly Arab immigrants.

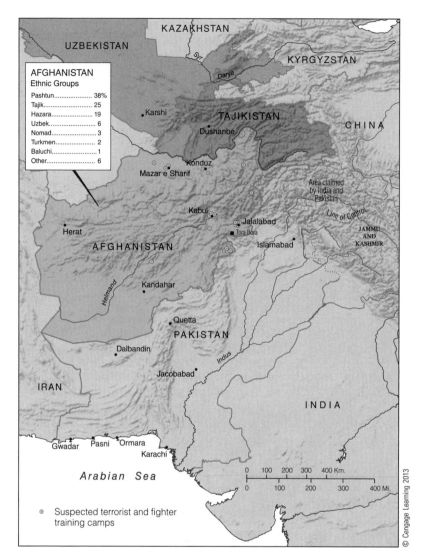

AFGHANISTAN
Ethnic Groups

Pashtun	38%
Tajik	25
Hazara	19
Uzbek	6
Nomad	3
Turkmen	2
Baluchi	1
Other	6

⊚ Suspected terrorist and fighter
   training camps

© Cengage Learning 2013

MAP 29.3 Afghanistan and Pakistan

After the attacks of September 11, 2001, U.S. and NATO forces attacked the terrorist organization al Qaeda, based in Afghanistan. The country's radical Islamist Taliban regime was overthrown, but many fighters retreated to the mountains along the Afghanistan-Pakistan border. Afghanistan remained violent and unsettled, and al Qaeda leader Osama bin Laden was still at large.

While Americans grappled with the enormity of the attacks, the Bush administration named **Al Qaeda**, a worldwide Islamic militant organization led by **Osama bin Laden**, as the organization responsible for the September 11 attacks. The son of a wealthy Saudi Arabian family, bin Laden had dedicated himself to freeing Muslim nations from outside control, especially American capitalist control. He announced in 1996 that it was the "duty of every Muslim" to "kill Americans and their allies." He and Al Qaeda were responsible for a series of attacks against American targets, including the 1996 bombing of a Saudi Arabian apartment complex that housed American servicemen and their families, and attacks on American embassies in Kenya and Tanzania in 1988.

President Bush quickly defined the new war on terrorism as a global effort, aimed not only against the "network of terrorists" but at any person or country that supported them. "Every nation in every region," he announced, had a choice to be "with us, or you are with the terrorists." Inside the White House, plans were being made for a military response against the **Taliban**, the Islamic fundamentalist government of Afghanistan, which supported bin Laden's operations. At the same time, Secretary of State Powell urged the president to first build an international coalition to support any American military action and to combat terrorism on a global basis. "We can't solve everything with one blow," stated a White House supporter of Powell's position.

Quickly, the Bush administration put in place a military campaign to remove the Taliban and worked to construct a global coalition against terrorism. While most nations agreed to eliminate and prevent terrorism in their own countries, several, including Britain, France, Germany, Australia, and Canada, agreed to join the campaign in Afghanistan. On October 7, 2001, the United States and its coalition began attacks on selected targets in Afghanistan. Accurate air and missile strikes effectively destroyed Taliban and Al Qaeda targets. They were followed by American ground forces, who joined existing anti-Taliban groups, especially the Northern Alliance, in an effort to remove the Taliban from power and kill or capture Osama bin Laden. Hundreds of Taliban and Al Qaeda fighters were captured and a new interim government headed by Hamid Kharzai was established, but Osama bin Laden and others had fled into the Tora Bora mountains bordering Pakistan and Afghanistan. To capture bin Laden, the military called for four thousand additional troops to search the mountains and pressured the Pakistani government to participate in the effort from their side of the border.

To defend against terrorism at home, Bush created a new cabinet department, Homeland Security, whose function would be to coordinate and direct various governmental agencies in preventing further acts of terrorism against the United States. He also asked Congress for large increases in spending for the military and for homeland defense. Bush accepted that the spending would create a deficit, maintaining that the price of freedom was "never too high."

The Bush administration, however, was shifting its focus away from Afghanistan toward Iraq. In November 2001, Bush rejected sending additional troops to hunt down bin Laden and had Secretary of Defense Donald Rumsfeld draw up secret plans to invade Iraq. In January, Bush defined what he termed an "axis of evil," saying that Iraq, Iran, and North Korea were threats to world peace. The administration also adopted a new strategy against terrorists and those who threatened world peace, the **preemptive strike**, also referred to as the Bush Doctrine. It stated that in the war on terrorism, the nation could not wait until an attack came; it had to take positive steps to halt such attacks before they occurred. Clinton's policy had been "reflexive pullback," said Rumsfeld, but the Bush policy would be "forward leaning."

The first preemptive strike would be against Iraq. The reasons for the focus on Iraq were varied. In part, it was personal. Saddam Hussein represented unfinished business left over from the war to liberate Kuwait. He was also a vile dictator who had used chemical and biological weapons against his enemies, including citizens of his own country. Finally, the administration maintained that he supported terrorism and Al Qaeda and possessed **weapons of mass destruction**. By March 2002, Bush and his closest advisers, Vice President Richard Cheney and Secretary of Defense Rumsfeld, had concluded that the United States should use force, if necessary, to remove Saddam. The hawks in the administration, however, were faced with opposition from Secretary of State Powell and most of the international community. They favored tightening of UN economic sanctions to force Saddam to allow UN weapons inspectors into Iraq to determine if he did have weapons of mass destruction.

The pressure from the United Nations appeared to work. Saddam agreed to allow the weapons inspectors into Iraq, but then he hindered their inspections efforts. The result was that they found no weapons of mass destruction, but said they could not rule out the possibility that Iraq had them. Claiming that it had intelligence proof that Saddam had such weapons, the Bush administration insisted the UN demand that Iraq allow full access to the inspectors or face dire consequences. Speaking just before the first anniversary of 9/11, Vice President Cheney stated that Iraq was reviving its "nuclear weapons program," that it "directly threatened the United States," and that "time is not on our side." Condoleezza Rice admitted that the status of Saddam Hussein's nuclear weapons was unknown, but added: "We don't want the smoking gun to be a mushroom cloud." Based on the administration's statements, a majority of the public and Congress agreed with a congressional resolution permitting the use of force against Iraq.

By March 2003, American troop strength in the Persian Gulf reached about 250,000 and Bush was tired of playing "patty-cake" with the United Nations and Iraq. He gave Saddam Hussein notice to leave the country within forty-eight hours or face a military onslaught that would "shock and awe" those who witnessed it. Even before the forty-eight hours was up, on March 20, 2003, Bush launched an attack on Baghdad designed to kill Saddam and members of his government. It failed but following an aerial barrage, a land offensive began advancing up the Tigris and Euphrates Rivers toward Baghdad, meeting only moderate resistance from regular and irregular Iraqi units. On April 9, Baghdad was in American hands. Saddam and his government fled into hiding. The official war ended without finding any weapons of mass destruction. Nonetheless, public opinion polls found that an overwhelming number of Americans considered the war a success and approved of Bush as president. But hostilities were not over,

---

weapons of mass destruction   Nuclear, chemical, and biological weapons that have the potential to injure or kill large numbers of people—civilians as well as military personnel.

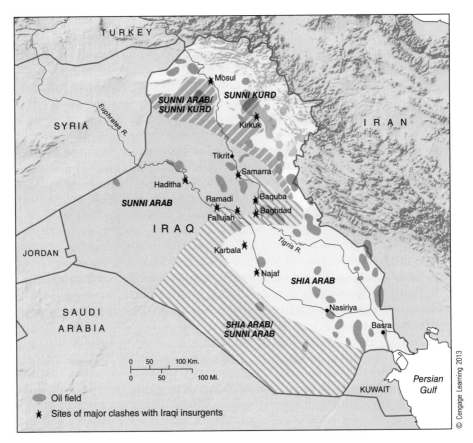

MAP 29.4 Iraq

With Saddam Hussein's overthrow by U.S.-led forces in 2003, violence erupted among Iraq's ethnic and religious groups, including the majority Shia Muslims concentrated in the southeast and the minority Sunni Muslims, who ruled the country under Saddam.

and the battle to remake Iraq would prove more difficult than toppling Saddam Hussein.

It quickly became apparent that the administration had made no plans for the occupation. The Department of State had proposed a complex plan to restore civil government and security forces, repair destroyed and damaged infrastructure, and provide food and other necessities for the Iraqis, but the White House had rejected the department's input. Consequently, there were not enough soldiers, equipment, or expertise to support a lengthy occupation. **Saboteurs** and

saboteurs Individuals who damage property or interfere with procedures to obstruct productivity and normal functions.

looters attacked Iraqi infrastructure, already extensively damaged by the war. Although most Iraqis thanked the United States for Saddam's removal—he was found hiding in a small "spider hole" in the ground on December 14, 2003, and taken into custody—they quickly grew impatient and angry with the occupation. They complained about the slow restoration of electricity, water, and other necessities, and they criticized the ominous lack of security. Many disagreed with the U.S.-selected interim government and called for the formation of an Islamic-based state.

Iraq became a new kind of war zone as occupation forces faced rapidly expanding violence not only from those resisting the occupation, but also from those fighting a sectarian civil war between Sunni and Shiite religious factions and from Al Qaeda forces. As casualties increased, the Bush administration admitted that an extensive search for weapons of mass destruction had failed to find any. Over the next two years, various investigatory commissions established to evaluate the intelligence reports and decisions leading to the war determined that the information claiming Saddam possessed such weapons and links to Al Qaeda were wrong. As critics of the war blamed the Bush administration for manipulating the nation into war, it seemed as if the United States was trapped in an expensive war with no effective plans to end the conflict and withdraw American troops.

War and Politics

Amid growing questions about the justification and conduct of the war, Bush ran for reelection. Although he received positive public approval rates for combating terrorism, the public gave him lesser marks on conducting the Iraq war, dealing with the economy, and controlling the deficit. Accordingly, the Democratic presidential candidate, Senator John Kerry of Massachusetts, focused on the economy and the war. Bush attacked Kerry and the Democrats as too liberal and claimed that their opposition to the war in Iraq undermined the U.S. effort and encouraged terrorism. When critics pointed to the misinformation on weapons of mass destruction that had been used to justify the invasion, Bush now argued that his true motive was to end Saddam Hussein's brutal dictatorship. He stressed that he had met the need for decisive leadership. "We acted. We led," stated Bush.

Although the economy was improving by the summer of 2004, spurred by low interest rates, tax cuts, and military spending, Democrats argued that it was a selective recovery and that for most Americans jobs were being lost and real wages were dropping. "We've declared victory over the recession," said a Democratic representative, but "we're still laying off a couple of hundred thousand workers a month." Republicans, meanwhile, were dusting off the culture war of previous campaigns, exploiting the issue of gay marriage. In November 2003, the Massachusetts Supreme Court had ruled that banning same-sex marriage violated the state's constitution and gave the state legislature 180 days to act on the court's decision. The following April, the Massachusetts legislature approved a constitutional amendment that defined marriage as a union only between a man and a woman, although it would permit same-sex **civil unions**. However, the amendment could not be ratified until 2006, and meanwhile, Massachusetts became the first state to issue marriage licenses to same-sex couples.

The response across the nation was generally negative. In most states, laws against same-sex marriage already existed, based on the 1996 federal **Defense of Marriage Act**, which bans federal recognition of same-sex marriages and allows states to ignore such marriages performed in other states. Nonetheless, thirty-five states hurried to strengthen their prohibitions of same-sex marriage. In addition, many opponents of same-sex marriage believed that civil unions should also be banned. In February 2004, President Bush endorsed the idea of a constitutional amendment that would disallow same-sex marriage. When pressed for his view, Kerry opposed such an amendment and argued that the issue should be left to the states to legislate. He also said that he personally opposed same-sex marriages but approved of civil unions.

Targeting "battleground" swing states, both parties poured vast amounts of time and campaign money into a few states, along with venomous campaign ads. Both also took new approaches to campaigning to woo supporters using the Internet. "Bloggers" created their own websites providing news, political analysis, and ads for and against the candidates. Days before the election, most polls showed the candidates tied in popular support.

On November 2, 2004, more Americans voted than ever before. They reelected Bush, giving him 51 percent of the vote. Bush had effectively mobilized his party's loyalists and won most of the battleground states. To the surprise of most observers, a majority of those supporting Bush stated that moral issues and family values were critical reasons for how they voted. Supporting this observation, in Ohio—which was critical to the president's reelection—and ten other states, voters affirmed their support for amendments to their state constitutions to prohibit same-sex marriages and civil unions. "Make no mistake—conservative Christians and 'value voters' won this election," stated one conservative observer.

Bush's Second Term   Referring to his victory as a public mandate for action and with Republican majorities in Congress, President Bush was eager to use his "political capital" to implement domestic goals that promoted an "ownership society," putting control in the hands of individuals regarding healthcare, Social Security retirement funds, and education. "Now comes the revolution," voiced some conservatives when the president announced that strengthening family values and reforming Social Security, tax codes, and education were agenda priorities. Bush's political capital fell apart within months when Congress and the public rejected his efforts to privatize Social Security and further reduce taxes. His leadership, which he had touted during the election campaign, suffered a serious blow following his lethargic response to the devastation caused by a category-four hurricane.

civil union Term for a civil status similar to marriage, allowing same-sex partners access to legal, medical, and financial and other benefits enjoyed by married heterosexuals.

On August 29, 2005, **Hurricane Katrina** battered New Orleans, much of which is below sea level, and the levees protecting the city broke. Flood waters poured in and submerged some sectors of New Orleans under 20 feet of water. Earlier, as the storm approached, most upper- and middle-class residents had boarded up their homes and left the city, but those without resources and transportation had no way out. Unable to leave, thousands who were able to escape the flood waters took refuge in the Superdome, the covered downtown stadium. Sheer numbers quickly overwhelmed its facilities. Television crews broadcast worldwide the horrid conditions in the Superdome, the bodies floating in the flooded streets, and the widespread destruction.

As conditions worsened, it became clear that government agencies were perilously slow to deal with the crisis. In fact, both President Bush and the Federal Emergency Management Administration (FEMA) appeared to ignore the stricken city and brush off the magnitude of the disaster. Four days passed before Bush took meaningful action. Only then, once Bush had belatedly ordered it, did FEMA begin to intensify its efforts in the region. The slow response caused many to question the administration's priorities and significantly damaged its aura of efficient management. "The rich escaped," conservative writer David Brooks editorialized, "while the poor were abandoned.... Leaving the poor in New Orleans was the moral equivalent of leaving the injured on the battlefield."

The inadequate response to Katrina was a huge blow to the public's confidence in Bush's leadership and policies. His popularity rating fell to under 50 percent, and criticism of the administration's war policies intensified. Despite the drafting of an Iraqi constitution and a large turnout to elect a parliamentary government in December 2005, conditions in Iraq failed to improve. The new government of Nouri al-Maliki was ineffective and unable even to limit the growing civil war between religious factions. Death tolls for both Americans and Iraqis soared—over three thousand American soldiers had died since the occupation started. For Iraqis, exact numbers are unknown, but estimates range from over half a million to less than 100,000. Bush's popularity ratings continued to fall, and polls disclosed that over 60 percent disapproved of his administration's handling of the war.

The 2006 congressional elections saw all 435 House seats and 33 Senate seats up for grabs. Democrats called for a "New Direction for America," and while they included the economy and protecting Social Security as important issues, nearly everyone considered the central issue to be Iraq. Democrats held that war policies needed to be changed and American troops withdrawn as soon as possible. They stressed that Bush and his advisers had lied about the reasons for going to war and had bungled the planning for a postwar Iraq, failing to establish a coherent policy to bring stability and security. The outcome was that American soldiers were being wounded and dying for no purpose. Bush and Republicans responded that they were better suited to protect the nation from terrorism and that to suggest withdrawing from Iraq would embolden the enemy and endanger American troops. Better, they argued, to increase the number of American troops in Iraq, especially in Baghdad, to enhance security and give the Iraqis time to take over their own battle.

Most observers believed that the Democrats would gain some congressional seats in the election, but that Republicans would maintain a slim majority. The results surprised nearly everyone. Democrats took a majority of 233 to 202 seats in the House of Representatives and a smaller majority of 51 to 49 in the Senate. Some saw the results as devastating for the Republican Party, sending a message to the administration to consider a timeline for the withdrawal of American forces in Iraq. With their majority confirmed, Democrats selected the first woman Speaker of the House, Congresswoman Nancy Pelosi from California. Upon taking office, she called her appointment "a historic moment" that women had been awaiting for more than two hundred years. "The marble ceiling" had been broken, Pelosi said.

Denying that the election indicated a clear "call to change" policy toward Iraq, Bush in December announced a 21,500-troop "surge" to boost security, reduce the violence, and allow the Iraqi forces to complete the training they were receiving from U.S. troops. It was the way to win the war, according to the administration, and Vice President Cheney stressed that efforts to block the president's plan would "undermine" the troops. Democrats responded by passing nonbinding resolutions opposing the troop increase and, in April, passed a bill that linked funding for the war to establishing a time frame for the removal of American forces. Bush vetoed the bill, and Republicans accused Democrats of trying to manage the war. They pointed out that the surge was working and had reduced violence.

Economic Crisis and "Remaking America" With the battle lines drawn over the war in Iraq, the 2008 presidential campaign started a year and a half before the election. The leading Democratic candidates, Senators Hillary Clinton of New York and Barack Obama of Illinois, were breaking historical traditions of gender and race, since neither a woman nor an African American had ever been nominated for the presidency by a major party. After a series of hard-fought primaries, Obama secured the nomination and selected Senator Joseph Biden of Delaware as his running mate. In a less bruising series of primaries, Arizona Senator John McCain overcame his Republican challengers and captured the nomination. Hoping to consolidate his support from conservative Republicans and to attract women voters, McCain surprised everyone by naming Alaska Governor Sarah Palin as his running mate. Many expected the war in Iraq and Obama's lesser political experience to dominate the campaign issues.

The campaign began nearly as expected. McCain, who called himself a maverick to distance himself from Bush's unpopular policies, touted his decades of government service and attacked Obama as inexperienced, too liberal, and weak on foreign policy, and wrong in his position on the Iraq war. Obama countered by offering innovation and change, asking the nation if they wanted four more years of the same failed Bush policies. Obama argued that Bush had fought the wrong war. Instead of invading Iraq, he should have continued the effort in Afghanistan to destroy Al Qaeda. American forces should be withdrawn from Iraq as soon as possible, he said, and used to establish a stable Afghanistan and hunt down terrorists. But as the summer arrived, so too did a new and critical issue—the start of the worldwide "Great Recession."

The debate over what caused the recession and how best to deal with it reshaped the campaign. Signs of an unsteady economy were visible, for those choosing to see them, as early as 2006. At the center of the brewing economic storm were extremely low interest rates, a boom in the housing market, inattentive government regulators, and greed. Banks and other lending institutions made housing loans, including **subprime loans,** to thousands of people who could normally not afford them. In many cases profit-seeking lenders actively marketed subprime and other special loan arrangements to high-risk borrowers with no concern for people's personal finances or the long-term consequences for the housing market. In one case a worker at McDonald's who earned $35,000 a year was able to get a half-million-dollar loan for a home.

Then housing values began to drop, leaving many owing more than the value of the house. A cascade of foreclosures began. Institutions that had either directly or indirectly invested in mortgages, once considered a safe investment, found themselves short of capital, unable to pay their investors, depositors, and creditors. As stock prices tumbled and banks and insurance and investment corporations tottered on the edge of bankruptcy, the fiscally conservative Bush administration concluded that a massive infusion of money was needed to prop up some of the nation's largest financial institutions. They were "too big" to fail, said one government official. Between July and December, the Bush administration asked Congress for financial bailouts to rescue the economy. In September, Federal Reserve Chairman Ben Bernanke and Treasury Secretary Henry M. Paulson Jr. asked Congress for $700 billion for the **Troubled Asset Relief Program** (TARP), saying that unless Congress acted immediately "we may not have an economy on Monday." Bush agreed, telling Congress to pass the rescue plan or see "this sucker [the economy] go down."

Congress approved the complex and controversial bill and Bush signed it on October 3. Responses to the TARP were mixed. Many people complained that it rewarded "Wall Street"—those who had caused the economic crisis—and did nothing for "Main Street," the hard-working Americans who were losing their jobs or homes, or both. Others voiced concerns about the TARP's effectiveness and cost and about the level of government intervention in buying the assets of private financial institutions. Even more controversial was the administration's request in December for more funds, $17.4 billion in loans to support failing American automobile manufacturers General Motors and Chrysler. Adding to the public's distrust and dissatisfaction with the behavior of CEOs and Wall Street financiers were revelations of elaborate illegal schemes by Bernard Madoff and R. Allen Stanford, whose actions epitomized the greedy quest for personal wealth

subprime loan   A loan that carries a higher-than-normal interest rate, generally used to make a loan to someone with a history of bad credit and default; between 2005 and 2006 such loans represented 20 percent of all housing loans.

that many believed was responsible for the nation's financial mess. Both used their role as financial advisers to steal millions of dollar from investors. Madoff, who bilked nearly $65 billion from investors in a massive **Ponzi scheme**, was found guilty and sentenced to 150 years in prison.

As the recession worsened, the central issue of the election campaign shifted away from McCain's comparative strength of experience and the war on terror. A mid-June Gallup Poll found that more than 56 percent of voters thought fixing the economy was more important than fighting terrorism; an almost equal number thought Obama was more qualified on economic issues than McCain. As Obama's popularity rose, Republicans intensified allegations that he lacked patriotism and was devoted to socialist-Marxist ideology. This time, their political attacks did not work. On Election Day more people voted than in any other presidential election, providing a decisive victory for Obama. While winning 53 percent of the popular vote, he received 365 electoral votes to McCain's 173. Democrats also added eight seats to their majority in the Senate and twenty-one to their margin in the House.

Around the world people waited to see what changes Obama would make in foreign and domestic policies. On January 20, 2009, President Obama gave his inaugural address to expectant listeners. Over a million people braved cold weather, descending on Washington, D.C., to watch the inauguration ceremonies, with many millions more watching television coverage around the world. Obama acknowledged the serious problems the nation confronted: "Our nation is at war against a far-reaching network of violence and hatred. Our economy is badly weakened, a consequence of greed and irresponsibility on the part of some but also our collective failure to make hard choices and prepare the nation for a new age." He added that meeting the challenges would not be easy or quickly accomplished, but that "starting today, we must pick ourselves up, dust ourselves off, and begin again the work of remaking America." He voiced the hope that the bitter polarization that had characterized politics would be laid aside for the common good.

Over the next months, Obama unfolded an ambitious agenda that not only sought to reshape the economy, but to implement a national healthcare system and to change the direction of the wars in Iraq and Afghanistan. Many argued the agenda was too ambitious and that the administration should focus on fixing the economy before tackling other issues. In turn, Obama argued that nearly all the issues were intertwined and that it made sense to deal with the complexities rather than focus on a single aspect of the problem. It was also immediately clear that personal and partisan politics would dominate nearly every issue.

Ponzi scheme A fraudulent investment operation in which the operator keeps the majority of investment money, making small payouts to investors from their own money or money paid by other investors; Madoff's scheme was the largest financial investor fraud in history committed by a single person.

Having won the Democratic nomination for president, Barack Obama easily defeated the Republican candidate John McCain. Receiving news of his victory, President-elect Obama addressed his supporters gathered in Chicago's Grant Park. On stage with him was the new first family: his wife Michelle and their two daughters Sasha and Malia.

During the campaign Obama had argued it was necessary to reach out to international adversaries and work more closely with allies and for the United States to regain its global moral authority. He also vowed to conduct the war on terrorism in a way that would ensure the safety of the American people and shift military priorities from Iraq to Afghanistan and Pakistan. In office, Obama and his foreign policy advisors established priorities based on the premise that American resources were limited and that the administration should focus on necessary problems. High on the list of those priorities were working with other industrial nations to confront the global economic crisis, improving trade relations with China, dealing with Afghanistan and Pakistan, and "resetting" the tone of American foreign policy.

By the end of the year, observers gave Obama mixed reviews. They gave him high marks for improving the image of American foreign policy and restoring the nation's moral authority. But on almost every other issue, there were serious objections and recognition that little had actually been accomplished. Both Democrats and Republicans objected to aspects of his conduct of the war on terrorism, to the failure to reduce the American military presence in Iraq, and to the deployment of nearly thirty thousand more American soldiers to Afghanistan. Some liberal critics argued that apart from his rhetoric, his policies paralleled those of Bush, while some conservatives warned that he was too soft in protecting American interests and that his actions and speeches made the nation's enemies stronger. Obama, however, gained more domestic and international approval in early 2010, for restructuring the **Strategic Arms Limitation Treaty** (START) that reduced the number of American and Russian nuclear warheads from 6,000 to 1,500.

The Politics of Filibuster   With significant Democratic majorities in the House and Senate, Republicans called for solid opposition to many Democratic domestic programs, thereby possibly forcing the administration to overcome a filibuster. If Republicans maintained solidarity, Democrats would need to muster sixty votes, every Democratic vote, to pass a bill in the Senate. The politics of filibuster not only put great pressure on Senate Democrats, but gave every Senator tremendous political leverage because one vote represented the margin of victory or defeat. Acting quickly to deal with the economic crisis, in February, with three Republicans in the Senate supporting the measure, Congress approved the **American Recovery and Reinvestment Act** to stimulate the economy. It provided $787 billion in federal spending and tax cuts to help the economy recover. Even as Obama watched his approval rating fall below 50 percent, Democrats pushed through bills creating national healthcare programs in the face of solid Republican opposition. The House passed a bill without any Republican support, while in the Senate, in late December 2009, Democrats needed every Democratic and Independent vote to avoid a Republican filibuster. Because the Senate bill differed from the House's version, the two bills needed to be reconciled. On March 23, the House, without a single Republican vote, accepted the Senate's version (219 to 212), approving the **Patient Protection Affordable Care Act**, and sent to the Senate the **Health Care and Education Reconciliation Act** that incorporated changes the House wanted to the Patient Protection Affordable Care Act. Through a simple majority vote, Senate Democrats quickly approved the measure. By March 30, Obama had signed two acts establishing an American system of national healthcare. Republicans immediately denounced "Obamacare" and called for its repeal. At the same time, officials in eighteen states filed motions in federal court arguing the acts were unconstitutional and infringed on states' rights. "The Constitution," their motion read, "nowhere authorizes the United States to mandate, either directly or under threat of penalty, that all citizens and legal residents have qualifying healthcare coverage." Unfazed, President Obama dismissed the constitutional challenges as pure politics and argued that as the provisions of the national healthcare took effect and the "Armageddon" promised by opponents did not occur, public support for the system would increase. He also continued to focus on further reviving the economy, which by spring appeared to be recovering. In July 2010, the administration won another victory when in the Senate three Republicans broke party ranks and voted for a sweeping reform bill that placed new and increased regulations on financial and investment institutions. Responding to opposition statements that the legislation would expand an already bloated federal bureaucracy and harm the banking system, the president said that it was needed to prevent the actions that led to the recession and that only those financial institutions that depended "on cutting corners or bilking … customers" had anything to fear. Still, other Democratic and administrative programs and bills remained captive to filibuster politics and continuing divisions within the Democratic Party.

The debates over the economy and healthcare sparked a political wave called the **Tea Party movement** that swept over the country. Focusing on taxes, the intrusive and "un-American" nature of big government and Obama programs, Tea Partiers leapt into state and congressional political races supporting the most conservative candidates, claiming victories in several state primaries. Buoyed by Obama's continued efforts to push programs that seemed to increase government spending and power and the surge of the Tea Party movement, Republicans projected significant political gains in the November congressional elections that would give them the ability to change the country's course.

Sharing the headlines with the Tea Party and partisan politics, on April 20, a BP deep-water drilling rig, the Deepwater Horizon, exploded in the Gulf of Mexico, killing eleven workers. Two days later the rig sank, releasing oil from its mile-deep well-head. Over the next few days, what was initially termed a small leak was recognized as a major oil spill, releasing thousands of gallons of oil into the Gulf each day. By June, after several efforts to stop the gushing oil had failed, the spill became the largest in American history and a major ecological disaster that threatened not only the marine and wildlife habitats along the coastlines of Louisiana, Alabama, Mississippi, and Florida, but also the livelihoods of Gulf Coast residents working in the fishing and tourism industries. In mid-July, BP capped the gushing well, choking off further releases of oil, but still leaving millions of gallons of oil still threatening the gulf coast. Amid growing criticism of BP's drilling techniques and responses, the oil company accepted "full responsibility for the spill," vowing to pay for the costs of the clean-up and to financially compensate those affected by the disaster. Some also criticized Obama and the government for not taking effective control of the crisis and actually obstructing efforts to deal with the gushing oil and its ecological and financial consequences. The administration, in response, argued that it held BP fully responsible and was requiring the company to create a $20 billion fund to pay for the consequences of the spill. "Make no mistake," President Obama stated, "we will fight this spill with everything we've got for as long as it takes." In 1974, Nixon said that the Santa Barbara oil spill "touched the conscience of the American people," helping awaken Americans to the ecological dangers facing the world and contributing to the establishment of the Environmental Protection Agency. Will the BP spill in the Gulf produce long- and short-term consequences having a similar role? How, as in earlier times, will disaster intersect with turbulent politics in the ongoing story of making America?

STUDY TOOLS

SUMMARY

During the last two decades, the economy has significantly shaped political and social issues. The changing American economy provided new opportunities for some, but for many, including much of the middle class, it heightened worries about their and their children's future. Bill Clinton exploited those concerns to help win the 1992 election and assumed the presidency determined to place the nation on a firm financial footing. His economic plan, while divisive, worked, and although facing a Republican-controlled Congress, by the end of his two terms, Clinton had balanced the budget, reduced the national debt, and weathered a Republican effort to remove him from office through the impeachment process.

The 2000 close presidential election between Gore and Bush was finally decided by the Supreme Court, which awarded Florida's electoral votes to Bush. President Bush began by implementing a tax cut and educational reform, but before he could push other agenda items, the nation was overwhelmed by the events of September 11, 2001, when terrorists affiliated with Osama bin Laden attacked the World Trade Center and the Pentagon, killing over three thousand people. As the nation rallied around the administration, it established an Office of Homeland Security and created a global coalition to fight terrorist organizations and their supporters. In that effort, the United States joined forces with others to conduct a successful war that brought down the Taliban government and much of the Al Qaeda organization in Afghanistan—although Osama bin Laden escaped.

In 2003, the Bush administration shifted its attention to Iraq, claiming that Saddam Hussein possessed weapons of mass destruction and was linked to Al Qaeda. In March, an American-led invasion toppled Saddam Hussein's government in less than three weeks. However, the occupation and efforts to transform Iraq into a stable democracy proved more difficult. As violence continued and American casualties increased, some Americans began to question Bush's justification and his conduct of the war.

Growing dissatisfaction with Bush's Iraq policy paralleled frustration with his handling of the economy. Both of these developments raised Democratic hopes of regaining the presidency in 2004. In November, however, voters reelected Bush and returned more Republicans to the House and Senate. Claiming a political mandate, Bush unsuccessfully tried to implement a conservative agenda. With an administration weakened by increasing frustration over the war in Iraq and its weak response to Hurricane Katrina, Democrats in the congressional elections of 2006 regained a majority in Congress.

The 2008 presidential campaign pitted a young, African American Illinois senator, Barack Obama, against the more experienced senator from Arizona, John McCain. With the start of a major recession, the economy displaced Iraq as the most important factor for the majority of voters. Obama offered change and seemed more capable of dealing with the economic crisis. A war-weary public, worried about the economy, overwhelmingly chose to put Obama in the White House.

In office, President Obama not only faced an economic crisis and wars in Iraq and Afghanistan, but put forward an ambitious agenda he said would remake America that included changing the tone of American foreign and domestic priorities and implementing a comprehensive healthcare system that would cover nearly every American. He hoped for bipartisan support to deal with the issues, but found that on almost every occasion, Republicans opted to oppose his efforts. Conservative critics argued that Obama's recovery programs and national health programs were too expensive and expanded the size and role of the federal government. In response to Obama, the economic stresses, and expansive government programs, a "Tea Party" movement arose that stressed reducing the size and reach of government, cutting taxes, and electing true conservatives. By a year and a half into his presidency, although the economy was improving, many Americans appeared to be increasingly unhappy with his leadership and policies, and Republicans looked forward to reasserting their political power in the 2010 congressional elections.

CHRONOLOGY

A NEW CENTURY WITH NEW CHALLENGES

1992   Bill Clinton elected president

1993   Congress ratifies North American Free Trade Agreement
Clinton's national healthcare package fails

1994   U.S. troops sent to Haiti
"Contract with America"

1995   Dayton Agreement

1996   Welfare reform passed
Clinton reelected

1998   Terrorists attack U.S. embassies in Kenya and Tanzania

1999   NATO bombs Serbia over Kosovo crisis
Effort to impeach Clinton fails

2000   George W. Bush elected president

2001   Terrorists associated with Al Qaeda attack World
      Trade towers and Pentagon
Office of Homeland Security established
U.S. launches operations in Afghanistan
USA Patriot Act

2002   Taliban regime collapses; replaced by interim government

2003   U.S. invades Iraq, removes Saddam Hussein regime
Massachusetts Supreme Court permits same-sex marriage

2004   George W. Bush reelected

2005   Hurricane Katrina strikes Gulf Coast

2006 Democrats regain majorities in Congress
2007 Nancy Pelosi becomes first woman Speaker of the House
of Representatives
2008 Barack H. Obama elected
2009 Congress passes economic stimulus bill
Congress approves financial aid package for American
automobile manufacturers, General Motors and Chrysler
2010 Congress passes a national healthcare bill
Strategic Arms Limitation Treaty negotiated between United States
and Russia
Accident on a Gulf off-shore oil platform releases millions of barrels
of oil, fouling wet lands of many Gulf states
Congress passes Wall Street financial regulation bill

Focus Questions

If you have mastered this chapter, you should be able to answer these questions and explain the terms that follow the questions.

1. What changes were taking place in the American economy in the 1990s?
2. How did economic changes shape society and politics?
3. In what ways did President Clinton's centrist agenda and personal behavior shape his presidency?
4. How did the Contract with America represent a conservative critique of liberalism and Democratic policies?
5. What actions did Clinton take to expand trade and support global stability?
6. What issues contributed to Bush's election and how did his policies differ from those of the Clinton years?
7. How did the events of September 11, 2001, affect politics, the public, and foreign policy?
8. How did the war in Iraq shape the issues Republicans wanted to highlight in the presidential elections of 2004 and 2008?
9. What major issues contributed to Barack Obama's election in 2008, and what constraints did he face in implementing his policies?

Key Terms

Nasdaq (*p.* 901)

Operation Rescue (*p.* 905)

Family and Medical Leave Act (*p.* 905)

North American Free Trade Agreement (*p.* 906)

General Agreement on Tariffs and Trade (*p.* 906)

Contract with America (*p.* 908)

judicial restraint (*p.* 908)

Monica Lewinsky (*p.* 910)

World Trade Organization (*p.* 912)

International Monetary Fund (*p.* 912)

Dayton Agreement (*p.* 914)

Kyoto Protocol (*p.* 915)

USA Patriot Act (*p.* 919)

Al Qaeda (*p.* 920)

Osama bin Laden (*p.* 920)

Taliban (*p.* 921)

preemptive strike (*p.* 921)

Defense of Marriage Act (*p.* 925)

Hurricane Katrina (*p.* 926)

Troubled Asset Relief Program (*p.* 928)

Strategic Arms Limitation Treaty (*p.* 931)

American Recovery and Reinvestment Act (*p.* 931)

Patient Protection Affordable Care Act (*p.* 931)

Health Care and Education Reconciliation Act (*p.* 931)

Tea Party movement (*p.* 932)

Appendix A

THE DECLARATION OF INDEPENDENCE

THE UNANIMOUS DECLARATION OF THE THIRTEEN UNITED STATES OF AMERICA

When in the Course of human events it becomes necessary for one people to dissolve the political bands which have connected them with another, and to assume among the Powers of the earth, the separate and equal station to which the Laws of Nature and of Nature's God entitle them, a decent respect to the opinions of mankind requires that they should declare the causes which impel them to the separation.

We hold these truths to be self-evident, that all men are created equal, that they are endowed by their Creator with certain unalienable Rights, that among these are Life, Liberty and the pursuit of Happiness. That to secure these rights, Governments are instituted among Men, deriving their just Powers from the consent of the governed. That whenever any Form of Government becomes destructive of these ends, it is the Right of the People to alter or to abolish it, and to institute new Government, laying its foundation on such principles and organizing its Powers in such form, as to them shall seem most likely to effect their Safety and Happiness. Prudence, indeed, will dictate that Governments long established should not be changed for light and transient causes; and accordingly all experience hath shewn, that mankind are more disposed to suffer, while evils are sufferable, than to right themselves by abolishing the forms to which they are accustomed. But when a long train of abuses and usurpations, pursuing invariably the same Object evinces a design to reduce them under absolute Despotism, it is their right, it is their duty, to throw off such Government, and to provide new Guards for their future security. Such has been the patient sufferance of these Colonies; and such is now the necessity which constrains them to alter their former Systems of Government. The history of the present King of Great Britain is a history of repeated injuries and usurpations, all having in direct object the establishment of an absolute Tyranny over these States. To prove this, let Facts be submitted to a candid world.

Text is reprinted from the facsimile of the engrossed copy in the National Archives. The original spelling, capitalization, and punctuation have been retained. Paragraphing has been added.

He has refused his Assent to Laws, the most wholesome and necessary for the public good.

He has forbidden his Governors to pass Laws of immediate and pressing importance, unless suspended in their operation till his Assent should be obtained; and when so suspended, he has utterly neglected to attend to them.

He has refused to pass other Laws for the accommodation of large districts of people, unless those people would relinquish the right of Representation in the Legislature, a right inestimable to them and formidable to tyrants only.

He has called together legislative bodies at places unusual, uncomfortable, and distant from the depository of their Public Records, for the sole Purpose of fatiguing them into compliance with his measures.

He has dissolved Representative Houses repeatedly, for opposing with manly firmness his invasions on the rights of the People.

He has refused for a long time, after such dissolutions, to cause others to be elected; whereby the Legislative Powers, incapable of Annihilation, have returned to the People at large for their exercise; the State remaining in the mean time exposed to all the dangers of invasion from without, and convulsions within.

He has endeavoured to prevent the Population of these States; for that purpose obstructing the Laws for Naturalization of Foreigners; refusing to pass others to encourage their migrations hither, and raising the conditions of new Appropriations of Lands.

He has obstructed the Administration of Justice, by refusing his Assent to Laws for establishing Judiciary Powers.

He has made Judges dependent on his Will alone, for the tenure of their offices, and the amount and payment of their salaries.

He has erected a multitude of New Offices, and sent hither swarms of Officers to harass our People, and eat out their substance.

He has kept among us, in times of peace, Standing Armies without the Consent of our legislatures.

He has affected to render the Military independent of and superior to the Civil Power.

He has combined with others to subject us to a jurisdiction foreign to our constitution, and unacknowledged by our laws; giving his Assent to their Acts of pretended Legislation:

For Quartering large bodies of armed troops among us:

For protecting them, by a mock Trial, from Punishment for any Murders which they should commit on the Inhabitants of these States:

For cutting off our Trade with all parts of the world:

For imposing Taxes on us without our Consent:

For depriving us in many cases, of the benefits of Trial by Jury:

For transporting us beyond Seas to be tried for pretended offences:

For abolishing the free System of English Laws in a neighbouring Province, establishing therein an Arbitrary government, and enlarging its Boundaries so as to render it at once an example and fit instrument for introducing the same absolute rule into these Colonies:

For taking away our Charters, abolishing our most valuable Laws, and altering fundamentally the Forms of our Governments:

For suspending our own Legislatures, and declaring themselves invested with Power to legislate for us in all cases whatsoever.

He has abdicated Government here, by declaring us out of his Protection, and waging War against us.

He has plundered our seas, ravaged our Coasts, burnt our towns, and destroyed the lives of our people.

He is at this time transporting large Armies of foreign Mercenaries to compleat the works of death, desolation and tyranny, already begun with circumstances of Cruelty and perfidy scarcely paralleled in the most barbarous ages, and totally unworthy the Head of a civilized nation.

He has constrained our fellow Citizens taken Captive on the high Seas to bear Arms against their Country, to become the executioners of their friends and Brethren, or to fall themselves by their Hands.

He has excited domestic insurrections amongst us, and has endeavoured to bring on the inhabitants of our frontiers, the merciless Indian Savages, whose known rule of warfare, is an undistinguished destruction of all ages, sexes and conditions.

In every stage of these Oppressions We have Petitioned for Redress in the most humble terms: Our repeated Petitions have been answered only by repeated injury. A Prince, whose character is thus marked by every act which may define a Tyrant, is unfit to be the ruler of a free People.

Nor have We been wanting in attentions to our British brethren. We have warned them from time to time of attempts by their legislature to extend an unwarrantable jurisdiction over us. We have reminded them of the circumstances of our emigration and settlement here. We have appealed to their native justice and magnanimity, and we have conjured them by the ties of our common kindred to disavow the usurpations, which, would inevitably interrupt our connections and correspondence. They too have been deaf to the voice of justice and of consanguinity. We must, therefore, acquiesce in the necessity, which denounces our Separation, and hold them, as we hold the rest of mankind, Enemies in War, in Peace Friends.

We, therefore, the Representatives of the United States of America, in General Congress, Assembled, appealing to the Supreme Judge of the world for the rectitude of our intentions, do, in the Name, and by Authority of the good People of these Colonies, solemnly publish and declare, That these United Colonies are, and of Right ought to be Free and Independent States; that they are Absolved from all Allegiance to the British Crown, and that all political connection between them and the State of Great Britain, is and ought to be totally dissolved; and that, as Free and Independent States, they have full Power to levy War, conclude Peace, contract Alliances, establish Commerce, and to do all other Acts and Things which Independent States may of right do. And for the support of this Declaration, with a firm reliance on the protection of divine Providence, we mutually pledge to each other our Lives, our Fortunes and our sacred Honor.

Appendix B

THE CONSTITUTION OF THE UNITED STATES OF AMERICA

We the People of the United States, in Order to form a more perfect Union, establish Justice, insure domestic Tranquility, provide for the common defence, promote the general Welfare, and secure the Blessings of Liberty to ourselves and our Posterity, do ordain and establish this Constitution for the United States of America.

Article I

Section 1 All legislative Powers herein granted shall be vested in a Congress of the United States, which shall consist of a Senate and House of Representatives.

Section 2 The House of Representatives shall be composed of Members chosen every second Year by the People of the several States, and the Electors in each State shall have the Qualifications requisite for Electors of the most numerous Branch of the State Legislature.

No Person shall be a Representative who shall not have attained to the Age of twenty five Years, and been seven Years a Citizen of the United States, and who shall not, when elected, be an Inhabitant of that State in which he shall be chosen.

Representatives and direct Taxes[1] shall be apportioned among the several States which may be included within this Union, according to their respective Numbers, which shall be determined by adding to the whole Number of free Persons, including those bound to Service for a Term of Years, and excluding Indians not taxed, three fifths of all other Persons.[2] The actual Enumeration shall be made within three Years after the first Meeting of the Congress of the United States, and within every subsequent Term of ten Years, in such Manner as they shall by Law direct. The Number of Representatives shall not exceed one for every thirty Thousand, but each State shall have at Least one Representative; and until such enumeration shall be made, the State of New Hampshire shall be entitled to chuse three; Massachusetts eight; Rhode Island and Providence Plantations one; Connecticut five; New York six; New Jersey four; Pennsylvania eight; Delaware one; Maryland six; Virginia ten; North Carolina five; South Carolina five; and Georgia three.

Text is from the engrossed copy in the National Archives. Original spelling, capitalization, and punctuation have been retained.

When vacancies happen in the Representation from any State, the Executive Authority thereof shall issue Writs of Election to fill such Vacancies.

The House of Representatives shall chuse their Speaker and other Officers; and shall have the sole Power of Impeachment.

Section 3   The Senate of the United States shall be composed of two Senators from each State, chosen by the Legislature thereof, for six Years; and each Senator shall have one Vote.[3]

Immediately after they shall be assembled in Consequence of the first Election, they shall be divided as equally as may be into three Classes. The Seats of the Senators of the first Class shall be vacated at the Expiration of the second Year, of the second Class at the Expiration of the fourth Year, and of the third Class at the Expiration of the sixth Year, so that one third may be chosen every second Year; and if Vacancies happen by Resignation, or otherwise, during the Recess of the Legislature of any State, the Executive thereof may make temporary Appointments until the next Meeting of the Legislature, which shall then fill such Vacancies.[4]

No Person shall be a Senator who shall not have attained to the Age of thirty Years, and been nine Years a Citizen of the United States, and who shall not, when elected, be an Inhabitant of that State for which he shall be chosen.

The Vice President of the United States shall be President of the Senate, but shall have no Vote, unless they be equally divided.

The Senate shall chuse their other Officers, and also a President pro tempore, in the Absence of the Vice President, or when he shall exercise the Office of President of the United States.

The Senate shall have the sole Power to try all Impeachments. When sitting for that Purpose, they shall be on Oath or Affirmation. When the President of the United States is tried, the Chief Justice shall preside: And no Person shall be convicted without the Concurrence of two thirds of the Members present.

Judgment in Cases of Impeachment shall not extend further than to removal from Office, and disqualification to hold and enjoy any Office of honor, Trust or Profit under the United States: but the Party convicted shall nevertheless be liable and subject to Indictment, Trial, Judgment and Punishment, according to Law.

Section 4   The Times, Places and Manner of holding Elections for Senators and Representatives, shall be prescribed in each State by the Legislature thereof, but the Congress may at any time by Law make or alter such Regulation, except as to the Places of chusing Senators.

The Congress shall assemble at least once in every Year, and such Meeting shall be on the first Monday in December, unless they shall by Law appoint a different Day.[5]

Section 5   Each House shall be the Judge of the Elections, Returns and Qualifications of its own Members, and a Majority of each shall constitute a Quorum to do Business; but a smaller Number may adjourn from day to day, and may be authorized to compel the Attendance of absent Members, in such Manner, and under such Penalties as each House may provide.

Each House may determine the Rules of its Proceedings, punish its Members for disorderly Behaviour, and, with the Concurrence of two thirds, expel a Member.

Each House shall keep a Journal of its Proceedings, and from time to time publish the same, excepting such Parts as may in their Judgment require Secrecy; and the Yeas and Nays of the Members of either House on any question shall, at the Desire of one fifth of those Present, be entered on the Journal.

Neither House, during the Session of Congress, shall, without the Consent of the other, adjourn for more than three days, nor to any other Place than that in which the two Houses shall be sitting.

Section 6   The Senators and Representatives shall receive a Compensation for their Services, to be ascertained by Law, and paid out of the Treasury of the United States. They shall in all Cases, except Treason, Felony and Breach of the Peace, be privileged from Arrest during their Attendance at the Session of their respective Houses, and in going to and returning from the same; and for any Speech or Debate in either House, they shall not be questioned in any other Place.

No Senator or Representative shall, during the Time for which he was elected, be appointed to any civil Office under the Authority of the United States, which shall have been created, or the Emoluments whereof shall have been encreased during such time; and no Person holding any Office under the United States, shall be a Member of either House during his Continuance in Office.

Section 7   All Bills for raising Revenue shall originate in the House of Representatives; but the Senate may propose or concur with Amendments as on other Bills.

Every Bill which shall have passed the House of Representatives and the Senate shall, before it become a Law, be presented to the President of the United States; If he approve he shall sign it, but if not he shall return it, with his Objections to that House in which it shall have originated, who shall enter the Objections at large on their Journal, and proceed to reconsider it. If after such Reconsideration two thirds of that House shall agree to pass the Bill, it shall be sent, together with the Objections, to the other House, by which it shall likewise be reconsidered, and if approved by two thirds of that House, it shall become a Law. But in all such Cases the Votes of both Houses shall be determined by yeas and Nays, and the Names of the Persons voting for and against the Bill shall be entered on the Journal of each House respectively. If any Bill shall not be returned by the President within ten Days (Sundays excepted) after it shall have been presented to him, the Same shall be a Law, in like Manner as if he had signed it, unless the Congress by their Adjournment prevent its Return, in which Case it shall not be a Law.

Every Order, Resolution, or Vote to which the Concurrence of the Senate and House of Representatives may be necessary (except on a question of Adjournment) shall be presented to the President of the United States; and before the Same shall take Effect, shall be approved by him, or being disapproved by him shall be repassed by two thirds of the Senate and House of Representatives, according to the Rules and Limitations prescribed in the Case of a Bill.

Section 8   The Congress shall have power To lay and collect Taxes, Duties, Imposts and Excises, to pay the Debts and provide for the common Defence and general Welfare of the United States; but all Duties, Imposts and Excises shall be uniform throughout the United States;

To borrow Money on the credit of the United States;

To regulate Commerce with foreign Nations, and among the several States, and with the Indian Tribes;

To establish an uniform Rule of Naturalization, and uniform Laws on the subject of Bankruptcies throughout the United States;

To coin Money, regulate the Value thereof, and of foreign Coin, and fix the Standard of Weights and Measures;

To provide for the Punishment of counterfeiting the Securities and current Coin of the United States;

To establish Post Offices and post Roads;

To promote the Progress of Science and useful Arts, by securing for limited Times to Authors and Inventors the exclusive Right to their respective Writings and Discoveries;

To constitute Tribunals inferior to the supreme Court;

To define and punish Piracies and Felonies committed on the high Seas, and Offences against the Law of Nations;

To declare War, grant Letters of Marque and Reprisal, and make Rules concerning Captures on Land and Water;

To raise and support Armies, but no Appropriation of Money to that Use shall be for a longer Term than two Years;

To provide and maintain a Navy;

To make Rules for the Government and Regulation of the land and naval Forces;

To provide for calling forth the Militia to execute the Laws of the Union, suppress Insurrections and repel Invasions;

To provide for organizing, arming, and disciplining, the Militia, and for governing such Part of them as may be employed in the Service of the United States, reserving to the States respectively, the Appointment of the Officers, and the Authority of training the Militia according to the discipline prescribed by Congress;

To exercise exclusive Legislation in all Cases whatsoever, over such District (not exceeding ten Miles square) as may, by Cession of particular States, and the Acceptance of Congress, become the Seat of the Government of the

United States, and to exercise like Authority over all Places purchased by the Consent of the Legislature of the State in which the Same shall be, for the Erection of Forts, Magazines, Arsenals, dock-Yards, and other needful Buildings;—And

To make all Laws which shall be necessary and proper for carrying into Execution the foregoing Powers, and all other Powers vested by this Constitution in the Government of the United States, or in any Department or Officer thereof.

Section 9   The Migration or Importation of such Persons as any of the States now existing shall think proper to admit, shall not be prohibited by the Congress prior to the Year one thousand eight hundred and eight, but a Tax or duty may be imposed on such Importation, not exceeding ten dollars for each Person.

The Privilege of the Writ of Habeas Corpus shall not be suspended, unless when in Cases of Rebellion or Invasion the public Safety may require it.

No Bill of Attainder or ex post facto Law shall be passed.

No Capitation, or other direct, Tax shall be laid, unless in Proportion to the Census or Enumeration herein before directed to be taken.

No Tax or Duty shall be laid on Articles exported from any State.

No Preference shall be given by any Regulation of Commerce or Revenue to the Ports of one State over those of another: nor shall Vessels bound to, or from, one State, be obliged to enter, clear, or pay Duties in another.

No Money shall be drawn from the Treasury, but in Consequence of Appropriations made by Law, and a regular Statement and Account of the Receipts and Expenditures of all public Money shall be published from time to time.

No Title of Nobility shall be granted by the United States: And no Person holding any Office of Profit or Trust under them, shall, without the Consent of the Congress, accept of any present, Emolument, Office, or Title, of any kind whatever, from any King, Prince, or foreign State.

Section 10   No State shall enter into any Treaty, Alliance, or Confederation; grant Letters of Marque and Reprisal; coin Money; emit Bills of Credit; make any Thing but gold and silver Coin a Tender in Payment of Debts; pass any Bill of Attainder, ex post facto Law, or Law impairing the Obligation of Contracts, or grant any Title of Nobility.

No State shall, without the Consent of the Congress, lay any Imposts or Duties on Imports or Exports, except what may be absolutely necessary for executing its inspection Laws: and the net Produce of all Duties and Imposts, laid by any State on Imports or Exports, shall be for the Use of the Treasury of the United States; and all such Laws shall be subject to the Revision and Controul of the Congress.

No State shall, without the Consent of Congress, lay any Duty of Tonnage, keep Troops, or Ships of War in time of Peace, enter into any Agreement or Compact with another State, or with a foreign Power, or engage in War, unless actually invaded, or in such imminent Danger as will not admit of delay.

Article II

Section 1   The executive Power shall be vested in a President of the United States of America. He shall hold his Office during the Term of four Years, and, together with the Vice President, chosen for the same Term, be elected, as follows:

Each State shall appoint, in such Manner as the Legislature thereof may direct, a Number of Electors, equal to the whole Number of Senators and Representatives to which the State may be entitled in the Congress: but no Senator or Representative, or Person holding an Office of Trust or Profit under the United States, shall be appointed an Elector.

The Electors shall meet in their respective States, and vote by Ballot for two Persons, of whom one at least shall not be an Inhabitant of the same State with themselves. And they shall make a List of all the Persons voted for, and of the Number of Votes for each; which List they shall sign and certify, and transmit sealed to the Seat of the Government of the United States, directed to the President of the Senate. The President of the Senate shall, in the Presence of the Senate and House of Representatives, open all the Certificates, and the Votes shall then be counted. The Person having the greatest Number of Votes shall be the President, if such Number be a Majority of the whole Number of Electors appointed; and if there be more than one who have such Majority, and have an equal Number of Votes, then the House of Representatives shall immediately chuse by Ballot one of them for President; and if no Person have a Majority, then from the five highest on the List the said House shall in like Manner chuse the President. But in chusing the President, the Votes shall be taken by States, the Representation from each State having one Vote; A quorum for this Purpose shall consist of a Member or Members from two thirds of the States, and a Majority of all the States shall be necessary to a Choice. In every Case, after the Choice of the President, the Person having the greatest Number of Votes of the Electors shall be the Vice President. But if there should remain two or more who have equal Votes, the Senate shall chuse from them by Ballot the Vice President.[6]

The Congress may determine the Time of chusing the Electors, and the Day on which they shall give their Votes; which Day shall be the same throughout the United States.

No Person except a natural born Citizen, or a Citizen of the United States, at the time of the Adoption of this Constitution, shall be eligible to the Office of President, neither shall any Person be eligible to that Office who shall not have attained to the Age of thirty five Years, and been fourteen Years a Resident within the United States.

In Case of the Removal of the President from Office, or of his Death, Resignation, or Inability to discharge the Powers and Duties of the said Office, the Same shall devolve on the Vice President, and the Congress may by Law provide for the Case of Removal, Death, Resignation or Inability, both of the President and Vice President, declaring what Officer shall then act as President, and such Officer shall act accordingly, until the Disability be removed, or a President shall be elected.[7]

The President shall, at stated Times, receive for his Services, a Compensation, which shall neither be encreased nor diminished during the Period for which he shall have been elected, and he shall not receive within that Period any other Emolument from the United States, or any of them.

Before he enter on the Execution of his Office, he shall take the following Oath or Affirmation:—"I do solemnly swear (or affirm) that I will faithfully execute the Office of President of the United States, and will to the best of my Ability, preserve, protect and defend the Constitution of the United States."

Section 2   The President shall be Commander in Chief of the Army and Navy of the United States, and of the Militia of the several States, when called into the actual Service of the United States; he may require the Opinion, in writing, of the principal Officer in each of the executive Departments, upon any Subject relating to the Duties of their respective Offices, and he shall have Power to grant Reprieves and Pardons for Offences against the United States, except in Cases of Impeachment.

He shall have Power, by and with the Advice and Consent of the Senate, to make Treaties, provided two thirds of the Senators present concur; and he shall nominate, and by and with the Advice and Consent of the Senate, shall appoint Ambassadors, other public Ministers and Consuls, Judges of the supreme Court, and all other Officers of the United States, whose Appointments are not herein otherwise provided for, and which shall be established by Law; but the Congress may by Law vest the Appointment of such inferior Officers, as they think proper, in the President alone, in the Courts of Law, or in the Heads of Departments.

The President shall have Power to fill up all Vacancies that may happen during the Recess of the Senate, by granting Commissions which shall expire at the End of their next Session.

Section 3   He shall from time to time give the Congress Information of the State of the Union, and recommend to their Consideration such Measures as he shall judge necessary and expedient; he may, on extraordinary Occasions, convene both Houses, or either of them, and in Case of Disagreement between them, with Respect to the Time of Adjournment, he may adjourn them to such Time as he shall think proper; he shall receive Ambassadors and other public Ministers; he shall take Care that the Laws be faithfully executed, and shall Commission all the Officers of the United States.

Section 4   The President, Vice President and all civil Officers of the United States, shall be removed from Office on Impeachment for, and Conviction of, Treason, Bribery, or other high Crimes and Misdemeanors.

Article III

Section 1   The judicial Power of the United States, shall be vested in one supreme Court, and in such inferior Courts as the Congress may from time to time ordain and establish. The Judges, both of the supreme and inferior Courts, shall hold their Offices during good Behaviour, and shall, at stated Times, receive for their Services, a Compensation, which shall not be diminished during their Continuance in Office.

Section 2   The judicial Power shall extend to all Cases, in Law and Equity, arising under this Constitution, the Laws of the United States, and Treaties made, or which shall be made, under their Authority;—to all Cases affecting Ambassadors, other public Ministers and Consuls;—to all Cases of admiralty and maritime Jurisdiction;—to Controversies to which the United States shall be a Party;—to Controversies between two or more States;—between a State and Citizens of another State;[8]—between Citizens of different States,—between Citizens of the same State claiming Lands under Grants of different States, and between a State, or the Citizens thereof, and foreign States, Citizens or Subjects.

In all Cases affecting Ambassadors, other public Ministers and Consuls, and those in which a State shall be Party, the supreme Court shall have original Jurisdiction. In all the other Cases before mentioned, the supreme Court shall have appellate Jurisdiction, both as to Law and Fact, with such Exceptions, and under such Regulations as the Congress shall make.

The Trial of all Crimes, except in Cases of Impeachment, shall be by Jury; and such Trial shall be held in the State where the said Crimes shall have been committed; but when not committed within any State, the Trial shall be at such Place or Places as the Congress may by Law have directed.

Section 3   Treason against the United States, shall consist only in levying War against them, or in adhering to their Enemies, giving them Aid and Comfort. No Person shall be convicted of Treason unless on the Testimony of two Witnesses to the same overt Act, or on Confession in open Court.

The Congress shall have Power to declare the Punishment of Treason, but no Attainder of Treason shall work Corruption of Blood, or Forfeiture except during the Life of the Person attainted.

Article IV

Section 1   Full Faith and Credit shall be given in each State to the public Acts, Records, and judicial Proceedings of every other State. And the Congress may by general Laws prescribe the Manner in which such Acts, Records and Proceedings shall be proved, and the Effect thereof.

Section 2   The Citizens of each State shall be entitled to all Privileges and Immunities of Citizens in the several States.

A Person charged in any State with Treason, Felony, or other Crime, who shall flee from Justice, and be found in another State, shall on Demand of the executive Authority of the State from which he fled, be delivered up, to be removed to the State having Jurisdiction of the Crime.

No Person held to Service or Labour in one State, under the Laws thereof, escaping into another, shall, in Consequence of any Law or Regulation therein, be discharged from such Service or Labour, but shall be delivered up on Claim of the Party to whom such Service or Labour may be due.

Section 3   New States may be admitted by the Congress into this Union; but no new State shall be formed or erected within the Jurisdiction of any other State, nor any State be formed by the Junction of two or more States, or Parts of States, without the Consent of the Legislatures of the States concerned as well as of the Congress.

The Congress shall have Power to dispose of and make all needful Rules and Regulations respecting the Territory or other Property belonging to the United States; and nothing in this Constitution shall be so construed as to Prejudice any Claims of the United States, or of any particular State.

Section 4   The United States shall guarantee to every State in this Union a Republican Form of Government, and shall protect each of them against Invasion; and on Application of the Legislature, or of the Executive (when the Legislature cannot be convened) against domestic Violence.

Article V

The Congress, whenever two thirds of both Houses shall deem it necessary, shall propose Amendments to this Constitution, or, on the Application of the Legislatures of two thirds of the several States, shall call a Convention for proposing Amendments, which, in either Case, shall be valid to all Intents and Purposes, as Part of this Constitution, when ratified by the Legislatures of three fourths of the several States, or by Conventions in three fourths thereof, as the one or the other Mode of Ratification may be proposed by the Congress; Provided that no Amendment which may be made prior to the Year One thousand eight hundred and eight shall in any Manner affect the first and fourth Clauses in the Ninth Section of the first Article; and that no State, without its Consent, shall be deprived of its equal Suffrage in the Senate.

Article VI

All Debts contracted and Engagements entered into, before the Adoption of this Constitution, shall be as valid against the United States under this Constitution, as under the Confederation.

This Constitution, and the Laws of the United States which shall be made in Pursuance thereof; and all Treaties made, or which shall be made, under the Authority of the United States, shall be the supreme Law of the Land; and the Judges in every State shall be bound thereby, any Thing in the Constitution or Laws of any State to the Contrary notwithstanding.

The Senators and Representatives before mentioned, and the Members of the several State Legislatures, and all executive and judicial Officers, both of the United States and of the several States, shall be bound by Oath or Affirmation, to support this Constitution; but no religious Test shall ever be required as a Qualification to any Office or public Trust under the United States.

Article VII

The Ratification of the Conventions of nine States, shall be sufficient for the Establishment of this Constitution between the States so ratifying the Same.

Done in Convention by the Unanimous Consent of the States present the Seventeenth Day of September in the Year of our Lord one thousand seven hundred and Eighty seven and of the Independence of the United States of America the Twelfth. In witness whereof We have hereunto subscribed our Names,

Articles in Addition to, and Amendment of, the Constitution of the United States of America, Proposed by Congress, and Ratified by the Legislatures of the Several States, Pursuant to the Fifth Article of the Original Constitution.

Amendment I[9]

Congress shall make no law respecting an establishment of religion, or prohibiting the free exercise there-of; or abridging the freedom of speech, or of the press; or the right of the people peaceably to assemble, and to petition the Government for a redress of grievances.

Amendment II

A well regulated Militia, being necessary to the security of a free State, the right of the people to keep and bear Arms shall not be infringed.

Amendment III

No Soldier shall, in time of peace, be quartered in any house, without the consent of the Owner, nor in time of war, but in a manner to be prescribed by law.

Amendment IV

The right of the people to be secure in their persons, houses, papers, and effects, against unreasonable searches and seizures, shall not be violated, and no

Warrants shall issue, but upon probable cause, supported by Oath or affirmation, and particularly describing the place to be searched, and the persons or things to be seized.

Amendment V

No person shall be held to answer for a capital or otherwise infamous crime, unless on a presentment or indictment of a Grand Jury, except in cases arising in the land or naval forces, or in the Militia, when in actual service in time of War or public danger; nor shall any person be subject for the same offence to be twice put in jeopardy of life or limb; nor shall be compelled in any criminal case to be a witness against himself, nor be deprived of life, liberty, or property, without due process of law; nor shall private property be taken for public use, without just compensation.

Amendment VI

In all criminal prosecutions, the accused shall enjoy the right to a speedy and public trial, by an impartial jury of the State and district wherein the crime shall have been committed, which district shall have been previously ascertained by law, and to be informed of the nature and cause of the accusation; to be confronted with the witnesses against him; to have compulsory process for obtaining witnesses in his favor, and to have the Assistance of Counsel for his defence.

Amendment VII

In suits at common law, where the value in controversy shall exceed twenty dollars, the right of trial by jury shall be preserved, and no fact tried by a jury, shall be otherwise reexamined in any Court of the United States, than according to the rules of the common law.

Amendment VIII

Excessive bail shall not be required, nor excessive fines imposed, nor cruel and unusual punishments inflicted.

Amendment IX

The enumeration in the Constitution, of certain rights, shall not be construed to deny or disparage others retained by the people.

Amendment X

The powers not delegated to the United States by the Constitution; nor prohibited by it to the States, are reserved to the States respectively, or to the people.

Amendment XI[10]

The Judicial power of the United States shall not be construed to extend to any suit in law or equity, commenced or prosecuted against one of the United States by Citizens of another State, or by Citizens or Subjects of any Foreign State.

Amendment XII[11]

The Electors shall meet in their respective States and vote by ballot for President and Vice-President, one of whom, at least, shall not be an inhabitant of the same State with themselves; they shall name in their ballots the person voted for as President, and in distinct ballots the person voted for as Vice-President, and they shall make distinct lists of all persons voted for as President, and of all persons voted for as Vice-President, and of the number of votes for each, which lists they shall sign and certify, and transmit sealed to the seat of the government of the United States, directed to the President of the Senate;—The President of the Senate shall, in the presence of the Senate and House of Representatives, open all the certificates and the votes shall then be counted;—The person having the greatest number of votes for President, shall be the President, if such number be a majority of the whole number of Electors appointed; and if no person have such majority, then from the persons having the highest numbers not exceeding three on the list of those voted for as President, the House of Representatives shall choose immediately, by ballot, the President. But in choosing the President, the votes shall be taken by states, the representation from each state having one vote; a quorum for this purpose shall consist of a member or members from two-thirds of the states, and a majority of all the states shall be necessary to a choice. And if the House of Representatives shall not choose a President whenever the right of choice shall devolve upon them, before the fourth day of March next following, then the Vice-President shall act as President, as in the case of the death or other constitutional disability of the President.—The person having the greatest number of votes as Vice-President, shall be the Vice-President, if such number be a majority of the whole number of Electors appointed, and if no person have a majority, then from the two highest numbers on the list, the Senate shall choose the Vice-President; a quorum for the purpose shall consist of two-thirds of the whole number of Senators, and a majority of the whole number shall be necessary to a choice. But no person constitutionally ineligible to the office of President shall be eligible to that of Vice-President of the United States.

Amendment XIII[12]

Section 1   Neither slavery nor involuntary servitude, except as a punishment for crime whereof the party shall have been duly convicted, shall exist within the United States, or any place subject to their jurisdiction.

Section 2   Congress shall have power to enforce this article by appropriate legislation.

Amendment XIV[13]

Section 1   All persons born or naturalized in the United States, and subject to the jurisdiction thereof, are citizens of the United States and of the State wherein they reside. No State shall make or enforce any law which shall abridge the privileges or immunities of citizens of the United States; nor shall any State deprive any person of life, liberty, or property, without due process of law; nor deny to any person within its jurisdiction the equal protection of the laws.

Section 2   Representatives shall be apportioned among the several States according to their respective numbers, counting the whole number of persons in each State, excluding Indians not taxed. But when the right to vote at any election for the choice of electors for President and Vice-President of the United States, Representatives in Congress, the Executive and Judicial officers of a State, or the members of the Legislature thereof, is denied to any of the male inhabitants of such State, being twenty-one years of age, and citizens of the United States, or in any way abridged, except for participation in rebellion, or other crime, the basis of representation therein shall be reduced in the proportion which the number of such male citizens shall bear to the whole number of male citizens twenty-one years of age in such State.

Section 3   No person shall be a Senator or Representative in Congress, or elector of President and Vice-President, or hold any office, civil or military, under the United States, or under any State, who, having previously taken an oath, as a member of Congress, or as an officer of the United States, or as a member of any State legislature, or as an executive or judicial officer of any State, to support the Constitution of the United States, shall have engaged in insurrection or rebellion against the same, or given aid or comfort to the enemies thereof. But Congress may by a vote of two-thirds of each House, remove such disability.

Section 4   The validity of the public debt of the United States, authorized by law, including debts incurred for payment of pensions and bounties for services in suppressing insurrection or rebellion, shall not be questioned. But neither the United States nor any State shall assume or pay any debt or obligation incurred in aid of insurrection or rebellion against the United States, or any claim for the loss or emancipation of any slave; but all such debts, obligations, and claims shall be held illegal and void.

Section 5   The Congress shall have the power to enforce, by appropriate legislation, the provisions of this article.

Amendment XV[14]

Section 1   The right of citizens of the United States to vote shall not be denied or abridged by the United States or by any State on account of race, color, or previous conditions of servitude—

Section 2   The Congress shall have power to enforce this article by appropriate legislation.

Amendment XVI[15]

The Congress shall have power to lay and collect taxes on incomes, from whatever source derived, without apportionment among the several States, and without regard to any census or enumeration.

Amendment XVII[16]

The Senate of the United States shall be composed of two Senators from each State, elected by the people thereof, for six years; and each Senator shall have one vote. The electors in each State shall have the qualifications requisite for electors of the most numerous branch of the State legislatures.

When vacancies happen in the representation of any State in the Senate, the executive authority of such State shall issue writs of election to fill such vacancies: *Provided*, That the legislature of any State may empower the executive thereof to make temporary appointments until the people fill the vacancies by election as the legislature may direct.

This amendment shall not be so construed as to affect the election or term of any Senator chosen before it becomes valid as part of the Constitution.

Amendment XVIII[17]

Section 1   After one year from the ratification of this article the manufacture, sale, or transportation of intoxicating liquors within, the importation thereof into, or the exportation thereof from the United States and all territory subject to the jurisdiction thereof for beverage purposes is hereby prohibited.

Section 2   The Congress and the several States shall have concurrent power to enforce this article by appropriate legislation.

Section 3   This article shall be inoperative unless it shall have been ratified as an amendment to the Constitution by the legislatures of the several States, as provided in the Constitution, within seven years from the date of the submission hereof to the States by the Congress.

Amendment XIX[18]

The right of citizens of the United States to vote shall not be denied or abridged by the United States or by any State on account of sex.

Congress shall have power to enforce this article by appropriate legislation.

Amendment XX[19]

Section 1   The terms of the President and Vice-President shall end at noon on the 20th day of January, and the terms of Senators and Representatives at noon on the 3rd day of January, of the years in which such terms would have ended if this article had not been ratified; and the terms of their successors shall then begin.

Section 2   The Congress shall assemble at least once in every year, and such meeting shall begin at noon on the 3rd day of January, unless they shall by law appoint a different day.

Section 3   If, at the time fixed for the beginning of the term of the President, the President elect shall have died, the Vice-President elect shall become President. If a President shall not have been chosen before the time fixed for the beginning of his term, or if the President elect shall have failed to qualify, then the Vice-President elect shall act as President until a President shall have qualified; and the Congress may by law provide for the case wherein neither a President elect nor a Vice-President elect shall have qualified, declaring who shall then act as President, or the manner in which one who is to act shall be selected, and such person shall act accordingly until a President or Vice-President shall have qualified.

Section 4   The Congress may by law provide for the case of the death of any of the persons from whom the House of Representatives may choose a President whenever the right of choice shall have devolved upon them, and for the case of the death of any of the persons from whom the Senate may choose a Vice-President whenever the right of choice shall have devolved upon them.

Section 5   Sections 1 and 2 shall take effect on the 15th day of October following the ratification of this article.

Section 6   This article shall be inoperative unless it shall have been ratified as an amendment to the Constitution by the legislatures of three-fourths of the several States within seven years from the date of its submission.

Amendment XXI[20]

Section 1   The eighteenth article of amendment to the Constitution of the United States is hereby repealed.

Section 2   The transportation or importation into any State, Territory, or possession of the United States for delivery or use therein of intoxicating liquors, in violation of the laws thereof, is hereby prohibited.

Section 3   This article shall be inoperative unless it shall have been ratified as an amendment to the Constitution by conventions in the several States, as provided in the Constitution, within seven years from the date of the submission hereof to the States by the Congress.

Amendment XXII[21]

No person shall be elected to the office of the President more than twice, and no person who has held the office of President, or acted as President, for more than two years of a term to which some other person was elected President shall be electesd to the office of the President more than once.

But this Article shall not apply to any person holding the office of President when this Article was proposed by the Congress, and shall not prevent any person who may be holding the office of President, or acting as President, during the term within which this Article becomes operative from holding the office of President or acting as President during the remainder of such term.

Amendment XXIII[22]

Section 1   The District constituting the seat of Government of the United States shall appoint in such manner as the Congress may direct:

A number of electors of President and Vice President equal to the whole number of Senators and Representatives in Congress to which the District would be entitled if it were a State, but in no event more than the least populous State; they shall be in addition to those appointed by the States, but they shall be considered, for the purposes of the election of President and Vice President, to be electors appointed by the State; and they shall meet in the District and perform such duties as provided by the twelfth article of amendment.

Section 2   The Congress shall have power to enforce this article by appropriate legislation.

Amendment XXIV[23]

Section 1   The right of citizens of the United States to vote in any primary or other election for President or Vice President, or for Senator or Representative in Congress, shall not be denied or abridged by the United States or any State by reason of failure to pay any poll tax or other tax.

Section 2   The Congress shall have power to enforce this article by appropriate legislation.

Amendment XXV[24]

Section 1   In case of the removal of the President from office or of his death or resignation, the Vice President shall become President.

Section 2   Whenever there is a vacancy in the office of the Vice President, the President shall nominate a Vice President who shall take office upon confirmation by a majority vote of both Houses of Congress.

Section 3   Whenever the President transmits to the President pro tempore of the Senate and the Speaker of the House of Representatives his written declaration that he is unable to discharge the powers and duties of his office, and until he transmits them a written declaration to the contrary, such powers and duties shall be discharged by the Vice President as Acting President.

Section 4   Whenever the Vice President and a majority of either the principal officers of the executive department or of such other body as Congress may by law provide, transmit to the President pro tempore of the Senate and the Speaker of the House of Representatives their written declaration that the President is unable to discharge the powers and duties of his office, the Vice President shall immediately assume the powers and duties of the office of Acting President.

Thereafter, when the President transmits to the President pro tempore of the Senate and the Speaker of the House of Representatives his written declaration that no inability exists, he shall resume the powers and duties of his office unless the Vice President and a majority of either the principal officers of the executive department or of such other body as Congress may by law provide, transmit within four days to the President pro tempore of the Senate and the Speaker of the House of Representatives their written declaration that the President is unable to discharge the powers and duties of his office. Thereupon Congress shall decide the issue, assembling within forty-eight hours for that purpose if not in session. If the Congress, within twenty-one days after receipt of the latter written declaration, or, if Congress is not in session, within twenty-one days after Congress is required to assemble, determines by two-thirds vote of both Houses that the President is unable to discharge the powers and duties of his office, the Vice President shall continue to discharge the same as Acting President; otherwise, the President shall resume the powers and duties of his office.

Amendment XXVI[25]

Section 1   The right of citizens of the United States, who are eighteen years of age or older, to vote shall not be denied or abridged by the United States or by any State on account of age.

Section 2   The Congress shall have power to enforce this article by appropriate legislation.

Amendment XXVII[26]

No law, varying the compensation for the service of the Senators and Representatives, shall take effect, until an election of Representatives shall have intervened.

NOTES

1. Modified by the Sixteenth Amendment.
2. Replaced by the Fourteenth Amendment.
3. Superseded by the Seventeenth Amendment.
4. Modified by the Seventeenth Amendment.
5. Superseded by the Twentieth Amendment.
6. Superseded by the Twelfth Amendment.
7. Modified by the Twenty-fifth Amendment.
8. Modified by the Eleventh Amendment.
9. The first ten amendments were passed by Congress September 25, 1789. They were ratified by three-fourths of the states December 15, 1791.
10. Passed March 4, 1794. Ratified January 23, 1795.
11. Passed December 9, 1803. Ratified June 15, 1804.
12. Passed January 31, 1865. Ratified December 6, 1865.
13. Passed June 13, 1866. Ratified July 9, 1868.
14. Passed February 26, 1869. Ratified February 2, 1870.
15. Passed July 12, 1909. Ratified February 3, 1913.
16. Passed May 13, 1912. Ratified April 8, 1913.
17. Passed December 18, 1917. Ratified January 16, 1919.

18. Passed June 4, 1919. Ratified August 18, 1920.
19. Passed March 2, 1932. Ratified January 23, 1933.
20. Passed February 20, 1933. Ratified December 5, 1933.
21. Passed March 12, 1947. Ratified March 1, 1951.
22. Passed June 16, 1960. Ratified April 3, 1961.
23. Passed August 27, 1962. Ratified January 23, 1964.
24. Passed July 6, 1965. Ratified February 11, 1967.
25. Passed March 23, 1971. Ratified July 5, 1971.
26. Passed September 25, 1789. Ratified May 7, 1992.

Index